A Chinese life

Published in English in 2012
by SelfMadeHero
5 Upper Wimpole Street
London WIG 6BP
www.selfmadehero.com

English translation © 2012 SelfMadeHero

Written by: Philippe Ôtié and Li Kunwu
Illustrated by: Li Kunwu
Translated from the French edition by: Edward Gauvin

INSTITUT FRANÇAIS

This book is supported by the Institut français
as part of the Burgess programme
(www.frenchbooknews.com)

Editorial Assistant and Lettering: Lizzie Kaye
Marketing Director: Doug Wallace
Publishing Director: Emma Hayley
With thanks to: Nick de Somogyi and Dan Lockwood

Published in French as *Une vie chinoise*
© 2009-2011 Li Kunwu – P. Ôtié
– KANA (DARGAUD-LOMBARD SA.)
www.mangakana.com

A CIP record for this book is available from the British Library

ISBN: 978-1-906838-55-3

10 9 8 7 6 5 4 3 2 1

Printed and bound in Slovenia

A Chinese Life

WRITTEN BY

PHILIPPE ÔTIÉ AND LI KUNWU

ILLUSTRATED BY

LI KUNWU

TRANSLATED BY

EDWARD GAUVIN

SELF MADE HERO

I have spent a thousand days and nights steeped in joys and hardships. A union of suffering and delight, pictures and words, which will come to form a significant part of my career as an artist.

Warm thanks to all my immediate family, as well as my friends in the art and literary worlds, in China and France alike, especially my co-writer P. Ôtié. I thank them for having unveiled the mysteries of the Western mind, and given me the strength to bring to light all the memories and feelings my subconscious had buried so deep inside. Also, I thank Cao Sibo, Shen Yue, Zhang Lijuan, Guo Honglian, Huang Rong, Zhang Bing and Shi Xiao for their help with this project. I can never thank the *Yunnan Daily* enough for their constant support, from the beginning of my professional career to the present. I dedicate Book II to my father.
LI KUNWU

To my loved ones, who for so many years put up with my time and mind being taken up by this project. Zhen, Mom, Lélé and Ninou, Lutin Lubrique, zch, Julien, Vivien, Gilles, Constance, Isabelle, Bertrand, Jean-Charles, Nicolas, Honglian: thanks to all who devoted their time to re-reading, dissecting and critiquing these pages so we could go on. Lao Li, I can never thank you enough for letting me tag along on the adventure I'd been waiting for since childhood.
P. ÔTIÉ

Lastly we would like to give special thanks to Lu Ming, Daisy Lee and the entire team at Kana: without you, this work would never have seen the light of day.
LI KUNWU & P. ÔTIÉ

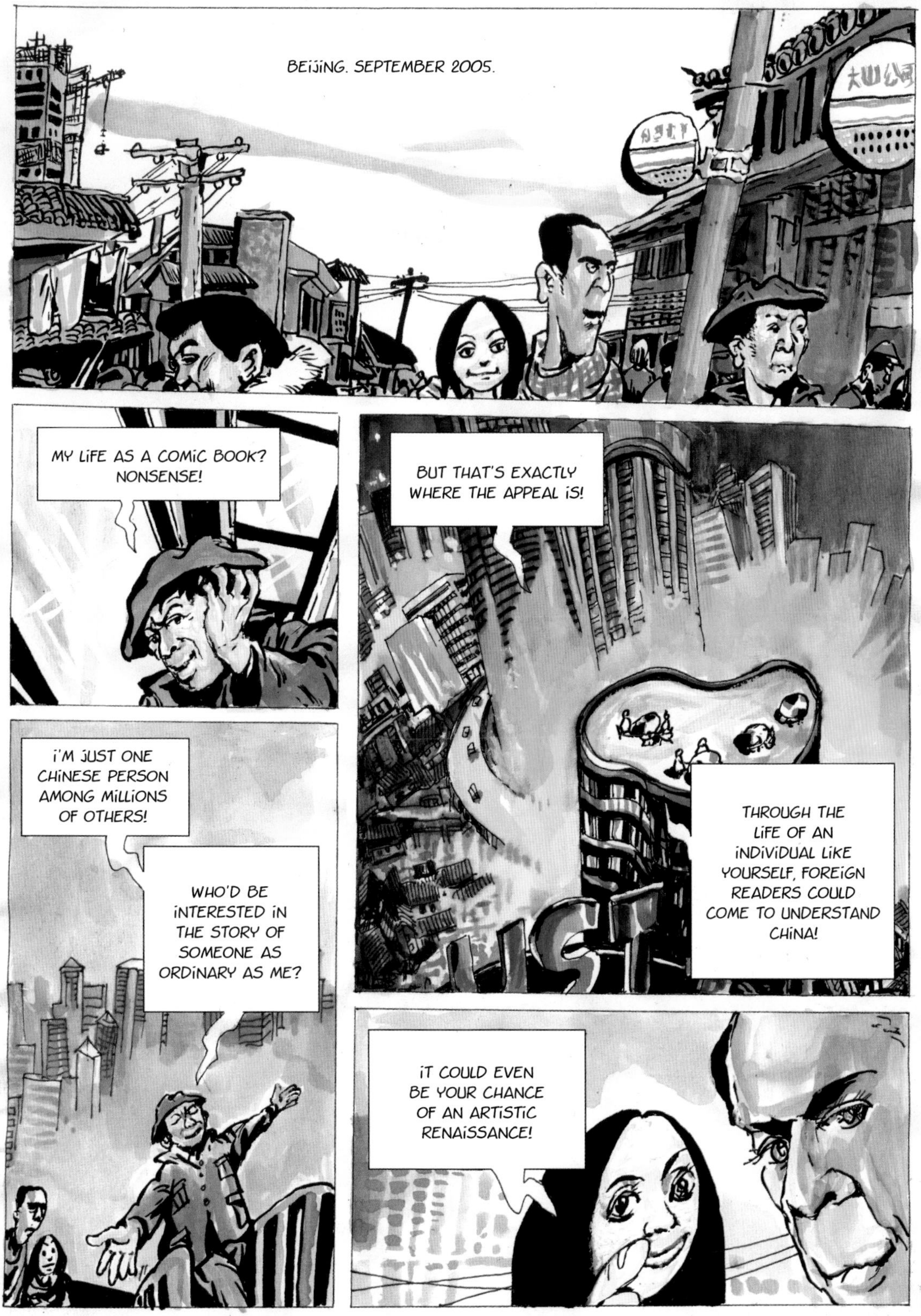
BEIJING. SEPTEMBER 2005.
MY LIFE AS A COMIC BOOK? NONSENSE!
BUT THAT'S EXACTLY WHERE THE APPEAL IS!
THROUGH THE LIFE OF AN INDIVIDUAL LIKE YOURSELF, FOREIGN READERS COULD COME TO UNDERSTAND CHINA!
I'M JUST ONE CHINESE PERSON AMONG MILLIONS OF OTHERS!
WHO'D BE INTERESTED IN THE STORY OF SOMEONE AS ORDINARY AS ME?
IT COULD EVEN BE YOUR CHANCE OF AN ARTISTIC RENAISSANCE!

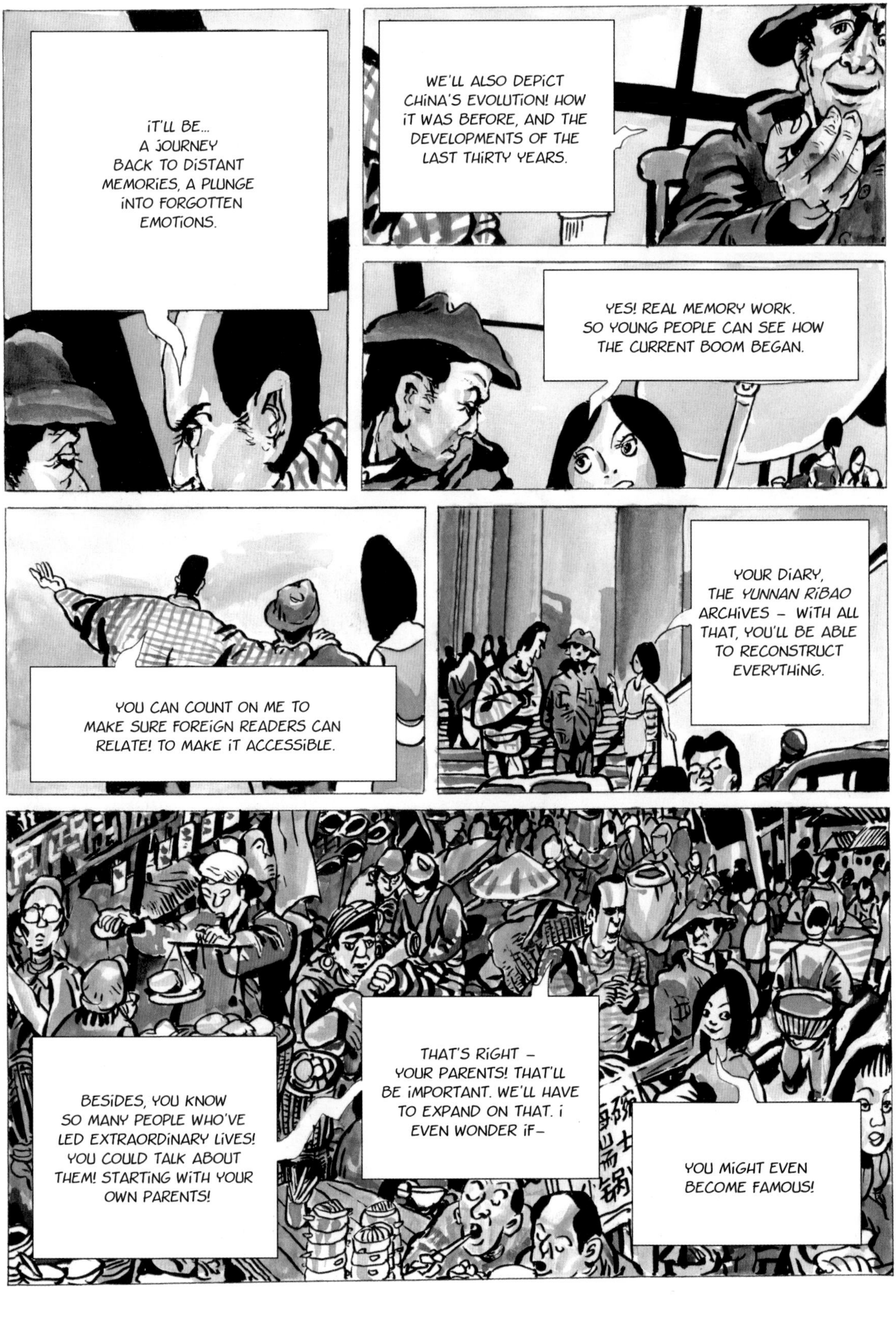
IT'LL BE... A JOURNEY BACK TO DISTANT MEMORIES, A PLUNGE INTO FORGOTTEN EMOTIONS.
WE'LL ALSO DEPICT CHINA'S EVOLUTION! HOW IT WAS BEFORE, AND THE DEVELOPMENTS OF THE LAST THIRTY YEARS.
YES! REAL MEMORY WORK. SO YOUNG PEOPLE CAN SEE HOW THE CURRENT BOOM BEGAN.
YOU CAN COUNT ON ME TO MAKE SURE FOREIGN READERS CAN RELATE! TO MAKE IT ACCESSIBLE.
YOUR DIARY, THE *YUNNAN RIBAO* ARCHIVES – WITH ALL THAT, YOU'LL BE ABLE TO RECONSTRUCT EVERYTHING.
BESIDES, YOU KNOW SO MANY PEOPLE WHO'VE LED EXTRAORDINARY LIVES! YOU COULD TALK ABOUT THEM! STARTING WITH YOUR OWN PARENTS!
THAT'S RIGHT – YOUR PARENTS! THAT'LL BE IMPORTANT. WE'LL HAVE TO EXPAND ON THAT. I EVEN WONDER IF–
YOU MIGHT EVEN BECOME FAMOUS!

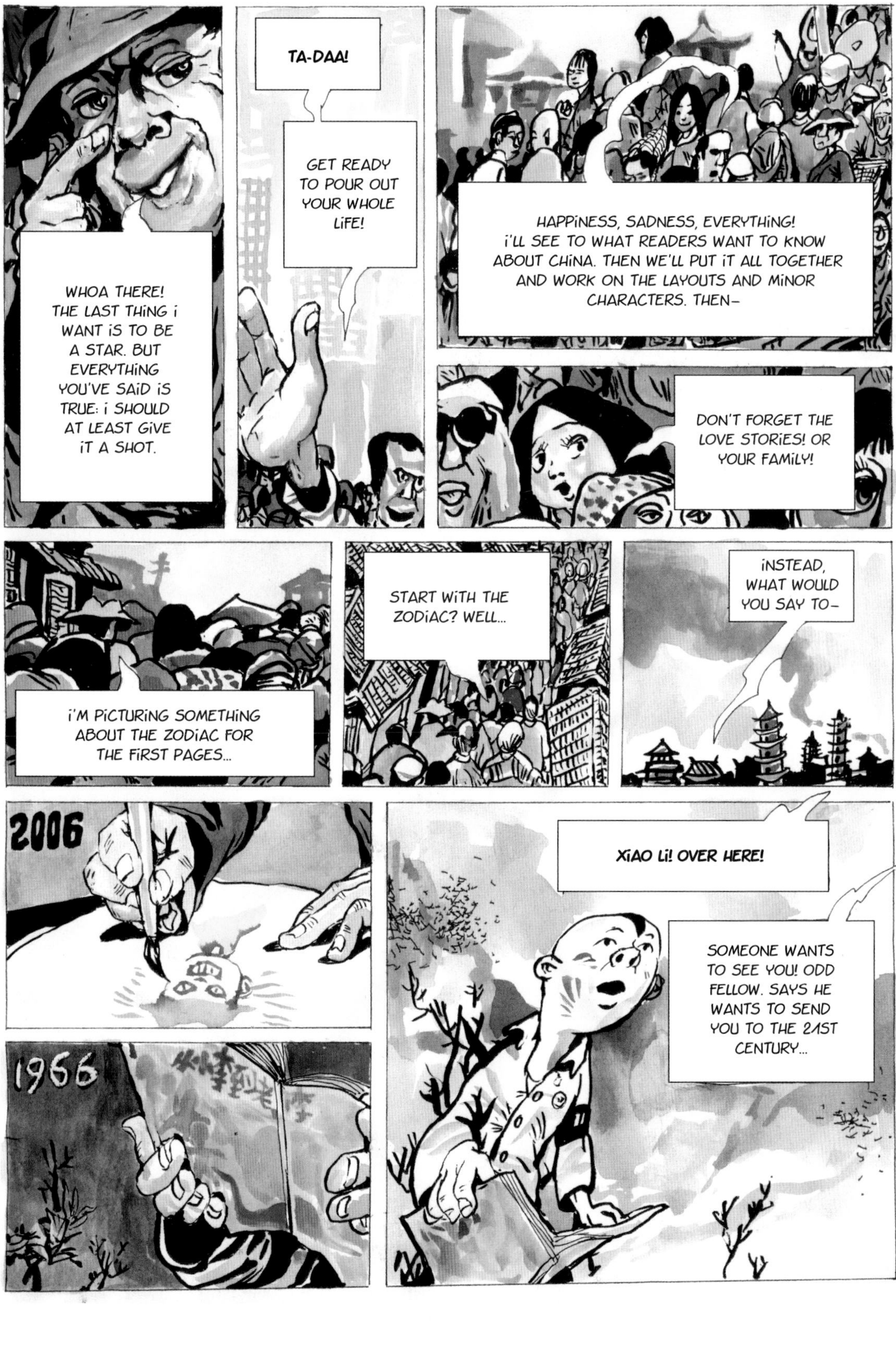
WHOA THERE! THE LAST THING I WANT IS TO BE A STAR. BUT EVERYTHING YOU'VE SAID IS TRUE: I SHOULD AT LEAST GIVE IT A SHOT.
TA-DAA!
GET READY TO POUR OUT YOUR WHOLE LIFE!
HAPPINESS, SADNESS, EVERYTHING! I'LL SEE TO WHAT READERS WANT TO KNOW ABOUT CHINA. THEN WE'LL PUT IT ALL TOGETHER AND WORK ON THE LAYOUTS AND MINOR CHARACTERS. THEN–
DON'T FORGET THE LOVE STORIES! OR YOUR FAMILY!
I'M PICTURING SOMETHING ABOUT THE ZODIAC FOR THE FIRST PAGES...
START WITH THE ZODIAC? WELL...
INSTEAD, WHAT WOULD YOU SAY TO–
2006
1966
XIAO LI! OVER HERE!
SOMEONE WANTS TO SEE YOU! ODD FELLOW. SAYS HE WANTS TO SEND YOU TO THE 21ST CENTURY...

I am not Lao Li ("Old Li", the friendly and respectful way I address Li Kunwu).

I haven't his years. His convictions. His talent. His past. The Party. His place in society. None of that.

I am not Lao Li, but I must think like him.

I'm not Chinese either, but I must think I am.

I must become Chinese, become Lao Li. I must be in his tongue, his brain, his heart, his soul. I must be more than Lao Li. A Lao Li who contains all the Lis, Zhangs and Chens of China.

A Lao Li who exposes himself, makes himself accessible to all non-Chinese people the world over who understand China so little. Even though China's in the middle of it all. Even though the Lis, Zhangs and Chengs see China so clearly.

In Lao Li's eyes, I am not only his friend "Lao Ou" ("Old Ou", the friendly and respectful way Li Kunwu addresses me), nor "my partner Ôtié": I am Dupont, Durand, Schmidt, Popov, Martin and Smith, all at once.

I am the Foreigner.

He who has everything to learn. Who sometimes annoys with his failure to understand things obvious to the Chinese. Who can't love China as much as the Chinese. Who worms out information, who wants to make Lao Li talk about what he won't talk about.

To dive into his life. To help him reconstruct it. To negotiate, with the real Lao Li, what inflections to give the dialogue, the story.

My story – no, his story.

In the beginning, Lao Li and I naïvely thought the project's biggest challenge would be sticking to its genre: memoir. And so what would count most was our ability to recount the actual life of its main character – Lao Li himself – as closely as possible, without betraying reality, or tiring the reader with details of too sedate a life led by a man who had neither the substance nor stature of a hero… but we knew nothing then.

We never expected that for foreign readers – or young Chinese people – who knew little about contemporary Chinese history, whatever happens to Xiao Li ("Young Li") would seem to have happened to all his fellow citizens in exactly the same way. Ditto with what he says. And thinks.

We thought Xiao Li would just be an example. But he changed on us completely, going from "average" all the way to "representative".

Lao Li and I found the resulting responsibility crushing. Everything got complicated. For example, how to approach this or that tragic episode in history without hurting this or that group? How to reconcile the vision the Chinese had of themselves with the sometimes very different one foreigners had? How to touch on political topics, which are so sensitive in China?

With every subject, we always had to walk a narrow ridge between critique and propaganda, with steep drops on either side. A path that remained faithful to Lao Li's life, even as it allowed the reader to make his or her own assessments and judgments.

And then there were the drawings, the invention of a style. For Lao Li didn't always draw like this. Before *A Chinese Life*, his lines were smooth, quick, airy, modest; his brush barely touched the paper. This was the style of the first few pages, the first few attempts. It didn't allow for digging deep, for spilling your guts. Like an actor who suddenly had to play himself, Lao Li let the masks drop and went looking deep inside himself for a style. His own style. Tortured. From the suffering of the first book to the fullness of the third.

That was five years ago, in Beijing.

"A biography, the life of a Chinese artist from Mao to the present day – I'd buy that in a flash!" It all started with those words, more or less, from editor Yves Schlirf, whom we'd met only moments before.

For Lao Li, it was the beginning of a deep plunge into his memories and his art. For me, it was a journey towards finding a friend and discovering a world, one that sometimes saw me on the verge of losing my own world, and myself.

– Philippe Ôtié

Book I

The Time of the Father

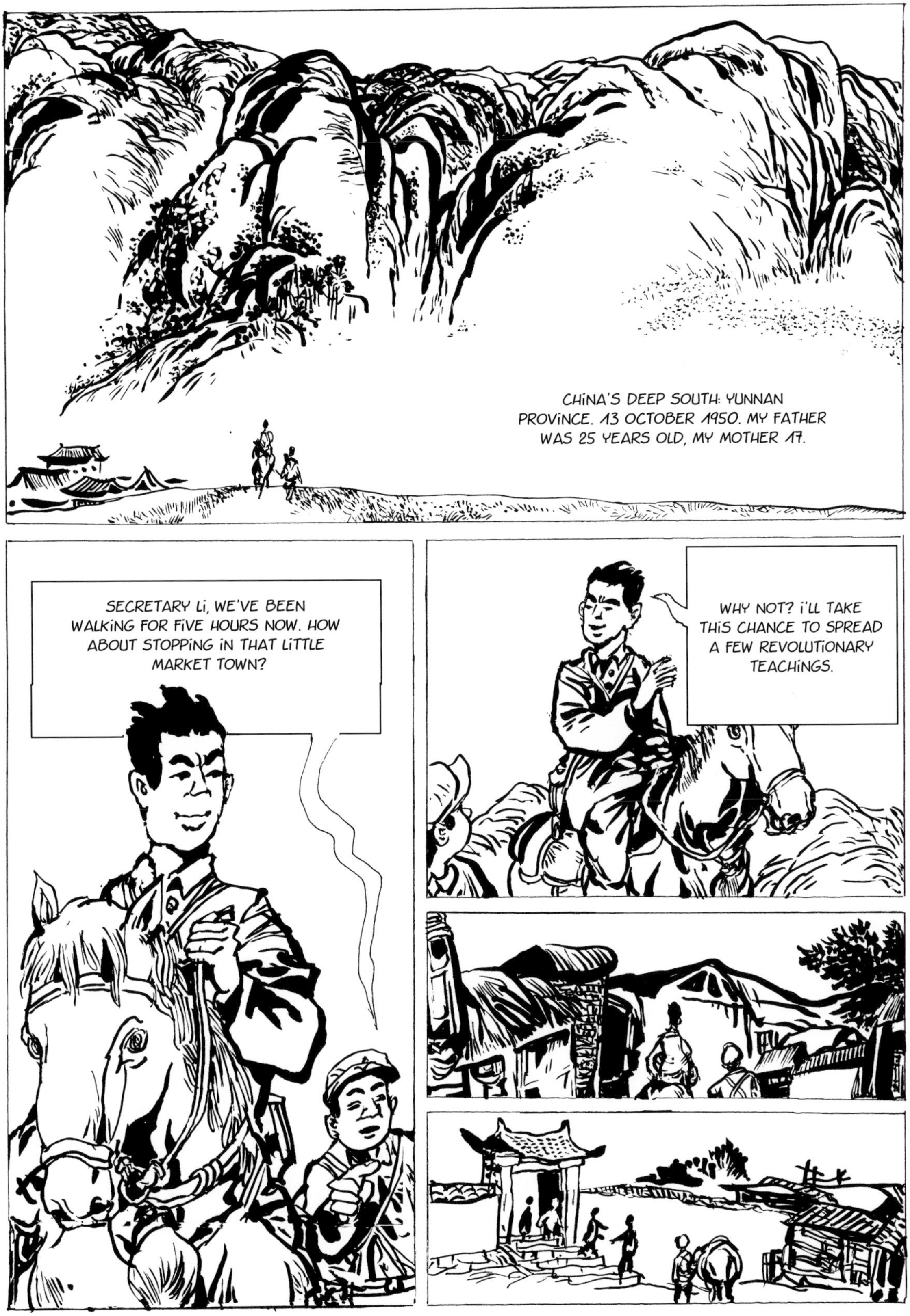
CHINA'S DEEP SOUTH: YUNNAN PROVINCE. 13 OCTOBER 1950. MY FATHER WAS 25 YEARS OLD, MY MOTHER 17.
SECRETARY LI, WE'VE BEEN WALKING FOR FIVE HOURS NOW. HOW ABOUT STOPPING IN THAT LITTLE MARKET TOWN?
WHY NOT? I'LL TAKE THIS CHANCE TO SPREAD A FEW REVOLUTIONARY TEACHINGS.

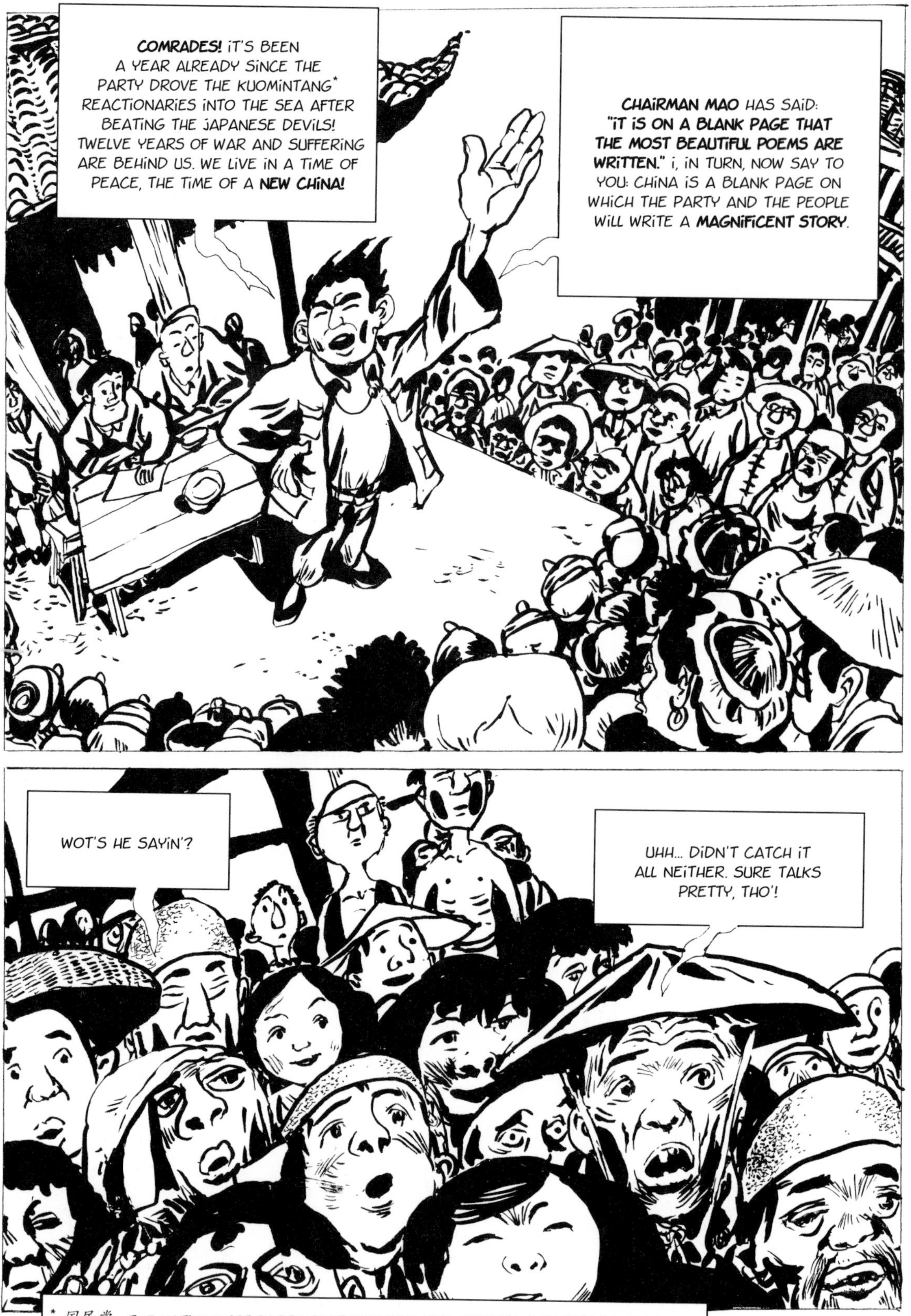
COMRADES! IT'S BEEN A YEAR ALREADY SINCE THE PARTY DROVE THE KUOMINTANG* REACTIONARIES INTO THE SEA AFTER BEATING THE JAPANESE DEVILS! TWELVE YEARS OF WAR AND SUFFERING ARE BEHIND US. WE LIVE IN A TIME OF PEACE, THE TIME OF A NEW CHINA!
CHAIRMAN MAO HAS SAID: "IT IS ON A BLANK PAGE THAT THE MOST BEAUTIFUL POEMS ARE WRITTEN." I, IN TURN, NOW SAY TO YOU: CHINA IS A BLANK PAGE ON WHICH THE PARTY AND THE PEOPLE WILL WRITE A MAGNIFICENT STORY.
WOT'S HE SAYIN'?
UHH... DIDN'T CATCH IT ALL NEITHER. SURE TALKS PRETTY, THO'!

* 国民党 : THE NATIONALIST PARTY THAT FOUNDED THE CHINESE REPUBLIC IN 1911.

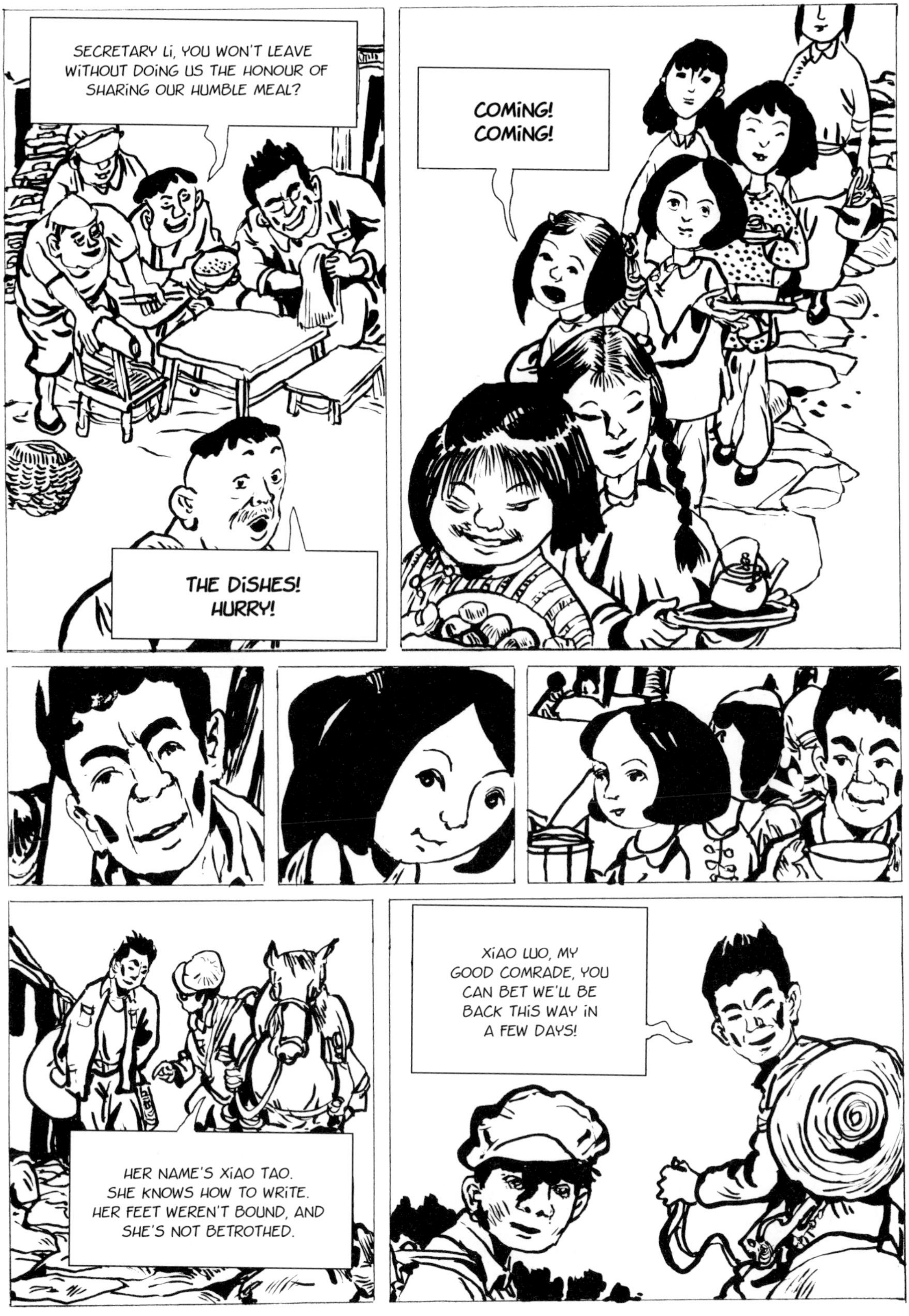
SECRETARY Li, YOU WON'T LEAVE WiTHOUT DOiNG US THE HONOUR OF SHARiNG OUR HUMBLE MEAL?
THE DiSHES! HURRY!
COMiNG! COMiNG!
HER NAME'S XiAO TAO. SHE KNOWS HOW TO WRiTE. HER FEET WEREN'T BOUND, AND SHE'S NOT BETROTHED.
XiAO LUO, MY GOOD COMRADE, YOU CAN BET WE'LL BE BACK THiS WAY iN A FEW DAYS!

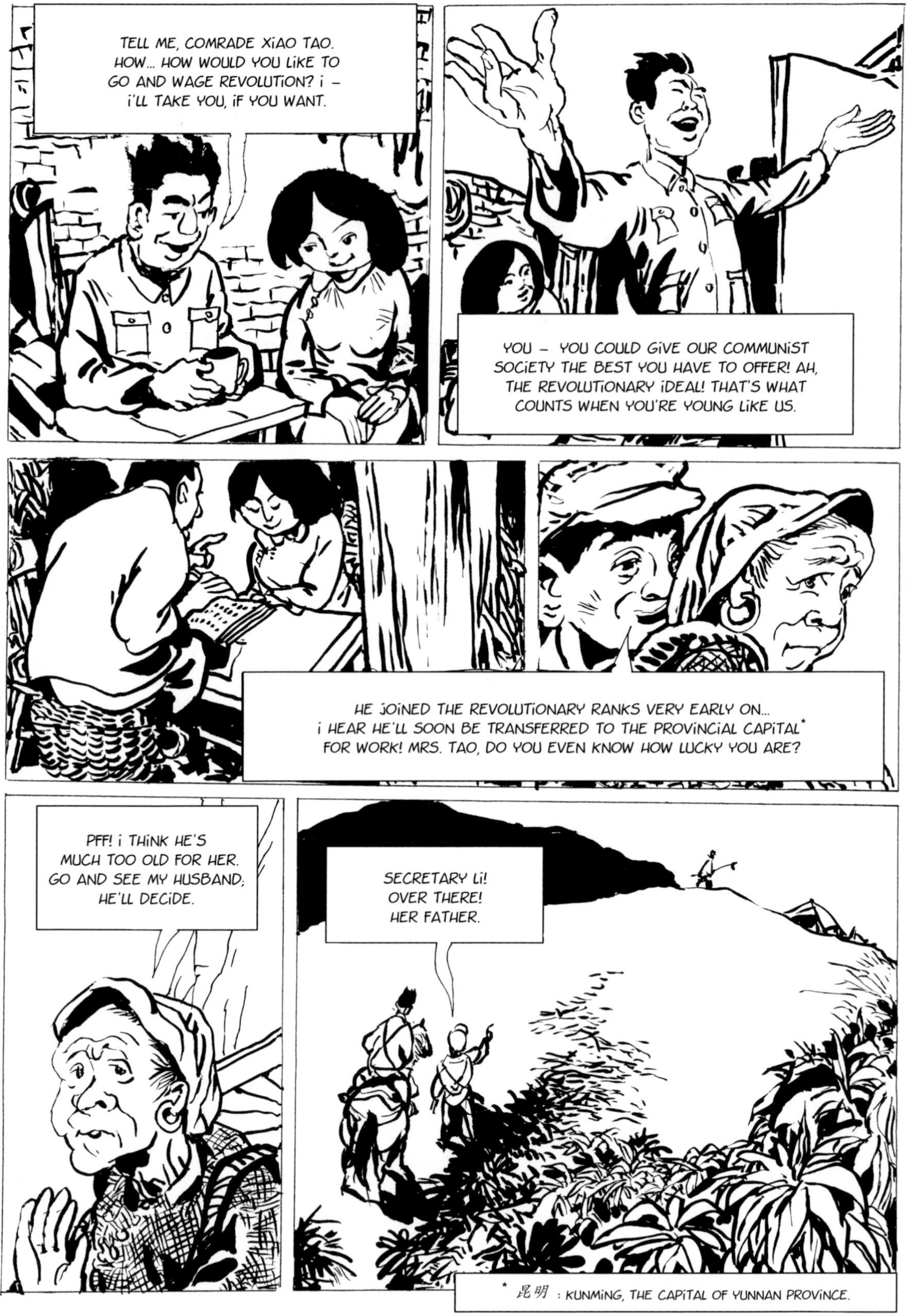
TELL ME, COMRADE XIAO TAO. HOW... HOW WOULD YOU LIKE TO GO AND WAGE REVOLUTION? I – I'LL TAKE YOU, IF YOU WANT.
YOU – YOU COULD GIVE OUR COMMUNIST SOCIETY THE BEST YOU HAVE TO OFFER! AH, THE REVOLUTIONARY IDEAL! THAT'S WHAT COUNTS WHEN YOU'RE YOUNG LIKE US.
HE JOINED THE REVOLUTIONARY RANKS VERY EARLY ON... I HEAR HE'LL SOON BE TRANSFERRED TO THE PROVINCIAL CAPITAL* FOR WORK! MRS. TAO, DO YOU EVEN KNOW HOW LUCKY YOU ARE?
PFF! I THINK HE'S MUCH TOO OLD FOR HER. GO AND SEE MY HUSBAND; HE'LL DECIDE.
SECRETARY LI! OVER THERE! HER FATHER.

* 昆明 : KUNMING, THE CAPITAL OF YUNNAN PROVINCE.

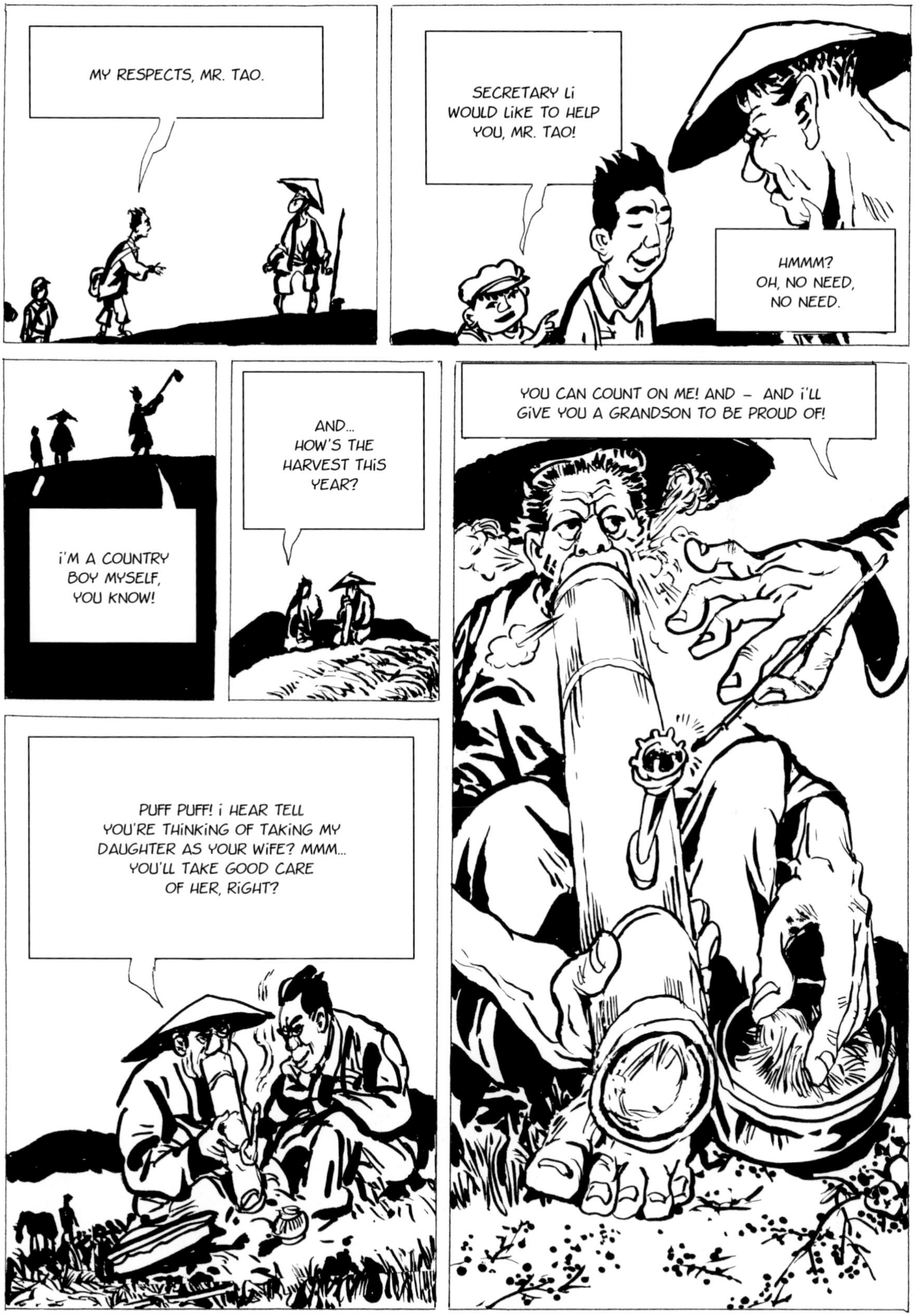
MY RESPECTS, MR. TAO.
SECRETARY Li WOULD LiKE TO HELP YOU, MR. TAO!
HMMM? OH, NO NEED, NO NEED.
i'M A COUNTRY BOY MYSELF, YOU KNOW!
AND... HOW'S THE HARVEST THiS YEAR?
PUFF PUFF! i HEAR TELL YOU'RE THiNKiNG OF TAKiNG MY DAUGHTER AS YOUR WiFE? MMM... YOU'LL TAKE GOOD CARE OF HER, RiGHT?
YOU CAN COUNT ON ME! AND – AND i'LL GiVE YOU A GRANDSON TO BE PROUD OF!

CHAPTER 1
Pure. Red.

GREAT AS ARE SKY AND EARTH,
THE BENEVOLENCE OF THE PARTY iS
GREATER.

DEAR AS ARE MOTHER AND FATHER, THE
LOVE OF CHAiRMAN MAO iS DEARER.

DEEP AS ARE SEAS AND RiVERS,
FRATERNiTY AMONG THE CLASSES iS
DEEPER.

A THOUSAND OR TEN THOUSAND
GOOD THiNGS ARE NOT BETTER THAN
SOCiALiSM.

THE PHiLOSOPHY OF MAO ZEDONG iS THE
JEWEL OF THE REVOLUTiON.

WHOSOEVER OPPOSES MAO, THAT MAN
iS OUR ENEMY.

(ELEMENTARY SCHOOL SONG)

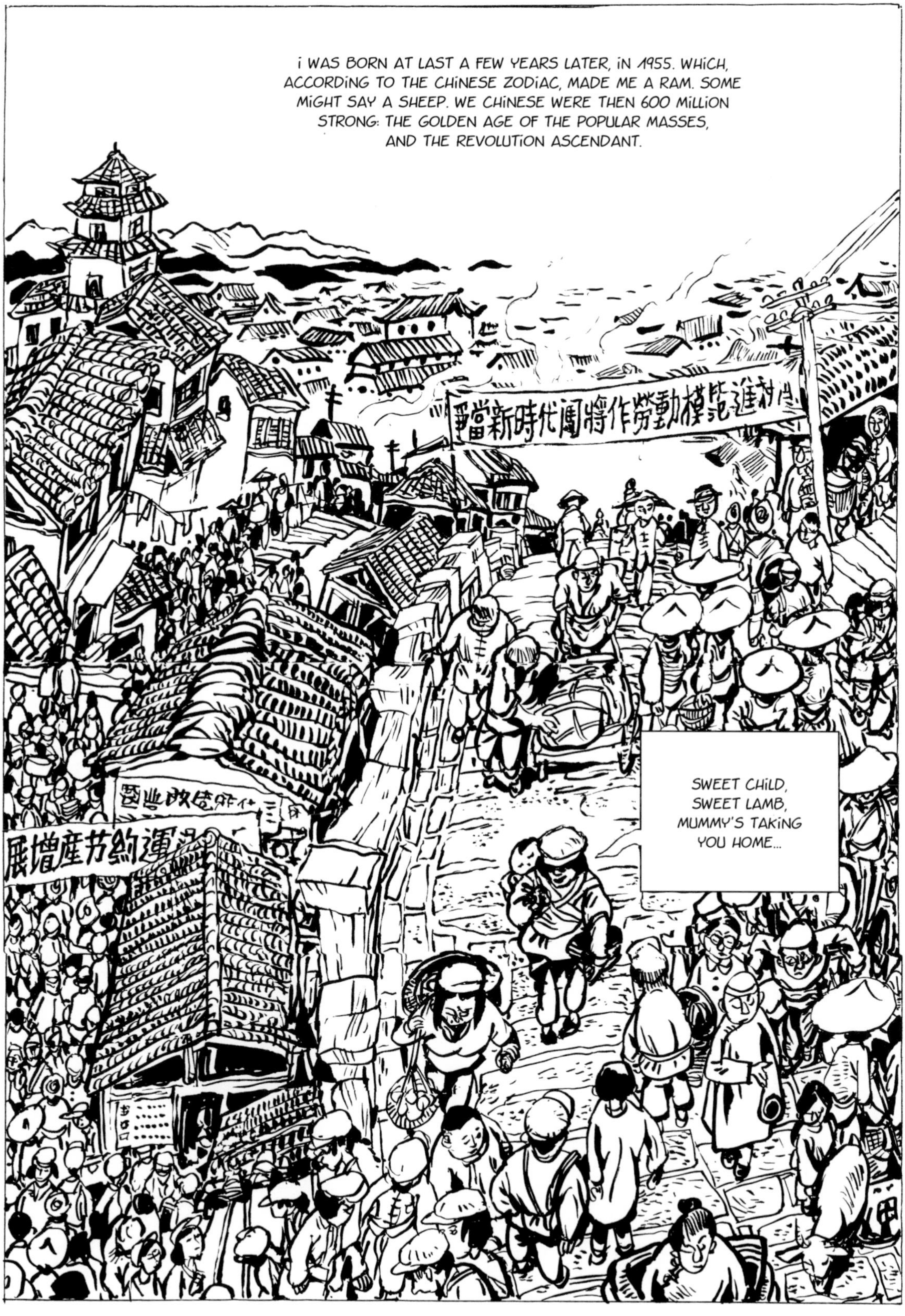
I WAS BORN AT LAST A FEW YEARS LATER, IN 1955. WHICH, ACCORDING TO THE CHINESE ZODIAC, MADE ME A RAM. SOME MIGHT SAY A SHEEP. WE CHINESE WERE THEN 600 MILLION STRONG: THE GOLDEN AGE OF THE POPULAR MASSES, AND THE REVOLUTION ASCENDANT.
SWEET CHILD, SWEET LAMB, MUMMY'S TAKING YOU HOME...

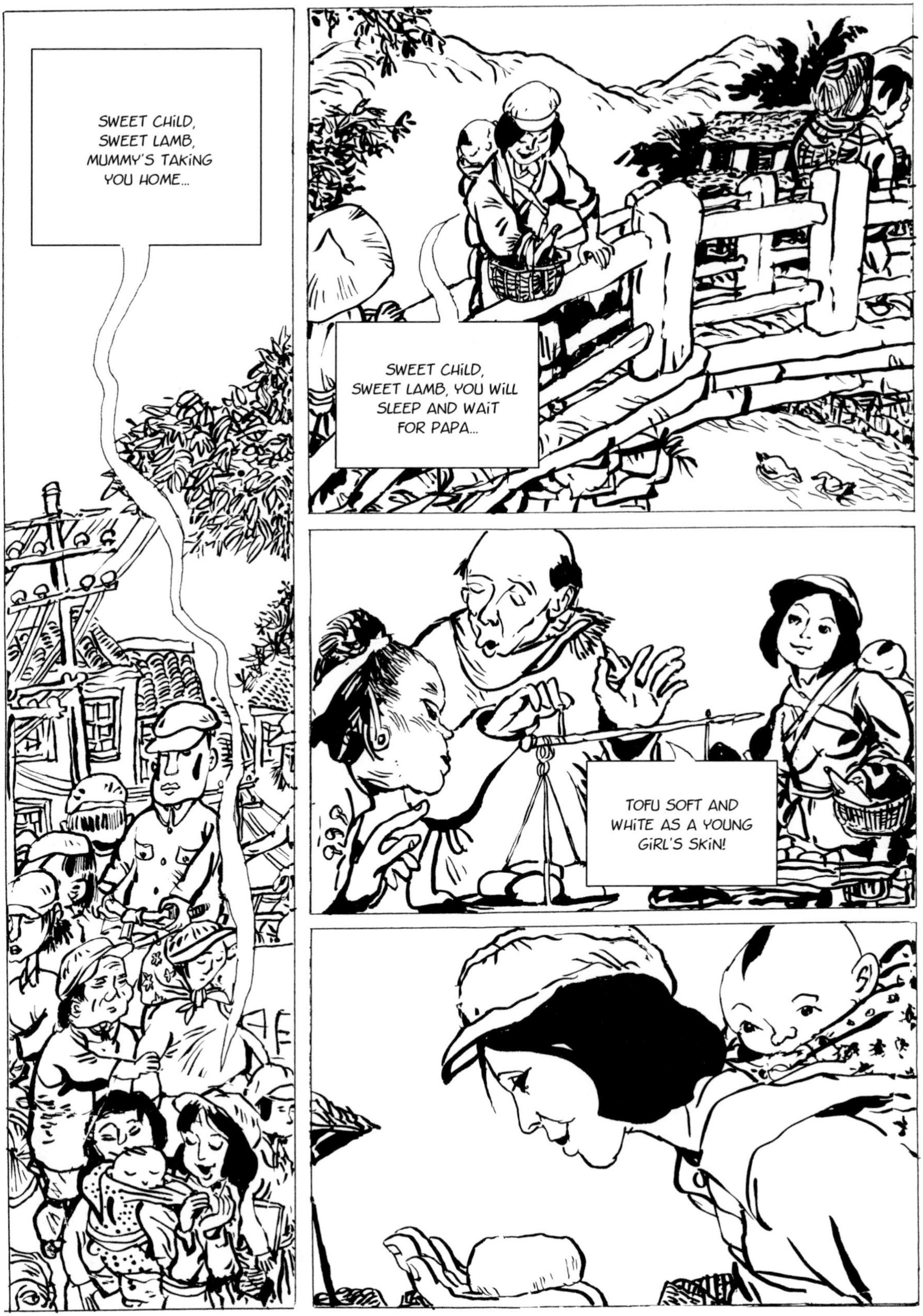
SWEET CHILD, SWEET LAMB, MUMMY'S TAKING YOU HOME...
SWEET CHILD, SWEET LAMB, YOU WILL SLEEP AND WAIT FOR PAPA...
TOFU SOFT AND WHITE AS A YOUNG GIRL'S SKIN!

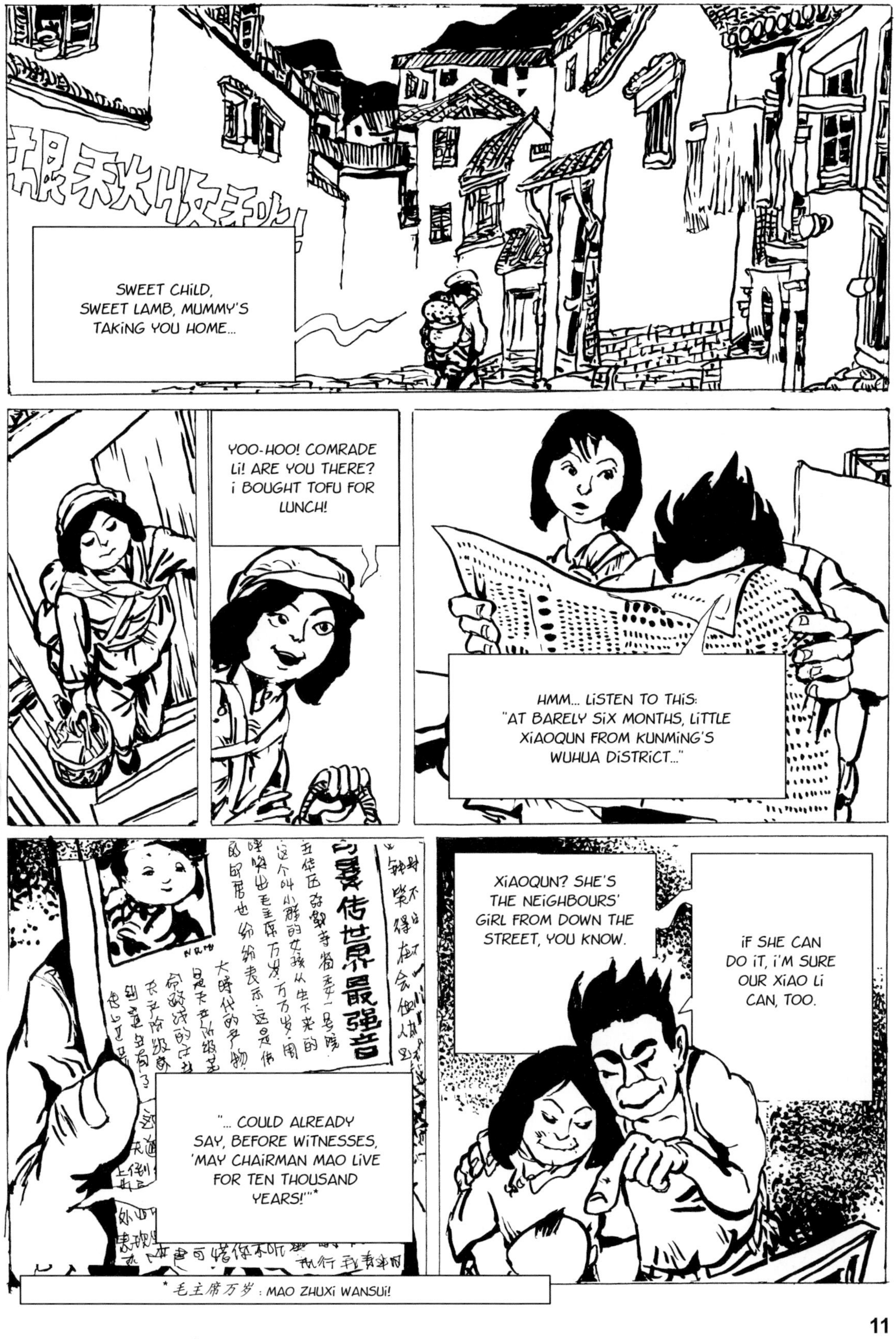
SWEET CHILD, SWEET LAMB, MUMMY'S TAKING YOU HOME...
YOO-HOO! COMRADE LI! ARE YOU THERE? I BOUGHT TOFU FOR LUNCH!
HMM... LISTEN TO THIS: "AT BARELY SIX MONTHS, LITTLE XIAOQUN FROM KUNMING'S WUHUA DISTRICT..."
"... COULD ALREADY SAY, BEFORE WITNESSES, 'MAY CHAIRMAN MAO LIVE FOR TEN THOUSAND YEARS!'"*
XIAOQUN? SHE'S THE NEIGHBOURS' GIRL FROM DOWN THE STREET, YOU KNOW.
IF SHE CAN DO IT, I'M SURE OUR XIAO LI CAN, TOO.

* 毛主席万岁 : MAO ZHUXI WANSUI!

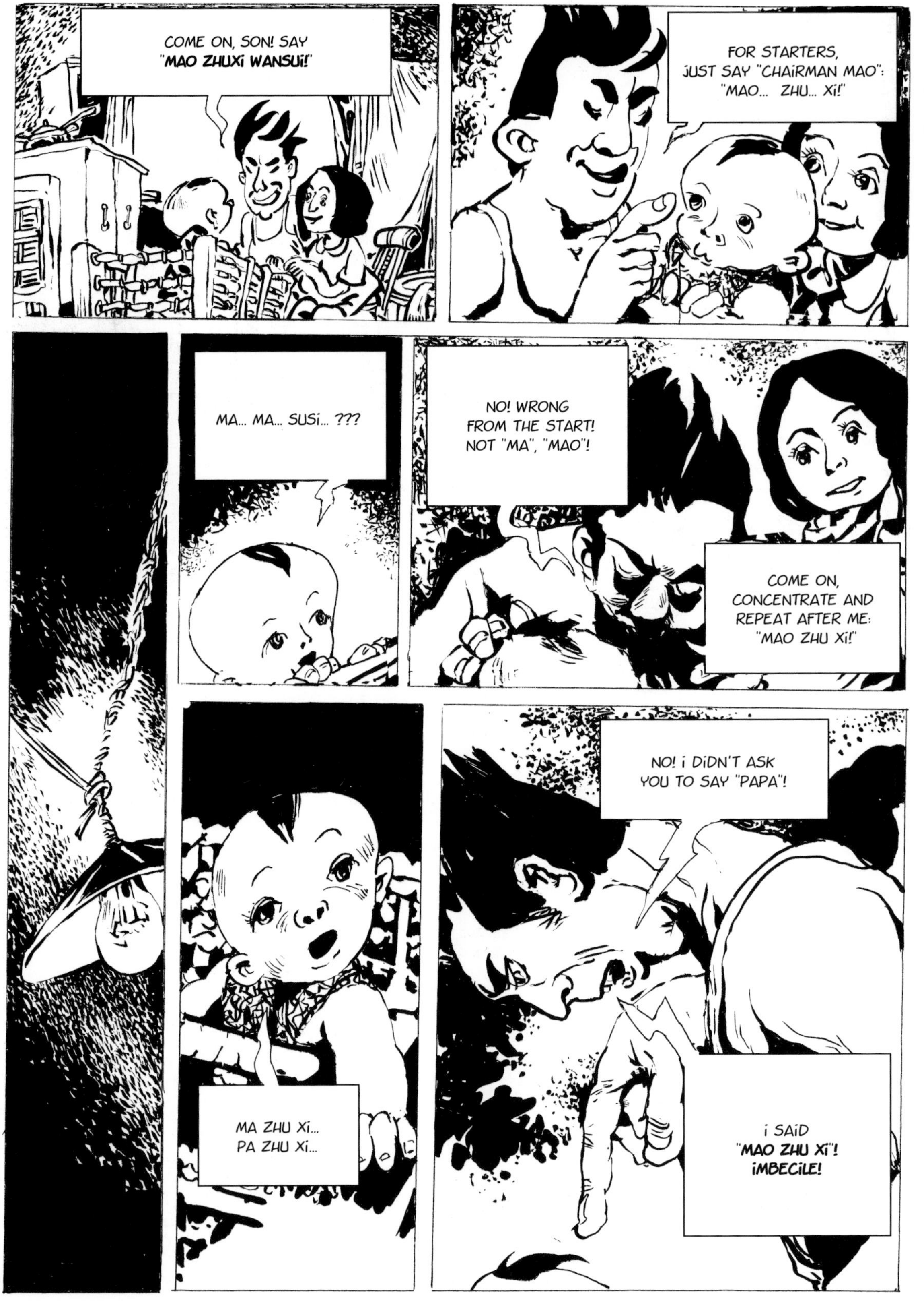
COME ON, SON! SAY "MAO ZHUXi WANSUi!"
FOR STARTERS, JUST SAY "CHAiRMAN MAO": "MAO... ZHU... Xi!"
MA... MA... SUSi... ???
NO! WRONG FROM THE START! NOT "MA", "MAO"!
COME ON, CONCENTRATE AND REPEAT AFTER ME: "MAO ZHU Xi!"
MA ZHU Xi... PA ZHU Xi...
NO! i DiDN'T ASK YOU TO SAY "PAPA"!
i SAiD "MAO ZHU Xi"! iMBECiLE!

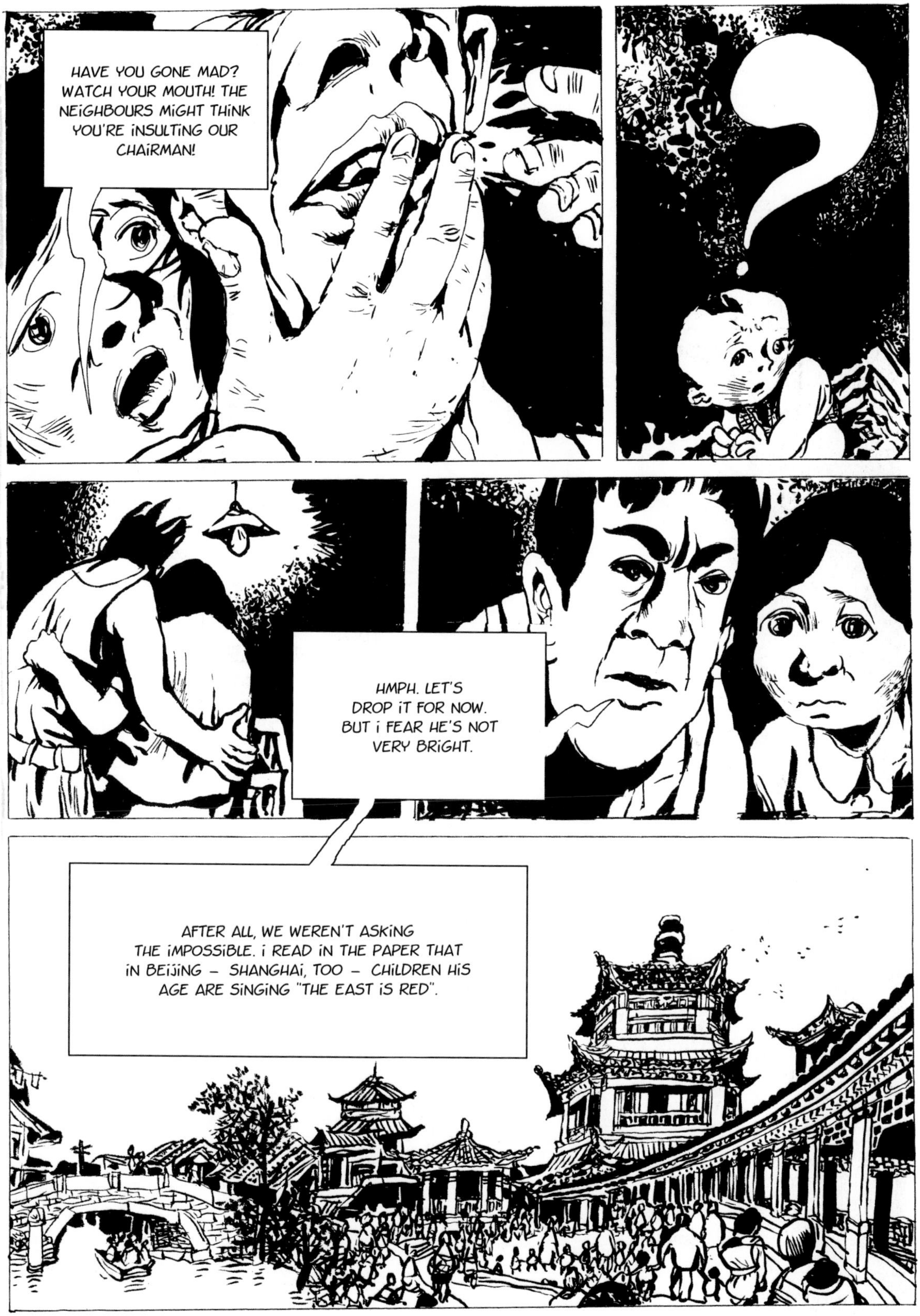
HAVE YOU GONE MAD? WATCH YOUR MOUTH! THE NEIGHBOURS MIGHT THINK YOU'RE INSULTING OUR CHAIRMAN!
?
HMPH. LET'S DROP IT FOR NOW. BUT I FEAR HE'S NOT VERY BRIGHT.
AFTER ALL, WE WEREN'T ASKING THE IMPOSSIBLE. I READ IN THE PAPER THAT IN BEIJING – SHANGHAI, TOO – CHILDREN HIS AGE ARE SINGING "THE EAST IS RED".

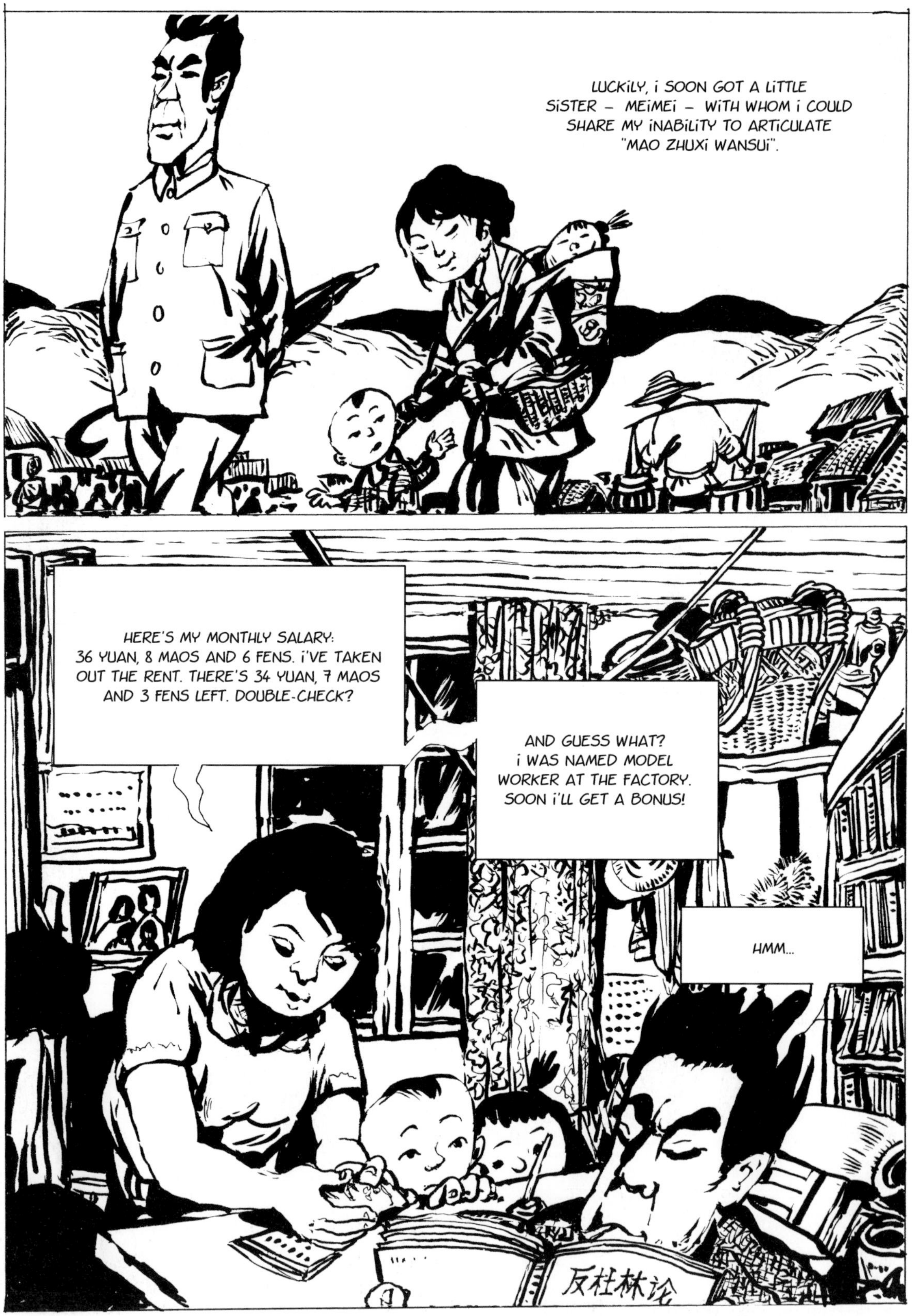
LUCKiLY, i SOON GOT A LiTTLE SiSTER – MEiMEi – WiTH WHOM i COULD SHARE MY iNABiLiTY TO ARTiCULATE "MAO ZHUXi WANSUi".
HERE'S MY MONTHLY SALARY: 36 YUAN, 8 MAOS AND 6 FENS. i'VE TAKEN OUT THE RENT. THERE'S 34 YUAN, 7 MAOS AND 3 FENS LEFT. DOUBLE-CHECK?
AND GUESS WHAT? i WAS NAMED MODEL WORKER AT THE FACTORY. SOON i'LL GET A BONUS!
HMM...
反杜林论

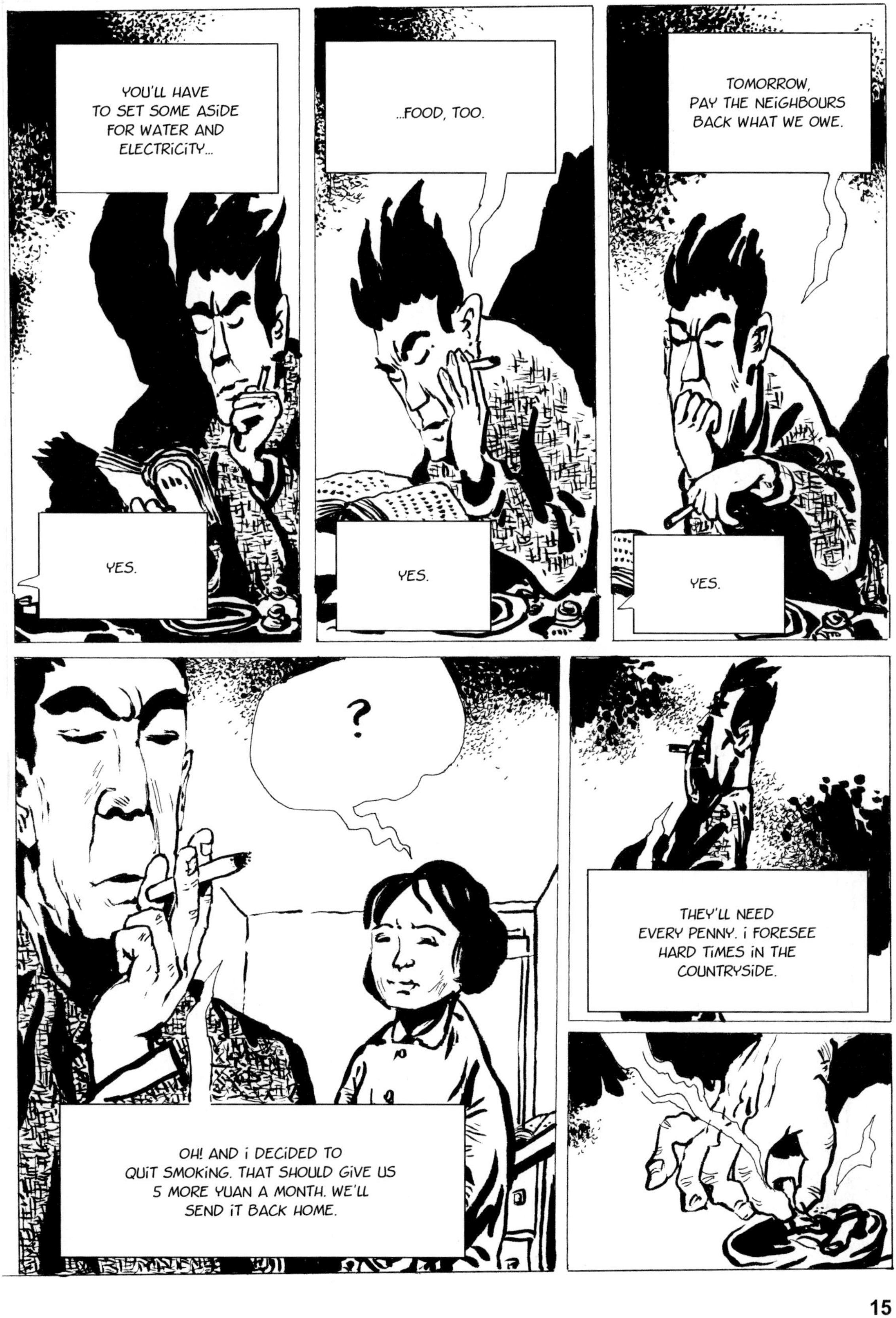
YOU'LL HAVE TO SET SOME ASIDE FOR WATER AND ELECTRICITY...
YES.
...FOOD, TOO.
YES.
TOMORROW, PAY THE NEIGHBOURS BACK WHAT WE OWE.
YES.
?
OH! AND I DECIDED TO QUIT SMOKING. THAT SHOULD GIVE US 5 MORE YUAN A MONTH. WE'LL SEND IT BACK HOME.
THEY'LL NEED EVERY PENNY. I FORESEE HARD TIMES IN THE COUNTRYSIDE.

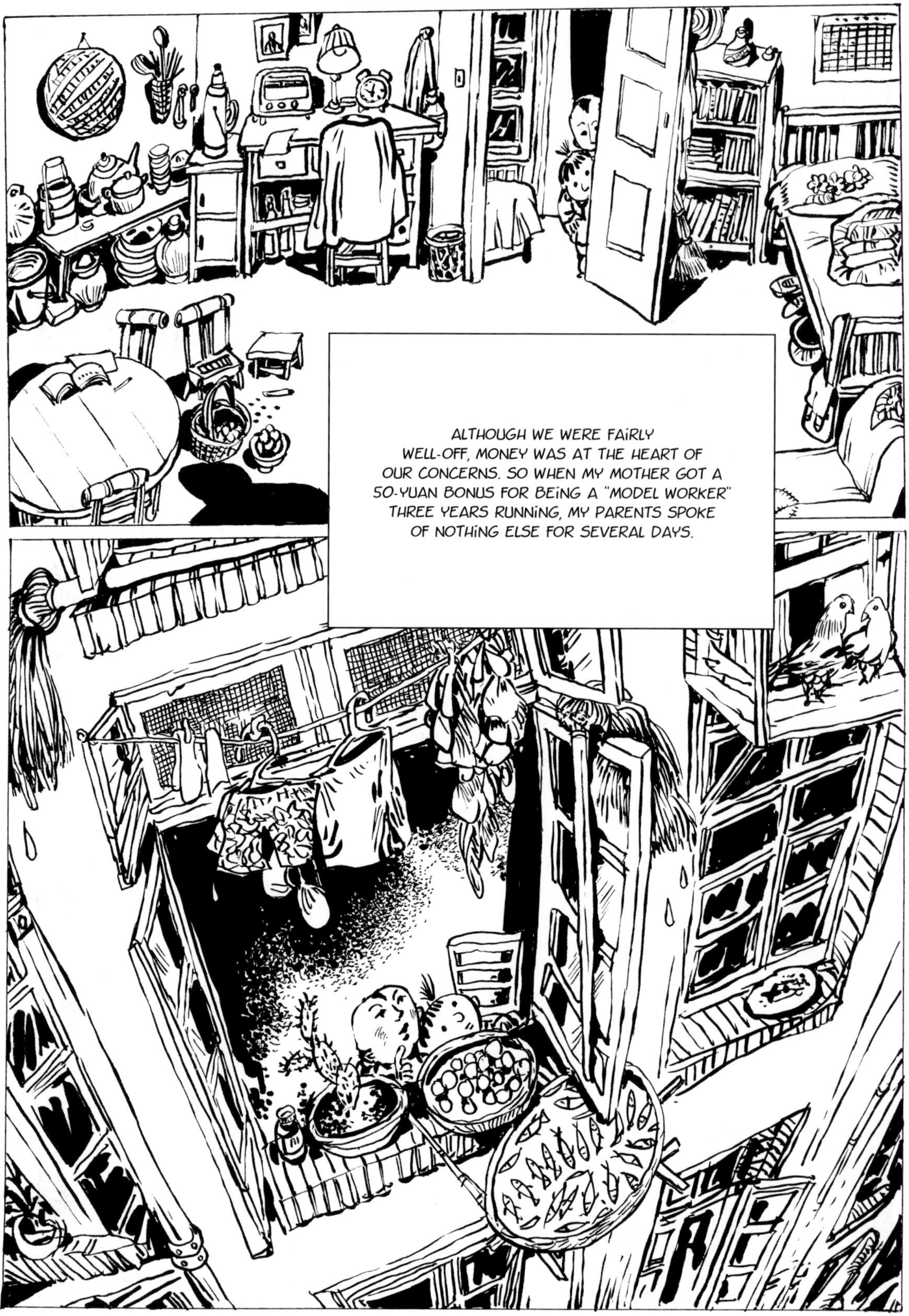
ALTHOUGH WE WERE FAIRLY WELL-OFF, MONEY WAS AT THE HEART OF OUR CONCERNS. SO WHEN MY MOTHER GOT A 50-YUAN BONUS FOR BEING A "MODEL WORKER" THREE YEARS RUNNING, MY PARENTS SPOKE OF NOTHING ELSE FOR SEVERAL DAYS.

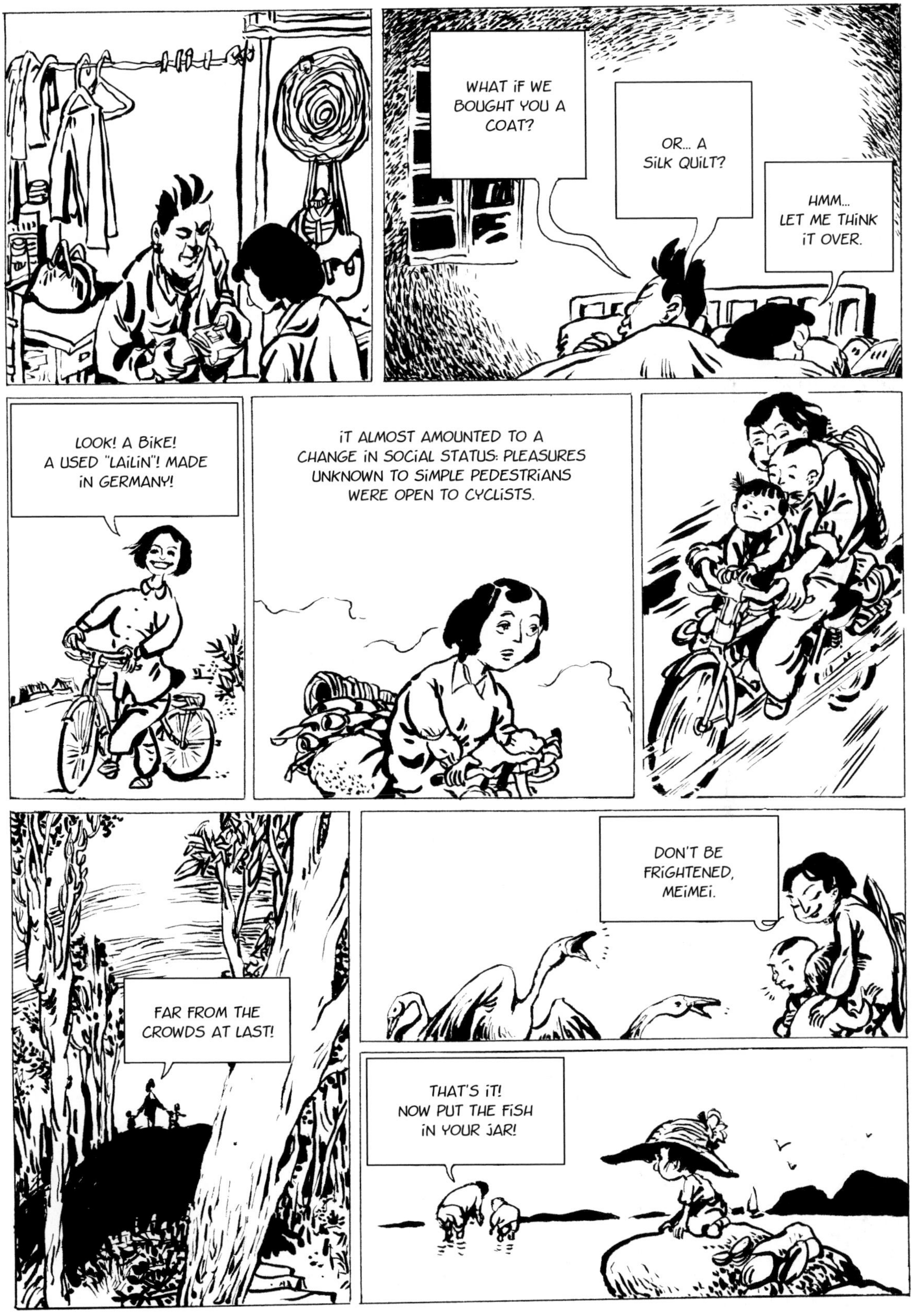
WHAT IF WE BOUGHT YOU A COAT?
OR... A SILK QUILT?
HMM... LET ME THINK IT OVER.
LOOK! A BIKE! A USED "LAILIN"! MADE IN GERMANY!
IT ALMOST AMOUNTED TO A CHANGE IN SOCIAL STATUS: PLEASURES UNKNOWN TO SIMPLE PEDESTRIANS WERE OPEN TO CYCLISTS.
FAR FROM THE CROWDS AT LAST!
DON'T BE FRIGHTENED, MEIMEI.
THAT'S IT! NOW PUT THE FISH IN YOUR JAR!

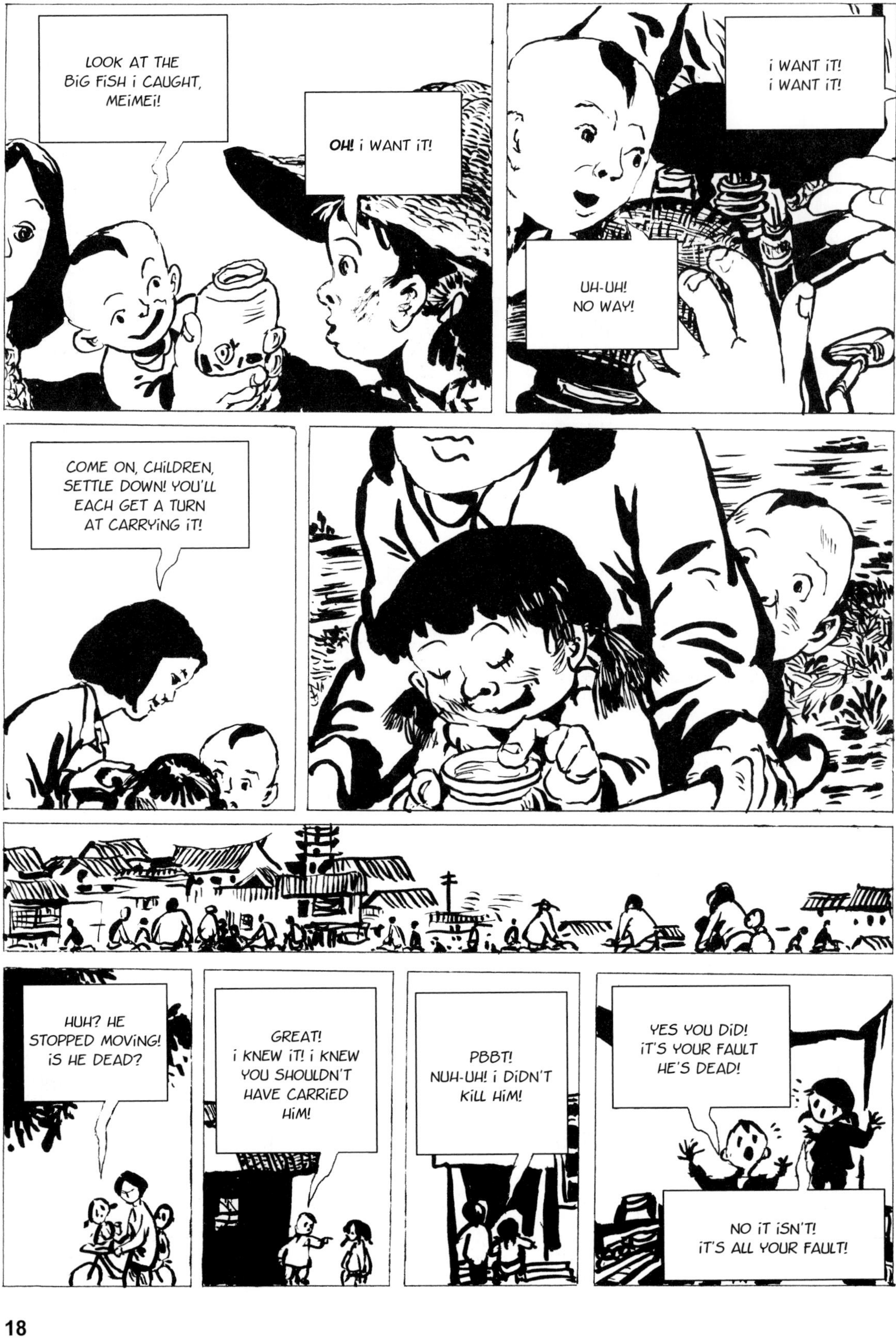
LOOK AT THE BIG FISH i CAUGHT, MEiMEi!
OH! i WANT iT!
i WANT iT! i WANT iT!
UH-UH! NO WAY!
COME ON, CHiLDREN, SETTLE DOWN! YOU'LL EACH GET A TURN AT CARRYiNG iT!
HUH? HE STOPPED MOViNG! iS HE DEAD?
GREAT! i KNEW iT! i KNEW YOU SHOULDN'T HAVE CARRiED HiM!
PBBT! NUH-UH! i DiDN'T KiLL HiM!
YES YOU DiD! iT'S YOUR FAULT HE'S DEAD!
NO iT iSN'T! iT'S ALL YOUR FAULT!

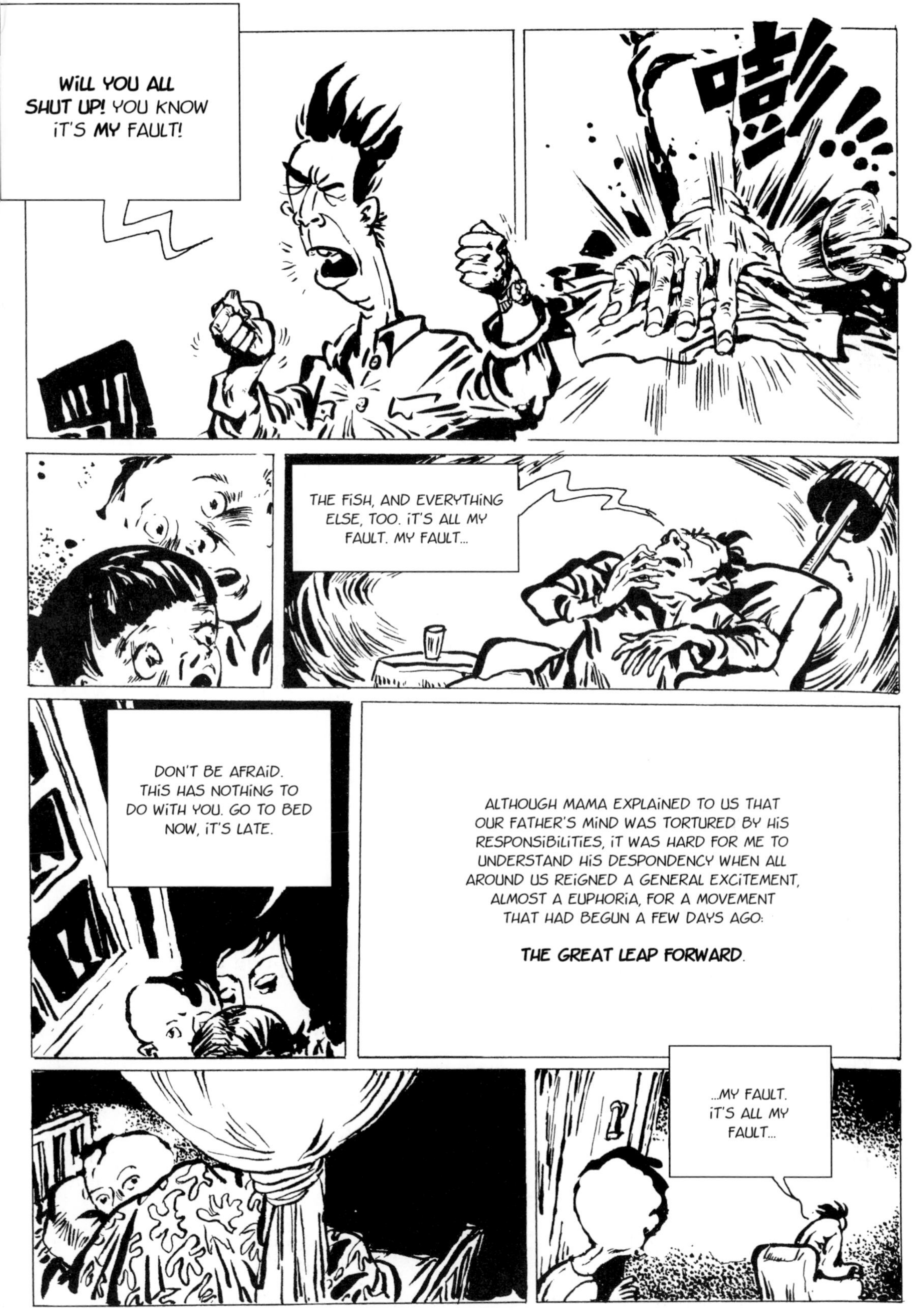
WILL YOU ALL SHUT UP! YOU KNOW IT'S MY FAULT!
THE FISH, AND EVERYTHING ELSE, TOO. IT'S ALL MY FAULT. MY FAULT...
DON'T BE AFRAID. THIS HAS NOTHING TO DO WITH YOU. GO TO BED NOW, IT'S LATE.
ALTHOUGH MAMA EXPLAINED TO US THAT OUR FATHER'S MIND WAS TORTURED BY HIS RESPONSIBILITIES, IT WAS HARD FOR ME TO UNDERSTAND HIS DESPONDENCY WHEN ALL AROUND US REIGNED A GENERAL EXCITEMENT, ALMOST A EUPHORIA, FOR A MOVEMENT THAT HAD BEGUN A FEW DAYS AGO:
THE GREAT LEAP FORWARD.
...MY FAULT. IT'S ALL MY FAULT...

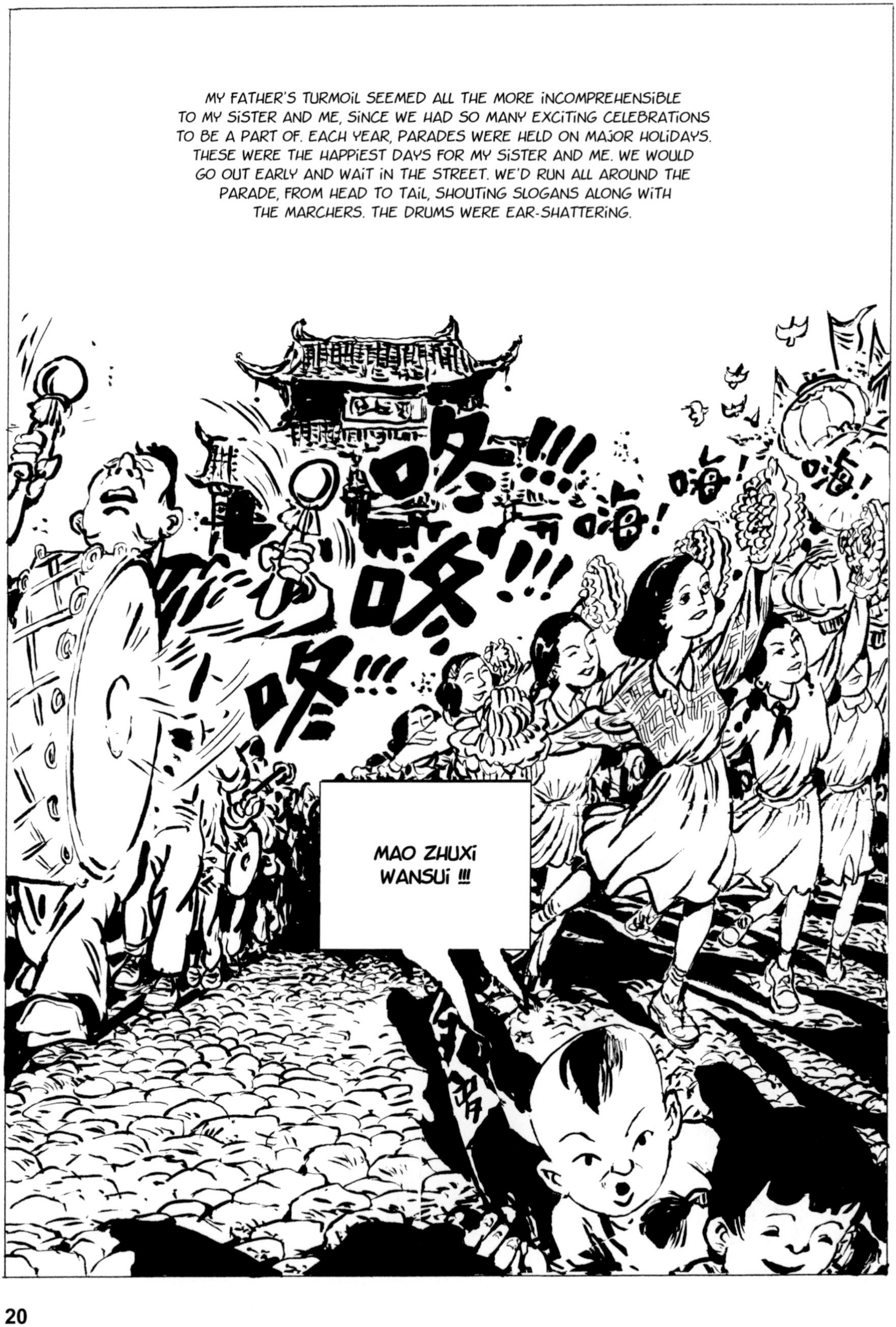
MY FATHER'S TURMOIL SEEMED ALL THE MORE INCOMPREHENSIBLE TO MY SISTER AND ME, SINCE WE HAD SO MANY EXCITING CELEBRATIONS TO BE A PART OF. EACH YEAR, PARADES WERE HELD ON MAJOR HOLIDAYS. THESE WERE THE HAPPIEST DAYS FOR MY SISTER AND ME. WE WOULD GO OUT EARLY AND WAIT IN THE STREET. WE'D RUN ALL AROUND THE PARADE, FROM HEAD TO TAIL, SHOUTING SLOGANS ALONG WITH THE MARCHERS. THE DRUMS WERE EAR-SHATTERING.
咚!!!
咚!!!
咚!!!
嗨!
嗨!
嗨!
MAO ZHUXI WANSUI !!!

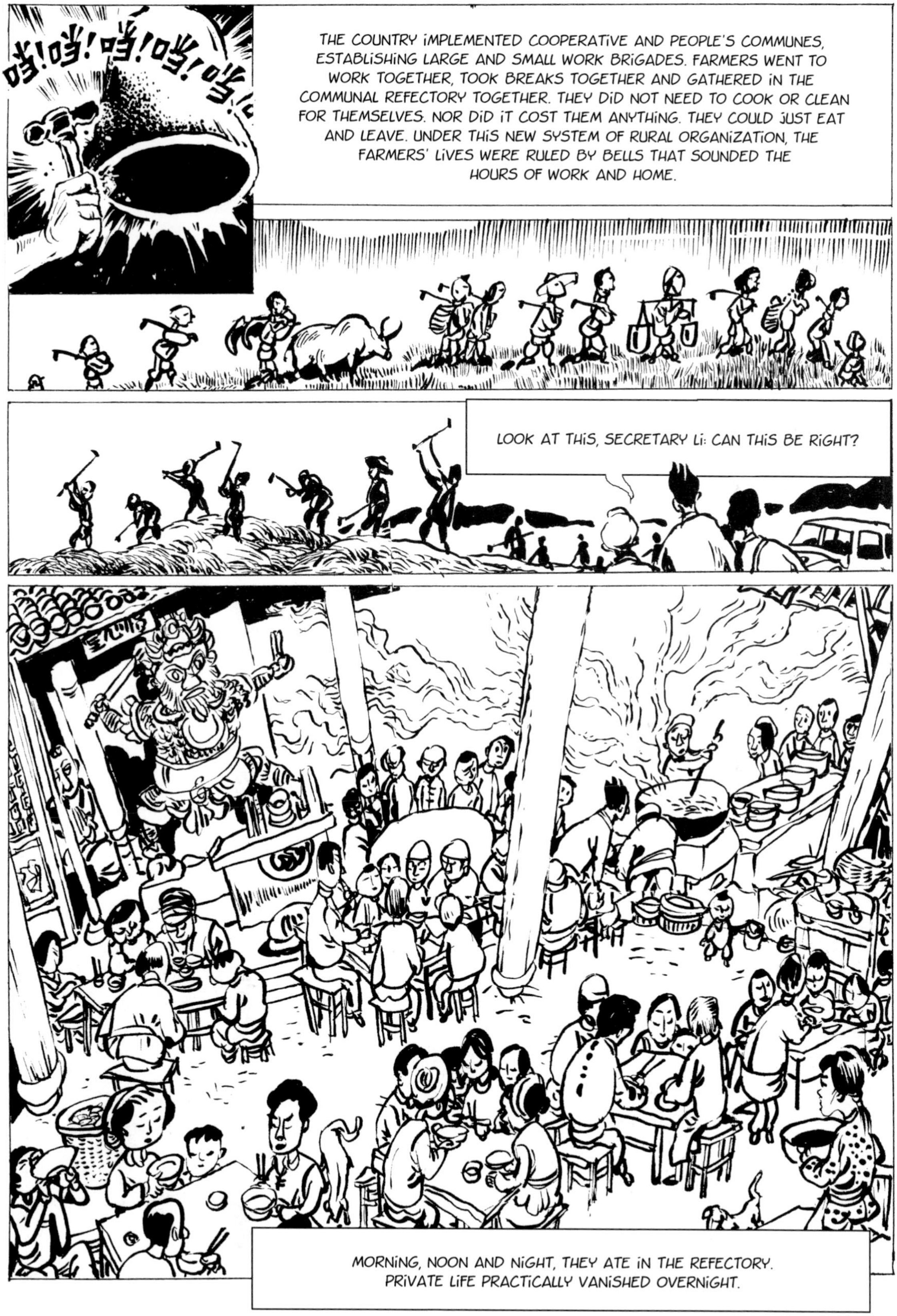
THE COUNTRY IMPLEMENTED COOPERATIVE AND PEOPLE'S COMMUNES, ESTABLISHING LARGE AND SMALL WORK BRIGADES. FARMERS WENT TO WORK TOGETHER, TOOK BREAKS TOGETHER AND GATHERED IN THE COMMUNAL REFECTORY TOGETHER. THEY DID NOT NEED TO COOK OR CLEAN FOR THEMSELVES. NOR DID IT COST THEM ANYTHING. THEY COULD JUST EAT AND LEAVE. UNDER THIS NEW SYSTEM OF RURAL ORGANIZATION, THE FARMERS' LIVES WERE RULED BY BELLS THAT SOUNDED THE HOURS OF WORK AND HOME.
LOOK AT THIS, SECRETARY LI: CAN THIS BE RIGHT?
MORNING, NOON AND NIGHT, THEY ATE IN THE REFECTORY. PRIVATE LIFE PRACTICALLY VANISHED OVERNIGHT.

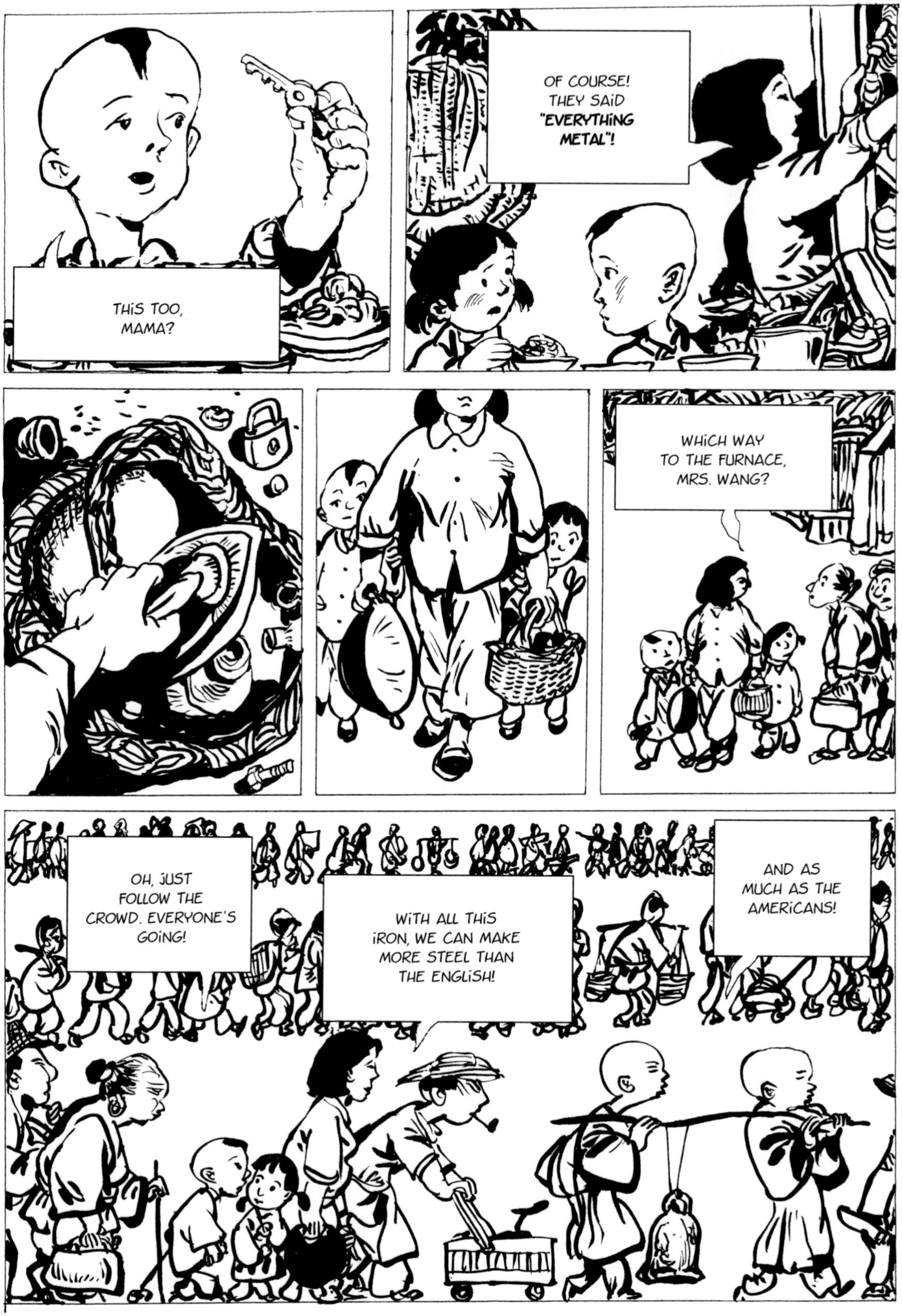
THIS TOO, MAMA?
OF COURSE! THEY SAID **"EVERYTHING METAL"!**
WHICH WAY TO THE FURNACE, MRS. WANG?
OH, JUST FOLLOW THE CROWD. EVERYONE'S GOING!
WITH ALL THIS IRON, WE CAN MAKE MORE STEEL THAN THE ENGLISH!
AND AS MUCH AS THE AMERICANS!

THIS WAS NO LITTLE LEAP, BUT A **GREAT** LEAP FORWARD. WE HAD **GREAT GOALS**.
FIRST AMONG THEM WAS FOR OUR STEEL PRODUCTION TO **"BEAT THE BRITS AND CATCH UP WITH THE AMERICANS."**

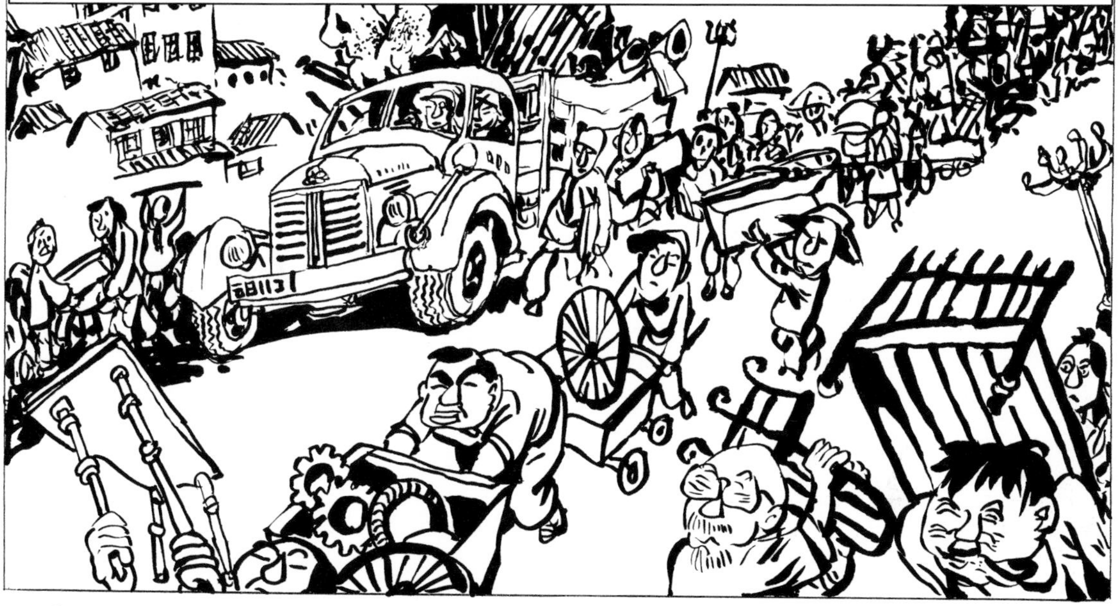

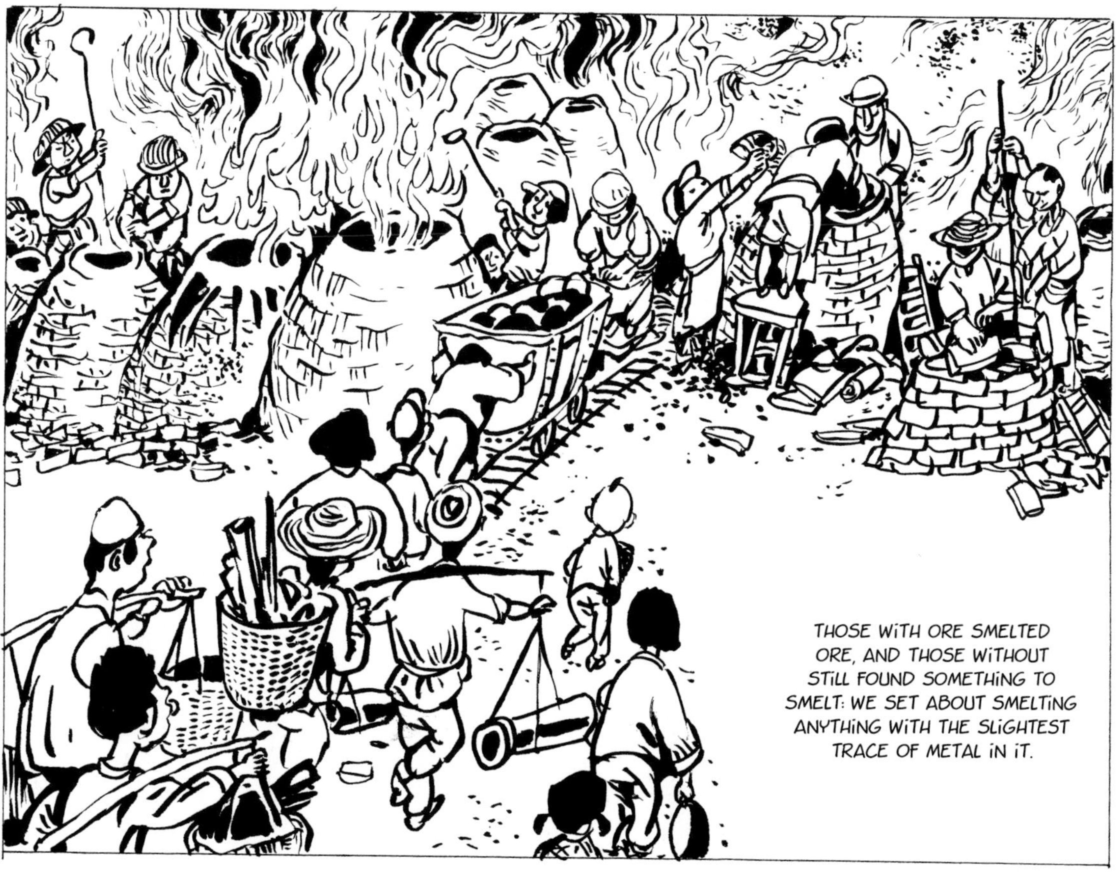
THOSE WITH ORE SMELTED ORE, AND THOSE WITHOUT STILL FOUND SOMETHING TO SMELT: WE SET ABOUT SMELTING ANYTHING WITH THE SLIGHTEST TRACE OF METAL IN IT.

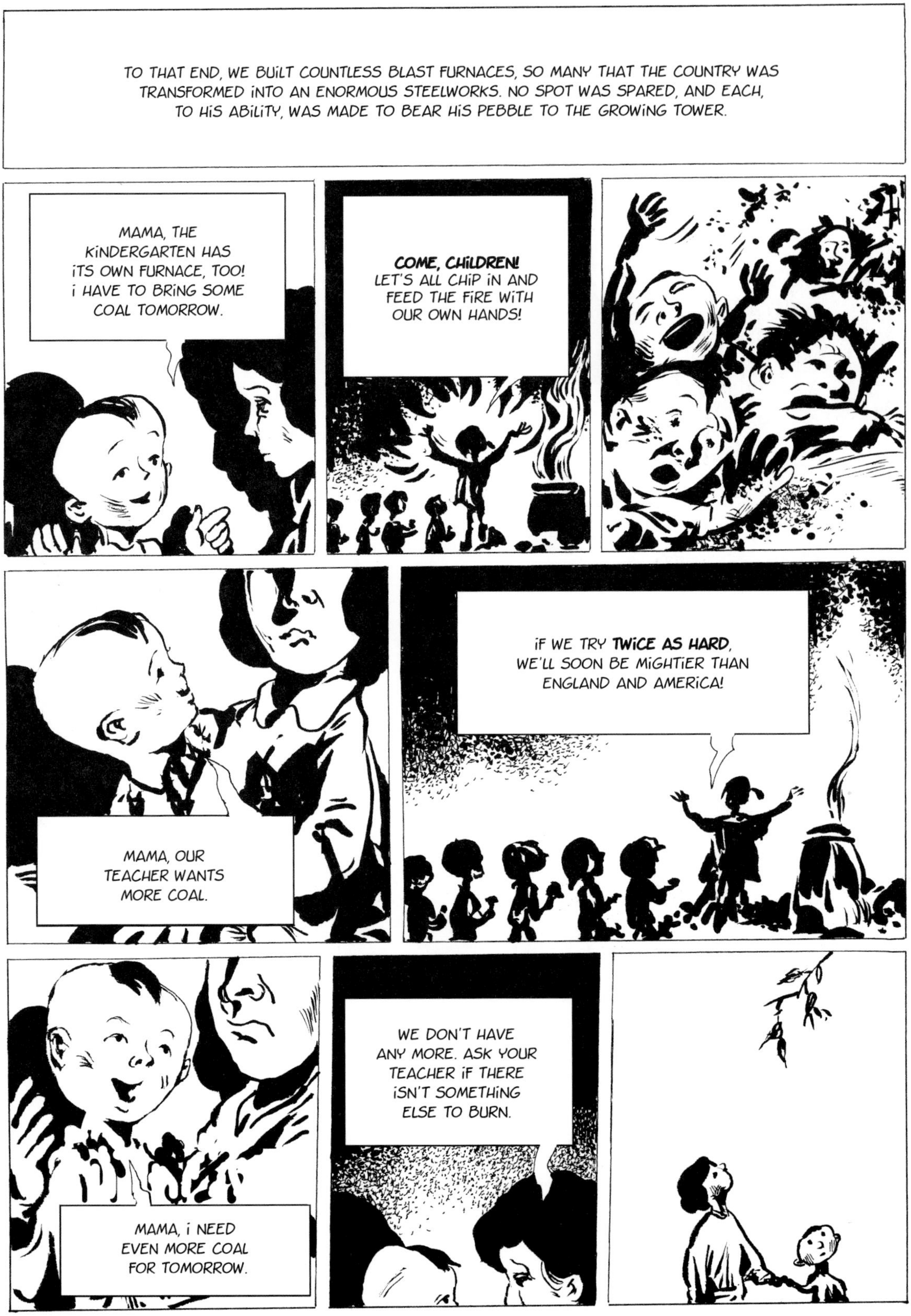
TO THAT END, WE BUILT COUNTLESS BLAST FURNACES, SO MANY THAT THE COUNTRY WAS TRANSFORMED INTO AN ENORMOUS STEELWORKS. NO SPOT WAS SPARED, AND EACH, TO HIS ABILITY, WAS MADE TO BEAR HIS PEBBLE TO THE GROWING TOWER.
MAMA, THE KINDERGARTEN HAS ITS OWN FURNACE, TOO! I HAVE TO BRING SOME COAL TOMORROW.
COME, CHILDREN! LET'S ALL CHIP IN AND FEED THE FIRE WITH OUR OWN HANDS!
MAMA, OUR TEACHER WANTS MORE COAL.
IF WE TRY **TWICE AS HARD**, WE'LL SOON BE MIGHTIER THAN ENGLAND AND AMERICA!
MAMA, I NEED EVEN MORE COAL FOR TOMORROW.
WE DON'T HAVE ANY MORE. ASK YOUR TEACHER IF THERE ISN'T SOMETHING ELSE TO BURN.

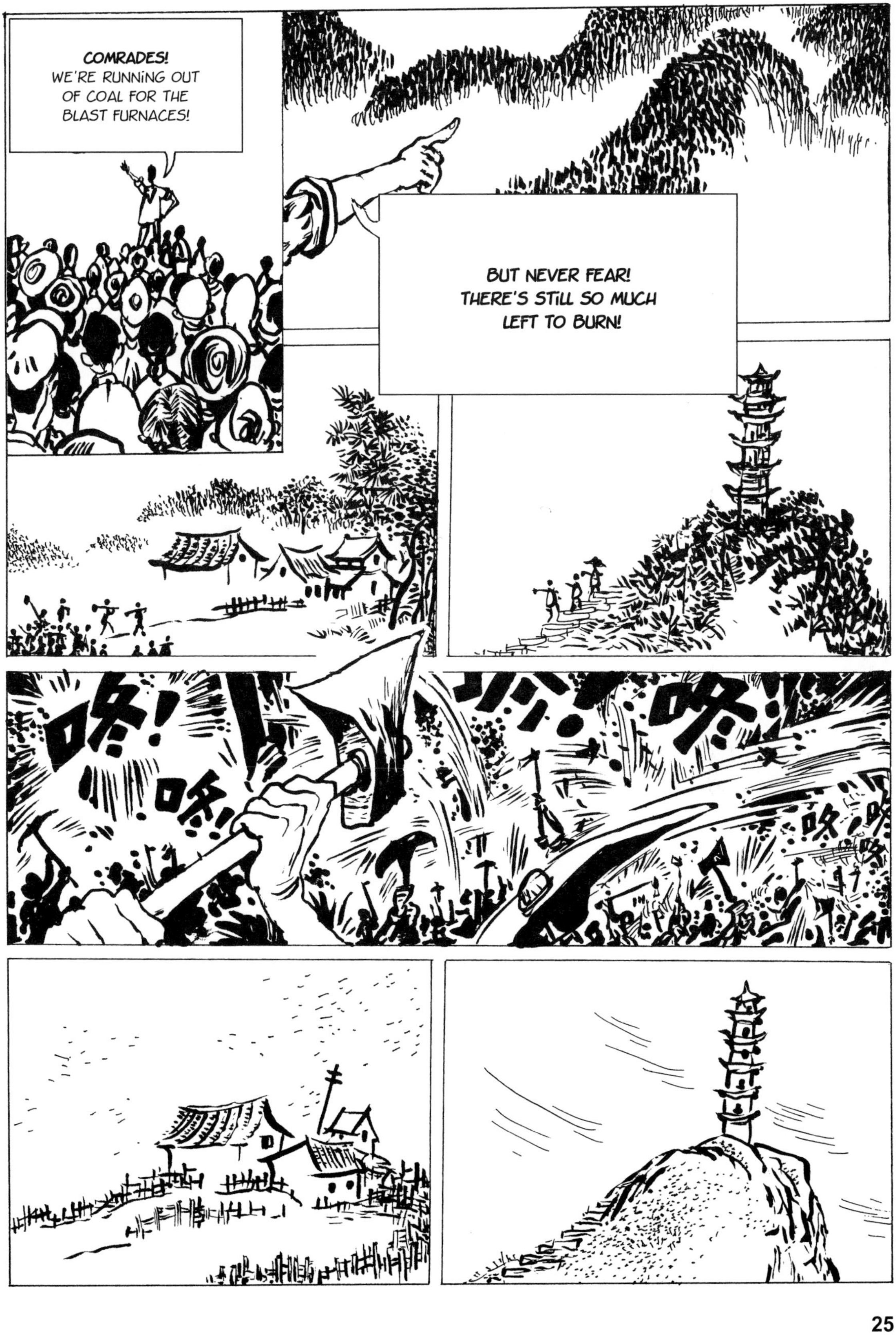
COMRADES!
WE'RE RUNNING OUT OF COAL FOR THE BLAST FURNACES!
BUT NEVER FEAR! THERE'S STILL SO MUCH LEFT TO BURN!
咚!
咚!
咚!

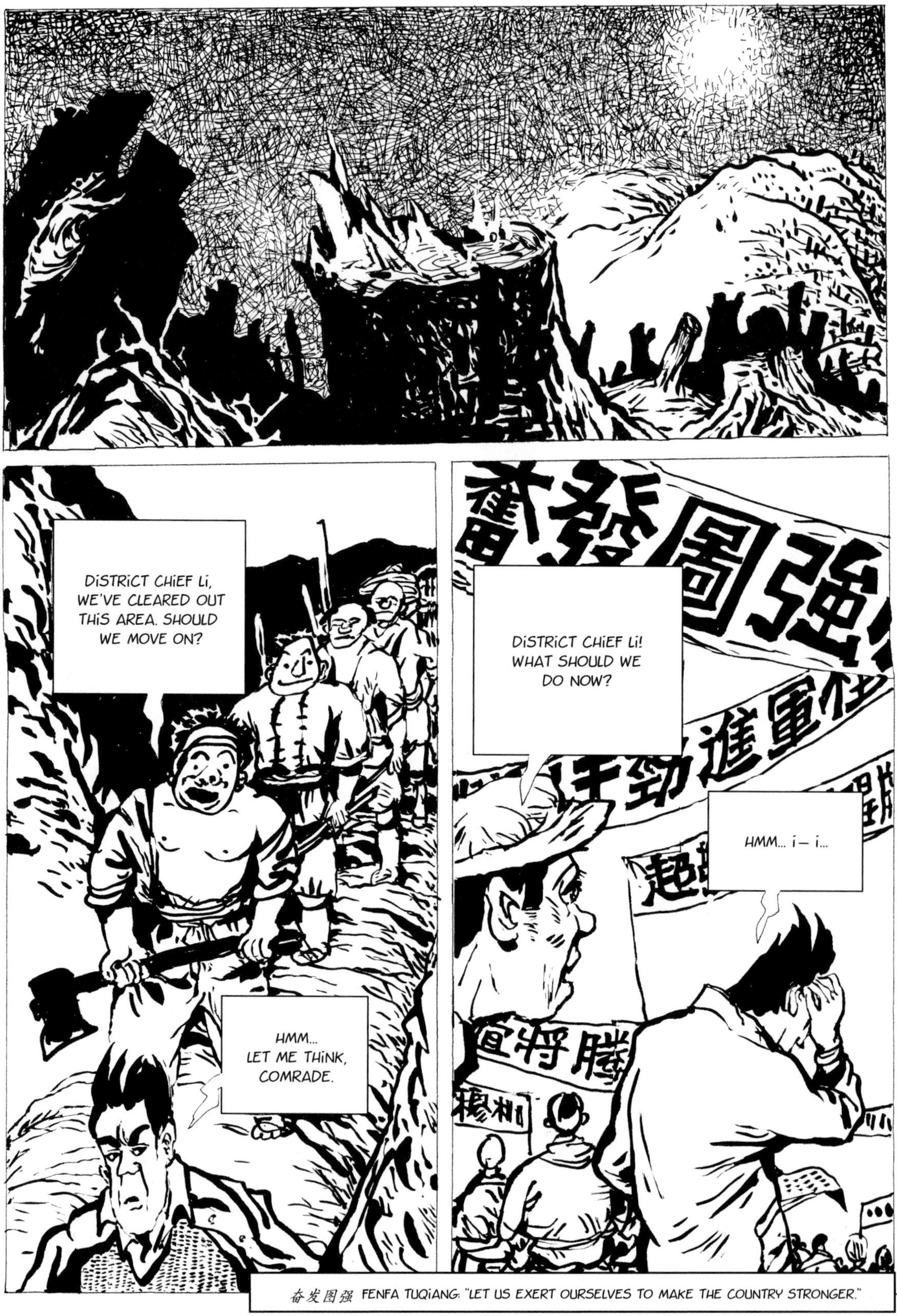
DISTRICT CHIEF LI, WE'VE CLEARED OUT THIS AREA. SHOULD WE MOVE ON?
HMM... LET ME THINK, COMRADE.
奮發圖強
DISTRICT CHIEF LI! WHAT SHOULD WE DO NOW?
HMM... I– I...

奋发图强 FENFA TUQIANG: "LET US EXERT OURSELVES TO MAKE THE COUNTRY STRONGER."

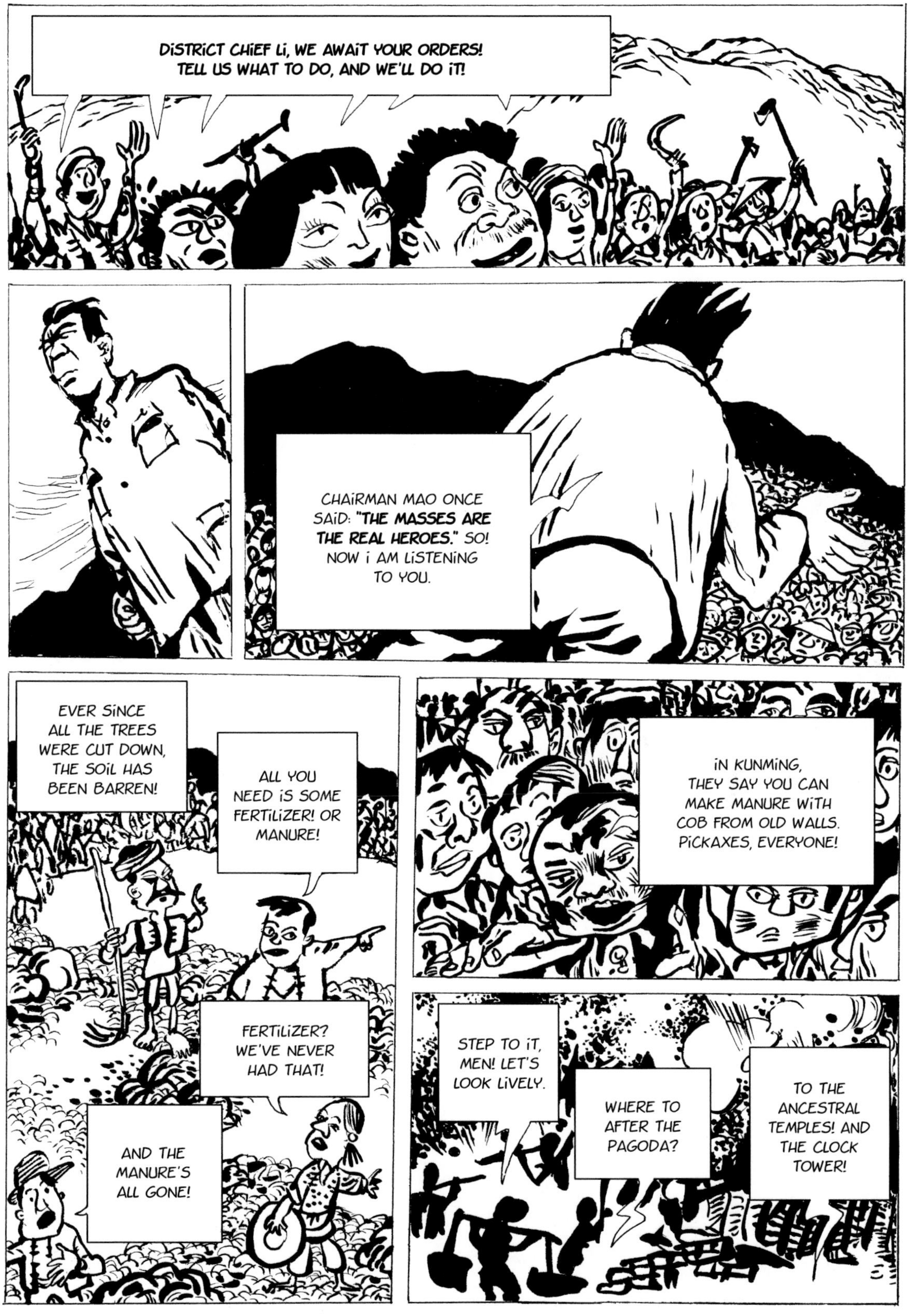
DISTRICT CHIEF LI, WE AWAIT YOUR ORDERS! TELL US WHAT TO DO, AND WE'LL DO IT!
CHAIRMAN MAO ONCE SAID: "THE MASSES ARE THE REAL HEROES." SO! NOW I AM LISTENING TO YOU.
EVER SINCE ALL THE TREES WERE CUT DOWN, THE SOIL HAS BEEN BARREN!
ALL YOU NEED IS SOME FERTILIZER! OR MANURE!
FERTILIZER? WE'VE NEVER HAD THAT!
AND THE MANURE'S ALL GONE!
IN KUNMING, THEY SAY YOU CAN MAKE MANURE WITH COB FROM OLD WALLS. PICKAXES, EVERYONE!
STEP TO IT, MEN! LET'S LOOK LIVELY.
WHERE TO AFTER THE PAGODA?
TO THE ANCESTRAL TEMPLES! AND THE CLOCK TOWER!

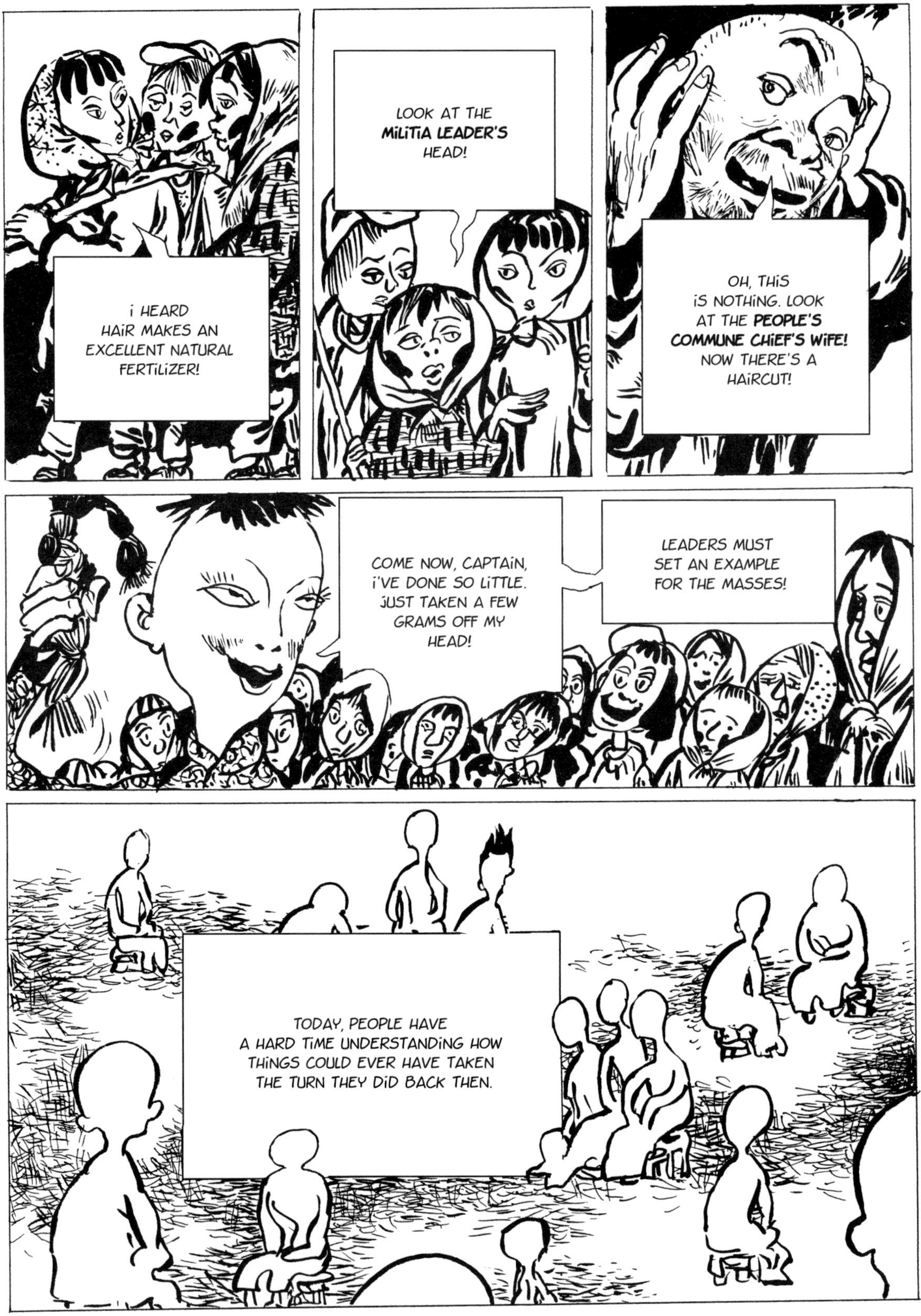
I HEARD HAIR MAKES AN EXCELLENT NATURAL FERTILIZER!
LOOK AT THE MILITIA LEADER'S HEAD!
OH, THIS IS NOTHING. LOOK AT THE PEOPLE'S COMMUNE CHIEF'S WIFE! NOW THERE'S A HAIRCUT!
COME NOW, CAPTAIN, I'VE DONE SO LITTLE. JUST TAKEN A FEW GRAMS OFF MY HEAD!
LEADERS MUST SET AN EXAMPLE FOR THE MASSES!
TODAY, PEOPLE HAVE A HARD TIME UNDERSTANDING HOW THINGS COULD EVER HAVE TAKEN THE TURN THEY DID BACK THEN.

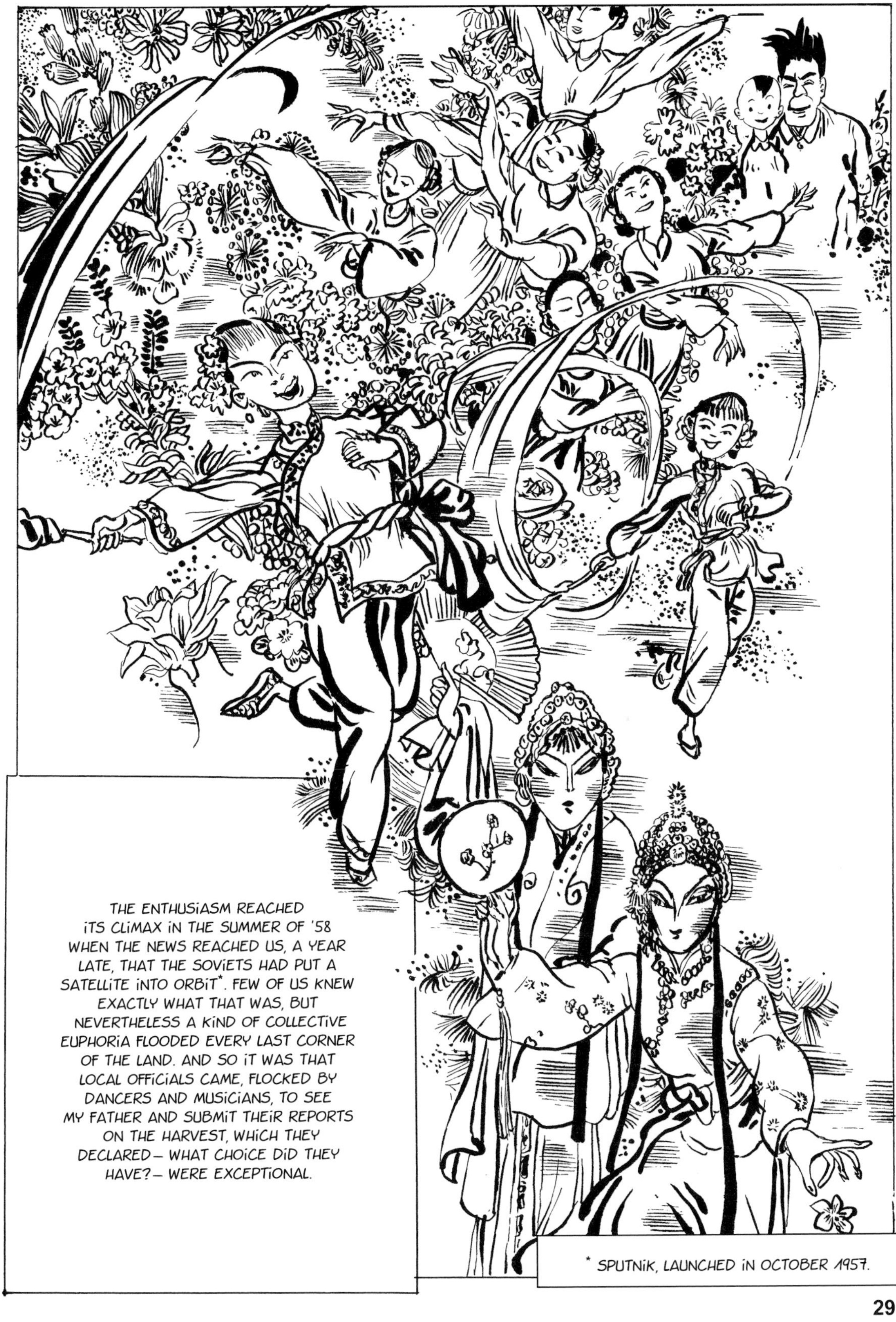
THE ENTHUSIASM REACHED ITS CLIMAX IN THE SUMMER OF '58 WHEN THE NEWS REACHED US, A YEAR LATE, THAT THE SOVIETS HAD PUT A SATELLITE INTO ORBIT*. FEW OF US KNEW EXACTLY WHAT THAT WAS, BUT NEVERTHELESS A KIND OF COLLECTIVE EUPHORIA FLOODED EVERY LAST CORNER OF THE LAND. AND SO IT WAS THAT LOCAL OFFICIALS CAME, FLOCKED BY DANCERS AND MUSICIANS, TO SEE MY FATHER AND SUBMIT THEIR REPORTS ON THE HARVEST, WHICH THEY DECLARED– WHAT CHOICE DID THEY HAVE?– WERE EXCEPTIONAL.
* SPUTNIK, LAUNCHED IN OCTOBER 1957.

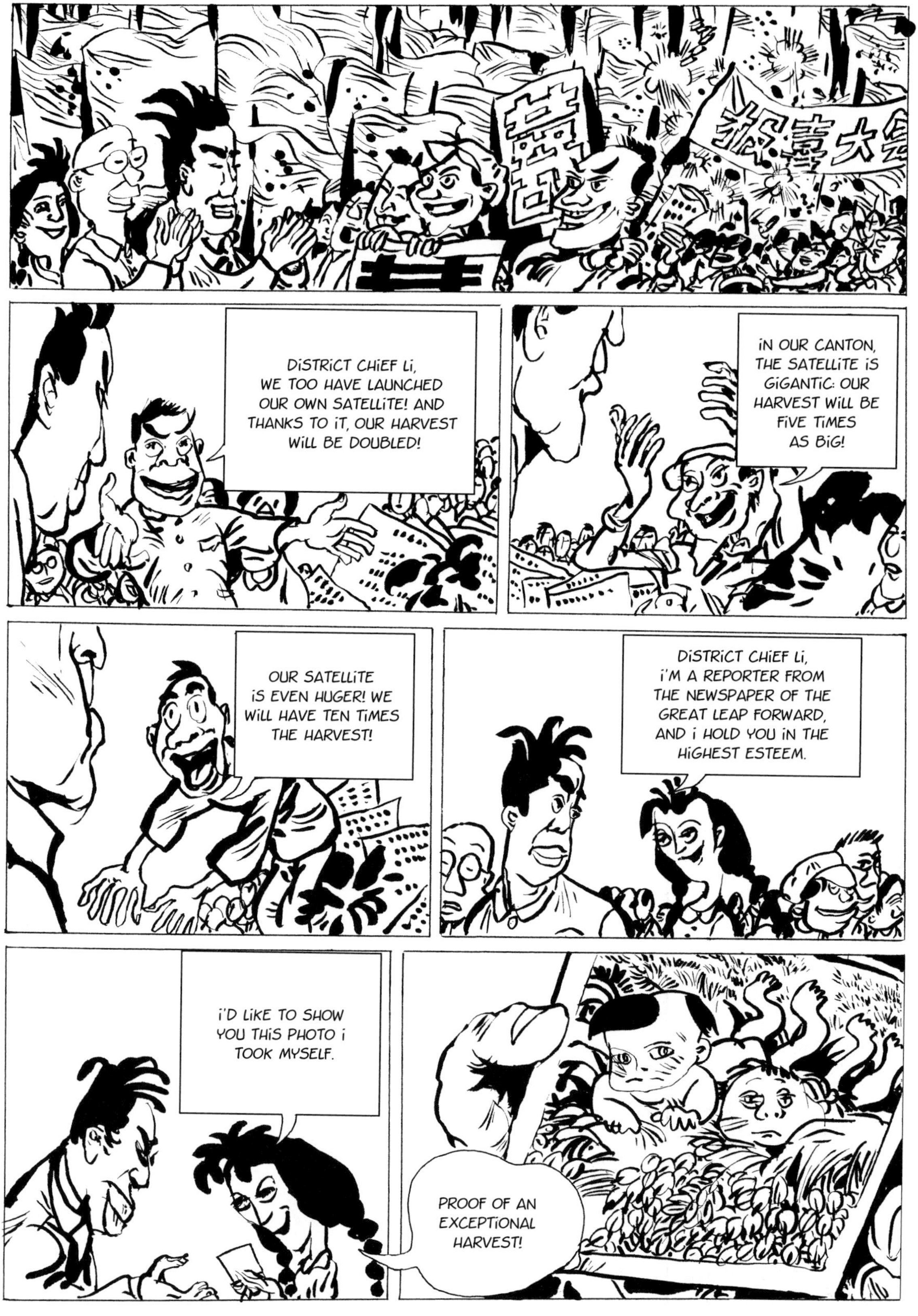
DISTRICT CHIEF LI, WE TOO HAVE LAUNCHED OUR OWN SATELLITE! AND THANKS TO IT, OUR HARVEST WILL BE DOUBLED!
IN OUR CANTON, THE SATELLITE IS GIGANTIC: OUR HARVEST WILL BE FIVE TIMES AS BIG!
OUR SATELLITE IS EVEN HUGER! WE WILL HAVE TEN TIMES THE HARVEST!
DISTRICT CHIEF LI, I'M A REPORTER FROM THE NEWSPAPER OF THE GREAT LEAP FORWARD, AND I HOLD YOU IN THE HIGHEST ESTEEM.
I'D LIKE TO SHOW YOU THIS PHOTO I TOOK MYSELF.
PROOF OF AN EXCEPTIONAL HARVEST!

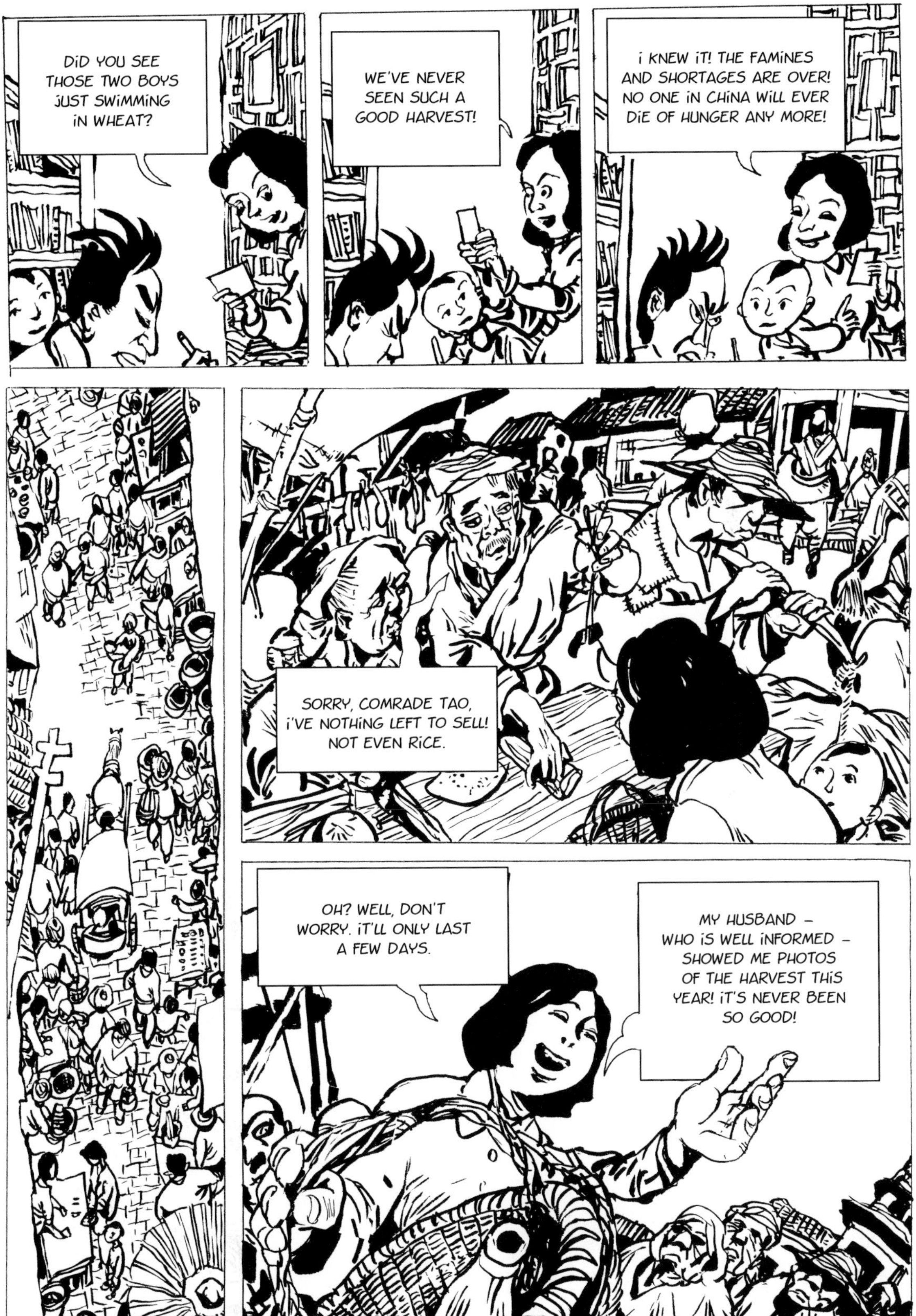
DID YOU SEE THOSE TWO BOYS JUST SWIMMING IN WHEAT?
WE'VE NEVER SEEN SUCH A GOOD HARVEST!
I KNEW IT! THE FAMINES AND SHORTAGES ARE OVER! NO ONE IN CHINA WILL EVER DIE OF HUNGER ANY MORE!
SORRY, COMRADE TAO, I'VE NOTHING LEFT TO SELL! NOT EVEN RICE.
OH? WELL, DON'T WORRY. IT'LL ONLY LAST A FEW DAYS.
MY HUSBAND – WHO IS WELL INFORMED – SHOWED ME PHOTOS OF THE HARVEST THIS YEAR! IT'S NEVER BEEN SO GOOD!

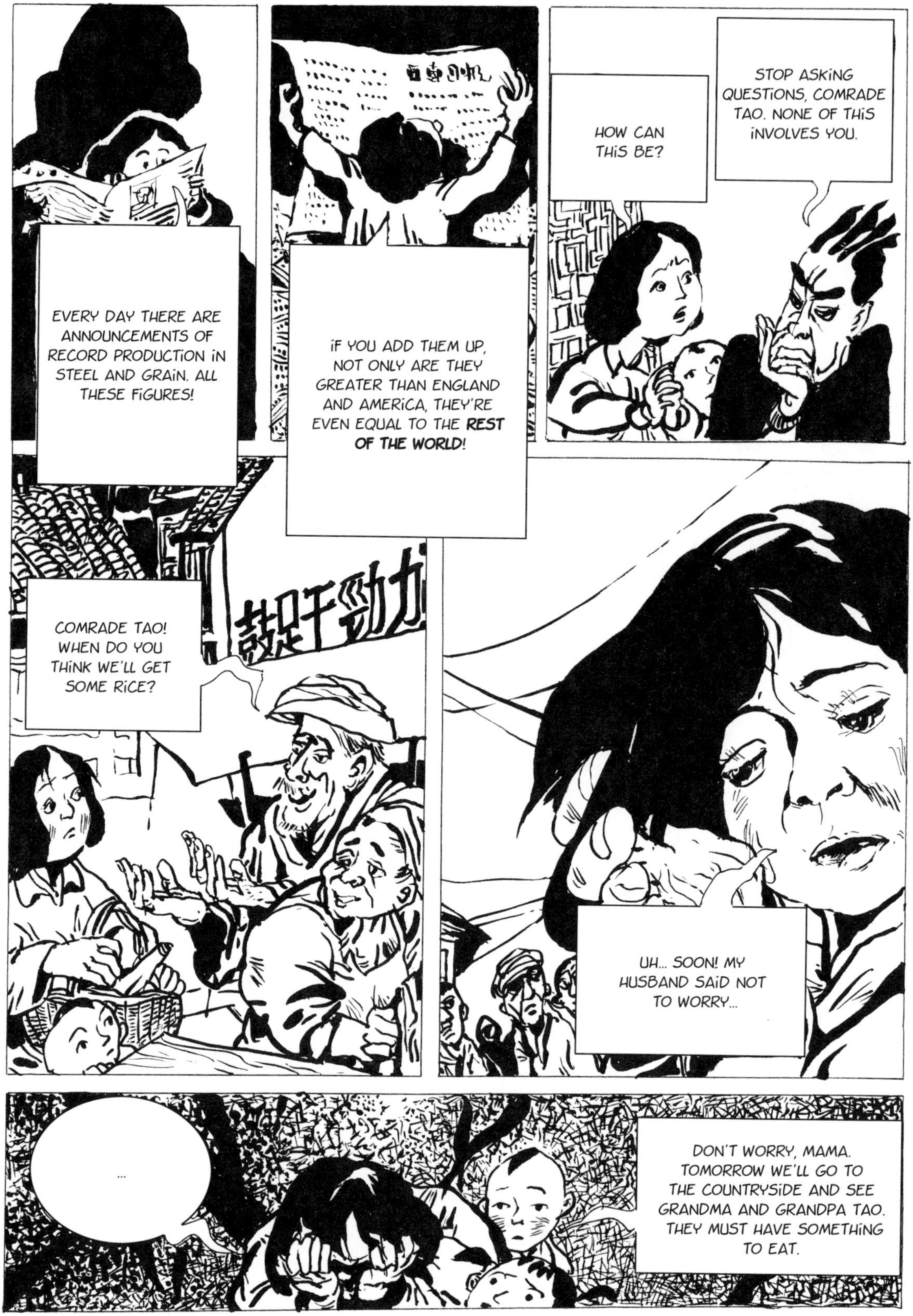
EVERY DAY THERE ARE ANNOUNCEMENTS OF RECORD PRODUCTION IN STEEL AND GRAIN. ALL THESE FIGURES!
IF YOU ADD THEM UP, NOT ONLY ARE THEY GREATER THAN ENGLAND AND AMERICA, THEY'RE EVEN EQUAL TO THE **REST OF THE WORLD**!
HOW CAN THIS BE?
STOP ASKING QUESTIONS, COMRADE TAO. NONE OF THIS INVOLVES YOU.
COMRADE TAO! WHEN DO YOU THINK WE'LL GET SOME RICE?
UH... SOON! MY HUSBAND SAID NOT TO WORRY...
...
DON'T WORRY, MAMA. TOMORROW WE'LL GO TO THE COUNTRYSIDE AND SEE GRANDMA AND GRANDPA TAO. THEY MUST HAVE SOMETHING TO EAT.

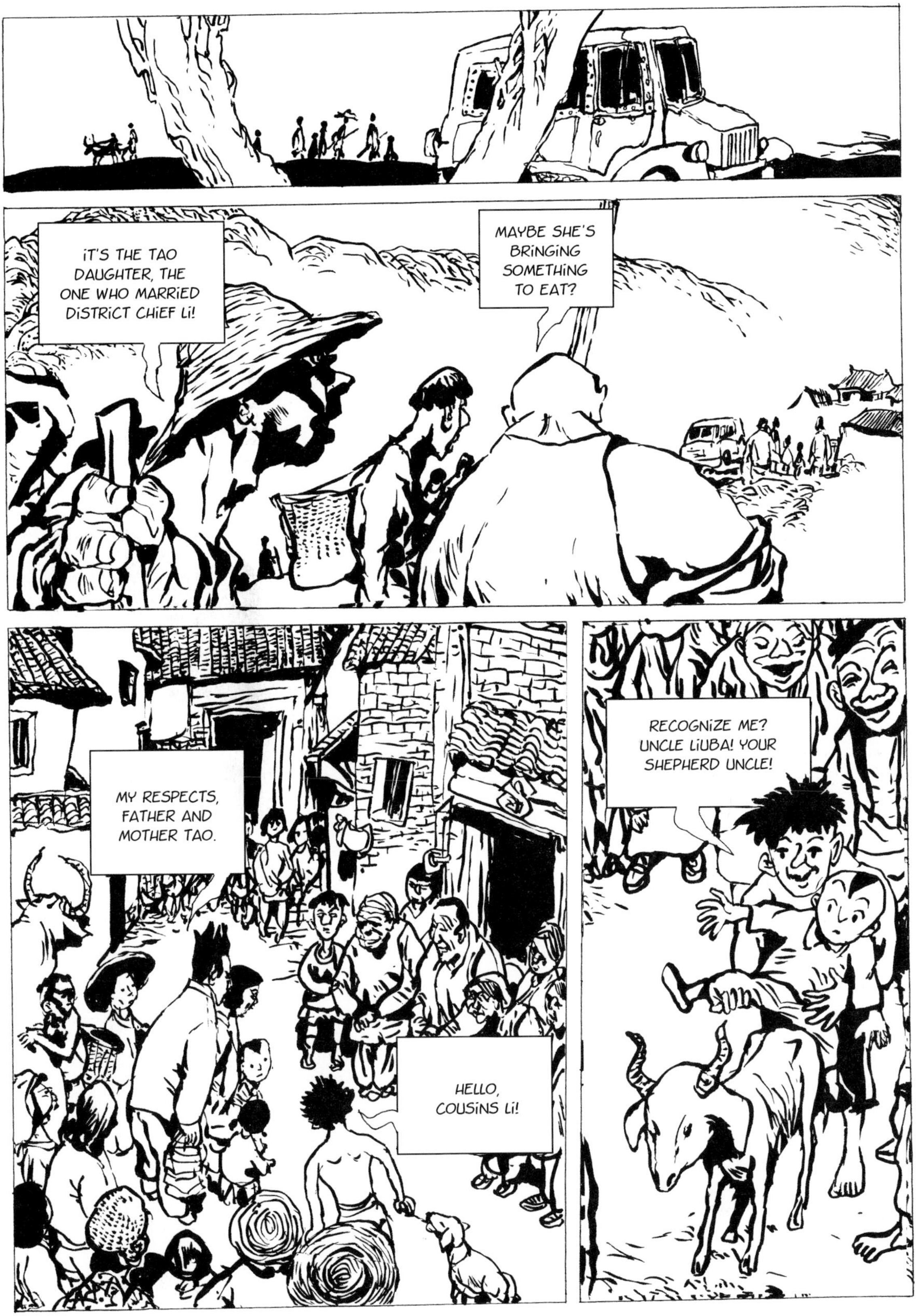
IT'S THE TAO DAUGHTER, THE ONE WHO MARRIED DISTRICT CHIEF LI!
MAYBE SHE'S BRINGING SOMETHING TO EAT?
MY RESPECTS, FATHER AND MOTHER TAO.
HELLO, COUSINS LI!
RECOGNIZE ME? UNCLE LIUBA! YOUR SHEPHERD UNCLE!

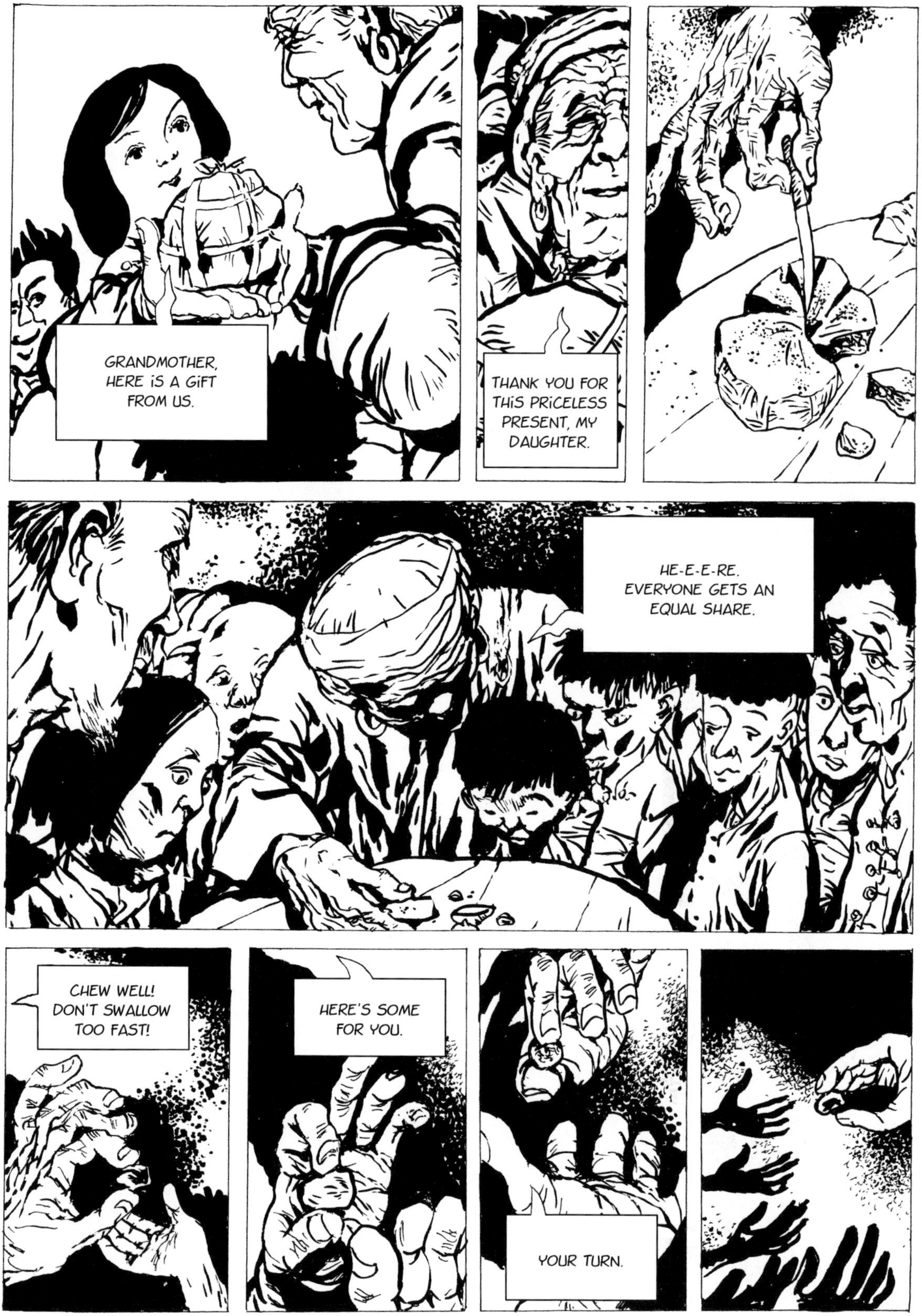
GRANDMOTHER, HERE IS A GIFT FROM US.
THANK YOU FOR THIS PRICELESS PRESENT, MY DAUGHTER.
HE-E-E-RE. EVERYONE GETS AN EQUAL SHARE.
CHEW WELL! DON'T SWALLOW TOO FAST!
HERE'S SOME FOR YOU.
YOUR TURN.

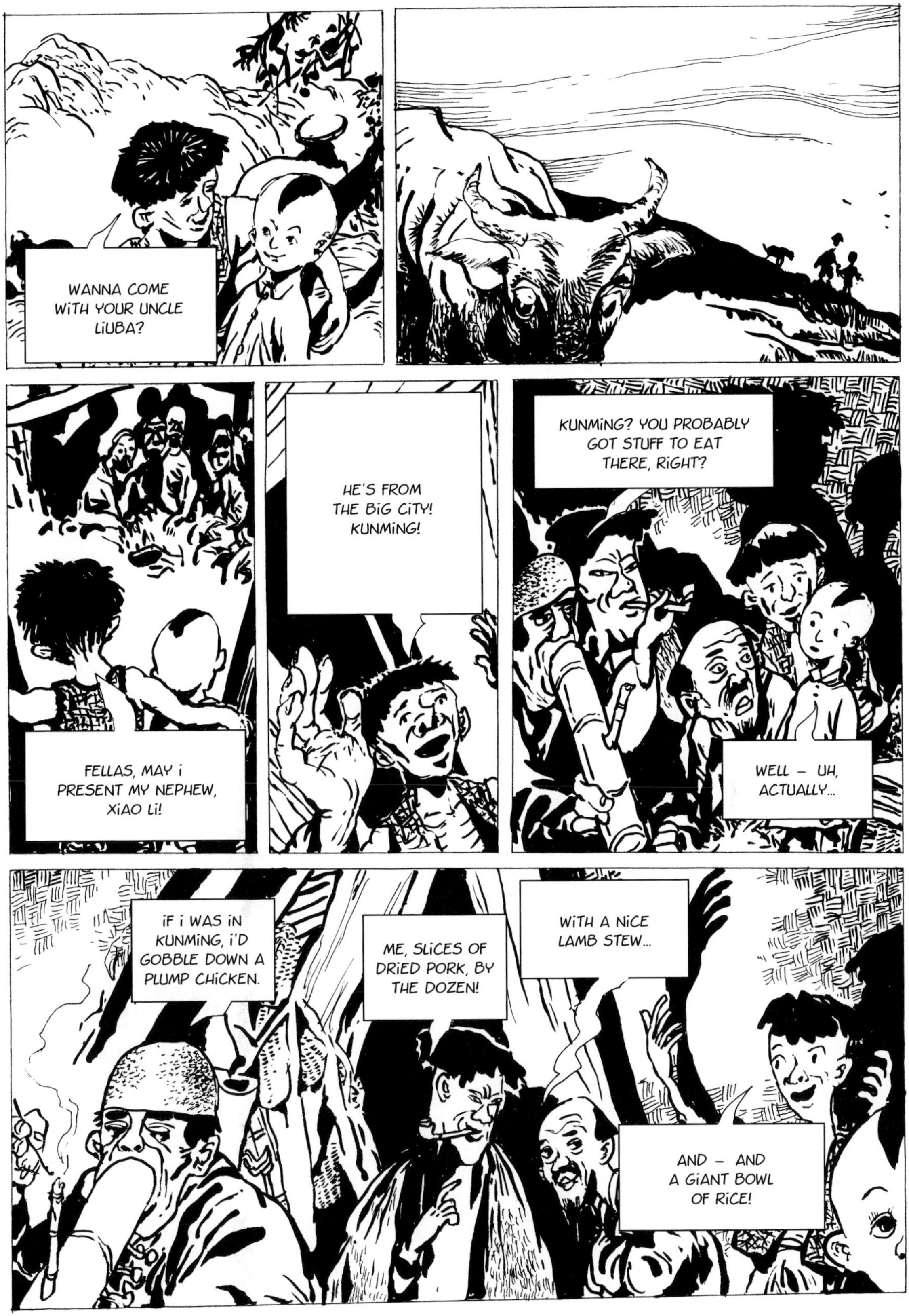

WANNA COME WITH YOUR UNCLE LIUBA?
FELLAS, MAY I PRESENT MY NEPHEW, XIAO LI!
HE'S FROM THE BIG CITY! KUNMING!
KUNMING? YOU PROBABLY GOT STUFF TO EAT THERE, RIGHT?
WELL – UH, ACTUALLY...
IF I WAS IN KUNMING, I'D GOBBLE DOWN A PLUMP CHICKEN.
ME, SLICES OF DRIED PORK, BY THE DOZEN!
WITH A NICE LAMB STEW...
AND – AND A GIANT BOWL OF RICE!

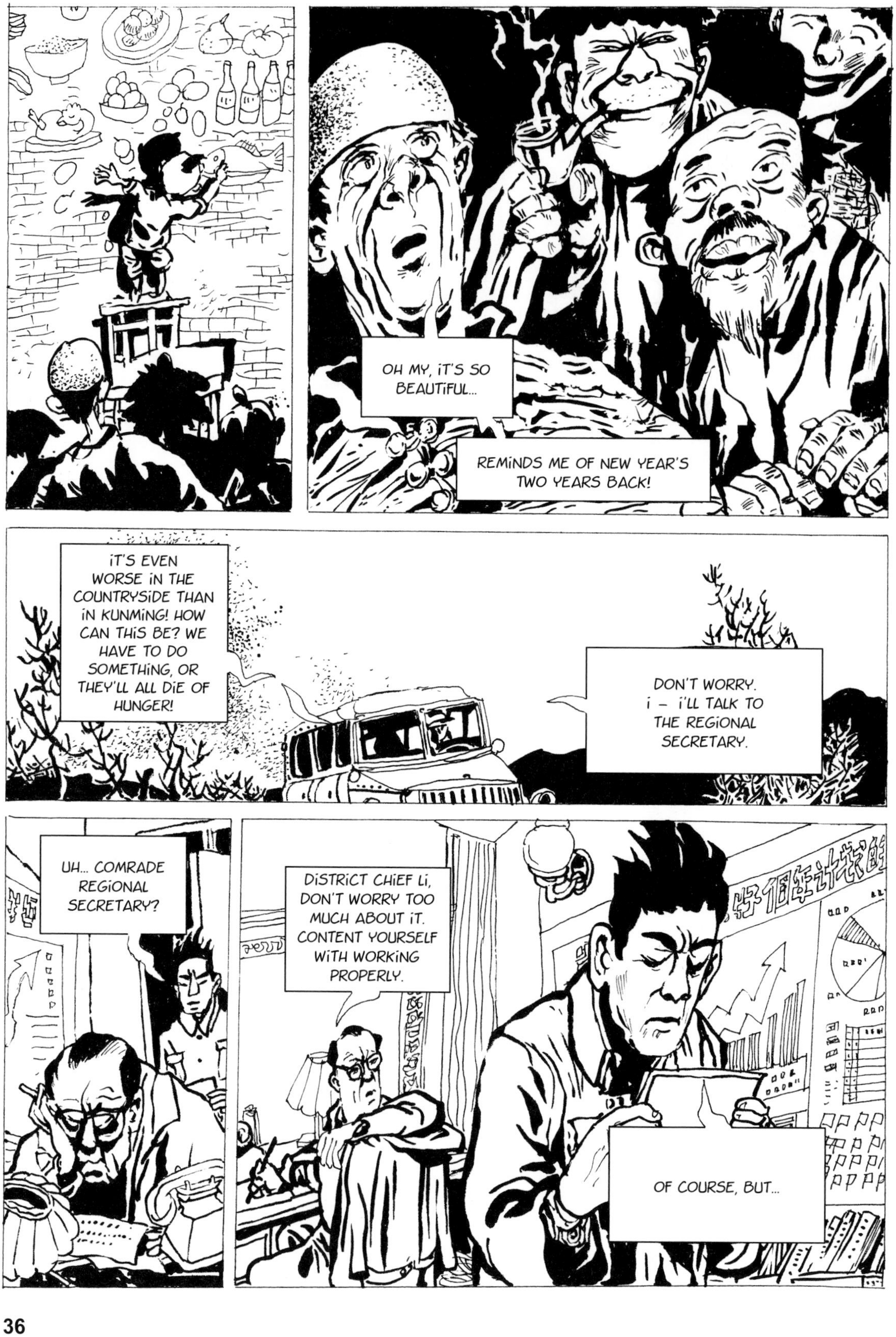

OH MY, iT'S SO BEAUTiFUL...
REMiNDS ME OF NEW YEAR'S TWO YEARS BACK!
iT'S EVEN WORSE iN THE COUNTRYSiDE THAN iN KUNMiNG! HOW CAN THiS BE? WE HAVE TO DO SOMETHiNG, OR THEY'LL ALL DiE OF HUNGER!
DON'T WORRY. i – i'LL TALK TO THE REGiONAL SECRETARY.
UH... COMRADE REGiONAL SECRETARY?
DiSTRiCT CHiEF Li, DON'T WORRY TOO MUCH ABOUT iT. CONTENT YOURSELF WiTH WORKiNG PROPERLY.
OF COURSE, BUT...

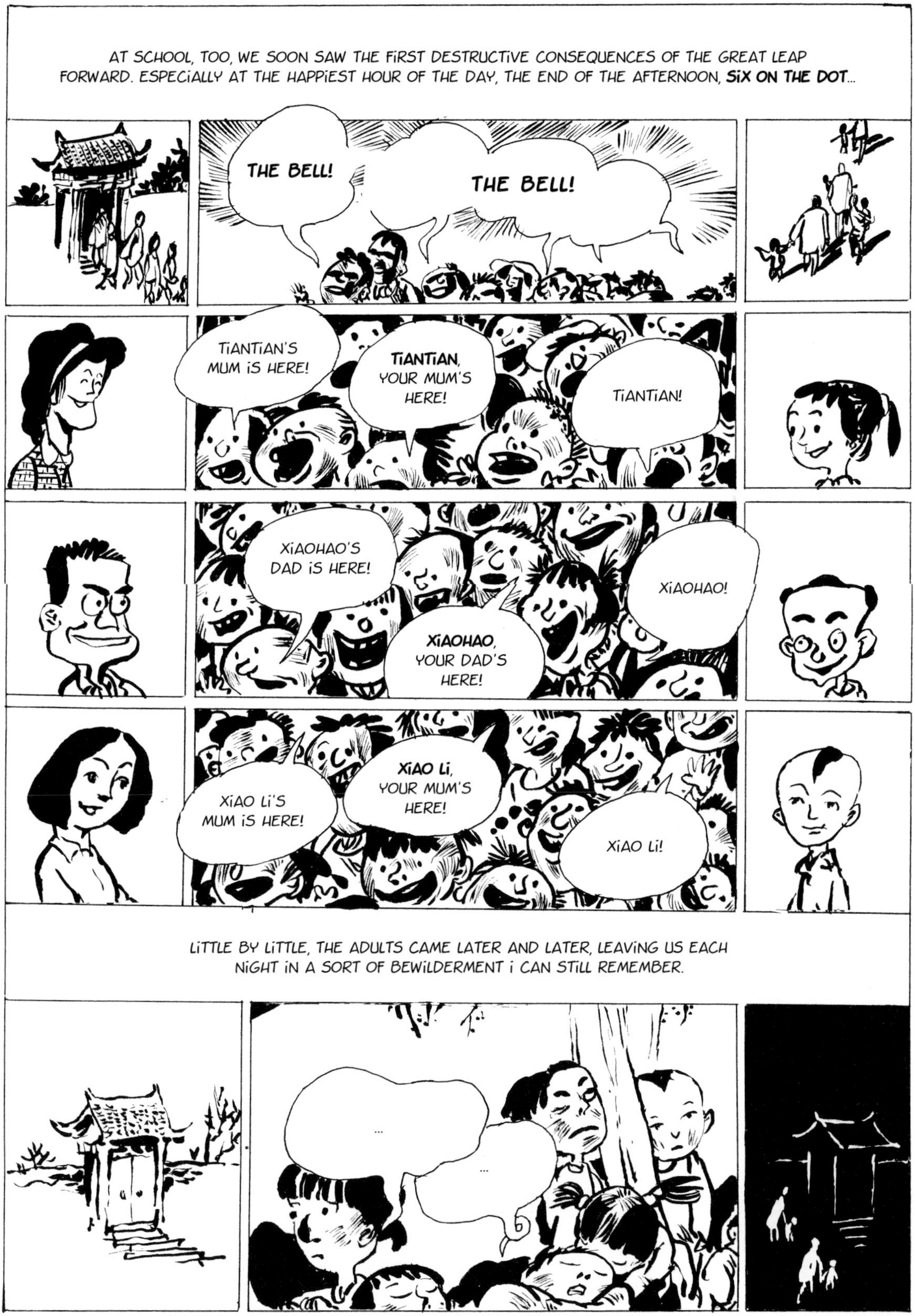
AT SCHOOL, TOO, WE SOON SAW THE FIRST DESTRUCTIVE CONSEQUENCES OF THE GREAT LEAP FORWARD. ESPECIALLY AT THE HAPPIEST HOUR OF THE DAY, THE END OF THE AFTERNOON, **SIX ON THE DOT**...
THE BELL!
THE BELL!
TIANTIAN'S MUM IS HERE!
TIANTIAN, YOUR MUM'S HERE!
TIANTIAN!
XIAOHAO'S DAD IS HERE!
XIAOHAO!
XIAOHAO, YOUR DAD'S HERE!
XIAO LI'S MUM IS HERE!
XIAO LI, YOUR MUM'S HERE!
XIAO LI!
LITTLE BY LITTLE, THE ADULTS CAME LATER AND LATER, LEAVING US EACH NIGHT IN A SORT OF BEWILDERMENT I CAN STILL REMEMBER.
...
...

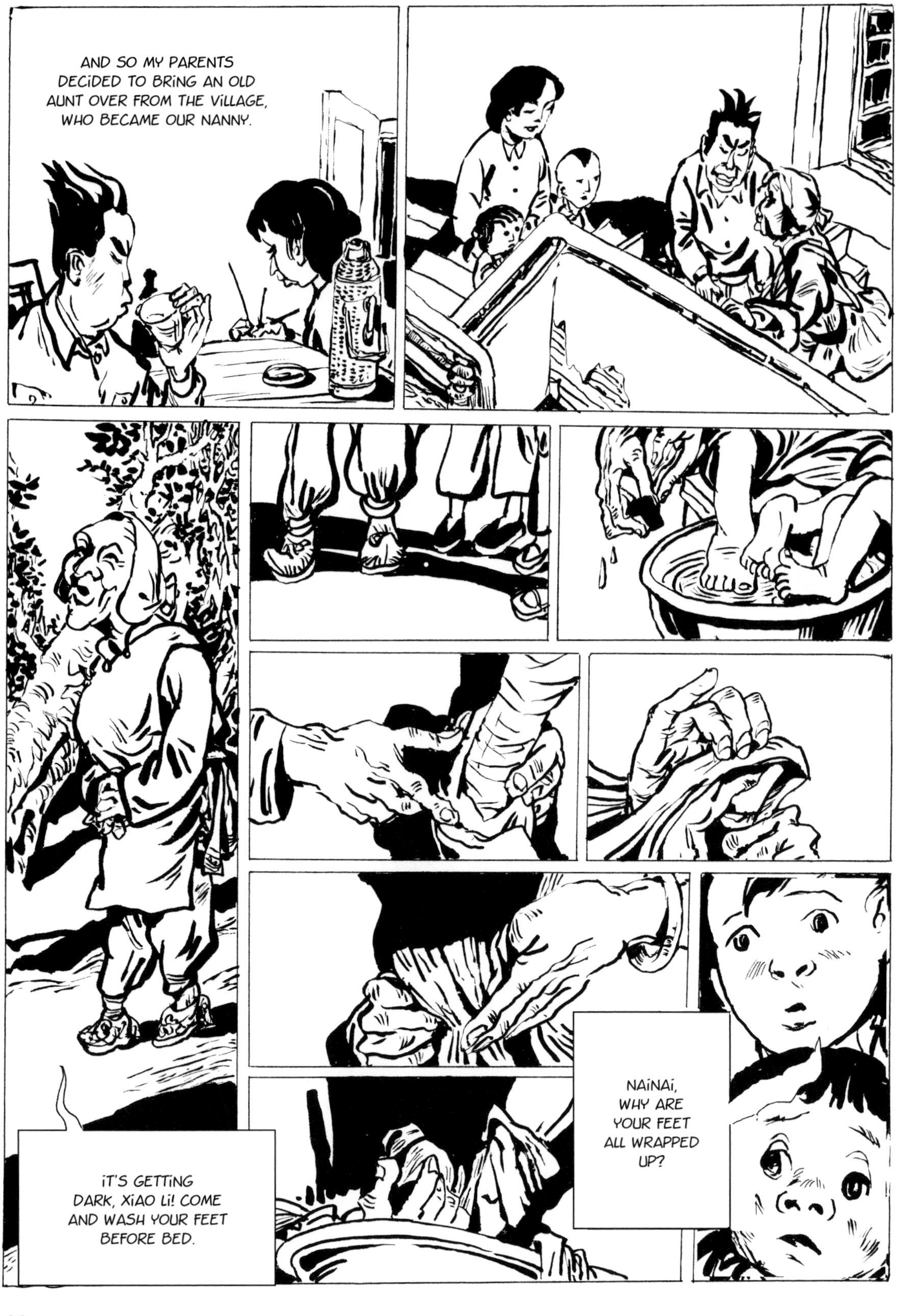
AND SO MY PARENTS DECIDED TO BRING AN OLD AUNT OVER FROM THE VILLAGE, WHO BECAME OUR NANNY.
IT'S GETTING DARK, XIAO LI! COME AND WASH YOUR FEET BEFORE BED.
NAINAI, WHY ARE YOUR FEET ALL WRAPPED UP?

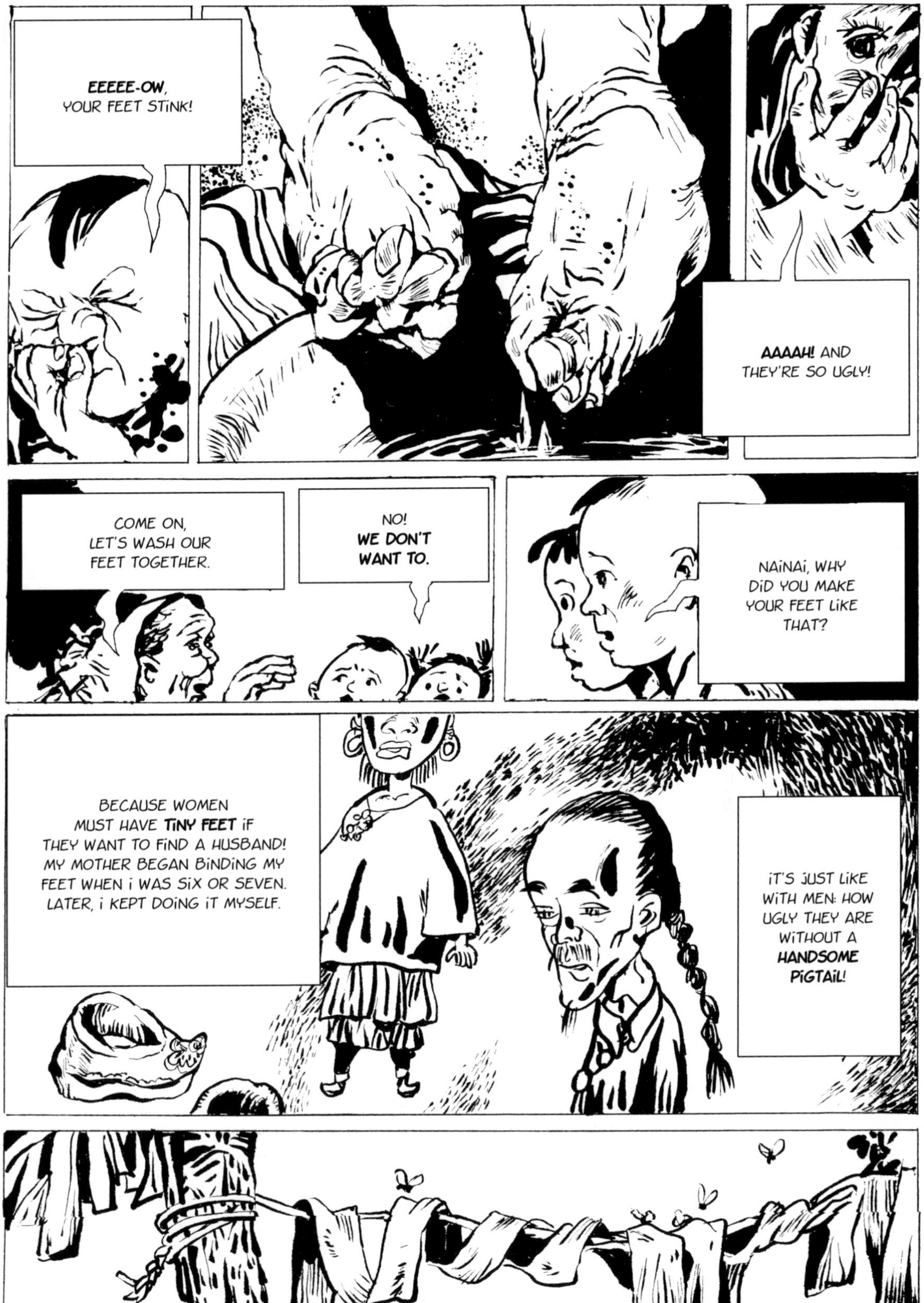
EEEEE-OW,
YOUR FEET STINK!
AAAAH! AND
THEY'RE SO UGLY!
COME ON,
LET'S WASH OUR
FEET TOGETHER.
NO!
WE DON'T
WANT TO.
NAINAI, WHY
DID YOU MAKE
YOUR FEET LIKE
THAT?
BECAUSE WOMEN
MUST HAVE TINY FEET IF
THEY WANT TO FIND A HUSBAND!
MY MOTHER BEGAN BINDING MY
FEET WHEN I WAS SIX OR SEVEN.
LATER, I KEPT DOING IT MYSELF.
IT'S JUST LIKE
WITH MEN: HOW
UGLY THEY ARE
WITHOUT A
HANDSOME
PIGTAIL!

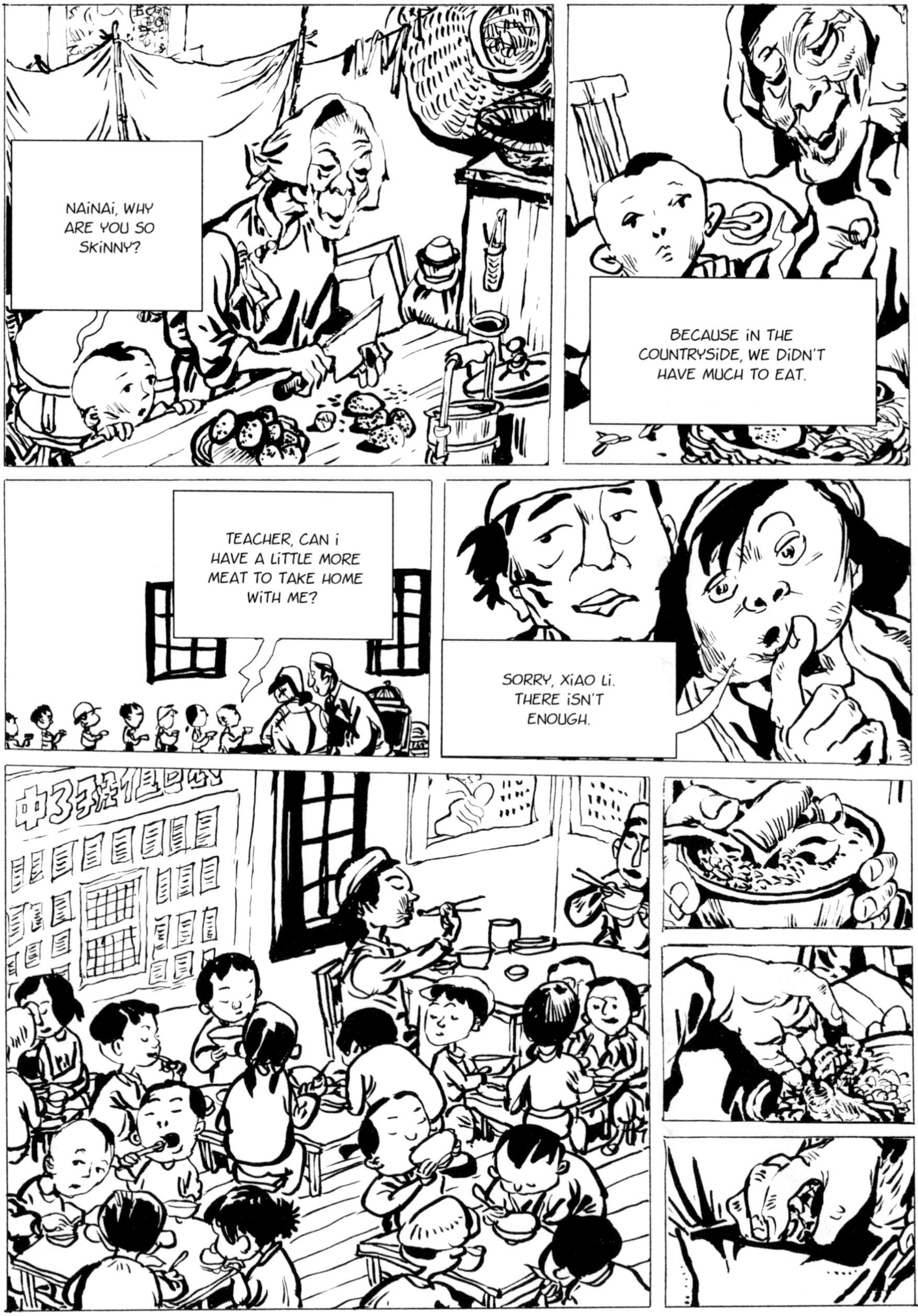
NAiNAi, WHY ARE YOU SO SKiNNY?
BECAUSE iN THE COUNTRYSiDE, WE DiDN'T HAVE MUCH TO EAT.
TEACHER, CAN i HAVE A LiTTLE MORE MEAT TO TAKE HOME WiTH ME?
SORRY, XiAO Li. THERE iSN'T ENOUGH.

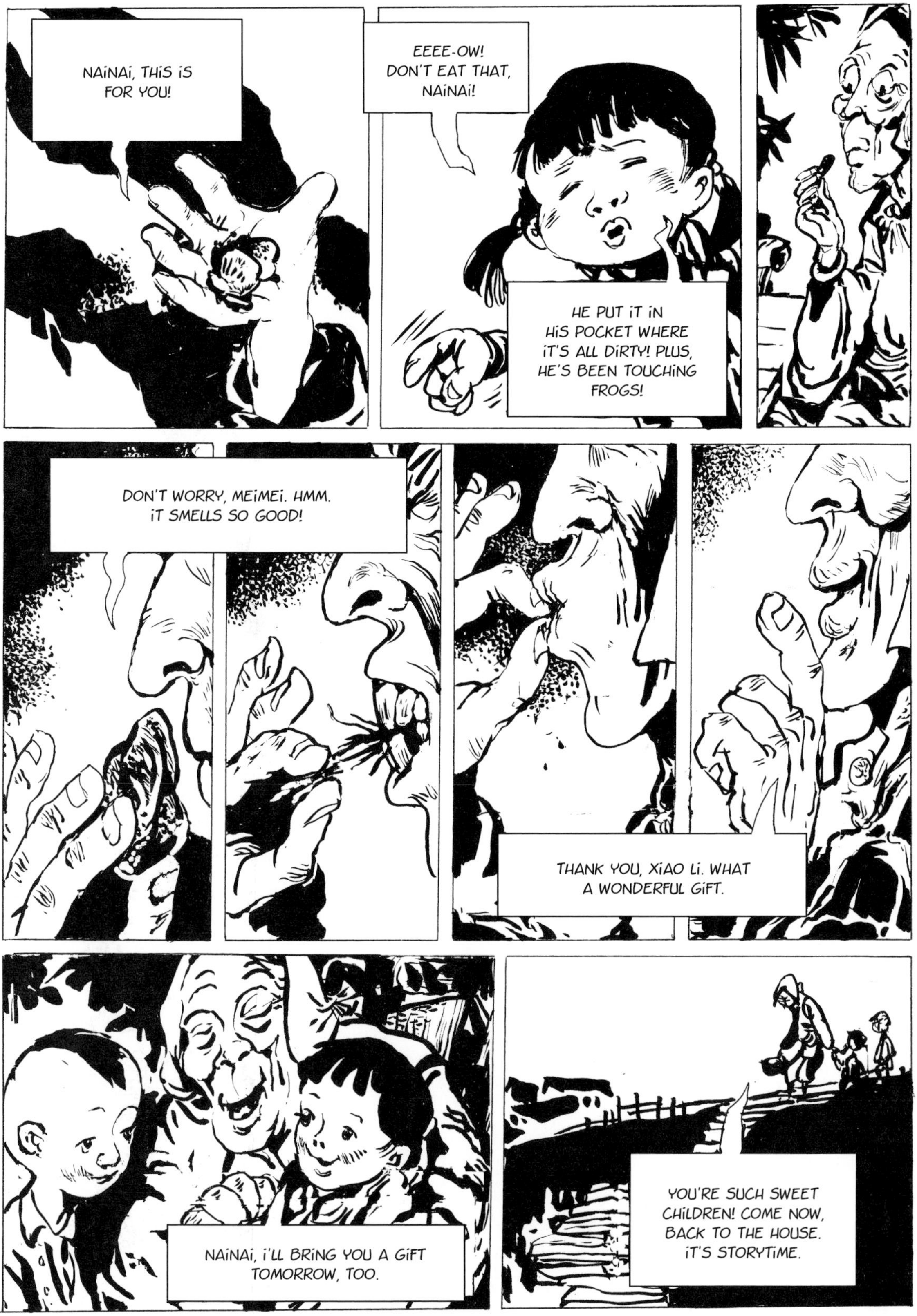
NAiNAi, THiS iS FOR YOU!
EEEE-OW! DON'T EAT THAT, NAiNAi!
HE PUT iT iN HiS POCKET WHERE iT'S ALL DiRTY! PLUS, HE'S BEEN TOUCHiNG FROGS!
DON'T WORRY, MEiMEi. HMM. iT SMELLS SO GOOD!
THANK YOU, XiAO Li. WHAT A WONDERFUL GiFT.
NAiNAi, i'LL BRiNG YOU A GiFT TOMORROW, TOO.
YOU'RE SUCH SWEET CHiLDREN! COME NOW, BACK TO THE HOUSE. iT'S STORYTiME.

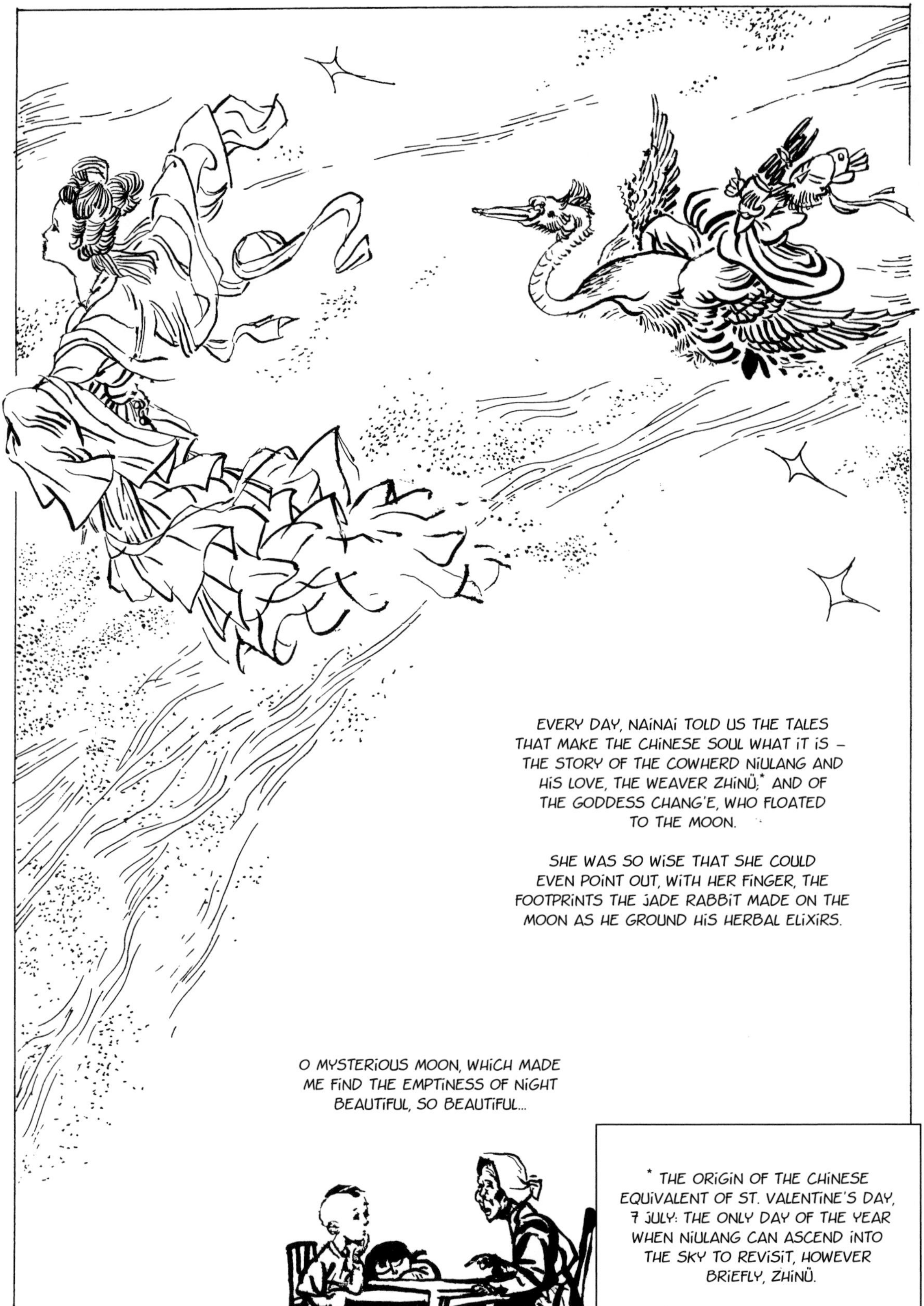
EVERY DAY, NAINAI TOLD US THE TALES THAT MAKE THE CHINESE SOUL WHAT IT IS – THE STORY OF THE COWHERD NIULANG AND HIS LOVE, THE WEAVER ZHINÜ;* AND OF THE GODDESS CHANG'E, WHO FLOATED TO THE MOON.
SHE WAS SO WISE THAT SHE COULD EVEN POINT OUT, WITH HER FINGER, THE FOOTPRINTS THE JADE RABBIT MADE ON THE MOON AS HE GROUND HIS HERBAL ELIXIRS.
O MYSTERIOUS MOON, WHICH MADE ME FIND THE EMPTINESS OF NIGHT BEAUTIFUL, SO BEAUTIFUL...
* THE ORIGIN OF THE CHINESE EQUIVALENT OF ST. VALENTINE'S DAY, 7 JULY: THE ONLY DAY OF THE YEAR WHEN NIULANG CAN ASCEND INTO THE SKY TO REVISIT, HOWEVER BRIEFLY, ZHINÜ.

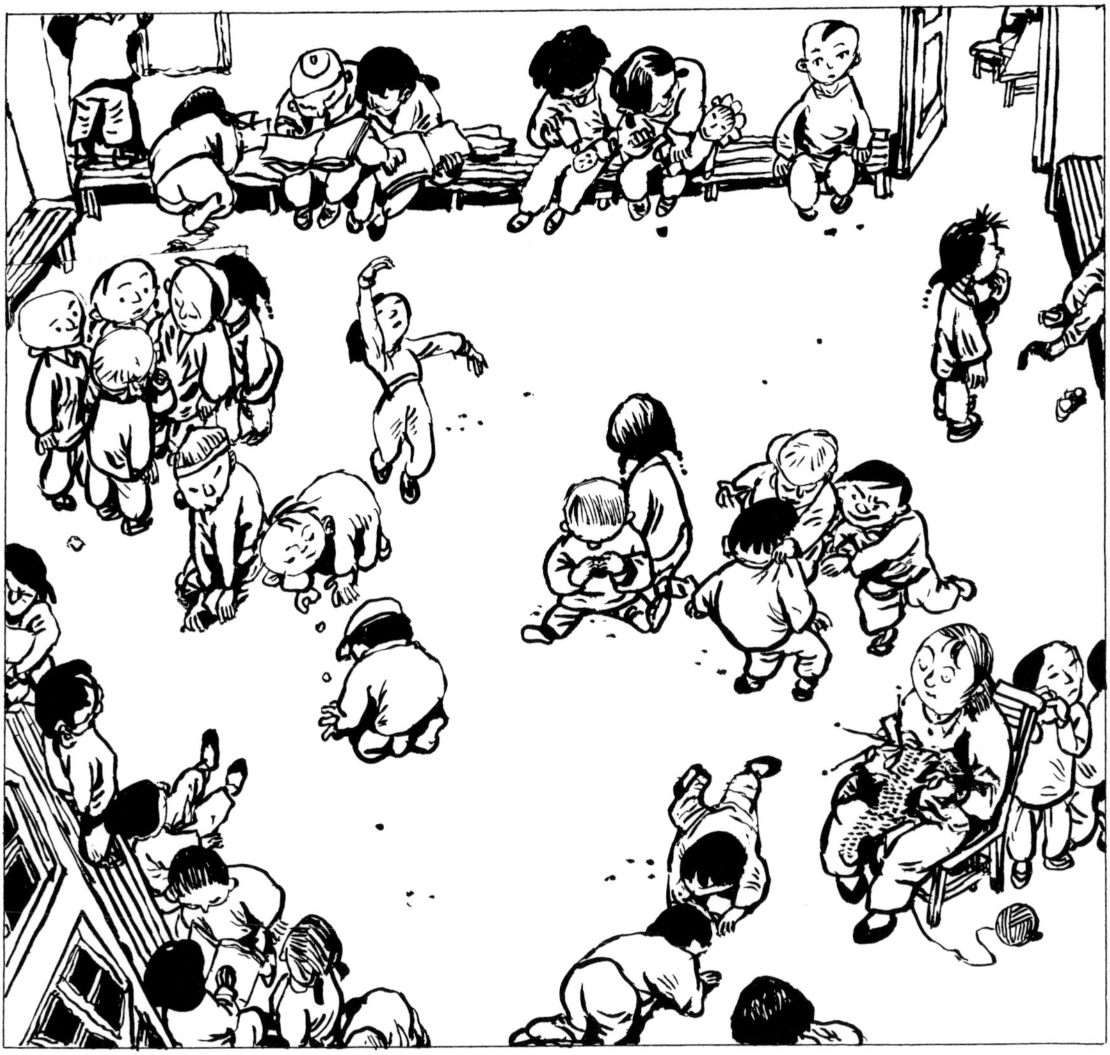

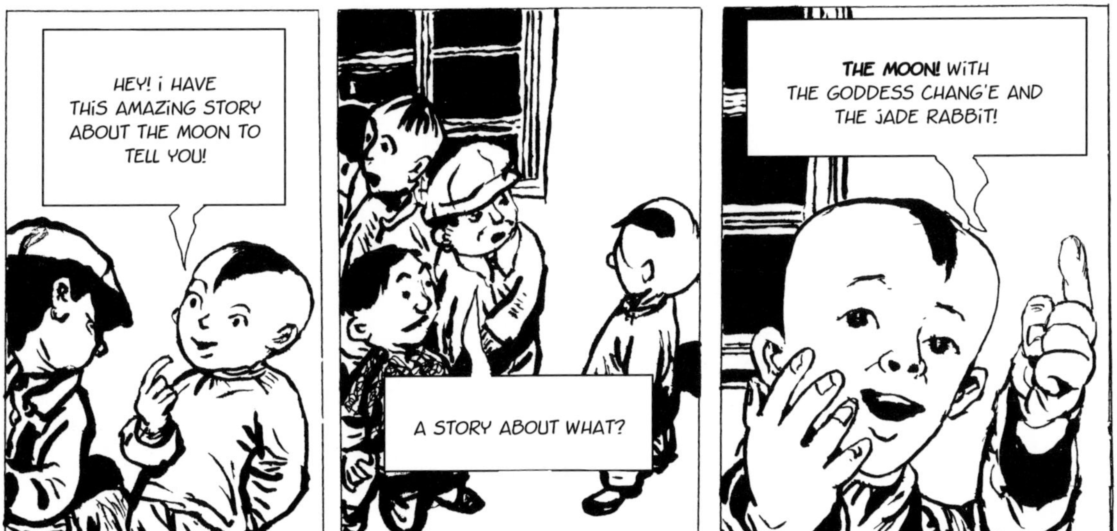
HEY! i HAVE THiS AMAZiNG STORY ABOUT THE MOON TO TELL YOU!
A STORY ABOUT WHAT?
THE MOON! WiTH THE GODDESS CHANG'E AND THE jADE RABBiT!

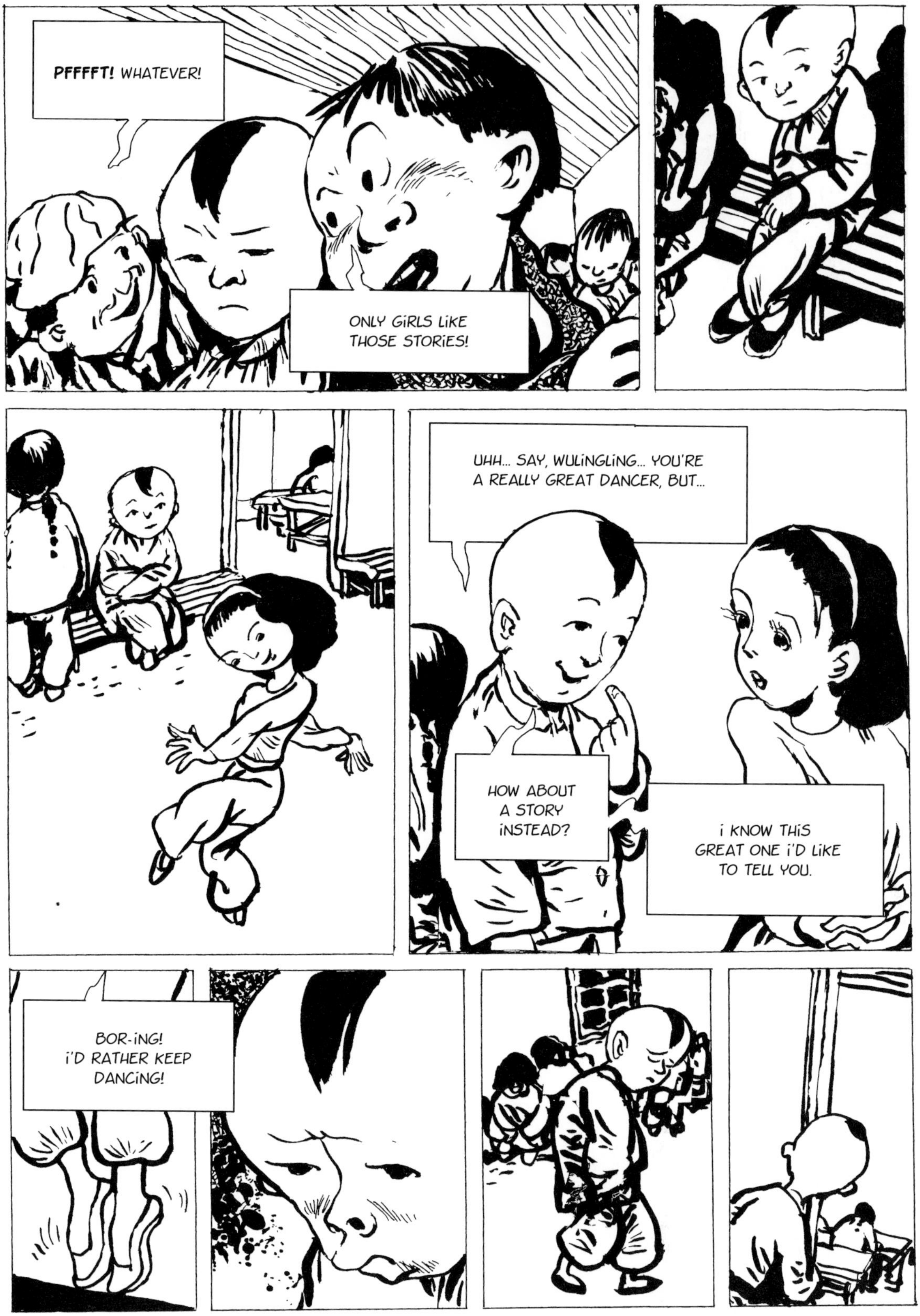
PFFFFT! WHATEVER!
ONLY GIRLS LIKE THOSE STORIES!
UHH... SAY, WULINGLING... YOU'RE A REALLY GREAT DANCER, BUT...
HOW ABOUT A STORY INSTEAD?
I KNOW THIS GREAT ONE I'D LIKE TO TELL YOU.
BOR-ING! I'D RATHER KEEP DANCING!

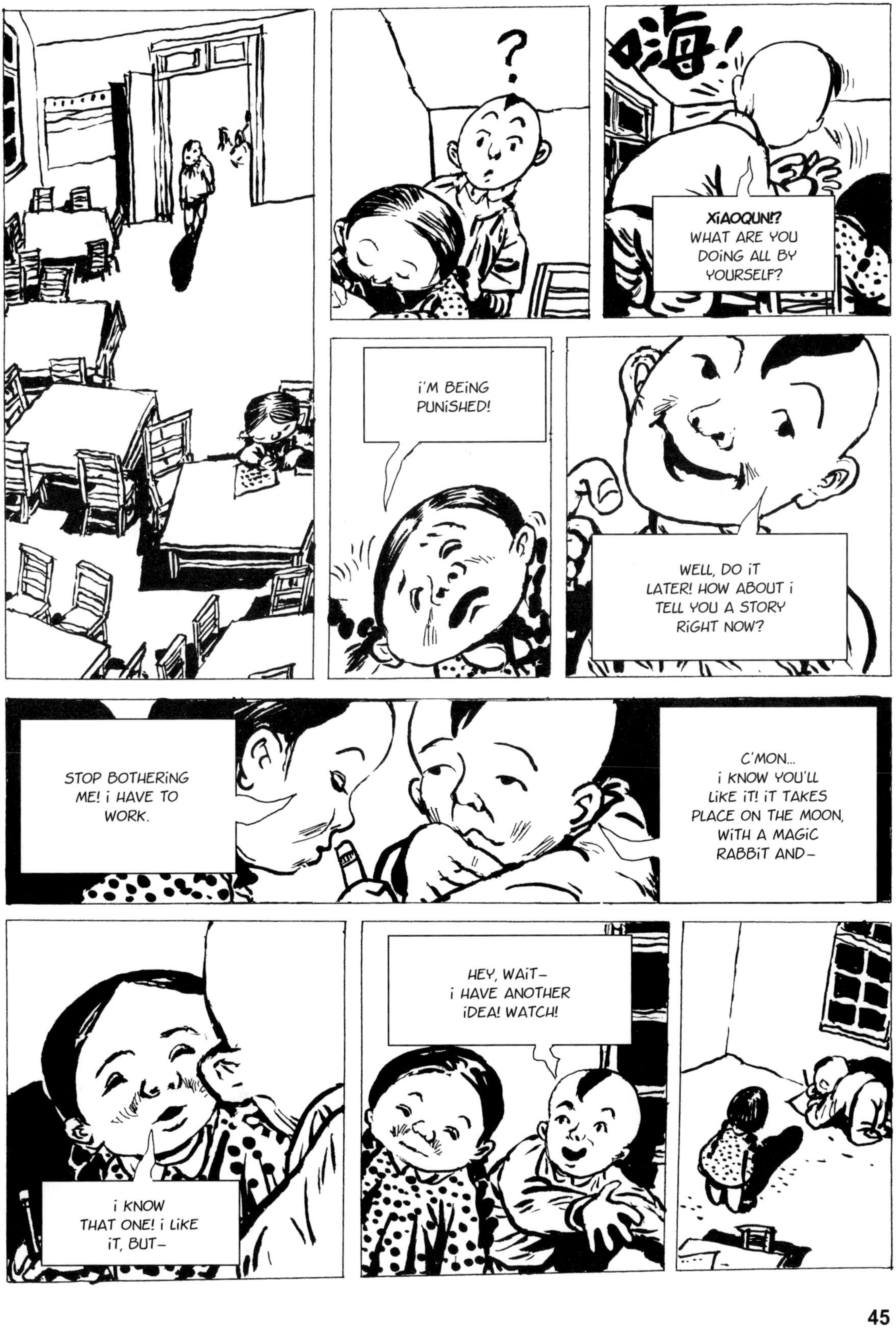
?
嗨!
XiAOQUN!? WHAT ARE YOU DOiNG ALL BY YOURSELF?
i'M BEiNG PUNiSHED!
WELL, DO iT LATER! HOW ABOUT i TELL YOU A STORY RiGHT NOW?
STOP BOTHERiNG ME! i HAVE TO WORK.
C'MON... i KNOW YOU'LL LiKE iT! iT TAKES PLACE ON THE MOON, WiTH A MAGiC RABBiT AND–
i KNOW THAT ONE! i LiKE iT, BUT–
HEY, WAiT– i HAVE ANOTHER iDEA! WATCH!

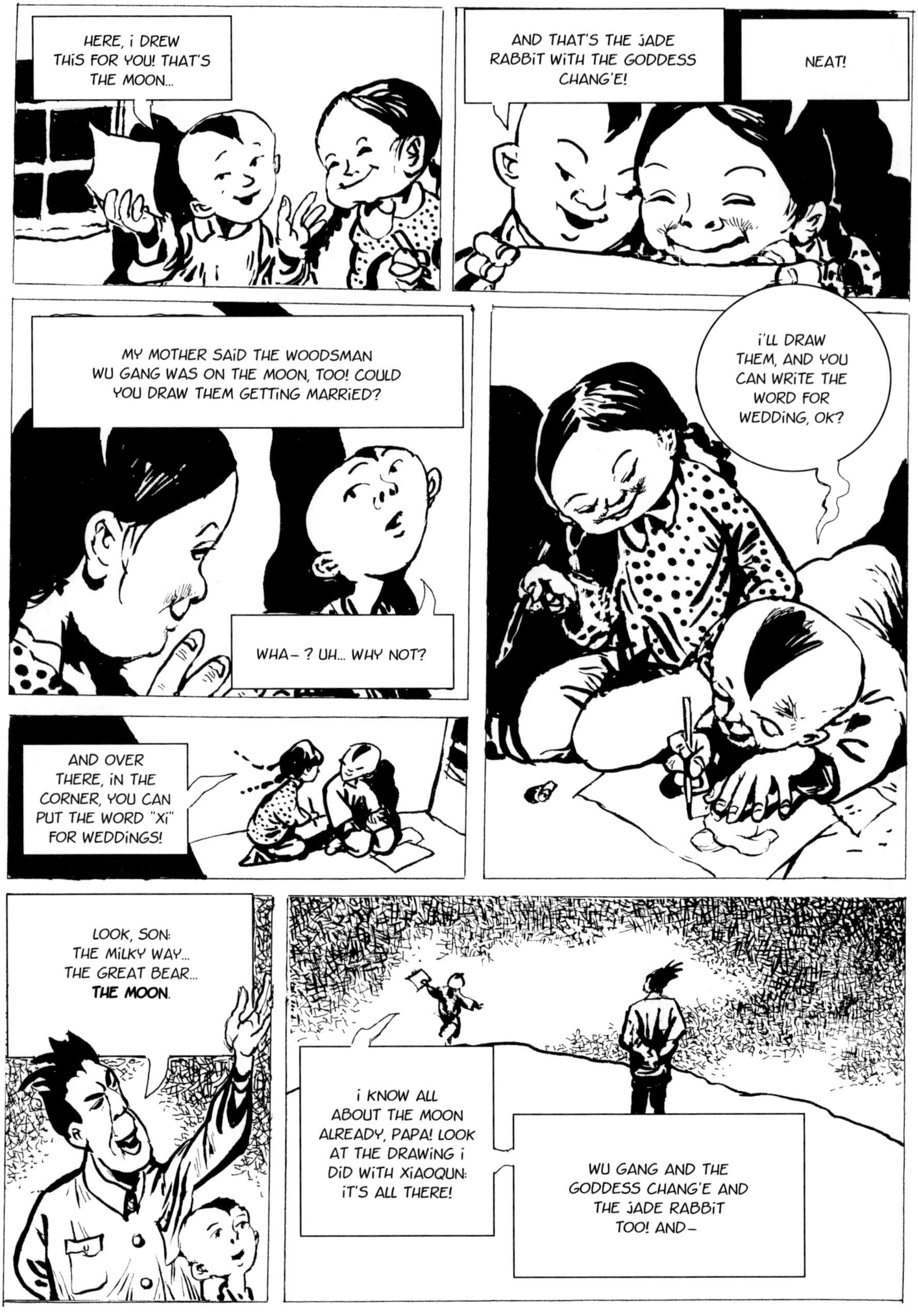
HERE, i DREW THIS FOR YOU! THAT'S THE MOON...
AND THAT'S THE JADE RABBiT WiTH THE GODDESS CHANG'E!
NEAT!
MY MOTHER SAiD THE WOODSMAN WU GANG WAS ON THE MOON, TOO! COULD YOU DRAW THEM GETTiNG MARRiED?
WHA– ? UH... WHY NOT?
i'LL DRAW THEM, AND YOU CAN WRiTE THE WORD FOR WEDDiNG, OK?
AND OVER THERE, iN THE CORNER, YOU CAN PUT THE WORD "Xi" FOR WEDDiNGS!
LOOK, SON: THE MiLKY WAY... THE GREAT BEAR... **THE MOON**.
i KNOW ALL ABOUT THE MOON ALREADY, PAPA! LOOK AT THE DRAWiNG i DiD WiTH XiAOQUN: iT'S ALL THERE!
WU GANG AND THE GODDESS CHANG'E AND THE JADE RABBiT TOO! AND–

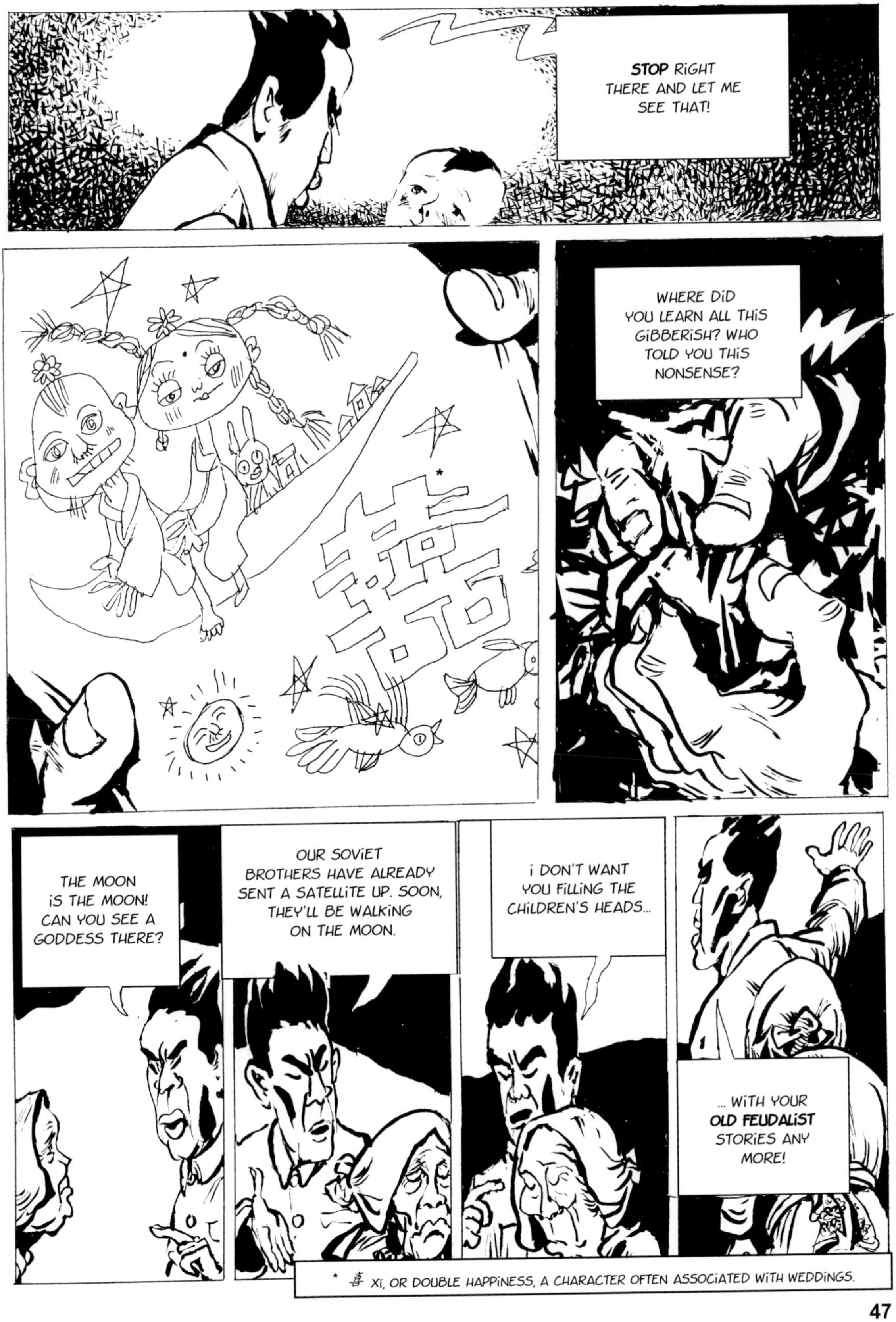
STOP RIGHT THERE AND LET ME SEE THAT!
WHERE DID YOU LEARN ALL THIS GIBBERISH? WHO TOLD YOU THIS NONSENSE?
THE MOON IS THE MOON! CAN YOU SEE A GODDESS THERE?
OUR SOVIET BROTHERS HAVE ALREADY SENT A SATELLITE UP. SOON, THEY'LL BE WALKING ON THE MOON.
I DON'T WANT YOU FILLING THE CHILDREN'S HEADS...
... WITH YOUR OLD FEUDALIST STORIES ANY MORE!
* 喜 XI, OR DOUBLE HAPPINESS, A CHARACTER OFTEN ASSOCIATED WITH WEDDINGS.

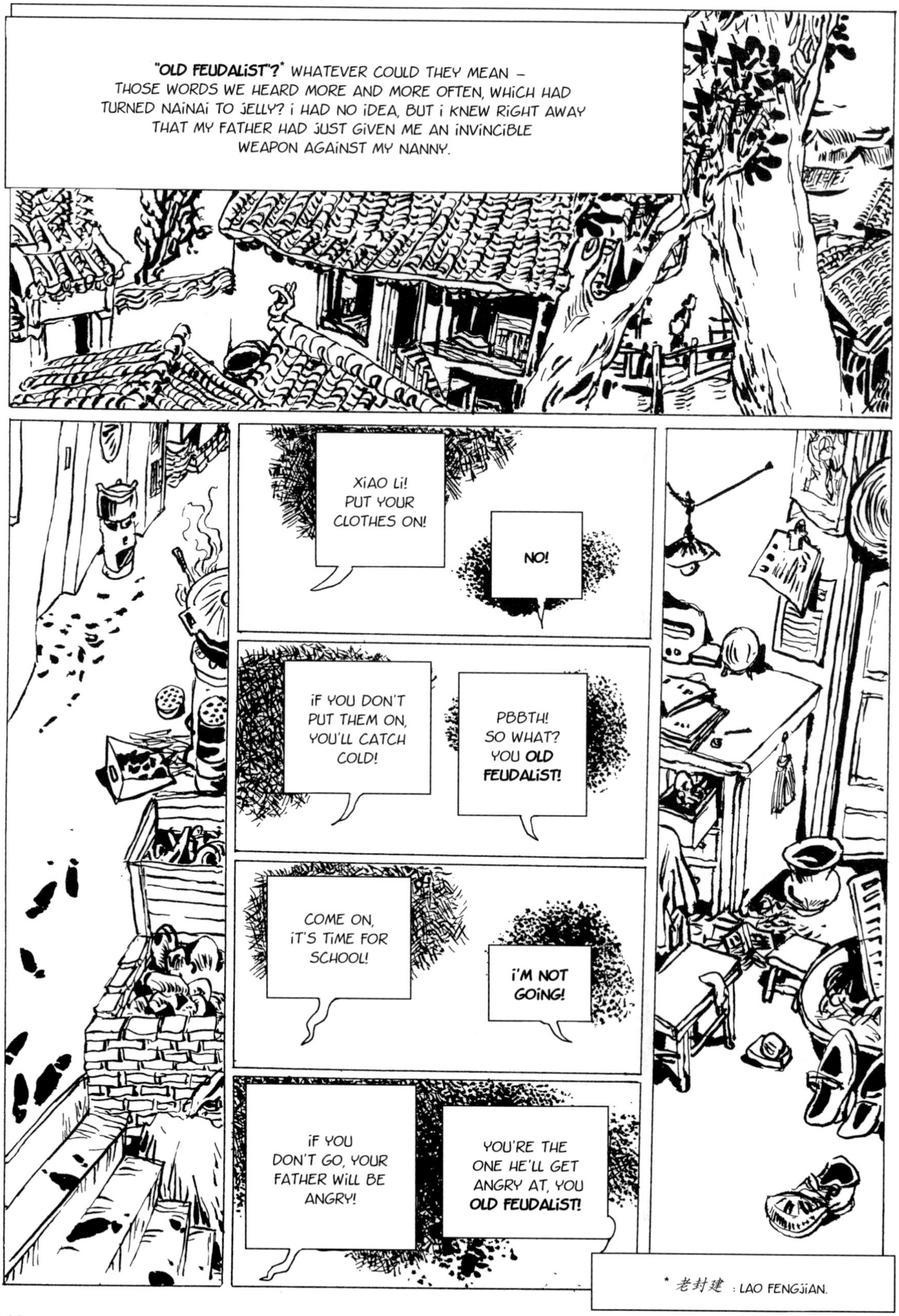
"OLD FEUDALIST"?* WHATEVER COULD THEY MEAN – THOSE WORDS WE HEARD MORE AND MORE OFTEN, WHICH HAD TURNED NAINAI TO JELLY? I HAD NO IDEA, BUT I KNEW RIGHT AWAY THAT MY FATHER HAD JUST GIVEN ME AN INVINCIBLE WEAPON AGAINST MY NANNY.
XIAO LI! PUT YOUR CLOTHES ON!
NO!
IF YOU DON'T PUT THEM ON, YOU'LL CATCH COLD!
PBBTH! SO WHAT? YOU OLD FEUDALIST!
COME ON, IT'S TIME FOR SCHOOL!
I'M NOT GOING!
IF YOU DON'T GO, YOUR FATHER WILL BE ANGRY!
YOU'RE THE ONE HE'LL GET ANGRY AT, YOU OLD FEUDALIST!

* 老封建 : LAO FENGJIAN.

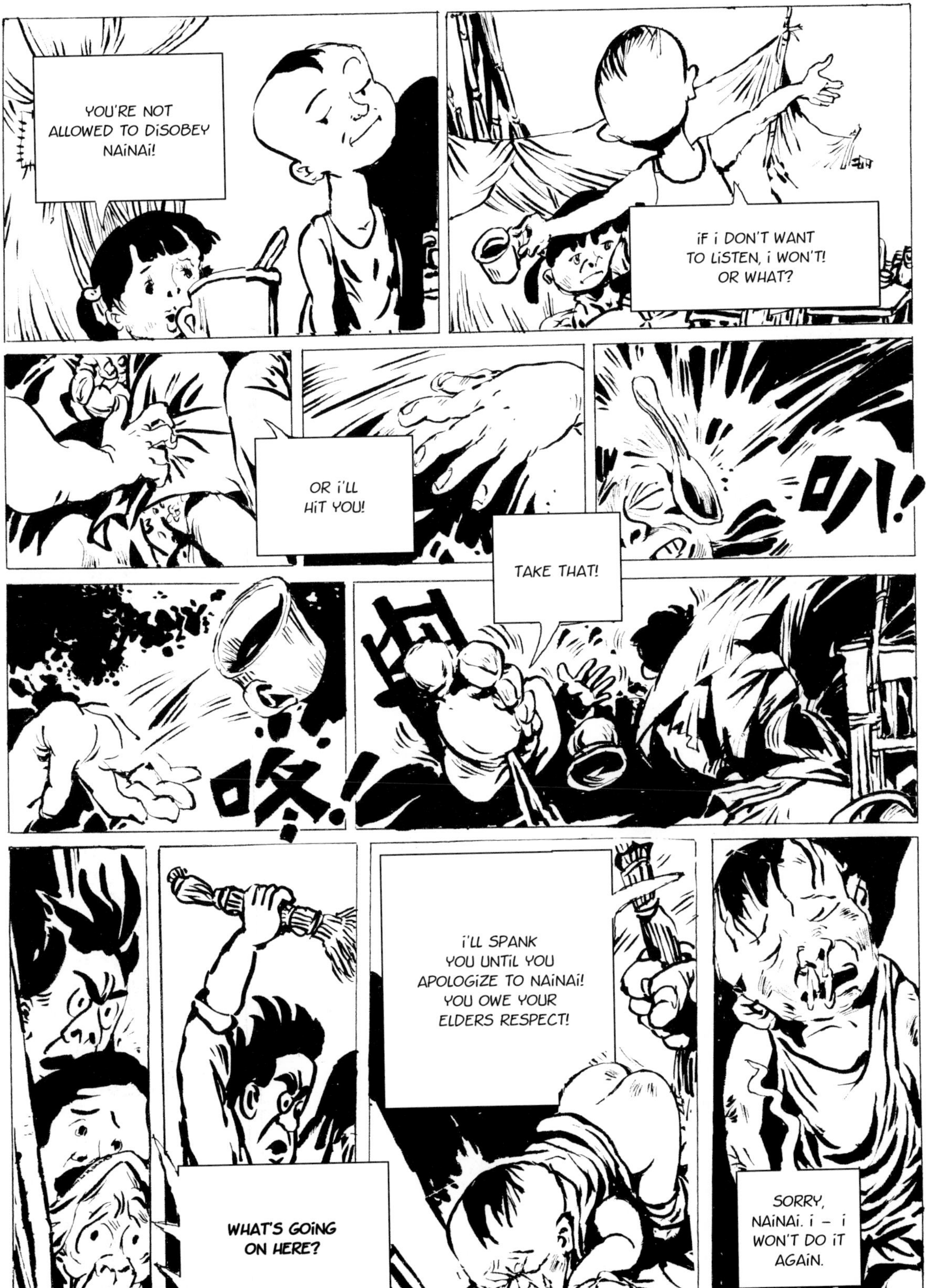
YOU'RE NOT ALLOWED TO DISOBEY NAINAI!
IF I DON'T WANT TO LISTEN, I WON'T! OR WHAT?
OR I'LL HIT YOU!
叭!
TAKE THAT!
咚!
WHAT'S GOING ON HERE?
I'LL SPANK YOU UNTIL YOU APOLOGIZE TO NAINAI! YOU OWE YOUR ELDERS RESPECT!
SORRY, NAINAI. I – I WON'T DO IT AGAIN.

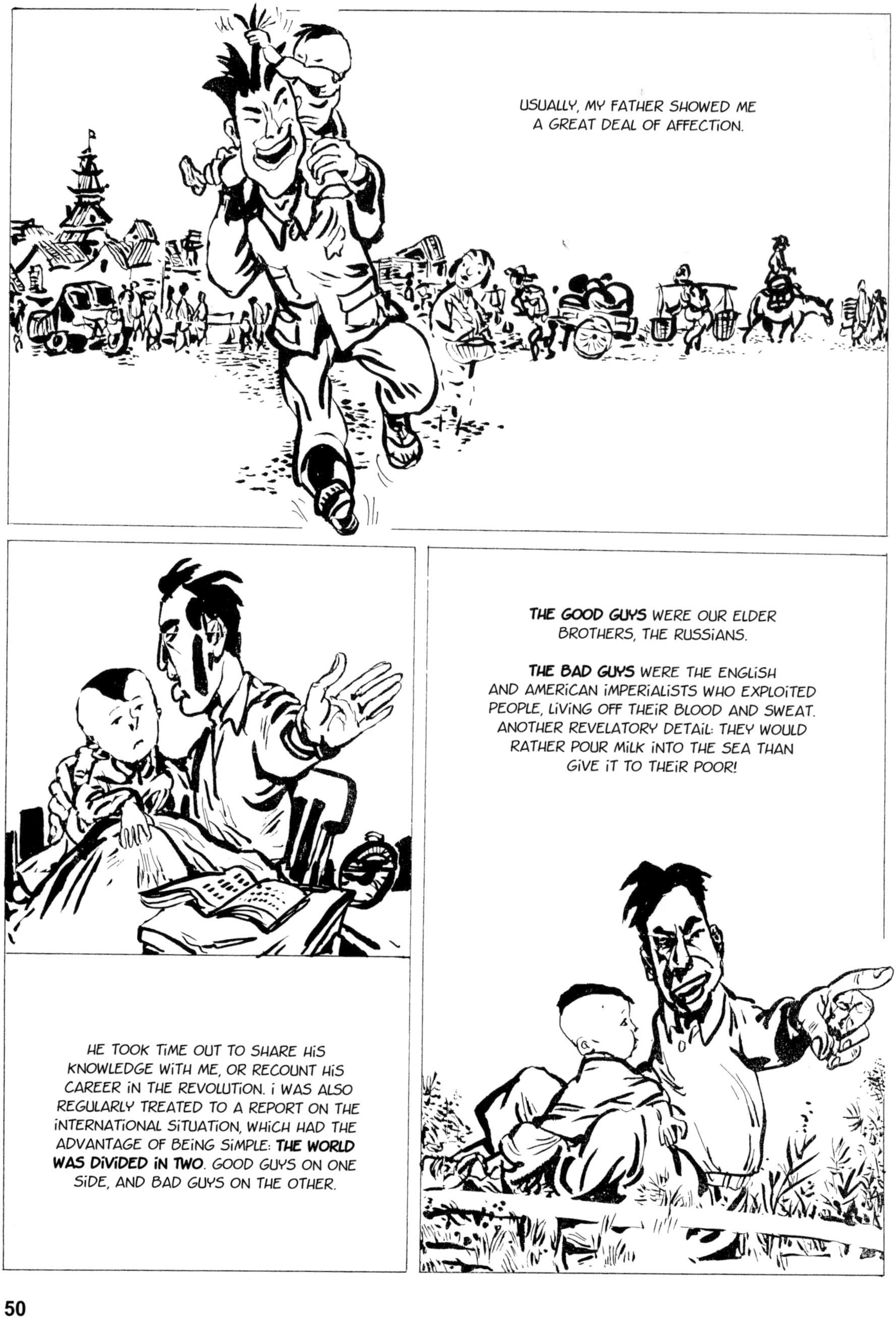
USUALLY, MY FATHER SHOWED ME A GREAT DEAL OF AFFECTION.
HE TOOK TIME OUT TO SHARE HIS KNOWLEDGE WITH ME, OR RECOUNT HIS CAREER IN THE REVOLUTION. I WAS ALSO REGULARLY TREATED TO A REPORT ON THE INTERNATIONAL SITUATION, WHICH HAD THE ADVANTAGE OF BEING SIMPLE: **THE WORLD WAS DIVIDED IN TWO**. GOOD GUYS ON ONE SIDE, AND BAD GUYS ON THE OTHER.
THE GOOD GUYS WERE OUR ELDER BROTHERS, THE RUSSIANS.
THE BAD GUYS WERE THE ENGLISH AND AMERICAN IMPERIALISTS WHO EXPLOITED PEOPLE, LIVING OFF THEIR BLOOD AND SWEAT. ANOTHER REVELATORY DETAIL: THEY WOULD RATHER POUR MILK INTO THE SEA THAN GIVE IT TO THEIR POOR!

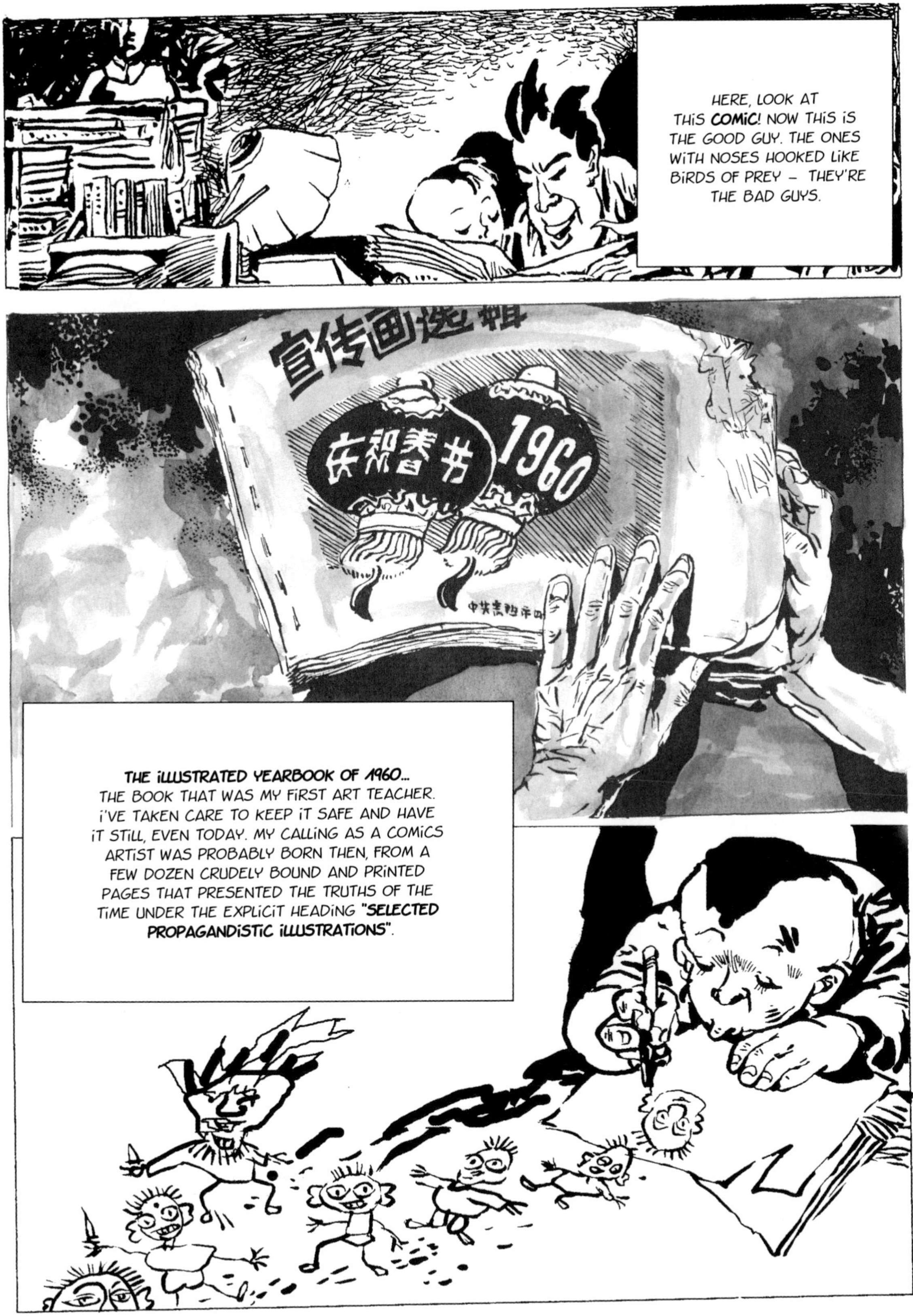
HERE, LOOK AT THIS **COMIC!** NOW THIS IS THE GOOD GUY. THE ONES WITH NOSES HOOKED LIKE BIRDS OF PREY – THEY'RE THE BAD GUYS.
宣传画选辑
庆祝春节
1960
THE ILLUSTRATED YEARBOOK OF 1960... THE BOOK THAT WAS MY FIRST ART TEACHER. I'VE TAKEN CARE TO KEEP IT SAFE AND HAVE IT STILL, EVEN TODAY. MY CALLING AS A COMICS ARTIST WAS PROBABLY BORN THEN, FROM A FEW DOZEN CRUDELY BOUND AND PRINTED PAGES THAT PRESENTED THE TRUTHS OF THE TIME UNDER THE EXPLICIT HEADING "**SELECTED PROPAGANDISTIC ILLUSTRATIONS**".

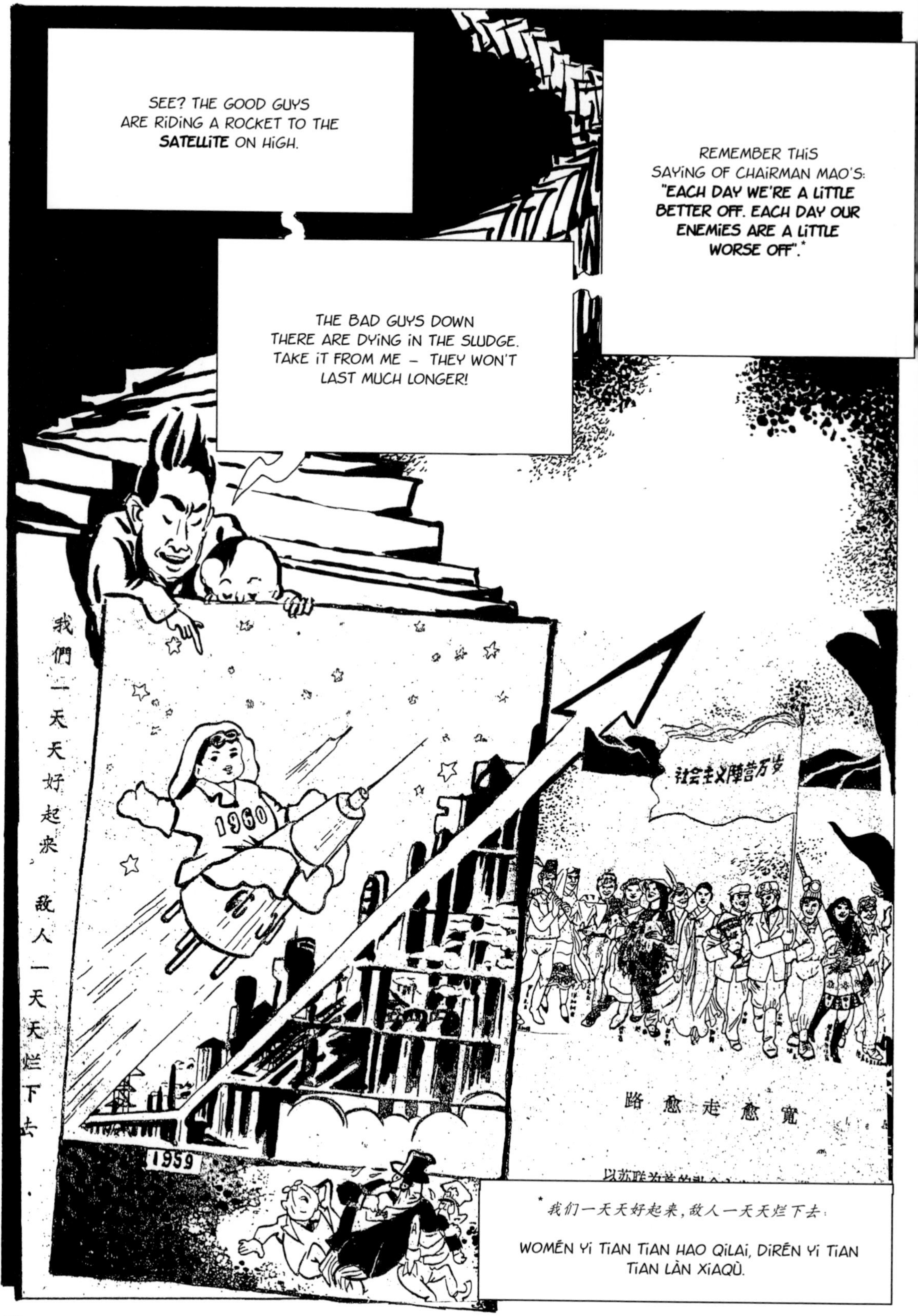
SEE? THE GOOD GUYS ARE RIDING A ROCKET TO THE **SATELLITE** ON HIGH.
THE BAD GUYS DOWN THERE ARE DYING IN THE SLUDGE. TAKE IT FROM ME – THEY WON'T LAST MUCH LONGER!
REMEMBER THIS SAYING OF CHAIRMAN MAO'S: **"EACH DAY WE'RE A LITTLE BETTER OFF. EACH DAY OUR ENEMIES ARE A LITTLE WORSE OFF".***
1960
1959
*我们一天天好起来，敌人一天天烂下去：
WOMĖN YI TIAN TIAN HAO QILAI, DIRĖN YI TIAN TIAN LÀN XIAQÙ.

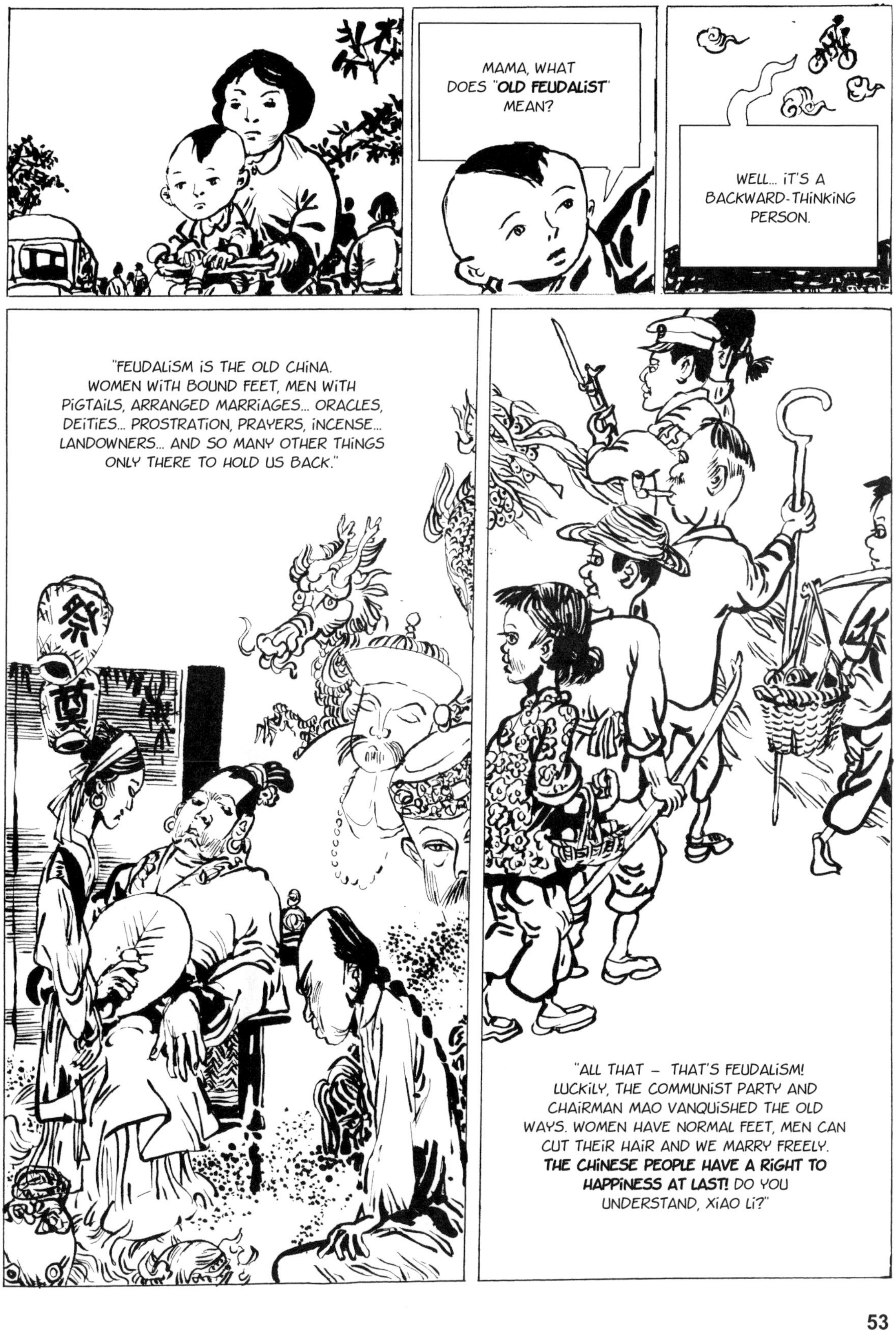

MAMA, WHAT DOES "OLD FEUDALIST" MEAN?
WELL... IT'S A BACKWARD-THINKING PERSON.
"FEUDALISM IS THE OLD CHINA. WOMEN WITH BOUND FEET, MEN WITH PIGTAILS, ARRANGED MARRIAGES... ORACLES, DEITIES... PROSTRATION, PRAYERS, INCENSE... LANDOWNERS... AND SO MANY OTHER THINGS ONLY THERE TO HOLD US BACK."
"ALL THAT – THAT'S FEUDALISM! LUCKILY, THE COMMUNIST PARTY AND CHAIRMAN MAO VANQUISHED THE OLD WAYS. WOMEN HAVE NORMAL FEET, MEN CAN CUT THEIR HAIR AND WE MARRY FREELY. THE CHINESE PEOPLE HAVE A RIGHT TO HAPPINESS AT LAST! DO YOU UNDERSTAND, XIAO LI?"

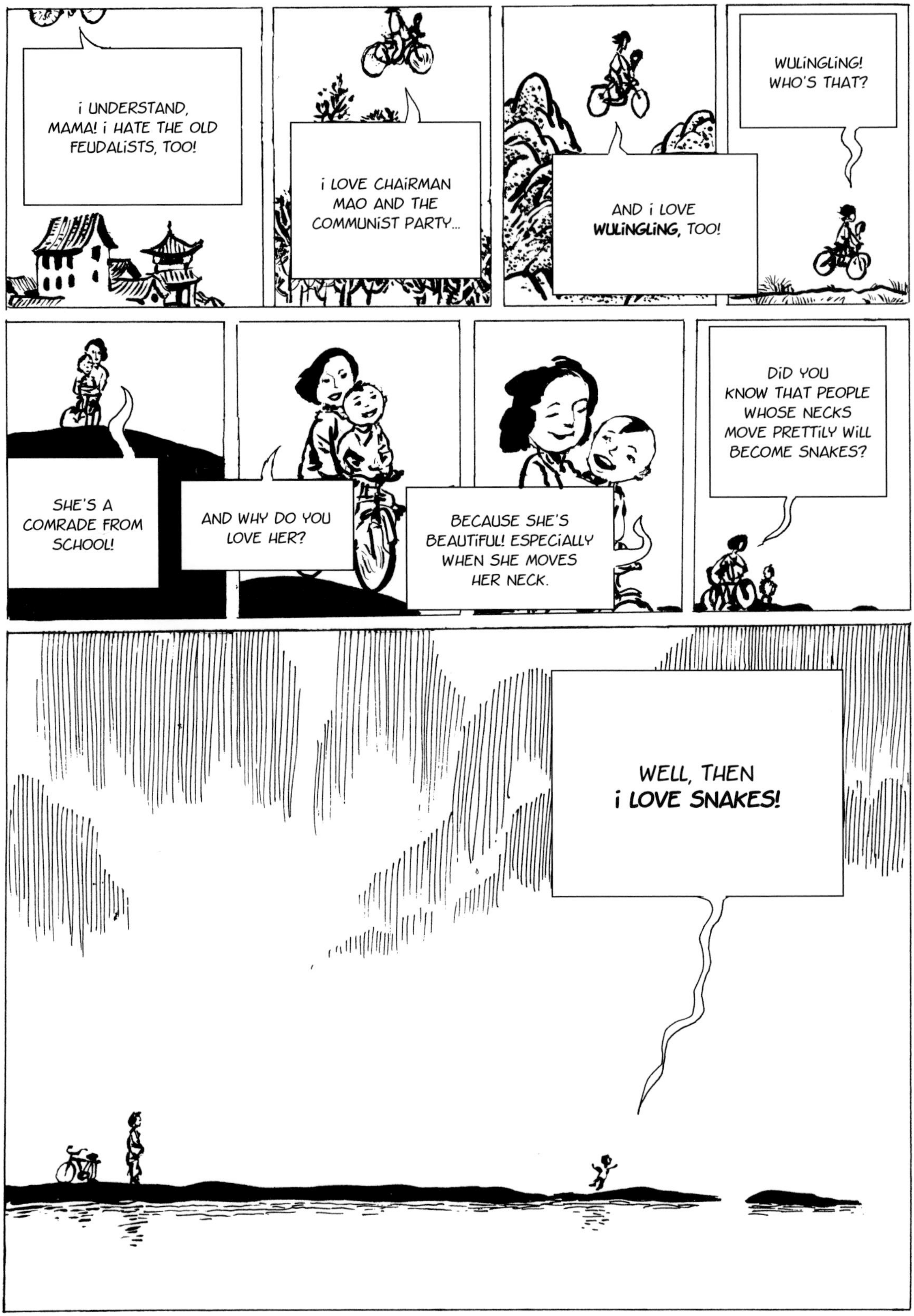
I UNDERSTAND, MAMA! I HATE THE OLD FEUDALISTS, TOO!
I LOVE CHAIRMAN MAO AND THE COMMUNIST PARTY...
AND I LOVE **WULINGLING**, TOO!
WULINGLING! WHO'S THAT?
SHE'S A COMRADE FROM SCHOOL!
AND WHY DO YOU LOVE HER?
BECAUSE SHE'S BEAUTIFUL! ESPECIALLY WHEN SHE MOVES HER NECK.
DID YOU KNOW THAT PEOPLE WHOSE NECKS MOVE PRETTILY WILL BECOME SNAKES?
WELL, THEN **I LOVE SNAKES!**

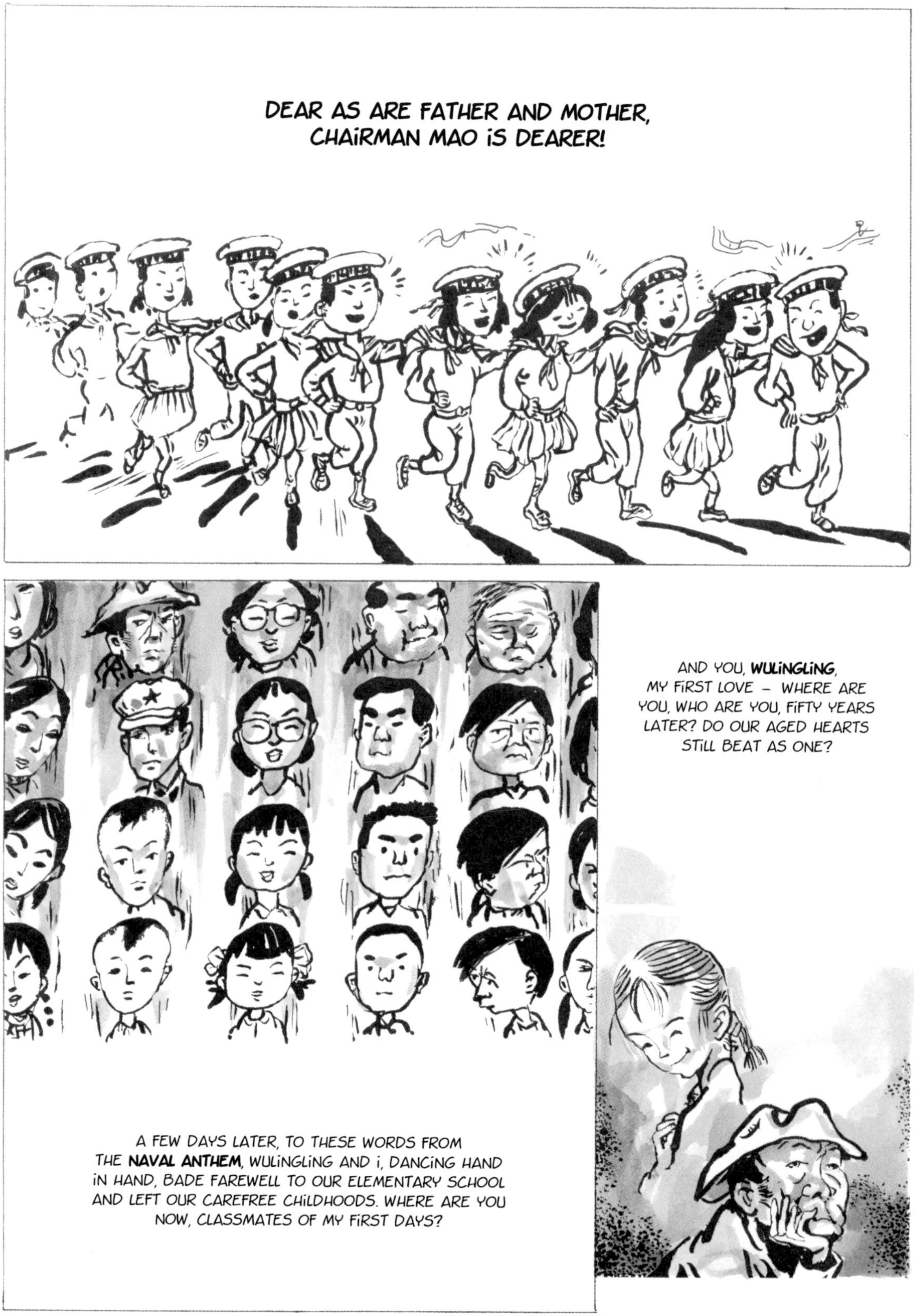
DEAR AS ARE FATHER AND MOTHER, CHAIRMAN MAO IS DEARER!
AND YOU, **WULINGLING**, MY FIRST LOVE – WHERE ARE YOU, WHO ARE YOU, FIFTY YEARS LATER? DO OUR AGED HEARTS STILL BEAT AS ONE?
A FEW DAYS LATER, TO THESE WORDS FROM THE **NAVAL ANTHEM**, WULINGLING AND I, DANCING HAND IN HAND, BADE FAREWELL TO OUR ELEMENTARY SCHOOL AND LEFT OUR CAREFREE CHILDHOODS. WHERE ARE YOU NOW, CLASSMATES OF MY FIRST DAYS?

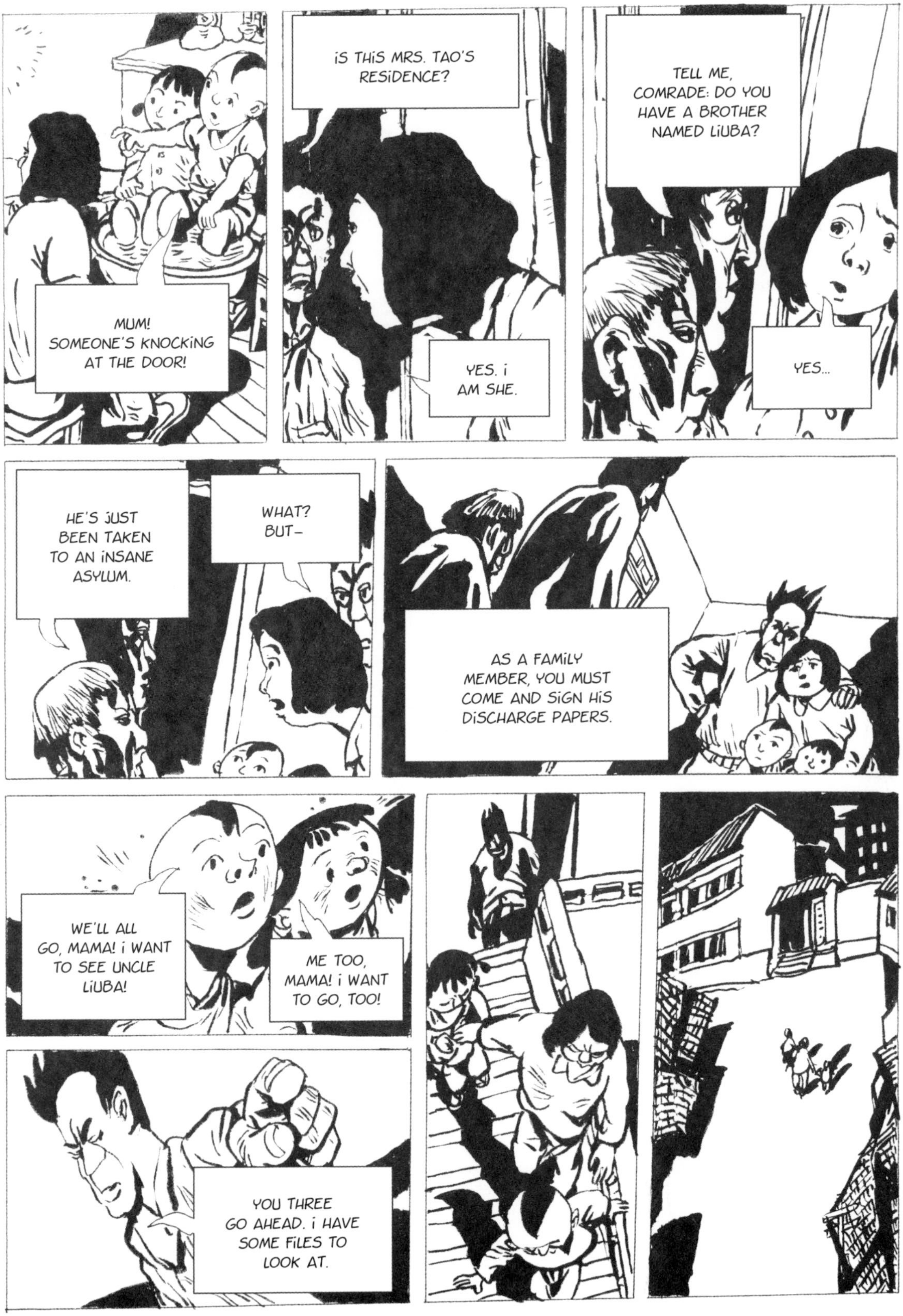
MUM! SOMEONE'S KNOCKING AT THE DOOR!
IS THIS MRS. TAO'S RESIDENCE?
YES. I AM SHE.
TELL ME, COMRADE: DO YOU HAVE A BROTHER NAMED LIUBA?
YES...
HE'S JUST BEEN TAKEN TO AN INSANE ASYLUM.
WHAT? BUT–
AS A FAMILY MEMBER, YOU MUST COME AND SIGN HIS DISCHARGE PAPERS.
WE'LL ALL GO, MAMA! I WANT TO SEE UNCLE LIUBA!
ME TOO, MAMA! I WANT TO GO, TOO!
YOU THREE GO AHEAD. I HAVE SOME FILES TO LOOK AT.

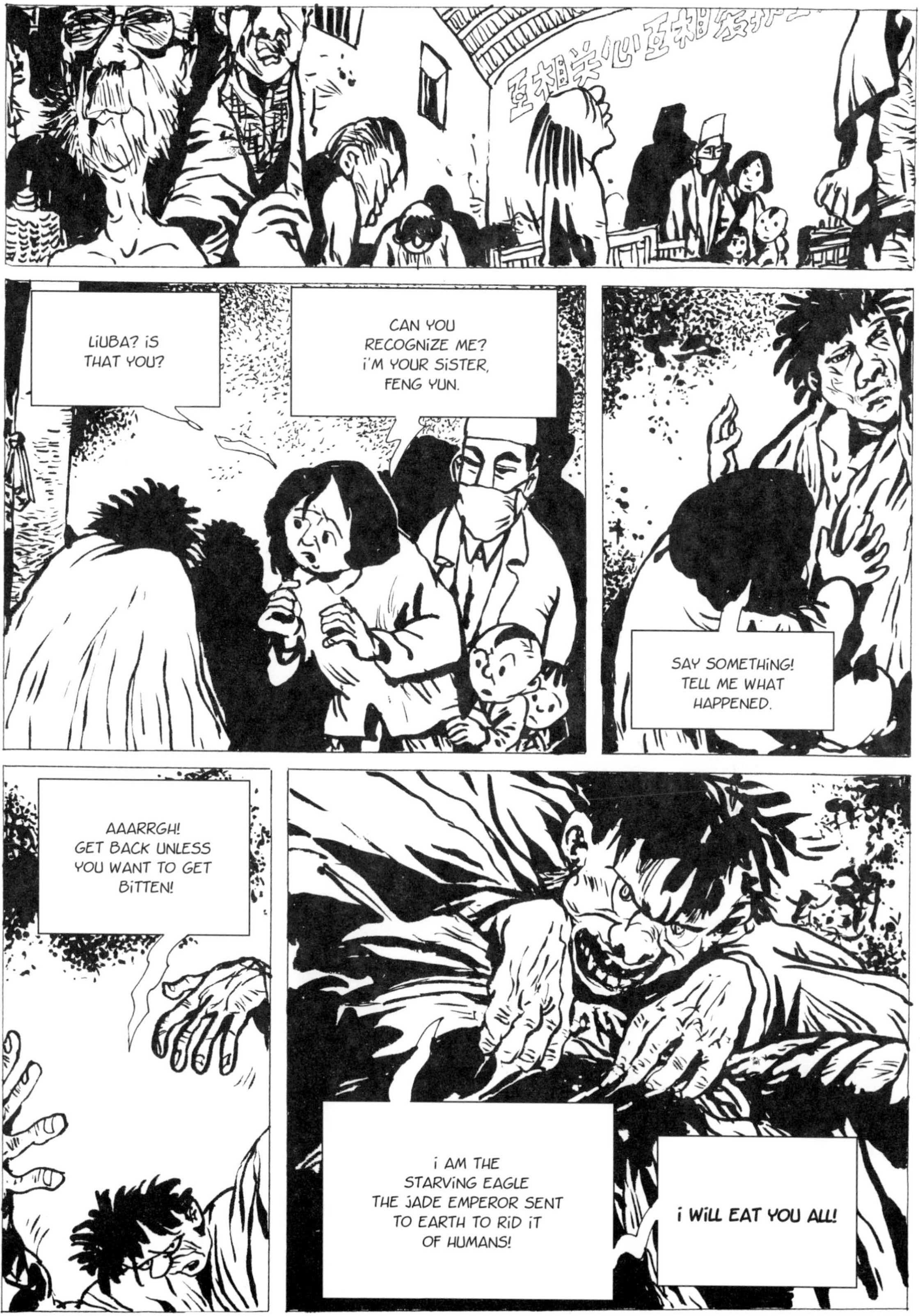
互相关心互相爱护
LiUBA? iS THAT YOU?
CAN YOU RECOGNiZE ME? i'M YOUR SiSTER, FENG YUN.
SAY SOMETHiNG! TELL ME WHAT HAPPENED.
AAARRGH! GET BACK UNLESS YOU WANT TO GET BiTTEN!
i AM THE STARViNG EAGLE THE JADE EMPEROR SENT TO EARTH TO RiD iT OF HUMANS!
i WiLL EAT YOU ALL!

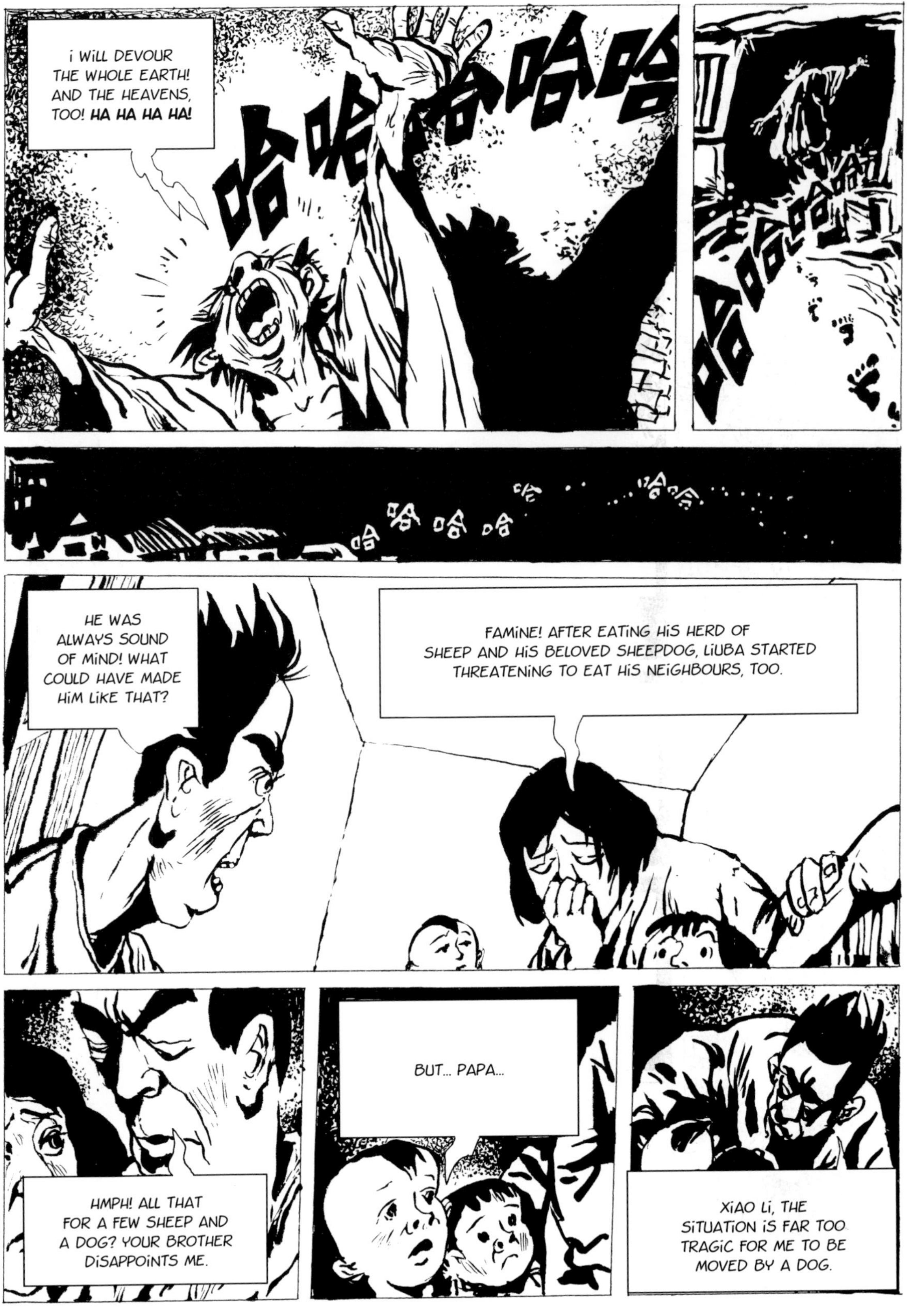
I WILL DEVOUR THE WHOLE EARTH! AND THE HEAVENS, TOO! **HA HA HA HA!**
哈哈哈哈哈
HE WAS ALWAYS SOUND OF MIND! WHAT COULD HAVE MADE HIM LIKE THAT?
FAMINE! AFTER EATING HIS HERD OF SHEEP AND HIS BELOVED SHEEPDOG, LIUBA STARTED THREATENING TO EAT HIS NEIGHBOURS, TOO.
HMPH! ALL THAT FOR A FEW SHEEP AND A DOG? YOUR BROTHER DISAPPOINTS ME.
BUT... PAPA...
XIAO LI, THE SITUATION IS FAR TOO TRAGIC FOR ME TO BE MOVED BY A DOG.

SADLY, MY FATHER WAS RIGHT: FAMINE HAD BEEN RAGING FOR TWO YEARS NOW... AND THE WORST WAS YET TO COME.

NO SOONER WAS i iN ELEMENTARY SCHOOL THAN A MASSiVE CAMPAIGN NAMED **"ELiMiNATE THE FOUR PESTS"*** WAS LAUNCHED TO ERADiCATE ALL CREATURES THAT MIGHT HARM THE HARVEST. WE APPLIED THE SAME FORMULA THAT HAD WORKED SO WELL WiTH STEEL, COAL, WOOD AND FERTiLiZER: MASS ACTiON.

COMRADE, YOUR SCHOOL MUST BE AN EXAMPLE!

COMRADE, YOUR CLASS MUST BE AN EXAMPLE!

YOU MUST BE AN EXAMPLE!

i'LL SHOW THEM AN EXAMPLE!

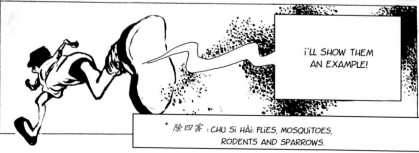

* 除四害 : CHU Si HÀi: FLiES, MOSQUiTOES, RODENTS AND SPARROWS.

59

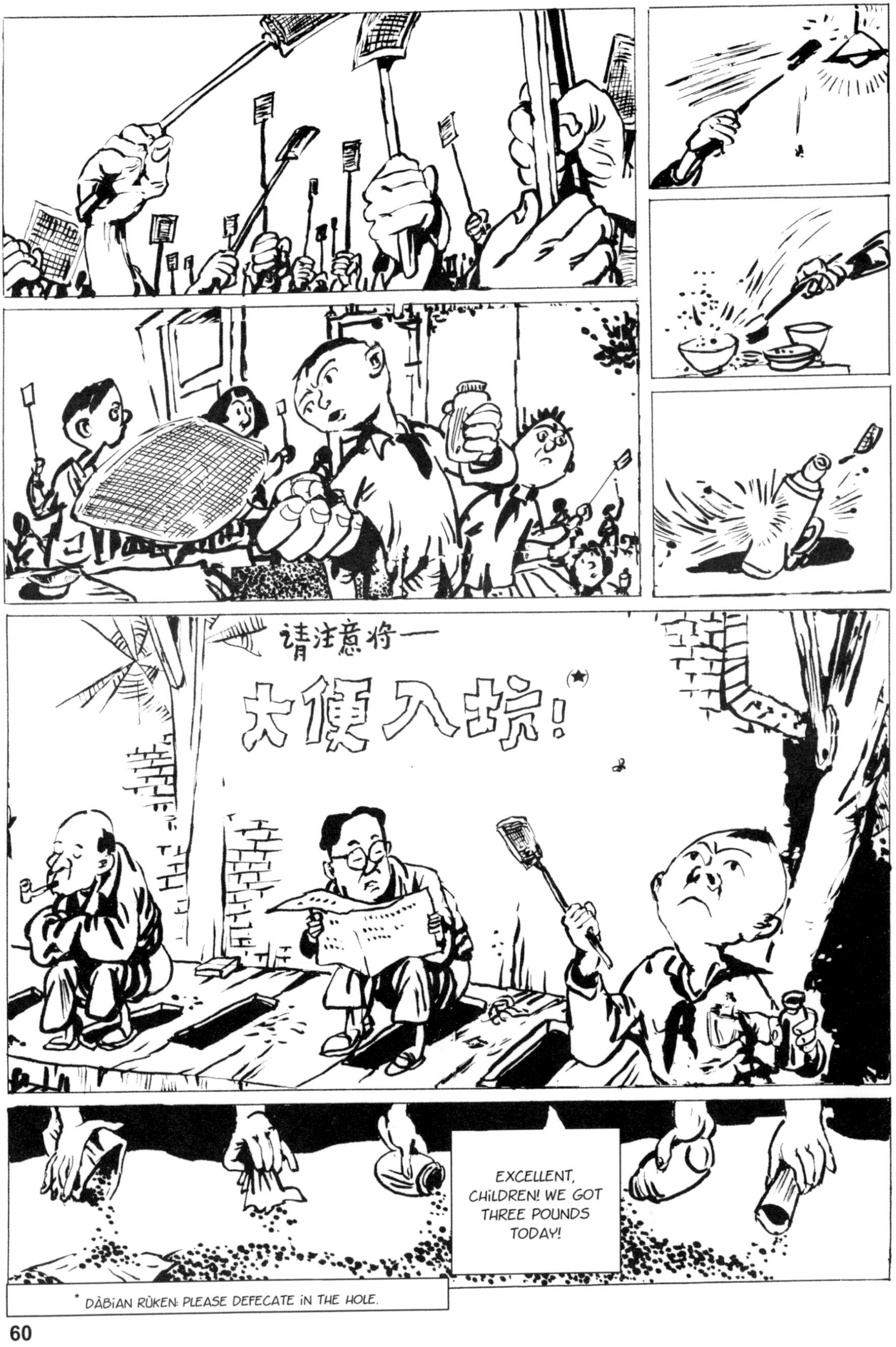

请注意将——
大便入坑!(★)
EXCELLENT, CHILDREN! WE GOT THREE POUNDS TODAY!

* DÀBIAN RÙKEN: PLEASE DEFECATE IN THE HOLE.

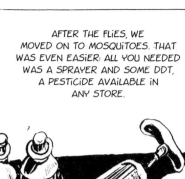

AFTER THE FLIES, WE MOVED ON TO MOSQUITOES. THAT WAS EVEN EASIER: ALL YOU NEEDED WAS A SPRAYER AND SOME DDT, A PESTICIDE AVAILABLE IN ANY STORE.

A CLASSMATE OF MINE, BAO BIANYUN, NURSED A GENUINE FASCINATION FOR THAT MYSTERIOUS FOG.

URRGH... MY STOMACH. IT HURTS. IT HUUUURTS!

I'M SURE OUR HOUSE IS HAUNTED!

HEY, GUYS, BAO BIANYUN'S SO STUPID WE HAVE TO GIVE HIM A NICKNAME!

HOW ABOUT "QIBAO"?

YEAH, THAT MEANS "ALL FOGGED-UP"!

AND "LADIES' DRESS"!

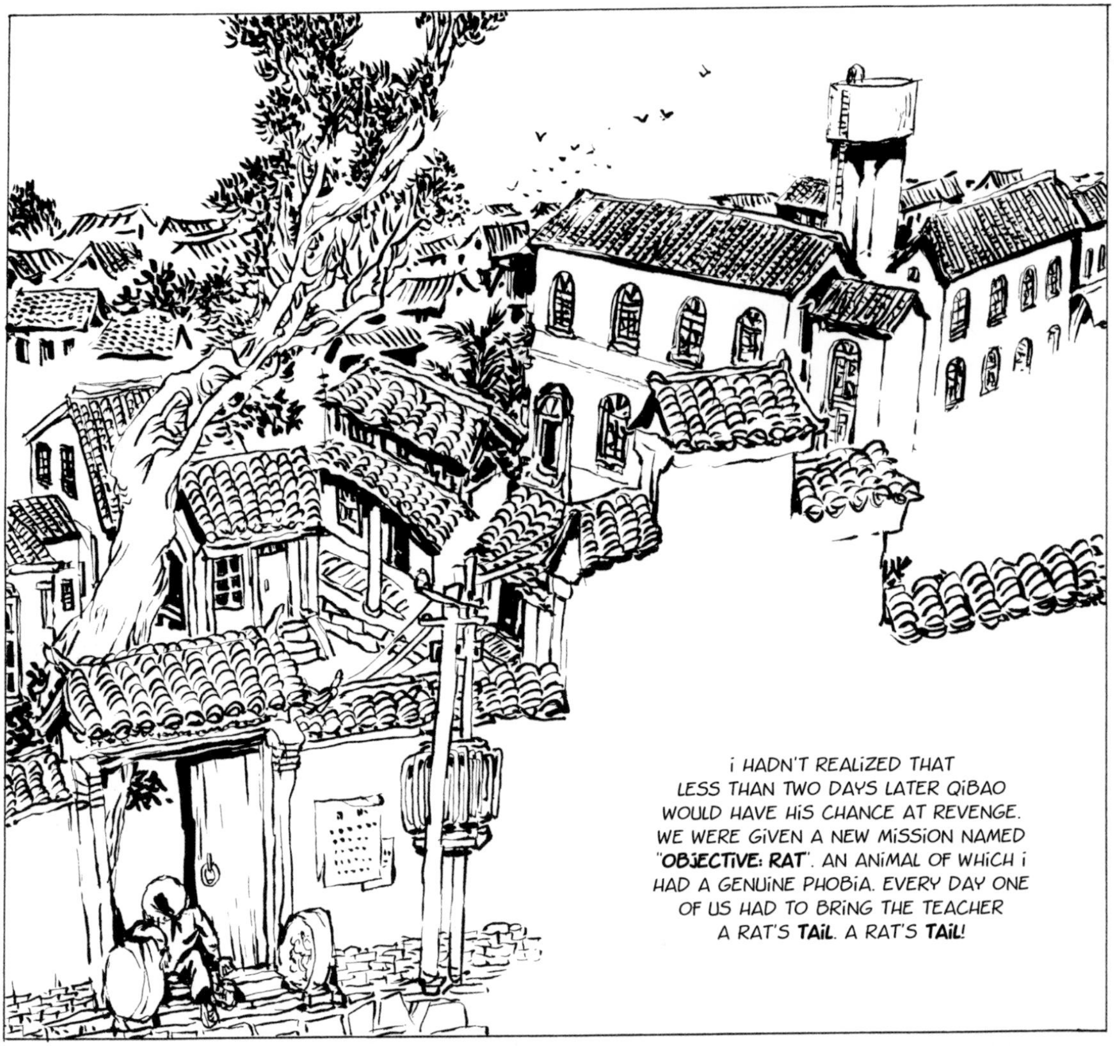
I HADN'T REALIZED THAT LESS THAN TWO DAYS LATER QIBAO WOULD HAVE HIS CHANCE AT REVENGE. WE WERE GIVEN A NEW MISSION NAMED "**OBJECTIVE: RAT**". AN ANIMAL OF WHICH I HAD A GENUINE PHOBIA. EVERY DAY ONE OF US HAD TO BRING THE TEACHER A RAT'S **TAIL**. A RAT'S **TAIL**!

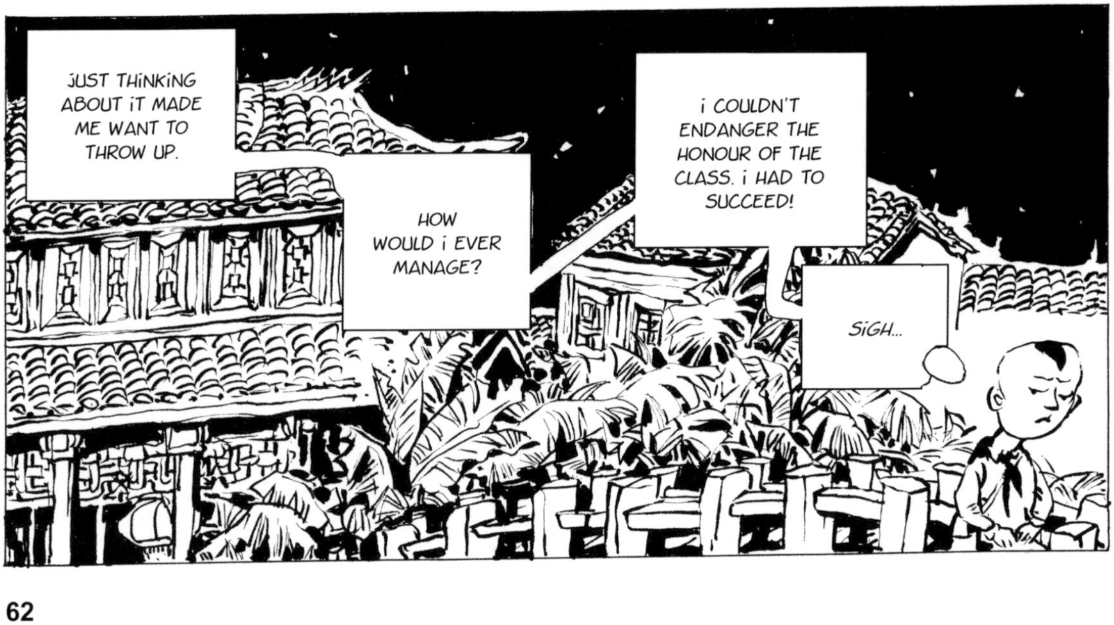
JUST THINKING ABOUT IT MADE ME WANT TO THROW UP.
HOW WOULD I EVER MANAGE?
I COULDN'T ENDANGER THE HONOUR OF THE CLASS. I HAD TO SUCCEED!
SIGH...

63

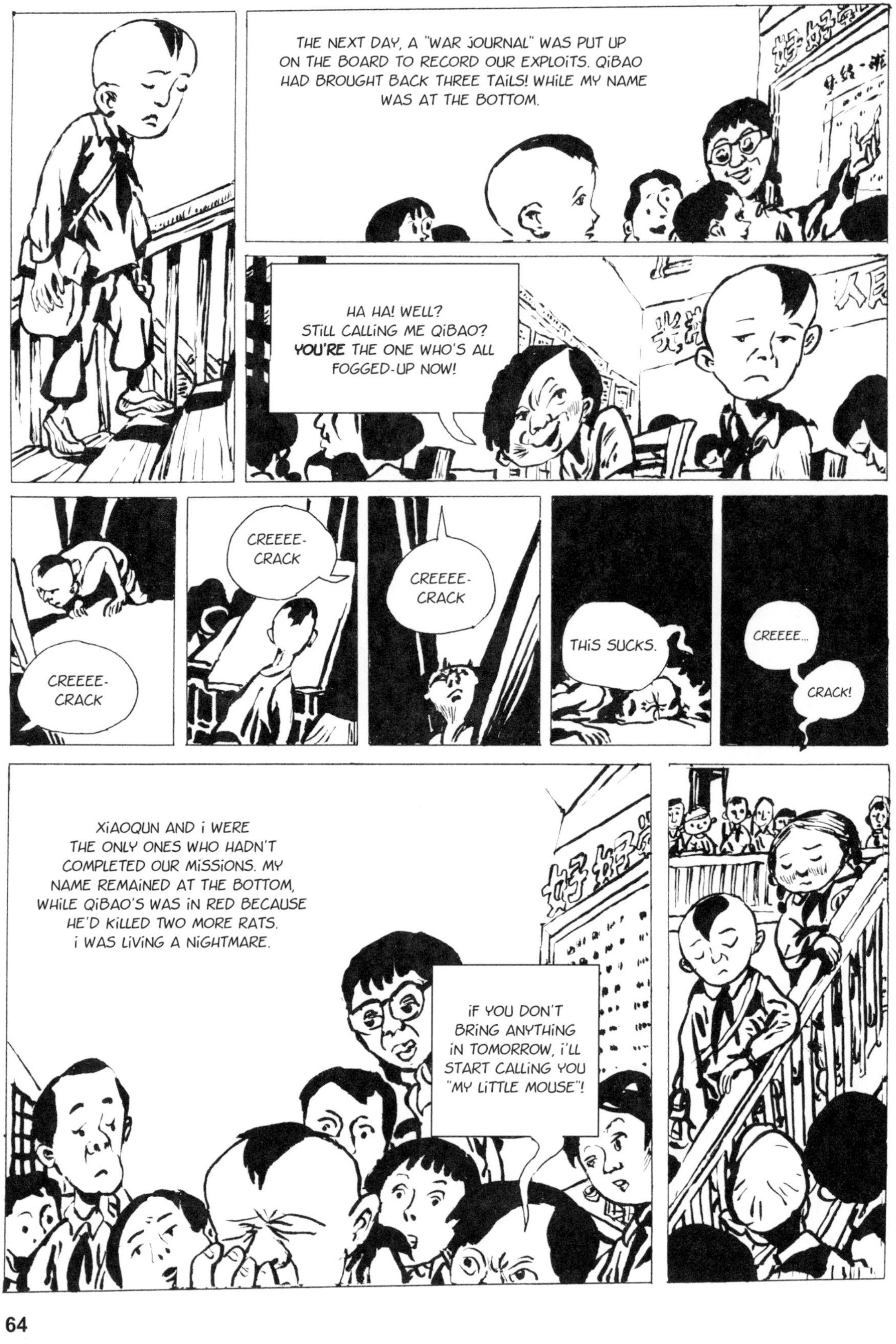
THE NEXT DAY, A "WAR JOURNAL" WAS PUT UP ON THE BOARD TO RECORD OUR EXPLOITS. QIBAO HAD BROUGHT BACK THREE TAILS! WHILE MY NAME WAS AT THE BOTTOM.
HA HA! WELL? STILL CALLING ME QIBAO? **YOU'RE** THE ONE WHO'S ALL FOGGED-UP NOW!
CREEEE-CRACK
CREEEE-CRACK
CREEEE-CRACK
THIS SUCKS.
CREEEE...
CRACK!
XIAOQUN AND I WERE THE ONLY ONES WHO HADN'T COMPLETED OUR MISSIONS. MY NAME REMAINED AT THE BOTTOM, WHILE QIBAO'S WAS IN RED BECAUSE HE'D KILLED TWO MORE RATS. I WAS LIVING A NIGHTMARE.
IF YOU DON'T BRING ANYTHING IN TOMORROW, I'LL START CALLING YOU "MY LITTLE MOUSE"!

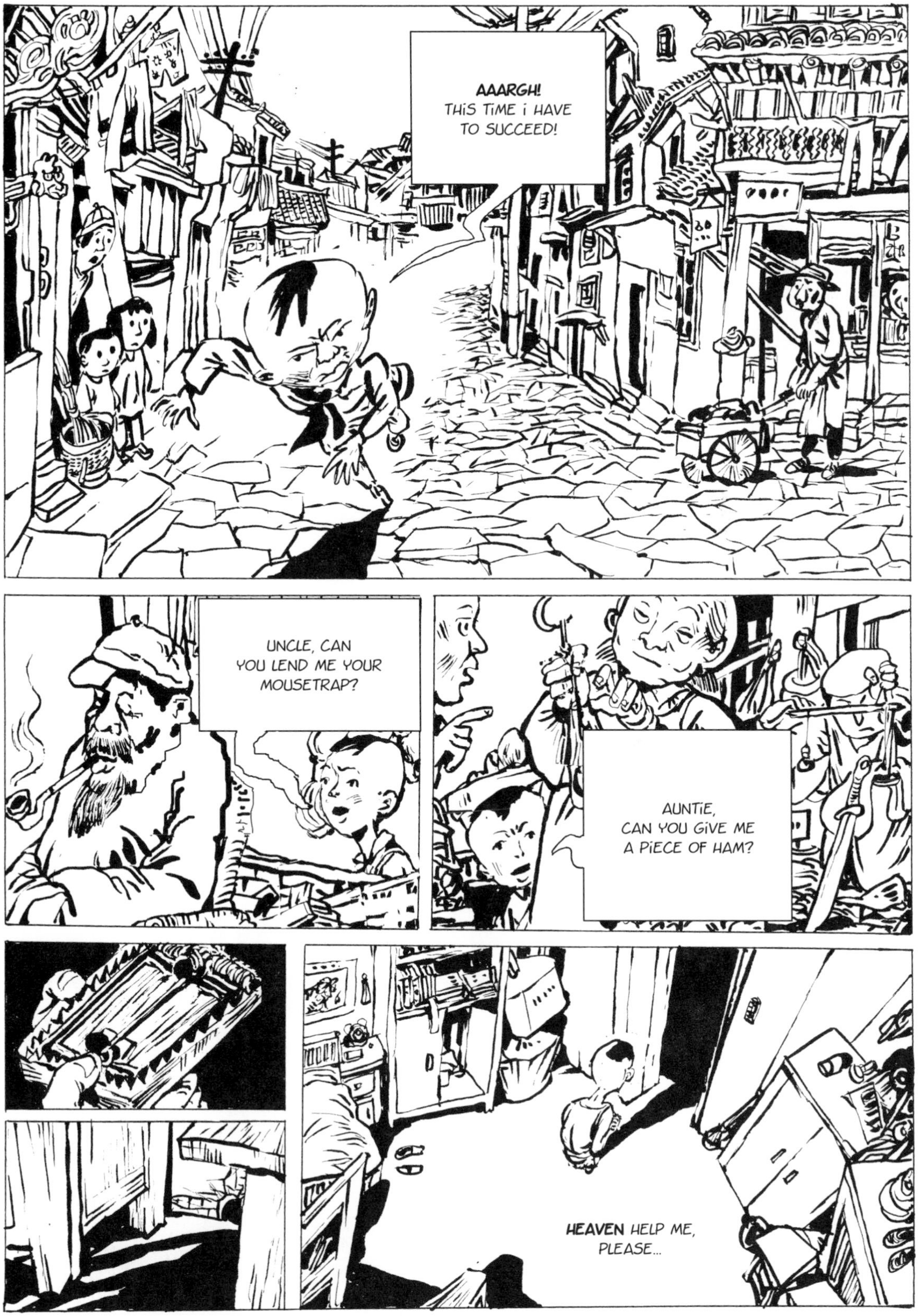

AAARGH!
THIS TIME I HAVE TO SUCCEED!
UNCLE, CAN YOU LEND ME YOUR MOUSETRAP?
AUNTIE, CAN YOU GIVE ME A PIECE OF HAM?
HEAVEN HELP ME, PLEASE...

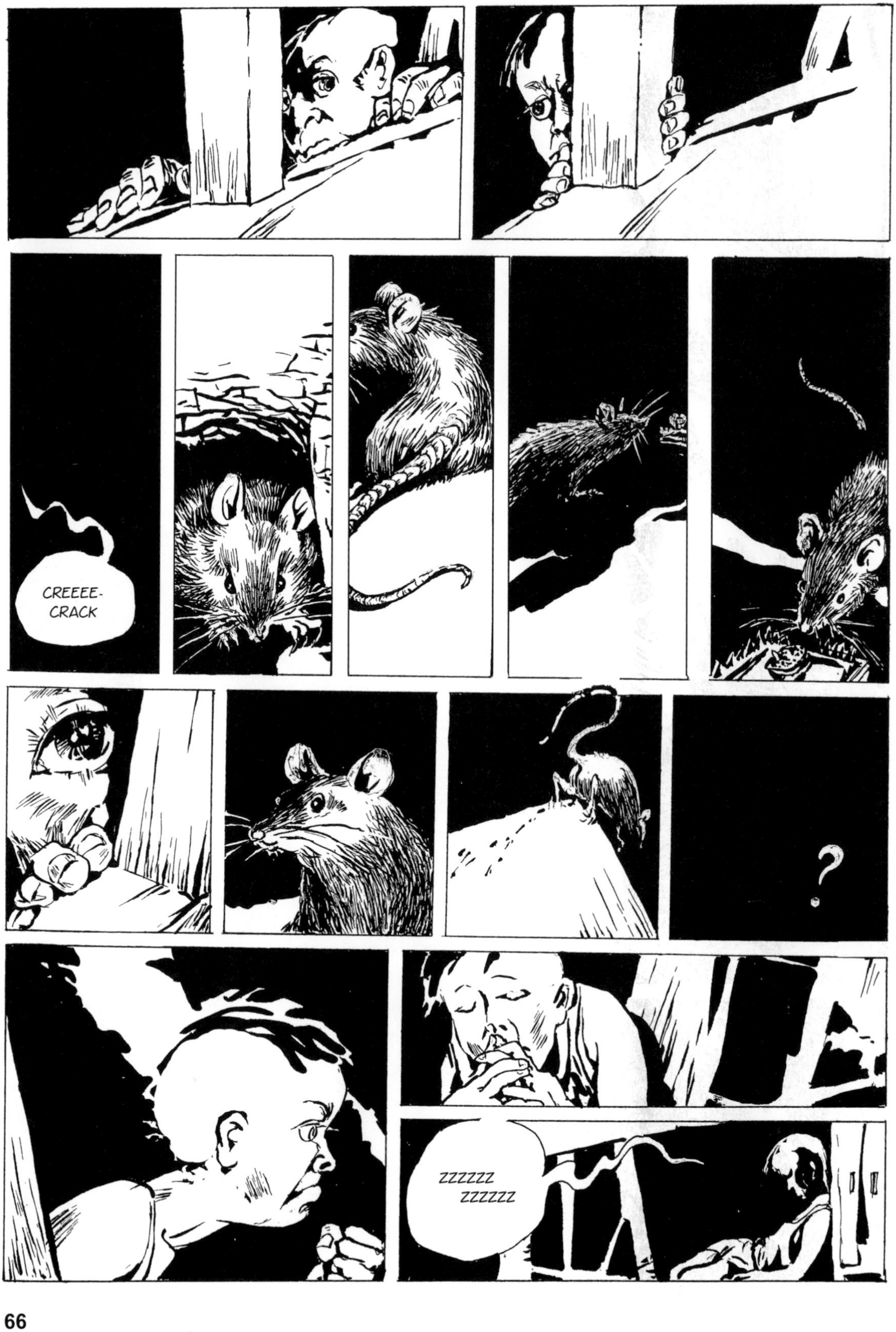
CREEEE-
CRACK
?
ZZZZZZ
ZZZZZZ

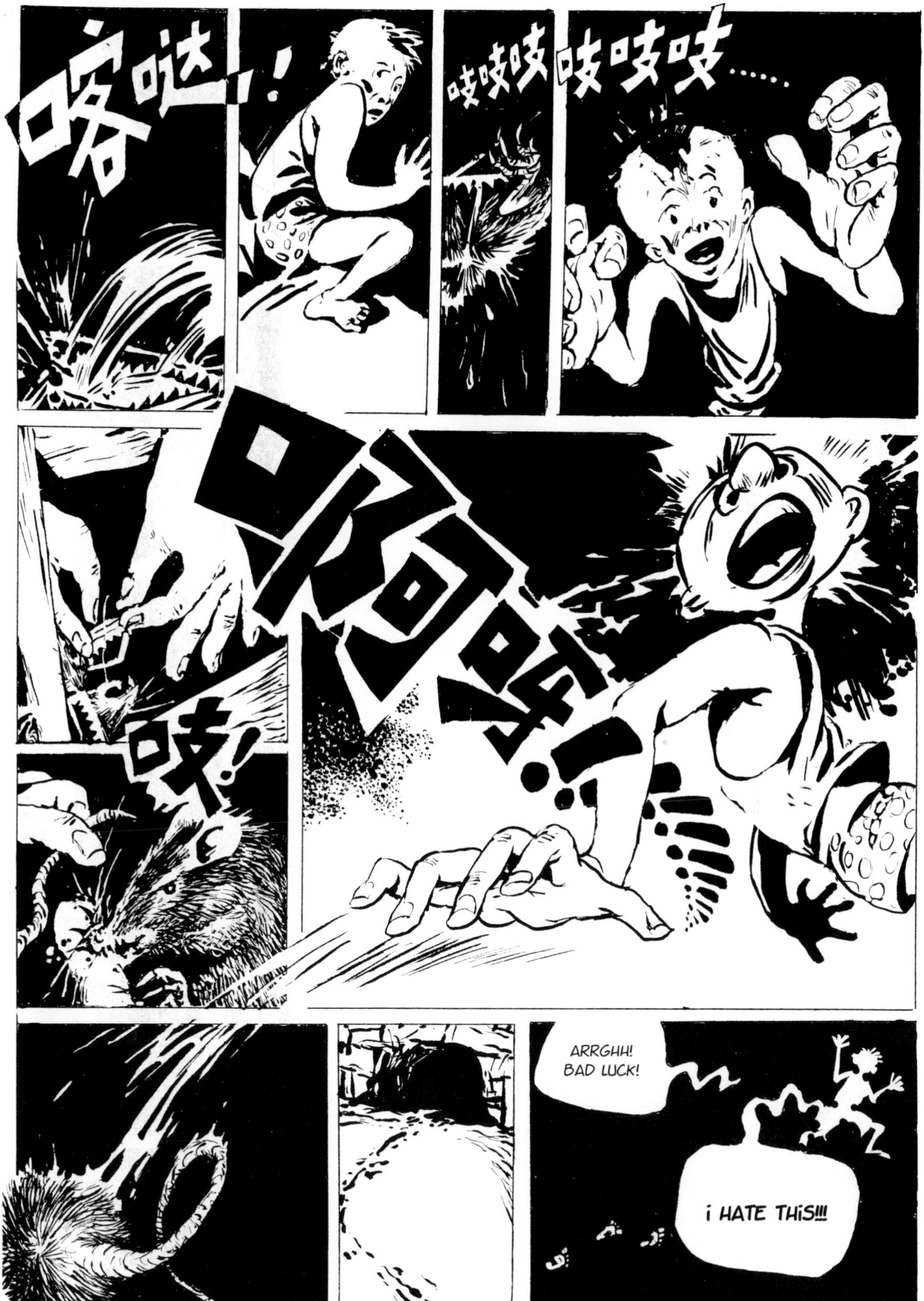
喀哒！！
吱吱吱吱吱吱……
啊呀！！
吱！
ARRGHH! BAD LUCK!
¡ HATE THIS!!!

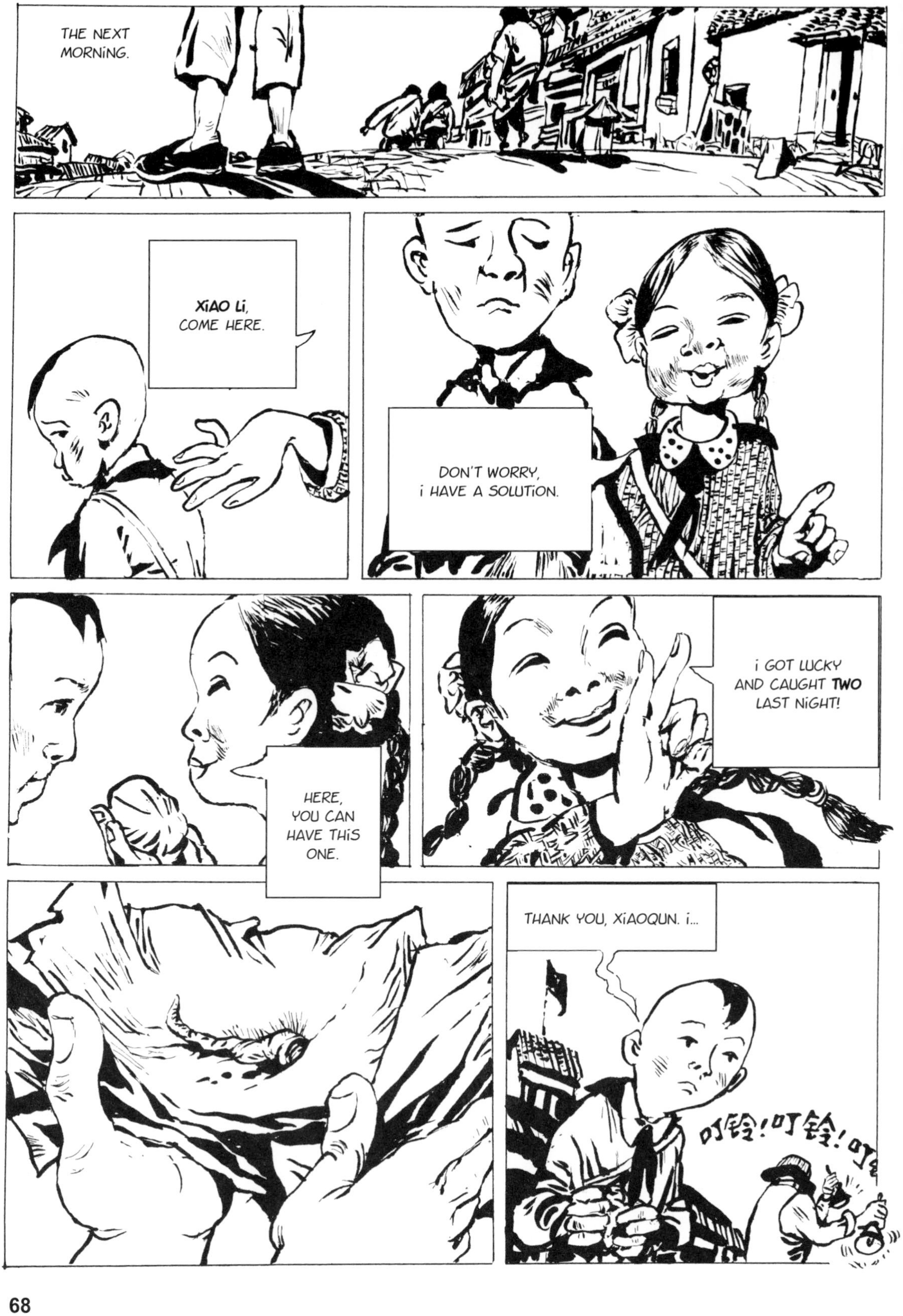
THE NEXT MORNING.
XIAO LI, COME HERE.
DON'T WORRY, I HAVE A SOLUTION.
HERE, YOU CAN HAVE THIS ONE.
I GOT LUCKY AND CAUGHT **TWO** LAST NIGHT!
THANK YOU, XIAOQUN. I...
叮铃！叮铃！叮铃

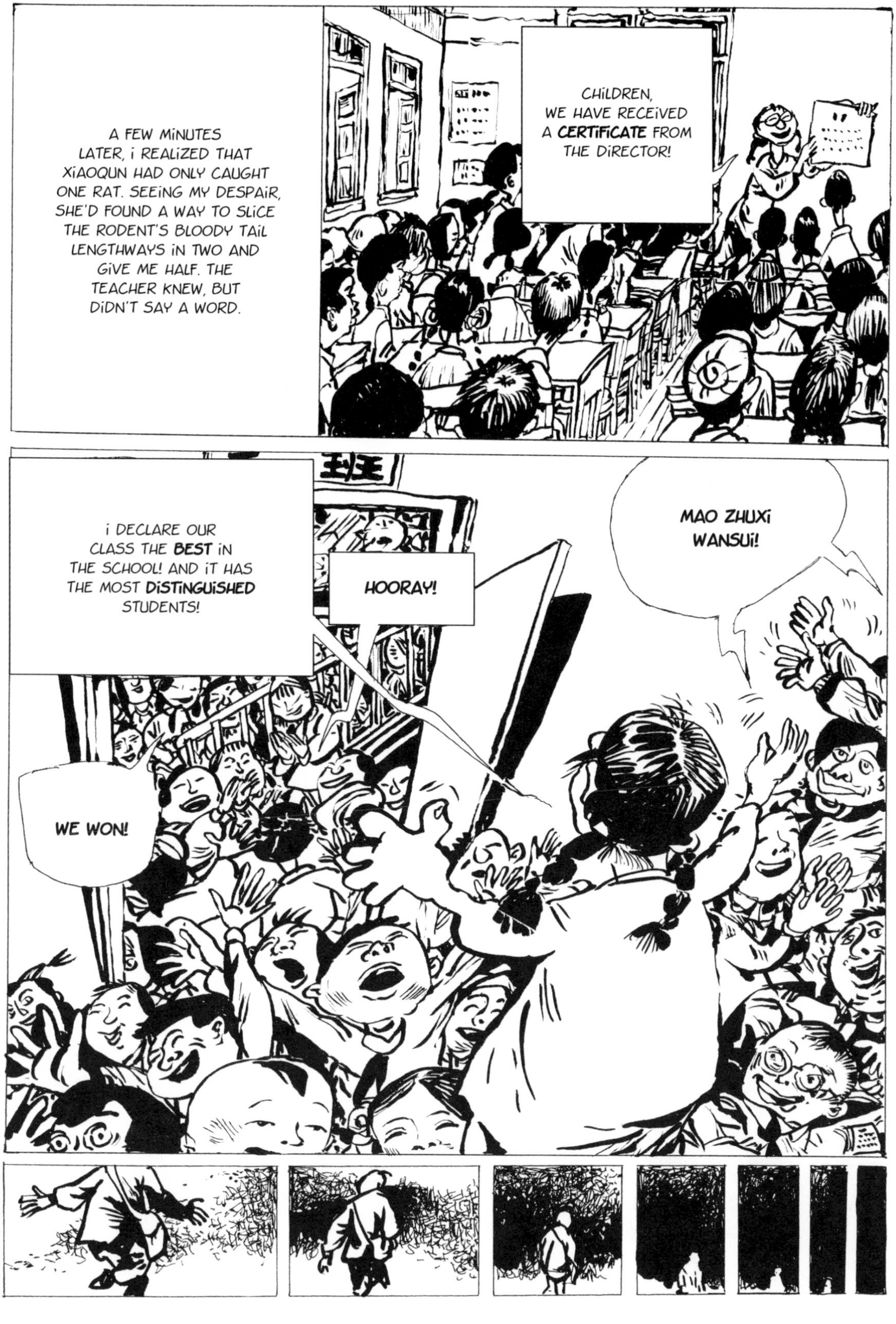
A FEW MINUTES LATER, I REALIZED THAT XIAOQUN HAD ONLY CAUGHT ONE RAT. SEEING MY DESPAIR, SHE'D FOUND A WAY TO SLICE THE RODENT'S BLOODY TAIL LENGTHWAYS IN TWO AND GIVE ME HALF. THE TEACHER KNEW, BUT DIDN'T SAY A WORD.
CHILDREN, WE HAVE RECEIVED A **CERTIFICATE** FROM THE DIRECTOR!
I DECLARE OUR CLASS THE **BEST** IN THE SCHOOL! AND IT HAS THE MOST **DISTINGUISHED** STUDENTS!
HOORAY!
MAO ZHUXI WANSUI!
WE WON!

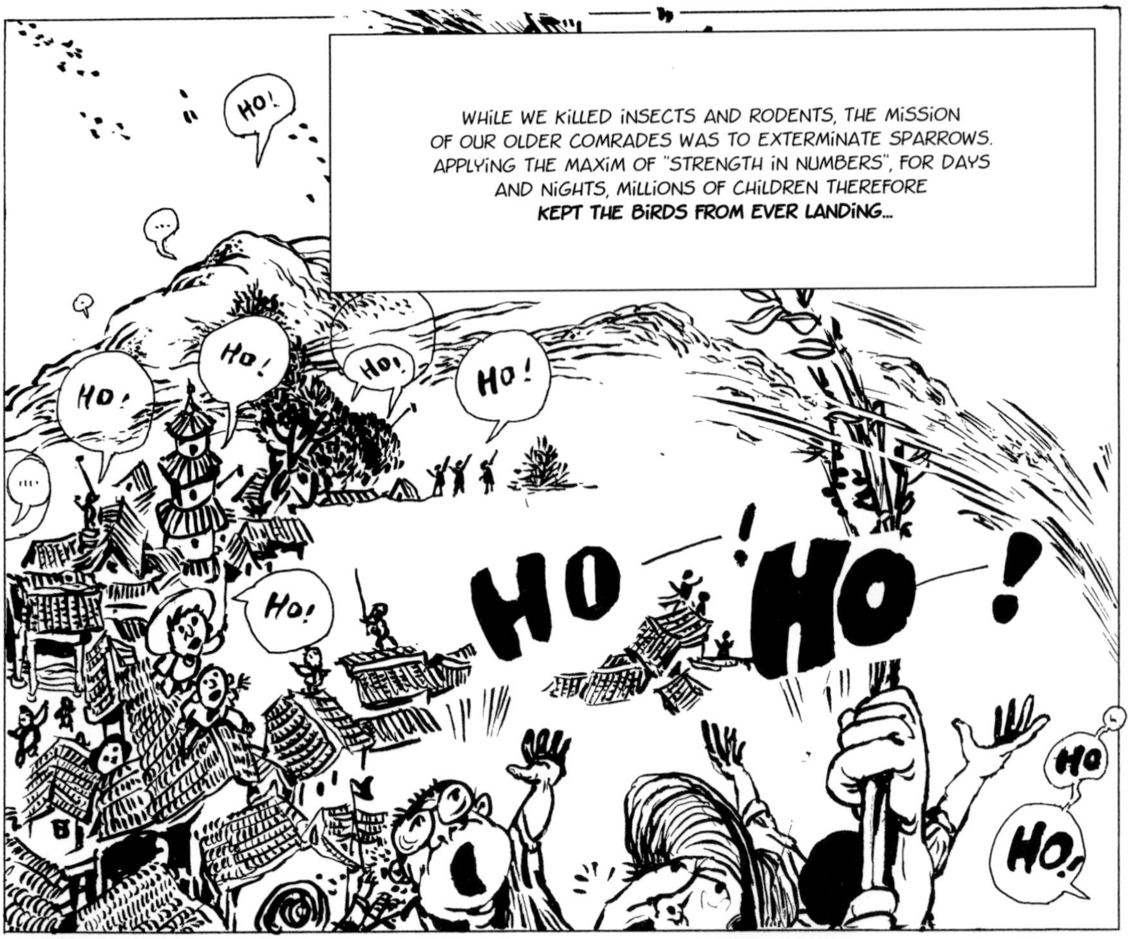
WHILE WE KILLED INSECTS AND RODENTS, THE MISSION OF OUR OLDER COMRADES WAS TO EXTERMINATE SPARROWS. APPLYING THE MAXIM OF "STRENGTH IN NUMBERS", FOR DAYS AND NIGHTS, MILLIONS OF CHILDREN THEREFORE **KEPT THE BIRDS FROM EVER LANDING...**
HO!
HO!
HO!
HO!
HO!
HO!
HO—!HO—!
HO
HO!

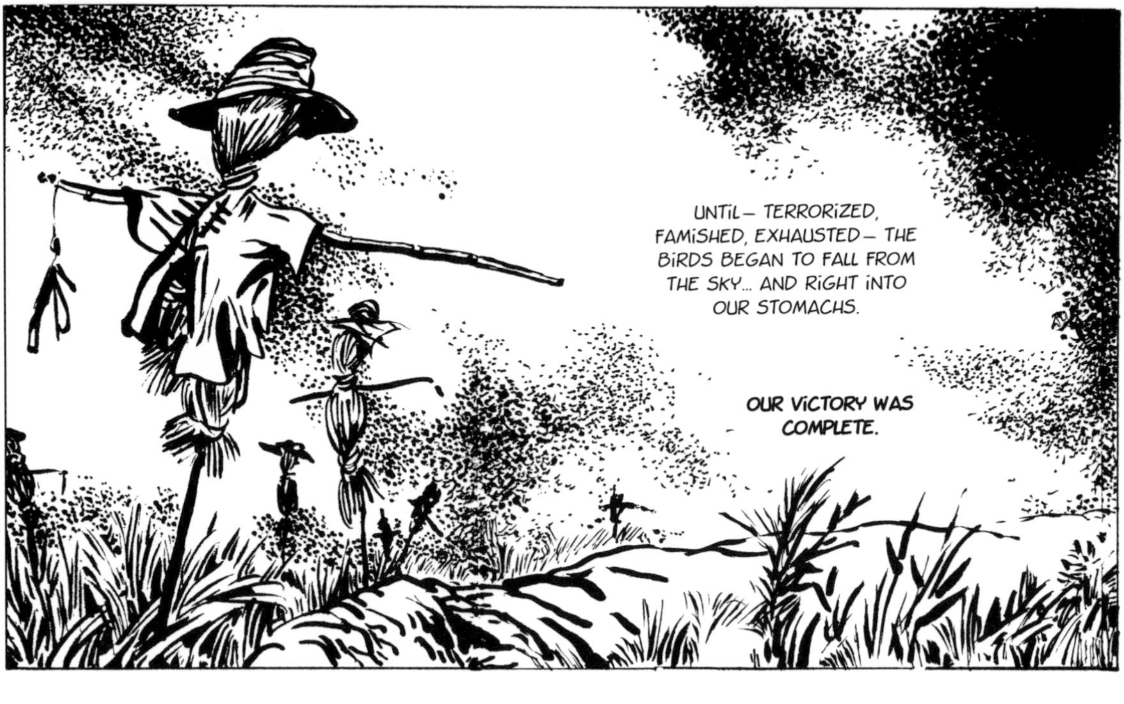
UNTIL— TERRORIZED, FAMISHED, EXHAUSTED— THE BIRDS BEGAN TO FALL FROM THE SKY... AND RIGHT INTO OUR STOMACHS.
OUR VICTORY WAS COMPLETE.

GREAT-AUNT?
WHY, WHAT ARE **YOU**
DOING IN KUNMING?

I—I CAME
SEEKING HELP. IN
THE VILLAGE, EVEN
THE ROACHES ARE
DYING OF HUNGER...

SIT DOWN. TAKE A
MOMENT TO RECOVER,
AND TELL ME WHAT'S
GOING ON IN THE VILLAGE.

IT'S HORRIBLE!
REMEMBER YOUR
COUSIN ZHANG, WHO
LIVED BY THE
WEST GATE?

WELL, A WEEK AGO, COUSIN
ZHANG SET OUT EARLY ONE
MORNING IN SEARCH OF A FEW
ROOTS OR WEEDS TO EAT.

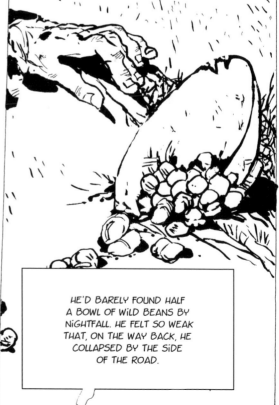

HE'D BARELY FOUND HALF
A BOWL OF WILD BEANS BY
NIGHTFALL. HE FELT SO WEAK
THAT, ON THE WAY BACK, HE
COLLAPSED BY THE SIDE
OF THE ROAD.

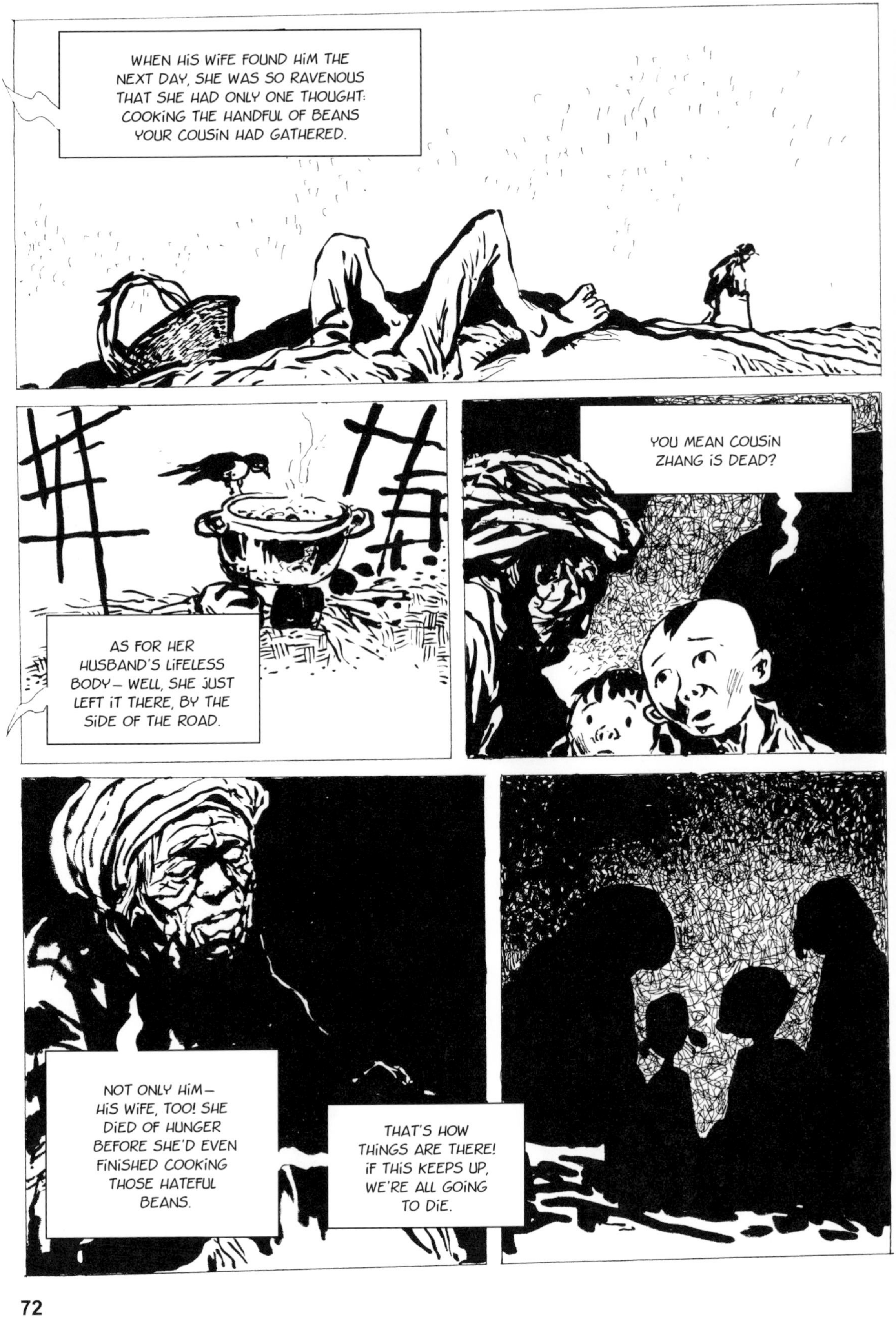
WHEN HIS WIFE FOUND HIM THE NEXT DAY, SHE WAS SO RAVENOUS THAT SHE HAD ONLY ONE THOUGHT: COOKING THE HANDFUL OF BEANS YOUR COUSIN HAD GATHERED.
AS FOR HER HUSBAND'S LIFELESS BODY— WELL, SHE JUST LEFT IT THERE, BY THE SIDE OF THE ROAD.
YOU MEAN COUSIN ZHANG IS DEAD?
NOT ONLY HIM— HIS WIFE, TOO! SHE DIED OF HUNGER BEFORE SHE'D EVEN FINISHED COOKING THOSE HATEFUL BEANS.
THAT'S HOW THINGS ARE THERE! IF THIS KEEPS UP, WE'RE ALL GOING TO DIE.

AND SO iT WAS. WE
HAD TURNED CHiNA iNTO A
BARREN LAND: A LAND WITHOUT
TREES, iNSECTS, RODENTS
OR BiRDS...

THERE WERE FEWER HUMAN
BEiNGS, TOO: iN THE THREE YEARS
FROM 1959 TO 1961, CHiNA SUFFERED
ONE OF THE WORST FAMiNES iN
iTS LONG HiSTORY.

iN MY iMMEDiATE FAMiLY,
ONE UNCLE WAS GORED TO DEATH WHiLE
TRYiNG TO STEAL FORAGE FROM A BUFFALO.
ANOTHER, WHO TRiED TO SURViVE BY EATiNG
DiRT, ALMOST DiED FROM CONSTiPATiON.
HE OWED HiS LiFE TO MY GREAT-GRANDMOTHER,
WHO SPENT DAYS AND DAYS CLEANiNG OUT
HiS ANUS WiTH HER FiNGER. TO SAVE HER
GREAT-GRANDSON, SHE SCRAPED AND PiCKED
UNTiL, EXHAUSTED AND STARViNG,
SHE DiED SHORTLY THEREAFTER.

HOW MANY MiLLiONS
PERiSHED? EVEN TODAY,
HiSTORiANS AREN'T iN AGREEMENT
ON A NUMBER: 5, 8, 10 MiLLiON DEAD?
OR EVEN MORE? NOR DiD THEY KNOW
WHAT NAME TO GiVE THiS **DARK ERA**:
"THE DEBiLiTATiON AFTER THE WiTHDRAWAL
OF SOViET AiD"? "THE THREE YEARS
OF NATURAL DiSASTERS"*? OR,
MORE PROSAiCALLY, "THE ERA OF
THE GREAT LEAP FORWARD
OF 1958"?

THE ONLY SURE
THiNG WAS THAT iN
1962, THE GREAT
LEAP FORWARD CAME
TO AN END.

BY THE SAME
TOKEN, THE "NATURAL
DiSASTERS" STOPPED.

---

* 三年自然灾害 : SAN NiAN ZiRAN ZAiHAi.

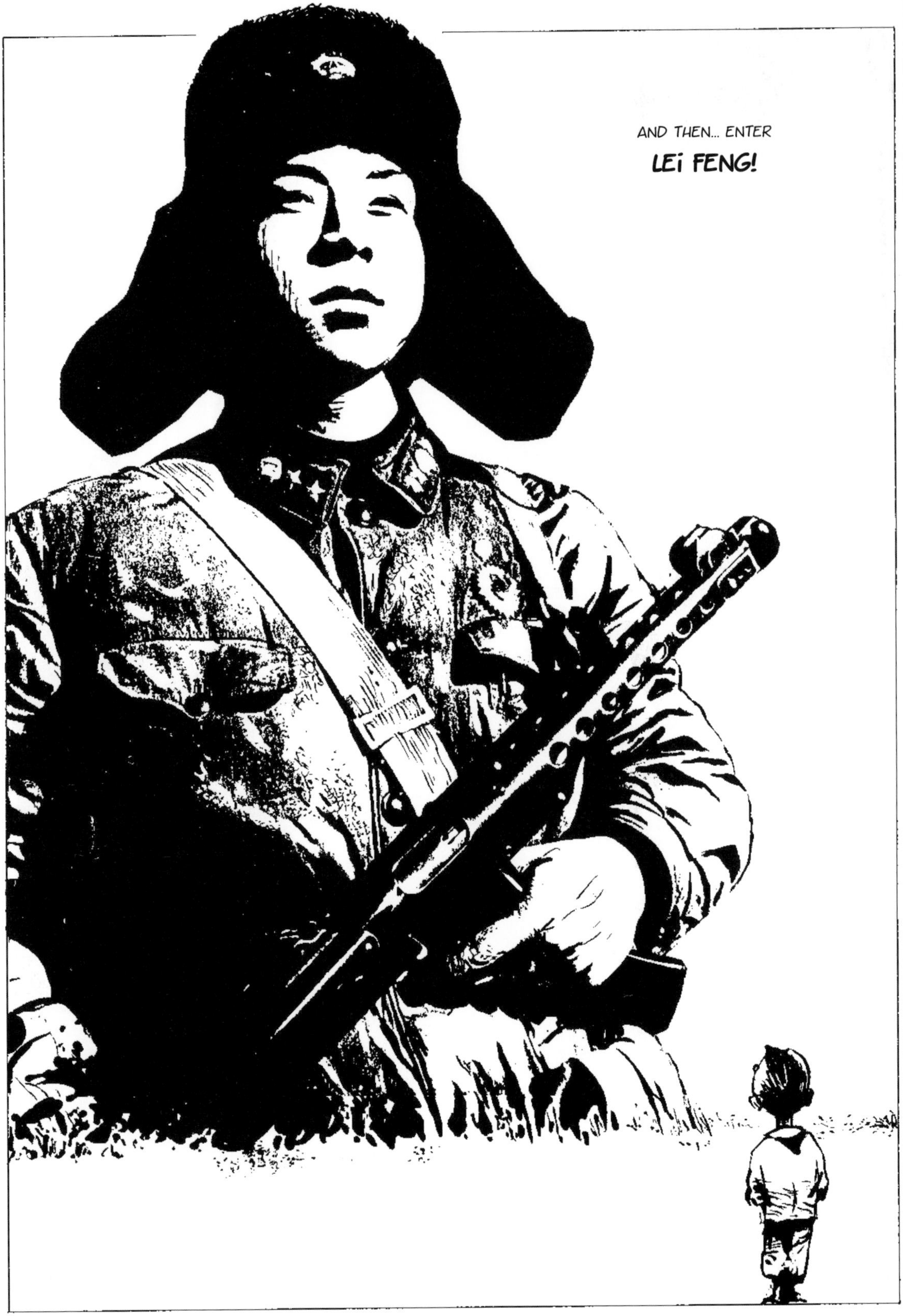
AND THEN... ENTER
LEi FENG!

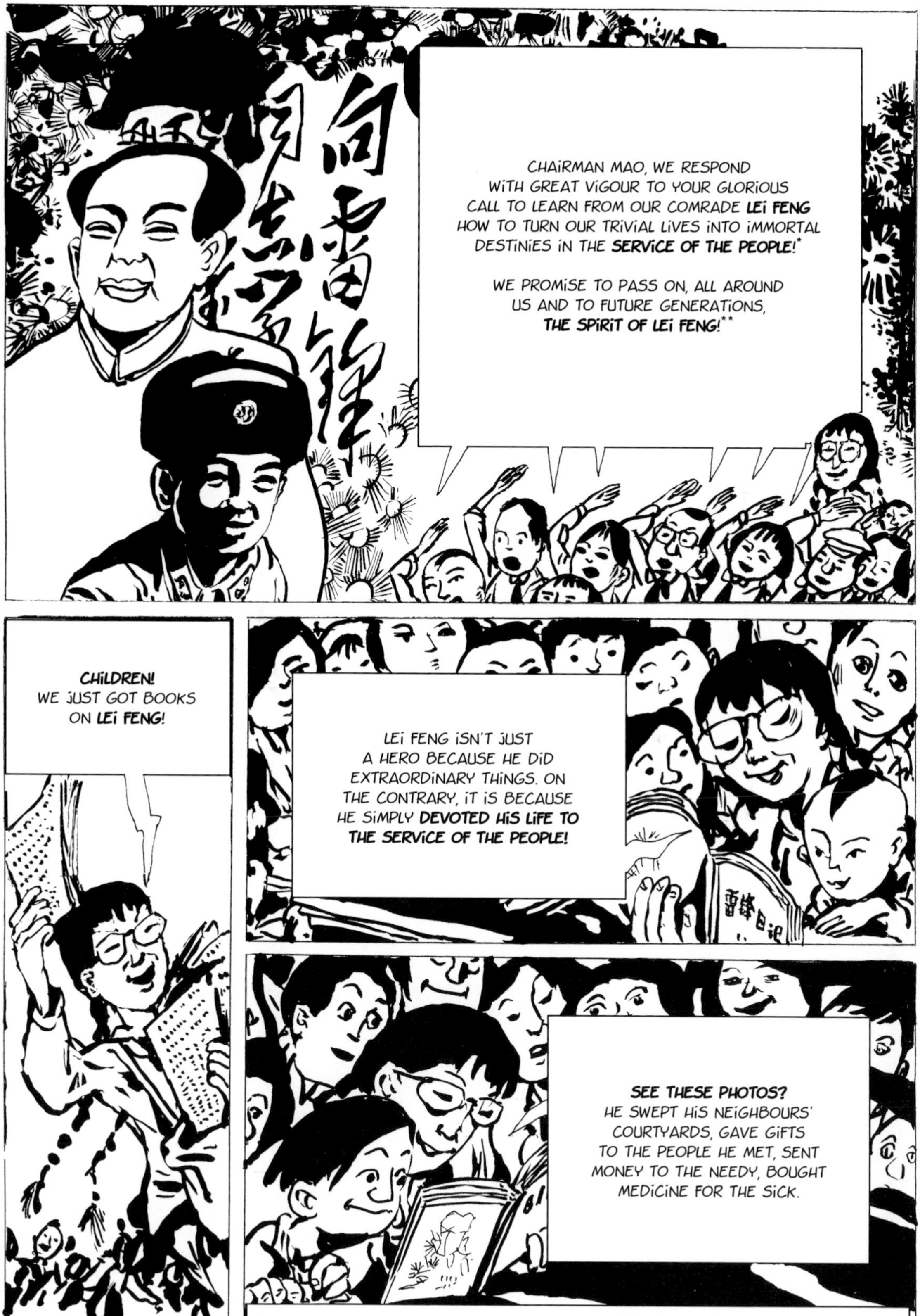
CHAIRMAN MAO, WE RESPOND WITH GREAT VIGOUR TO YOUR GLORIOUS CALL TO LEARN FROM OUR COMRADE **LEI FENG** HOW TO TURN OUR TRIVIAL LIVES INTO IMMORTAL DESTINIES IN THE **SERVICE OF THE PEOPLE!***
WE PROMISE TO PASS ON, ALL AROUND US AND TO FUTURE GENERATIONS, **THE SPIRIT OF LEI FENG!****
CHILDREN! WE JUST GOT BOOKS ON **LEI FENG!**
LEI FENG ISN'T JUST A HERO BECAUSE HE DID EXTRAORDINARY THINGS. ON THE CONTRARY, IT IS BECAUSE HE SIMPLY **DEVOTED HIS LIFE TO THE SERVICE OF THE PEOPLE!**
雷锋日记
SEE THESE PHOTOS? HE SWEPT HIS NEIGHBOURS' COURTYARDS, GAVE GIFTS TO THE PEOPLE HE MET, SENT MONEY TO THE NEEDY, BOUGHT MEDICINE FOR THE SICK.

* 为人民服务 : WÈI RÉNMÍN FÚWÙ. ** 雷锋精神 : LÉI FĒNG JĪNGSHÉN.

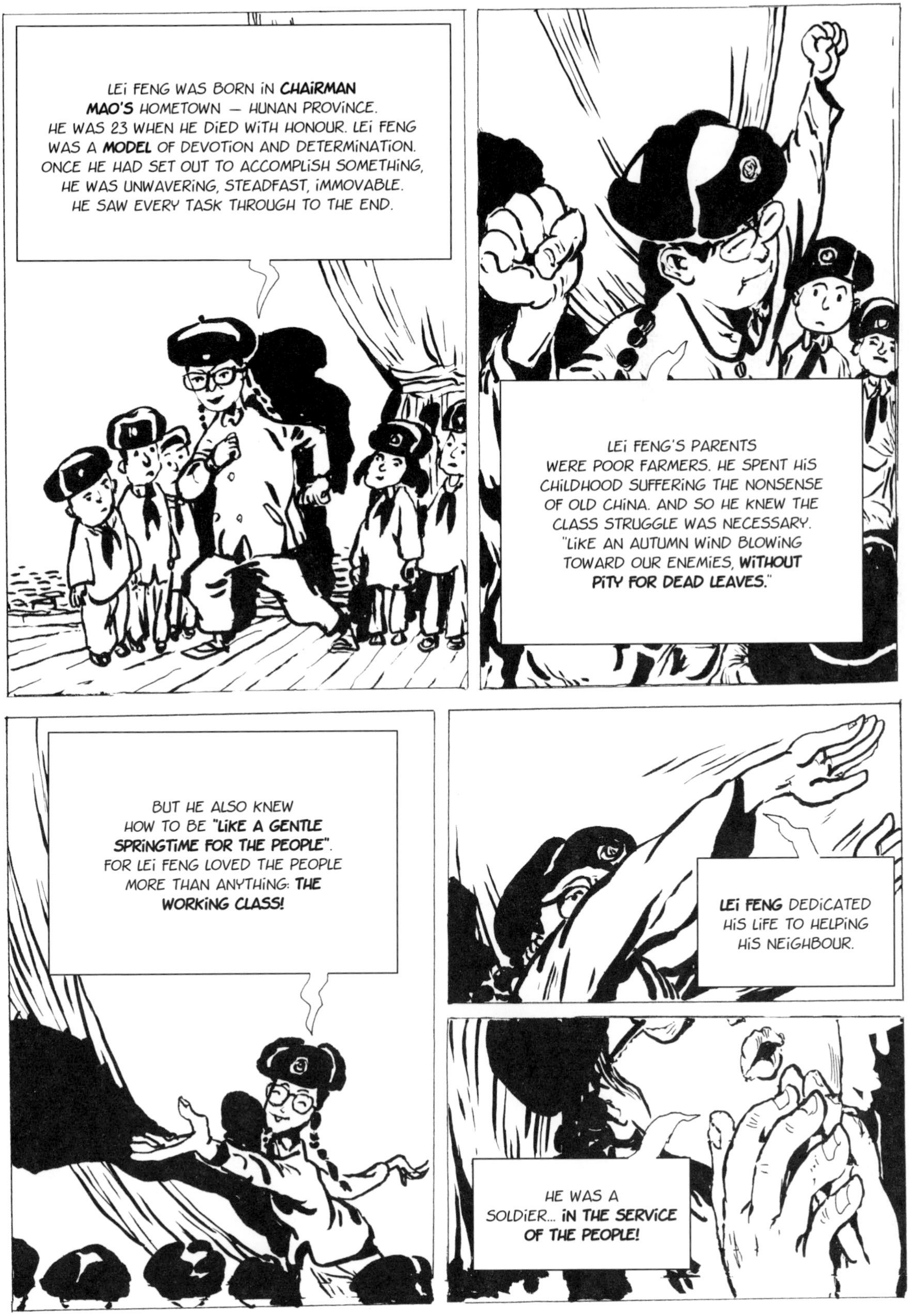
LEi FENG WAS BORN iN CHAiRMAN MAO'S HOMETOWN – HUNAN PROViNCE. HE WAS 23 WHEN HE DiED WiTH HONOUR. LEi FENG WAS A MODEL OF DEVOTiON AND DETERMiNATiON. ONCE HE HAD SET OUT TO ACCOMPLiSH SOMETHiNG, HE WAS UNWAVERiNG, STEADFAST, iMMOVABLE. HE SAW EVERY TASK THROUGH TO THE END.
LEi FENG'S PARENTS WERE POOR FARMERS. HE SPENT HiS CHiLDHOOD SUFFERiNG THE NONSENSE OF OLD CHiNA. AND SO HE KNEW THE CLASS STRUGGLE WAS NECESSARY. "LiKE AN AUTUMN WiND BLOWiNG TOWARD OUR ENEMiES, WiTHOUT PiTY FOR DEAD LEAVES."
BUT HE ALSO KNEW HOW TO BE "LiKE A GENTLE SPRiNGTiME FOR THE PEOPLE". FOR LEi FENG LOVED THE PEOPLE MORE THAN ANYTHiNG: THE WORKiNG CLASS!
LEi FENG DEDiCATED HiS LiFE TO HELPiNG HiS NEiGHBOUR.
HE WAS A SOLDiER... iN THE SERViCE OF THE PEOPLE!

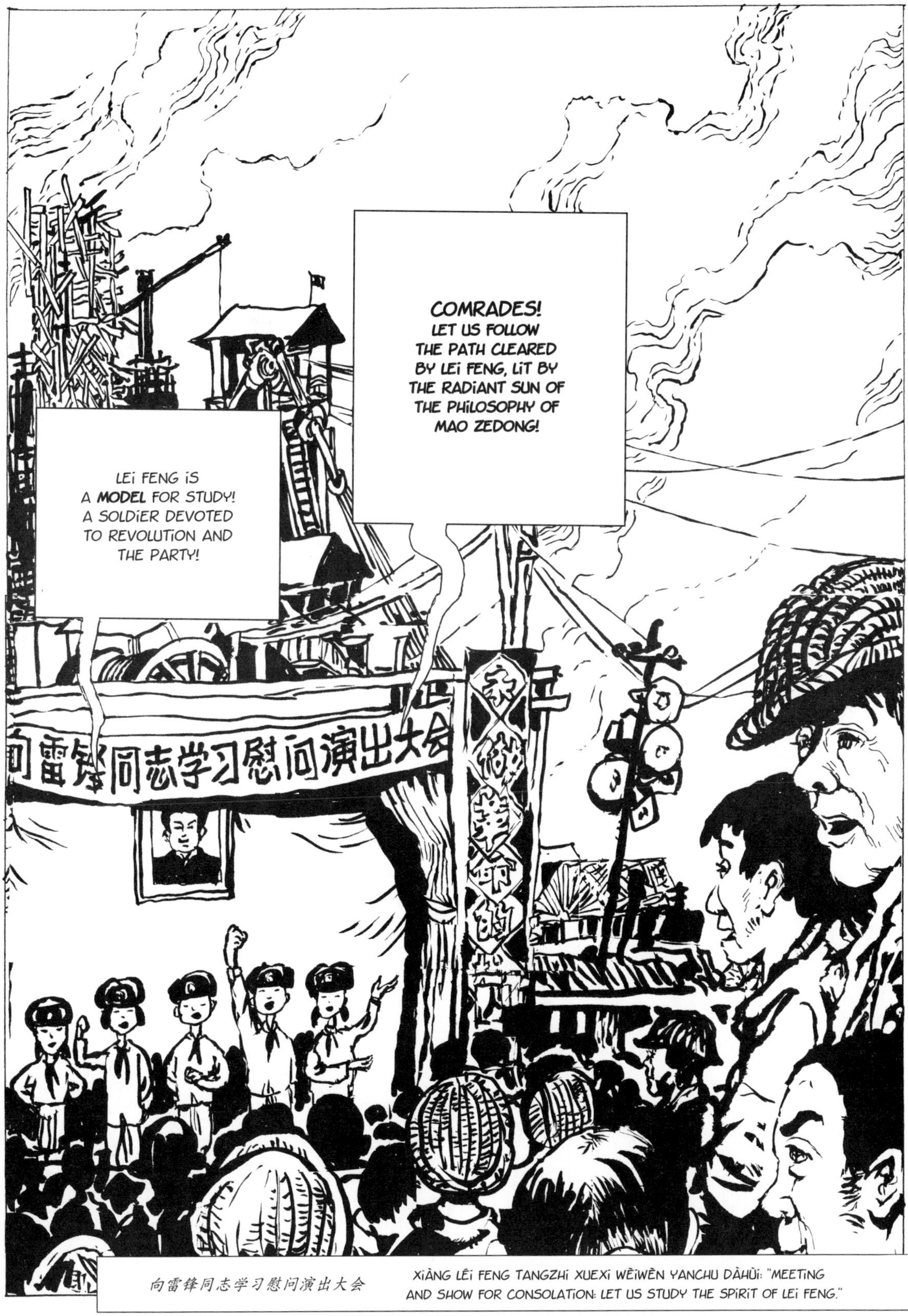
LEi FENG iS A **MODEL** FOR STUDY! A SOLDiER DEVOTED TO REVOLUTiON AND THE PARTY!
COMRADES! LET US FOLLOW THE PATH CLEARED BY LEi FENG, LiT BY THE RADiANT SUN OF THE PHiLOSOPHY OF MAO ZEDONG!
向雷锋同志学习慰问演出大会

向雷锋同志学习慰问演出大会 XiÀNG LĚi FENG TANGZHi XUEXi WĚiWĚN YANCHU DÀHÙi: "MEETiNG AND SHOW FOR CONSOLATiON: LET US STUDY THE SPiRiT OF LEi FENG."

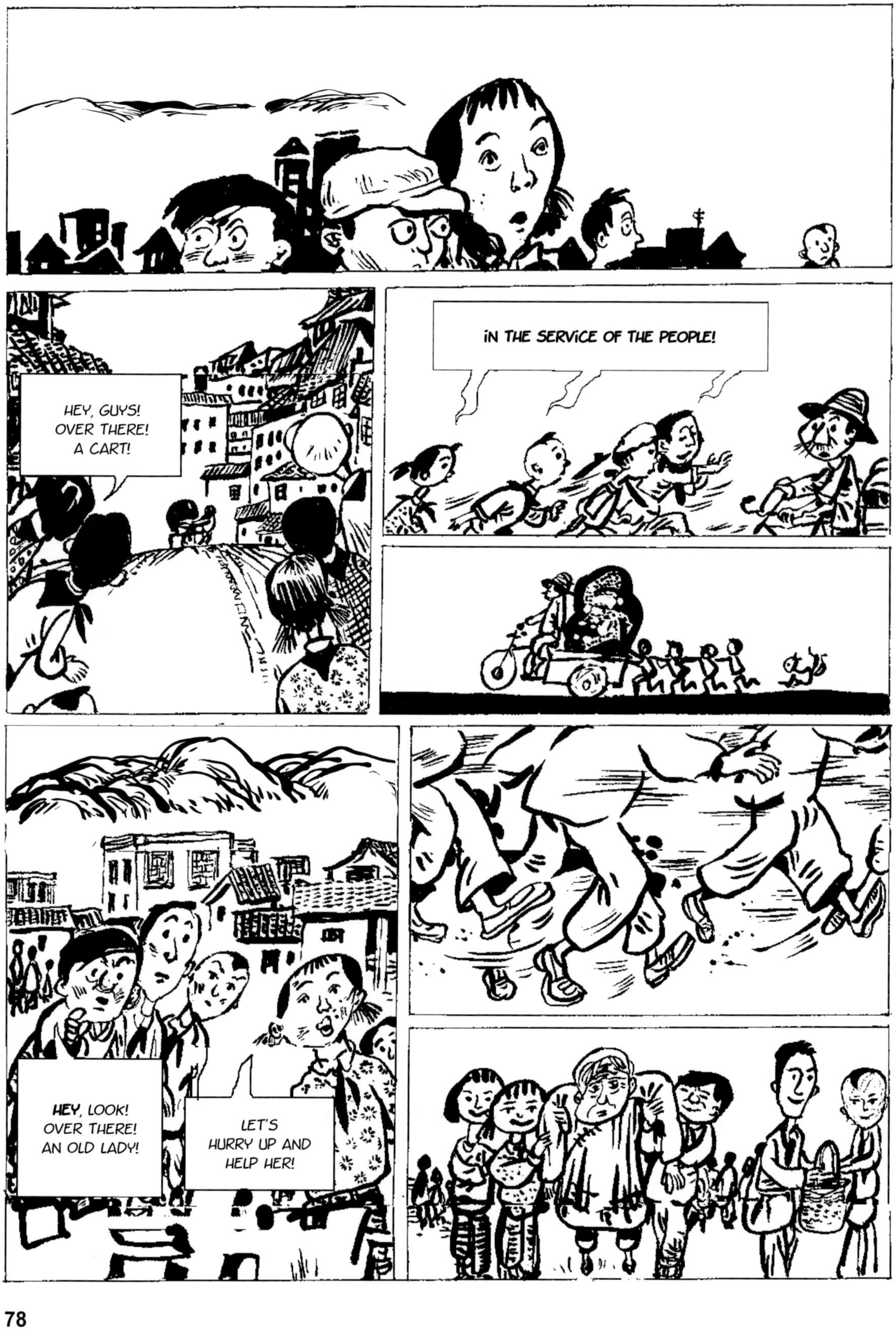
HEY, GUYS! OVER THERE! A CART!
iN THE SERViCE OF THE PEOPLE!
HEY, LOOK! OVER THERE! AN OLD LADY!
LET'S HURRY UP AND HELP HER!

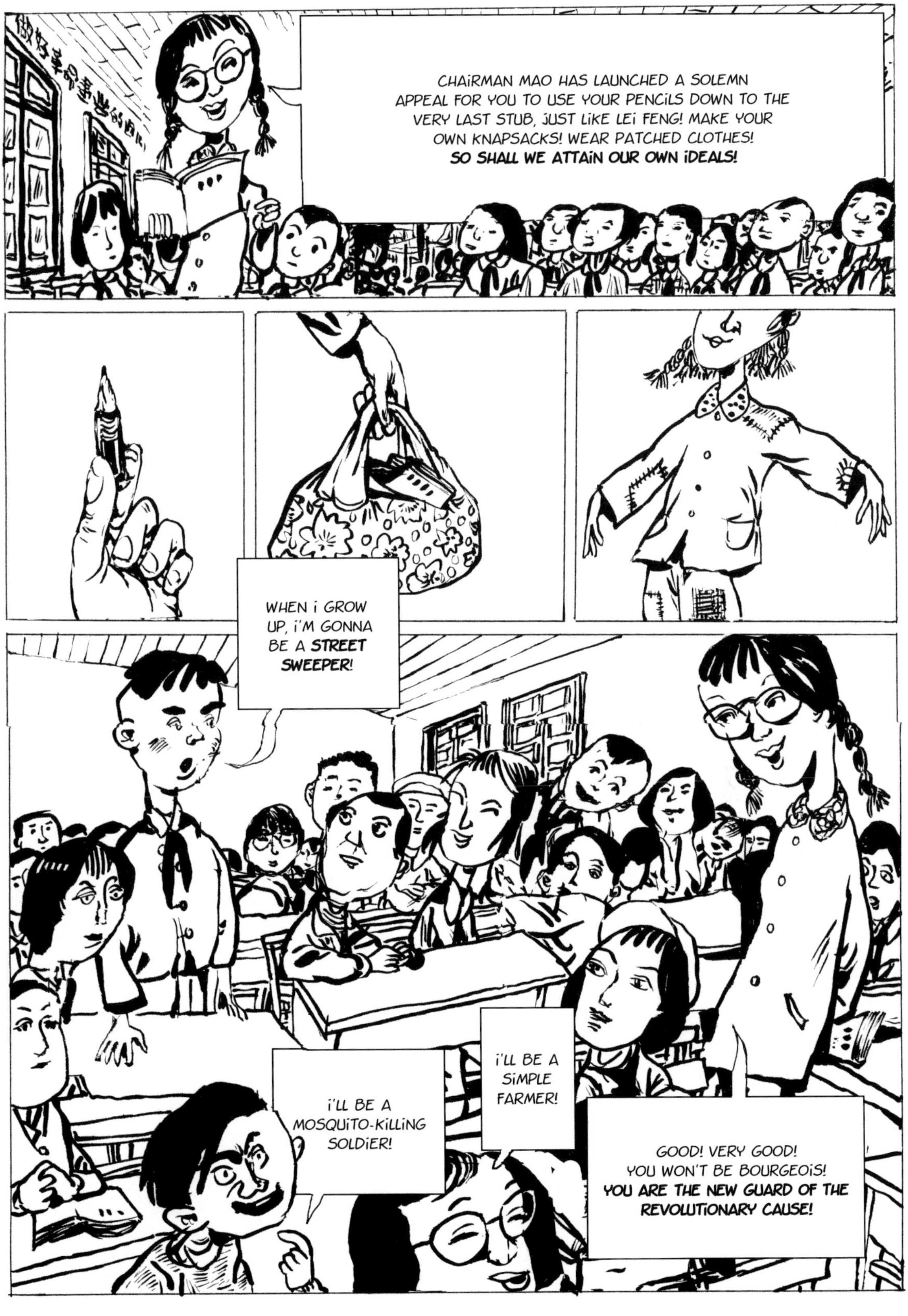
CHAIRMAN MAO HAS LAUNCHED A SOLEMN APPEAL FOR YOU TO USE YOUR PENCILS DOWN TO THE VERY LAST STUB, JUST LIKE LEI FENG! MAKE YOUR OWN KNAPSACKS! WEAR PATCHED CLOTHES! **SO SHALL WE ATTAIN OUR OWN IDEALS!**
WHEN I GROW UP, I'M GONNA BE A **STREET SWEEPER!**
I'LL BE A MOSQUITO-KILLING SOLDIER!
I'LL BE A SIMPLE FARMER!
GOOD! VERY GOOD! YOU WON'T BE BOURGEOIS! **YOU ARE THE NEW GUARD OF THE REVOLUTIONARY CAUSE!**

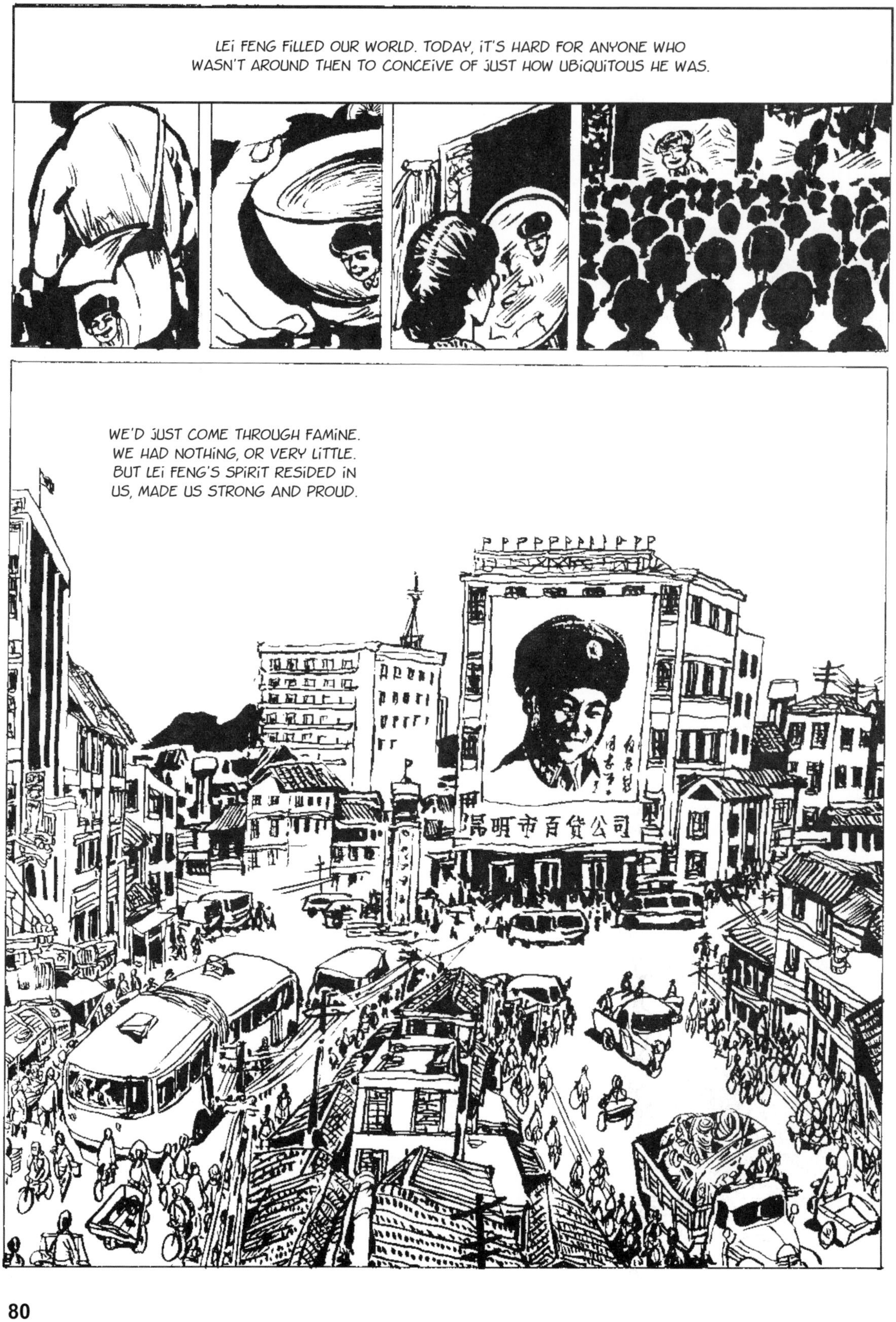
LEi FENG FiLLED OUR WORLD. TODAY, iT'S HARD FOR ANYONE WHO WASN'T AROUND THEN TO CONCEiVE OF JUST HOW UBiQUiTOUS HE WAS.
WE'D JUST COME THROUGH FAMiNE. WE HAD NOTHiNG, OR VERY LiTTLE. BUT LEi FENG'S SPiRiT RESiDED iN US, MADE US STRONG AND PROUD.
昆明市百货公司

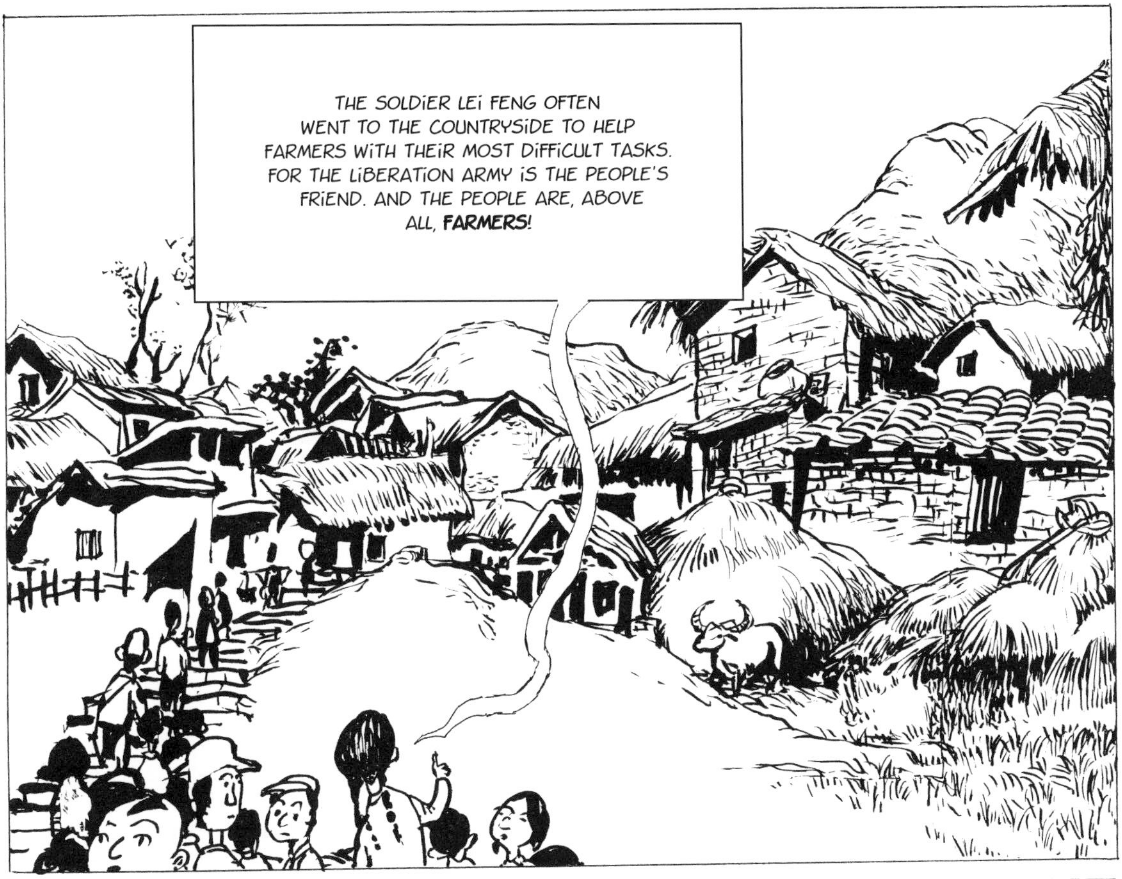
THE SOLDIER LEI FENG OFTEN WENT TO THE COUNTRYSIDE TO HELP FARMERS WITH THEIR MOST DIFFICULT TASKS. FOR THE LIBERATION ARMY IS THE PEOPLE'S FRIEND. AND THE PEOPLE ARE, ABOVE ALL, **FARMERS**!

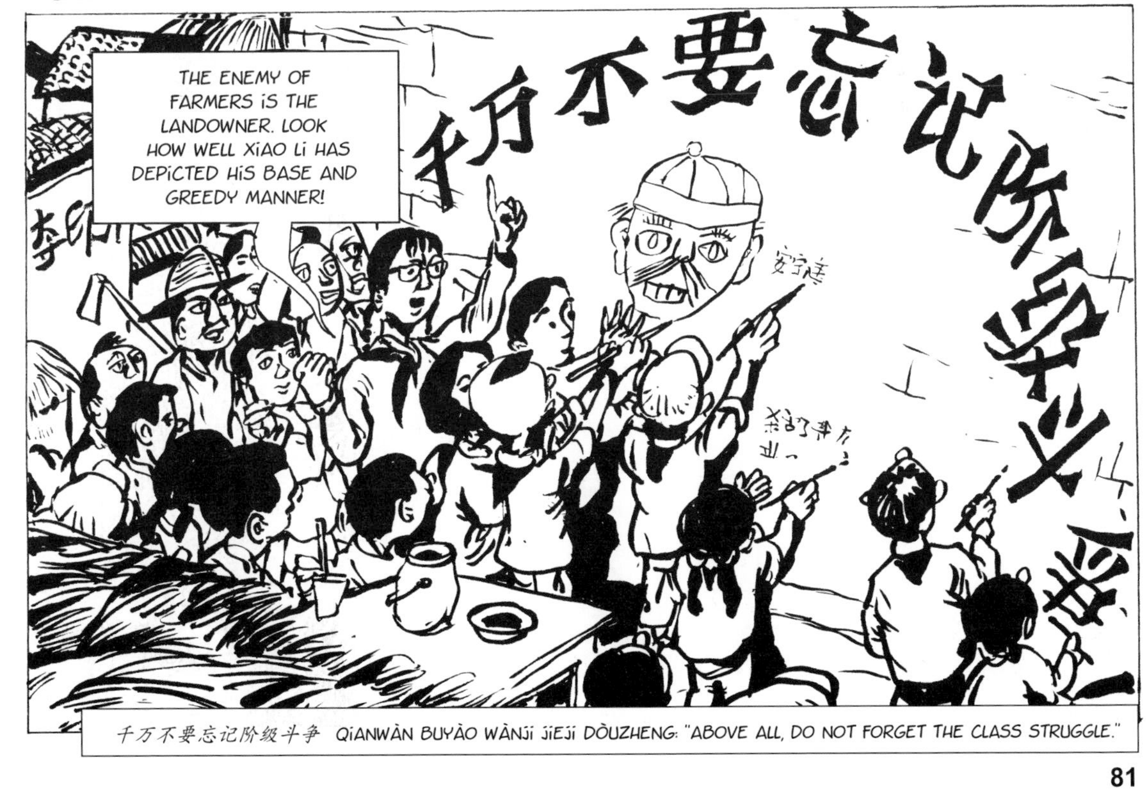
THE ENEMY OF FARMERS IS THE LANDOWNER. LOOK HOW WELL XIAO LI HAS DEPICTED HIS BASE AND GREEDY MANNER!
千万不要忘记阶级斗争

千万不要忘记阶级斗争 QIANWÀN BUYÀO WÀNJI JIEJI DÒUZHENG: "ABOVE ALL, DO NOT FORGET THE CLASS STRUGGLE."

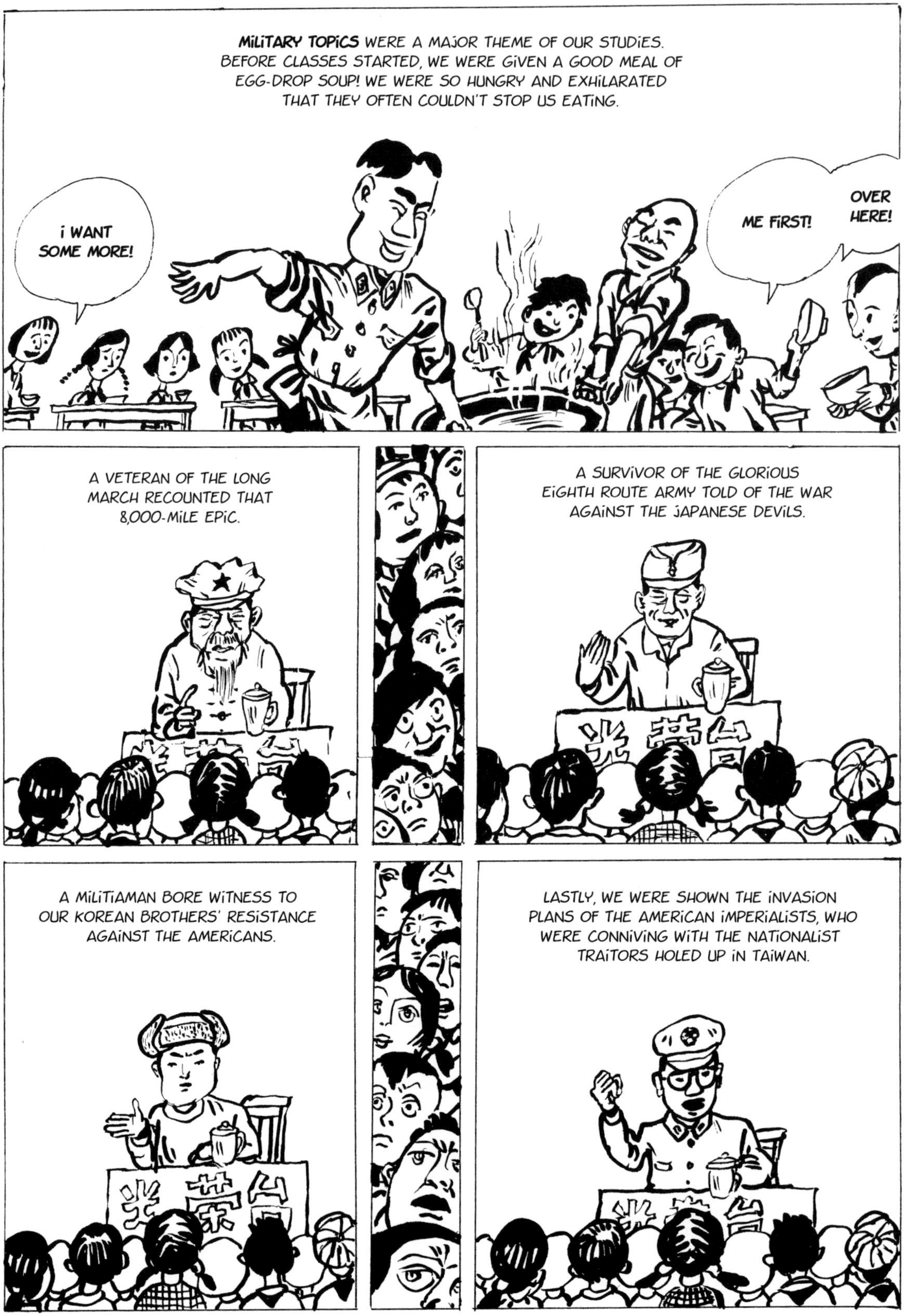
MILITARY TOPICS WERE A MAJOR THEME OF OUR STUDIES. BEFORE CLASSES STARTED, WE WERE GIVEN A GOOD MEAL OF EGG-DROP SOUP! WE WERE SO HUNGRY AND EXHILARATED THAT THEY OFTEN COULDN'T STOP US EATING.
I WANT SOME MORE!
ME FIRST!
OVER HERE!
A VETERAN OF THE LONG MARCH RECOUNTED THAT 8,000-MILE EPIC.
A SURVIVOR OF THE GLORIOUS EIGHTH ROUTE ARMY TOLD OF THE WAR AGAINST THE JAPANESE DEVILS.
光荣台
A MILITIAMAN BORE WITNESS TO OUR KOREAN BROTHERS' RESISTANCE AGAINST THE AMERICANS.
光荣台
LASTLY, WE WERE SHOWN THE INVASION PLANS OF THE AMERICAN IMPERIALISTS, WHO WERE CONNIVING WITH THE NATIONALIST TRAITORS HOLED UP IN TAIWAN.

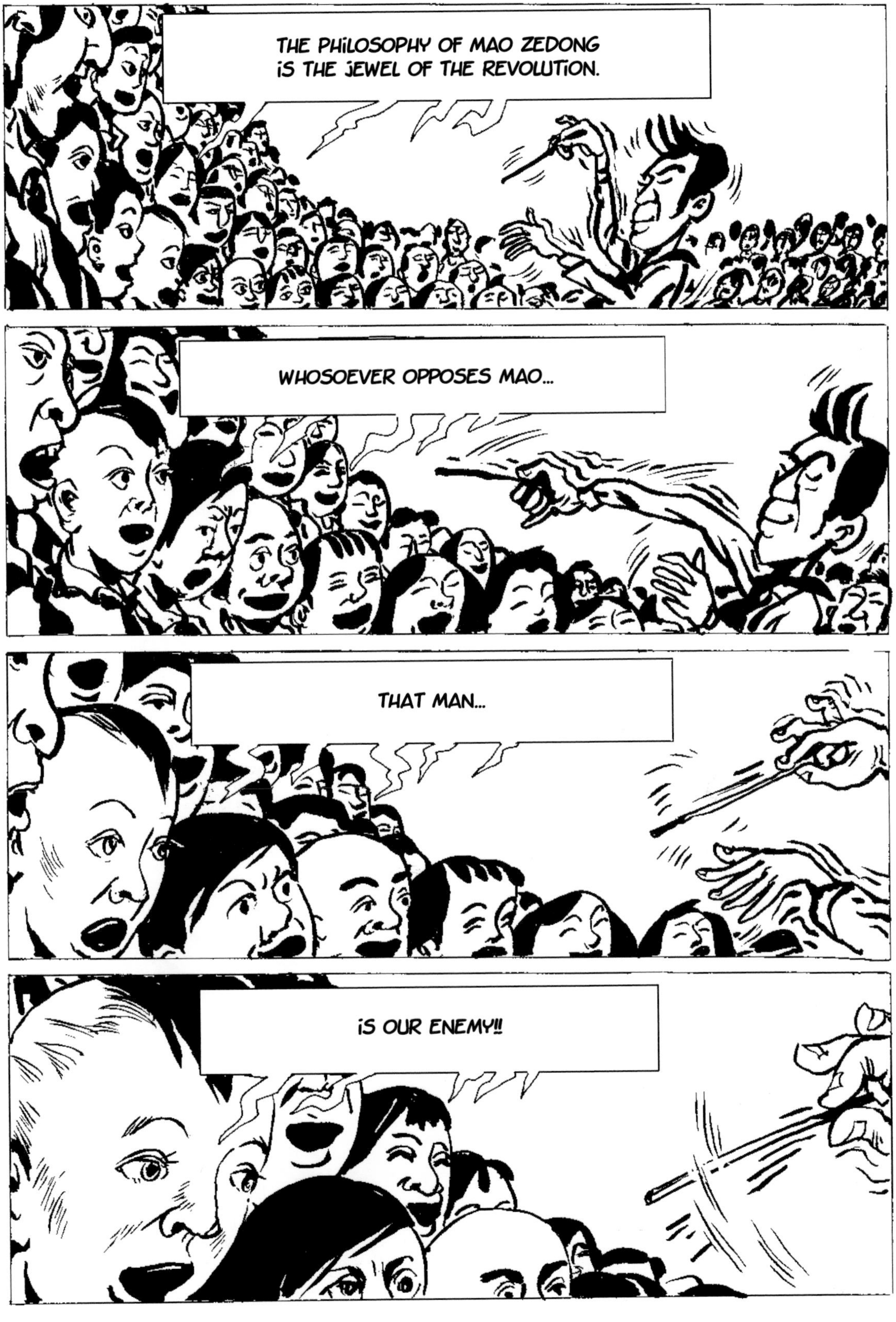
THE PHILOSOPHY OF MAO ZEDONG IS THE JEWEL OF THE REVOLUTION.
WHOSOEVER OPPOSES MAO...
THAT MAN...
IS OUR ENEMY!!

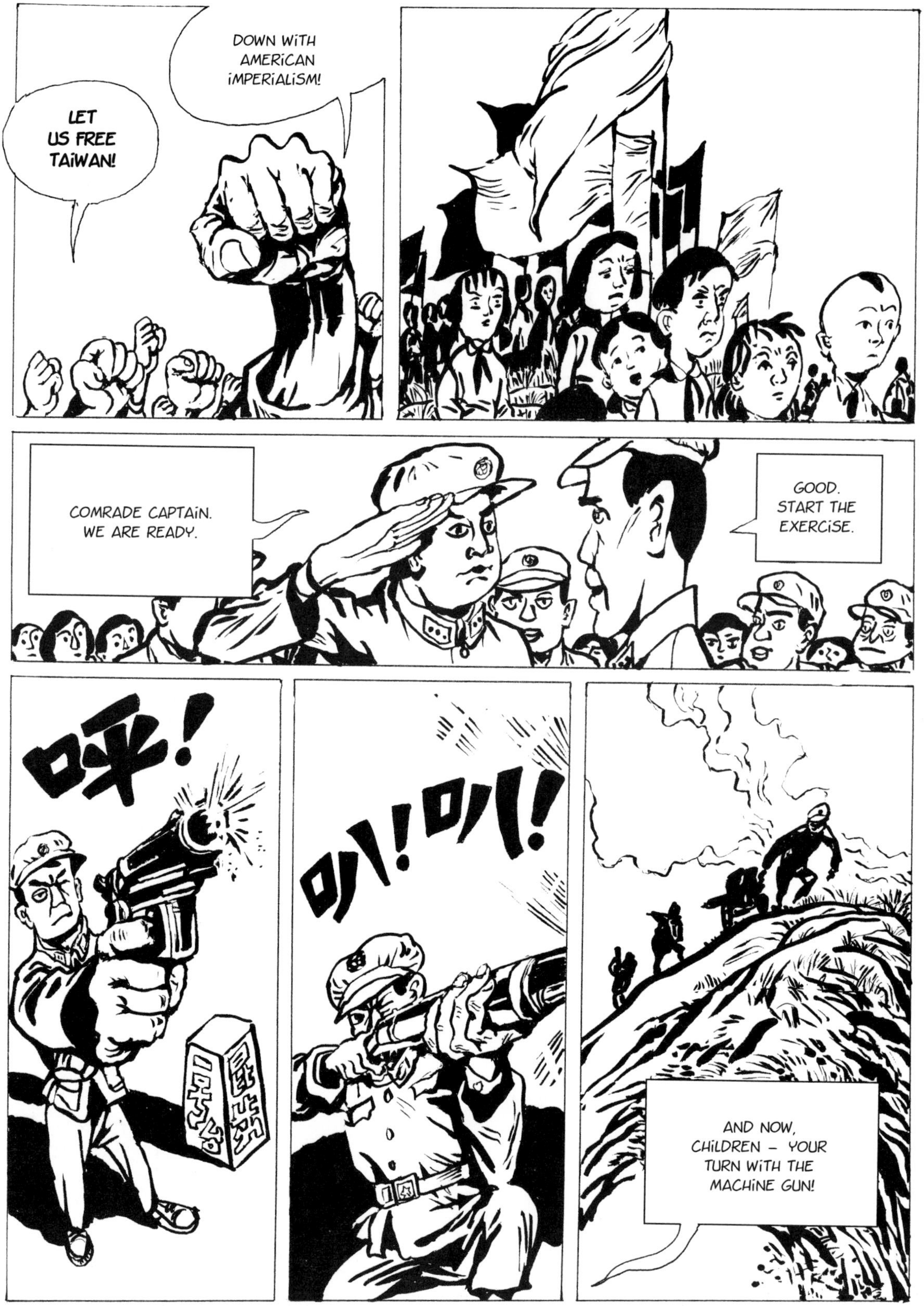
DOWN WITH AMERICAN IMPERIALISM!
LET US FREE TAIWAN!
COMRADE CAPTAIN. WE ARE READY.
GOOD. START THE EXERCISE.
呼!
叭!叭!
AND NOW, CHILDREN – YOUR TURN WITH THE MACHINE GUN!

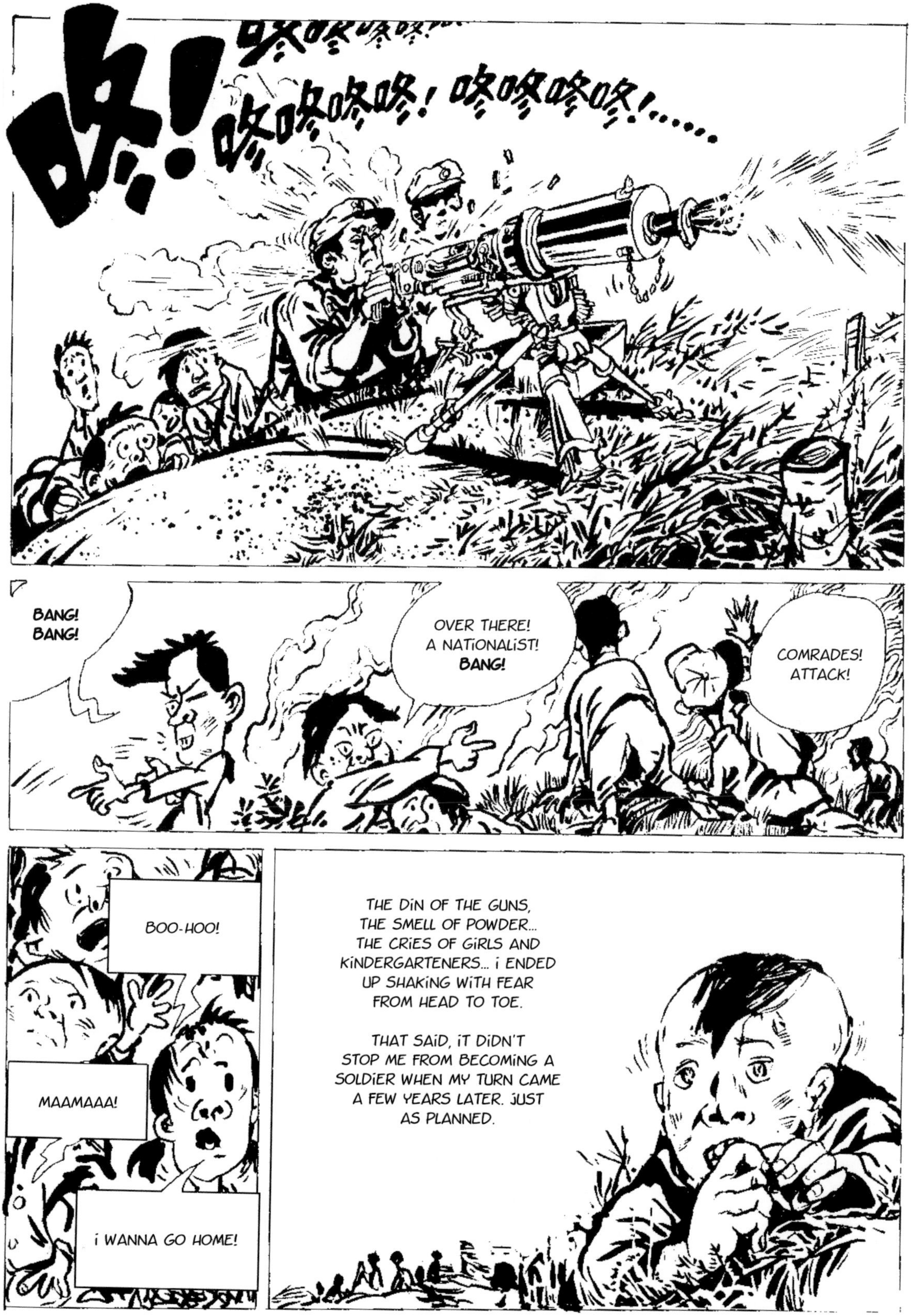
咚!
咚咚咚咚! 咚咚咚咚!......
BANG! BANG!
OVER THERE! A NATIONALIST! BANG!
COMRADES! ATTACK!
BOO-HOO!
MAAMAAA!
I WANNA GO HOME!
THE DIN OF THE GUNS, THE SMELL OF POWDER... THE CRIES OF GIRLS AND KINDERGARTENERS... I ENDED UP SHAKING WITH FEAR FROM HEAD TO TOE.
THAT SAID, IT DIDN'T STOP ME FROM BECOMING A SOLDIER WHEN MY TURN CAME A FEW YEARS LATER. JUST AS PLANNED.

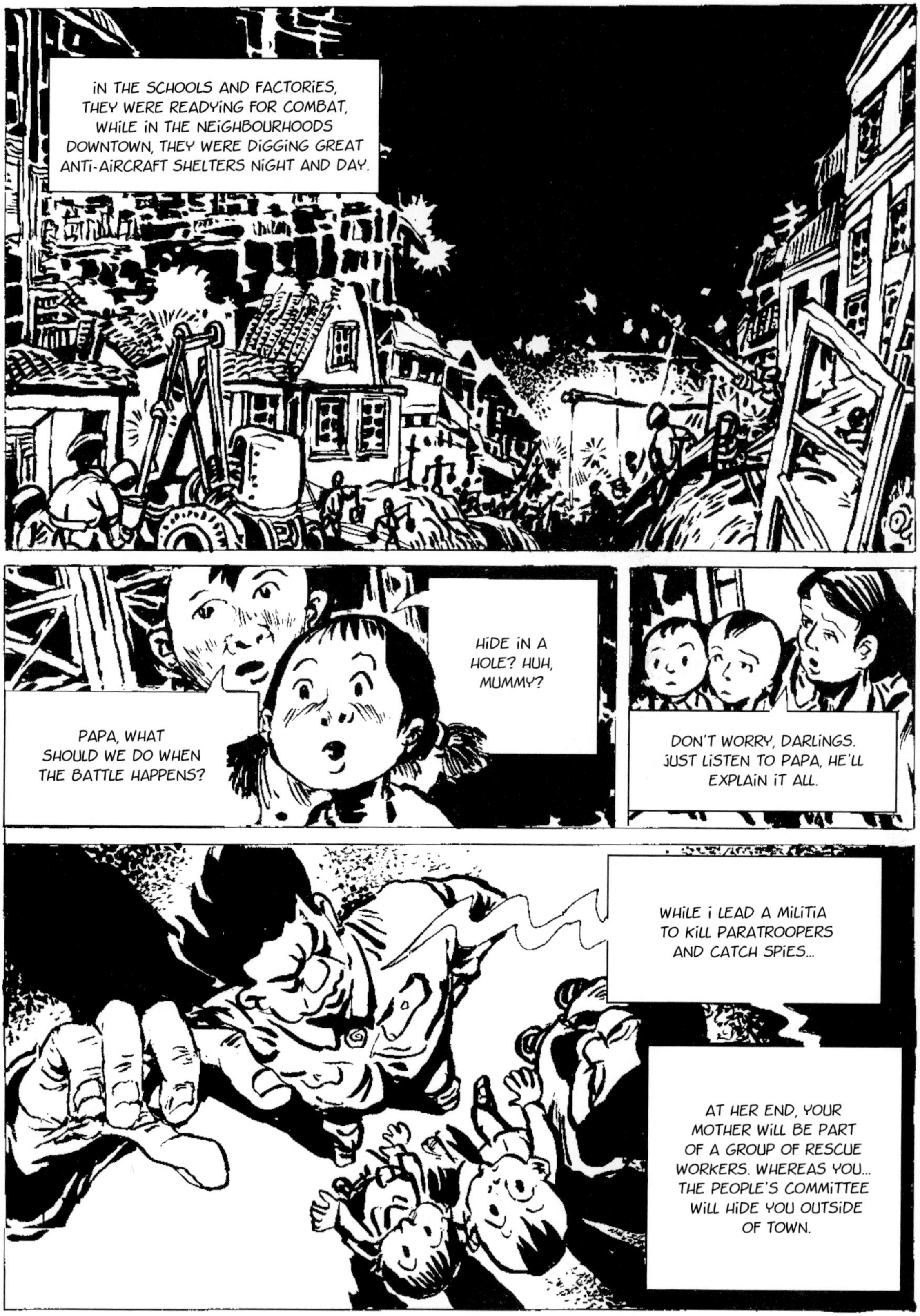
IN THE SCHOOLS AND FACTORIES, THEY WERE READYING FOR COMBAT, WHILE IN THE NEIGHBOURHOODS DOWNTOWN, THEY WERE DIGGING GREAT ANTI-AIRCRAFT SHELTERS NIGHT AND DAY.
PAPA, WHAT SHOULD WE DO WHEN THE BATTLE HAPPENS?
HIDE IN A HOLE? HUH, MUMMY?
DON'T WORRY, DARLINGS. JUST LISTEN TO PAPA, HE'LL EXPLAIN IT ALL.
WHILE I LEAD A MILITIA TO KILL PARATROOPERS AND CATCH SPIES...
AT HER END, YOUR MOTHER WILL BE PART OF A GROUP OF RESCUE WORKERS. WHEREAS YOU... THE PEOPLE'S COMMITTEE WILL HIDE YOU OUTSIDE OF TOWN.

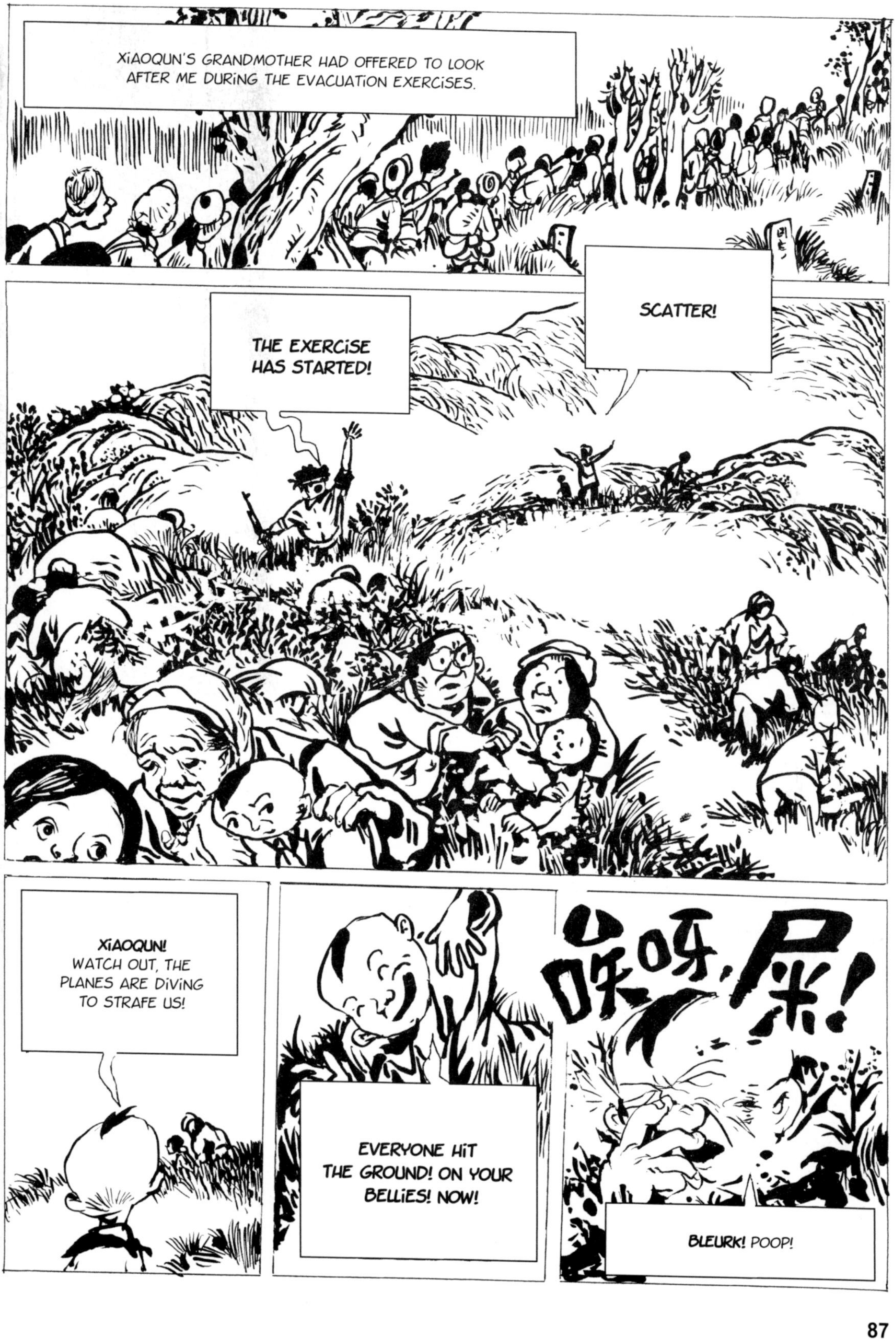
XIAOQUN'S GRANDMOTHER HAD OFFERED TO LOOK AFTER ME DURING THE EVACUATION EXERCISES.
THE EXERCISE HAS STARTED!
SCATTER!
XIAOQUN! WATCH OUT, THE PLANES ARE DIVING TO STRAFE US!
EVERYONE HIT THE GROUND! ON YOUR BELLIES! NOW!
唉呀，屎！
BLEURK! POOP!

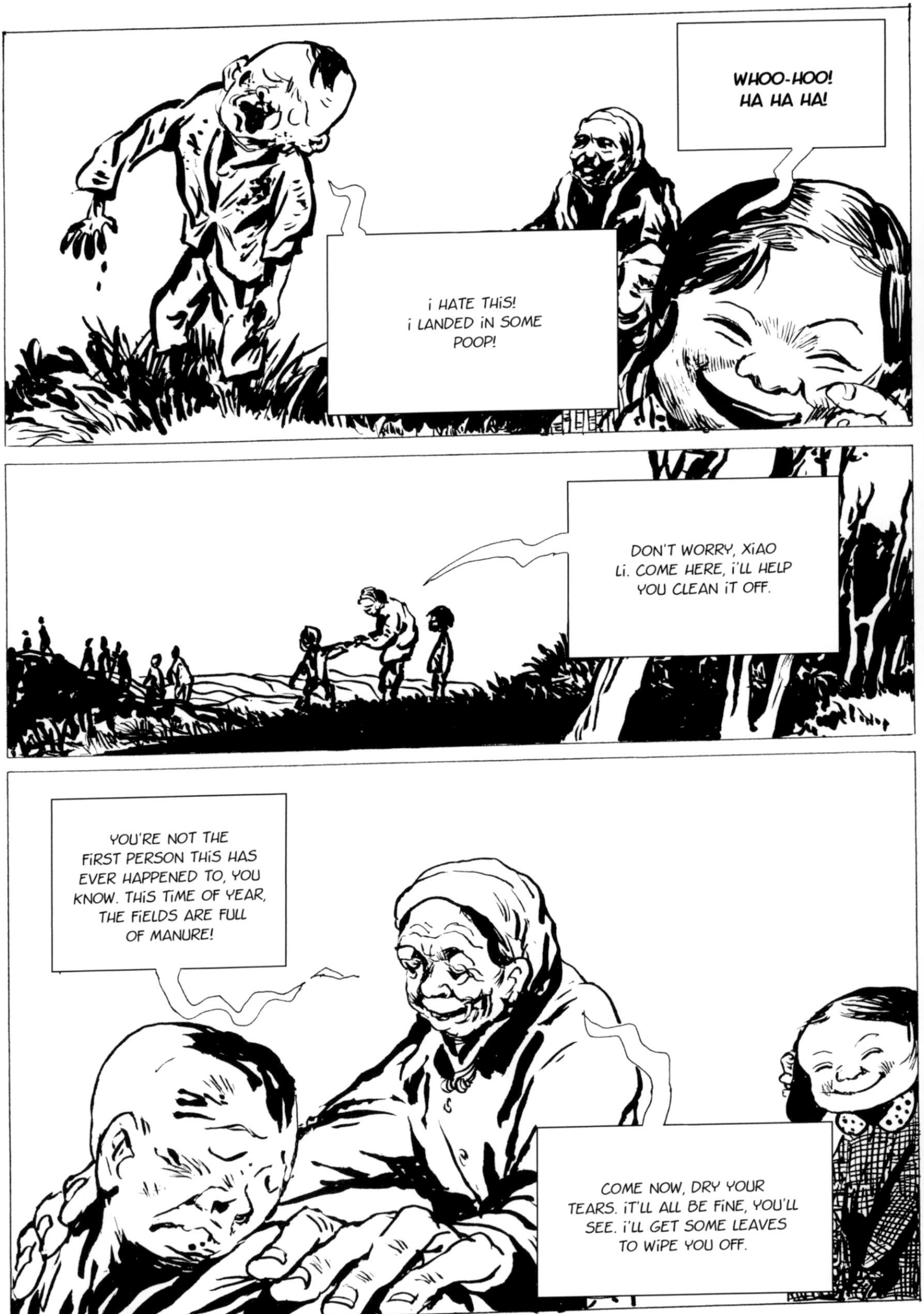
WHOO-HOO! HA HA HA!
I HATE THIS! I LANDED IN SOME POOP!
DON'T WORRY, XIAO LI. COME HERE, I'LL HELP YOU CLEAN IT OFF.
YOU'RE NOT THE FIRST PERSON THIS HAS EVER HAPPENED TO, YOU KNOW. THIS TIME OF YEAR, THE FIELDS ARE FULL OF MANURE!
COME NOW, DRY YOUR TEARS. IT'LL ALL BE FINE, YOU'LL SEE. I'LL GET SOME LEAVES TO WIPE YOU OFF.

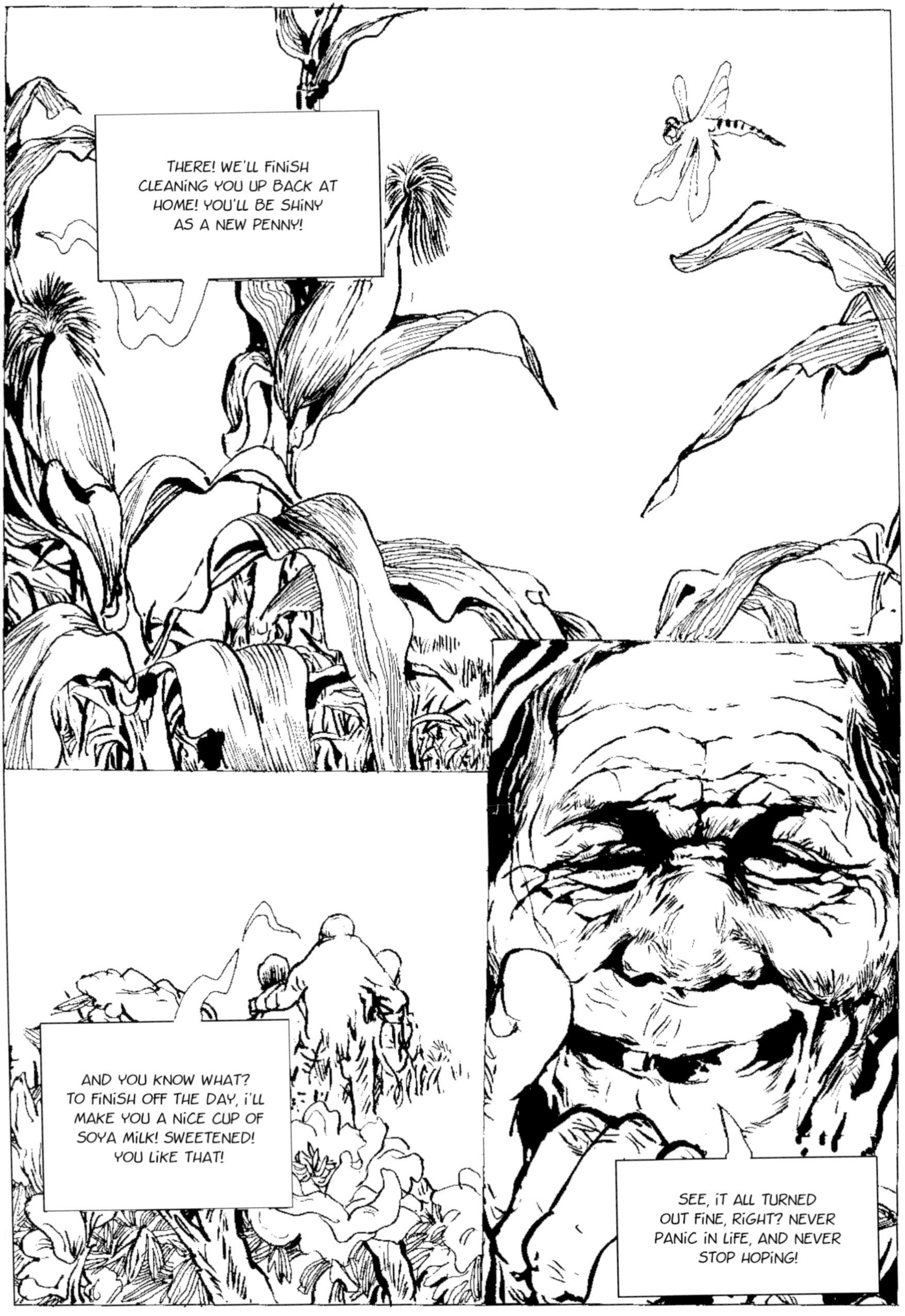
THERE! WE'LL FINISH CLEANING YOU UP BACK AT HOME! YOU'LL BE SHINY AS A NEW PENNY!
AND YOU KNOW WHAT? TO FINISH OFF THE DAY, I'LL MAKE YOU A NICE CUP OF SOYA MILK! SWEETENED! YOU LIKE THAT!
SEE, IT ALL TURNED OUT FINE, RIGHT? NEVER PANIC IN LIFE, AND NEVER STOP HOPING!

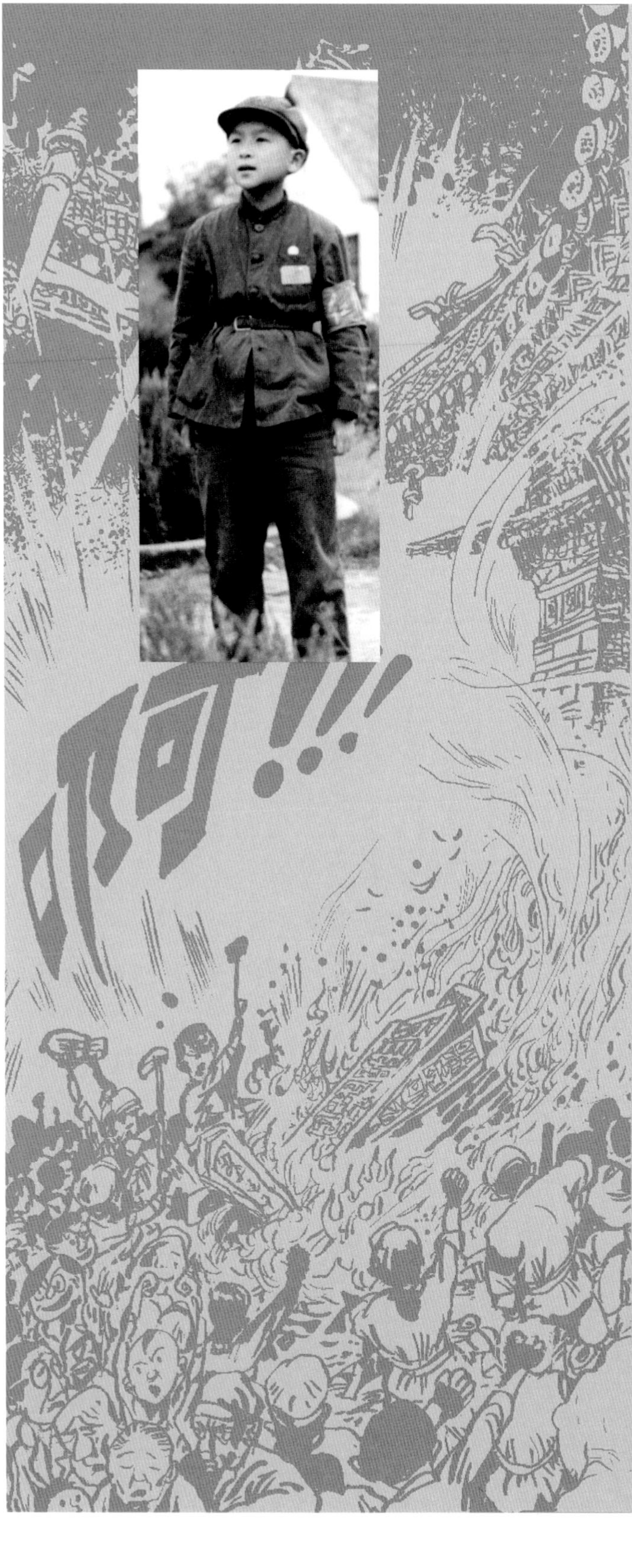
啊!!!

CHAPTER 2
The Little Red Book

LET US STAY DETERMINED,
LET US FEAR NO SACRIFICE.

LET US OVERCOME
10,000 OBSTACLES
IN OUR QUEST FOR VICTORY.

下定决心，不怕牺牲，

排除万难，去争取胜利

("SONG OF THE RED GUARD")

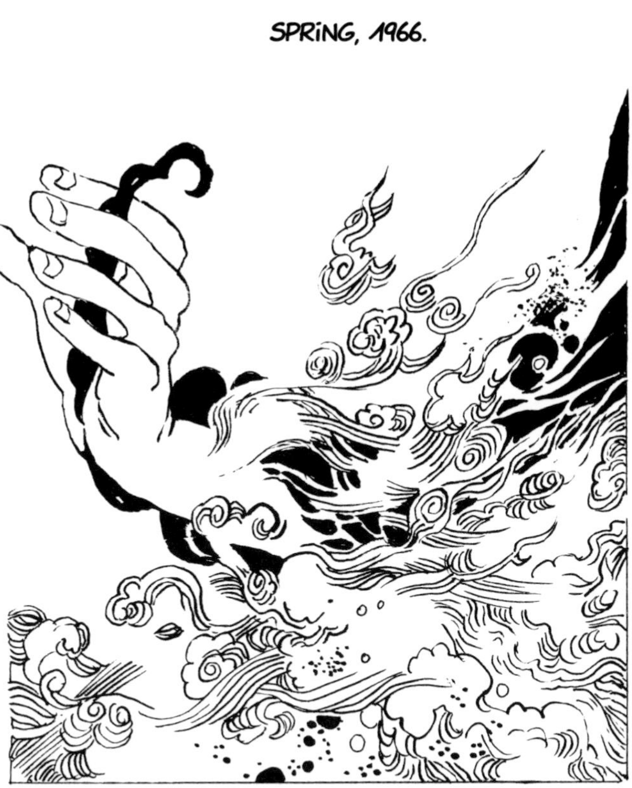
SPRiNG, 1966.

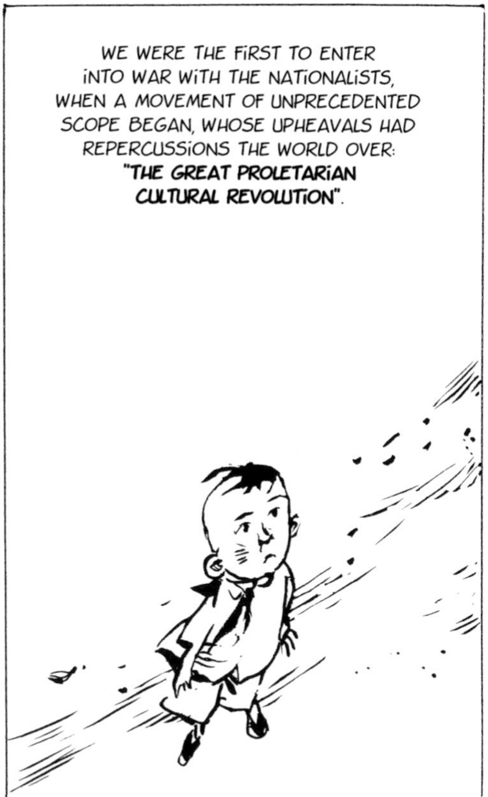
WE WERE THE FIRST TO ENTER INTO WAR WITH THE NATIONALISTS, WHEN A MOVEMENT OF UNPRECEDENTED SCOPE BEGAN, WHOSE UPHEAVALS HAD REPERCUSSIONS THE WORLD OVER: "THE GREAT PROLETARIAN CULTURAL REVOLUTION".

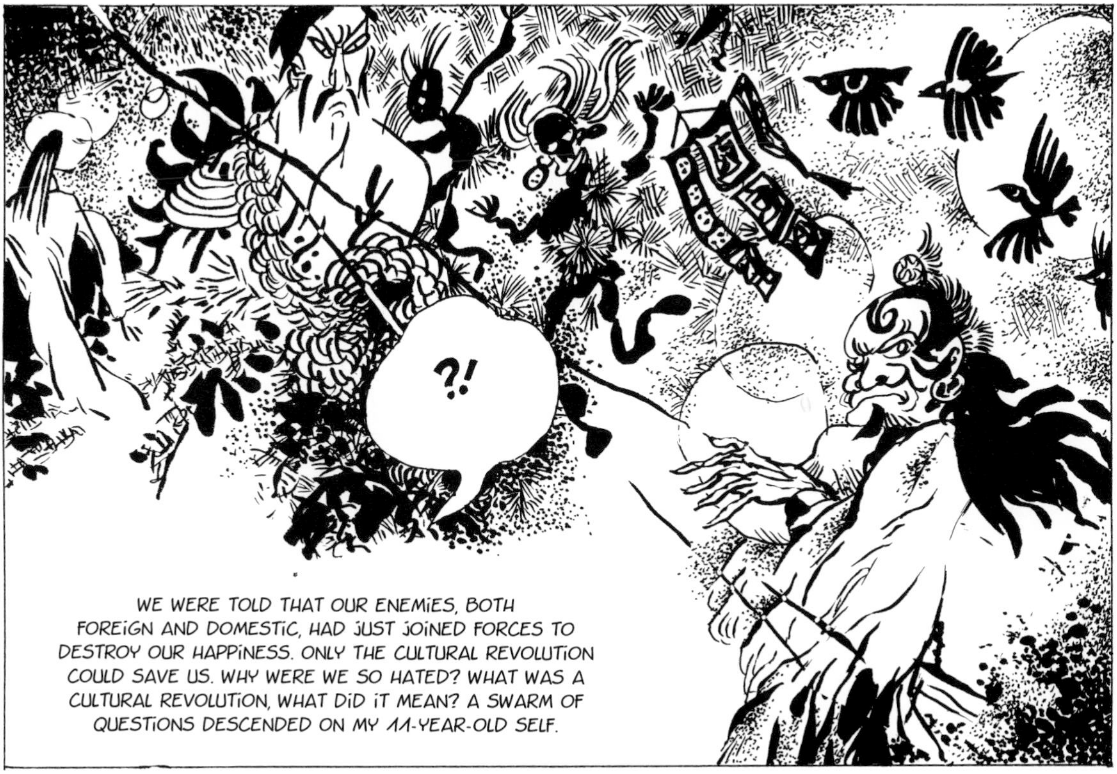
?!
WE WERE TOLD THAT OUR ENEMIES, BOTH FOREIGN AND DOMESTIC, HAD JUST JOINED FORCES TO DESTROY OUR HAPPINESS. ONLY THE CULTURAL REVOLUTION COULD SAVE US. WHY WERE WE SO HATED? WHAT WAS A CULTURAL REVOLUTION, WHAT DID IT MEAN? A SWARM OF QUESTIONS DESCENDED ON MY 11-YEAR-OLD SELF.

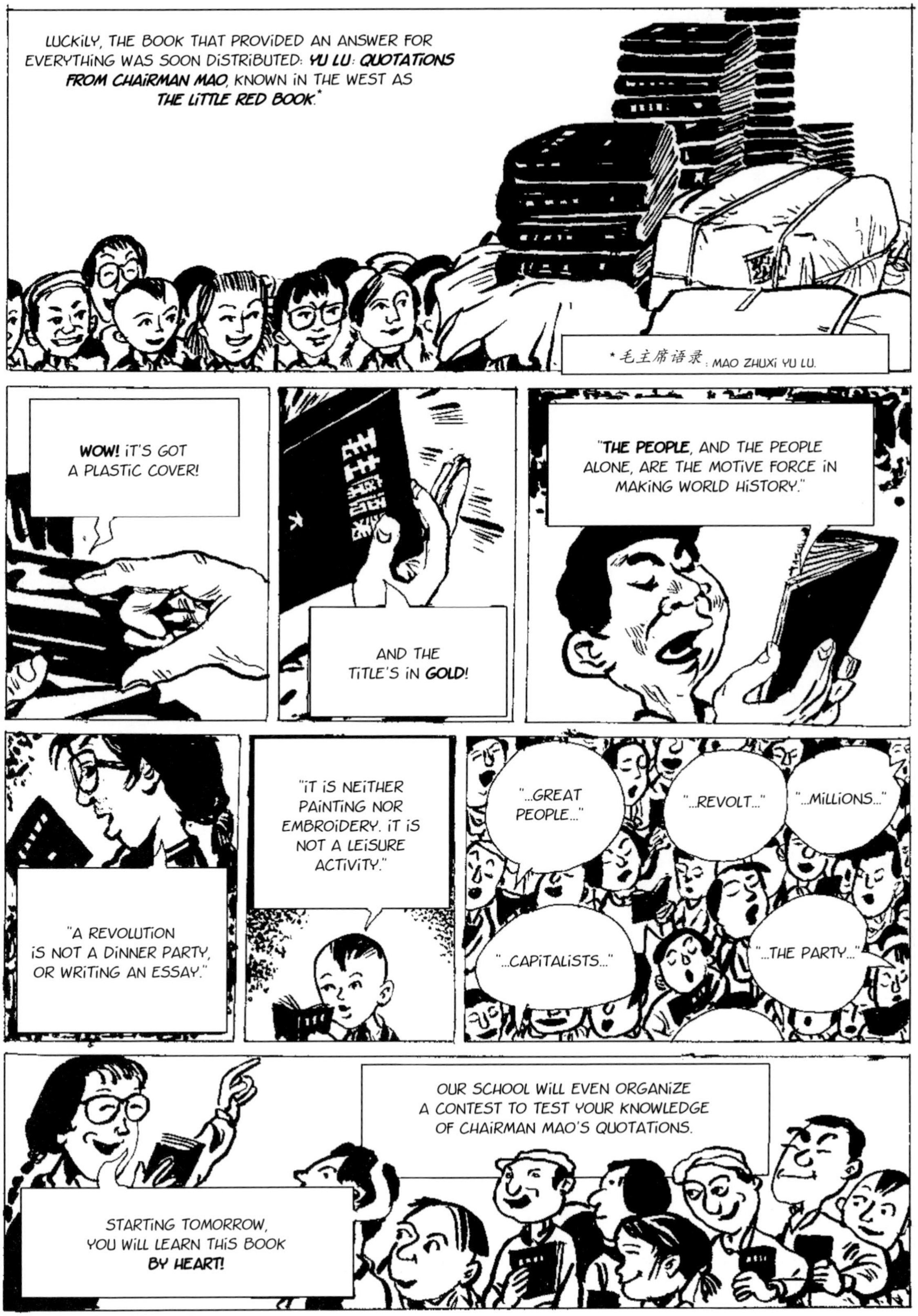
LUCKILY, THE BOOK THAT PROVIDED AN ANSWER FOR EVERYTHING WAS SOON DISTRIBUTED: YU LU: QUOTATIONS FROM CHAIRMAN MAO, KNOWN IN THE WEST AS THE LITTLE RED BOOK.*
* 毛主席语录: MAO ZHUXI YU LU.
WOW! IT'S GOT A PLASTIC COVER!
AND THE TITLE'S IN GOLD!
"THE PEOPLE, AND THE PEOPLE ALONE, ARE THE MOTIVE FORCE IN MAKING WORLD HISTORY."
"A REVOLUTION IS NOT A DINNER PARTY, OR WRITING AN ESSAY."
"IT IS NEITHER PAINTING NOR EMBROIDERY. IT IS NOT A LEISURE ACTIVITY."
"...GREAT PEOPLE..."
"...REVOLT..."
"...MILLIONS..."
"...CAPITALISTS..."
"...THE PARTY..."
OUR SCHOOL WILL EVEN ORGANIZE A CONTEST TO TEST YOUR KNOWLEDGE OF CHAIRMAN MAO'S QUOTATIONS.
STARTING TOMORROW, YOU WILL LEARN THIS BOOK BY HEART!

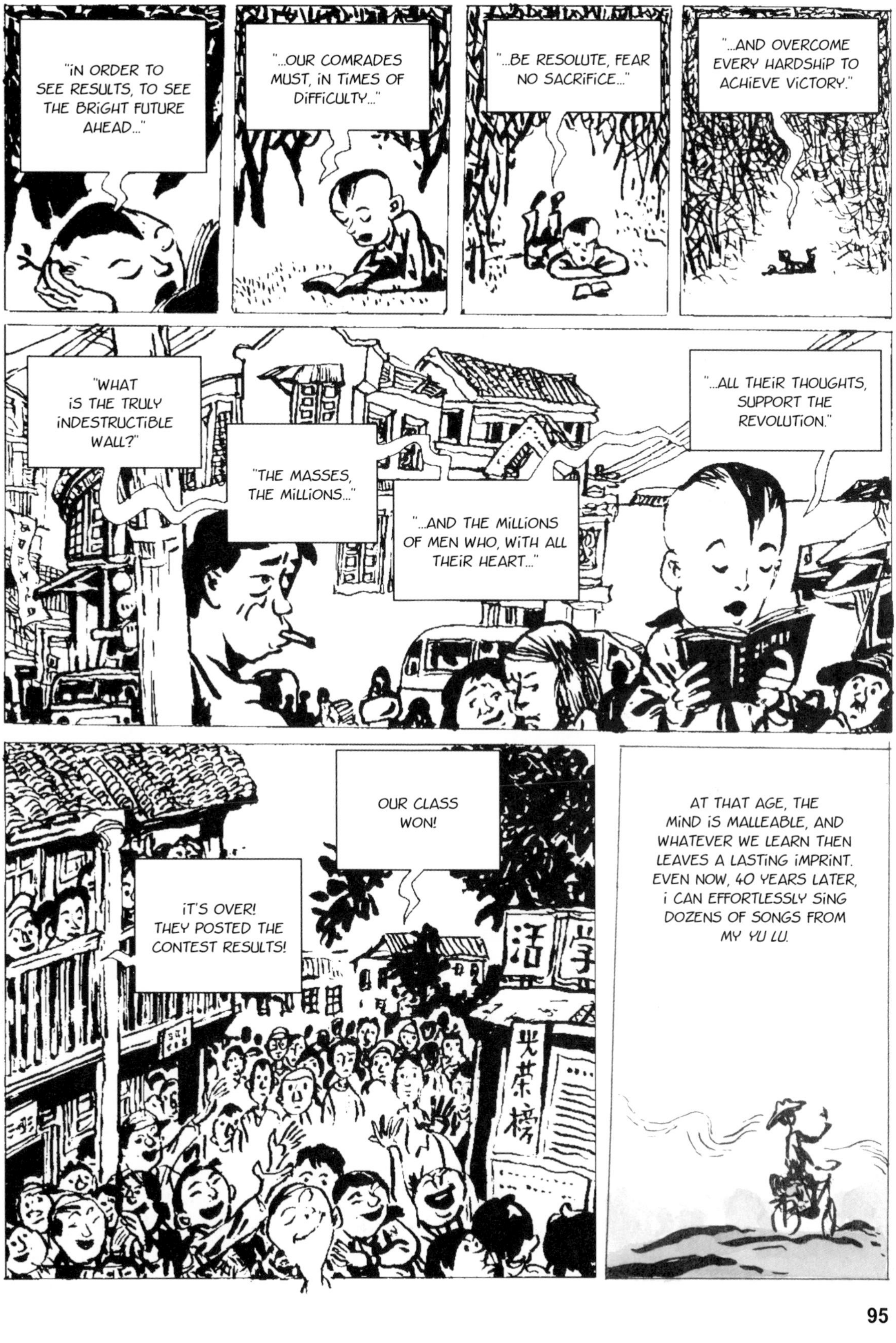
"iN ORDER TO SEE RESULTS, TO SEE THE BRiGHT FUTURE AHEAD..."
"...OUR COMRADES MUST, iN TiMES OF DiFFiCULTY..."
"...BE RESOLUTE, FEAR NO SACRiFiCE..."
"...AND OVERCOME EVERY HARDSHiP TO ACHiEVE ViCTORY."
"WHAT iS THE TRULY iNDESTRUCTiBLE WALL?"
"THE MASSES, THE MiLLiONS..."
"...AND THE MiLLiONS OF MEN WHO, WiTH ALL THEiR HEART..."
"...ALL THEiR THOUGHTS, SUPPORT THE REVOLUTiON."
iT'S OVER! THEY POSTED THE CONTEST RESULTS!
OUR CLASS WON!
活
学
光荣榜
AT THAT AGE, THE MiND iS MALLEABLE, AND WHATEVER WE LEARN THEN LEAVES A LASTiNG iMPRiNT. EVEN NOW, 40 YEARS LATER, i CAN EFFORTLESSLY SiNG DOZENS OF SONGS FROM MY YU LU.

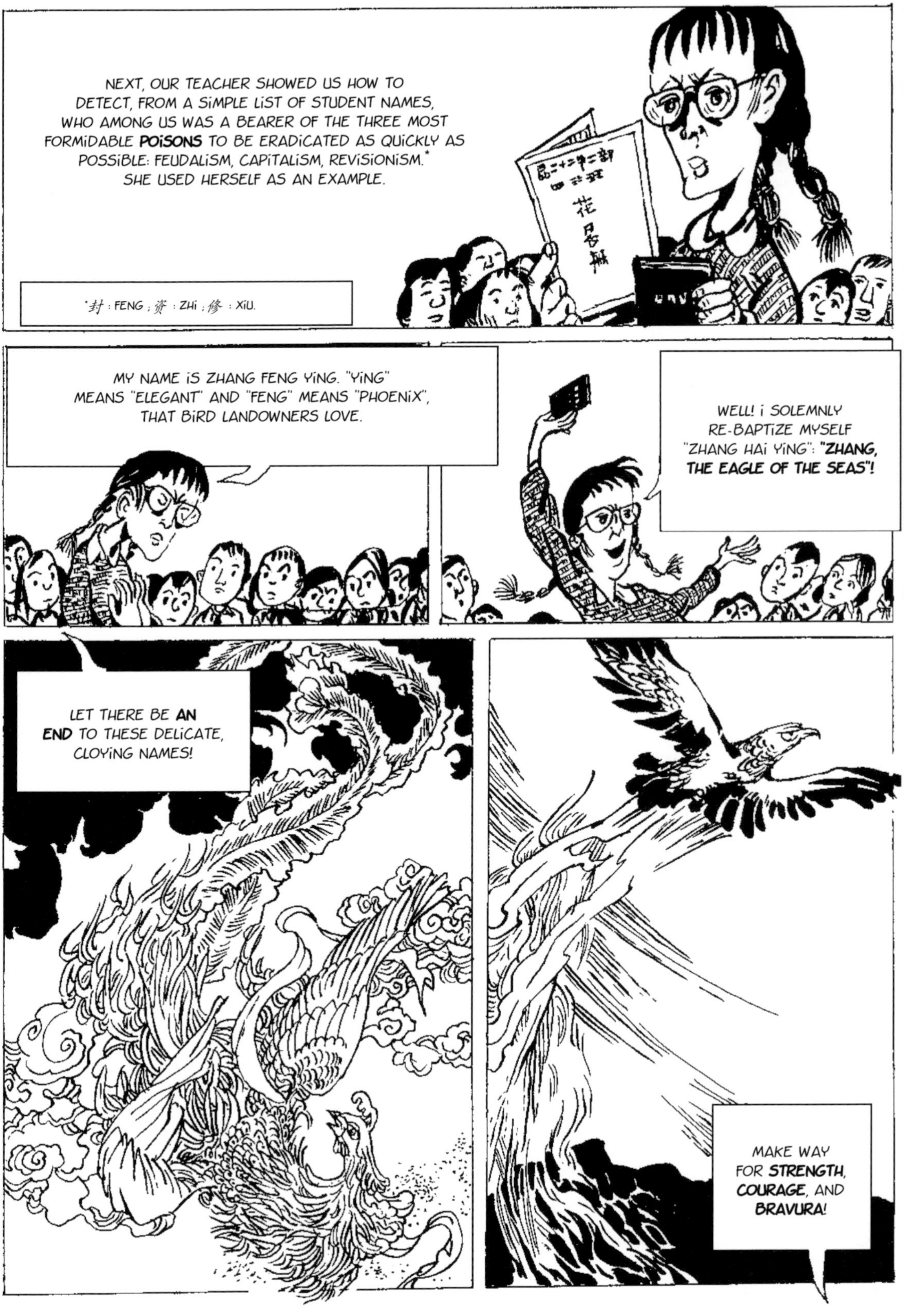
NEXT, OUR TEACHER SHOWED US HOW TO DETECT, FROM A SIMPLE LIST OF STUDENT NAMES, WHO AMONG US WAS A BEARER OF THE THREE MOST FORMIDABLE **POISONS** TO BE ERADICATED AS QUICKLY AS POSSIBLE: FEUDALISM, CAPITALISM, REVISIONISM.* SHE USED HERSELF AS AN EXAMPLE.
*封 : FENG ; 资 : ZHI ; 修 : XIU.
花
MY NAME IS ZHANG FENG YING. "YING" MEANS "ELEGANT" AND "FENG" MEANS "PHOENIX", THAT BIRD LANDOWNERS LOVE.
WELL! I SOLEMNLY RE-BAPTIZE MYSELF "ZHANG HAI YING": **"ZHANG, THE EAGLE OF THE SEAS"!**
LET THERE BE **AN END** TO THESE DELICATE, CLOYING NAMES!
MAKE WAY FOR **STRENGTH, COURAGE,** AND **BRAVURA!**

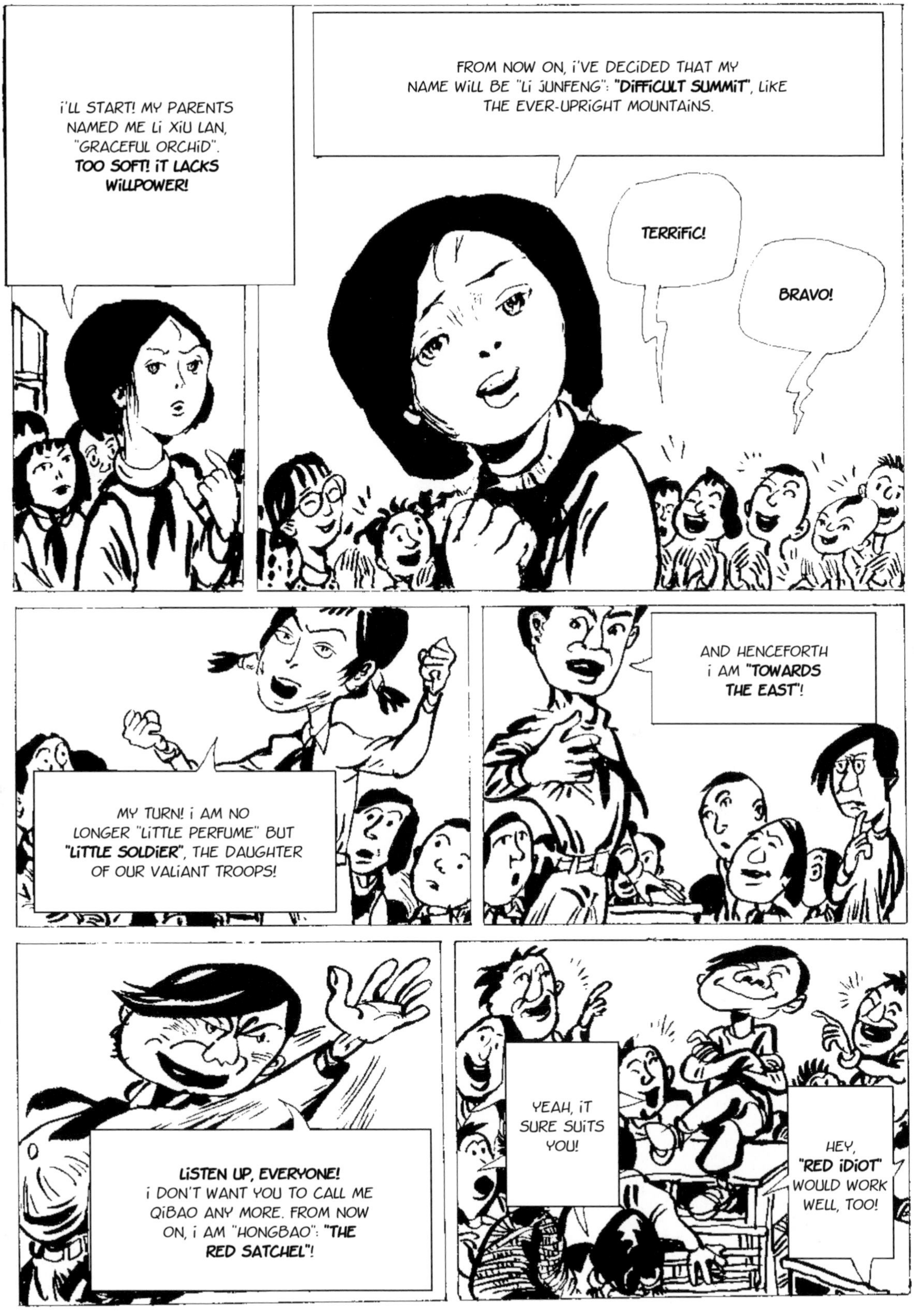

I'LL START! MY PARENTS NAMED ME LI XIU LAN, "GRACEFUL ORCHID". **TOO SOFT! IT LACKS WILLPOWER!**
FROM NOW ON, I'VE DECIDED THAT MY NAME WILL BE "LI JUNFENG": **"DIFFICULT SUMMIT"**, LIKE THE EVER-UPRIGHT MOUNTAINS.
TERRIFIC!
BRAVO!
MY TURN! I AM NO LONGER "LITTLE PERFUME" BUT **"LITTLE SOLDIER"**, THE DAUGHTER OF OUR VALIANT TROOPS!
AND HENCEFORTH I AM **"TOWARDS THE EAST"**!
LISTEN UP, EVERYONE! I DON'T WANT YOU TO CALL ME QIBAO ANY MORE. FROM NOW ON, I AM "HONGBAO": **"THE RED SATCHEL"**!
YEAH, IT SURE SUITS YOU!
HEY, **"RED IDIOT"** WOULD WORK WELL, TOO!

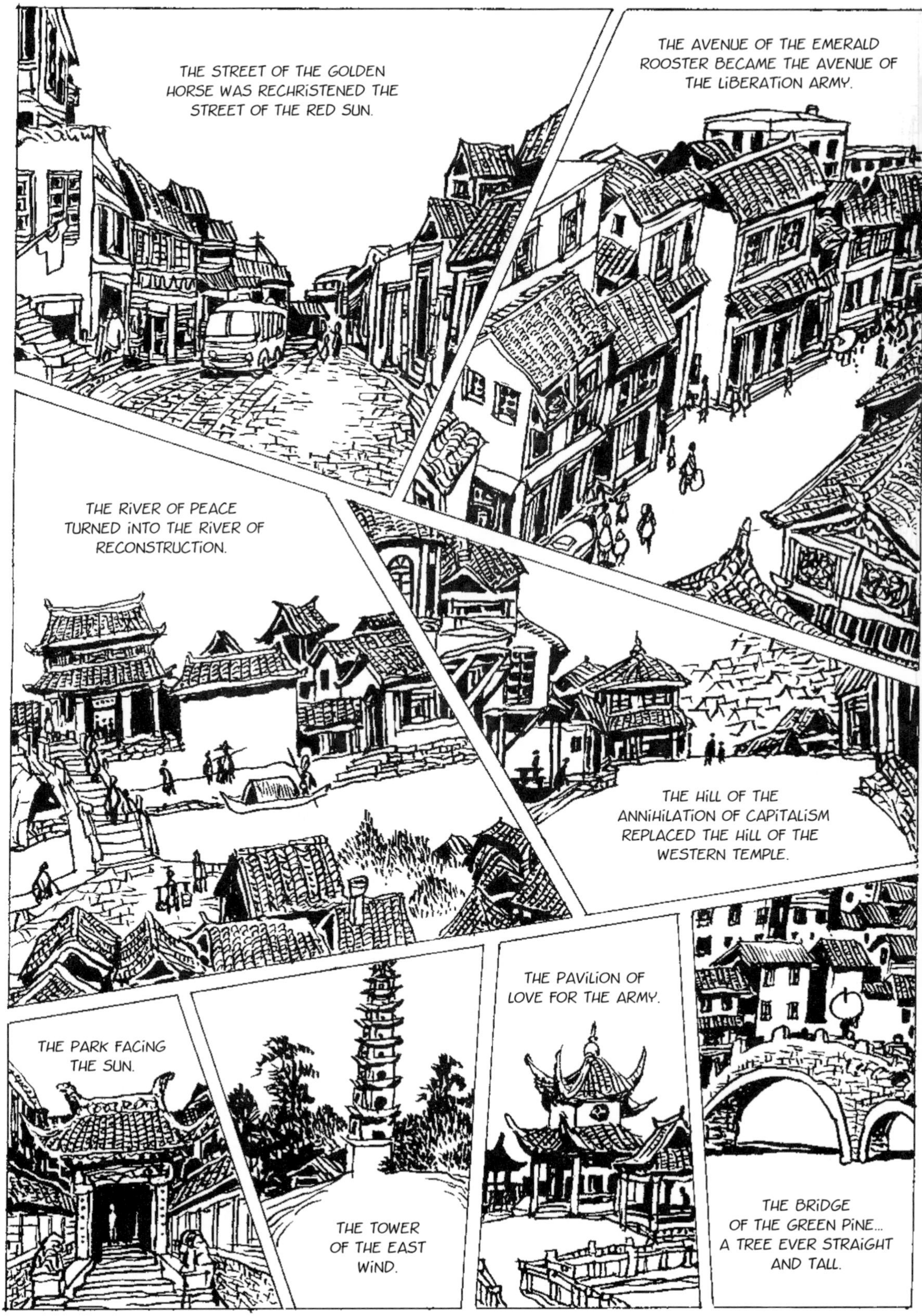
THE STREET OF THE GOLDEN HORSE WAS RECHRISTENED THE STREET OF THE RED SUN.
THE AVENUE OF THE EMERALD ROOSTER BECAME THE AVENUE OF THE LIBERATION ARMY.
THE RIVER OF PEACE TURNED INTO THE RIVER OF RECONSTRUCTION.
THE HILL OF THE ANNIHILATION OF CAPITALISM REPLACED THE HILL OF THE WESTERN TEMPLE.
THE PARK FACING THE SUN.
THE TOWER OF THE EAST WIND.
THE PAVILION OF LOVE FOR THE ARMY.
THE BRIDGE OF THE GREEN PINE... A TREE EVER STRAIGHT AND TALL.

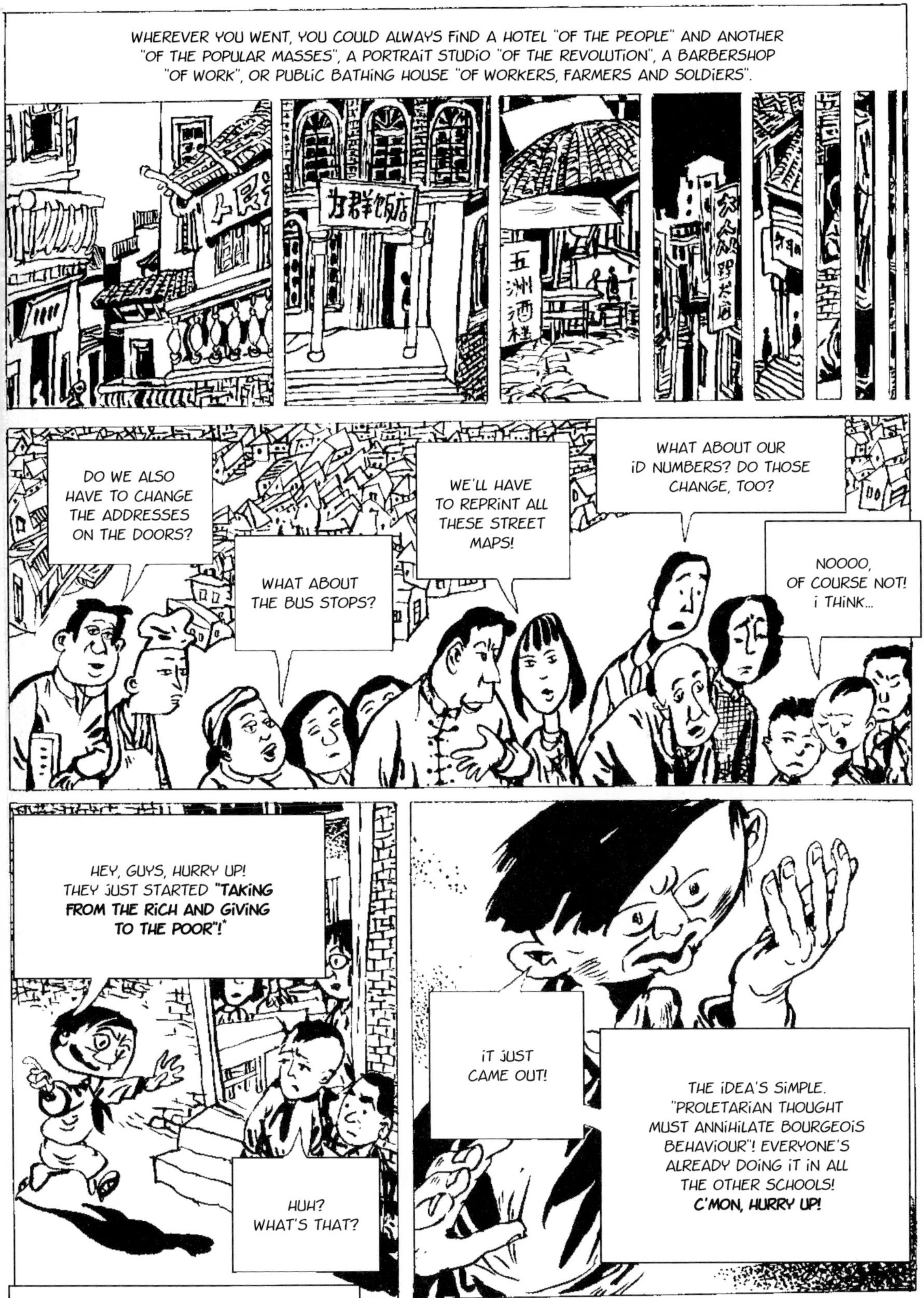
WHEREVER YOU WENT, YOU COULD ALWAYS FiND A HOTEL "OF THE PEOPLE" AND ANOTHER "OF THE POPULAR MASSES", A PORTRAiT STUDiO "OF THE REVOLUTiON", A BARBERSHOP "OF WORK", OR PUBLiC BATHiNG HOUSE "OF WORKERS, FARMERS AND SOLDiERS".
DO WE ALSO HAVE TO CHANGE THE ADDRESSES ON THE DOORS?
WHAT ABOUT THE BUS STOPS?
WE'LL HAVE TO REPRiNT ALL THESE STREET MAPS!
WHAT ABOUT OUR iD NUMBERS? DO THOSE CHANGE, TOO?
NOOOO, OF COURSE NOT! i THiNK...
HEY, GUYS, HURRY UP! THEY JUST STARTED "**TAKiNG FROM THE RiCH AND GiViNG TO THE POOR**"!*
HUH? WHAT'S THAT?
iT JUST CAME OUT!
THE iDEA'S SiMPLE. "PROLETARiAN THOUGHT MUST ANNiHiLATE BOURGEOiS BEHAViOUR"! EVERYONE'S ALREADY DOiNG iT iN ALL THE OTHER SCHOOLS! **C'MON, HURRY UP!**

* 兴无灭资 XiNGWUMiEZi.

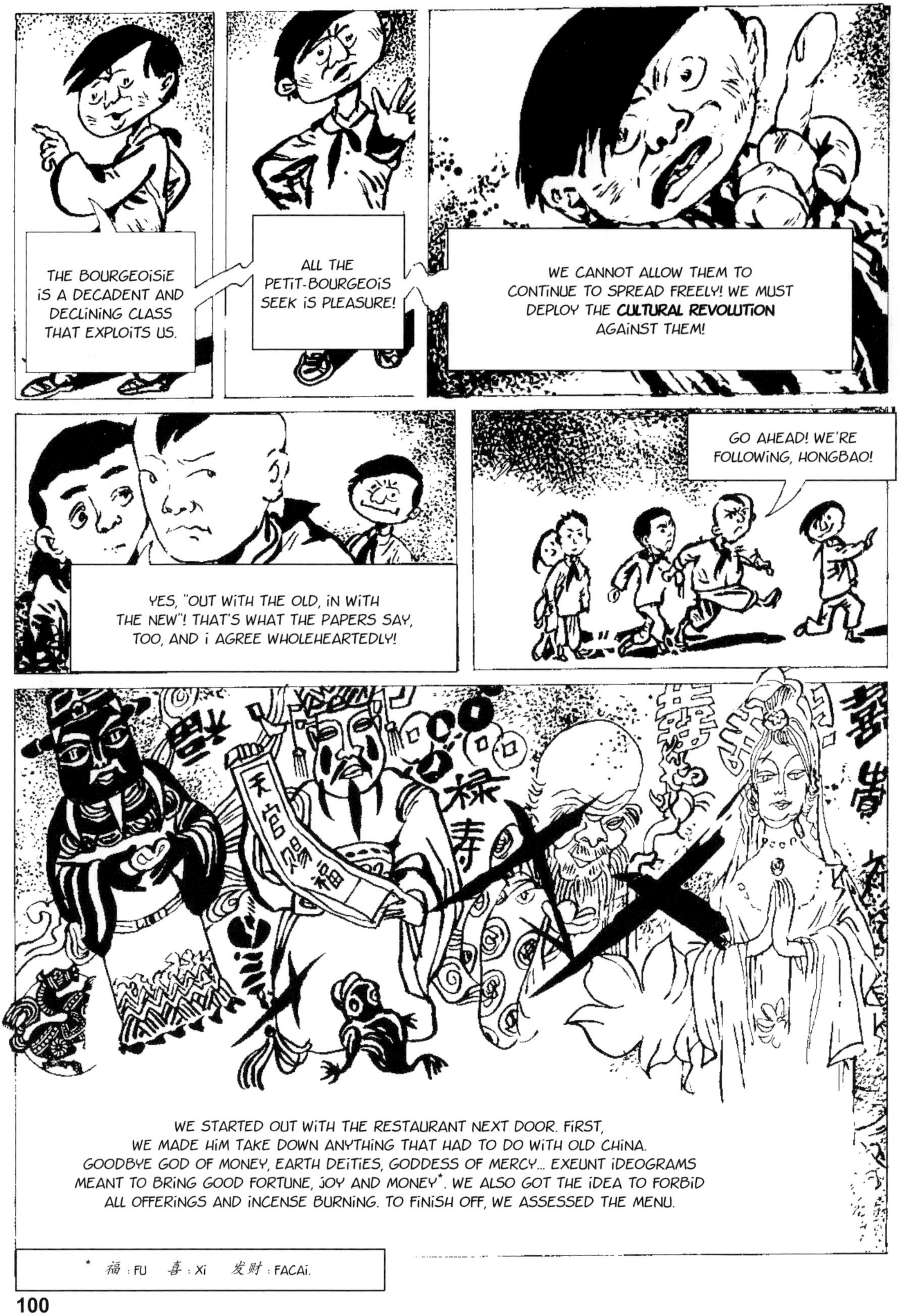
THE BOURGEOISIE IS A DECADENT AND DECLINING CLASS THAT EXPLOITS US.
ALL THE PETIT-BOURGEOIS SEEK IS PLEASURE!
WE CANNOT ALLOW THEM TO CONTINUE TO SPREAD FREELY! WE MUST DEPLOY THE **CULTURAL REVOLUTION** AGAINST THEM!
YES, "OUT WITH THE OLD, IN WITH THE NEW"! THAT'S WHAT THE PAPERS SAY, TOO, AND I AGREE WHOLEHEARTEDLY!
GO AHEAD! WE'RE FOLLOWING, HONGBAO!
WE STARTED OUT WITH THE RESTAURANT NEXT DOOR. FIRST, WE MADE HIM TAKE DOWN ANYTHING THAT HAD TO DO WITH OLD CHINA. GOODBYE GOD OF MONEY, EARTH DEITIES, GODDESS OF MERCY... EXEUNT IDEOGRAMS MEANT TO BRING GOOD FORTUNE, JOY AND MONEY*. WE ALSO GOT THE IDEA TO FORBID ALL OFFERINGS AND INCENSE BURNING. TO FINISH OFF, WE ASSESSED THE MENU.

* 福 : FU 喜 : XI 发财 : FACAI.

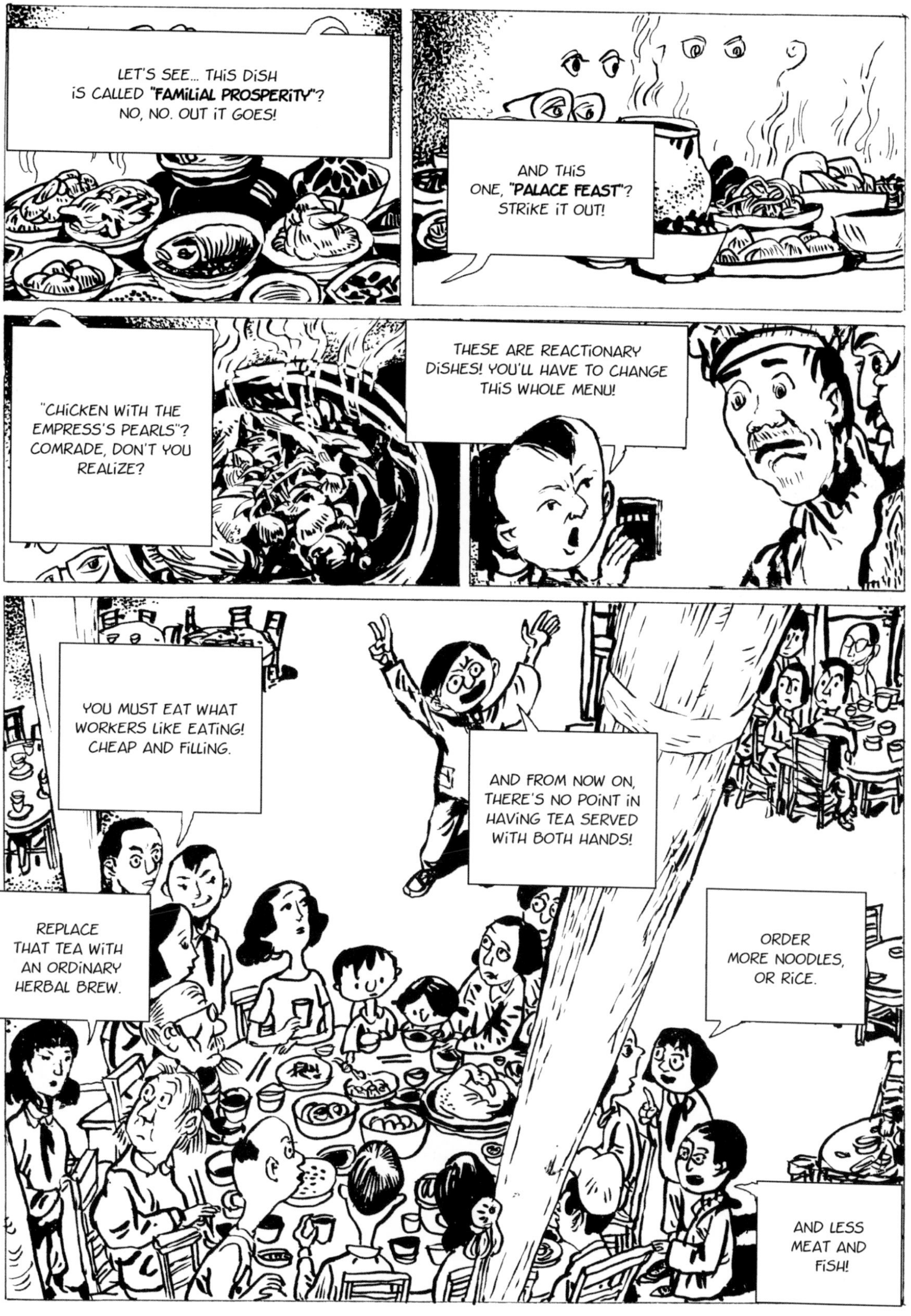
LET'S SEE... THIS DISH IS CALLED "FAMILIAL PROSPERITY"? NO, NO. OUT IT GOES!
AND THIS ONE, "PALACE FEAST"? STRIKE IT OUT!
"CHICKEN WITH THE EMPRESS'S PEARLS"? COMRADE, DON'T YOU REALIZE?
THESE ARE REACTIONARY DISHES! YOU'LL HAVE TO CHANGE THIS WHOLE MENU!
YOU MUST EAT WHAT WORKERS LIKE EATING! CHEAP AND FILLING.
AND FROM NOW ON, THERE'S NO POINT IN HAVING TEA SERVED WITH BOTH HANDS!
REPLACE THAT TEA WITH AN ORDINARY HERBAL BREW.
ORDER MORE NOODLES, OR RICE.
AND LESS MEAT AND FISH!

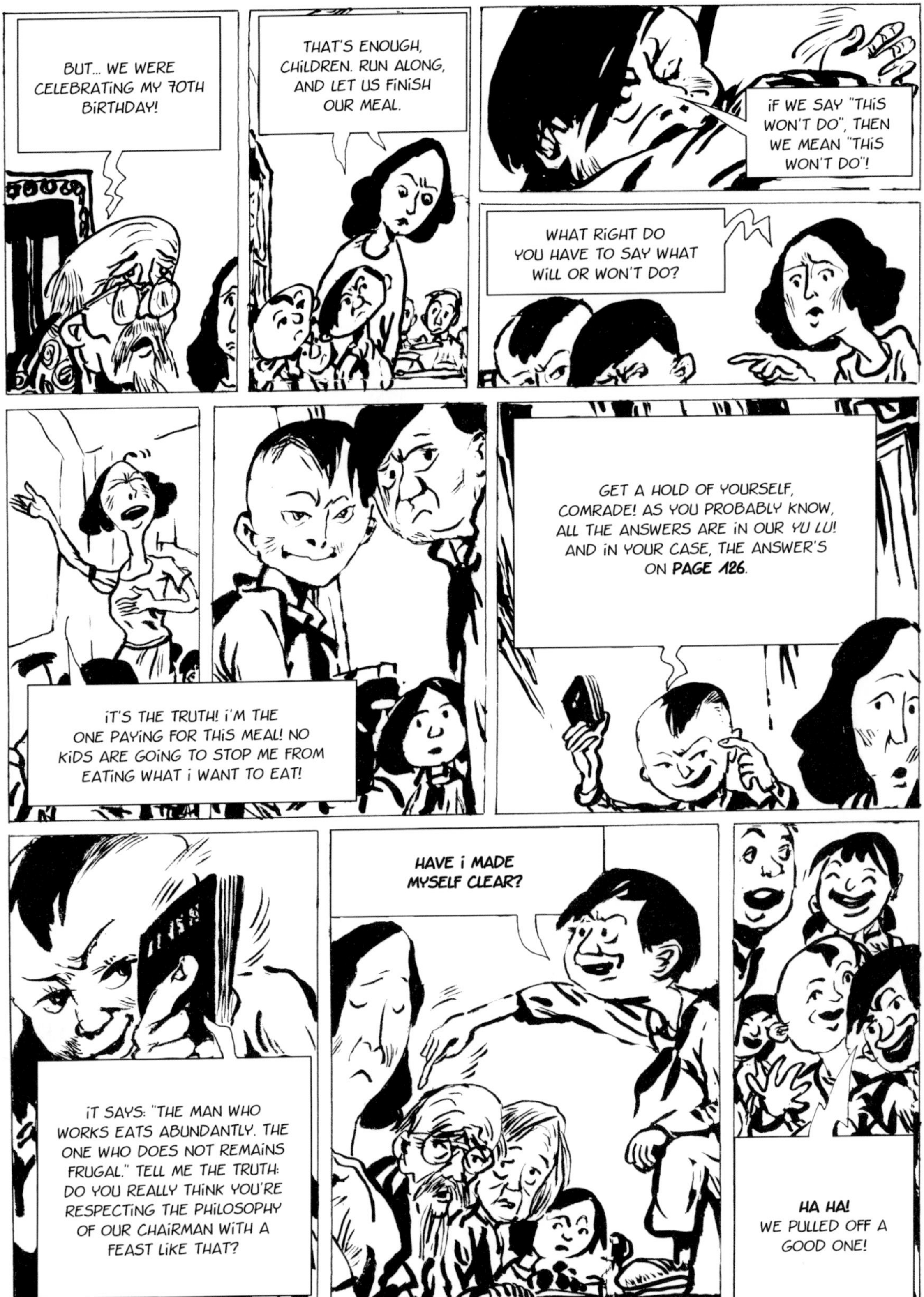
BUT... WE WERE CELEBRATING MY 70TH BIRTHDAY!
THAT'S ENOUGH, CHILDREN. RUN ALONG, AND LET US FINISH OUR MEAL.
IF WE SAY "THIS WON'T DO", THEN WE MEAN "THIS WON'T DO"!
WHAT RIGHT DO YOU HAVE TO SAY WHAT WILL OR WON'T DO?
IT'S THE TRUTH! I'M THE ONE PAYING FOR THIS MEAL! NO KIDS ARE GOING TO STOP ME FROM EATING WHAT I WANT TO EAT!
GET A HOLD OF YOURSELF, COMRADE! AS YOU PROBABLY KNOW, ALL THE ANSWERS ARE IN OUR *YU LU*! AND IN YOUR CASE, THE ANSWER'S ON **PAGE 126**.
IT SAYS: "THE MAN WHO WORKS EATS ABUNDANTLY. THE ONE WHO DOES NOT REMAINS FRUGAL." TELL ME THE TRUTH: DO YOU REALLY THINK YOU'RE RESPECTING THE PHILOSOPHY OF OUR CHAIRMAN WITH A FEAST LIKE THAT?
HAVE I MADE MYSELF CLEAR?
HA HA! WE PULLED OFF A GOOD ONE!

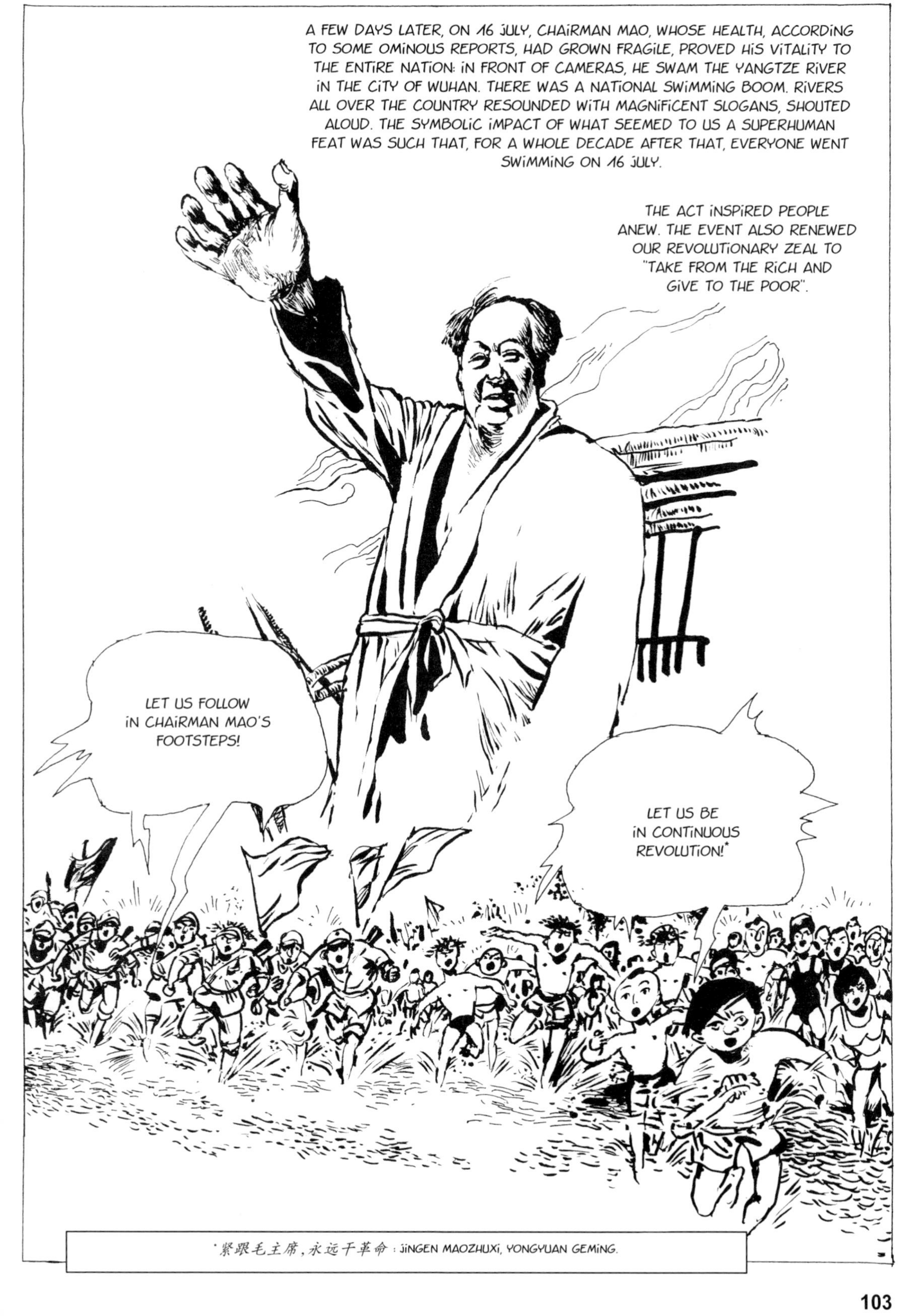
A FEW DAYS LATER, ON 16 JULY, CHAIRMAN MAO, WHOSE HEALTH, ACCORDING TO SOME OMINOUS REPORTS, HAD GROWN FRAGILE, PROVED HIS VITALITY TO THE ENTIRE NATION: IN FRONT OF CAMERAS, HE SWAM THE YANGTZE RIVER IN THE CITY OF WUHAN. THERE WAS A NATIONAL SWIMMING BOOM. RIVERS ALL OVER THE COUNTRY RESOUNDED WITH MAGNIFICENT SLOGANS, SHOUTED ALOUD. THE SYMBOLIC IMPACT OF WHAT SEEMED TO US A SUPERHUMAN FEAT WAS SUCH THAT, FOR A WHOLE DECADE AFTER THAT, EVERYONE WENT SWIMMING ON 16 JULY.
THE ACT INSPIRED PEOPLE ANEW. THE EVENT ALSO RENEWED OUR REVOLUTIONARY ZEAL TO "TAKE FROM THE RICH AND GIVE TO THE POOR".
LET US FOLLOW IN CHAIRMAN MAO'S FOOTSTEPS!
LET US BE IN CONTINUOUS REVOLUTION!*

*紧跟毛主席，永远干革命：JINGEN MAOZHUXI, YONGYUAN GEMING.

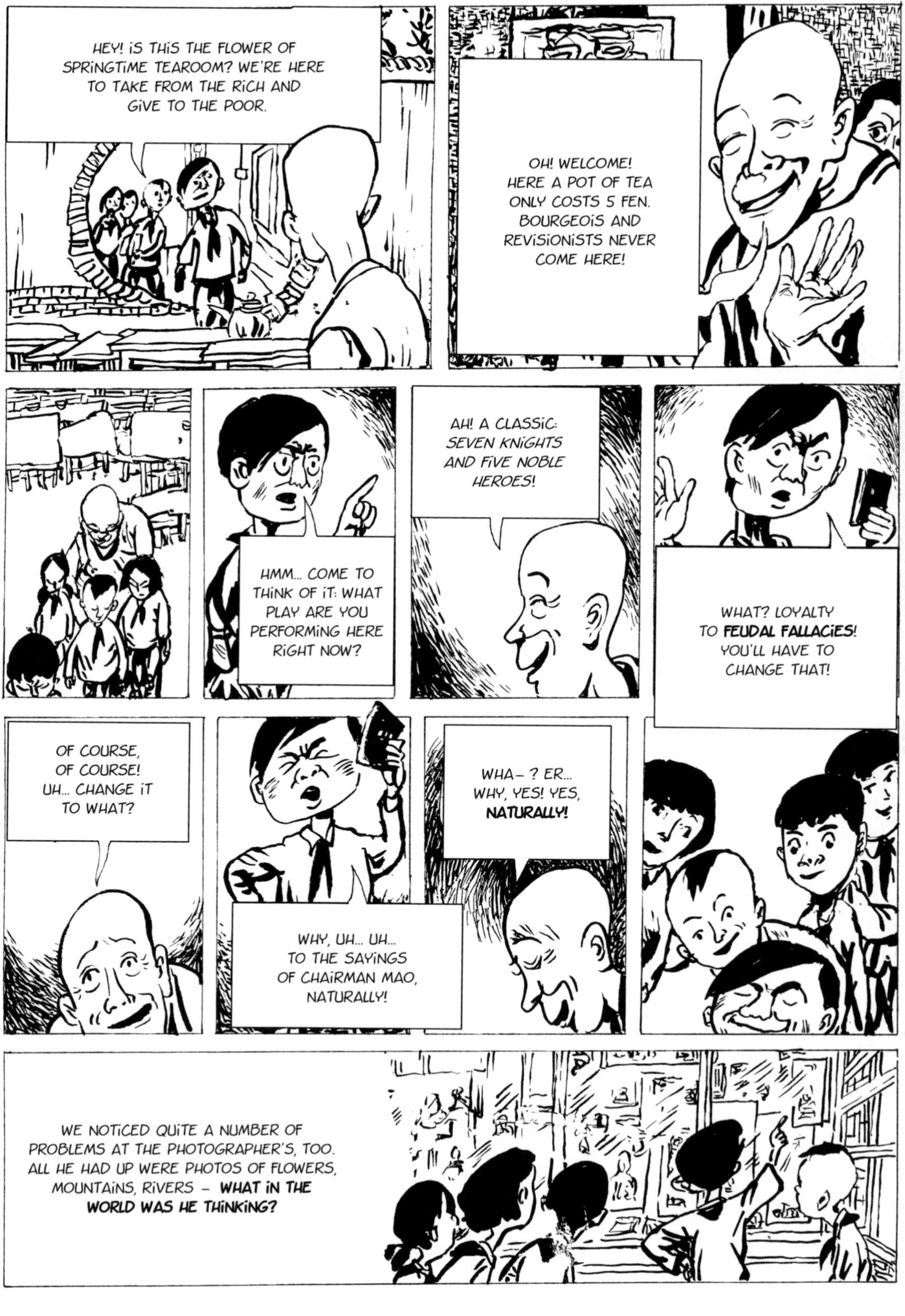
HEY! IS THIS THE FLOWER OF SPRINGTIME TEAROOM? WE'RE HERE TO TAKE FROM THE RICH AND GIVE TO THE POOR.
OH! WELCOME! HERE A POT OF TEA ONLY COSTS 5 FEN. BOURGEOIS AND REVISIONISTS NEVER COME HERE!
HMM... COME TO THINK OF IT: WHAT PLAY ARE YOU PERFORMING HERE RIGHT NOW?
AH! A CLASSIC: SEVEN KNIGHTS AND FIVE NOBLE HEROES!
WHAT? LOYALTY TO FEUDAL FALLACIES! YOU'LL HAVE TO CHANGE THAT!
OF COURSE, OF COURSE! UH... CHANGE IT TO WHAT?
WHY, UH... UH... TO THE SAYINGS OF CHAIRMAN MAO, NATURALLY!
WHA- ? ER... WHY, YES! YES, NATURALLY!
WE NOTICED QUITE A NUMBER OF PROBLEMS AT THE PHOTOGRAPHER'S, TOO. ALL HE HAD UP WERE PHOTOS OF FLOWERS, MOUNTAINS, RIVERS – WHAT IN THE WORLD WAS HE THINKING?

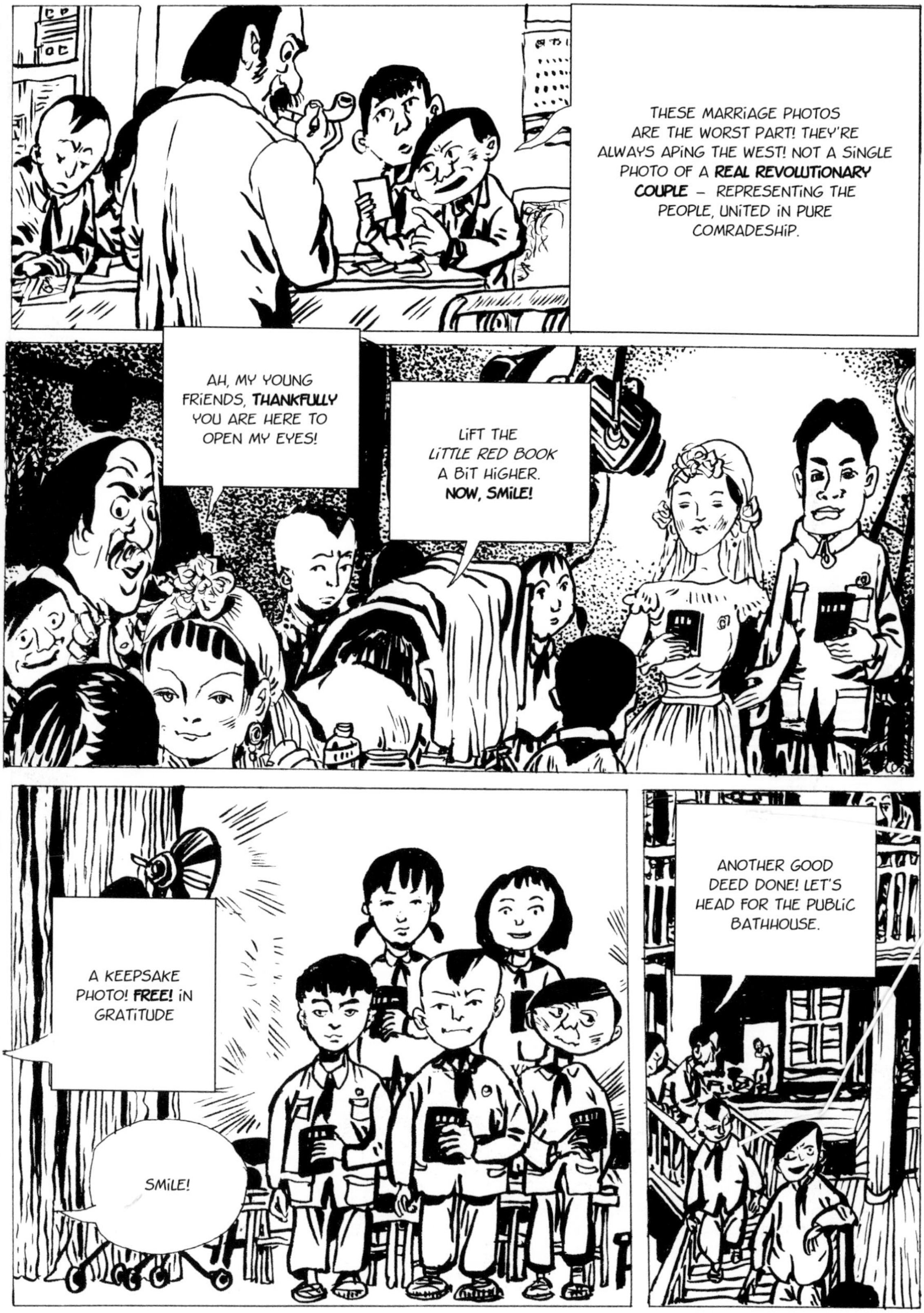
THESE MARRIAGE PHOTOS ARE THE WORST PART! THEY'RE ALWAYS APING THE WEST! NOT A SINGLE PHOTO OF A **REAL REVOLUTIONARY COUPLE** – REPRESENTING THE PEOPLE, UNITED IN PURE COMRADESHIP.
AH, MY YOUNG FRIENDS, **THANKFULLY** YOU ARE HERE TO OPEN MY EYES!
LIFT THE LITTLE RED BOOK A BIT HIGHER. **NOW, SMILE!**
A KEEPSAKE PHOTO! **FREE!** IN GRATITUDE
SMILE!
ANOTHER GOOD DEED DONE! LET'S HEAD FOR THE PUBLIC BATHHOUSE.

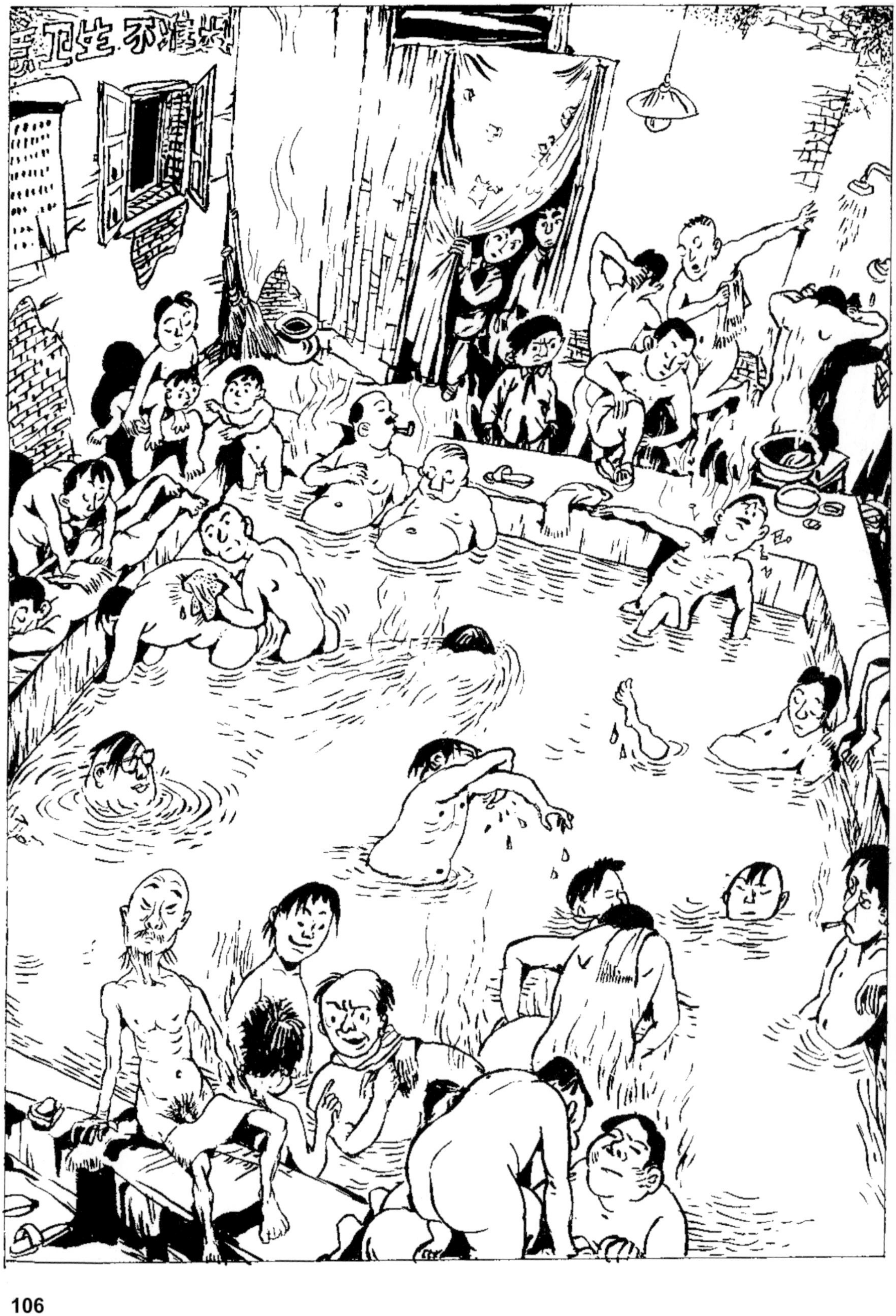
卫生 不

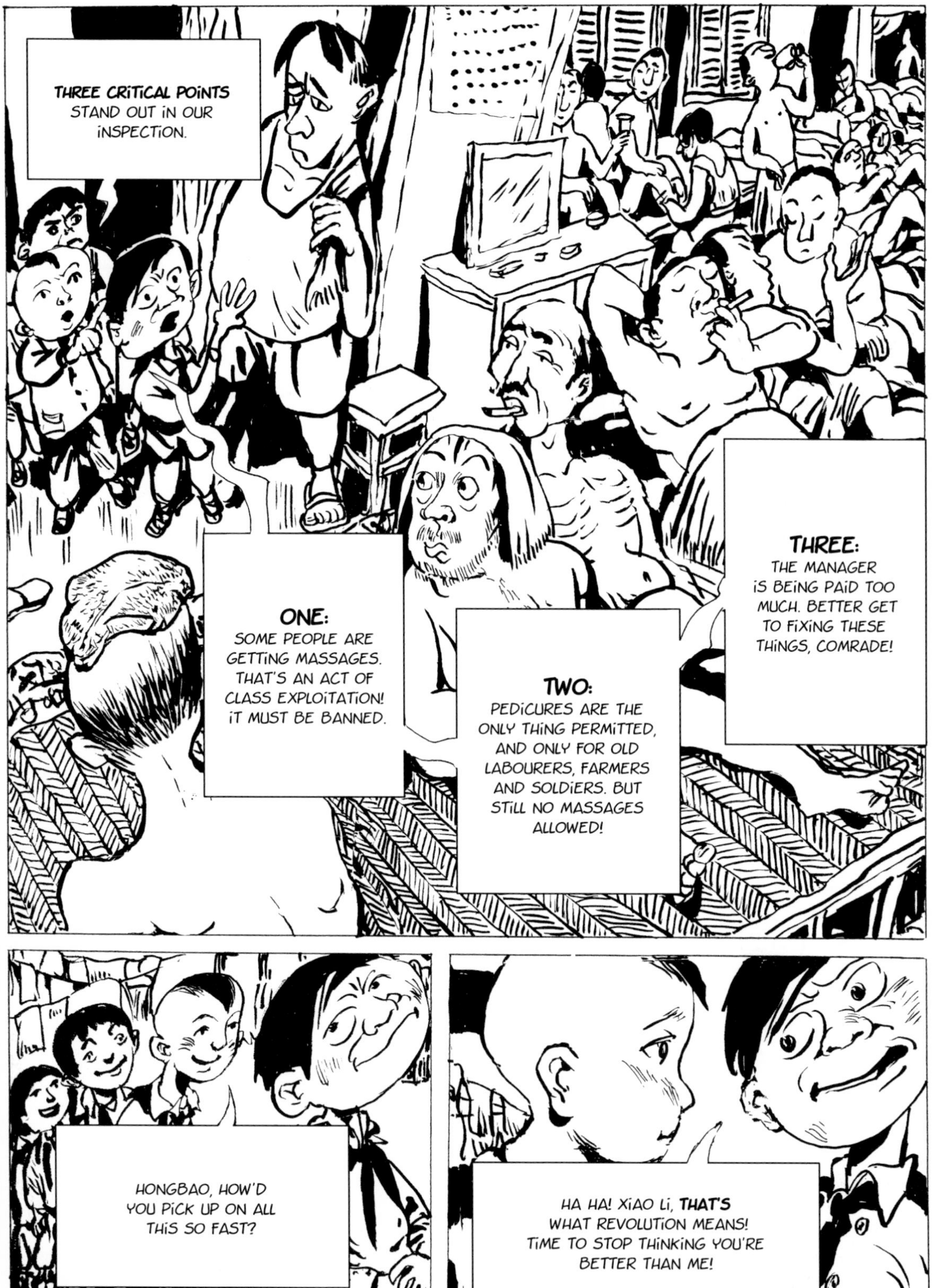
THREE CRITICAL POINTS STAND OUT IN OUR INSPECTION.
ONE: SOME PEOPLE ARE GETTING MASSAGES. THAT'S AN ACT OF CLASS EXPLOITATION! IT MUST BE BANNED.
TWO: PEDICURES ARE THE ONLY THING PERMITTED, AND ONLY FOR OLD LABOURERS, FARMERS AND SOLDIERS. BUT STILL NO MASSAGES ALLOWED!
THREE: THE MANAGER IS BEING PAID TOO MUCH. BETTER GET TO FIXING THESE THINGS, COMRADE!
HONGBAO, HOW'D YOU PICK UP ON ALL THIS SO FAST?
HA HA! XIAO LI, THAT'S WHAT REVOLUTION MEANS! TIME TO STOP THINKING YOU'RE BETTER THAN ME!

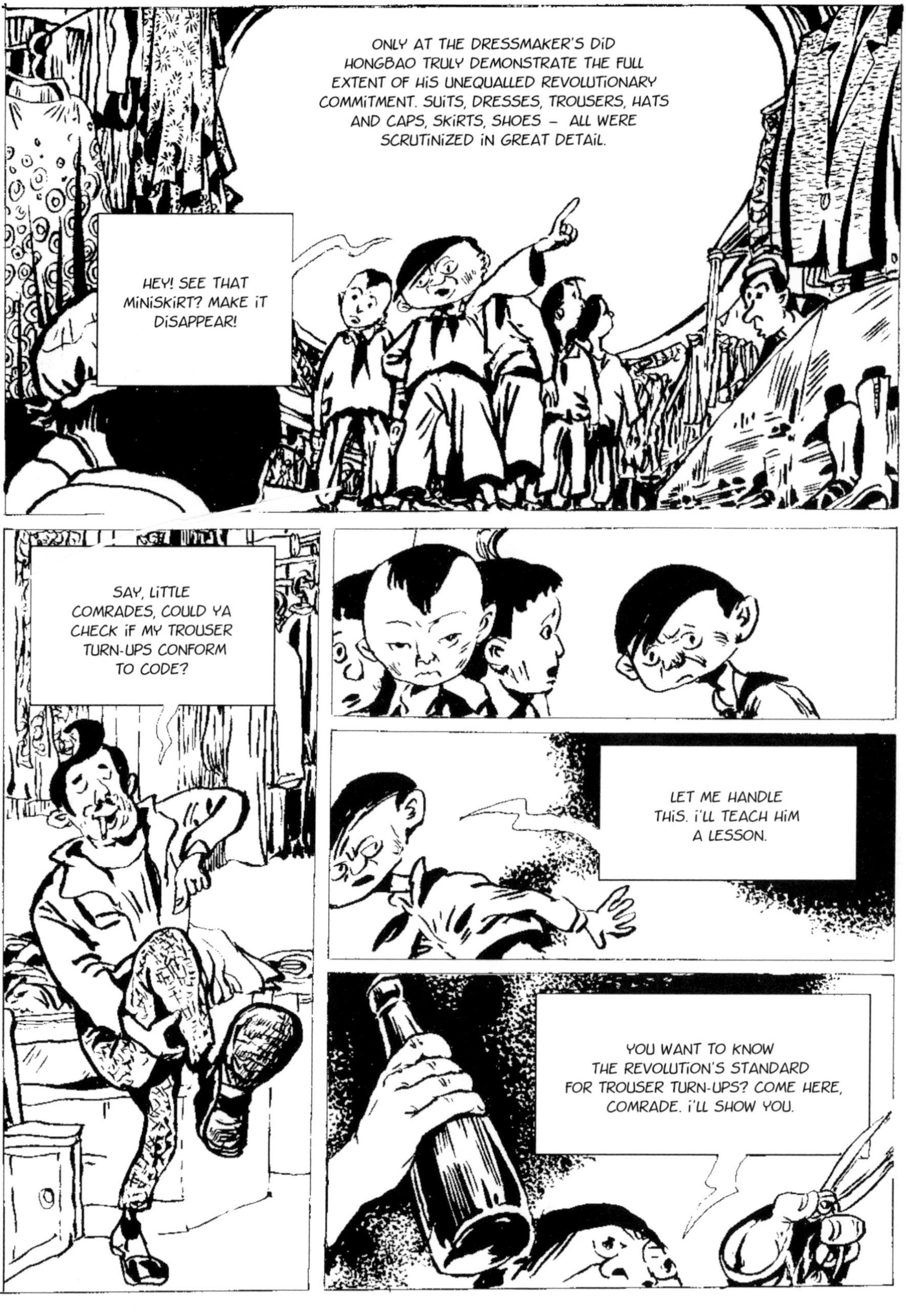
ONLY AT THE DRESSMAKER'S DID HONGBAO TRULY DEMONSTRATE THE FULL EXTENT OF HIS UNEQUALLED REVOLUTIONARY COMMITMENT. SUITS, DRESSES, TROUSERS, HATS AND CAPS, SKIRTS, SHOES – ALL WERE SCRUTINIZED IN GREAT DETAIL.
HEY! SEE THAT MINISKIRT? MAKE IT DISAPPEAR!
SAY, LITTLE COMRADES, COULD YA CHECK IF MY TROUSER TURN-UPS CONFORM TO CODE?
LET ME HANDLE THIS. I'LL TEACH HIM A LESSON.
YOU WANT TO KNOW THE REVOLUTION'S STANDARD FOR TROUSER TURN-UPS? COME HERE, COMRADE. I'LL SHOW YOU.

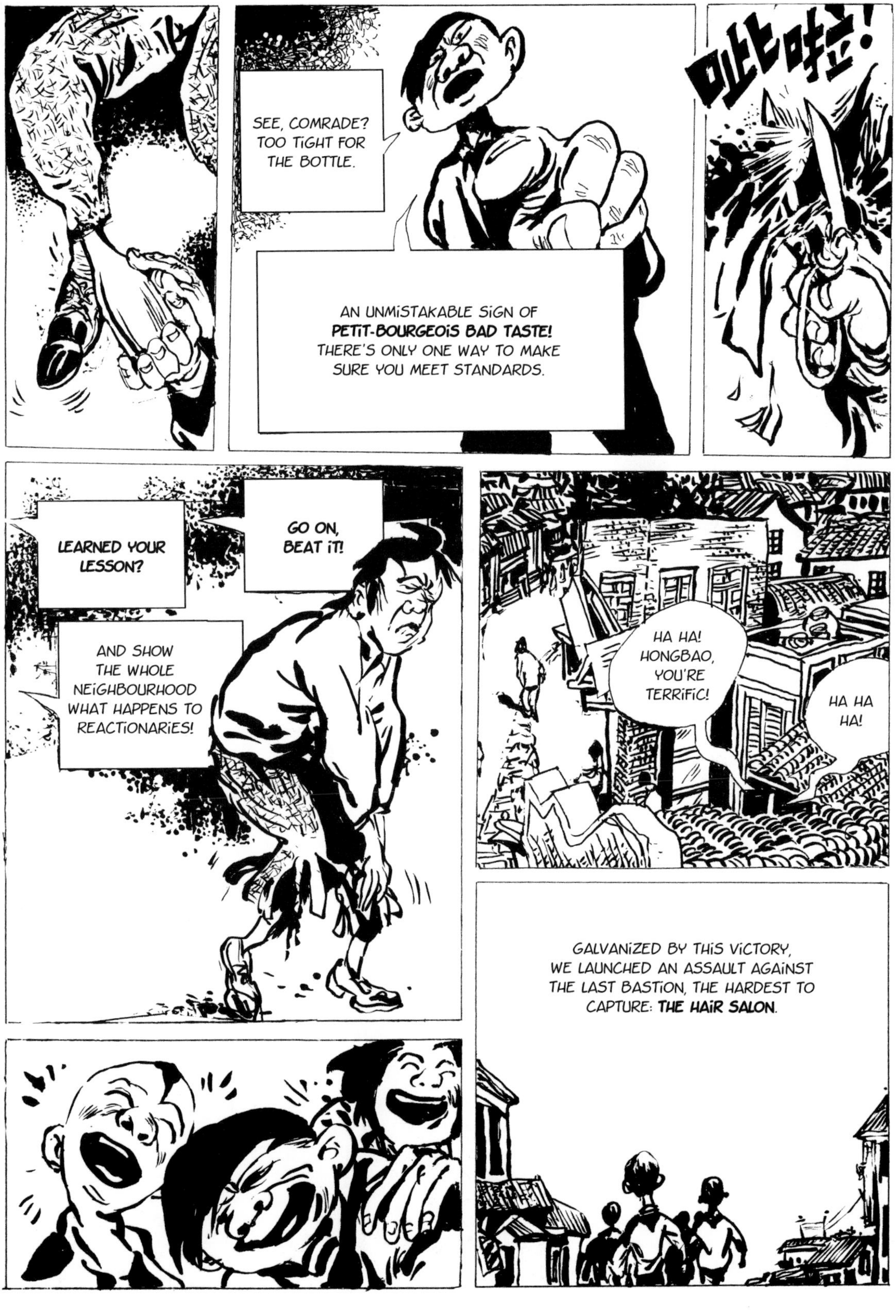
SEE, COMRADE? TOO TIGHT FOR THE BOTTLE.
AN UNMISTAKABLE SIGN OF **PETIT-BOURGEOIS BAD TASTE!** THERE'S ONLY ONE WAY TO MAKE SURE YOU MEET STANDARDS.
LEARNED YOUR LESSON?
GO ON, BEAT IT!
AND SHOW THE WHOLE NEIGHBOURHOOD WHAT HAPPENS TO REACTIONARIES!
HA HA! HONGBAO, YOU'RE TERRIFIC!
HA HA HA!
GALVANIZED BY THIS VICTORY, WE LAUNCHED AN ASSAULT AGAINST THE LAST BASTION, THE HARDEST TO CAPTURE: **THE HAIR SALON**.

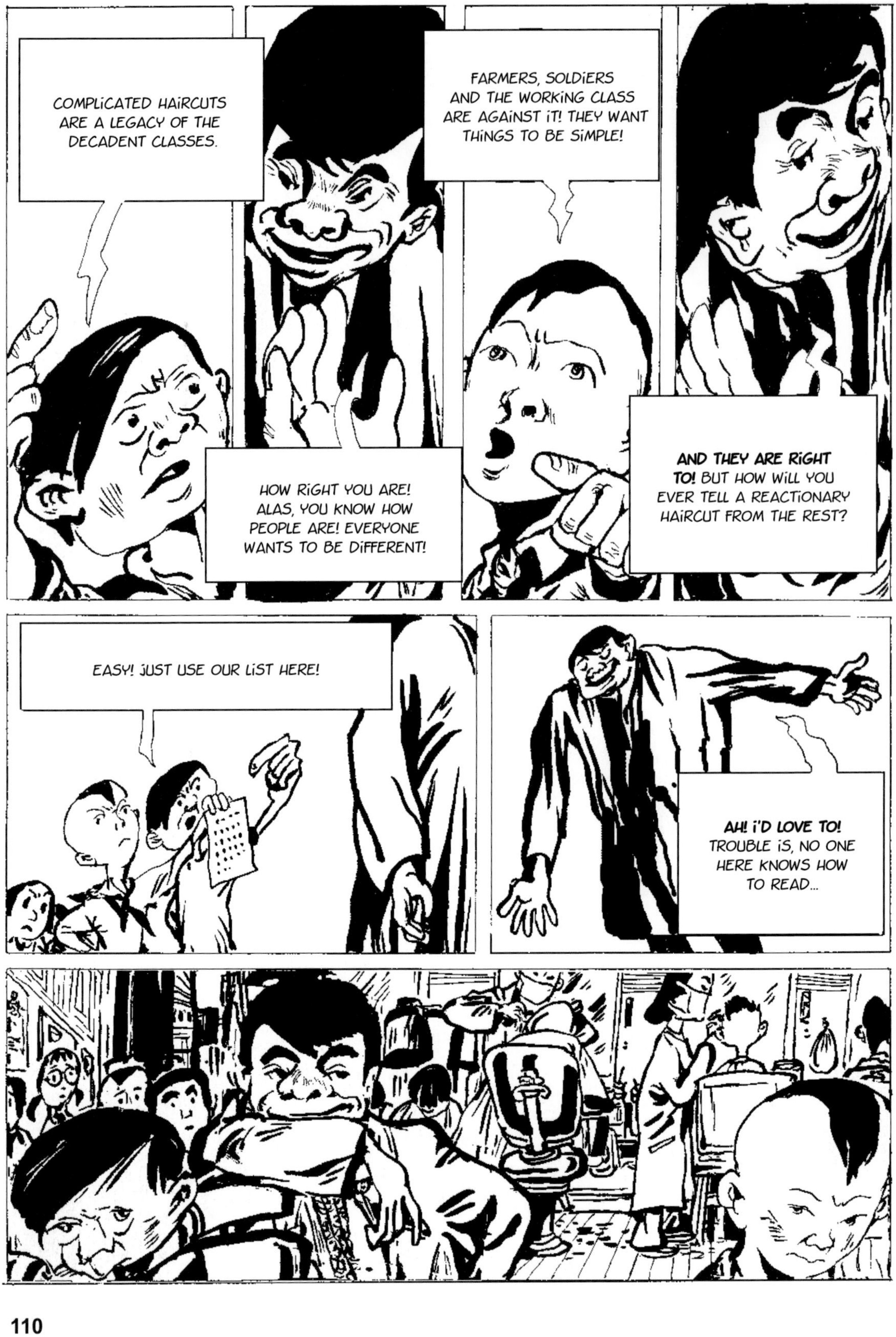
COMPLICATED HAIRCUTS ARE A LEGACY OF THE DECADENT CLASSES.
HOW RIGHT YOU ARE! ALAS, YOU KNOW HOW PEOPLE ARE! EVERYONE WANTS TO BE DIFFERENT!
FARMERS, SOLDIERS AND THE WORKING CLASS ARE AGAINST IT! THEY WANT THINGS TO BE SIMPLE!
AND THEY ARE RIGHT TO! BUT HOW WILL YOU EVER TELL A REACTIONARY HAIRCUT FROM THE REST?
EASY! JUST USE OUR LIST HERE!
AH! I'D LOVE TO! TROUBLE IS, NO ONE HERE KNOWS HOW TO READ...

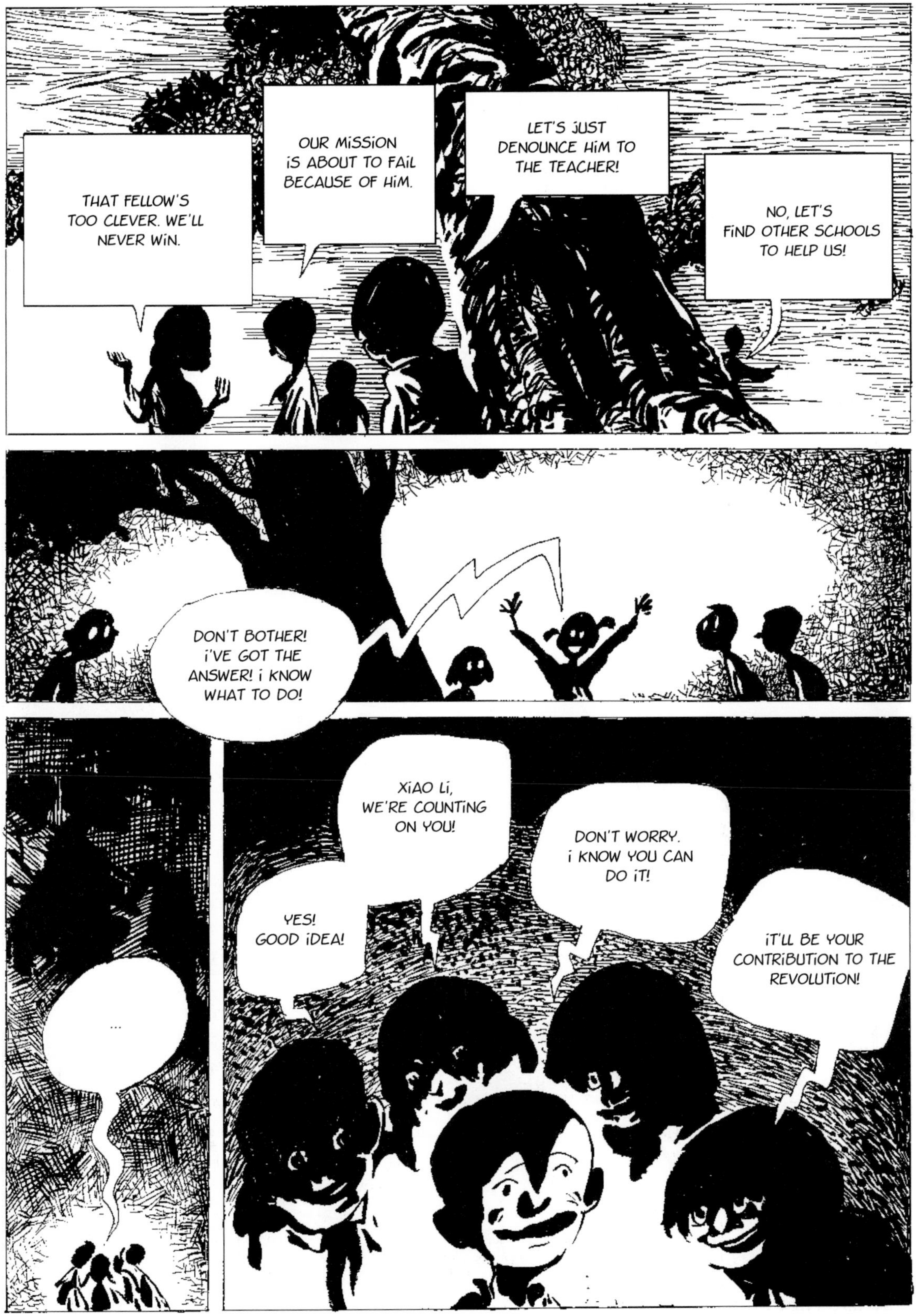
THAT FELLOW'S TOO CLEVER. WE'LL NEVER WIN.
OUR MISSION IS ABOUT TO FAIL BECAUSE OF HIM.
LET'S JUST DENOUNCE HIM TO THE TEACHER!
NO, LET'S FIND OTHER SCHOOLS TO HELP US!
DON'T BOTHER! I'VE GOT THE ANSWER! I KNOW WHAT TO DO!
...
XIAO LI, WE'RE COUNTING ON YOU!
YES! GOOD IDEA!
DON'T WORRY. I KNOW YOU CAN DO IT!
IT'LL BE YOUR CONTRIBUTION TO THE REVOLUTION!

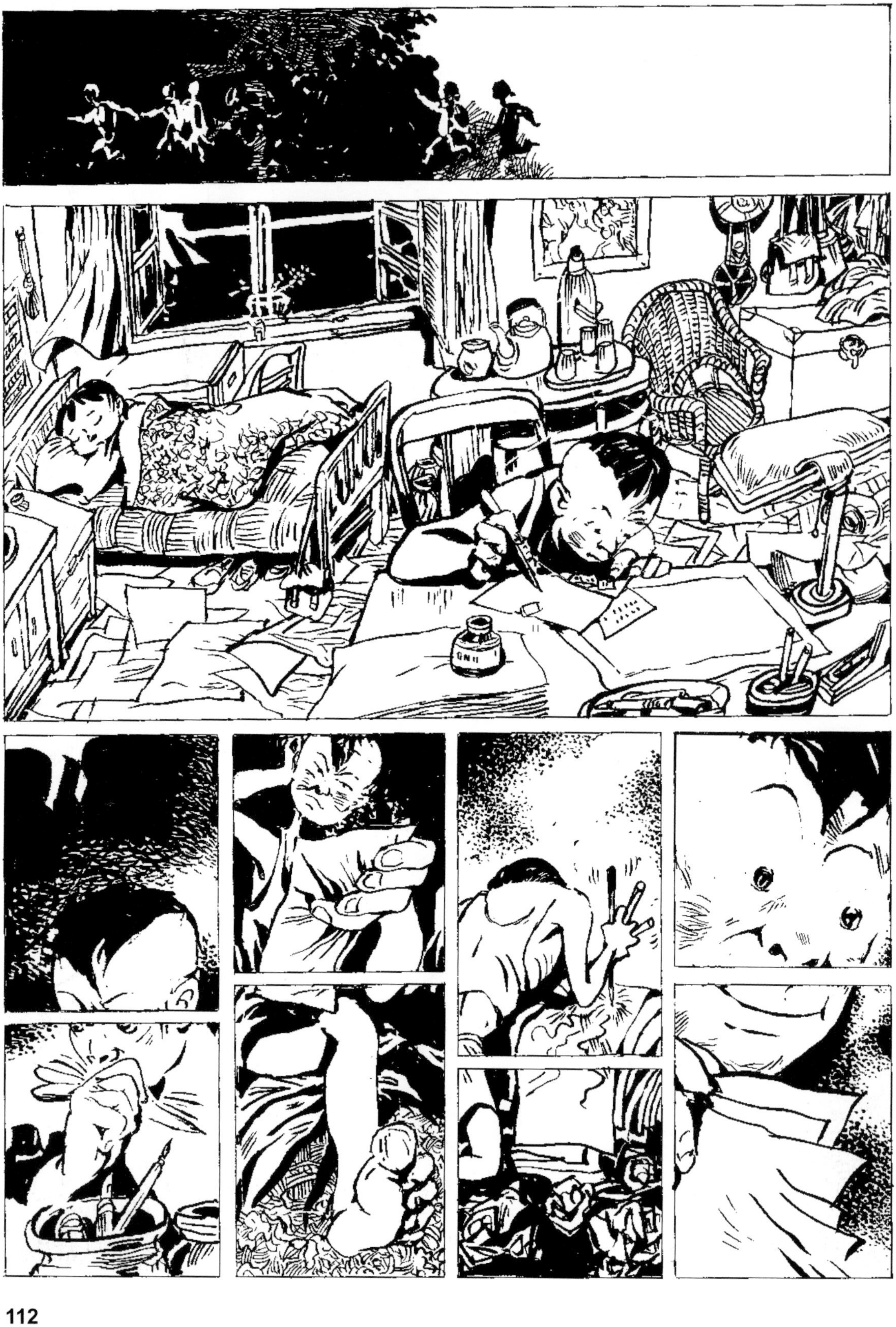

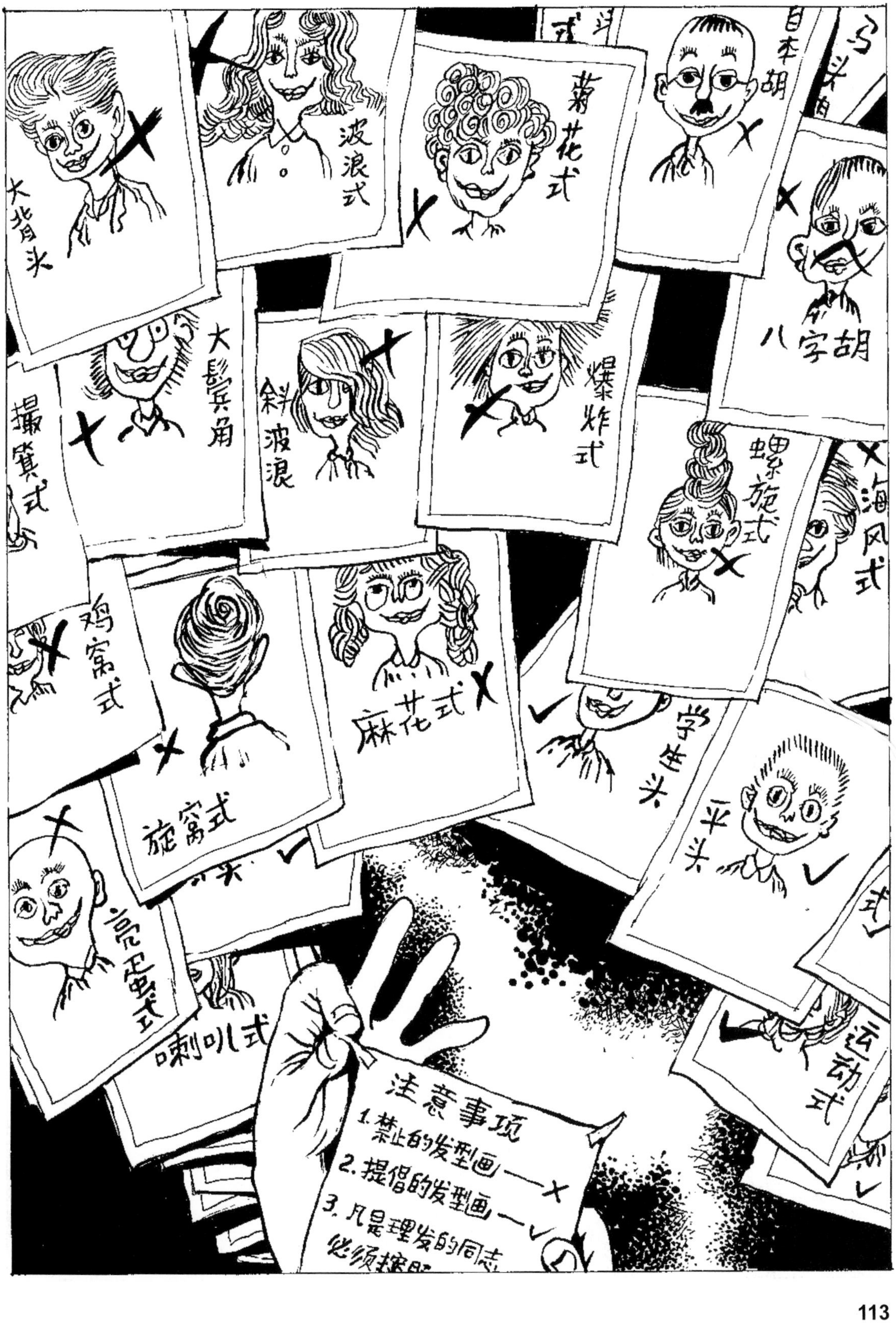
大背头
波浪式
菊花式
日本胡
八字胡
大鬓角
斜波浪
爆炸式
撮箕式
螺旋式
海风式
鸡窝式
旋窝式
麻花式
学生头
平头
亮蛋式
喇叭式
运动式
注意事项
1.禁止的发型画
2.提倡的发型画—×
3.凡是理发的同志—✓
必须

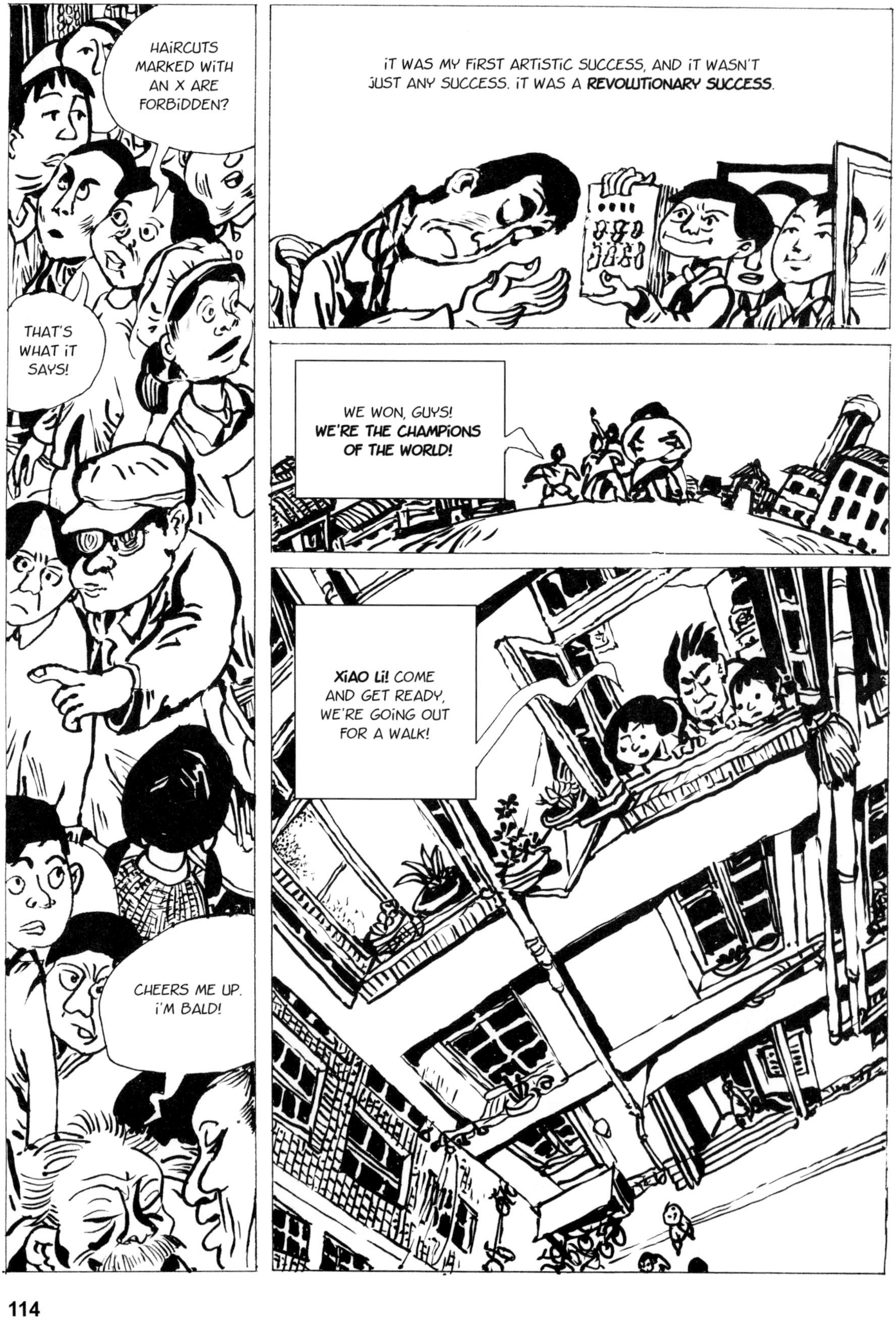
HAIRCUTS MARKED WITH AN X ARE FORBIDDEN?
THAT'S WHAT IT SAYS!
CHEERS ME UP. I'M BALD!
IT WAS MY FIRST ARTISTIC SUCCESS, AND IT WASN'T JUST ANY SUCCESS. IT WAS A **REVOLUTIONARY SUCCESS**.
WE WON, GUYS! **WE'RE THE CHAMPIONS OF THE WORLD!**
XIAO LI! COME AND GET READY, WE'RE GOING OUT FOR A WALK!

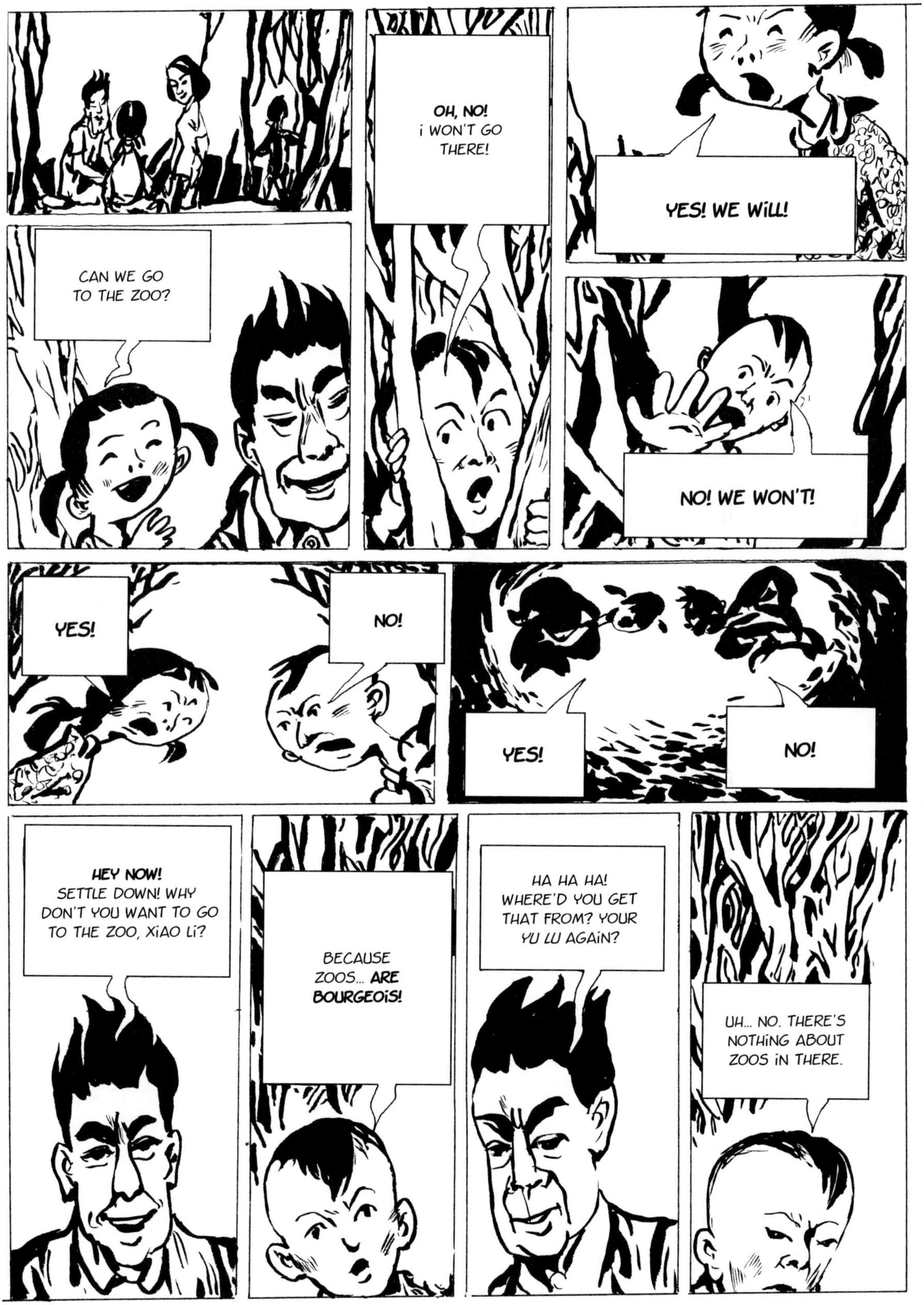
OH, NO! I WON'T GO THERE!
CAN WE GO TO THE ZOO?
YES! WE WILL!
NO! WE WON'T!
YES!
NO!
YES!
NO!
HEY NOW! SETTLE DOWN! WHY DON'T YOU WANT TO GO TO THE ZOO, XIAO LI?
BECAUSE ZOOS... ARE BOURGEOIS!
HA HA HA! WHERE'D YOU GET THAT FROM? YOUR YU LU AGAIN?
UH... NO. THERE'S NOTHING ABOUT ZOOS IN THERE.

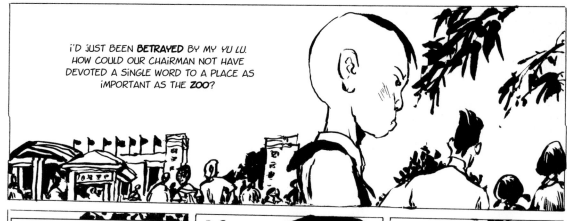

I'D JUST BEEN **BETRAYED** BY MY *YU LU*. HOW COULD OUR CHAIRMAN NOT HAVE DEVOTED A SINGLE WORD TO A PLACE AS IMPORTANT AS THE **ZOO**?

YOO-HOO! OVER HERE, YOU DIRTY STINKIN' ANIMAL!

OVER HERE, I GOT A GIFT FOR YA!

OK!

TSK. ANOTHER ILL-BRED PEASANT!

PAPA! COME HERE! I MUST SPEAK WITH YOU!

IT WOULDN'T HURT IF YOU STUDIED MAO'S WORDS A LITTLE MORE CLOSELY!

IN MY *YU LU*, IT SAYS: "WITHOUT FARMERS, THERE WOULD BE NO REVOLUTION. TO CRITICIZE THE FARMER IS TO CRITICIZE THE REVOLUTION." **GOT IT?**

116

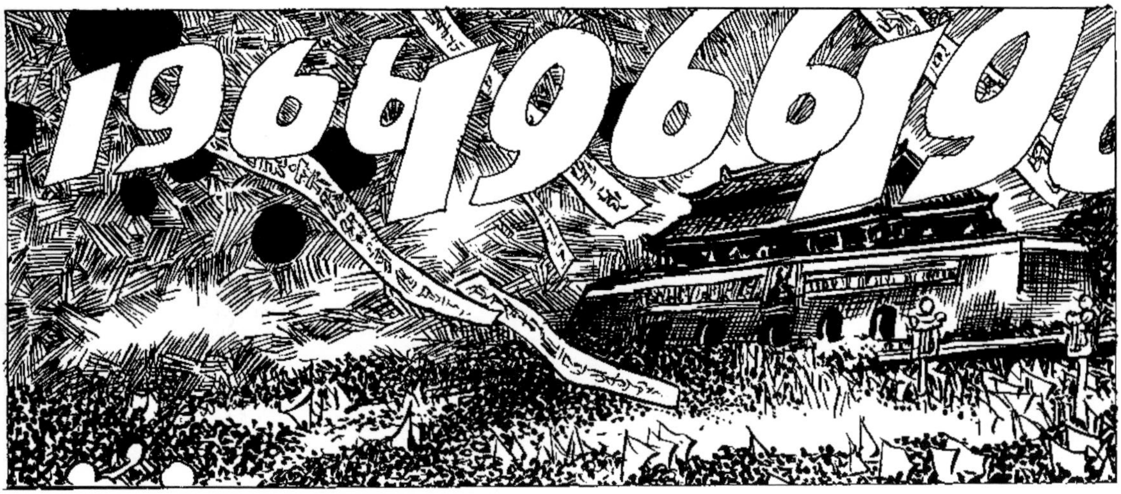
1966 1966 196

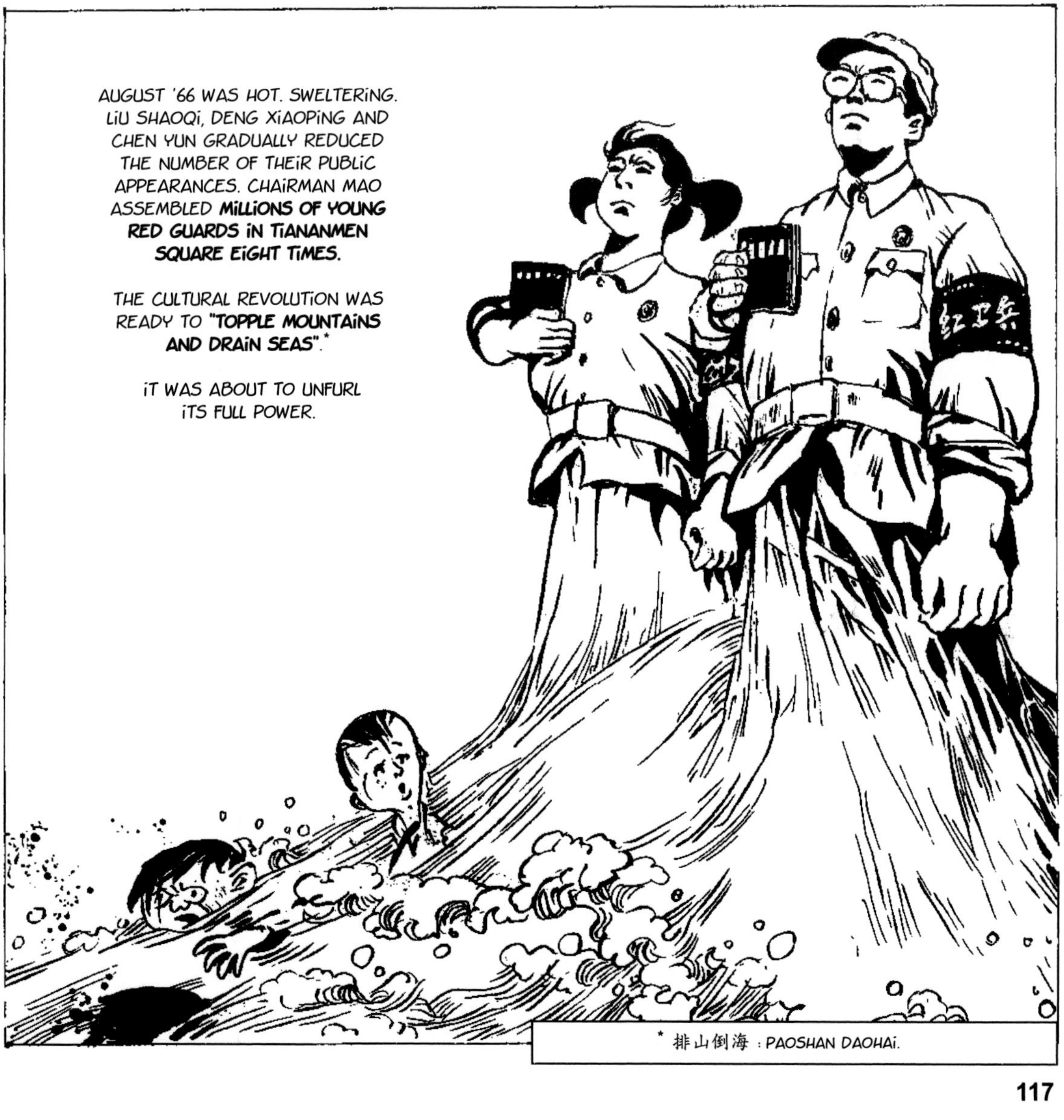
AUGUST '66 WAS HOT. SWELTERING. LIU SHAOQI, DENG XIAOPING AND CHEN YUN GRADUALLY REDUCED THE NUMBER OF THEIR PUBLIC APPEARANCES. CHAIRMAN MAO ASSEMBLED **MILLIONS OF YOUNG RED GUARDS IN TIANANMEN SQUARE EIGHT TIMES.**
THE CULTURAL REVOLUTION WAS READY TO "**TOPPLE MOUNTAINS AND DRAIN SEAS**".*
IT WAS ABOUT TO UNFURL ITS FULL POWER.
红卫兵

* 排山倒海 : PAOSHAN DAOHAI.

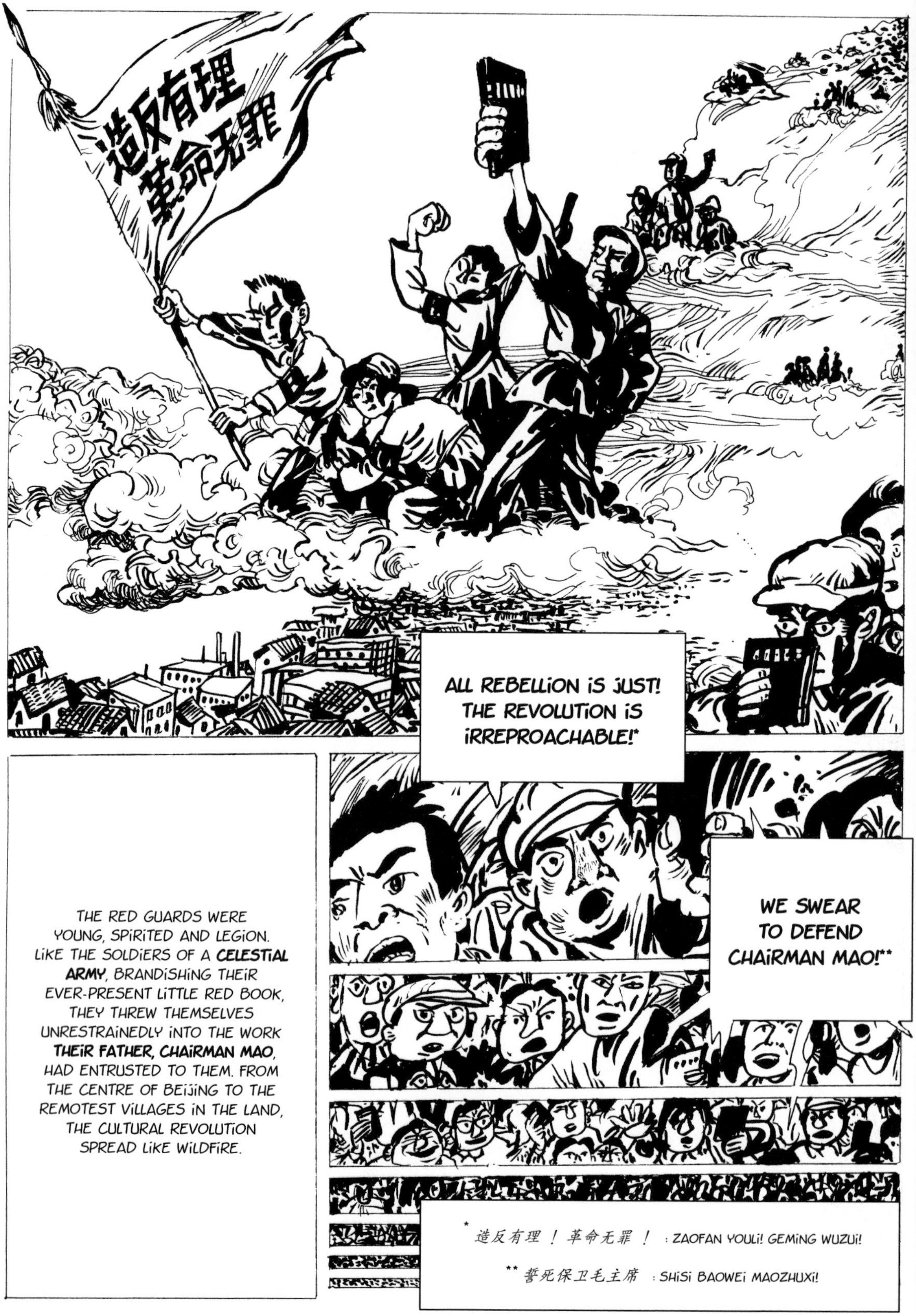
造反有理
革命无罪
ALL REBELLION IS JUST! THE REVOLUTION IS IRREPROACHABLE!*
THE RED GUARDS WERE YOUNG, SPIRITED AND LEGION. LIKE THE SOLDIERS OF A **CELESTIAL ARMY**, BRANDISHING THEIR EVER-PRESENT LITTLE RED BOOK, THEY THREW THEMSELVES UNRESTRAINEDLY INTO THE WORK **THEIR FATHER, CHAIRMAN MAO**, HAD ENTRUSTED TO THEM. FROM THE CENTRE OF BEIJING TO THE REMOTEST VILLAGES IN THE LAND, THE CULTURAL REVOLUTION SPREAD LIKE WILDFIRE.
WE SWEAR TO DEFEND CHAIRMAN MAO!**
* 造反有理 ！ 革命无罪 ！ : ZAOFAN YOULI! GEMING WUZUI!
** 誓死保卫毛主席 : SHISI BAOWEI MAOZHUXI!

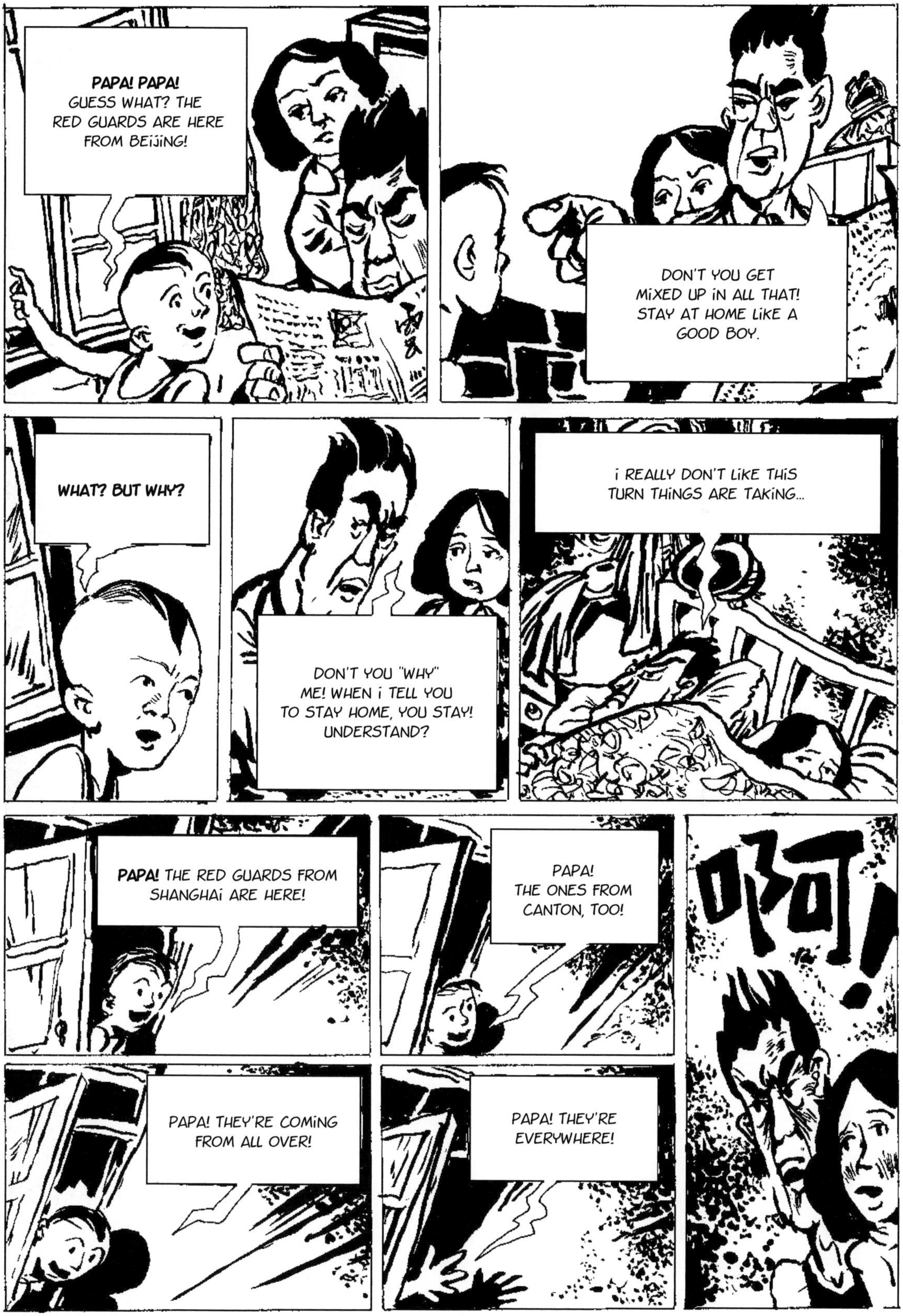
PAPA! PAPA! GUESS WHAT? THE RED GUARDS ARE HERE FROM BEIJING!
DON'T YOU GET MIXED UP IN ALL THAT! STAY AT HOME LIKE A GOOD BOY.
WHAT? BUT WHY?
DON'T YOU "WHY" ME! WHEN I TELL YOU TO STAY HOME, YOU STAY! UNDERSTAND?
I REALLY DON'T LIKE THIS TURN THINGS ARE TAKING...
PAPA! THE RED GUARDS FROM SHANGHAI ARE HERE!
PAPA! THE ONES FROM CANTON, TOO!
PAPA! THEY'RE COMING FROM ALL OVER!
PAPA! THEY'RE EVERYWHERE!
哆可!

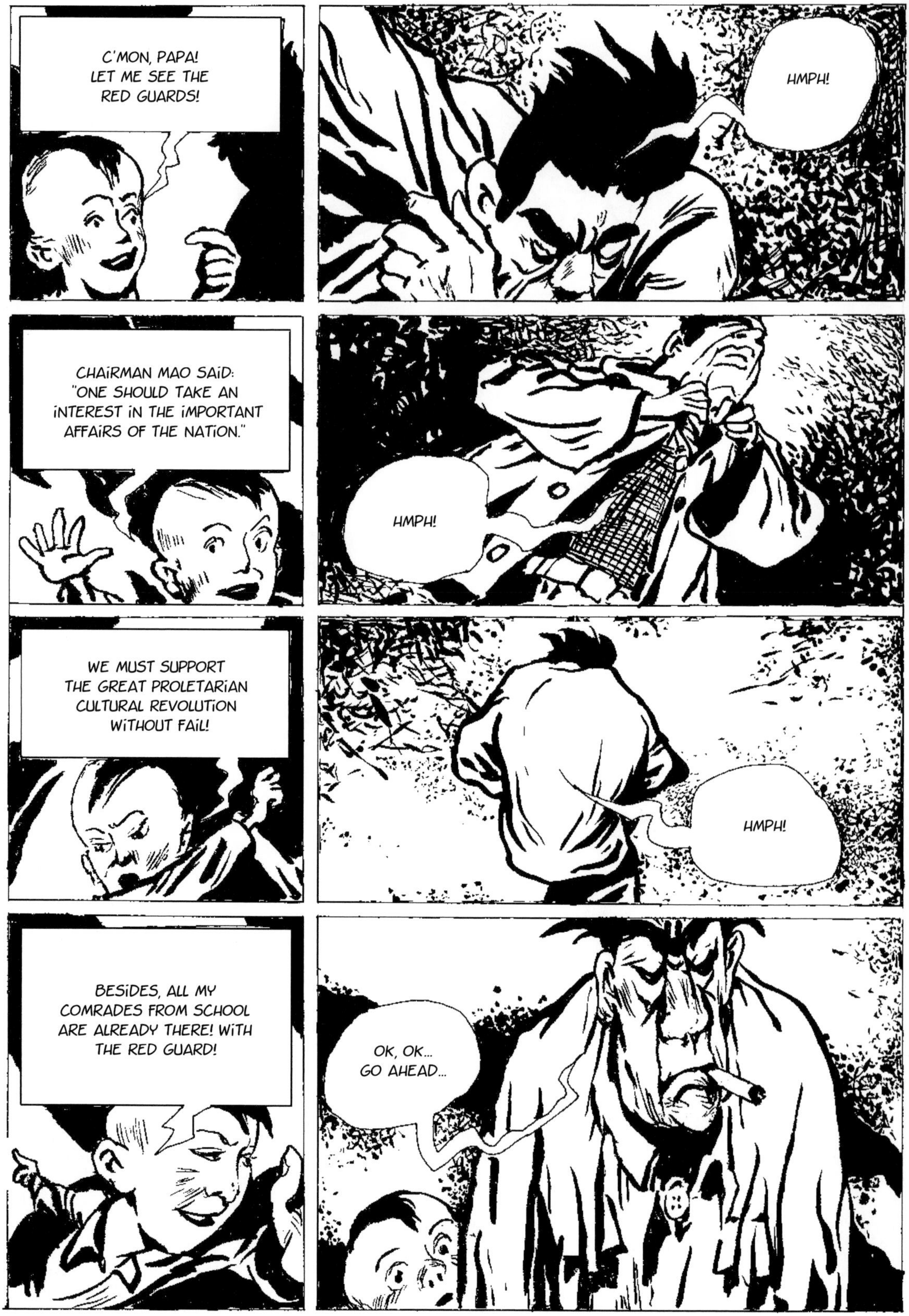
C'MON, PAPA! LET ME SEE THE RED GUARDS!
HMPH!
CHAIRMAN MAO SAID: "ONE SHOULD TAKE AN INTEREST IN THE IMPORTANT AFFAIRS OF THE NATION."
HMPH!
WE MUST SUPPORT THE GREAT PROLETARIAN CULTURAL REVOLUTION WITHOUT FAIL!
HMPH!
BESIDES, ALL MY COMRADES FROM SCHOOL ARE ALREADY THERE! WITH THE RED GUARD!
OK, OK... GO AHEAD...

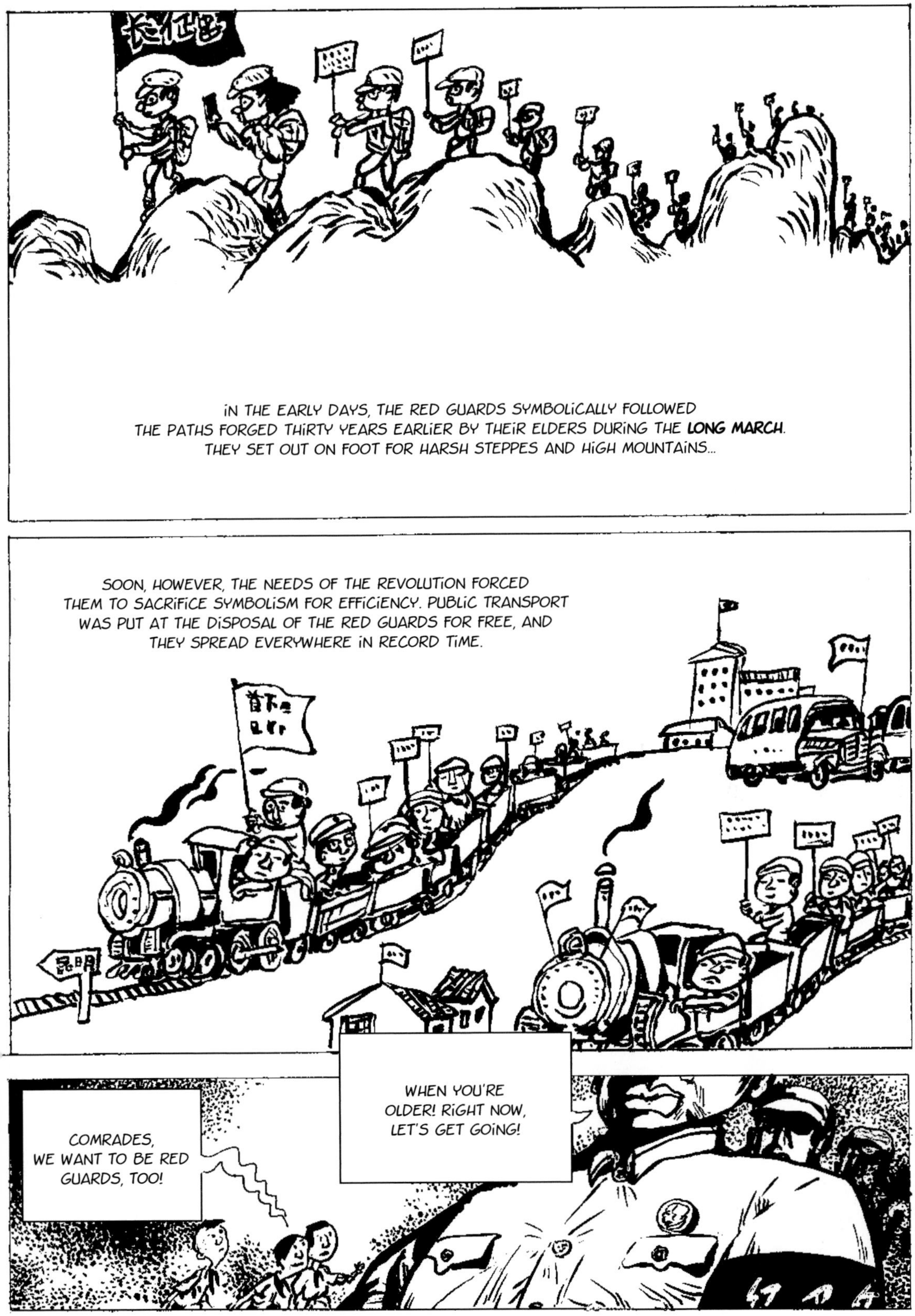
IN THE EARLY DAYS, THE RED GUARDS SYMBOLICALLY FOLLOWED THE PATHS FORGED THIRTY YEARS EARLIER BY THEIR ELDERS DURING THE **LONG MARCH**. THEY SET OUT ON FOOT FOR HARSH STEPPES AND HIGH MOUNTAINS...
SOON, HOWEVER, THE NEEDS OF THE REVOLUTION FORCED THEM TO SACRIFICE SYMBOLISM FOR EFFICIENCY. PUBLIC TRANSPORT WAS PUT AT THE DISPOSAL OF THE RED GUARDS FOR FREE, AND THEY SPREAD EVERYWHERE IN RECORD TIME.
COMRADES, WE WANT TO BE RED GUARDS, TOO!
WHEN YOU'RE OLDER! RIGHT NOW, LET'S GET GOING!

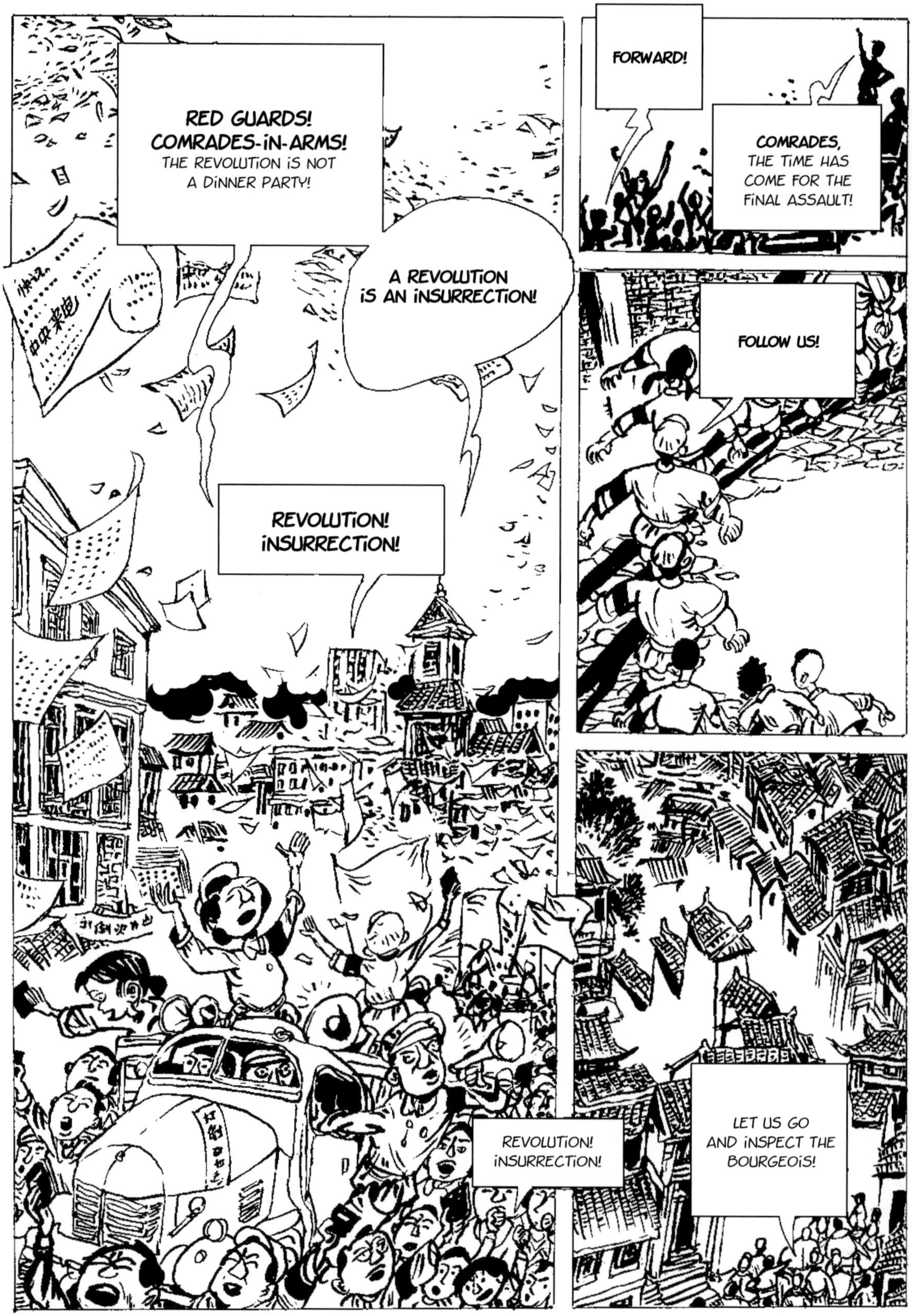
RED GUARDS! COMRADES-IN-ARMS!
THE REVOLUTION IS NOT A DINNER PARTY!
A REVOLUTION IS AN INSURRECTION!
REVOLUTION! INSURRECTION!
REVOLUTION! INSURRECTION!
FORWARD!
COMRADES, THE TIME HAS COME FOR THE FINAL ASSAULT!
FOLLOW US!
LET US GO AND INSPECT THE BOURGEOIS!

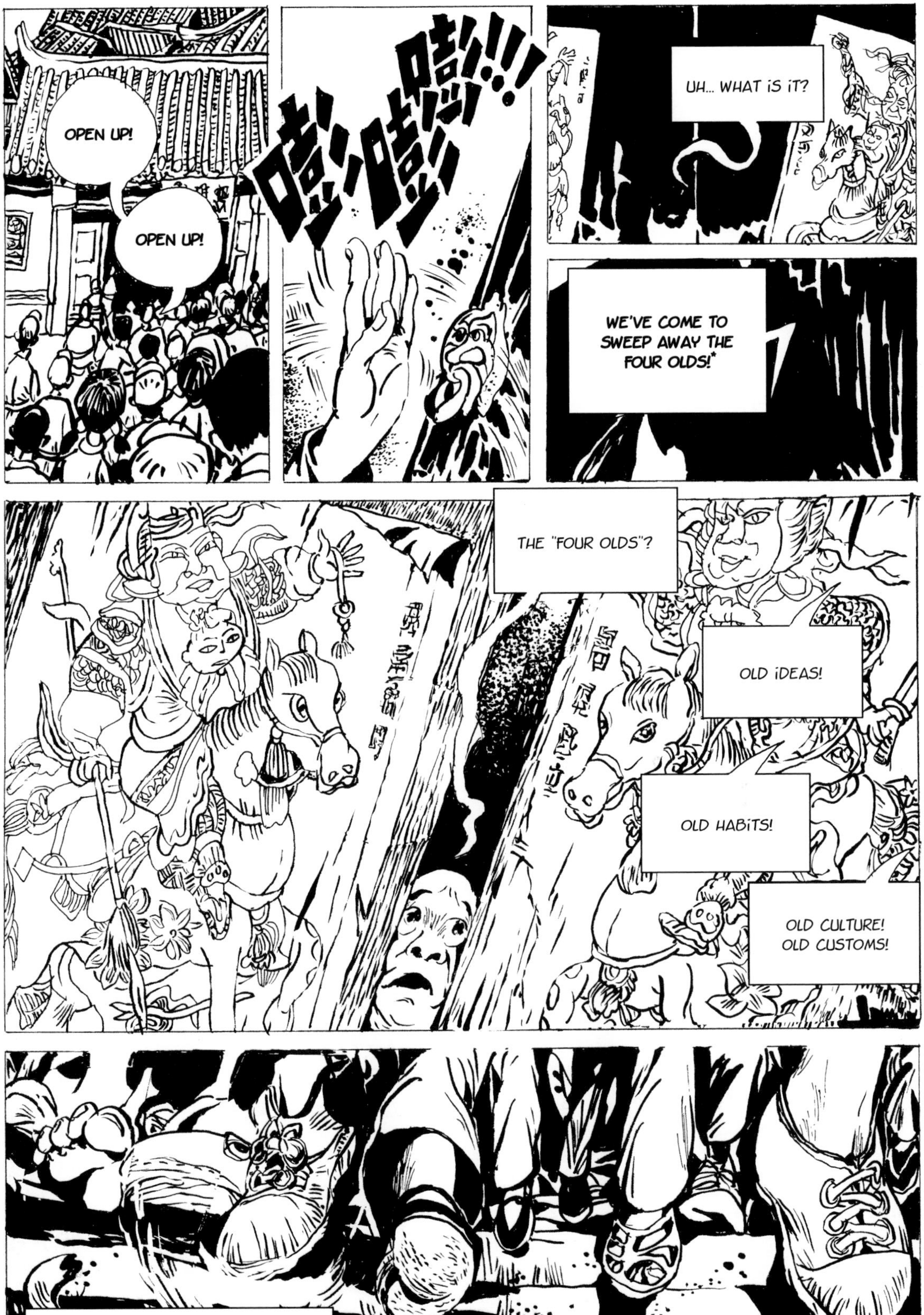
OPEN UP!
OPEN UP!
UH... WHAT IS IT?
WE'VE COME TO SWEEP AWAY THE FOUR OLDS!*
THE "FOUR OLDS"?
OLD IDEAS!
OLD HABITS!
OLD CULTURE! OLD CUSTOMS!

*扫四旧: SAO SI JIU.

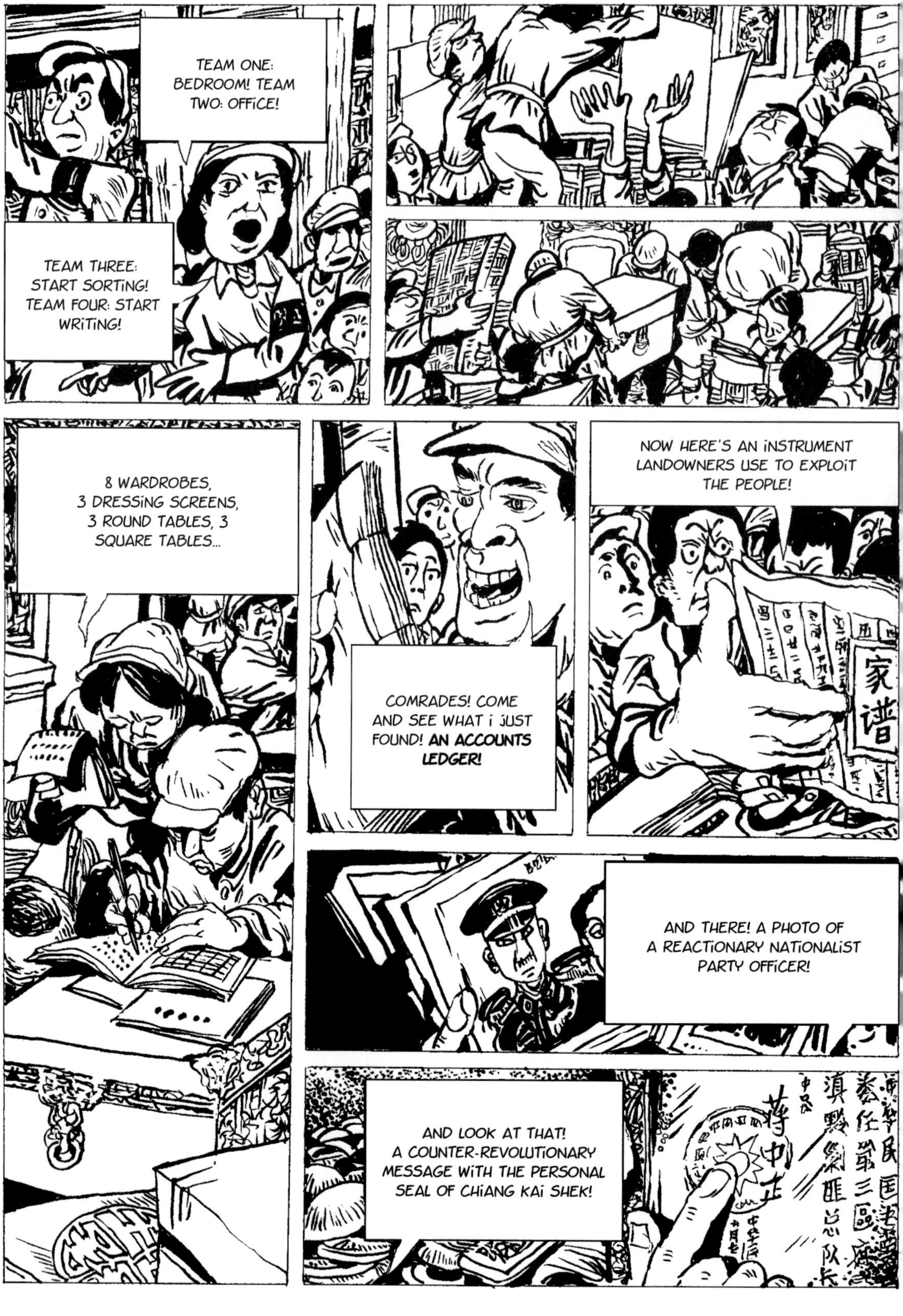
TEAM ONE: BEDROOM! TEAM TWO: OFFICE!
TEAM THREE: START SORTING! TEAM FOUR: START WRITING!
8 WARDROBES, 3 DRESSING SCREENS, 3 ROUND TABLES, 3 SQUARE TABLES...
COMRADES! COME AND SEE WHAT I JUST FOUND! **AN ACCOUNTS LEDGER!**
NOW HERE'S AN INSTRUMENT LANDOWNERS USE TO EXPLOIT THE PEOPLE!
家谱
AND THERE! A PHOTO OF A REACTIONARY NATIONALIST PARTY OFFICER!
AND LOOK AT THAT! A COUNTER-REVOLUTIONARY MESSAGE WITH THE PERSONAL SEAL OF CHIANG KAI SHEK!

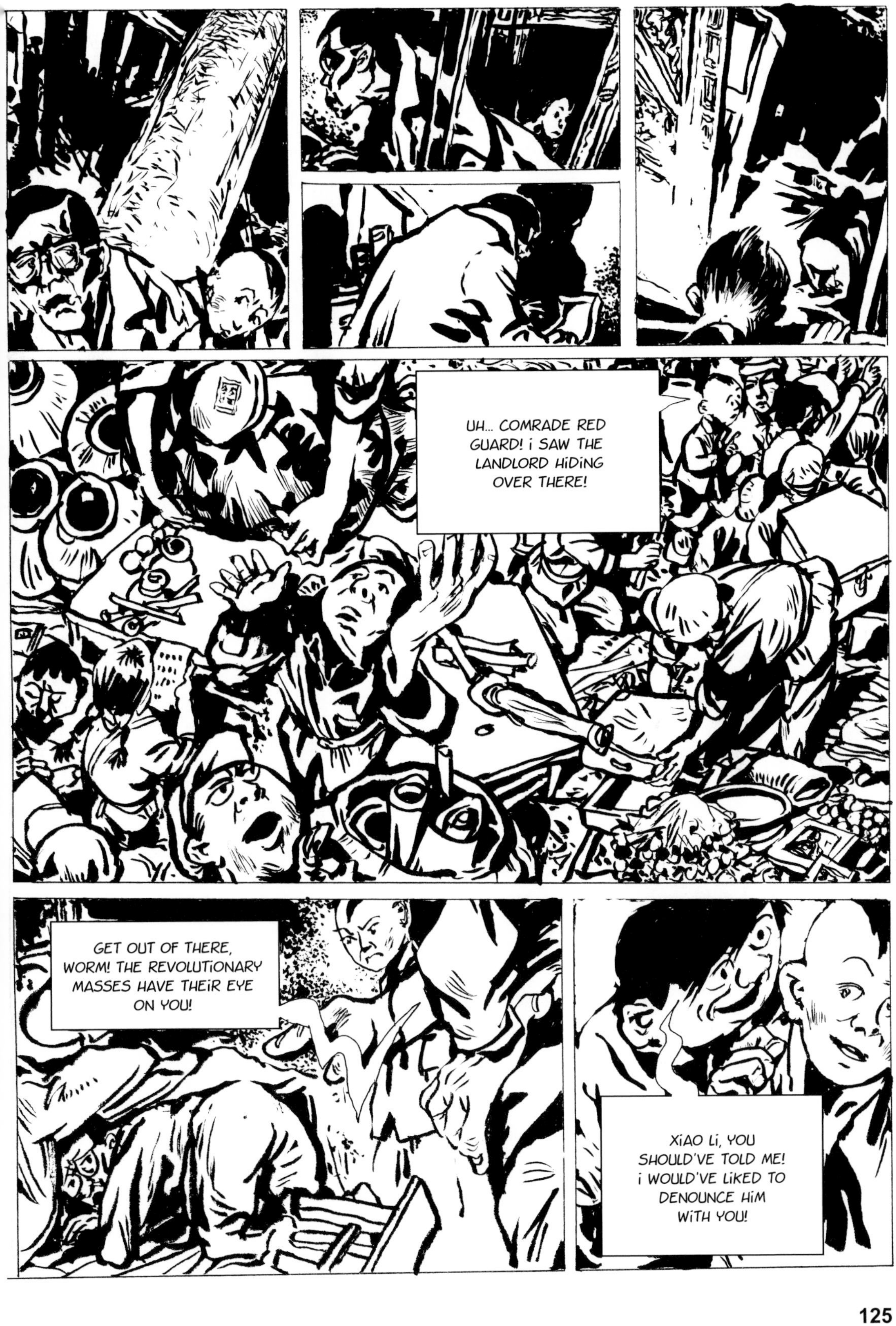
UH... COMRADE RED GUARD! i SAW THE LANDLORD HiDiNG OVER THERE!
GET OUT OF THERE, WORM! THE REVOLUTiONARY MASSES HAVE THEiR EYE ON YOU!
XiAO Li, YOU SHOULD'VE TOLD ME! i WOULD'VE LiKED TO DENOUNCE HiM WiTH YOU!

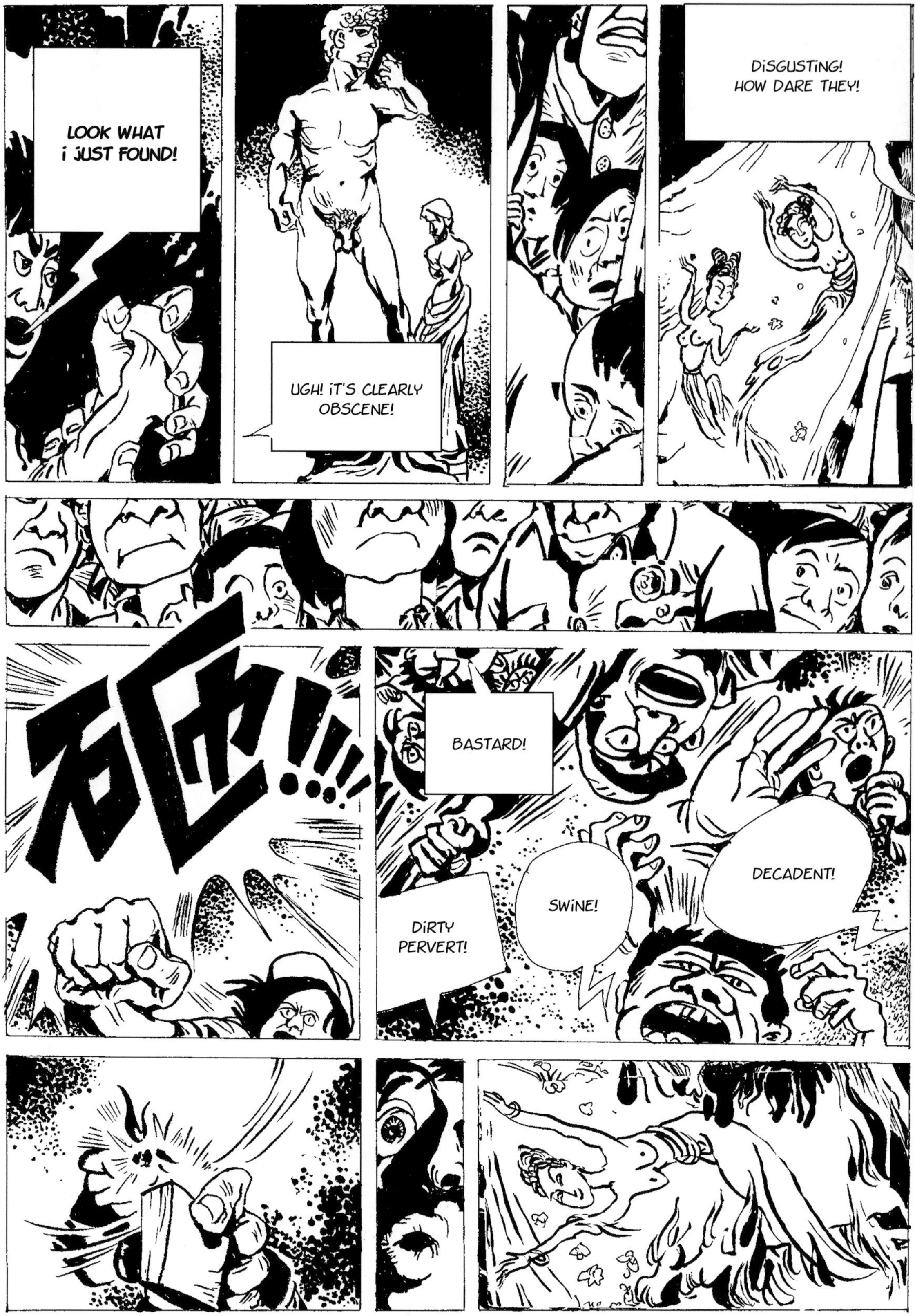

LOOK WHAT i JUST FOUND!
UGH! iT'S CLEARLY OBSCENE!
DiSGUSTiNG! HOW DARE THEY!
BASTARD!
DECADENT!
SWiNE!
DiRTY PERVERT!

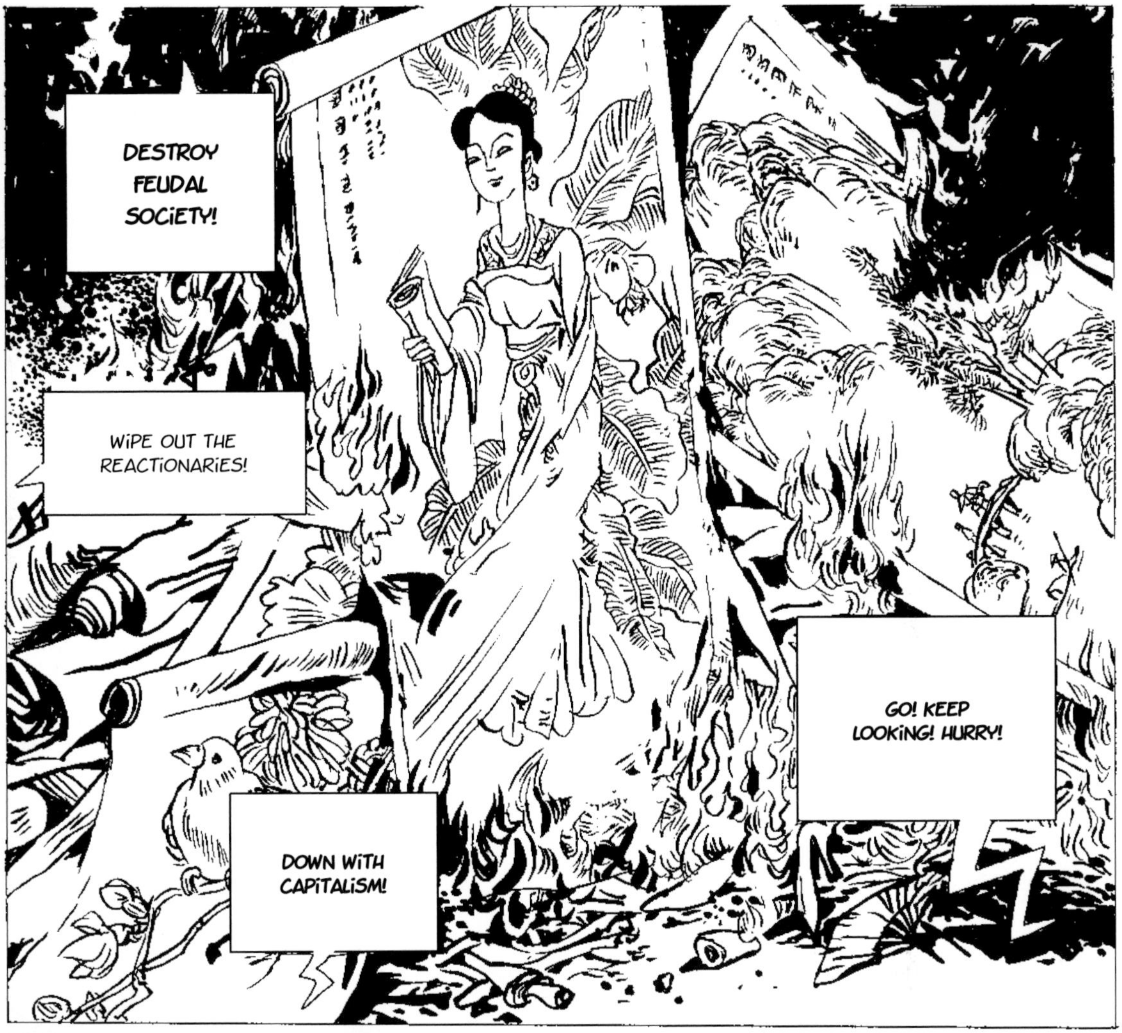
DESTROY FEUDAL SOCiETY!
WiPE OUT THE REACTiONARiES!
DOWN WiTH CAPiTALiSM!
GO! KEEP LOOKiNG! HURRY!

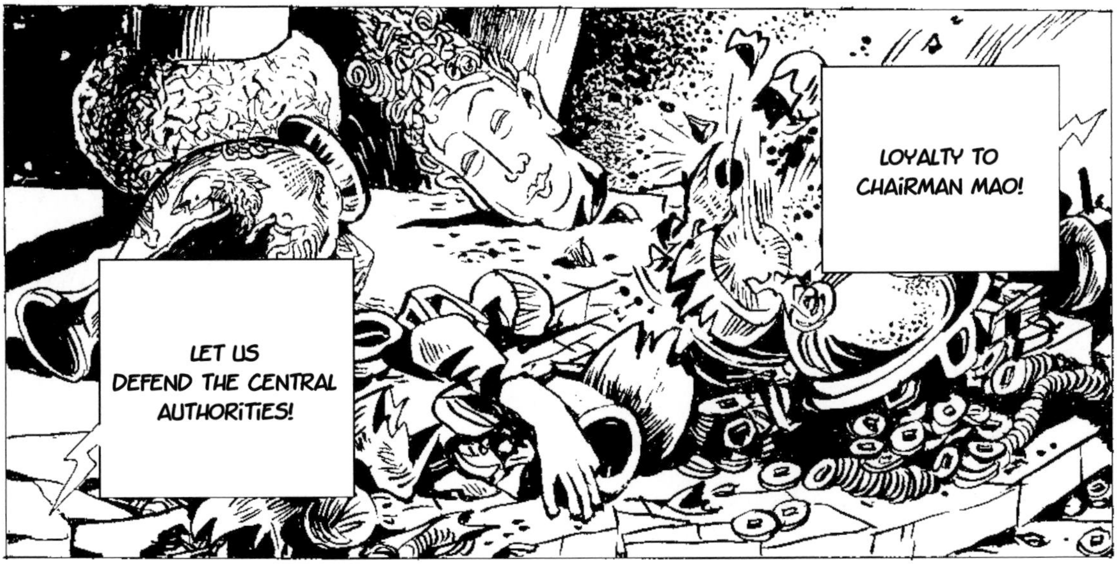
LOYALTY TO CHAiRMAN MAO!
LET US DEFEND THE CENTRAL AUTHORiTiES!

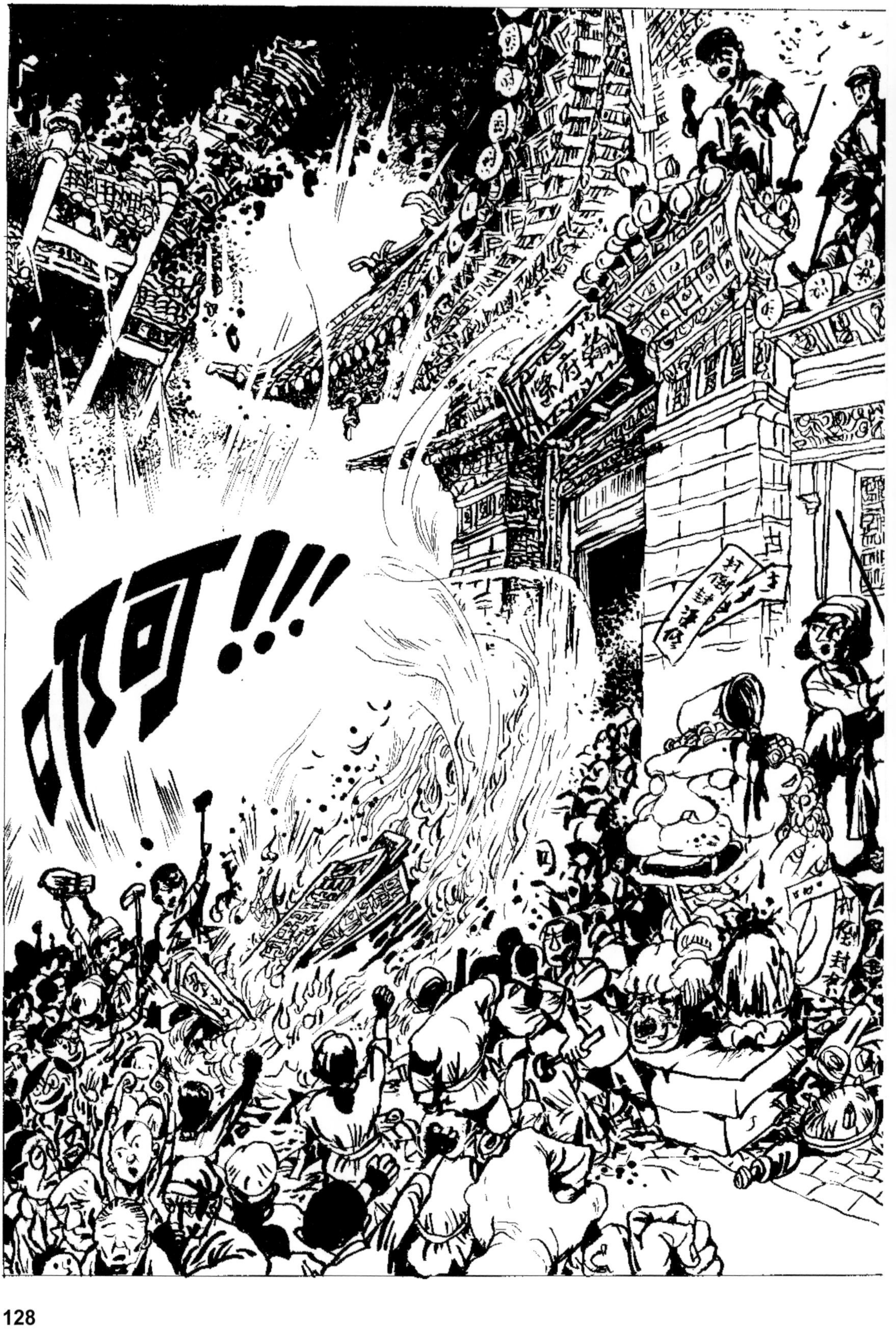
啊!!!
打倒封

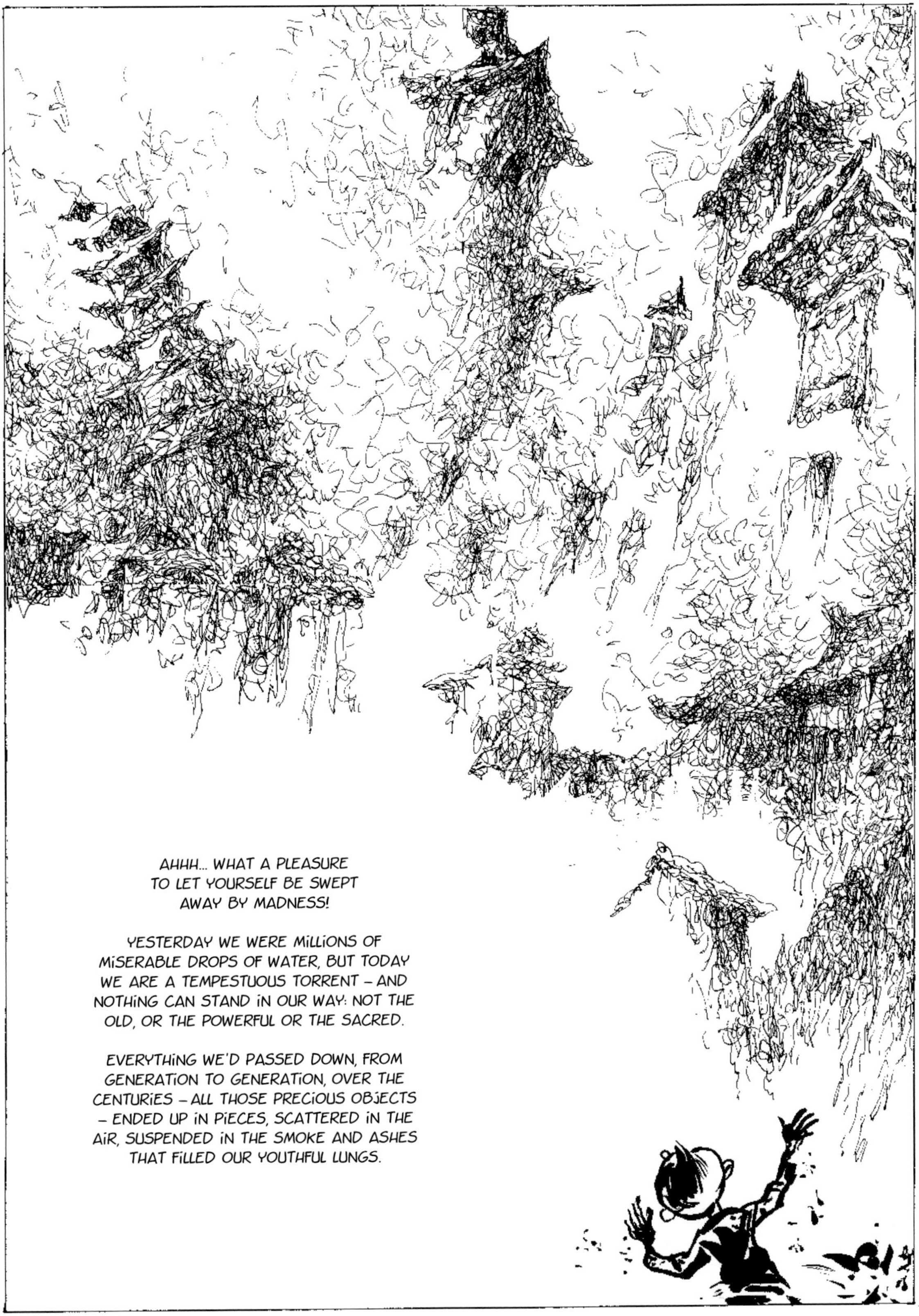
AHHH... WHAT A PLEASURE TO LET YOURSELF BE SWEPT AWAY BY MADNESS!
YESTERDAY WE WERE MILLIONS OF MISERABLE DROPS OF WATER, BUT TODAY WE ARE A TEMPESTUOUS TORRENT – AND NOTHING CAN STAND IN OUR WAY: NOT THE OLD, OR THE POWERFUL OR THE SACRED.
EVERYTHING WE'D PASSED DOWN, FROM GENERATION TO GENERATION, OVER THE CENTURIES – ALL THOSE PRECIOUS OBJECTS – ENDED UP IN PIECES, SCATTERED IN THE AIR, SUSPENDED IN THE SMOKE AND ASHES THAT FILLED OUR YOUTHFUL LUNGS.

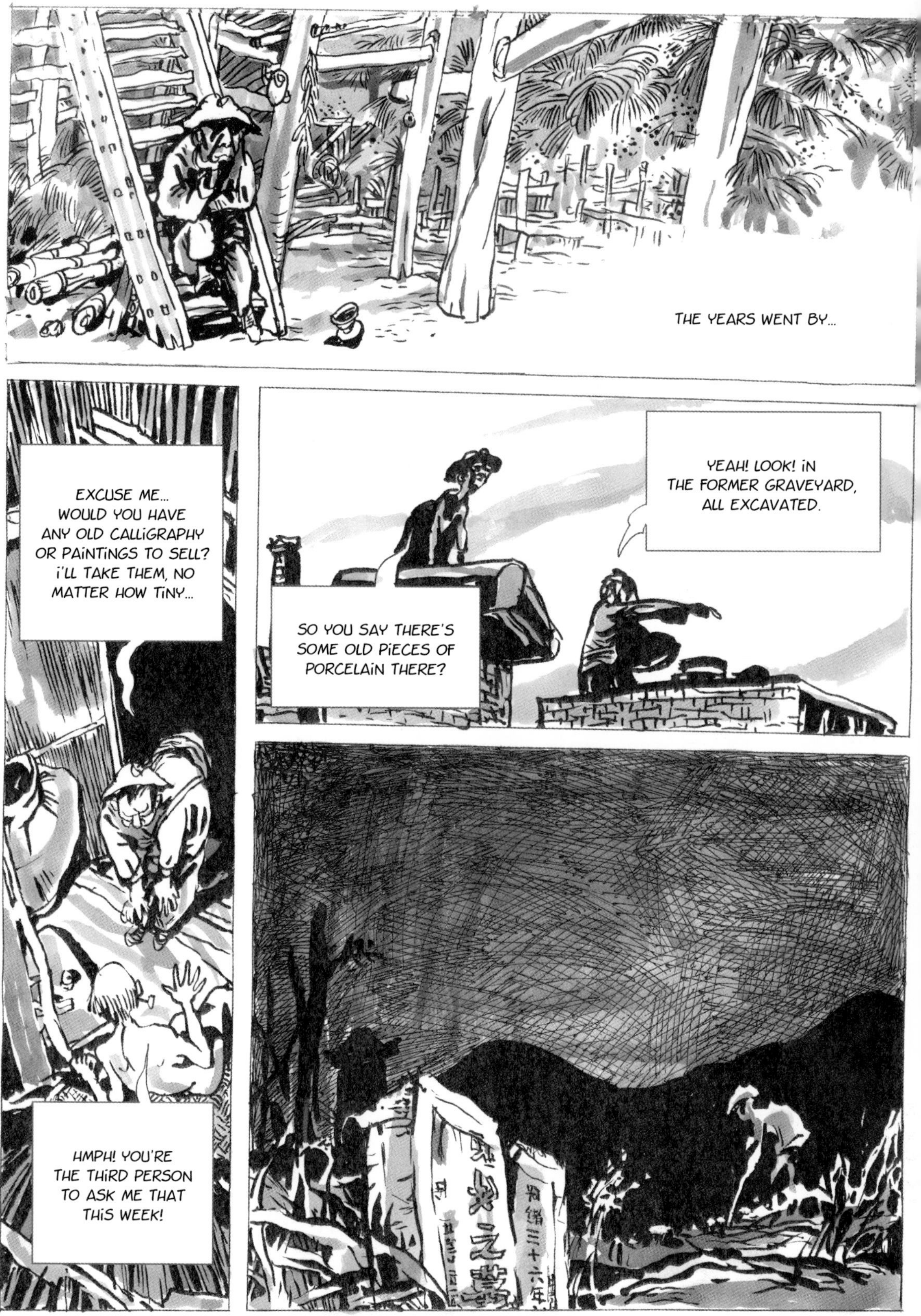
THE YEARS WENT BY...
EXCUSE ME... WOULD YOU HAVE ANY OLD CALLIGRAPHY OR PAINTINGS TO SELL? I'LL TAKE THEM, NO MATTER HOW TINY...
HMPH! YOU'RE THE THIRD PERSON TO ASK ME THAT THIS WEEK!
SO YOU SAY THERE'S SOME OLD PIECES OF PORCELAIN THERE?
YEAH! LOOK! IN THE FORMER GRAVEYARD, ALL EXCAVATED.

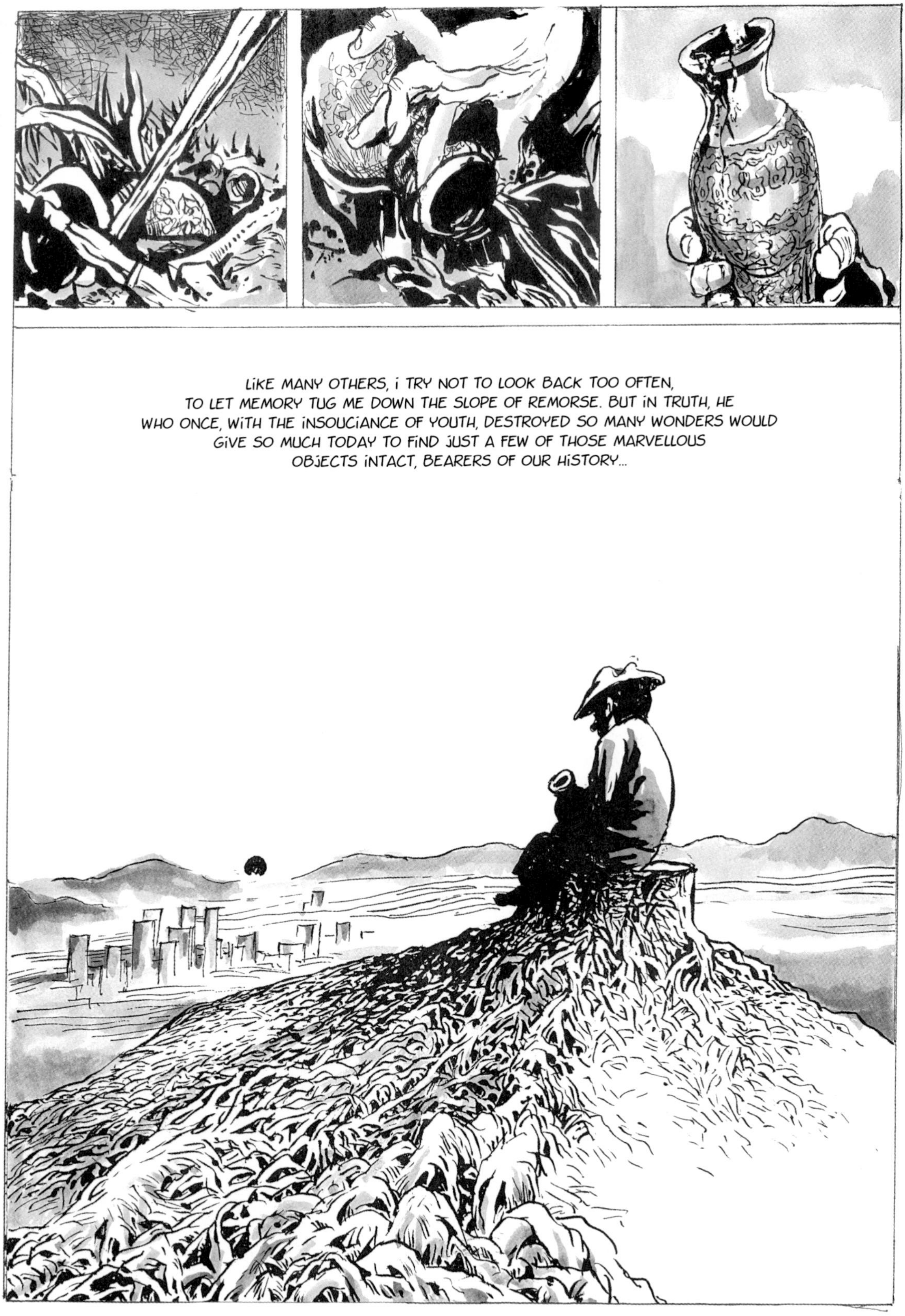
LIKE MANY OTHERS, I TRY NOT TO LOOK BACK TOO OFTEN, TO LET MEMORY TUG ME DOWN THE SLOPE OF REMORSE. BUT IN TRUTH, HE WHO ONCE, WITH THE INSOUCIANCE OF YOUTH, DESTROYED SO MANY WONDERS WOULD GIVE SO MUCH TODAY TO FIND JUST A FEW OF THOSE MARVELLOUS OBJECTS INTACT, BEARERS OF OUR HISTORY...

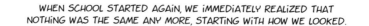

WHEN SCHOOL STARTED AGAIN, WE IMMEDIATELY REALIZED THAT NOTHING WAS THE SAME ANY MORE, STARTING WITH HOW WE LOOKED.

NICE RED ARMBAND! HOW'D YOU GET INTO A COMBAT BRIGADE?

BAH! JUST MAKE UP YOUR OWN BRIGADE!

YOU MEAN I CAN HAVE MY OWN COMBAT BRIGADE?

SURE! JUST MAKE SURE YOU'RE NOT IN ONE OF THE "FIVE BLACK CATEGORIES":* LANDOWNERS, RICH FARMERS, REACTIONARIES, WRONGDOERS AND RIGHTISTS.

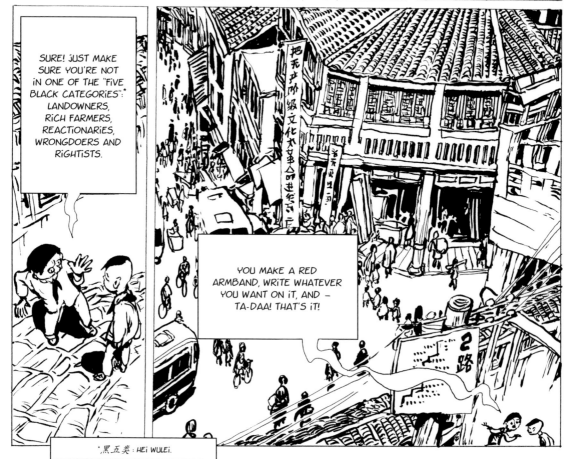

YOU MAKE A RED ARMBAND, WRITE WHATEVER YOU WANT ON IT, AND — TA-DAA! THAT'S IT!

*黑五类: HEI WULEi.

132

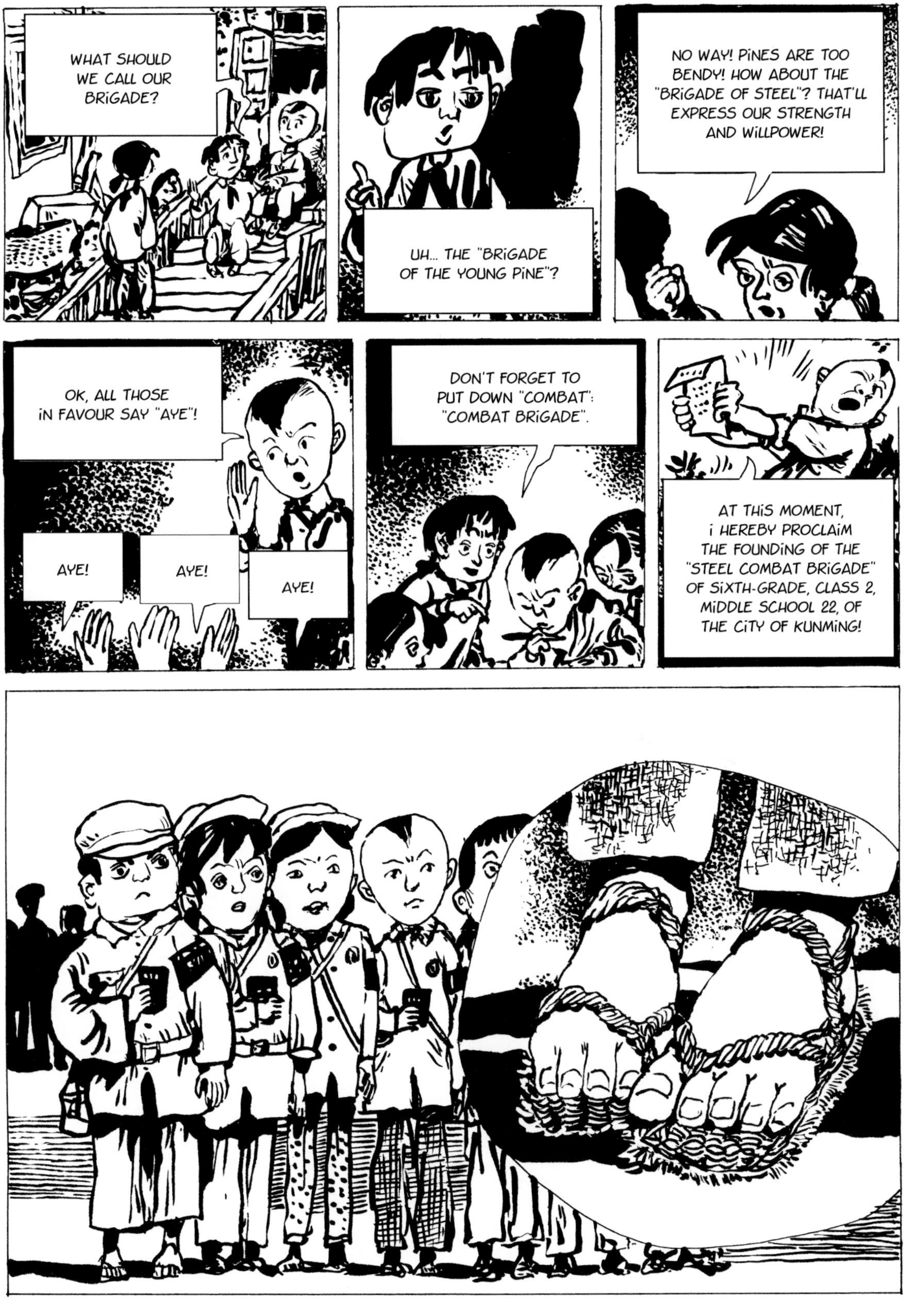
WHAT SHOULD WE CALL OUR BRIGADE?
UH... THE "BRIGADE OF THE YOUNG PINE"?
NO WAY! PINES ARE TOO BENDY! HOW ABOUT THE "BRIGADE OF STEEL"? THAT'LL EXPRESS OUR STRENGTH AND WILLPOWER!
OK, ALL THOSE IN FAVOUR SAY "AYE"!
AYE!
AYE!
AYE!
DON'T FORGET TO PUT DOWN "COMBAT": "COMBAT BRIGADE".
AT THIS MOMENT, I HEREBY PROCLAIM THE FOUNDING OF THE "STEEL COMBAT BRIGADE" OF SIXTH-GRADE, CLASS 2, MIDDLE SCHOOL 22, OF THE CITY OF KUNMING!

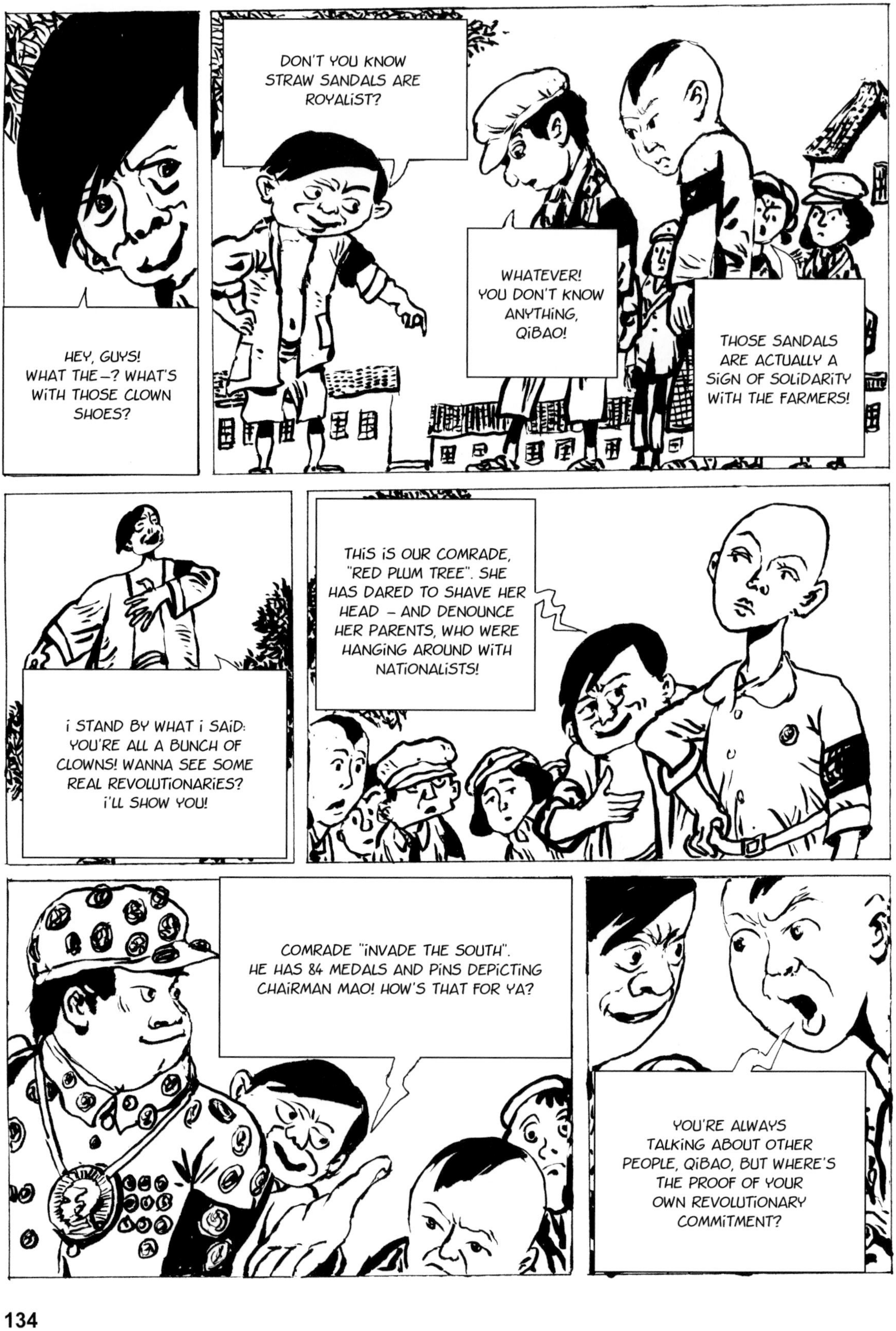
HEY, GUYS! WHAT THE–? WHAT'S WITH THOSE CLOWN SHOES?
DON'T YOU KNOW STRAW SANDALS ARE ROYALIST?
WHATEVER! YOU DON'T KNOW ANYTHING, QIBAO!
THOSE SANDALS ARE ACTUALLY A SIGN OF SOLIDARITY WITH THE FARMERS!
I STAND BY WHAT I SAID: YOU'RE ALL A BUNCH OF CLOWNS! WANNA SEE SOME REAL REVOLUTIONARIES? I'LL SHOW YOU!
THIS IS OUR COMRADE, "RED PLUM TREE". SHE HAS DARED TO SHAVE HER HEAD – AND DENOUNCE HER PARENTS, WHO WERE HANGING AROUND WITH NATIONALISTS!
COMRADE "INVADE THE SOUTH". HE HAS 84 MEDALS AND PINS DEPICTING CHAIRMAN MAO! HOW'S THAT FOR YA?
YOU'RE ALWAYS TALKING ABOUT OTHER PEOPLE, QIBAO, BUT WHERE'S THE PROOF OF YOUR OWN REVOLUTIONARY COMMITMENT?

WHAT'S THAT? DOUBTING MY LOVE FOR THE REVOLUTION?

THAT'S RIGHT! AND I SAY YOU'RE THE CLOWN AROUND HERE!

OH YEAH? TAKE A GOOD LOOK AT THIS!

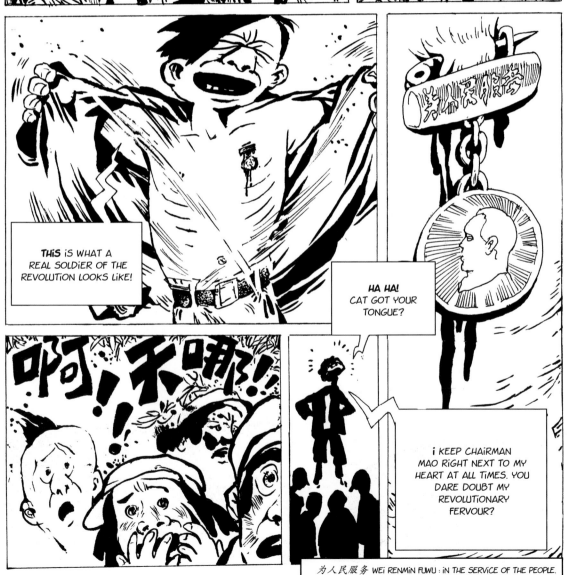

THIS IS WHAT A REAL SOLDIER OF THE REVOLUTION LOOKS LIKE!

HA HA! CAT GOT YOUR TONGUE?

啊呵！！不哪？！！

I KEEP CHAIRMAN MAO RIGHT NEXT TO MY HEART AT ALL TIMES. YOU DARE DOUBT MY REVOLUTIONARY FERVOUR?

为人民服务 WEI RENMIN FUWU : IN THE SERVICE OF THE PEOPLE.

135

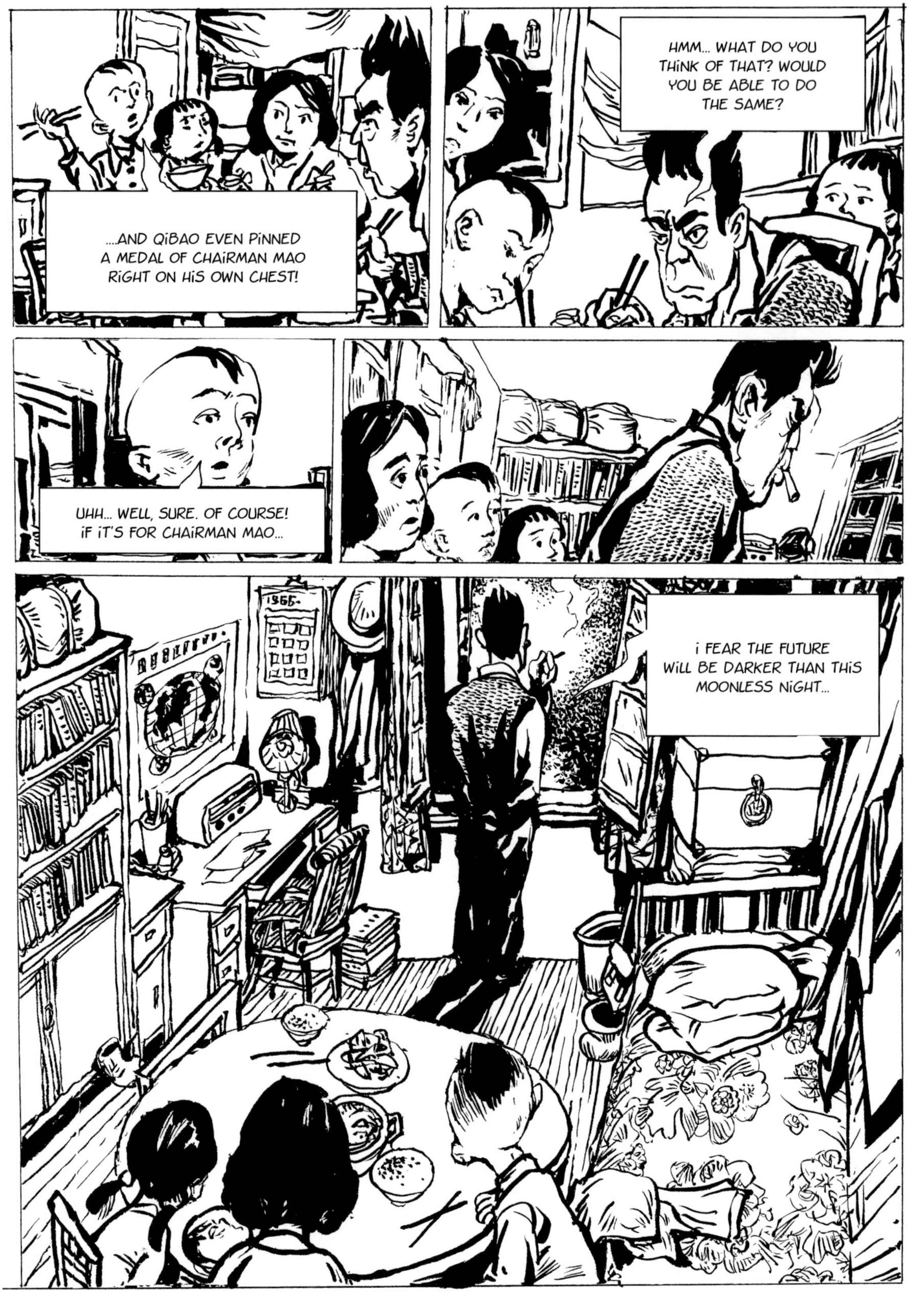
...AND QIBAO EVEN PINNED A MEDAL OF CHAIRMAN MAO RIGHT ON HIS OWN CHEST!
HMM... WHAT DO YOU THINK OF THAT? WOULD YOU BE ABLE TO DO THE SAME?
UHH... WELL, SURE. OF COURSE! IF IT'S FOR CHAIRMAN MAO...
1966
I FEAR THE FUTURE WILL BE DARKER THAN THIS MOONLESS NIGHT...

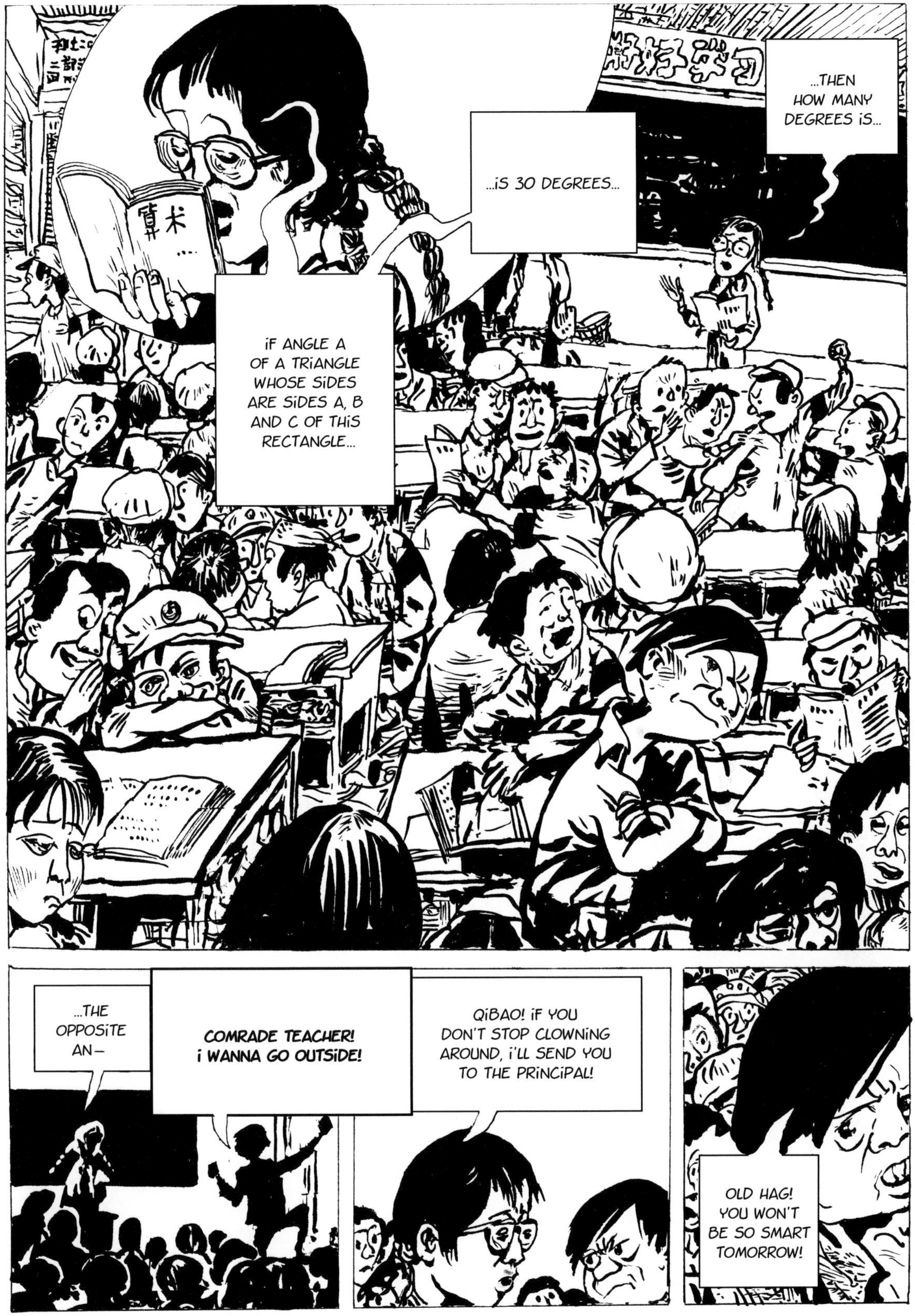
算术
iF ANGLE A OF A TRiANGLE WHOSE SiDES ARE SiDES A, B AND C OF THiS RECTANGLE...
...iS 30 DEGREES...
...THEN HOW MANY DEGREES iS...
...THE OPPOSiTE AN—
COMRADE TEACHER! i WANNA GO OUTSiDE!
QiBAO! iF YOU DON'T STOP CLOWNiNG AROUND, i'LL SEND YOU TO THE PRiNCiPAL!
OLD HAG! YOU WON'T BE SO SMART TOMORROW!

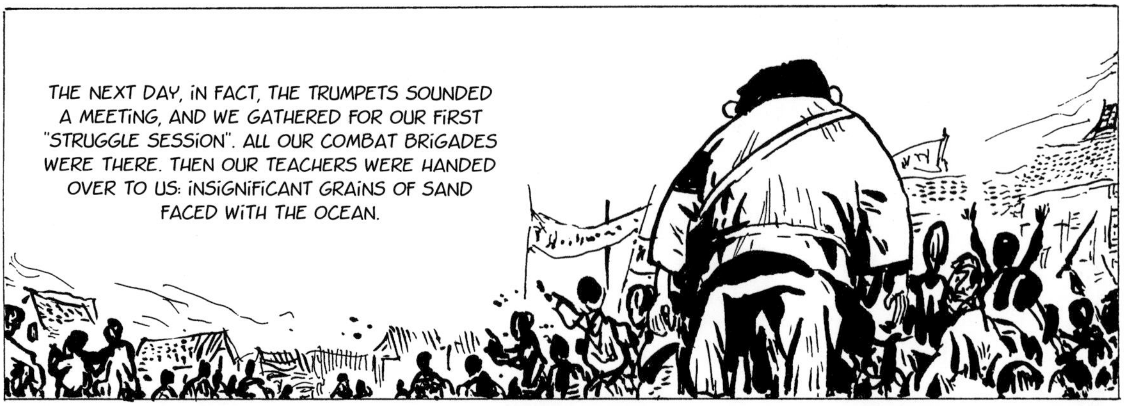
THE NEXT DAY, IN FACT, THE TRUMPETS SOUNDED A MEETING, AND WE GATHERED FOR OUR FIRST "STRUGGLE SESSION". ALL OUR COMBAT BRIGADES WERE THERE. THEN OUR TEACHERS WERE HANDED OVER TO US: INSIGNIFICANT GRAINS OF SAND FACED WITH THE OCEAN.

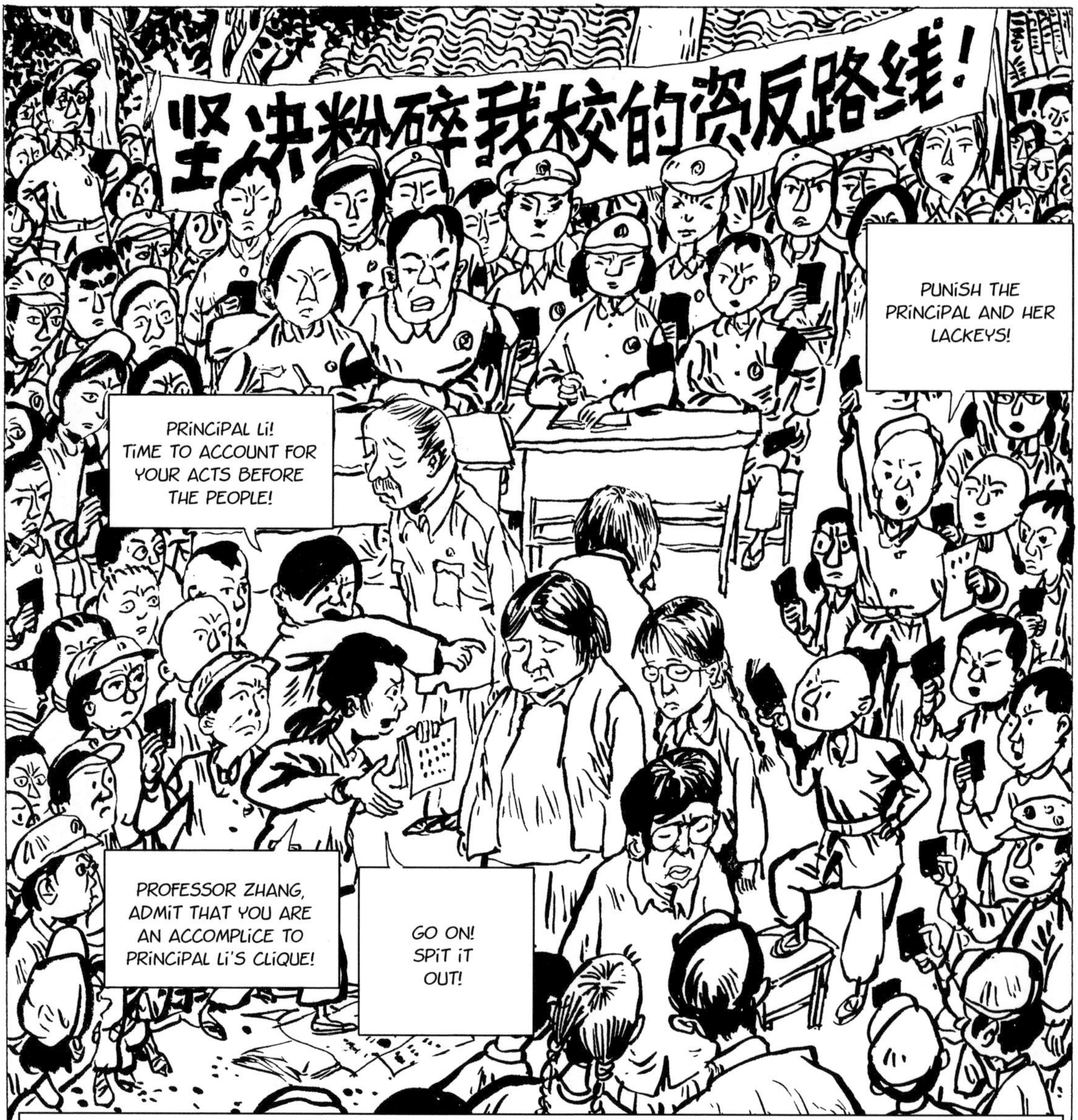
坚决粉碎我校的资反路线！
PUNISH THE PRINCIPAL AND HER LACKEYS!
PRINCIPAL LI! TIME TO ACCOUNT FOR YOUR ACTS BEFORE THE PEOPLE!
PROFESSOR ZHANG, ADMIT THAT YOU ARE AN ACCOMPLICE TO PRINCIPAL LI'S CLIQUE!
GO ON! SPIT IT OUT!

坚决粉碎我校的资反路线 JIANJUE FENSUI WO XIAODE ZIFAN LUXIAN : CUT OUR SCHOOL'S CAPITALIST REBELS TO PIECES!

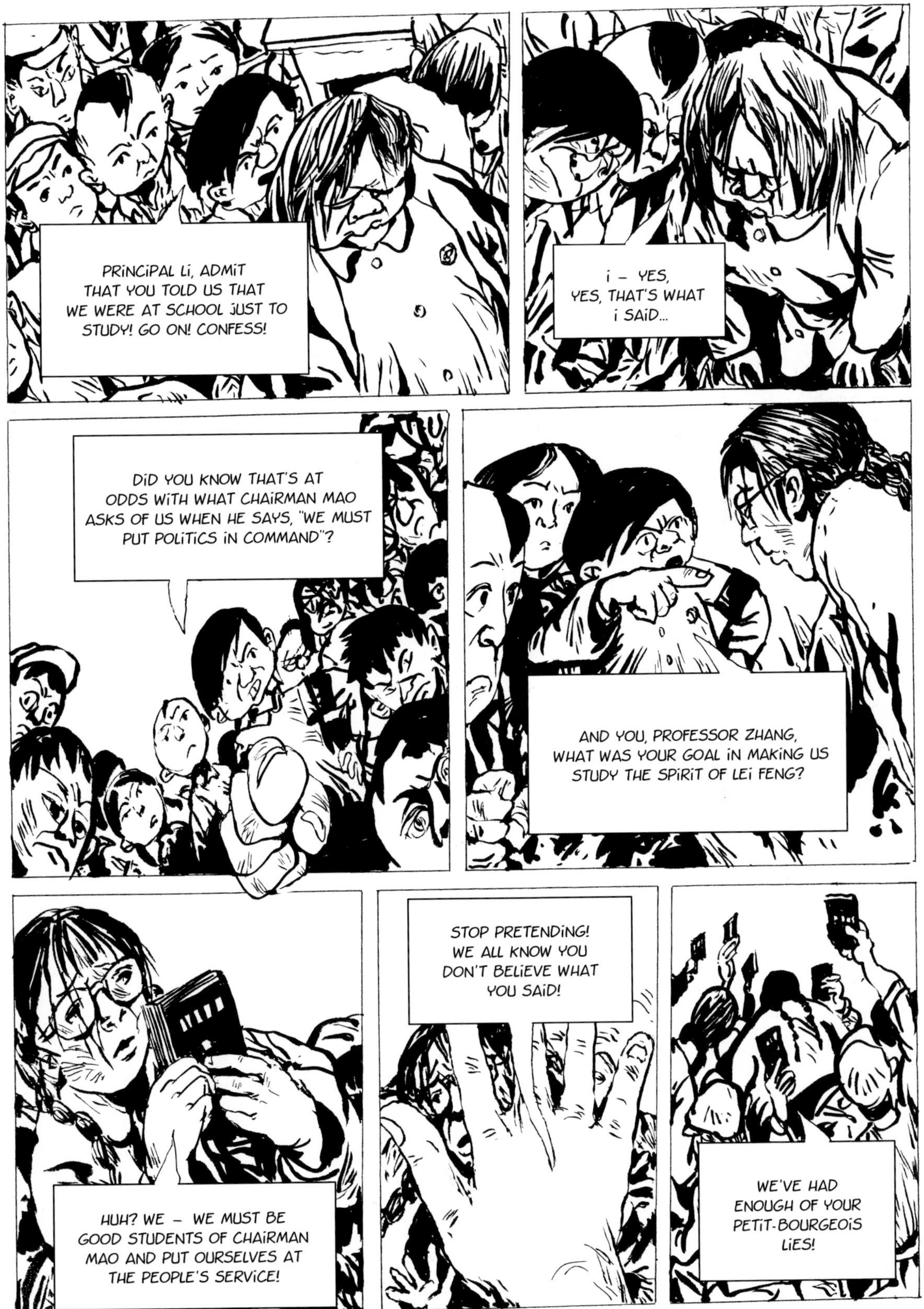
PRINCIPAL LI, ADMIT THAT YOU TOLD US THAT WE WERE AT SCHOOL JUST TO STUDY! GO ON! CONFESS!
I – YES, YES, THAT'S WHAT I SAID...
DID YOU KNOW THAT'S AT ODDS WITH WHAT CHAIRMAN MAO ASKS OF US WHEN HE SAYS, "WE MUST PUT POLITICS IN COMMAND"?
AND YOU, PROFESSOR ZHANG, WHAT WAS YOUR GOAL IN MAKING US STUDY THE SPIRIT OF LEI FENG?
HUH? WE – WE MUST BE GOOD STUDENTS OF CHAIRMAN MAO AND PUT OURSELVES AT THE PEOPLE'S SERVICE!
STOP PRETENDING! WE ALL KNOW YOU DON'T BELIEVE WHAT YOU SAID!
WE'VE HAD ENOUGH OF YOUR PETIT-BOURGEOIS LIES!

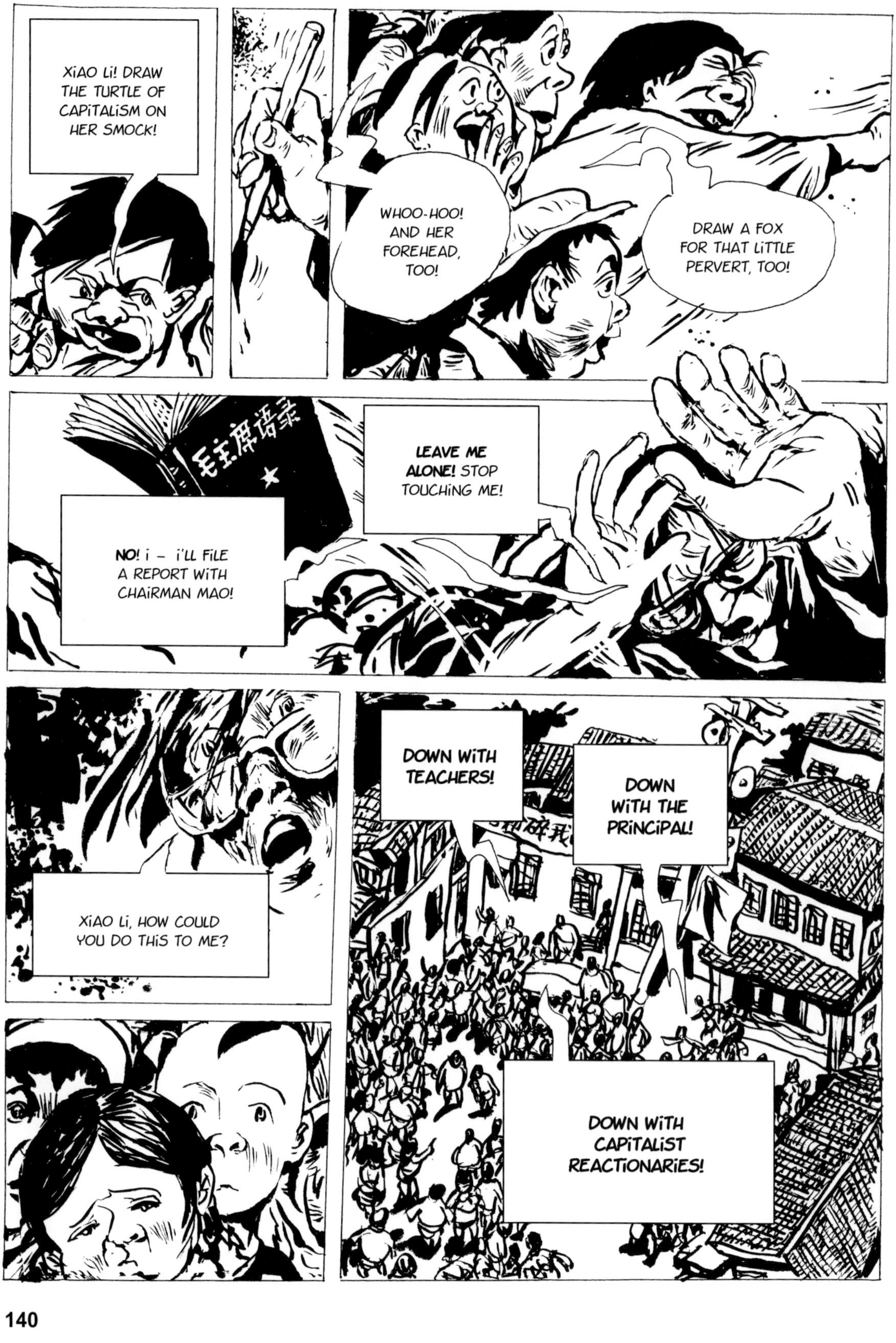
XIAO LI! DRAW THE TURTLE OF CAPITALISM ON HER SMOCK!
WHOO-HOO! AND HER FOREHEAD, TOO!
DRAW A FOX FOR THAT LITTLE PERVERT, TOO!
毛主席语录
LEAVE ME ALONE! STOP TOUCHING ME!
NO! I – I'LL FILE A REPORT WITH CHAIRMAN MAO!
XIAO LI, HOW COULD YOU DO THIS TO ME?
DOWN WITH TEACHERS!
DOWN WITH THE PRINCIPAL!
DOWN WITH CAPITALIST REACTIONARIES!

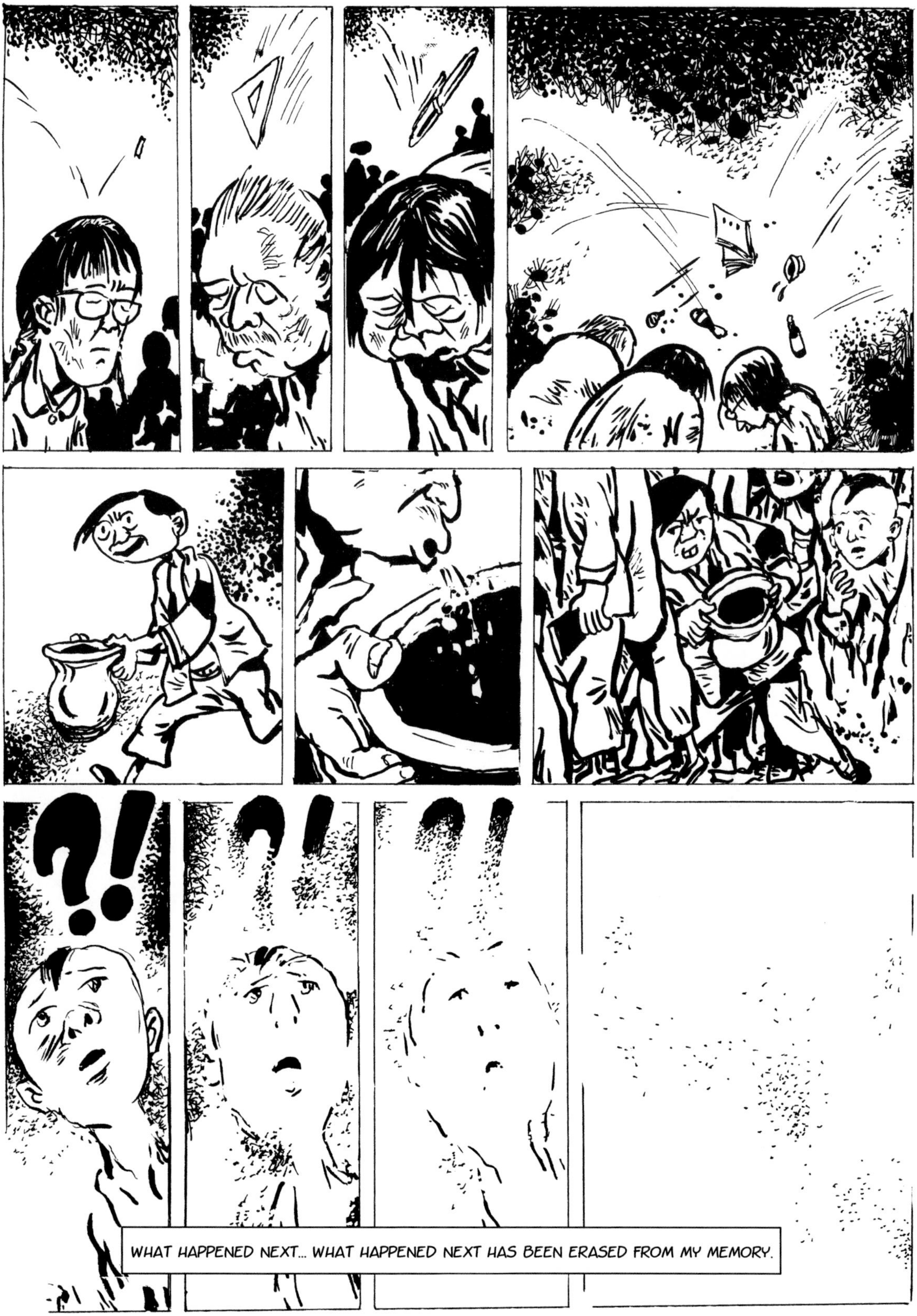
?!
!
!
WHAT HAPPENED NEXT... WHAT HAPPENED NEXT HAS BEEN ERASED FROM MY MEMORY.

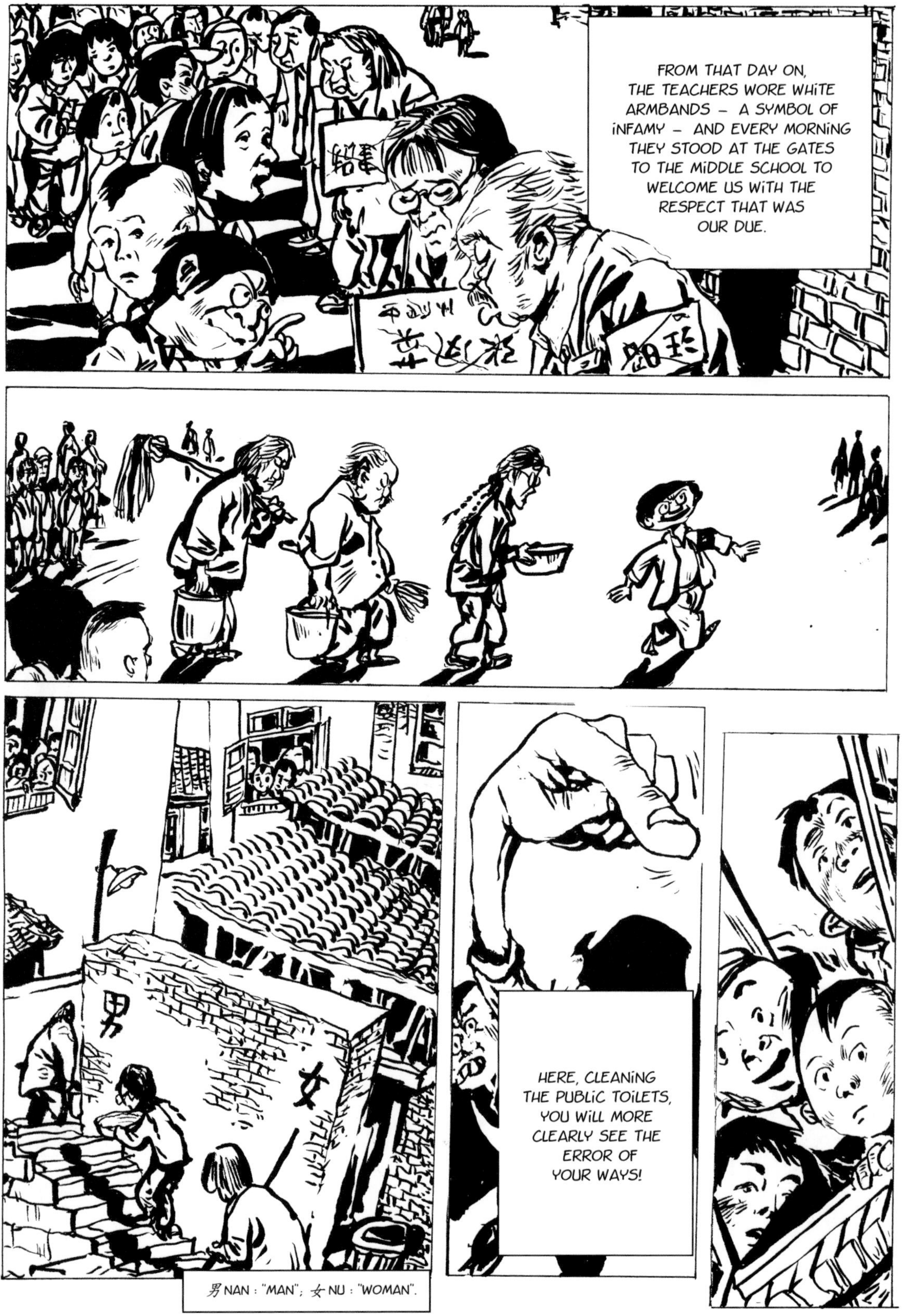
FROM THAT DAY ON, THE TEACHERS WORE WHITE ARMBANDS – A SYMBOL OF INFAMY – AND EVERY MORNING THEY STOOD AT THE GATES TO THE MIDDLE SCHOOL TO WELCOME US WITH THE RESPECT THAT WAS OUR DUE.
男
女
HERE, CLEANING THE PUBLIC TOILETS, YOU WILL MORE CLEARLY SEE THE ERROR OF YOUR WAYS!
男 NAN : "MAN"; 女 NU : "WOMAN".

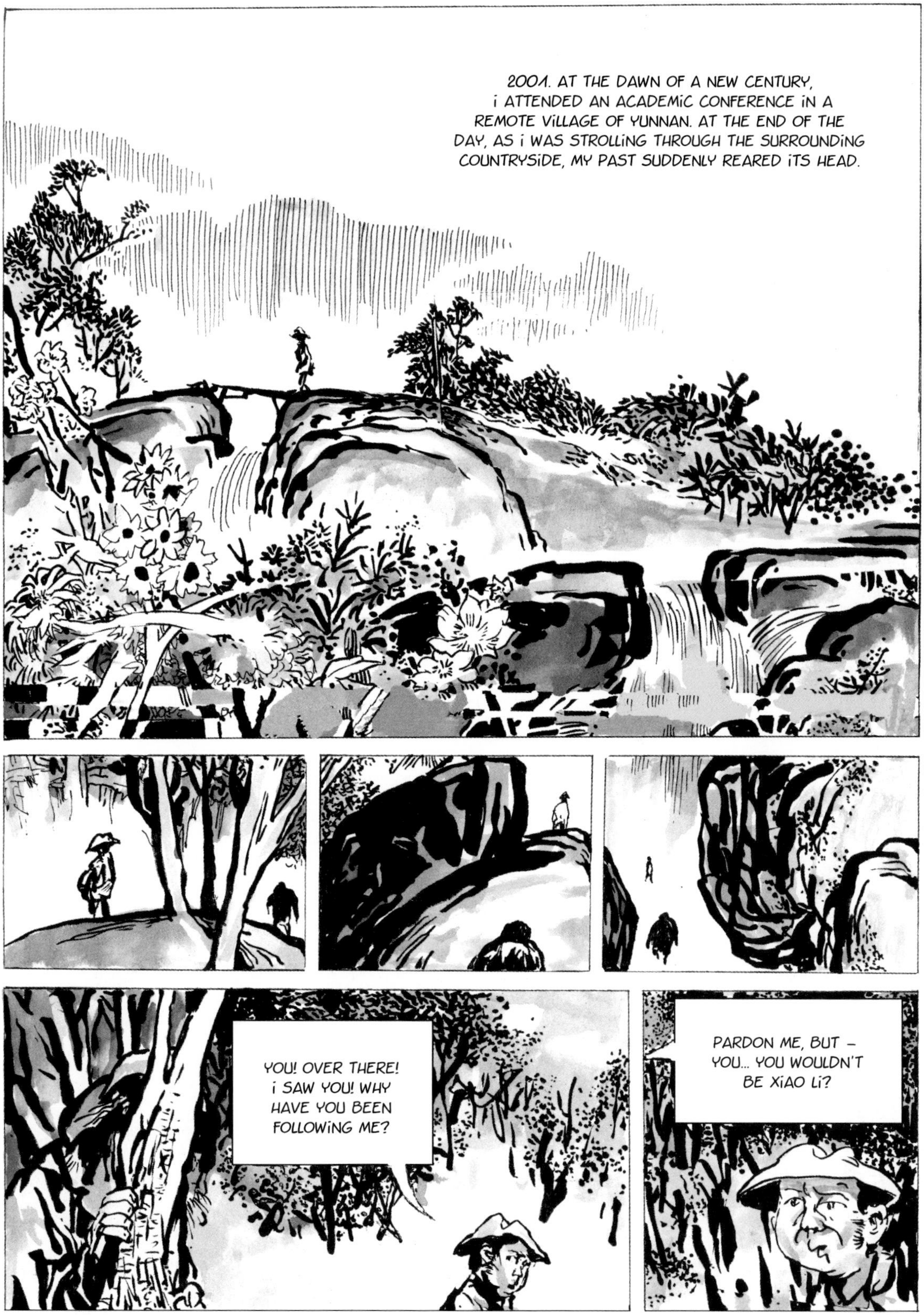
2001. AT THE DAWN OF A NEW CENTURY, I ATTENDED AN ACADEMIC CONFERENCE IN A REMOTE VILLAGE OF YUNNAN. AT THE END OF THE DAY, AS I WAS STROLLING THROUGH THE SURROUNDING COUNTRYSIDE, MY PAST SUDDENLY REARED ITS HEAD.
YOU! OVER THERE! I SAW YOU! WHY HAVE YOU BEEN FOLLOWING ME?
PARDON ME, BUT – YOU... YOU WOULDN'T BE XIAO LI?

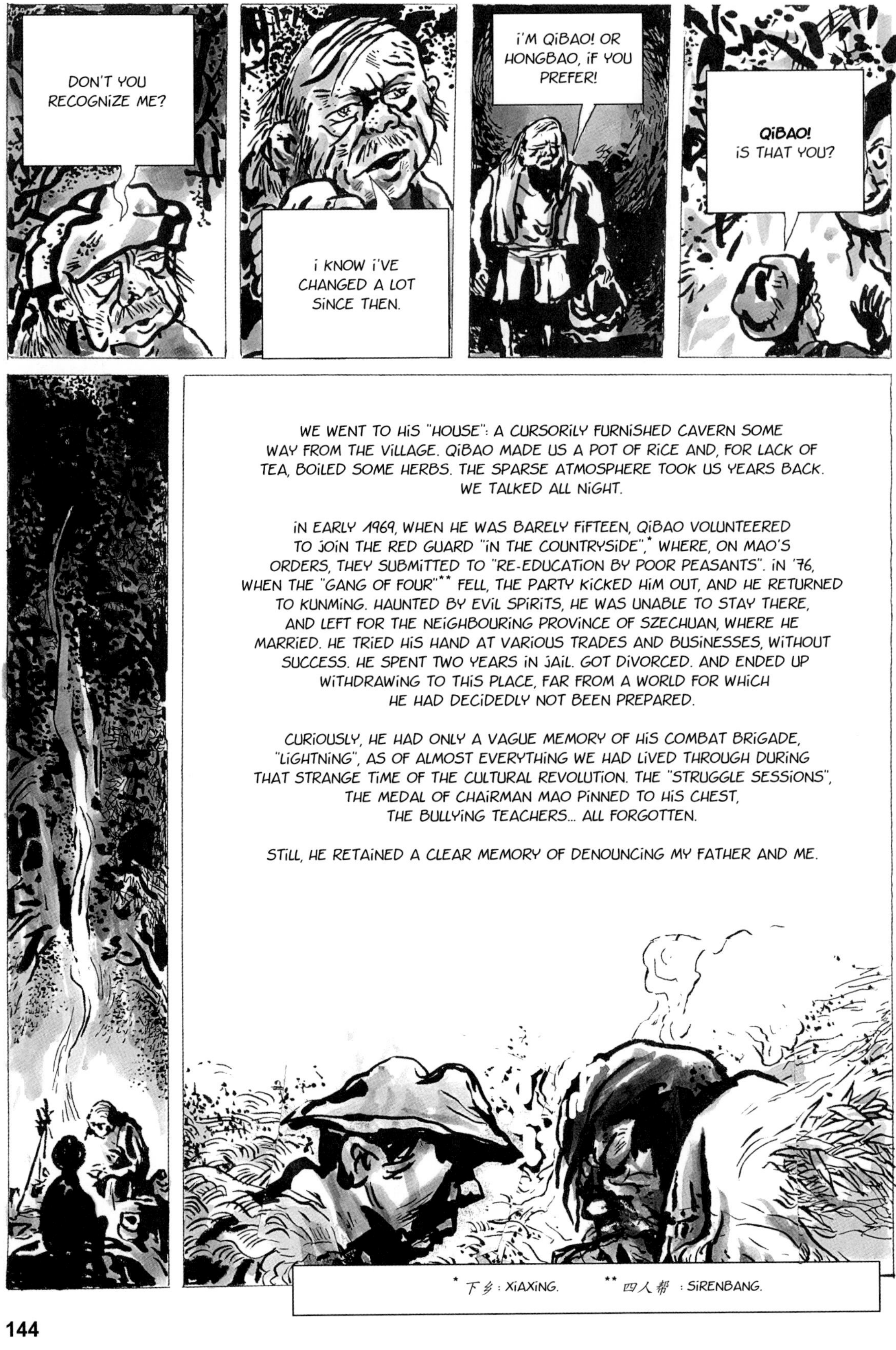
DON'T YOU RECOGNIZE ME?
I KNOW I'VE CHANGED A LOT SINCE THEN.
I'M QIBAO! OR HONGBAO, IF YOU PREFER!
QIBAO! IS THAT YOU?
WE WENT TO HIS "HOUSE": A CURSORILY FURNISHED CAVERN SOME WAY FROM THE VILLAGE. QIBAO MADE US A POT OF RICE AND, FOR LACK OF TEA, BOILED SOME HERBS. THE SPARSE ATMOSPHERE TOOK US YEARS BACK. WE TALKED ALL NIGHT.
IN EARLY 1969, WHEN HE WAS BARELY FIFTEEN, QIBAO VOLUNTEERED TO JOIN THE RED GUARD "IN THE COUNTRYSIDE",* WHERE, ON MAO'S ORDERS, THEY SUBMITTED TO "RE-EDUCATION BY POOR PEASANTS". IN '76, WHEN THE "GANG OF FOUR"** FELL, THE PARTY KICKED HIM OUT, AND HE RETURNED TO KUNMING. HAUNTED BY EVIL SPIRITS, HE WAS UNABLE TO STAY THERE, AND LEFT FOR THE NEIGHBOURING PROVINCE OF SZECHUAN, WHERE HE MARRIED. HE TRIED HIS HAND AT VARIOUS TRADES AND BUSINESSES, WITHOUT SUCCESS. HE SPENT TWO YEARS IN JAIL. GOT DIVORCED. AND ENDED UP WITHDRAWING TO THIS PLACE, FAR FROM A WORLD FOR WHICH HE HAD DECIDEDLY NOT BEEN PREPARED.
CURIOUSLY, HE HAD ONLY A VAGUE MEMORY OF HIS COMBAT BRIGADE, "LIGHTNING", AS OF ALMOST EVERYTHING WE HAD LIVED THROUGH DURING THAT STRANGE TIME OF THE CULTURAL REVOLUTION. THE "STRUGGLE SESSIONS", THE MEDAL OF CHAIRMAN MAO PINNED TO HIS CHEST, THE BULLYING TEACHERS... ALL FORGOTTEN.
STILL, HE RETAINED A CLEAR MEMORY OF DENOUNCING MY FATHER AND ME.
* 下乡 : XIAXING. ** 四人帮 : SIRENBANG.

QIBAO MANAGED — I DON'T KNOW HOW — TO OBTAIN MY PERSONAL FILE, MY HU KOU. LIABLE AS WE WERE FOR OUR ANCESTORS UP TO THREE GENERATIONS BACK, MY FATHER AND I WERE IMPLICATED BY QIBAO'S DISCOVERIES.

THEY'RE A TYPICAL **"BLACK-BASTARD"** FAMILY! PURE-BLOOD REACTIONARIES! TRYING TO MAKE US THINK THEY'VE CHANGED!

BUT IN TRUTH, THEY'VE STAYED THE SAME! **LIKE FATHER, LIKE SON!**

THEY'VE INFILTRATED THE RANKS OF THE REVOLUTION!

THEY'RE HIDING THEIR TRUE FACE!

BUT I UNMASKED THEM! AND BROUGHT THEM BEFORE **THE PEOPLE!**

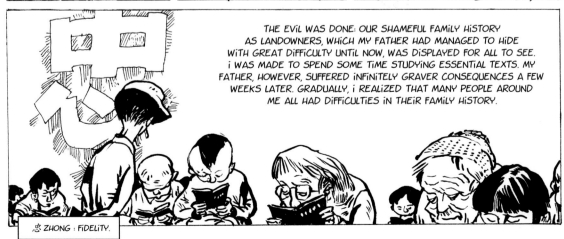

THE EVIL WAS DONE: OUR SHAMEFUL FAMILY HISTORY AS LANDOWNERS, WHICH MY FATHER HAD MANAGED TO HIDE WITH GREAT DIFFICULTY UNTIL NOW, WAS DISPLAYED FOR ALL TO SEE. I WAS MADE TO SPEND SOME TIME STUDYING ESSENTIAL TEXTS. MY FATHER, HOWEVER, SUFFERED INFINITELY GRAVER CONSEQUENCES A FEW WEEKS LATER. GRADUALLY, I REALIZED THAT MANY PEOPLE AROUND ME ALL HAD DIFFICULTIES IN THEIR FAMILY HISTORY.

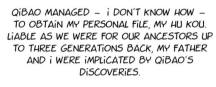

忠 ZHONG : FIDELITY.

145

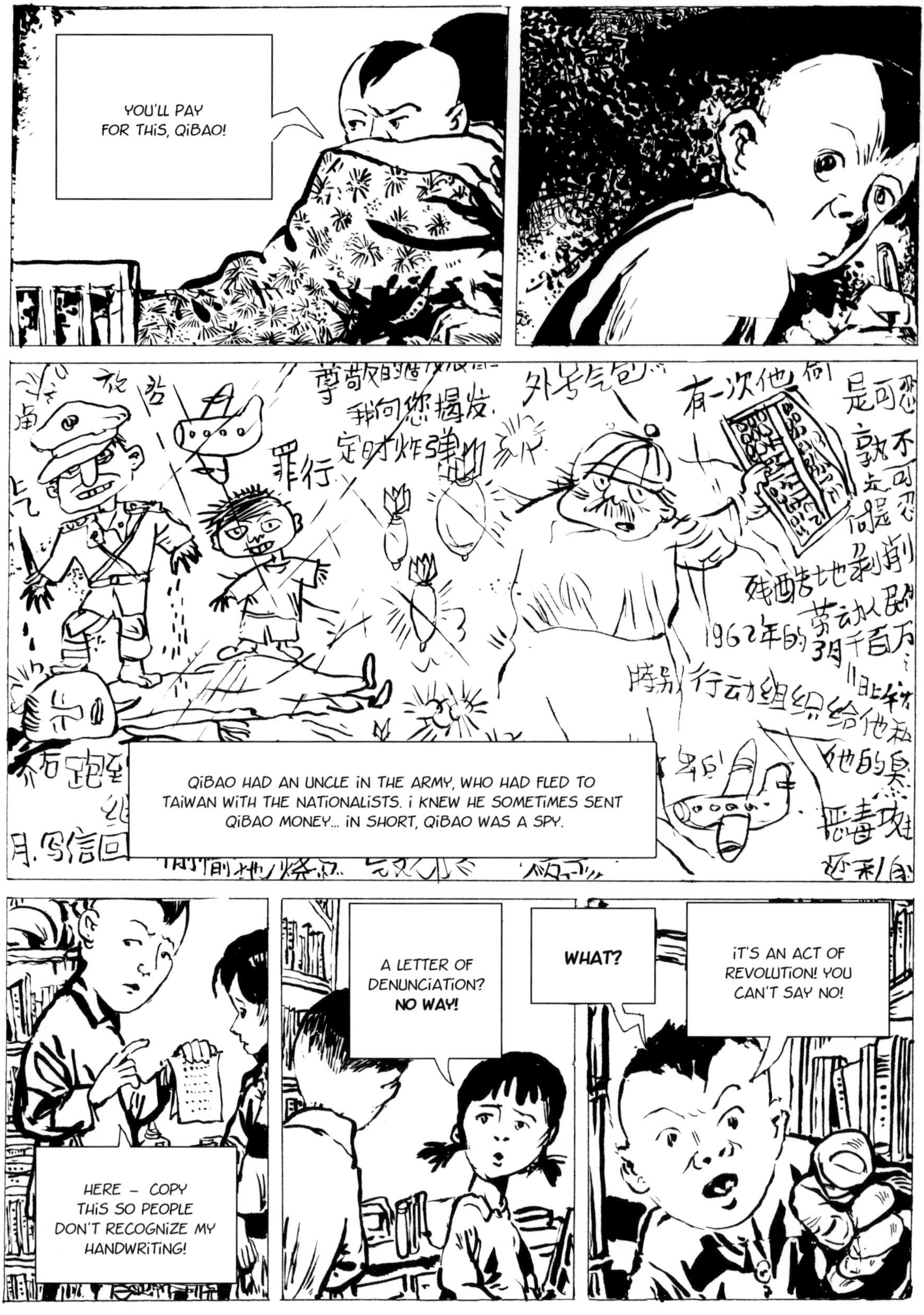

YOU'LL PAY FOR THIS, QIBAO!
我向您揭发
罪行
定时炸弹
有一次他
残酷地剥削
QIBAO HAD AN UNCLE IN THE ARMY, WHO HAD FLED TO TAIWAN WITH THE NATIONALISTS. I KNEW HE SOMETIMES SENT QIBAO MONEY... IN SHORT, QIBAO WAS A SPY.
HERE – COPY THIS SO PEOPLE DON'T RECOGNIZE MY HANDWRITING!
A LETTER OF DENUNCIATION? **NO WAY!**
WHAT?
IT'S AN ACT OF REVOLUTION! YOU CAN'T SAY NO!

"THE YOUNG MUST CRITICIZE CADRES ENGAGED IN RESTORING CAPITALISM, THE CHINESE KHRUSHCHEVS AND THEIR ACCOMPLICES." CHAIRMAN MAO'S TEACHINGS WERE MISINTERPRETED: THE SKIES FILLED WITH MALICIOUS GOSSIP, AND THE WALLS WITH DA ZI BAOS.* THESE LARGE-SCALE CHARACTER POSTERS IN THE STREETS, WHICH ALLOWED EVERYONE TO OPENLY EXPRESS THEIR FEELINGS ABOUT THEIR NEIGHBOURS, WERE PROBABLY THE FREEST, MOST UNRESTRICTED MEANS OF EXPRESSION EVER USED IN CHINA. THE DAMAGE WAS CONSIDERABLE.

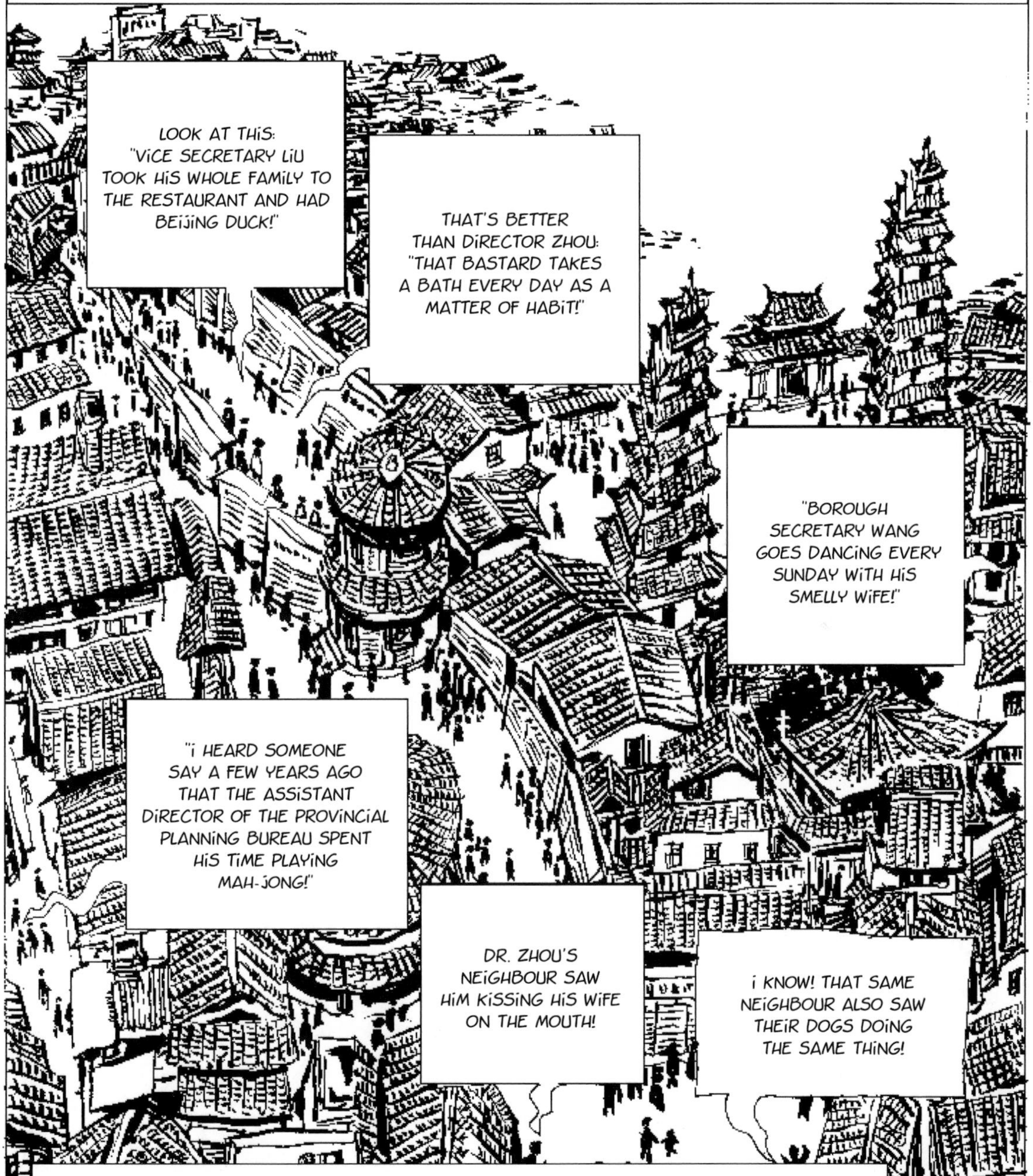

LOOK AT THIS: "VICE SECRETARY LIU TOOK HIS WHOLE FAMILY TO THE RESTAURANT AND HAD BEIJING DUCK!"
THAT'S BETTER THAN DIRECTOR ZHOU: "THAT BASTARD TAKES A BATH EVERY DAY AS A MATTER OF HABIT!"
"BOROUGH SECRETARY WANG GOES DANCING EVERY SUNDAY WITH HIS SMELLY WIFE!"
"I HEARD SOMEONE SAY A FEW YEARS AGO THAT THE ASSISTANT DIRECTOR OF THE PROVINCIAL PLANNING BUREAU SPENT HIS TIME PLAYING MAH-JONG!"
DR. ZHOU'S NEIGHBOUR SAW HIM KISSING HIS WIFE ON THE MOUTH!
I KNOW! THAT SAME NEIGHBOUR ALSO SAW THEIR DOGS DOING THE SAME THING!

* 大字报 DAZIBAO : LARGE-CHARACTER PUBLIC DENOUNCIATIONS.

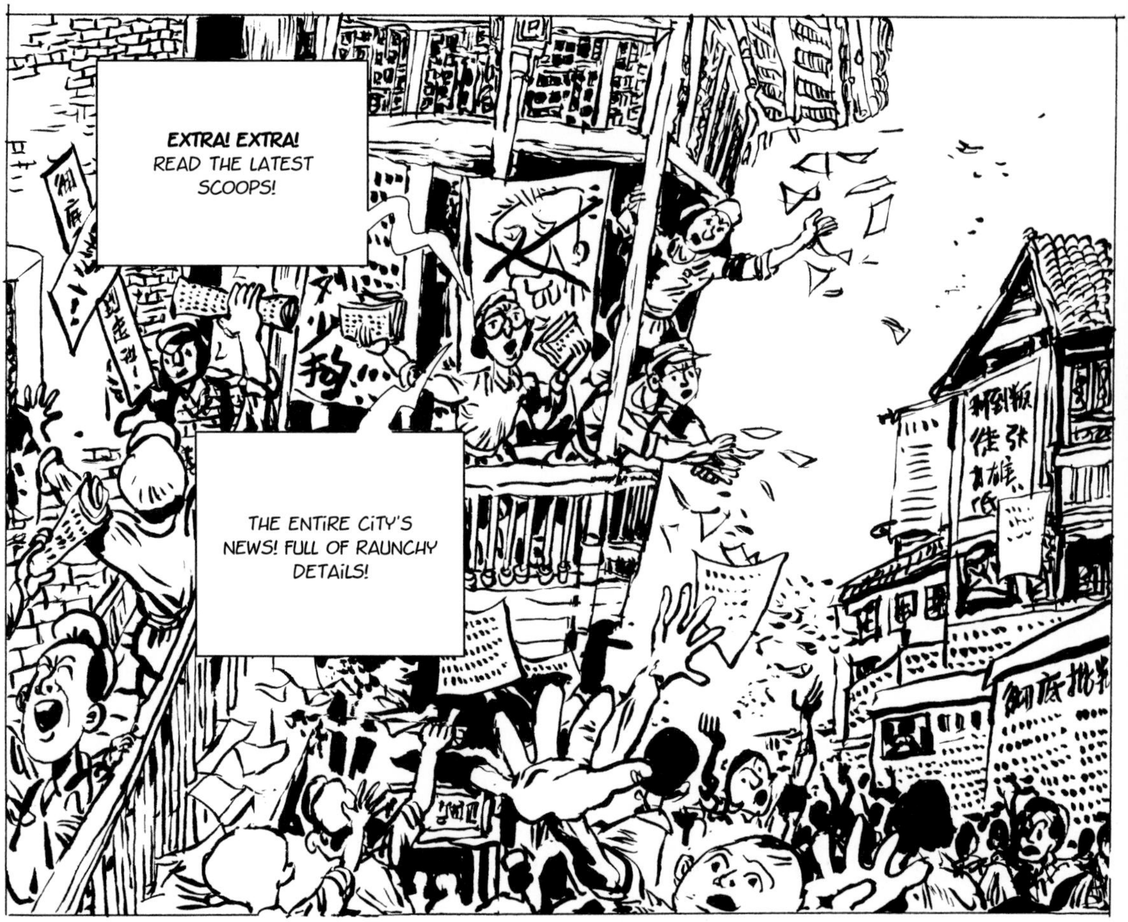
EXTRA! EXTRA!
READ THE LATEST SCOOPS!
THE ENTIRE CITY'S NEWS! FULL OF RAUNCHY DETAILS!

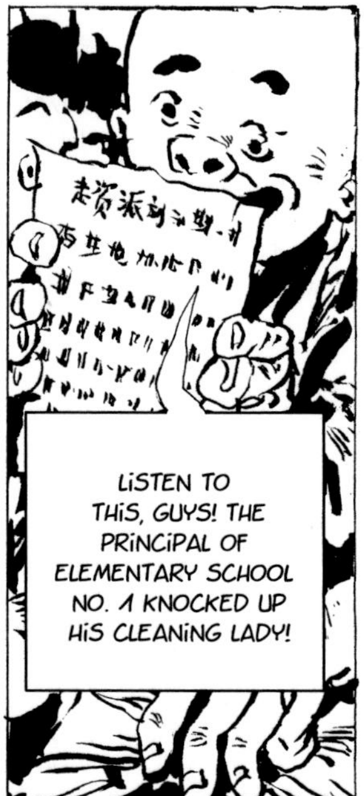
LISTEN TO THIS, GUYS! THE PRINCIPAL OF ELEMENTARY SCHOOL NO. 1 KNOCKED UP HIS CLEANING LADY!

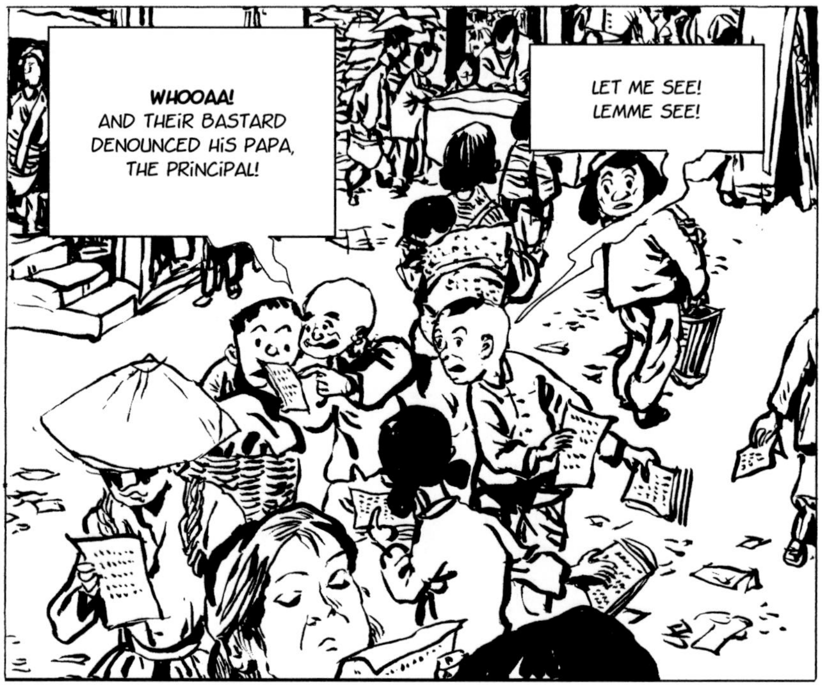
WHOOAA!
AND THEIR BASTARD DENOUNCED HIS PAPA, THE PRINCIPAL!
LET ME SEE! LEMME SEE!

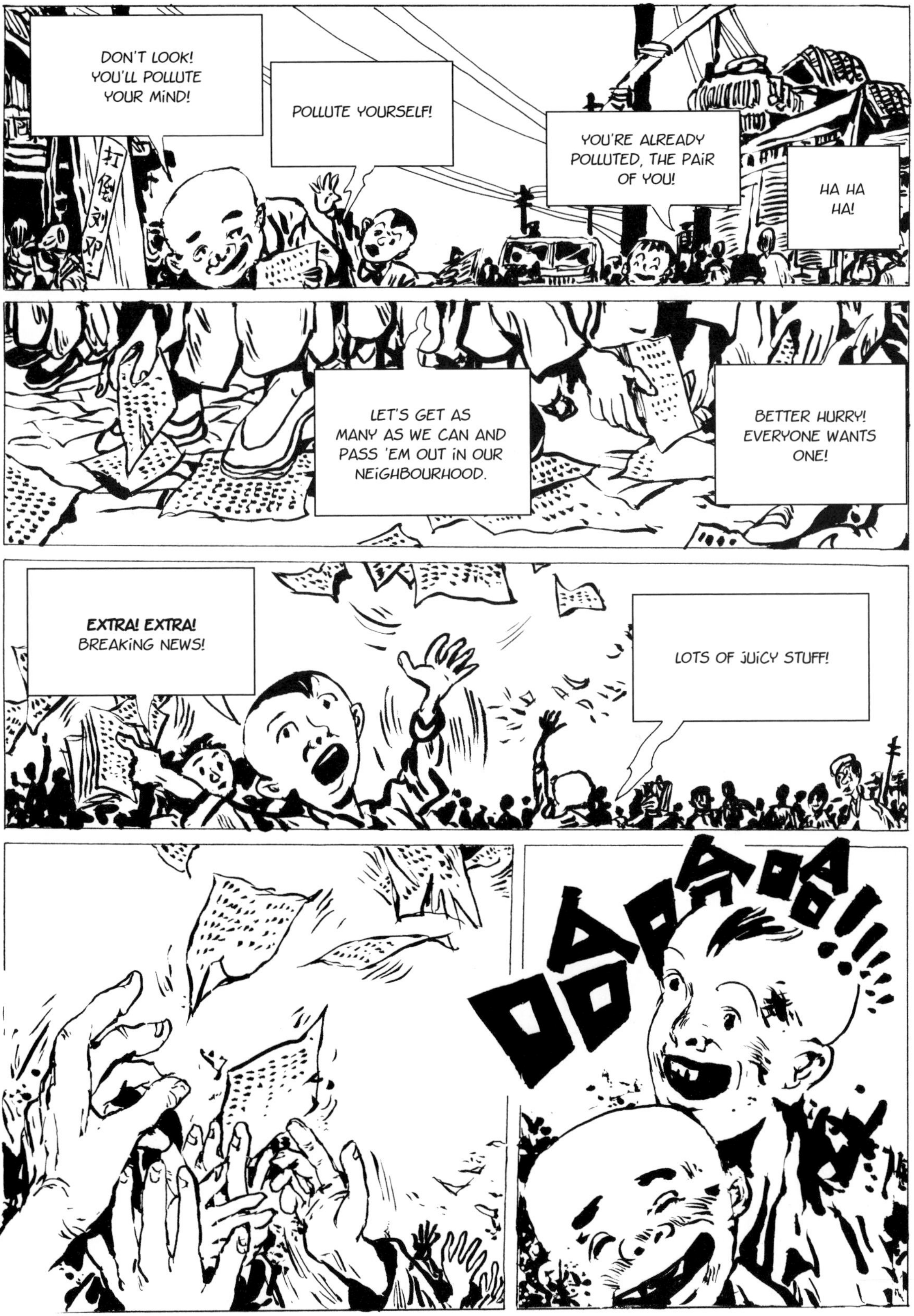
DON'T LOOK! YOU'LL POLLUTE YOUR MIND!
打倒刘邓
POLLUTE YOURSELF!
YOU'RE ALREADY POLLUTED, THE PAIR OF YOU!
HA HA HA!
LET'S GET AS MANY AS WE CAN AND PASS 'EM OUT IN OUR NEIGHBOURHOOD.
BETTER HURRY! EVERYONE WANTS ONE!
EXTRA! EXTRA! BREAKING NEWS!
LOTS OF JUICY STUFF!

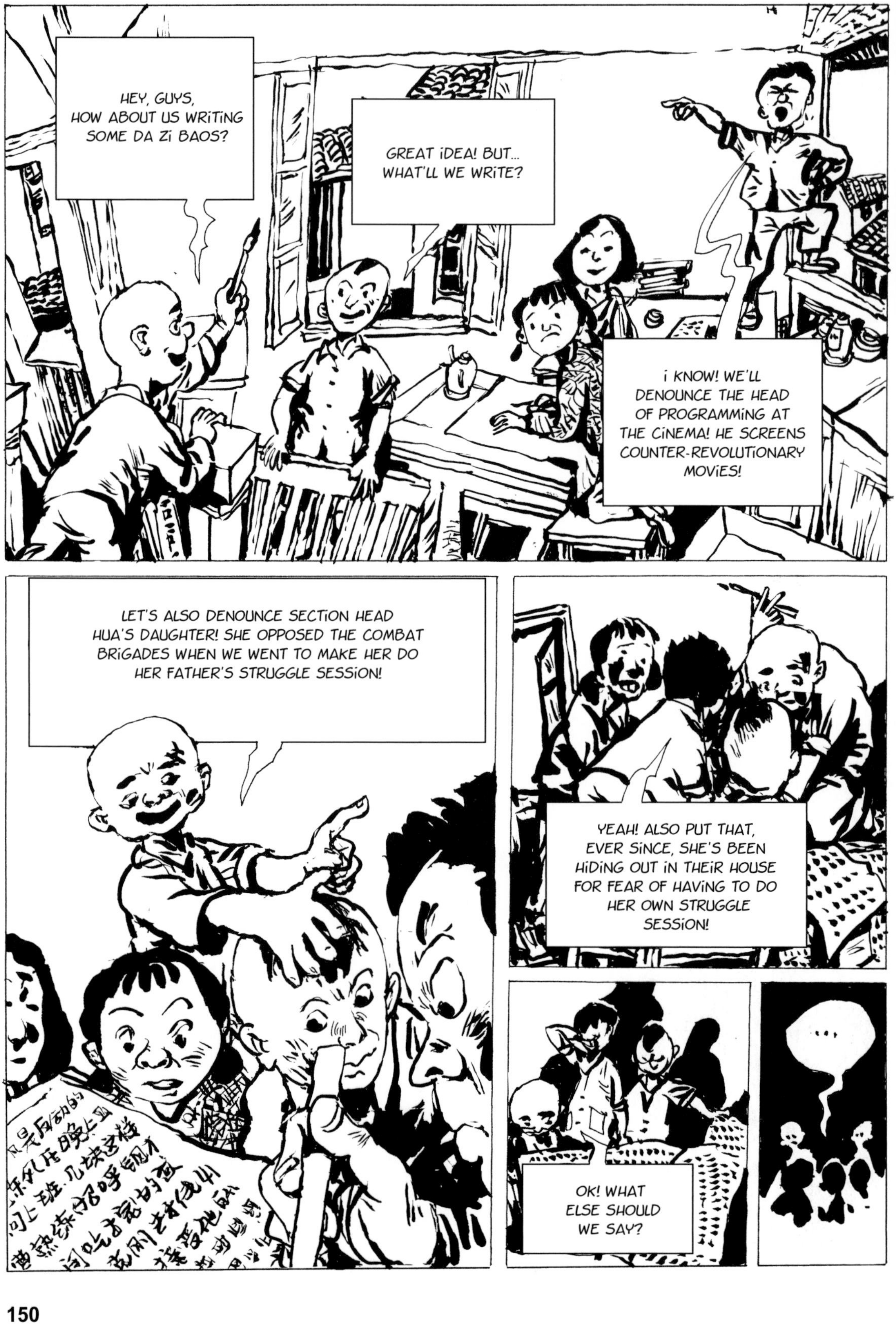
HEY, GUYS, HOW ABOUT US WRITING SOME DA ZI BAOS?
GREAT IDEA! BUT... WHAT'LL WE WRITE?
I KNOW! WE'LL DENOUNCE THE HEAD OF PROGRAMMING AT THE CINEMA! HE SCREENS COUNTER-REVOLUTIONARY MOVIES!
LET'S ALSO DENOUNCE SECTION HEAD HUA'S DAUGHTER! SHE OPPOSED THE COMBAT BRIGADES WHEN WE WENT TO MAKE HER DO HER FATHER'S STRUGGLE SESSION!
YEAH! ALSO PUT THAT, EVER SINCE, SHE'S BEEN HIDING OUT IN THEIR HOUSE FOR FEAR OF HAVING TO DO HER OWN STRUGGLE SESSION!
OK! WHAT ELSE SHOULD WE SAY?
...

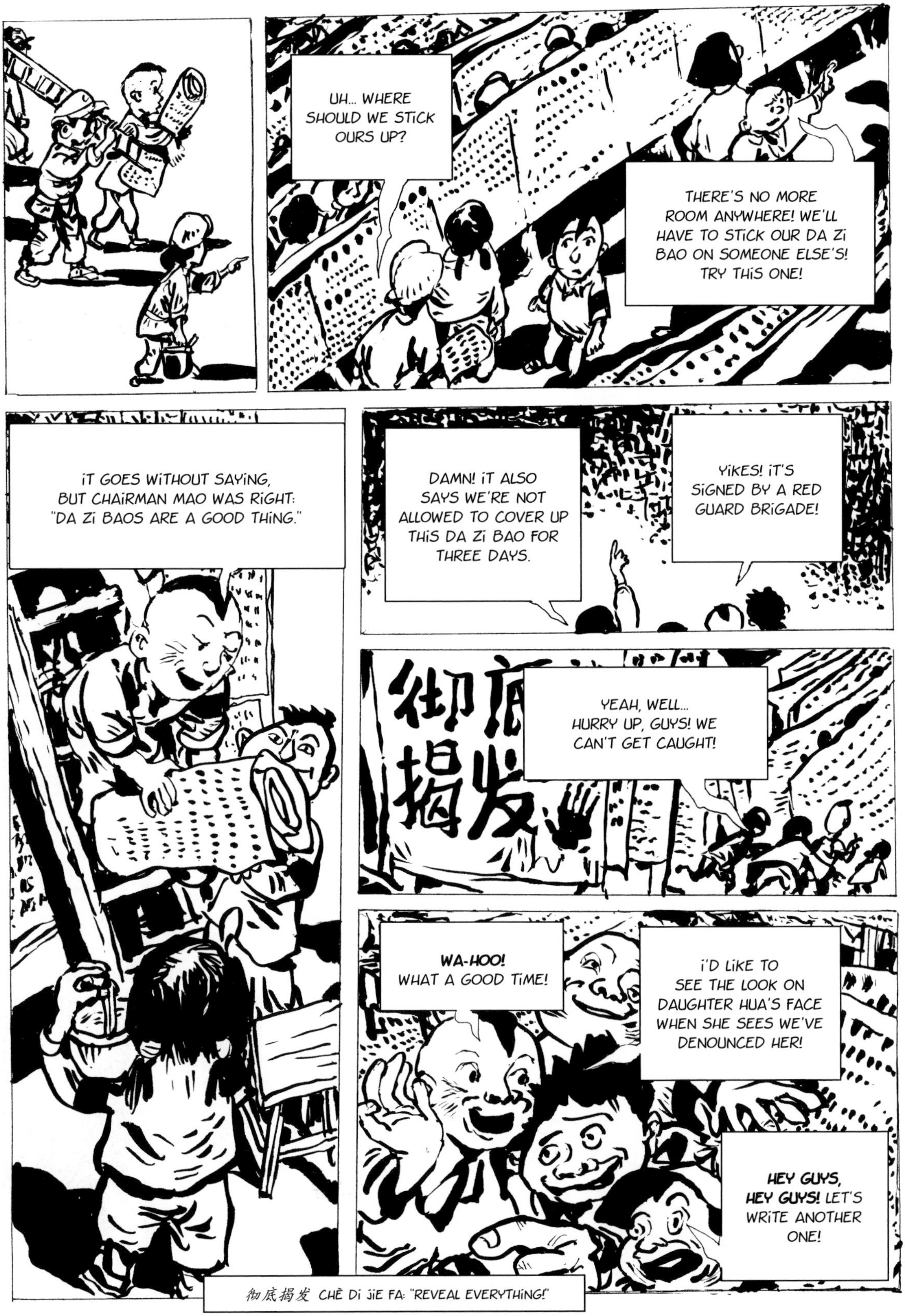
UH... WHERE SHOULD WE STICK OURS UP?
THERE'S NO MORE ROOM ANYWHERE! WE'LL HAVE TO STICK OUR DA ZI BAO ON SOMEONE ELSE'S! TRY THIS ONE!
IT GOES WITHOUT SAYING, BUT CHAIRMAN MAO WAS RIGHT: "DA ZI BAOS ARE A GOOD THING."
DAMN! IT ALSO SAYS WE'RE NOT ALLOWED TO COVER UP THIS DA ZI BAO FOR THREE DAYS.
YIKES! IT'S SIGNED BY A RED GUARD BRIGADE!
彻底揭发
YEAH, WELL... HURRY UP, GUYS! WE CAN'T GET CAUGHT!
WA-HOO! WHAT A GOOD TIME!
I'D LIKE TO SEE THE LOOK ON DAUGHTER HUA'S FACE WHEN SHE SEES WE'VE DENOUNCED HER!
HEY GUYS, HEY GUYS! LET'S WRITE ANOTHER ONE!
彻底揭发 CHÈ DI JIE FA: "REVEAL EVERYTHING!"

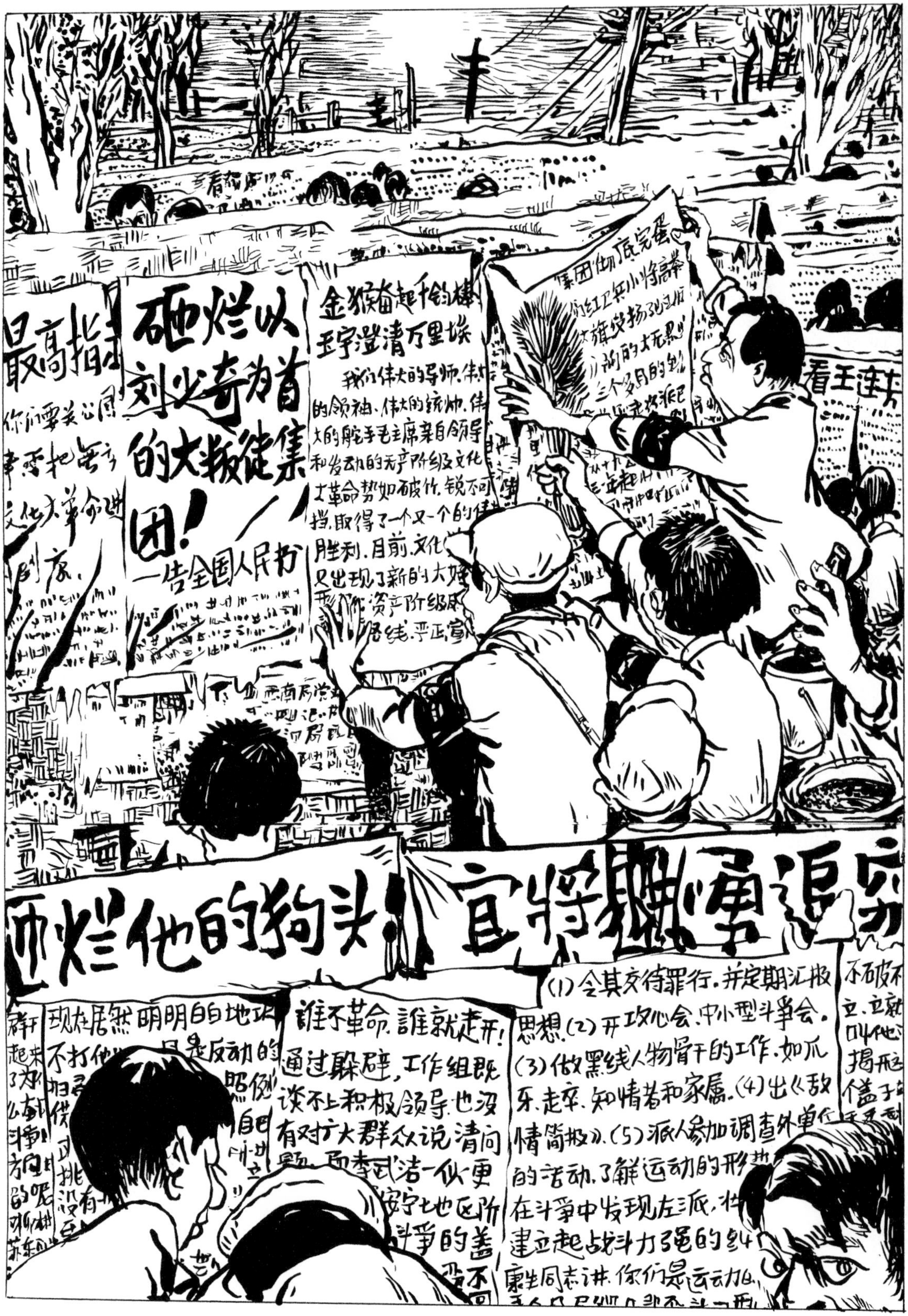
最高指
你们要关心国
事要把无产
文化大革命进
到底
砸烂以
刘少奇为首
的大叛徒集
团！
—告全国人民书
金猴奋起千钧棒
玉宇澄清万里埃
我们伟大的导师、伟大
的领袖、伟大的统帅、伟
大的舵手毛主席亲自领导
和发动的无产阶级文化
大革命势如破竹，锐不可
挡，取得了一个又一个的伟
胜利。目前，文化
又出现了新的大好
形势，资产阶级反
路线，严正宣
集团彻底完蛋
向红卫兵小将学
大旗发扬
看王连
砸烂他的狗头
宜将剩勇追穷
(1)令其交待罪行，并定期汇报
思想。(2)开攻心会、中小型斗争会。
(3)做黑线人物骨干的工作，如爪
牙、走卒、知情者和家属。(4)出《敌
情简报》。(5)派人参加调查外单位
的活动，了解运动的形势
在斗争中发现左派，并
建立起战斗力强的
康生同志讲：你们是运动
谁不革命，谁就走开！
通过躲避，工作组既
谈不上积极领导，也没
有对广大群众说清问
题，而李武洁一伙更
安宁地区
斗争的盖
现在居然明明白白地
不打他
是反动的
不破不
立、立就
叫他
揭开
盖子

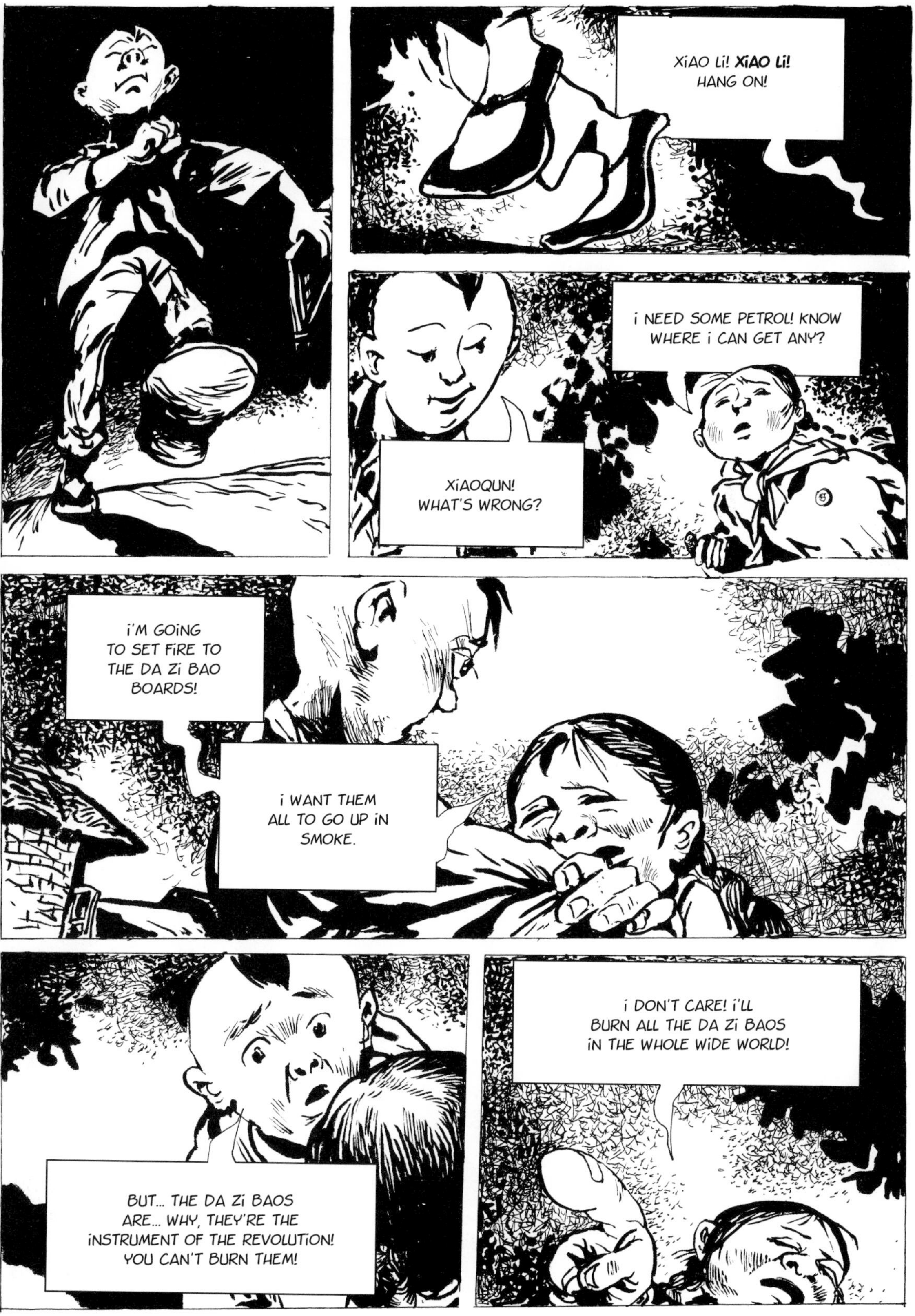
XiAO Li! XiAO Li!
HANG ON!
i NEED SOME PETROL! KNOW WHERE i CAN GET ANY?
XiAOQUN! WHAT'S WRONG?
i'M GOiNG TO SET FiRE TO THE DA Zi BAO BOARDS!
i WANT THEM ALL TO GO UP iN SMOKE.
BUT... THE DA Zi BAOS ARE... WHY, THEY'RE THE iNSTRUMENT OF THE REVOLUTiON! YOU CAN'T BURN THEM!
i DON'T CARE! i'LL BURN ALL THE DA Zi BAOS iN THE WHOLE WiDE WORLD!

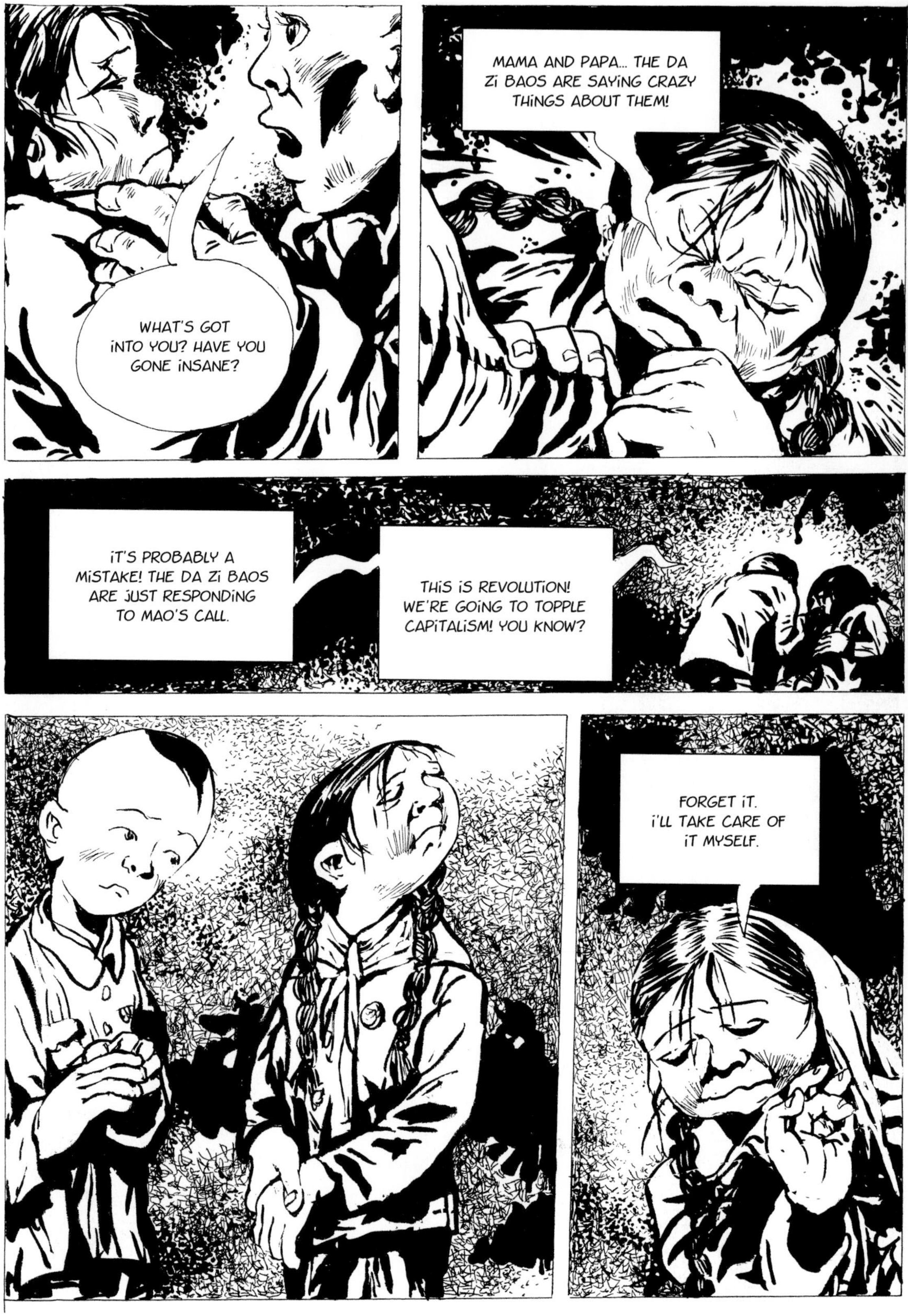
WHAT'S GOT INTO YOU? HAVE YOU GONE INSANE?
MAMA AND PAPA... THE DA ZI BAOS ARE SAYING CRAZY THINGS ABOUT THEM!
IT'S PROBABLY A MISTAKE! THE DA ZI BAOS ARE JUST RESPONDING TO MAO'S CALL.
THIS IS REVOLUTION! WE'RE GOING TO TOPPLE CAPITALISM! YOU KNOW?
FORGET IT. I'LL TAKE CARE OF IT MYSELF.

I HOPE FOR YOUR SAKE THAT YOUR FATHER DOESN'T GET ACCUSED LIKE MINE WAS TODAY.

MY FATHER? WHY SHOULD HE WORRY?

MY FATHER'S THE VERY MODEL OF LOYALTY TO CHAIRMAN MAO! BESIDES, I LOVE HIM AS MUCH AS I LOVE CHAIRMAN MAO!

YOU'LL SEE...

XIAOQUN! XIAOQUN! WAIT!

I HAD SOMETHING ELSE TO SAY TO YOU...

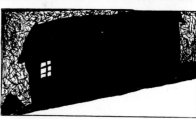

155

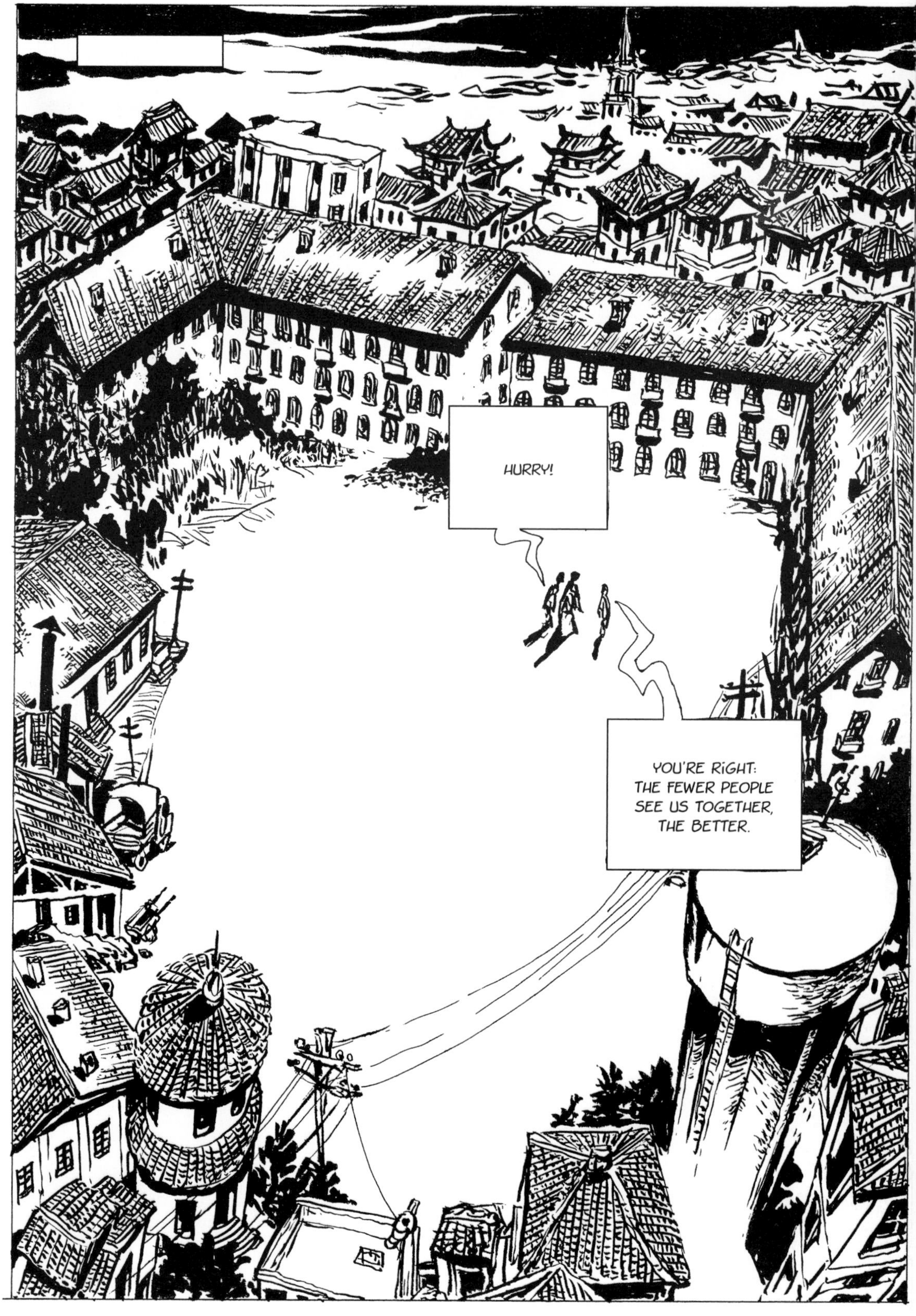
HURRY!
YOU'RE RIGHT: THE FEWER PEOPLE SEE US TOGETHER, THE BETTER.

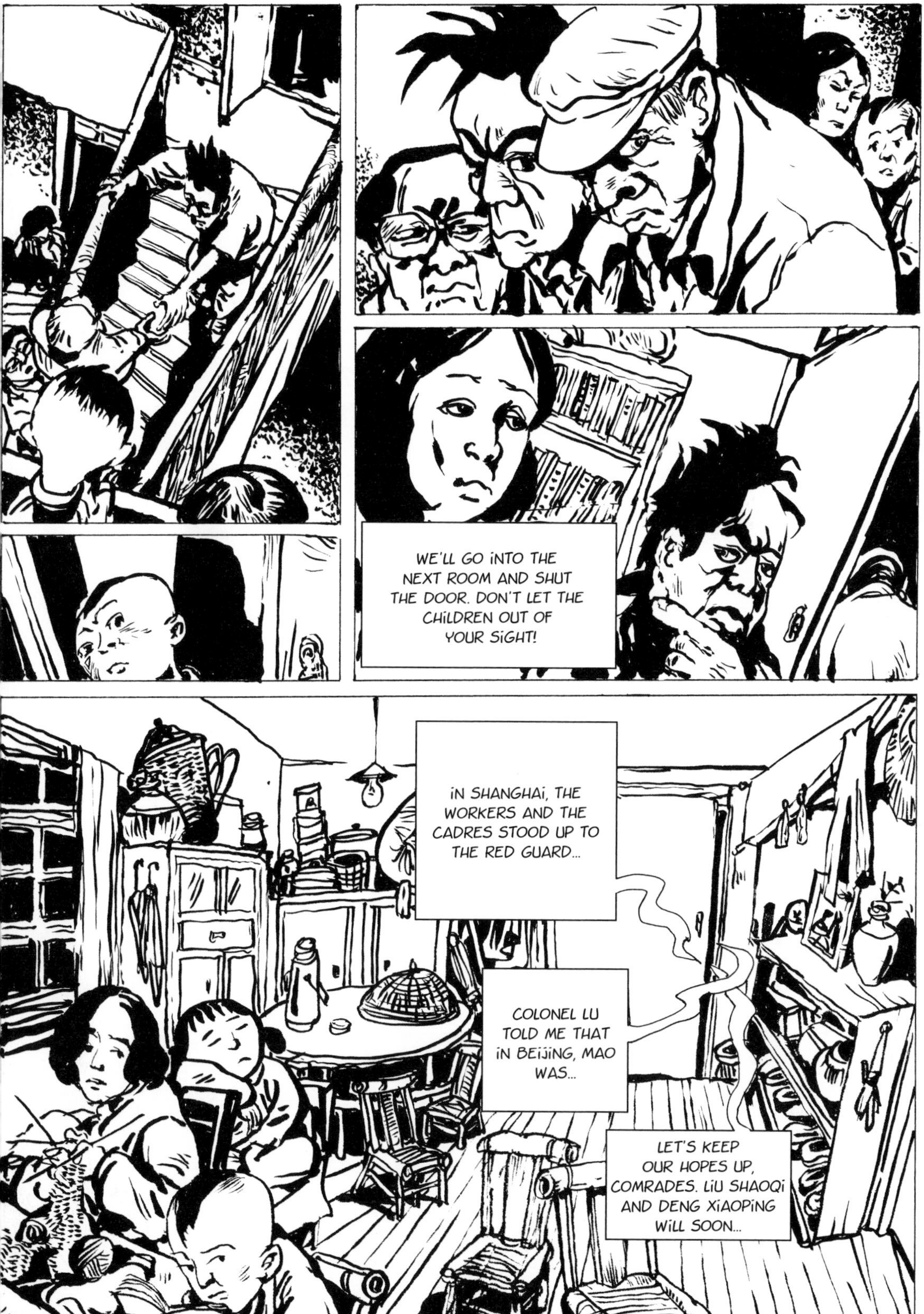
WE'LL GO INTO THE NEXT ROOM AND SHUT THE DOOR. DON'T LET THE CHILDREN OUT OF YOUR SIGHT!
IN SHANGHAI, THE WORKERS AND THE CADRES STOOD UP TO THE RED GUARD...
COLONEL LU TOLD ME THAT IN BEIJING, MAO WAS...
LET'S KEEP OUR HOPES UP, COMRADES. LIU SHAOQI AND DENG XIAOPING WILL SOON...

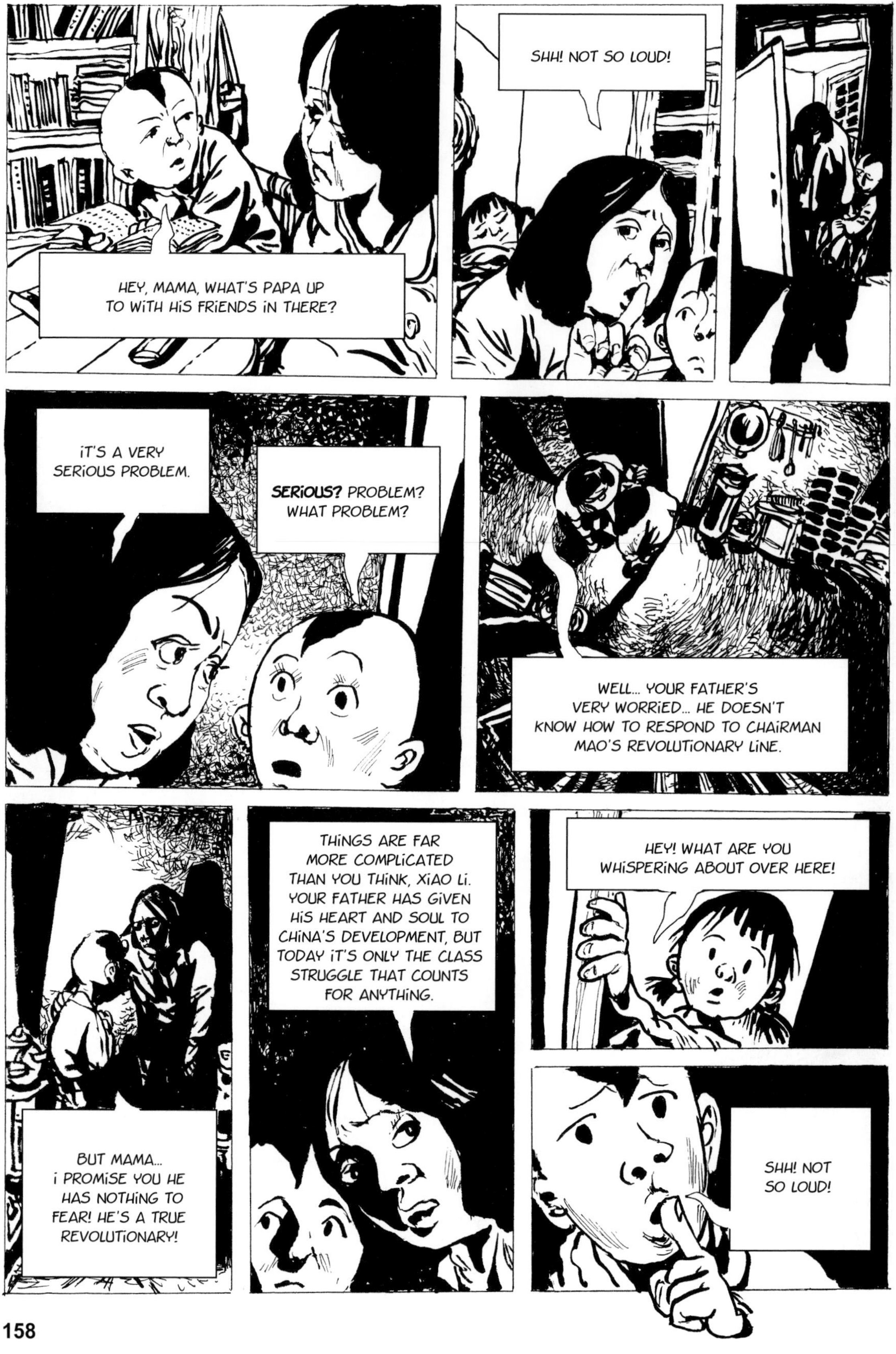
HEY, MAMA, WHAT'S PAPA UP TO WITH HIS FRIENDS IN THERE?
SHH! NOT SO LOUD!
IT'S A VERY SERIOUS PROBLEM.
SERIOUS? PROBLEM? WHAT PROBLEM?
WELL... YOUR FATHER'S VERY WORRIED... HE DOESN'T KNOW HOW TO RESPOND TO CHAIRMAN MAO'S REVOLUTIONARY LINE.
BUT MAMA... I PROMISE YOU HE HAS NOTHING TO FEAR! HE'S A TRUE REVOLUTIONARY!
THINGS ARE FAR MORE COMPLICATED THAN YOU THINK, XIAO LI. YOUR FATHER HAS GIVEN HIS HEART AND SOUL TO CHINA'S DEVELOPMENT, BUT TODAY IT'S ONLY THE CLASS STRUGGLE THAT COUNTS FOR ANYTHING.
HEY! WHAT ARE YOU WHISPERING ABOUT OVER HERE!
SHH! NOT SO LOUD!

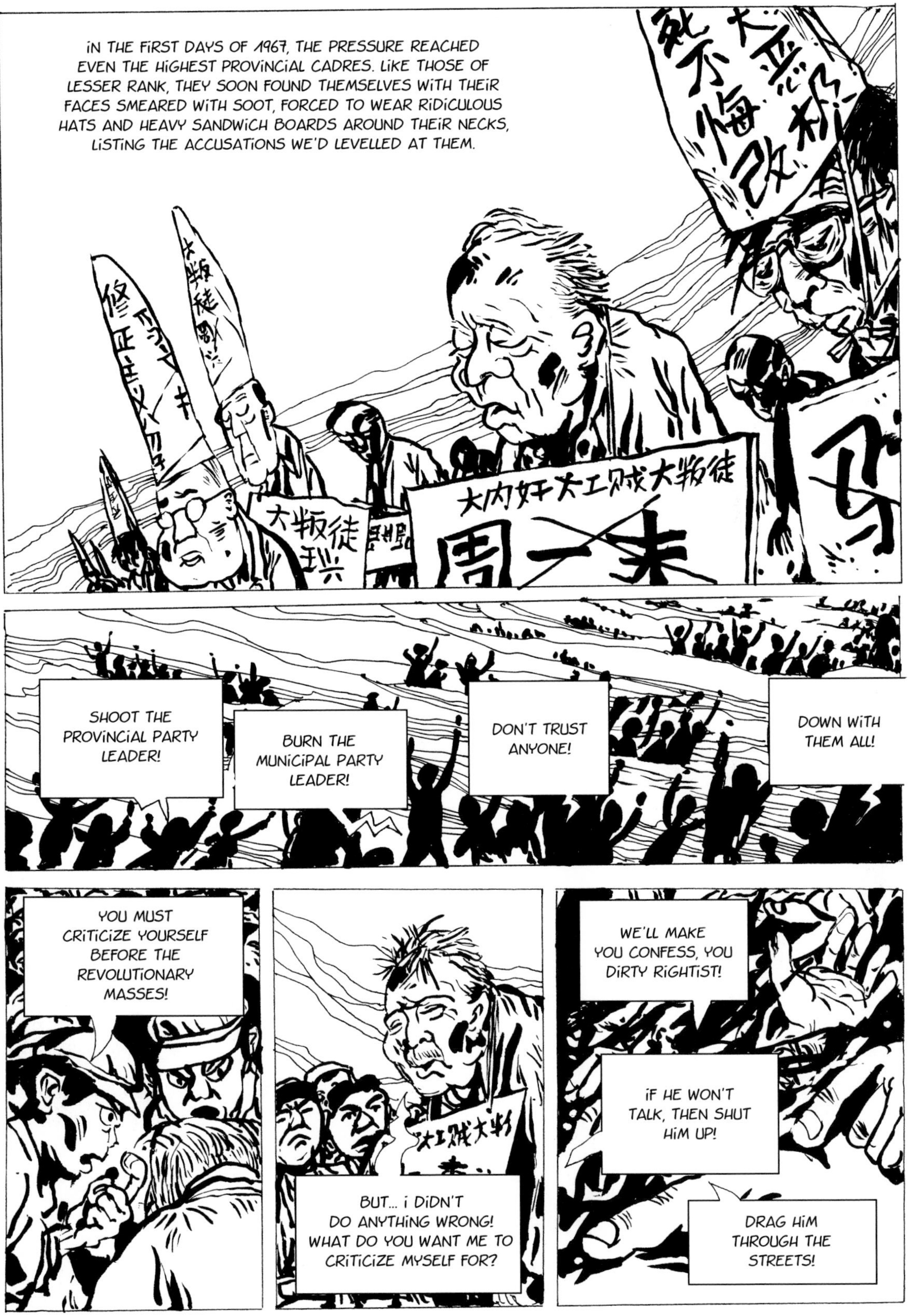
IN THE FIRST DAYS OF 1967, THE PRESSURE REACHED EVEN THE HIGHEST PROVINCIAL CADRES. LIKE THOSE OF LESSER RANK, THEY SOON FOUND THEMSELVES WITH THEIR FACES SMEARED WITH SOOT, FORCED TO WEAR RIDICULOUS HATS AND HEAVY SANDWICH BOARDS AROUND THEIR NECKS, LISTING THE ACCUSATIONS WE'D LEVELLED AT THEM.
大内奸大工贼大叛徒
大叛徒
SHOOT THE PROVINCIAL PARTY LEADER!
BURN THE MUNICIPAL PARTY LEADER!
DON'T TRUST ANYONE!
DOWN WITH THEM ALL!
YOU MUST CRITICIZE YOURSELF BEFORE THE REVOLUTIONARY MASSES!
BUT... I DIDN'T DO ANYTHING WRONG! WHAT DO YOU WANT ME TO CRITICIZE MYSELF FOR?
WE'LL MAKE YOU CONFESS, YOU DIRTY RIGHTIST!
IF HE WON'T TALK, THEN SHUT HIM UP!
DRAG HIM THROUGH THE STREETS!

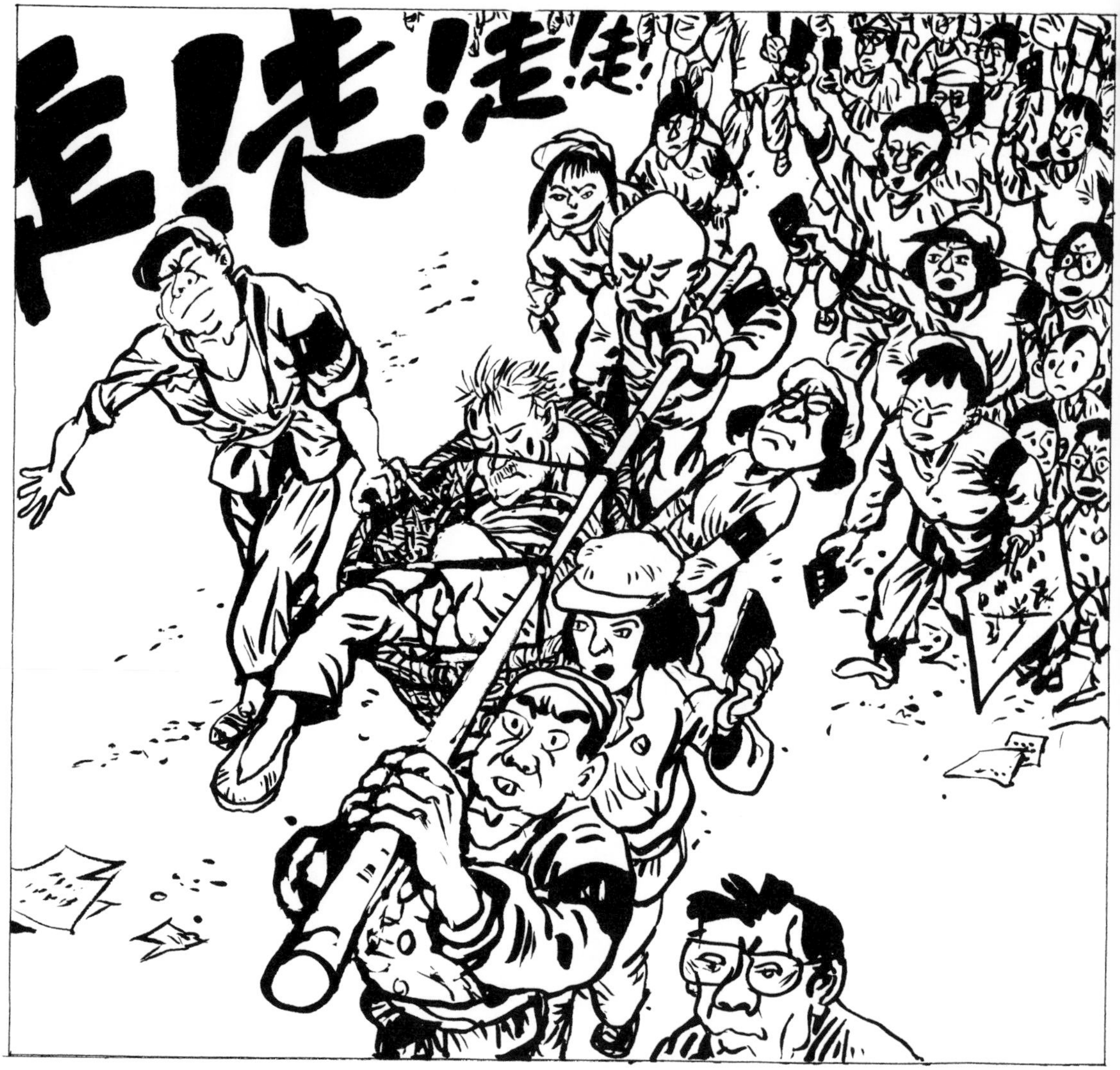
走!走!走!走!

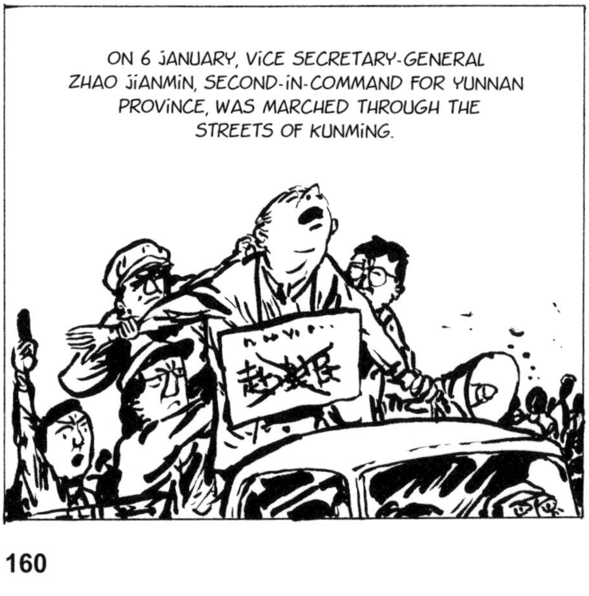
ON 6 JANUARY, VICE SECRETARY-GENERAL ZHAO JIANMIN, SECOND-IN-COMMAND FOR YUNNAN PROVINCE, WAS MARCHED THROUGH THE STREETS OF KUNMING.

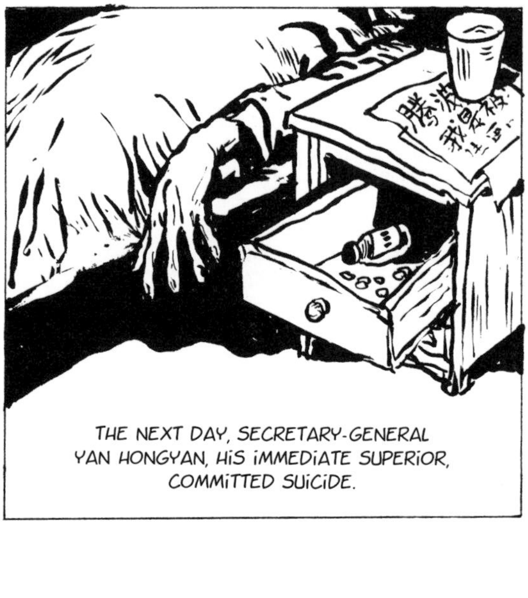
THE NEXT DAY, SECRETARY-GENERAL YAN HONGYAN, HIS IMMEDIATE SUPERIOR, COMMITTED SUICIDE.

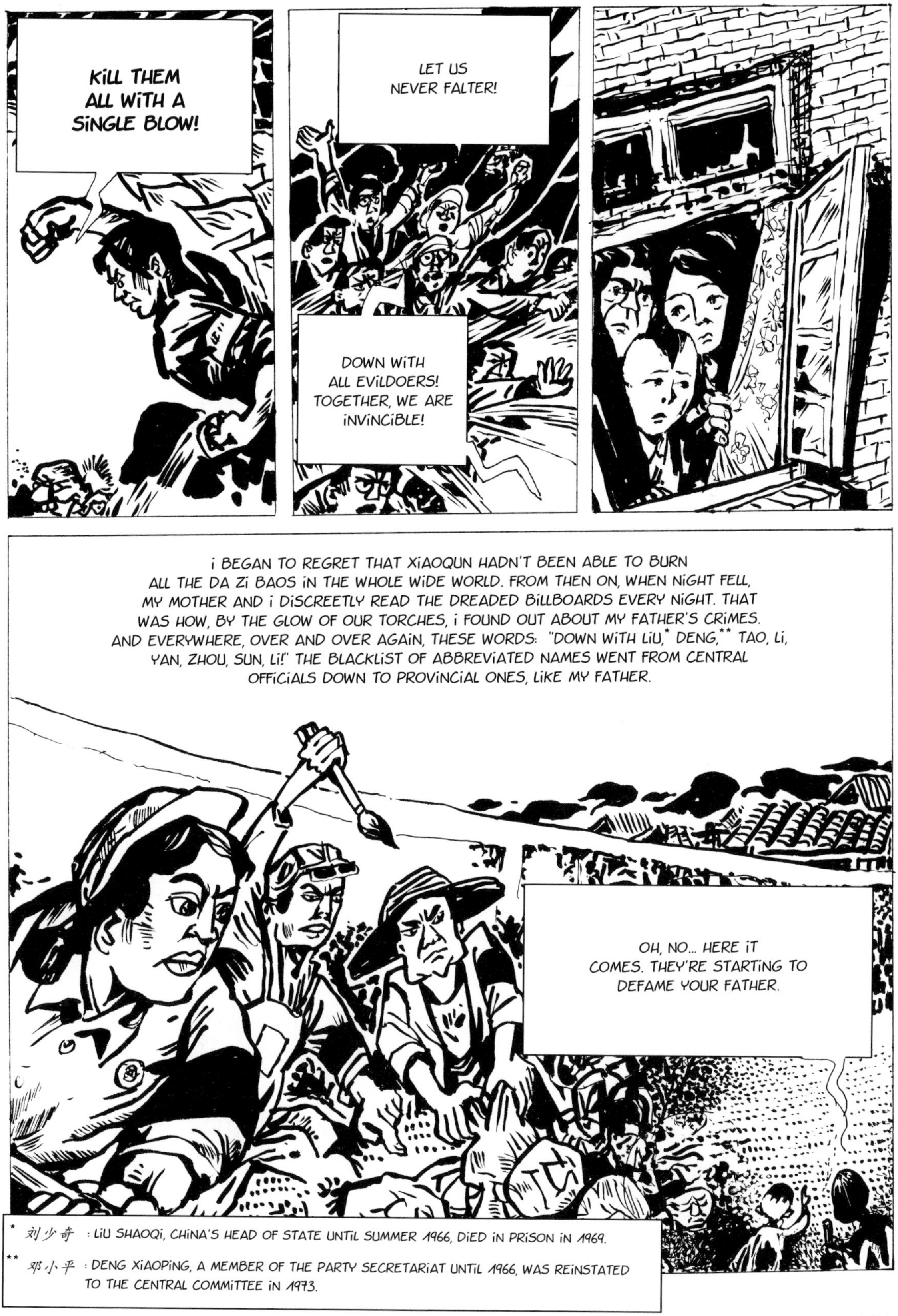
KILL THEM ALL WITH A SINGLE BLOW!
LET US NEVER FALTER!
DOWN WITH ALL EVILDOERS! TOGETHER, WE ARE INVINCIBLE!
I BEGAN TO REGRET THAT XIAOQUN HADN'T BEEN ABLE TO BURN ALL THE DA ZI BAOS IN THE WHOLE WIDE WORLD. FROM THEN ON, WHEN NIGHT FELL, MY MOTHER AND I DISCREETLY READ THE DREADED BILLBOARDS EVERY NIGHT. THAT WAS HOW, BY THE GLOW OF OUR TORCHES, I FOUND OUT ABOUT MY FATHER'S CRIMES. AND EVERYWHERE, OVER AND OVER AGAIN, THESE WORDS: "DOWN WITH LIU,* DENG,** TAO, LI, YAN, ZHOU, SUN, LI!" THE BLACKLIST OF ABBREVIATED NAMES WENT FROM CENTRAL OFFICIALS DOWN TO PROVINCIAL ONES, LIKE MY FATHER.
OH, NO... HERE IT COMES. THEY'RE STARTING TO DEFAME YOUR FATHER.

* 刘少奇 : LIU SHAOQI, CHINA'S HEAD OF STATE UNTIL SUMMER 1966, DIED IN PRISON IN 1969.

** 邓小平 : DENG XIAOPING, A MEMBER OF THE PARTY SECRETARIAT UNTIL 1966, WAS REINSTATED TO THE CENTRAL COMMITTEE IN 1973.

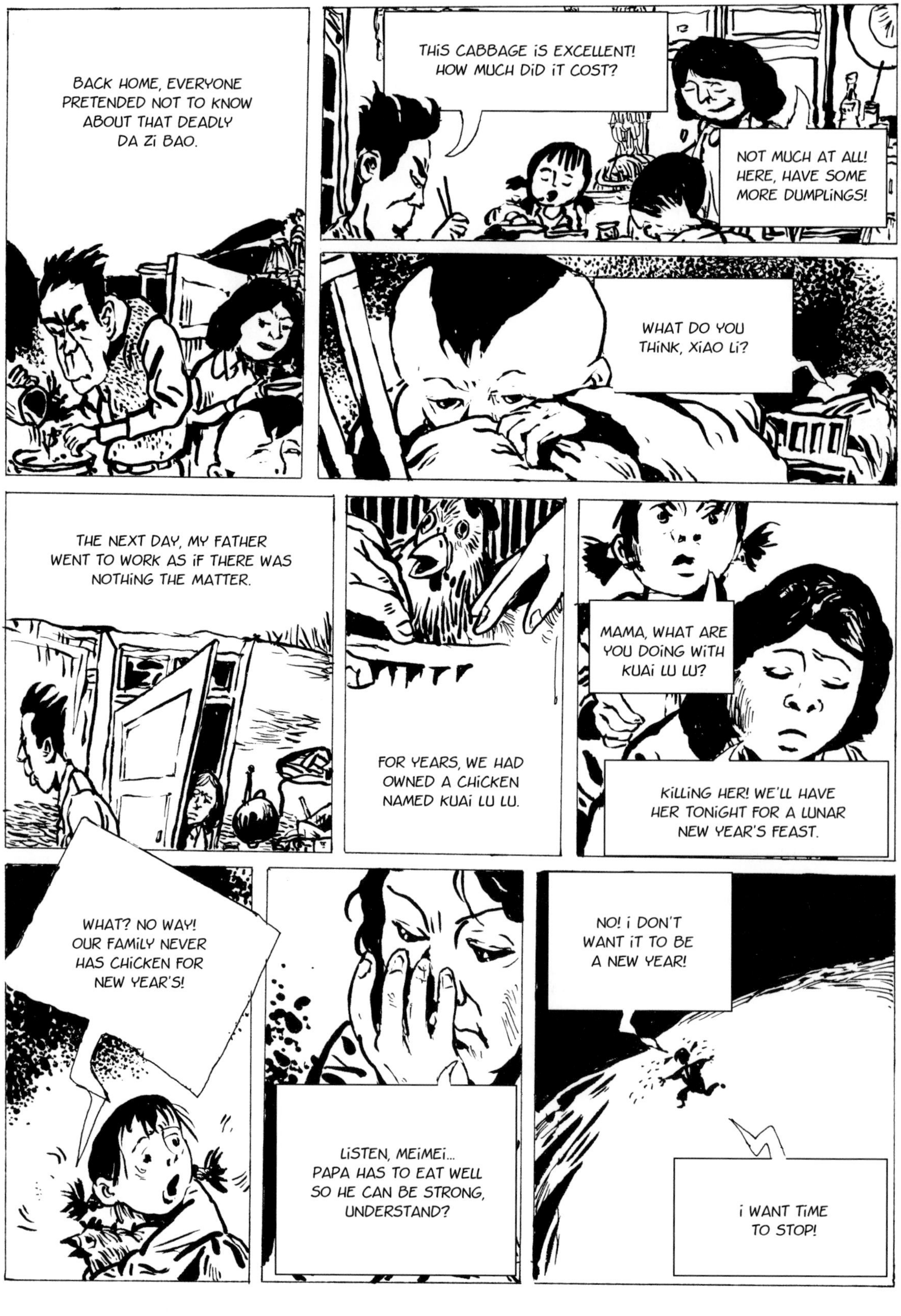
BACK HOME, EVERYONE PRETENDED NOT TO KNOW ABOUT THAT DEADLY DA ZI BAO.
THIS CABBAGE IS EXCELLENT! HOW MUCH DID IT COST?
NOT MUCH AT ALL! HERE, HAVE SOME MORE DUMPLINGS!
WHAT DO YOU THINK, XIAO LI?
THE NEXT DAY, MY FATHER WENT TO WORK AS IF THERE WAS NOTHING THE MATTER.
FOR YEARS, WE HAD OWNED A CHICKEN NAMED KUAI LU LU.
MAMA, WHAT ARE YOU DOING WITH KUAI LU LU?
KILLING HER! WE'LL HAVE HER TONIGHT FOR A LUNAR NEW YEAR'S FEAST.
WHAT? NO WAY! OUR FAMILY NEVER HAS CHICKEN FOR NEW YEAR'S!
LISTEN, MEIMEI... PAPA HAS TO EAT WELL SO HE CAN BE STRONG, UNDERSTAND?
NO! I DON'T WANT IT TO BE A NEW YEAR!
I WANT TIME TO STOP!

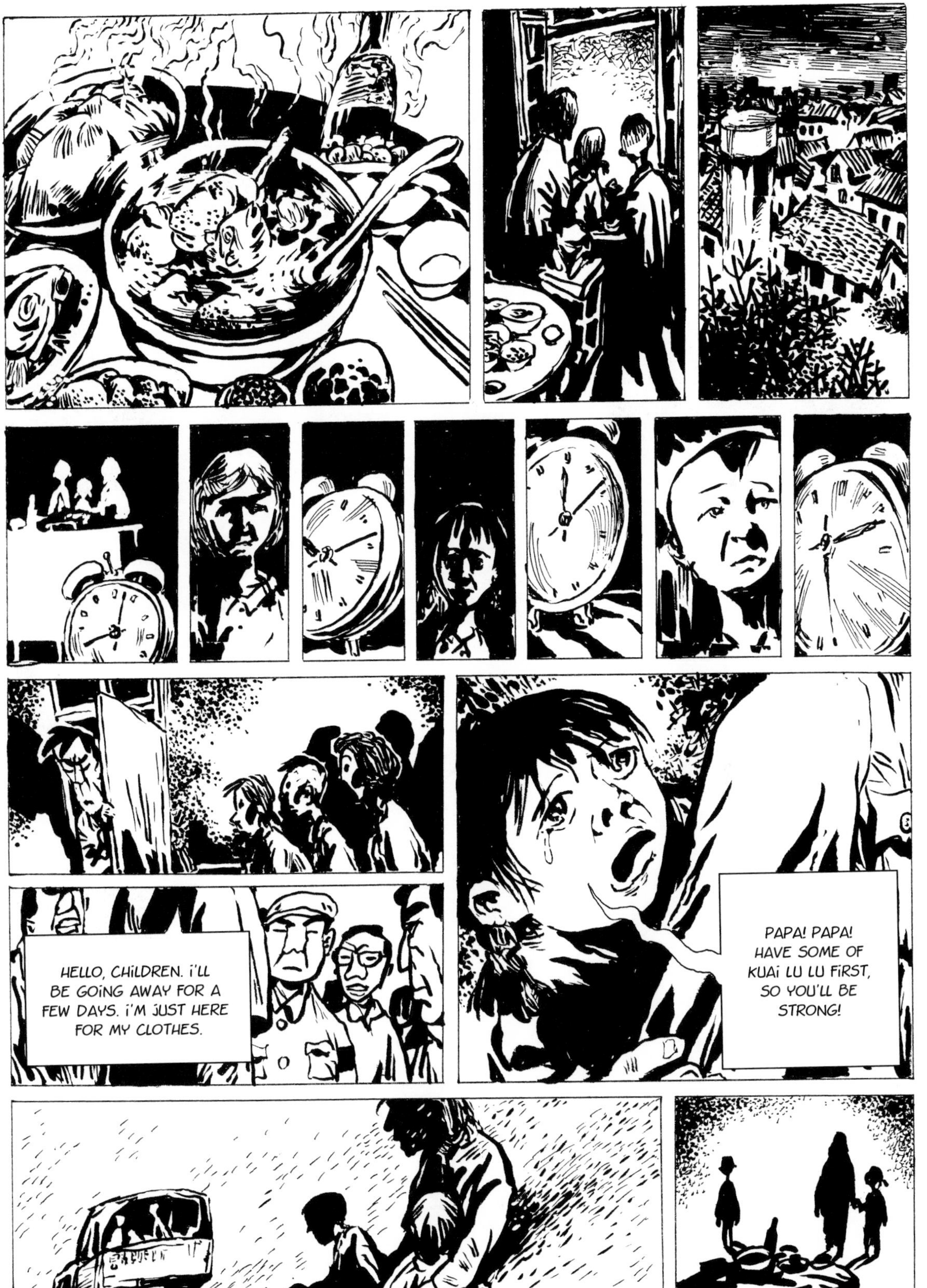
HELLO, CHILDREN. I'LL BE GOING AWAY FOR A FEW DAYS. I'M JUST HERE FOR MY CLOTHES.
PAPA! PAPA! HAVE SOME OF KUAI LU LU FIRST, SO YOU'LL BE STRONG!

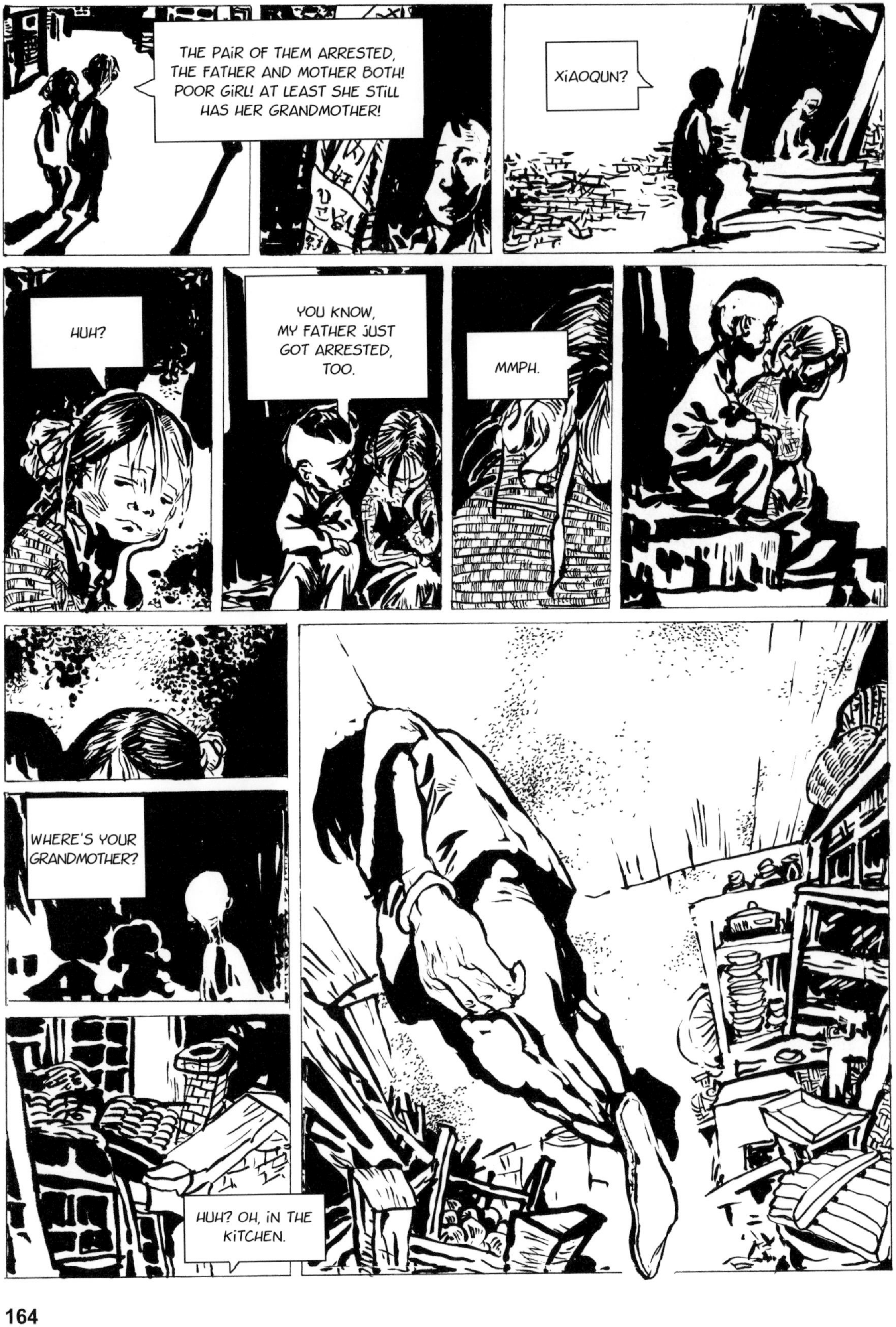
THE PAIR OF THEM ARRESTED, THE FATHER AND MOTHER BOTH! POOR GIRL! AT LEAST SHE STILL HAS HER GRANDMOTHER!
XIAOQUN?
HUH?
YOU KNOW, MY FATHER JUST GOT ARRESTED, TOO.
MMPH.
WHERE'S YOUR GRANDMOTHER?
HUH? OH, IN THE KITCHEN.

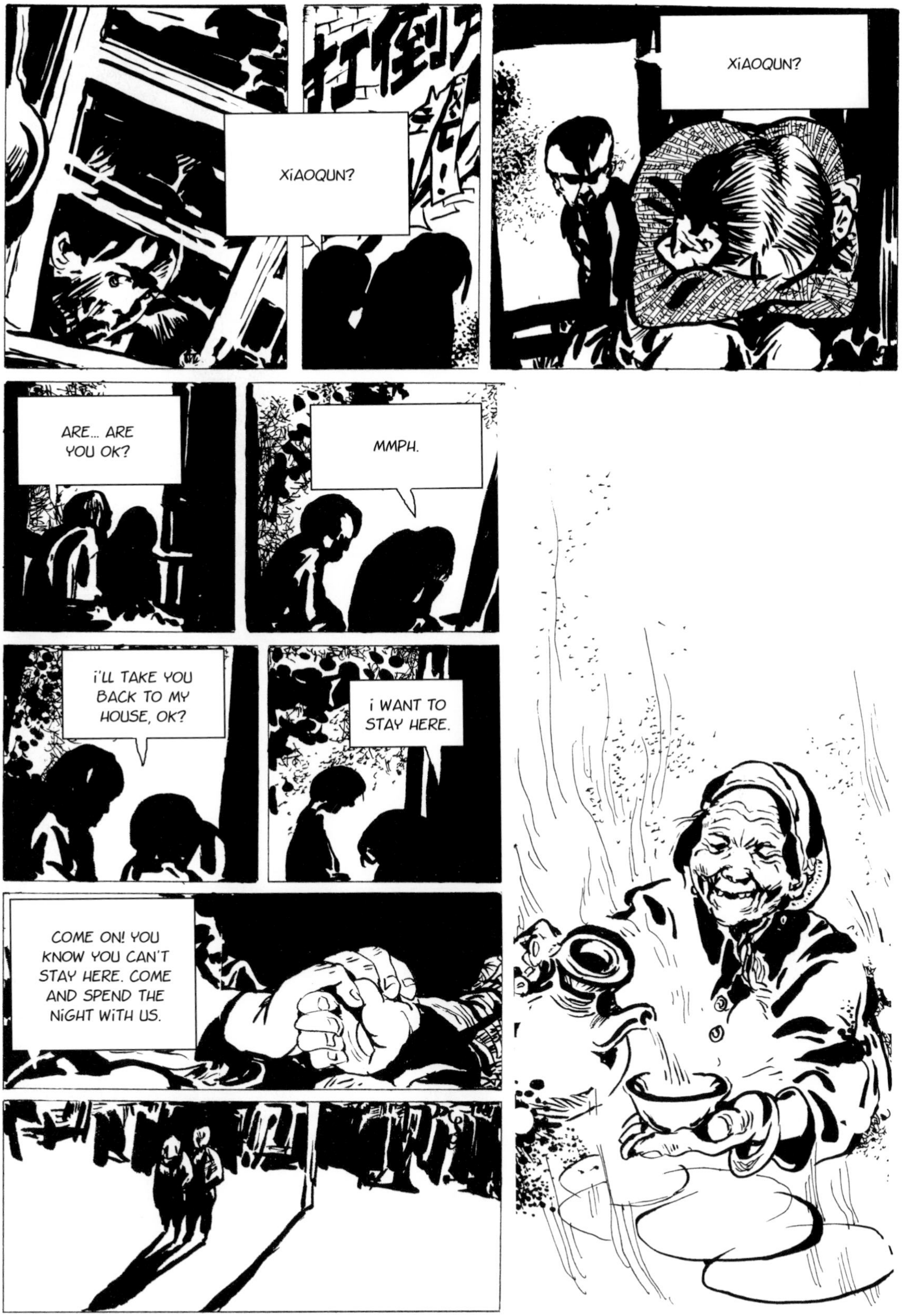
XiAOQUN?
XiAOQUN?
ARE... ARE YOU OK?
MMPH.
i'LL TAKE YOU BACK TO MY HOUSE, OK?
i WANT TO STAY HERE.
COME ON! YOU KNOW YOU CAN'T STAY HERE. COME AND SPEND THE NiGHT WiTH US.

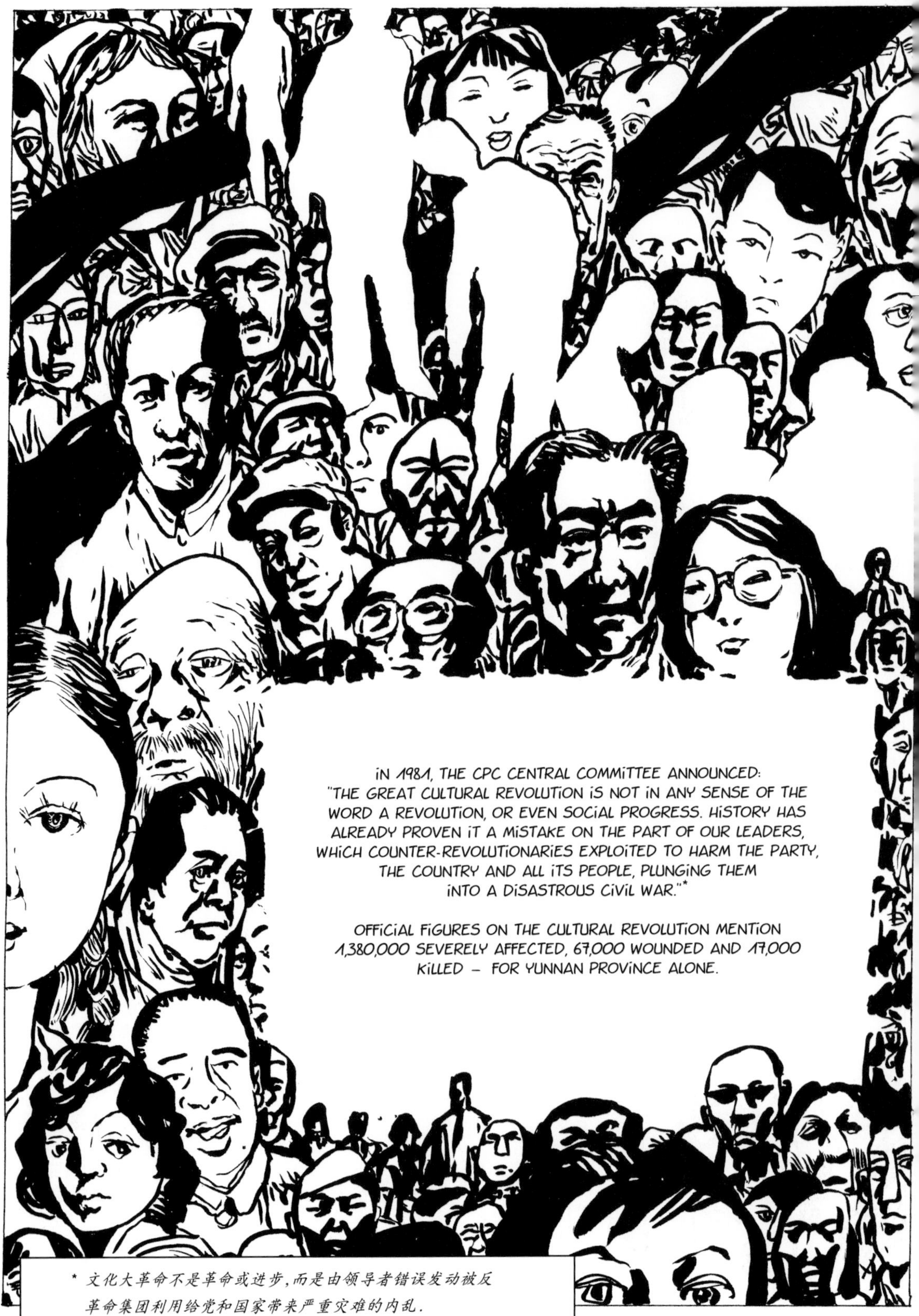
IN 1981, THE CPC CENTRAL COMMITTEE ANNOUNCED:
"THE GREAT CULTURAL REVOLUTION IS NOT IN ANY SENSE OF THE WORD A REVOLUTION, OR EVEN SOCIAL PROGRESS. HISTORY HAS ALREADY PROVEN IT A MISTAKE ON THE PART OF OUR LEADERS, WHICH COUNTER-REVOLUTIONARIES EXPLOITED TO HARM THE PARTY, THE COUNTRY AND ALL ITS PEOPLE, PLUNGING THEM INTO A DISASTROUS CIVIL WAR."*
OFFICIAL FIGURES ON THE CULTURAL REVOLUTION MENTION 1,380,000 SEVERELY AFFECTED, 67,000 WOUNDED AND 17,000 KILLED – FOR YUNNAN PROVINCE ALONE.

* 文化大革命不是革命或进步,而是由领导者错误发动被反革命集团利用给党和国家带来严重灾难的内乱.

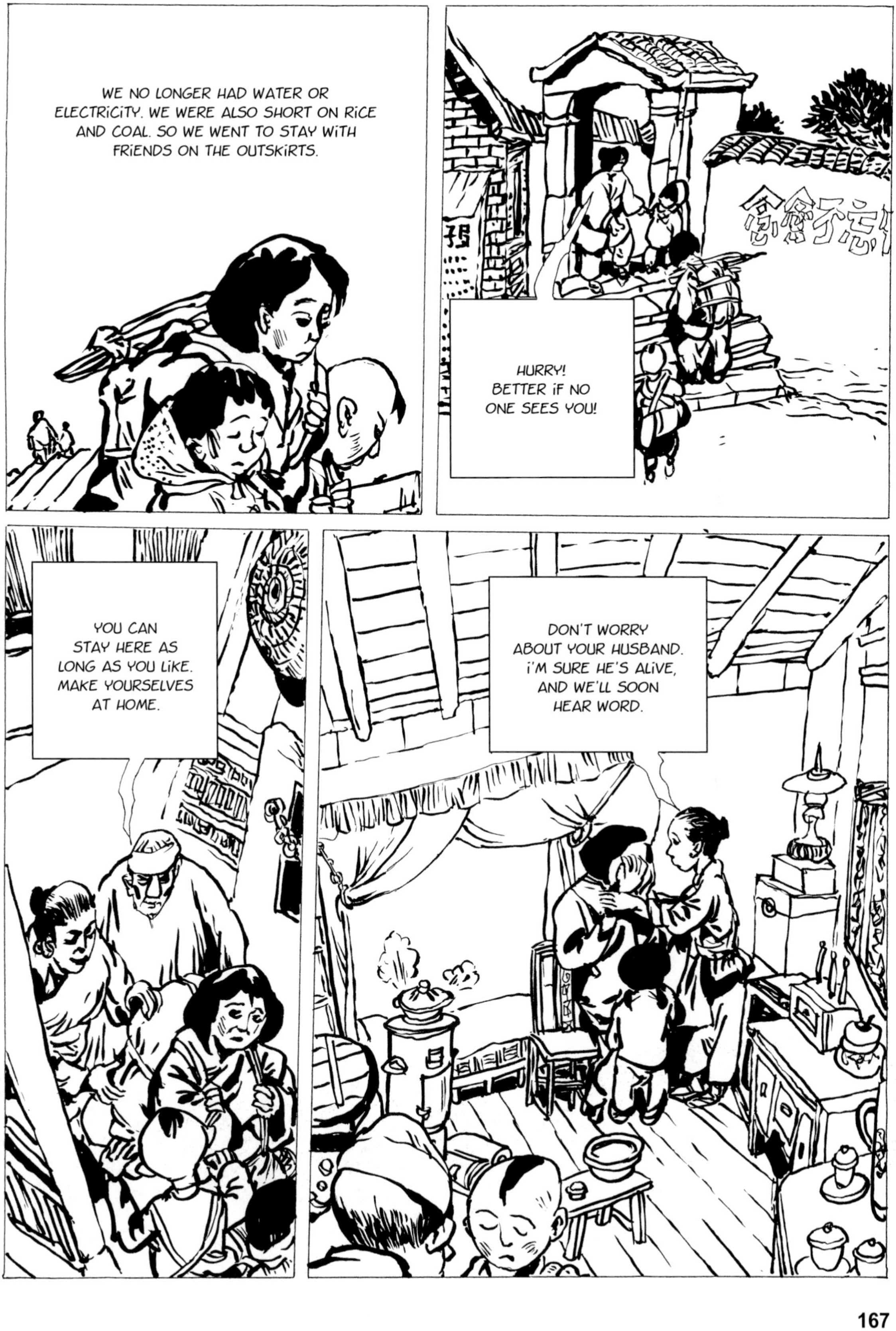
WE NO LONGER HAD WATER OR ELECTRICITY. WE WERE ALSO SHORT ON RICE AND COAL. SO WE WENT TO STAY WITH FRIENDS ON THE OUTSKIRTS.
念念不忘
HURRY! BETTER IF NO ONE SEES YOU!
YOU CAN STAY HERE AS LONG AS YOU LIKE. MAKE YOURSELVES AT HOME.
DON'T WORRY ABOUT YOUR HUSBAND. I'M SURE HE'S ALIVE, AND WE'LL SOON HEAR WORD.

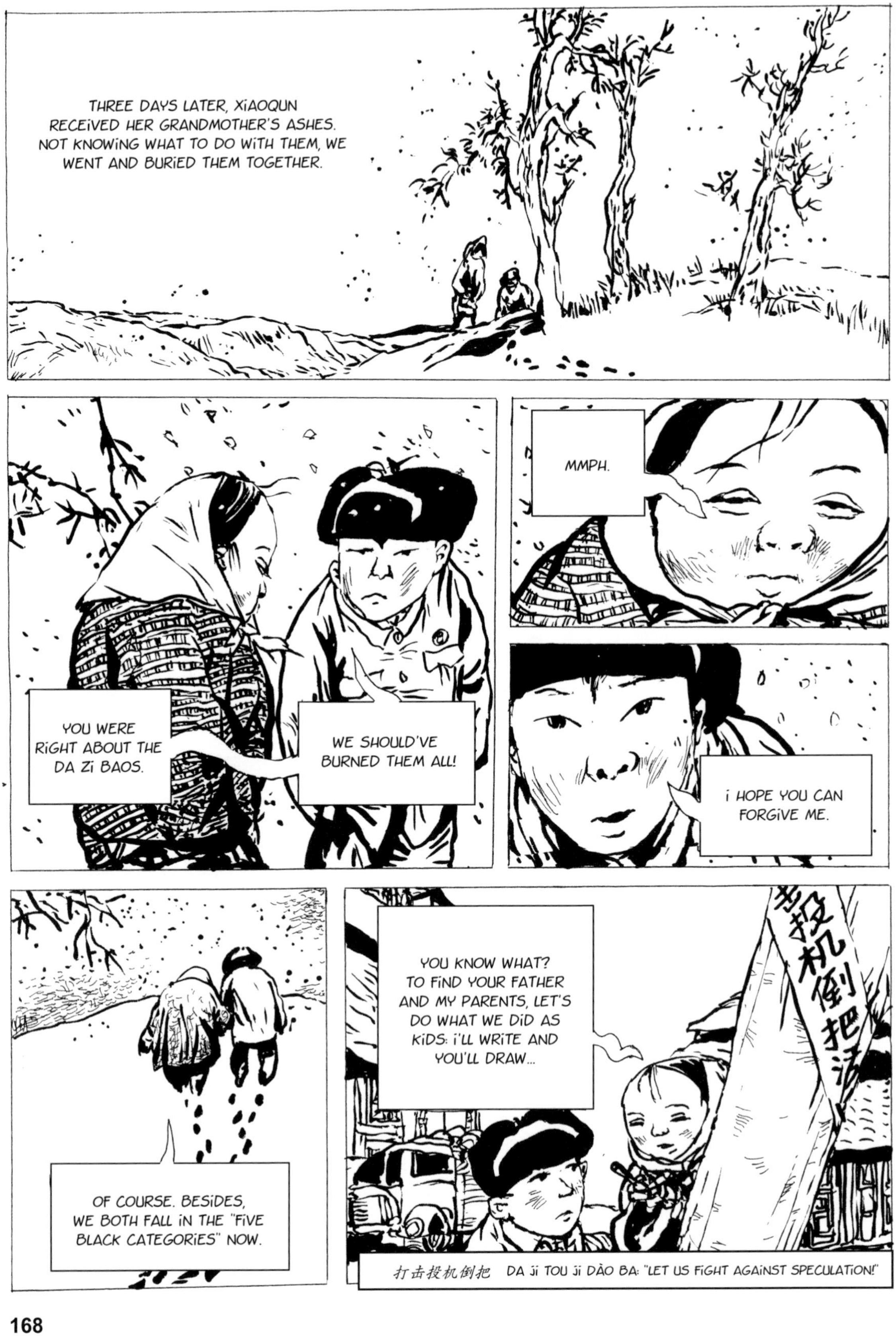
THREE DAYS LATER, XIAOQUN RECEIVED HER GRANDMOTHER'S ASHES. NOT KNOWING WHAT TO DO WITH THEM, WE WENT AND BURIED THEM TOGETHER.
YOU WERE RIGHT ABOUT THE DA ZI BAOS.
WE SHOULD'VE BURNED THEM ALL!
MMPH.
I HOPE YOU CAN FORGIVE ME.
OF COURSE. BESIDES, WE BOTH FALL IN THE "FIVE BLACK CATEGORIES" NOW.
YOU KNOW WHAT? TO FIND YOUR FATHER AND MY PARENTS, LET'S DO WHAT WE DID AS KIDS: I'LL WRITE AND YOU'LL DRAW...
投机倒把
打击投机倒把 DA JI TOU JI DÀO BA: "LET US FIGHT AGAINST SPECULATION!"

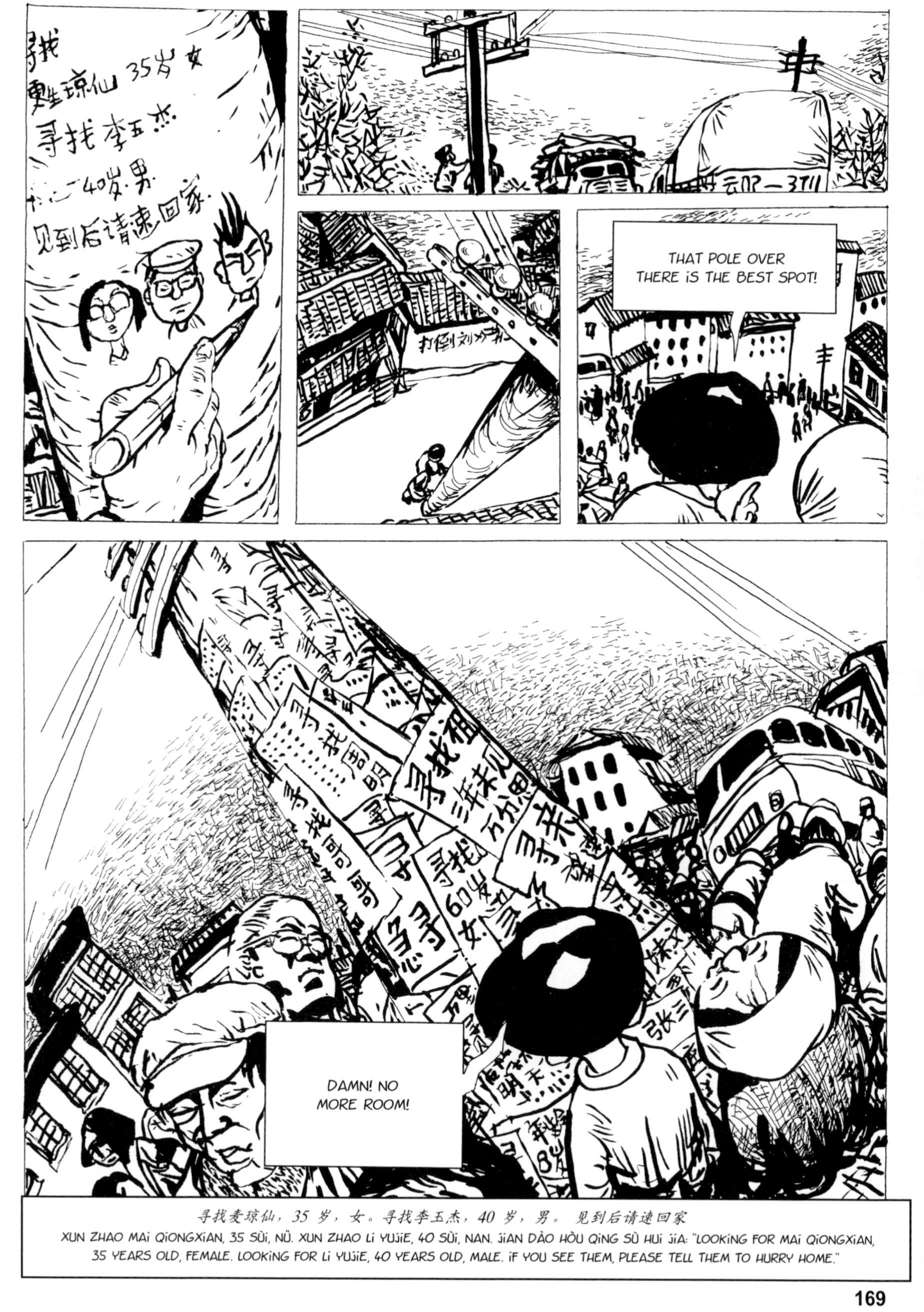
寻找李玉杰
见到后请速回家
THAT POLE OVER THERE iS THE BEST SPOT!
DAMN! NO MORE ROOM!

寻找麦琼仙，35 岁，女。寻找李玉杰，40 岁，男。 见到后请速回家

XUN ZHAO MAi QiONGXiAN, 35 SÙi, NÜ. XUN ZHAO Li YUJiE, 40 SÙi, NAN. JiAN DÀO HÒU QiNG SÙ HUi JiA: "LOOKiNG FOR MAi QiONGXiAN, 35 YEARS OLD, FEMALE. LOOKiNG FOR Li YUJiE, 40 YEARS OLD, MALE. iF YOU SEE THEM, PLEASE TELL THEM TO HURRY HOME."

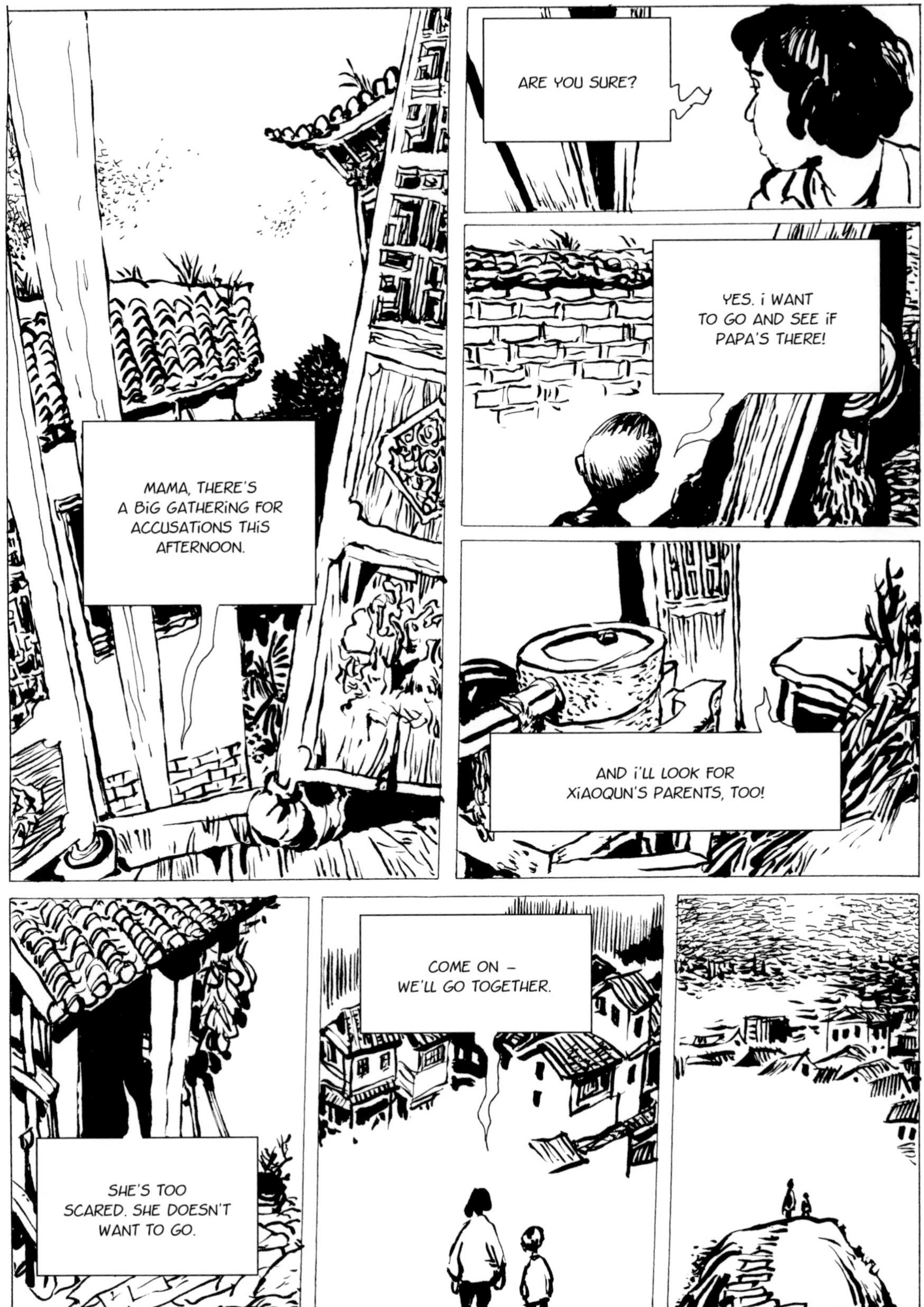
MAMA, THERE'S A BiG GATHERiNG FOR ACCUSATiONS THiS AFTERNOON.
ARE YOU SURE?
YES. i WANT TO GO AND SEE iF PAPA'S THERE!
AND i'LL LOOK FOR XiAOQUN'S PARENTS, TOO!
SHE'S TOO SCARED. SHE DOESN'T WANT TO GO.
COME ON – WE'LL GO TOGETHER.

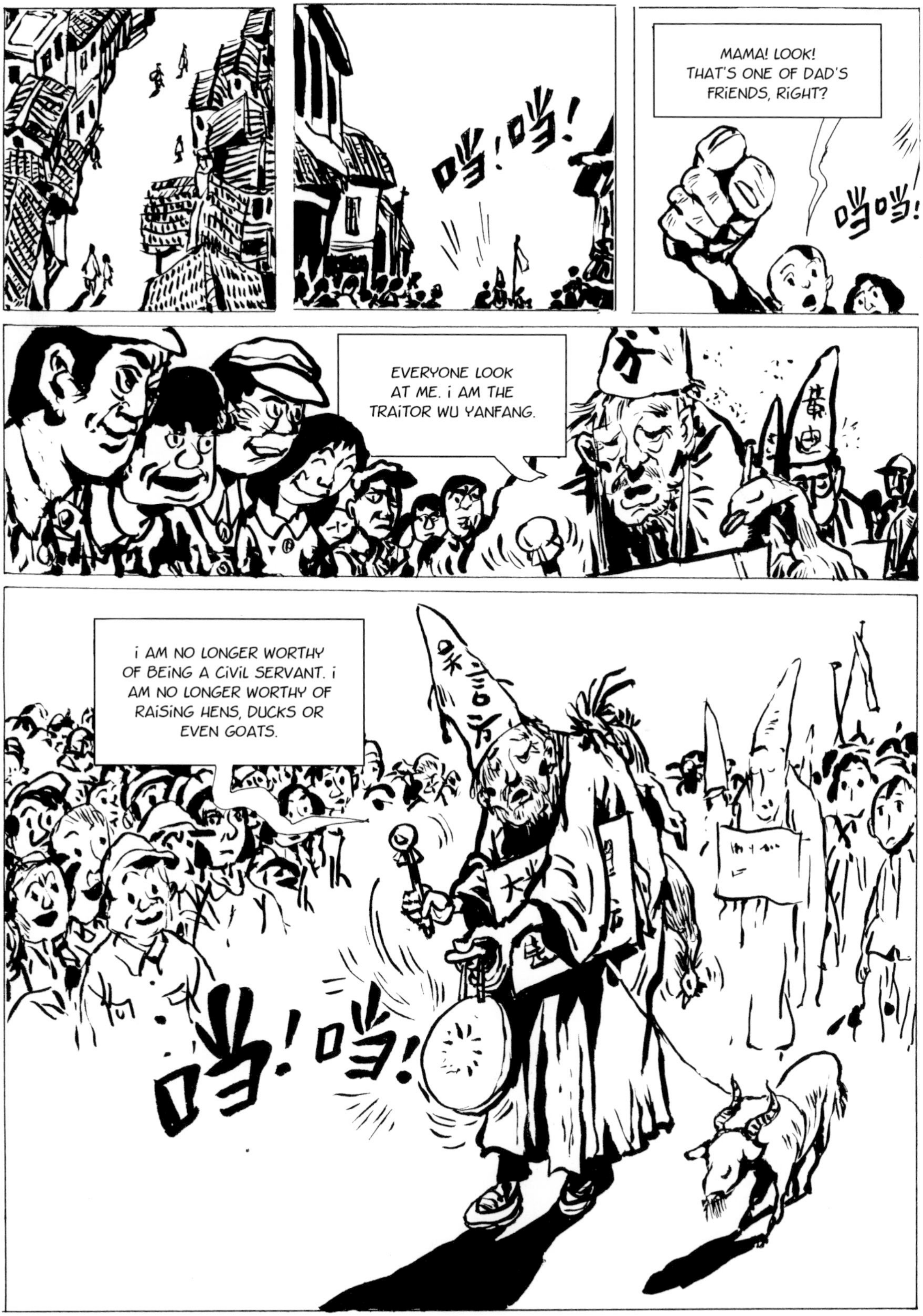
MAMA! LOOK! THAT'S ONE OF DAD'S FRIENDS, RIGHT?
EVERYONE LOOK AT ME. I AM THE TRAITOR WU YANFANG.
I AM NO LONGER WORTHY OF BEING A CIVIL SERVANT. I AM NO LONGER WORTHY OF RAISING HENS, DUCKS OR EVEN GOATS.

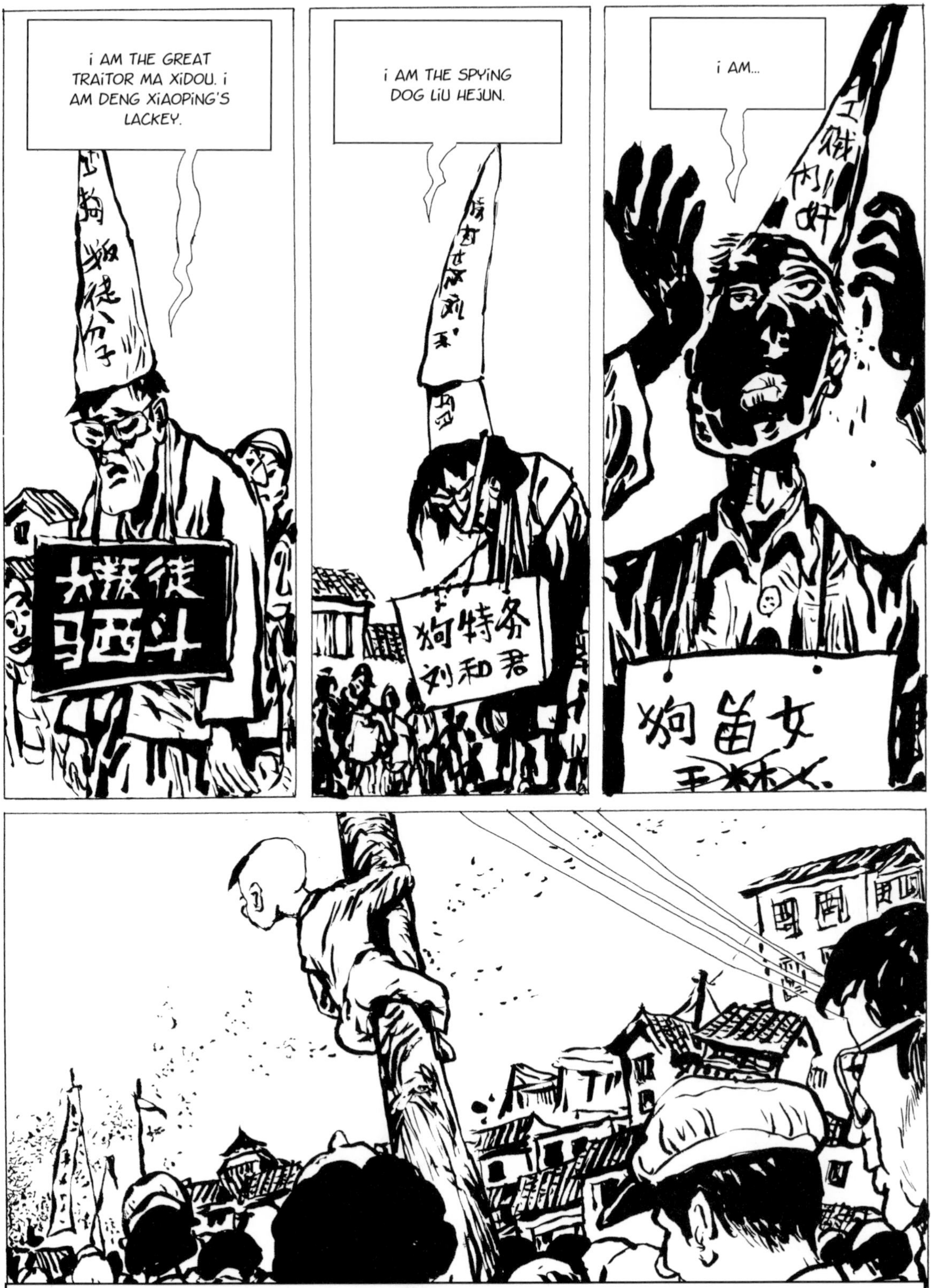

i AM THE GREAT TRAiTOR MA XiDOU. i AM DENG XiAOPiNG'S LACKEY.
i AM THE SPYiNG DOG LiU HEJUN.
狗特务
刘和君
i AM...

大叛徒 马西斗 DÀ PÀN TU MA XiDOU: THE GREAT TRAiTOR MA XiDOU. 狗特务刘和君 GOU TÈ WÙ LiU HEJUN: SPYiNG DOG LiU HEJUN.
狗男女 王林义 GOU NAN NÜ WANG LiNYi: THE MAD DOG WANG LiNYi.

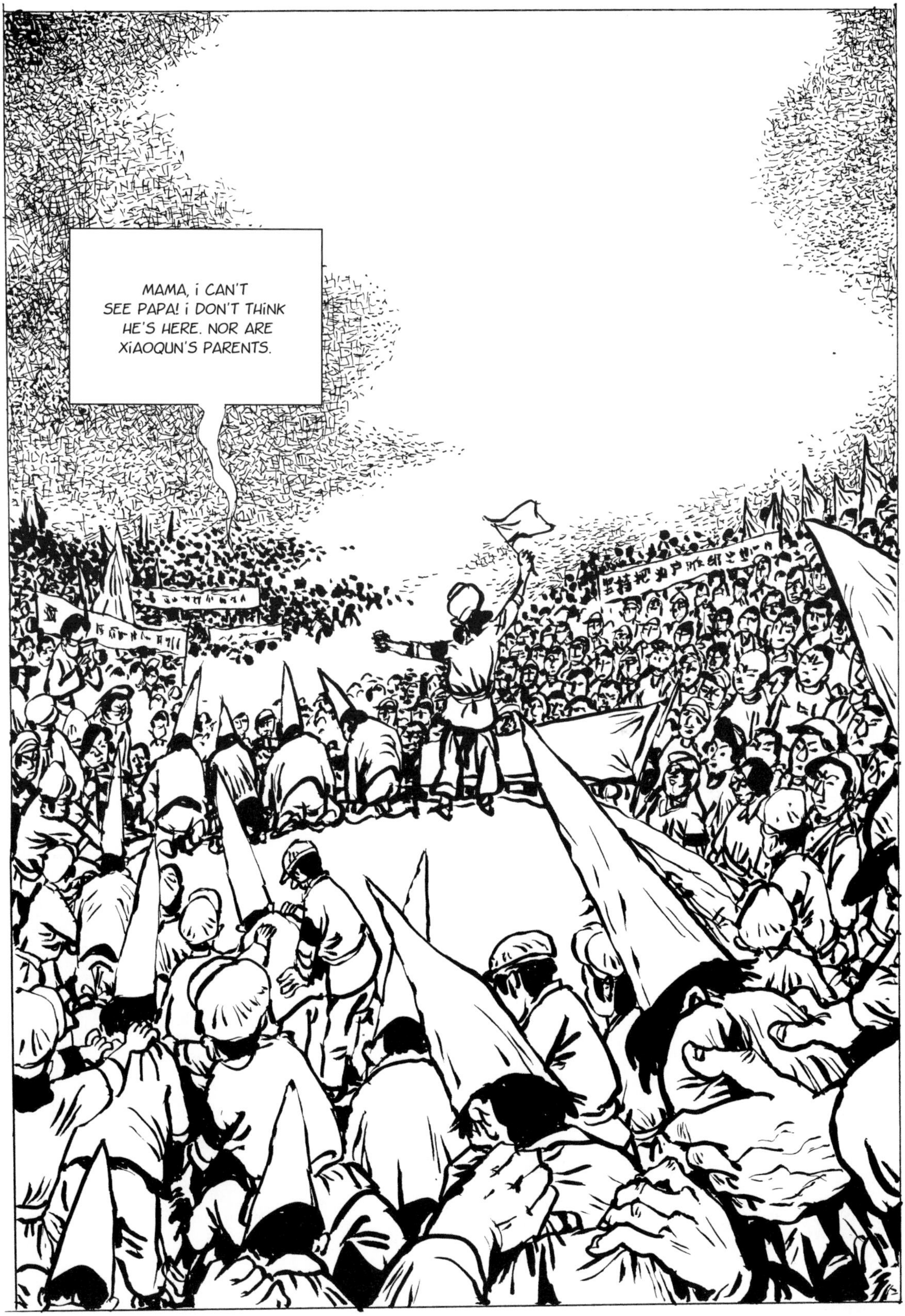
MAMA, i CAN'T SEE PAPA! i DON'T THiNK HE'S HERE. NOR ARE XiAOQUN'S PARENTS.

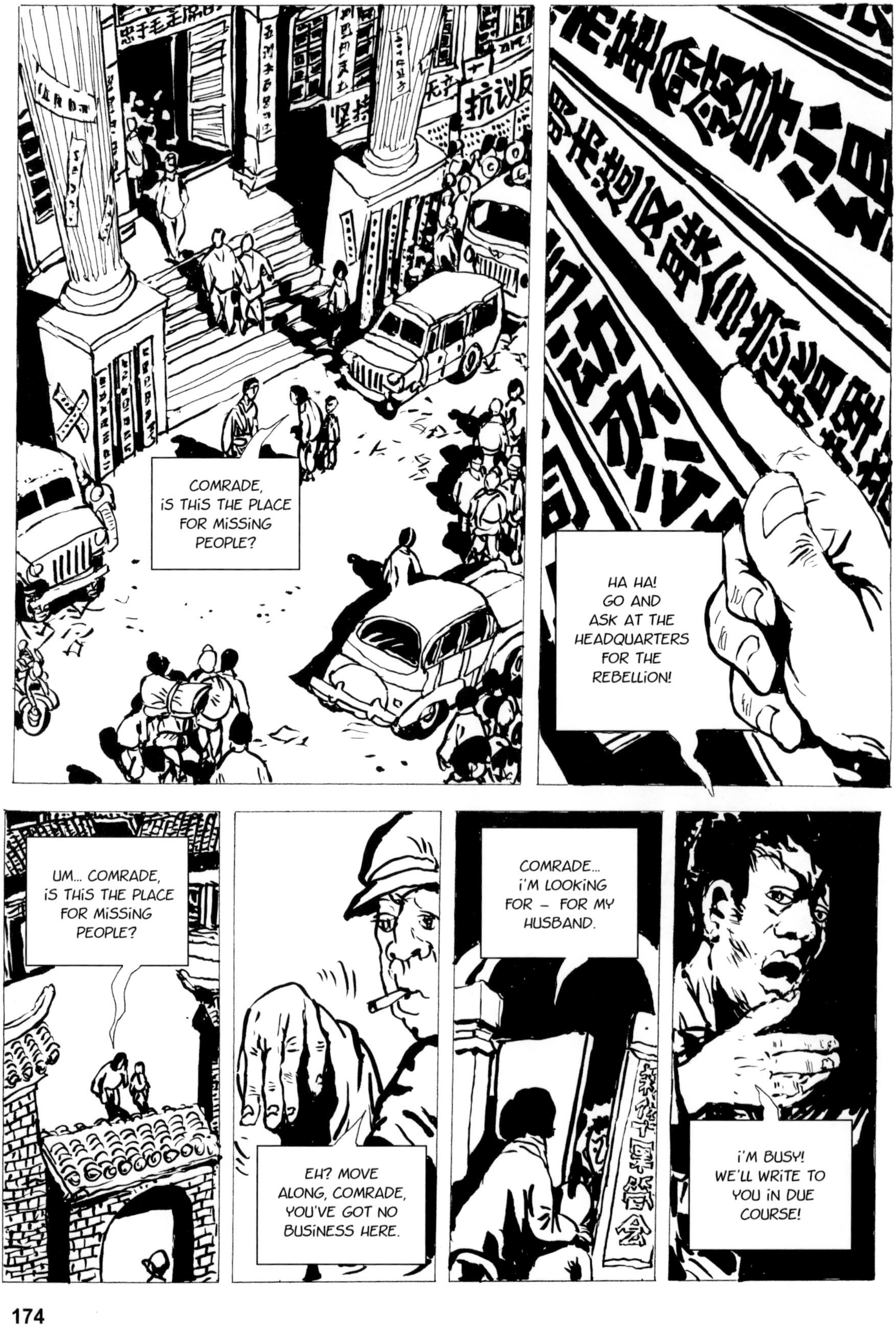
COMRADE, IS THIS THE PLACE FOR MISSING PEOPLE?
HA HA! GO AND ASK AT THE HEADQUARTERS FOR THE REBELLION!
UM... COMRADE, IS THIS THE PLACE FOR MISSING PEOPLE?
EH? MOVE ALONG, COMRADE, YOU'VE GOT NO BUSINESS HERE.
COMRADE... I'M LOOKING FOR – FOR MY HUSBAND.
I'M BUSY! WE'LL WRITE TO YOU IN DUE COURSE!

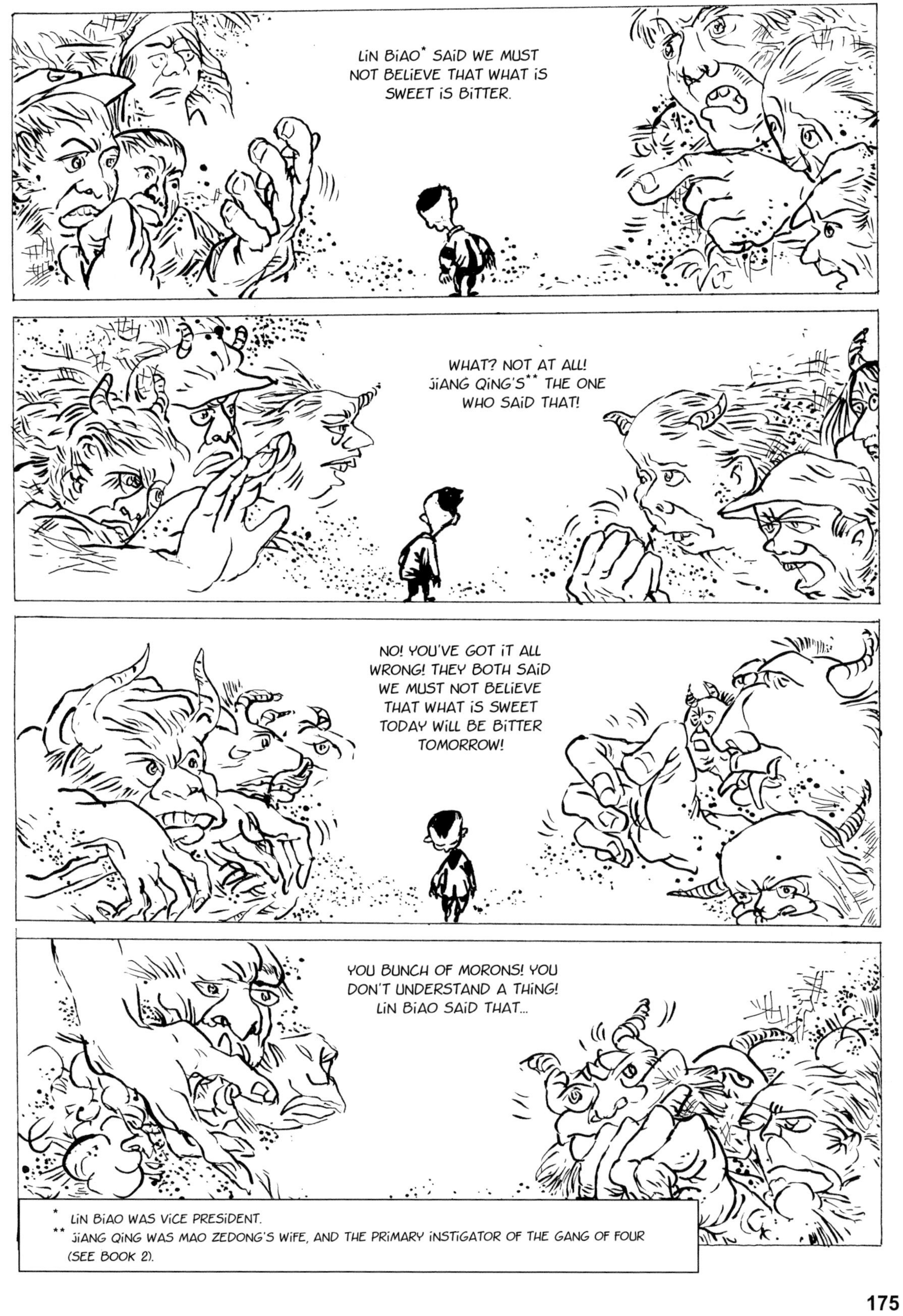
LIN BIAO* SAID WE MUST NOT BELIEVE THAT WHAT IS SWEET IS BITTER.
WHAT? NOT AT ALL! JIANG QING'S** THE ONE WHO SAID THAT!
NO! YOU'VE GOT IT ALL WRONG! THEY BOTH SAID WE MUST NOT BELIEVE THAT WHAT IS SWEET TODAY WILL BE BITTER TOMORROW!
YOU BUNCH OF MORONS! YOU DON'T UNDERSTAND A THING! LIN BIAO SAID THAT...

* LIN BIAO WAS VICE PRESIDENT.

** JIANG QING WAS MAO ZEDONG'S WIFE, AND THE PRIMARY INSTIGATOR OF THE GANG OF FOUR (SEE BOOK 2).

LIKE MANY OTHERS, I NO LONGER UNDERSTOOD THE TURN THAT EVENTS HAD TAKEN. NO ONE AGREED WITH ANYONE ELSE. EVERYONE WAS READY TO MURDER HIS NEIGHBOUR FOR AN ENIGMATIC PHRASE UTTERED THOUSANDS OF MILES AWAY, BY PEOPLE I DIDN'T KNOW, WHOM CHAIRMAN MAO HAD NOT MANAGED TO SILENCE. FISTS CLENCHED AT THE READY HAD GIVEN WAY TO MEAT CLEAVERS, WHICH IN TURN MADE WAY FOR GUNS AND RIFLES. ANARCHY BECAME CIVIL WAR. I SAW MY FIRST DEAD BODIES, MY FIRST DISEMBOWELLED CORPSES, THE GUTS IN OPEN VIEW...

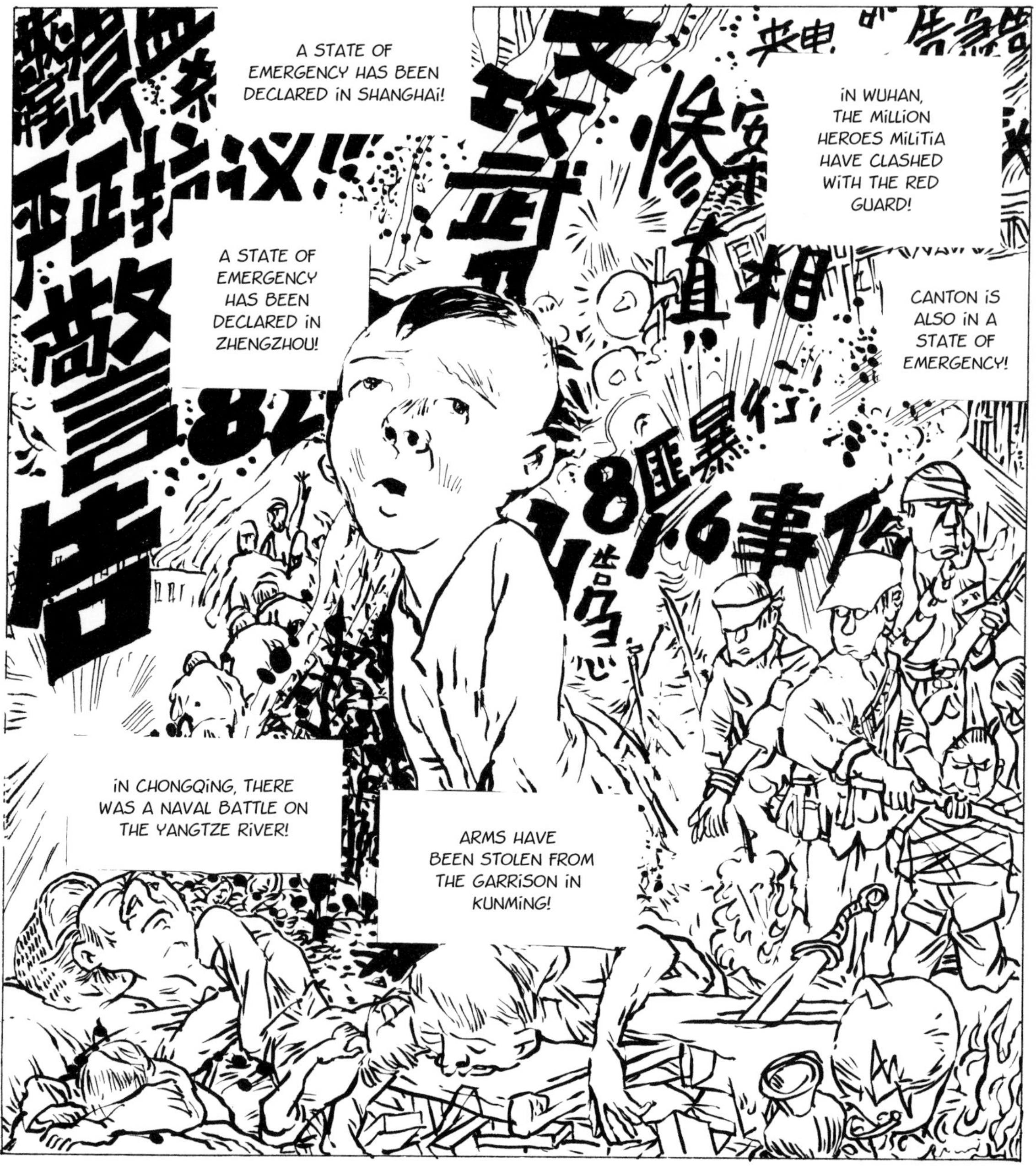

A STATE OF EMERGENCY HAS BEEN DECLARED IN SHANGHAI!
IN WUHAN, THE MILLION HEROES MILITIA HAVE CLASHED WITH THE RED GUARD!
A STATE OF EMERGENCY HAS BEEN DECLARED IN ZHENGZHOU!
CANTON IS ALSO IN A STATE OF EMERGENCY!
IN CHONGQING, THERE WAS A NAVAL BATTLE ON THE YANGTZE RIVER!
ARMS HAVE BEEN STOLEN FROM THE GARRISON IN KUNMING!

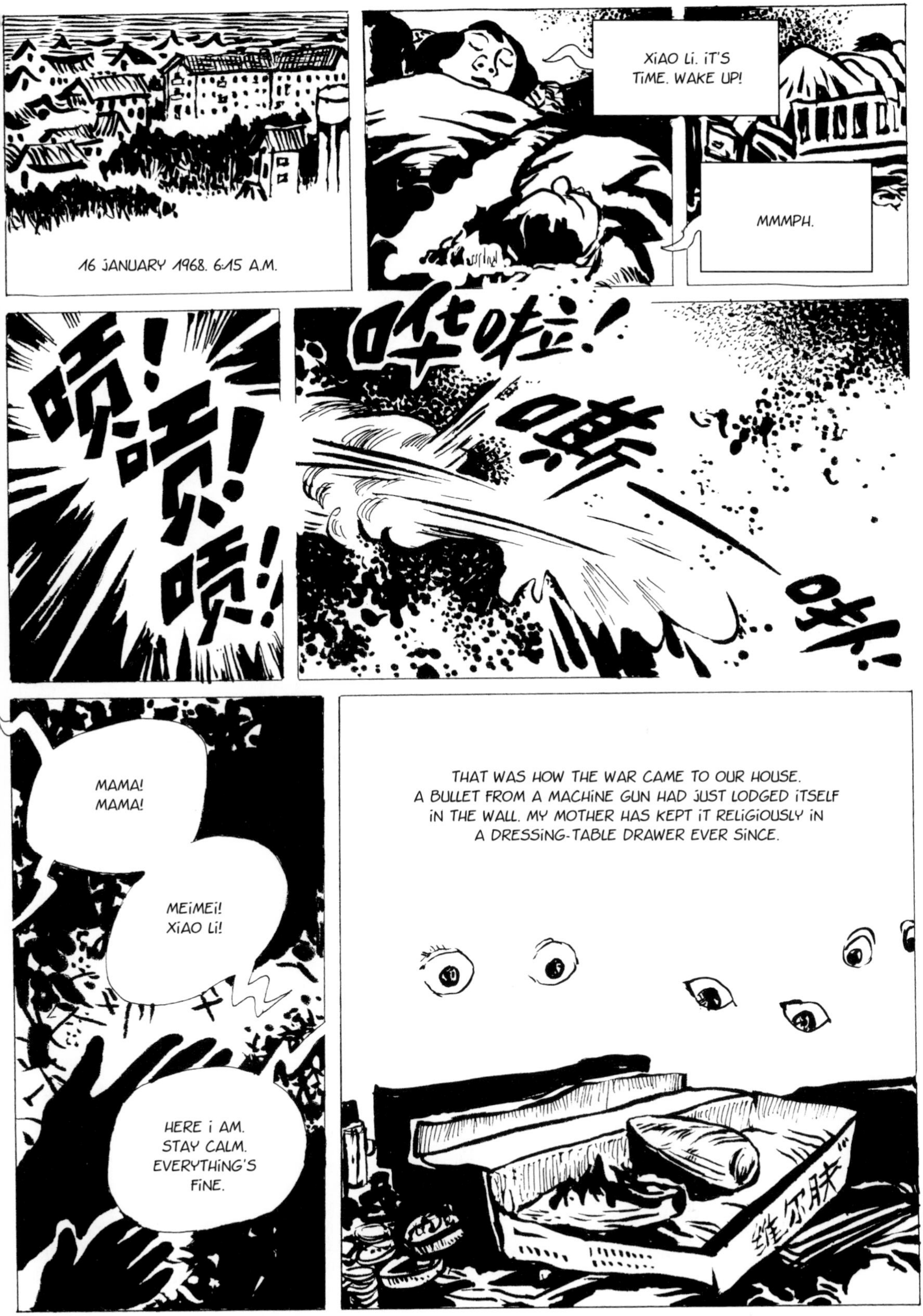
16 JANUARY 1968. 6:15 A.M.
XiAO Li. iT'S TiME. WAKE UP!
MMMPH.
喷！喷！喷！
哗啦！
MAMA! MAMA!
MEiMEi! XiAO Li!
HERE i AM. STAY CALM. EVERYTHiNG'S FiNE.
THAT WAS HOW THE WAR CAME TO OUR HOUSE. A BULLET FROM A MACHiNE GUN HAD JUST LODGED iTSELF iN THE WALL. MY MOTHER HAS KEPT iT RELiGiOUSLY iN A DRESSiNG-TABLE DRAWER EVER SiNCE.
维尔肤

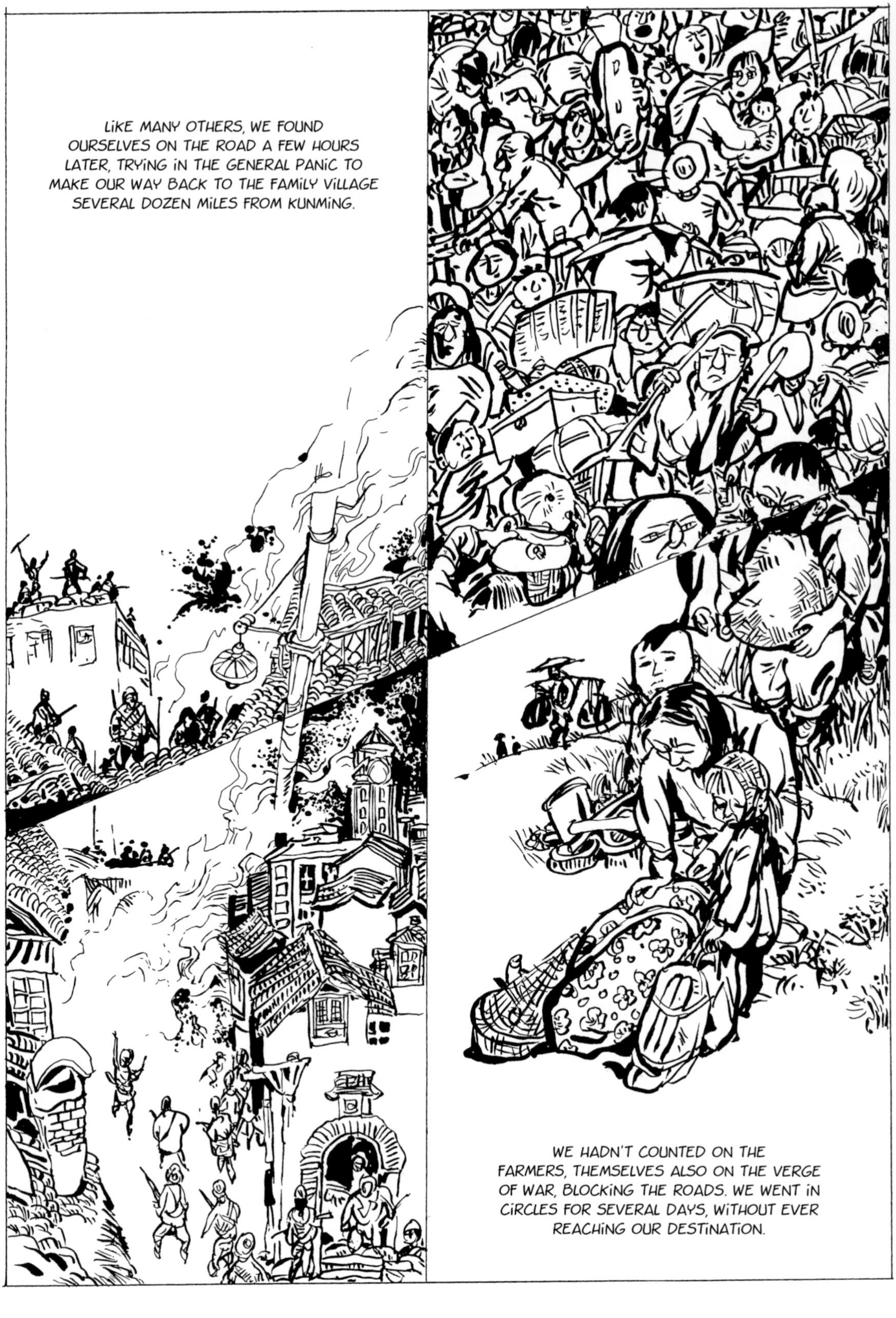
LIKE MANY OTHERS, WE FOUND OURSELVES ON THE ROAD A FEW HOURS LATER, TRYING IN THE GENERAL PANIC TO MAKE OUR WAY BACK TO THE FAMILY VILLAGE SEVERAL DOZEN MILES FROM KUNMING.
WE HADN'T COUNTED ON THE FARMERS, THEMSELVES ALSO ON THE VERGE OF WAR, BLOCKING THE ROADS. WE WENT IN CIRCLES FOR SEVERAL DAYS, WITHOUT EVER REACHING OUR DESTINATION.

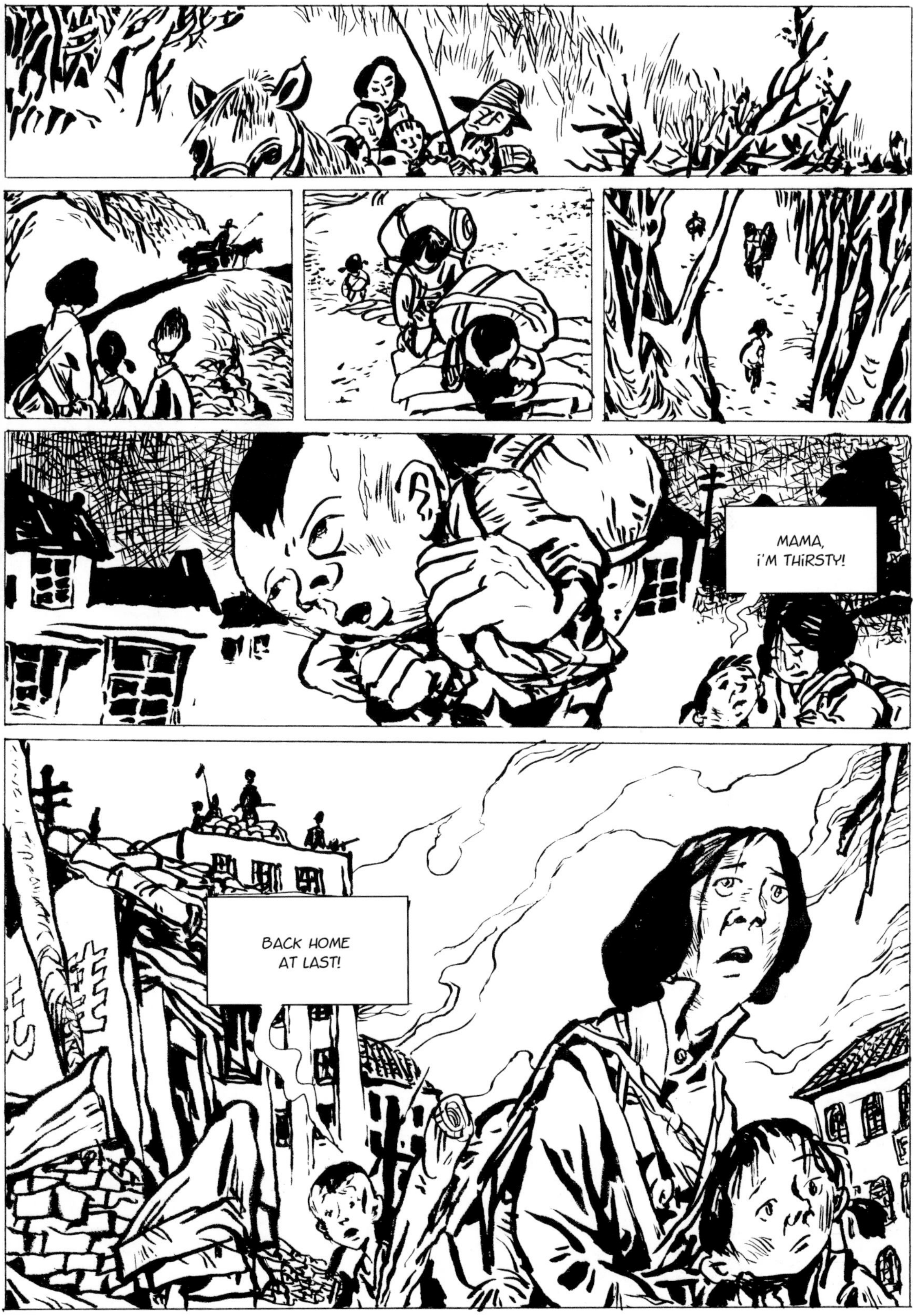
MAMA, I'M THIRSTY!
BACK HOME AT LAST!

XIAO LI'S FOREHEAD IS BURNING.

MAMA... MY HEAD... IT HURTS ALL OVER!

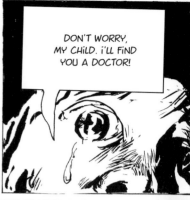

DON'T WORRY, MY CHILD. I'LL FIND YOU A DOCTOR!

THERE ARE NO MORE DOCTORS IN THE WHOLE TOWN! BUT MEIMEI HAS LUCKILY FOUND SOME HERBS.

WE MADE YOU SOME HERBAL TEA. HERE, XIAO LI! DRINK. DRINK!

DON'T CRY, MAMA!

FIGHT IT, MY SON. SOON YOU'LL FEEL BETTER, YOU'LL SEE. DON'T LEAVE US. YOU TWO ARE ALL I HAVE LEFT.

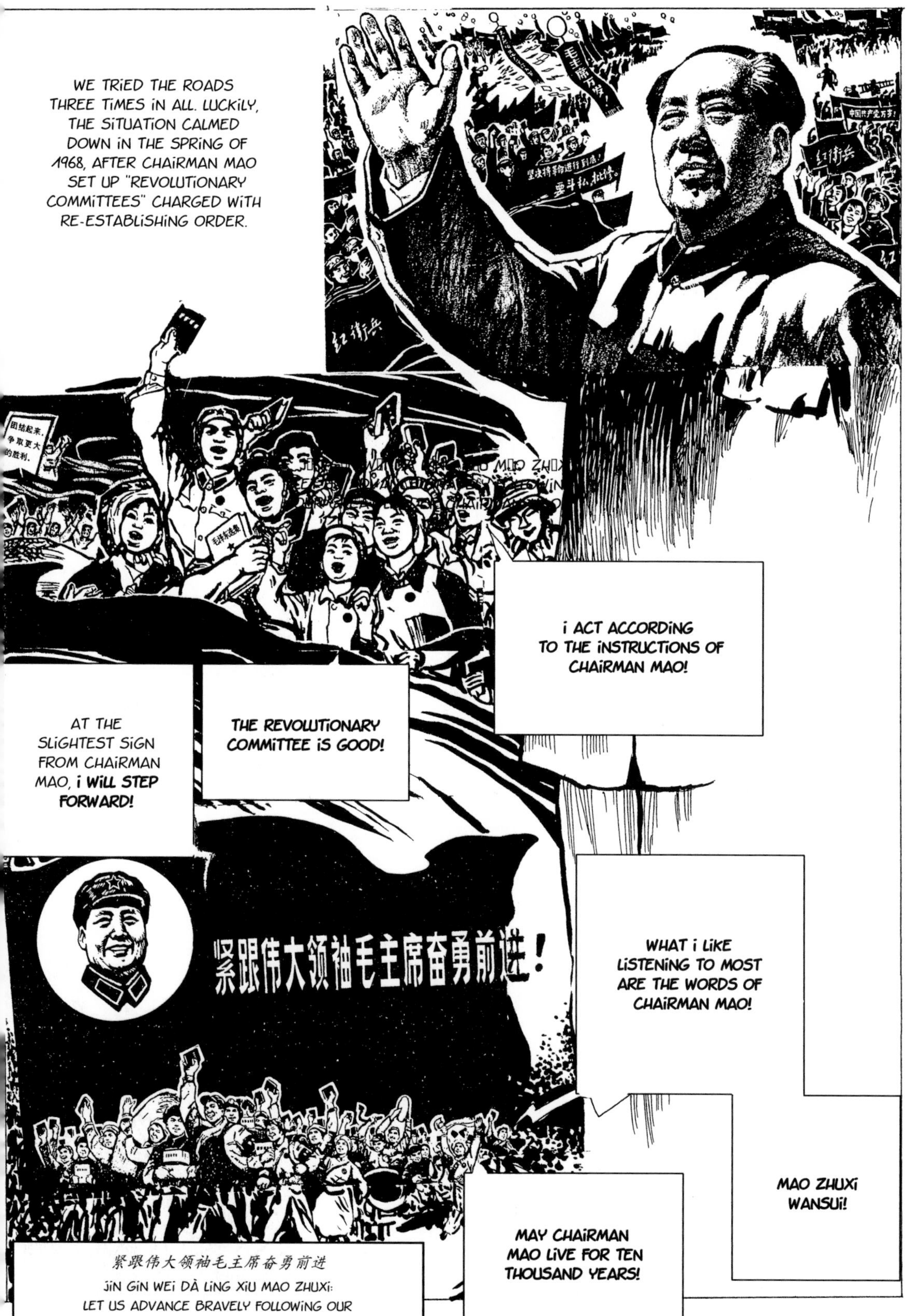
WE TRIED THE ROADS THREE TIMES IN ALL. LUCKILY, THE SITUATION CALMED DOWN IN THE SPRING OF 1968, AFTER CHAIRMAN MAO SET UP "REVOLUTIONARY COMMITTEES" CHARGED WITH RE-ESTABLISHING ORDER.
毛主席万岁
中国共产党万岁!
红卫兵
要斗私,批修。
团结起来,争取更大的胜利。
毛泽东选集
I ACT ACCORDING TO THE INSTRUCTIONS OF CHAIRMAN MAO!
AT THE SLIGHTEST SIGN FROM CHAIRMAN MAO, I WILL STEP FORWARD!
THE REVOLUTIONARY COMMITTEE IS GOOD!
紧跟伟大领袖毛主席奋勇前进!
WHAT I LIKE LISTENING TO MOST ARE THE WORDS OF CHAIRMAN MAO!
MAO ZHUXI WANSUI!
MAY CHAIRMAN MAO LIVE FOR TEN THOUSAND YEARS!
紧跟伟大领袖毛主席奋勇前进
JIN GIN WEI DÀ LING XIU MAO ZHUXI: LET US ADVANCE BRAVELY FOLLOWING OUR GREAT LEADER CHAIRMAN MAO!

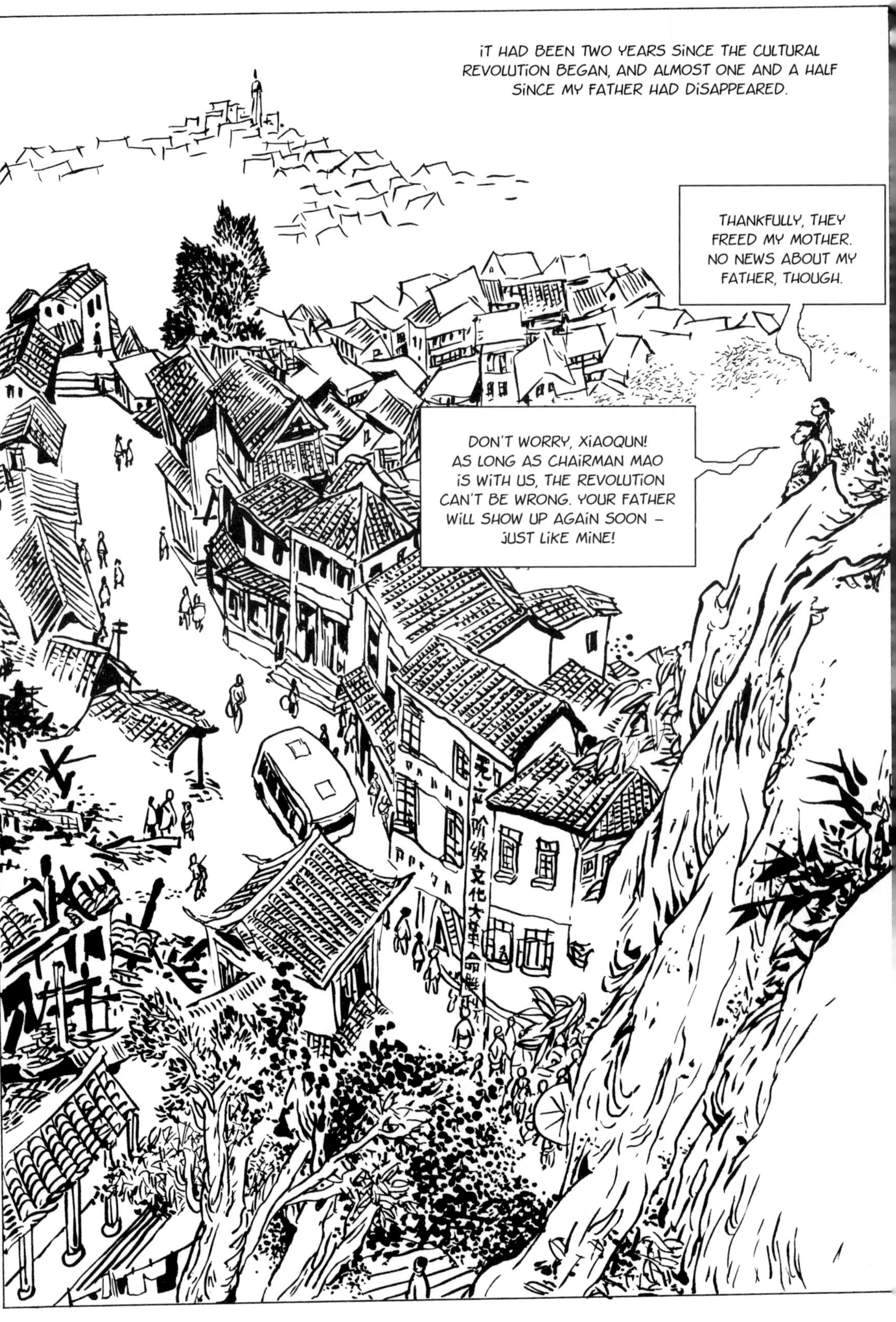
IT HAD BEEN TWO YEARS SINCE THE CULTURAL REVOLUTION BEGAN, AND ALMOST ONE AND A HALF SINCE MY FATHER HAD DISAPPEARED.
THANKFULLY, THEY FREED MY MOTHER. NO NEWS ABOUT MY FATHER, THOUGH.
DON'T WORRY, XIAOQUN! AS LONG AS CHAIRMAN MAO IS WITH US, THE REVOLUTION CAN'T BE WRONG. YOUR FATHER WILL SHOW UP AGAIN SOON – JUST LIKE MINE!

MAMA, WHAT DO YOU THINK HAPPENED TO PAPA?

PSST! COMRADE TAO?

I'M XIAO LUO. REMEMBER ME? SECRETARY LI'S ASSISTANT?

REMEMBER BACK IN '50, WHEN YOU MET YOUR HUSBAND?

LISTEN: YOUR HUSBAND'S ALIVE! HE'S IN A "SEVENTH-OF-MAY CADRE SCHOOL"* IN THE SOUTH PART OF THE PROVINCE.

GO TO THE XIBA MARKET ELEVEN DAYS FROM NOW, AT NOON. I'LL HAVE NEWS!

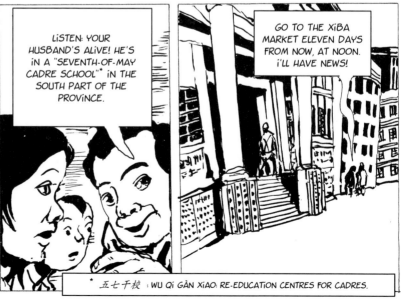

* 五七干校 : WU QI GÀN XIAO: RE-EDUCATION CENTRES FOR CADRES.

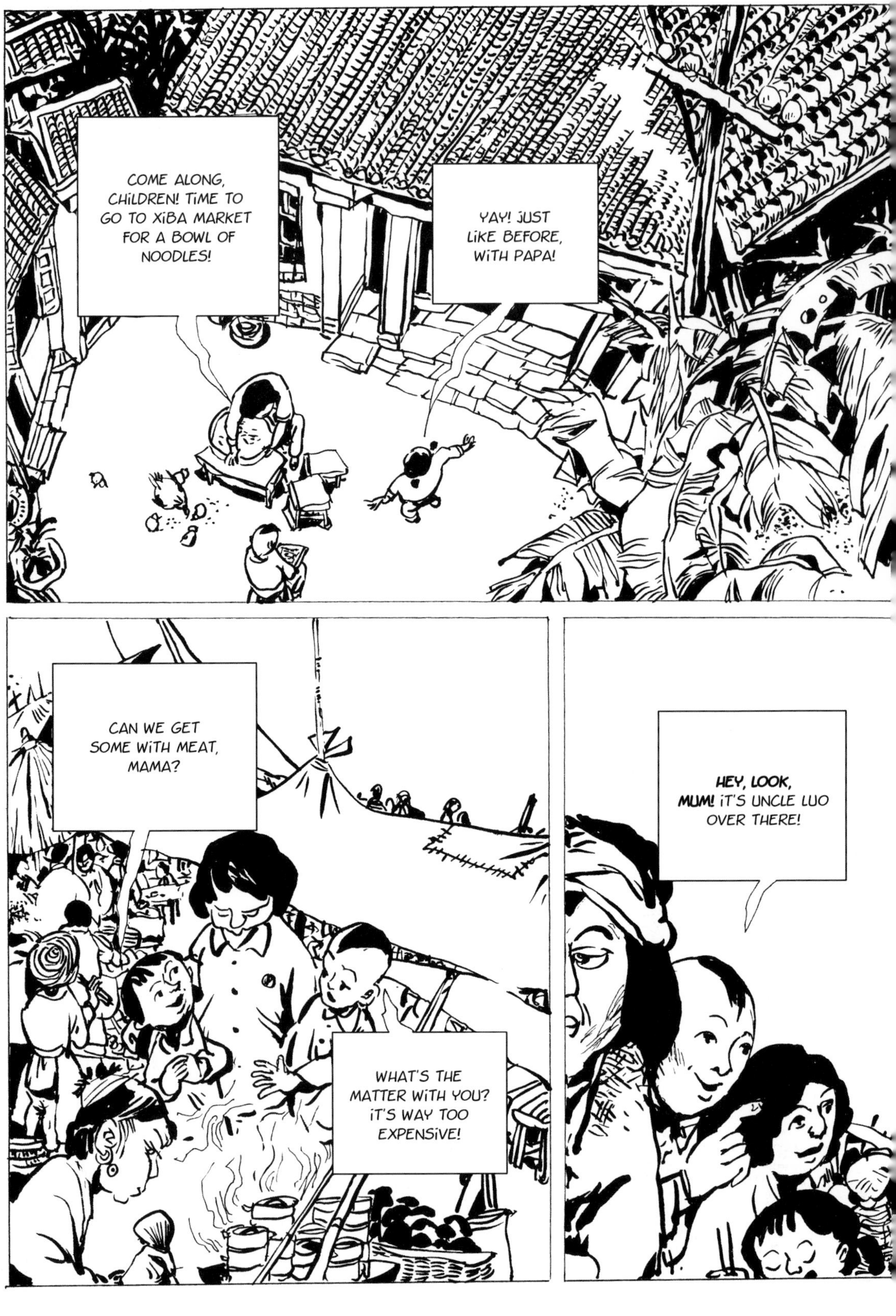
COME ALONG, CHILDREN! TIME TO GO TO XIBA MARKET FOR A BOWL OF NOODLES!
YAY! JUST LIKE BEFORE, WITH PAPA!
CAN WE GET SOME WITH MEAT, MAMA?
WHAT'S THE MATTER WITH YOU? IT'S WAY TOO EXPENSIVE!
HEY, LOOK, MUM! IT'S UNCLE LUO OVER THERE!

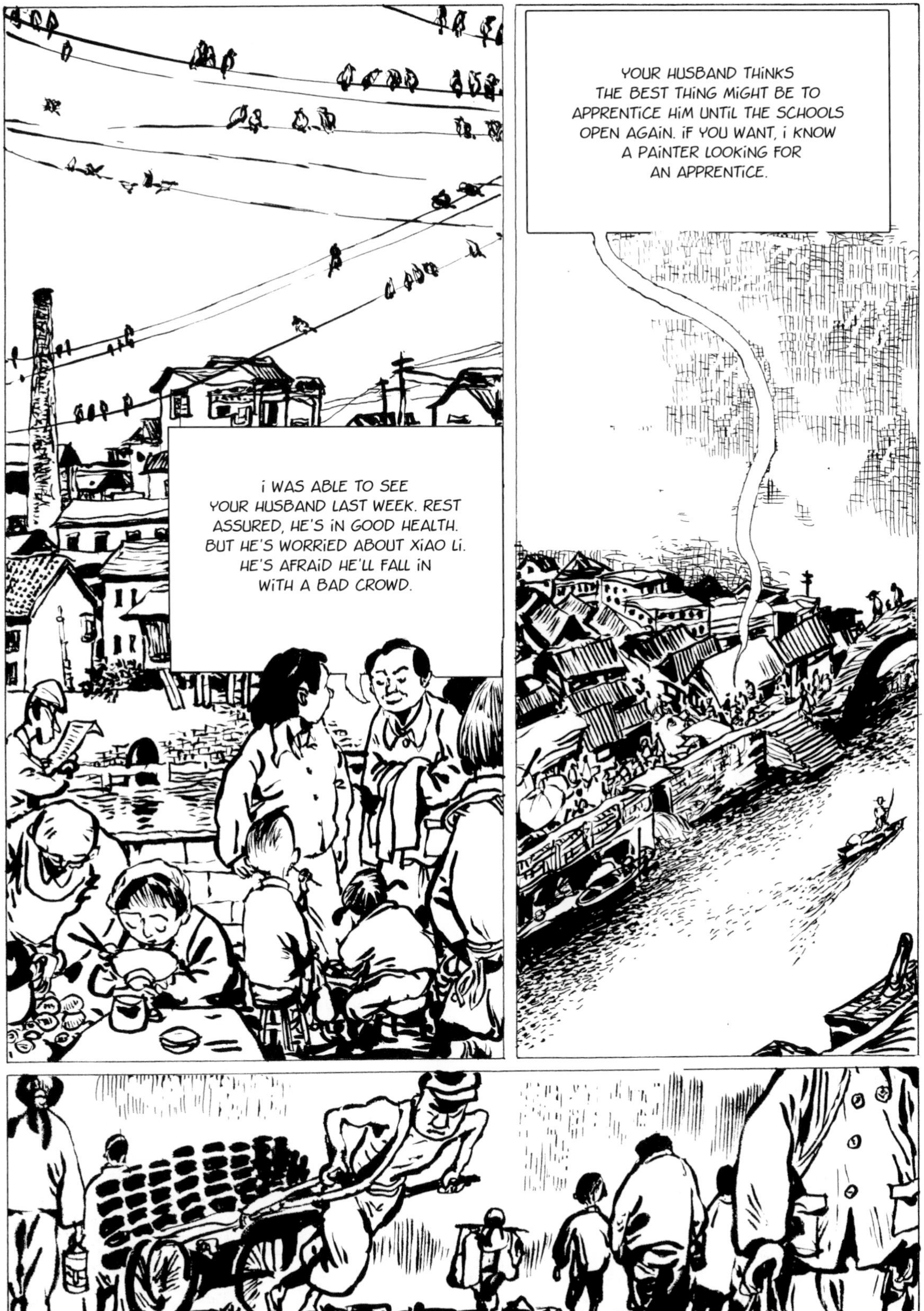
i WAS ABLE TO SEE YOUR HUSBAND LAST WEEK. REST ASSURED, HE'S iN GOOD HEALTH. BUT HE'S WORRiED ABOUT XiAO Li. HE'S AFRAiD HE'LL FALL iN WiTH A BAD CROWD.
YOUR HUSBAND THiNKS THE BEST THiNG MiGHT BE TO APPRENTiCE HiM UNTiL THE SCHOOLS OPEN AGAiN. iF YOU WANT, i KNOW A PAiNTER LOOKiNG FOR AN APPRENTiCE.

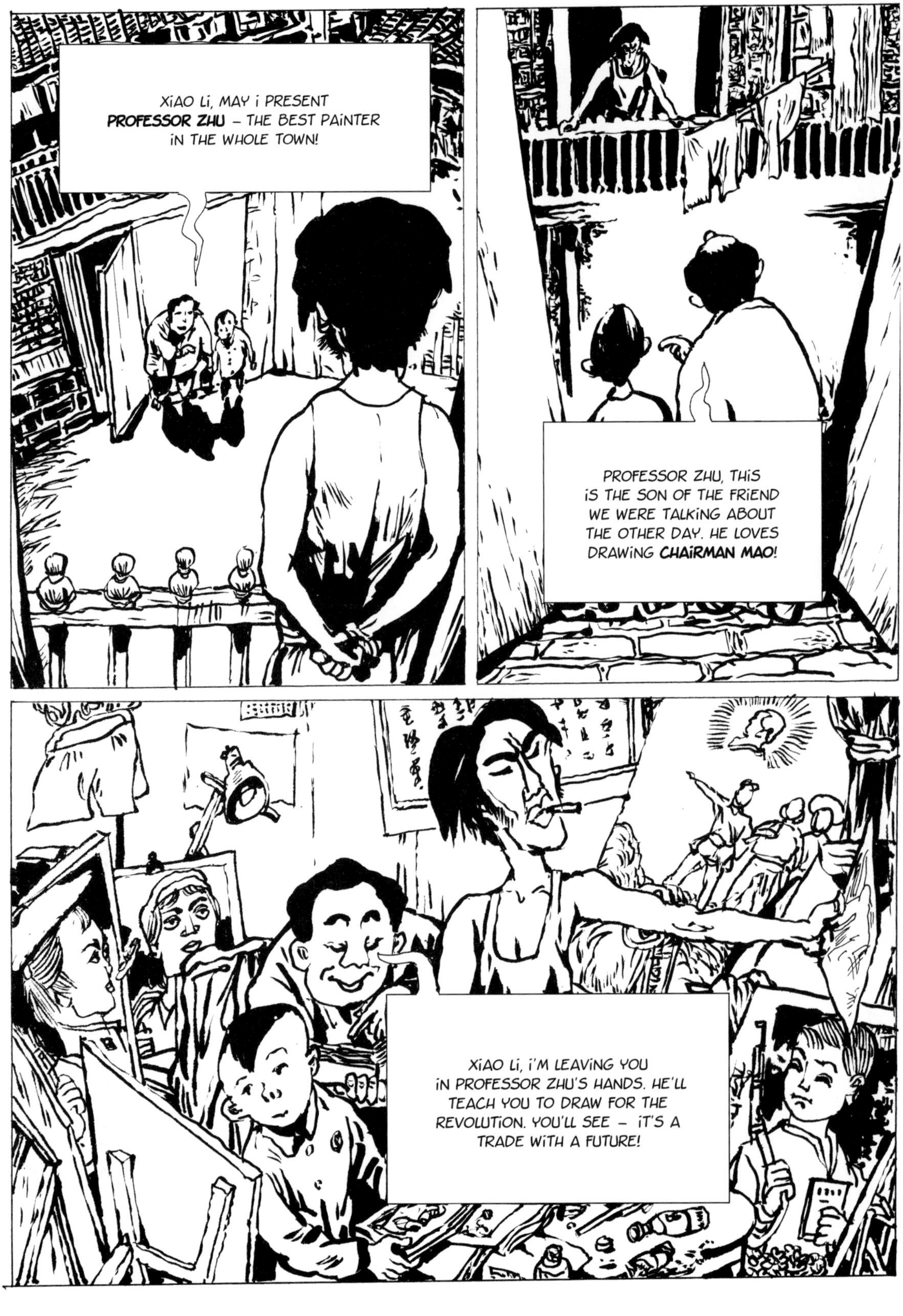
XIAO LI, MAY I PRESENT PROFESSOR ZHU – THE BEST PAINTER IN THE WHOLE TOWN!
PROFESSOR ZHU, THIS IS THE SON OF THE FRIEND WE WERE TALKING ABOUT THE OTHER DAY. HE LOVES DRAWING CHAIRMAN MAO!
XIAO LI, I'M LEAVING YOU IN PROFESSOR ZHU'S HANDS. HE'LL TEACH YOU TO DRAW FOR THE REVOLUTION. YOU'LL SEE – IT'S A TRADE WITH A FUTURE!

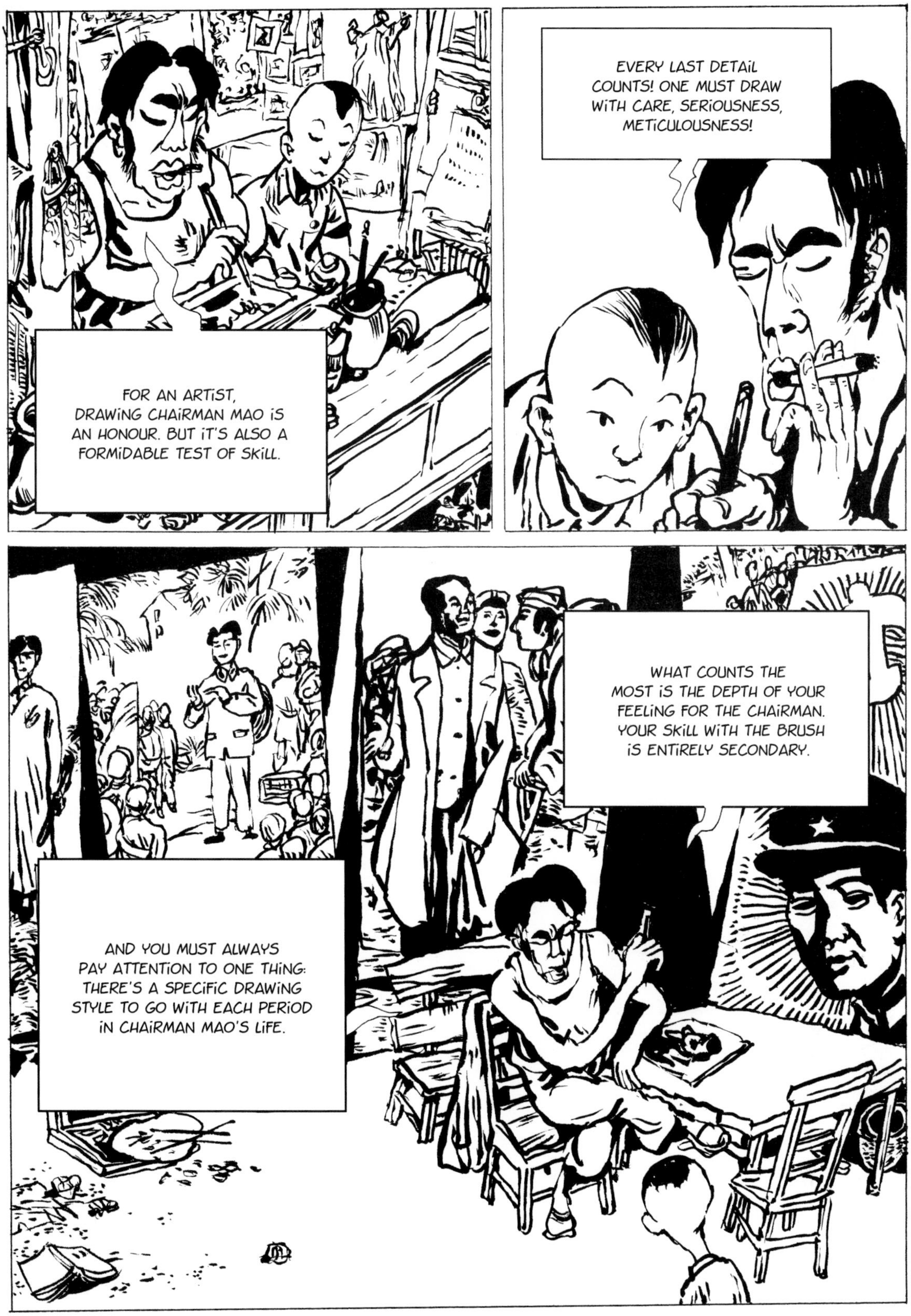
FOR AN ARTIST, DRAWING CHAIRMAN MAO IS AN HONOUR. BUT IT'S ALSO A FORMIDABLE TEST OF SKILL.
EVERY LAST DETAIL COUNTS! ONE MUST DRAW WITH CARE, SERIOUSNESS, METICULOUSNESS!
WHAT COUNTS THE MOST IS THE DEPTH OF YOUR FEELING FOR THE CHAIRMAN. YOUR SKILL WITH THE BRUSH IS ENTIRELY SECONDARY.
AND YOU MUST ALWAYS PAY ATTENTION TO ONE THING: THERE'S A SPECIFIC DRAWING STYLE TO GO WITH EACH PERIOD IN CHAIRMAN MAO'S LIFE.

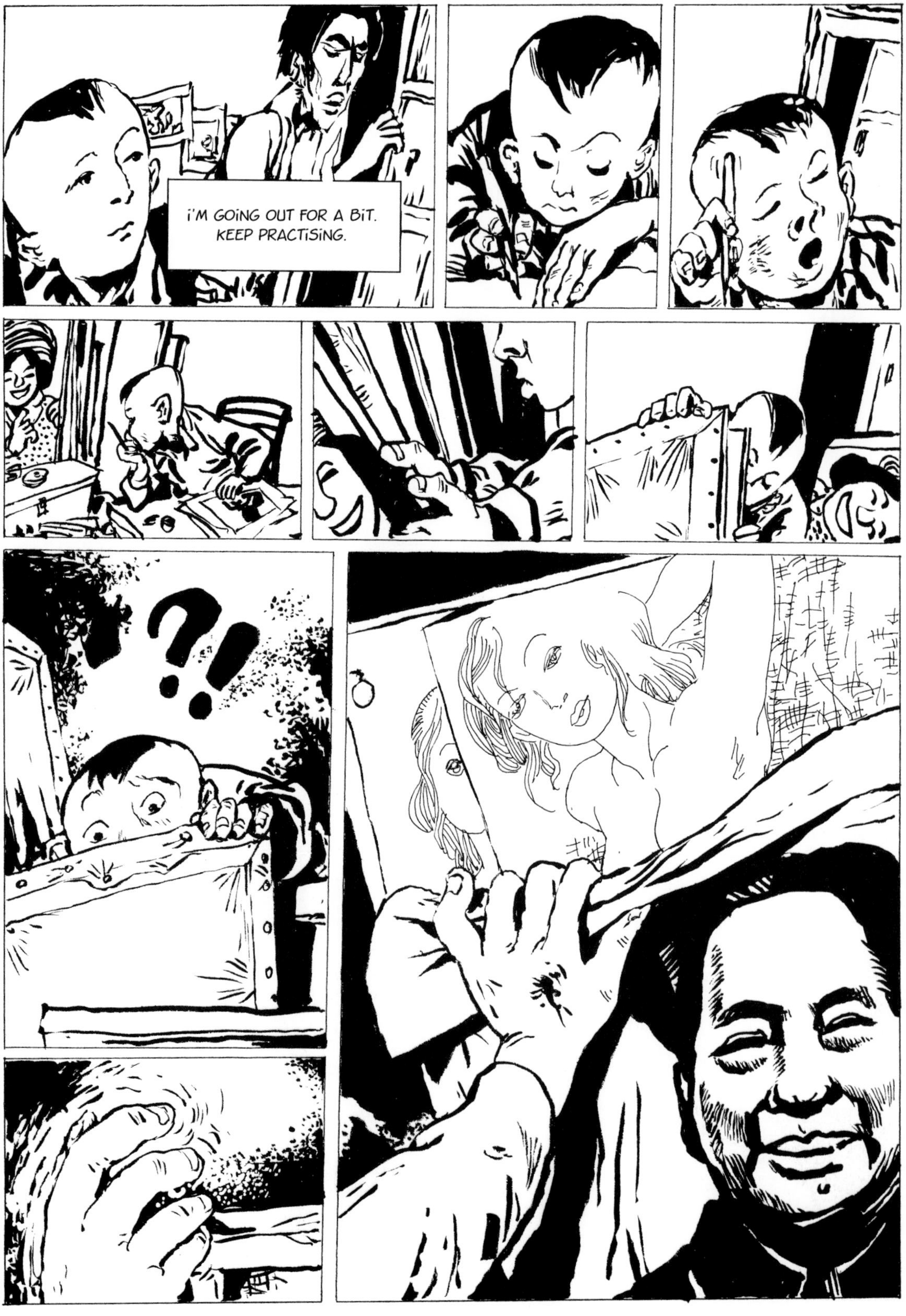
I'M GOING OUT FOR A BIT.
KEEP PRACTISING.
?!

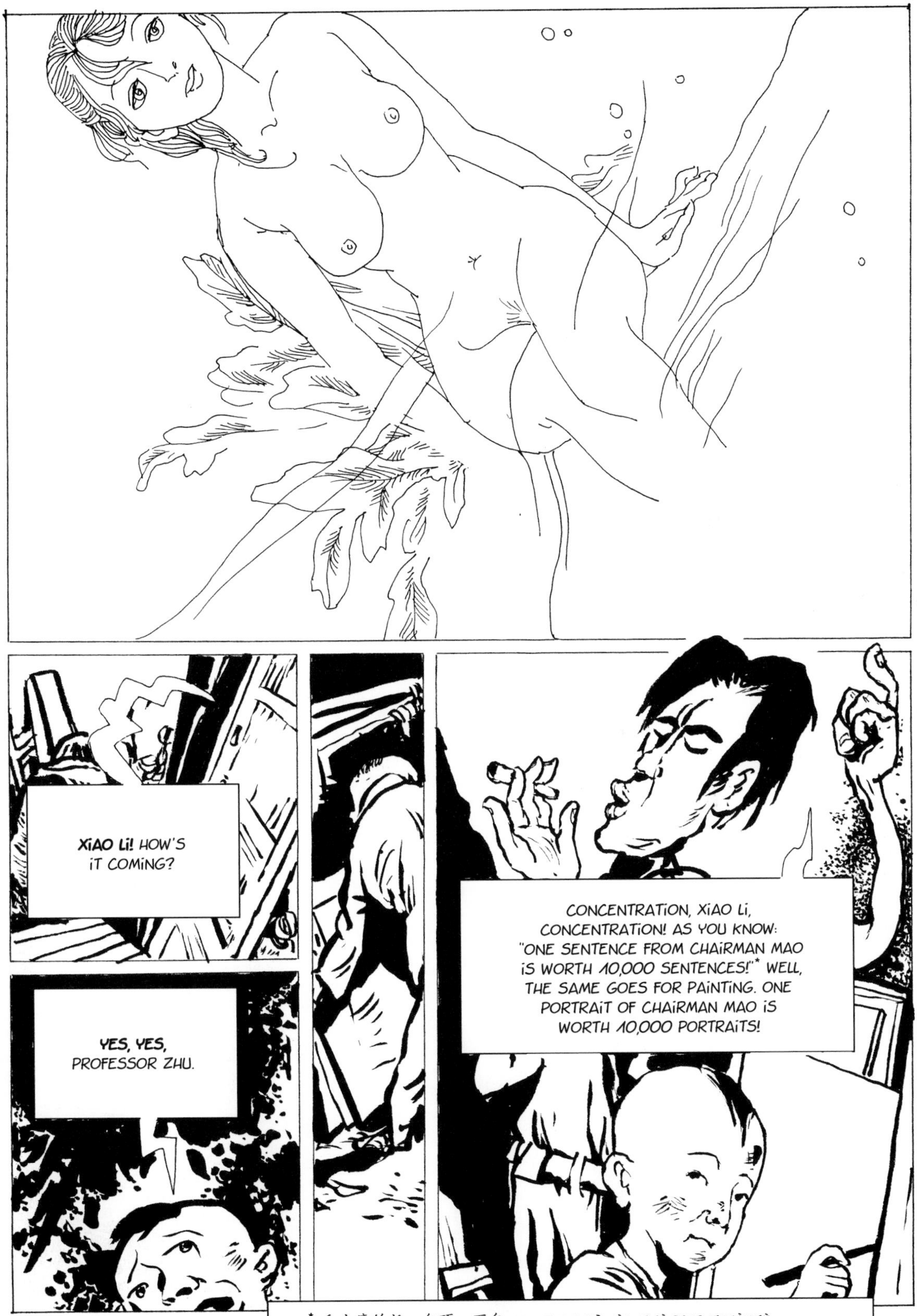
XiAO Li! HOW'S iT COMiNG?
YES, YES, PROFESSOR ZHU.
CONCENTRATiON, XiAO Li, CONCENTRATiON! AS YOU KNOW: "ONE SENTENCE FROM CHAiRMAN MAO iS WORTH 10,000 SENTENCES!"* WELL, THE SAME GOES FOR PAiNTiNG. ONE PORTRAiT OF CHAiRMAN MAO iS WORTH 10,000 PORTRAiTS!

* 毛主席的话一句顶一万句 MAO ZHUXi DÈ HÙA Yi JÙ DiNG Yi WÀN JÙ.

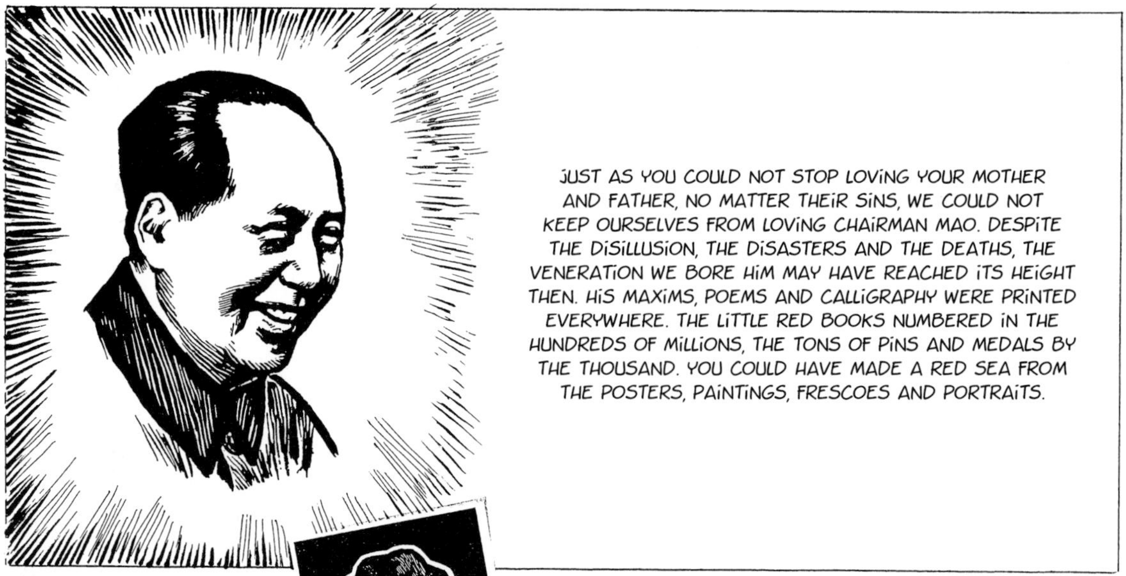
JUST AS YOU COULD NOT STOP LOVING YOUR MOTHER AND FATHER, NO MATTER THEIR SINS, WE COULD NOT KEEP OURSELVES FROM LOVING CHAIRMAN MAO. DESPITE THE DISILLUSION, THE DISASTERS AND THE DEATHS, THE VENERATION WE BORE HIM MAY HAVE REACHED ITS HEIGHT THEN. HIS MAXIMS, POEMS AND CALLIGRAPHY WERE PRINTED EVERYWHERE. THE LITTLE RED BOOKS NUMBERED IN THE HUNDREDS OF MILLIONS, THE TONS OF PINS AND MEDALS BY THE THOUSAND. YOU COULD HAVE MADE A RED SEA FROM THE POSTERS, PAINTINGS, FRESCOES AND PORTRAITS.

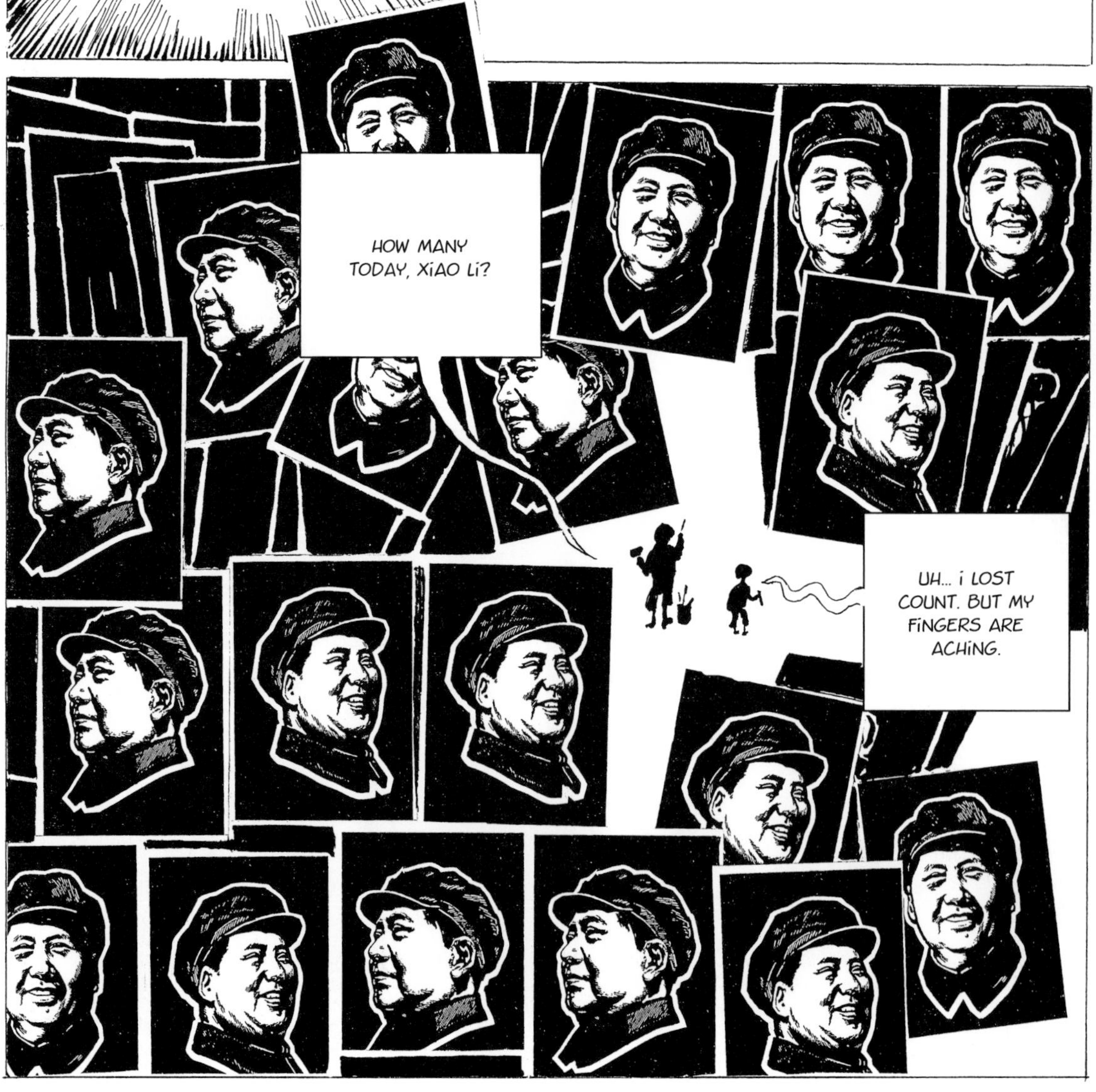
HOW MANY TODAY, XIAO LI?
UH... I LOST COUNT. BUT MY FINGERS ARE ACHING.

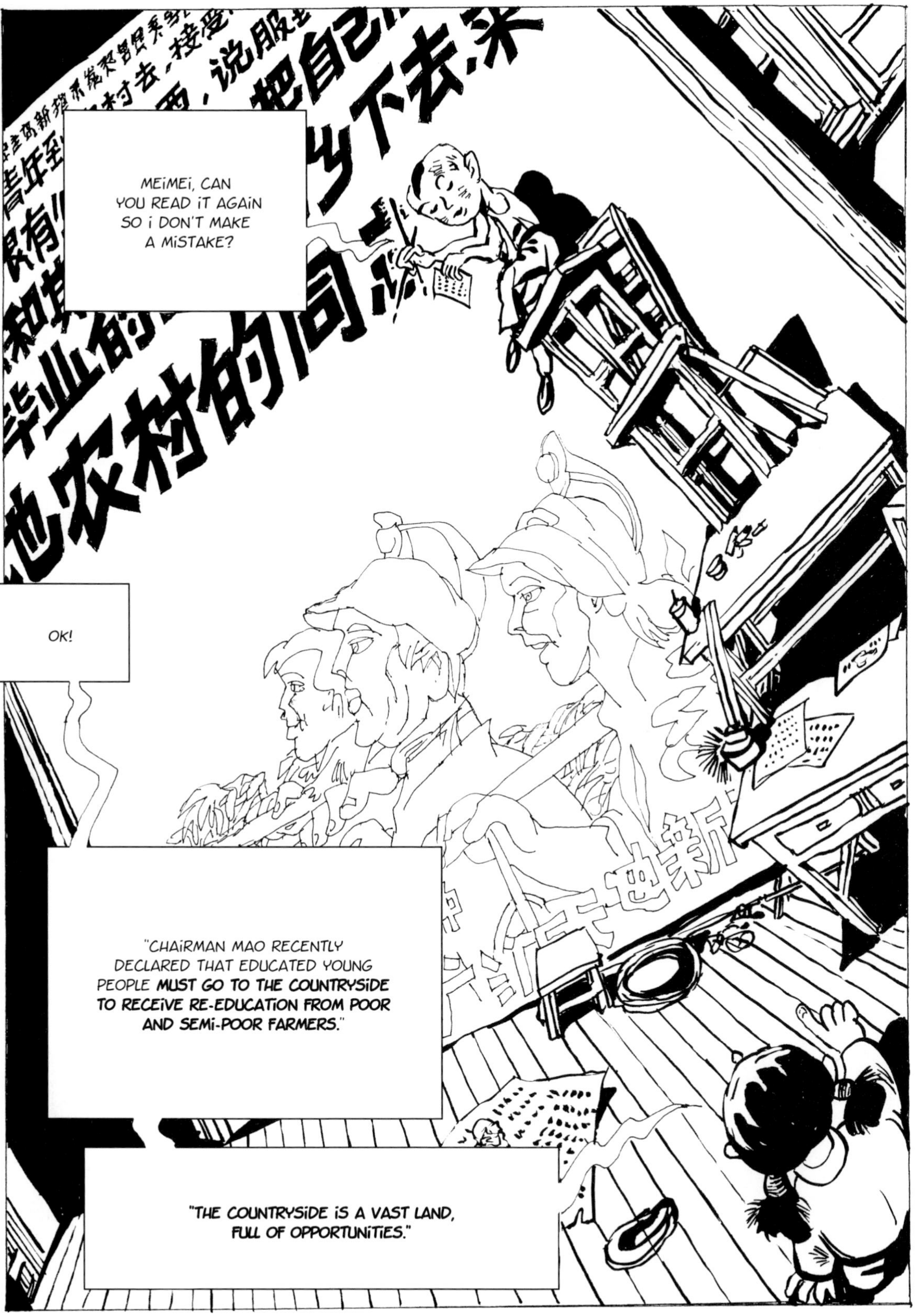
MEiMEi, CAN YOU READ iT AGAiN SO i DON'T MAKE A MiSTAKE?
OK!
"CHAiRMAN MAO RECENTLY DECLARED THAT EDUCATED YOUNG PEOPLE **MUST GO TO THE COUNTRYSiDE TO RECEiVE RE-EDUCATiON FROM POOR AND SEMi-POOR FARMERS.**"
"THE COUNTRYSiDE iS A VAST LAND, FULL OF OPPORTUNiTiES."

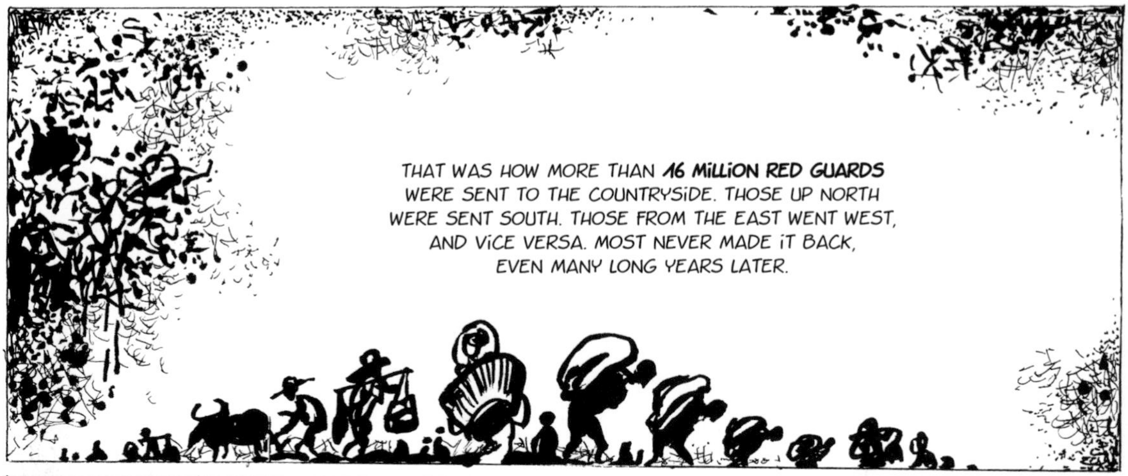
THAT WAS HOW MORE THAN **16 MILLION RED GUARDS** WERE SENT TO THE COUNTRYSIDE. THOSE UP NORTH WERE SENT SOUTH. THOSE FROM THE EAST WENT WEST, AND VICE VERSA. MOST NEVER MADE IT BACK, EVEN MANY LONG YEARS LATER.

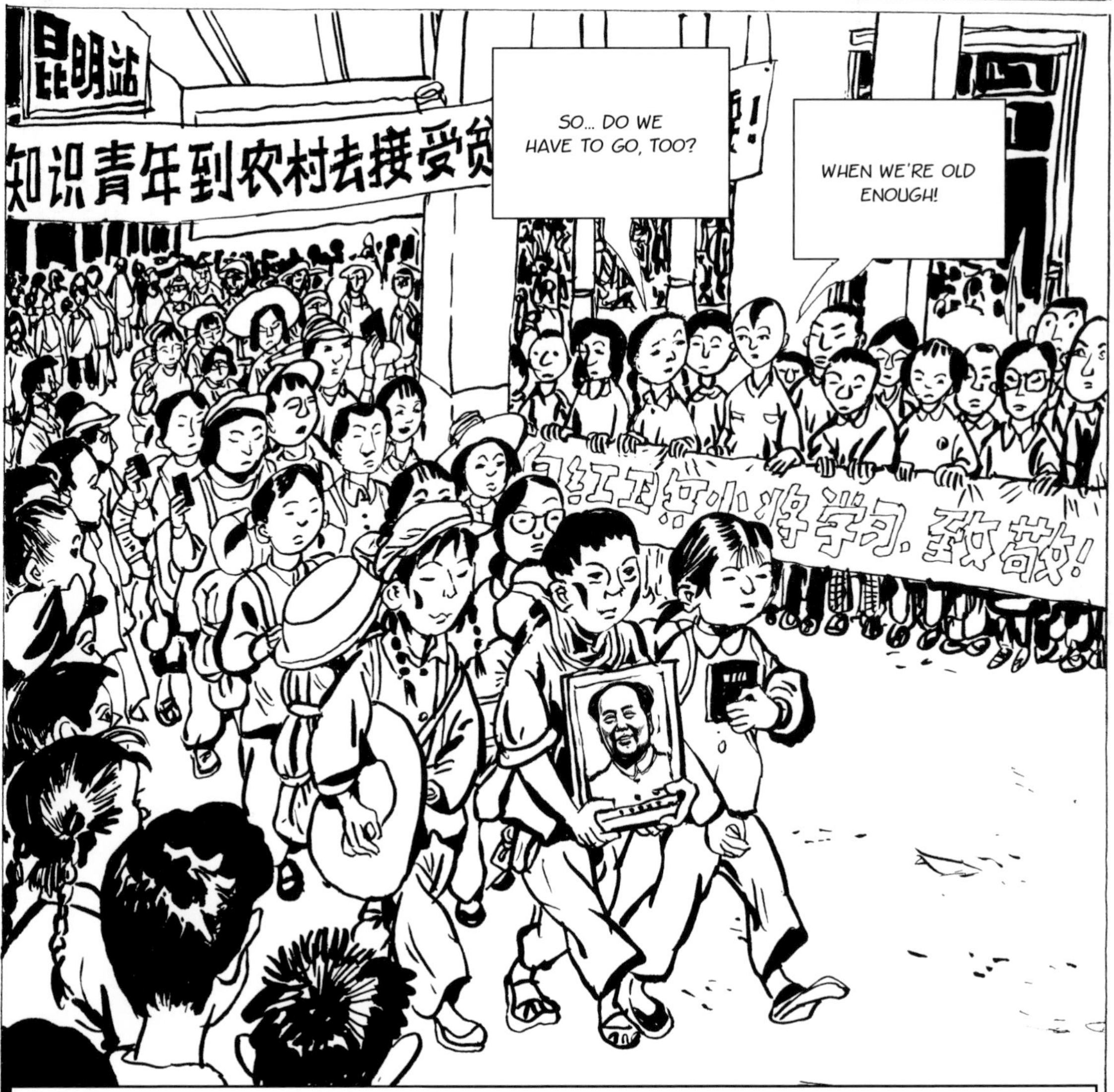
昆明站
知识青年到农村去接受
SO... DO WE HAVE TO GO, TOO?
WHEN WE'RE OLD ENOUGH!
红卫兵小将学习，致敬!

向红卫兵小将学习。致敬 XIANG HONG WEI BING XIAO JIANG XIE XU ZHI JING: "LET US STUDY THE LITTLE GENERAL OF THE RED GUARD. RESPECT!"

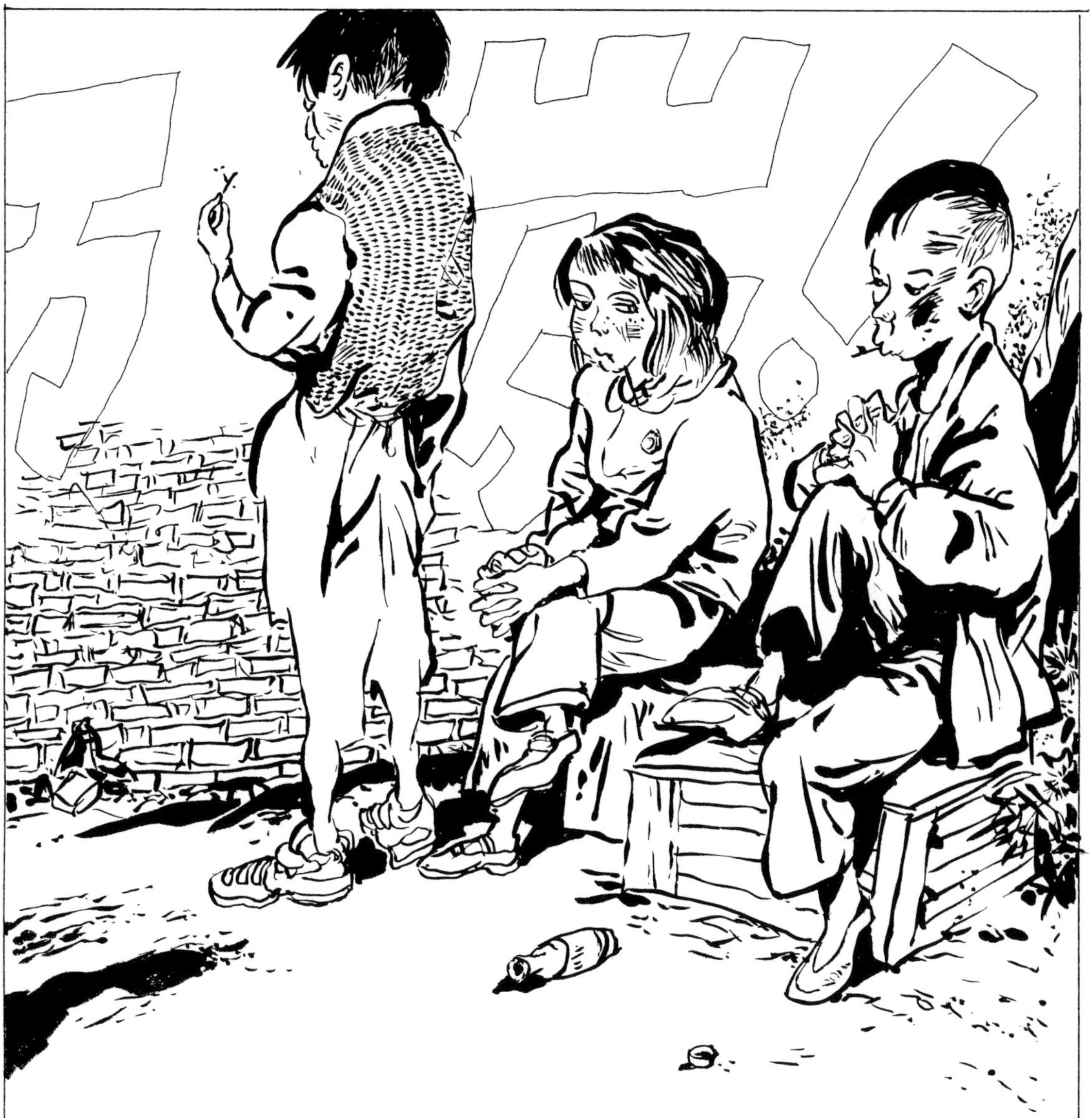

WITH THE RED GUARDS IN THE COUNTRYSIDE, AND THE CADRES KILLED OR IN RE-EDUCATION CAMPS, THE CITY WAS OURS, MORE OR LESS.

THERE HAD BEEN NO AUTHORITY IN OUR LIVES FOR THREE YEARS RUNNING. WE HAD GROWN UP WITHOUT REALIZING IT, AND WITHOUT LEARNING ANYTHING OF MUCH USE...

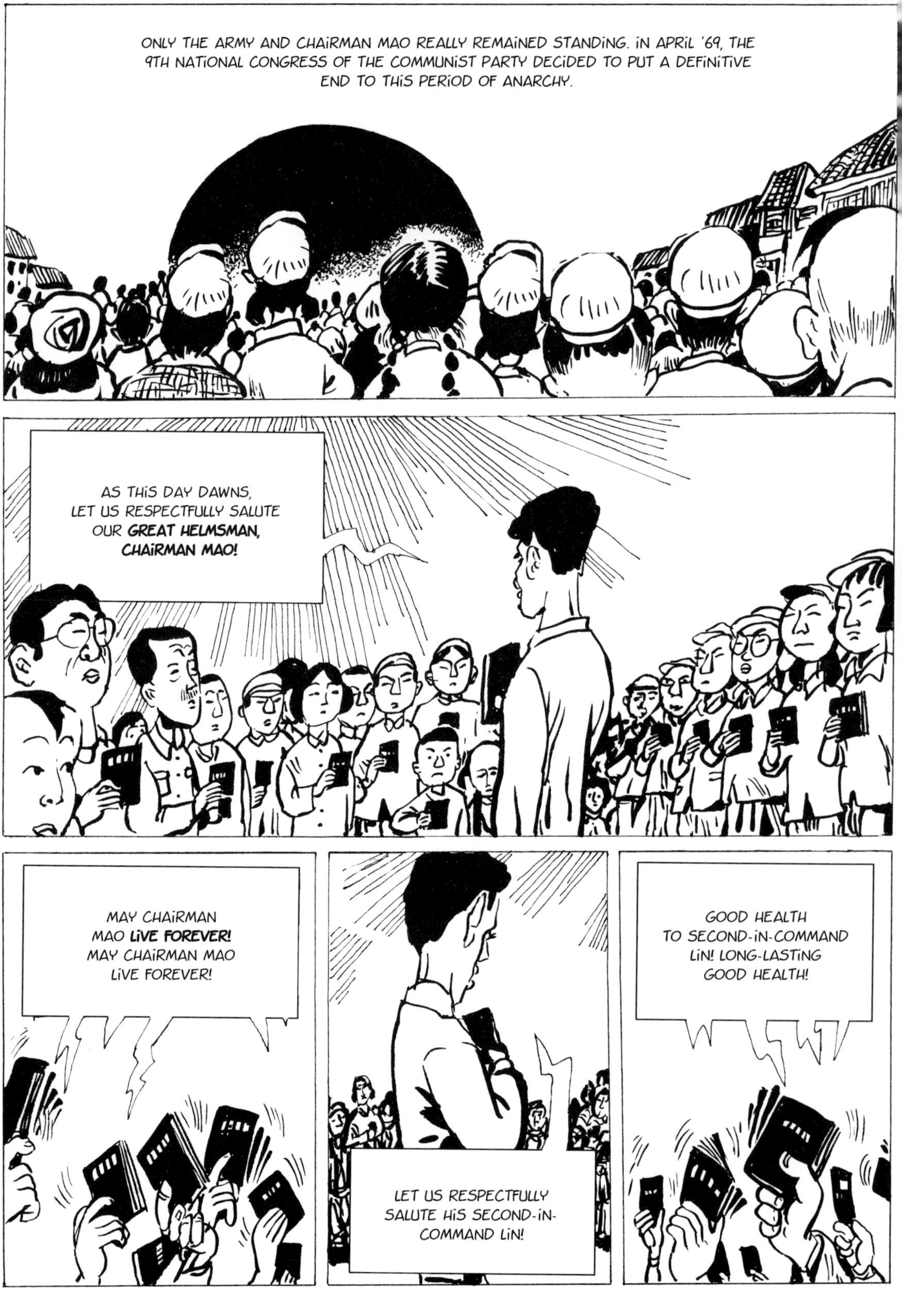
ONLY THE ARMY AND CHAIRMAN MAO REALLY REMAINED STANDING. IN APRIL '69, THE 9TH NATIONAL CONGRESS OF THE COMMUNIST PARTY DECIDED TO PUT A DEFINITIVE END TO THIS PERIOD OF ANARCHY.
AS THIS DAY DAWNS, LET US RESPECTFULLY SALUTE OUR **GREAT HELMSMAN, CHAIRMAN MAO!**
MAY CHAIRMAN MAO **LIVE FOREVER!** MAY CHAIRMAN MAO LIVE FOREVER!
LET US RESPECTFULLY SALUTE HIS SECOND-IN-COMMAND LIN!
GOOD HEALTH TO SECOND-IN-COMMAND LIN! LONG-LASTING GOOD HEALTH!

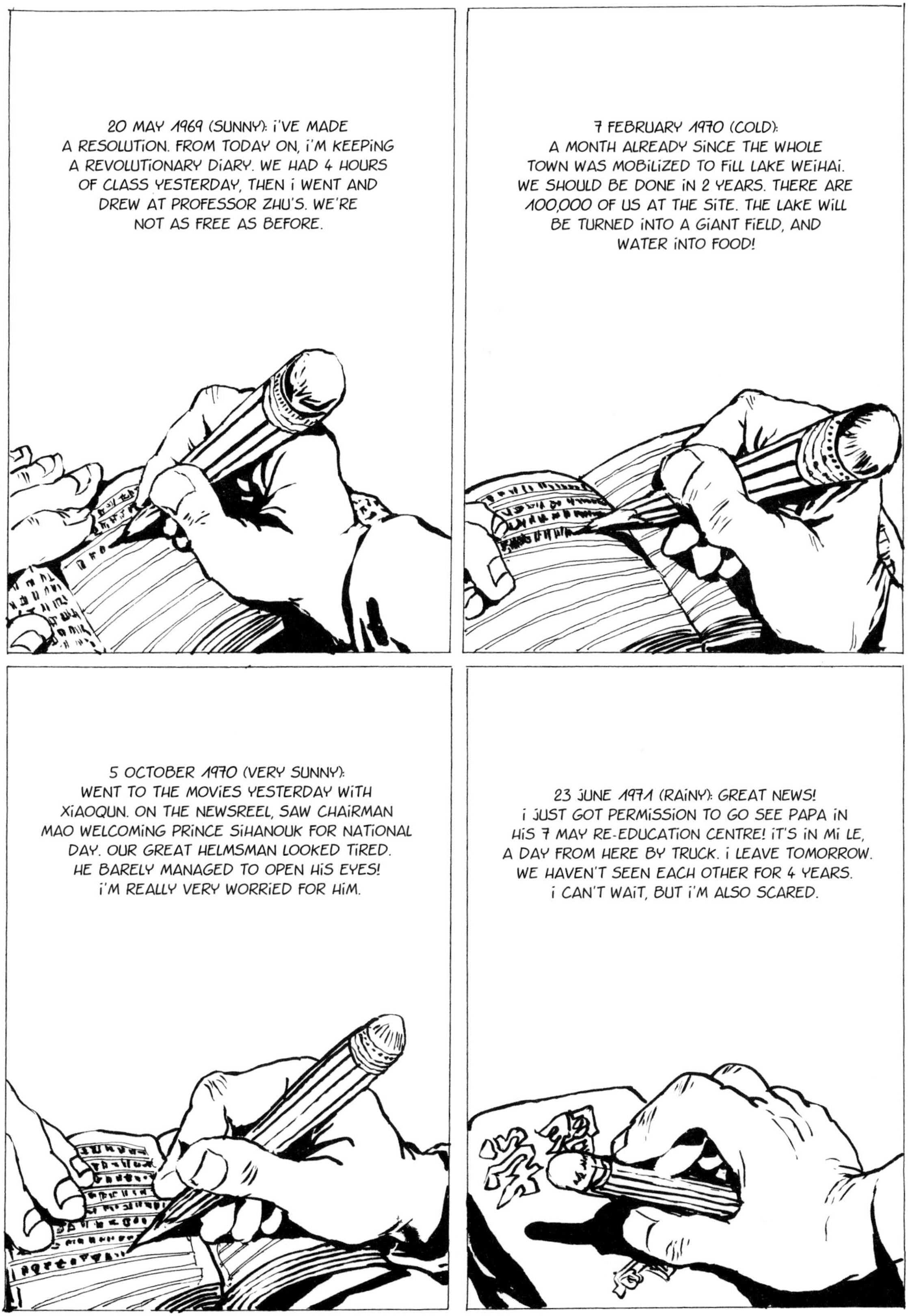

20 MAY 1969 (SUNNY): I'VE MADE A RESOLUTION. FROM TODAY ON, I'M KEEPING A REVOLUTIONARY DIARY. WE HAD 4 HOURS OF CLASS YESTERDAY, THEN I WENT AND DREW AT PROFESSOR ZHU'S. WE'RE NOT AS FREE AS BEFORE.

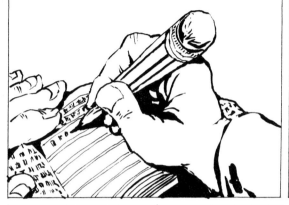

7 FEBRUARY 1970 (COLD): A MONTH ALREADY SINCE THE WHOLE TOWN WAS MOBILIZED TO FILL LAKE WEIHAI. WE SHOULD BE DONE IN 2 YEARS. THERE ARE 100,000 OF US AT THE SITE. THE LAKE WILL BE TURNED INTO A GIANT FIELD, AND WATER INTO FOOD!

5 OCTOBER 1970 (VERY SUNNY): WENT TO THE MOVIES YESTERDAY WITH XIAOQUN. ON THE NEWSREEL, SAW CHAIRMAN MAO WELCOMING PRINCE SIHANOUK FOR NATIONAL DAY. OUR GREAT HELMSMAN LOOKED TIRED. HE BARELY MANAGED TO OPEN HIS EYES! I'M REALLY VERY WORRIED FOR HIM.

23 JUNE 1971 (RAINY): GREAT NEWS! I JUST GOT PERMISSION TO GO SEE PAPA IN HIS 7 MAY RE-EDUCATION CENTRE! IT'S IN MI LE, A DAY FROM HERE BY TRUCK. I LEAVE TOMORROW. WE HAVEN'T SEEN EACH OTHER FOR 4 YEARS. I CAN'T WAIT, BUT I'M ALSO SCARED.

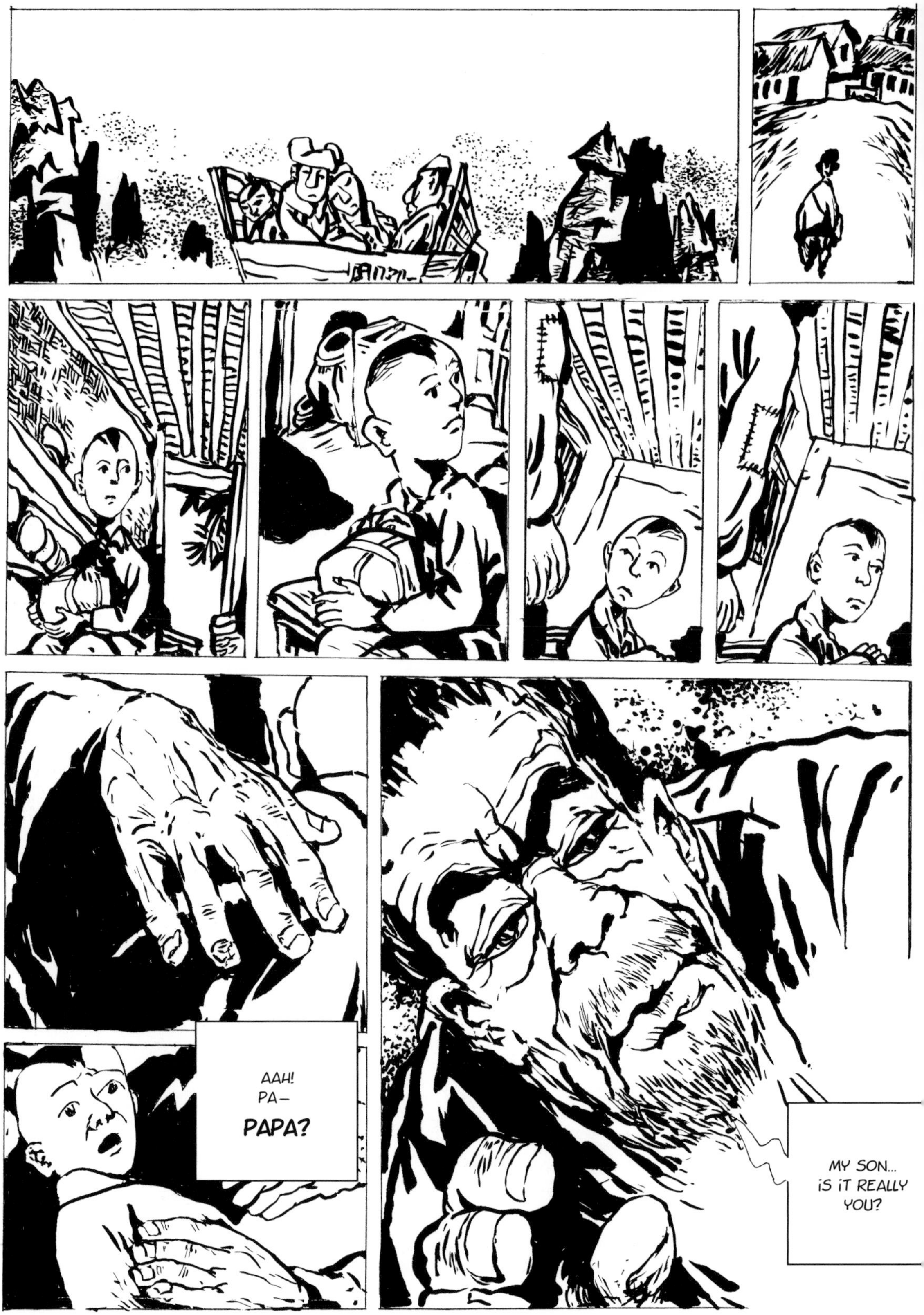
AAH!
PA–
PAPA?
MY SON...
IS IT REALLY
YOU?

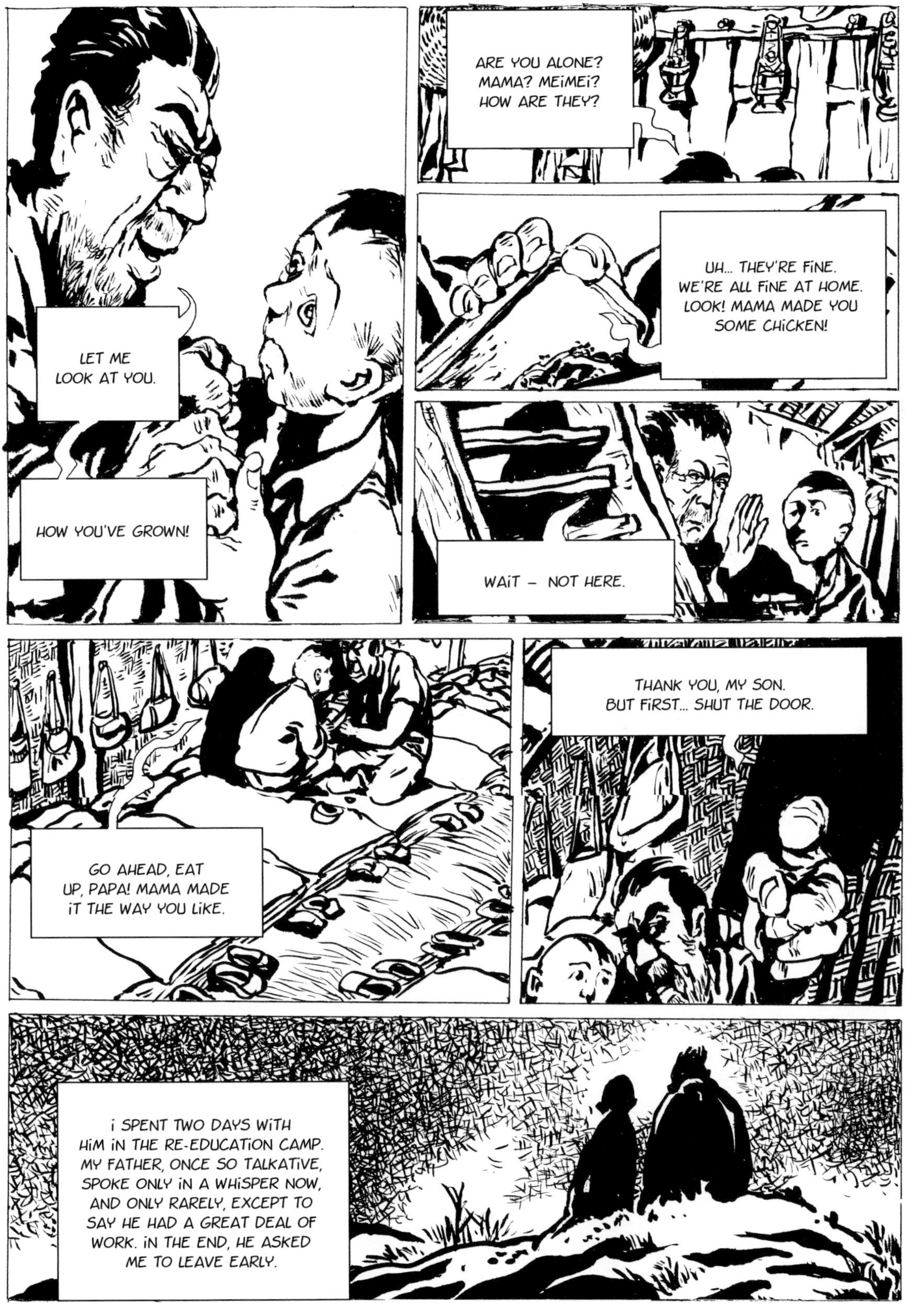
LET ME LOOK AT YOU.
HOW YOU'VE GROWN!
ARE YOU ALONE? MAMA? MEIMEI? HOW ARE THEY?
UH... THEY'RE FINE. WE'RE ALL FINE AT HOME. LOOK! MAMA MADE YOU SOME CHICKEN!
WAIT – NOT HERE.
GO AHEAD, EAT UP, PAPA! MAMA MADE IT THE WAY YOU LIKE.
THANK YOU, MY SON. BUT FIRST... SHUT THE DOOR.
I SPENT TWO DAYS WITH HIM IN THE RE-EDUCATION CAMP. MY FATHER, ONCE SO TALKATIVE, SPOKE ONLY IN A WHISPER NOW, AND ONLY RARELY, EXCEPT TO SAY HE HAD A GREAT DEAL OF WORK. IN THE END, HE ASKED ME TO LEAVE EARLY.

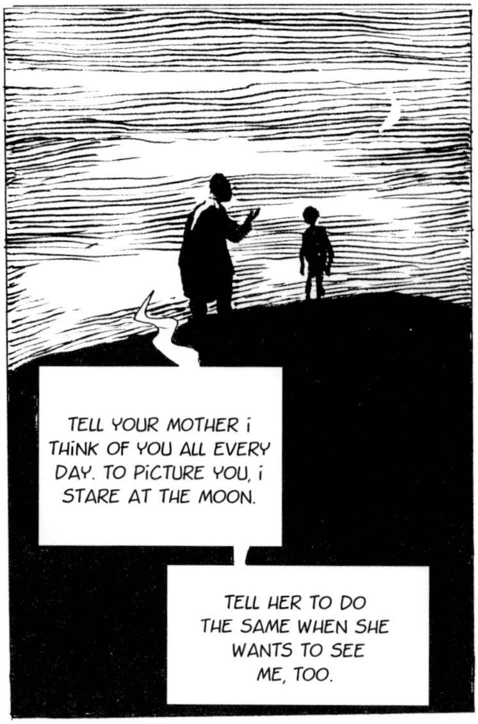
TELL YOUR MOTHER i THINK OF YOU ALL EVERY DAY. TO PICTURE YOU, i STARE AT THE MOON.
TELL HER TO DO THE SAME WHEN SHE WANTS TO SEE ME, TOO.

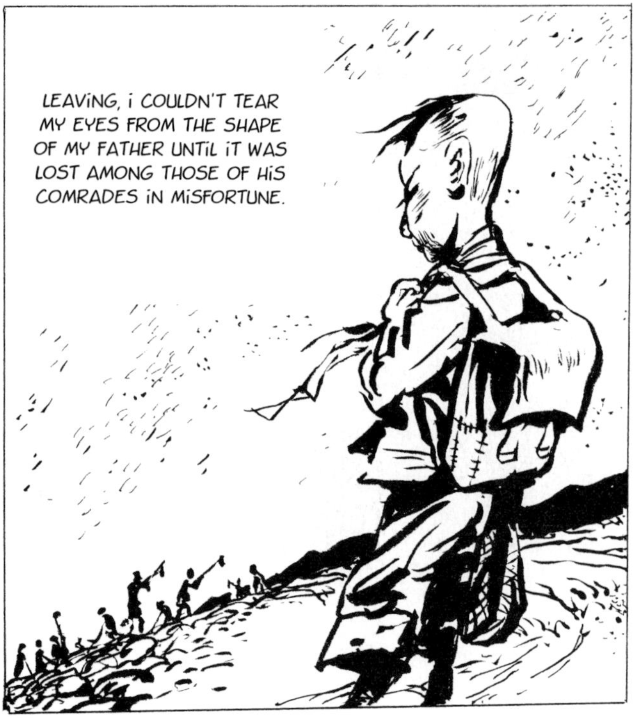
LEAVING, i COULDN'T TEAR MY EYES FROM THE SHAPE OF MY FATHER UNTIL IT WAS LOST AMONG THOSE OF HIS COMRADES IN MISFORTUNE.

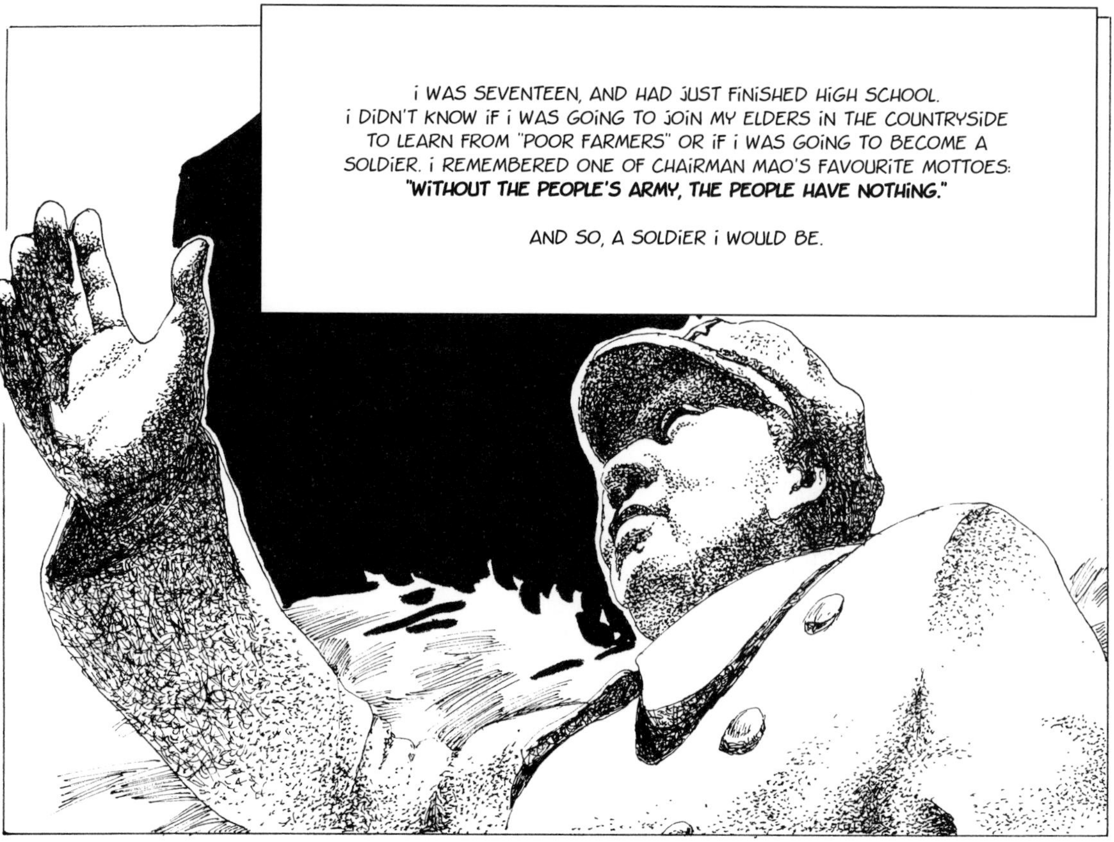
i WAS SEVENTEEN, AND HAD JUST FINISHED HIGH SCHOOL. i DIDN'T KNOW IF i WAS GOING TO JOIN MY ELDERS IN THE COUNTRYSIDE TO LEARN FROM "POOR FARMERS" OR IF i WAS GOING TO BECOME A SOLDIER. i REMEMBERED ONE OF CHAIRMAN MAO'S FAVOURITE MOTTOES: **"WITHOUT THE PEOPLE'S ARMY, THE PEOPLE HAVE NOTHING."**
AND SO, A SOLDIER i WOULD BE.

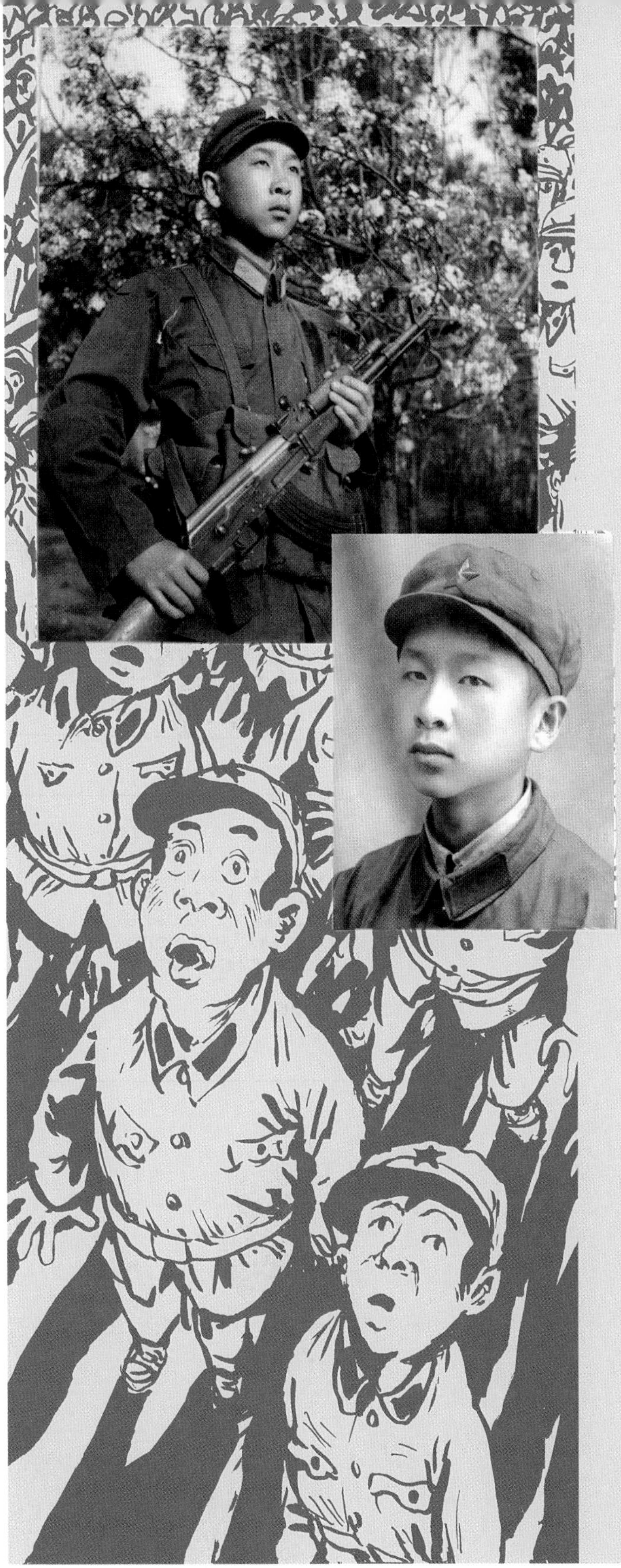

CHAPTER 3
Red Army

I AM A SOLDIER.

I LOVE THE NATION.
I LOVE THE PEOPLE.

FORGED IN THE ORDEALS
OF THE REVOLUTION,

I AM THE MOST DETERMINED
IN MY ACTIONS.

我是一个兵，
爱国爱人民，
革命 战争 考验
我 立场最 坚定。

(ARMY SONG)

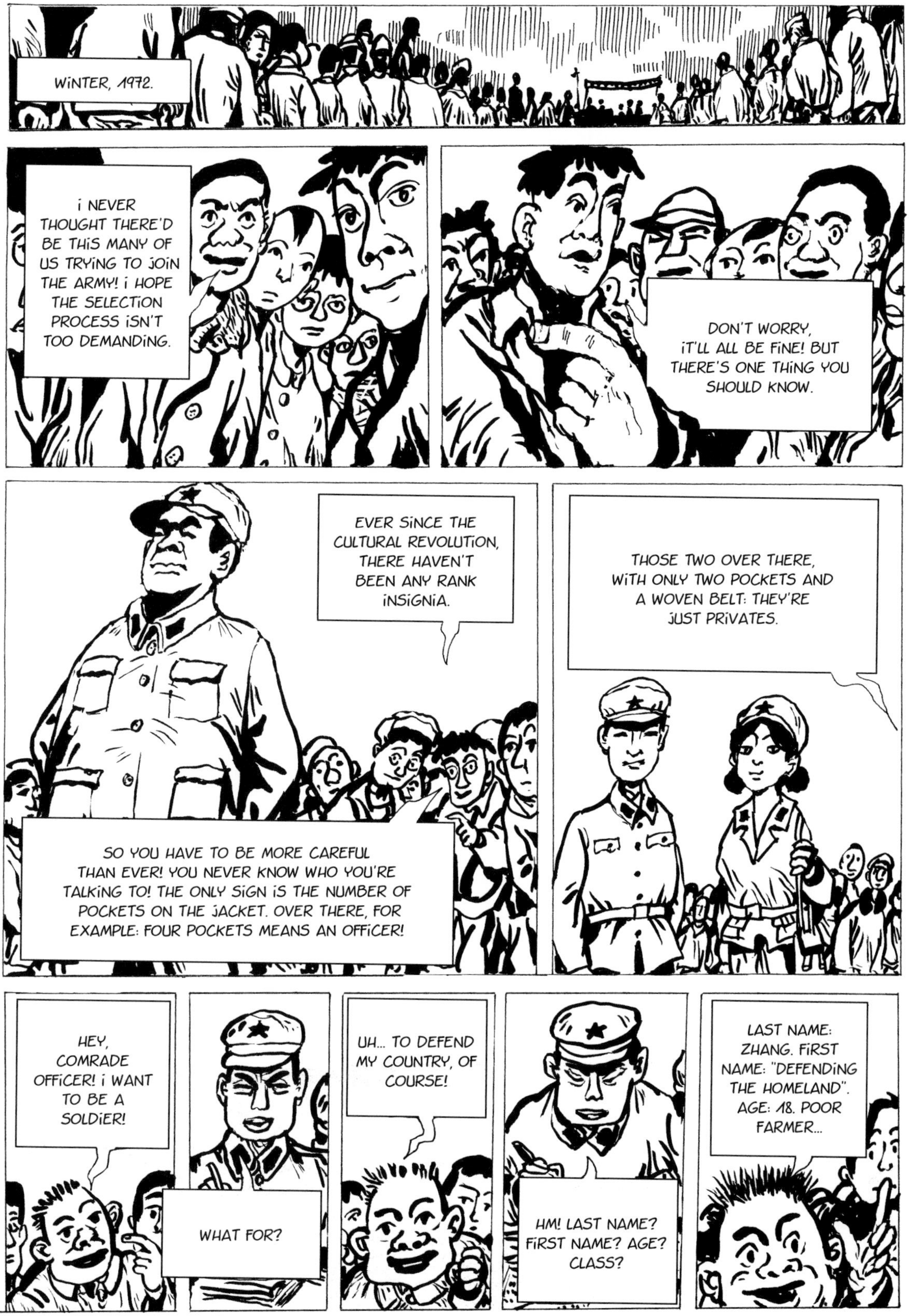
WINTER, 1972.
I NEVER THOUGHT THERE'D BE THIS MANY OF US TRYING TO JOIN THE ARMY! I HOPE THE SELECTION PROCESS ISN'T TOO DEMANDING.
DON'T WORRY, IT'LL ALL BE FINE! BUT THERE'S ONE THING YOU SHOULD KNOW.
EVER SINCE THE CULTURAL REVOLUTION, THERE HAVEN'T BEEN ANY RANK INSIGNIA.
SO YOU HAVE TO BE MORE CAREFUL THAN EVER! YOU NEVER KNOW WHO YOU'RE TALKING TO! THE ONLY SIGN IS THE NUMBER OF POCKETS ON THE JACKET. OVER THERE, FOR EXAMPLE: FOUR POCKETS MEANS AN OFFICER!
THOSE TWO OVER THERE, WITH ONLY TWO POCKETS AND A WOVEN BELT: THEY'RE JUST PRIVATES.
HEY, COMRADE OFFICER! I WANT TO BE A SOLDIER!
WHAT FOR?
UH... TO DEFEND MY COUNTRY, OF COURSE!
HM! LAST NAME? FIRST NAME? AGE? CLASS?
LAST NAME: ZHANG. FIRST NAME: "DEFENDING THE HOMELAND". AGE: 18. POOR FARMER...

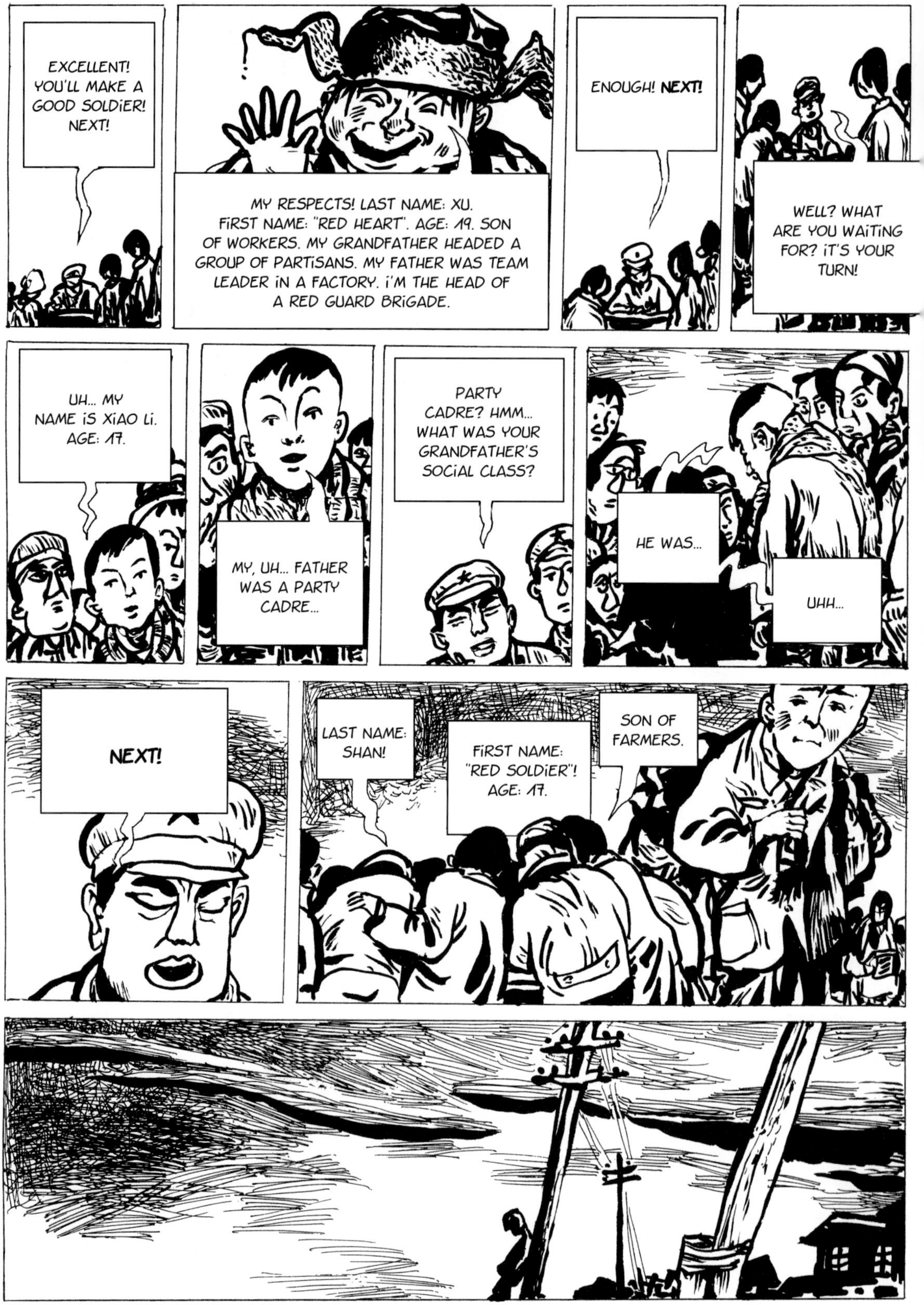
EXCELLENT! YOU'LL MAKE A GOOD SOLDIER! NEXT!
MY RESPECTS! LAST NAME: XU. FIRST NAME: "RED HEART". AGE: 19. SON OF WORKERS. MY GRANDFATHER HEADED A GROUP OF PARTISANS. MY FATHER WAS TEAM LEADER IN A FACTORY. I'M THE HEAD OF A RED GUARD BRIGADE.
ENOUGH! NEXT!
WELL? WHAT ARE YOU WAITING FOR? IT'S YOUR TURN!
UH... MY NAME IS XIAO LI. AGE: 17.
MY, UH... FATHER WAS A PARTY CADRE...
PARTY CADRE? HMM... WHAT WAS YOUR GRANDFATHER'S SOCIAL CLASS?
HE WAS...
UHH...
NEXT!
LAST NAME: SHAN!
FIRST NAME: "RED SOLDIER"! AGE: 17.
SON OF FARMERS.

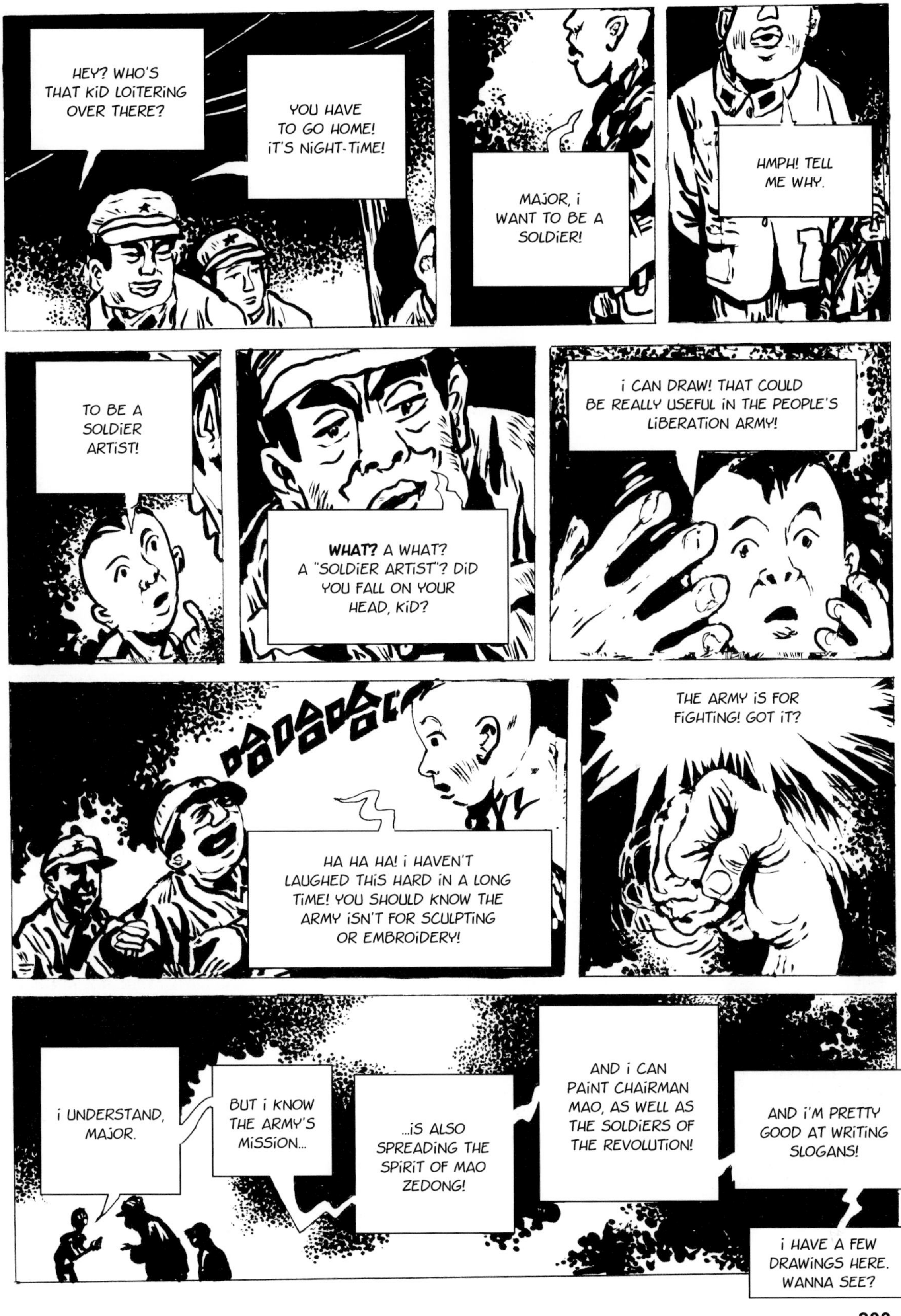
HEY? WHO'S THAT KID LOITERING OVER THERE?
YOU HAVE TO GO HOME! IT'S NIGHT-TIME!
MAJOR, I WANT TO BE A SOLDIER!
HMPH! TELL ME WHY.
TO BE A SOLDIER ARTIST!
WHAT? A WHAT? A "SOLDIER ARTIST"? DID YOU FALL ON YOUR HEAD, KID?
I CAN DRAW! THAT COULD BE REALLY USEFUL IN THE PEOPLE'S LIBERATION ARMY!
哈哈哈
HA HA HA! I HAVEN'T LAUGHED THIS HARD IN A LONG TIME! YOU SHOULD KNOW THE ARMY ISN'T FOR SCULPTING OR EMBROIDERY!
THE ARMY IS FOR FIGHTING! GOT IT?
I UNDERSTAND, MAJOR.
BUT I KNOW THE ARMY'S MISSION...
...IS ALSO SPREADING THE SPIRIT OF MAO ZEDONG!
AND I CAN PAINT CHAIRMAN MAO, AS WELL AS THE SOLDIERS OF THE REVOLUTION!
AND I'M PRETTY GOOD AT WRITING SLOGANS!
I HAVE A FEW DRAWINGS HERE. WANNA SEE?

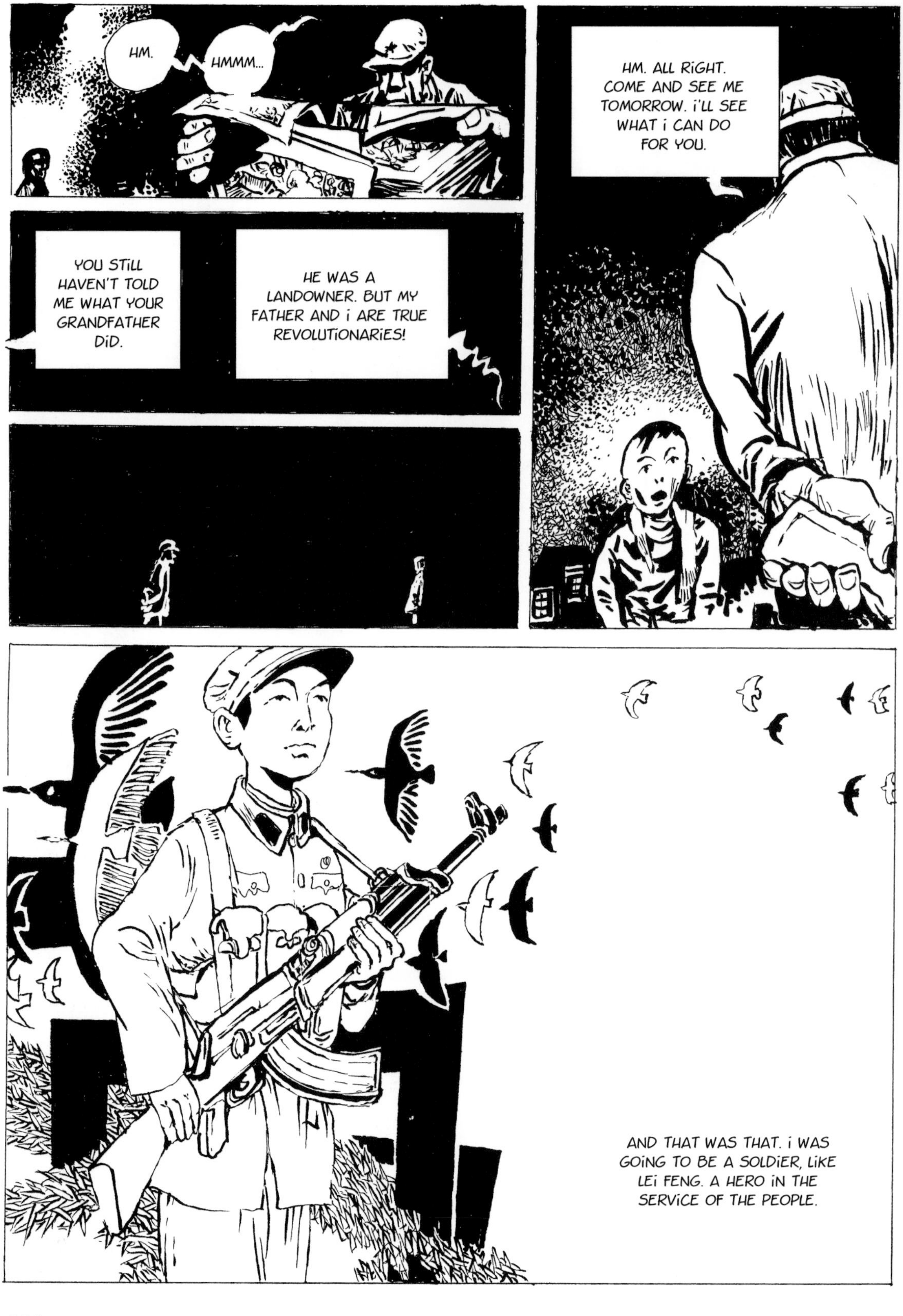
HM.
HMMM...
YOU STILL HAVEN'T TOLD ME WHAT YOUR GRANDFATHER DID.
HE WAS A LANDOWNER. BUT MY FATHER AND I ARE TRUE REVOLUTIONARIES!
HM. ALL RIGHT. COME AND SEE ME TOMORROW. I'LL SEE WHAT I CAN DO FOR YOU.
AND THAT WAS THAT. I WAS GOING TO BE A SOLDIER, LIKE LEI FENG. A HERO IN THE SERVICE OF THE PEOPLE.

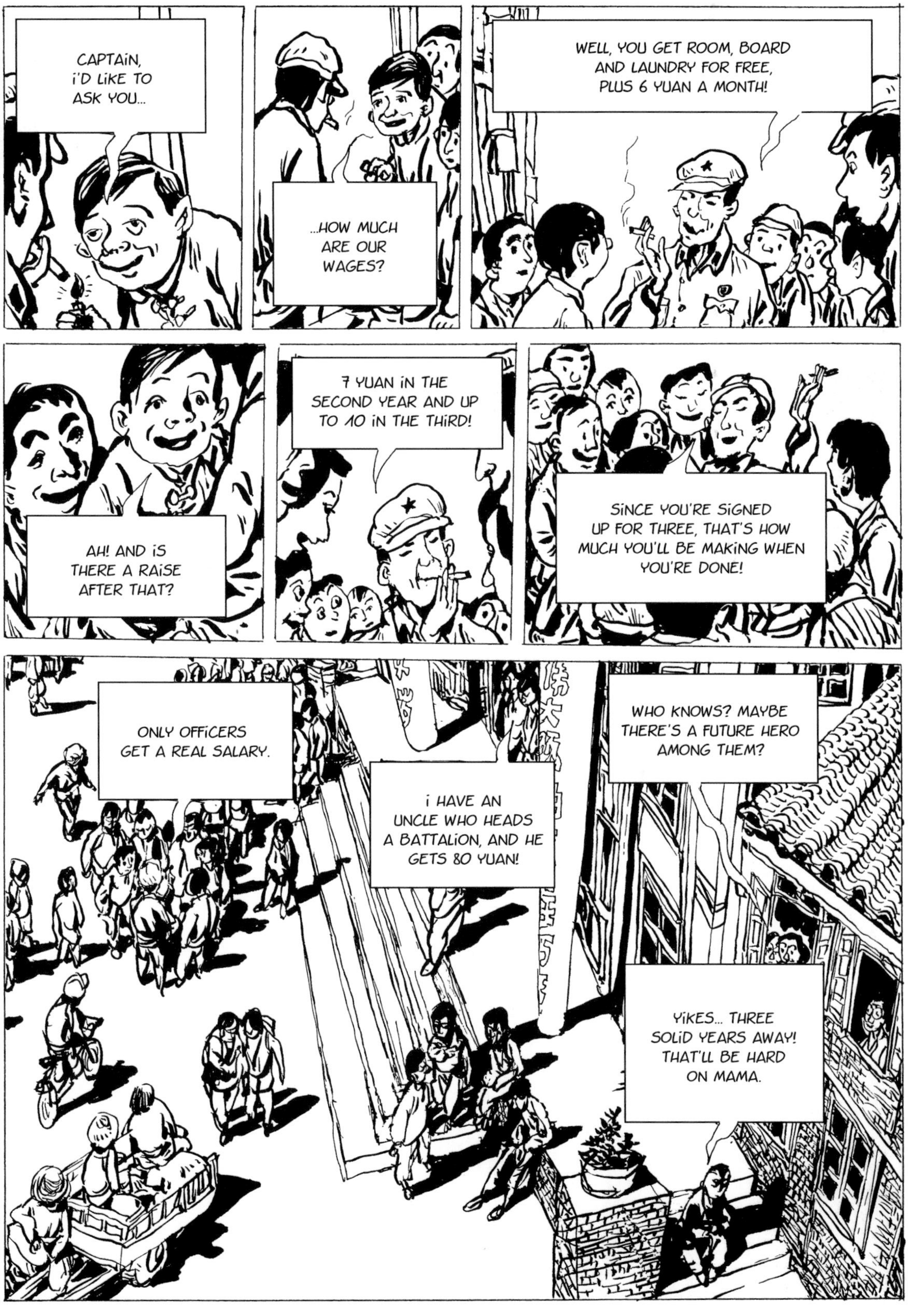
CAPTAIN, I'D LIKE TO ASK YOU...
...HOW MUCH ARE OUR WAGES?
WELL, YOU GET ROOM, BOARD AND LAUNDRY FOR FREE, PLUS 6 YUAN A MONTH!
AH! AND IS THERE A RAISE AFTER THAT?
7 YUAN IN THE SECOND YEAR AND UP TO 10 IN THE THIRD!
SINCE YOU'RE SIGNED UP FOR THREE, THAT'S HOW MUCH YOU'LL BE MAKING WHEN YOU'RE DONE!
ONLY OFFICERS GET A REAL SALARY.
I HAVE AN UNCLE WHO HEADS A BATTALION, AND HE GETS 80 YUAN!
WHO KNOWS? MAYBE THERE'S A FUTURE HERO AMONG THEM?
YIKES... THREE SOLID YEARS AWAY! THAT'LL BE HARD ON MAMA.

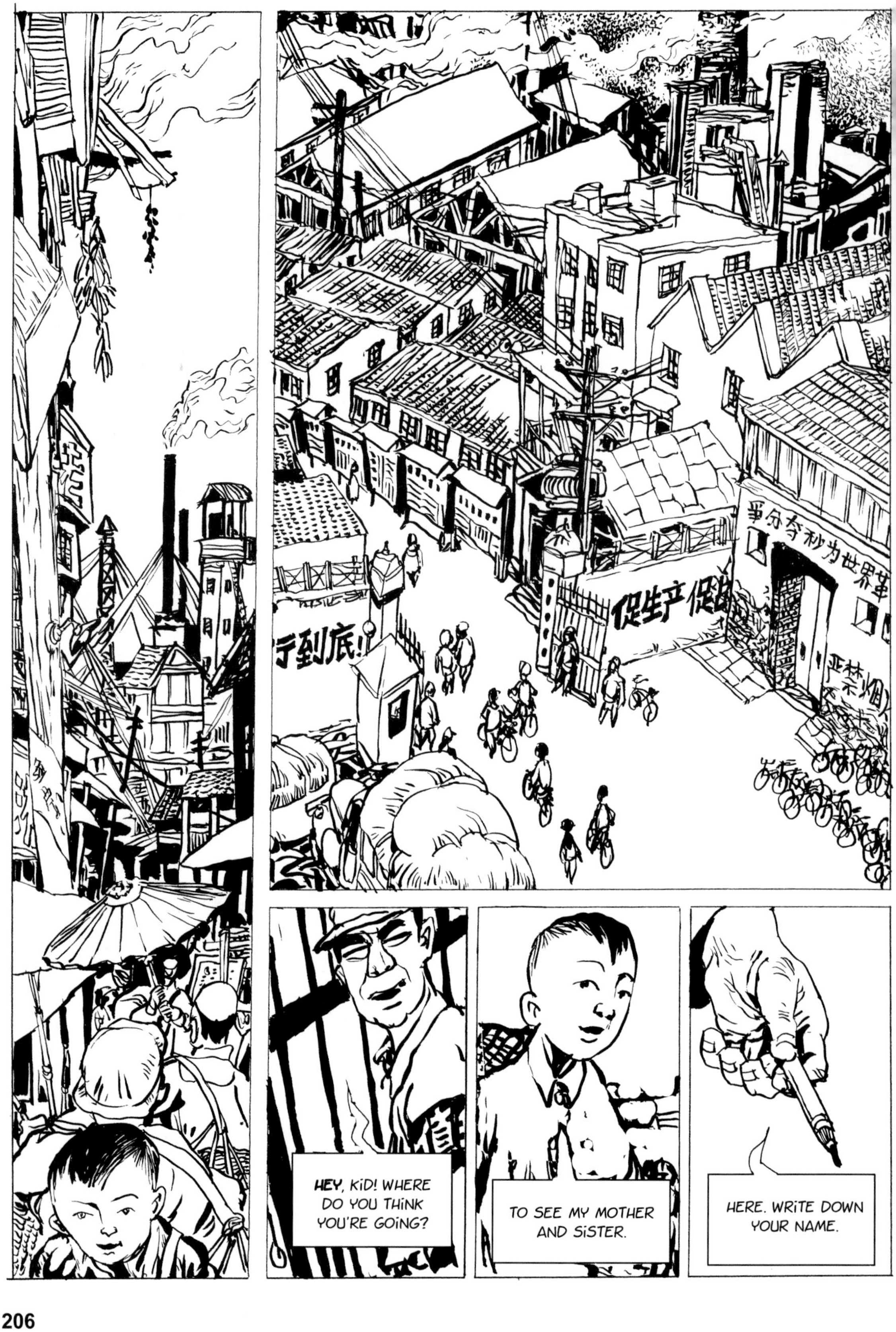
促生产
到底!
争分夺秒为世界革
严禁烟
HEY, KID! WHERE DO YOU THINK YOU'RE GOING?
TO SEE MY MOTHER AND SISTER.
HERE. WRITE DOWN YOUR NAME.

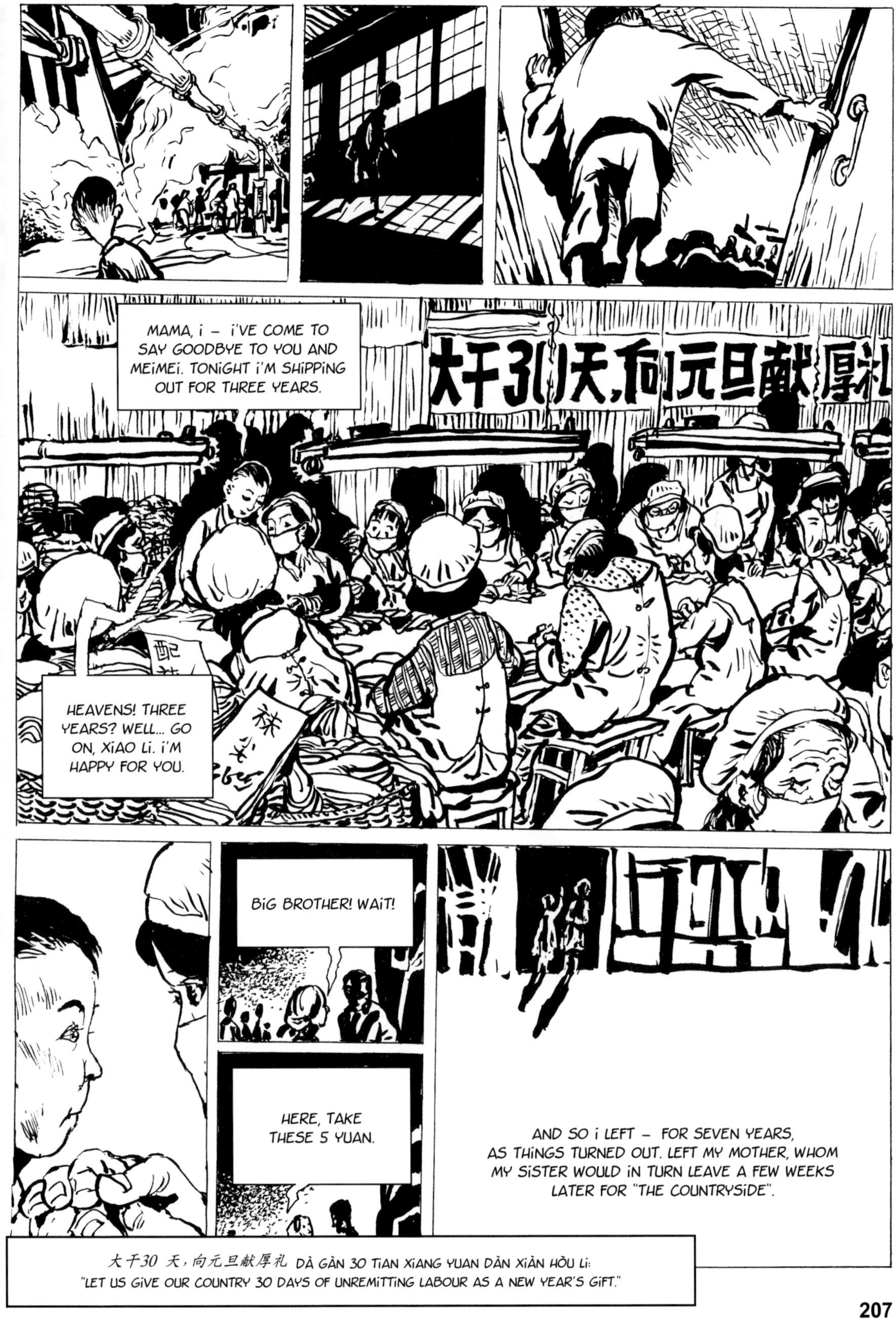
MAMA, i – i'VE COME TO SAY GOODBYE TO YOU AND MEiMEi. TONiGHT i'M SHiPPiNG OUT FOR THREE YEARS.
大干30天，向元旦献厚礼
HEAVENS! THREE YEARS? WELL... GO ON, XiAO Li. i'M HAPPY FOR YOU.
BiG BROTHER! WAiT!
HERE, TAKE THESE 5 YUAN.
AND SO i LEFT – FOR SEVEN YEARS, AS THiNGS TURNED OUT. LEFT MY MOTHER, WHOM MY SiSTER WOULD iN TURN LEAVE A FEW WEEKS LATER FOR "THE COUNTRYSiDE".

大干30 天，向元旦献厚礼 DÀ GÀN 30 TiAN XiANG YUAN DÀN XiÀN HÒU Lǐ:
"LET US GiVE OUR COUNTRY 30 DAYS OF UNREMiTTiNG LABOUR AS A NEW YEAR'S GiFT."

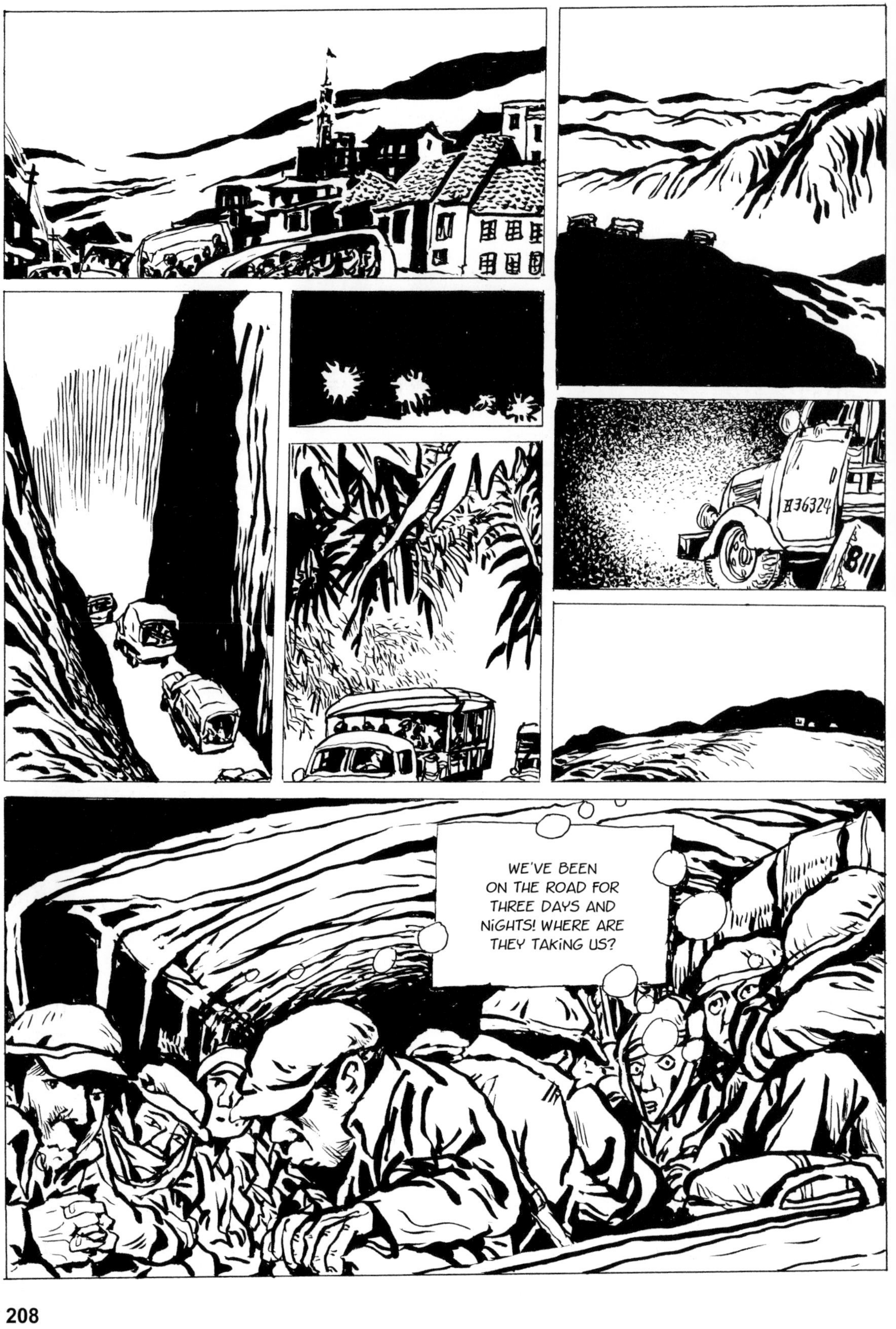
WE'VE BEEN ON THE ROAD FOR THREE DAYS AND NIGHTS! WHERE ARE THEY TAKING US?

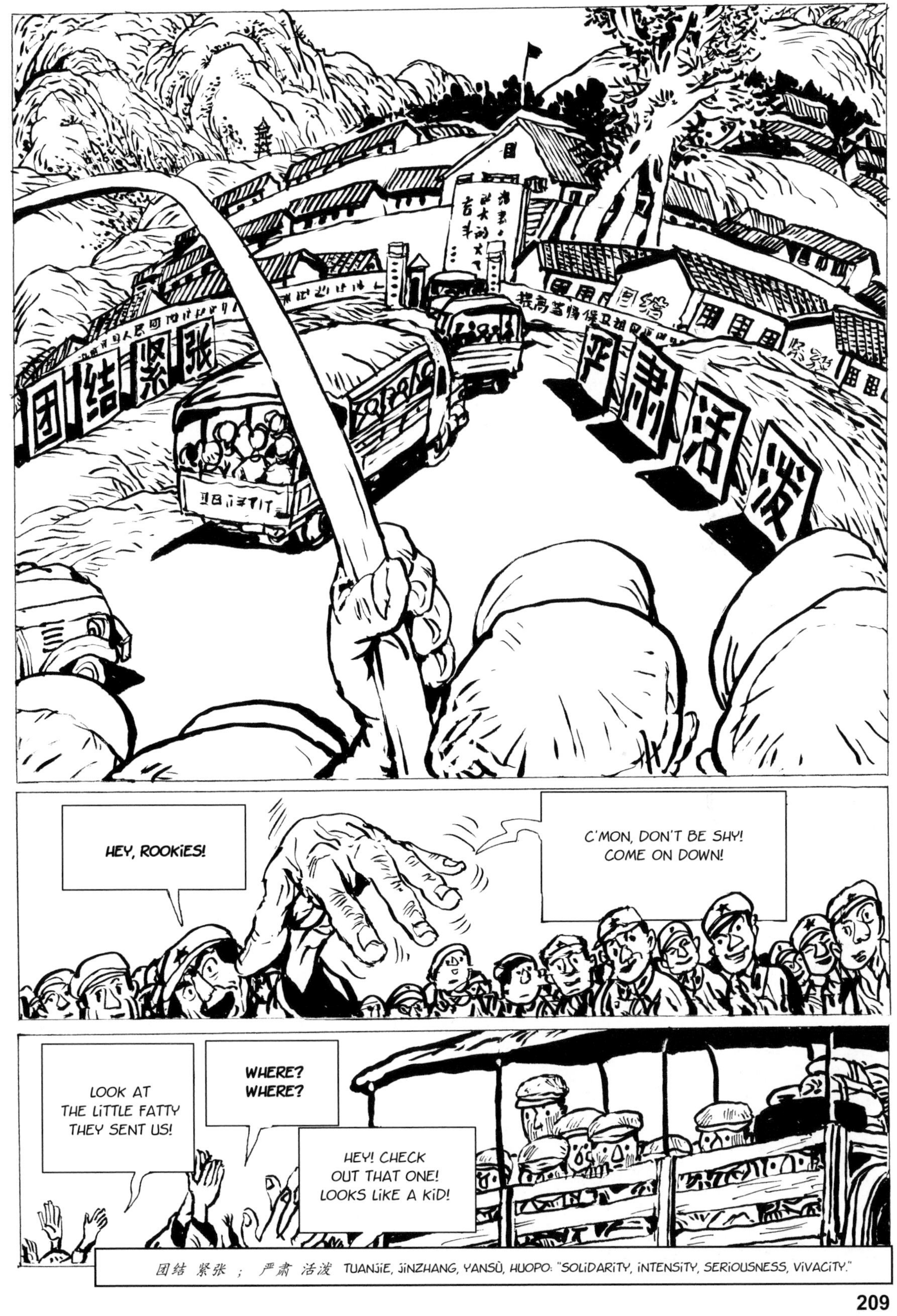
团结紧张
严肃活泼
HEY, ROOKIES!
C'MON, DON'T BE SHY!
COME ON DOWN!
LOOK AT THE LITTLE FATTY THEY SENT US!
WHERE? WHERE?
HEY! CHECK OUT THAT ONE! LOOKS LIKE A KID!

团结 紧张 ； 严肃 活泼 TUANJIE, JINZHANG, YANSÙ, HUOPO: "SOLIDARITY, INTENSITY, SERIOUSNESS, VIVACITY."

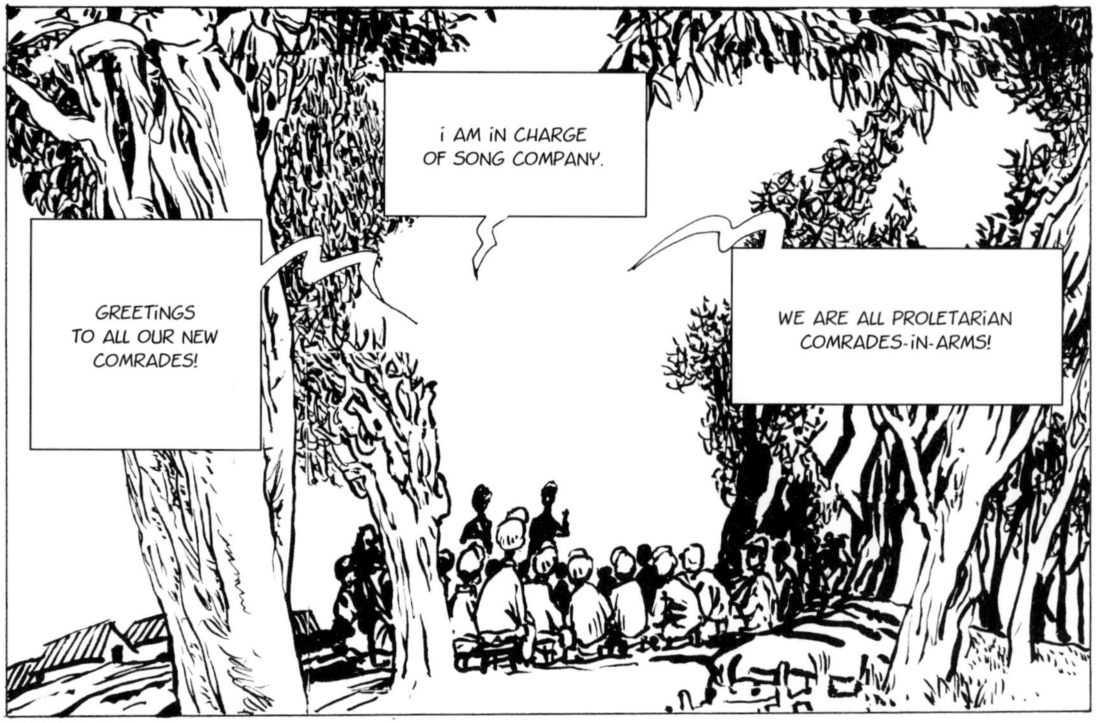
GREETINGS TO ALL OUR NEW COMRADES!
I AM IN CHARGE OF SONG COMPANY.
WE ARE ALL PROLETARIAN COMRADES-IN-ARMS!

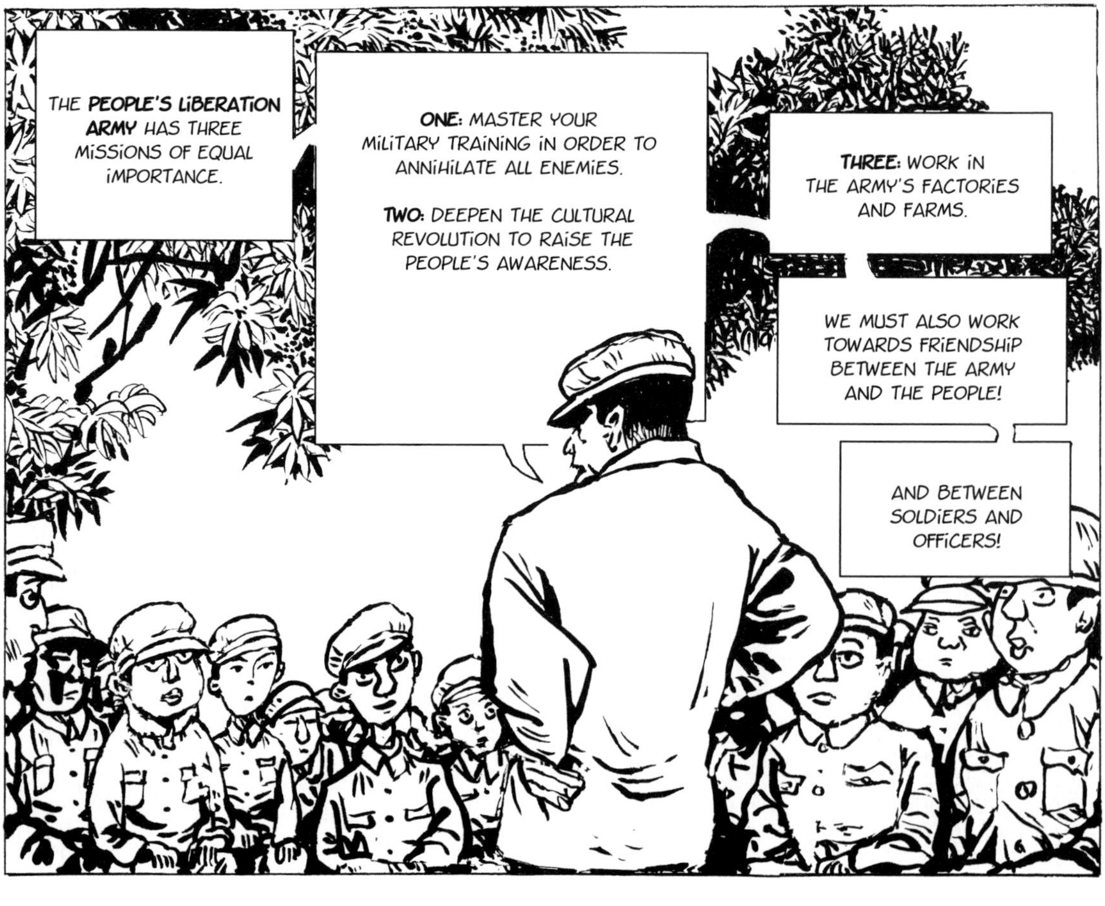
THE **PEOPLE'S LIBERATION ARMY** HAS THREE MISSIONS OF EQUAL IMPORTANCE.
ONE: MASTER YOUR MILITARY TRAINING IN ORDER TO ANNIHILATE ALL ENEMIES.
TWO: DEEPEN THE CULTURAL REVOLUTION TO RAISE THE PEOPLE'S AWARENESS.
THREE: WORK IN THE ARMY'S FACTORIES AND FARMS.
WE MUST ALSO WORK TOWARDS FRIENDSHIP BETWEEN THE ARMY AND THE PEOPLE!
AND BETWEEN SOLDIERS AND OFFICERS!

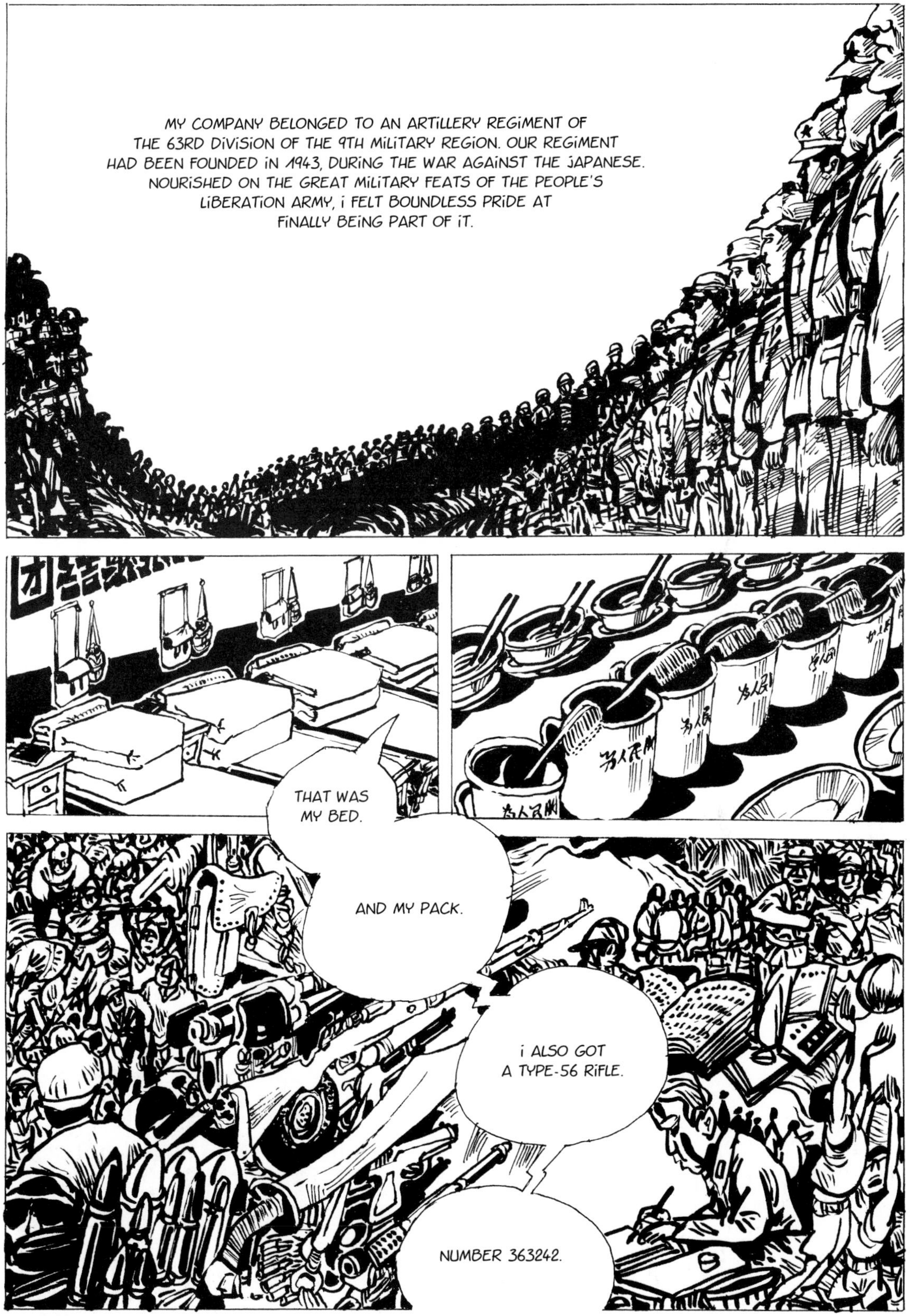
MY COMPANY BELONGED TO AN ARTILLERY REGIMENT OF THE 63RD DIVISION OF THE 9TH MILITARY REGION. OUR REGIMENT HAD BEEN FOUNDED IN 1943, DURING THE WAR AGAINST THE JAPANESE. NOURISHED ON THE GREAT MILITARY FEATS OF THE PEOPLE'S LIBERATION ARMY, I FELT BOUNDLESS PRIDE AT FINALLY BEING PART OF IT.
THAT WAS MY BED.
AND MY PACK.
I ALSO GOT A TYPE-56 RIFLE.
NUMBER 363242.

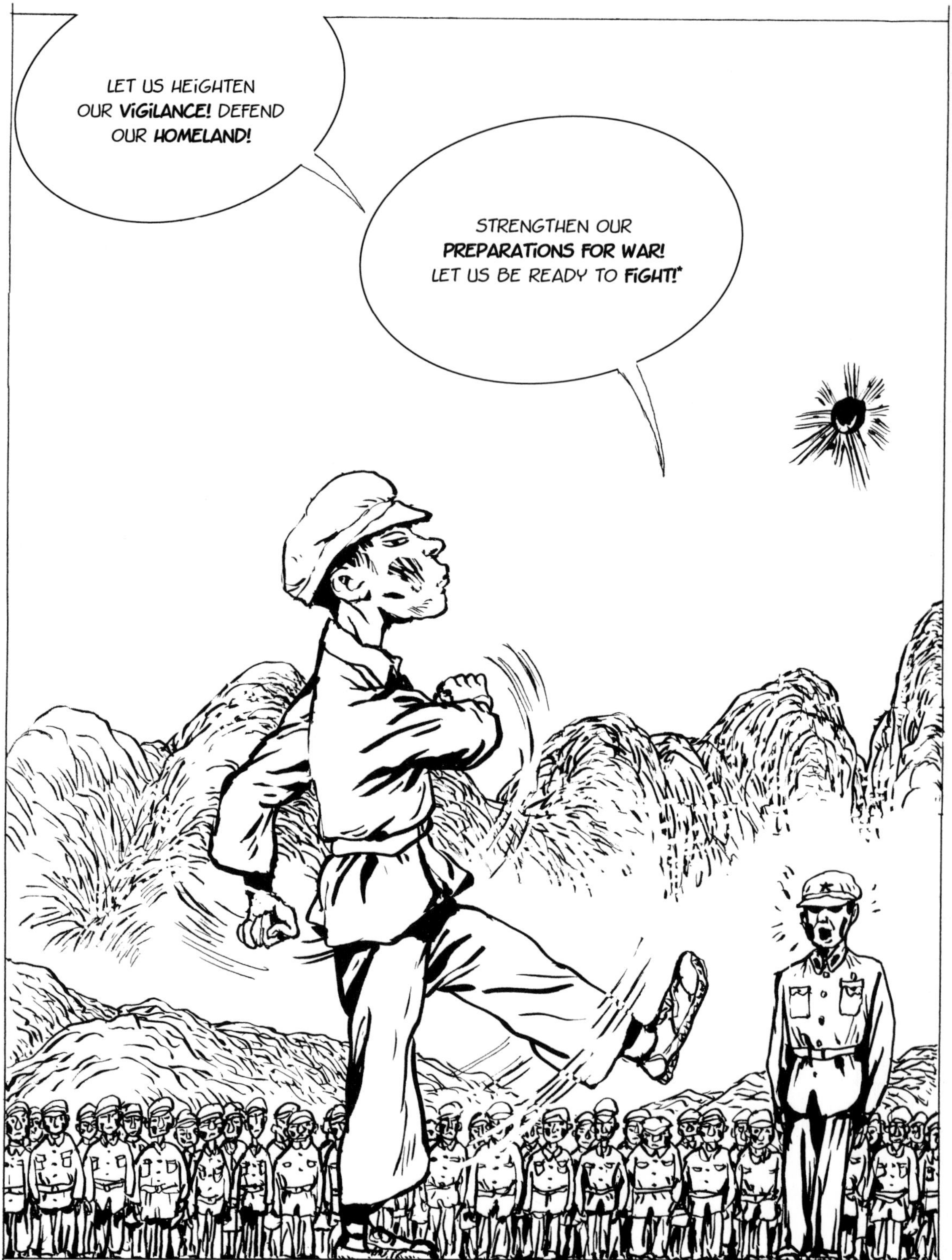
LET US HEIGHTEN OUR VIGILANCE! DEFEND OUR HOMELAND!
STRENGTHEN OUR PREPARATIONS FOR WAR! LET US BE READY TO FIGHT!*

*提高警惕，保卫祖国，加强战备，准备打仗！

FROM A MILITARY SONG : TIGAO JINGTI, AOWEI ZUGUO, JIAQANG ZHANBEI, ZHUNBEI DAZHANG!

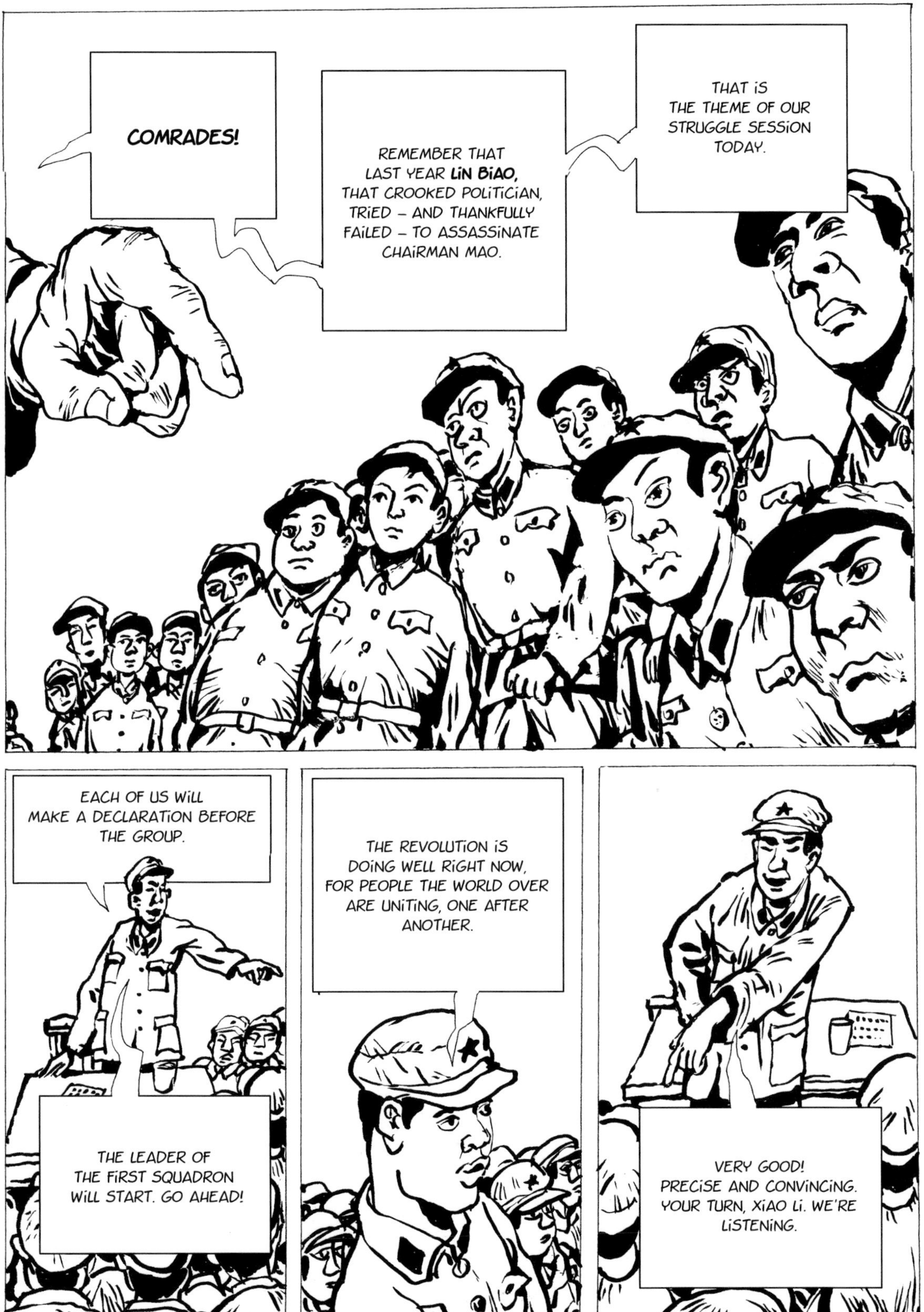
COMRADES!
REMEMBER THAT LAST YEAR LIN BIAO, THAT CROOKED POLITICIAN, TRIED – AND THANKFULLY FAILED – TO ASSASSINATE CHAIRMAN MAO.
THAT IS THE THEME OF OUR STRUGGLE SESSION TODAY.
EACH OF US WILL MAKE A DECLARATION BEFORE THE GROUP.
THE LEADER OF THE FIRST SQUADRON WILL START. GO AHEAD!
THE REVOLUTION IS DOING WELL RIGHT NOW, FOR PEOPLE THE WORLD OVER ARE UNITING, ONE AFTER ANOTHER.
VERY GOOD! PRECISE AND CONVINCING. YOUR TURN, XIAO LI. WE'RE LISTENING.

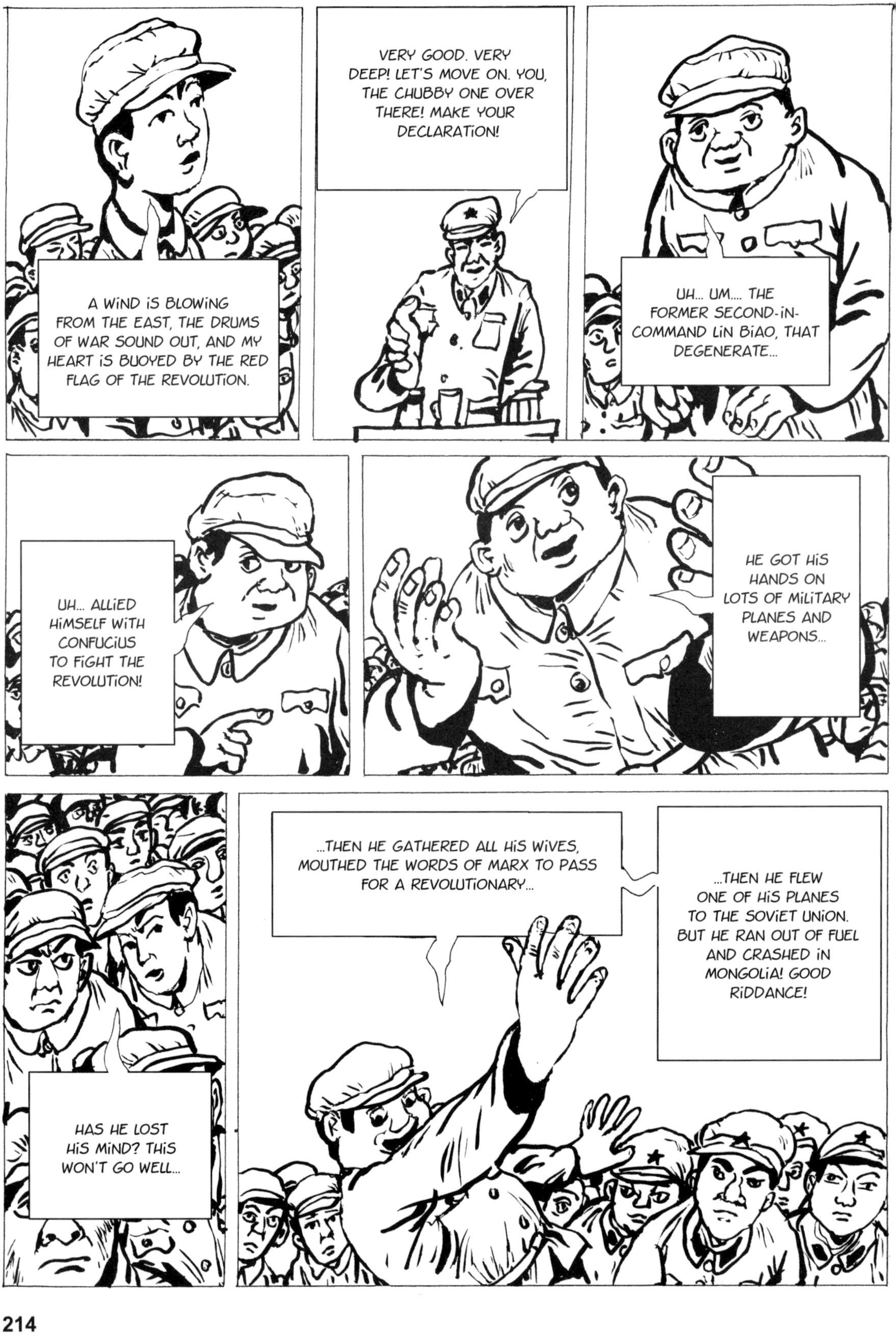
A WIND IS BLOWING FROM THE EAST, THE DRUMS OF WAR SOUND OUT, AND MY HEART IS BUOYED BY THE RED FLAG OF THE REVOLUTION.
VERY GOOD. VERY DEEP! LET'S MOVE ON. YOU, THE CHUBBY ONE OVER THERE! MAKE YOUR DECLARATION!
UH... UM.... THE FORMER SECOND-IN-COMMAND LIN BIAO, THAT DEGENERATE...
UH... ALLIED HIMSELF WITH CONFUCIUS TO FIGHT THE REVOLUTION!
HE GOT HIS HANDS ON LOTS OF MILITARY PLANES AND WEAPONS...
HAS HE LOST HIS MIND? THIS WON'T GO WELL...
...THEN HE GATHERED ALL HIS WIVES, MOUTHED THE WORDS OF MARX TO PASS FOR A REVOLUTIONARY...
...THEN HE FLEW ONE OF HIS PLANES TO THE SOVIET UNION. BUT HE RAN OUT OF FUEL AND CRASHED IN MONGOLIA! GOOD RIDDANCE!

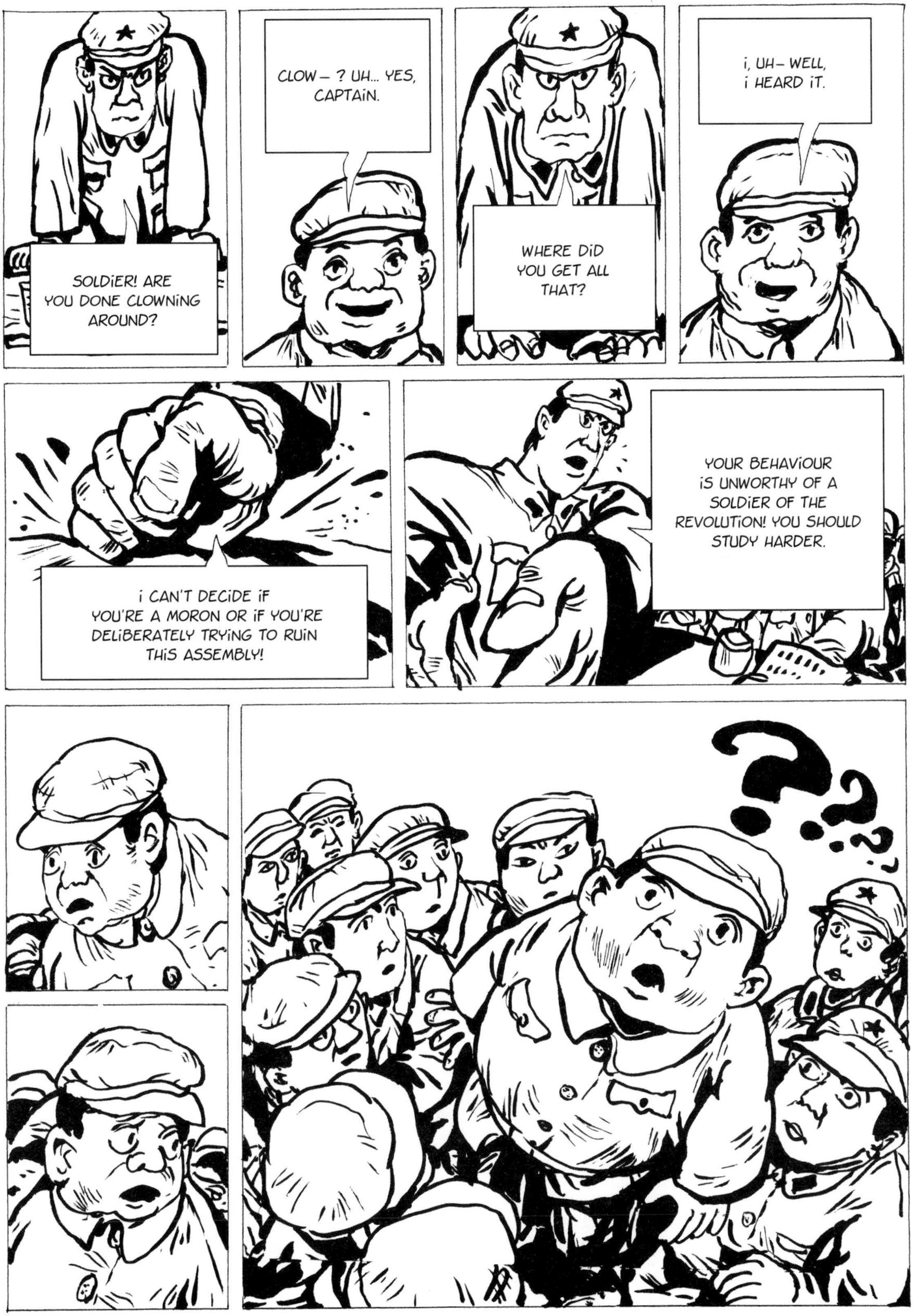
SOLDIER! ARE YOU DONE CLOWNING AROUND?
CLOW – ? UH... YES, CAPTAIN.
WHERE DID YOU GET ALL THAT?
I, UH– WELL, I HEARD IT.
I CAN'T DECIDE IF YOU'RE A MORON OR IF YOU'RE DELIBERATELY TRYING TO RUIN THIS ASSEMBLY!
YOUR BEHAVIOUR IS UNWORTHY OF A SOLDIER OF THE REVOLUTION! YOU SHOULD STUDY HARDER.

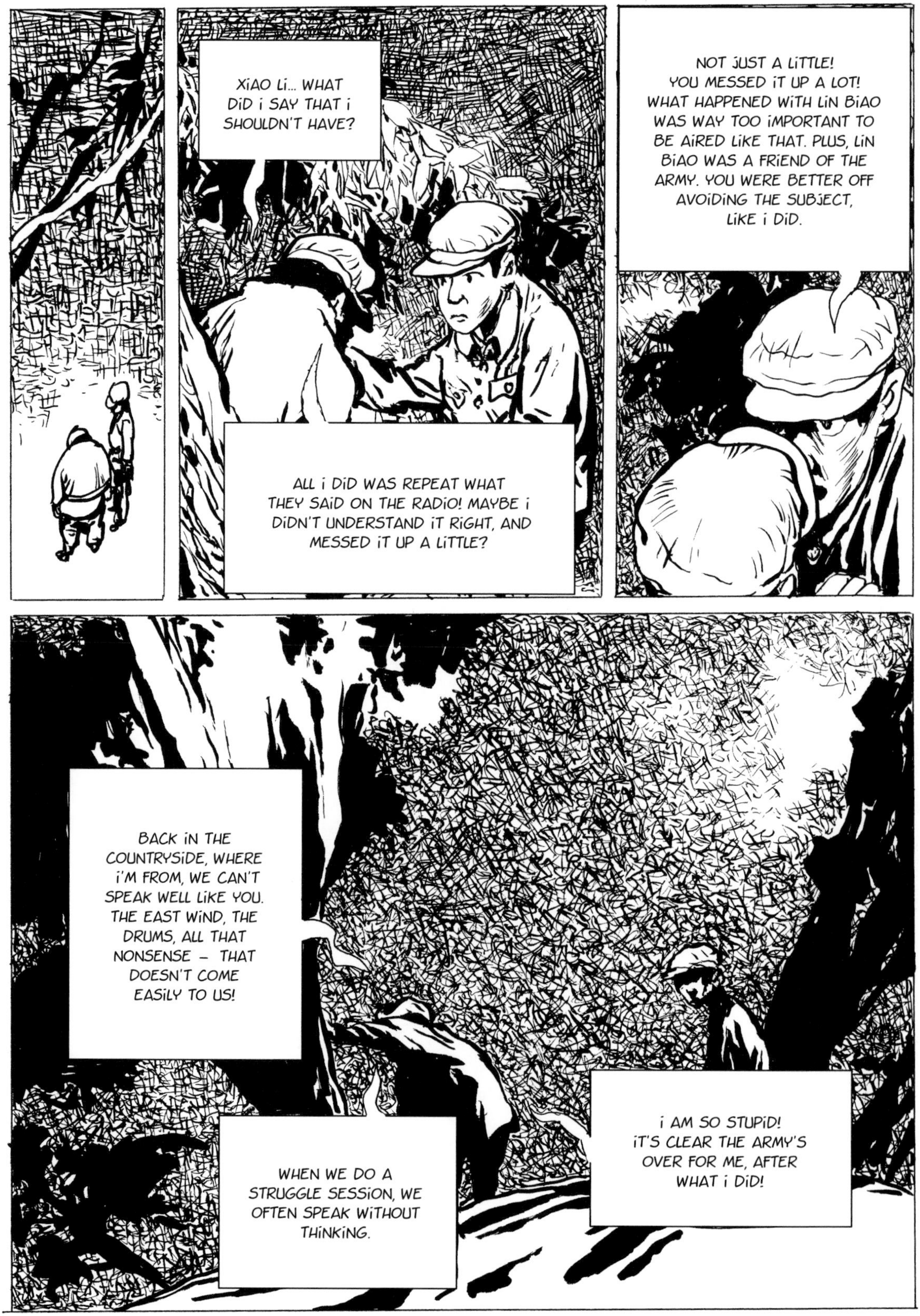
XIAO LI... WHAT DID I SAY THAT I SHOULDN'T HAVE?
ALL I DID WAS REPEAT WHAT THEY SAID ON THE RADIO! MAYBE I DIDN'T UNDERSTAND IT RIGHT, AND MESSED IT UP A LITTLE?
NOT JUST A LITTLE! YOU MESSED IT UP A LOT! WHAT HAPPENED WITH LIN BIAO WAS WAY TOO IMPORTANT TO BE AIRED LIKE THAT. PLUS, LIN BIAO WAS A FRIEND OF THE ARMY. YOU WERE BETTER OFF AVOIDING THE SUBJECT, LIKE I DID.
BACK IN THE COUNTRYSIDE, WHERE I'M FROM, WE CAN'T SPEAK WELL LIKE YOU. THE EAST WIND, THE DRUMS, ALL THAT NONSENSE – THAT DOESN'T COME EASILY TO US!
WHEN WE DO A STRUGGLE SESSION, WE OFTEN SPEAK WITHOUT THINKING.
I AM SO STUPID! IT'S CLEAR THE ARMY'S OVER FOR ME, AFTER WHAT I DID!

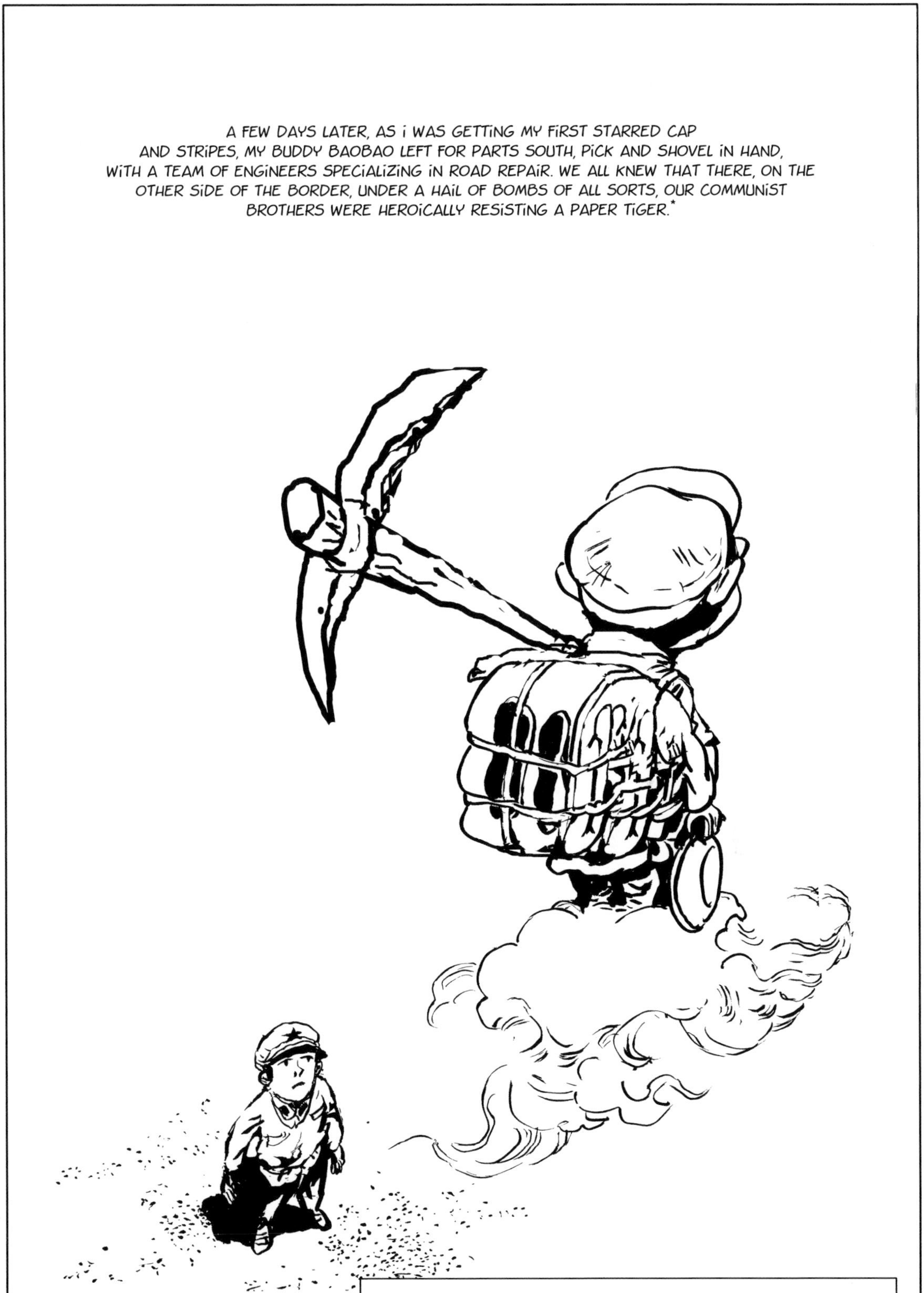
A FEW DAYS LATER, AS I WAS GETTING MY FIRST STARRED CAP AND STRIPES, MY BUDDY BAOBAO LEFT FOR PARTS SOUTH, PICK AND SHOVEL IN HAND, WITH A TEAM OF ENGINEERS SPECIALIZING IN ROAD REPAIR. WE ALL KNEW THAT THERE, ON THE OTHER SIDE OF THE BORDER, UNDER A HAIL OF BOMBS OF ALL SORTS, OUR COMMUNIST BROTHERS WERE HEROICALLY RESISTING A PAPER TIGER.*

* 纸老虎 ZHI LAO HU: THE UNITED STATES OF AMERICA.

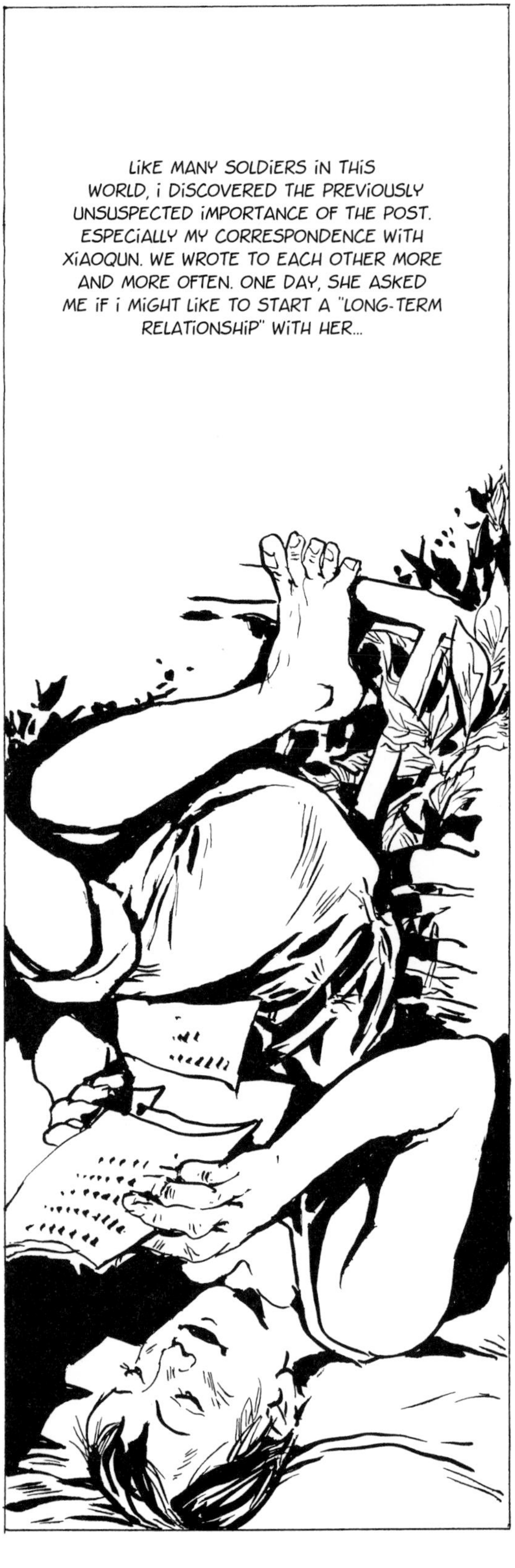
LIKE MANY SOLDIERS IN THIS WORLD, I DISCOVERED THE PREVIOUSLY UNSUSPECTED IMPORTANCE OF THE POST. ESPECIALLY MY CORRESPONDENCE WITH XIAOQUN. WE WROTE TO EACH OTHER MORE AND MORE OFTEN. ONE DAY, SHE ASKED ME IF I MIGHT LIKE TO START A "LONG-TERM RELATIONSHIP" WITH HER...

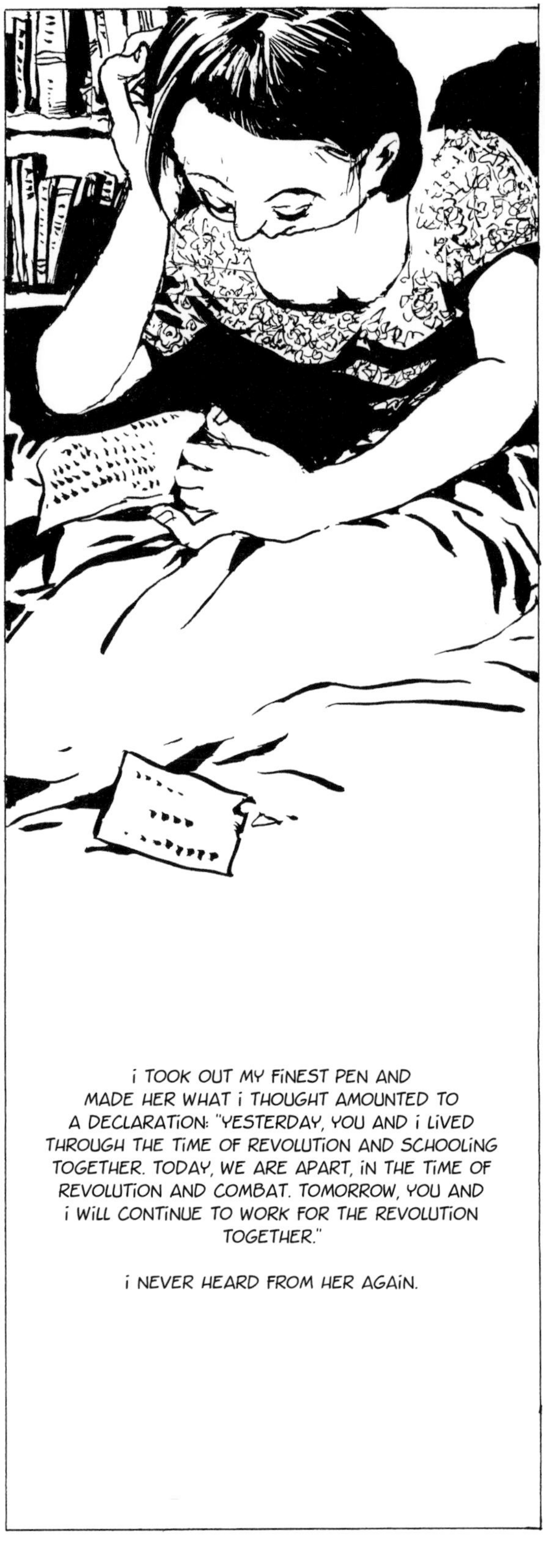
I TOOK OUT MY FINEST PEN AND MADE HER WHAT I THOUGHT AMOUNTED TO A DECLARATION: "YESTERDAY, YOU AND I LIVED THROUGH THE TIME OF REVOLUTION AND SCHOOLING TOGETHER. TODAY, WE ARE APART, IN THE TIME OF REVOLUTION AND COMBAT. TOMORROW, YOU AND I WILL CONTINUE TO WORK FOR THE REVOLUTION TOGETHER."
I NEVER HEARD FROM HER AGAIN.

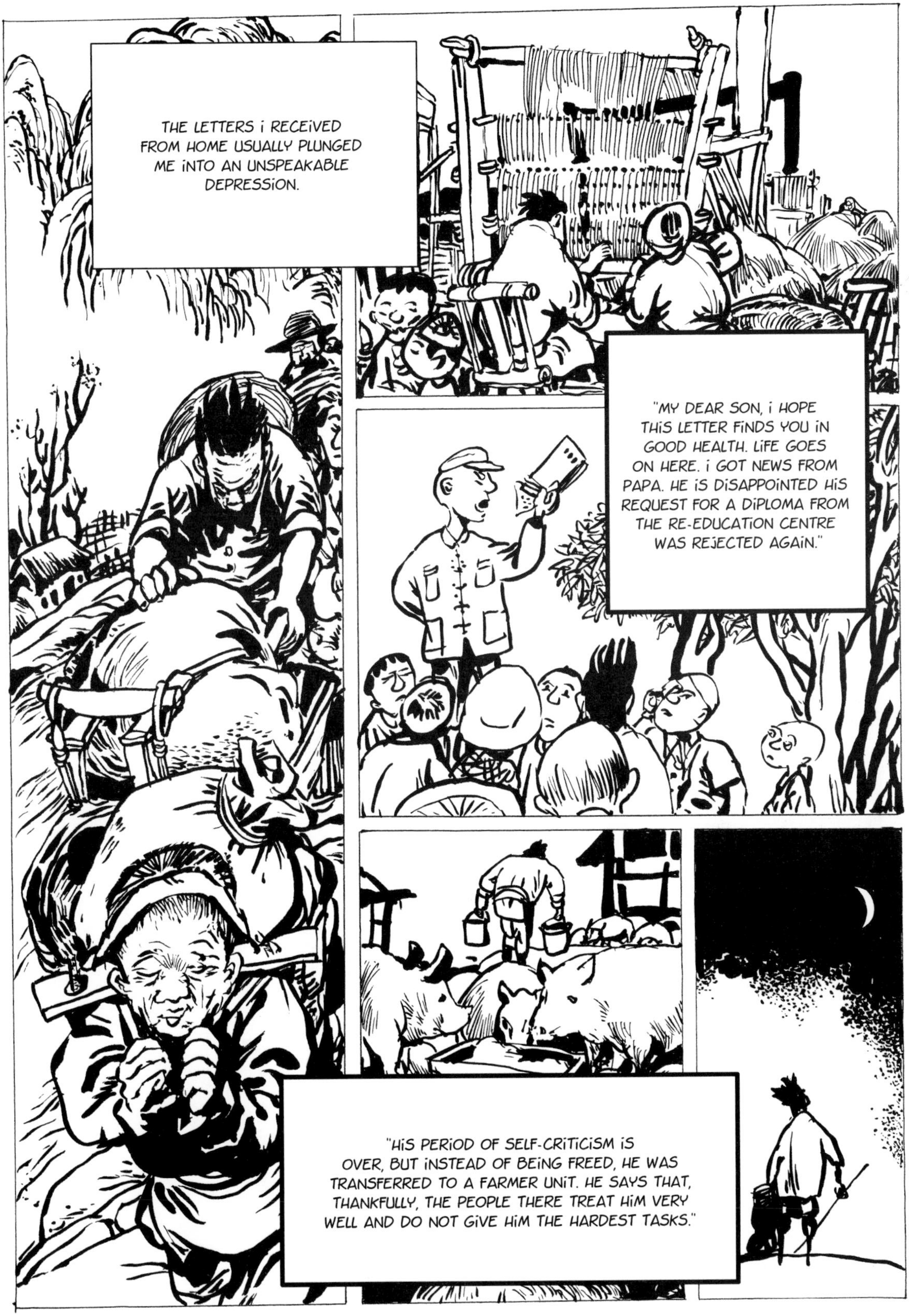
THE LETTERS I RECEIVED FROM HOME USUALLY PLUNGED ME INTO AN UNSPEAKABLE DEPRESSION.
"MY DEAR SON, I HOPE THIS LETTER FINDS YOU IN GOOD HEALTH. LIFE GOES ON HERE. I GOT NEWS FROM PAPA. HE IS DISAPPOINTED HIS REQUEST FOR A DIPLOMA FROM THE RE-EDUCATION CENTRE WAS REJECTED AGAIN."
"HIS PERIOD OF SELF-CRITICISM IS OVER, BUT INSTEAD OF BEING FREED, HE WAS TRANSFERRED TO A FARMER UNIT. HE SAYS THAT, THANKFULLY, THE PEOPLE THERE TREAT HIM VERY WELL AND DO NOT GIVE HIM THE HARDEST TASKS."

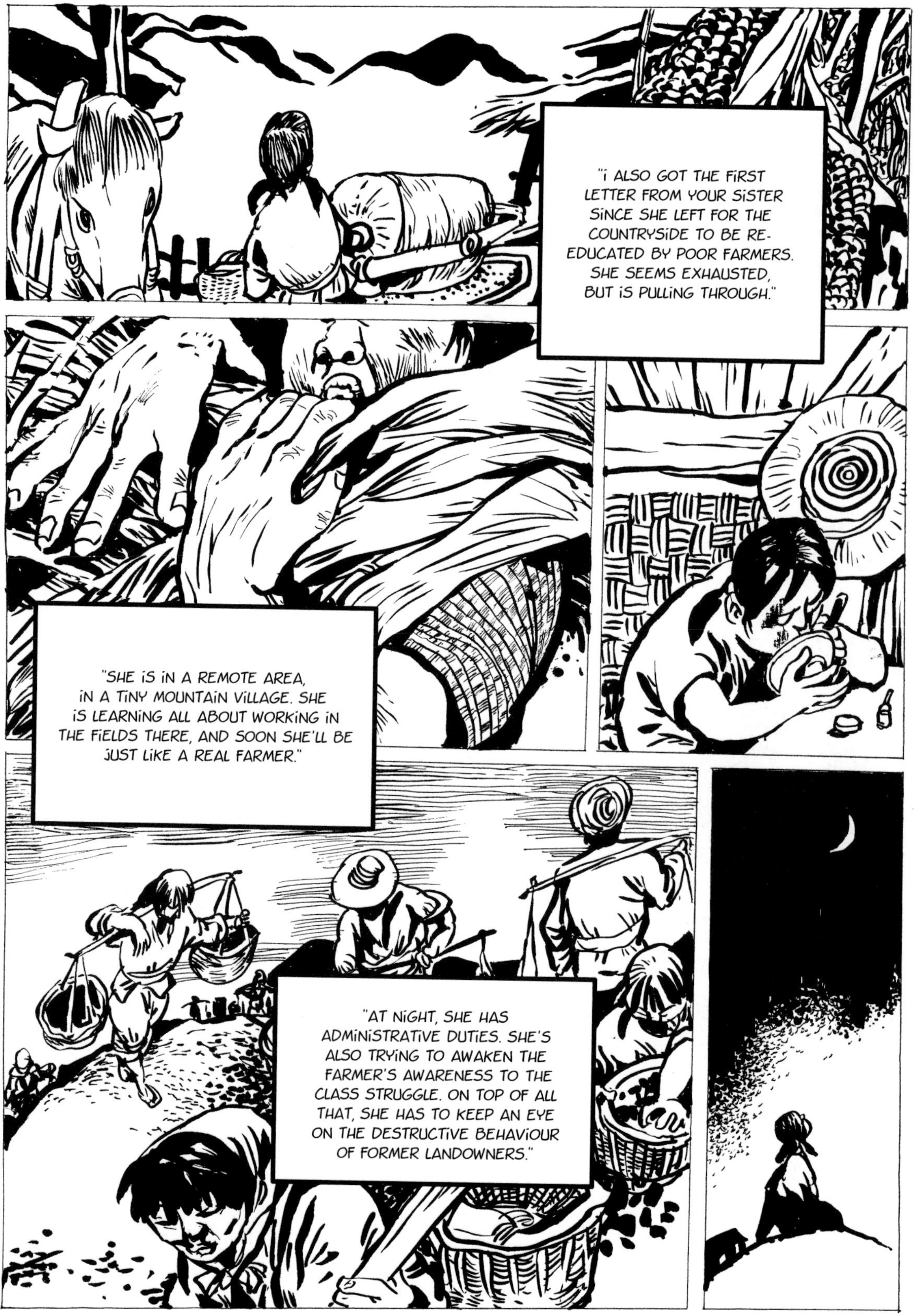
"I ALSO GOT THE FIRST LETTER FROM YOUR SISTER SINCE SHE LEFT FOR THE COUNTRYSIDE TO BE RE-EDUCATED BY POOR FARMERS. SHE SEEMS EXHAUSTED, BUT IS PULLING THROUGH."
"SHE IS IN A REMOTE AREA, IN A TINY MOUNTAIN VILLAGE. SHE IS LEARNING ALL ABOUT WORKING IN THE FIELDS THERE, AND SOON SHE'LL BE JUST LIKE A REAL FARMER."
"AT NIGHT, SHE HAS ADMINISTRATIVE DUTIES. SHE'S ALSO TRYING TO AWAKEN THE FARMER'S AWARENESS TO THE CLASS STRUGGLE. ON TOP OF ALL THAT, SHE HAS TO KEEP AN EYE ON THE DESTRUCTIVE BEHAVIOUR OF FORMER LANDOWNERS."

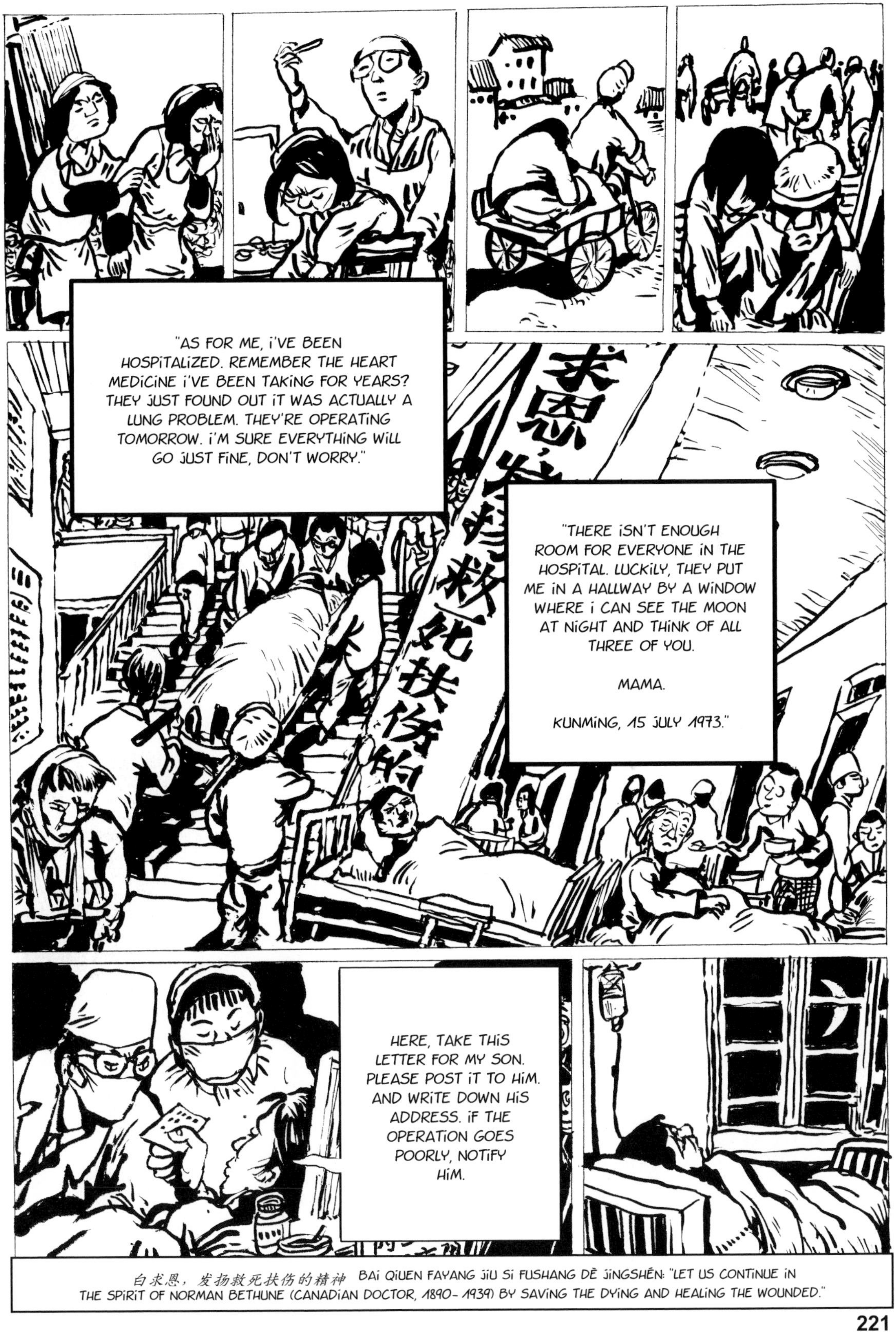
"AS FOR ME, I'VE BEEN HOSPITALIZED. REMEMBER THE HEART MEDICINE I'VE BEEN TAKING FOR YEARS? THEY JUST FOUND OUT IT WAS ACTUALLY A LUNG PROBLEM. THEY'RE OPERATING TOMORROW. I'M SURE EVERYTHING WILL GO JUST FINE, DON'T WORRY."
"THERE ISN'T ENOUGH ROOM FOR EVERYONE IN THE HOSPITAL. LUCKILY, THEY PUT ME IN A HALLWAY BY A WINDOW WHERE I CAN SEE THE MOON AT NIGHT AND THINK OF ALL THREE OF YOU.
MAMA.
KUNMING, 15 JULY 1973."
HERE, TAKE THIS LETTER FOR MY SON. PLEASE POST IT TO HIM. AND WRITE DOWN HIS ADDRESS. IF THE OPERATION GOES POORLY, NOTIFY HIM.

白求恩，发扬救死扶伤的精神 BAI QIUEN FAYANG JIU SI FUSHANG DE JINGSHÉN: "LET US CONTINUE IN THE SPIRIT OF NORMAN BETHUNE (CANADIAN DOCTOR, 1890- 1939) BY SAVING THE DYING AND HEALING THE WOUNDED."

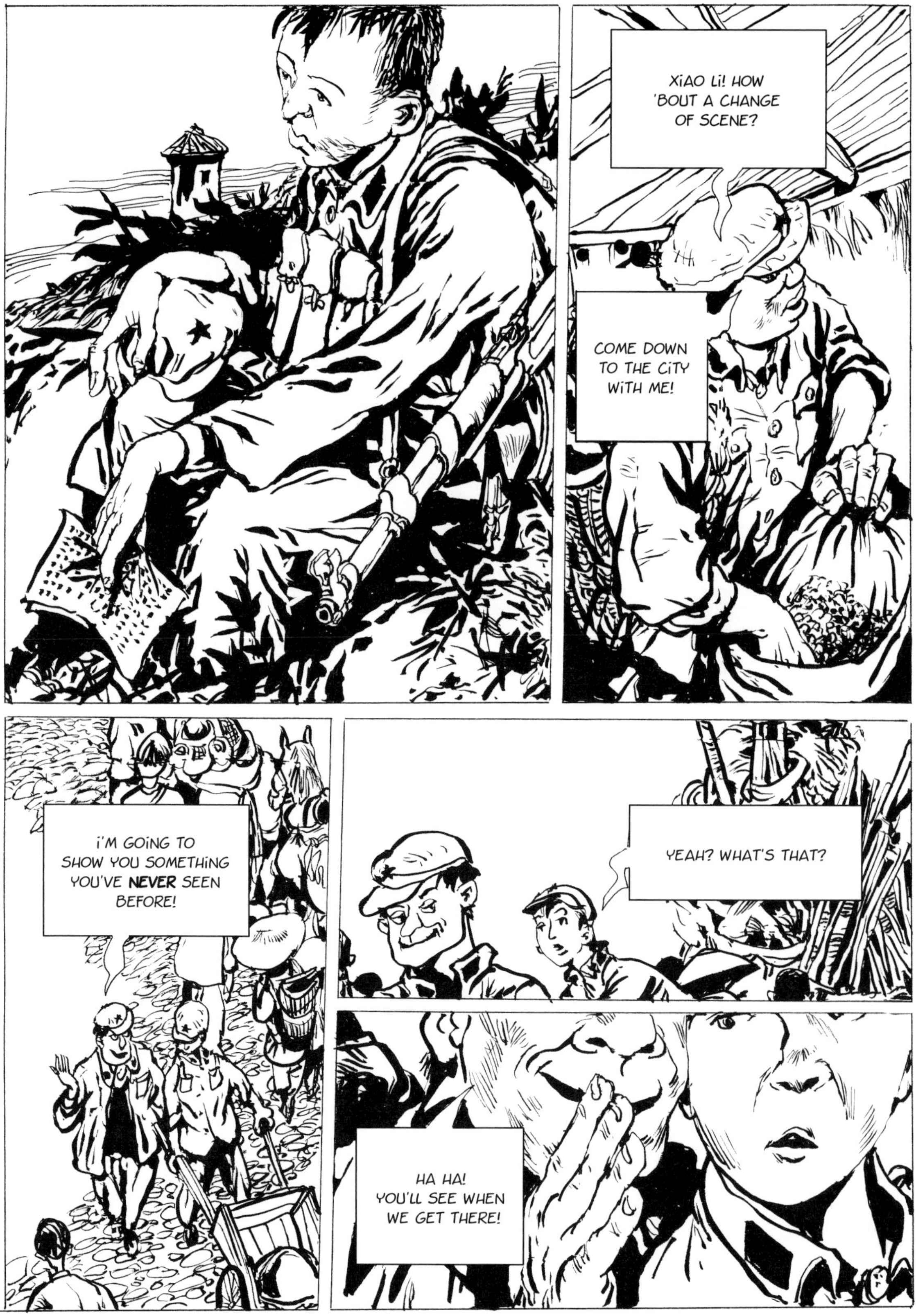
XiAO Li! HOW 'BOUT A CHANGE OF SCENE?
COME DOWN TO THE CiTY WiTH ME!
i'M GOiNG TO SHOW YOU SOMETHiNG YOU'VE **NEVER** SEEN BEFORE!
YEAH? WHAT'S THAT?
HA HA! YOU'LL SEE WHEN WE GET THERE!

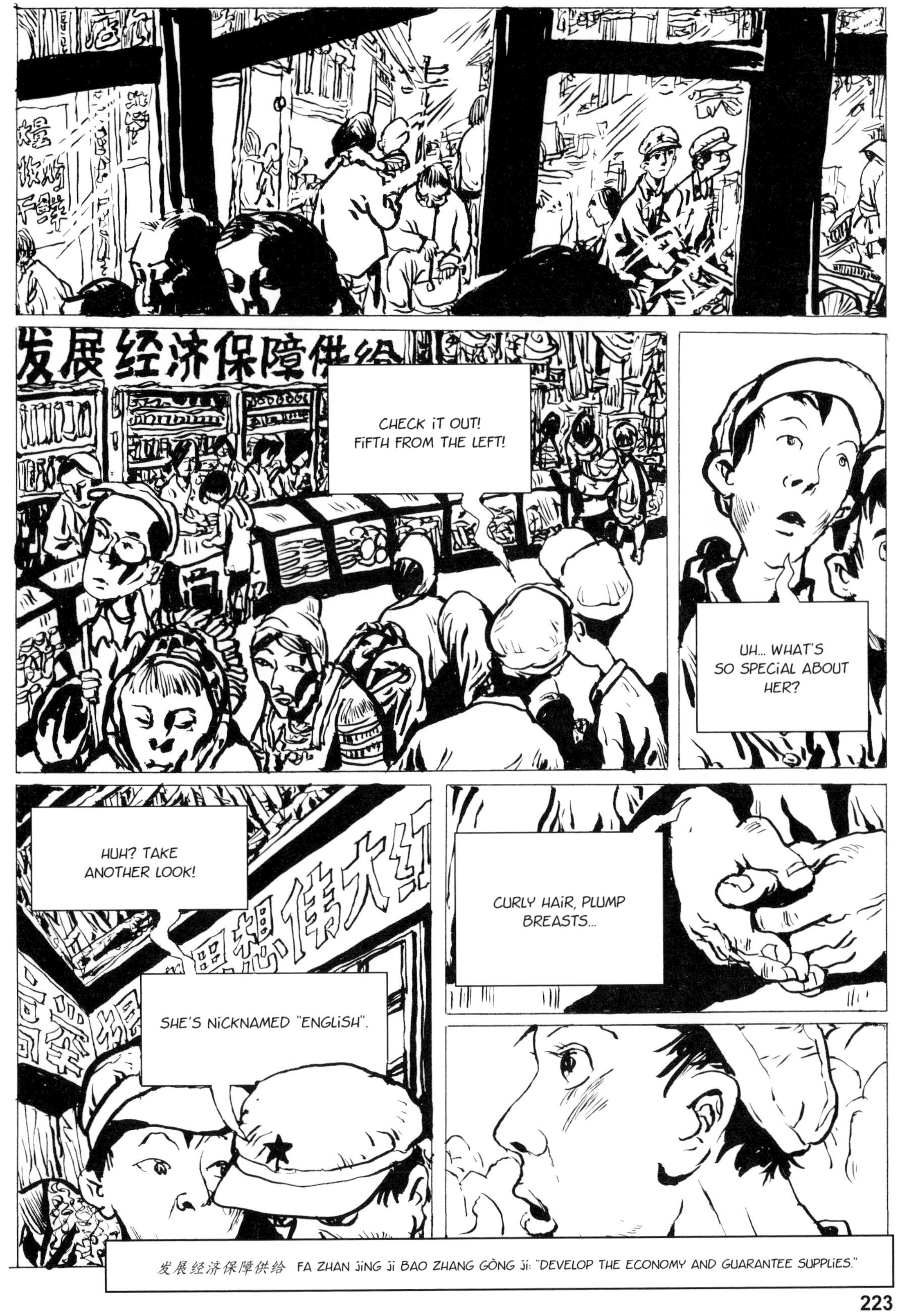
发展经济保障供给
CHECK iT OUT! FiFTH FROM THE LEFT!
UH... WHAT'S SO SPECiAL ABOUT HER?
HUH? TAKE ANOTHER LOOK!
SHE'S NiCKNAMED "ENGLiSH".
CURLY HAiR, PLUMP BREASTS...

发展经济保障供给 FA ZHAN JiNG Ji BAO ZHANG GÒNG Ji: "DEVELOP THE ECONOMY AND GUARANTEE SUPPLiES."

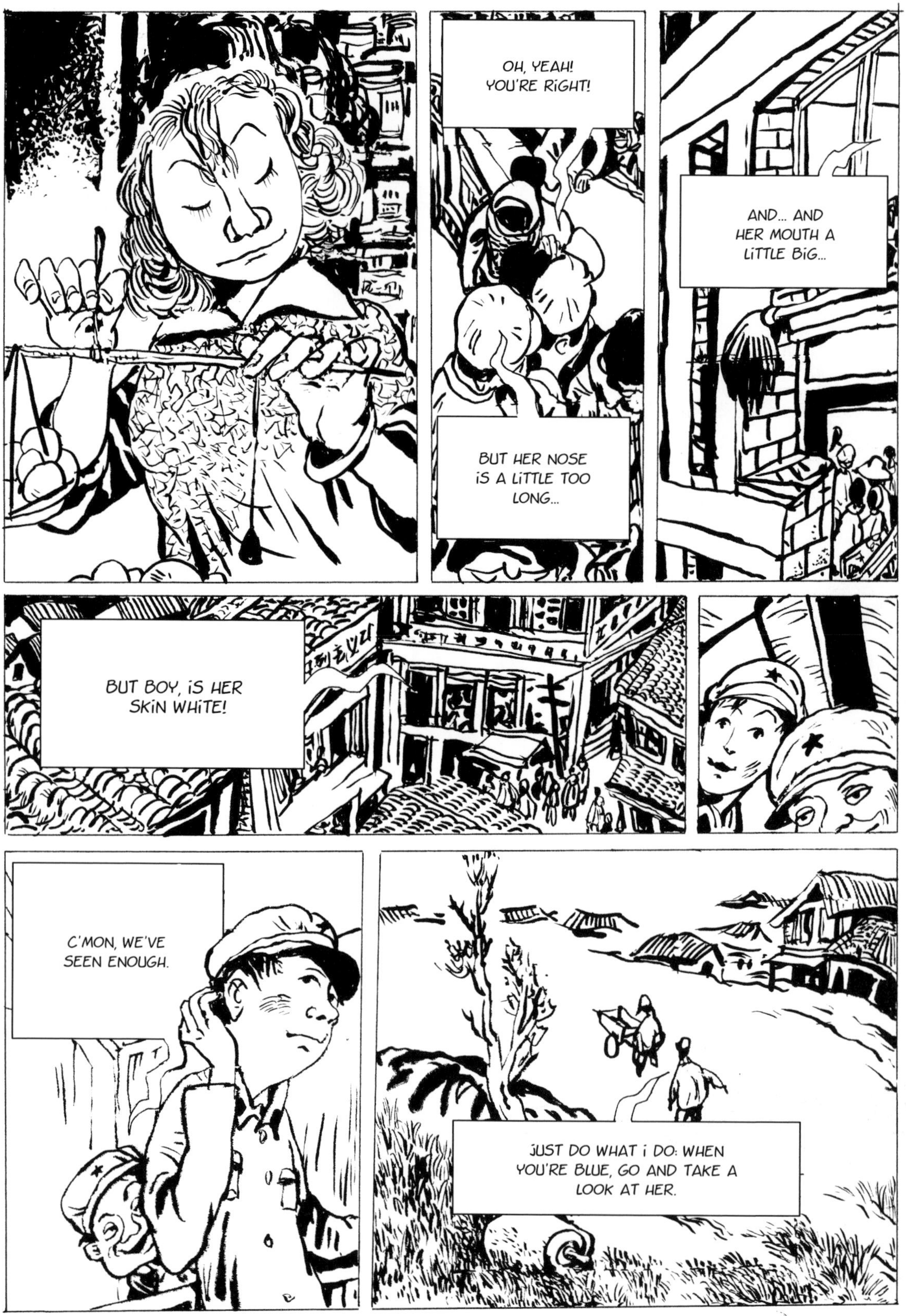
OH, YEAH! YOU'RE RIGHT!
BUT HER NOSE IS A LITTLE TOO LONG...
AND... AND HER MOUTH A LITTLE BIG...
BUT BOY, IS HER SKIN WHITE!
C'MON, WE'VE SEEN ENOUGH.
JUST DO WHAT I DO: WHEN YOU'RE BLUE, GO AND TAKE A LOOK AT HER.

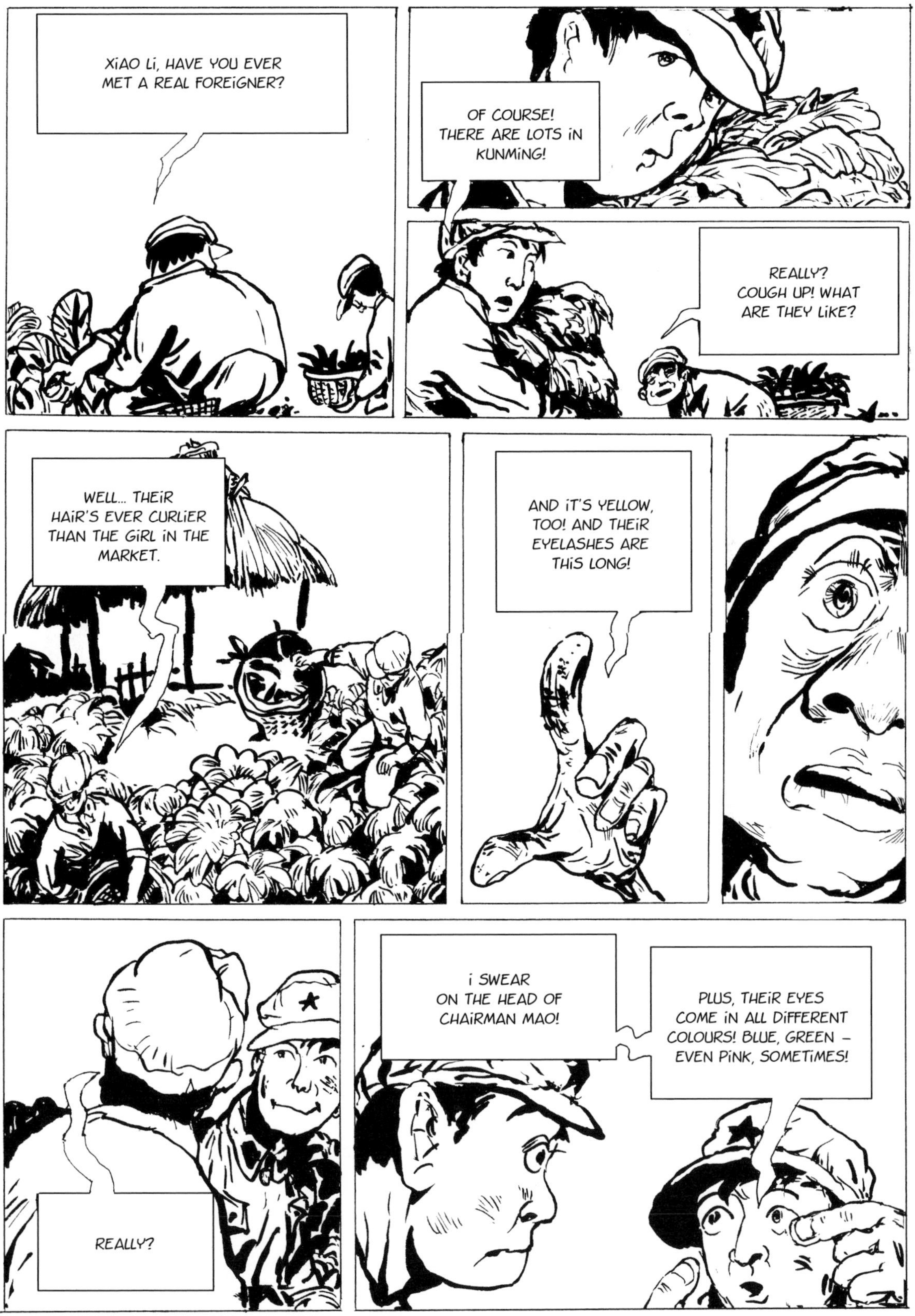
XiAO Li, HAVE YOU EVER MET A REAL FOREiGNER?
OF COURSE! THERE ARE LOTS iN KUNMiNG!
REALLY? COUGH UP! WHAT ARE THEY LiKE?
WELL... THEiR HAiR'S EVER CURLiER THAN THE GiRL iN THE MARKET.
AND iT'S YELLOW, TOO! AND THEiR EYELASHES ARE THiS LONG!
REALLY?
i SWEAR ON THE HEAD OF CHAiRMAN MAO!
PLUS, THEiR EYES COME iN ALL DiFFERENT COLOURS! BLUE, GREEN – EVEN PiNK, SOMETiMES!

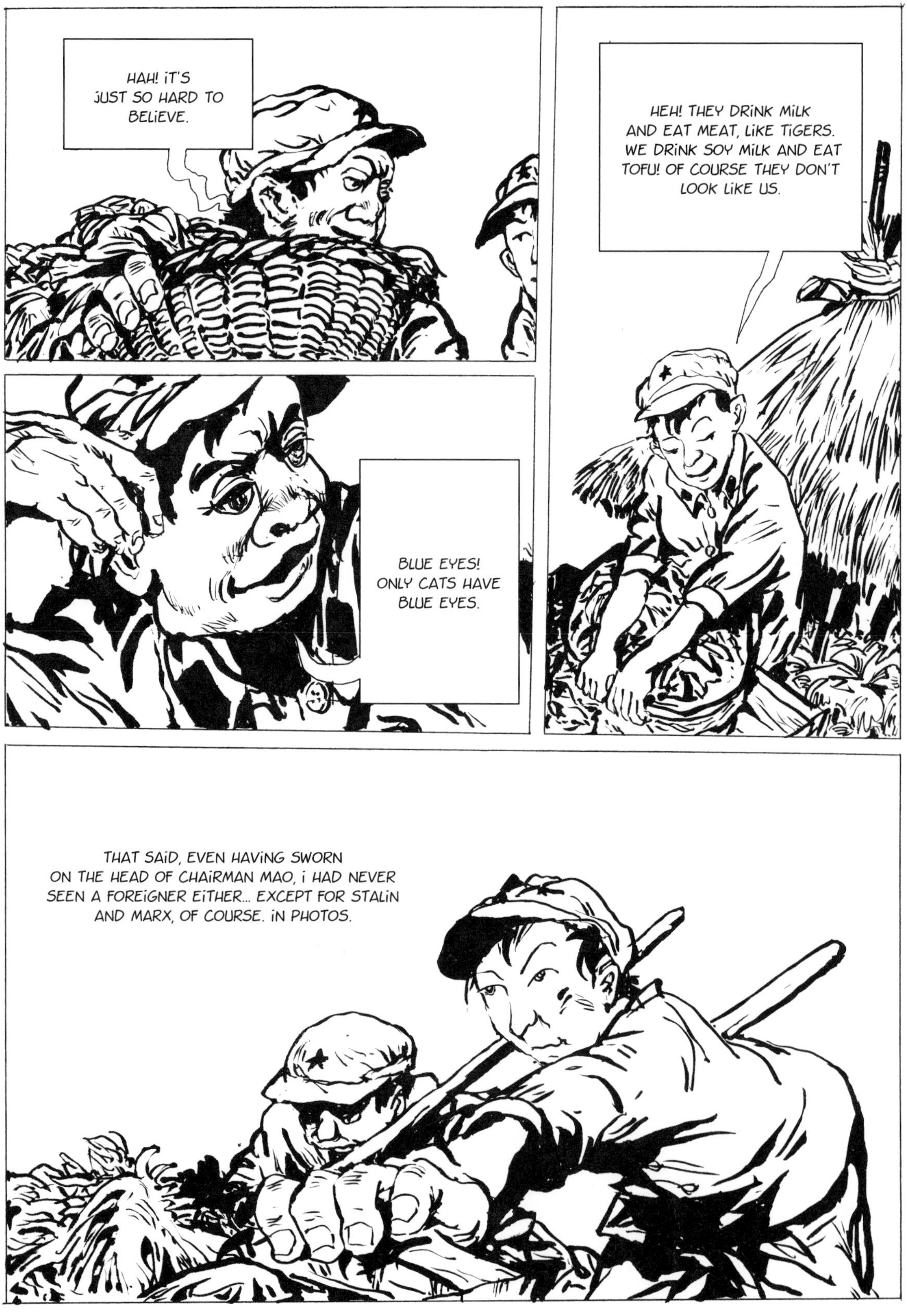
HAH! IT'S JUST SO HARD TO BELIEVE.
HEH! THEY DRINK MILK AND EAT MEAT, LIKE TIGERS. WE DRINK SOY MILK AND EAT TOFU! OF COURSE THEY DON'T LOOK LIKE US.
BLUE EYES! ONLY CATS HAVE BLUE EYES.
THAT SAID, EVEN HAVING SWORN ON THE HEAD OF CHAIRMAN MAO, I HAD NEVER SEEN A FOREIGNER EITHER... EXCEPT FOR STALIN AND MARX, OF COURSE. IN PHOTOS.

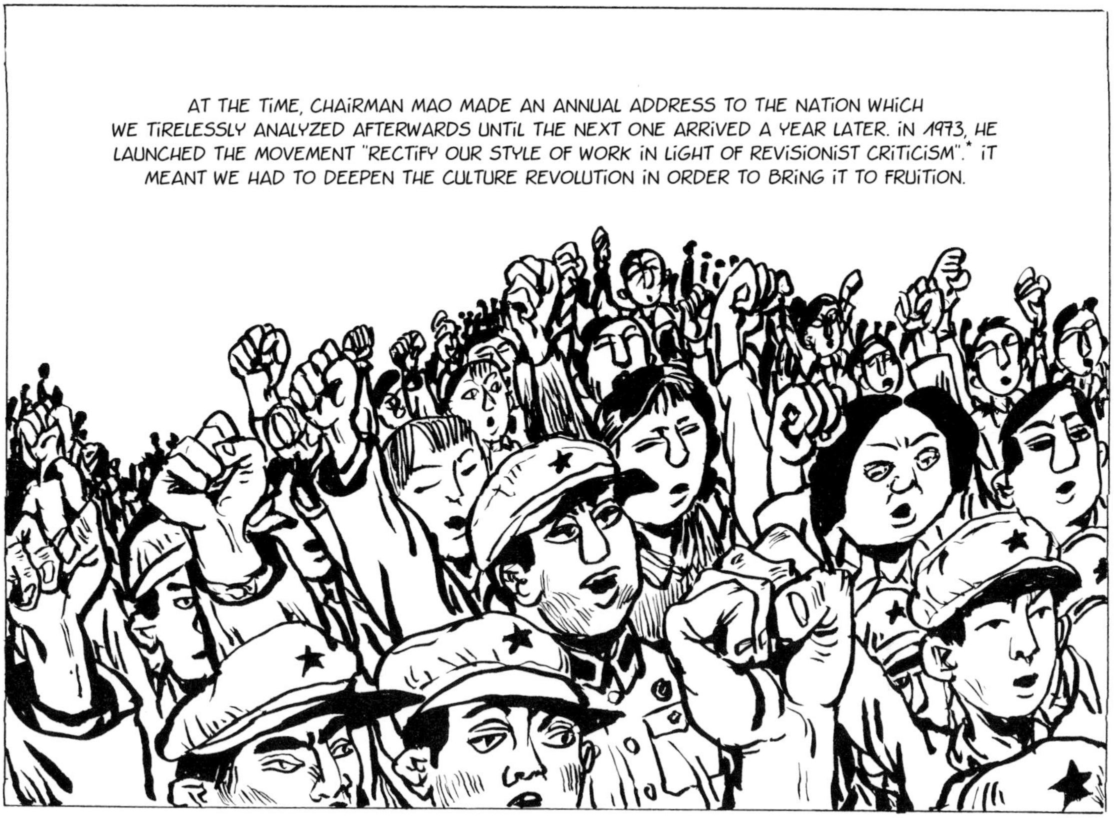
AT THE TIME, CHAIRMAN MAO MADE AN ANNUAL ADDRESS TO THE NATION WHICH WE TIRELESSLY ANALYZED AFTERWARDS UNTIL THE NEXT ONE ARRIVED A YEAR LATER. IN 1973, HE LAUNCHED THE MOVEMENT "RECTIFY OUR STYLE OF WORK IN LIGHT OF REVISIONIST CRITICISM".* IT MEANT WE HAD TO DEEPEN THE CULTURE REVOLUTION IN ORDER TO BRING IT TO FRUITION.

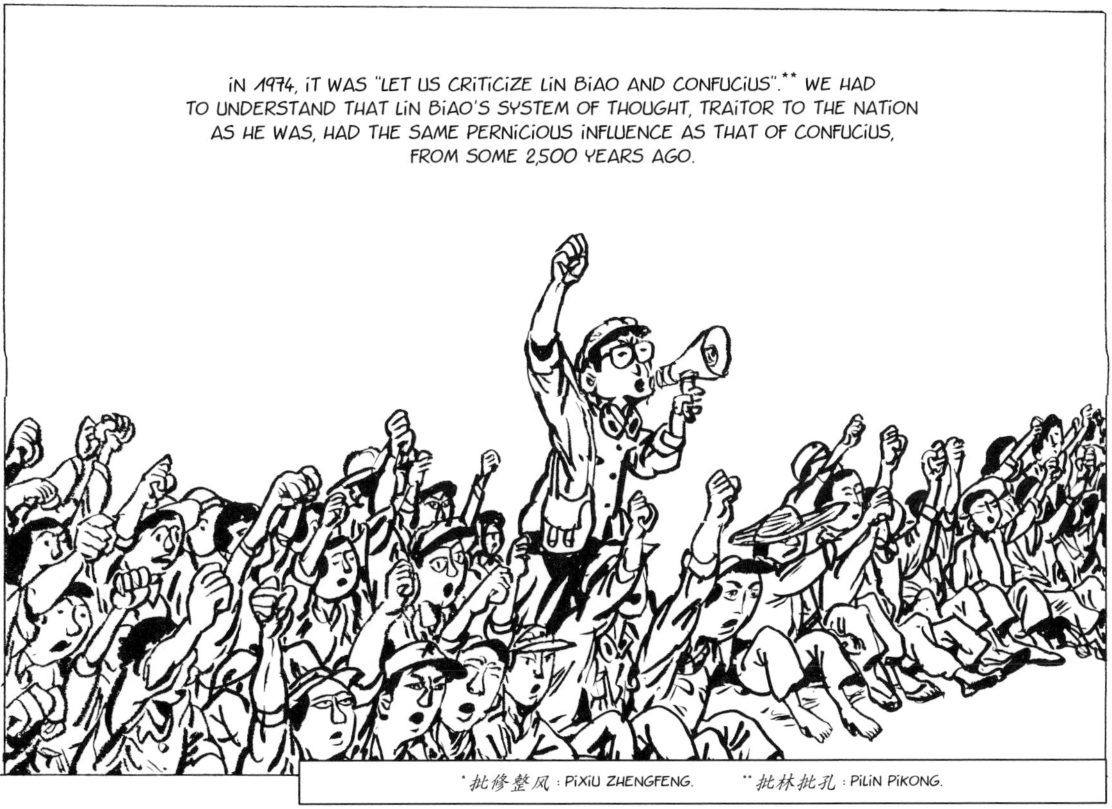
IN 1974, IT WAS "LET US CRITICIZE LIN BIAO AND CONFUCIUS".** WE HAD TO UNDERSTAND THAT LIN BIAO'S SYSTEM OF THOUGHT, TRAITOR TO THE NATION AS HE WAS, HAD THE SAME PERNICIOUS INFLUENCE AS THAT OF CONFUCIUS, FROM SOME 2,500 YEARS AGO.

* 批修整风 : PIXIU ZHENGFENG. ** 批林批孔 : PILIN PIKONG.

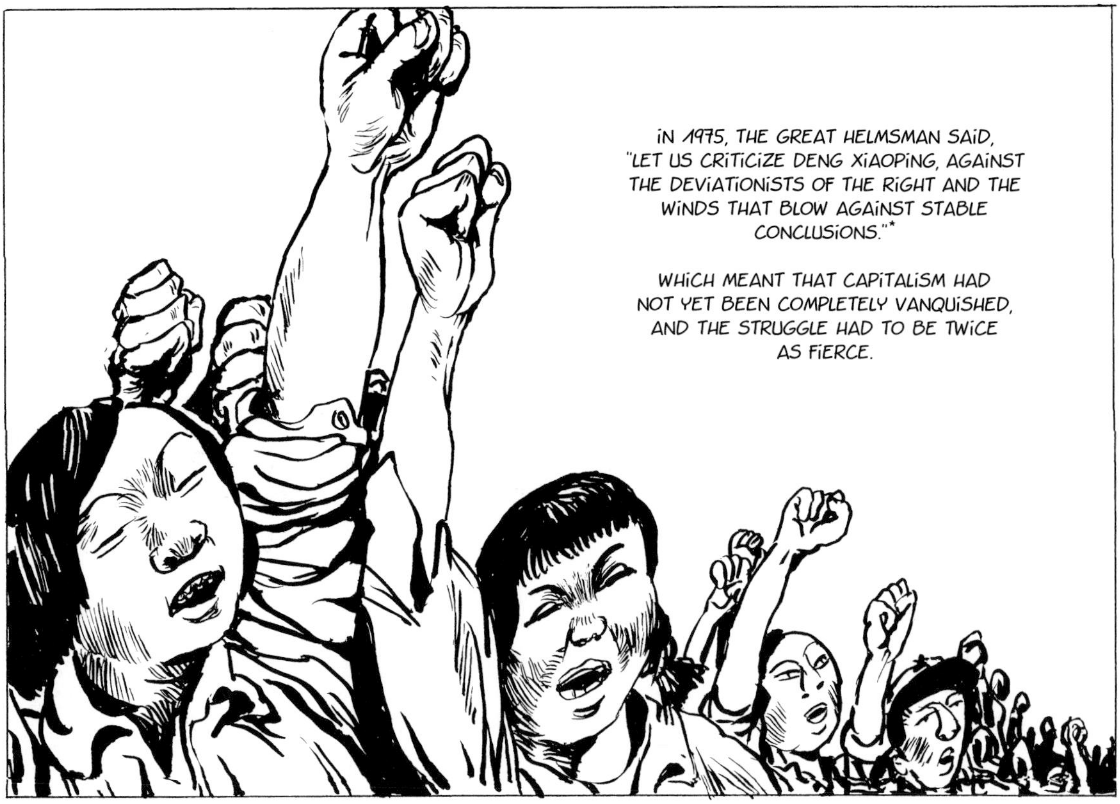
IN 1975, THE GREAT HELMSMAN SAID, "LET US CRITICIZE DENG XIAOPING, AGAINST THE DEVIATIONISTS OF THE RIGHT AND THE WINDS THAT BLOW AGAINST STABLE CONCLUSIONS."*
WHICH MEANT THAT CAPITALISM HAD NOT YET BEEN COMPLETELY VANQUISHED, AND THE STRUGGLE HAD TO BE TWICE AS FIERCE.

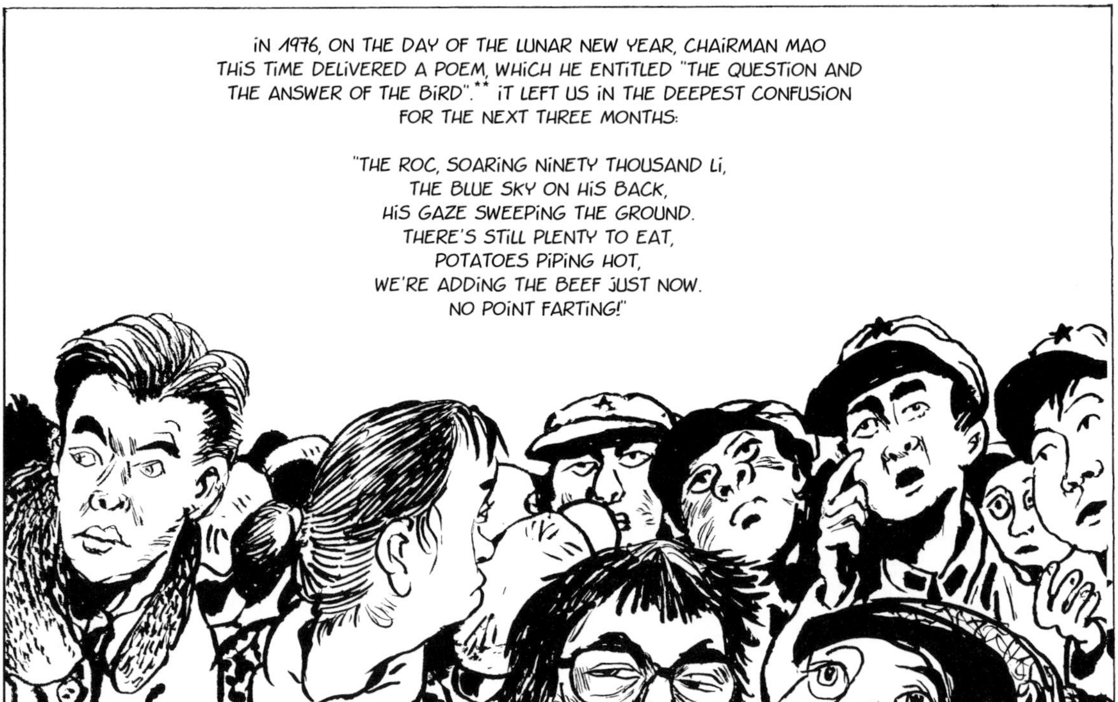
IN 1976, ON THE DAY OF THE LUNAR NEW YEAR, CHAIRMAN MAO THIS TIME DELIVERED A POEM, WHICH HE ENTITLED "THE QUESTION AND THE ANSWER OF THE BIRD".** IT LEFT US IN THE DEEPEST CONFUSION FOR THE NEXT THREE MONTHS:
"THE ROC, SOARING NINETY THOUSAND LI,
THE BLUE SKY ON HIS BACK,
HIS GAZE SWEEPING THE GROUND.
THERE'S STILL PLENTY TO EAT,
POTATOES PIPING HOT,
WE'RE ADDING THE BEEF JUST NOW.
NO POINT FARTING!"

* 批邓反击右倾翻案风: PIDENG, FANJI YOUQING, FANANFENG.

** 鸟儿问答 – 鲲鹏展翅九万里，背负青天，朝下看，还有吃的，土豆烧熟了，再加牛肉，不须放屁.

9 SEPTEMBER 1976.

"NO POINT **FARTING**."

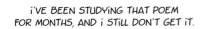

I'VE BEEN STUDYING THAT POEM FOR MONTHS, AND I STILL DON'T GET IT.

DON'T BE SO NEGATIVE, COMRADE. CHAIRMAN MAO MUST HAVE HIS REASONS: IT'S UP TO US TO FIND AND UNDERSTAND THEM!

"HE HAS HIS REASONS"? I'M NOT SO SURE ABOUT THAT ANY MORE. IN FACT, LOTS OF US ARE WONDERING IF HE HASN'T LOST HIS MARBLES!

HEY! WATCH YOUR MOUTH, COMRADE! YOU CAN'T TALK ABOUT THE GREAT HELMSMAN LIKE THAT! THAT'S AS SERIOUS AS INSULTING YOUR OWN FATHER.

229

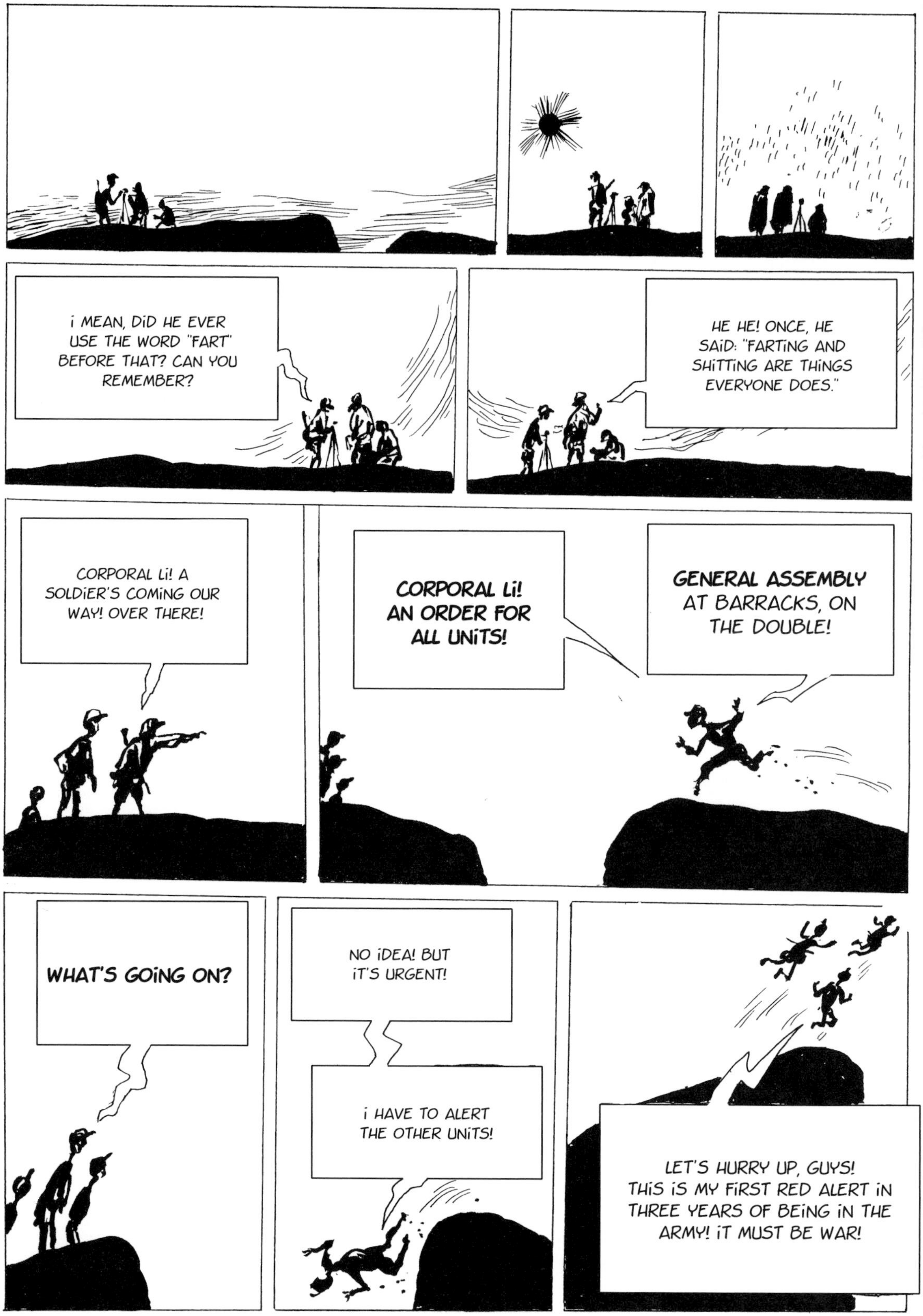

I MEAN, DID HE EVER USE THE WORD "FART" BEFORE THAT? CAN YOU REMEMBER?
HE HE! ONCE, HE SAID: "FARTING AND SHITTING ARE THINGS EVERYONE DOES."
CORPORAL LI! A SOLDIER'S COMING OUR WAY! OVER THERE!
CORPORAL LI! AN ORDER FOR ALL UNITS!
GENERAL ASSEMBLY AT BARRACKS, ON THE DOUBLE!
WHAT'S GOING ON?
NO IDEA! BUT IT'S URGENT!
I HAVE TO ALERT THE OTHER UNITS!
LET'S HURRY UP, GUYS! THIS IS MY FIRST RED ALERT IN THREE YEARS OF BEING IN THE ARMY! IT MUST BE WAR!

WHAT'S GOING ON, MAJOR?

ASSEMBLE BEFORE THE LOUDSPEAKERS. WE'VE PLUGGED THEM INTO THE RADIO.

THE RADIO?

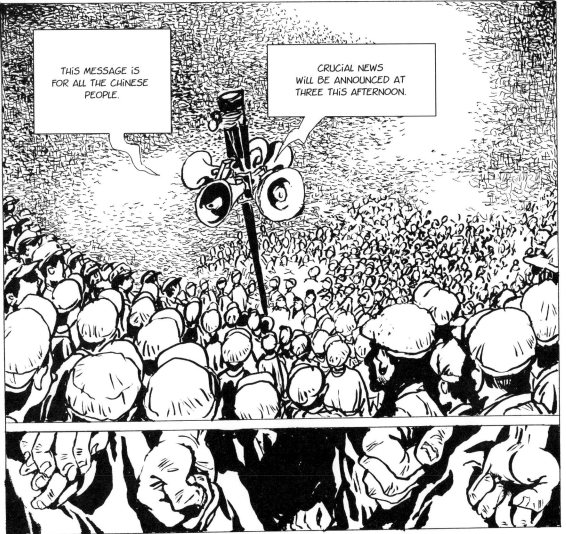

THIS MESSAGE IS FOR ALL THE CHINESE PEOPLE.

CRUCIAL NEWS WILL BE ANNOUNCED AT THREE THIS AFTERNOON.

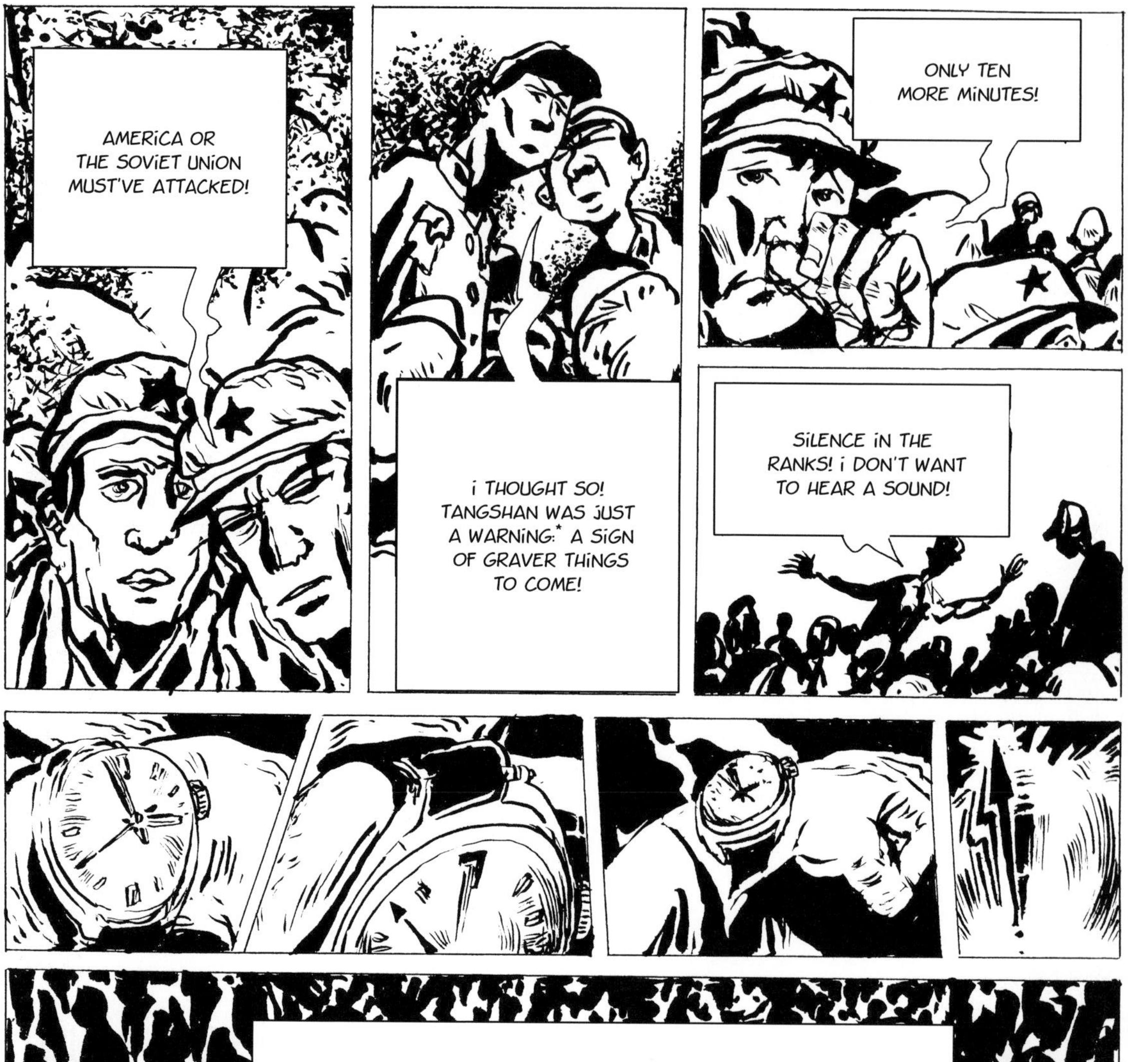
AMERICA OR THE SOVIET UNION MUST'VE ATTACKED!
I THOUGHT SO! TANGSHAN WAS JUST A WARNING:* A SIGN OF GRAVER THINGS TO COME!
ONLY TEN MORE MINUTES!
SILENCE IN THE RANKS! I DON'T WANT TO HEAR A SOUND!
IT IS WITH GREAT SADNESS THAT THE CENTRAL COMMITTEE OF THE CHINESE COMMUNIST PARTY ANNOUNCES TO ALL ITS MEMBERS, THE ARMY AND THE CHINESE PEOPLE THAT UNFORTUNATELY, THIS MORNING AT DAWN, OUR GREAT HELMSMAN, CHAIRMAN MAO, PASSED AWAY...

* ON 28 JULY 1976, AN EARTHQUAKE IN TANGSHAN TOOK 242,000 LIVES.

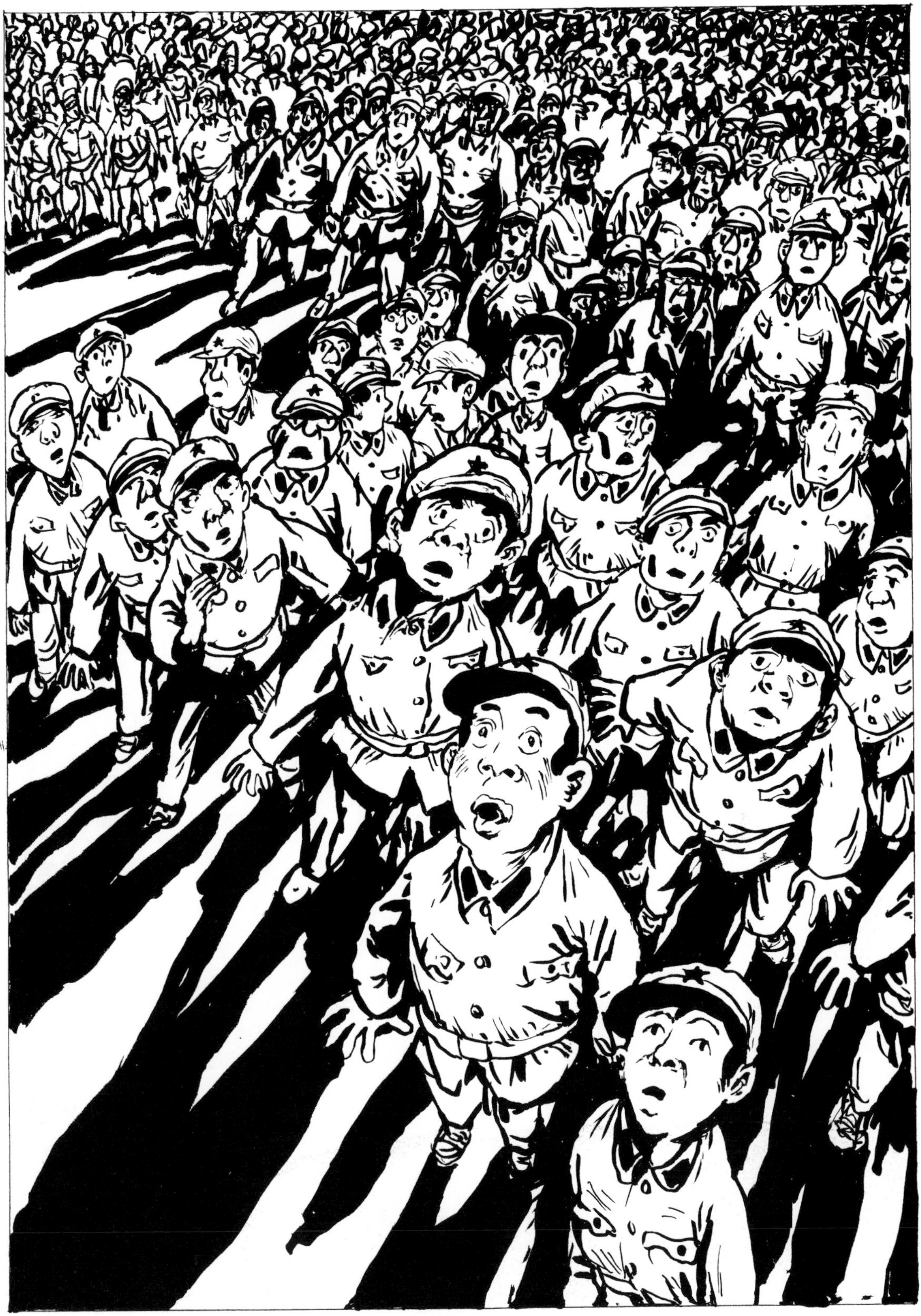

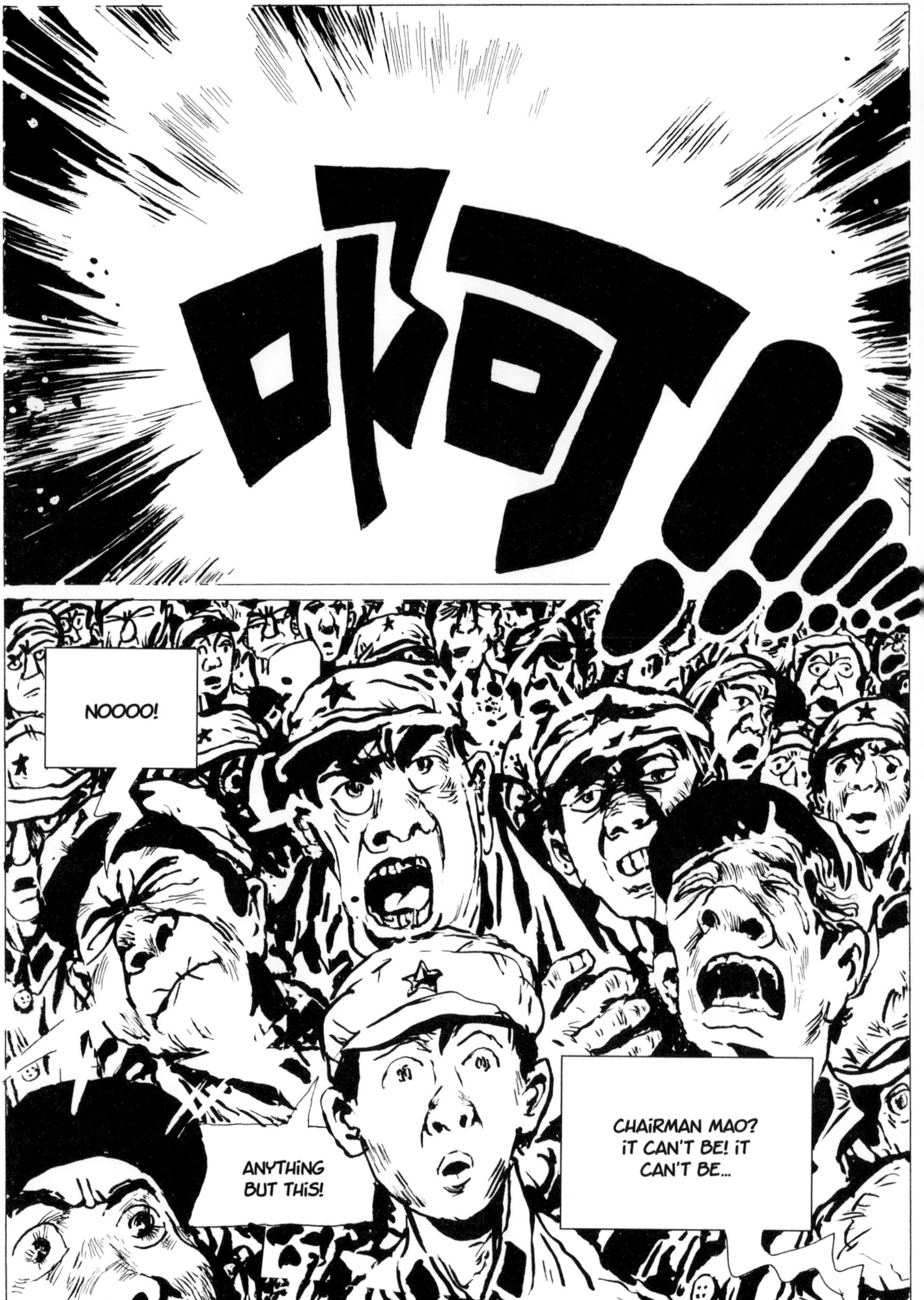
啊!!!!!!
NOOOO!
ANYTHING BUT THIS!
CHAIRMAN MAO? IT CAN'T BE! IT CAN'T BE...

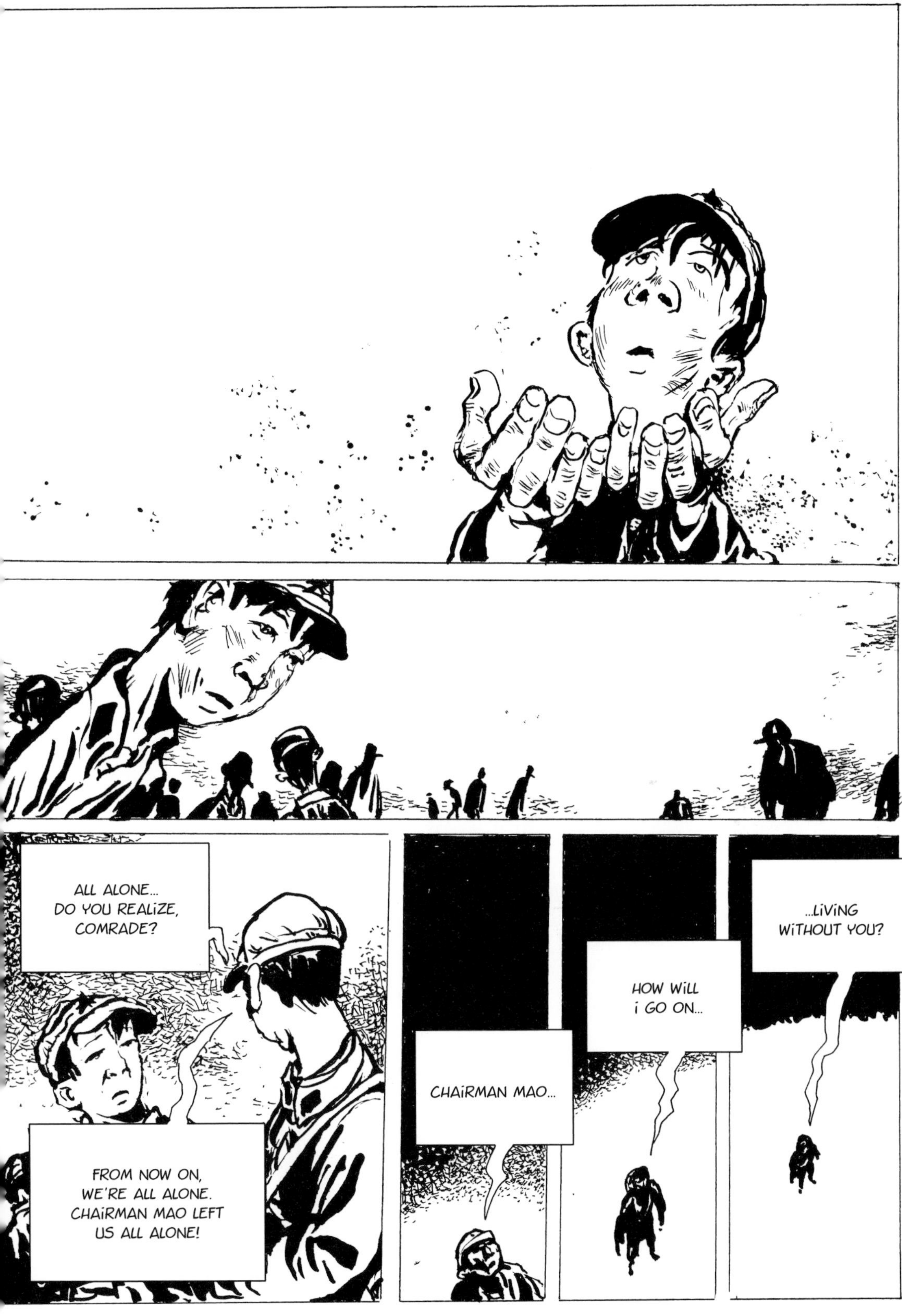
ALL ALONE... DO YOU REALIZE, COMRADE?
FROM NOW ON, WE'RE ALL ALONE. CHAIRMAN MAO LEFT US ALL ALONE!
CHAIRMAN MAO...
HOW WILL I GO ON...
...LIVING WITHOUT YOU?

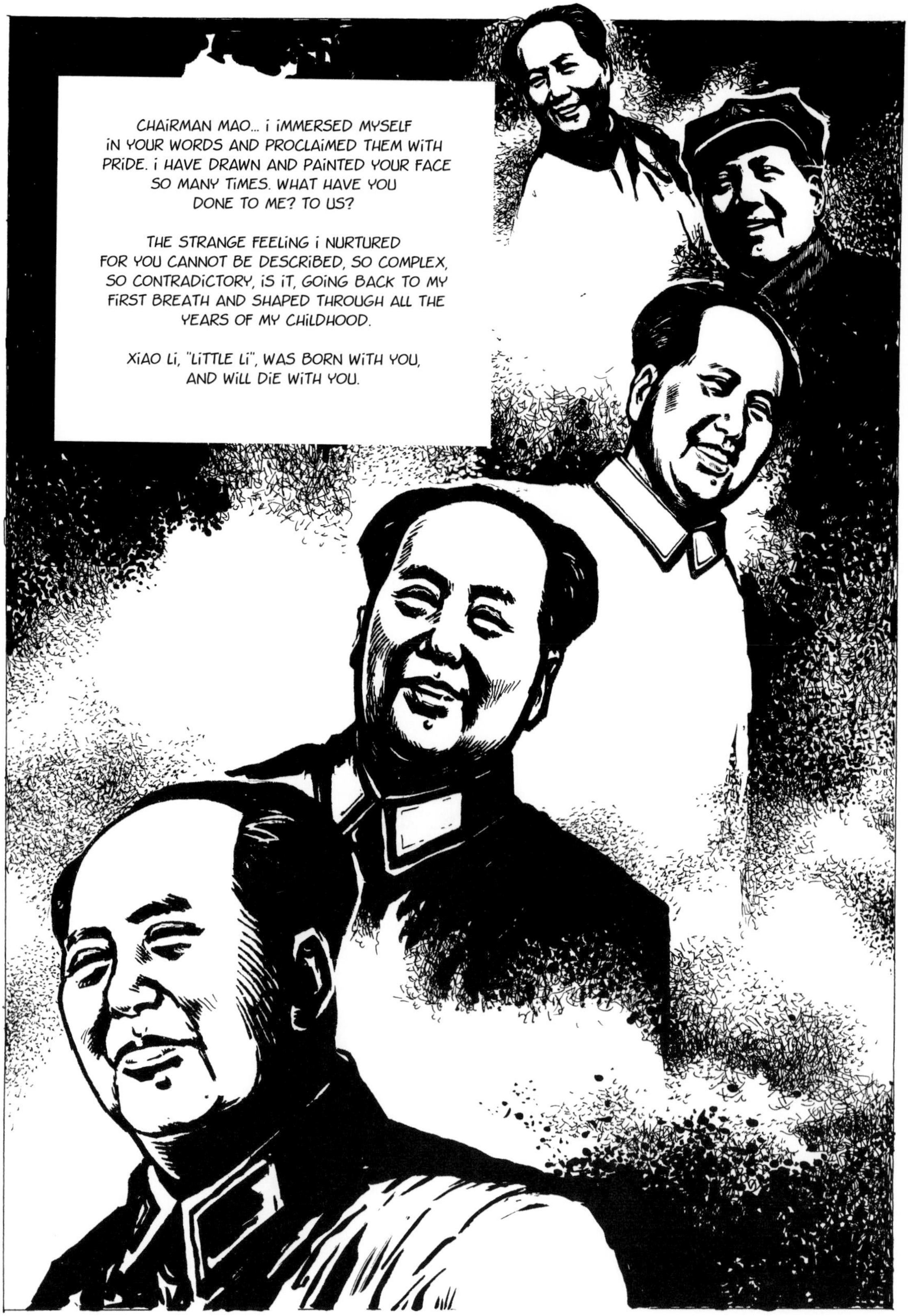
CHAIRMAN MAO... I IMMERSED MYSELF IN YOUR WORDS AND PROCLAIMED THEM WITH PRIDE. I HAVE DRAWN AND PAINTED YOUR FACE SO MANY TIMES. WHAT HAVE YOU DONE TO ME? TO US?
THE STRANGE FEELING I NURTURED FOR YOU CANNOT BE DESCRIBED, SO COMPLEX, SO CONTRADICTORY, IS IT, GOING BACK TO MY FIRST BREATH AND SHAPED THROUGH ALL THE YEARS OF MY CHILDHOOD.
XIAO LI, "LITTLE LI", WAS BORN WITH YOU, AND WILL DIE WITH YOU.

BOOK II

The Time of the Party

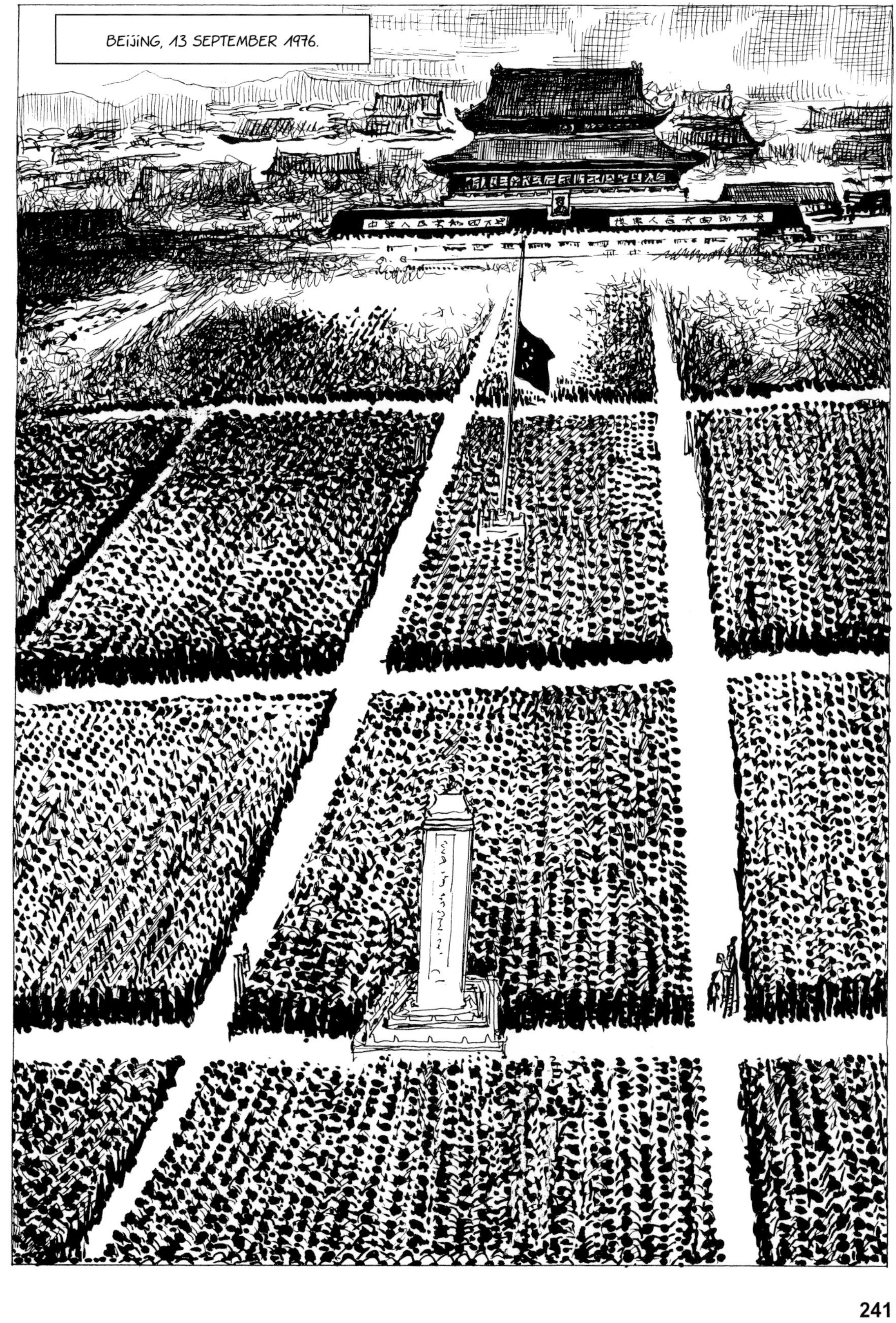
BEIJING, 13 SEPTEMBER 1976.

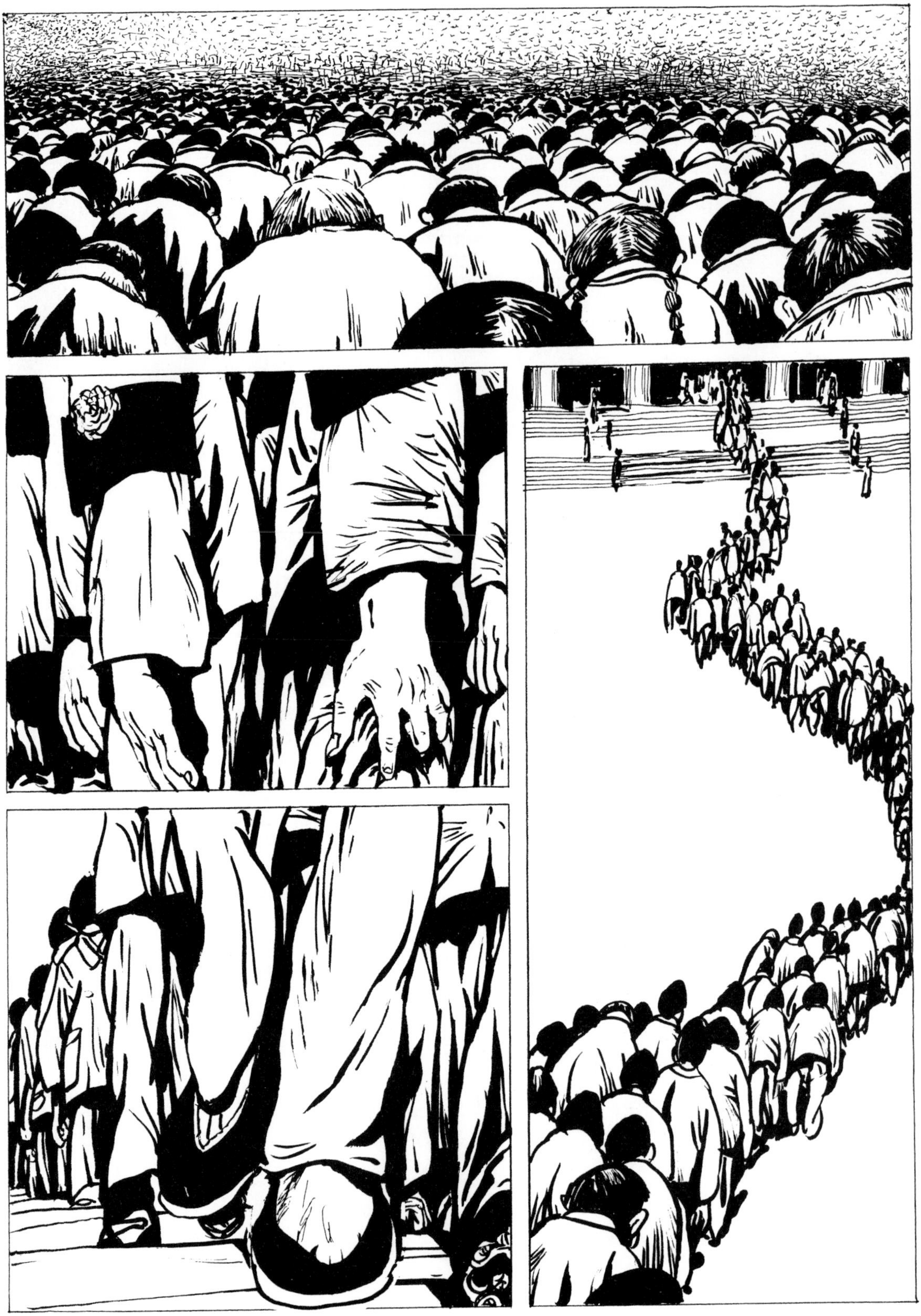

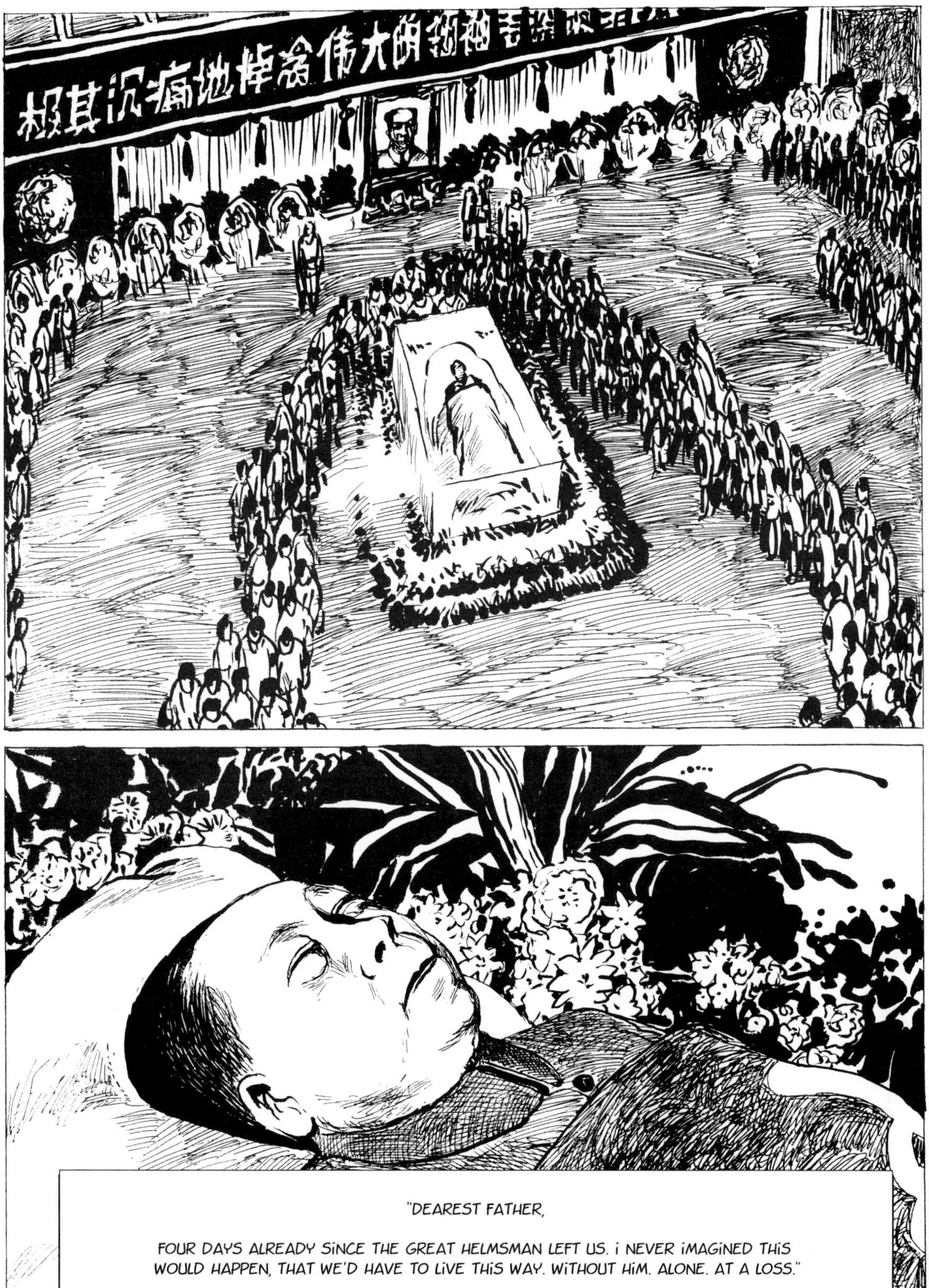
"DEAREST FATHER,
FOUR DAYS ALREADY SINCE THE GREAT HELMSMAN LEFT US. I NEVER IMAGINED THIS WOULD HAPPEN, THAT WE'D HAVE TO LIVE THIS WAY. WITHOUT HIM. ALONE. AT A LOSS."

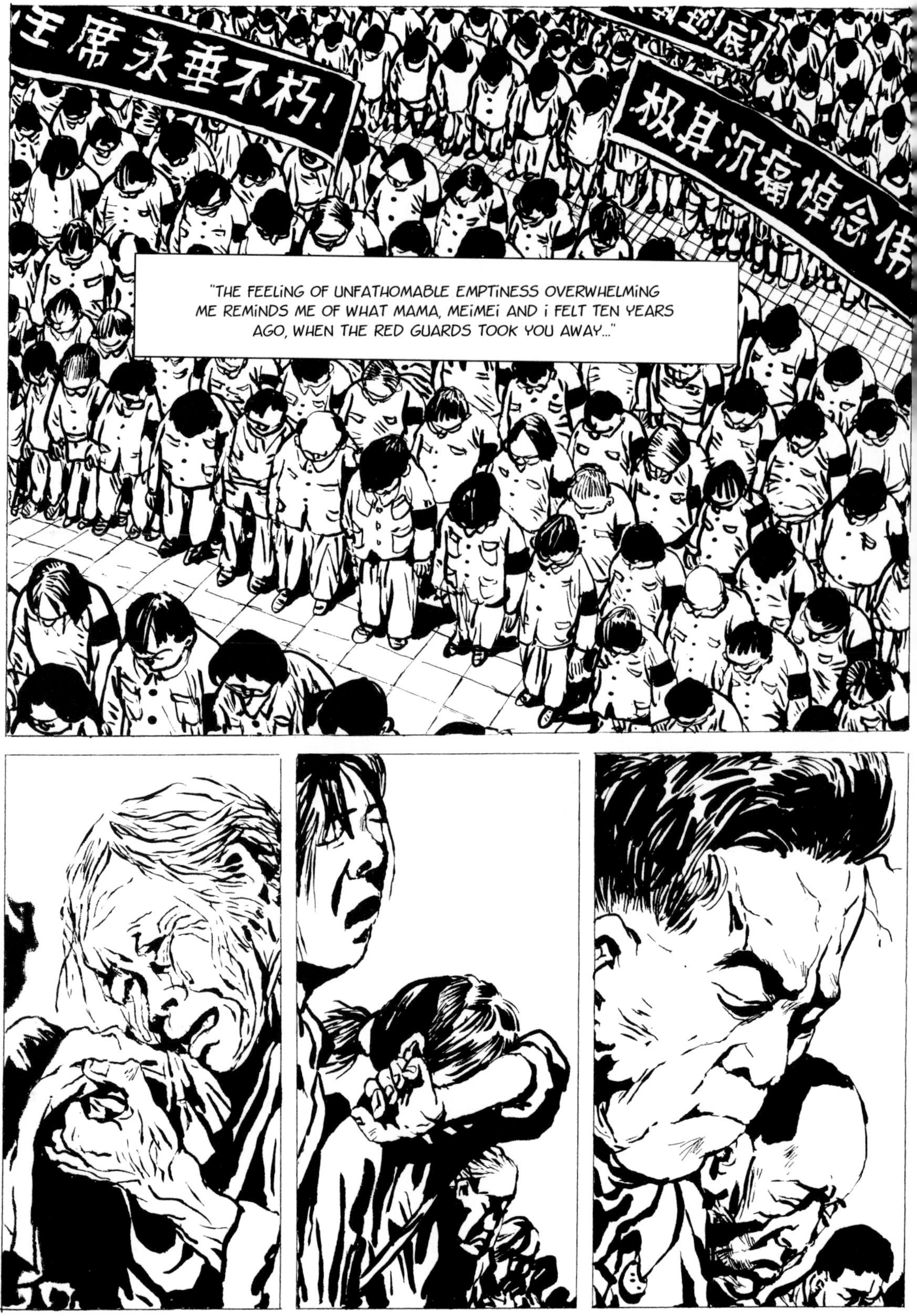

主席永垂不朽!
极其沉痛悼念伟
"THE FEELING OF UNFATHOMABLE EMPTINESS OVERWHELMING ME REMINDS ME OF WHAT MAMA, MEIMEI AND I FELT TEN YEARS AGO, WHEN THE RED GUARDS TOOK YOU AWAY..."

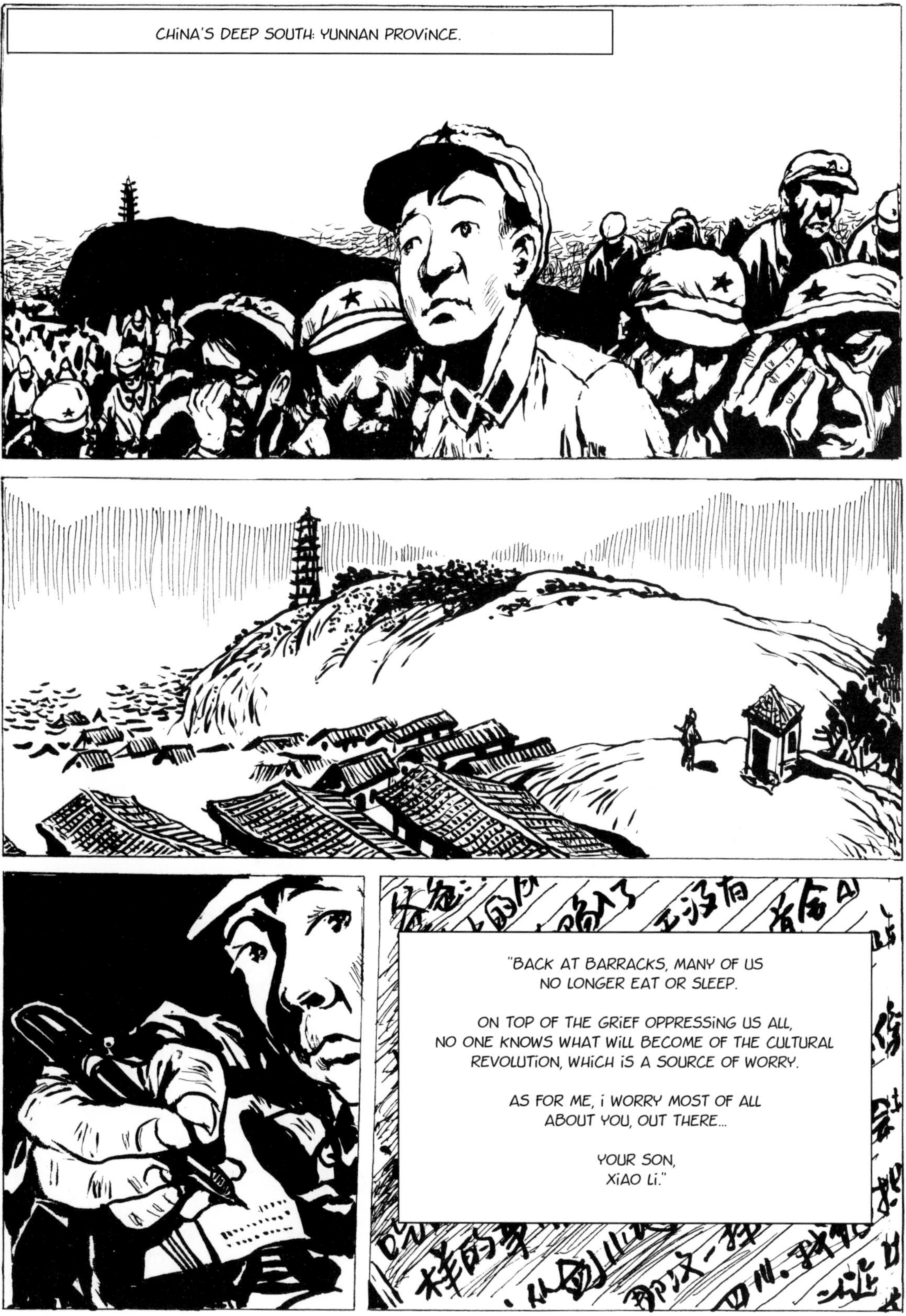
CHINA'S DEEP SOUTH: YUNNAN PROVINCE.
"BACK AT BARRACKS, MANY OF US NO LONGER EAT OR SLEEP.
ON TOP OF THE GRIEF OPPRESSING US ALL, NO ONE KNOWS WHAT WILL BECOME OF THE CULTURAL REVOLUTION, WHICH IS A SOURCE OF WORRY.
AS FOR ME, I WORRY MOST OF ALL ABOUT YOU, OUT THERE...
YOUR SON, XIAO LI."

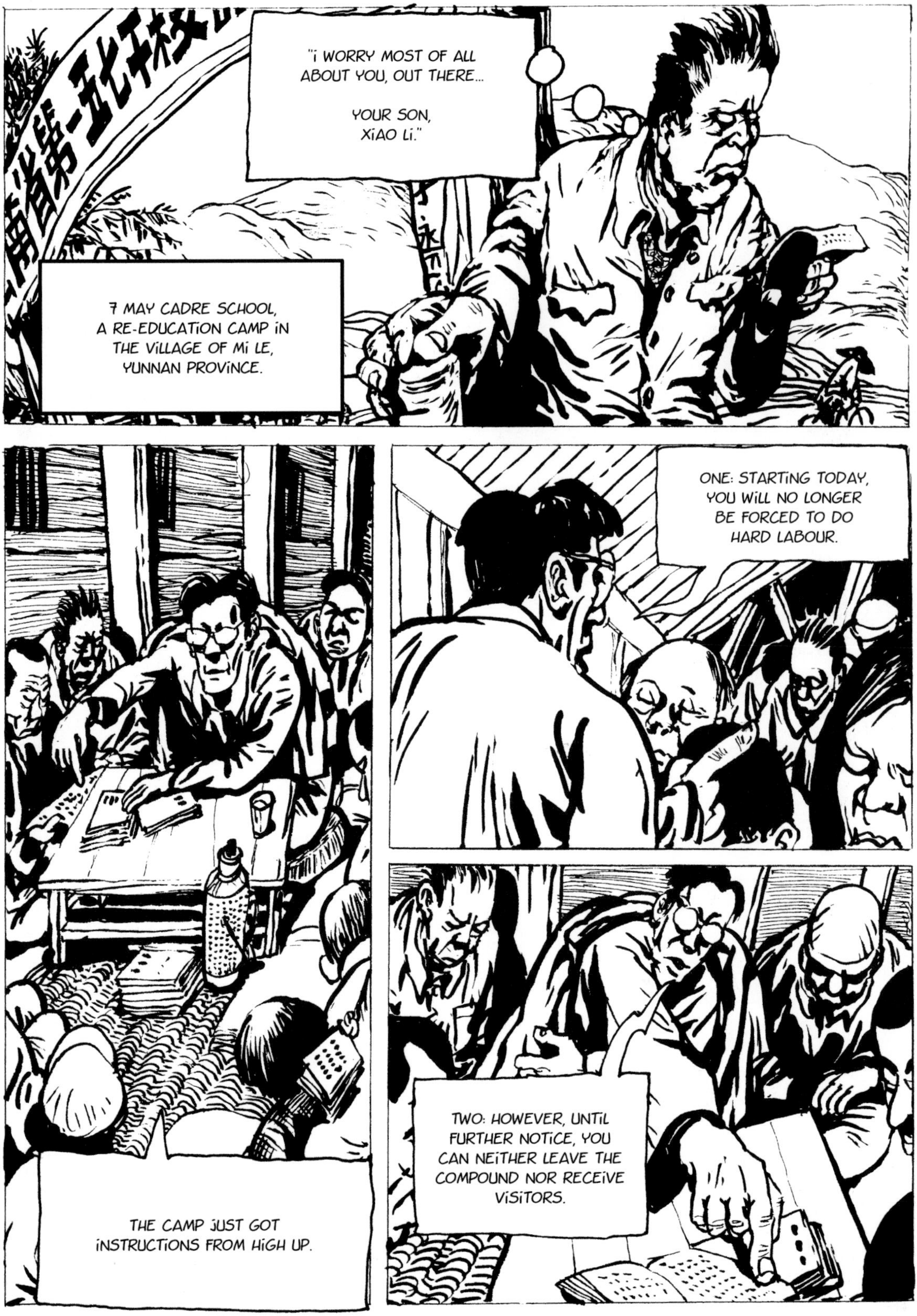
"i WORRY MOST OF ALL ABOUT YOU, OUT THERE...
YOUR SON, XiAO Li."
7 MAY CADRE SCHOOL, A RE-EDUCATION CAMP iN THE ViLLAGE OF Mi LE, YUNNAN PROViNCE.
THE CAMP JUST GOT iNSTRUCTiONS FROM HiGH UP.
ONE: STARTiNG TODAY, YOU WiLL NO LONGER BE FORCED TO DO HARD LABOUR.
TWO: HOWEVER, UNTiL FURTHER NOTiCE, YOU CAN NEiTHER LEAVE THE COMPOUND NOR RECEiVE ViSiTORS.

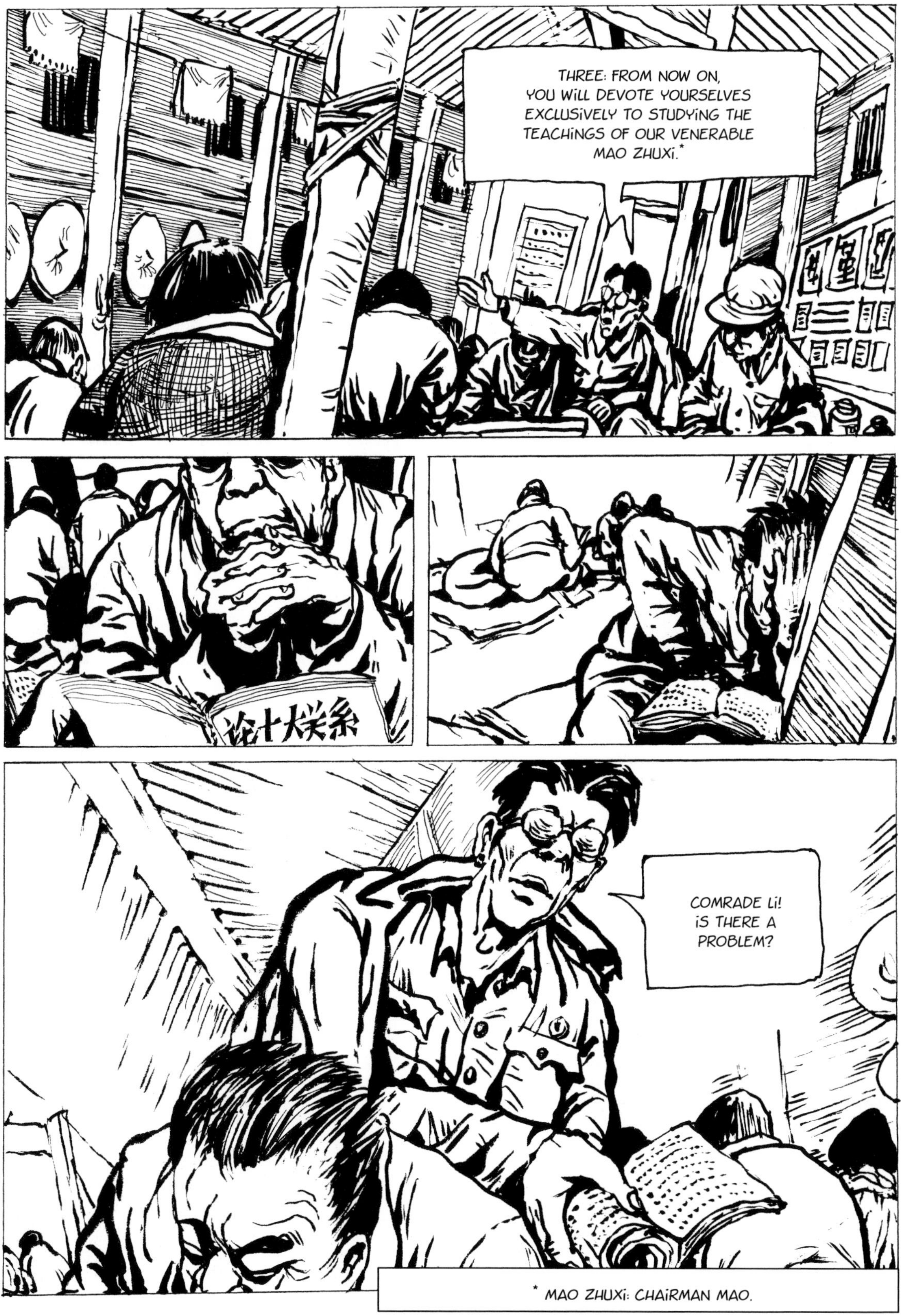
THREE: FROM NOW ON, YOU WILL DEVOTE YOURSELVES EXCLUSIVELY TO STUDYING THE TEACHINGS OF OUR VENERABLE MAO ZHUXI.*
论十大关系
COMRADE LI! IS THERE A PROBLEM?

* MAO ZHUXI: CHAIRMAN MAO.

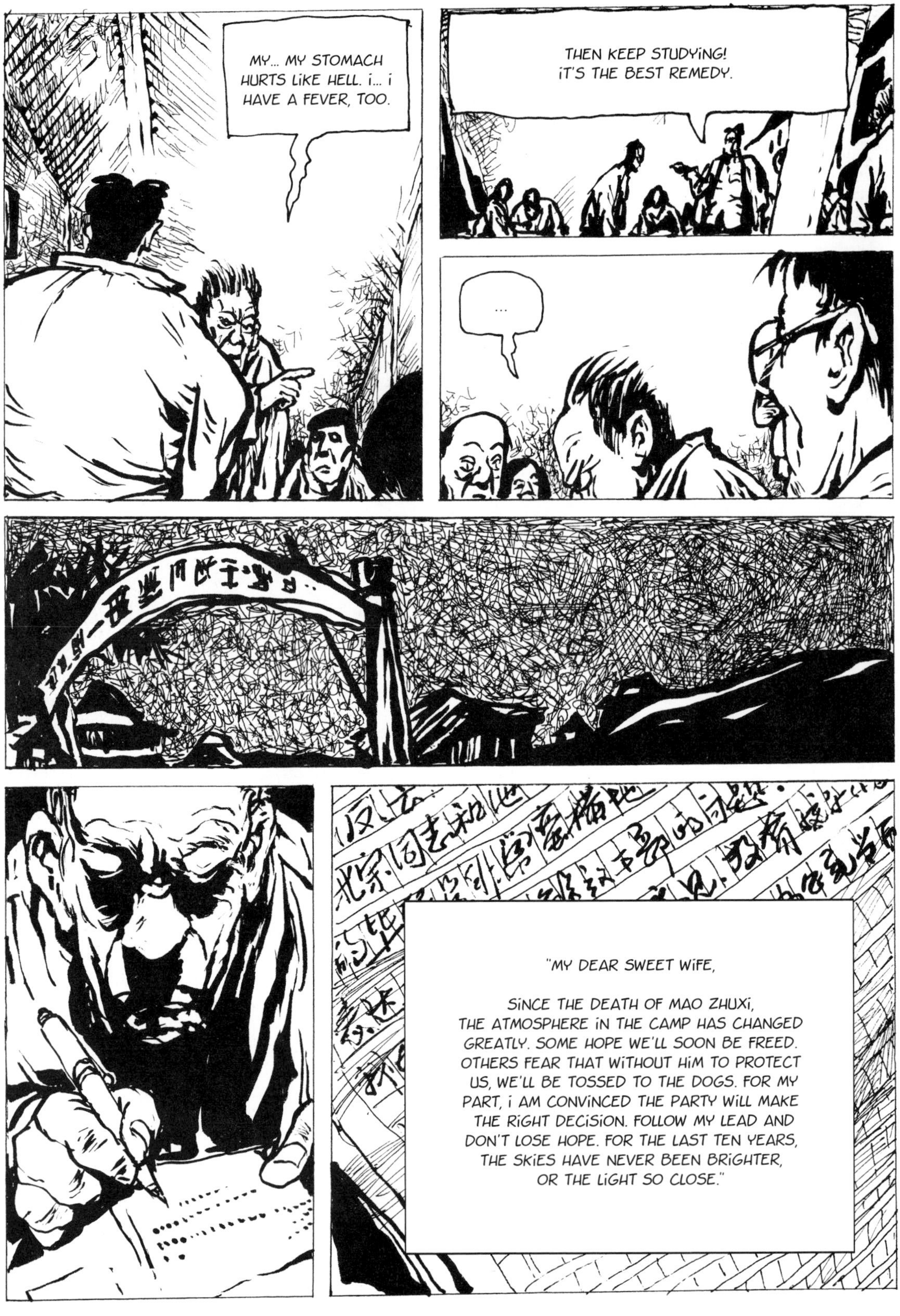
MY... MY STOMACH HURTS LIKE HELL. I... I HAVE A FEVER, TOO.
THEN KEEP STUDYING! IT'S THE BEST REMEDY.
...
"MY DEAR SWEET WIFE,
SINCE THE DEATH OF MAO ZHUXI, THE ATMOSPHERE IN THE CAMP HAS CHANGED GREATLY. SOME HOPE WE'LL SOON BE FREED. OTHERS FEAR THAT WITHOUT HIM TO PROTECT US, WE'LL BE TOSSED TO THE DOGS. FOR MY PART, I AM CONVINCED THE PARTY WILL MAKE THE RIGHT DECISION. FOLLOW MY LEAD AND DON'T LOSE HOPE. FOR THE LAST TEN YEARS, THE SKIES HAVE NEVER BEEN BRIGHTER, OR THE LIGHT SO CLOSE."

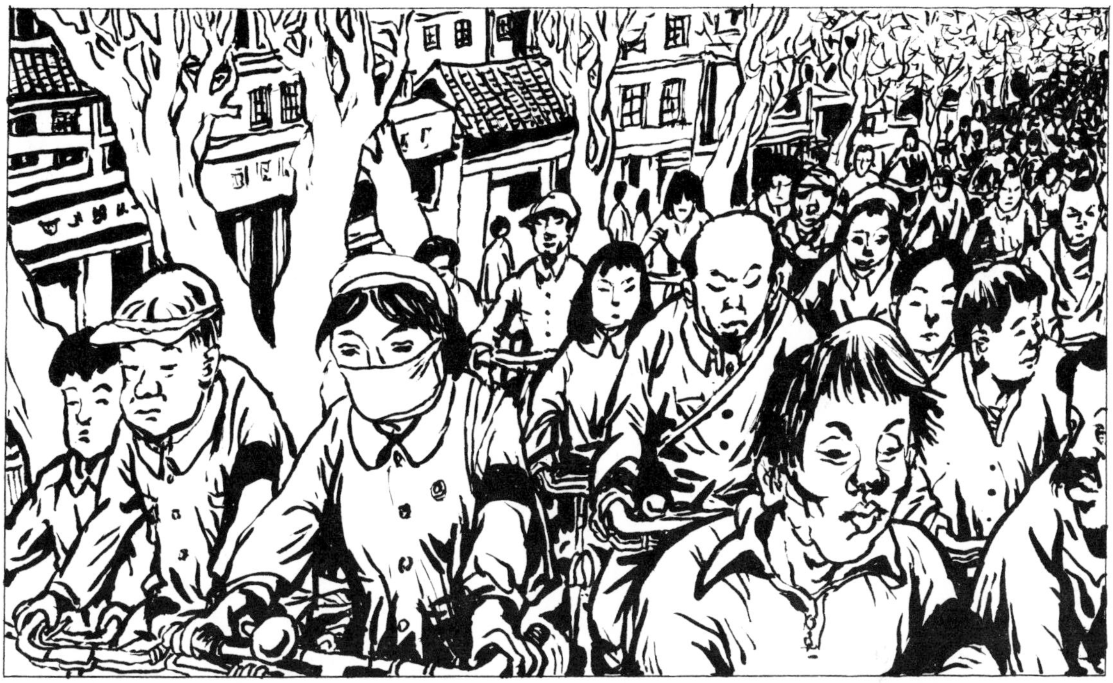

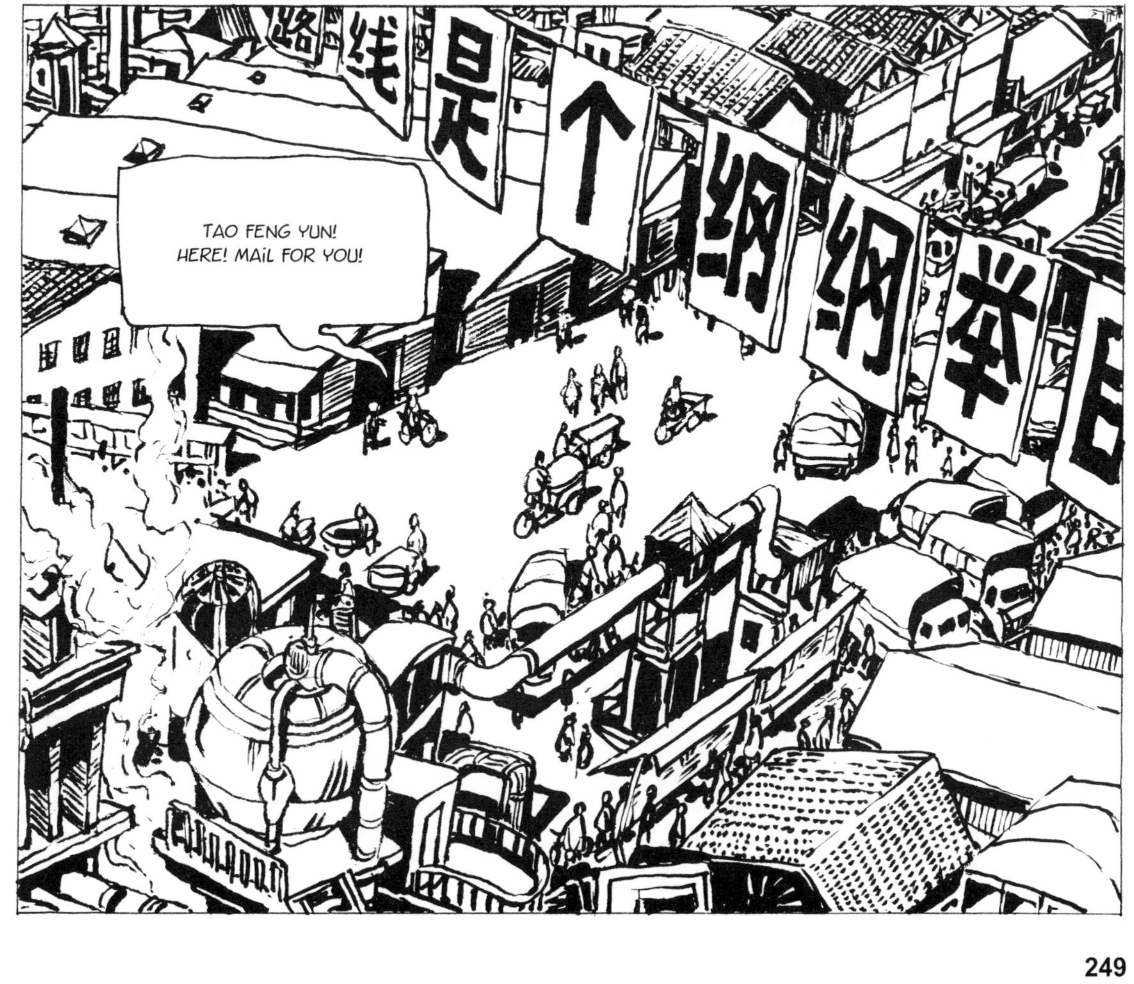
路线是个纲纲举
TAO FENG YUN!
HERE! MAIL FOR YOU!

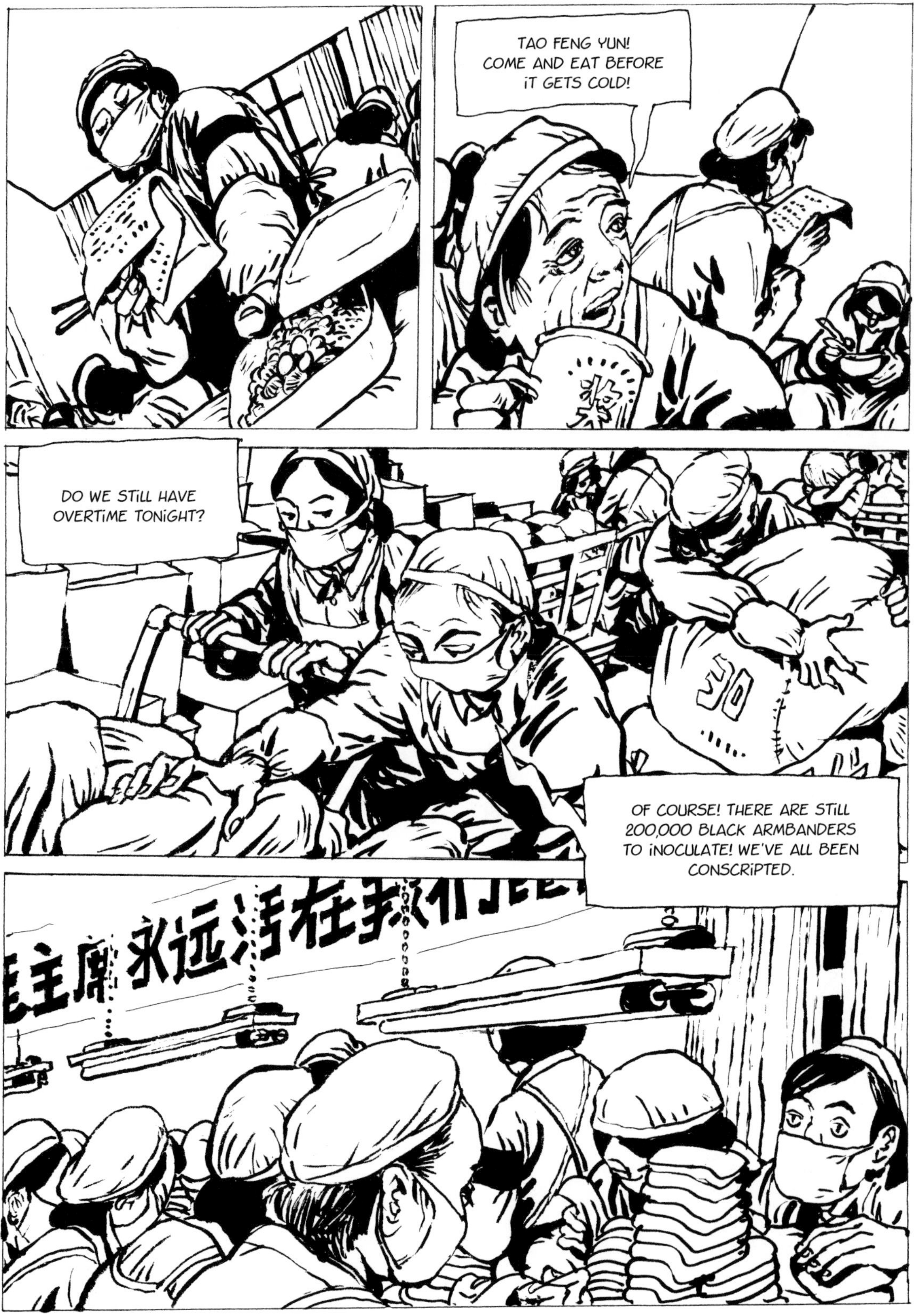

TAO FENG YUN!
COME AND EAT BEFORE
iT GETS COLD!
DO WE STiLL HAVE
OVERTiME TONiGHT?
OF COURSE! THERE ARE STiLL
200,000 BLACK ARMBANDERS
TO iNOCULATE! WE'VE ALL BEEN
CONSCRiPTED.

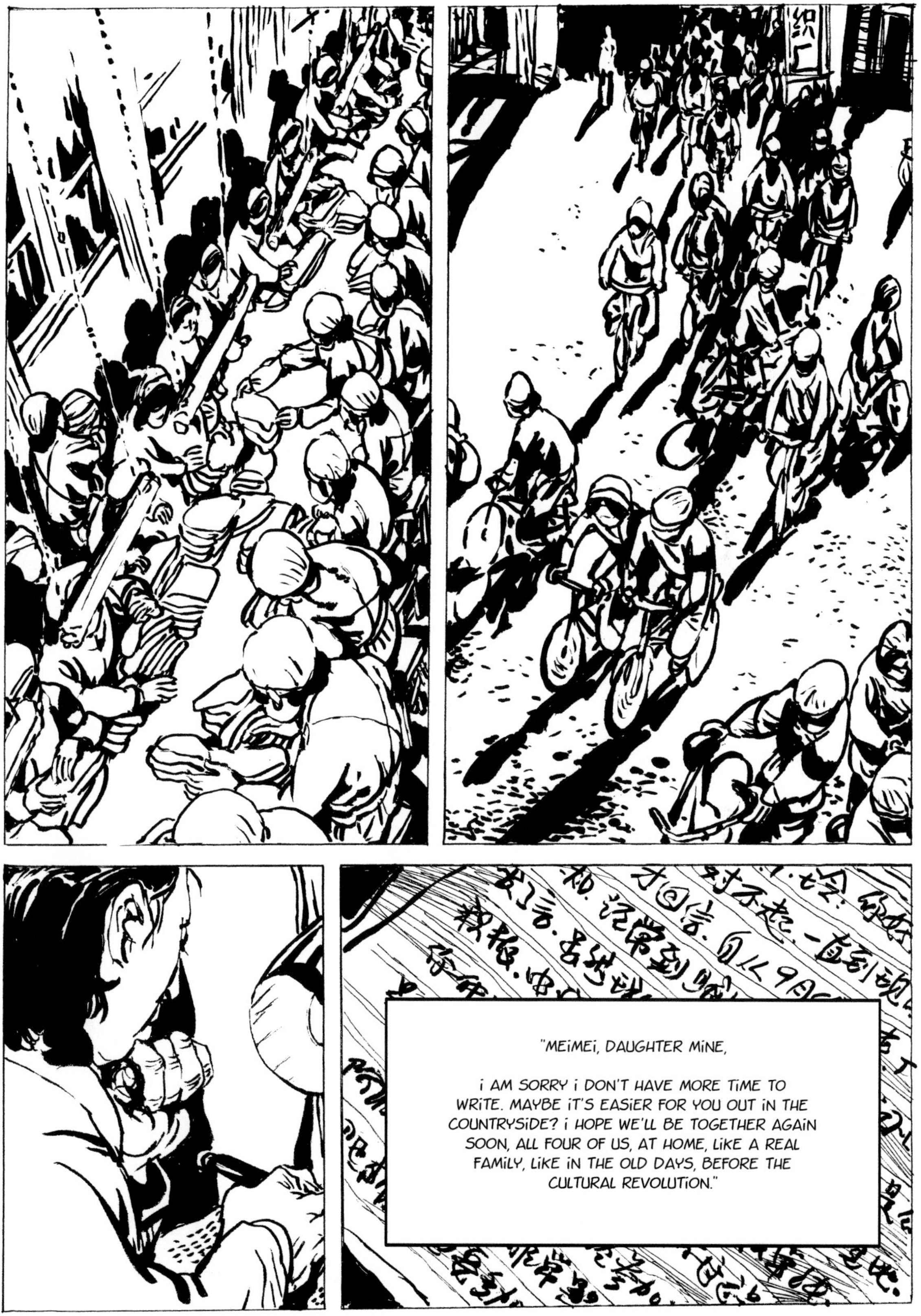
"MEIMEI, DAUGHTER MINE,
I AM SORRY I DON'T HAVE MORE TIME TO WRITE. MAYBE IT'S EASIER FOR YOU OUT IN THE COUNTRYSIDE? I HOPE WE'LL BE TOGETHER AGAIN SOON, ALL FOUR OF US, AT HOME, LIKE A REAL FAMILY, LIKE IN THE OLD DAYS, BEFORE THE CULTURAL REVOLUTION."

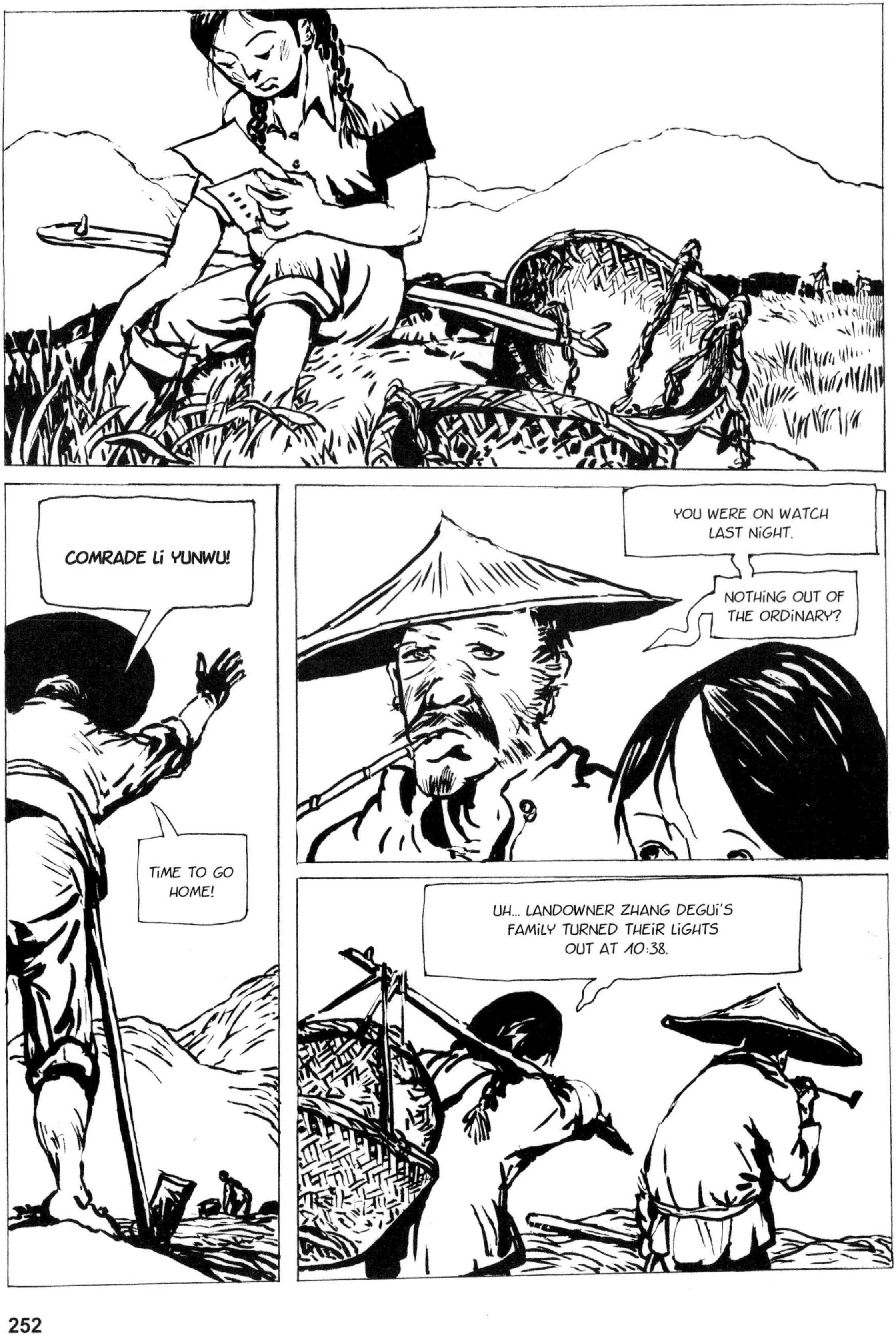
COMRADE Li YUNWU!
TiME TO GO HOME!
YOU WERE ON WATCH LAST NiGHT.
NOTHiNG OUT OF THE ORDiNARY?
UH... LANDOWNER ZHANG DEGUi'S FAMiLY TURNED THEiR LiGHTS OUT AT 10:38.

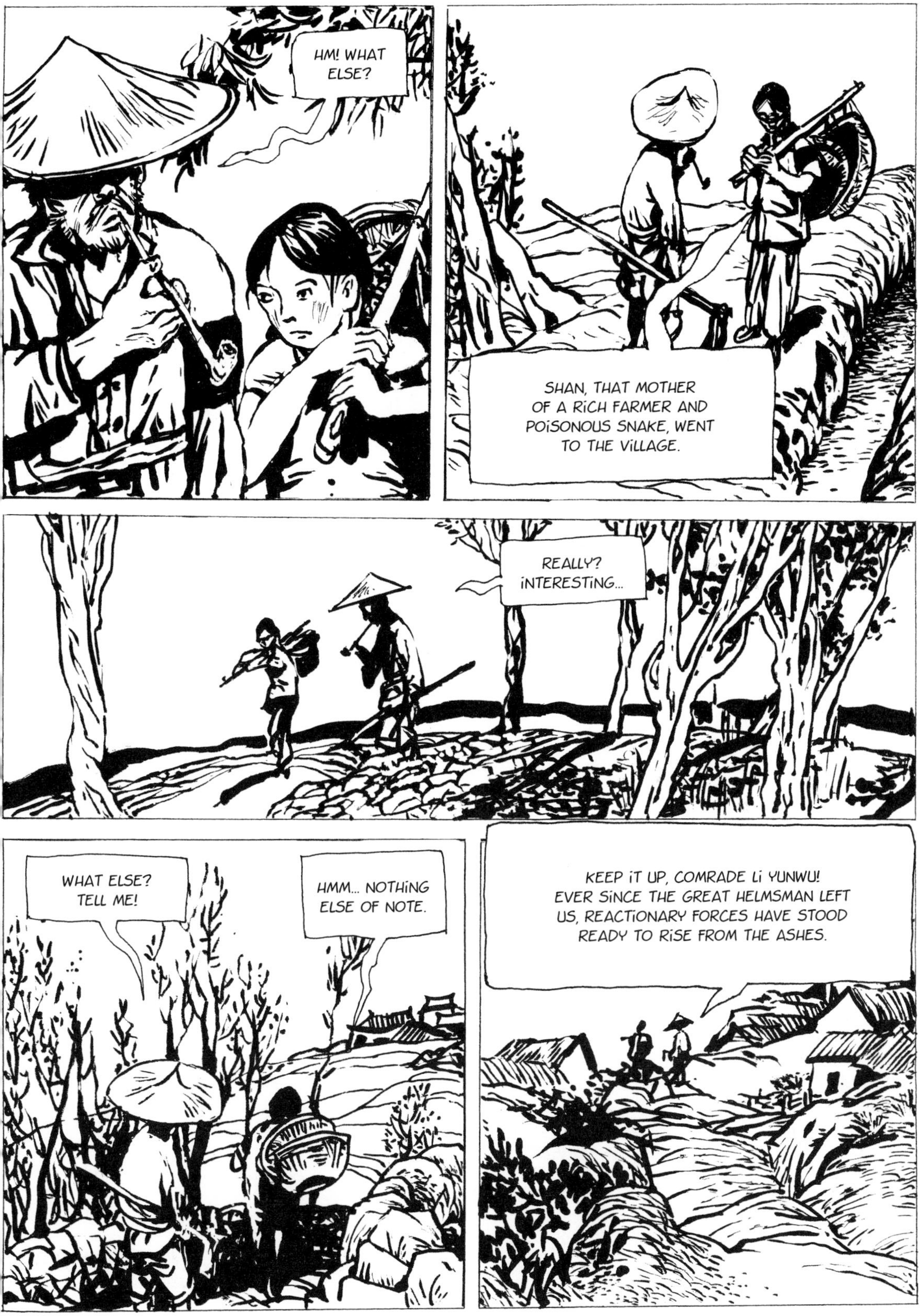
HM! WHAT ELSE?
SHAN, THAT MOTHER OF A RICH FARMER AND POISONOUS SNAKE, WENT TO THE VILLAGE.
REALLY? INTERESTING...
WHAT ELSE? TELL ME!
HMM... NOTHING ELSE OF NOTE.
KEEP IT UP, COMRADE LI YUNWU! EVER SINCE THE GREAT HELMSMAN LEFT US, REACTIONARY FORCES HAVE STOOD READY TO RISE FROM THE ASHES.

THE PARTY NEEDS PEOPLE LIKE YOU! YOUNG PEOPLE AT THE READY, PREPARED TO DEFEND THE REVOLUTION! NOT LIKE YOUR RED GUARD FRIENDS. ALL THEY'RE GOOD FOR IS PLAYING MAH-JONG.

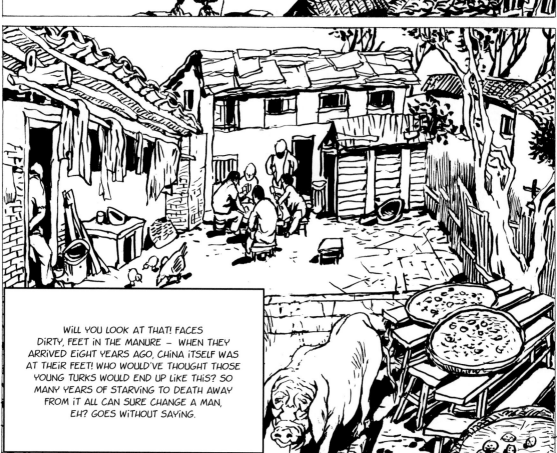

WILL YOU LOOK AT THAT! FACES DIRTY, FEET IN THE MANURE — WHEN THEY ARRIVED EIGHT YEARS AGO, CHINA ITSELF WAS AT THEIR FEET! WHO WOULD'VE THOUGHT THOSE YOUNG TURKS WOULD END UP LIKE THIS? SO MANY YEARS OF STARVING TO DEATH AWAY FROM IT ALL CAN SURE CHANGE A MAN, EH? GOES WITHOUT SAYING.

"XIAO LI, DEAREST BROTHER,

IT'S BEEN ALMOST THREE WEEKS SINCE MAO ZHUXI LEFT US, AND I MISS HIM TERRIBLY. ON TOP OF WORKING IN THE FIELDS, I SPEND A LOT OF TIME BEING VIGILANT ABOUT DEFENDING OUR COUNTRY (LIKE YOU). OUR PURE RED HEARTS WILL TRIUMPH OVER THE REACTIONARIES! STAY STRONG, BROTHER MINE; WE HAVE GREAT RESPONSIBILITIES."

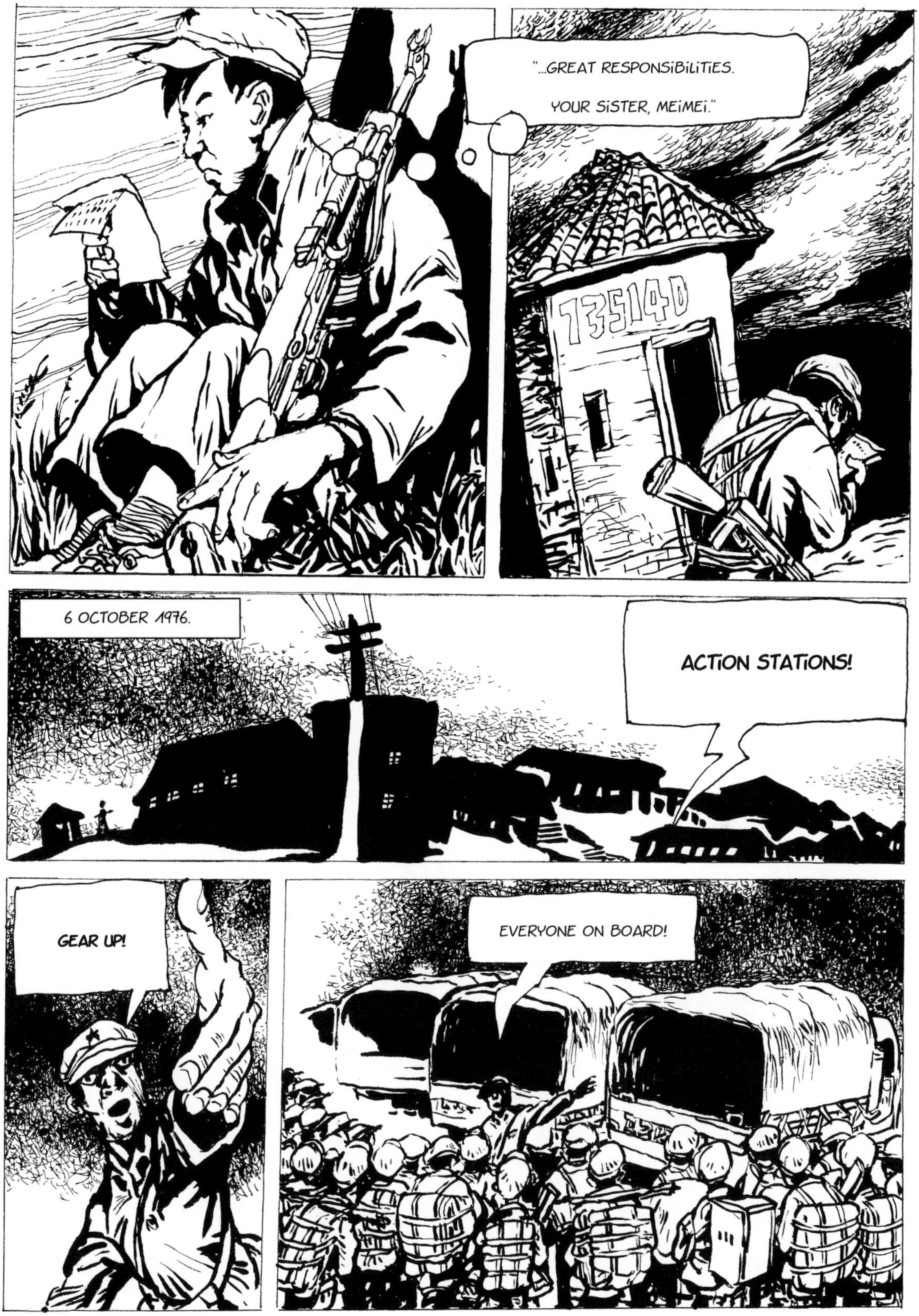
"...GREAT RESPONSIBILITIES.
YOUR SISTER, MEIMEI."
735140
6 OCTOBER 1976.
ACTION STATIONS!
GEAR UP!
EVERYONE ON BOARD!

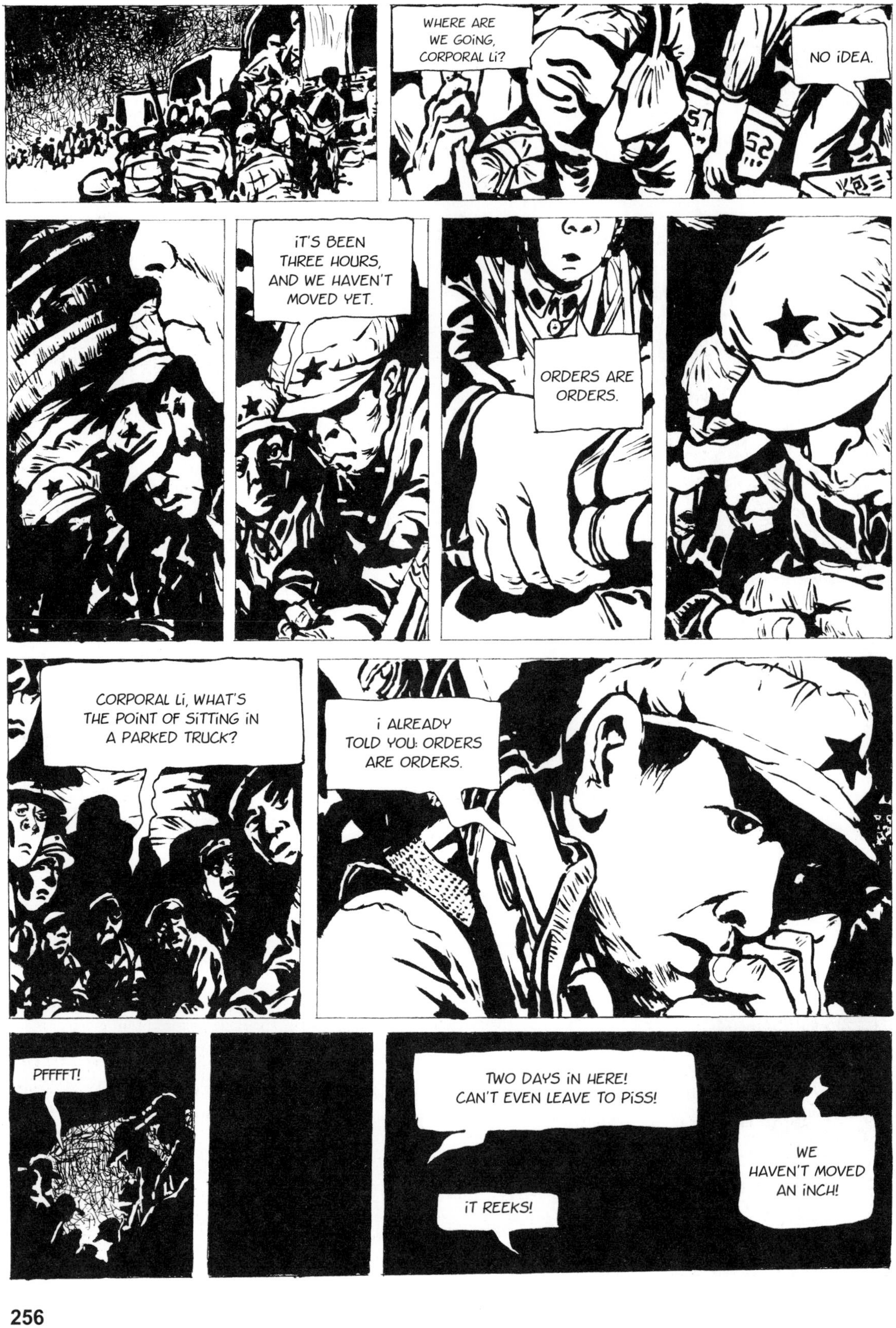
WHERE ARE WE GOiNG, CORPORAL Li?
NO iDEA.
iT'S BEEN THREE HOURS, AND WE HAVEN'T MOVED YET.
ORDERS ARE ORDERS.
CORPORAL Li, WHAT'S THE POINT OF SiTTiNG iN A PARKED TRUCK?
i ALREADY TOLD YOU: ORDERS ARE ORDERS.
PFFFFT!
TWO DAYS iN HERE! CAN'T EVEN LEAVE TO PiSS!
iT REEKS!
WE HAVEN'T MOVED AN iNCH!

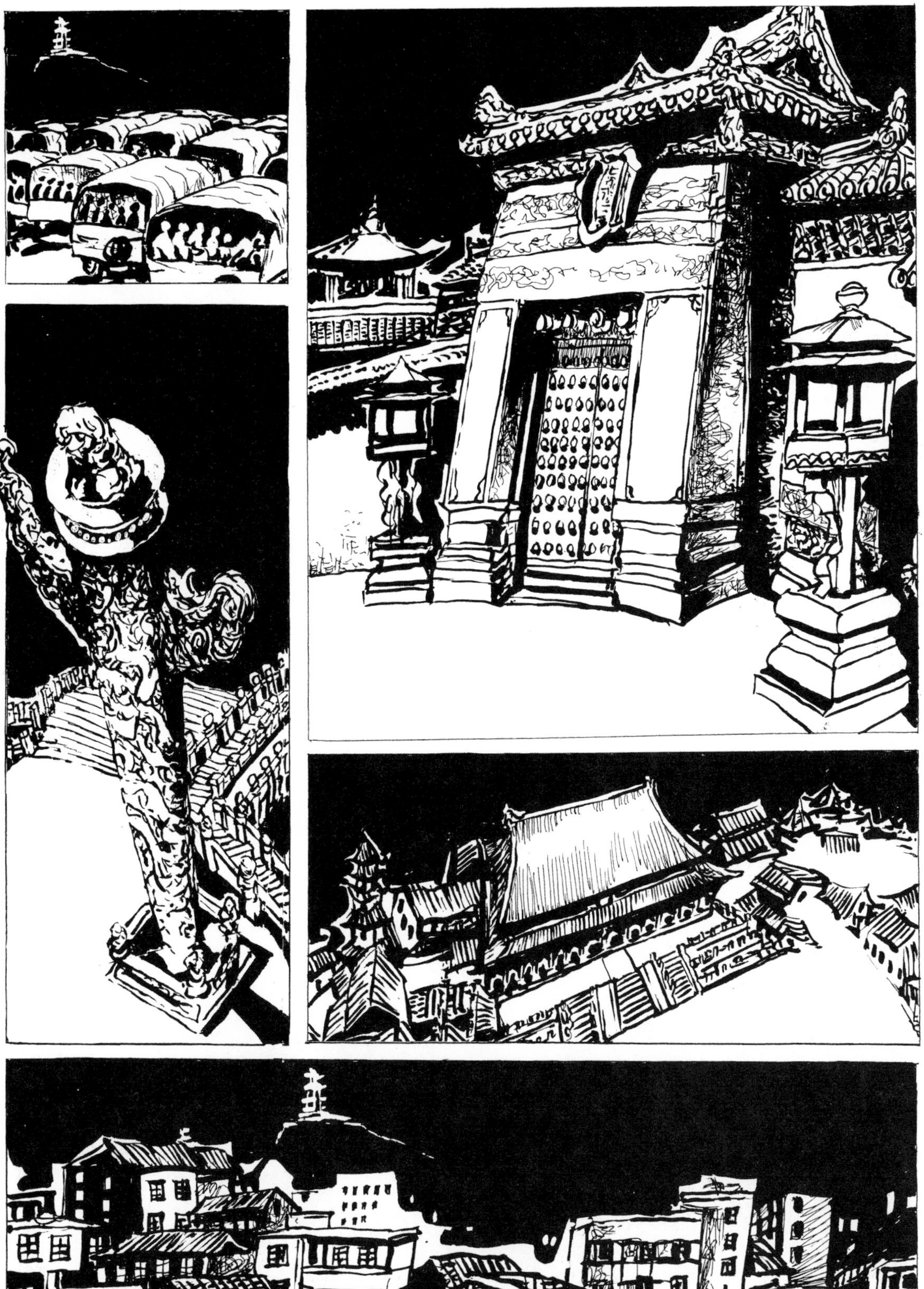

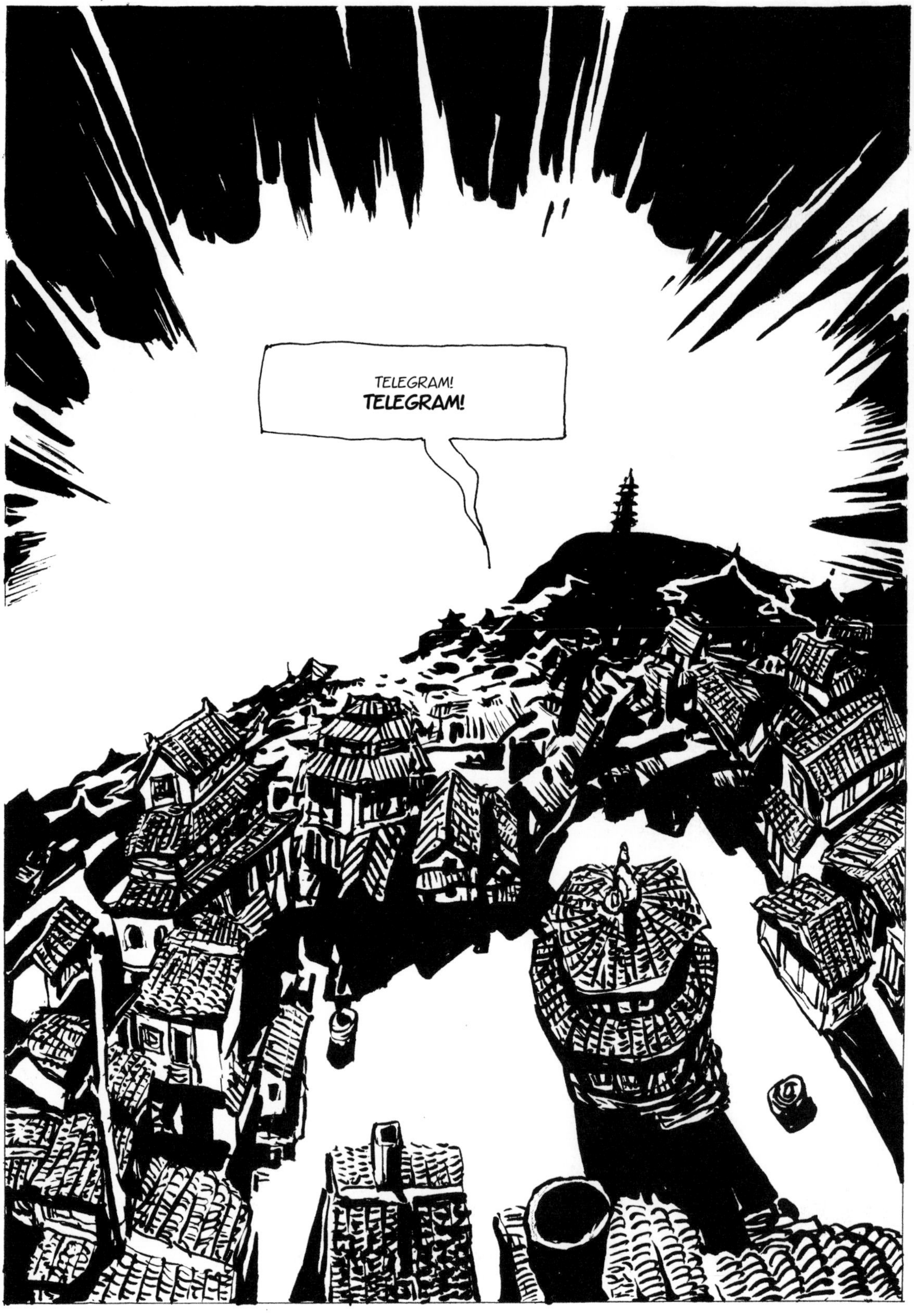
TELEGRAM!
TELEGRAM!

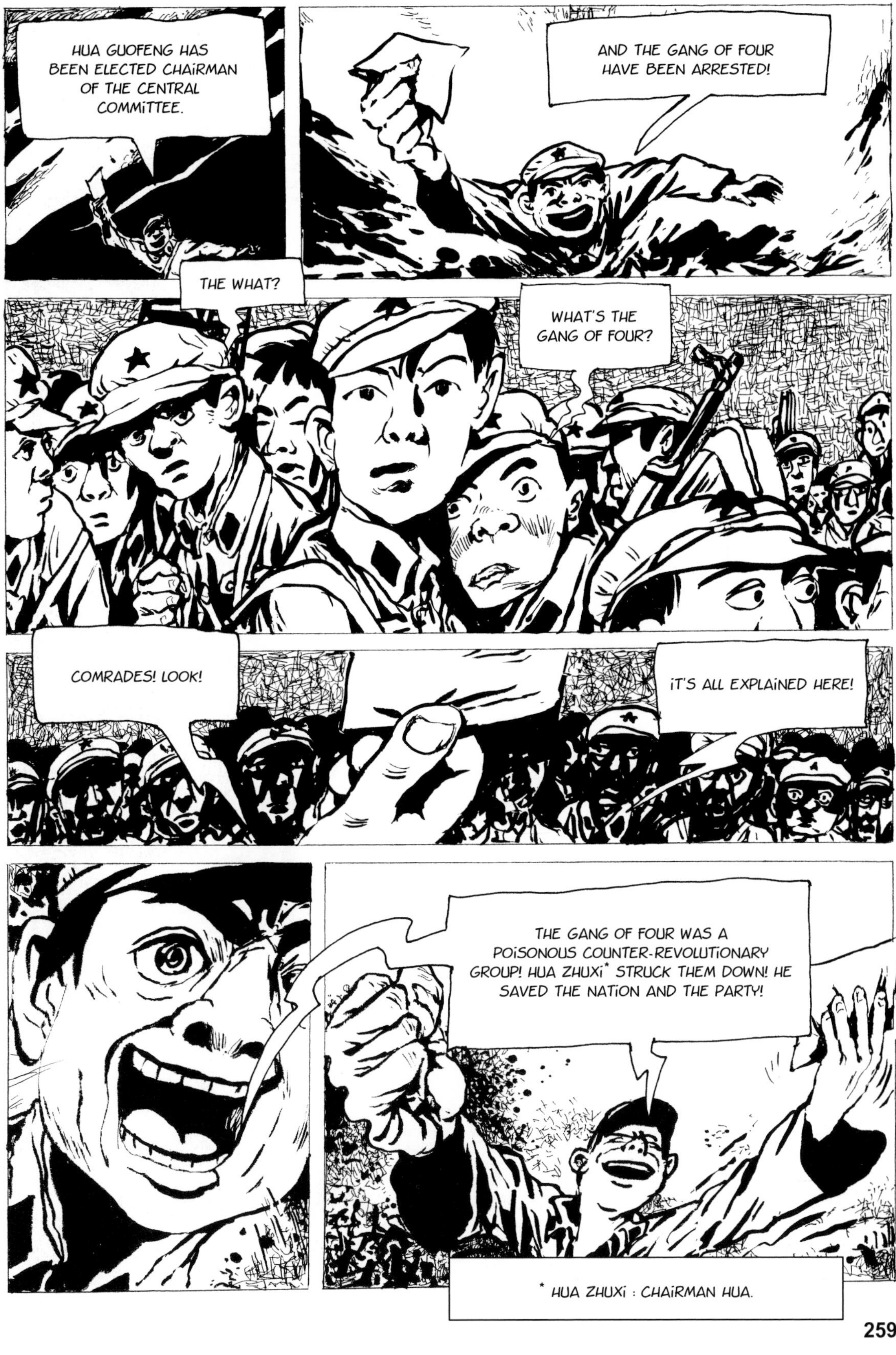
HUA GUOFENG HAS BEEN ELECTED CHAIRMAN OF THE CENTRAL COMMITTEE.
AND THE GANG OF FOUR HAVE BEEN ARRESTED!
THE WHAT?
WHAT'S THE GANG OF FOUR?
COMRADES! LOOK!
IT'S ALL EXPLAINED HERE!
THE GANG OF FOUR WAS A POISONOUS COUNTER-REVOLUTIONARY GROUP! HUA ZHUXI* STRUCK THEM DOWN! HE SAVED THE NATION AND THE PARTY!
* HUA ZHUXI : CHAIRMAN HUA.

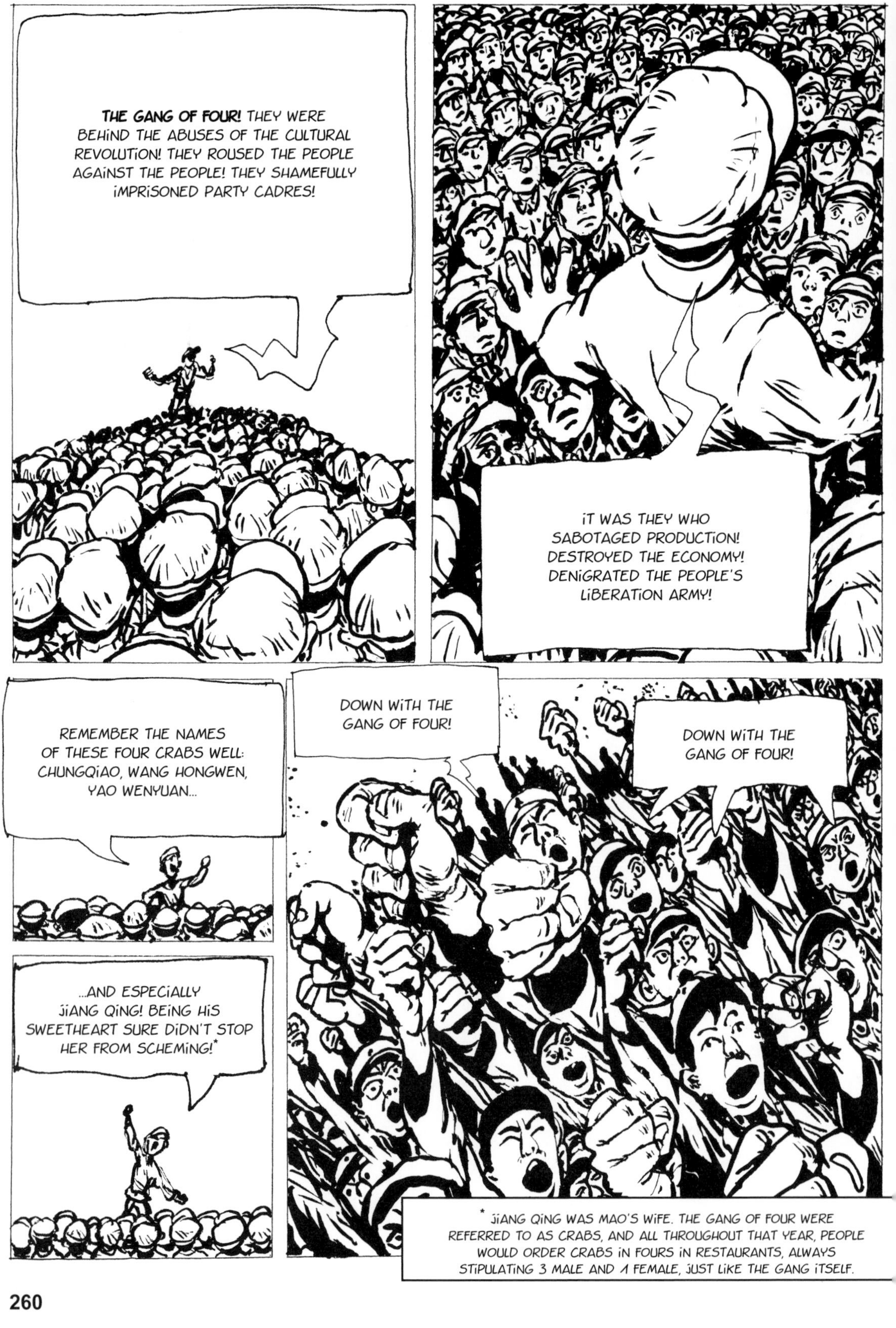
THE GANG OF FOUR! THEY WERE BEHIND THE ABUSES OF THE CULTURAL REVOLUTION! THEY ROUSED THE PEOPLE AGAINST THE PEOPLE! THEY SHAMEFULLY IMPRISONED PARTY CADRES!
IT WAS THEY WHO SABOTAGED PRODUCTION! DESTROYED THE ECONOMY! DENIGRATED THE PEOPLE'S LIBERATION ARMY!
REMEMBER THE NAMES OF THESE FOUR CRABS WELL: CHUNGQIAO, WANG HONGWEN, YAO WENYUAN...
...AND ESPECIALLY JIANG QING! BEING HIS SWEETHEART SURE DIDN'T STOP HER FROM SCHEMING!*
DOWN WITH THE GANG OF FOUR!
DOWN WITH THE GANG OF FOUR!
* JIANG QING WAS MAO'S WIFE. THE GANG OF FOUR WERE REFERRED TO AS CRABS, AND ALL THROUGHOUT THAT YEAR, PEOPLE WOULD ORDER CRABS IN FOURS IN RESTAURANTS, ALWAYS STIPULATING 3 MALE AND 1 FEMALE, JUST LIKE THE GANG ITSELF.

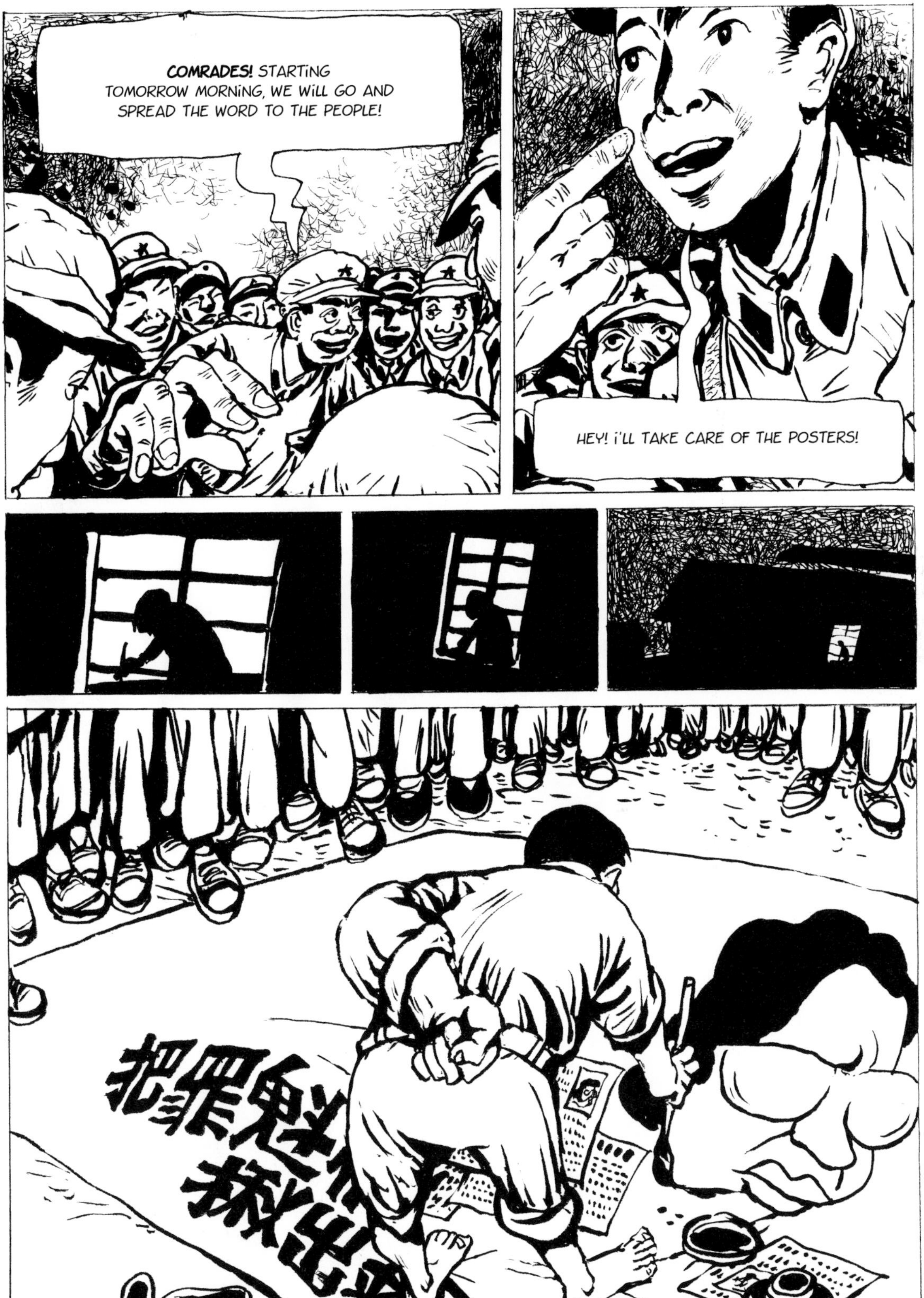
COMRADES! STARTING TOMORROW MORNING, WE WILL GO AND SPREAD THE WORD TO THE PEOPLE!
HEY! I'LL TAKE CARE OF THE POSTERS!

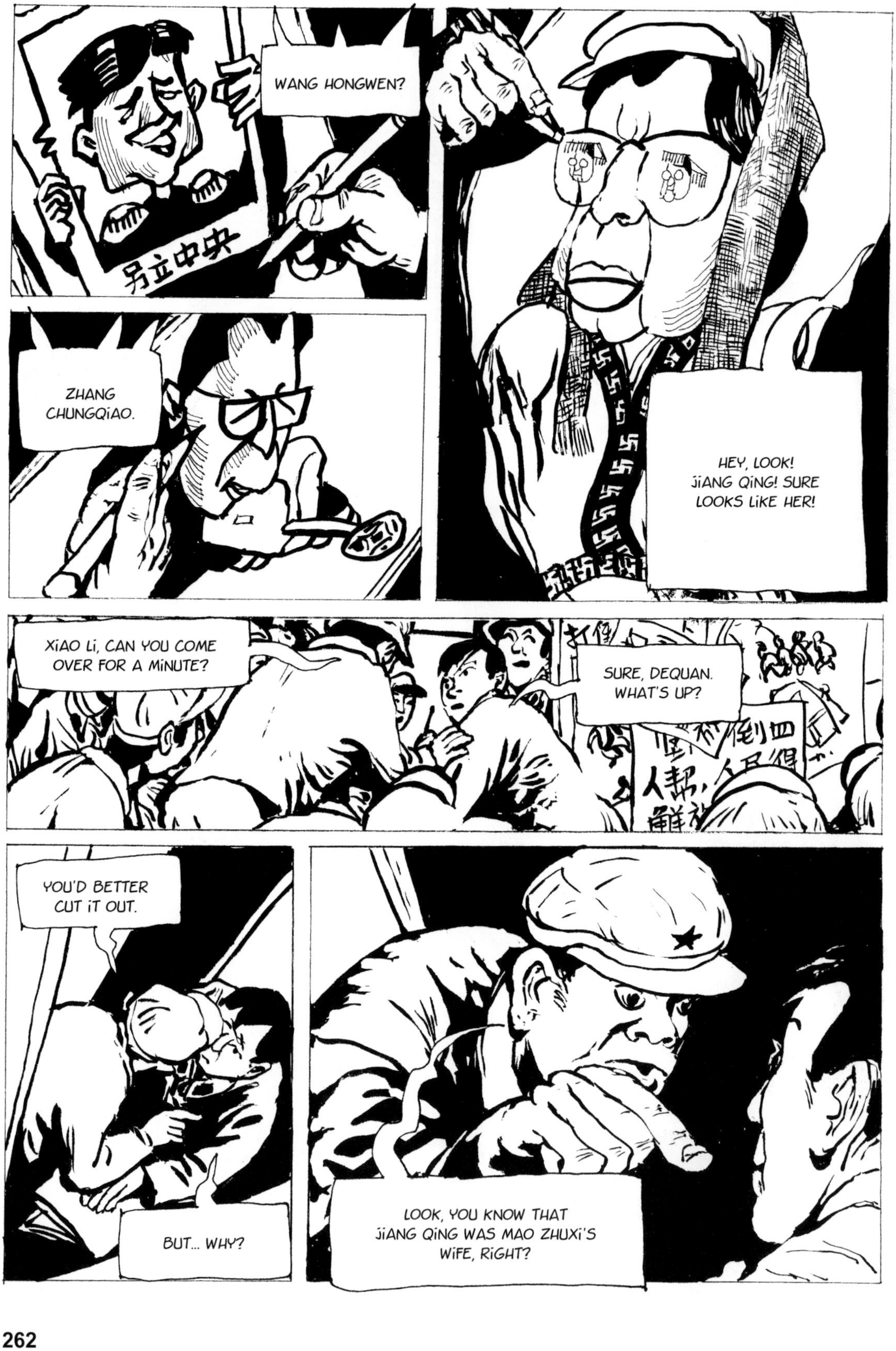
另立中央
WANG HONGWEN?
ZHANG CHUNGQIAO.
HEY, LOOK! JIANG QING! SURE LOOKS LIKE HER!
XIAO LI, CAN YOU COME OVER FOR A MINUTE?
SURE, DEQUAN. WHAT'S UP?
YOU'D BETTER CUT IT OUT.
BUT... WHY?
LOOK, YOU KNOW THAT JIANG QING WAS MAO ZHUXI'S WIFE, RIGHT?

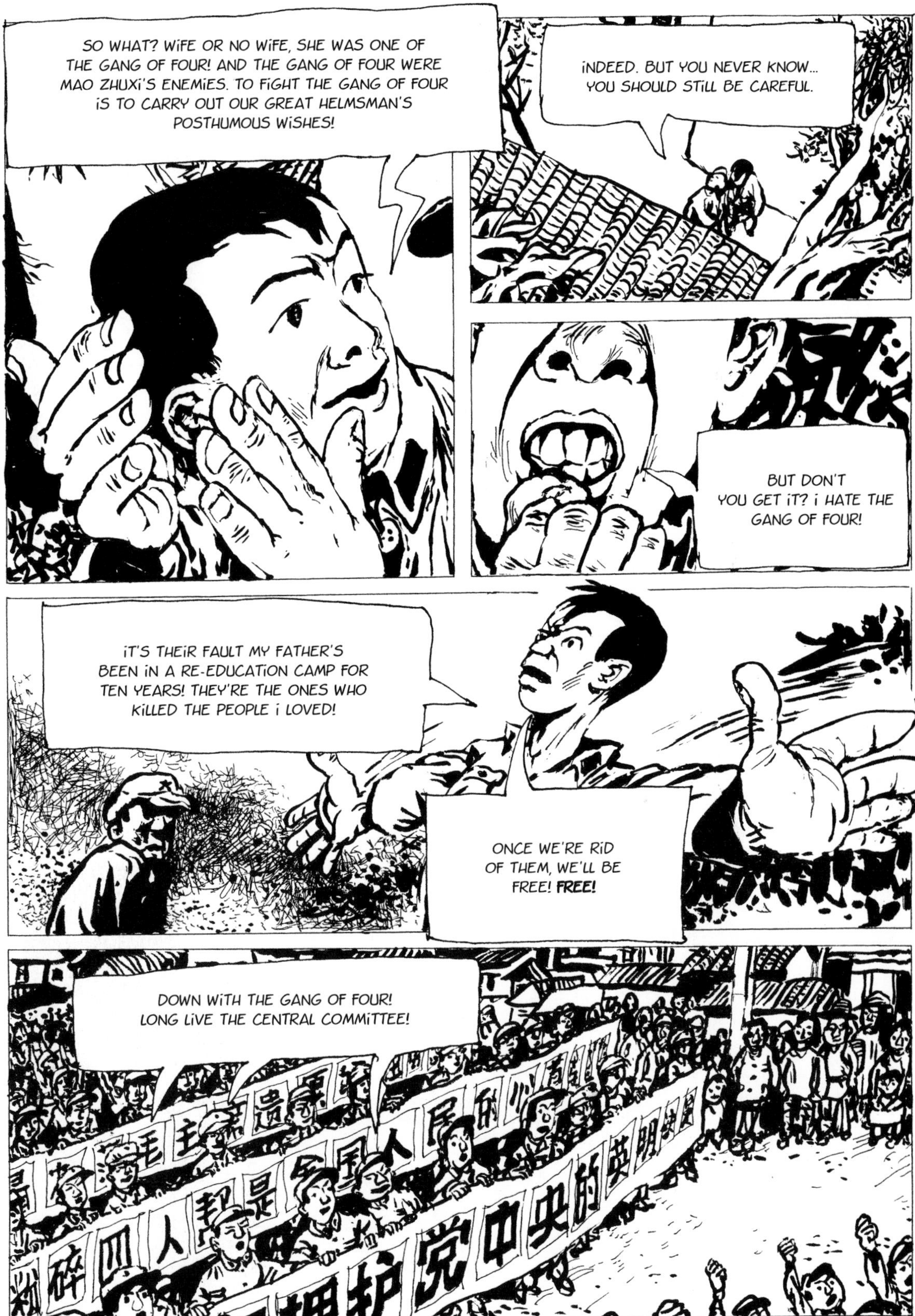
SO WHAT? WIFE OR NO WIFE, SHE WAS ONE OF THE GANG OF FOUR! AND THE GANG OF FOUR WERE MAO ZHUXI'S ENEMIES. TO FIGHT THE GANG OF FOUR IS TO CARRY OUT OUR GREAT HELMSMAN'S POSTHUMOUS WISHES!
INDEED. BUT YOU NEVER KNOW... YOU SHOULD STILL BE CAREFUL.
BUT DON'T YOU GET IT? I HATE THE GANG OF FOUR!
IT'S THEIR FAULT MY FATHER'S BEEN IN A RE-EDUCATION CAMP FOR TEN YEARS! THEY'RE THE ONES WHO KILLED THE PEOPLE I LOVED!
ONCE WE'RE RID OF THEM, WE'LL BE FREE! **FREE!**
DOWN WITH THE GANG OF FOUR! LONG LIVE THE CENTRAL COMMITTEE!

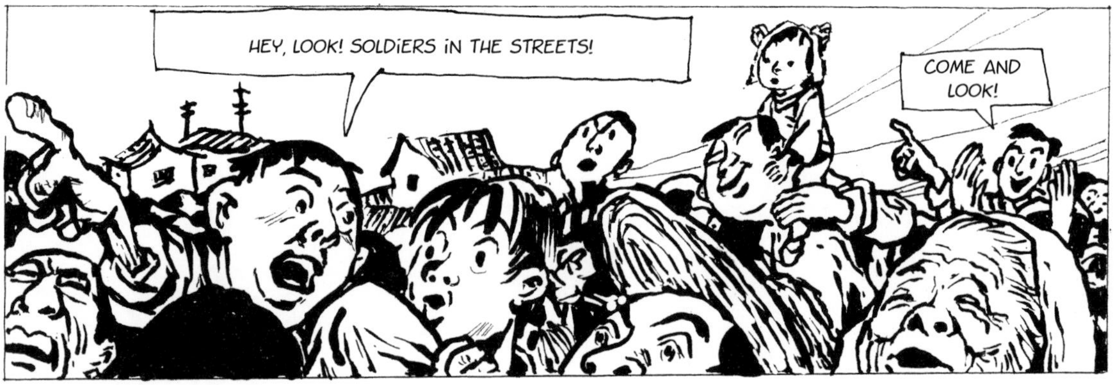
HEY, LOOK! SOLDIERS IN THE STREETS!
COME AND LOOK!

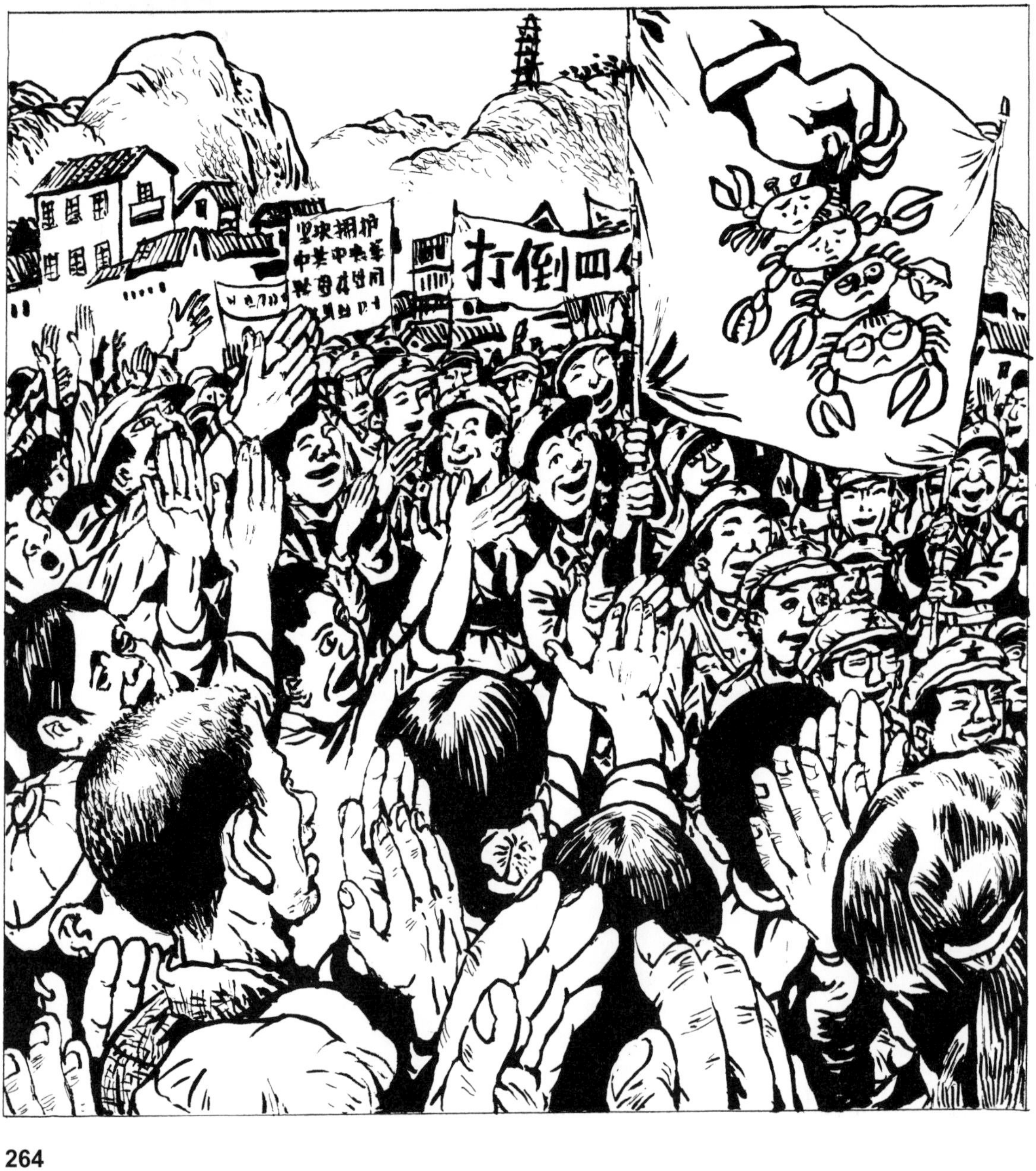
坚决拥护
中共中央华
打倒四

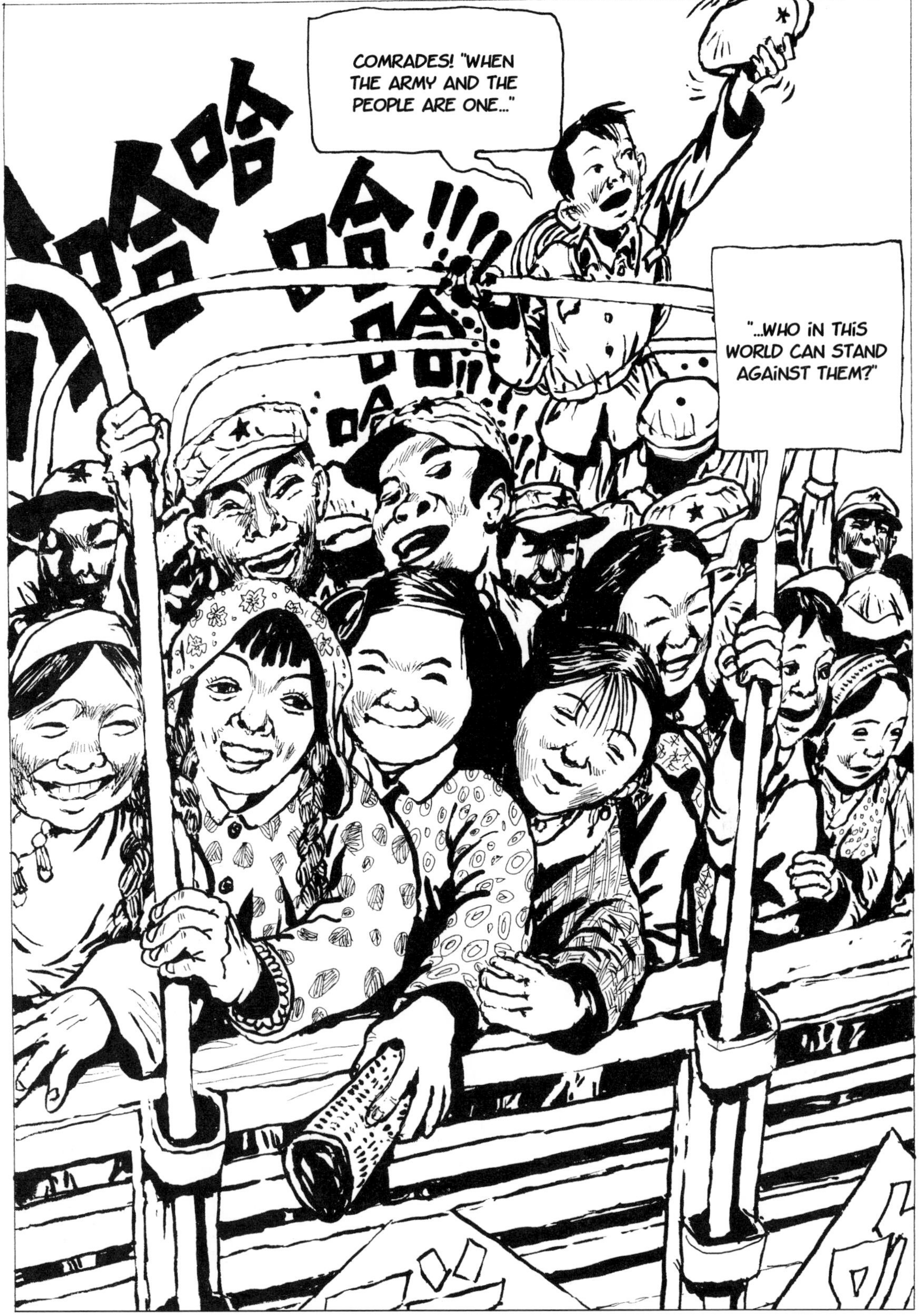
COMRADES! "WHEN THE ARMY AND THE PEOPLE ARE ONE..."
"...WHO IN THIS WORLD CAN STAND AGAINST THEM?"

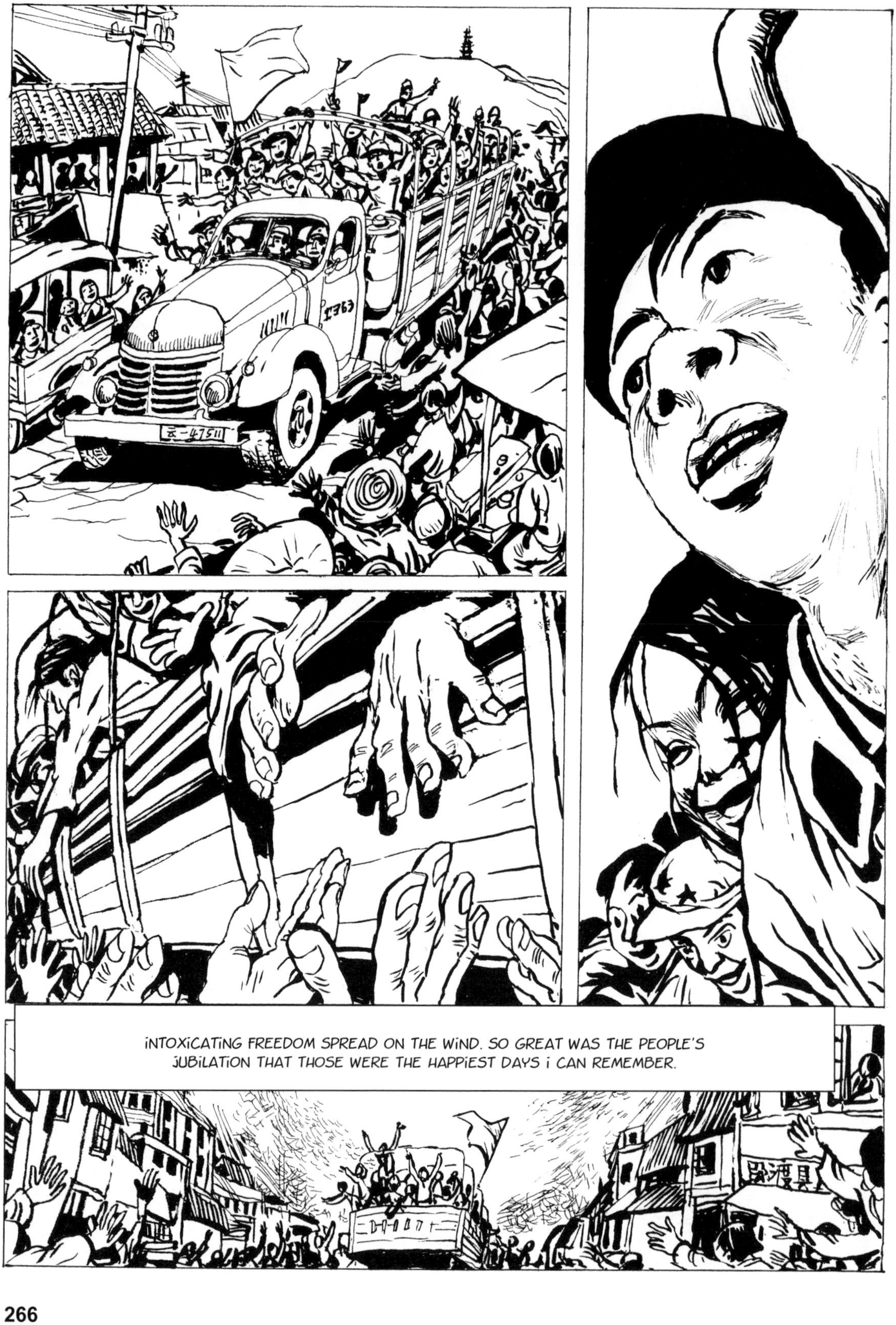
INTOXICATING FREEDOM SPREAD ON THE WIND. SO GREAT WAS THE PEOPLE'S JUBILATION THAT THOSE WERE THE HAPPIEST DAYS I CAN REMEMBER.

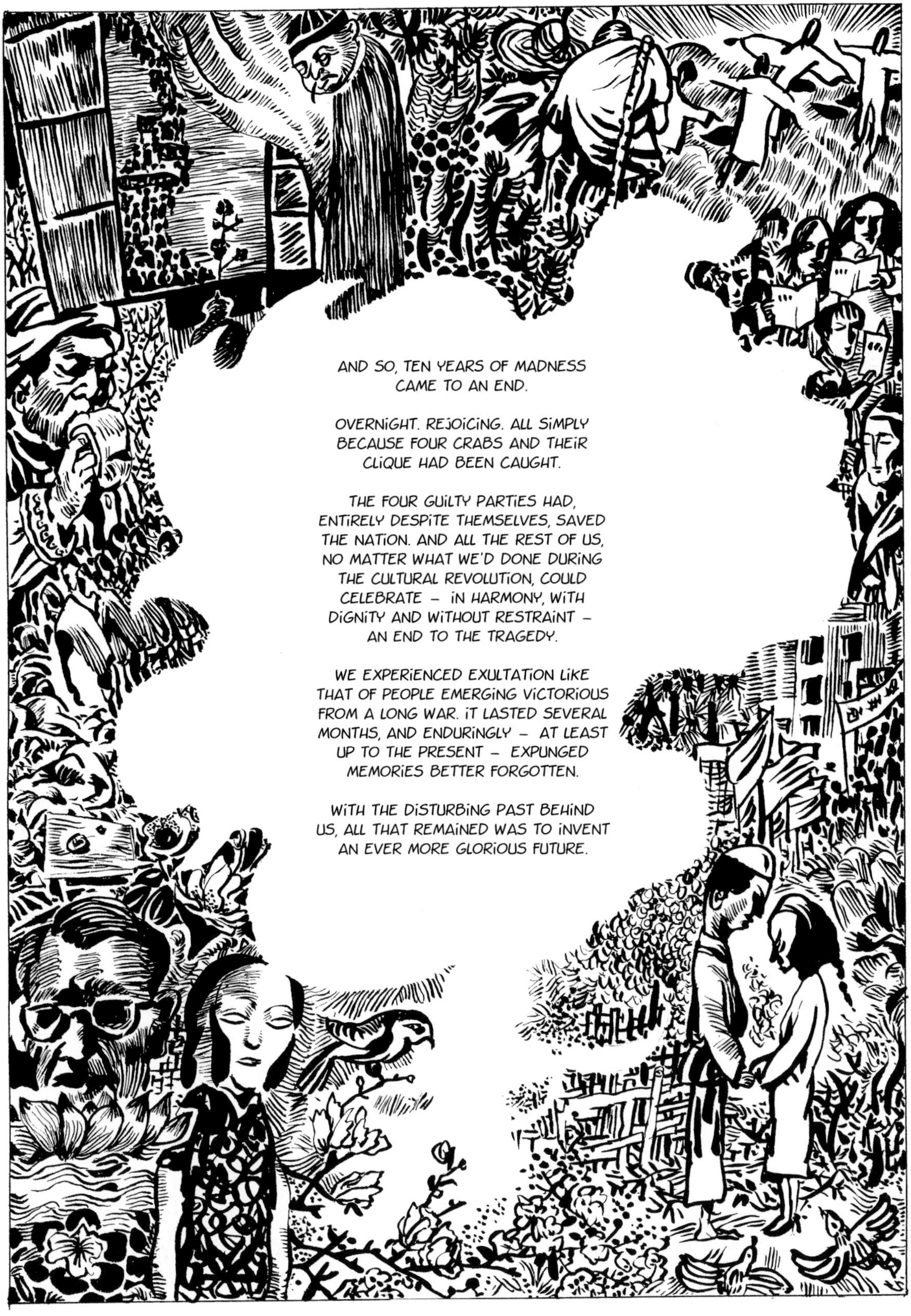
AND SO, TEN YEARS OF MADNESS CAME TO AN END.
OVERNIGHT. REJOICING. ALL SIMPLY BECAUSE FOUR CRABS AND THEIR CLIQUE HAD BEEN CAUGHT.
THE FOUR GUILTY PARTIES HAD, ENTIRELY DESPITE THEMSELVES, SAVED THE NATION. AND ALL THE REST OF US, NO MATTER WHAT WE'D DONE DURING THE CULTURAL REVOLUTION, COULD CELEBRATE – IN HARMONY, WITH DIGNITY AND WITHOUT RESTRAINT – AN END TO THE TRAGEDY.
WE EXPERIENCED EXULTATION LIKE THAT OF PEOPLE EMERGING VICTORIOUS FROM A LONG WAR. IT LASTED SEVERAL MONTHS, AND ENDURINGLY – AT LEAST UP TO THE PRESENT – EXPUNGED MEMORIES BETTER FORGOTTEN.
WITH THE DISTURBING PAST BEHIND US, ALL THAT REMAINED WAS TO INVENT AN EVER MORE GLORIOUS FUTURE.

CHAPTER 4
The Party

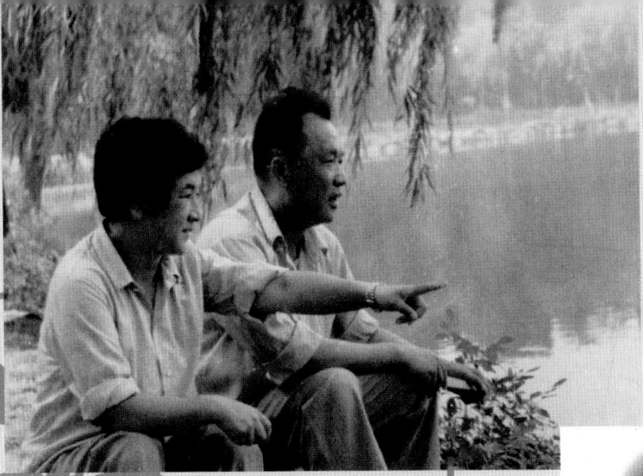

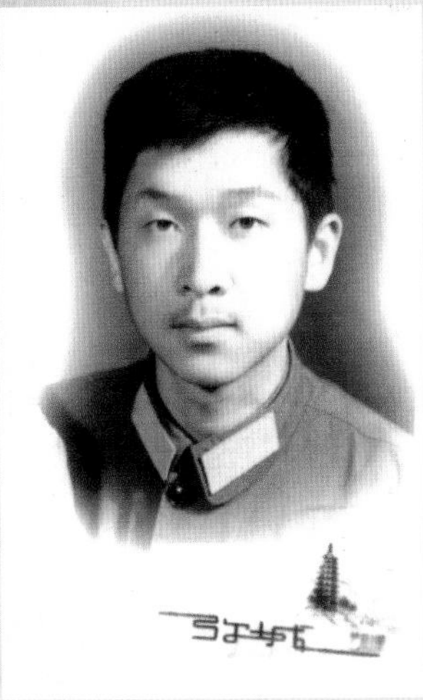

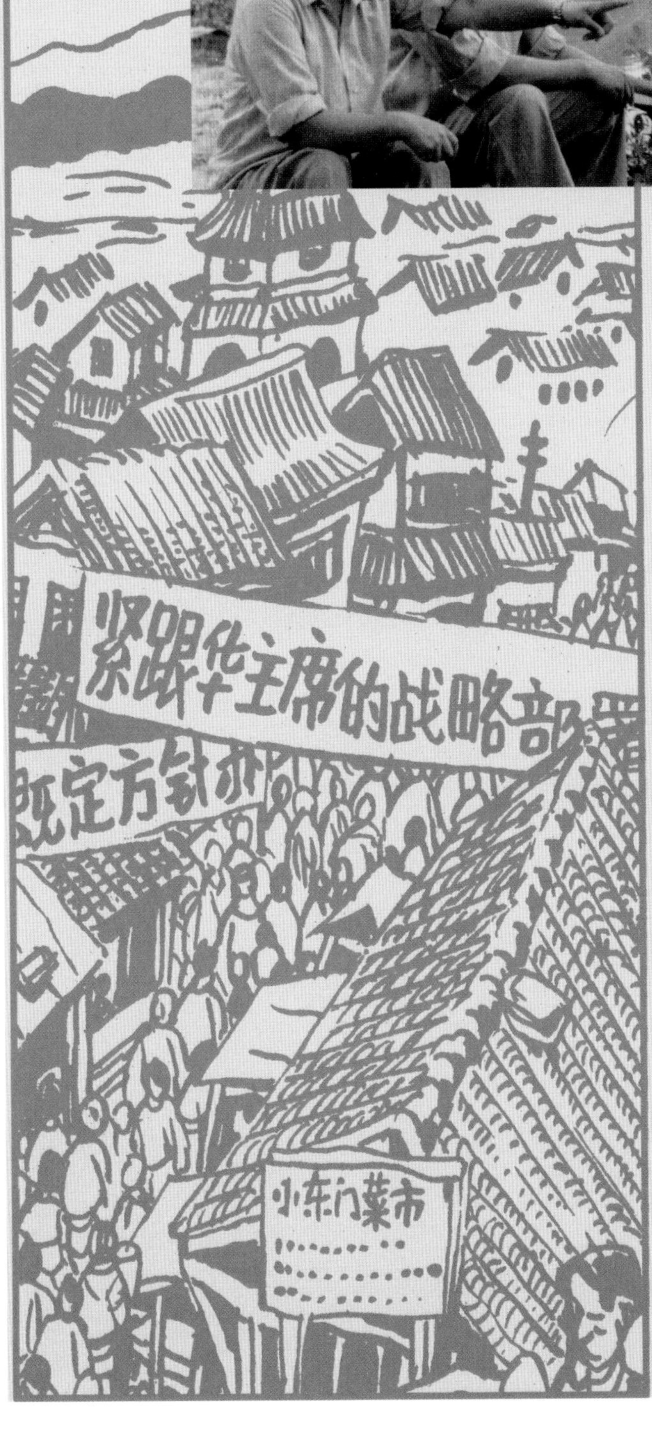
紧跟华主席的战略部
小东门菜市

一 条大河波浪宽，
风吹稻花香两岸，
我家就在岸上住
听惯了艄公的号子

THE RIVER, WIDE
AS AN OCEAN WAVE,

THE BANKS BENEATH THE WIND
FRAGRANT WITH RICE FLOWERS.

THAT IS WHERE I LIVE,
ON THAT BANK,

WHERE I LISTEN TO
THE ORDERS OF THE HELMSMEN.

(A SONG OF THE PEOPLE)

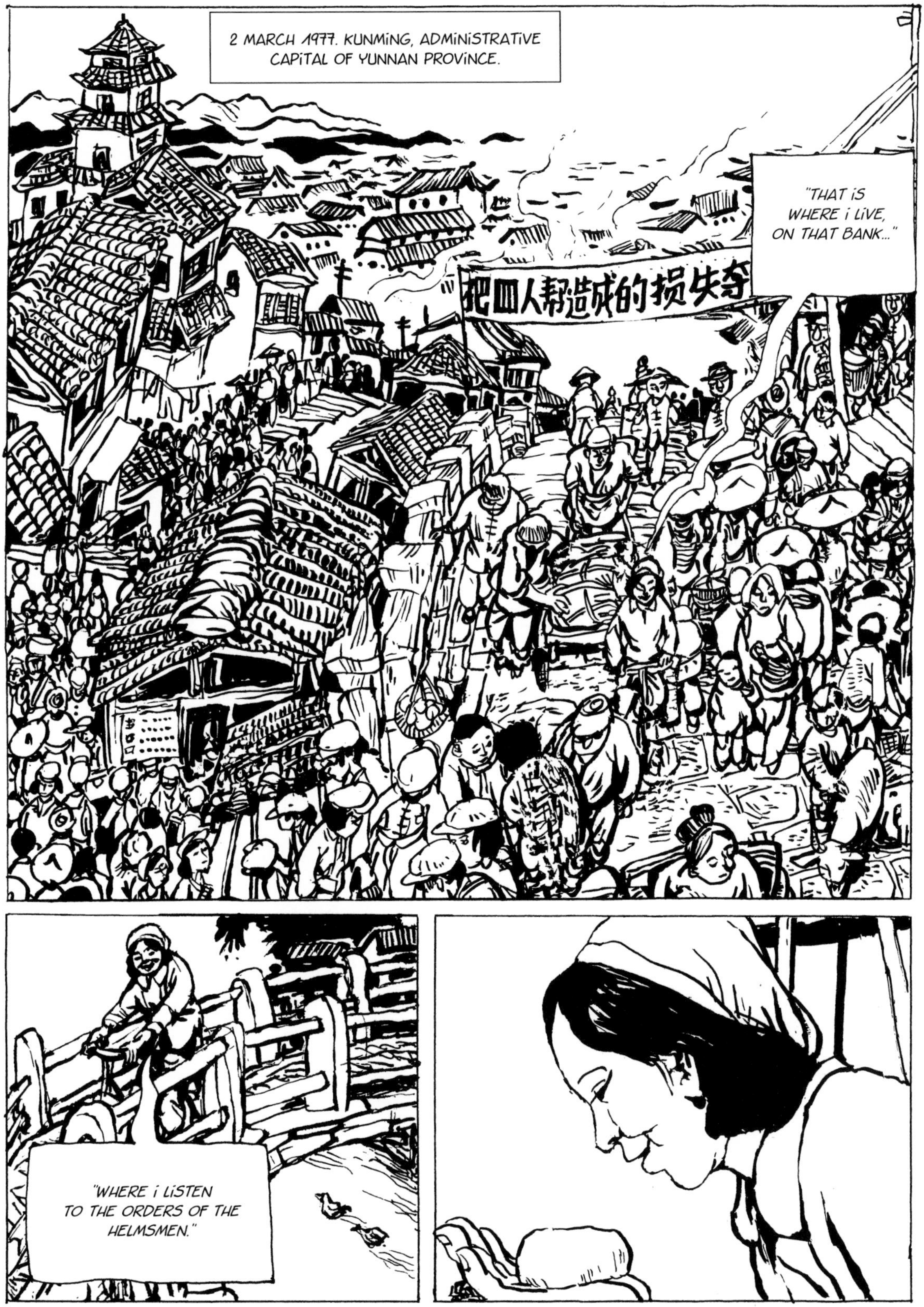
2 MARCH 1977. KUNMING, ADMINISTRATIVE CAPITAL OF YUNNAN PROVINCE.
把四人帮造成的损失夺
"THAT IS WHERE I LIVE, ON THAT BANK..."
"WHERE I LISTEN TO THE ORDERS OF THE HELMSMEN."

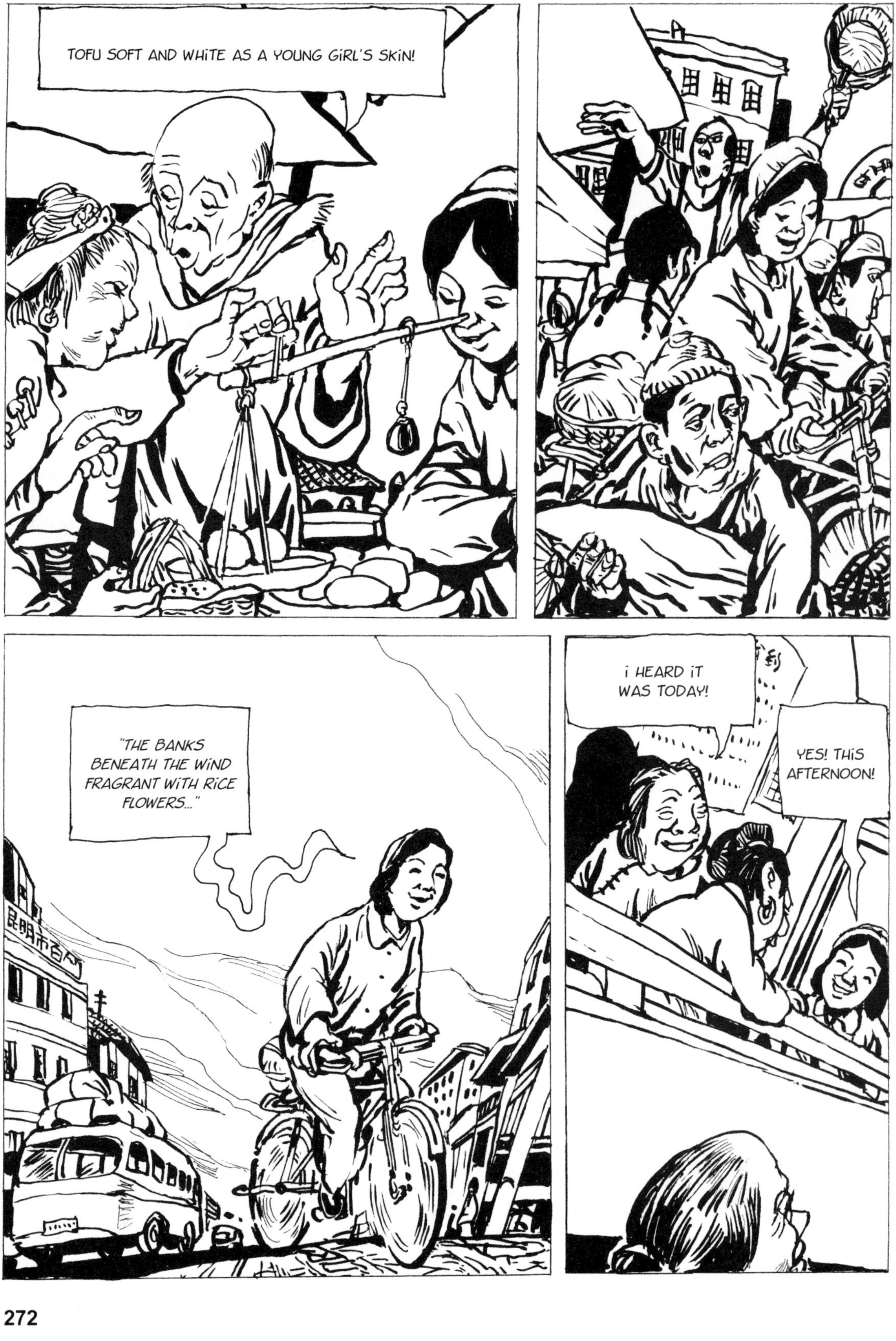
TOFU SOFT AND WHITE AS A YOUNG GIRL'S SKIN!
"THE BANKS BENEATH THE WIND FRAGRANT WITH RICE FLOWERS..."
I HEARD IT WAS TODAY!
YES! THIS AFTERNOON!

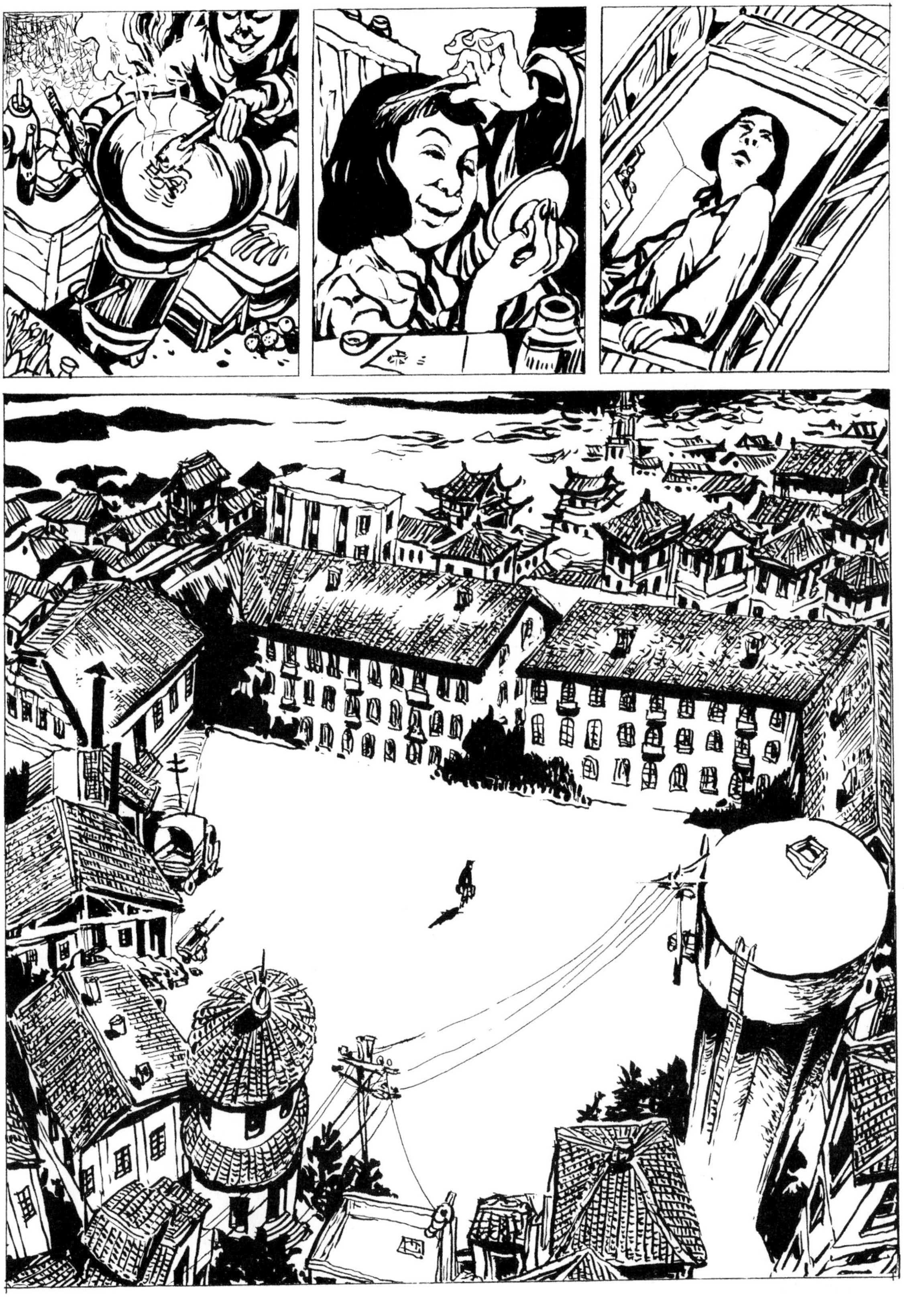

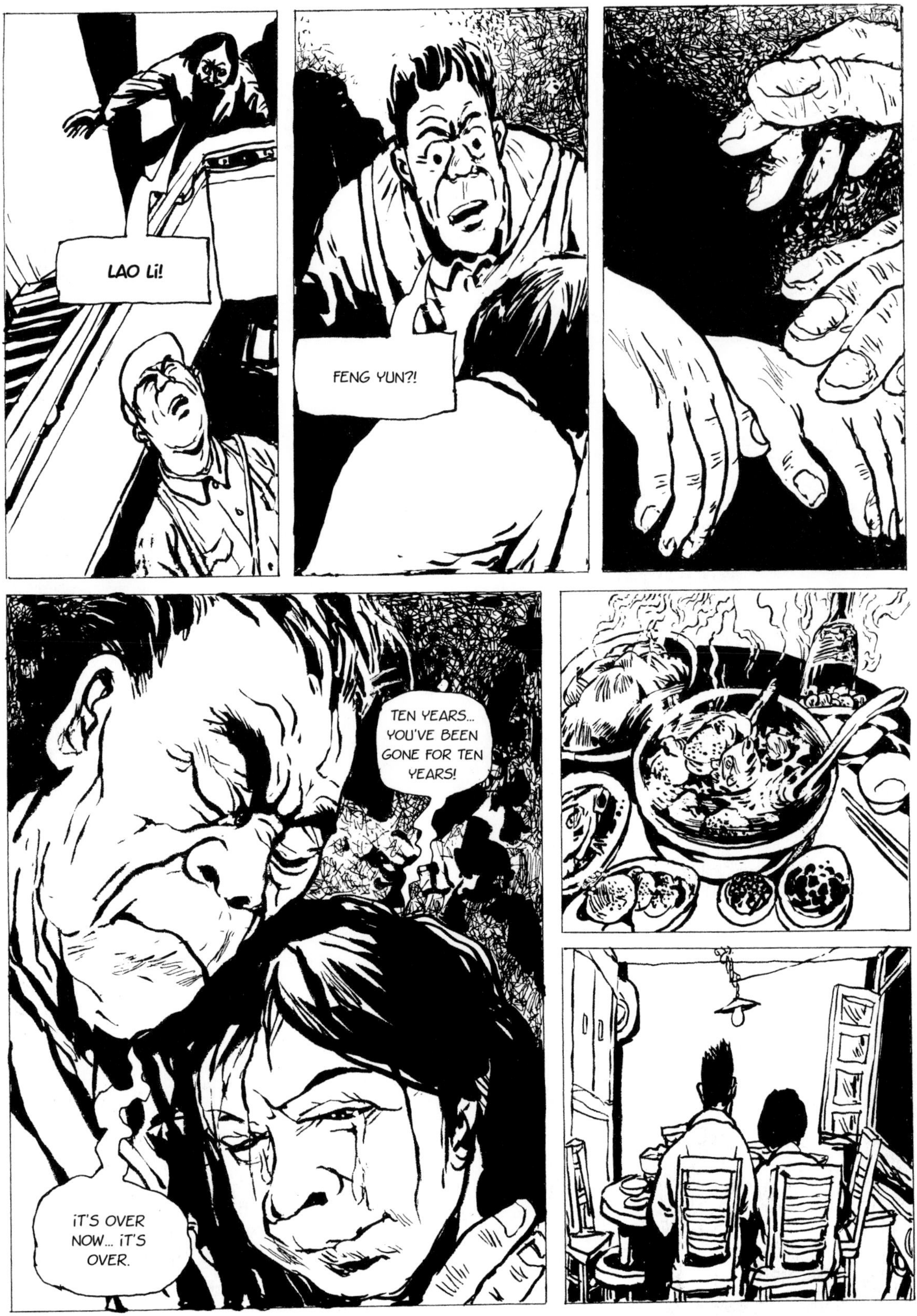
LAO LI!
FENG YUN?!
TEN YEARS... YOU'VE BEEN GONE FOR TEN YEARS!
IT'S OVER NOW... IT'S OVER.

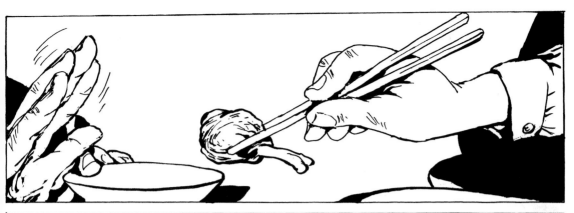

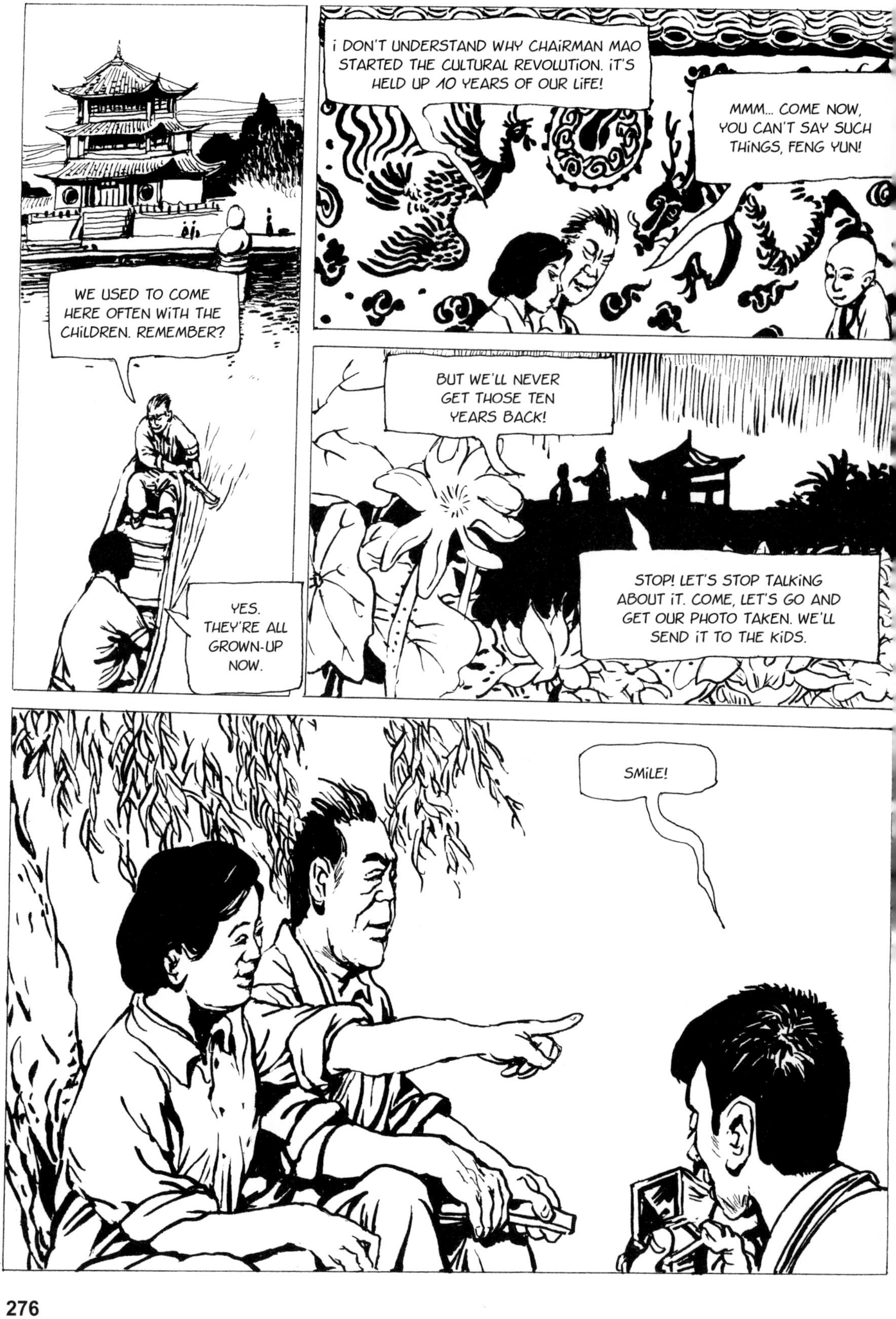
WE USED TO COME HERE OFTEN WITH THE CHILDREN. REMEMBER?
YES. THEY'RE ALL GROWN-UP NOW.
I DON'T UNDERSTAND WHY CHAIRMAN MAO STARTED THE CULTURAL REVOLUTION. IT'S HELD UP 10 YEARS OF OUR LIFE!
MMM... COME NOW, YOU CAN'T SAY SUCH THINGS, FENG YUN!
BUT WE'LL NEVER GET THOSE TEN YEARS BACK!
STOP! LET'S STOP TALKING ABOUT IT. COME, LET'S GO AND GET OUR PHOTO TAKEN. WE'LL SEND IT TO THE KIDS.
SMILE!

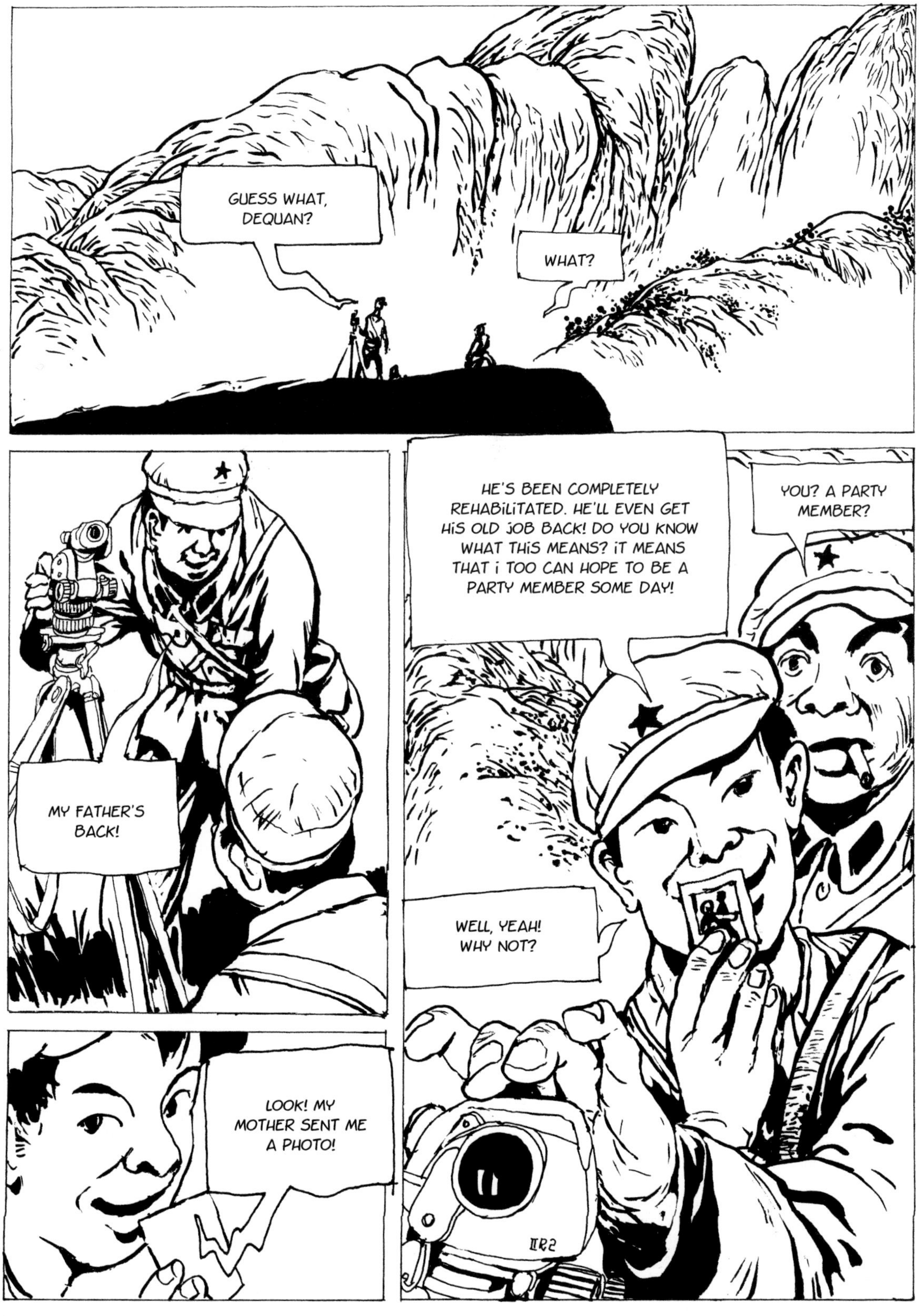
GUESS WHAT, DEQUAN?
WHAT?
MY FATHER'S BACK!
HE'S BEEN COMPLETELY REHABILITATED. HE'LL EVEN GET HIS OLD JOB BACK! DO YOU KNOW WHAT THIS MEANS? IT MEANS THAT I TOO CAN HOPE TO BE A PARTY MEMBER SOME DAY!
YOU? A PARTY MEMBER?
WELL, YEAH! WHY NOT?
LOOK! MY MOTHER SENT ME A PHOTO!

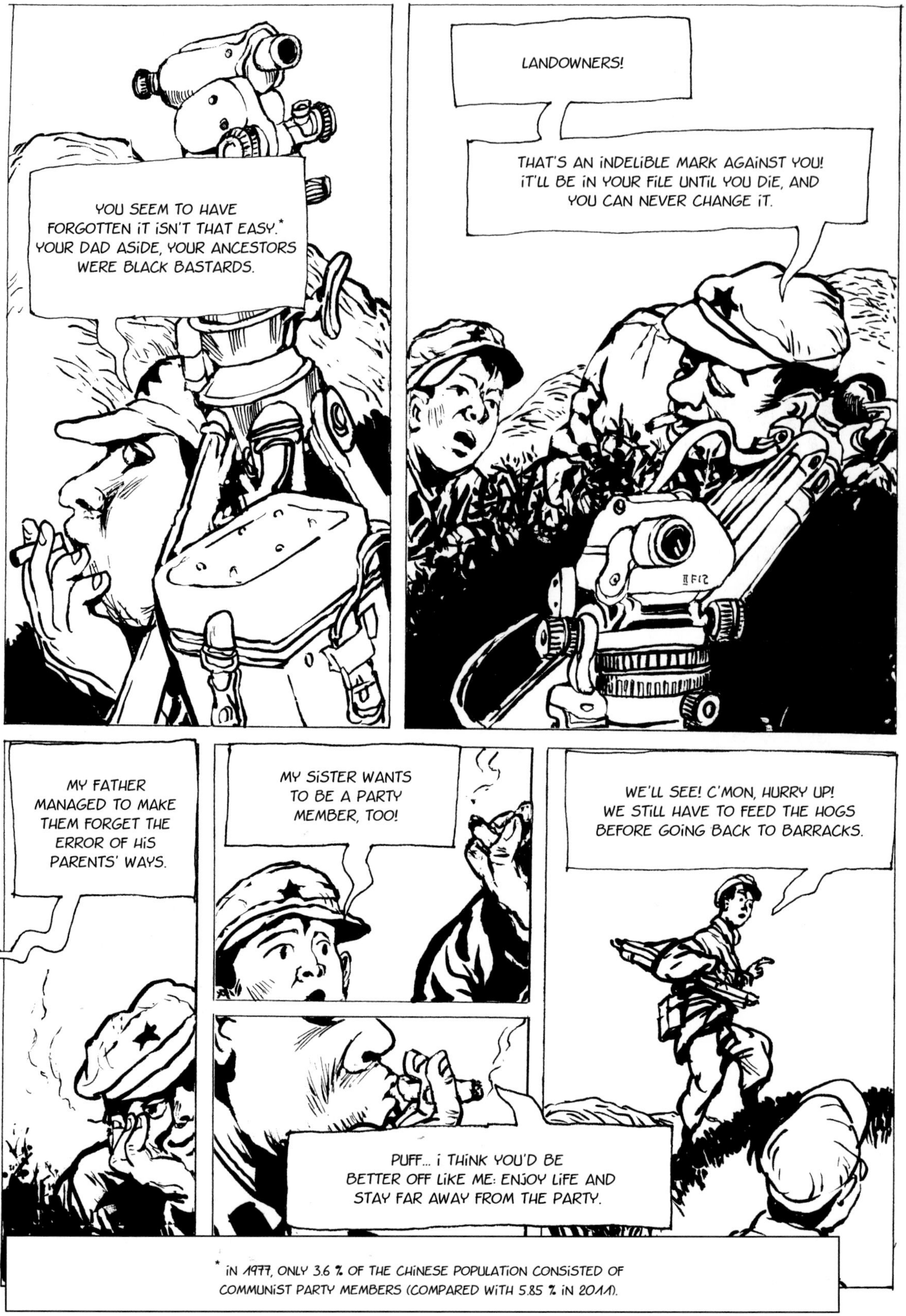
YOU SEEM TO HAVE FORGOTTEN iT iSN'T THAT EASY.* YOUR DAD ASiDE, YOUR ANCESTORS WERE BLACK BASTARDS.
LANDOWNERS!
THAT'S AN iNDELiBLE MARK AGAiNST YOU! iT'LL BE iN YOUR FiLE UNTiL YOU DiE, AND YOU CAN NEVER CHANGE iT.
MY FATHER MANAGED TO MAKE THEM FORGET THE ERROR OF HiS PARENTS' WAYS.
MY SiSTER WANTS TO BE A PARTY MEMBER, TOO!
PUFF... i THiNK YOU'D BE BETTER OFF LiKE ME: ENJOY LiFE AND STAY FAR AWAY FROM THE PARTY.
WE'LL SEE! C'MON, HURRY UP! WE STiLL HAVE TO FEED THE HOGS BEFORE GOiNG BACK TO BARRACKS.

* iN 1977, ONLY 3.6 % OF THE CHiNESE POPULATiON CONSiSTED OF COMMUNiST PARTY MEMBERS (COMPARED WiTH 5.85 % iN 2011).

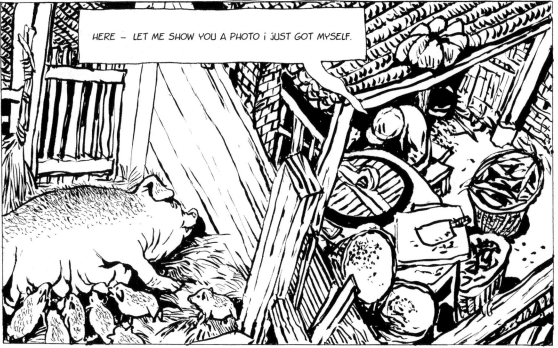

HERE — LET ME SHOW YOU A PHOTO I JUST GOT MYSELF.

WHOA! IS THAT CUIXIAN, THE FIANCÉE YOU TOLD ME ABOUT?

YUP! BEAUTIFUL, RIGHT?

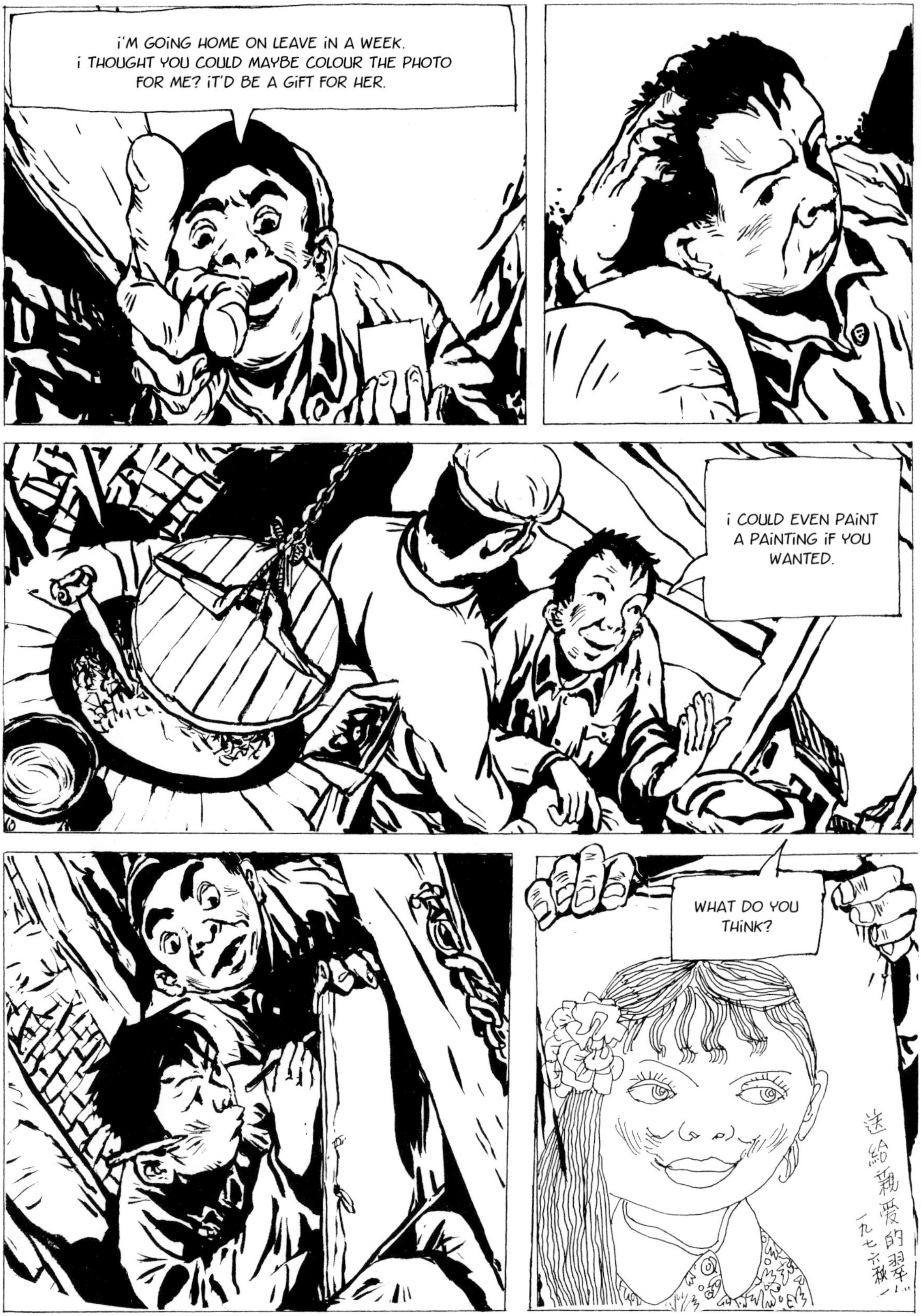
i'M GOING HOME ON LEAVE iN A WEEK. i THOUGHT YOU COULD MAYBE COLOUR THE PHOTO FOR ME? iT'D BE A GiFT FOR HER.
i COULD EVEN PAiNT A PAiNTiNG iF YOU WANTED.
WHAT DO YOU THiNK?
送給親愛的翠
一九七六秋

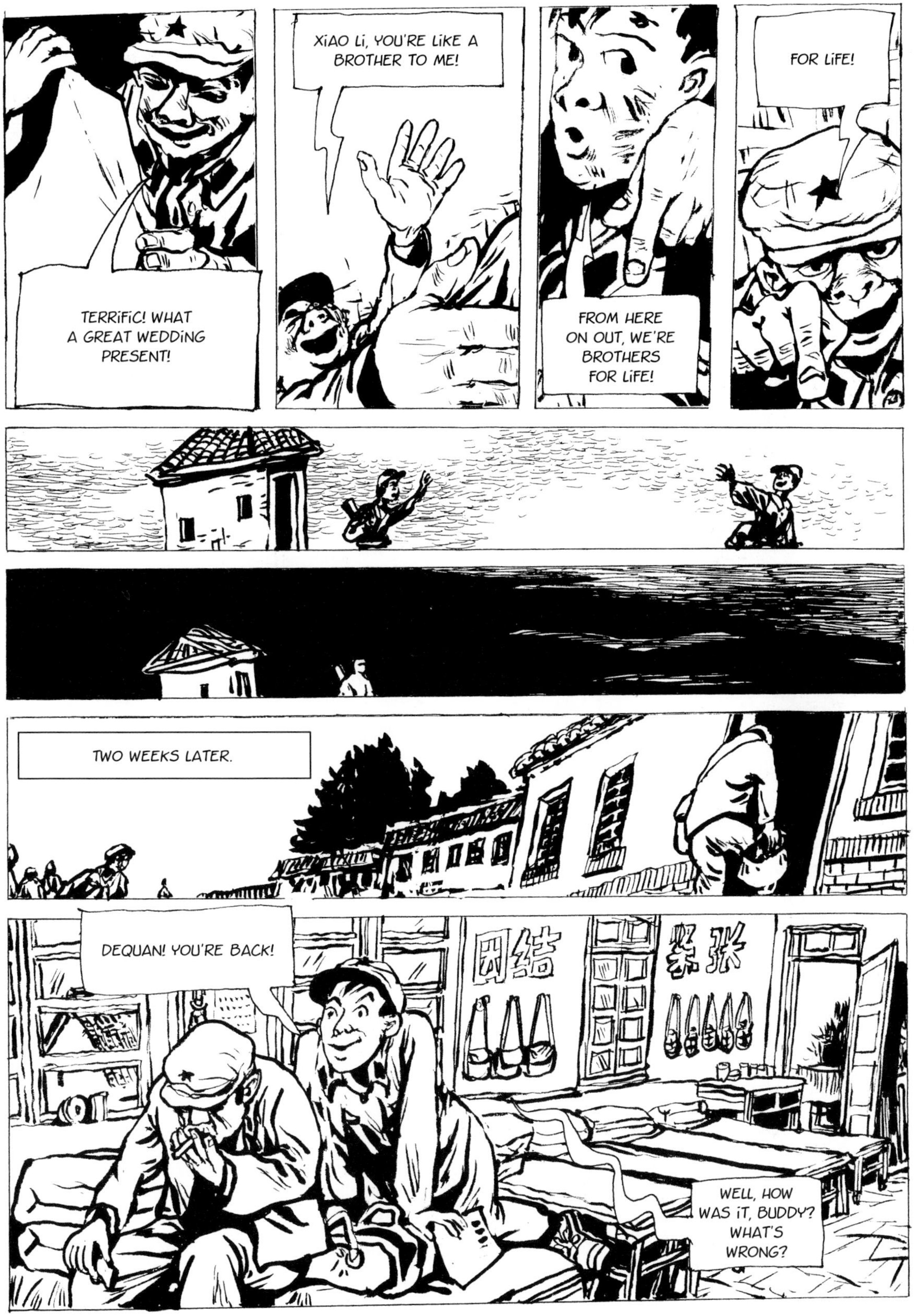
TERRIFIC! WHAT A GREAT WEDDING PRESENT!
XIAO LI, YOU'RE LIKE A BROTHER TO ME!
FROM HERE ON OUT, WE'RE BROTHERS FOR LIFE!
FOR LIFE!
TWO WEEKS LATER.
DEQUAN! YOU'RE BACK!
团结
紧张
WELL, HOW WAS IT, BUDDY? WHAT'S WRONG?

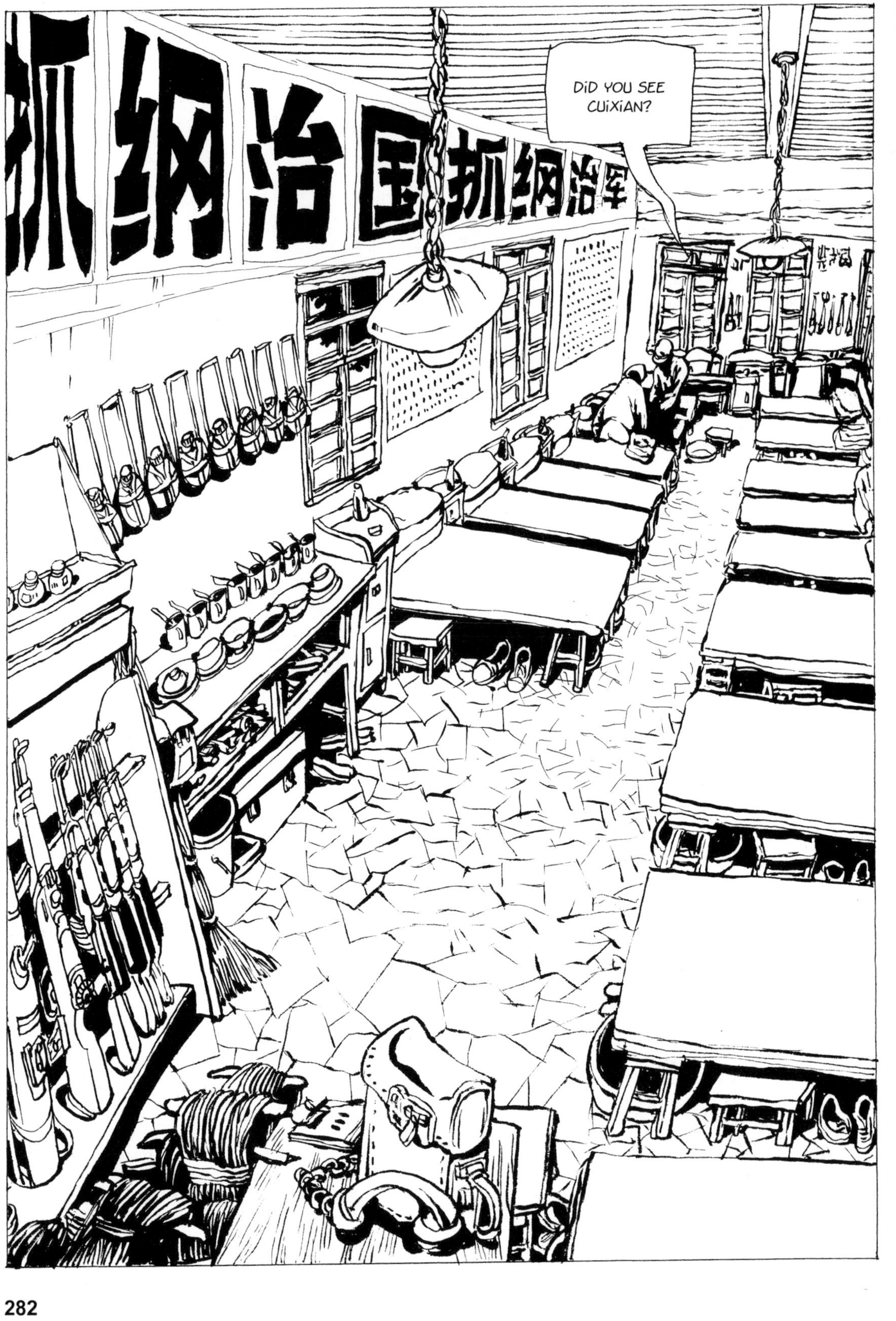
抓纲治国抓纲治军
DID YOU SEE CUIXIAN?

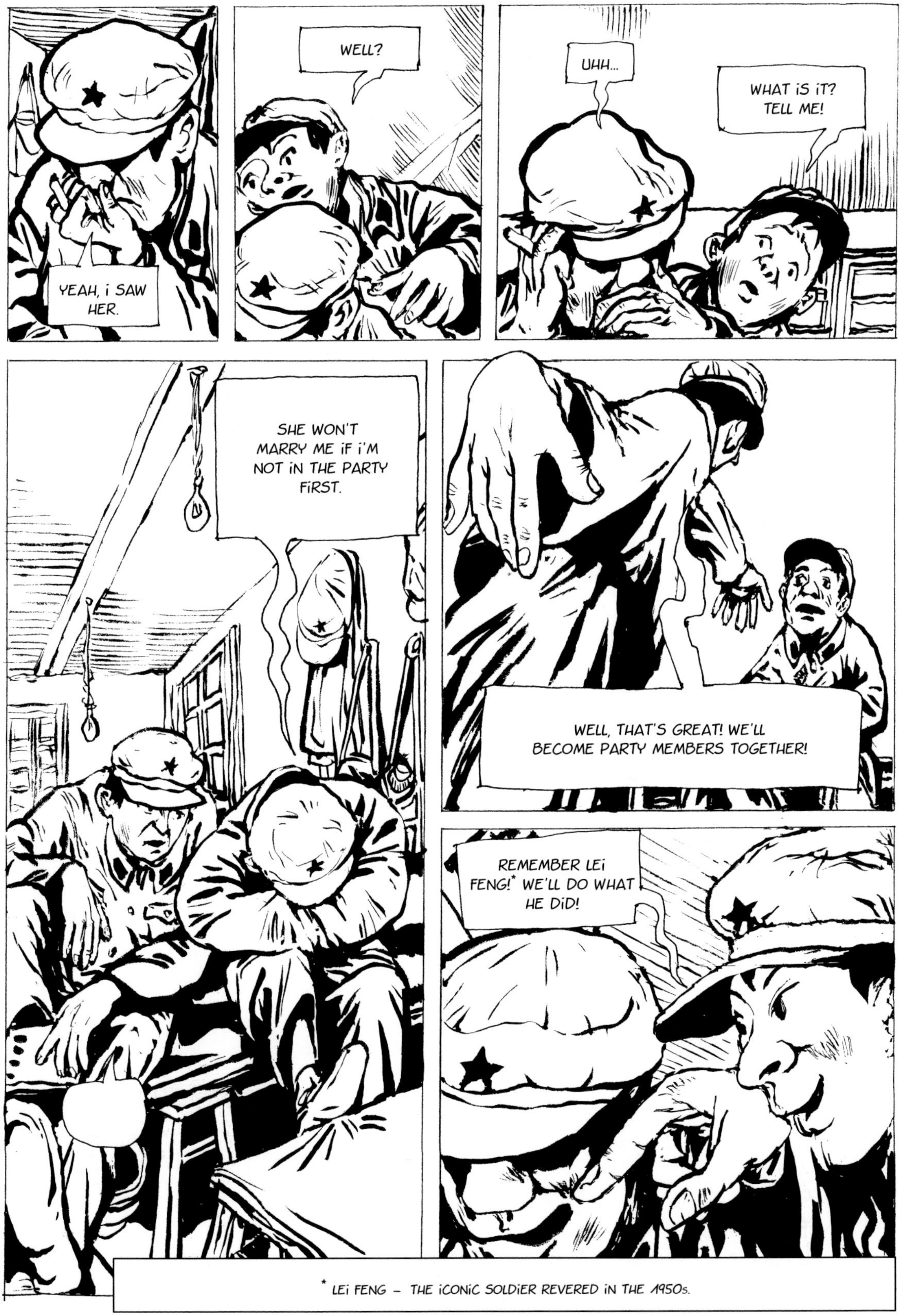
YEAH, i SAW HER.
WELL?
UHH...
WHAT iS iT? TELL ME!
SHE WON'T MARRY ME iF i'M NOT iN THE PARTY FiRST.
WELL, THAT'S GREAT! WE'LL BECOME PARTY MEMBERS TOGETHER!
REMEMBER LEi FENG!* WE'LL DO WHAT HE DiD!

* LEi FENG – THE iCONiC SOLDiER REVERED iN THE 1950s.

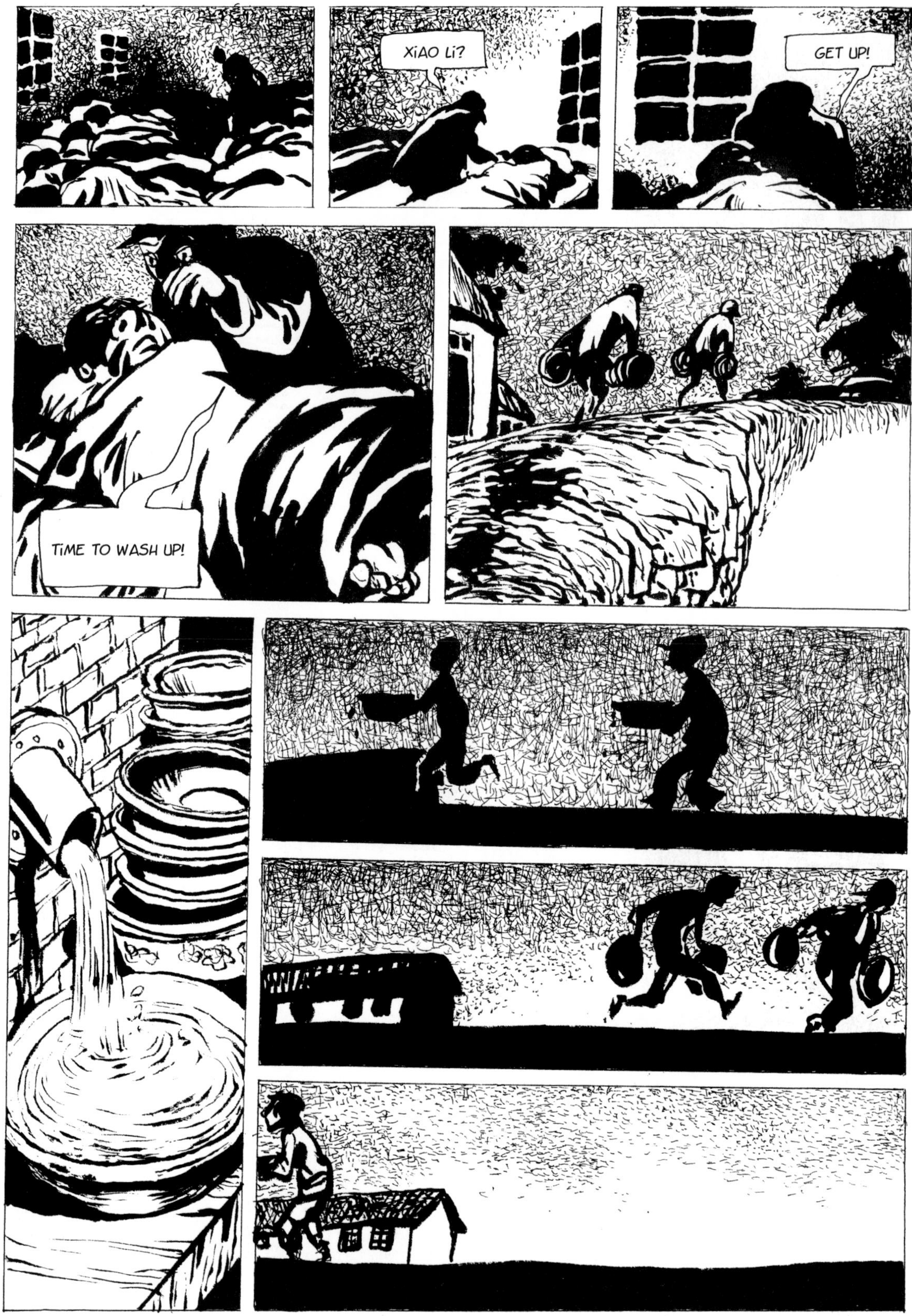
XIAO LI?
GET UP!
TIME TO WASH UP!

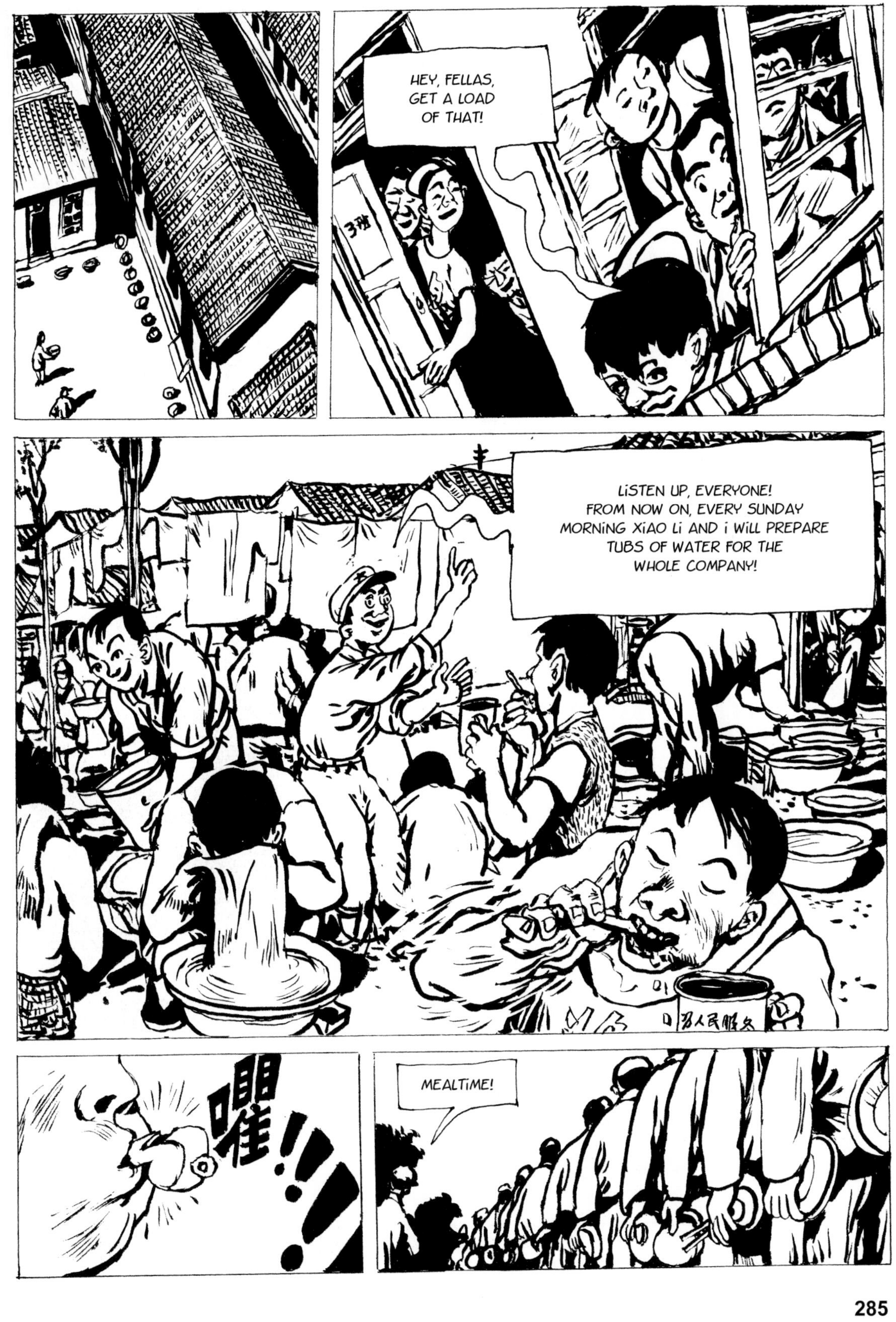

HEY, FELLAS, GET A LOAD OF THAT!
LISTEN UP, EVERYONE! FROM NOW ON, EVERY SUNDAY MORNING XIAO LI AND I WILL PREPARE TUBS OF WATER FOR THE WHOLE COMPANY!
MEALTIME!

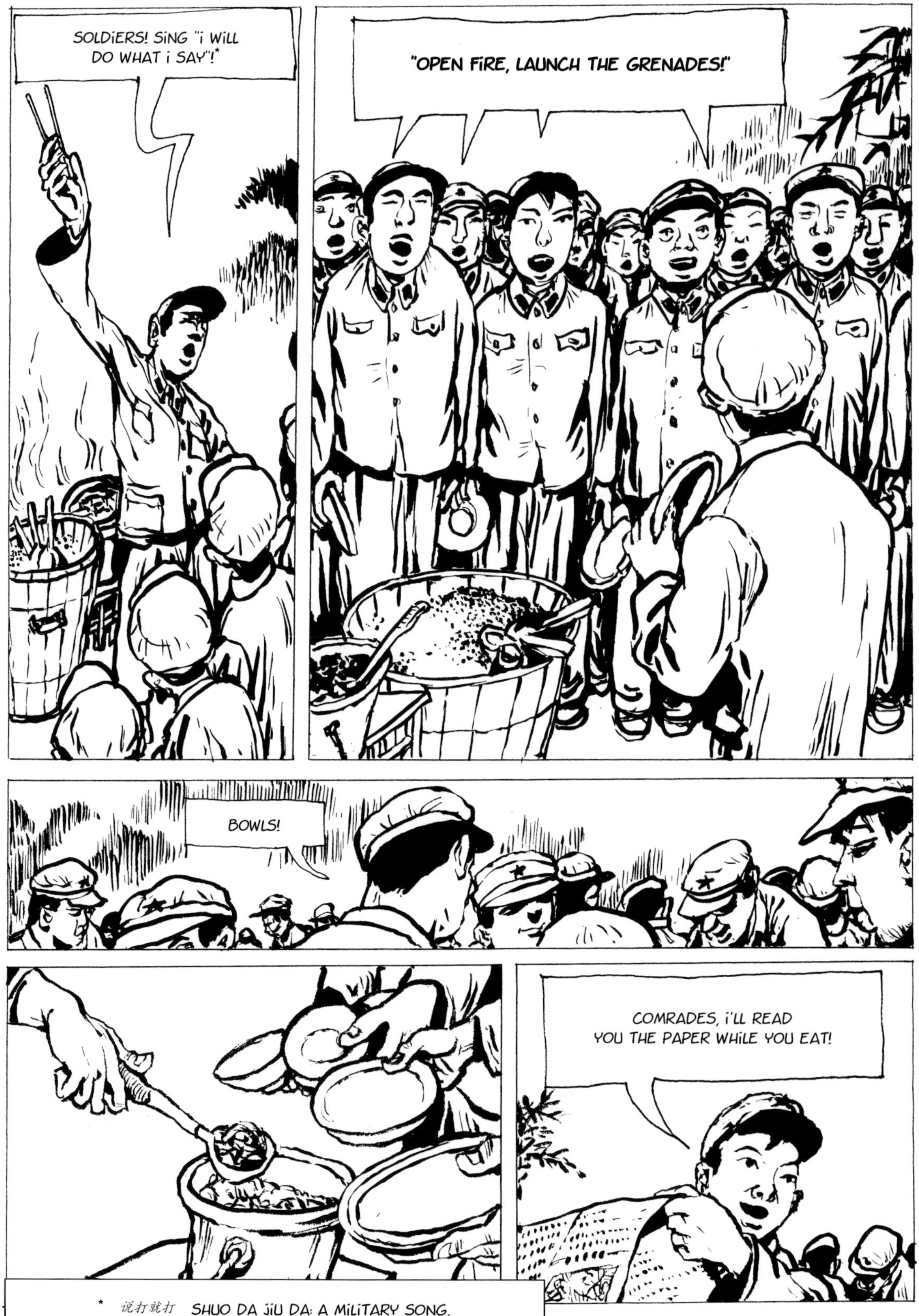
SOLDIERS! SING "I WILL DO WHAT I SAY"!*
"OPEN FIRE, LAUNCH THE GRENADES!"
BOWLS!
COMRADES, I'LL READ YOU THE PAPER WHILE YOU EAT!

* 说打就打 SHUO DA JIU DA: A MILITARY SONG.

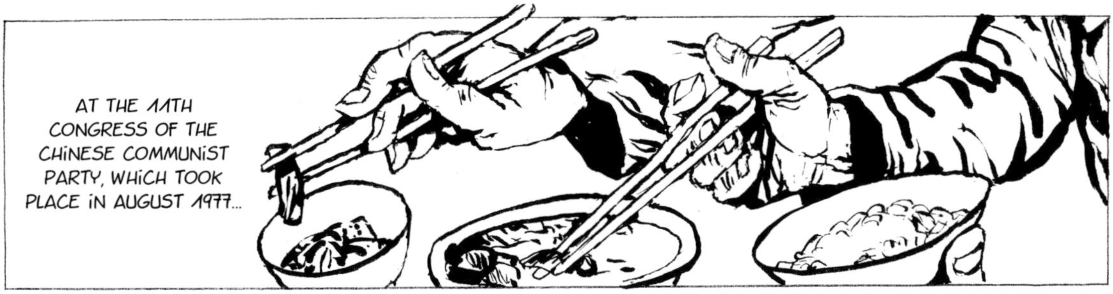
AT THE 11TH CONGRESS OF THE CHINESE COMMUNIST PARTY, WHICH TOOK PLACE IN AUGUST 1977...

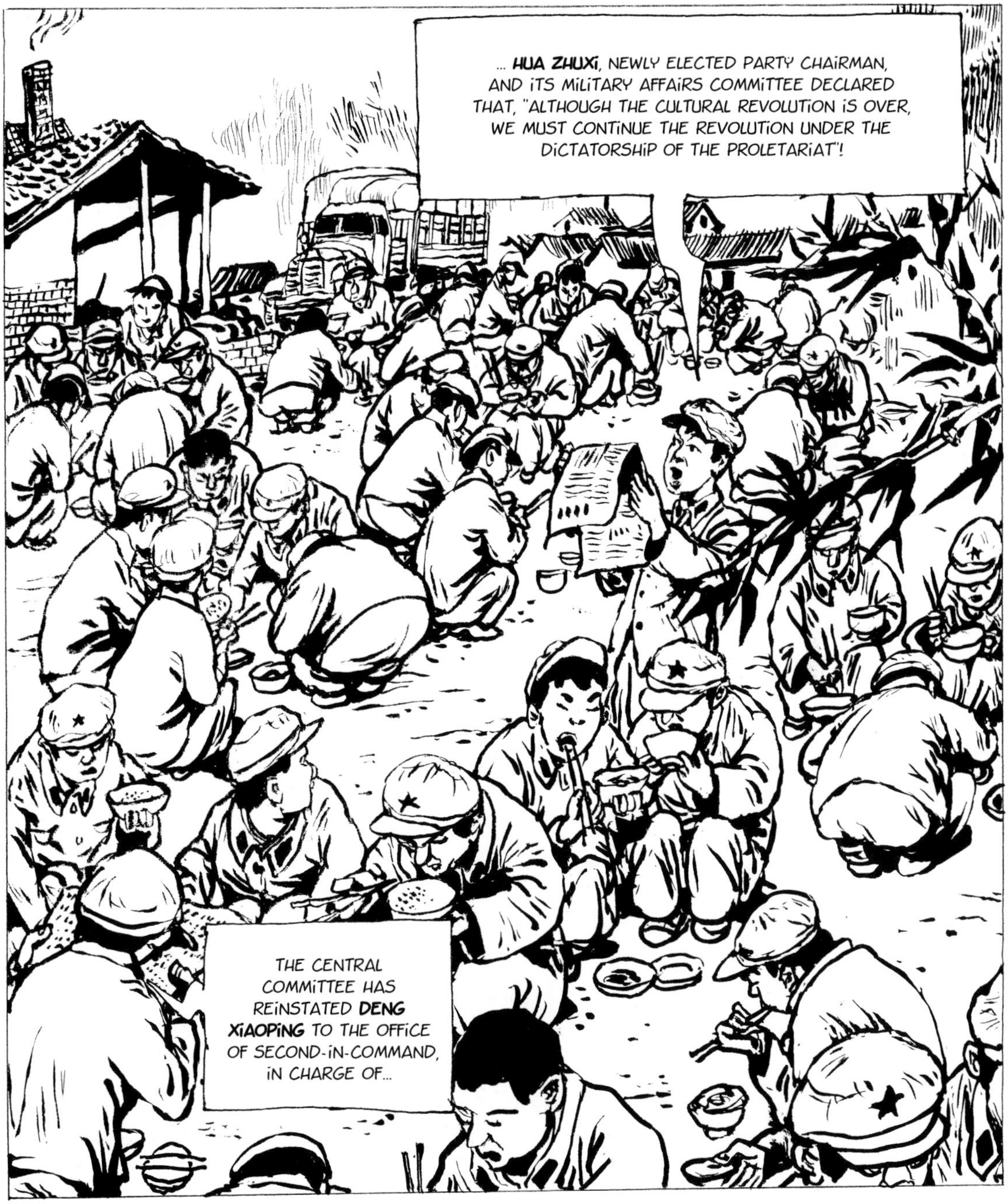
... HUA ZHUXI, NEWLY ELECTED PARTY CHAIRMAN, AND ITS MILITARY AFFAIRS COMMITTEE DECLARED THAT, "ALTHOUGH THE CULTURAL REVOLUTION IS OVER, WE MUST CONTINUE THE REVOLUTION UNDER THE DICTATORSHIP OF THE PROLETARIAT"!
THE CENTRAL COMMITTEE HAS REINSTATED DENG XIAOPING TO THE OFFICE OF SECOND-IN-COMMAND, IN CHARGE OF...

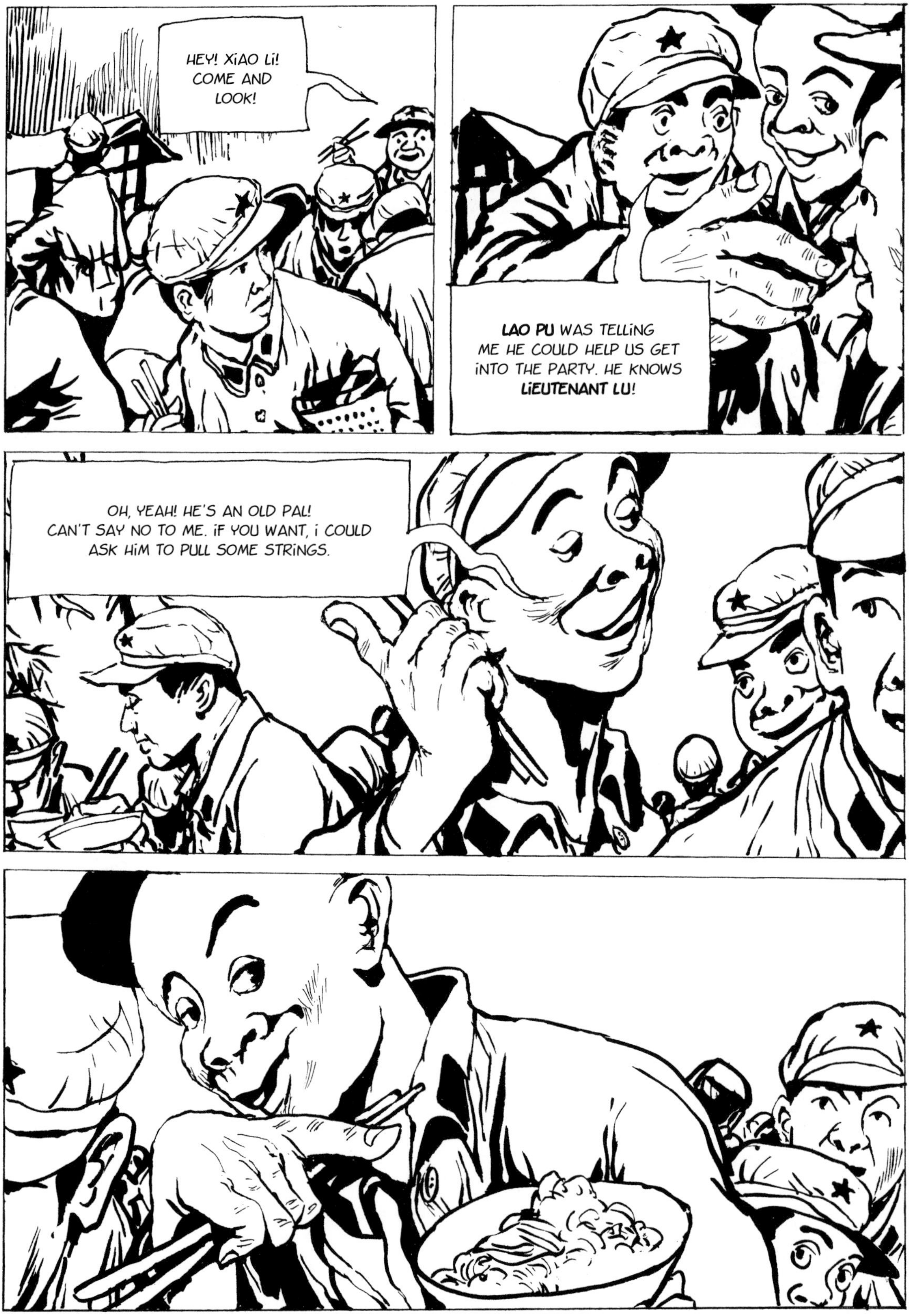
HEY! XiAO Li! COME AND LOOK!
LAO PU WAS TELLiNG ME HE COULD HELP US GET iNTO THE PARTY. HE KNOWS LiEUTENANT LU!
OH, YEAH! HE'S AN OLD PAL! CAN'T SAY NO TO ME. iF YOU WANT, i COULD ASK HiM TO PULL SOME STRiNGS.

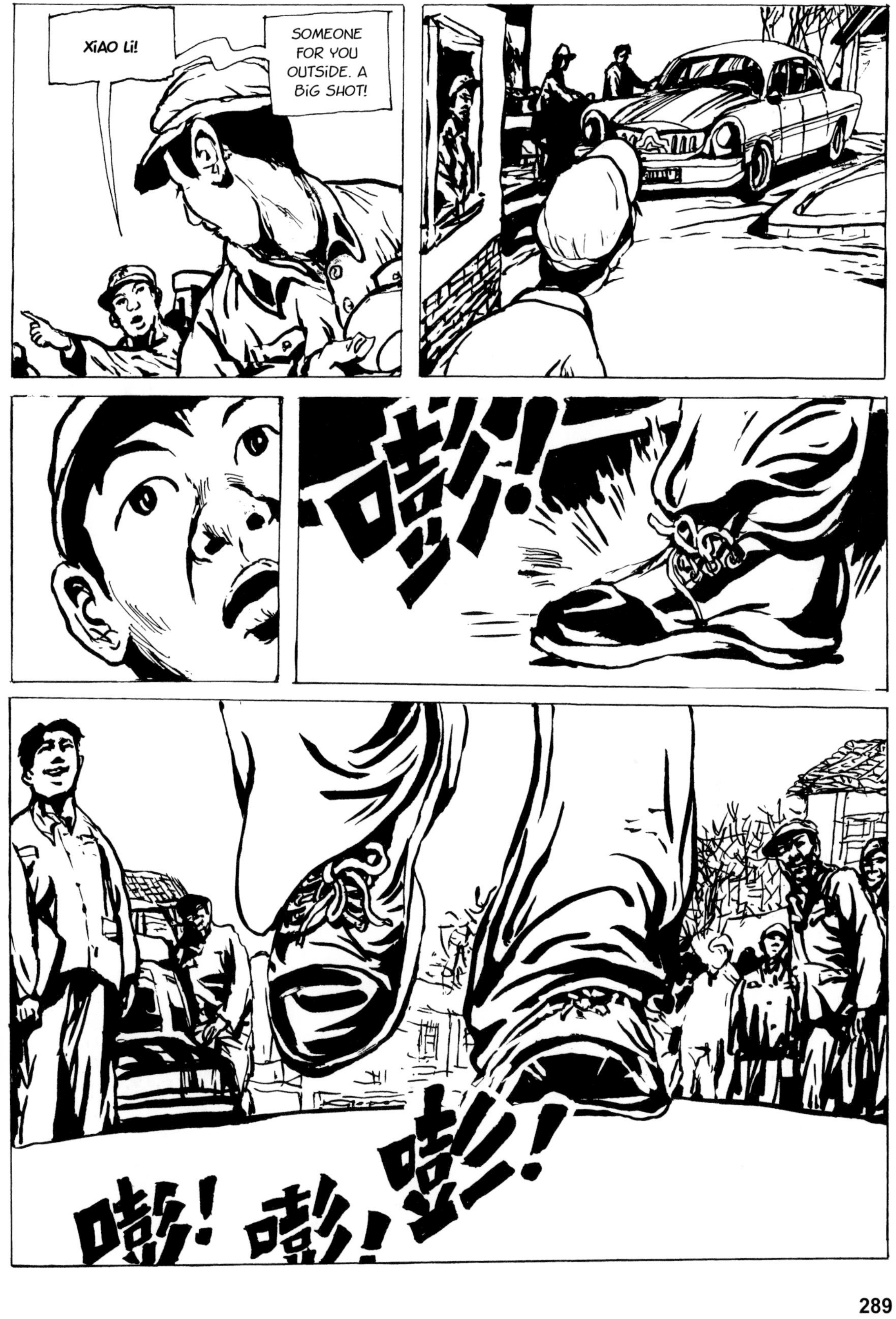
XiAO Li!
SOMEONE FOR YOU OUTSiDE. A BiG SHOT!
嘭!
嘭! 嘭! 嘭!

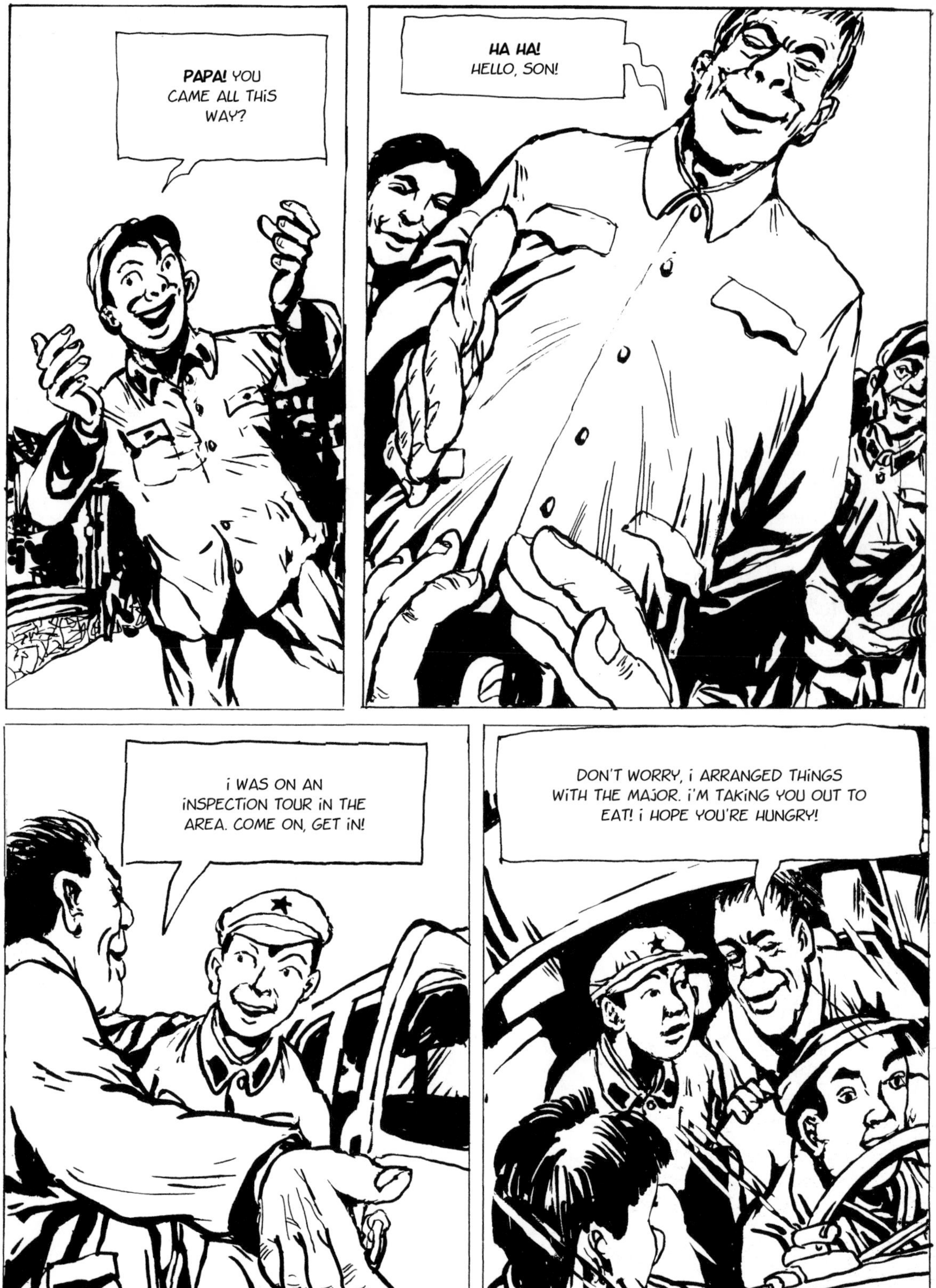
PAPA! YOU CAME ALL THIS WAY?
HA HA! HELLO, SON!
I WAS ON AN INSPECTION TOUR IN THE AREA. COME ON, GET IN!
DON'T WORRY, I ARRANGED THINGS WITH THE MAJOR. I'M TAKING YOU OUT TO EAT! I HOPE YOU'RE HUNGRY!

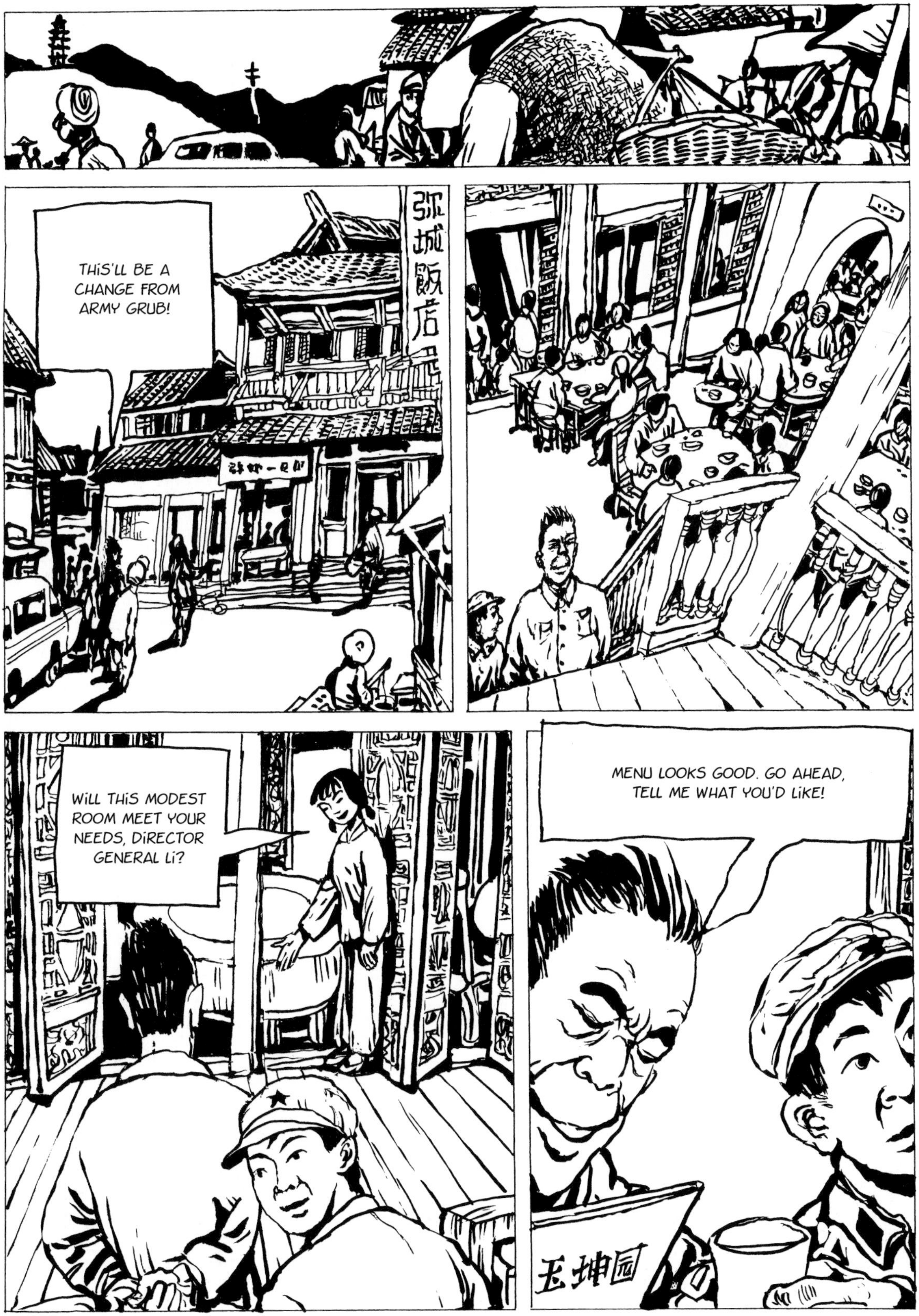
THIS'LL BE A CHANGE FROM ARMY GRUB!
弥城饭店
WILL THIS MODEST ROOM MEET YOUR NEEDS, DIRECTOR GENERAL LI?
MENU LOOKS GOOD. GO AHEAD, TELL ME WHAT YOU'D LIKE!
玉坤园

SO! i REMEMBER READiNG iN YOUR LETTER THAT YOU WANT TO JOiN THE PARTY.

THAT'S GOOD, SON. THE REVOLUTiON NEEDS YOUNG PEOPLE LiKE YOU TO TAKE THE REiNS.

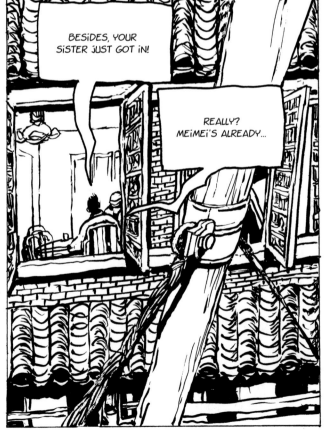

BESiDES, YOUR SiSTER JUST GOT iN!

REALLY? MEiMEi'S ALREADY...

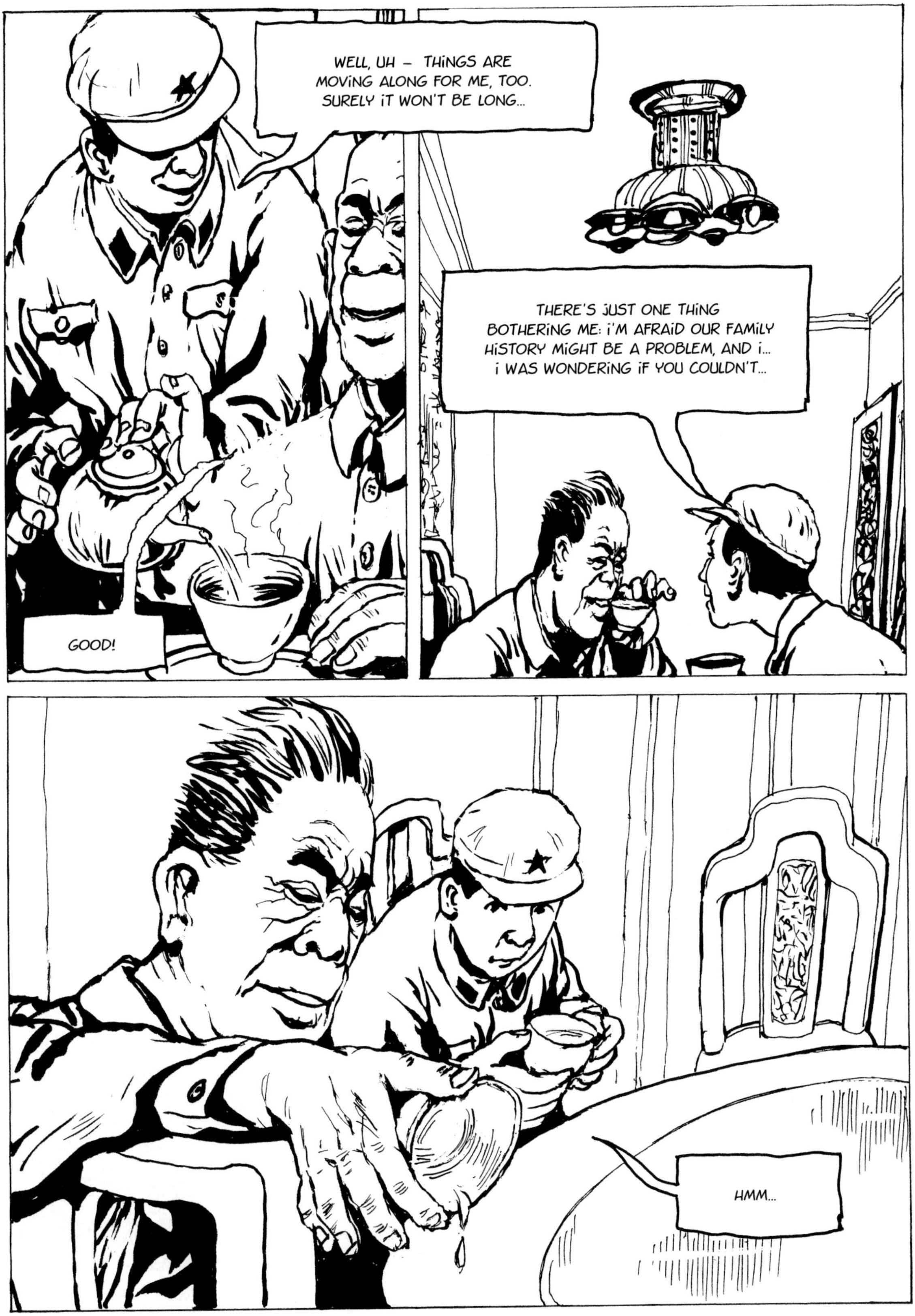
WELL, UH – THINGS ARE MOVING ALONG FOR ME, TOO. SURELY IT WON'T BE LONG...
GOOD!
THERE'S JUST ONE THING BOTHERING ME: I'M AFRAID OUR FAMILY HISTORY MIGHT BE A PROBLEM, AND I... I WAS WONDERING IF YOU COULDN'T...
HMM...

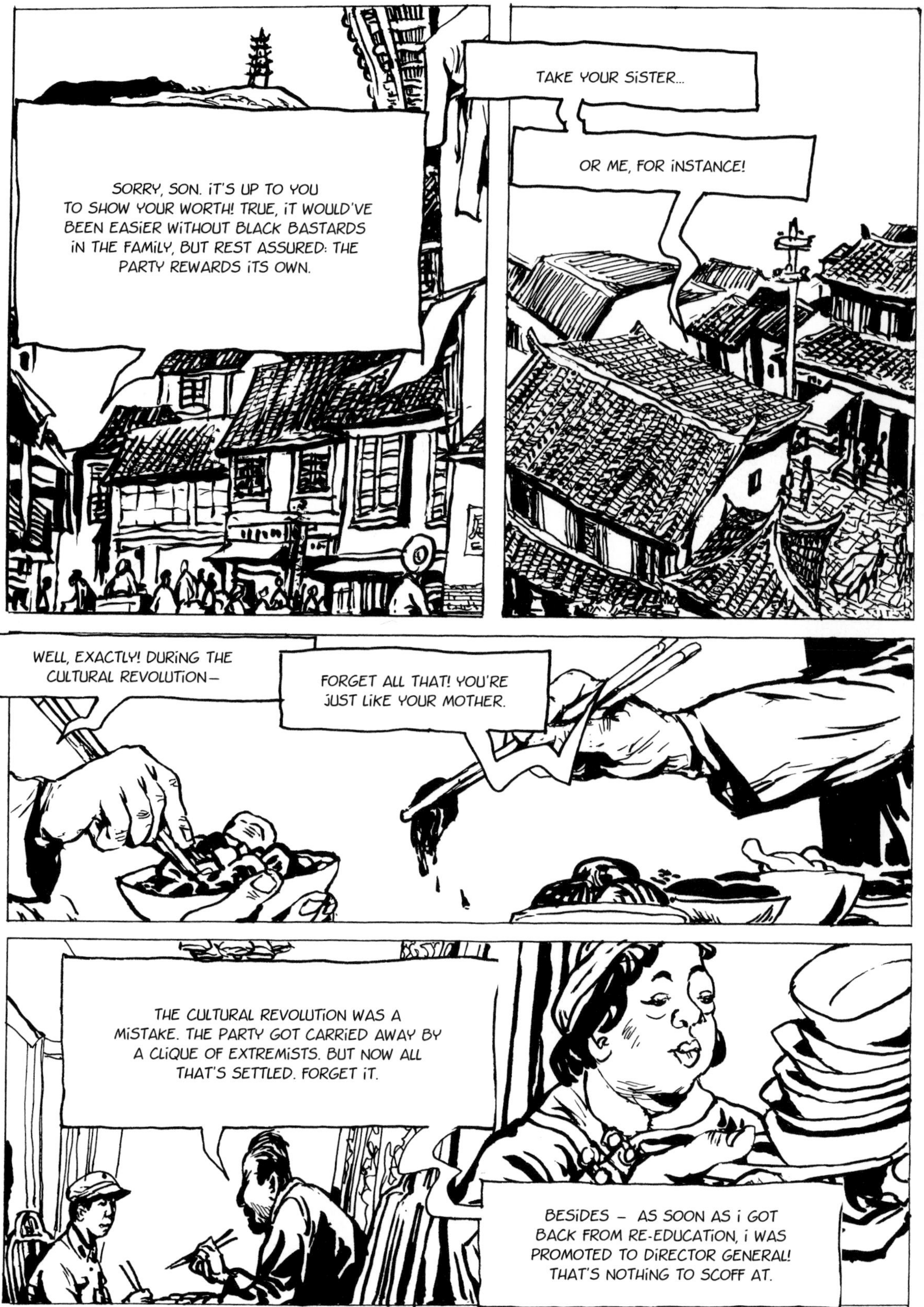
SORRY, SON. IT'S UP TO YOU TO SHOW YOUR WORTH! TRUE, IT WOULD'VE BEEN EASIER WITHOUT BLACK BASTARDS IN THE FAMILY, BUT REST ASSURED: THE PARTY REWARDS ITS OWN.
TAKE YOUR SISTER...
OR ME, FOR INSTANCE!
WELL, EXACTLY! DURING THE CULTURAL REVOLUTION—
FORGET ALL THAT! YOU'RE JUST LIKE YOUR MOTHER.
THE CULTURAL REVOLUTION WAS A MISTAKE. THE PARTY GOT CARRIED AWAY BY A CLIQUE OF EXTREMISTS. BUT NOW ALL THAT'S SETTLED. FORGET IT.
BESIDES – AS SOON AS I GOT BACK FROM RE-EDUCATION, I WAS PROMOTED TO DIRECTOR GENERAL! THAT'S NOTHING TO SCOFF AT.

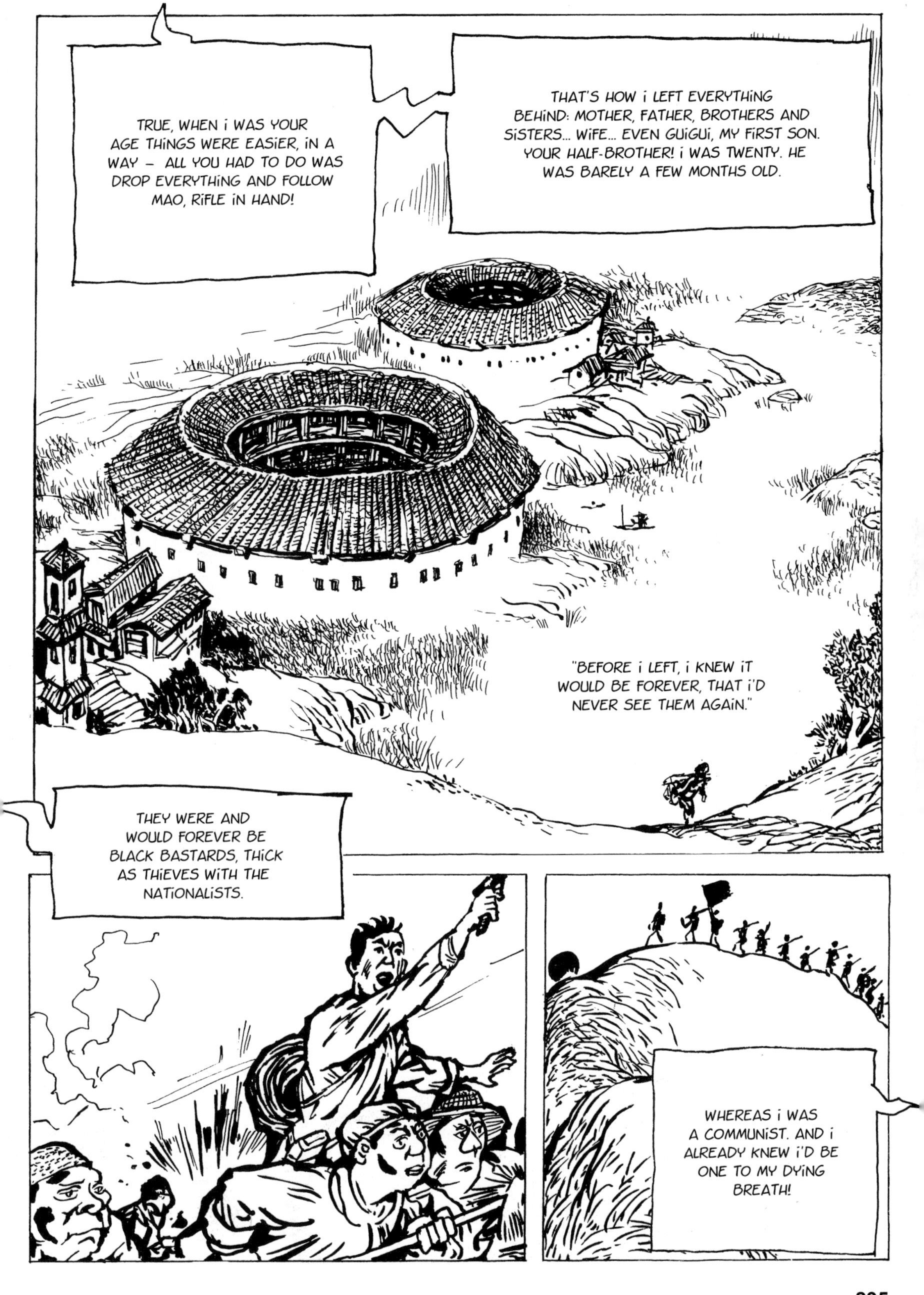
TRUE, WHEN i WAS YOUR AGE THINGS WERE EASIER, IN A WAY – ALL YOU HAD TO DO WAS DROP EVERYTHING AND FOLLOW MAO, RIFLE IN HAND!
THAT'S HOW i LEFT EVERYTHING BEHIND: MOTHER, FATHER, BROTHERS AND SISTERS... WIFE... EVEN GUIGUI, MY FIRST SON. YOUR HALF-BROTHER! i WAS TWENTY. HE WAS BARELY A FEW MONTHS OLD.
"BEFORE i LEFT, i KNEW iT WOULD BE FOREVER, THAT i'D NEVER SEE THEM AGAiN."
THEY WERE AND WOULD FOREVER BE BLACK BASTARDS, THICK AS THIEVES WITH THE NATIONALISTS.
WHEREAS i WAS A COMMUNIST. AND i ALREADY KNEW i'D BE ONE TO MY DYING BREATH!

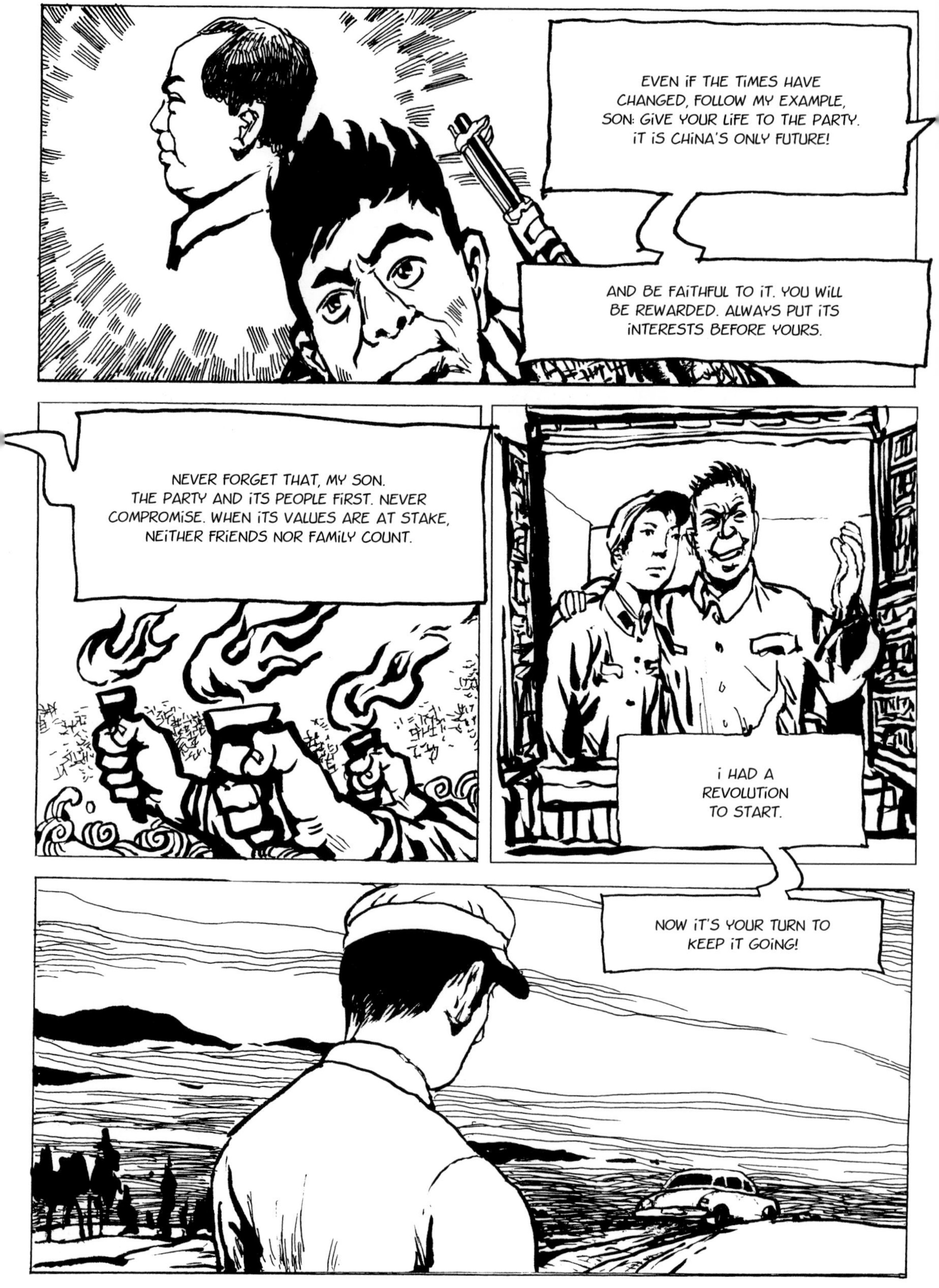
EVEN IF THE TIMES HAVE CHANGED, FOLLOW MY EXAMPLE, SON: GIVE YOUR LIFE TO THE PARTY. IT IS CHINA'S ONLY FUTURE!
AND BE FAITHFUL TO IT. YOU WILL BE REWARDED. ALWAYS PUT ITS INTERESTS BEFORE YOURS.
NEVER FORGET THAT, MY SON. THE PARTY AND ITS PEOPLE FIRST. NEVER COMPROMISE. WHEN ITS VALUES ARE AT STAKE, NEITHER FRIENDS NOR FAMILY COUNT.
I HAD A REVOLUTION TO START.
NOW IT'S YOUR TURN TO KEEP IT GOING!

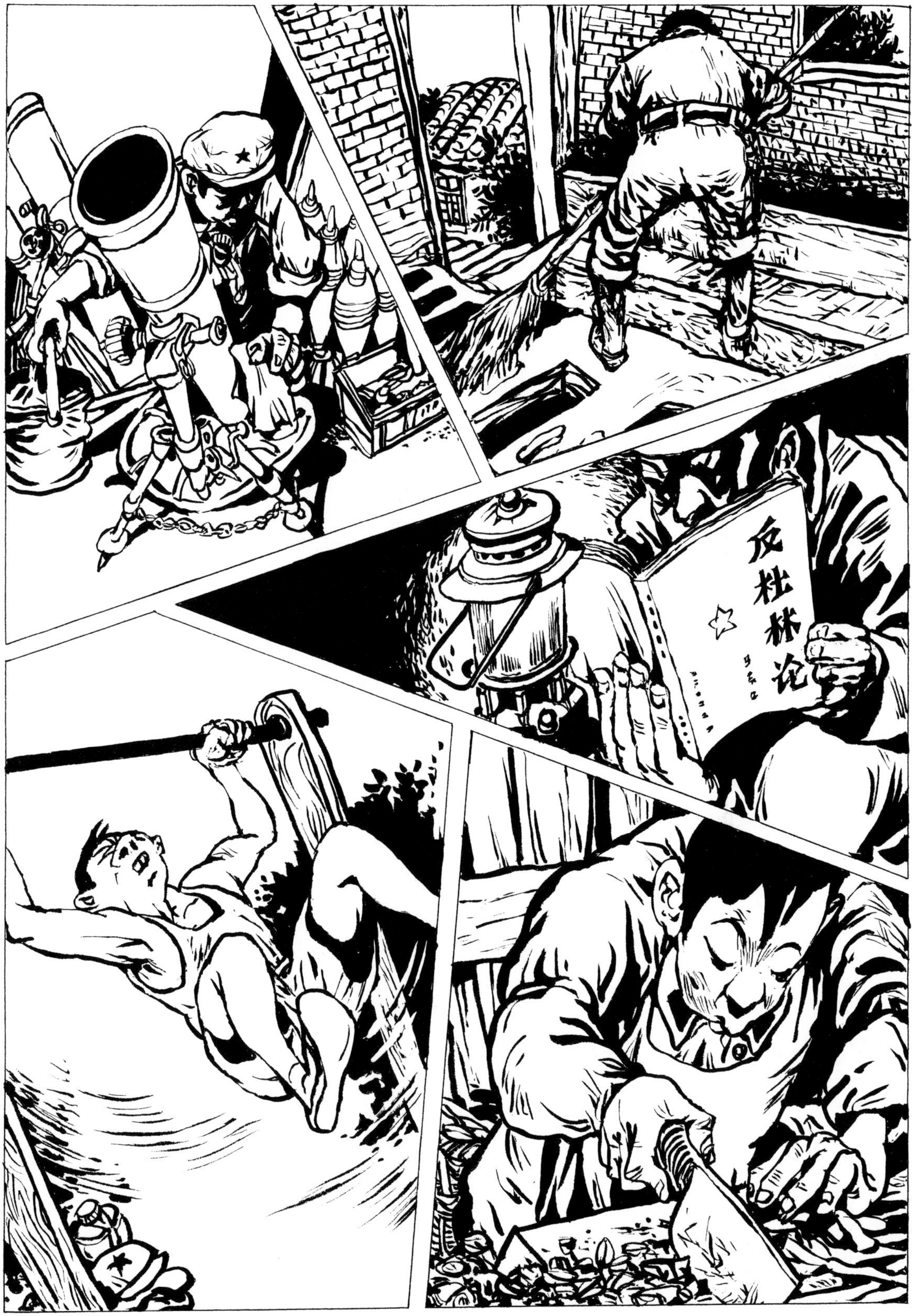
反杜林论

COMRADES! IF YOU NEED PHOTOGRAPHS HAND-TINTED FOR FREE, I'M AT YOUR DISPOSAL!

TEN PHOTOS EVERY SUNDAY!

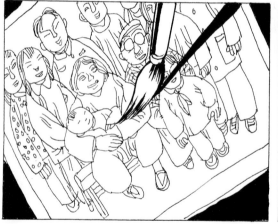

HEY, I HAVE AN IDEA...

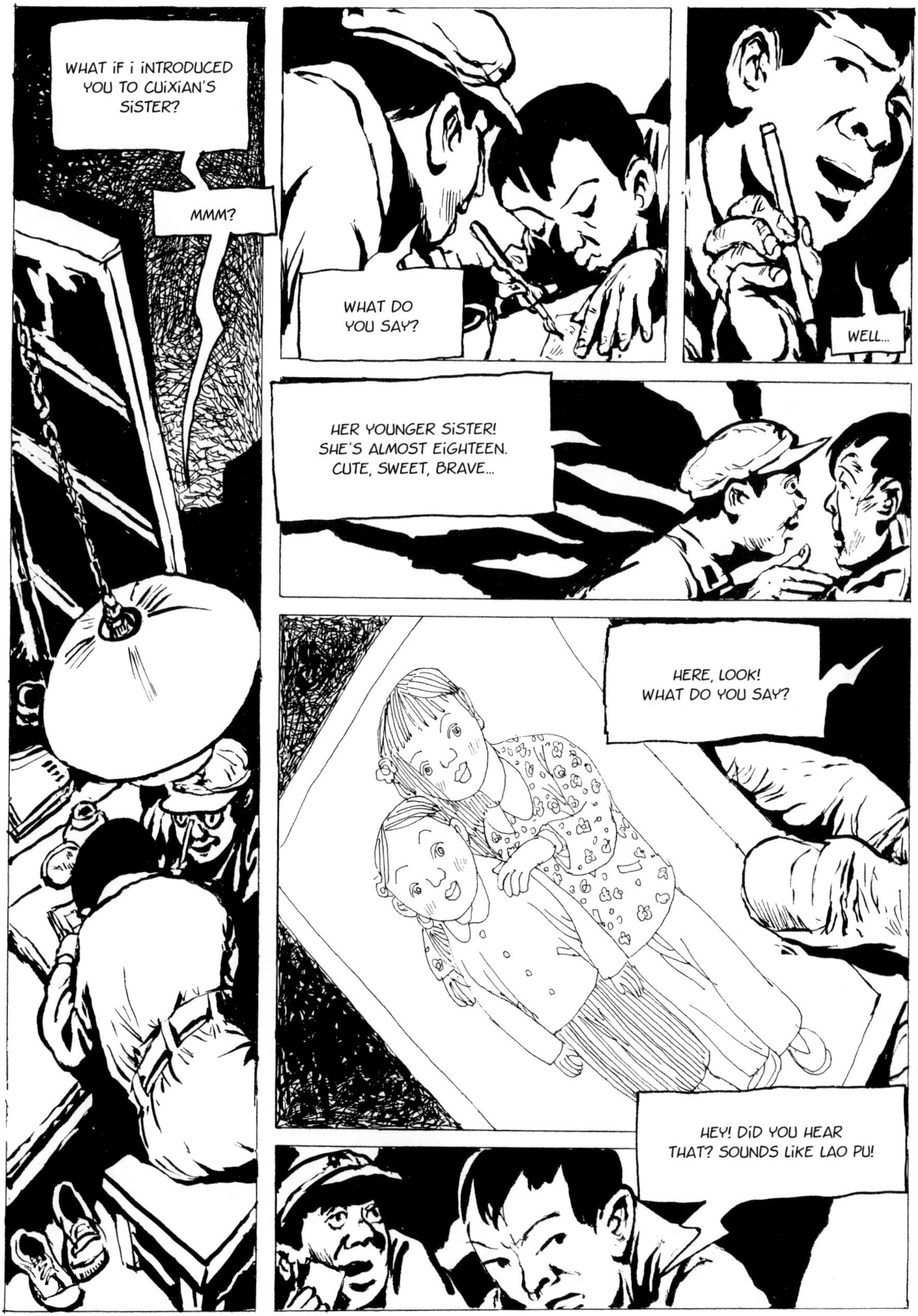
WHAT IF I INTRODUCED YOU TO CUIXIAN'S SISTER?
MMM?
WHAT DO YOU SAY?
WELL...
HER YOUNGER SISTER! SHE'S ALMOST EIGHTEEN. CUTE, SWEET, BRAVE...
HERE, LOOK! WHAT DO YOU SAY?
HEY! DID YOU HEAR THAT? SOUNDS LIKE LAO PU!

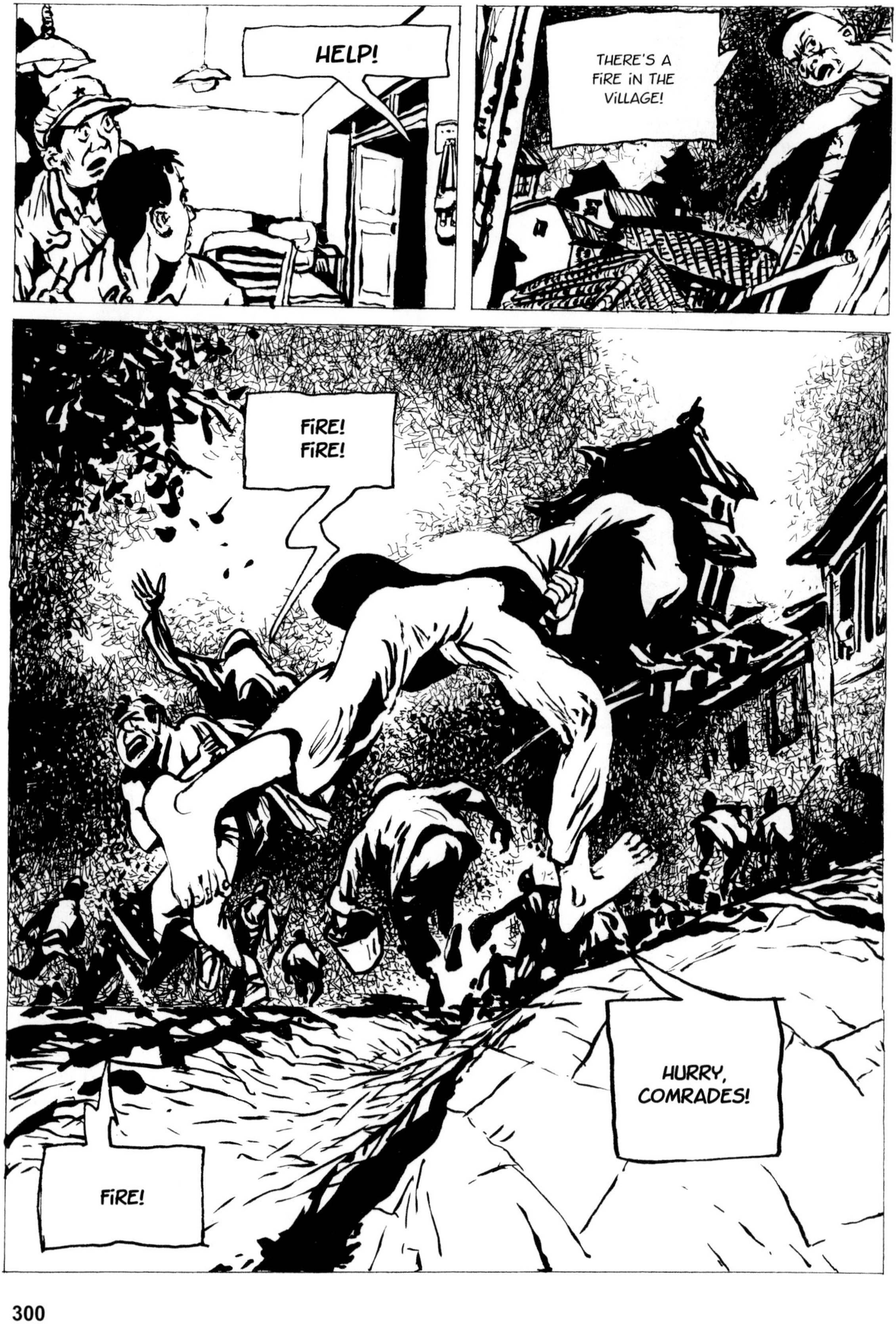
HELP!
THERE'S A FIRE IN THE VILLAGE!
FIRE! FIRE!
FIRE!
HURRY, COMRADES!

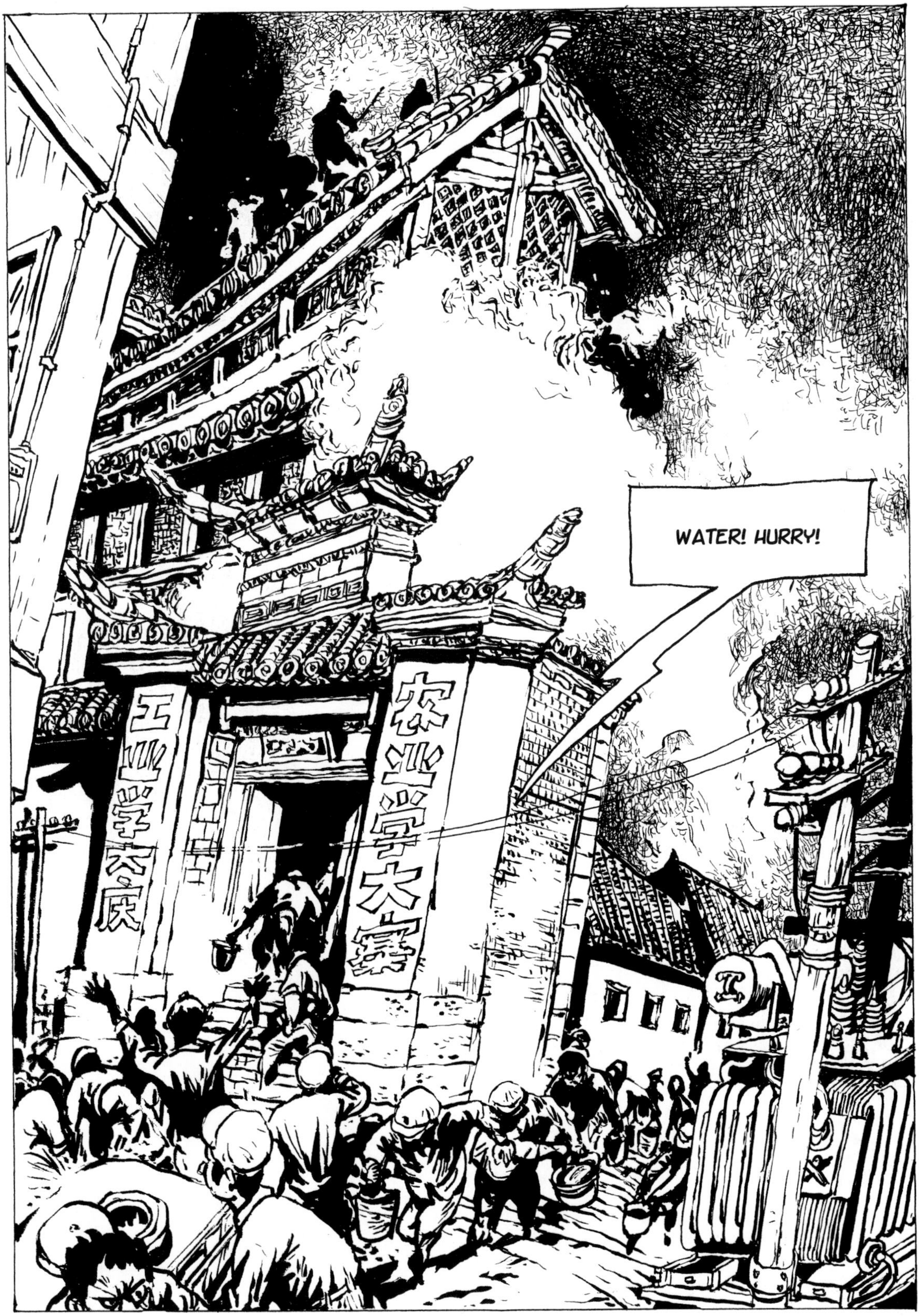
工业学大庆
农业学大寨
WATER! HURRY!

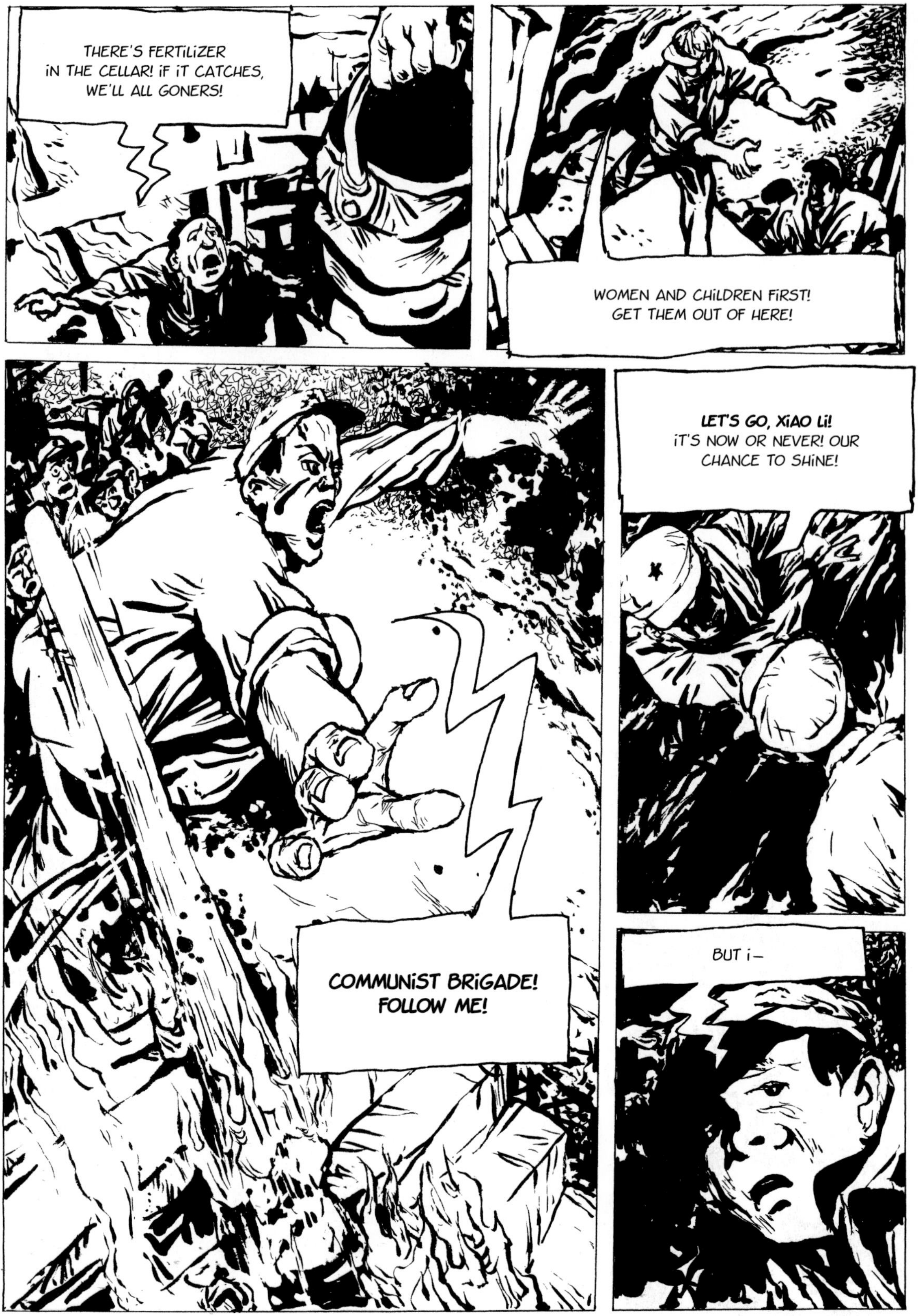

THERE'S FERTILIZER IN THE CELLAR! IF IT CATCHES, WE'LL ALL GONERS!
WOMEN AND CHILDREN FIRST! GET THEM OUT OF HERE!
COMMUNIST BRIGADE! FOLLOW ME!
LET'S GO, XIAO LI! IT'S NOW OR NEVER! OUR CHANCE TO SHINE!
BUT I–

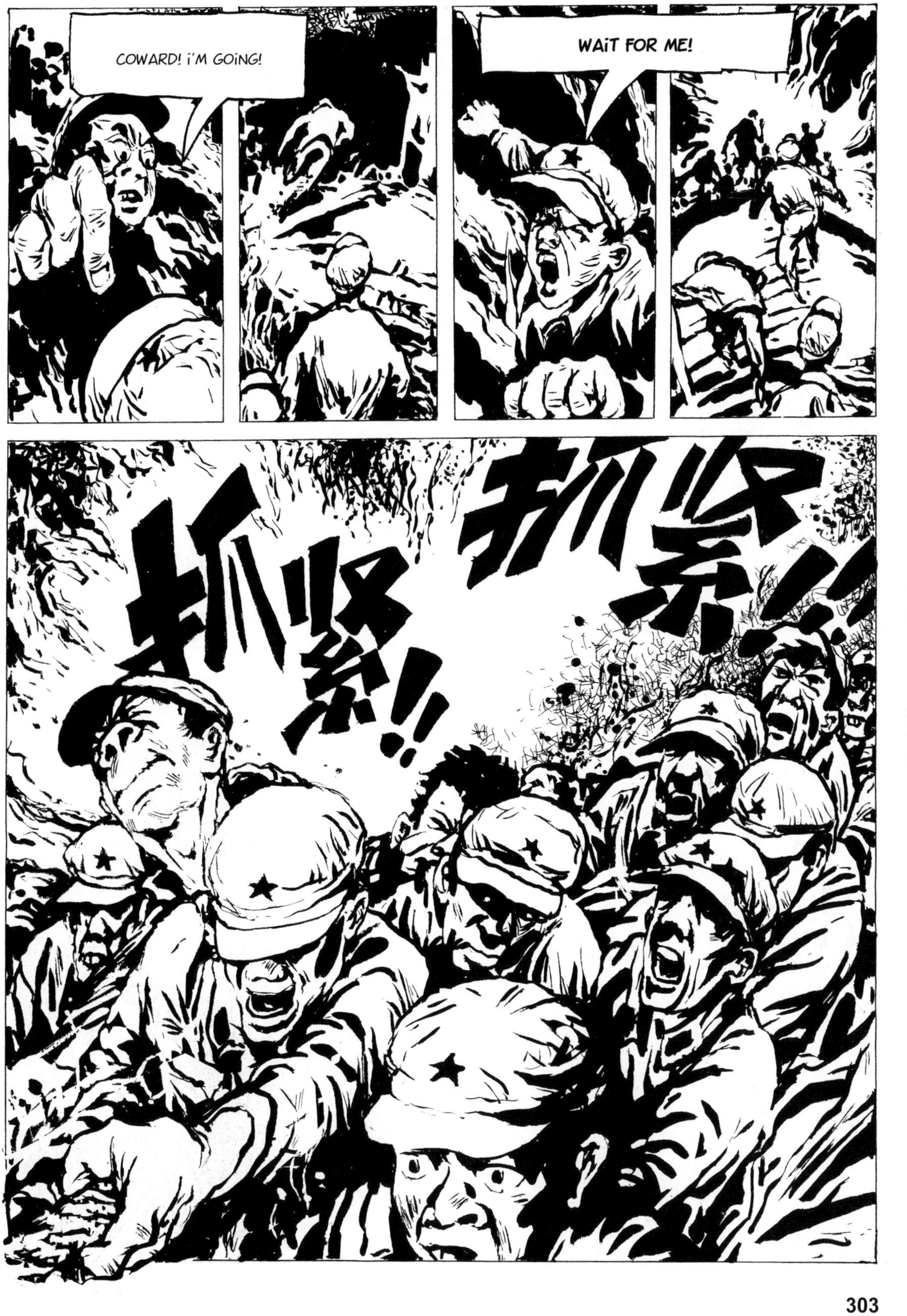
COWARD! i'M GOiNG!
WAiT FOR ME!
抓紧!!
抓紧!!

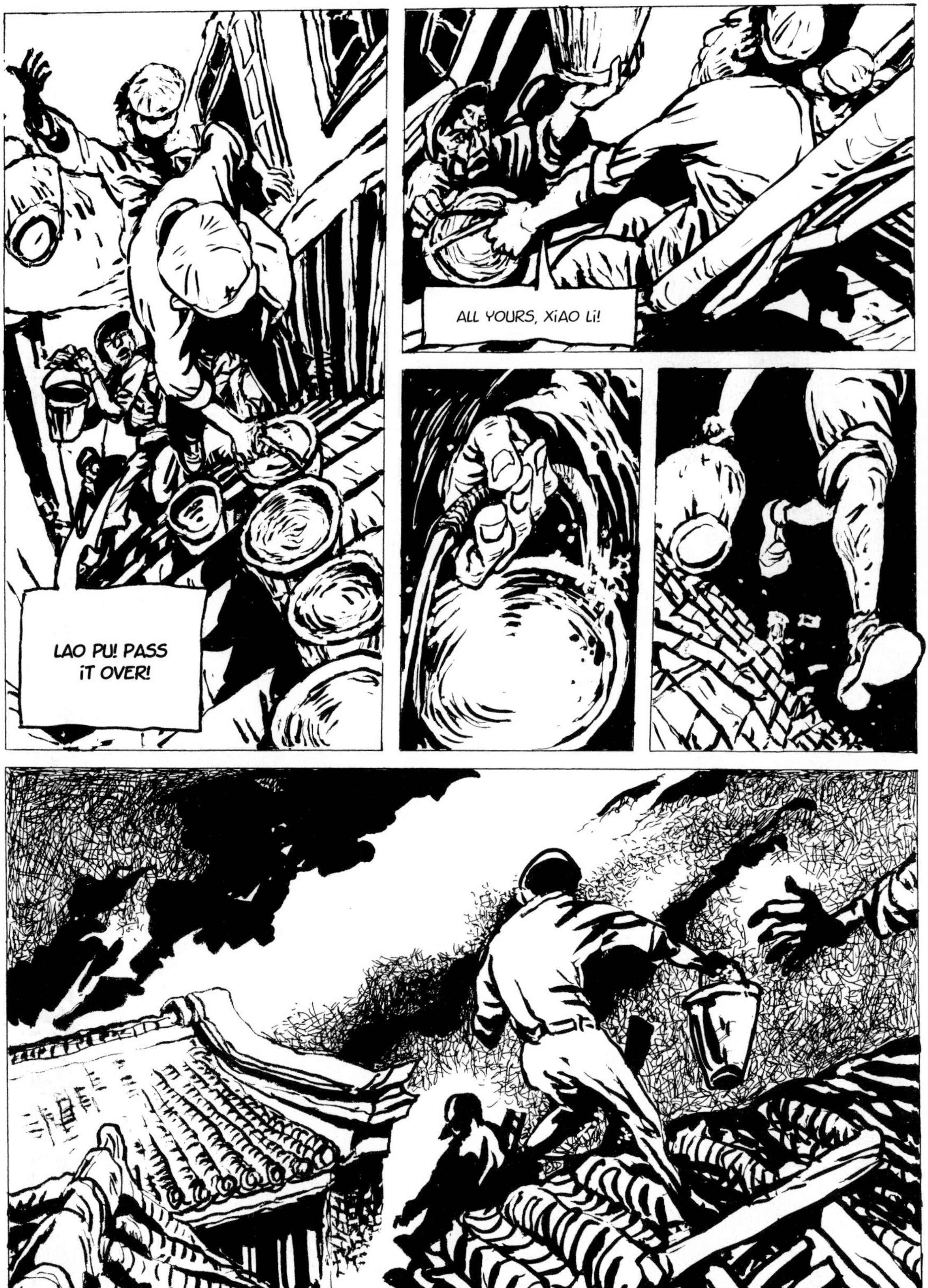
LAO PU! PASS IT OVER!
ALL YOURS, XIAO LI!

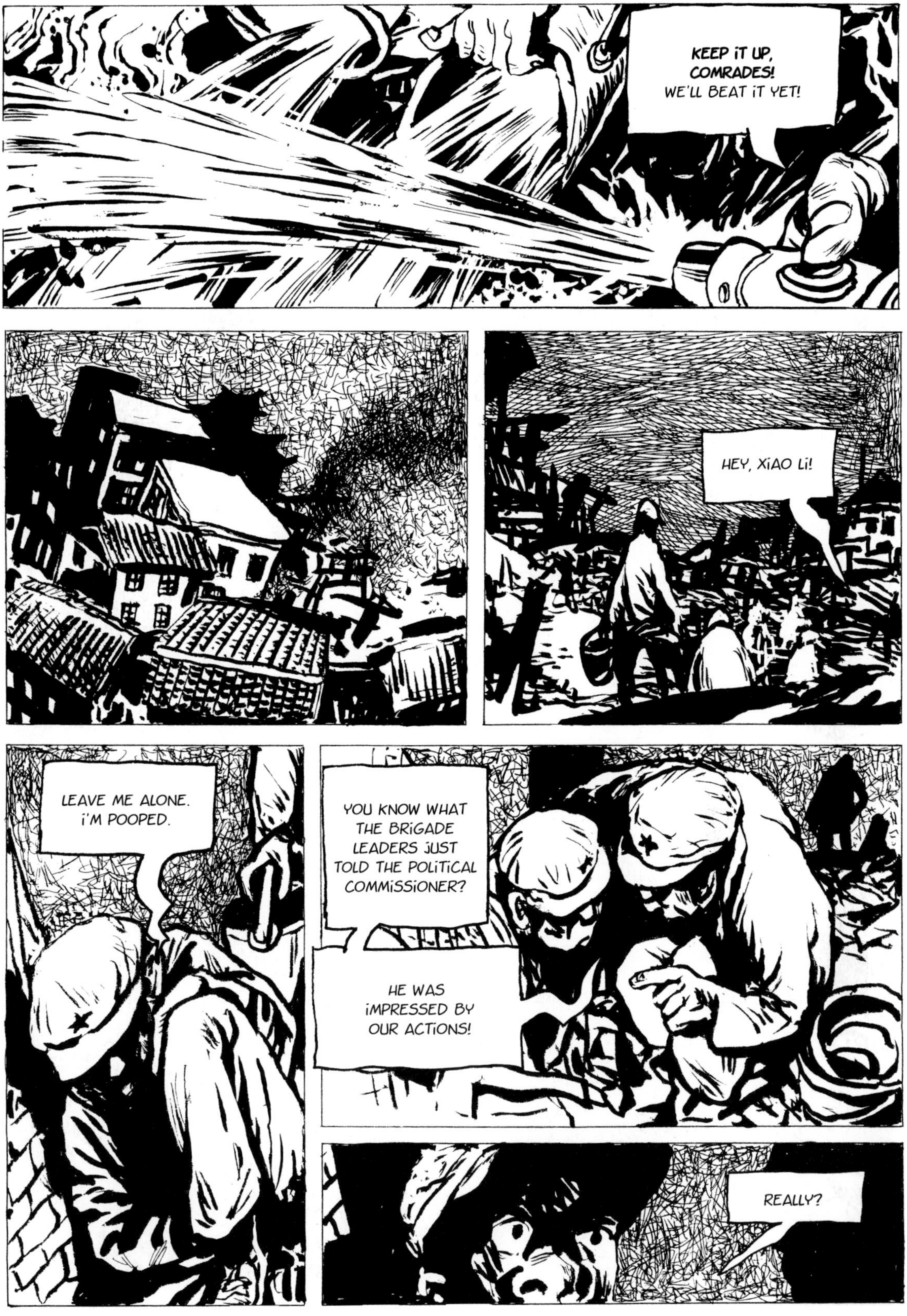
KEEP iT UP, COMRADES! WE'LL BEAT iT YET!
HEY, XiAO Li!
LEAVE ME ALONE. i'M POOPED.
YOU KNOW WHAT THE BRiGADE LEADERS JUST TOLD THE POLiTiCAL COMMiSSiONER?
HE WAS iMPRESSED BY OUR ACTiONS!
REALLY?

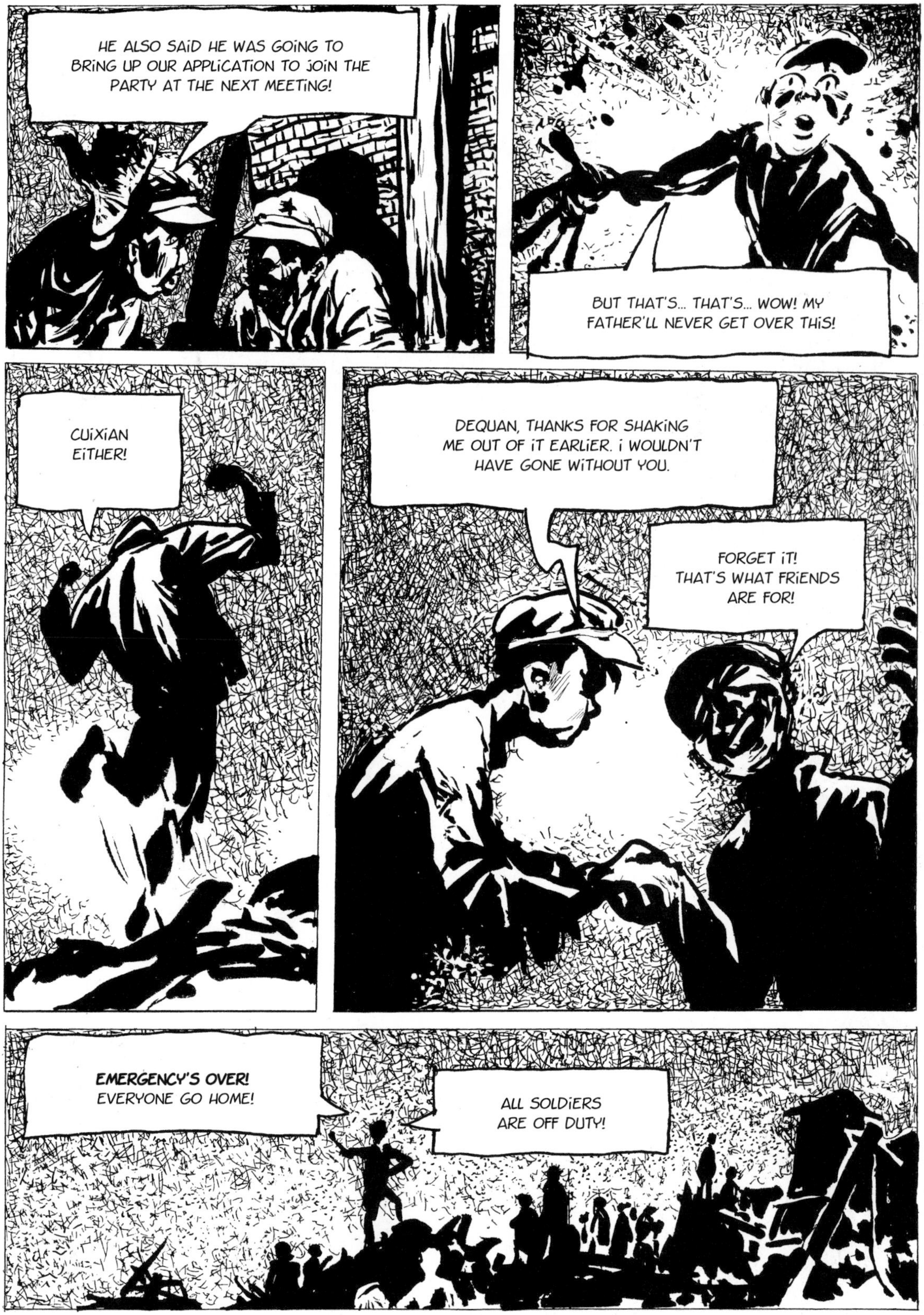
HE ALSO SAID HE WAS GOING TO BRING UP OUR APPLICATION TO JOIN THE PARTY AT THE NEXT MEETING!
BUT THAT'S... THAT'S... WOW! MY FATHER'LL NEVER GET OVER THIS!
CUIXIAN EITHER!
DEQUAN, THANKS FOR SHAKING ME OUT OF IT EARLIER. I WOULDN'T HAVE GONE WITHOUT YOU.
FORGET IT! THAT'S WHAT FRIENDS ARE FOR!
EMERGENCY'S OVER! EVERYONE GO HOME!
ALL SOLDIERS ARE OFF DUTY!

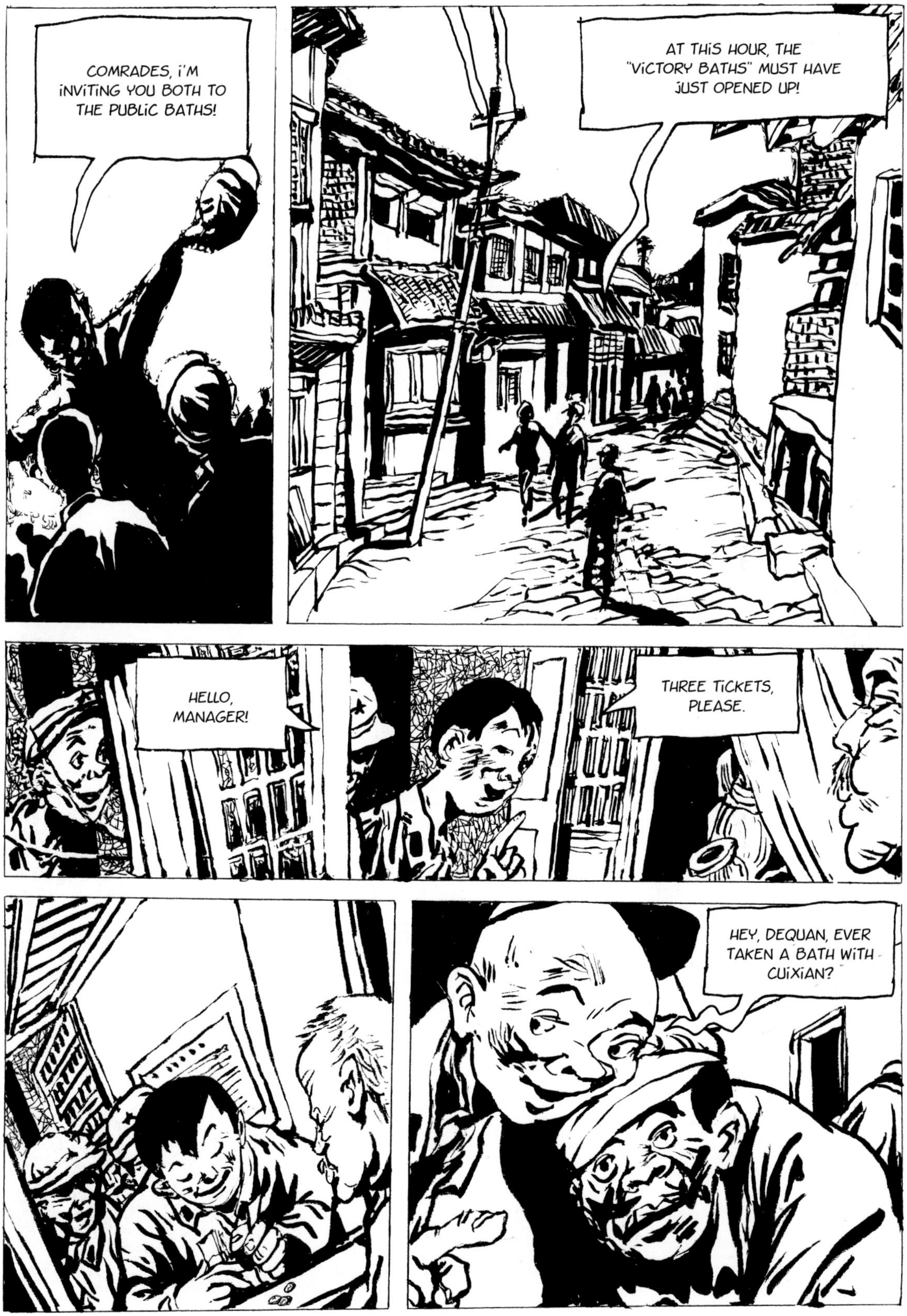
COMRADES, I'M INVITING YOU BOTH TO THE PUBLIC BATHS!
AT THIS HOUR, THE "VICTORY BATHS" MUST HAVE JUST OPENED UP!
HELLO, MANAGER!
THREE TICKETS, PLEASE.
HEY, DEQUAN, EVER TAKEN A BATH WITH CUIXIAN?

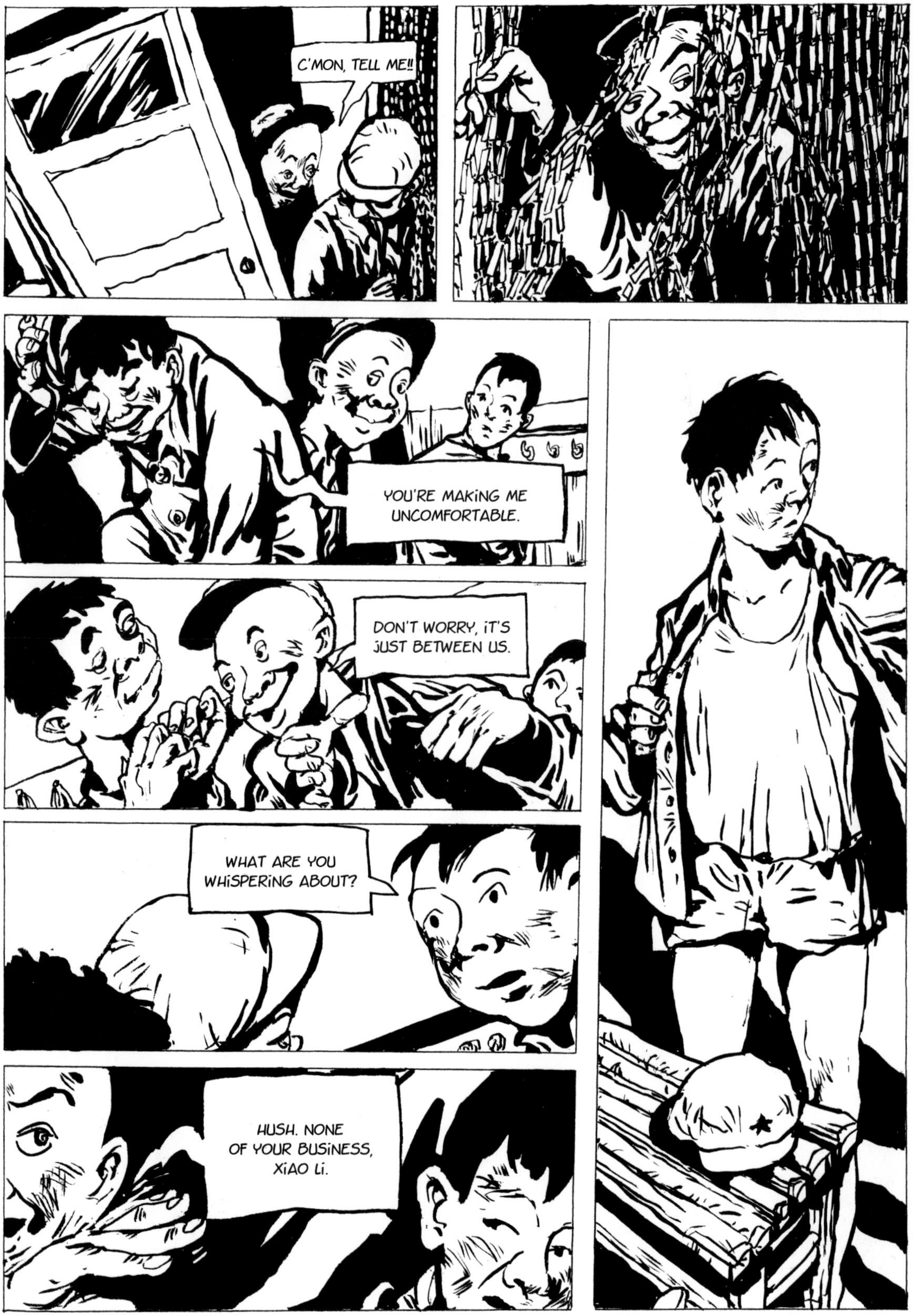
C'MON, TELL ME!!
YOU'RE MAKiNG ME UNCOMFORTABLE.
DON'T WORRY, iT'S JUST BETWEEN US.
WHAT ARE YOU WHiSPERiNG ABOUT?
HUSH. NONE OF YOUR BUSiNESS, XiAO Li.

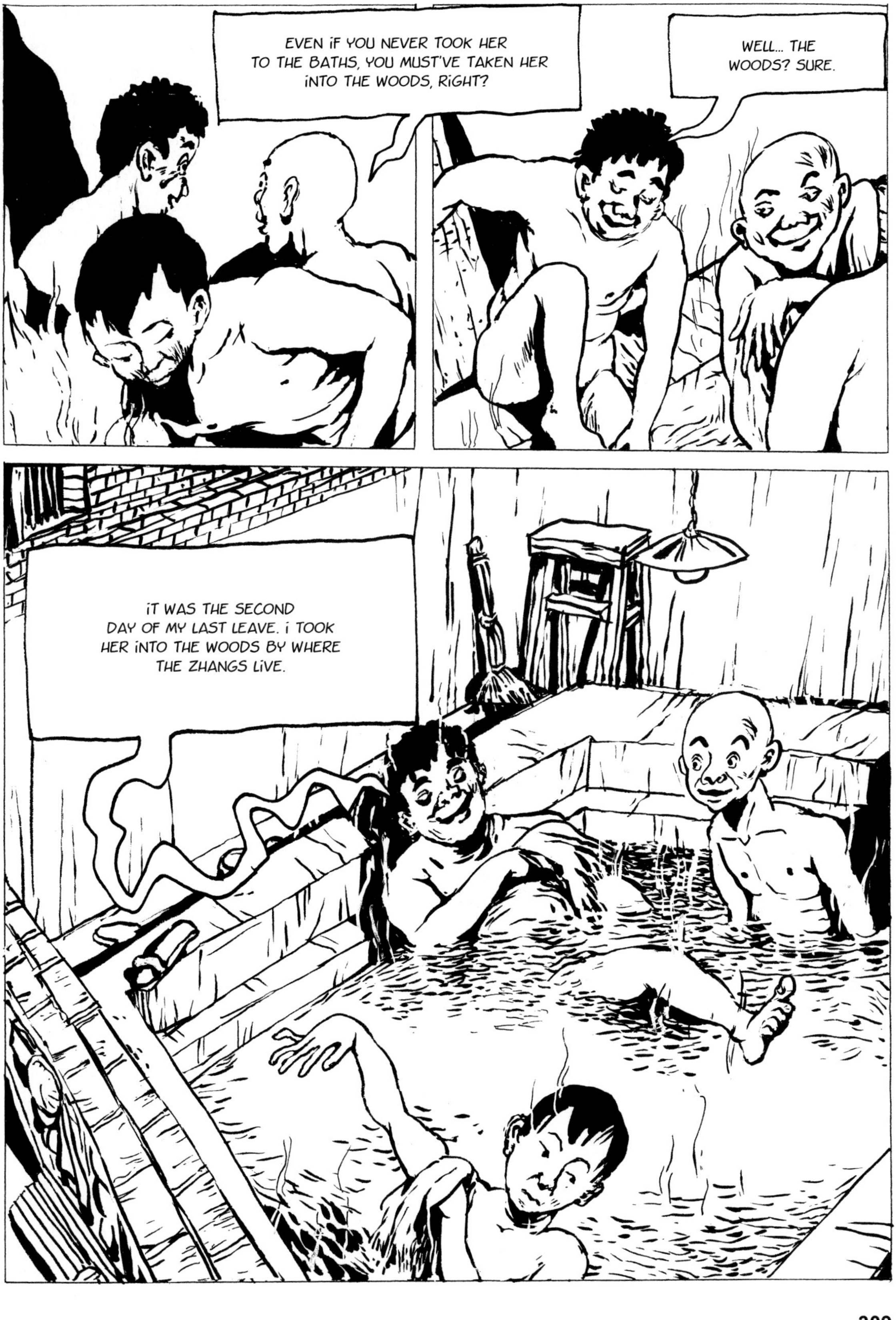
EVEN iF YOU NEVER TOOK HER TO THE BATHS, YOU MUST'VE TAKEN HER iNTO THE WOODS, RiGHT?
WELL... THE WOODS? SURE.
iT WAS THE SECOND DAY OF MY LAST LEAVE. i TOOK HER iNTO THE WOODS BY WHERE THE ZHANGS LiVE.

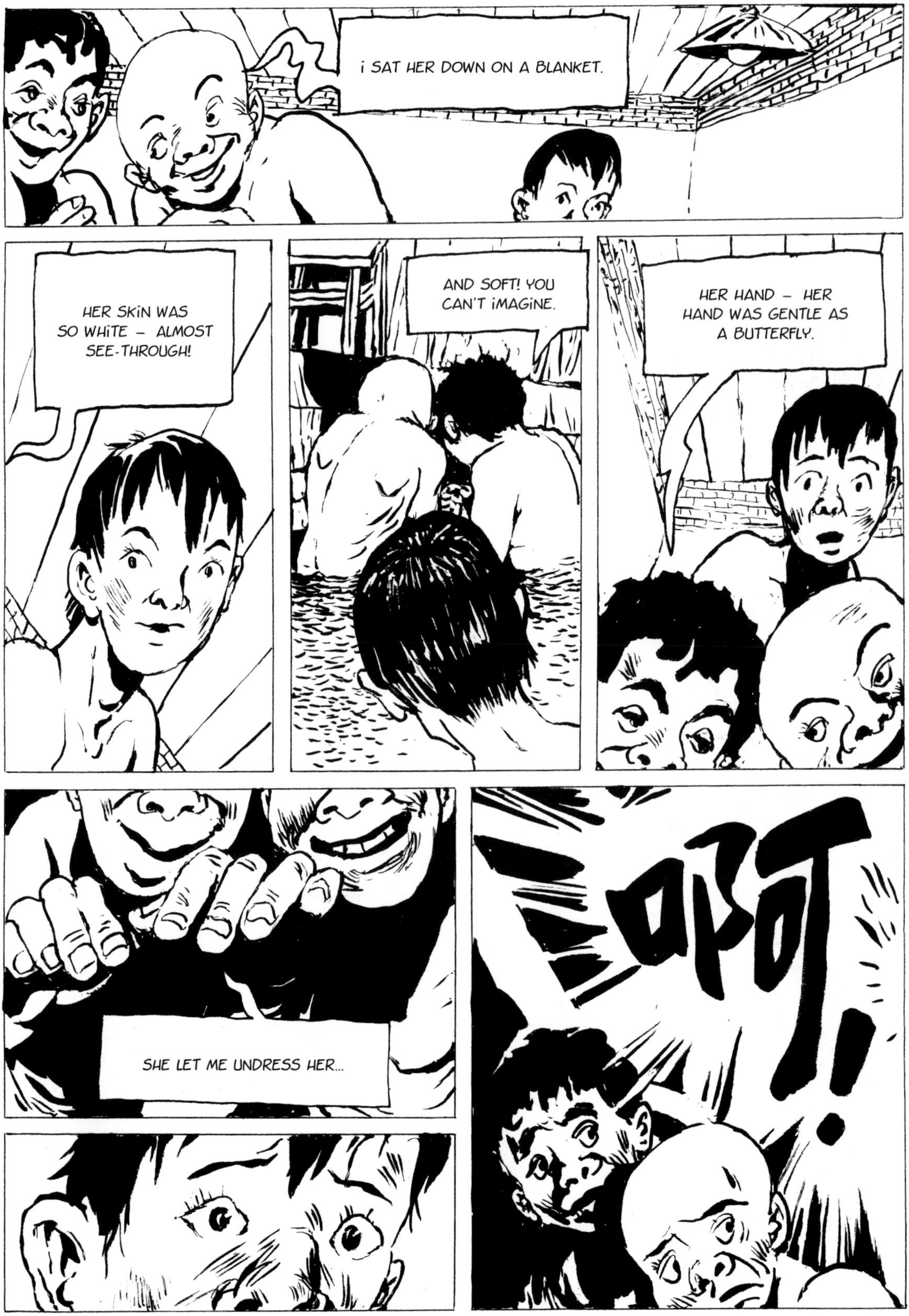
I SAT HER DOWN ON A BLANKET.
HER SKIN WAS SO WHITE – ALMOST SEE-THROUGH!
AND SOFT! YOU CAN'T IMAGINE.
HER HAND – HER HAND WAS GENTLE AS A BUTTERFLY.
SHE LET ME UNDRESS HER...

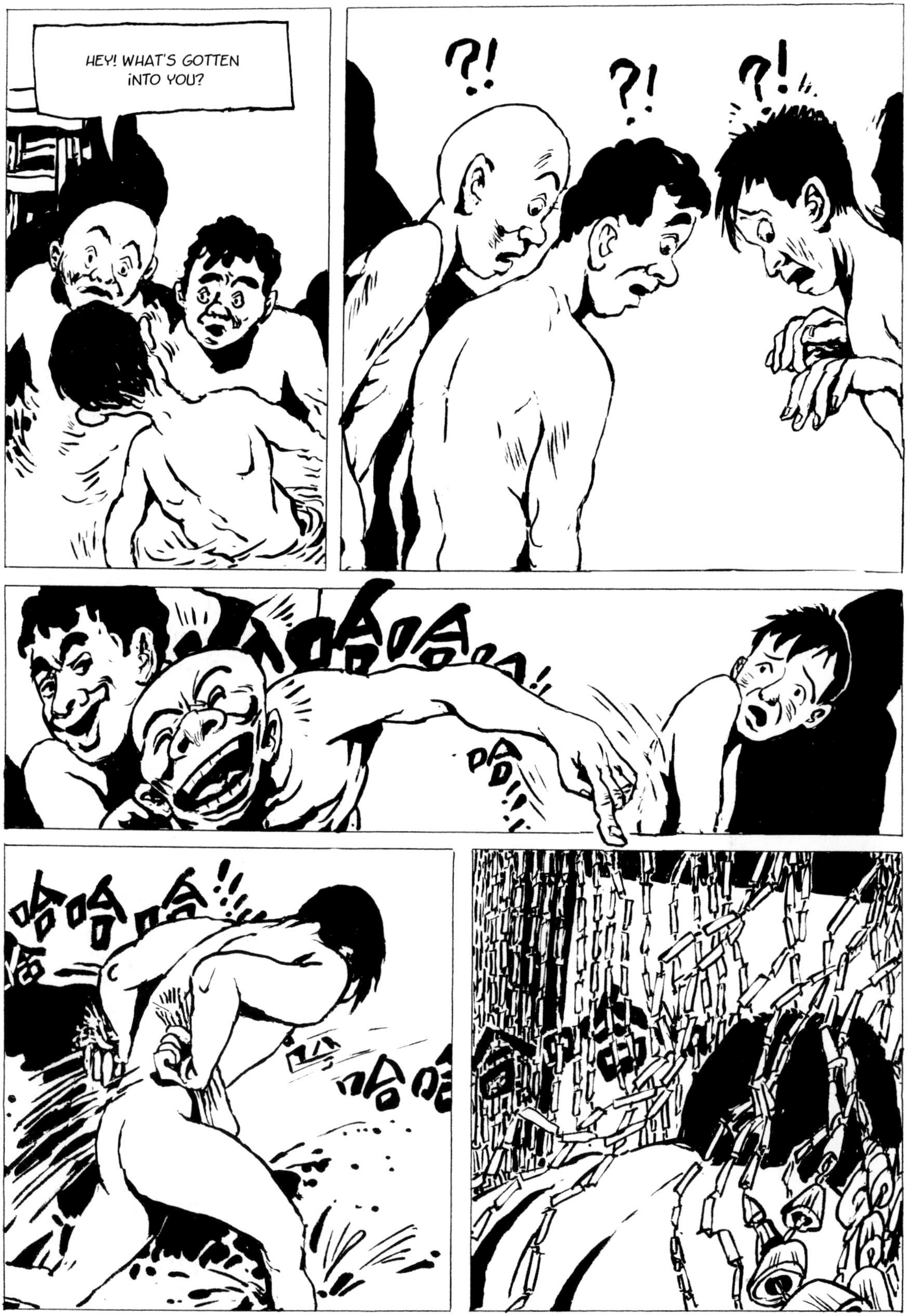
HEY! WHAT'S GOTTEN INTO YOU?
?!
?!
?!
哈!!
哈哈哈!!
哈哈哈

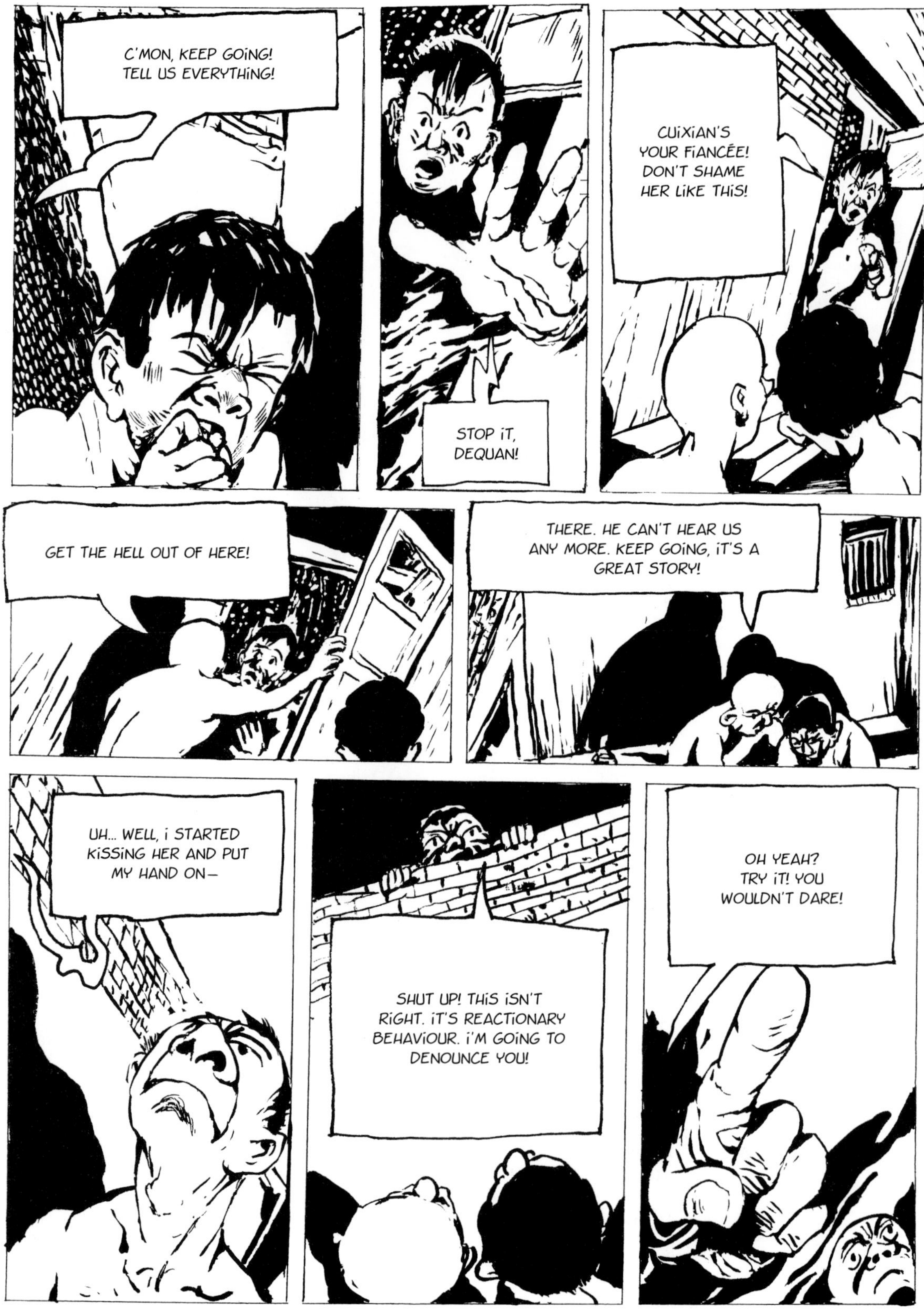
C'MON, KEEP GOiNG! TELL US EVERYTHiNG!
STOP iT, DEQUAN!
CUiXiAN'S YOUR FiANCÉE! DON'T SHAME HER LiKE THiS!
GET THE HELL OUT OF HERE!
THERE. HE CAN'T HEAR US ANY MORE. KEEP GOiNG, iT'S A GREAT STORY!
UH... WELL, i STARTED KiSSiNG HER AND PUT MY HAND ON—
SHUT UP! THiS iSN'T RiGHT. iT'S REACTIONARY BEHAViOUR. i'M GOiNG TO DENOUNCE YOU!
OH YEAH? TRY iT! YOU WOULDN'T DARE!

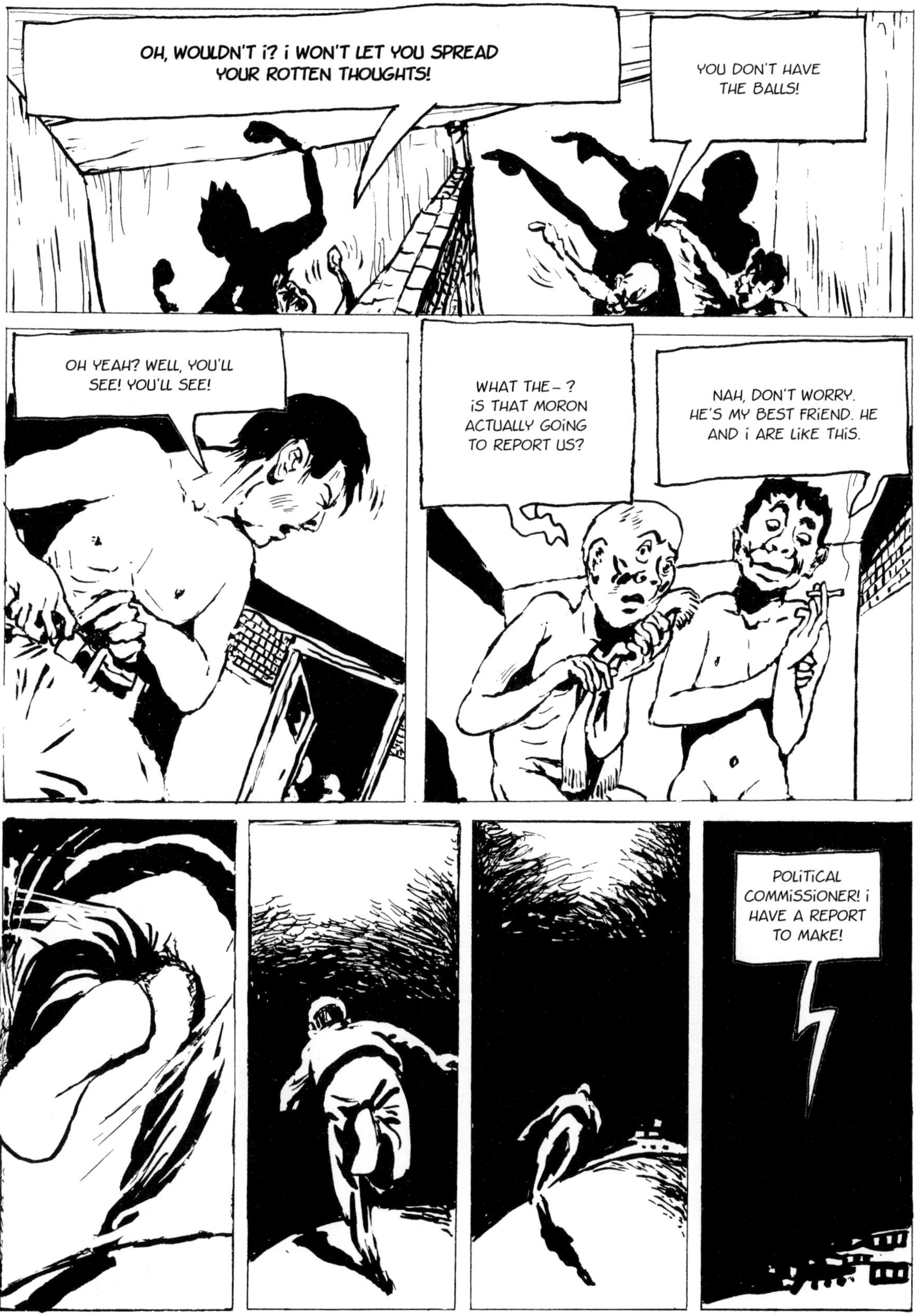
OH, WOULDN'T i? i WON'T LET YOU SPREAD YOUR ROTTEN THOUGHTS!
YOU DON'T HAVE THE BALLS!
OH YEAH? WELL, YOU'LL SEE! YOU'LL SEE!
WHAT THE– ? iS THAT MORON ACTUALLY GOiNG TO REPORT US?
NAH, DON'T WORRY. HE'S MY BEST FRiEND. HE AND i ARE LiKE THiS.
POLiTiCAL COMMiSSiONER! i HAVE A REPORT TO MAKE!

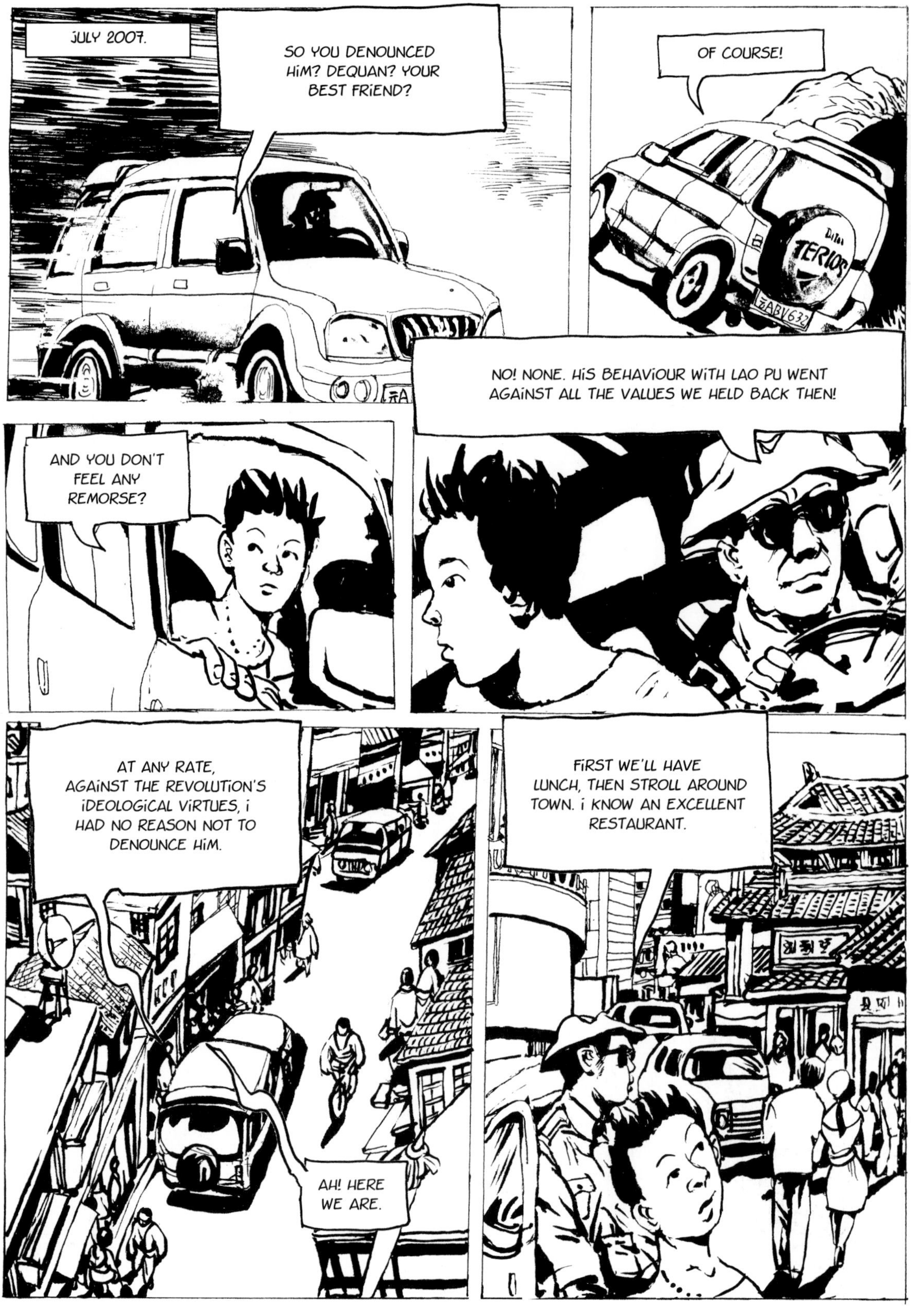
JULY 2007.
SO YOU DENOUNCED HIM? DEQUAN? YOUR BEST FRIEND?
OF COURSE!
TERIOS
AND YOU DON'T FEEL ANY REMORSE?
NO! NONE. HIS BEHAVIOUR WITH LAO PU WENT AGAINST ALL THE VALUES WE HELD BACK THEN!
AT ANY RATE, AGAINST THE REVOLUTION'S IDEOLOGICAL VIRTUES, I HAD NO REASON NOT TO DENOUNCE HIM.
AH! HERE WE ARE.
FIRST WE'LL HAVE LUNCH, THEN STROLL AROUND TOWN. I KNOW AN EXCELLENT RESTAURANT.

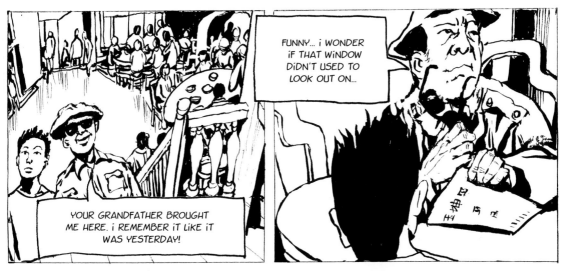

FUNNY... I WONDER IF THAT WINDOW DIDN'T USED TO LOOK OUT ON...

YOUR GRANDFATHER BROUGHT ME HERE. I REMEMBER IT LIKE IT WAS YESTERDAY!

AHA! I THOUGHT SO! SEE THAT POOL? THIRTY YEARS AGO, THOSE WERE THE PUBLIC BATHS! THE "VICTORY BATHS"!

THAT WAS WHERE THE STORY I JUST TOLD YOU ABOUT TOOK PLACE.

C'MON, PAPA, DON'T THINK ABOUT THAT ANY MORE. IT'S IN THE PAST NOW...

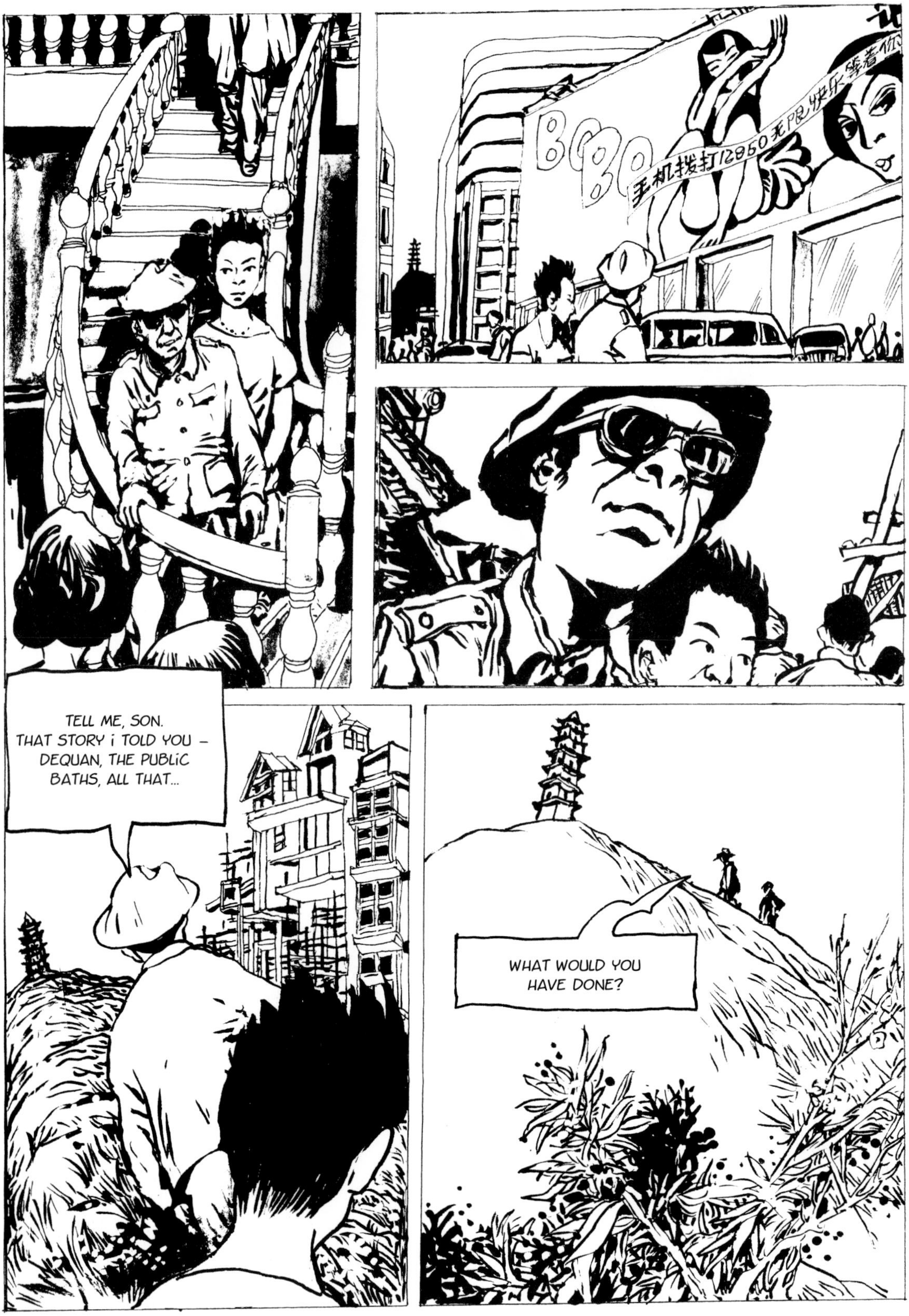
BOBO
手机拨打12850无限快乐等着你
TELL ME, SON. THAT STORY i TOLD YOU – DEQUAN, THE PUBLiC BATHS, ALL THAT...
WHAT WOULD YOU HAVE DONE?

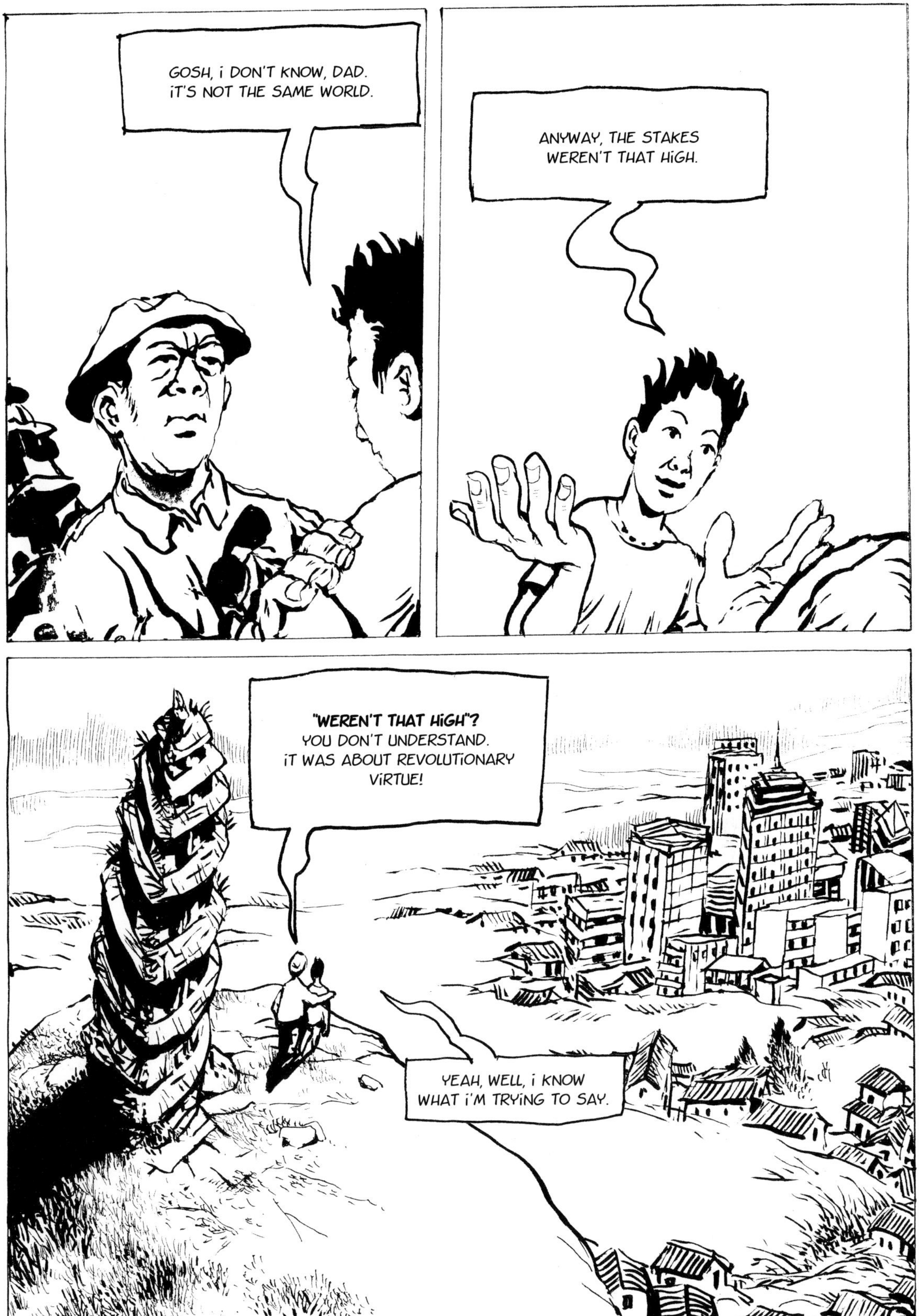
GOSH, i DON'T KNOW, DAD. iT'S NOT THE SAME WORLD.
ANYWAY, THE STAKES WEREN'T THAT HiGH.
"WEREN'T THAT HiGH"? YOU DON'T UNDERSTAND. iT WAS ABOUT REVOLUTiONARY ViRTUE!
YEAH, WELL, i KNOW WHAT i'M TRYiNG TO SAY.

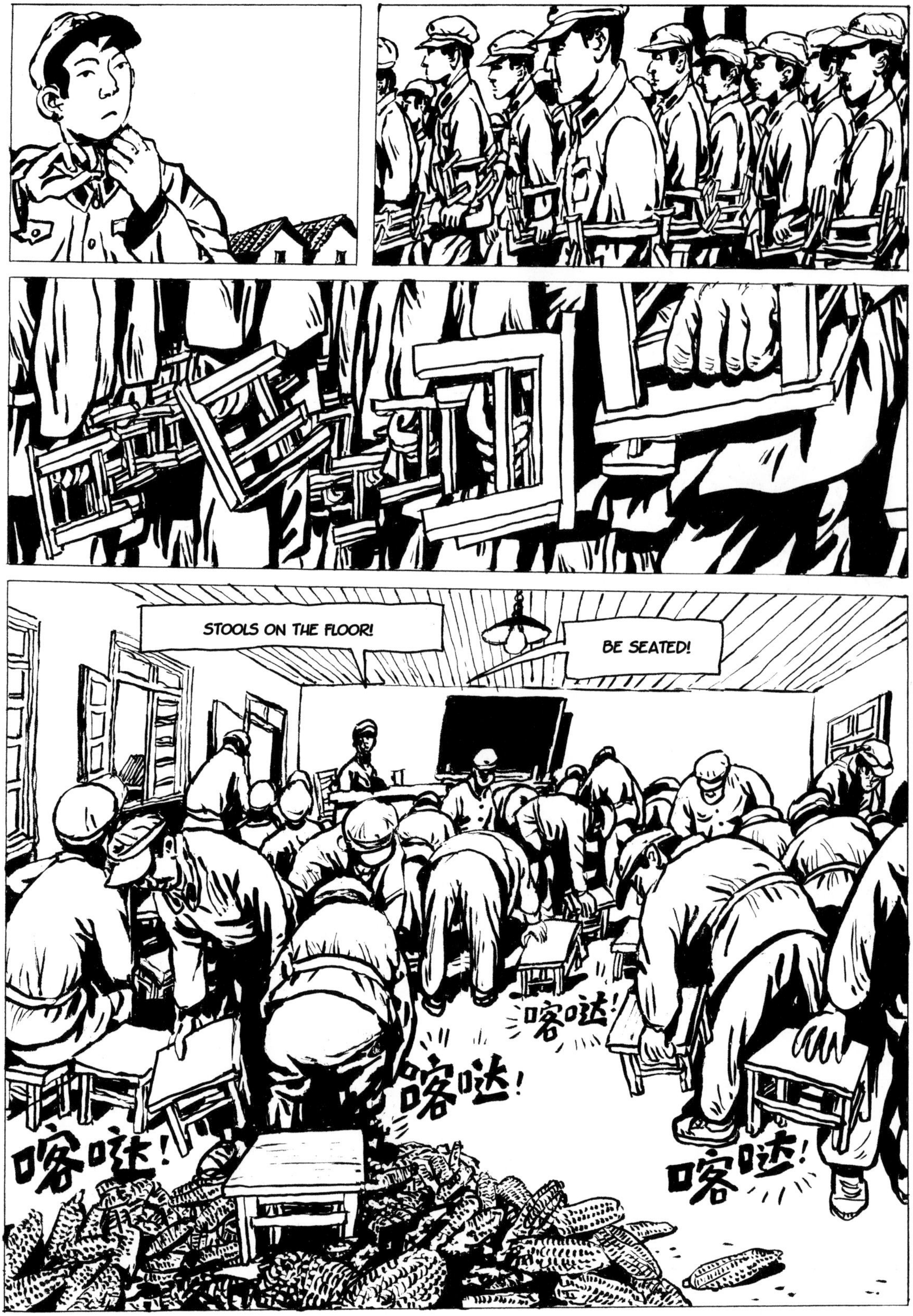
STOOLS ON THE FLOOR!
BE SEATED!
喀哒!
喀哒!
喀哒!
喀哒!

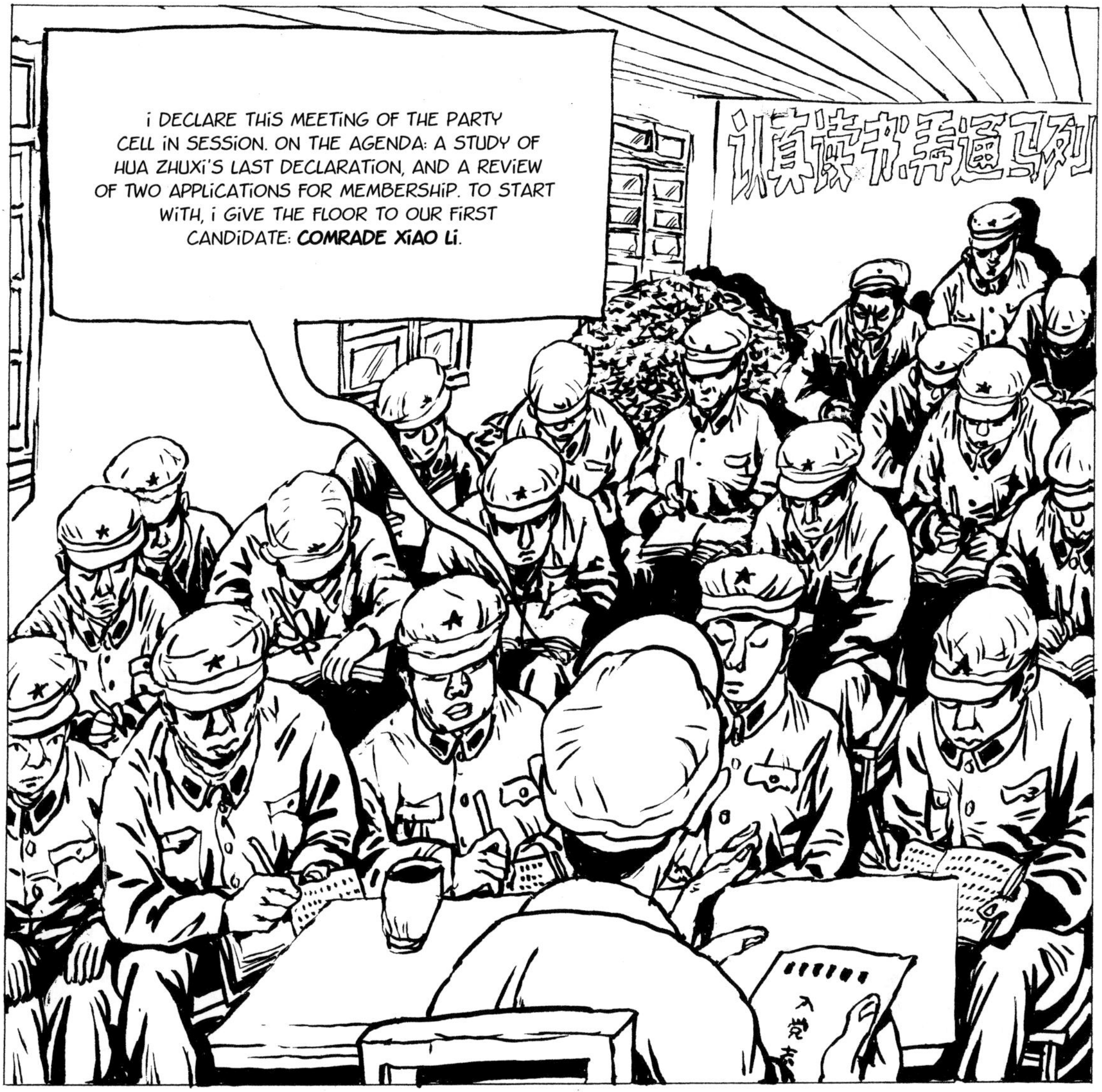
I DECLARE THIS MEETING OF THE PARTY CELL IN SESSION. ON THE AGENDA: A STUDY OF HUA ZHUXI'S LAST DECLARATION, AND A REVIEW OF TWO APPLICATIONS FOR MEMBERSHIP. TO START WITH, I GIVE THE FLOOR TO OUR FIRST CANDIDATE: **COMRADE XIAO LI**.
认真读书，弄通马列

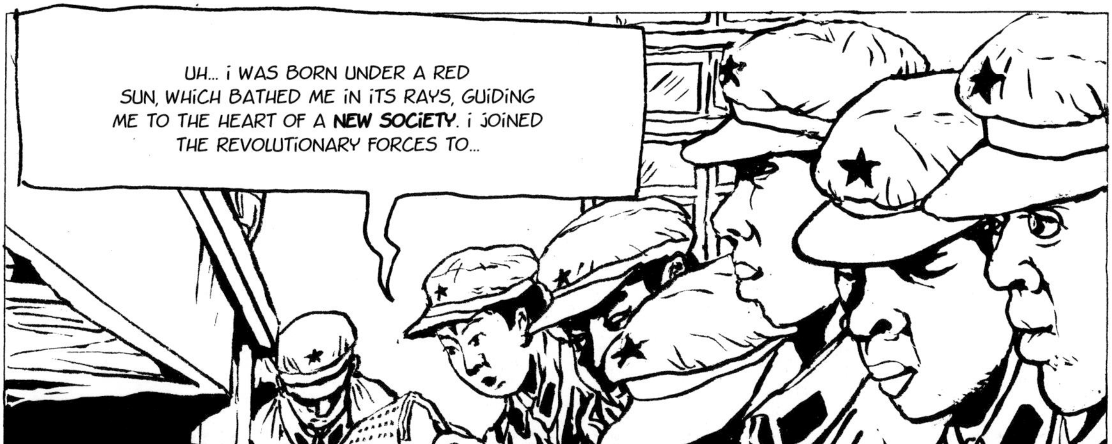
UH... I WAS BORN UNDER A RED SUN, WHICH BATHED ME IN ITS RAYS, GUIDING ME TO THE HEART OF A **NEW SOCIETY**. I JOINED THE REVOLUTIONARY FORCES TO...

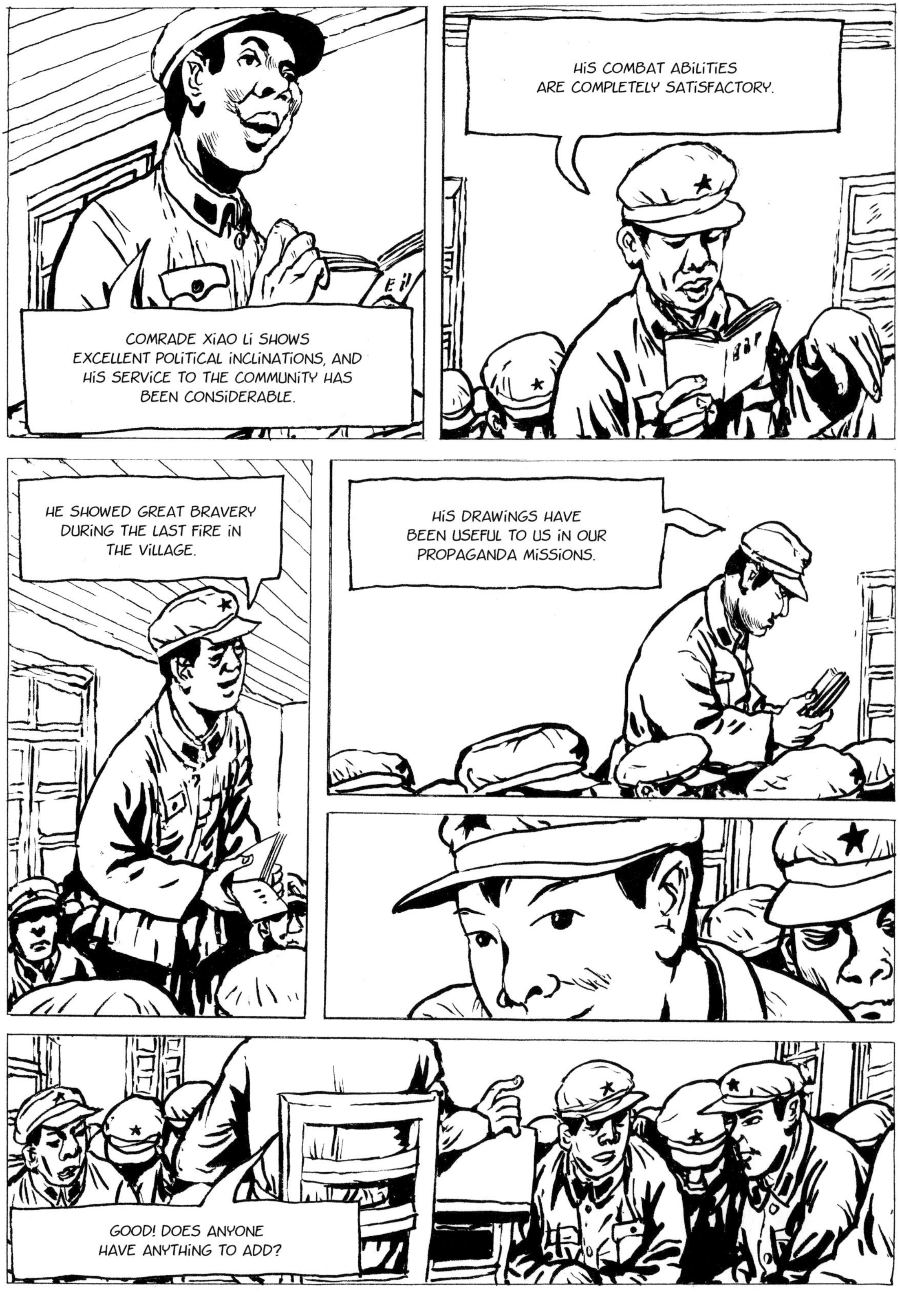
COMRADE XIAO LI SHOWS EXCELLENT POLITICAL INCLINATIONS, AND HIS SERVICE TO THE COMMUNITY HAS BEEN CONSIDERABLE.
HIS COMBAT ABILITIES ARE COMPLETELY SATISFACTORY.
HE SHOWED GREAT BRAVERY DURING THE LAST FIRE IN THE VILLAGE.
HIS DRAWINGS HAVE BEEN USEFUL TO US IN OUR PROPAGANDA MISSIONS.
GOOD! DOES ANYONE HAVE ANYTHING TO ADD?

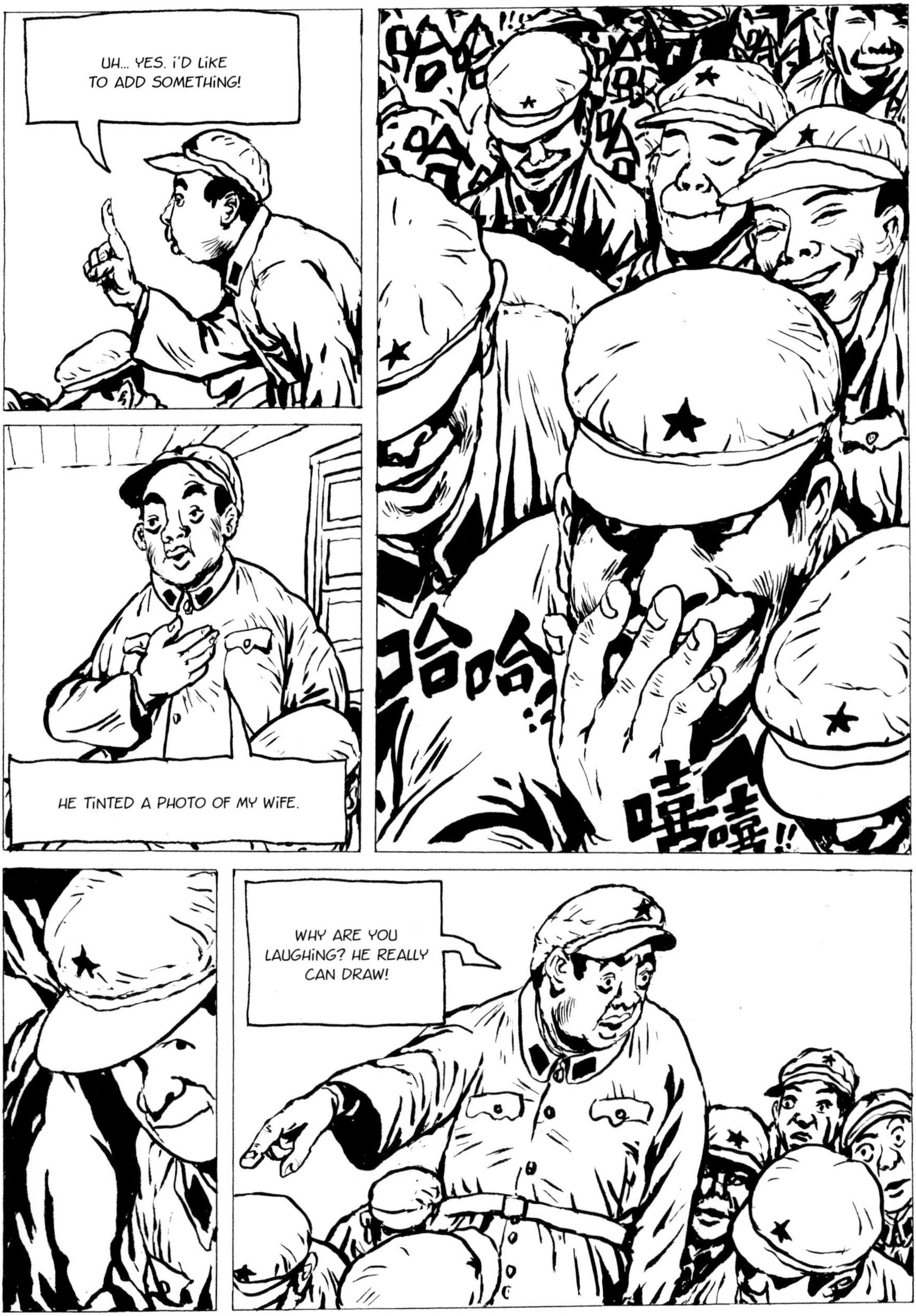
UH... YES. I'D LIKE TO ADD SOMETHING!
HE TINTED A PHOTO OF MY WIFE.
哈哈!!
嘻嘻!!
WHY ARE YOU LAUGHING? HE REALLY CAN DRAW!

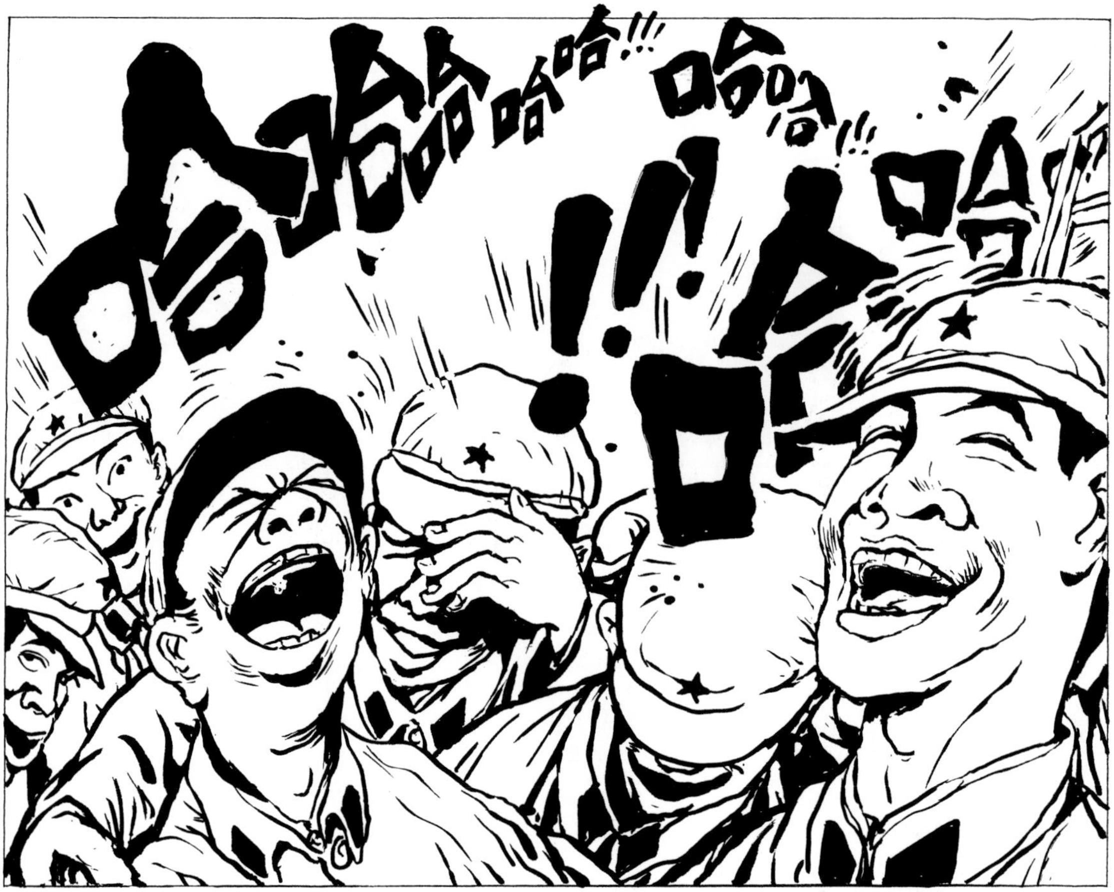
哈哈哈哈哈!!!
哈哈!!!
!!!哈哈
哈

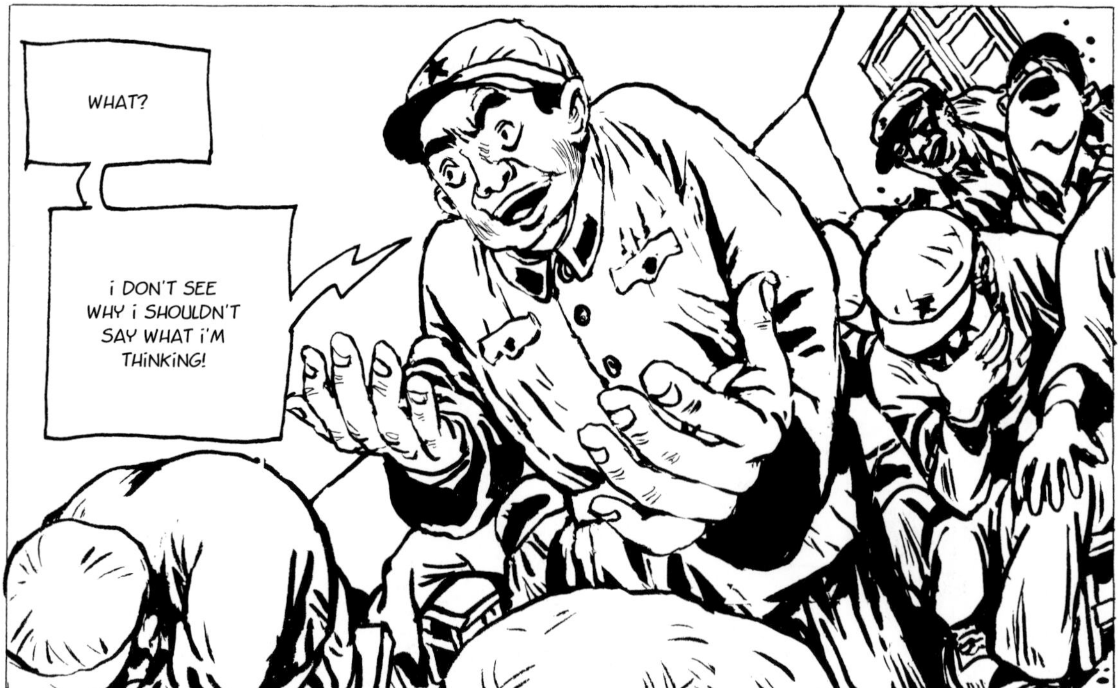
WHAT?
i DON'T SEE WHY i SHOULDN'T SAY WHAT i'M THINKiNG!

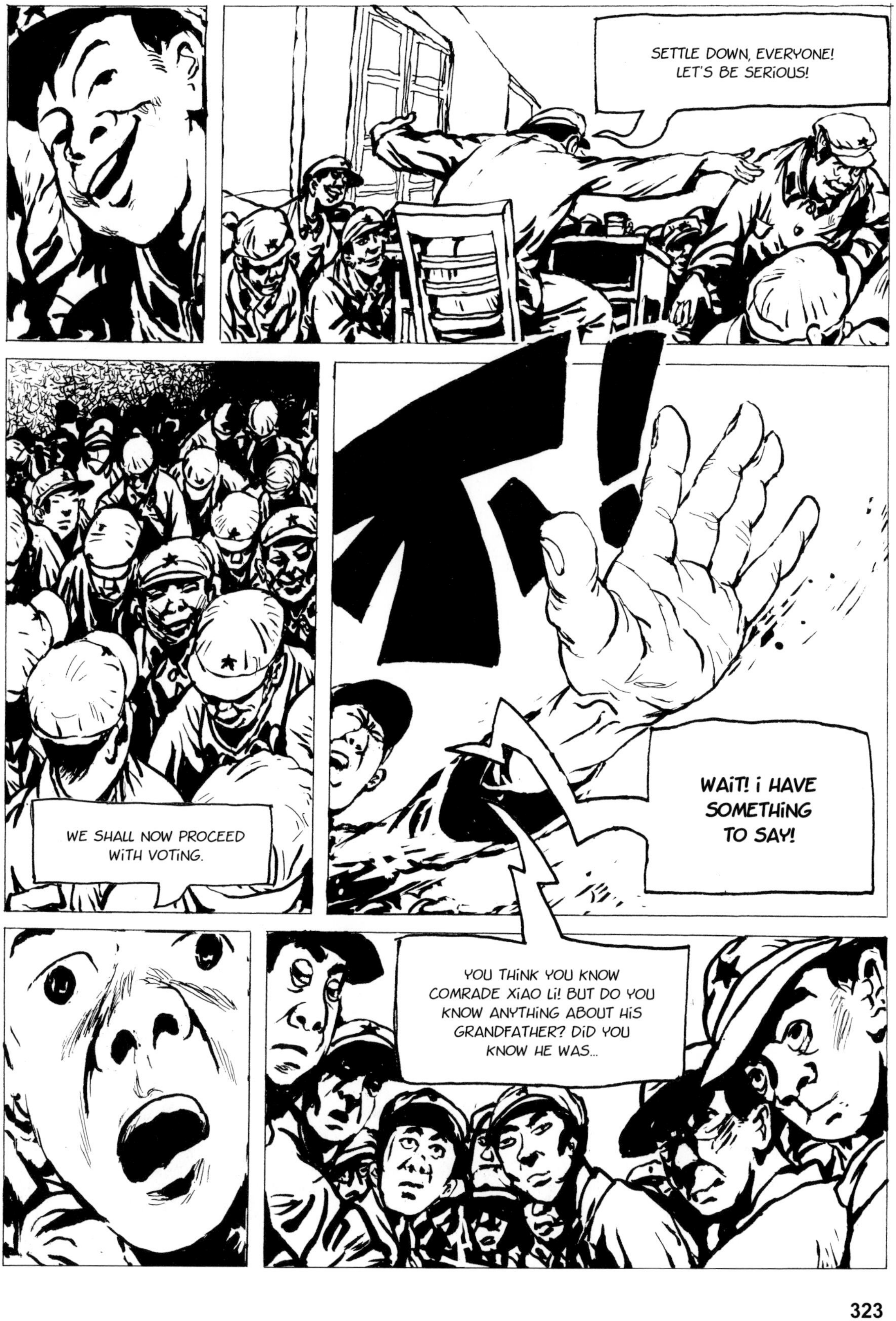
SETTLE DOWN, EVERYONE! LET'S BE SERIOUS!
WE SHALL NOW PROCEED WITH VOTING.
WAIT! I HAVE SOMETHING TO SAY!
YOU THINK YOU KNOW COMRADE XIAO LI! BUT DO YOU KNOW ANYTHING ABOUT HIS GRANDFATHER? DID YOU KNOW HE WAS...

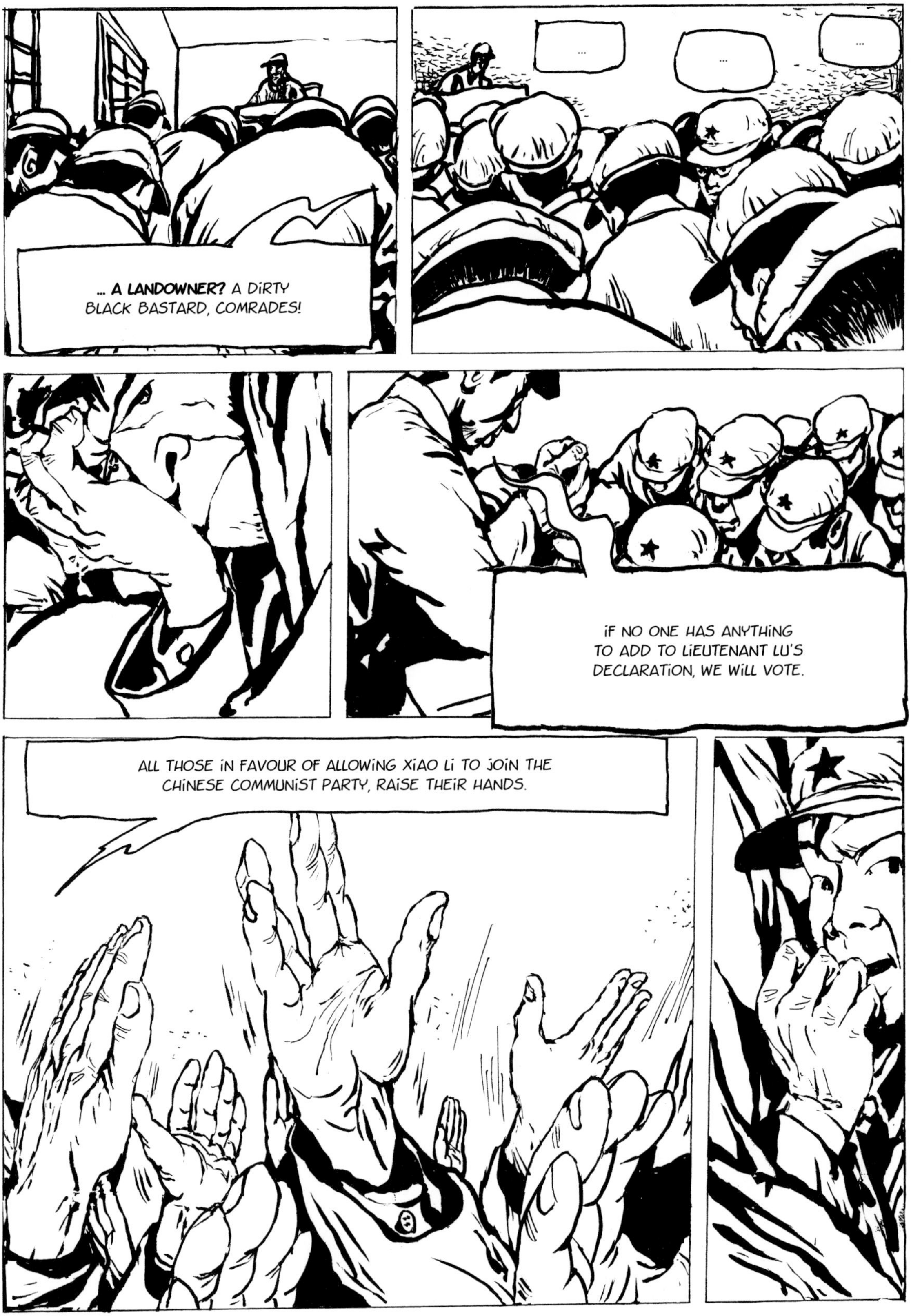
... A LANDOWNER? A DIRTY BLACK BASTARD, COMRADES!
...
...
...
IF NO ONE HAS ANYTHING TO ADD TO LIEUTENANT LU'S DECLARATION, WE WILL VOTE.
ALL THOSE IN FAVOUR OF ALLOWING XIAO LI TO JOIN THE CHINESE COMMUNIST PARTY, RAISE THEIR HANDS.

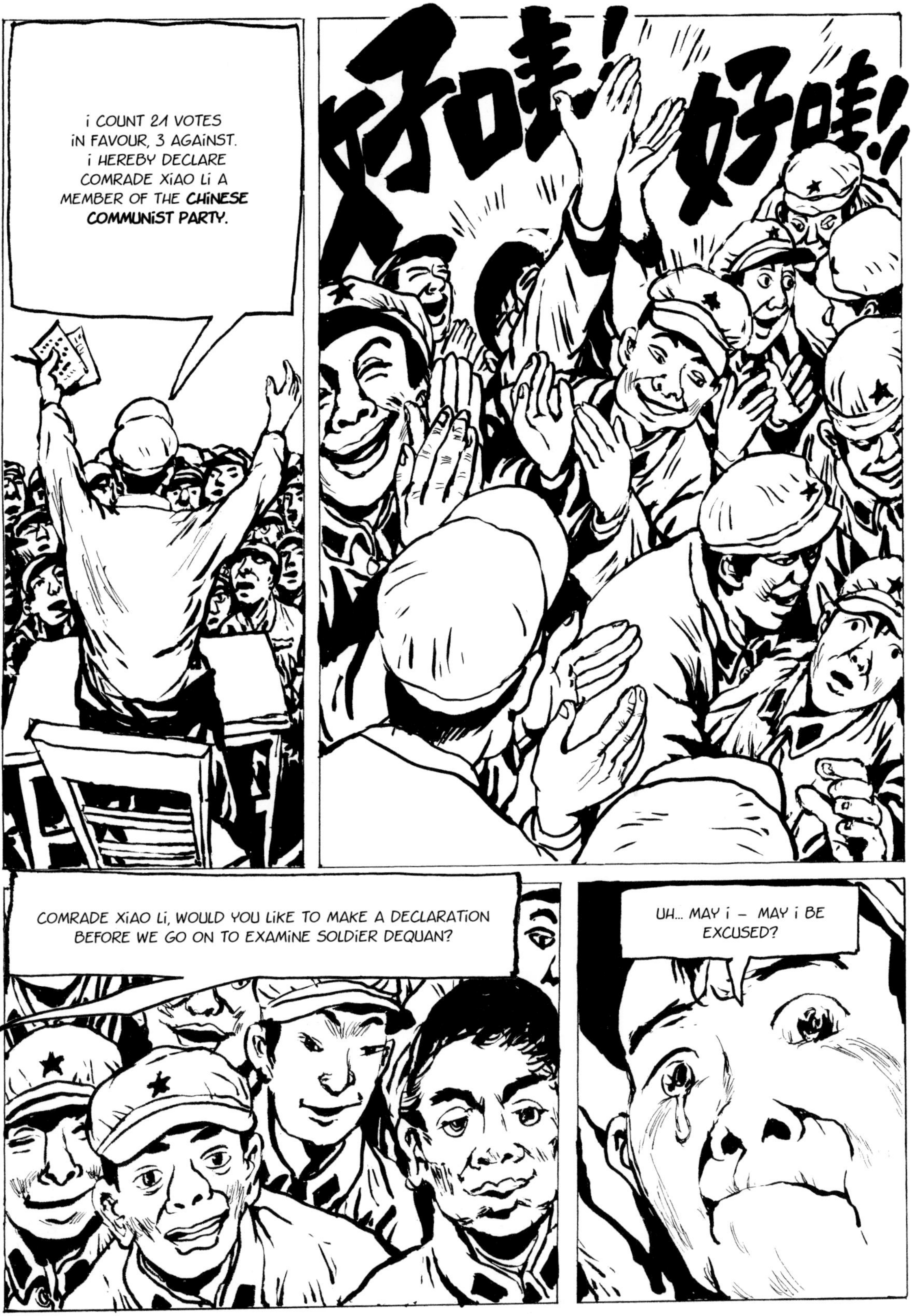
I COUNT 21 VOTES IN FAVOUR, 3 AGAINST. I HEREBY DECLARE COMRADE XIAO LI A MEMBER OF THE **CHINESE COMMUNIST PARTY.**
好哇！ 好哇！！
COMRADE XIAO LI, WOULD YOU LIKE TO MAKE A DECLARATION BEFORE WE GO ON TO EXAMINE SOLDIER DEQUAN?
UH... MAY I – MAY I BE EXCUSED?

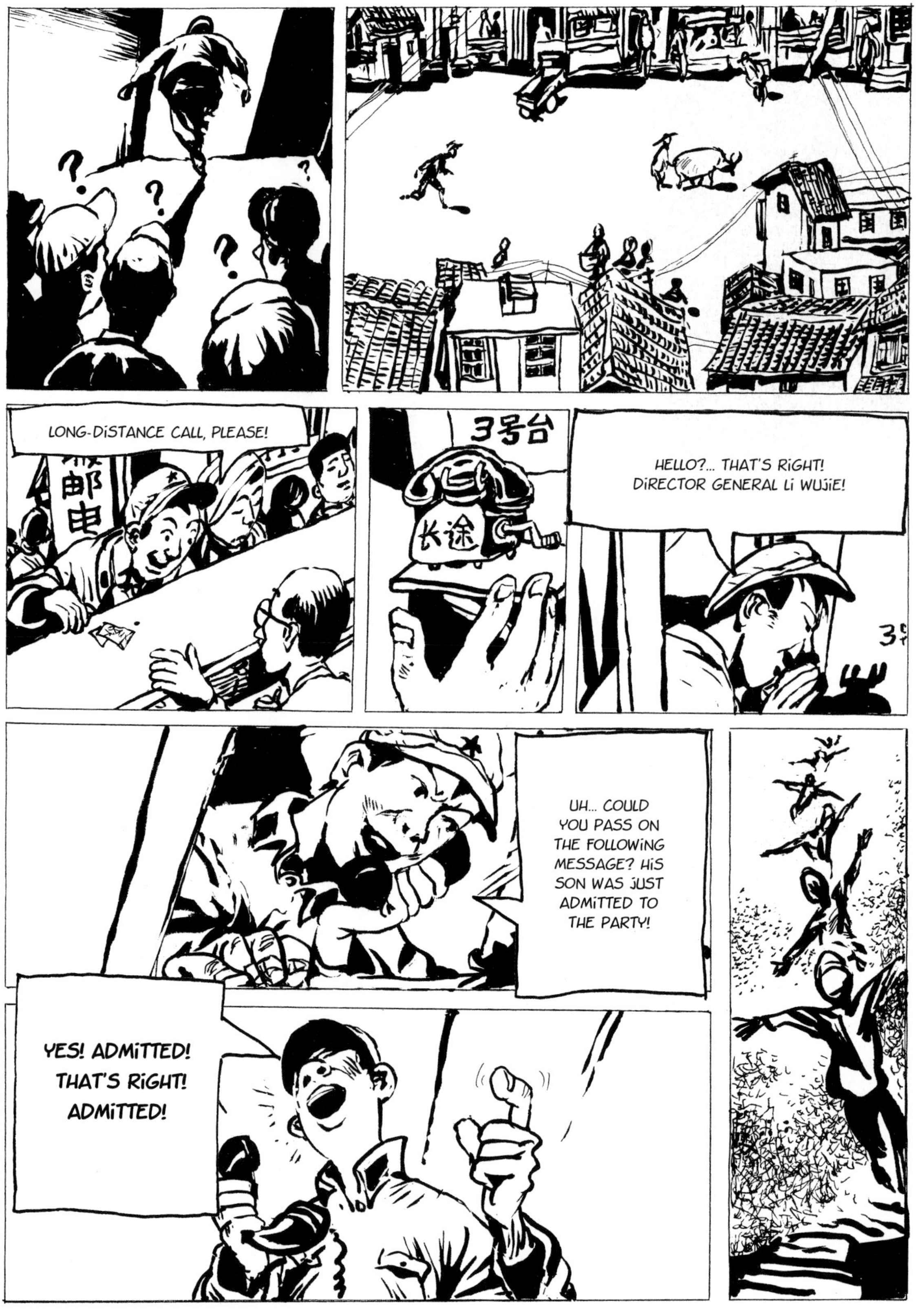
LONG-DISTANCE CALL, PLEASE!
邮电
3号台
长途
HELLO?... THAT'S RIGHT! DIRECTOR GENERAL LI WUJIE!
UH... COULD YOU PASS ON THE FOLLOWING MESSAGE? HIS SON WAS JUST ADMITTED TO THE PARTY!
YES! ADMITTED! THAT'S RIGHT! ADMITTED!

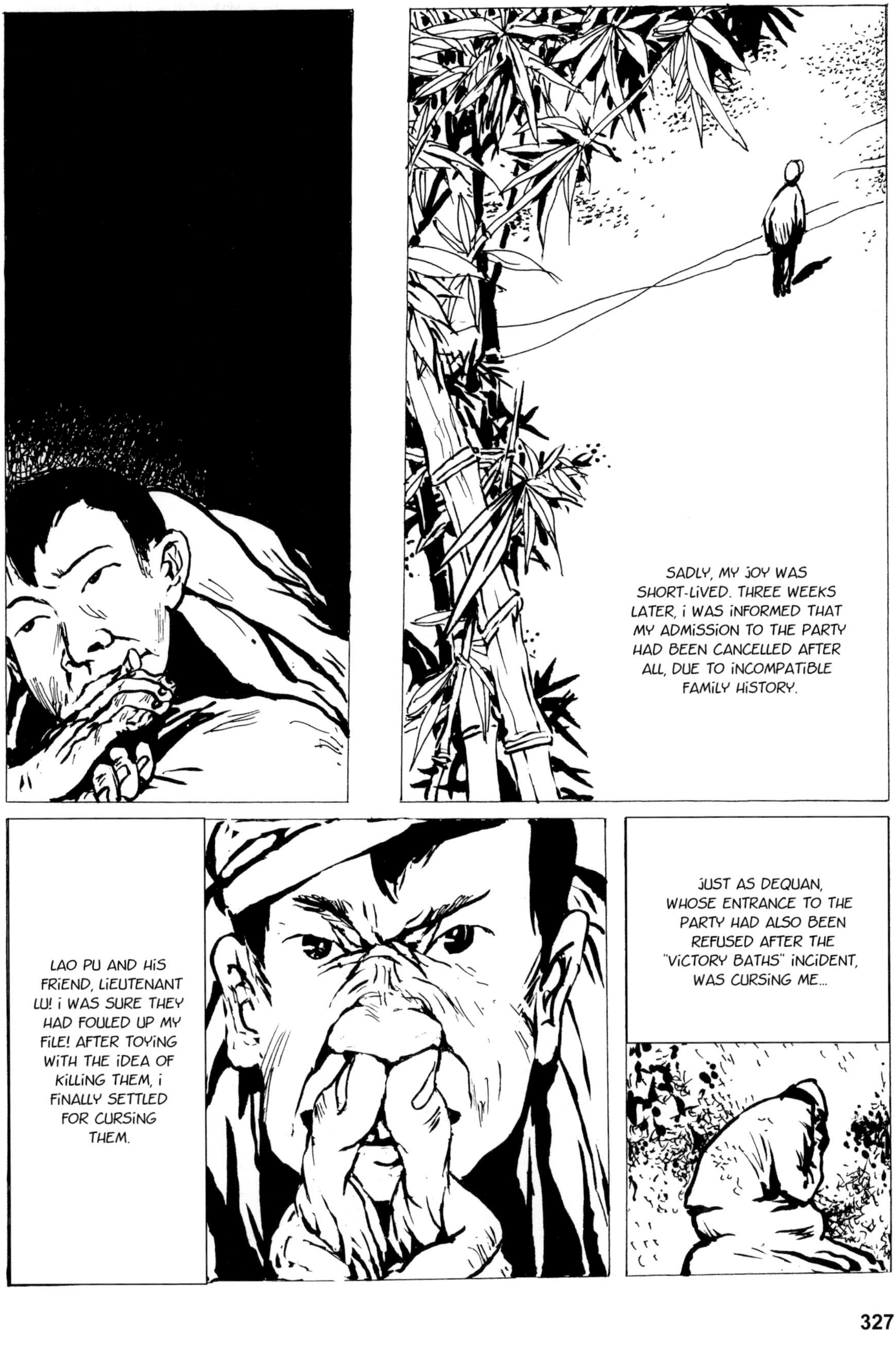

SADLY, MY JOY WAS SHORT-LIVED. THREE WEEKS LATER, I WAS INFORMED THAT MY ADMISSION TO THE PARTY HAD BEEN CANCELLED AFTER ALL, DUE TO INCOMPATIBLE FAMILY HISTORY.
LAO PU AND HIS FRIEND, LIEUTENANT LU! I WAS SURE THEY HAD FOULED UP MY FILE! AFTER TOYING WITH THE IDEA OF KILLING THEM, I FINALLY SETTLED FOR CURSING THEM.
JUST AS DEQUAN, WHOSE ENTRANCE TO THE PARTY HAD ALSO BEEN REFUSED AFTER THE "VICTORY BATHS" INCIDENT, WAS CURSING ME...

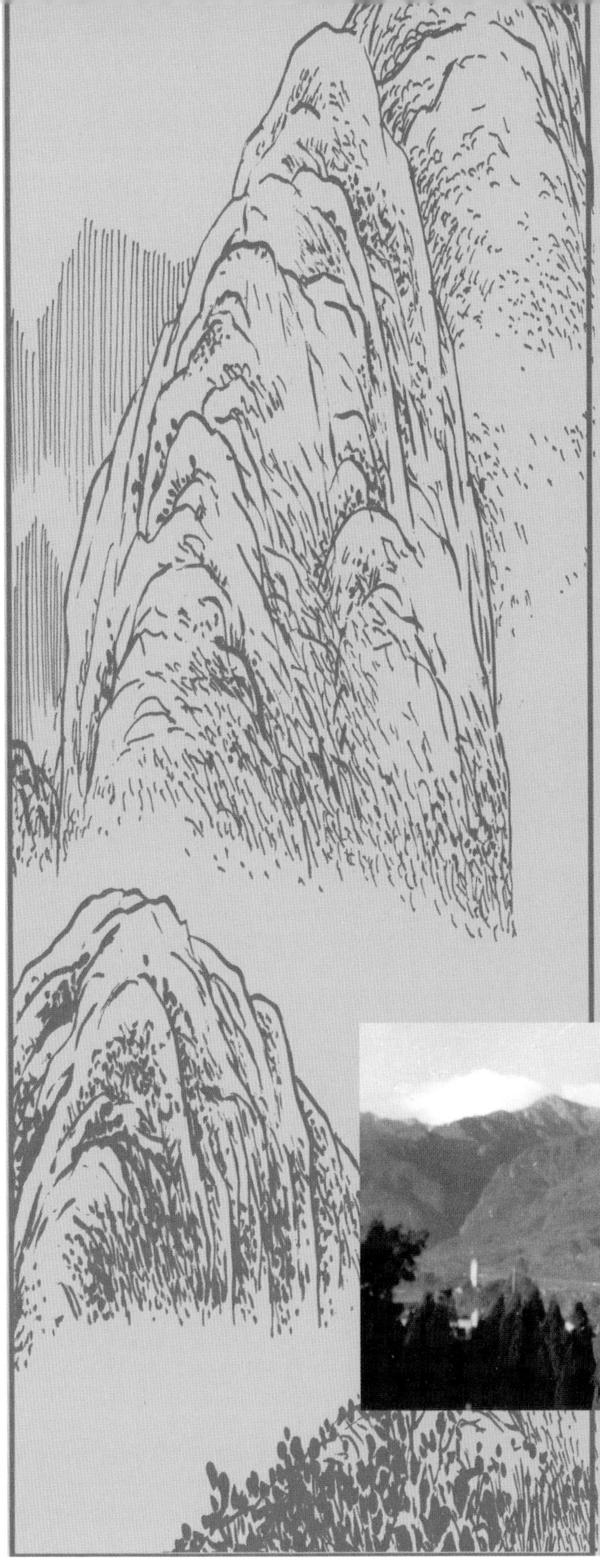

CHAPTER 5
Red Earth

二月里来好风光，
家家户户种田忙，
种豆的得豆，
种瓜的得瓜，
多打五谷充军粮

FEBRUARY, THE LAND
IS REBORN. EVERYONE
IS PLANTING.

WHO SOWS PEAS
SHALL REAP PEAS.
WHO SOWS MELONS
SHALL REAP MELONS.

LET US ALL SOW THE
FIVE GRAINS TO
SUPPLY THE ARMY.

(POPULAR SONG)

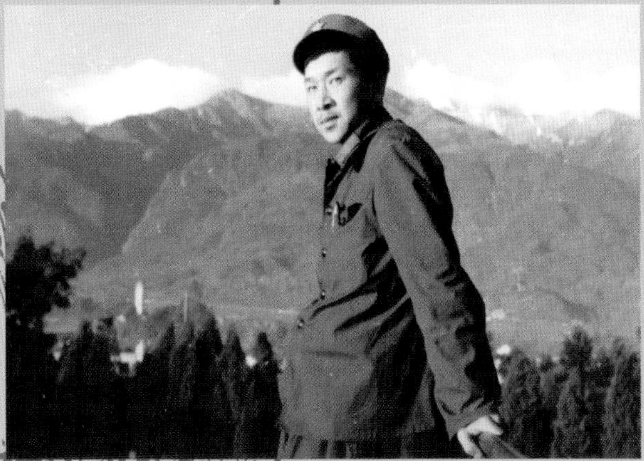

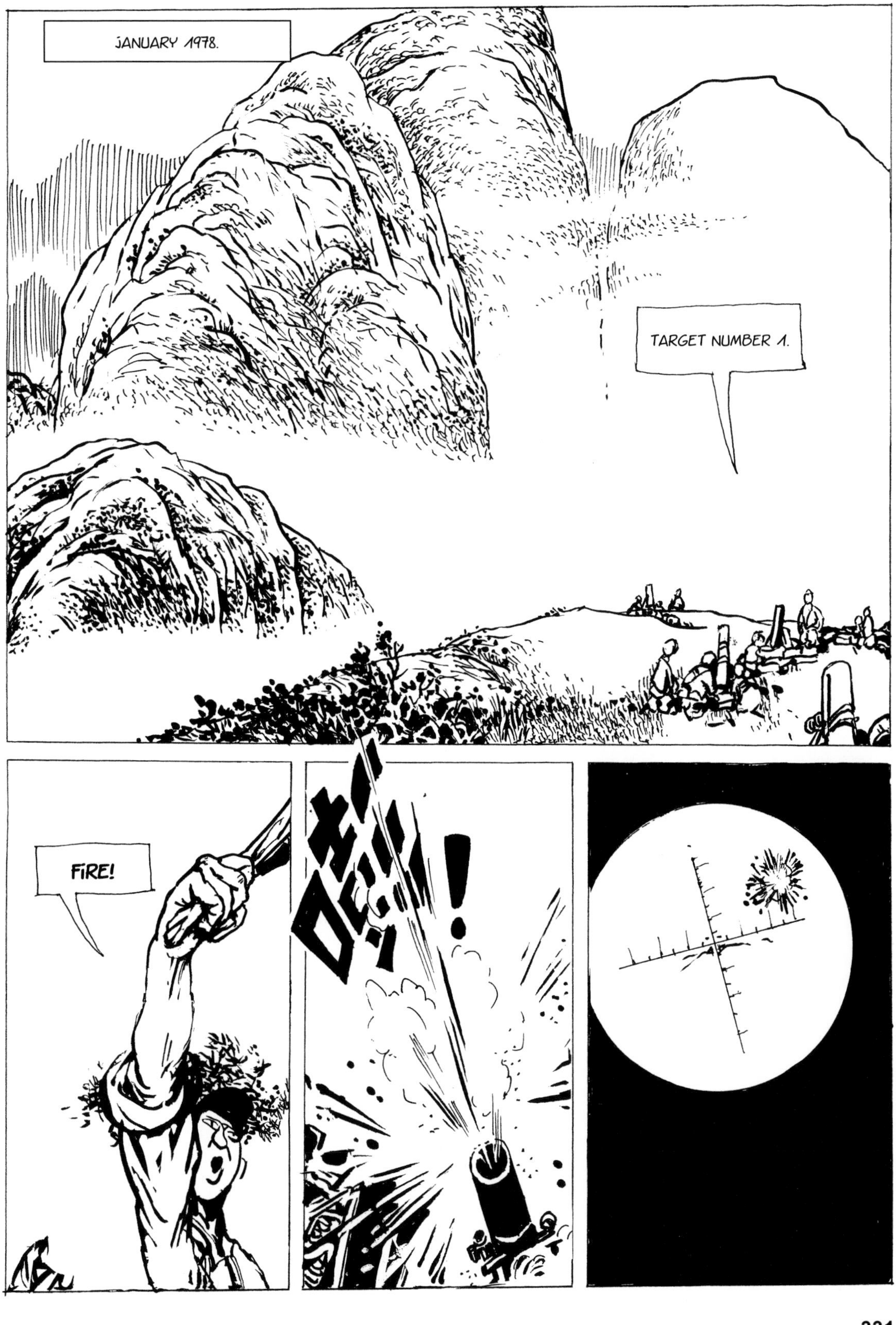
JANUARY 1978.
TARGET NUMBER 1.
FIRE!

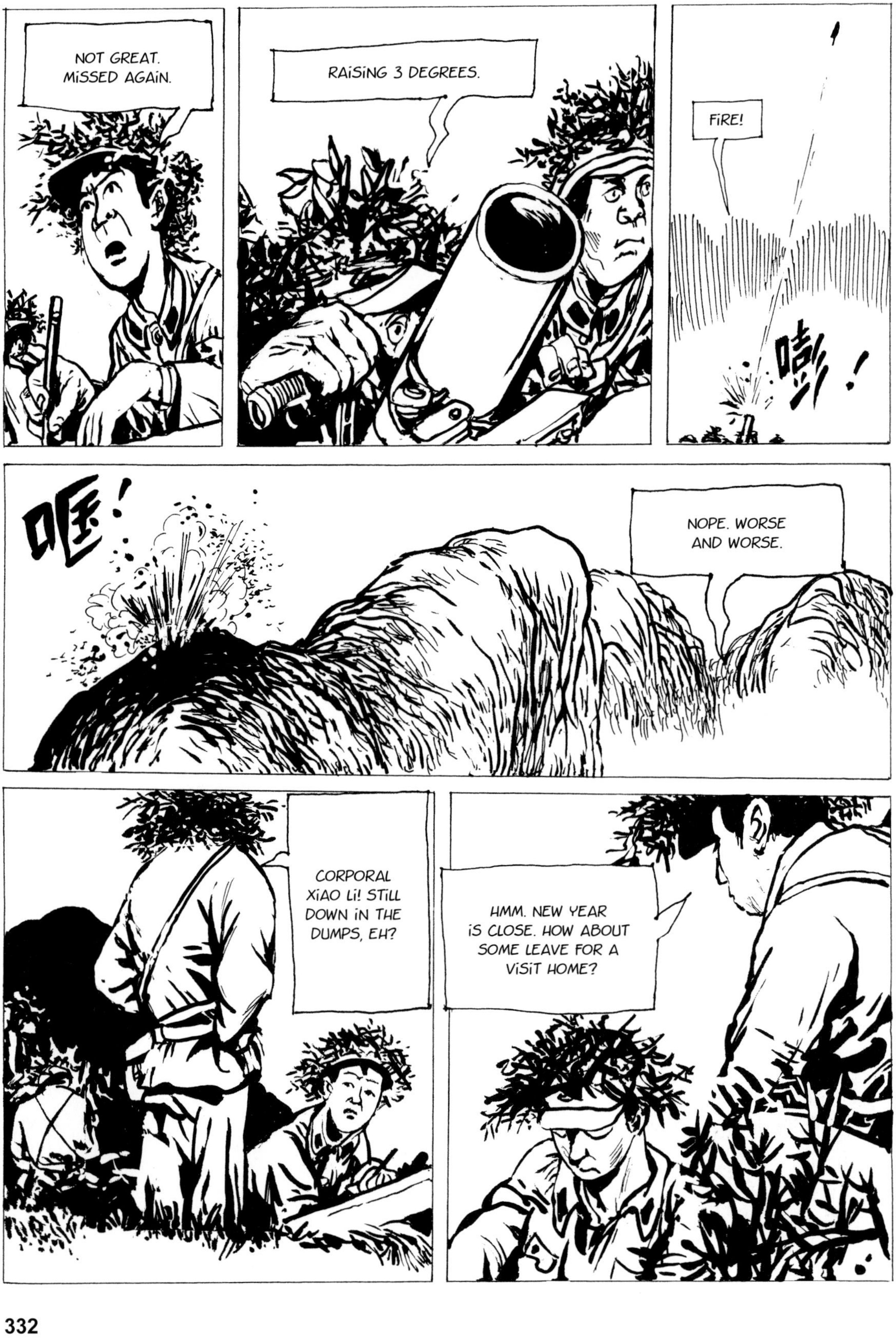
NOT GREAT. MISSED AGAIN.
RAISING 3 DEGREES.
FIRE!
嘭!
哐!
NOPE. WORSE AND WORSE.
CORPORAL XIAO LI! STILL DOWN IN THE DUMPS, EH?
HMM. NEW YEAR IS CLOSE. HOW ABOUT SOME LEAVE FOR A VISIT HOME?

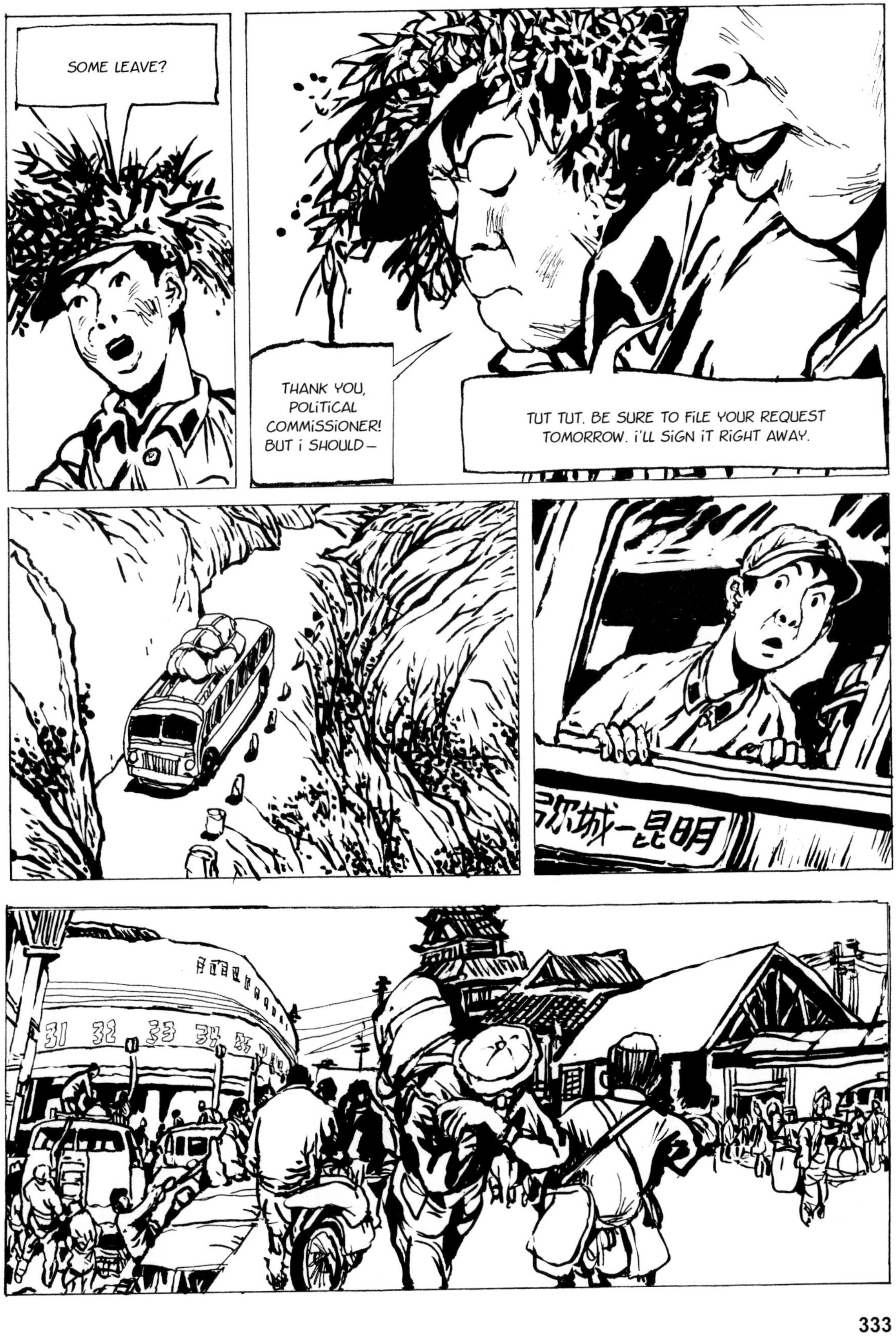
SOME LEAVE?
THANK YOU, POLITICAL COMMISSIONER! BUT I SHOULD—
TUT TUT. BE SURE TO FILE YOUR REQUEST TOMORROW. I'LL SIGN IT RIGHT AWAY.
弥城—昆明
31 32 33 34

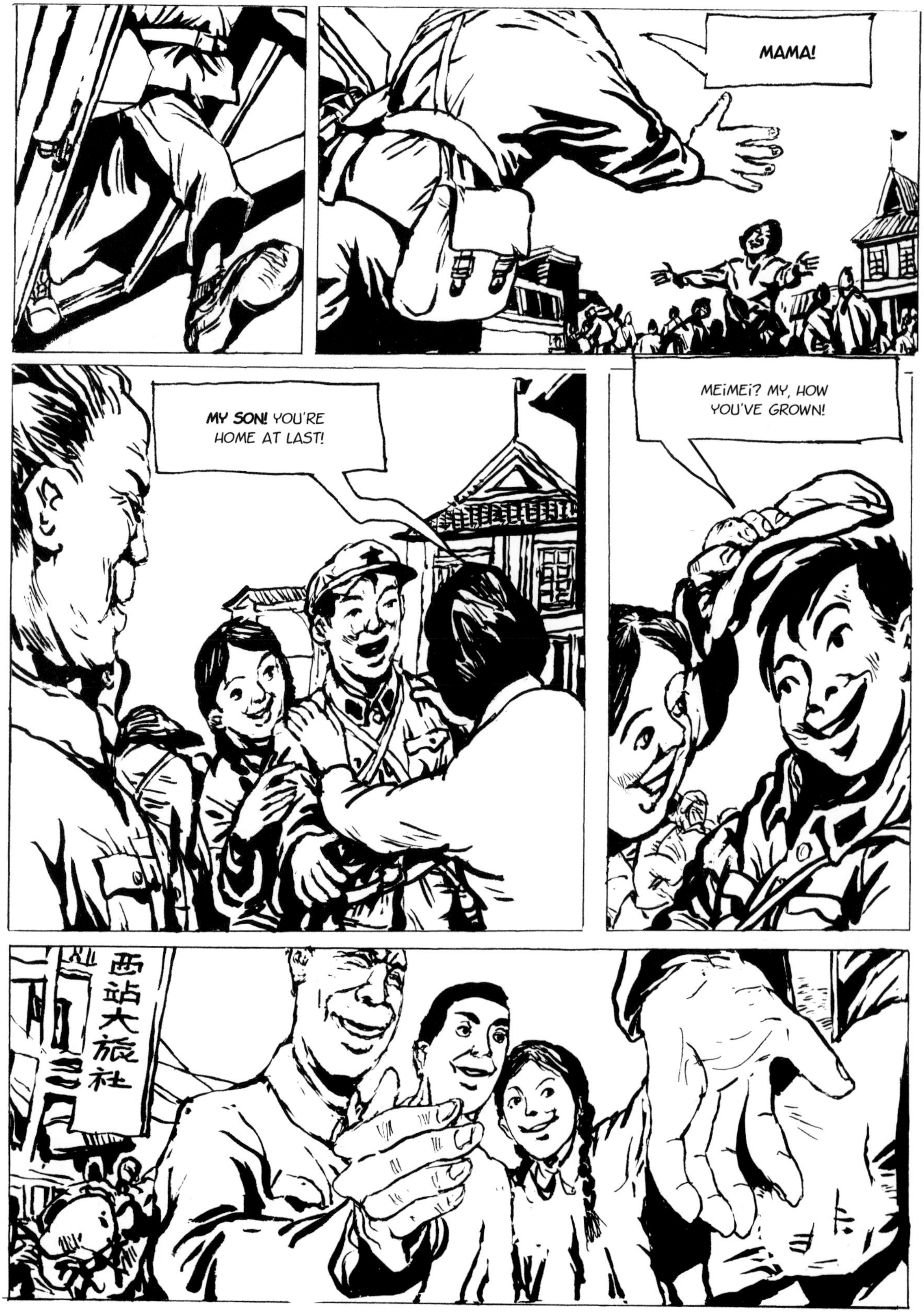
MAMA!
MY SON! YOU'RE HOME AT LAST!
MEiMEi? MY, HOW YOU'VE GROWN!
西站大旅社

UH... XIAO LI, DO YOU REMEMBER YOUR **BIG BROTHER**, GUIGUI, WHO I MENTIONED SO OFTEN?

WELL... HE'S REJOINED US AT LAST.

THERE HE WAS: GUIGUI... MY MYSTERIOUS OLDER BROTHER. MY FATHER'S FIRST WIFE HAD RAISED HIM AS BEST SHE COULD WITH A SIDE OF THE FAMILY I DIDN'T KNOW AND MY FATHER SPOKE OF ONLY RARELY.

ALTHOUGH WE HADN'T HAD THE SAME CHILDHOOD — FAR FROM IT — WE SHARED WITH ALL OUR COUNTRYMEN THE SAME CHAOTIC HISTORY — HE AS A BLACK BASTARD, AND I A YOUNG REVOLUTIONARY — WHICH PARADOXICALLY HAD THE VIRTUE OF BRINGING US CLOSER TOGETHER RIGHT FROM THE START.

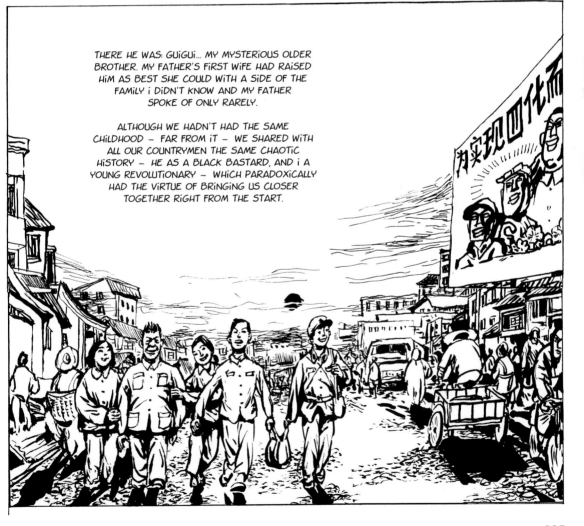

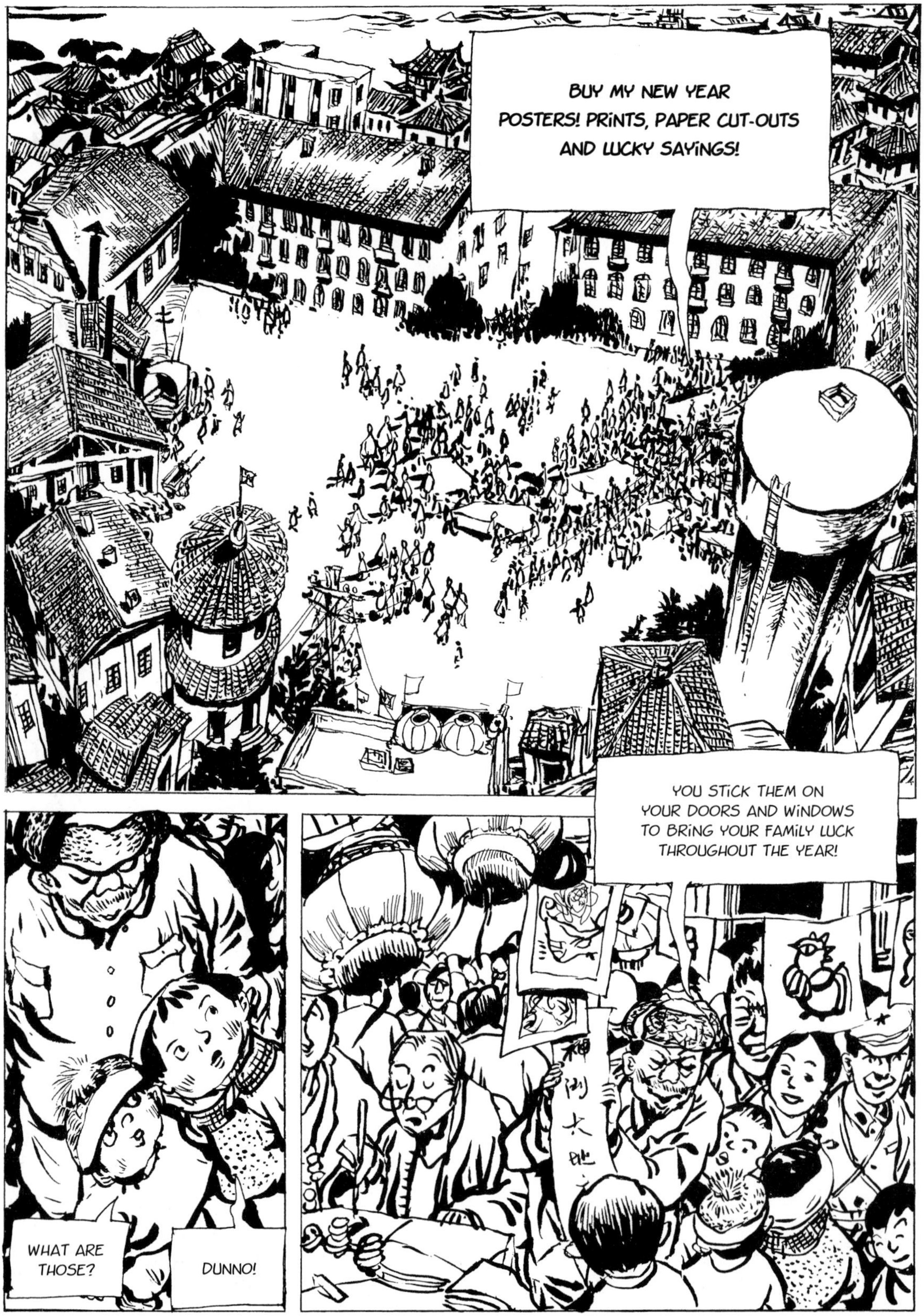
BUY MY NEW YEAR POSTERS! PRINTS, PAPER CUT-OUTS AND LUCKY SAYINGS!
YOU STICK THEM ON YOUR DOORS AND WINDOWS TO BRING YOUR FAMILY LUCK THROUGHOUT THE YEAR!
WHAT ARE THOSE?
DUNNO!

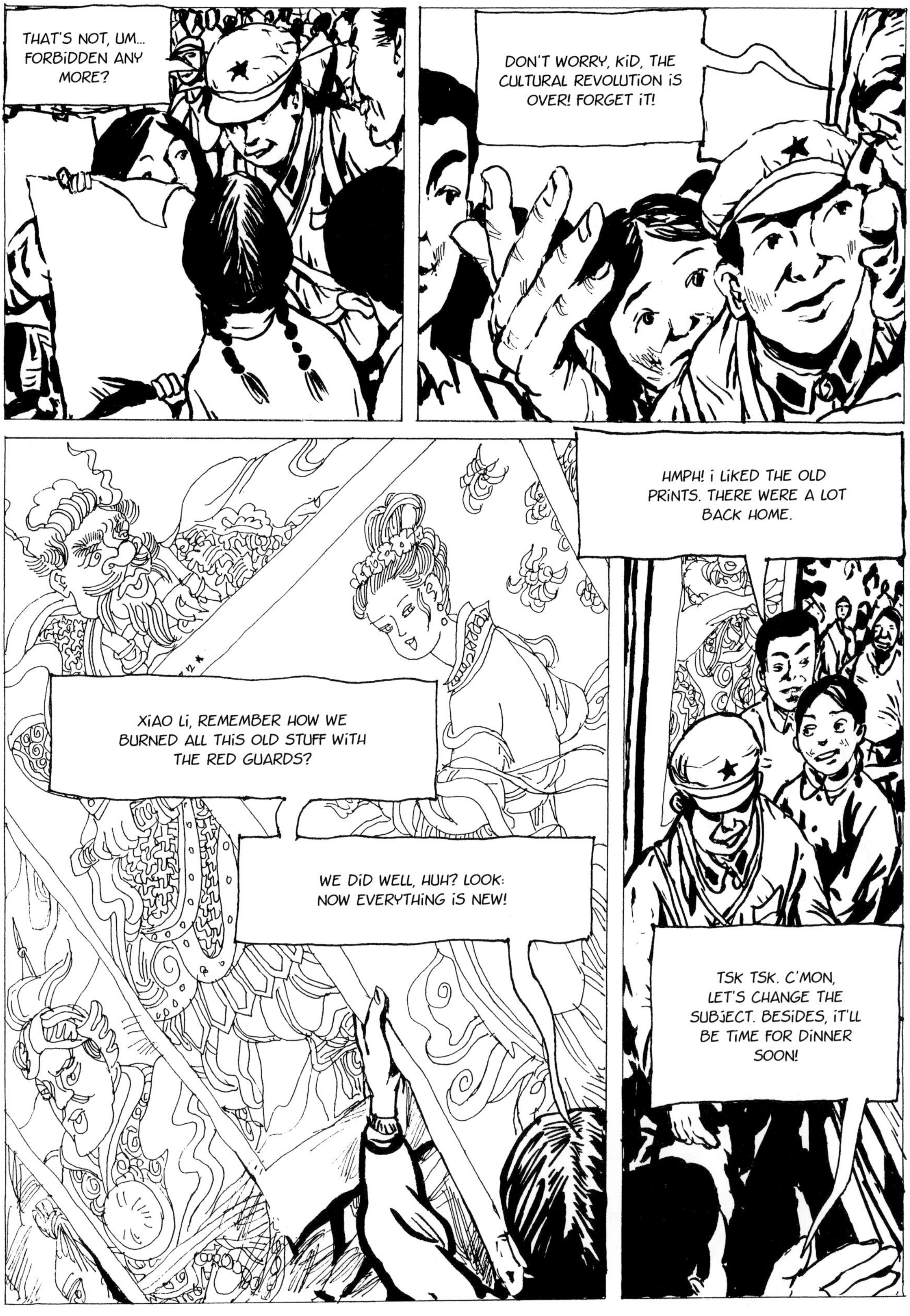
THAT'S NOT, UM... FORBIDDEN ANY MORE?
DON'T WORRY, KID, THE CULTURAL REVOLUTION IS OVER! FORGET IT!
XIAO LI, REMEMBER HOW WE BURNED ALL THIS OLD STUFF WITH THE RED GUARDS?
WE DID WELL, HUH? LOOK: NOW EVERYTHING IS NEW!
HMPH! I LIKED THE OLD PRINTS. THERE WERE A LOT BACK HOME.
TSK TSK. C'MON, LET'S CHANGE THE SUBJECT. BESIDES, IT'LL BE TIME FOR DINNER SOON!

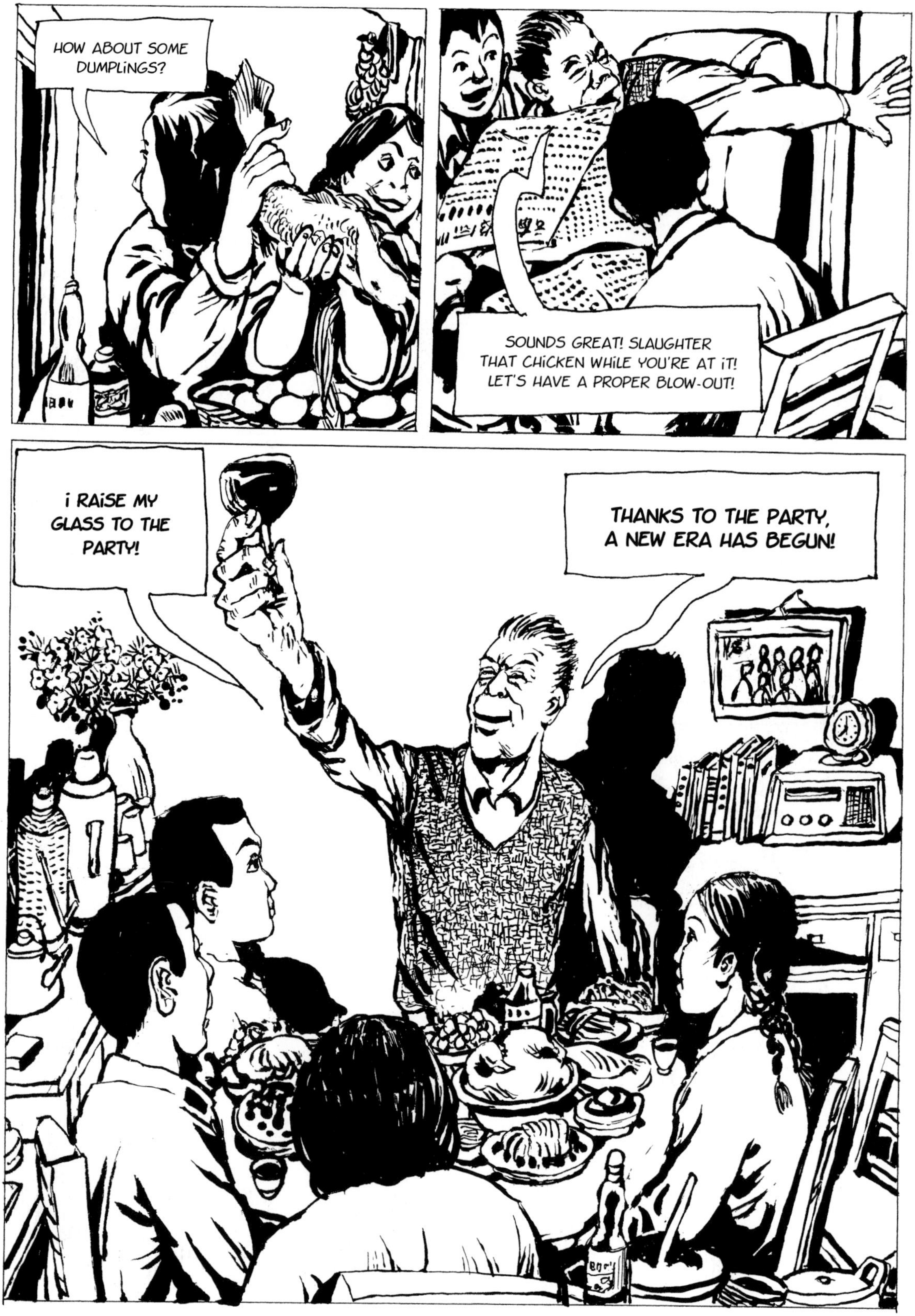
HOW ABOUT SOME DUMPLINGS?
SOUNDS GREAT! SLAUGHTER THAT CHICKEN WHILE YOU'RE AT IT! LET'S HAVE A PROPER BLOW-OUT!
I RAISE MY GLASS TO THE PARTY!
THANKS TO THE PARTY, A NEW ERA HAS BEGUN!

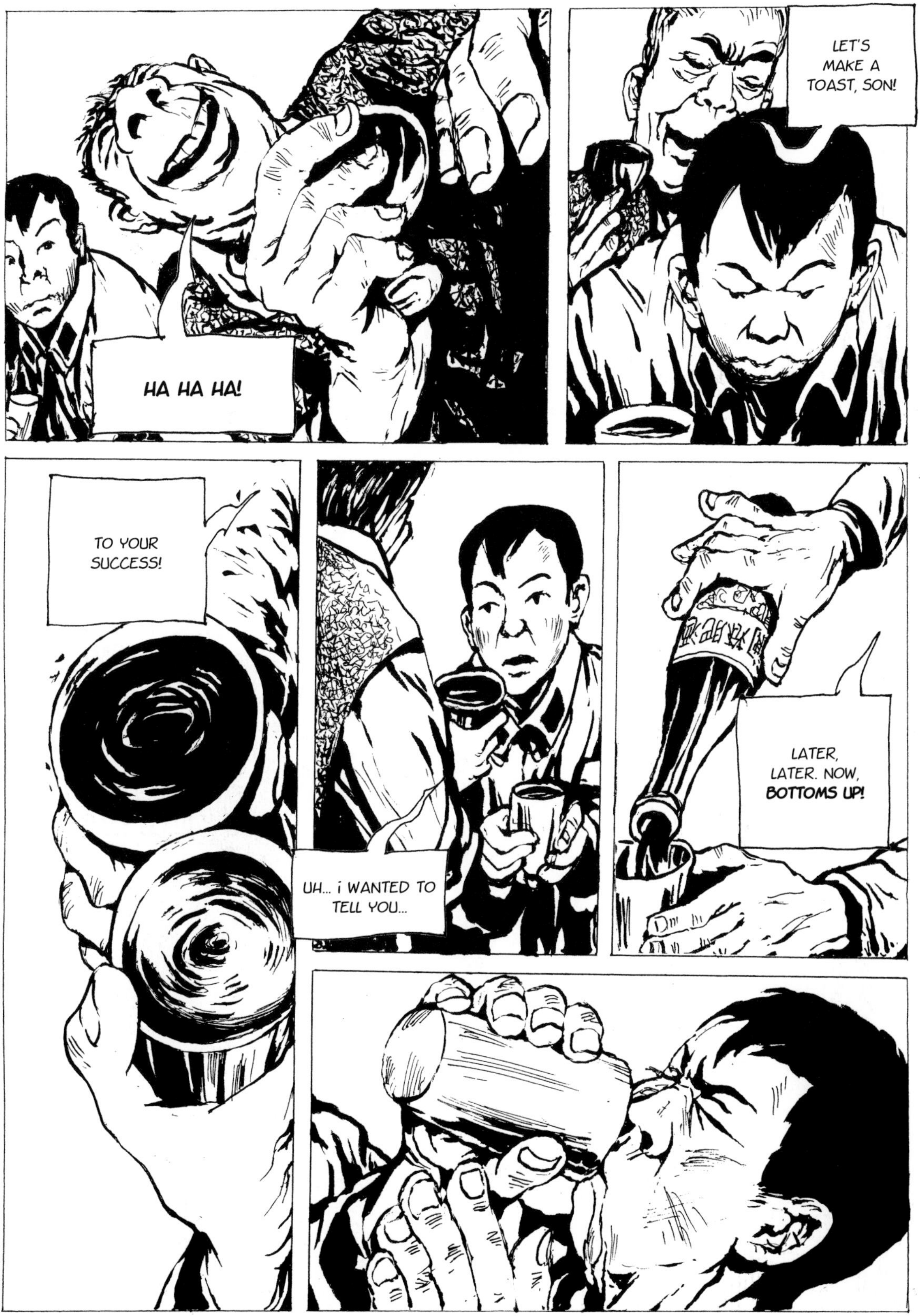
HA HA HA!
LET'S MAKE A TOAST, SON!
TO YOUR SUCCESS!
UH... I WANTED TO TELL YOU...
LATER, LATER. NOW, **BOTTOMS UP!**

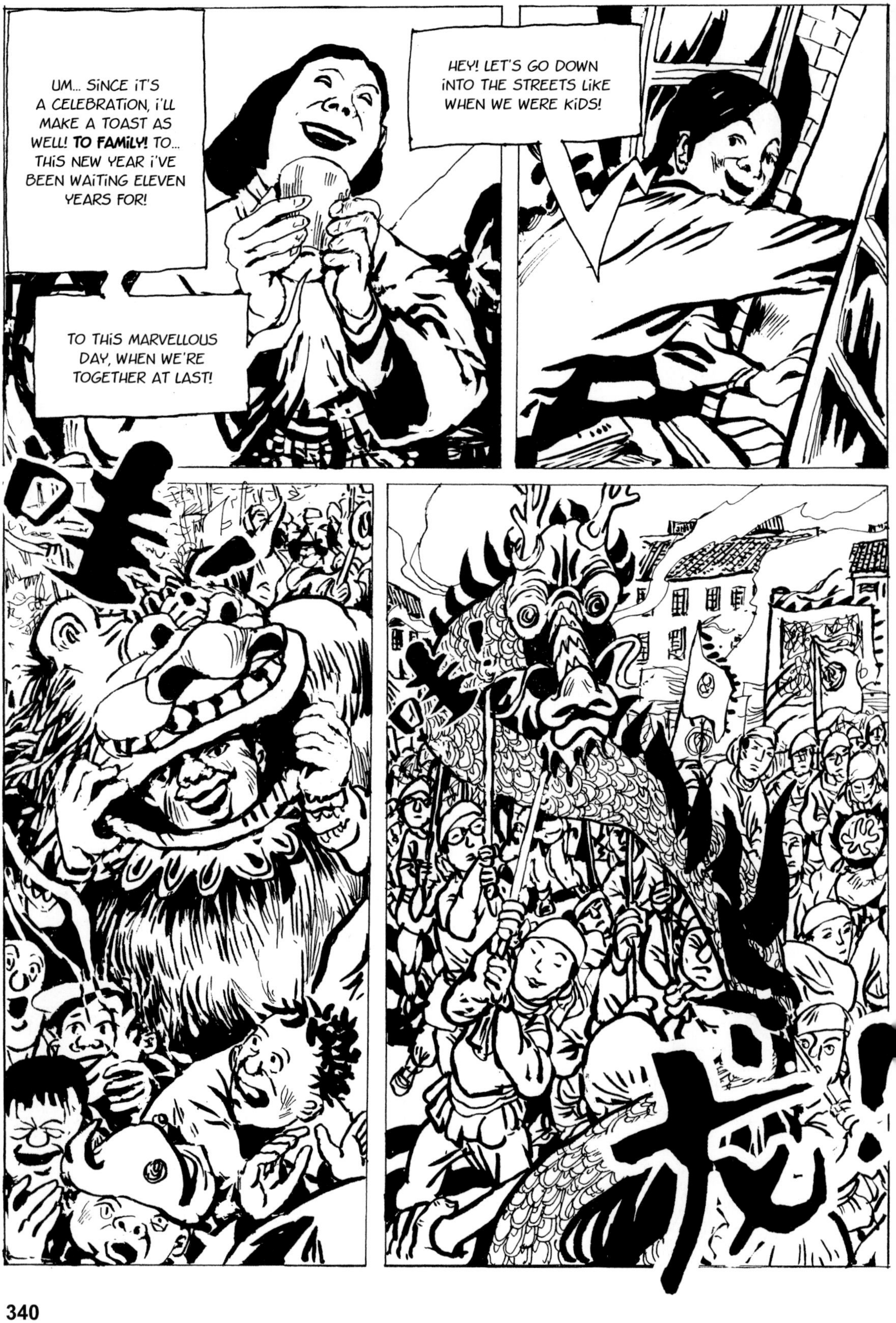
UM... SINCE IT'S A CELEBRATION, I'LL MAKE A TOAST AS WELL! **TO FAMILY!** TO... THIS NEW YEAR I'VE BEEN WAITING ELEVEN YEARS FOR!
TO THIS MARVELLOUS DAY, WHEN WE'RE TOGETHER AT LAST!
HEY! LET'S GO DOWN INTO THE STREETS LIKE WHEN WE WERE KIDS!

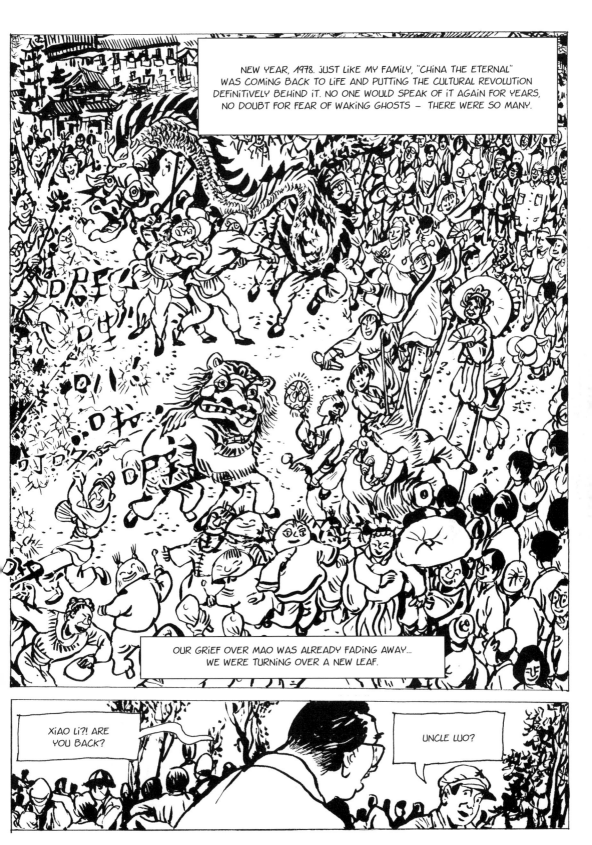

NEW YEAR, 1978. JUST LIKE MY FAMILY, "CHINA THE ETERNAL" WAS COMING BACK TO LIFE AND PUTTING THE CULTURAL REVOLUTION DEFINITIVELY BEHIND IT. NO ONE WOULD SPEAK OF IT AGAIN FOR YEARS, NO DOUBT FOR FEAR OF WAKING GHOSTS — THERE WERE SO MANY.

OUR GRIEF OVER MAO WAS ALREADY FADING AWAY... WE WERE TURNING OVER A NEW LEAF.

XIAO LI?! ARE YOU BACK?

UNCLE LUO?

341

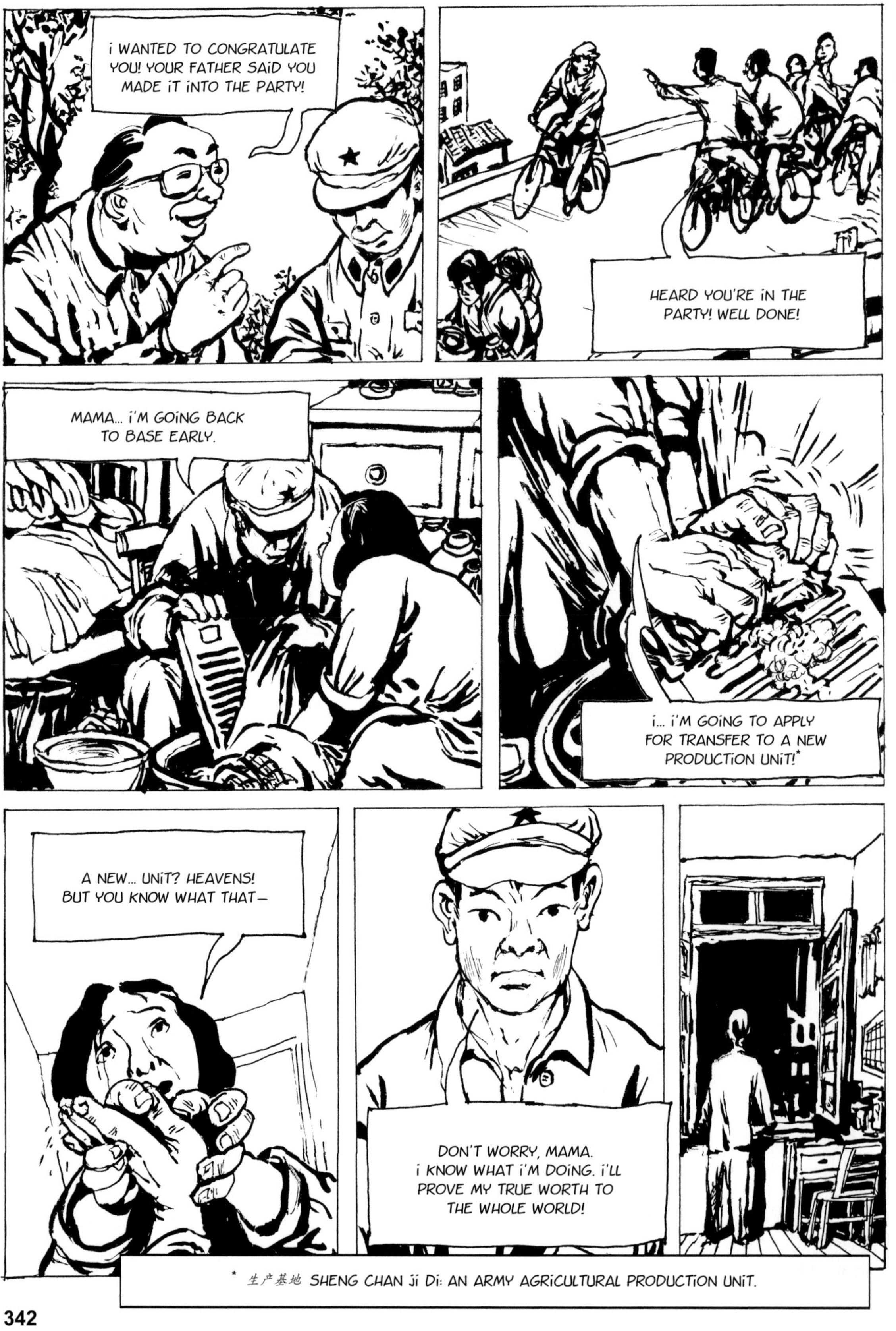
I WANTED TO CONGRATULATE YOU! YOUR FATHER SAID YOU MADE IT INTO THE PARTY!
HEARD YOU'RE IN THE PARTY! WELL DONE!
MAMA... I'M GOING BACK TO BASE EARLY.
I... I'M GOING TO APPLY FOR TRANSFER TO A NEW PRODUCTION UNIT!*
A NEW... UNIT? HEAVENS! BUT YOU KNOW WHAT THAT–
DON'T WORRY, MAMA. I KNOW WHAT I'M DOING. I'LL PROVE MY TRUE WORTH TO THE WHOLE WORLD!

* 生产基地 SHENG CHAN JI DI: AN ARMY AGRICULTURAL PRODUCTION UNIT.

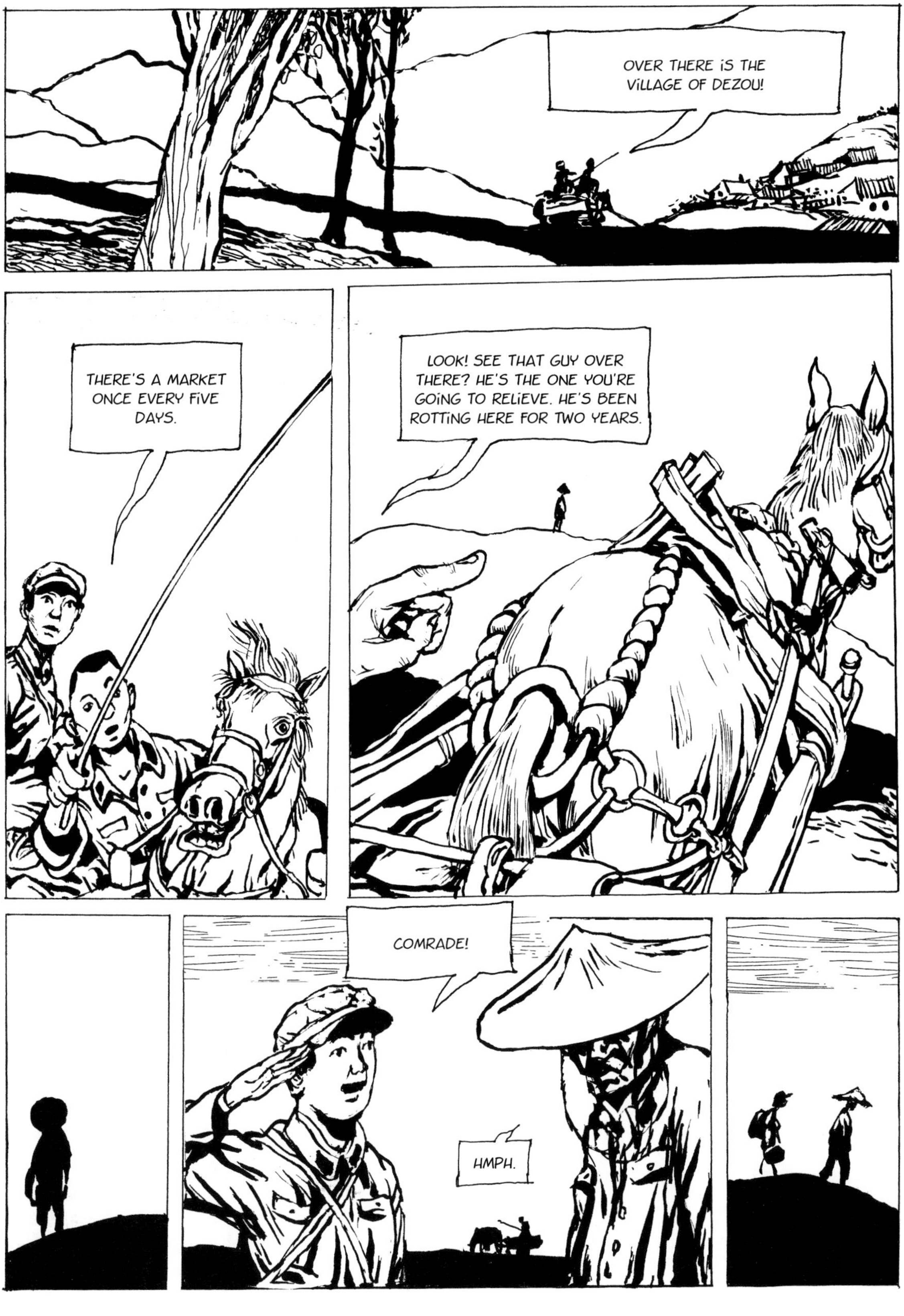
OVER THERE iS THE VILLAGE OF DEZOU!
THERE'S A MARKET ONCE EVERY FiVE DAYS.
LOOK! SEE THAT GUY OVER THERE? HE'S THE ONE YOU'RE GOiNG TO RELiEVE. HE'S BEEN ROTTiNG HERE FOR TWO YEARS.
COMRADE!
HMPH.

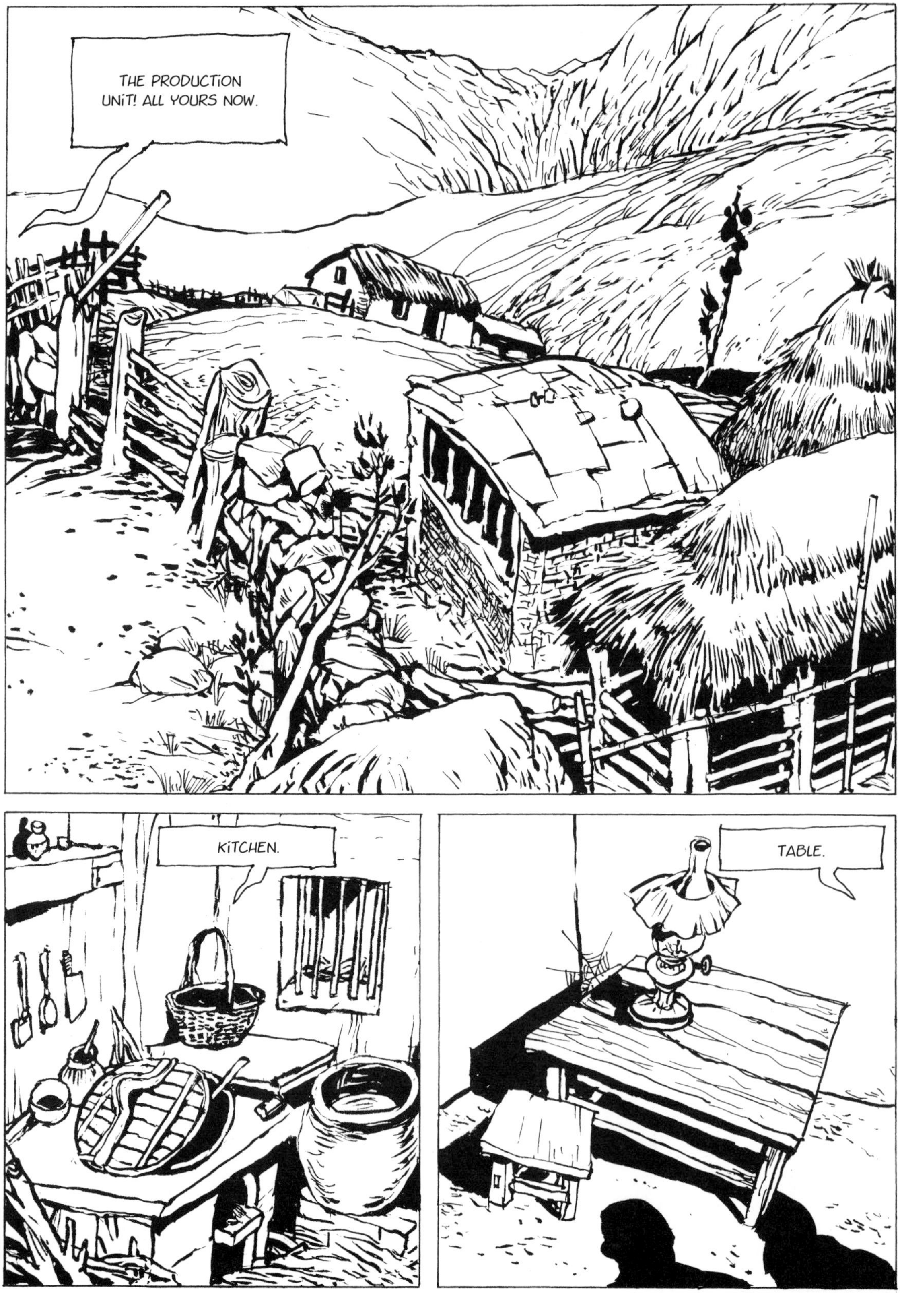
THE PRODUCTION UNIT! ALL YOURS NOW.
KITCHEN.
TABLE.

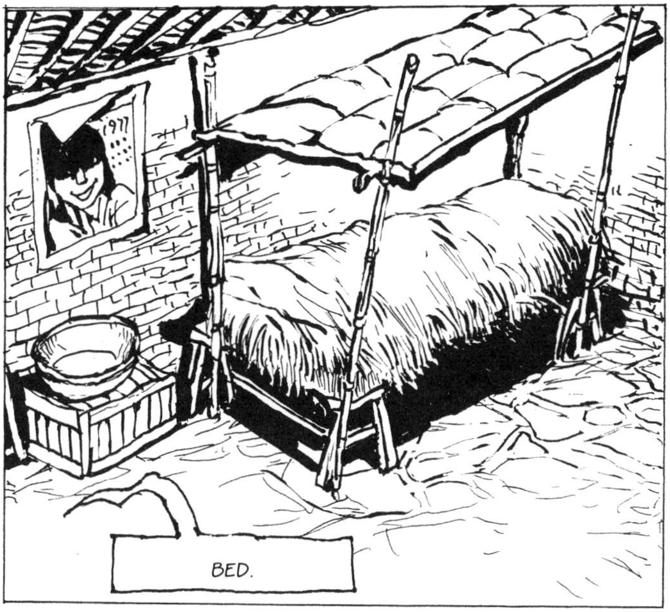
BED.

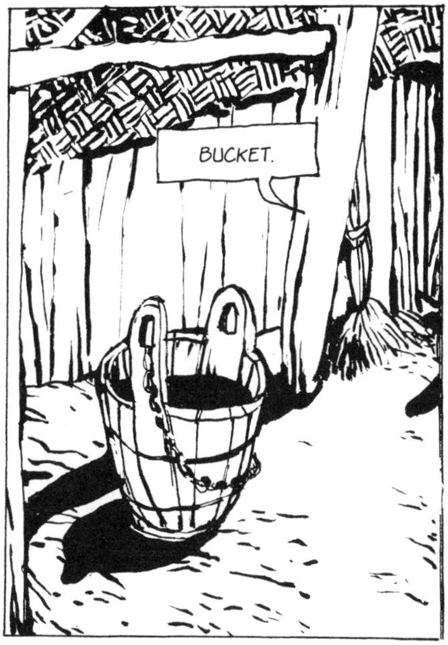
BUCKET.

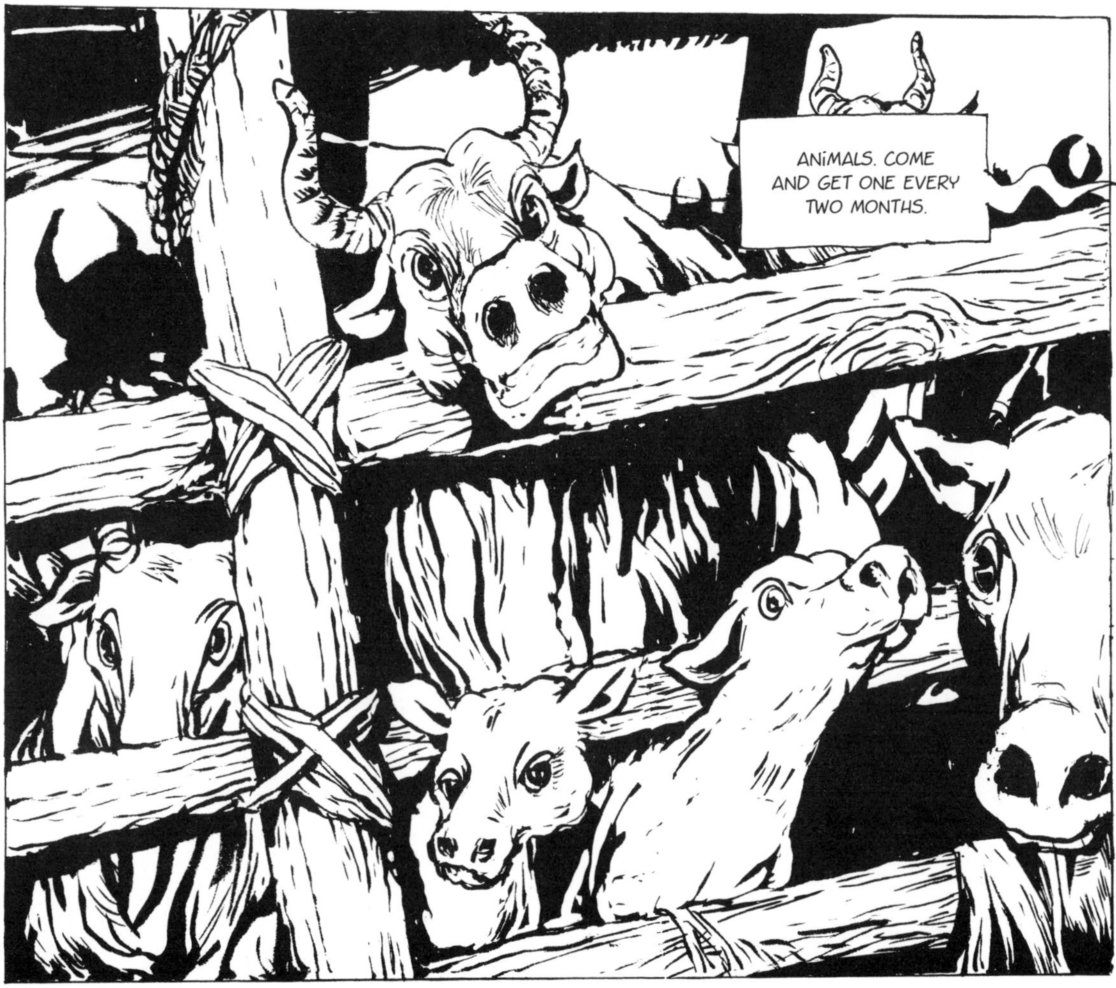
ANIMALS. COME AND GET ONE EVERY TWO MONTHS.

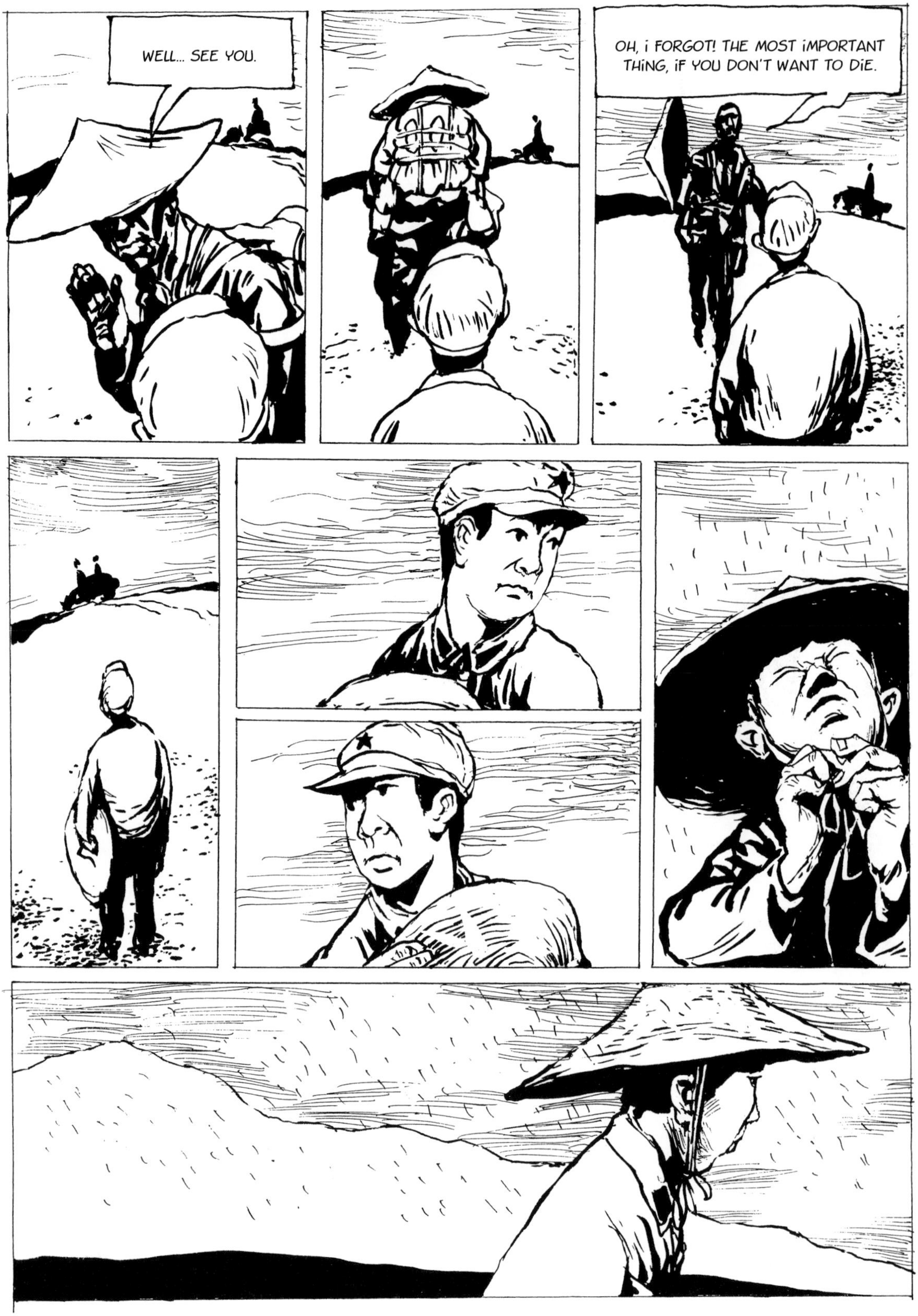

WELL... SEE YOU.
OH, i FORGOT! THE MOST iMPORTANT THiNG, iF YOU DON'T WANT TO DiE.

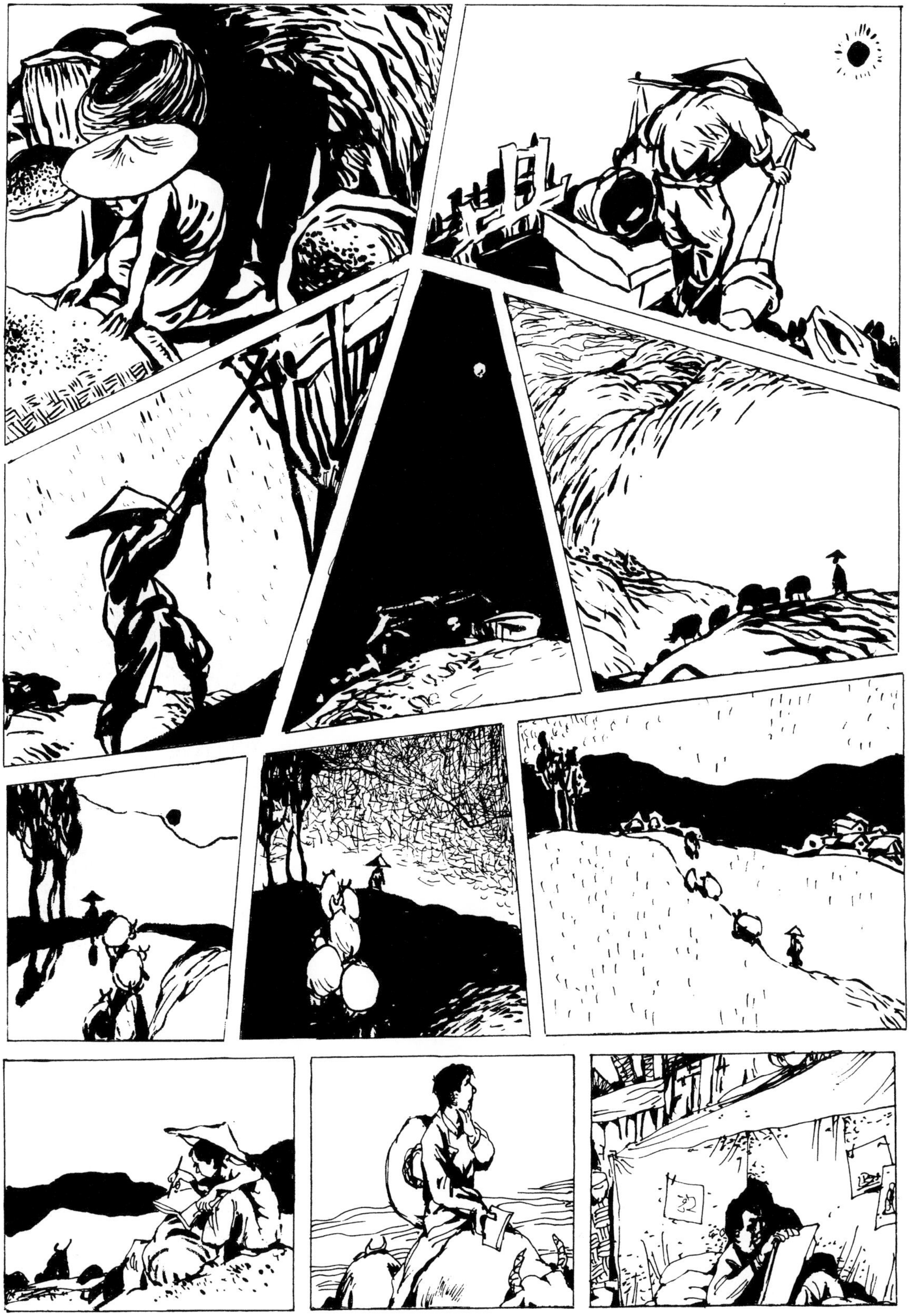

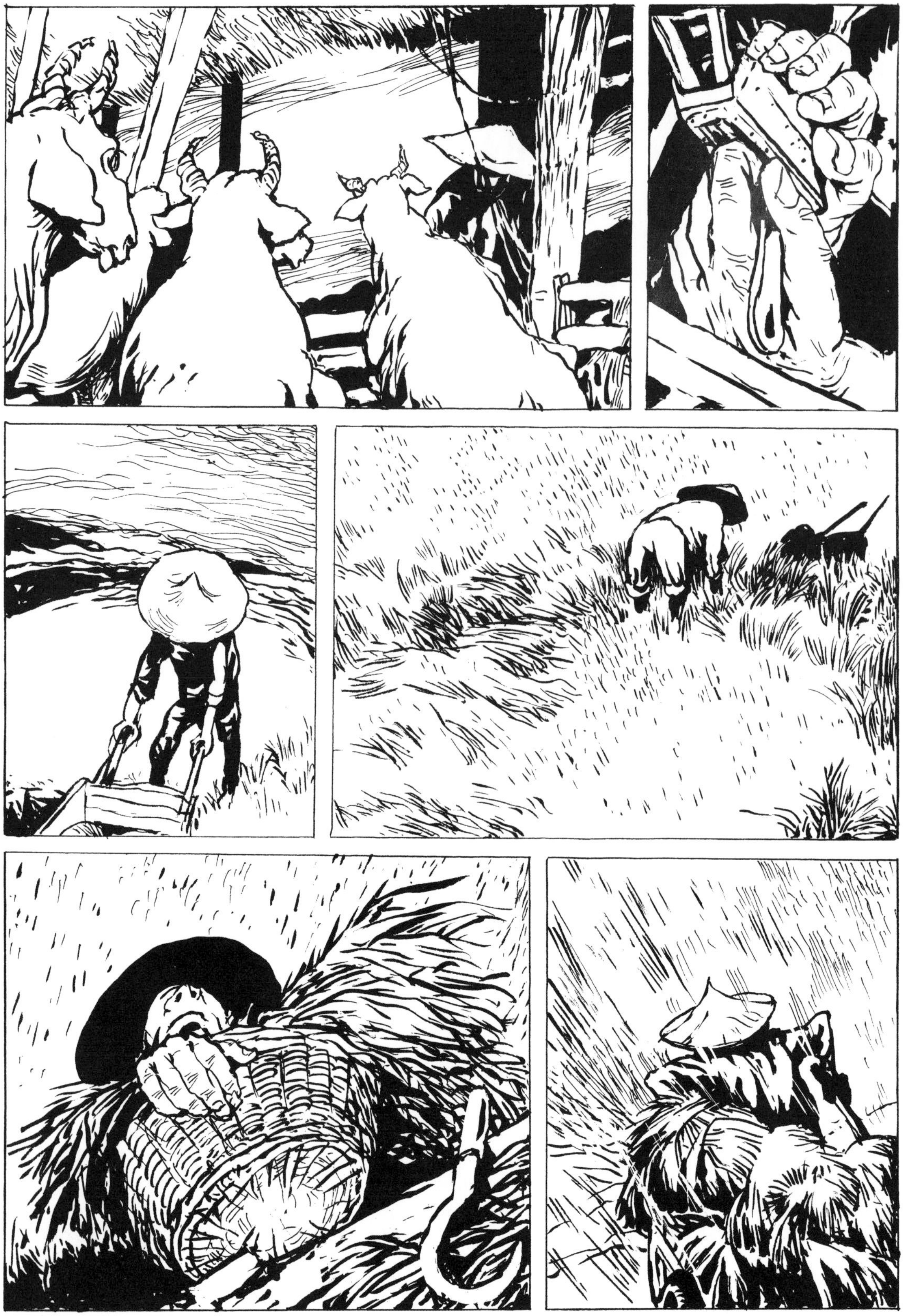

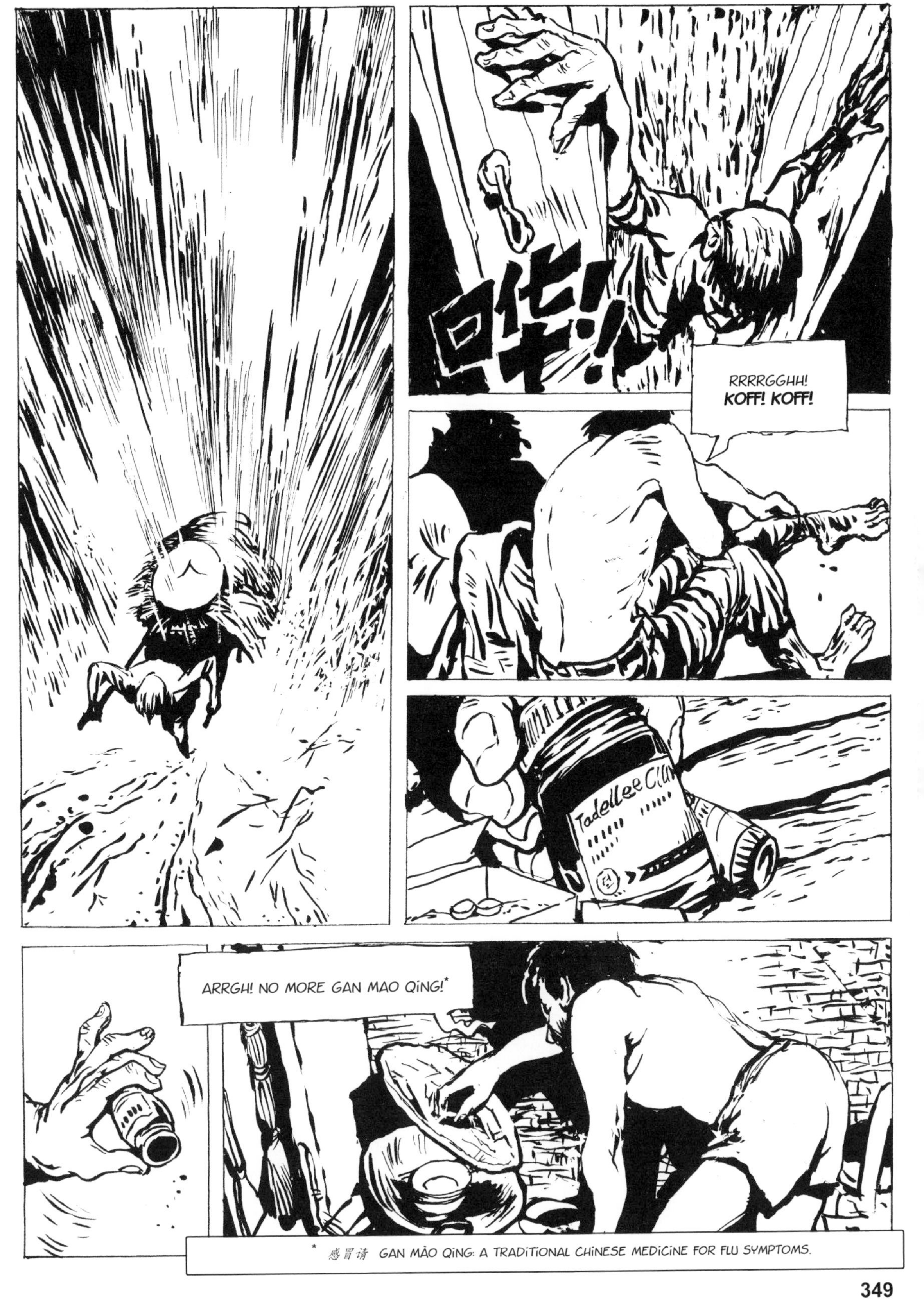
咔!!
RRRRGGHH!
KOFF! KOFF!
Tadellee
ARRGH! NO MORE GAN MAO QING!*

* 感冒请 GAN MÀO QING: A TRADITIONAL CHINESE MEDICINE FOR FLU SYMPTOMS.

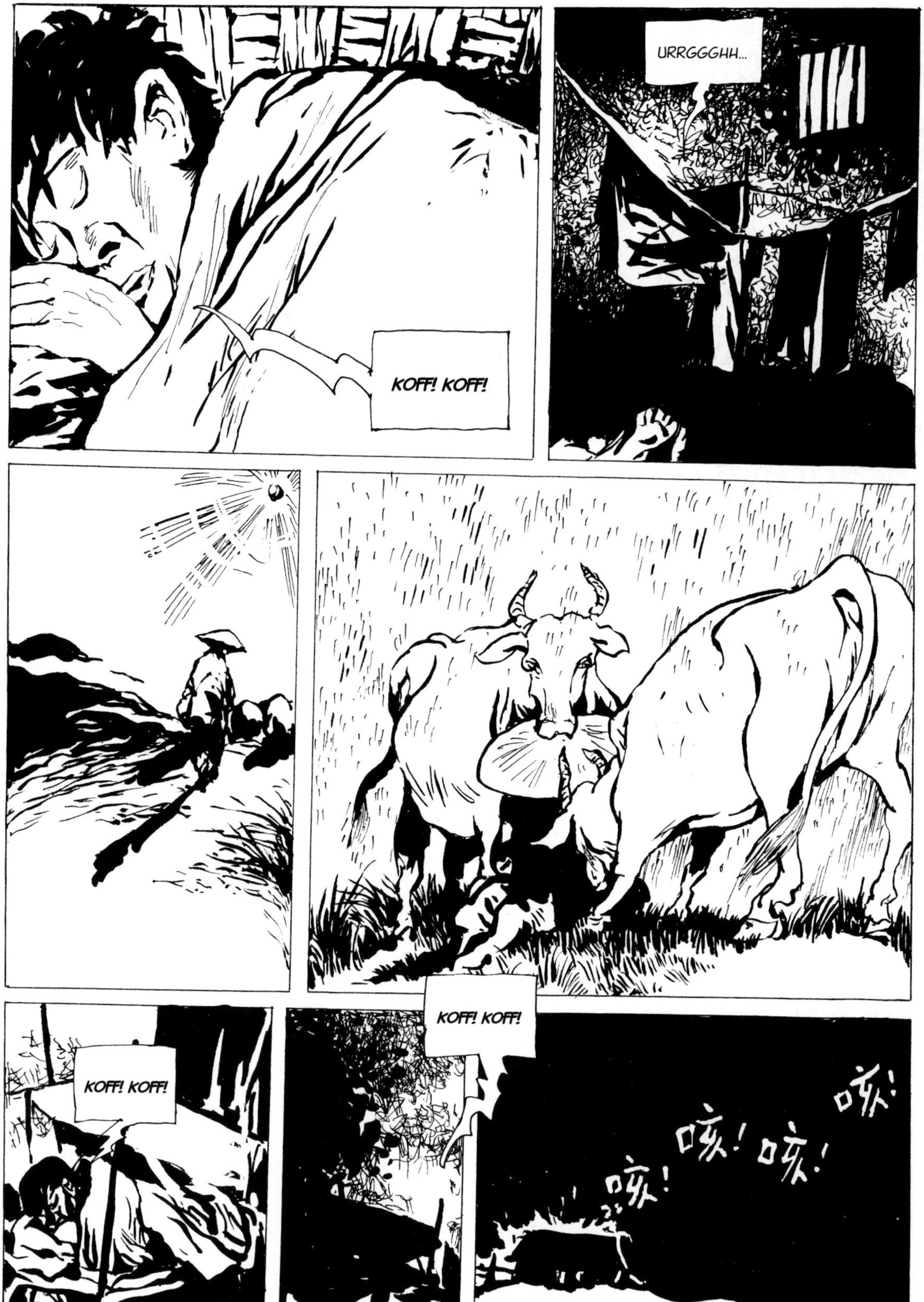
KOFF! KOFF!
URRGGGHH...
KOFF! KOFF!
KOFF! KOFF!
咳! 咳! 咳! 咳!

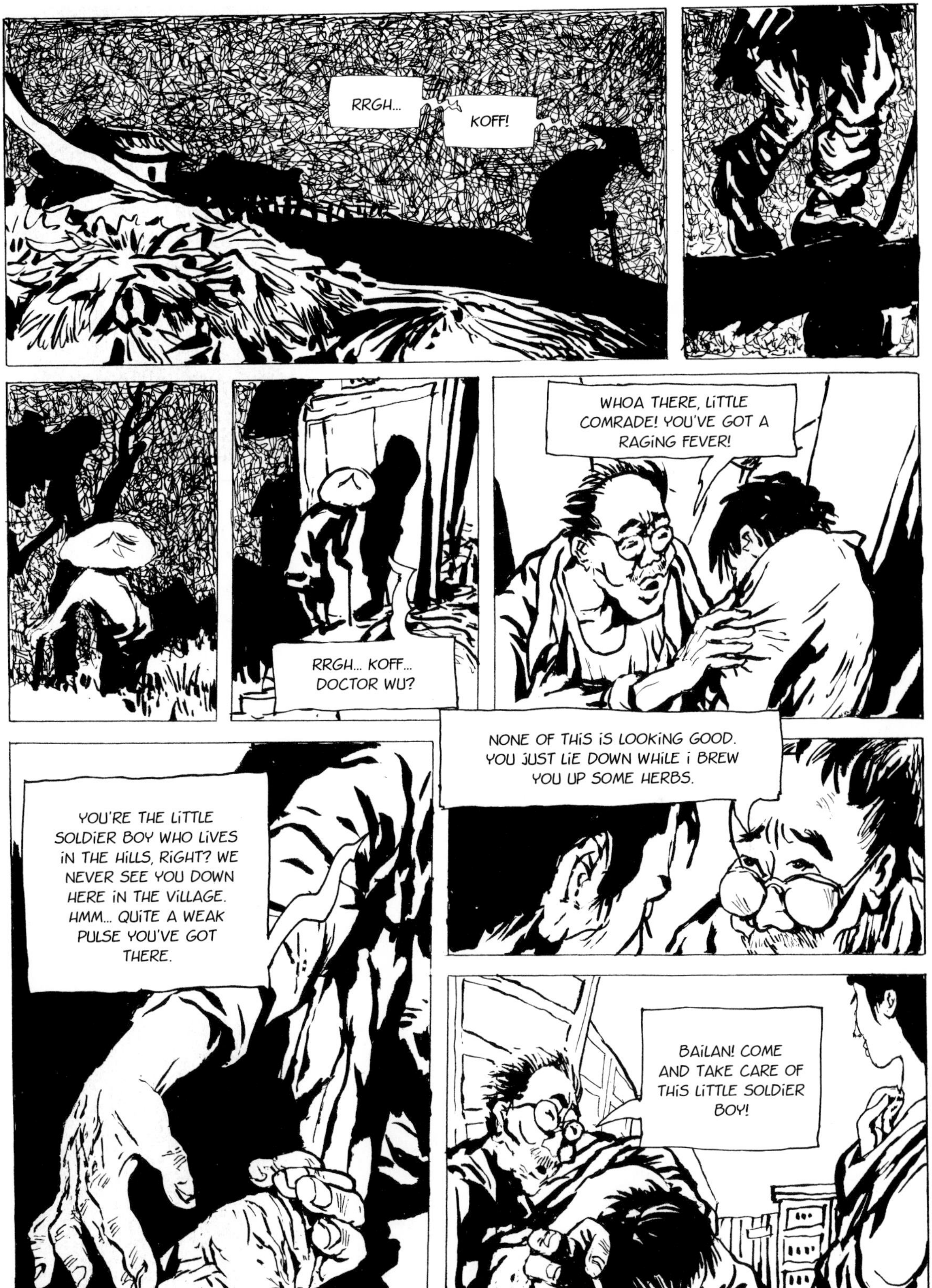
RRGH...
KOFF!
RRGH... KOFF... DOCTOR WU?
WHOA THERE, LITTLE COMRADE! YOU'VE GOT A RAGING FEVER!
YOU'RE THE LITTLE SOLDIER BOY WHO LIVES IN THE HILLS, RIGHT? WE NEVER SEE YOU DOWN HERE IN THE VILLAGE. HMM... QUITE A WEAK PULSE YOU'VE GOT THERE.
NONE OF THIS IS LOOKING GOOD. YOU JUST LIE DOWN WHILE I BREW YOU UP SOME HERBS.
BAILAN! COME AND TAKE CARE OF THIS LITTLE SOLDIER BOY!

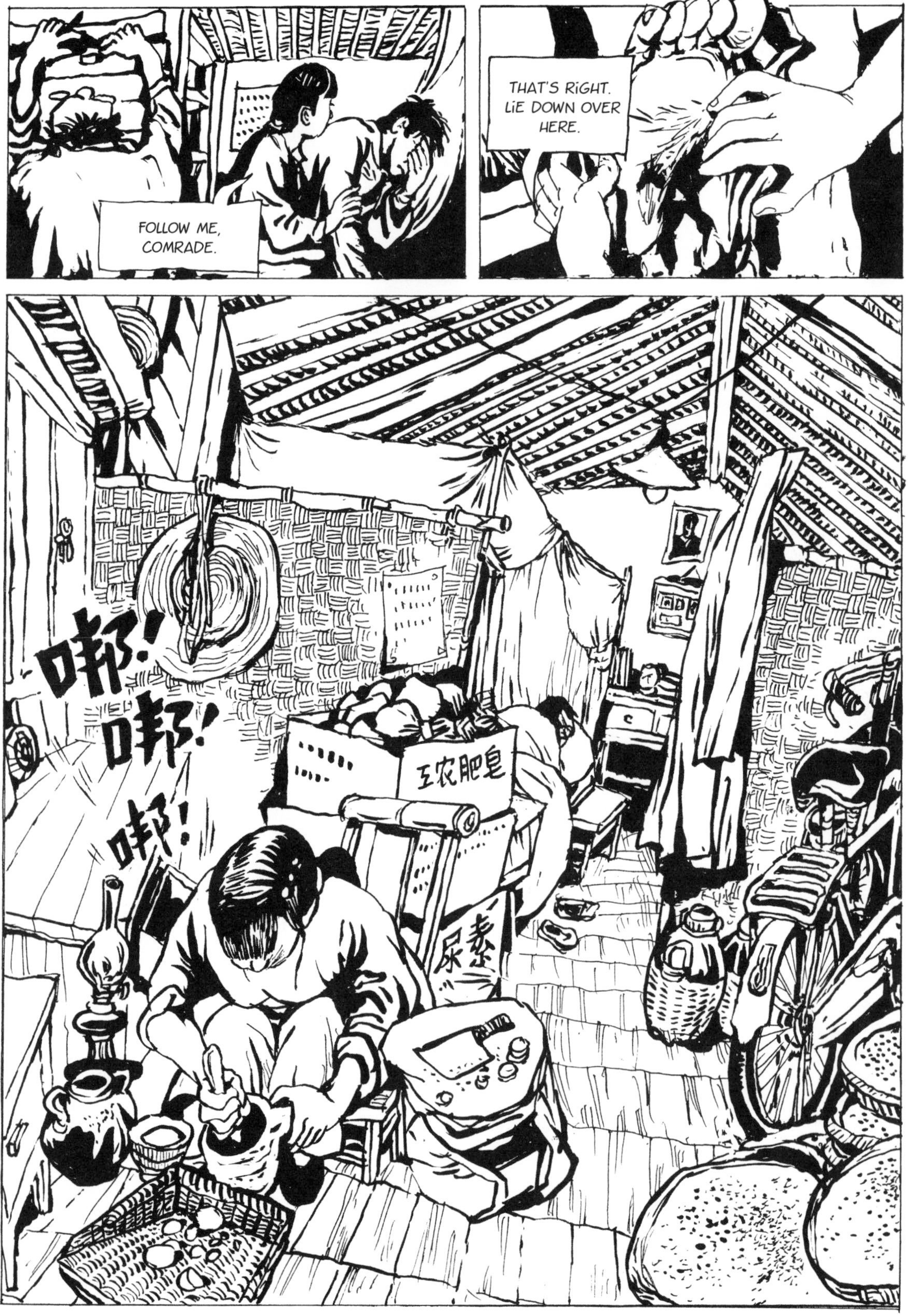
FOLLOW ME, COMRADE.
THAT'S RIGHT. LIE DOWN OVER HERE.
尿素

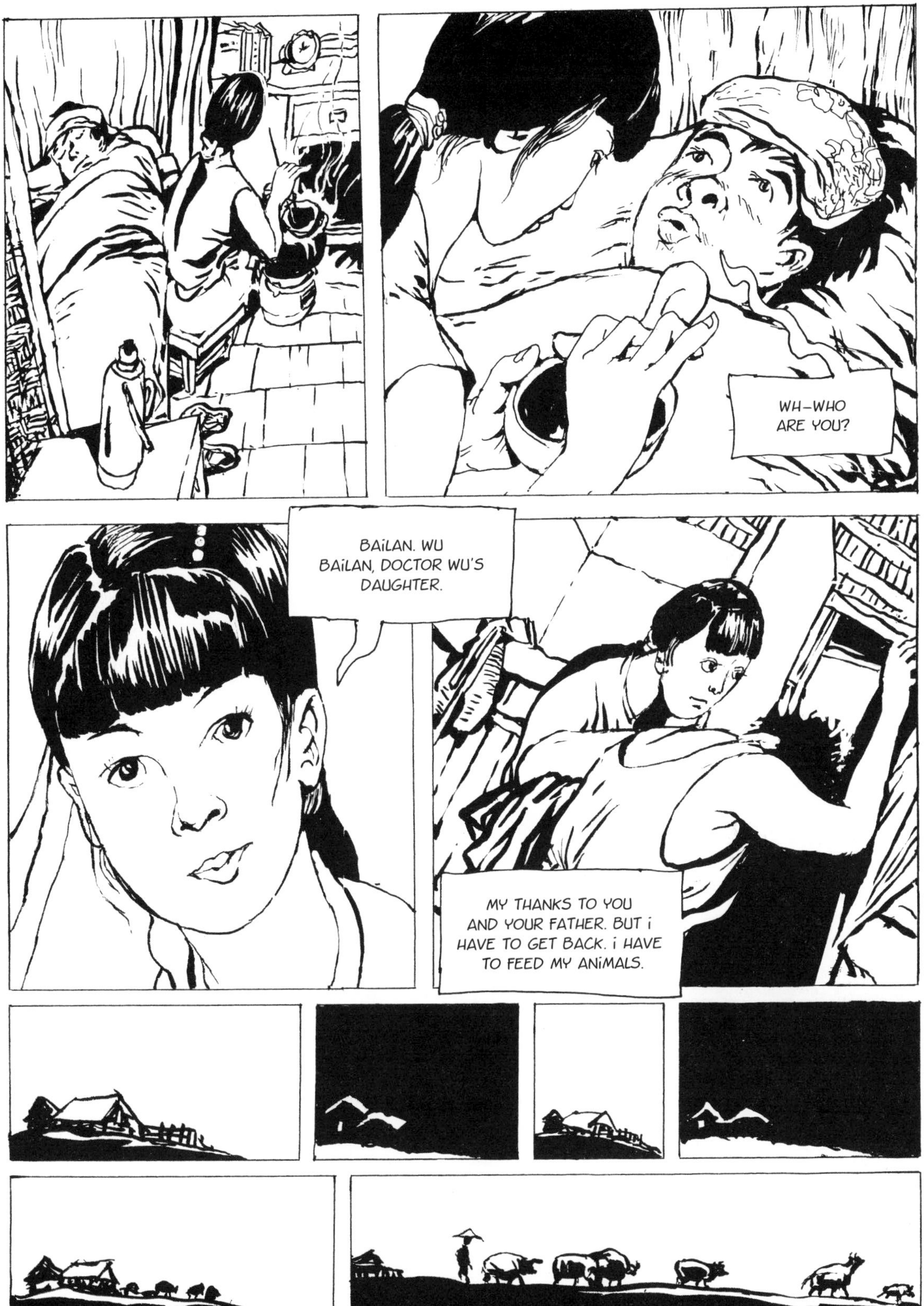
WH-WHO ARE YOU?
BAiLAN. WU BAiLAN, DOCTOR WU'S DAUGHTER.
MY THANKS TO YOU AND YOUR FATHER. BUT i HAVE TO GET BACK. i HAVE TO FEED MY ANiMALS.

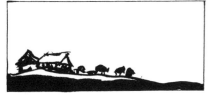

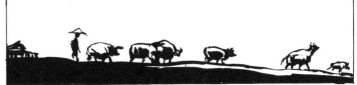

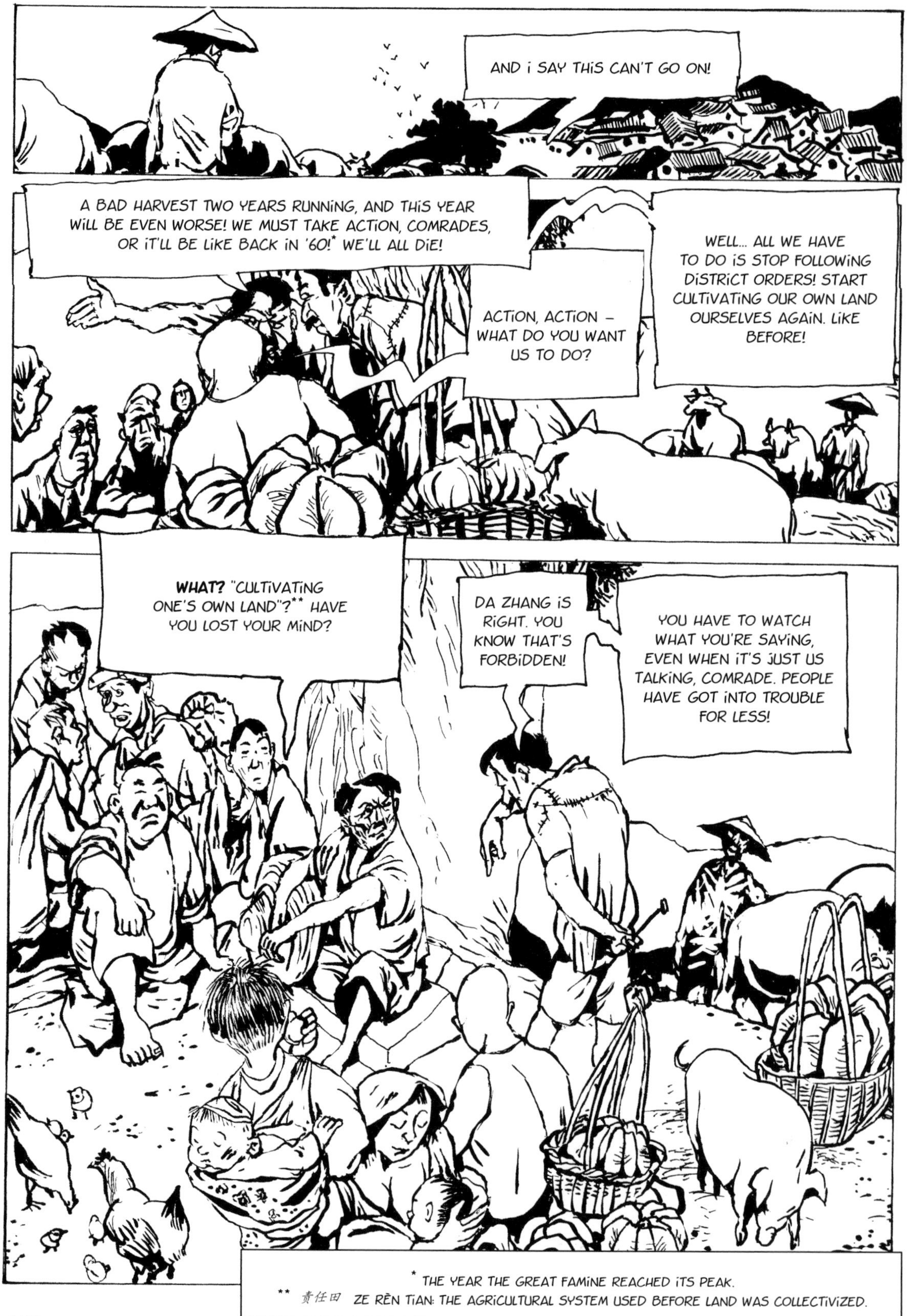
AND I SAY THIS CAN'T GO ON!
A BAD HARVEST TWO YEARS RUNNING, AND THIS YEAR WILL BE EVEN WORSE! WE MUST TAKE ACTION, COMRADES, OR IT'LL BE LIKE BACK IN '60!* WE'LL ALL DIE!
ACTION, ACTION – WHAT DO YOU WANT US TO DO?
WELL... ALL WE HAVE TO DO IS STOP FOLLOWING DISTRICT ORDERS! START CULTIVATING OUR OWN LAND OURSELVES AGAIN. LIKE BEFORE!
WHAT? "CULTIVATING ONE'S OWN LAND"?** HAVE YOU LOST YOUR MIND?
DA ZHANG IS RIGHT. YOU KNOW THAT'S FORBIDDEN!
YOU HAVE TO WATCH WHAT YOU'RE SAYING, EVEN WHEN IT'S JUST US TALKING, COMRADE. PEOPLE HAVE GOT INTO TROUBLE FOR LESS!

* THE YEAR THE GREAT FAMINE REACHED ITS PEAK.

** 责任田 ZE RÈN TIAN: THE AGRICULTURAL SYSTEM USED BEFORE LAND WAS COLLECTIVIZED.

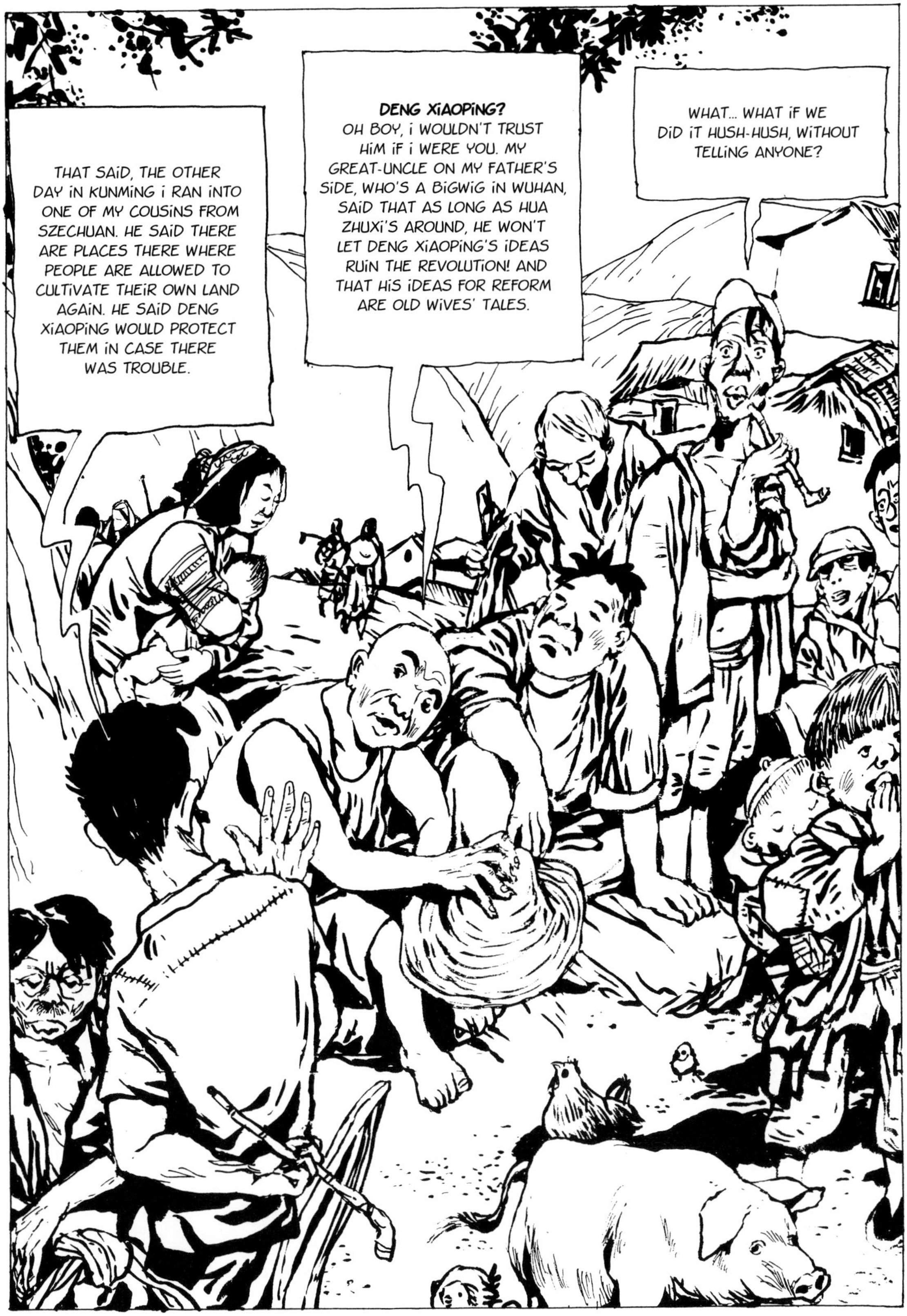
THAT SAID, THE OTHER DAY IN KUNMING I RAN INTO ONE OF MY COUSINS FROM SZECHUAN. HE SAID THERE ARE PLACES THERE WHERE PEOPLE ARE ALLOWED TO CULTIVATE THEIR OWN LAND AGAIN. HE SAID DENG XIAOPING WOULD PROTECT THEM IN CASE THERE WAS TROUBLE.
DENG XIAOPING? OH BOY, I WOULDN'T TRUST HIM IF I WERE YOU. MY GREAT-UNCLE ON MY FATHER'S SIDE, WHO'S A BIGWIG IN WUHAN, SAID THAT AS LONG AS HUA ZHUXI'S AROUND, HE WON'T LET DENG XIAOPING'S IDEAS RUIN THE REVOLUTION! AND THAT HIS IDEAS FOR REFORM ARE OLD WIVES' TALES.
WHAT... WHAT IF WE DID IT HUSH-HUSH, WITHOUT TELLING ANYONE?

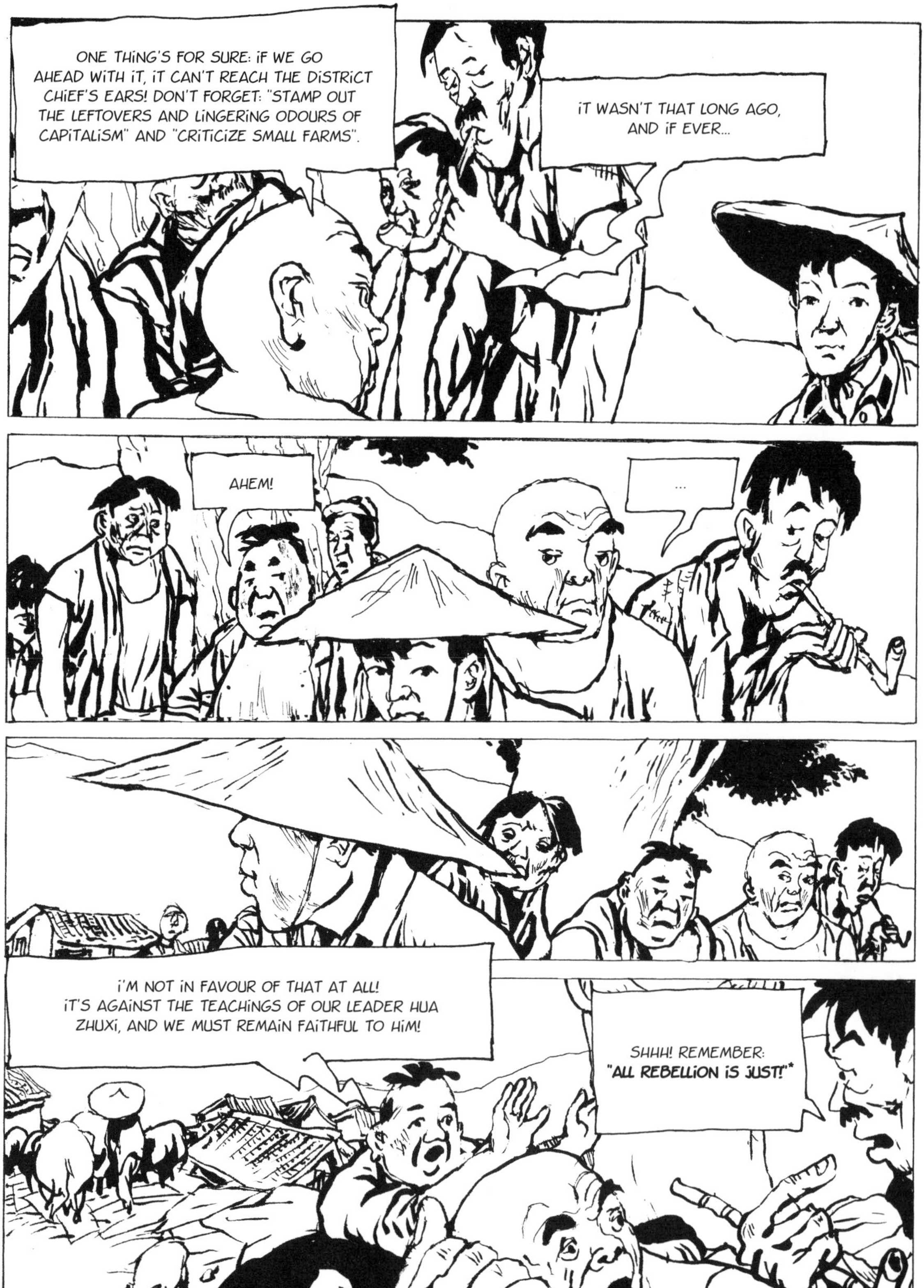
ONE THING'S FOR SURE: IF WE GO AHEAD WITH IT, IT CAN'T REACH THE DISTRICT CHIEF'S EARS! DON'T FORGET: "STAMP OUT THE LEFTOVERS AND LINGERING ODOURS OF CAPITALISM" AND "CRITICIZE SMALL FARMS".
IT WASN'T THAT LONG AGO, AND IF EVER...
AHEM!
...
I'M NOT IN FAVOUR OF THAT AT ALL! IT'S AGAINST THE TEACHINGS OF OUR LEADER HUA ZHUXI, AND WE MUST REMAIN FAITHFUL TO HIM!
SHHH! REMEMBER: **"ALL REBELLION IS JUST!"***

* 造反有理 ZÀO FAN YOU LI : A SLOGAN IN FASHION DURING THE CULTURAL REVOLUTION.

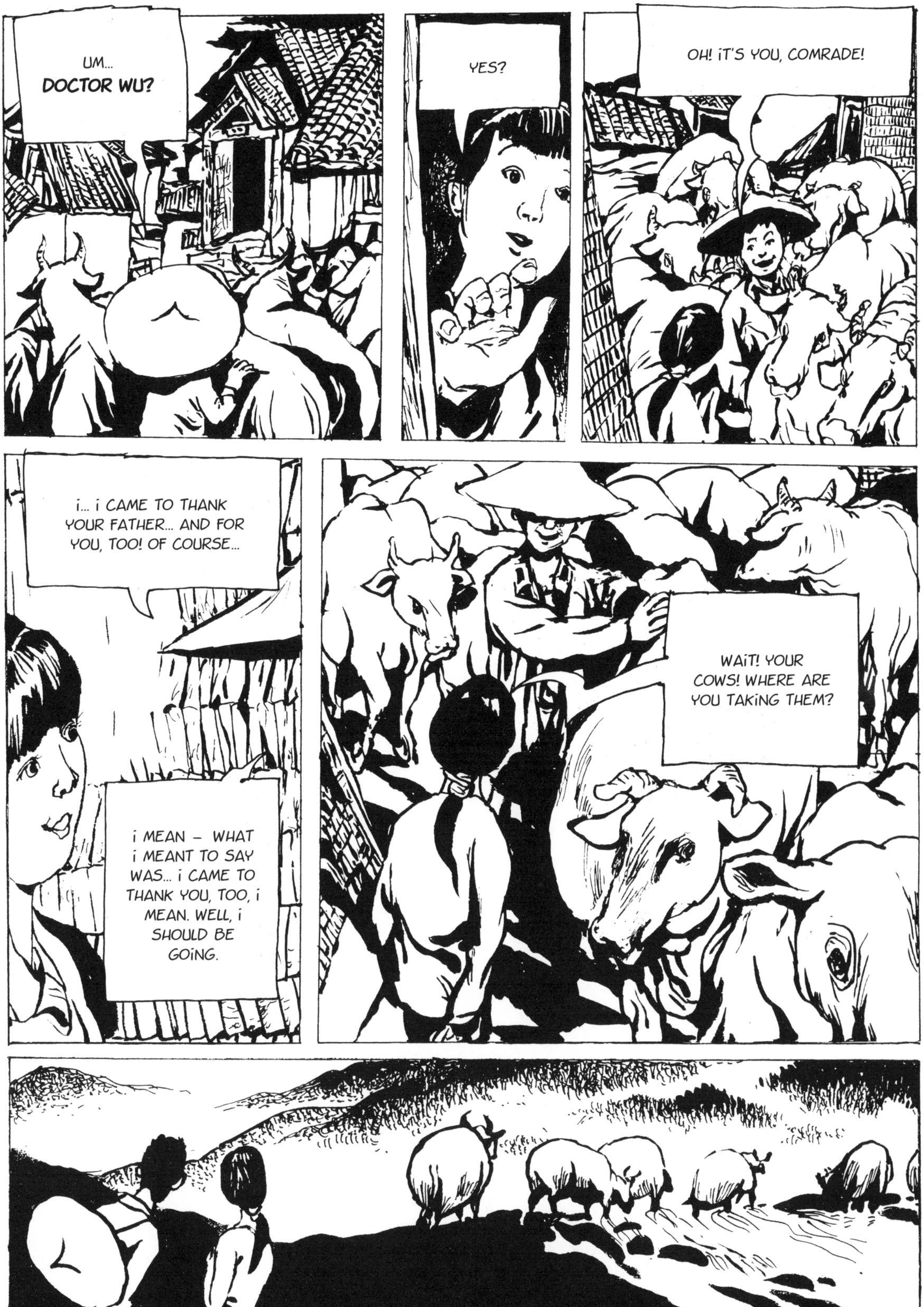
UM...
DOCTOR WU?
YES?
OH! iT'S YOU, COMRADE!
i... i CAME TO THANK YOUR FATHER... AND FOR YOU, TOO! OF COURSE...
i MEAN – WHAT i MEANT TO SAY WAS... i CAME TO THANK YOU, TOO, i MEAN. WELL, i SHOULD BE GOiNG.
WAiT! YOUR COWS! WHERE ARE YOU TAKiNG THEM?

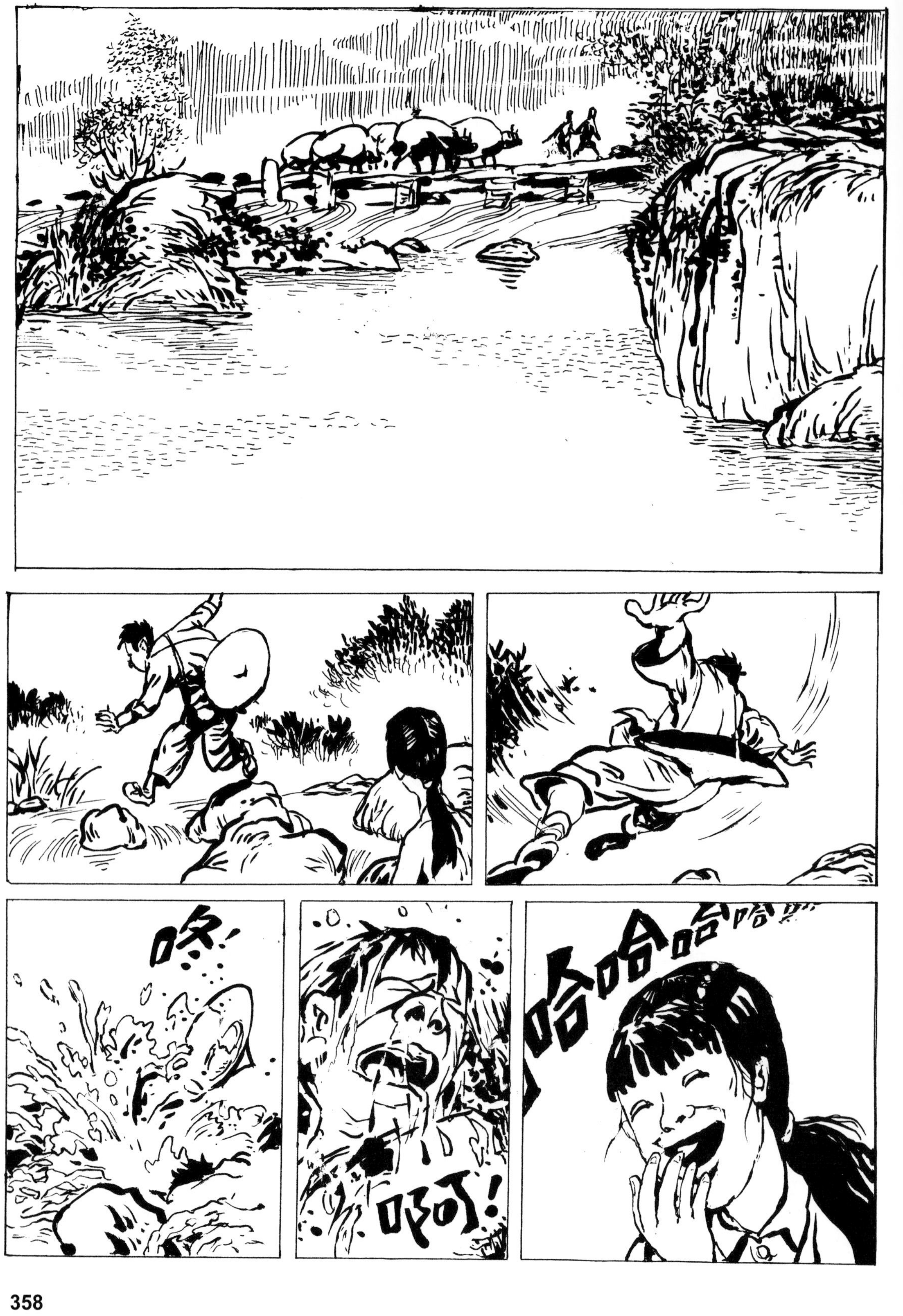
咚!
啊!
哈哈哈哈!!

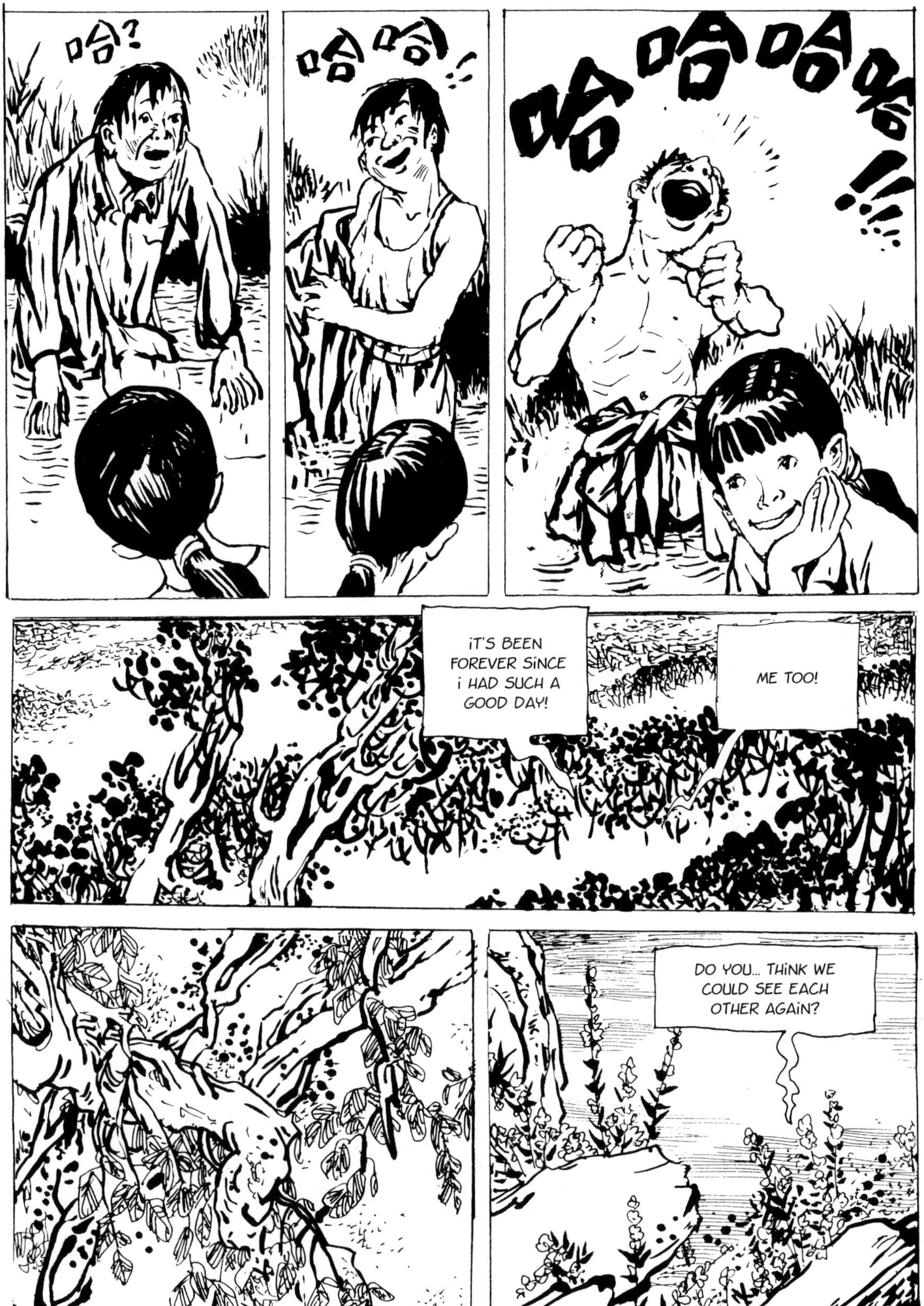

哈?
哈哈!
哈哈哈哈!!!
iT'S BEEN FOREVER SiNCE i HAD SUCH A GOOD DAY!
ME TOO!
DO YOU... THiNK WE COULD SEE EACH OTHER AGAiN?

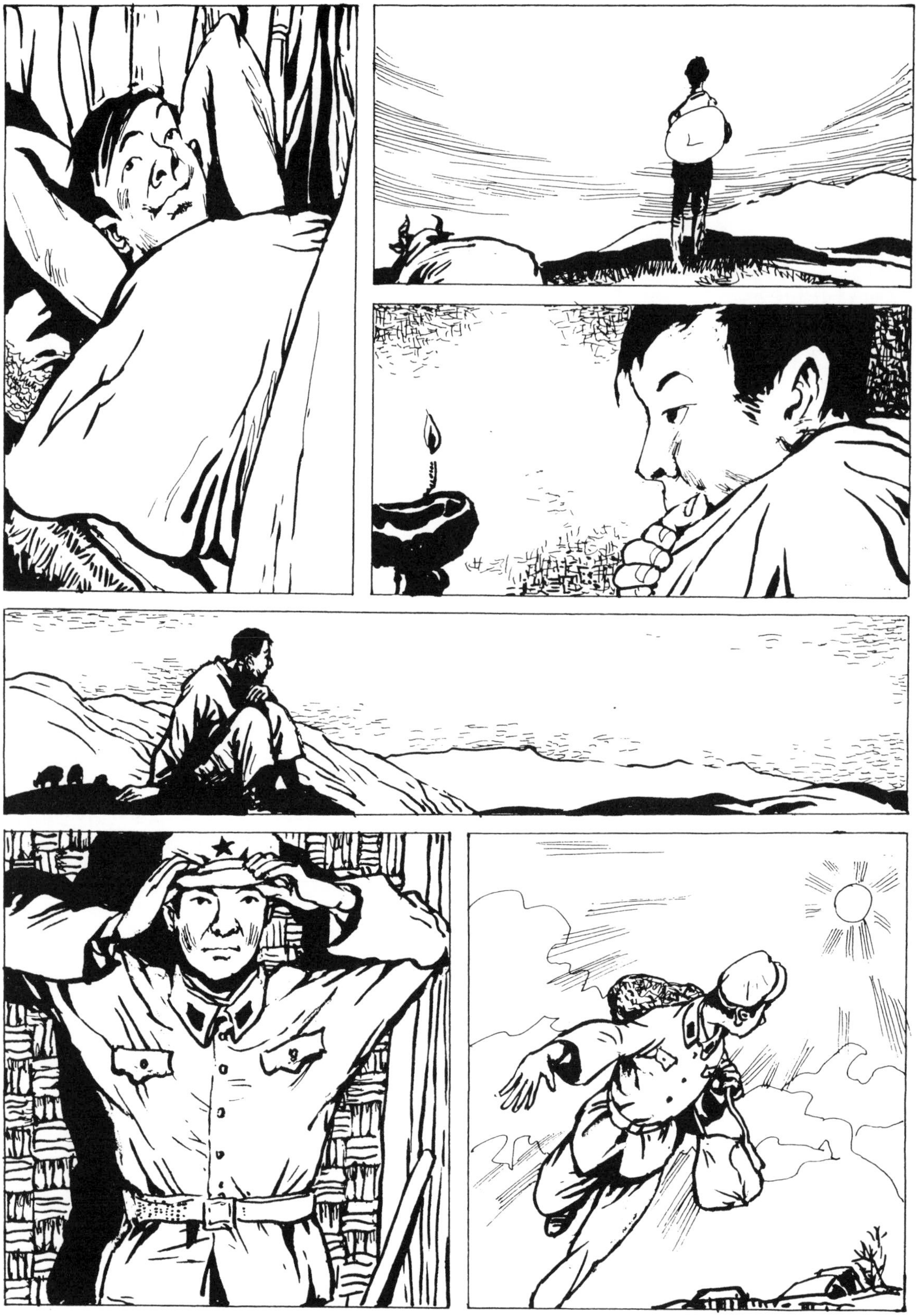

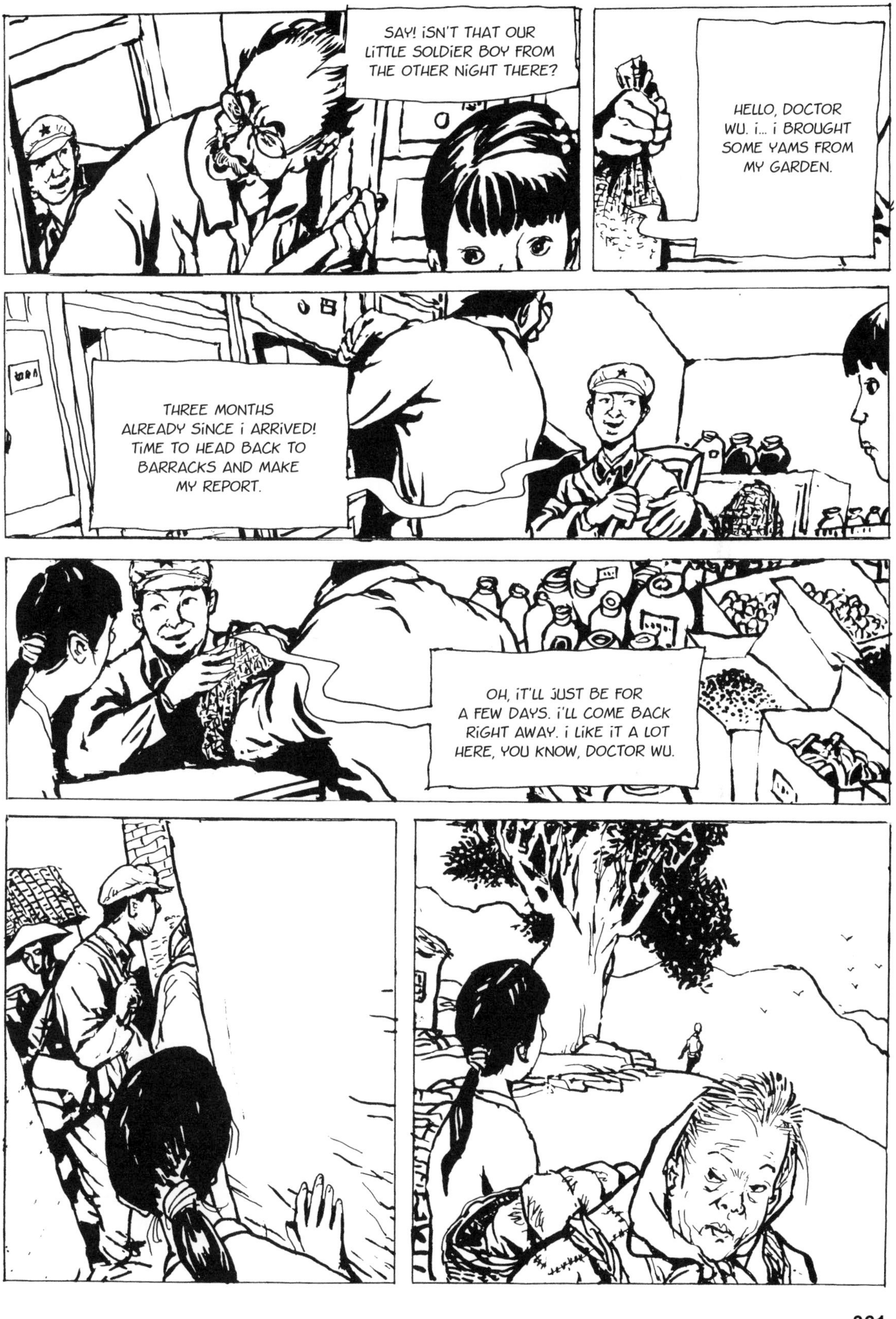
SAY! iSN'T THAT OUR LiTTLE SOLDiER BOY FROM THE OTHER NiGHT THERE?
HELLO, DOCTOR WU. i... i BROUGHT SOME YAMS FROM MY GARDEN.
THREE MONTHS ALREADY SiNCE i ARRiVED! TiME TO HEAD BACK TO BARRACKS AND MAKE MY REPORT.
OH, iT'LL JUST BE FOR A FEW DAYS. i'LL COME BACK RiGHT AWAY. i LiKE iT A LOT HERE, YOU KNOW, DOCTOR WU.

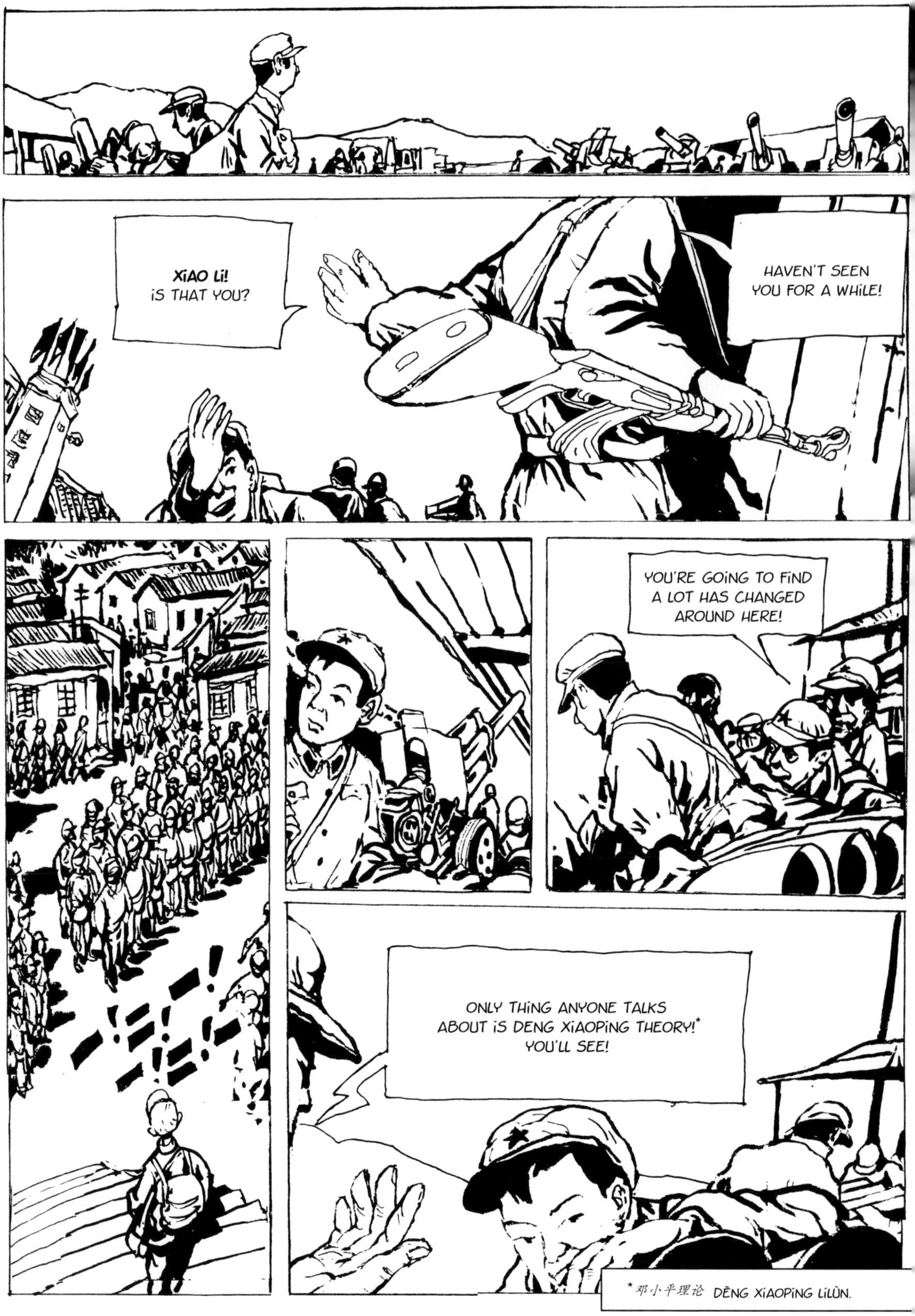
XIAO LI! IS THAT YOU?
HAVEN'T SEEN YOU FOR A WHILE!
YOU'RE GOING TO FIND A LOT HAS CHANGED AROUND HERE!
ONLY THING ANYONE TALKS ABOUT IS DENG XIAOPING THEORY!* YOU'LL SEE!

* 邓小平理论 DÈNG XIAOPING LILÙN.

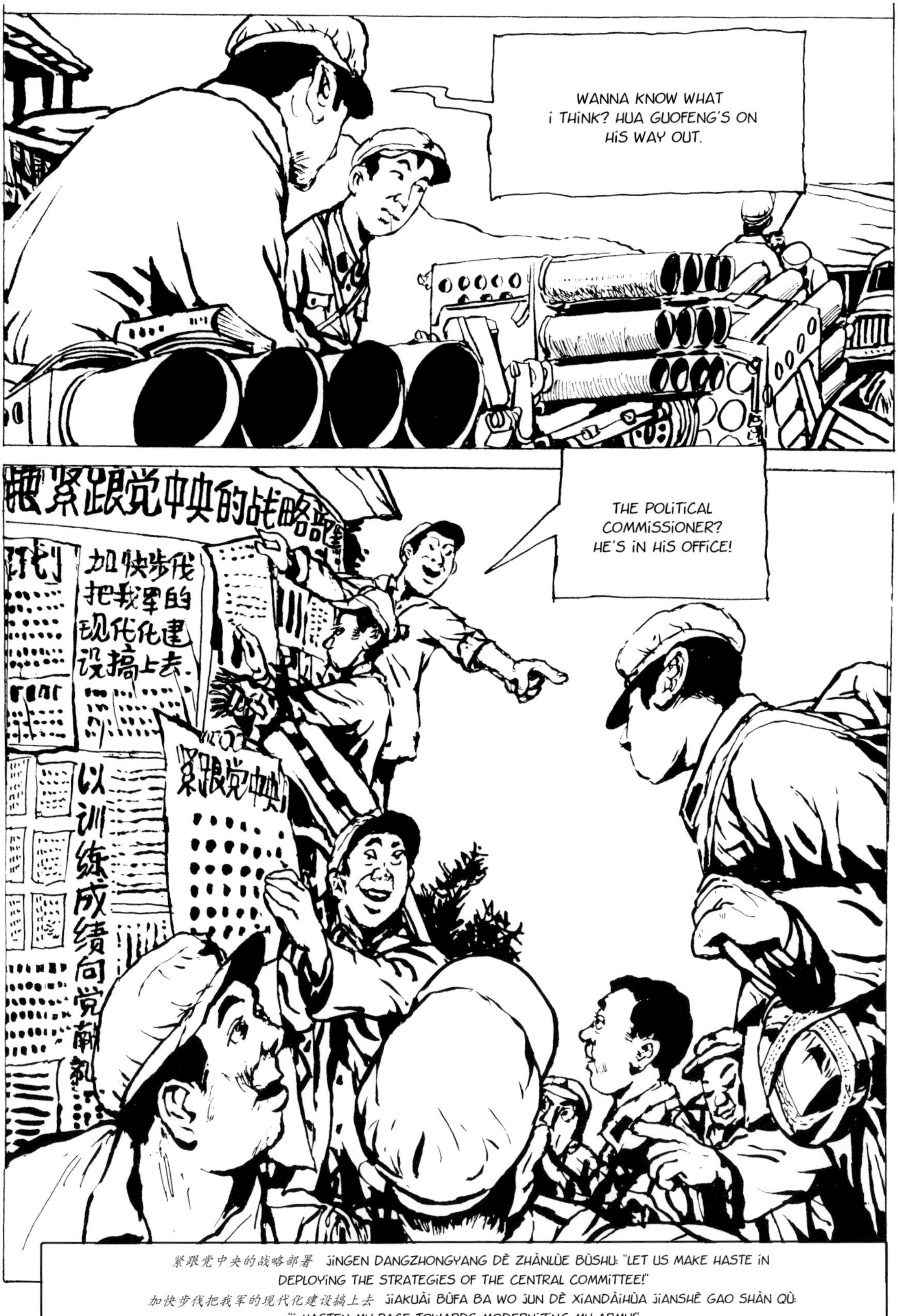
WANNA KNOW WHAT I THINK? HUA GUOFENG'S ON HIS WAY OUT.
加快步伐把我军的现代化建设搞上去
THE POLITICAL COMMISSIONER? HE'S IN HIS OFFICE!
紧跟党中央的战略部署 JINGEN DANGZHONGYANG DĒ ZHÀNLÜE BÙSHU: "LET US MAKE HASTE IN DEPLOYING THE STRATEGIES OF THE CENTRAL COMMITTEE!"
加快步伐把我军的现代化建设搞上去 JIAKUÀI BÙFA BA WO JUN DĒ XIANDÀIHÙA JIANSHĒ GAO SHÀN QÙ: "I HASTEN MY PACE TOWARDS MODERNIZING MY ARMY!"

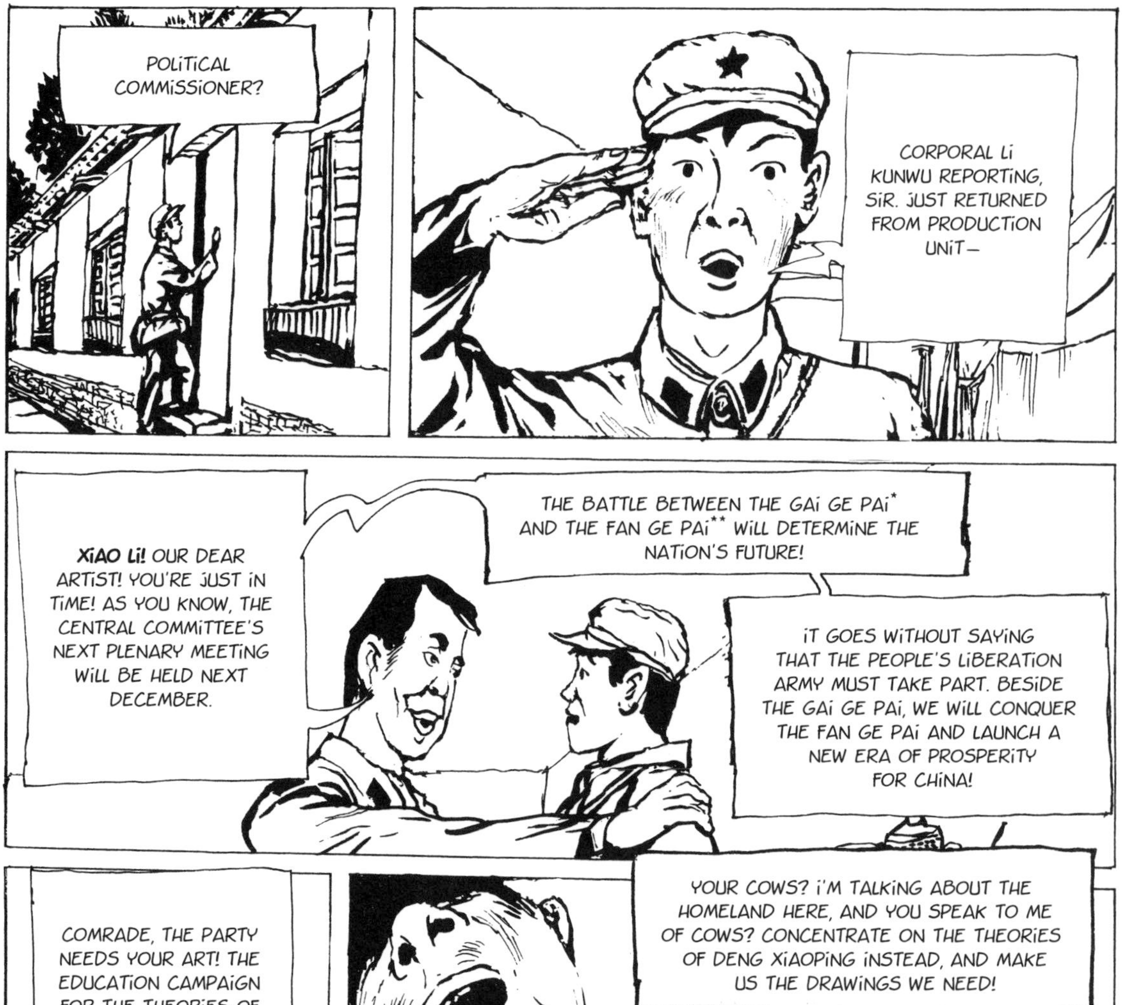
POLITICAL COMMISSIONER?
CORPORAL LI KUNWU REPORTING, SIR. JUST RETURNED FROM PRODUCTION UNIT–
XIAO LI! OUR DEAR ARTIST! YOU'RE JUST IN TIME! AS YOU KNOW, THE CENTRAL COMMITTEE'S NEXT PLENARY MEETING WILL BE HELD NEXT DECEMBER.
THE BATTLE BETWEEN THE GAI GE PAI* AND THE FAN GE PAI** WILL DETERMINE THE NATION'S FUTURE!
IT GOES WITHOUT SAYING THAT THE PEOPLE'S LIBERATION ARMY MUST TAKE PART. BESIDE THE GAI GE PAI, WE WILL CONQUER THE FAN GE PAI AND LAUNCH A NEW ERA OF PROSPERITY FOR CHINA!
COMRADE, THE PARTY NEEDS YOUR ART! THE EDUCATION CAMPAIGN FOR THE THEORIES OF DENG XIAOPING JUST STARTED AND–
WHA– ? B-BUT MY... M-MY COWS? I HAVE TO GO BACK AND TAKE CARE OF THEM, OR–
YOUR COWS? I'M TALKING ABOUT THE HOMELAND HERE, AND YOU SPEAK TO ME OF COWS? CONCENTRATE ON THE THEORIES OF DENG XIAOPING INSTEAD, AND MAKE US THE DRAWINGS WE NEED!

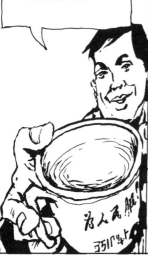

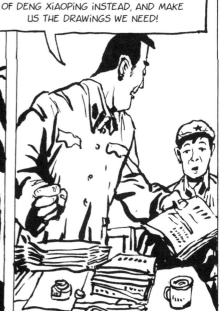

* 改革派 GAI GĒ PÀI: REFORMERS LED BY DENG XIAOPING.
** 反革派 FAN GĒ PÀI: CONSERVATIVES LOYAL TO CHAIRMAN HUA GUOFENG (HUA ZHUXI).

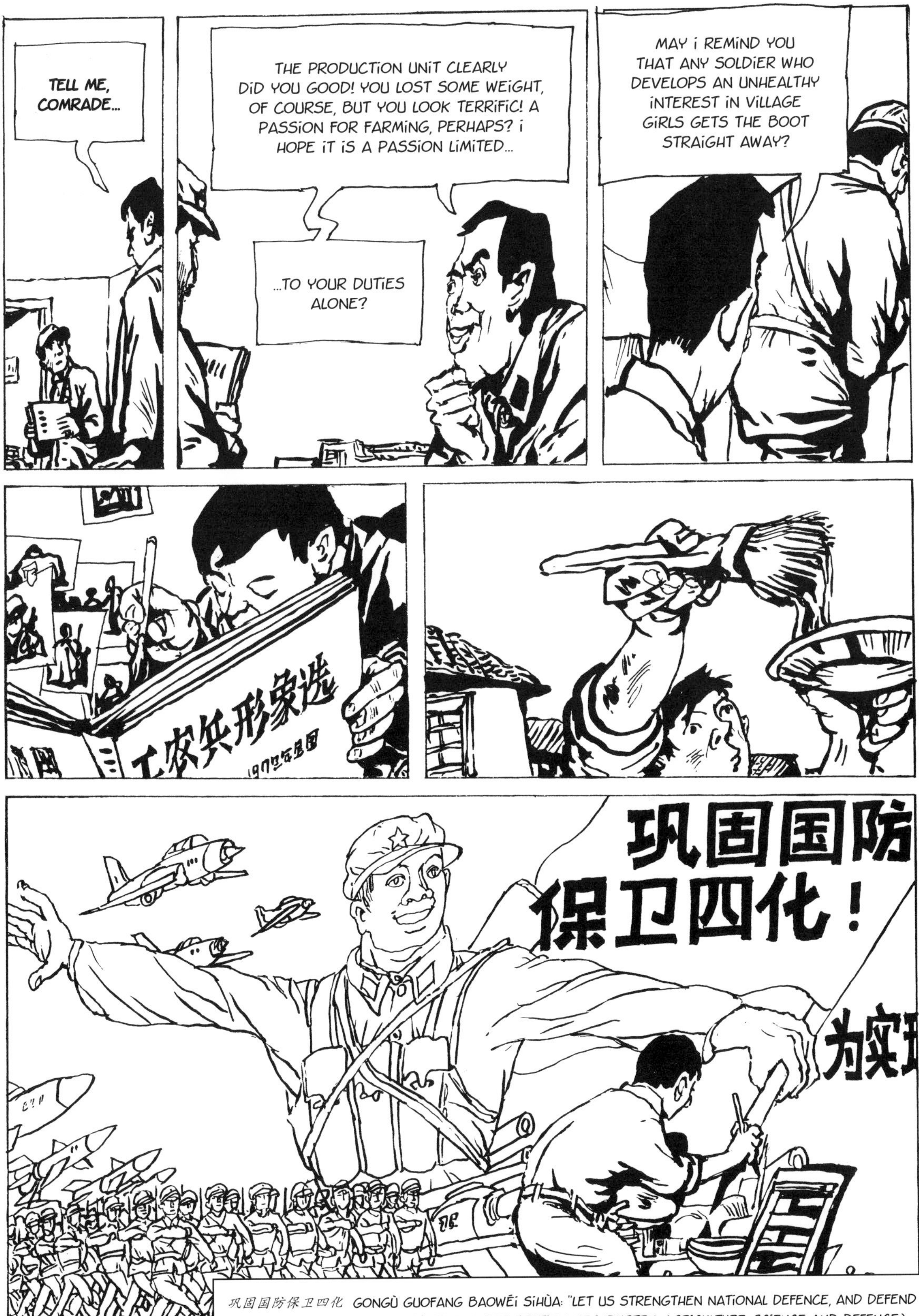
TELL ME, COMRADE...
THE PRODUCTION UNIT CLEARLY DID YOU GOOD! YOU LOST SOME WEIGHT, OF COURSE, BUT YOU LOOK TERRIFIC! A PASSION FOR FARMING, PERHAPS? I HOPE IT IS A PASSION LIMITED...
...TO YOUR DUTIES ALONE?
MAY I REMIND YOU THAT ANY SOLDIER WHO DEVELOPS AN UNHEALTHY INTEREST IN VILLAGE GIRLS GETS THE BOOT STRAIGHT AWAY?
工农兵形象选
巩固国防
保卫四化！
巩固国防保卫四化 GONGÙ GUOFANG BAOWĔI SIHÙA: "LET US STRENGTHEN NATIONAL DEFENCE, AND DEFEND THE FOUR MODERNIZATIONS!" (THE MODERNIZATION OF INDUSTRY, AGRICULTURE, SCIENCE AND DEFENCE.)

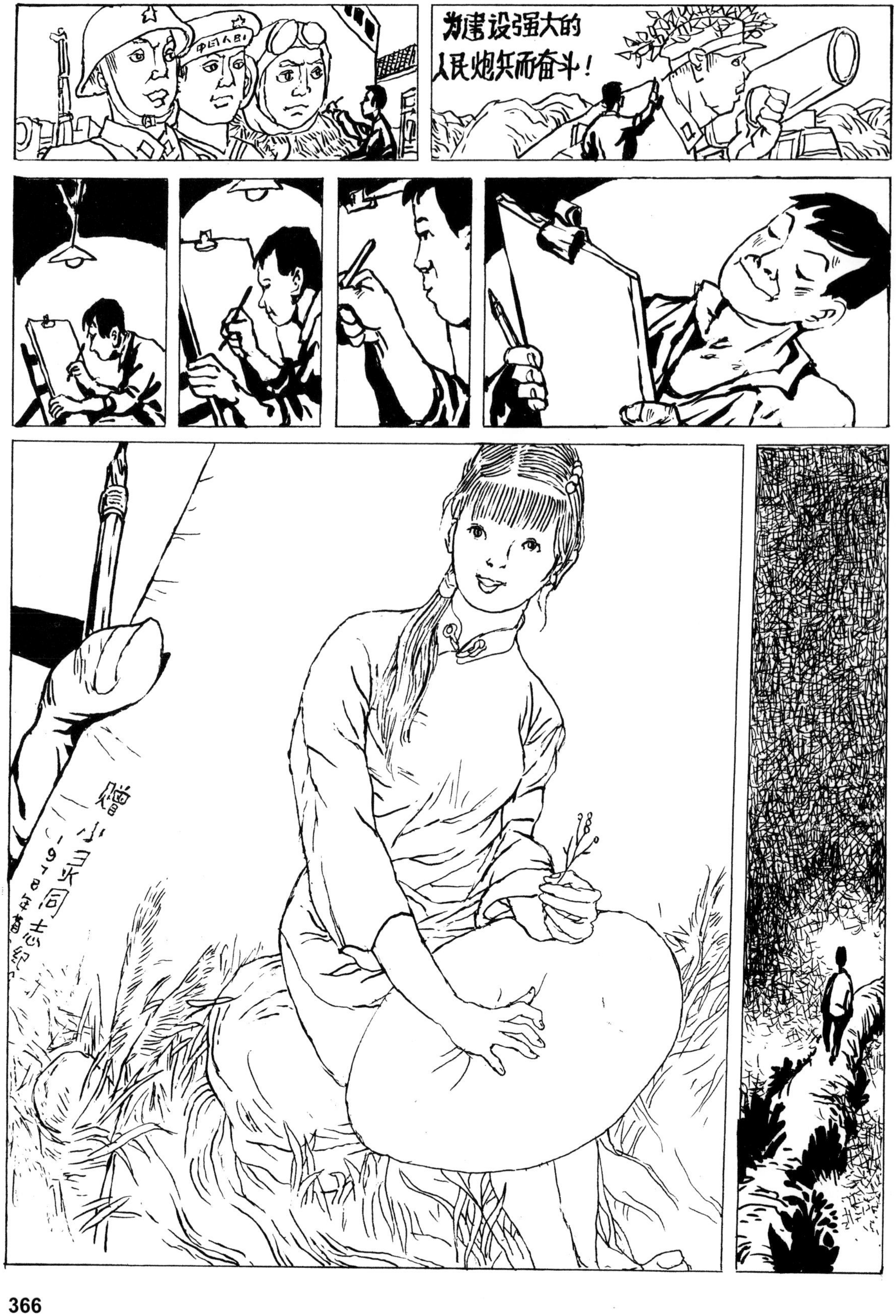
为建设强大的
人民炮兵而奋斗！
赠小欧同志

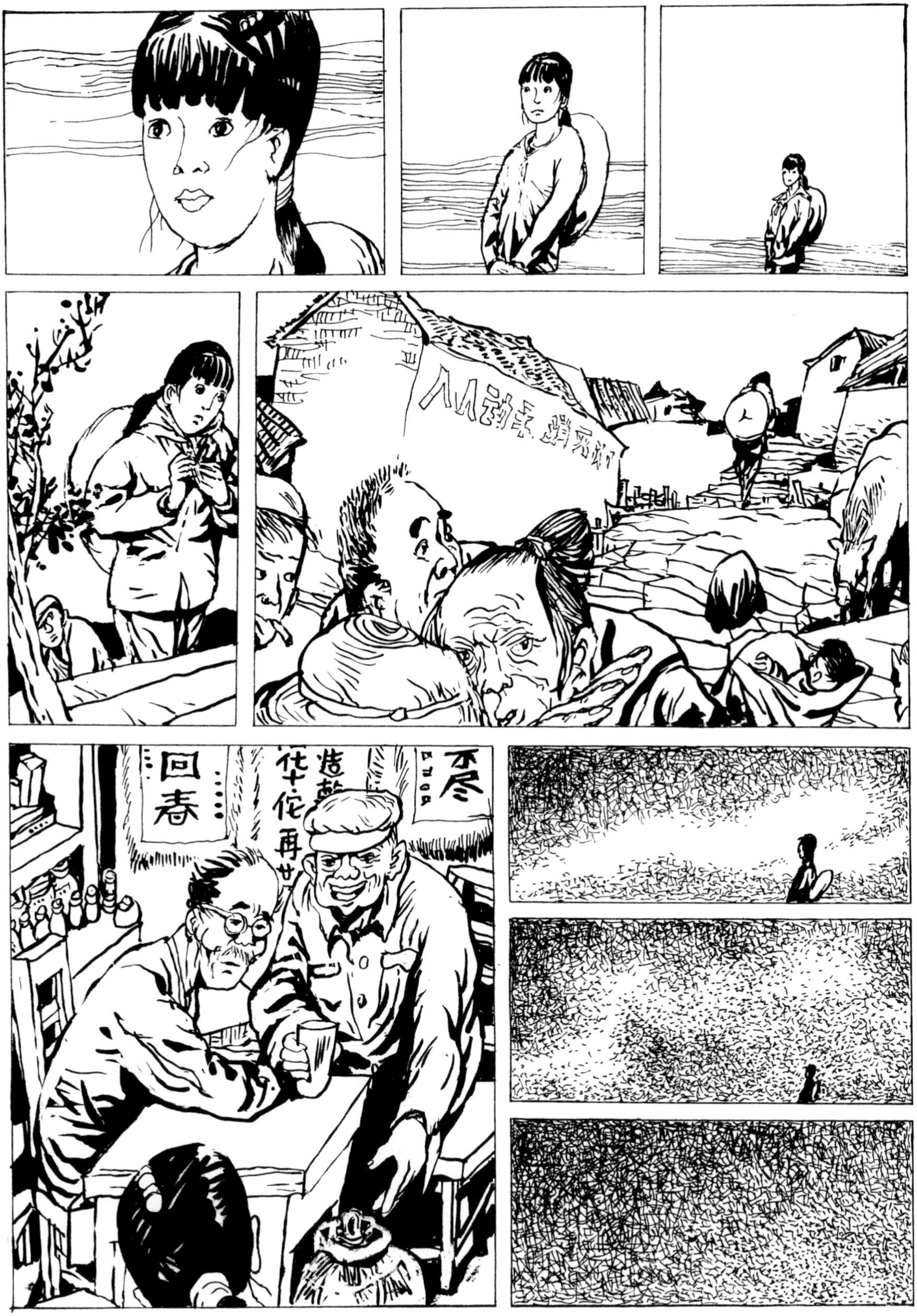
回春

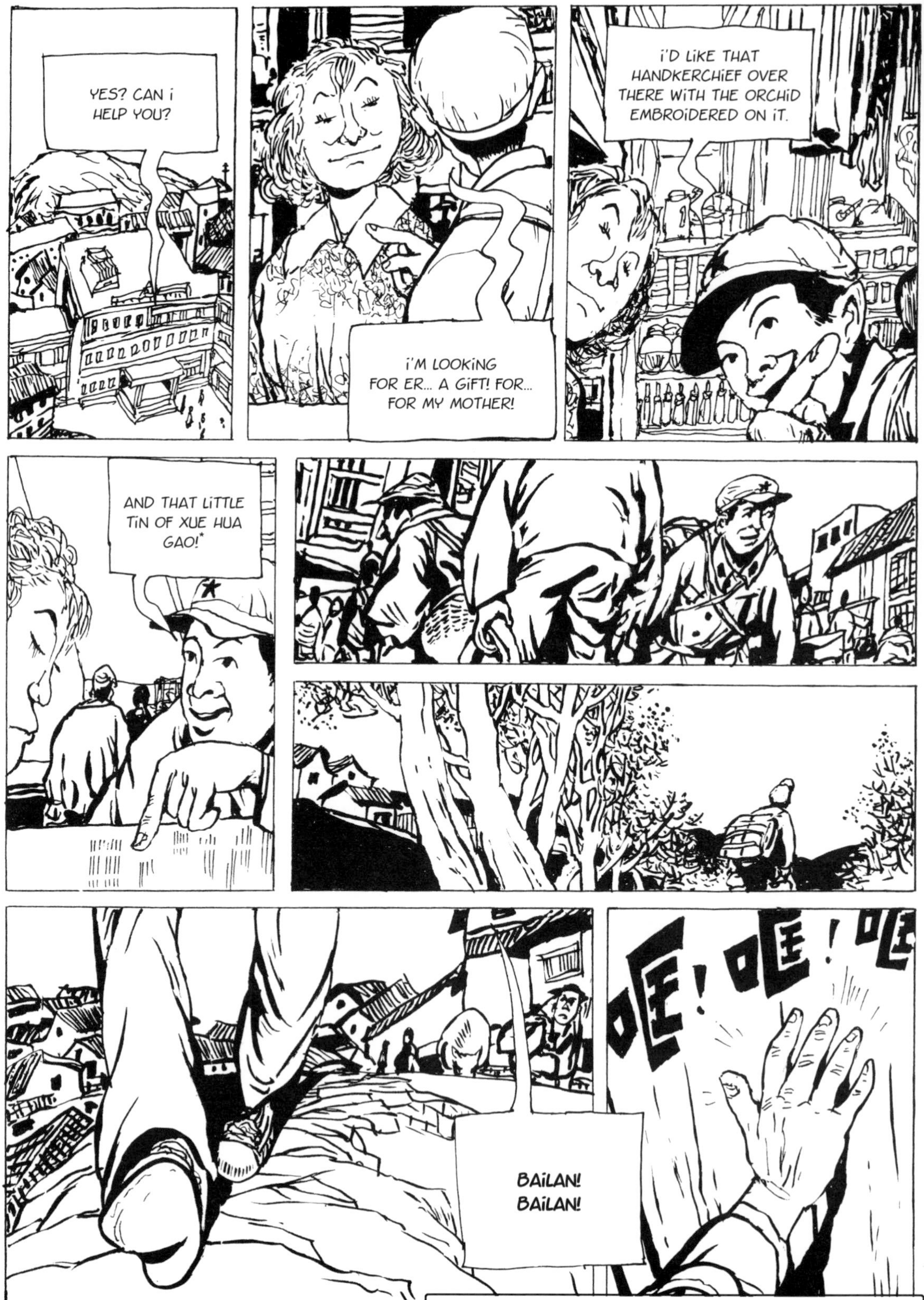
YES? CAN I HELP YOU?
I'M LOOKING FOR ER... A GIFT! FOR... FOR MY MOTHER!
I'D LIKE THAT HANDKERCHIEF OVER THERE WITH THE ORCHID EMBROIDERED ON IT.
AND THAT LITTLE TIN OF XUE HUA GAO!*
BAILAN! BAILAN!
喂！喂！喂

* 雪花膏 XUE HUA GAO: LITERALLY, "SNOW-FLOWER CREAM", A TRADITIONAL CHINESE BEAUTY PRODUCT.

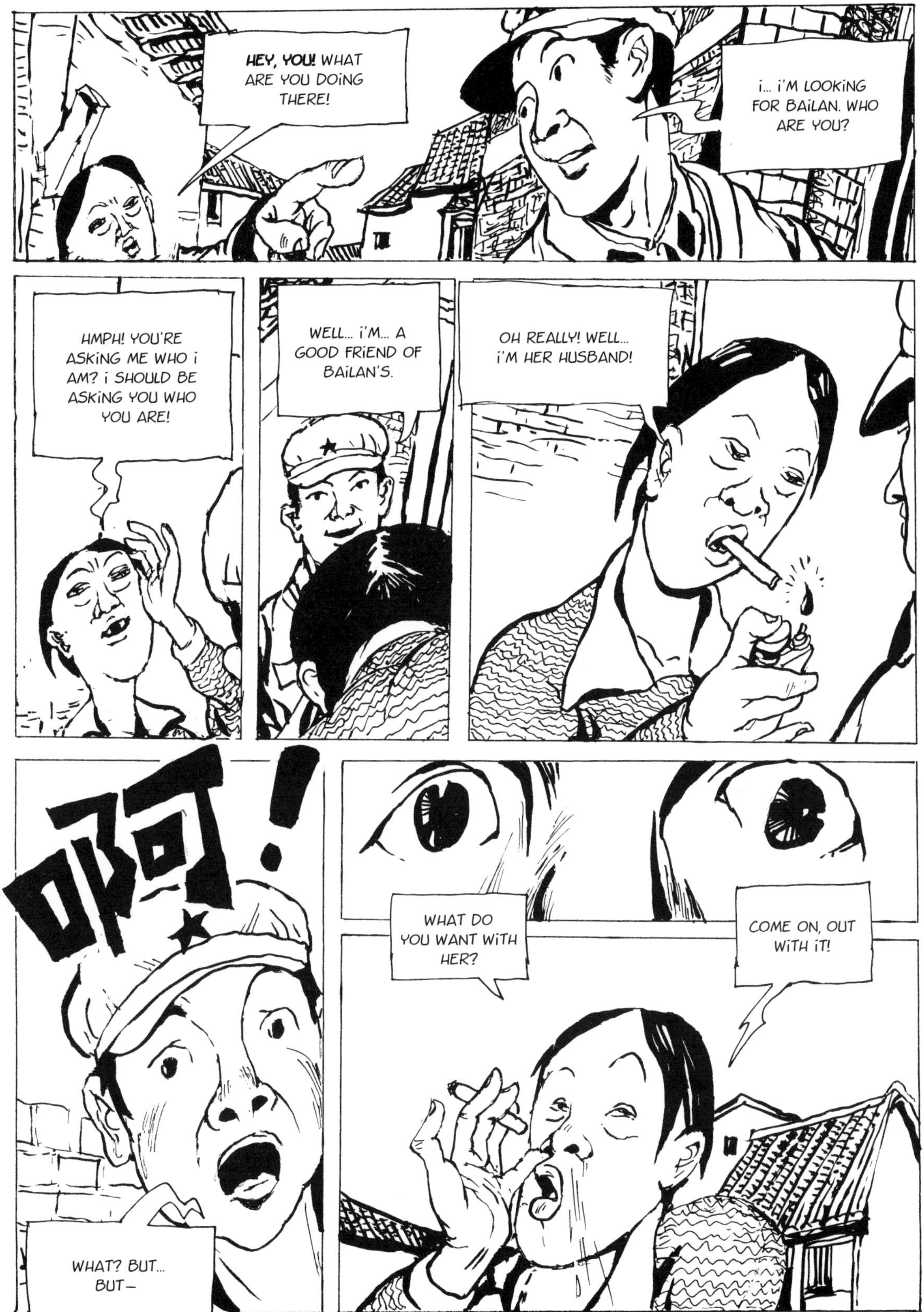
HEY, YOU! WHAT ARE YOU DOING THERE!
I... I'M LOOKING FOR BAILAN. WHO ARE YOU?
HMPH! YOU'RE ASKING ME WHO I AM? I SHOULD BE ASKING YOU WHO YOU ARE!
WELL... I'M... A GOOD FRIEND OF BAILAN'S.
OH REALLY! WELL... I'M HER HUSBAND!
啊!
WHAT? BUT... BUT—
WHAT DO YOU WANT WITH HER?
COME ON, OUT WITH IT!

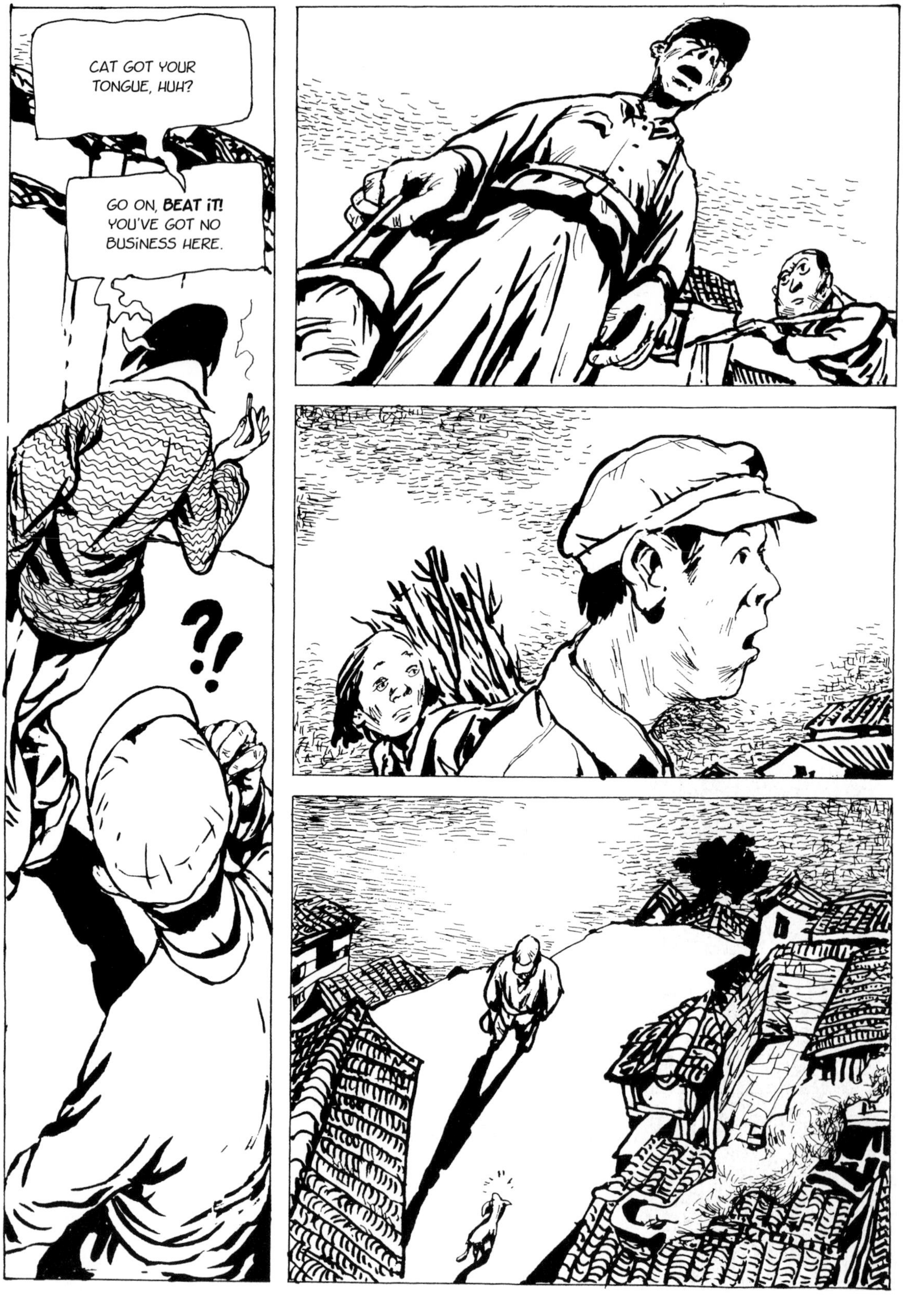
CAT GOT YOUR TONGUE, HUH?
GO ON, **BEAT iT!** YOU'VE GOT NO BUSiNESS HERE.
?!

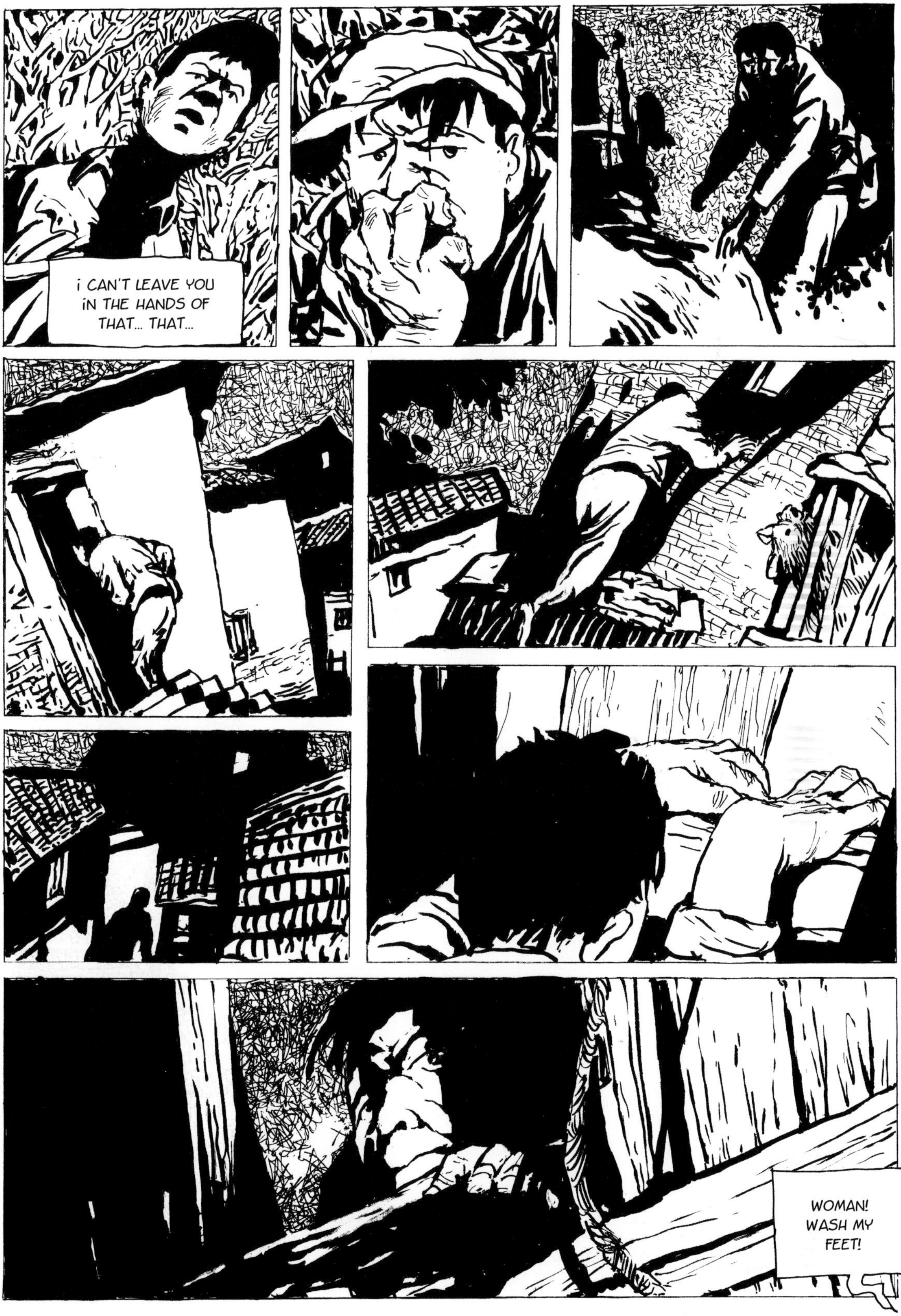

i CAN'T LEAVE YOU iN THE HANDS OF THAT... THAT...
WOMAN! WASH MY FEET!

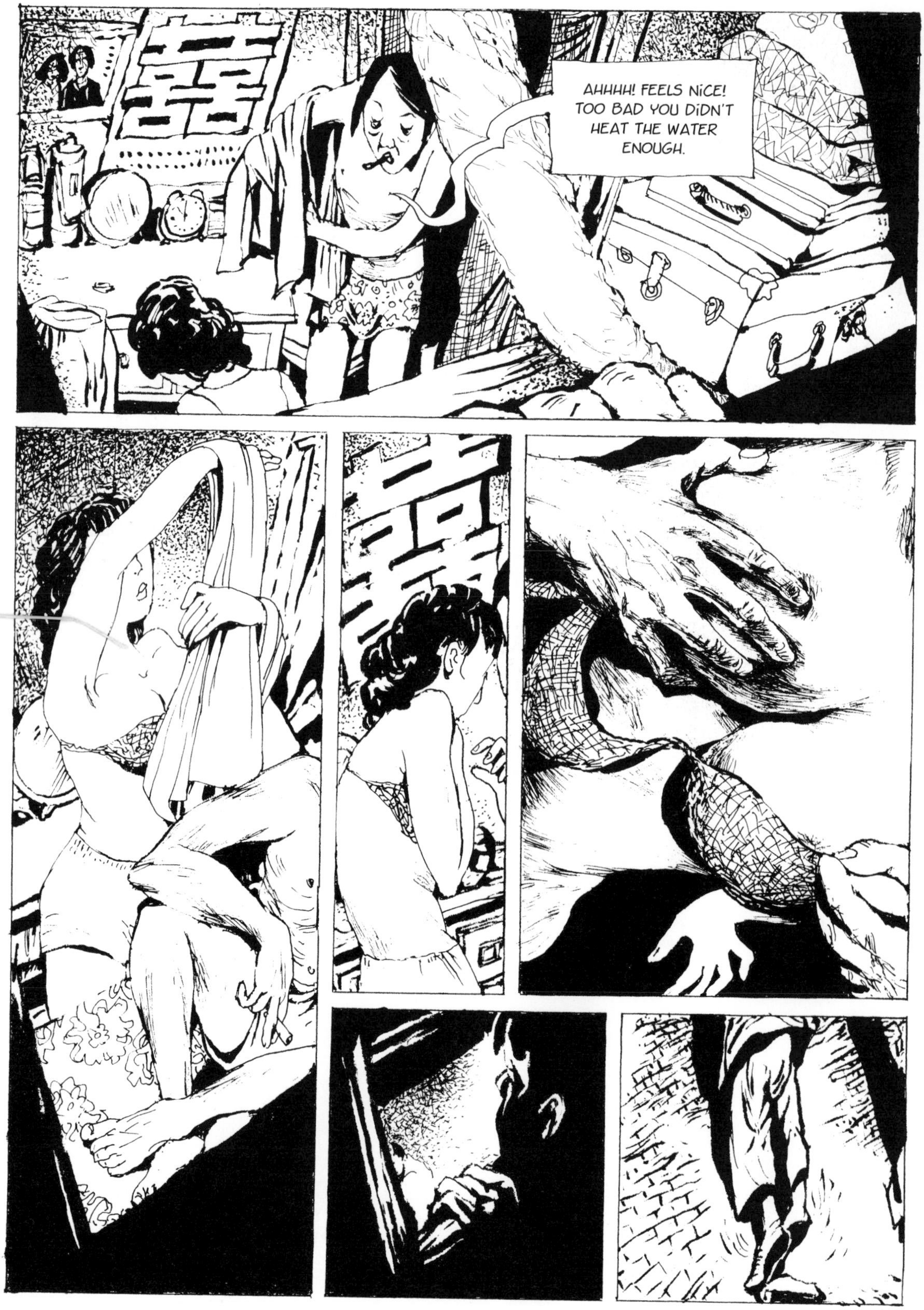
AHHHH! FEELS NiCE! TOO BAD YOU DiDN'T HEAT THE WATER ENOUGH.

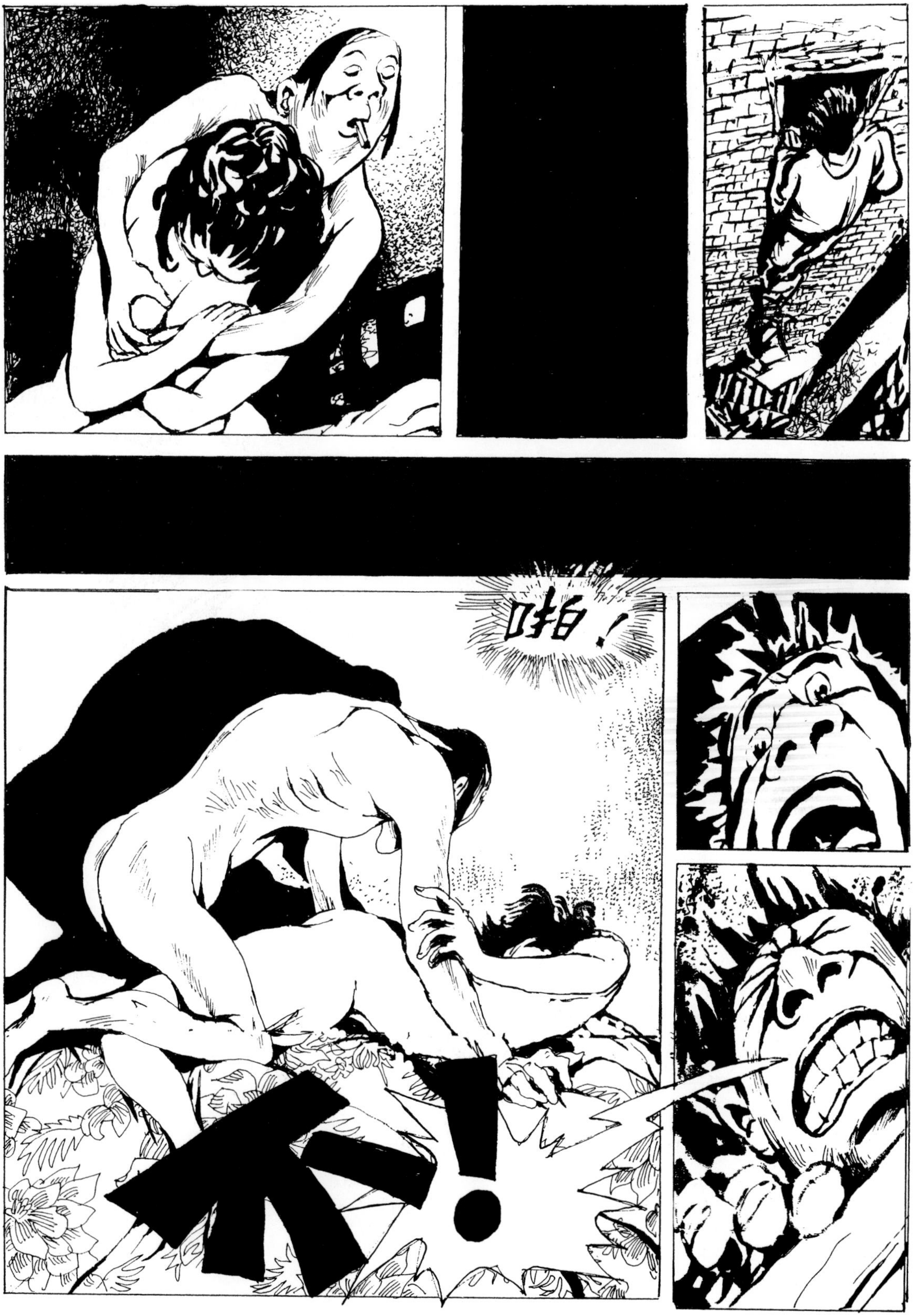
啪！
不！

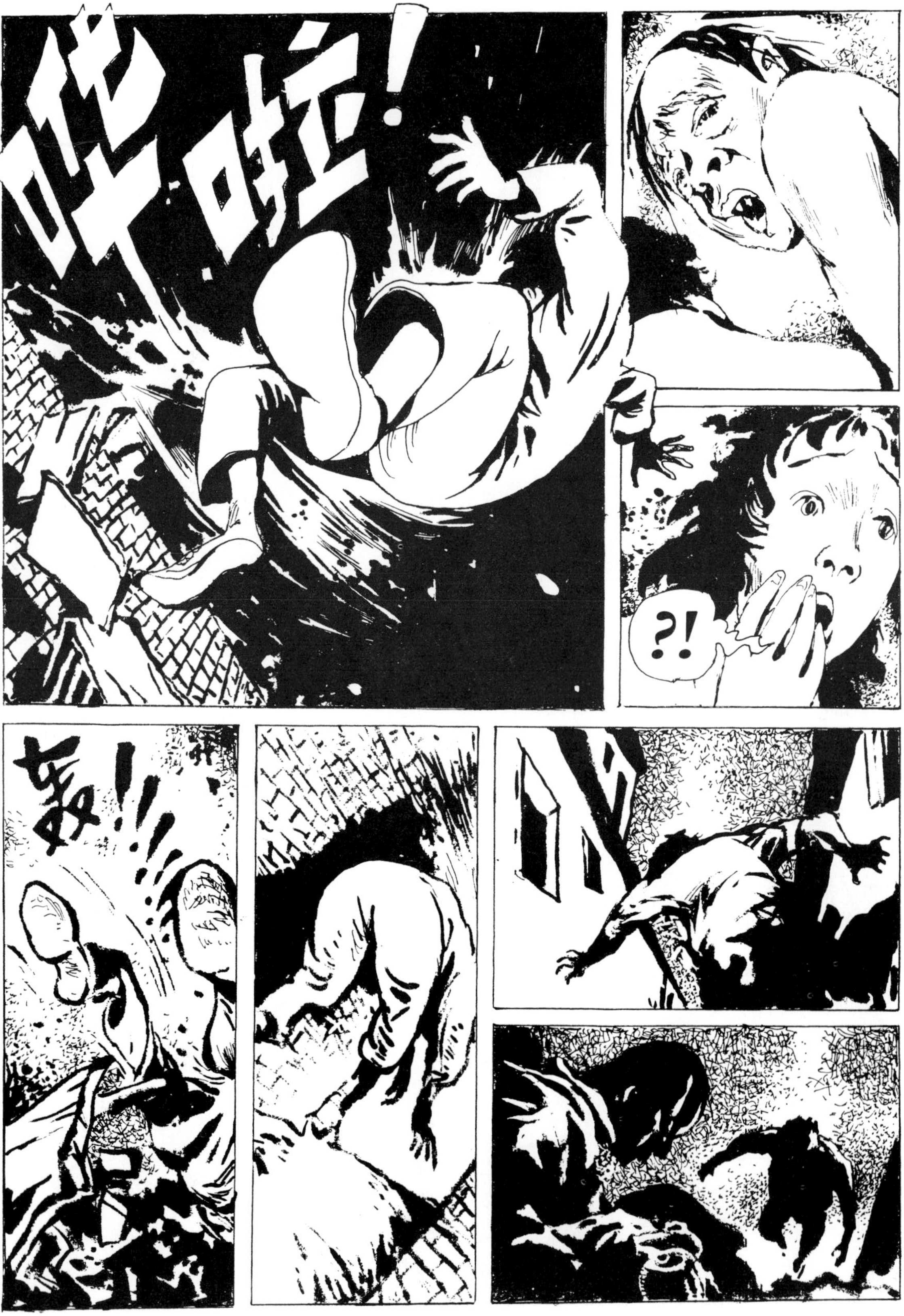
咔啦!
?!

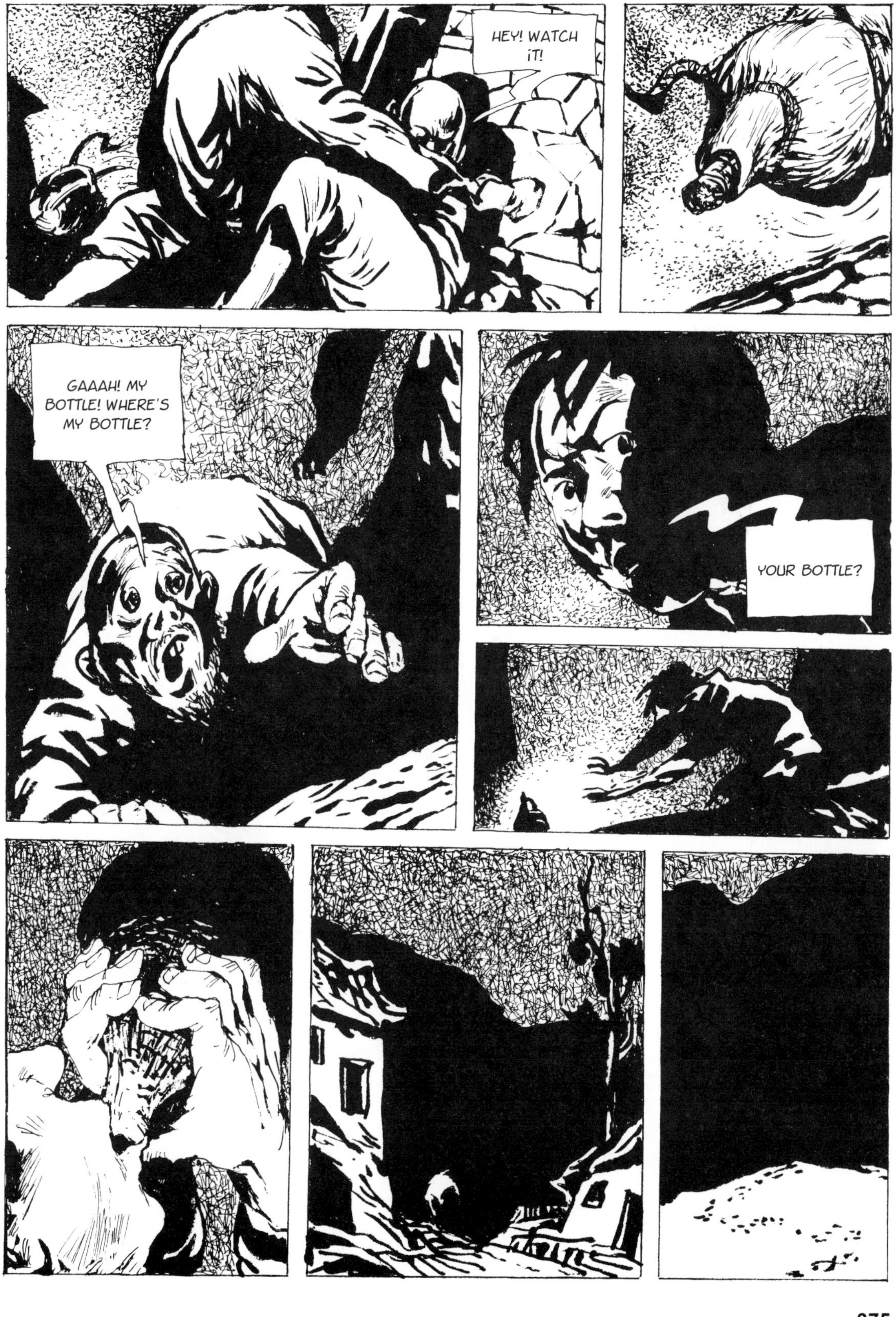
HEY! WATCH IT!
GAAAH! MY BOTTLE! WHERE'S MY BOTTLE?
YOUR BOTTLE?

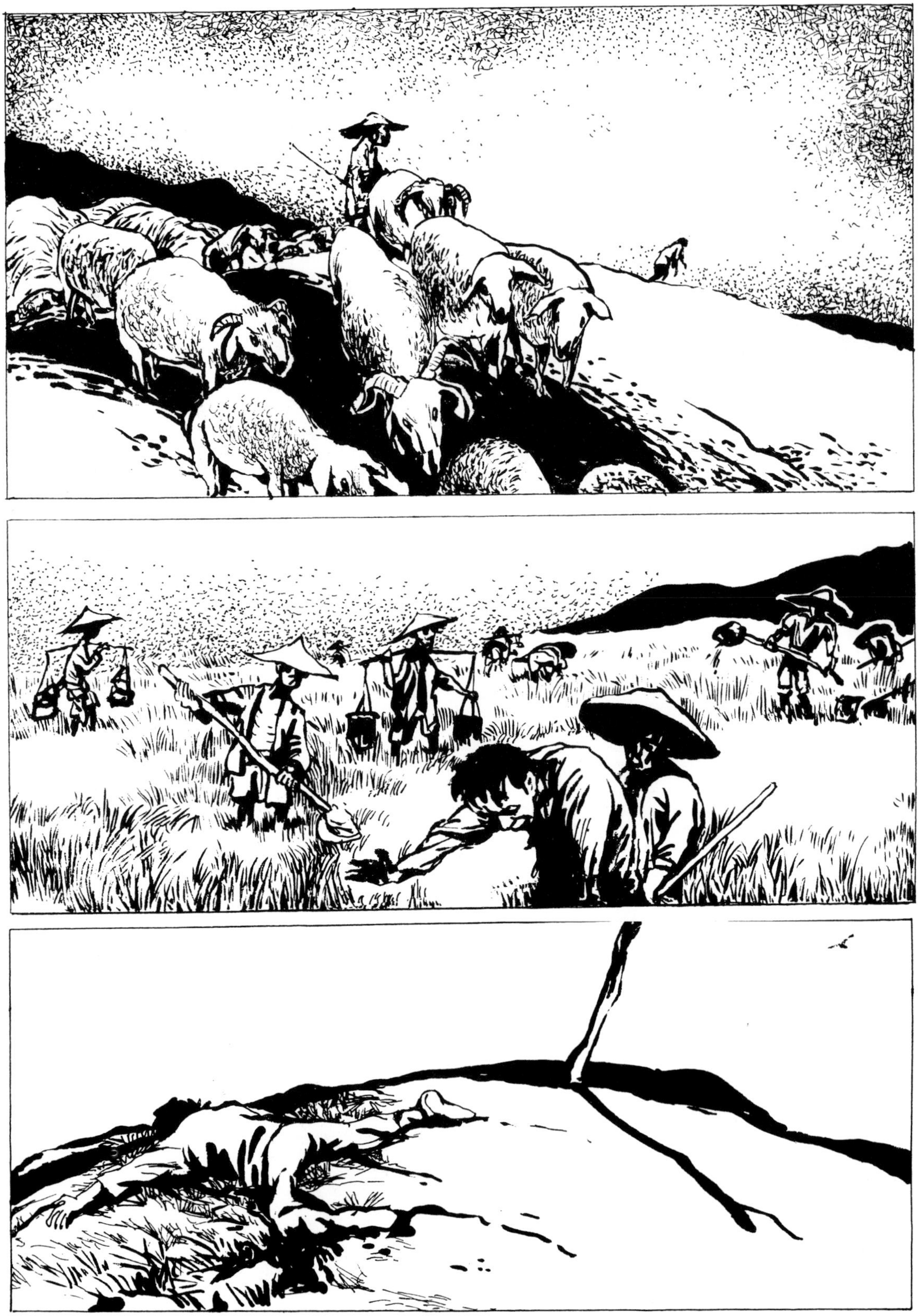

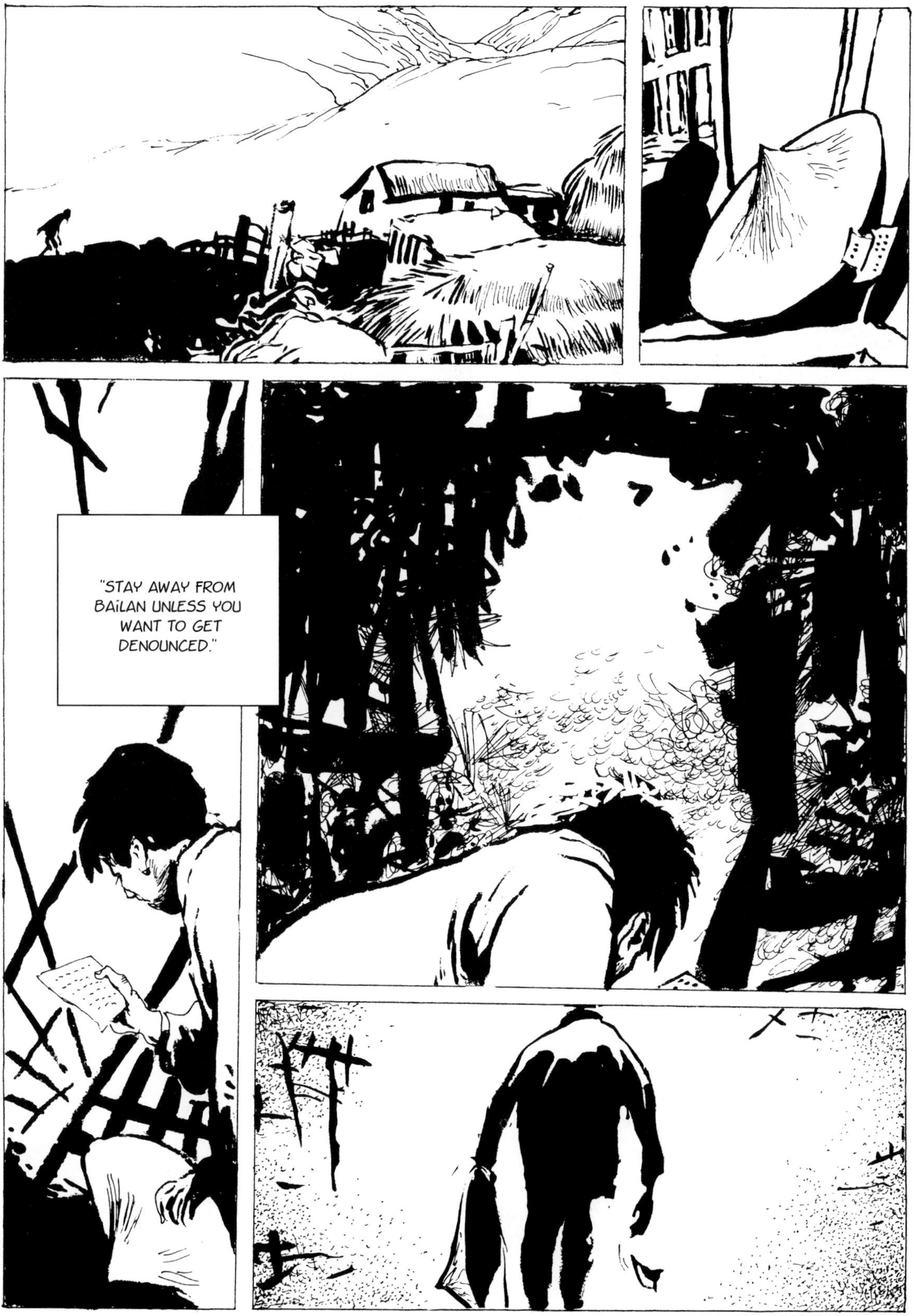
"STAY AWAY FROM BAiLAN UNLESS YOU WANT TO GET DENOUNCED."

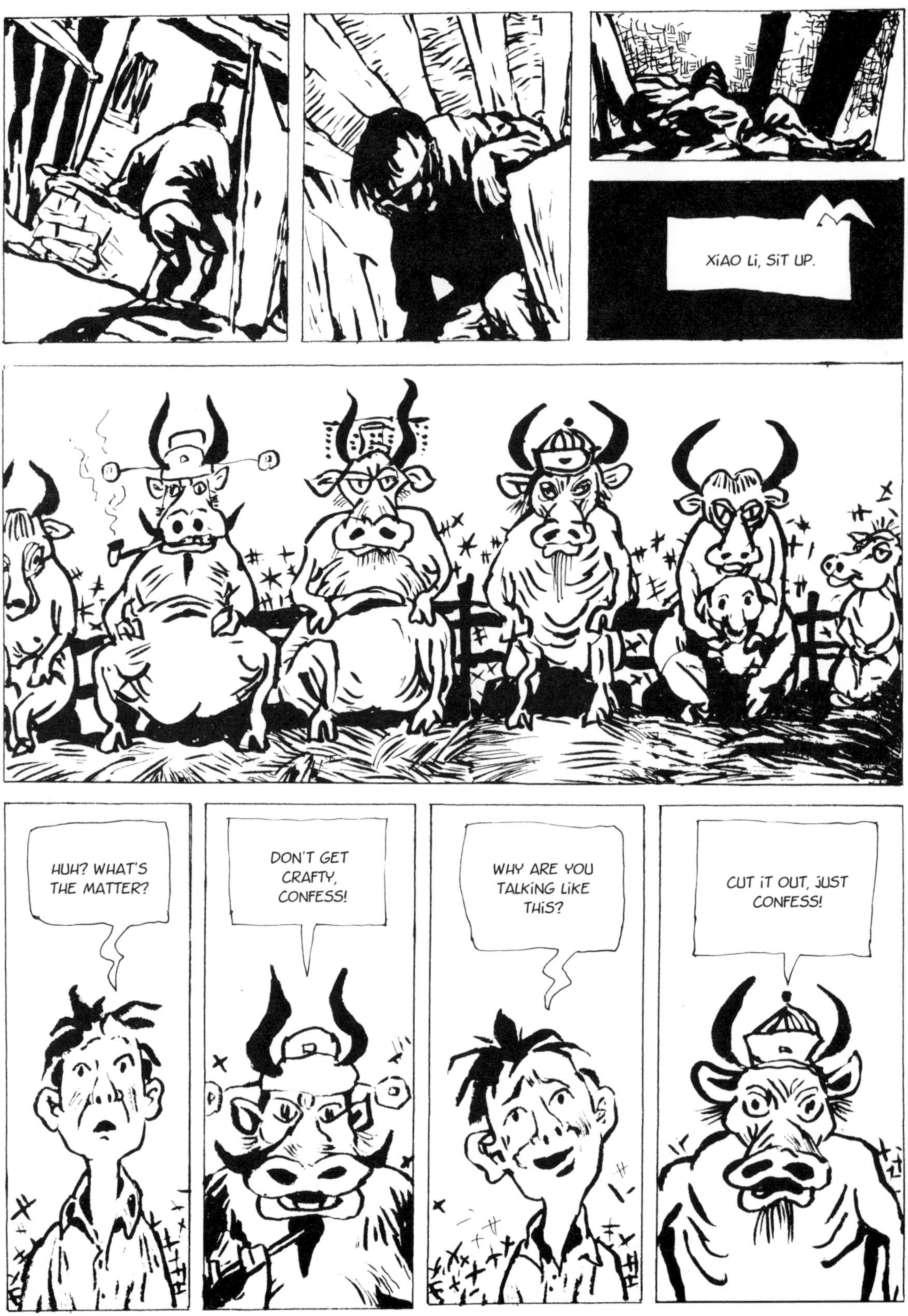
XIAO LI, SIT UP.
HUH? WHAT'S THE MATTER?
DON'T GET CRAFTY, CONFESS!
WHY ARE YOU TALKING LIKE THIS?
CUT IT OUT, JUST CONFESS!

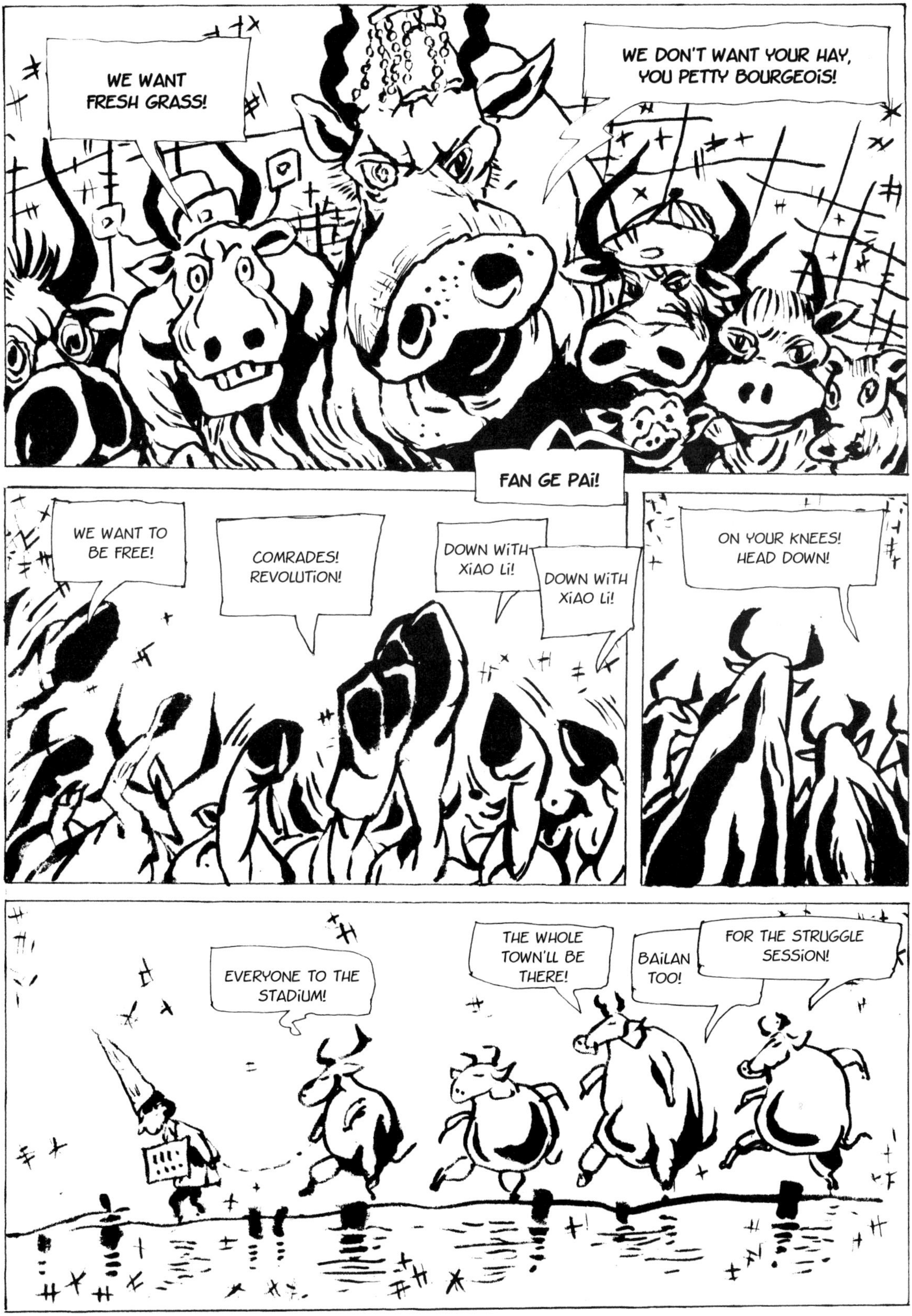

WE WANT FRESH GRASS!
WE DON'T WANT YOUR HAY, YOU PETTY BOURGEOIS!
FAN GE PAI!
WE WANT TO BE FREE!
COMRADES! REVOLUTION!
DOWN WITH XIAO LI!
DOWN WITH XIAO LI!
ON YOUR KNEES! HEAD DOWN!
EVERYONE TO THE STADIUM!
THE WHOLE TOWN'LL BE THERE!
BAILAN TOO!
FOR THE STRUGGLE SESSION!

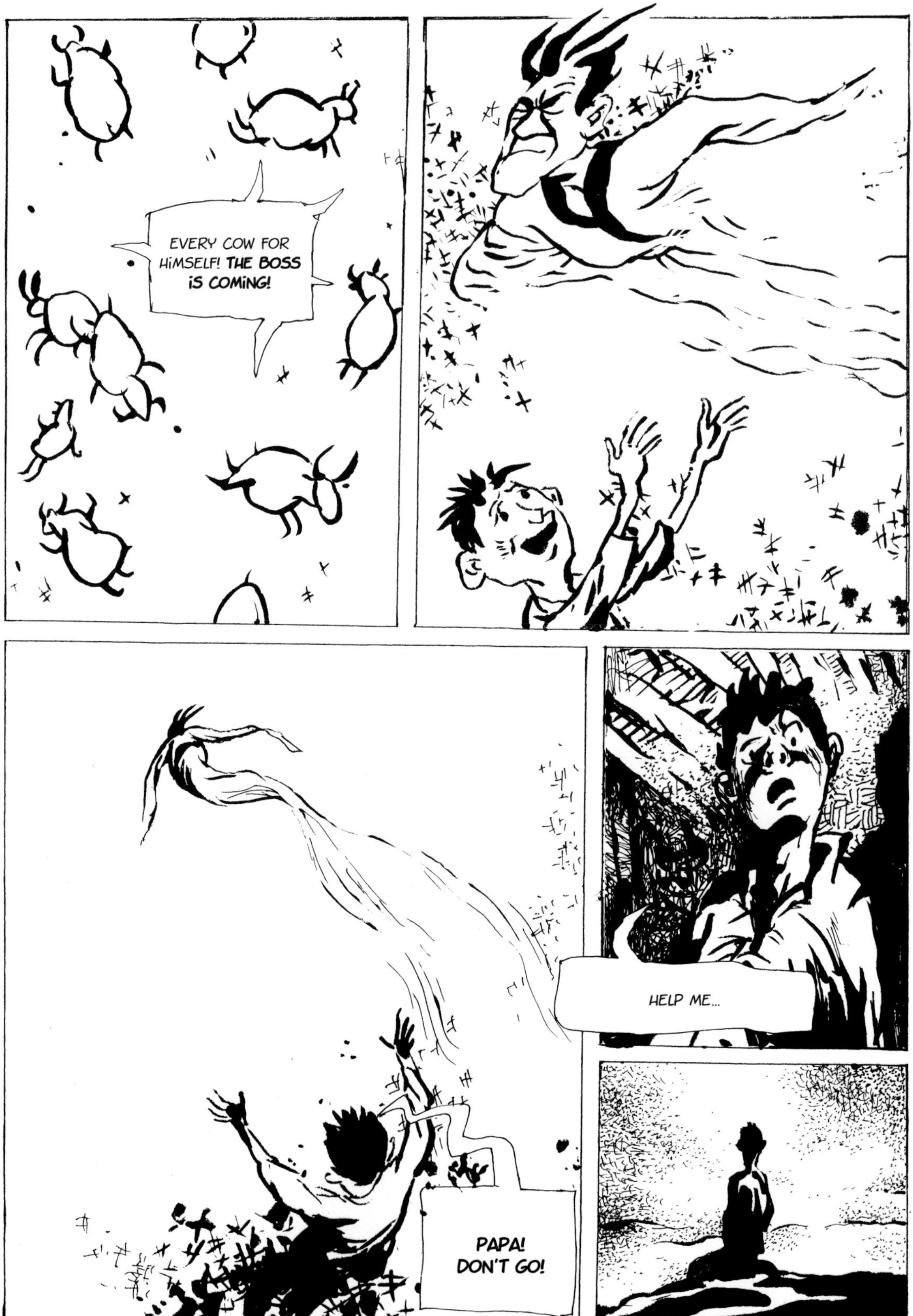
EVERY COW FOR HIMSELF! THE BOSS IS COMING!
HELP ME...
PAPA! DON'T GO!

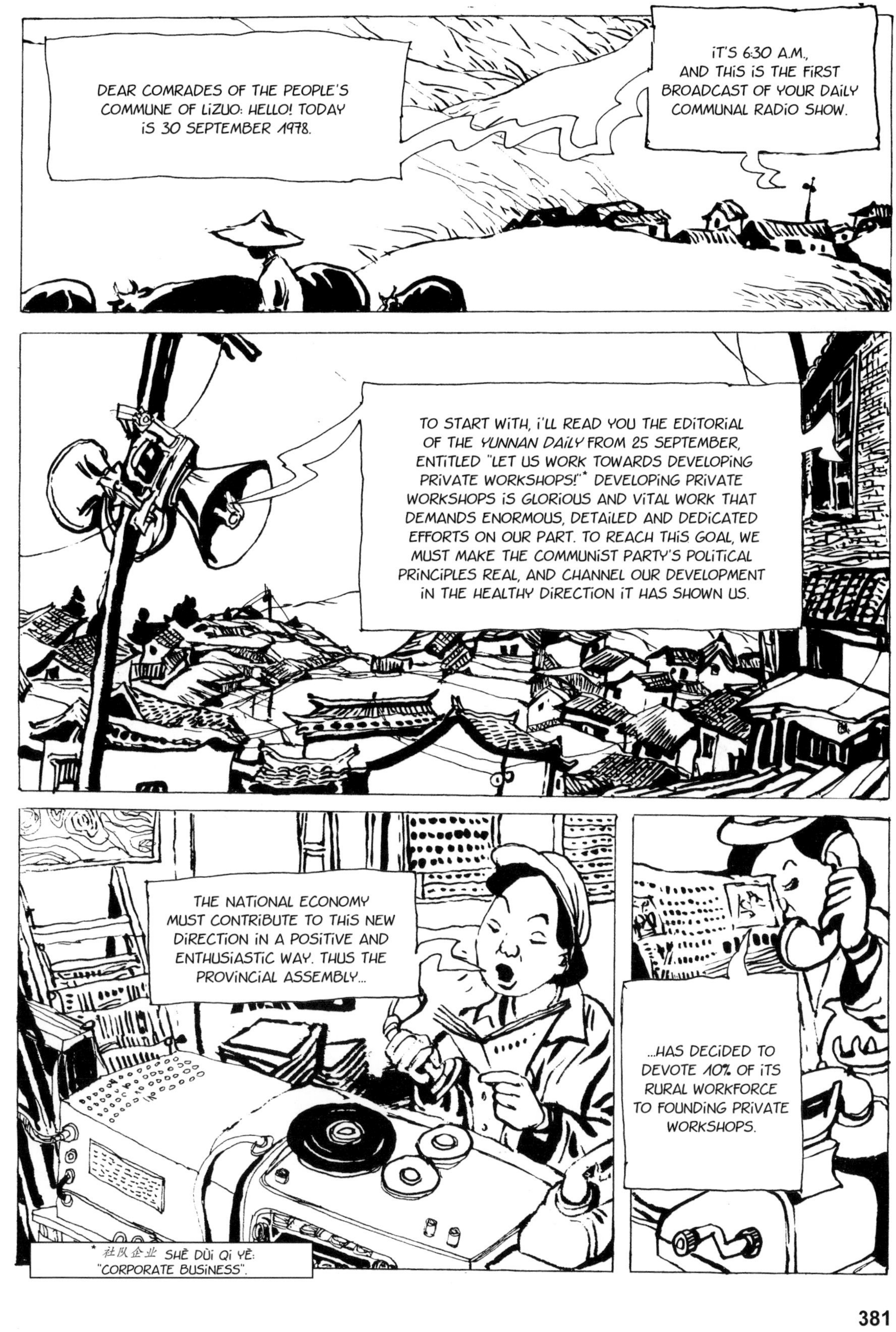
DEAR COMRADES OF THE PEOPLE'S COMMUNE OF LIZUO: HELLO! TODAY IS 30 SEPTEMBER 1978.
IT'S 6:30 A.M., AND THIS IS THE FIRST BROADCAST OF YOUR DAILY COMMUNAL RADIO SHOW.
TO START WITH, I'LL READ YOU THE EDITORIAL OF THE *YUNNAN DAILY* FROM 25 SEPTEMBER, ENTITLED "LET US WORK TOWARDS DEVELOPING PRIVATE WORKSHOPS!"* DEVELOPING PRIVATE WORKSHOPS IS GLORIOUS AND VITAL WORK THAT DEMANDS ENORMOUS, DETAILED AND DEDICATED EFFORTS ON OUR PART. TO REACH THIS GOAL, WE MUST MAKE THE COMMUNIST PARTY'S POLITICAL PRINCIPLES REAL, AND CHANNEL OUR DEVELOPMENT IN THE HEALTHY DIRECTION IT HAS SHOWN US.
THE NATIONAL ECONOMY MUST CONTRIBUTE TO THIS NEW DIRECTION IN A POSITIVE AND ENTHUSIASTIC WAY. THUS THE PROVINCIAL ASSEMBLY...
...HAS DECIDED TO DEVOTE 10% OF ITS RURAL WORKFORCE TO FOUNDING PRIVATE WORKSHOPS.

* 社队企业 SHÈ DÙI QI YÈ: "CORPORATE BUSINESS".

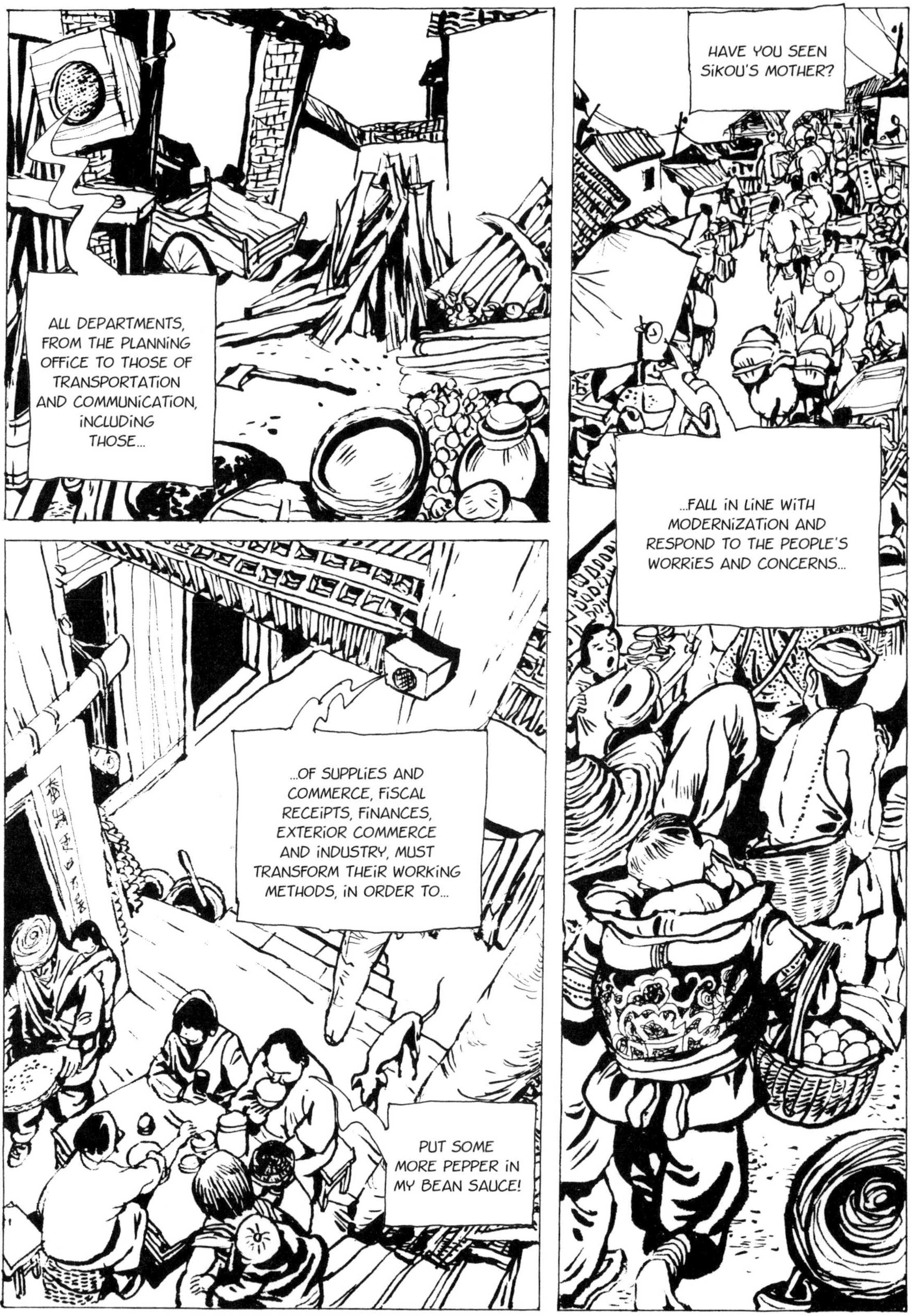
ALL DEPARTMENTS, FROM THE PLANNING OFFICE TO THOSE OF TRANSPORTATION AND COMMUNICATION, INCLUDING THOSE...
...OF SUPPLIES AND COMMERCE, FISCAL RECEIPTS, FINANCES, EXTERIOR COMMERCE AND INDUSTRY, MUST TRANSFORM THEIR WORKING METHODS, IN ORDER TO...
PUT SOME MORE PEPPER IN MY BEAN SAUCE!
HAVE YOU SEEN SIKOU'S MOTHER?
...FALL IN LINE WITH MODERNIZATION AND RESPOND TO THE PEOPLE'S WORRIES AND CONCERNS...

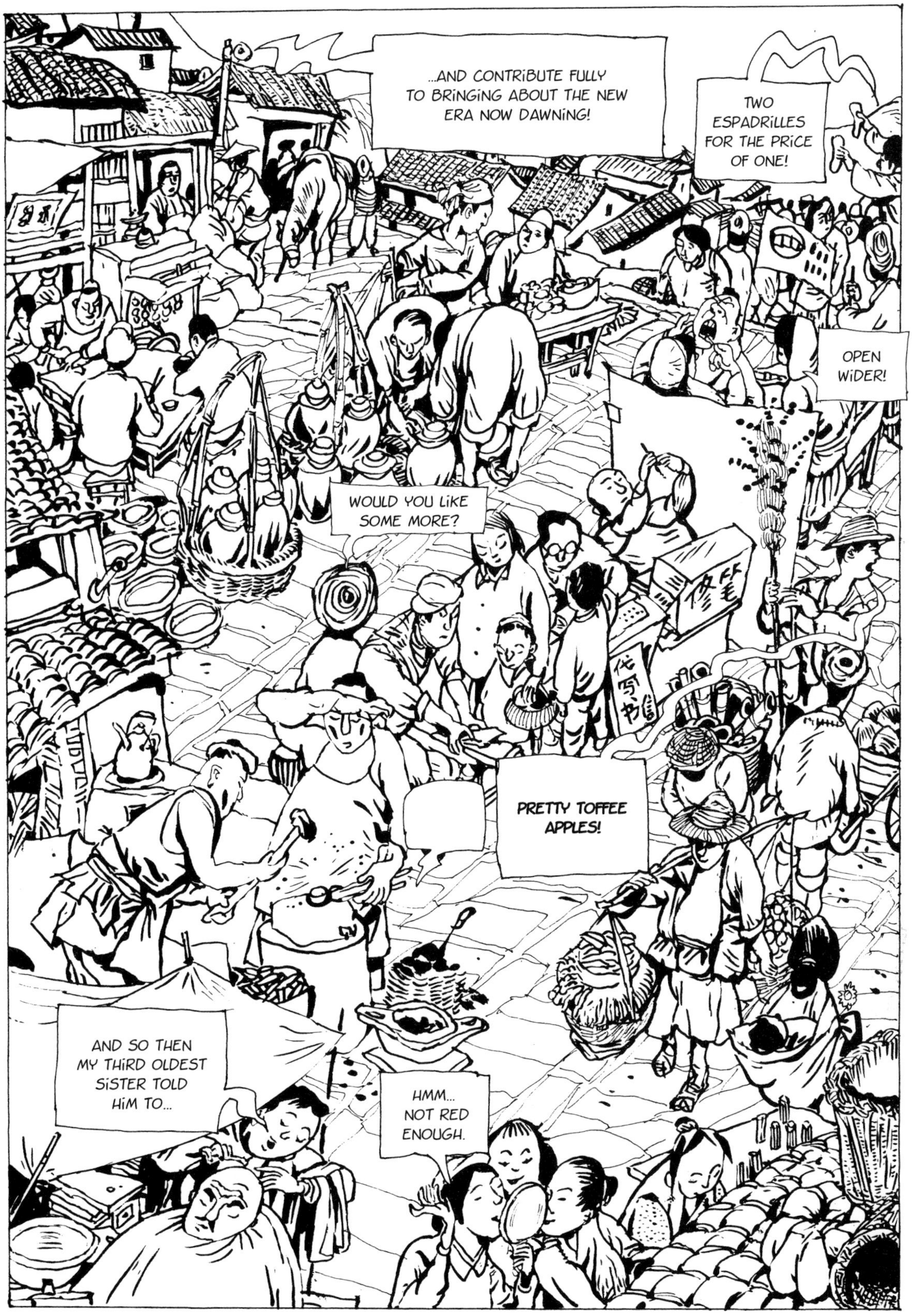
...AND CONTRIBUTE FULLY TO BRINGING ABOUT THE NEW ERA NOW DAWNING!
TWO ESPADRILLES FOR THE PRICE OF ONE!
OPEN WIDER!
WOULD YOU LIKE SOME MORE?
PRETTY TOFFEE APPLES!
AND SO THEN MY THIRD OLDEST SISTER TOLD HIM TO...
HMM... NOT RED ENOUGH.

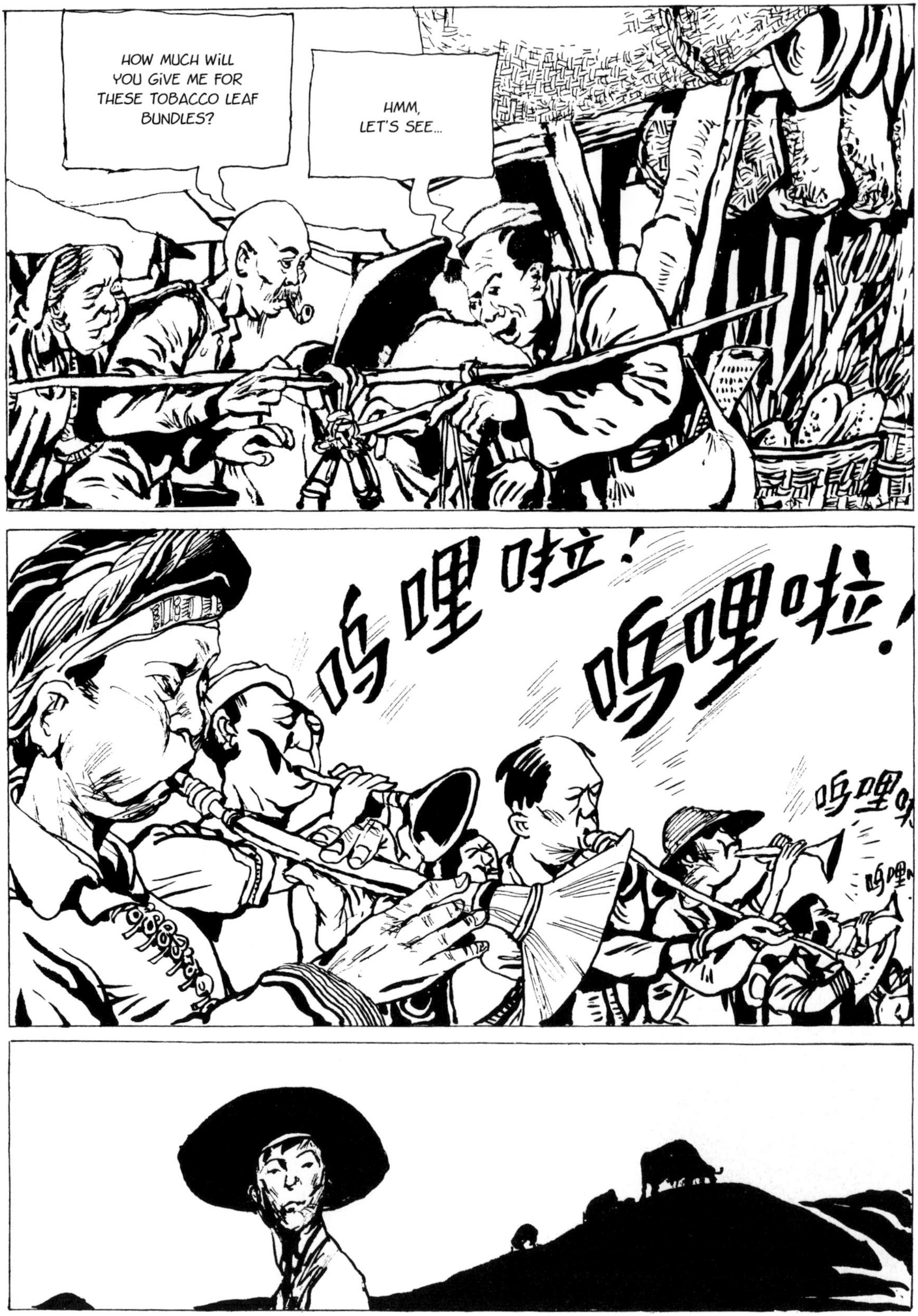

HOW MUCH WiLL YOU GiVE ME FOR THESE TOBACCO LEAF BUNDLES?
HMM, LET'S SEE...
呜哩啦！
呜哩啦！

HEAR THAT, GIRLS? QUITE A COMMOTION DOWN AT THE VILLAGE THESE DAYS!

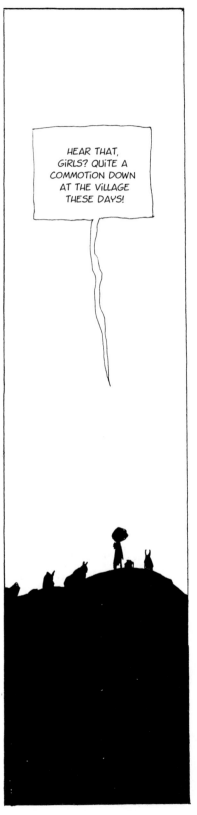

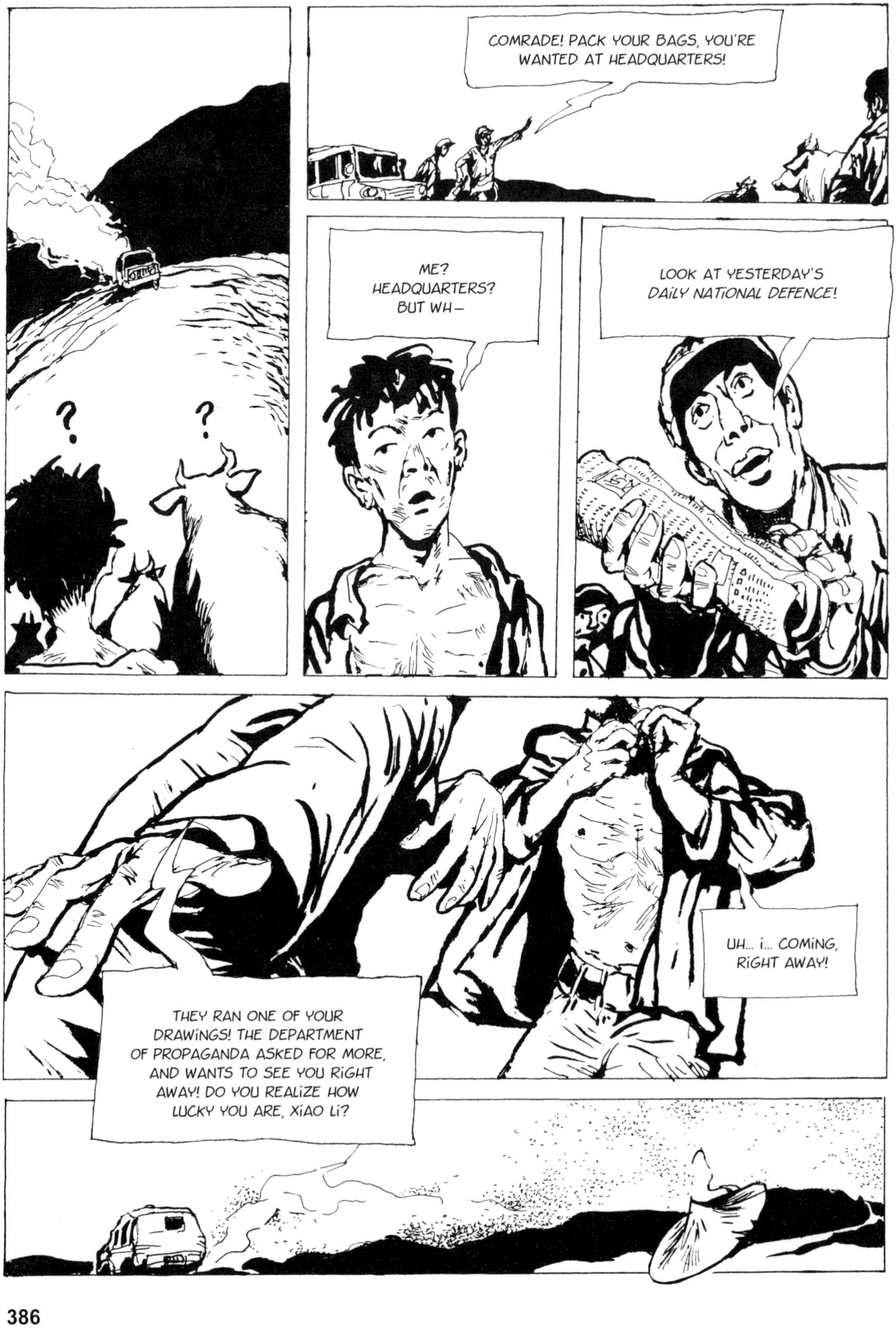
COMRADE! PACK YOUR BAGS, YOU'RE WANTED AT HEADQUARTERS!
ME? HEADQUARTERS? BUT WH—
LOOK AT YESTERDAY'S *DAILY NATIONAL DEFENCE*!
THEY RAN ONE OF YOUR DRAWINGS! THE DEPARTMENT OF PROPAGANDA ASKED FOR MORE, AND WANTS TO SEE YOU RIGHT AWAY! DO YOU REALIZE HOW LUCKY YOU ARE, XIAO LI?
UH... I... COMING, RIGHT AWAY!

AH! XIAO LI! COME IN, MY LITTLE COMRADE, COME IN!

WE'RE SO HAPPY TO HAVE YOU AMONG US!

REVOLUTIONARY ART NEEDS COMRADES LIKE YOU: BRAVE, UPSTANDING SOLDIERS WITH ON-THE-GROUND EXPERIENCE!

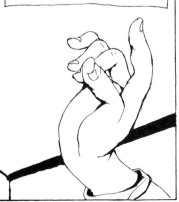

ESPECIALLY WITH THE 3RD PLENARY SESSION OF THE CENTRAL COMMITTEE DURING THE 11TH CONGRESS NEXT DECEMBER!

GUIDED BY DENG XIAOPING THEORY, YOUR MIND AND BRUSH WILL SHOW THE MASSES THE WAY!

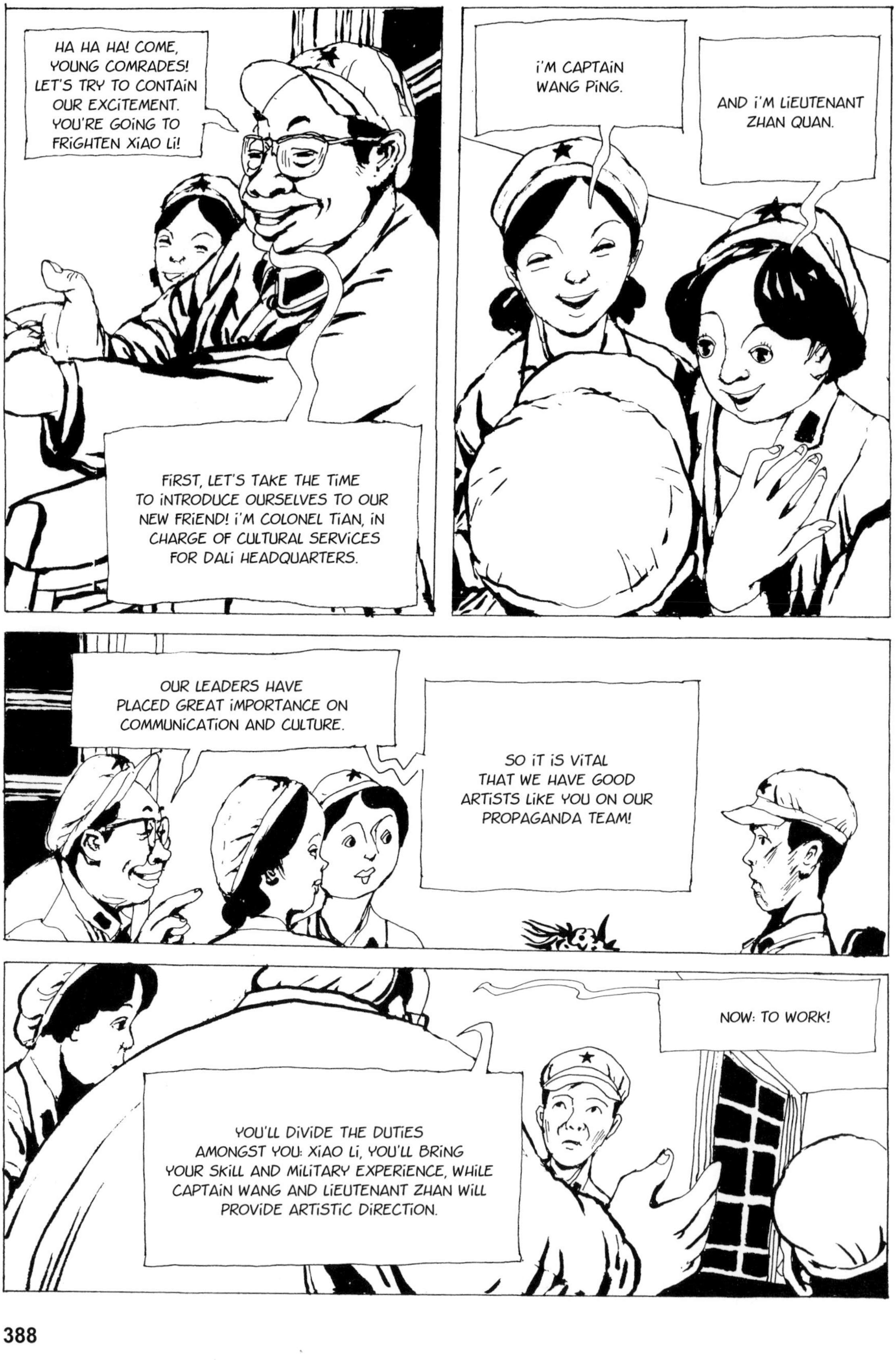
HA HA HA! COME, YOUNG COMRADES! LET'S TRY TO CONTAIN OUR EXCITEMENT. YOU'RE GOING TO FRIGHTEN XIAO LI!
FIRST, LET'S TAKE THE TIME TO INTRODUCE OURSELVES TO OUR NEW FRIEND! I'M COLONEL TIAN, IN CHARGE OF CULTURAL SERVICES FOR DALI HEADQUARTERS.
I'M CAPTAIN WANG PING.
AND I'M LIEUTENANT ZHAN QUAN.
OUR LEADERS HAVE PLACED GREAT IMPORTANCE ON COMMUNICATION AND CULTURE.
SO IT IS VITAL THAT WE HAVE GOOD ARTISTS LIKE YOU ON OUR PROPAGANDA TEAM!
YOU'LL DIVIDE THE DUTIES AMONGST YOU: XIAO LI, YOU'LL BRING YOUR SKILL AND MILITARY EXPERIENCE, WHILE CAPTAIN WANG AND LIEUTENANT ZHAN WILL PROVIDE ARTISTIC DIRECTION.
NOW: TO WORK!

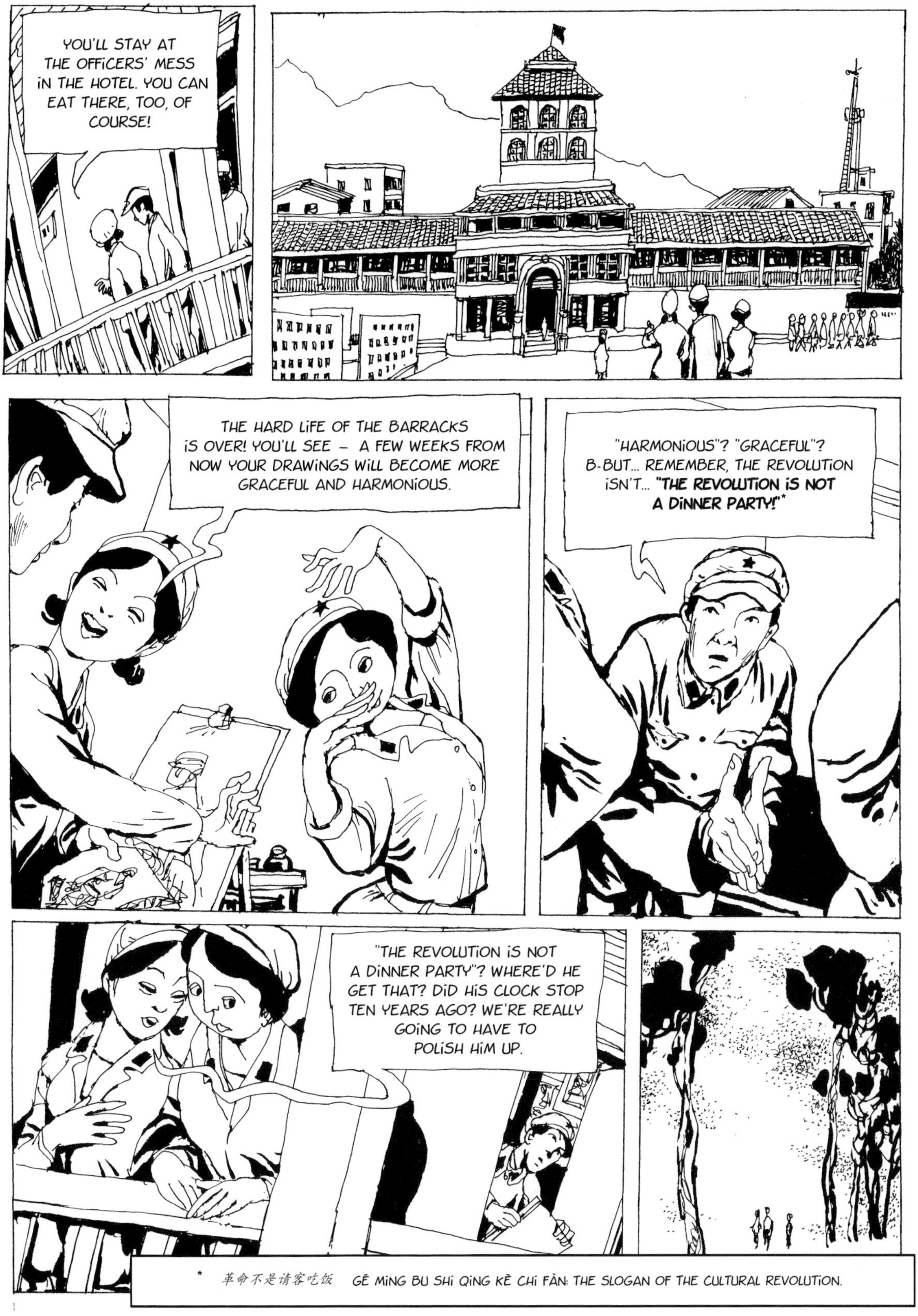
YOU'LL STAY AT THE OFFICERS' MESS IN THE HOTEL. YOU CAN EAT THERE, TOO, OF COURSE!
THE HARD LIFE OF THE BARRACKS IS OVER! YOU'LL SEE – A FEW WEEKS FROM NOW YOUR DRAWINGS WILL BECOME MORE GRACEFUL AND HARMONIOUS.
"HARMONIOUS"? "GRACEFUL"? B-BUT... REMEMBER, THE REVOLUTION ISN'T... **"THE REVOLUTION IS NOT A DINNER PARTY!"***
"THE REVOLUTION IS NOT A DINNER PARTY"? WHERE'D HE GET THAT? DID HIS CLOCK STOP TEN YEARS AGO? WE'RE REALLY GOING TO HAVE TO POLISH HIM UP.

* 革命不是请客吃饭 GĒ MING BU SHI QING KĚ CHI FÀN: THE SLOGAN OF THE CULTURAL REVOLUTION.

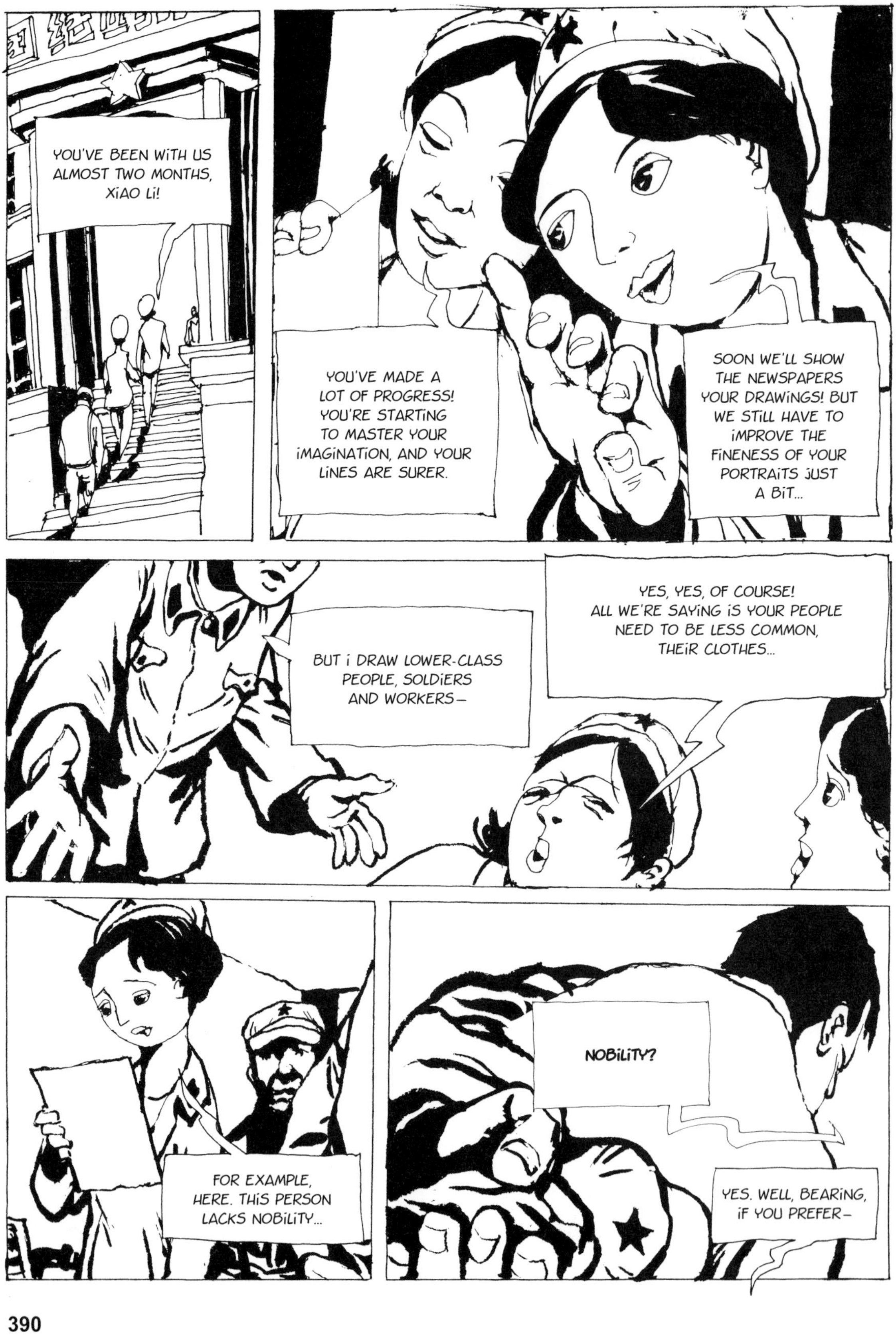
YOU'VE BEEN WITH US ALMOST TWO MONTHS, XIAO LI!
YOU'VE MADE A LOT OF PROGRESS! YOU'RE STARTING TO MASTER YOUR IMAGINATION, AND YOUR LINES ARE SURER.
SOON WE'LL SHOW THE NEWSPAPERS YOUR DRAWINGS! BUT WE STILL HAVE TO IMPROVE THE FINENESS OF YOUR PORTRAITS JUST A BIT...
BUT I DRAW LOWER-CLASS PEOPLE, SOLDIERS AND WORKERS–
YES, YES, OF COURSE! ALL WE'RE SAYING IS YOUR PEOPLE NEED TO BE LESS COMMON, THEIR CLOTHES...
FOR EXAMPLE, HERE. THIS PERSON LACKS NOBILITY...
NOBILITY?
YES. WELL, BEARING, IF YOU PREFER–

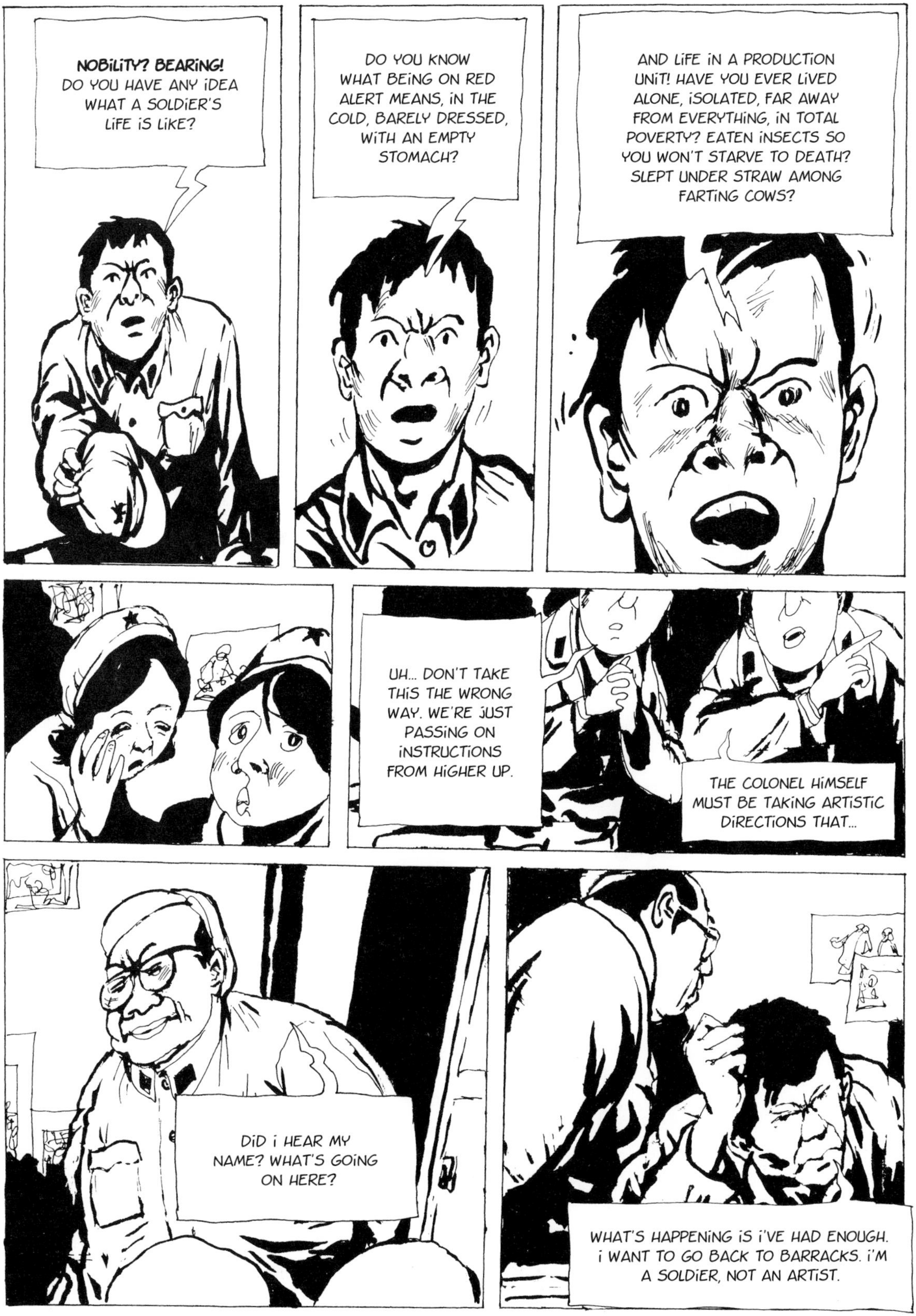
NOBILITY? BEARING! DO YOU HAVE ANY IDEA WHAT A SOLDIER'S LIFE IS LIKE?
DO YOU KNOW WHAT BEING ON RED ALERT MEANS, IN THE COLD, BARELY DRESSED, WITH AN EMPTY STOMACH?
AND LIFE IN A PRODUCTION UNIT! HAVE YOU EVER LIVED ALONE, ISOLATED, FAR AWAY FROM EVERYTHING, IN TOTAL POVERTY? EATEN INSECTS SO YOU WON'T STARVE TO DEATH? SLEPT UNDER STRAW AMONG FARTING COWS?
UH... DON'T TAKE THIS THE WRONG WAY. WE'RE JUST PASSING ON INSTRUCTIONS FROM HIGHER UP.
THE COLONEL HIMSELF MUST BE TAKING ARTISTIC DIRECTIONS THAT...
DID I HEAR MY NAME? WHAT'S GOING ON HERE?
WHAT'S HAPPENING IS I'VE HAD ENOUGH. I WANT TO GO BACK TO BARRACKS. I'M A SOLDIER, NOT AN ARTIST.

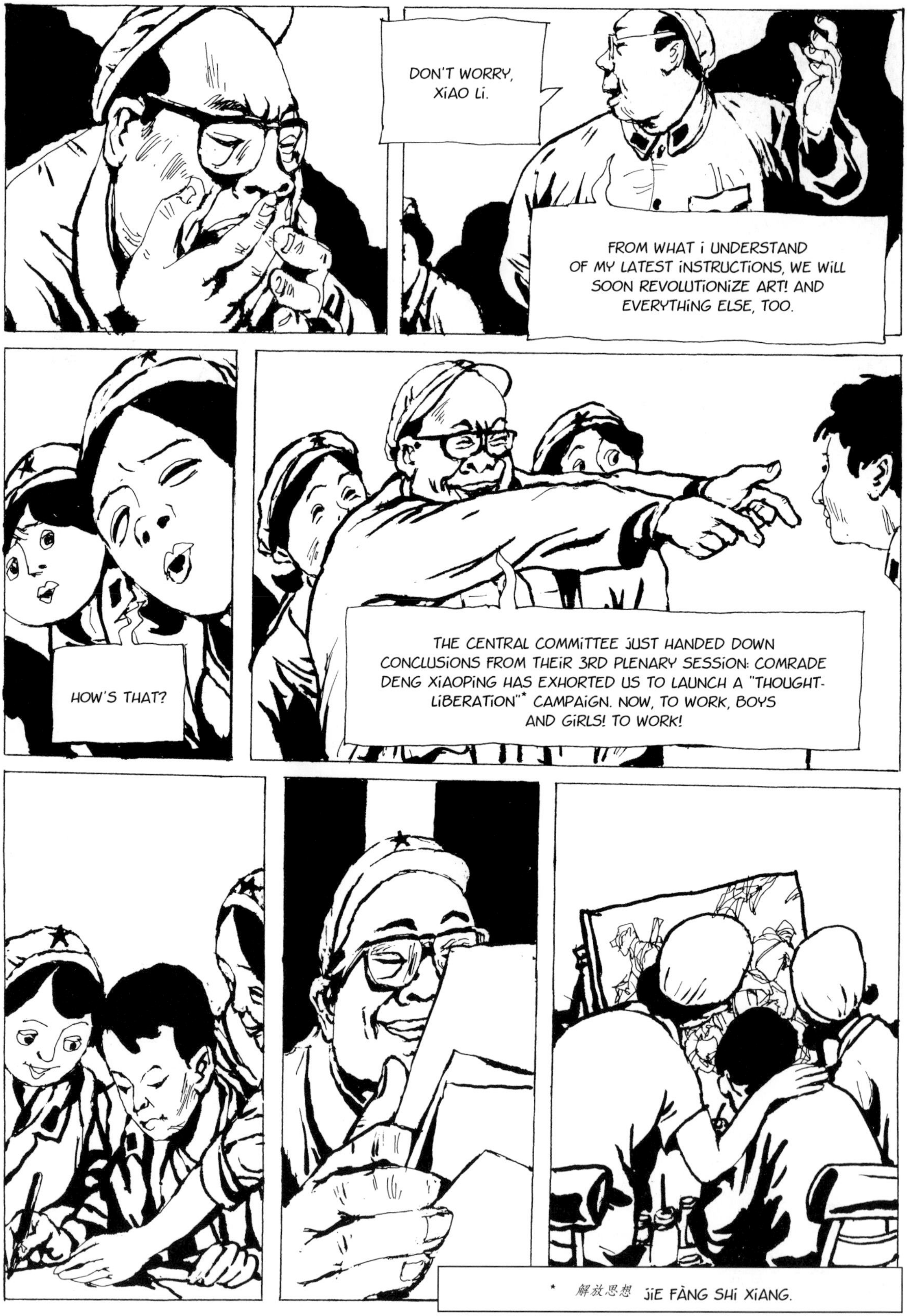
DON'T WORRY, XiAO Li.
FROM WHAT i UNDERSTAND OF MY LATEST iNSTRUCTiONS, WE WiLL SOON REVOLUTiONiZE ART! AND EVERYTHiNG ELSE, TOO.
HOW'S THAT?
THE CENTRAL COMMiTTEE JUST HANDED DOWN CONCLUSiONS FROM THEiR 3RD PLENARY SESSiON: COMRADE DENG XiAOPiNG HAS EXHORTED US TO LAUNCH A "THOUGHT-LiBERATiON"* CAMPAiGN. NOW, TO WORK, BOYS AND GiRLS! TO WORK!
* 解放思想 JiE FÀNG SHi XiANG.

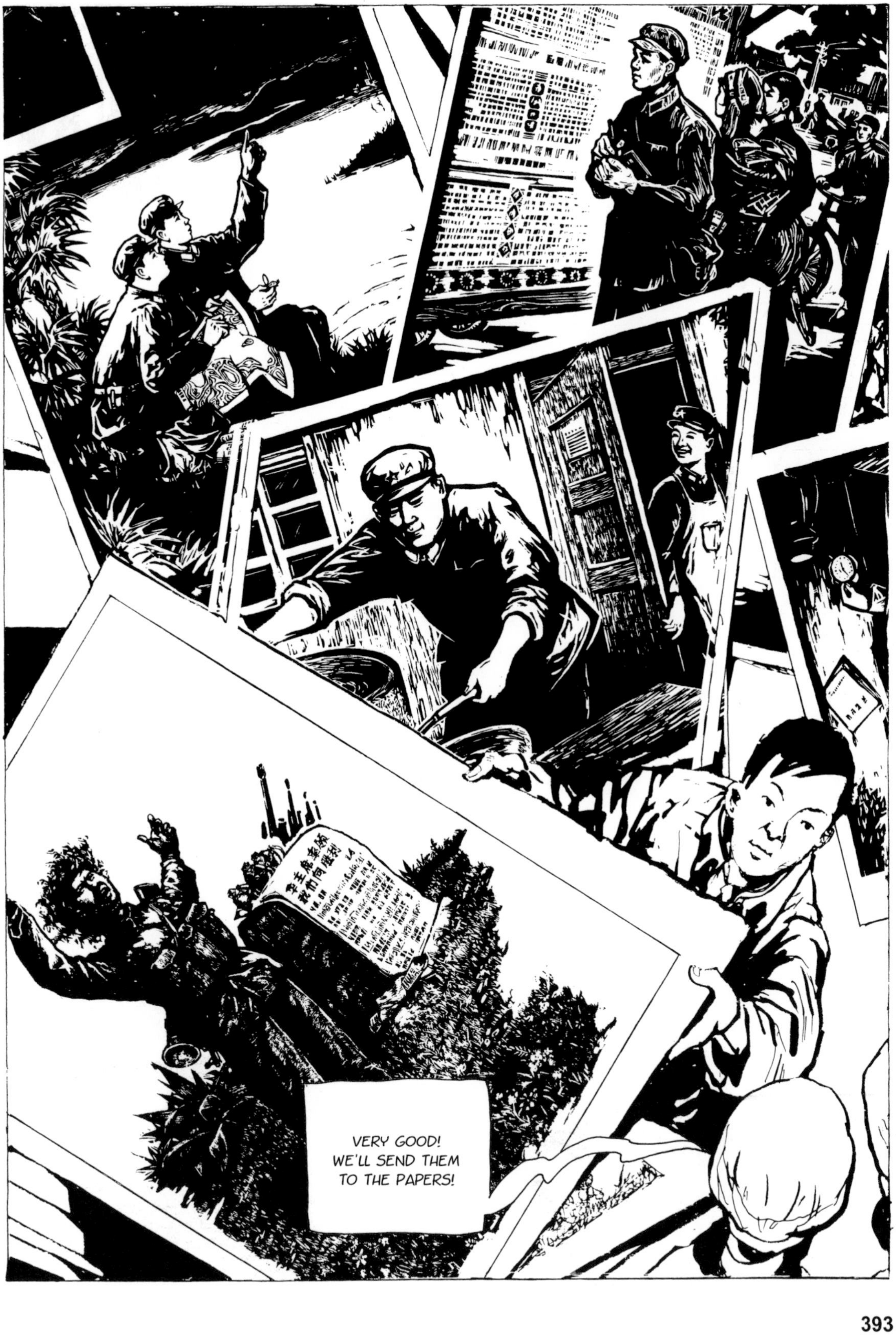
VERY GOOD! WE'LL SEND THEM TO THE PAPERS!

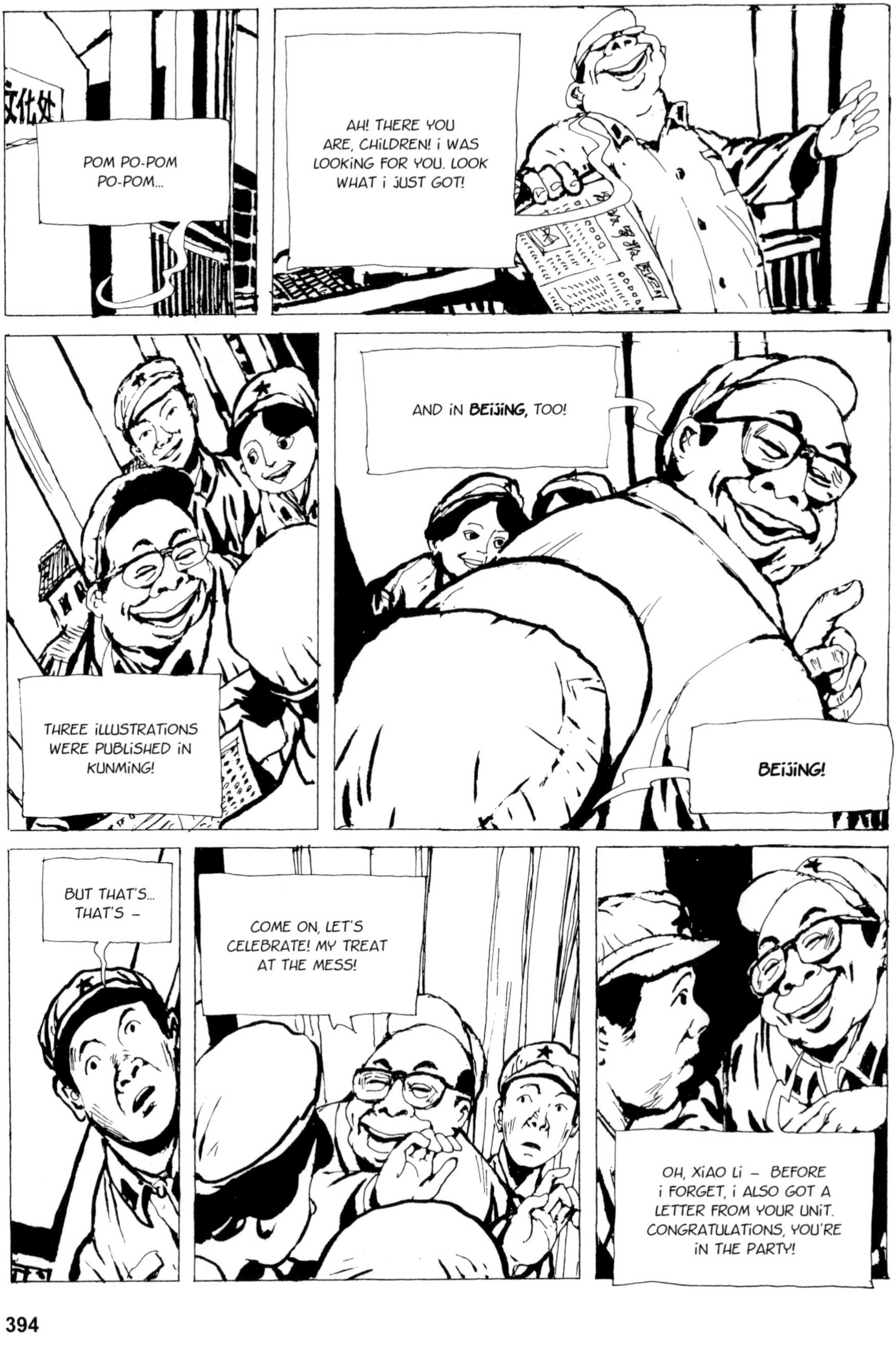
POM PO-POM PO-POM...
AH! THERE YOU ARE, CHILDREN! i WAS LOOKiNG FOR YOU. LOOK WHAT i JUST GOT!
THREE iLLUSTRATiONS WERE PUBLiSHED iN KUNMiNG!
AND iN **BEiJiNG,** TOO!
BEiJiNG!
BUT THAT'S... THAT'S –
COME ON, LET'S CELEBRATE! MY TREAT AT THE MESS!
OH, XiAO Li – BEFORE i FORGET, i ALSO GOT A LETTER FROM YOUR UNiT. CONGRATULATiONS, YOU'RE iN THE PARTY!

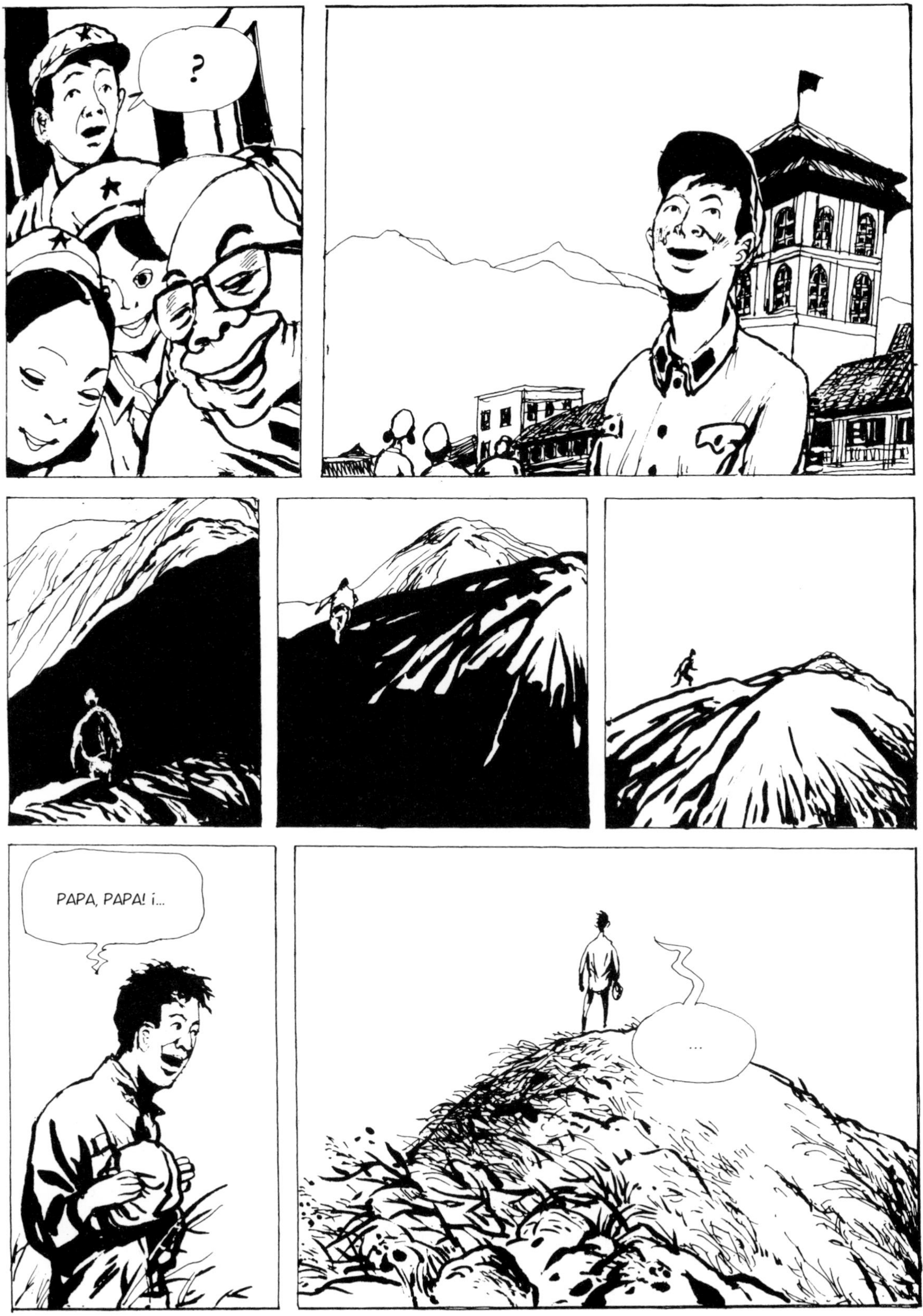
?
PAPA, PAPA! ¡...
...

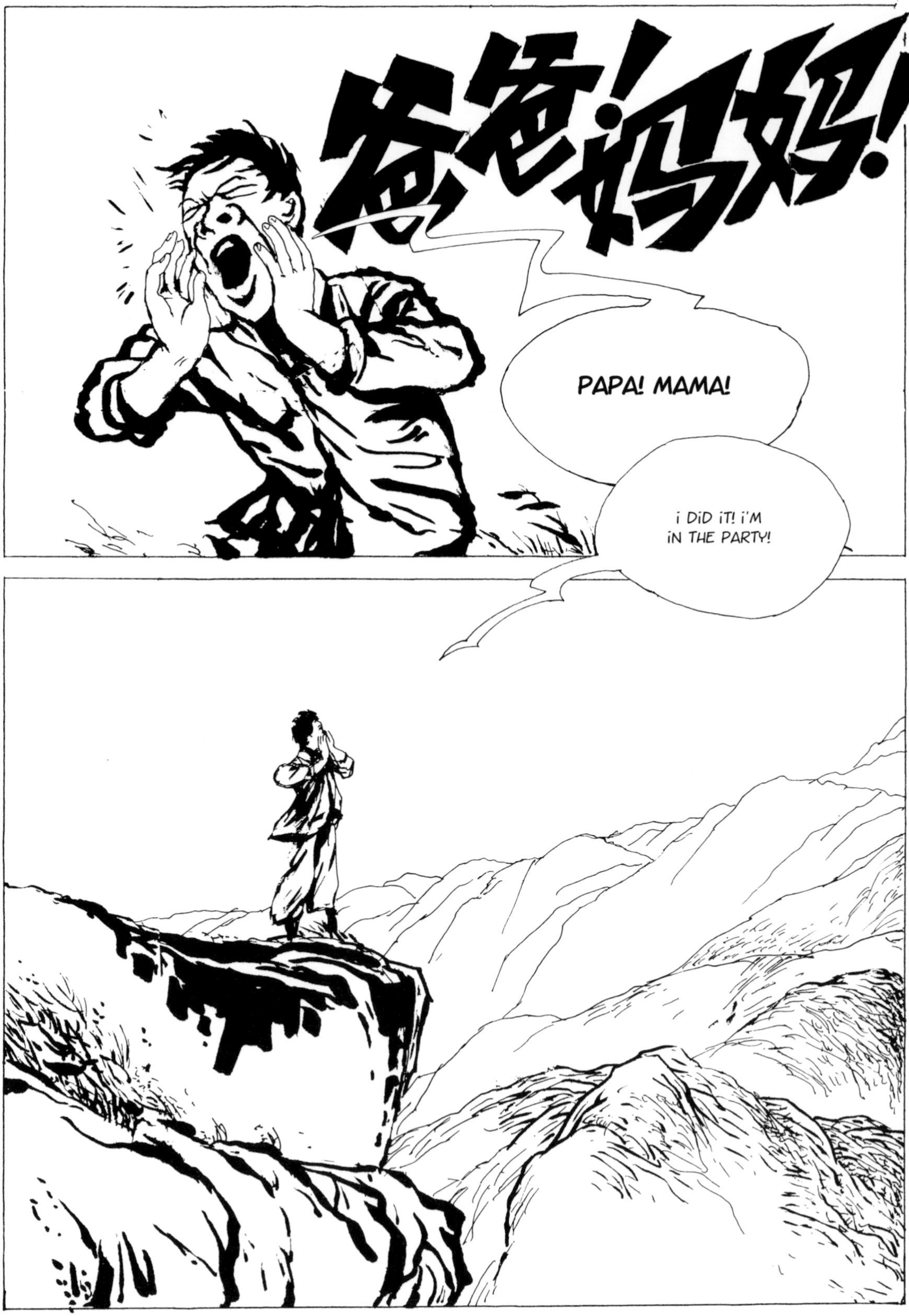
爸爸妈妈!
PAPA! MAMA!
I DID IT! I'M IN THE PARTY!

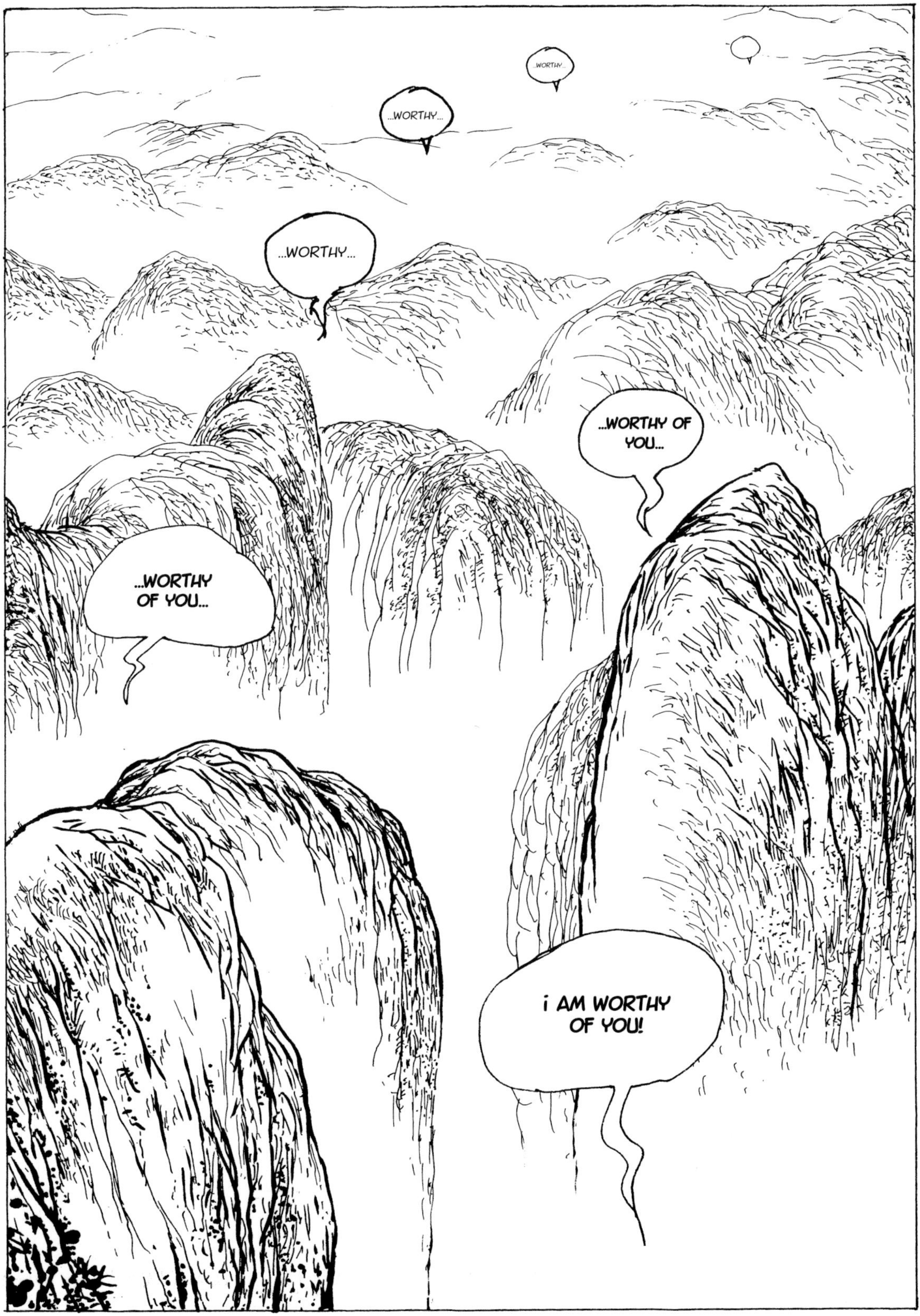
...WORTHY...
...WORTHY...
...WORTHY...
...WORTHY OF YOU...
...WORTHY OF YOU...
I AM WORTHY OF YOU!

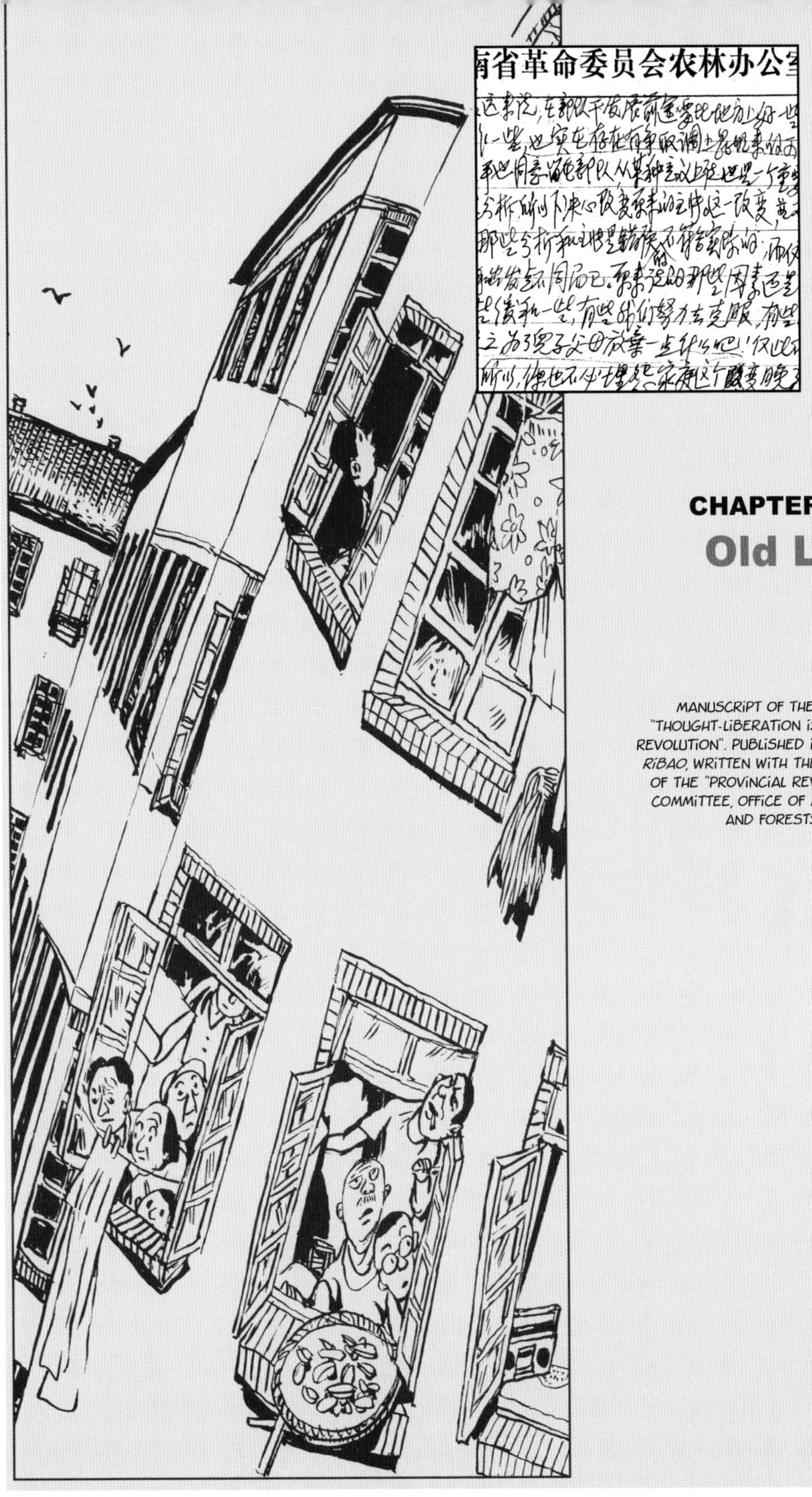
省革命委员会农林办公

CHAPTER 6
Old Li

MANUSCRIPT OF THE ARTICLE "THOUGHT-LIBERATION IS A FORM OF REVOLUTION". PUBLISHED IN THE *YUNNAN RIBAO*, WRITTEN WITH THE LETTERHEAD OF THE "PROVINCIAL REVOLUTIONARY COMMITTEE, OFFICE OF AGRICULTURE AND FORESTS".

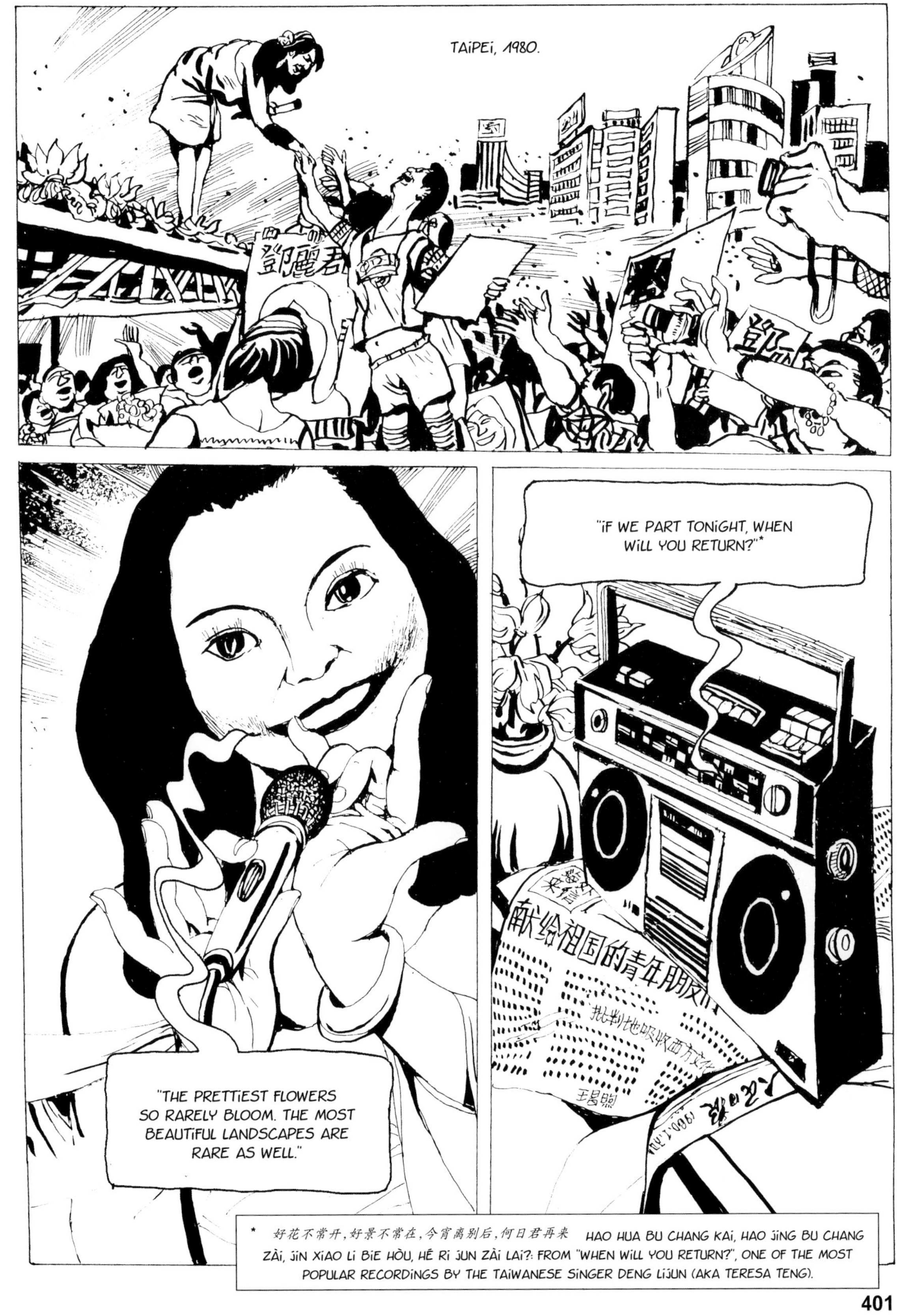
TAIPEI, 1980.
鄧麗君
"IF WE PART TONIGHT, WHEN WILL YOU RETURN?"*
献给祖国的青年朋友
"THE PRETTIEST FLOWERS SO RARELY BLOOM. THE MOST BEAUTIFUL LANDSCAPES ARE RARE AS WELL."

* 好花不常开，好景不常在，今宵离别后，何日君再来 HAO HUA BU CHANG KAI, HAO JING BU CHANG ZÀI, JIN XIAO LI BIE HÒU, HÉ RI JUN ZÀI LAI?: FROM "WHEN WILL YOU RETURN?", ONE OF THE MOST POPULAR RECORDINGS BY THE TAIWANESE SINGER DENG LIJUN (AKA TERESA TENG).

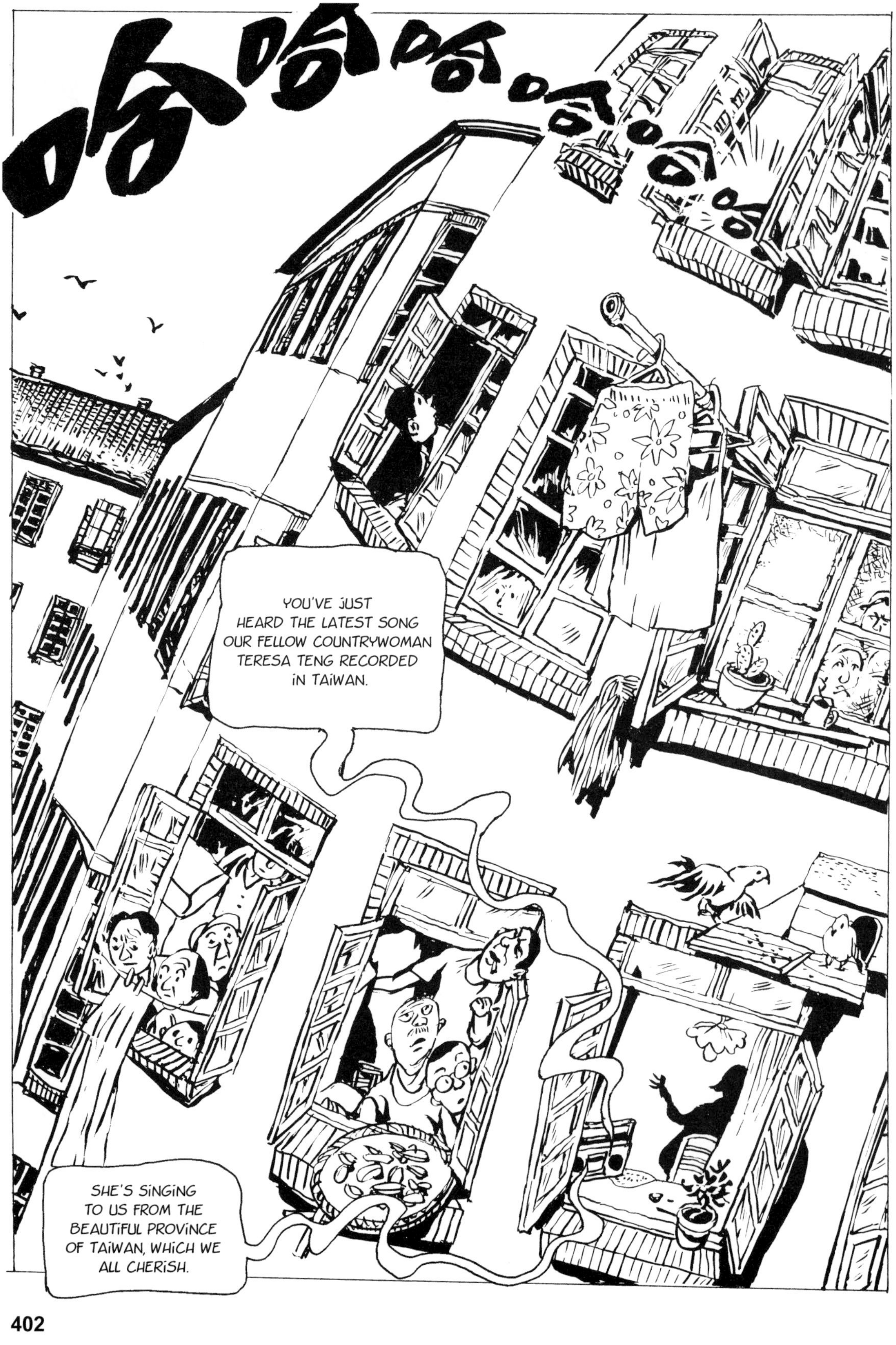
YOU'VE JUST HEARD THE LATEST SONG OUR FELLOW COUNTRYWOMAN TERESA TENG RECORDED IN TAIWAN.
SHE'S SINGING TO US FROM THE BEAUTIFUL PROVINCE OF TAIWAN, WHICH WE ALL CHERISH.

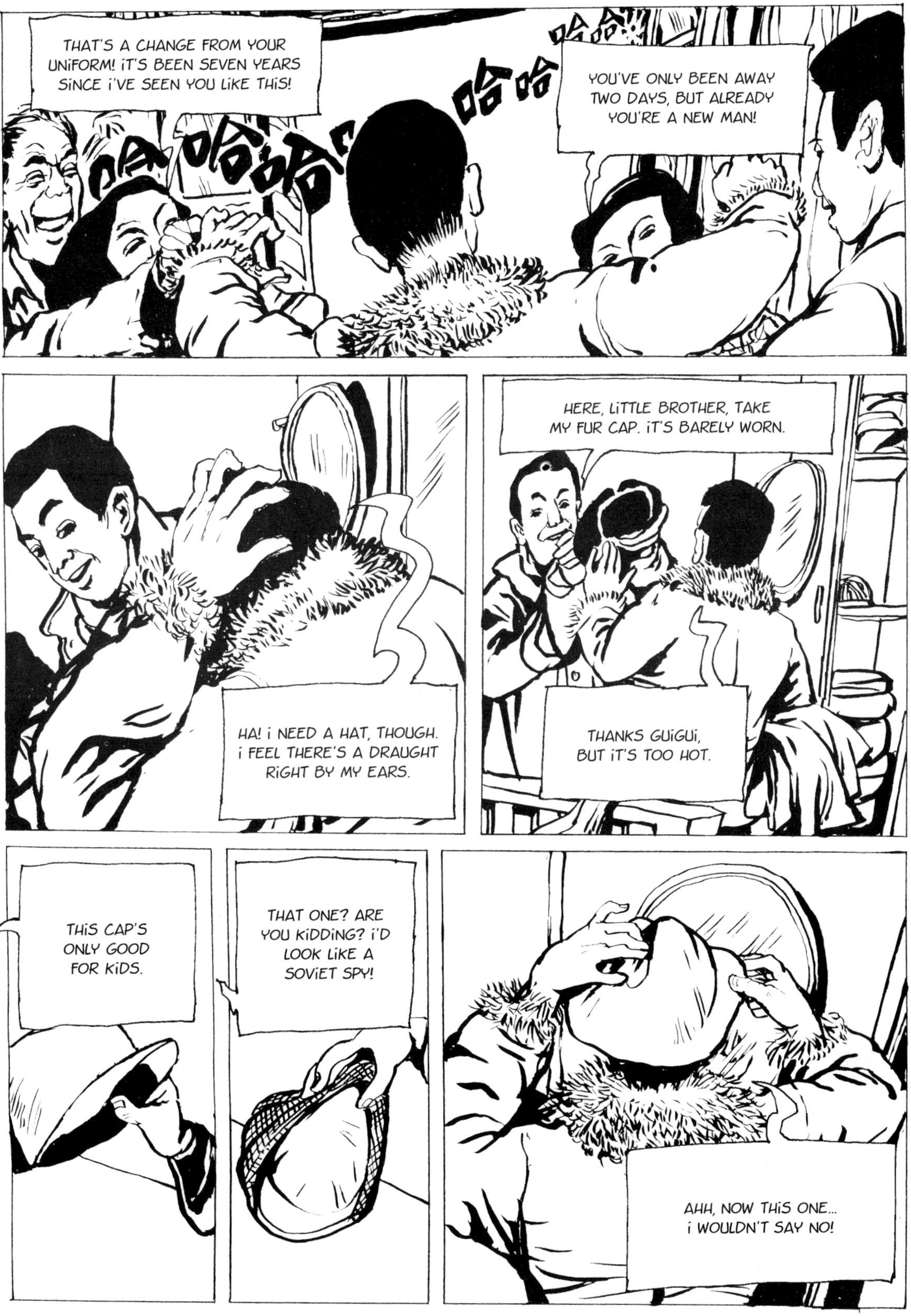
THAT'S A CHANGE FROM YOUR UNIFORM! IT'S BEEN SEVEN YEARS SINCE I'VE SEEN YOU LIKE THIS!
哈哈哈
哈哈
哈哈
YOU'VE ONLY BEEN AWAY TWO DAYS, BUT ALREADY YOU'RE A NEW MAN!
HA! I NEED A HAT, THOUGH. I FEEL THERE'S A DRAUGHT RIGHT BY MY EARS.
HERE, LITTLE BROTHER, TAKE MY FUR CAP. IT'S BARELY WORN.
THANKS GUIGUI, BUT IT'S TOO HOT.
THIS CAP'S ONLY GOOD FOR KIDS.
THAT ONE? ARE YOU KIDDING? I'D LOOK LIKE A SOVIET SPY!
AHH, NOW THIS ONE... I WOULDN'T SAY NO!

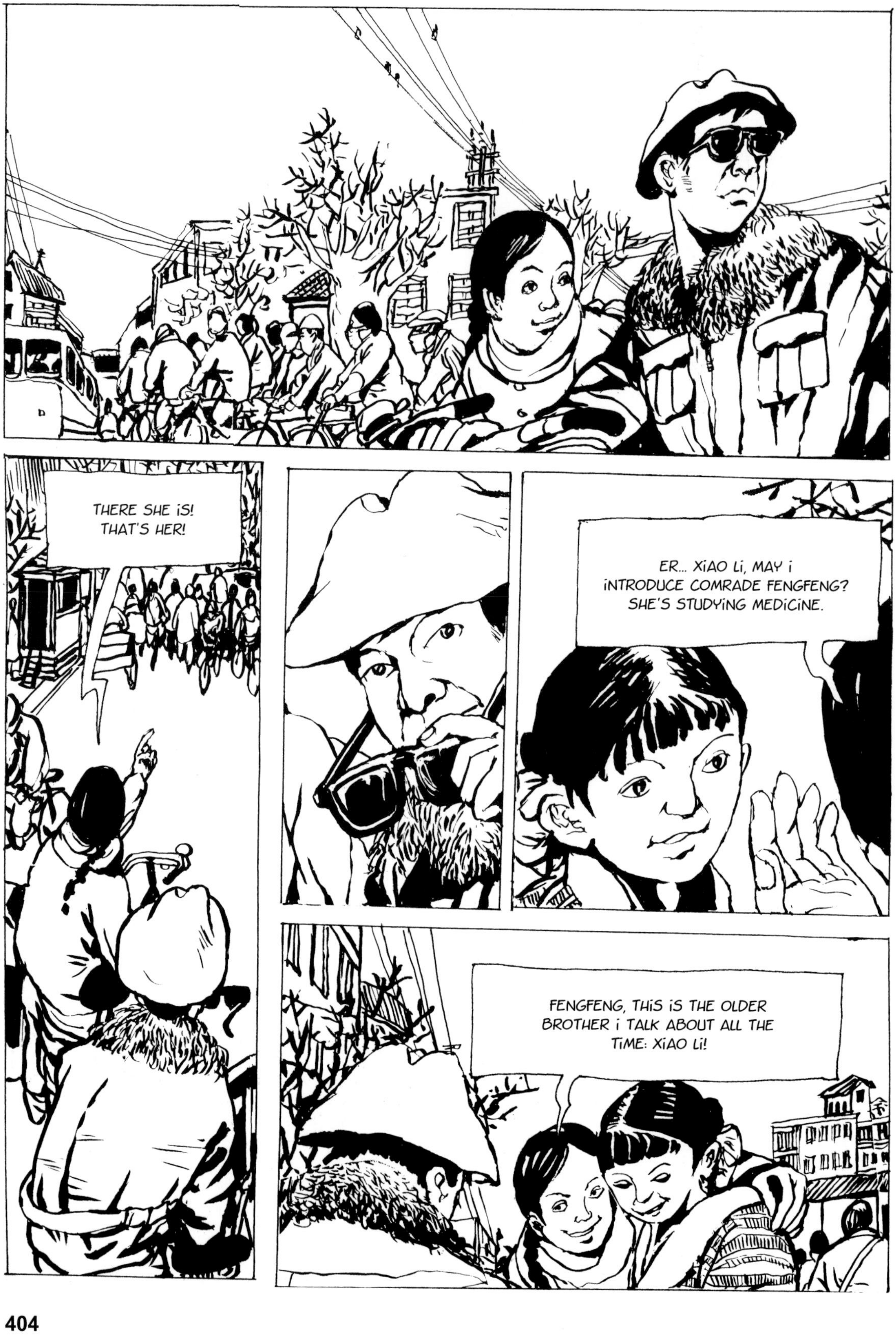
THERE SHE iS! THAT'S HER!
ER... XiAO Li, MAY i iNTRODUCE COMRADE FENGFENG? SHE'S STUDYiNG MEDiCiNE.
FENGFENG, THiS iS THE OLDER BROTHER i TALK ABOUT ALL THE TiME: XiAO Li!

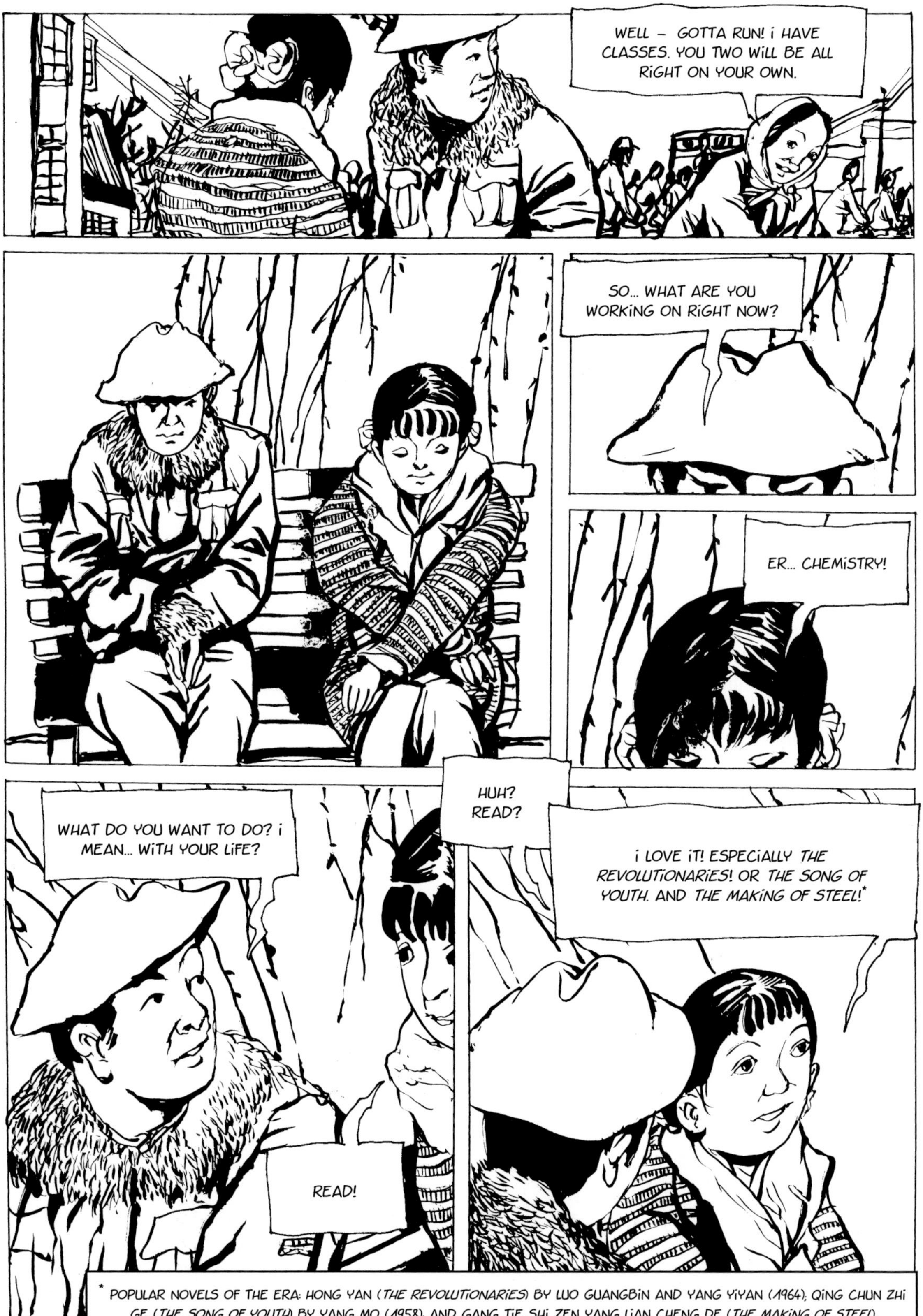
WELL – GOTTA RUN! i HAVE CLASSES. YOU TWO WiLL BE ALL RiGHT ON YOUR OWN.
SO... WHAT ARE YOU WORKiNG ON RiGHT NOW?
ER... CHEMiSTRY!
WHAT DO YOU WANT TO DO? i MEAN... WiTH YOUR LiFE?
READ!
HUH? READ?
i LOVE iT! ESPECiALLY THE REVOLUTiONARiES! OR THE SONG OF YOUTH. AND THE MAKiNG OF STEEL!*

* POPULAR NOVELS OF THE ERA: HONG YAN (*THE REVOLUTiONARiES*) BY LUO GUANGBiN AND YANG YiYAN (1964); QiNG CHUN ZHi GE (*THE SONG OF YOUTH*) BY YANG MO (1958); AND GANG TiE SHi ZEN YANG LiAN CHENG DE (*THE MAKiNG OF STEEL*) BY THE SOViET NOVELiST NiKOLAi OSTROVSKii (1936), WHiCH WAS TRANSLATED iNTO CHiNESE iN 1952.

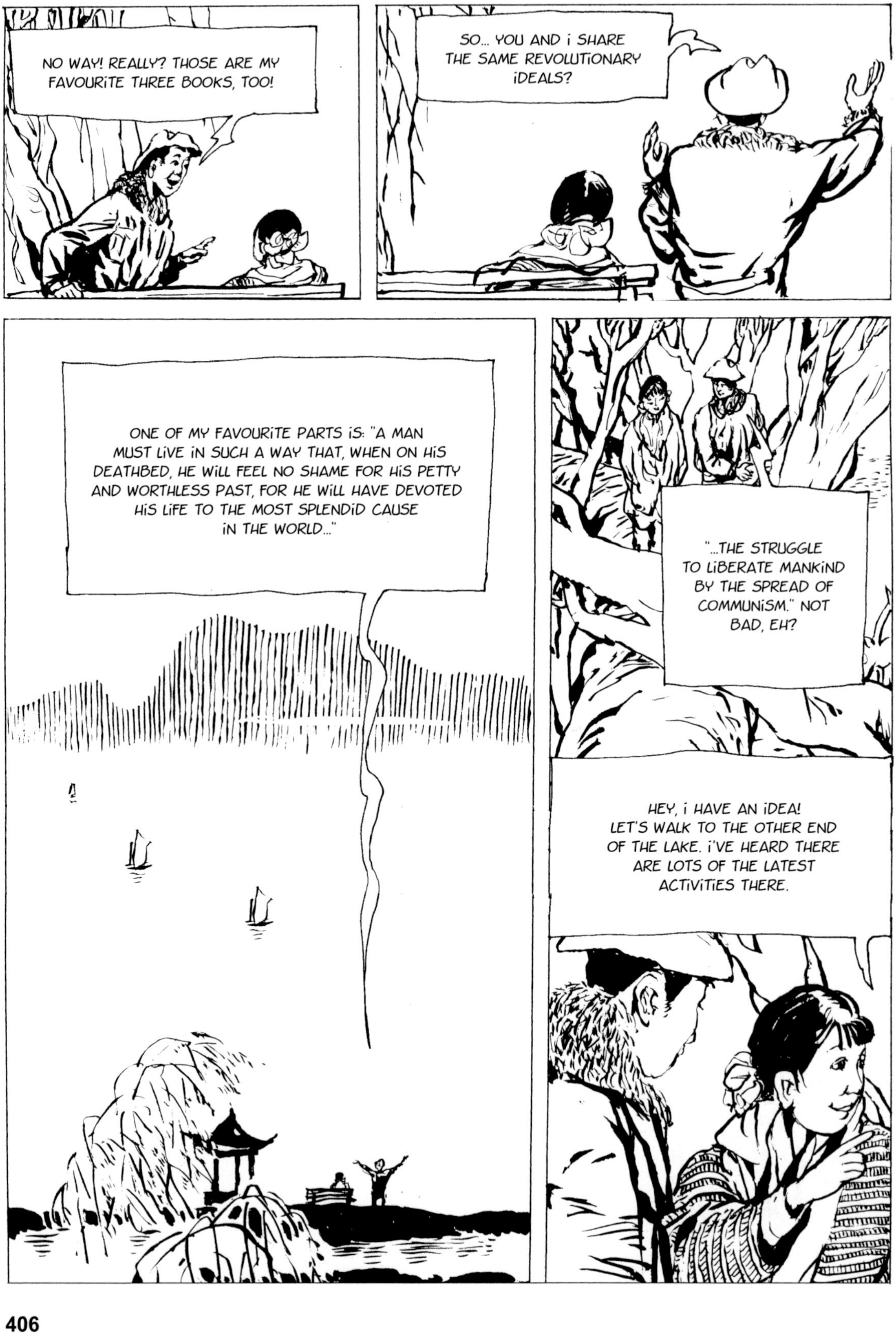
NO WAY! REALLY? THOSE ARE MY FAVOURITE THREE BOOKS, TOO!
SO... YOU AND I SHARE THE SAME REVOLUTIONARY IDEALS?
ONE OF MY FAVOURITE PARTS IS: "A MAN MUST LIVE IN SUCH A WAY THAT, WHEN ON HIS DEATHBED, HE WILL FEEL NO SHAME FOR HIS PETTY AND WORTHLESS PAST, FOR HE WILL HAVE DEVOTED HIS LIFE TO THE MOST SPLENDID CAUSE IN THE WORLD..."
"...THE STRUGGLE TO LIBERATE MANKIND BY THE SPREAD OF COMMUNISM." NOT BAD, EH?
HEY, I HAVE AN IDEA! LET'S WALK TO THE OTHER END OF THE LAKE. I'VE HEARD THERE ARE LOTS OF THE LATEST ACTIVITIES THERE.

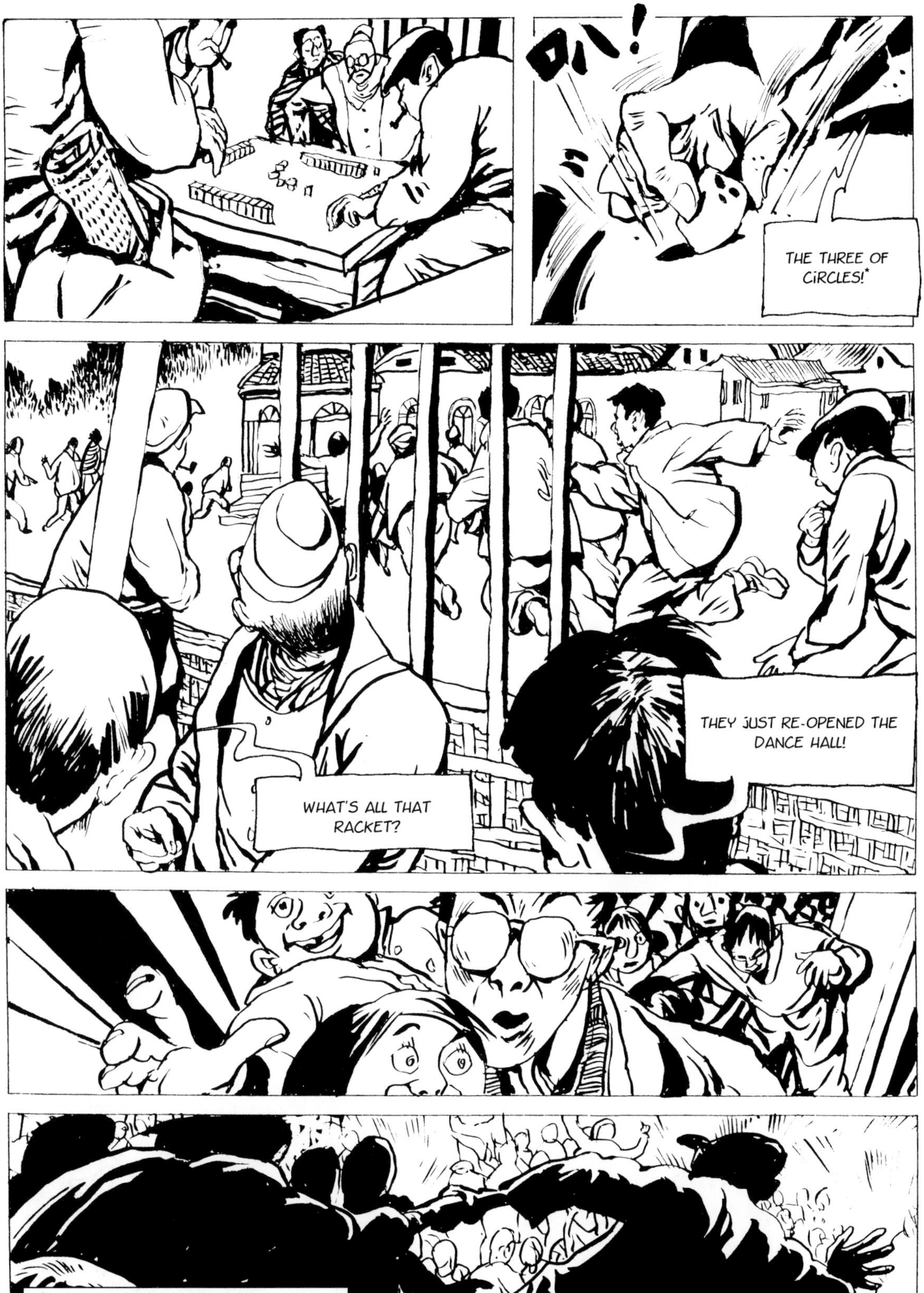
THE THREE OF CIRCLES!*
WHAT'S ALL THAT RACKET?
THEY JUST RE-OPENED THE DANCE HALL!
* SAN BING: A THREE OF THE "CIRCLE" SUIT IN MAH-JONG TILES (REPRESENTING COPPER COINS).

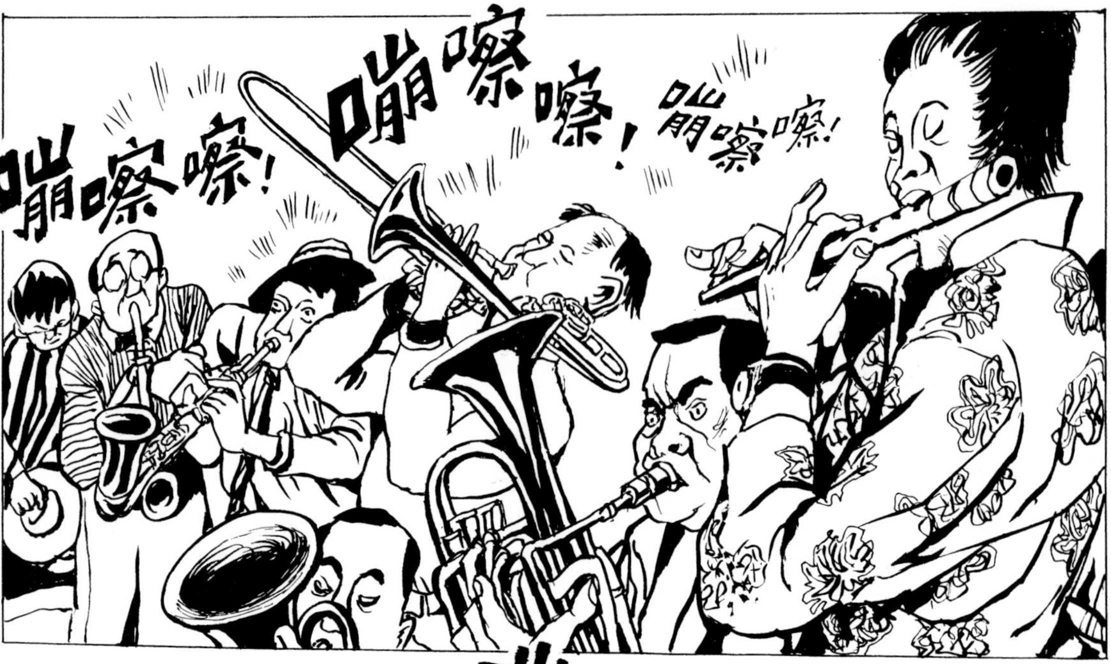
嘣嚓嚓!
嘣嚓嚓!
嘣嚓嚓!

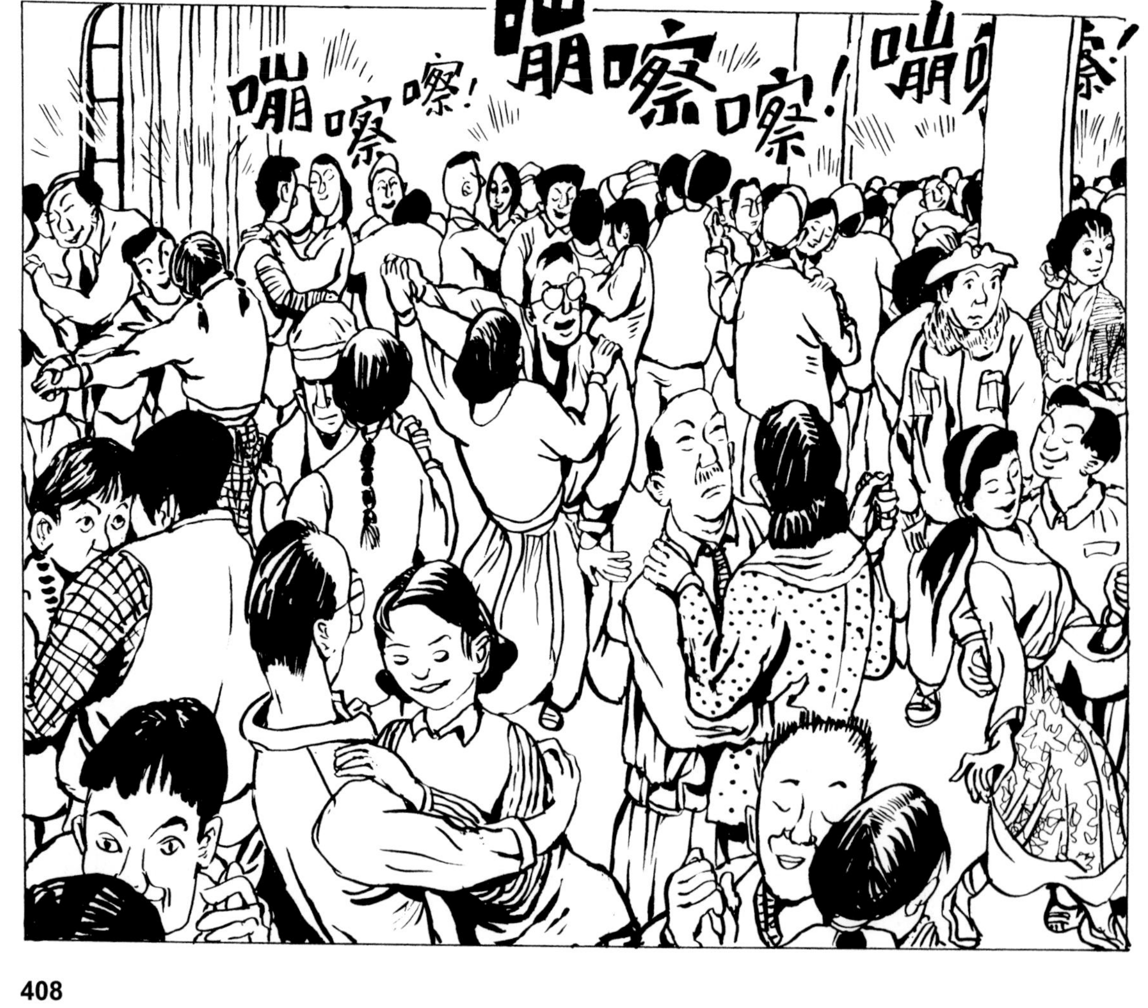
嘣嚓嚓!
嘣嚓嚓!

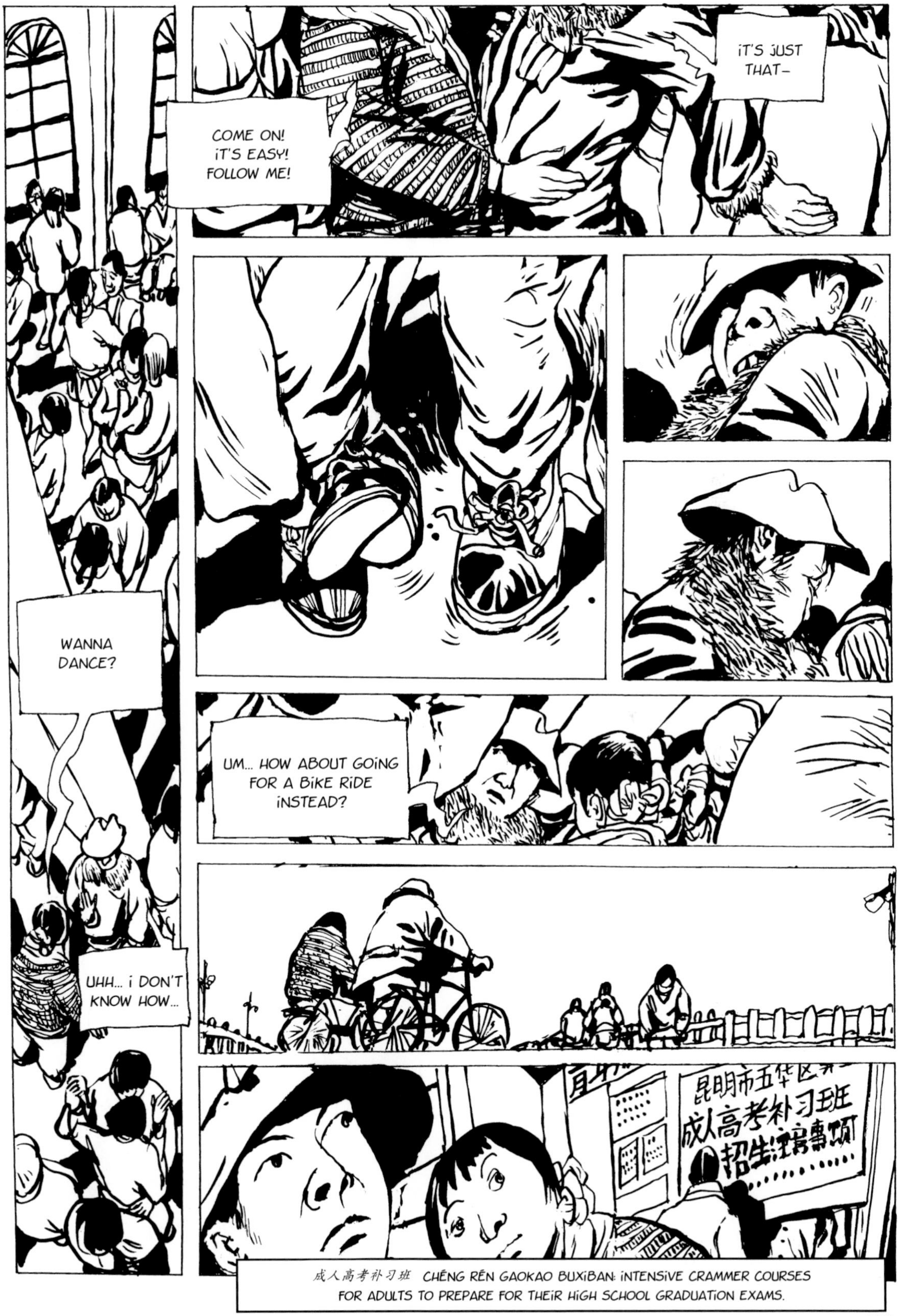
WANNA DANCE?
UHH... i DON'T KNOW HOW...
COME ON! iT'S EASY! FOLLOW ME!
iT'S JUST THAT–
UM... HOW ABOUT GOiNG FOR A BiKE RiDE iNSTEAD?
成人高考补习班 CHÉNG RÉN GAOKAO BUXiBAN: iNTENSiVE CRAMMER COURSES FOR ADULTS TO PREPARE FOR THEiR HiGH SCHOOL GRADUATiON EXAMS.

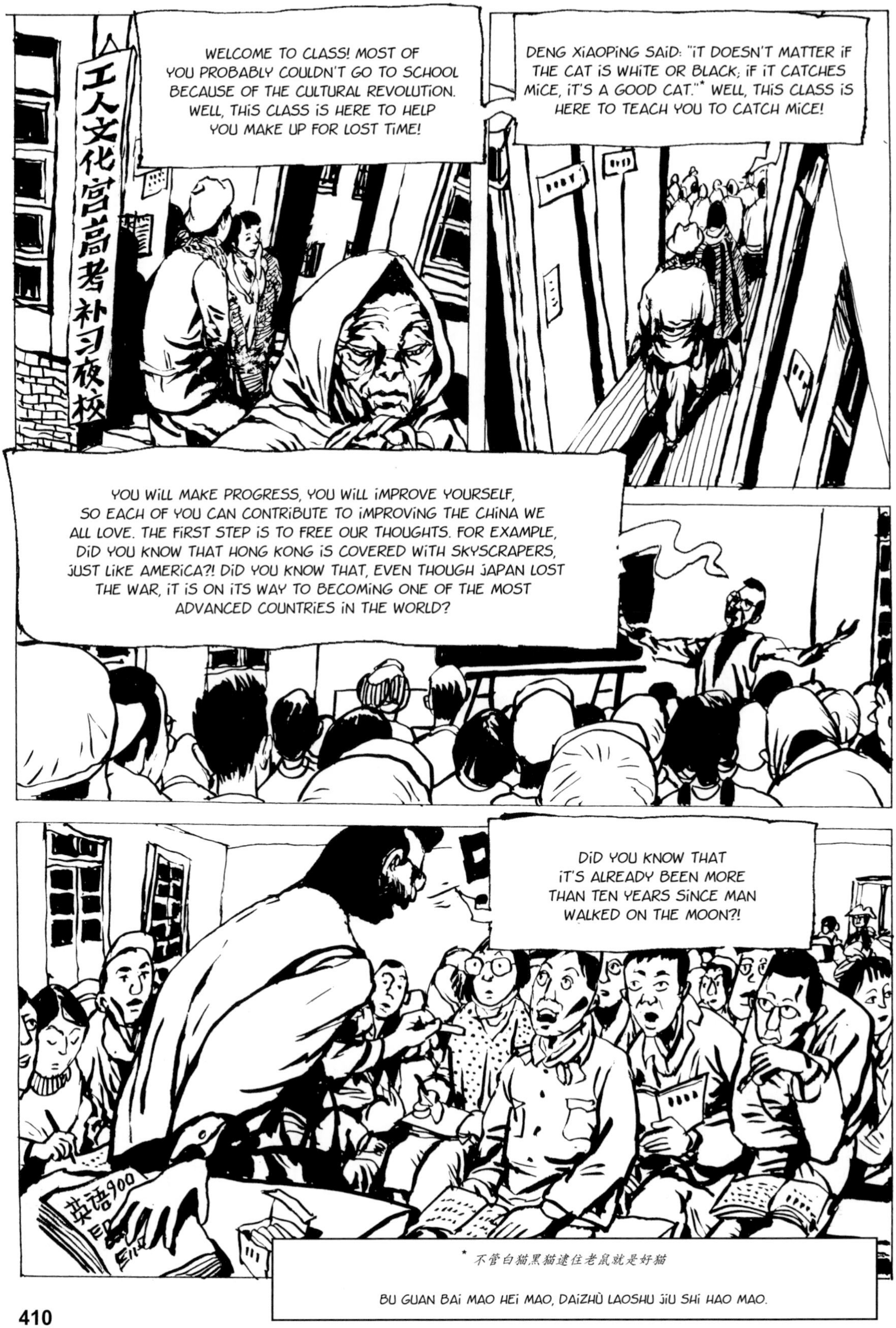
WELCOME TO CLASS! MOST OF YOU PROBABLY COULDN'T GO TO SCHOOL BECAUSE OF THE CULTURAL REVOLUTION. WELL, THIS CLASS IS HERE TO HELP YOU MAKE UP FOR LOST TIME!
工人文化宫高考补习夜校
DENG XIAOPING SAID: "IT DOESN'T MATTER IF THE CAT IS WHITE OR BLACK; IF IT CATCHES MICE, IT'S A GOOD CAT."* WELL, THIS CLASS IS HERE TO TEACH YOU TO CATCH MICE!
YOU WILL MAKE PROGRESS, YOU WILL IMPROVE YOURSELF, SO EACH OF YOU CAN CONTRIBUTE TO IMPROVING THE CHINA WE ALL LOVE. THE FIRST STEP IS TO FREE OUR THOUGHTS. FOR EXAMPLE, DID YOU KNOW THAT HONG KONG IS COVERED WITH SKYSCRAPERS, JUST LIKE AMERICA?! DID YOU KNOW THAT, EVEN THOUGH JAPAN LOST THE WAR, IT IS ON ITS WAY TO BECOMING ONE OF THE MOST ADVANCED COUNTRIES IN THE WORLD?
DID YOU KNOW THAT IT'S ALREADY BEEN MORE THAN TEN YEARS SINCE MAN WALKED ON THE MOON?!
英语900

* 不管白猫黑猫逮住老鼠就是好猫

BU GUAN BAI MAO HEI MAO, DAIZHÙ LAOSHU JIU SHI HAO MAO.

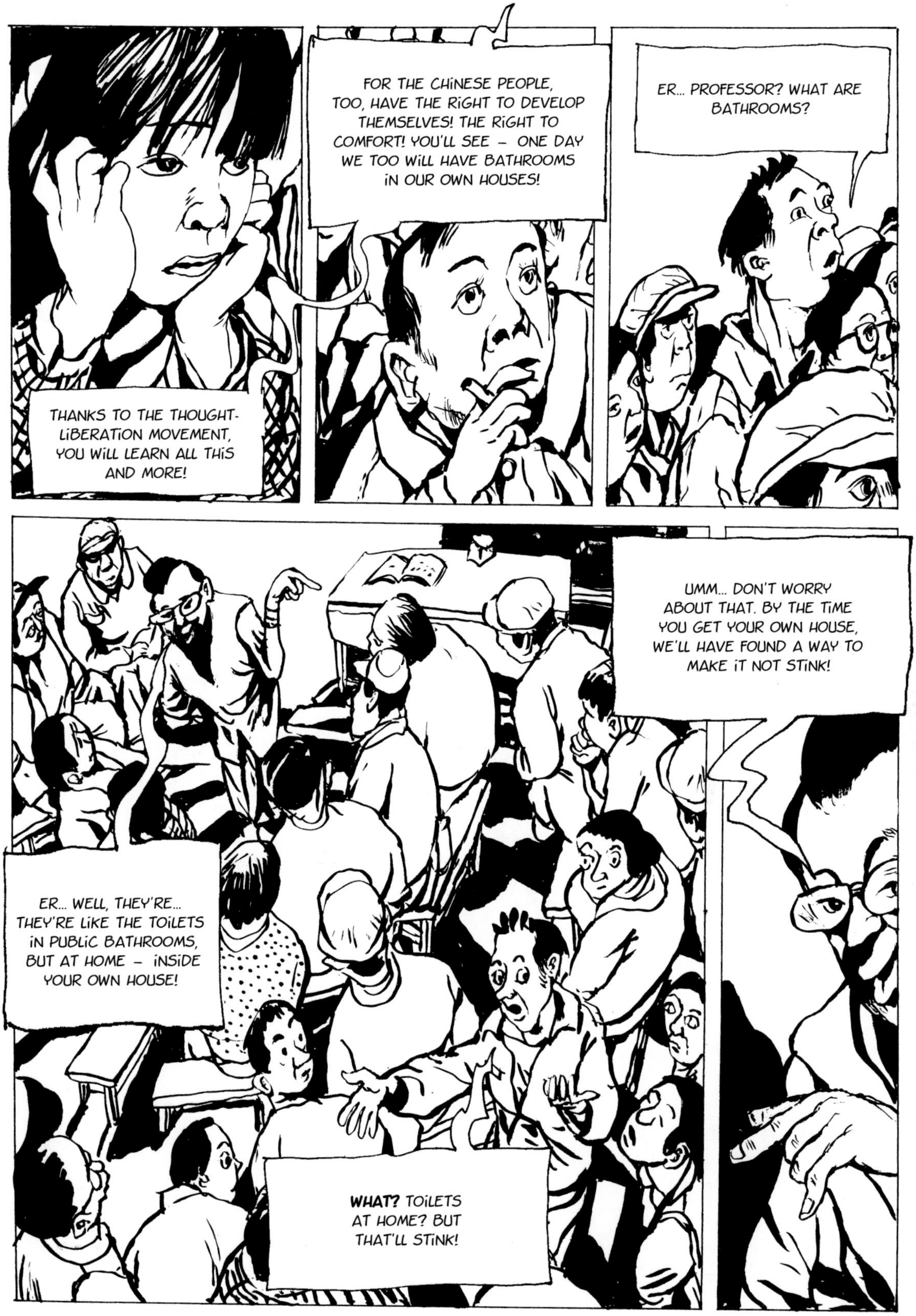
THANKS TO THE THOUGHT-LIBERATION MOVEMENT, YOU WILL LEARN ALL THIS AND MORE!
FOR THE CHINESE PEOPLE, TOO, HAVE THE RIGHT TO DEVELOP THEMSELVES! THE RIGHT TO COMFORT! YOU'LL SEE – ONE DAY WE TOO WILL HAVE BATHROOMS IN OUR OWN HOUSES!
ER… PROFESSOR? WHAT ARE BATHROOMS?
ER… WELL, THEY'RE… THEY'RE LIKE THE TOILETS IN PUBLIC BATHROOMS, BUT AT HOME – INSIDE YOUR OWN HOUSE!
WHAT? TOILETS AT HOME? BUT THAT'LL STINK!
UMM… DON'T WORRY ABOUT THAT. BY THE TIME YOU GET YOUR OWN HOUSE, WE'LL HAVE FOUND A WAY TO MAKE IT NOT STINK!

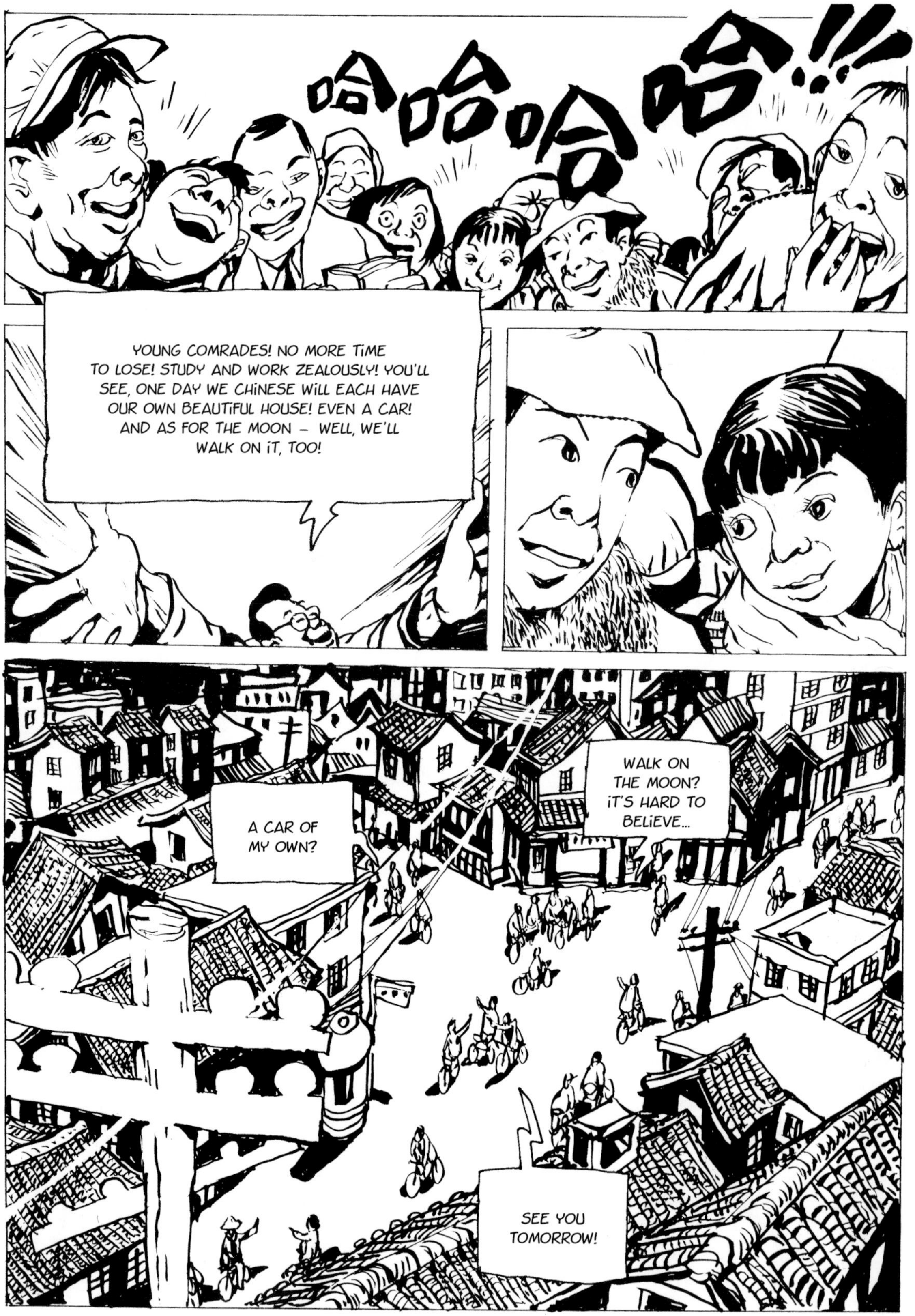
哈哈哈哈!!!
YOUNG COMRADES! NO MORE TIME TO LOSE! STUDY AND WORK ZEALOUSLY! YOU'LL SEE, ONE DAY WE CHINESE WILL EACH HAVE OUR OWN BEAUTIFUL HOUSE! EVEN A CAR! AND AS FOR THE MOON – WELL, WE'LL WALK ON IT, TOO!
A CAR OF MY OWN?
WALK ON THE MOON? IT'S HARD TO BELIEVE...
SEE YOU TOMORROW!

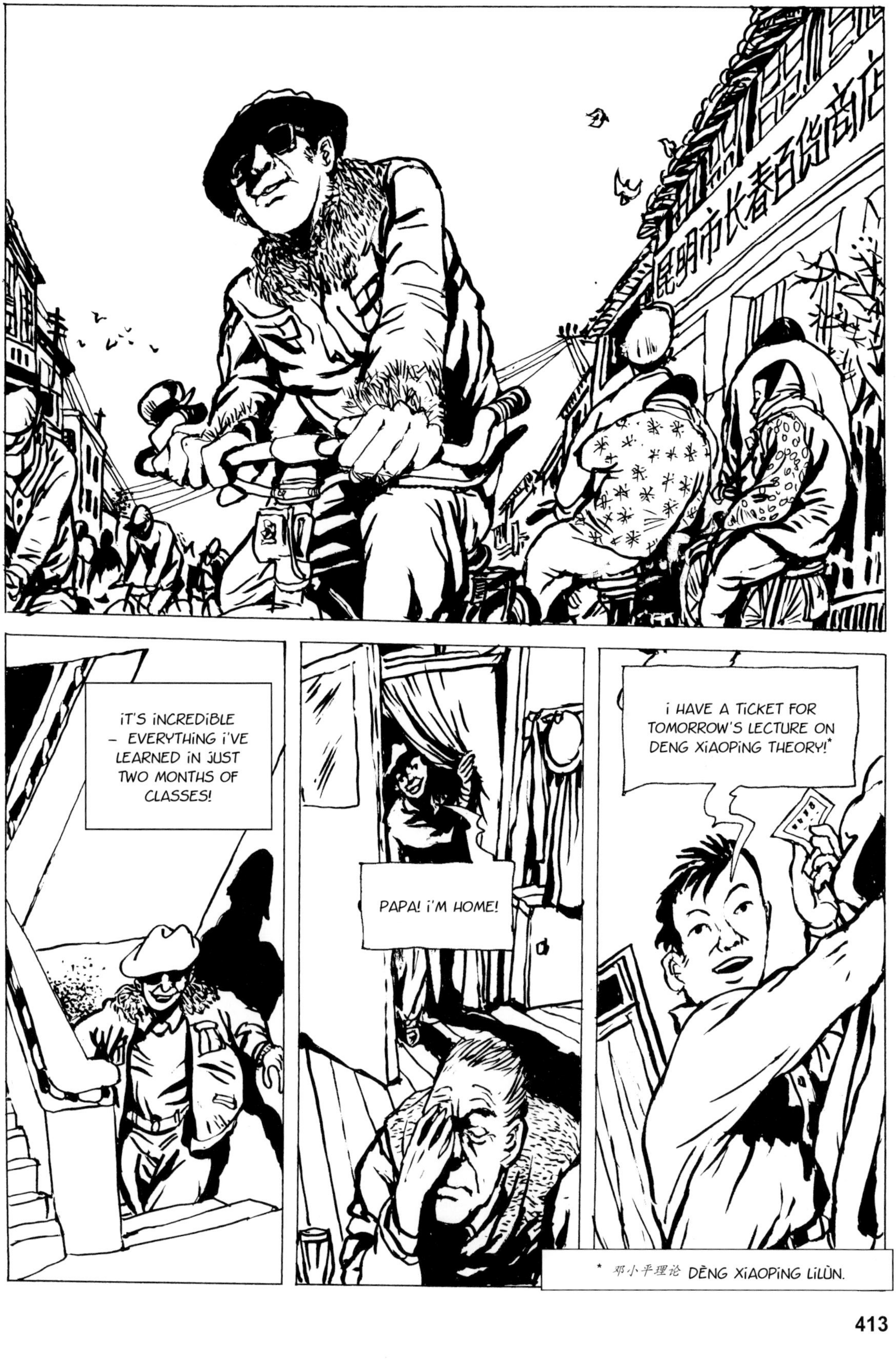
昆明市长春百货商店
iT'S iNCREDiBLE – EVERYTHiNG i'VE LEARNED iN JUST TWO MONTHS OF CLASSES!
PAPA! i'M HOME!
i HAVE A TiCKET FOR TOMORROW'S LECTURE ON DENG XiAOPiNG THEORY!*

* 邓小平理论 DĚNG XiAOPiNG LiLÙN.

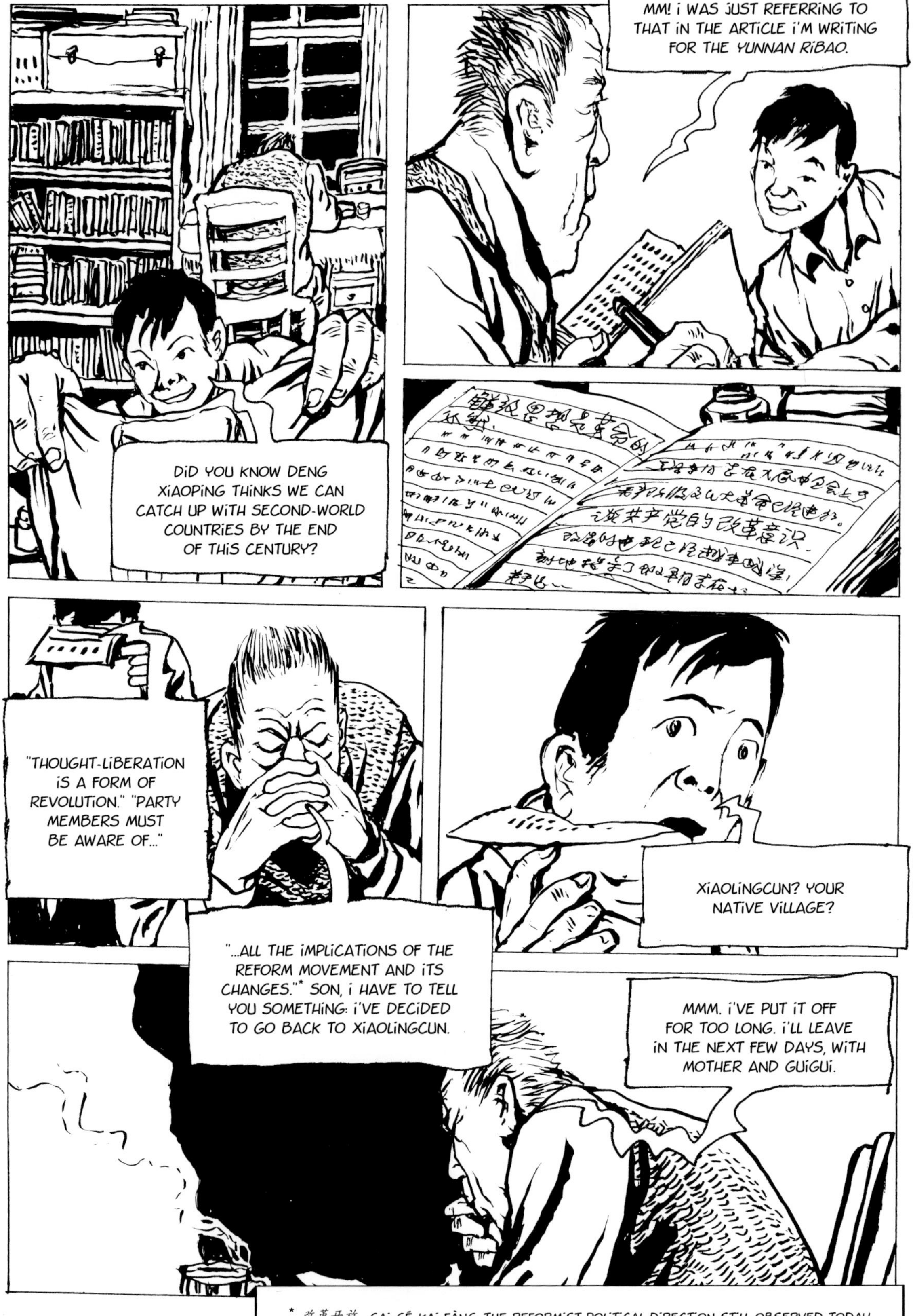
DID YOU KNOW DENG XIAOPING THINKS WE CAN CATCH UP WITH SECOND-WORLD COUNTRIES BY THE END OF THIS CENTURY?
MM! I WAS JUST REFERRING TO THAT IN THE ARTICLE I'M WRITING FOR THE *YUNNAN RIBAO*.
"THOUGHT-LIBERATION IS A FORM OF REVOLUTION." "PARTY MEMBERS MUST BE AWARE OF..."
"...ALL THE IMPLICATIONS OF THE REFORM MOVEMENT AND ITS CHANGES."* SON, I HAVE TO TELL YOU SOMETHING: I'VE DECIDED TO GO BACK TO XIAOLINGCUN.
XIAOLINGCUN? YOUR NATIVE VILLAGE?
MMM. I'VE PUT IT OFF FOR TOO LONG. I'LL LEAVE IN THE NEXT FEW DAYS, WITH MOTHER AND GUIGUI.

* 改革开放 GAI GĒ KAI FÀNG: THE REFORMIST POLITICAL DIRECTION STILL OBSERVED TODAY.

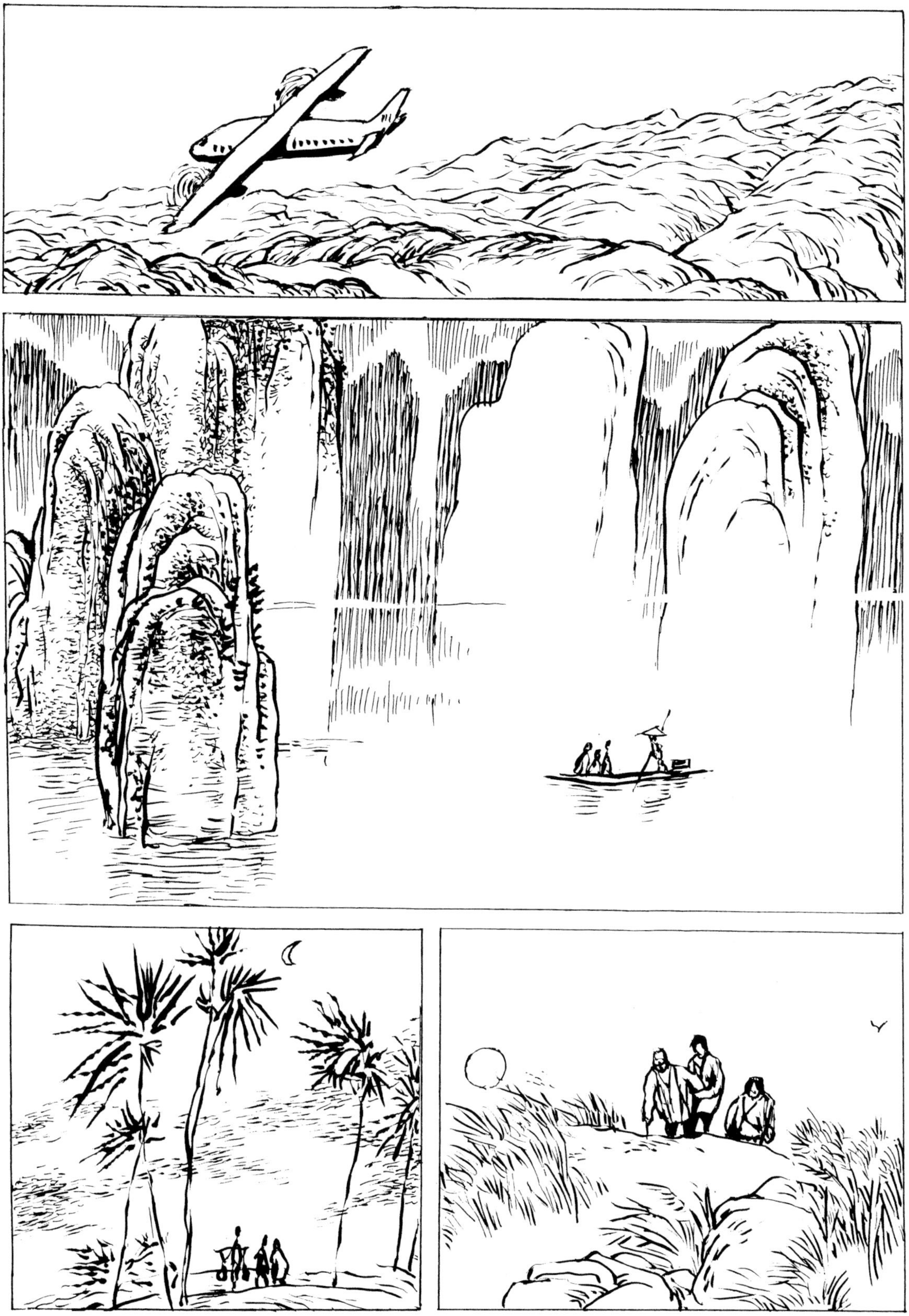

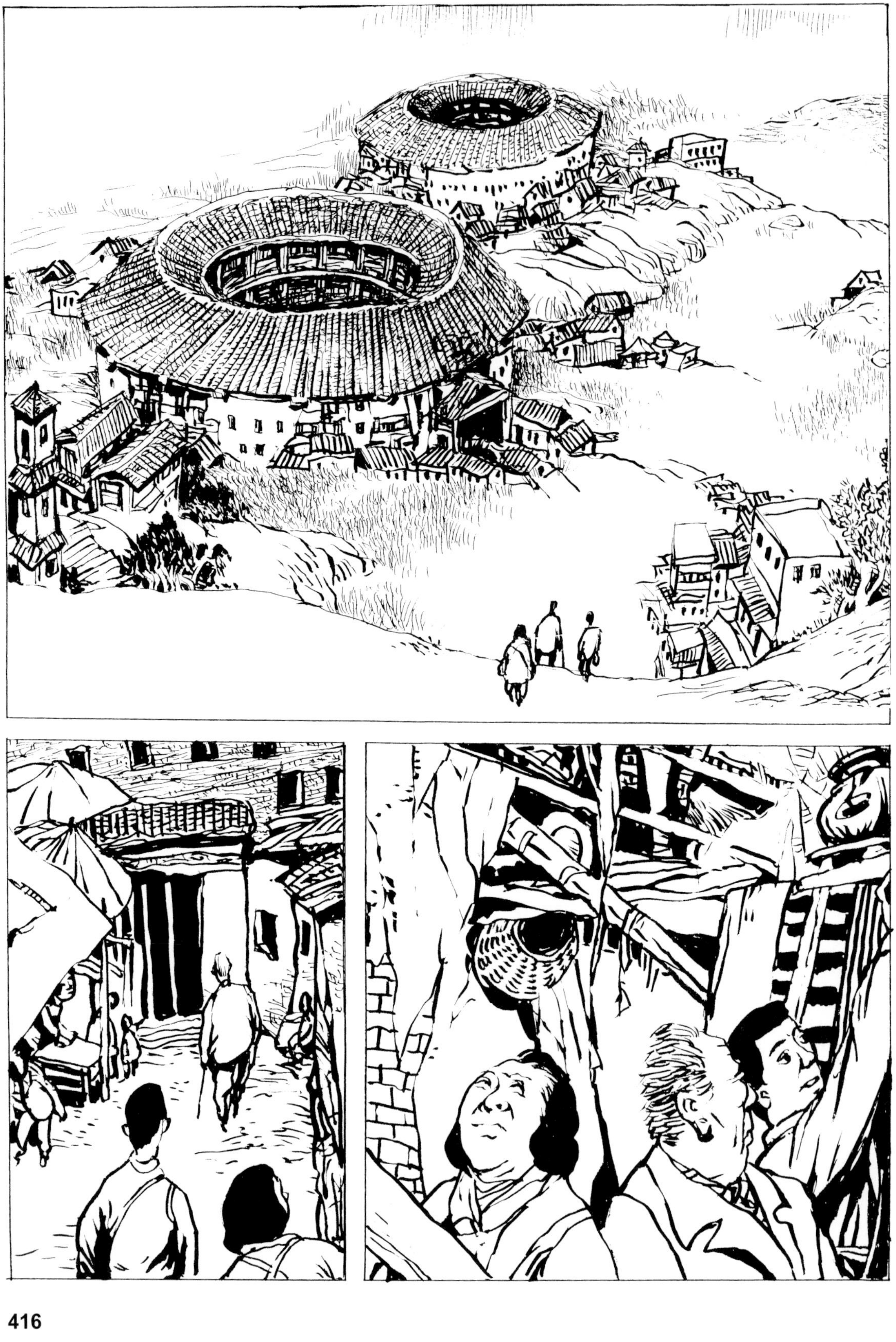

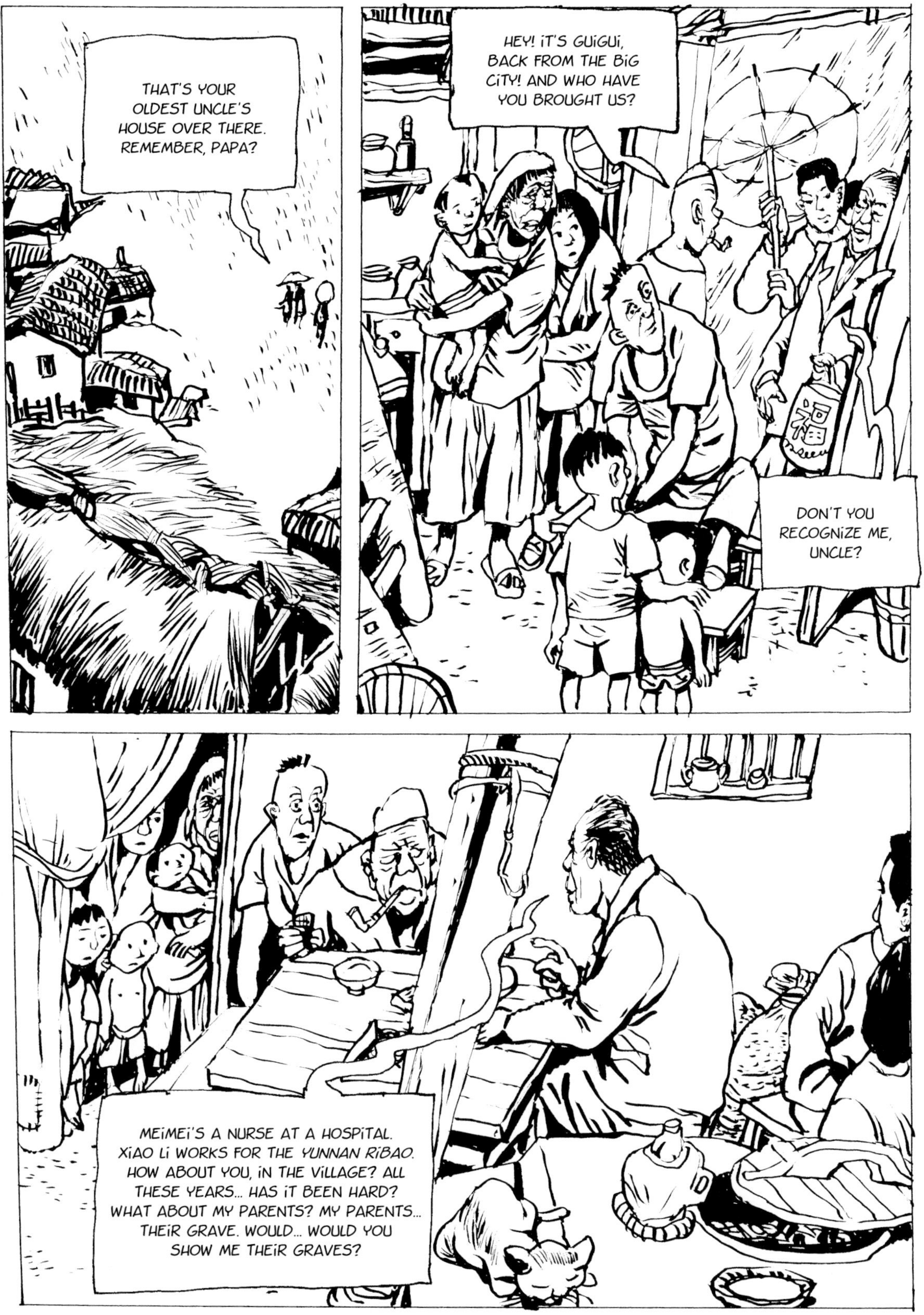
THAT'S YOUR OLDEST UNCLE'S HOUSE OVER THERE. REMEMBER, PAPA?
HEY! IT'S GUIGUI, BACK FROM THE BIG CITY! AND WHO HAVE YOU BROUGHT US?
DON'T YOU RECOGNIZE ME, UNCLE?
MEIMEI'S A NURSE AT A HOSPITAL. XIAO LI WORKS FOR THE *YUNNAN RIBAO*. HOW ABOUT YOU, IN THE VILLAGE? ALL THESE YEARS... HAS IT BEEN HARD? WHAT ABOUT MY PARENTS? MY PARENTS... THEIR GRAVE. WOULD... WOULD YOU SHOW ME THEIR GRAVES?

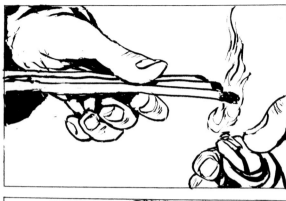

THERE, ON THE HILL!

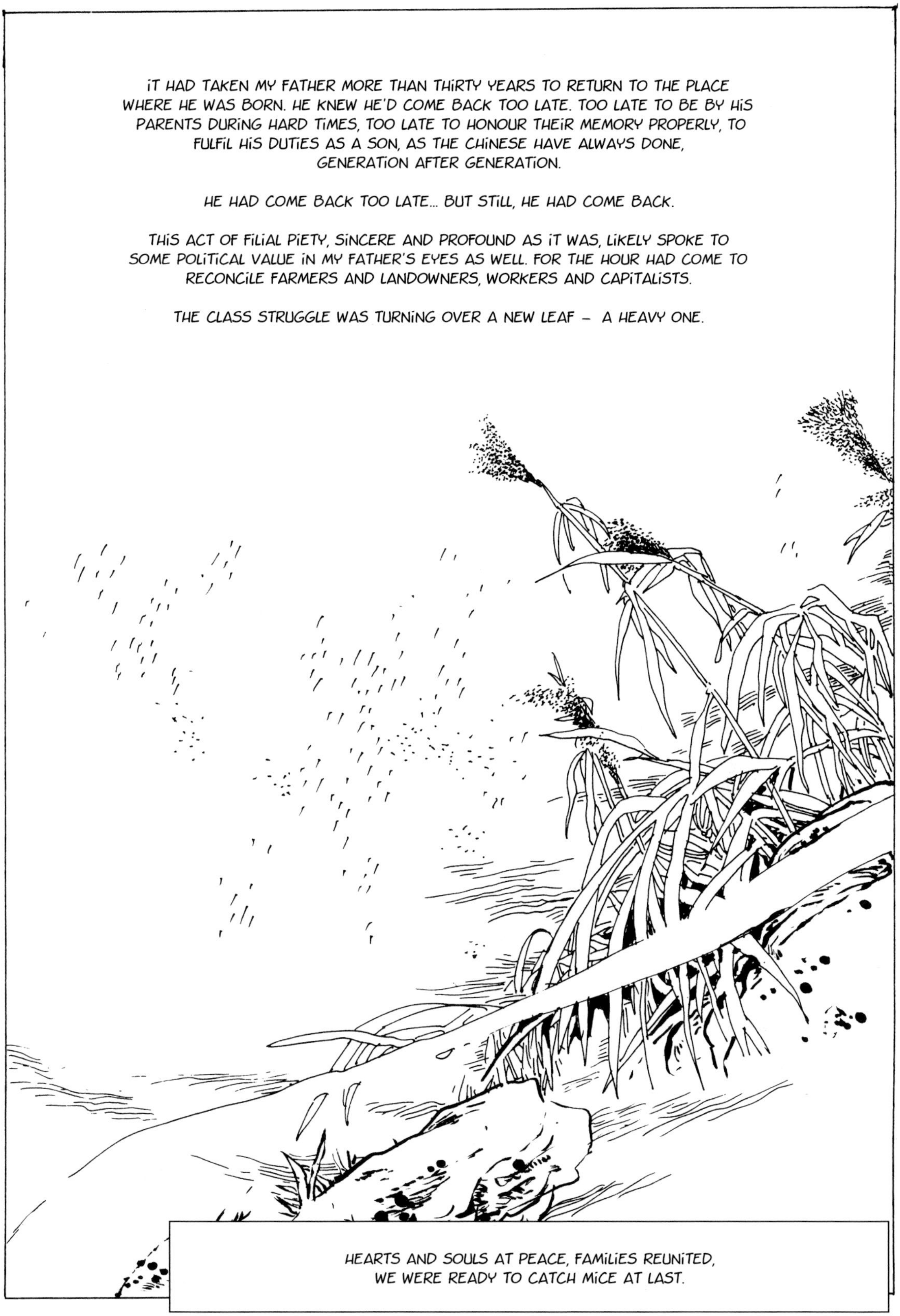
IT HAD TAKEN MY FATHER MORE THAN THIRTY YEARS TO RETURN TO THE PLACE WHERE HE WAS BORN. HE KNEW HE'D COME BACK TOO LATE. TOO LATE TO BE BY HIS PARENTS DURING HARD TIMES, TOO LATE TO HONOUR THEIR MEMORY PROPERLY, TO FULFIL HIS DUTIES AS A SON, AS THE CHINESE HAVE ALWAYS DONE, GENERATION AFTER GENERATION.
HE HAD COME BACK TOO LATE... BUT STILL, HE HAD COME BACK.
THIS ACT OF FILIAL PIETY, SINCERE AND PROFOUND AS IT WAS, LIKELY SPOKE TO SOME POLITICAL VALUE IN MY FATHER'S EYES AS WELL. FOR THE HOUR HAD COME TO RECONCILE FARMERS AND LANDOWNERS, WORKERS AND CAPITALISTS.
THE CLASS STRUGGLE WAS TURNING OVER A NEW LEAF – A HEAVY ONE.
HEARTS AND SOULS AT PEACE, FAMILIES REUNITED, WE WERE READY TO CATCH MICE AT LAST.

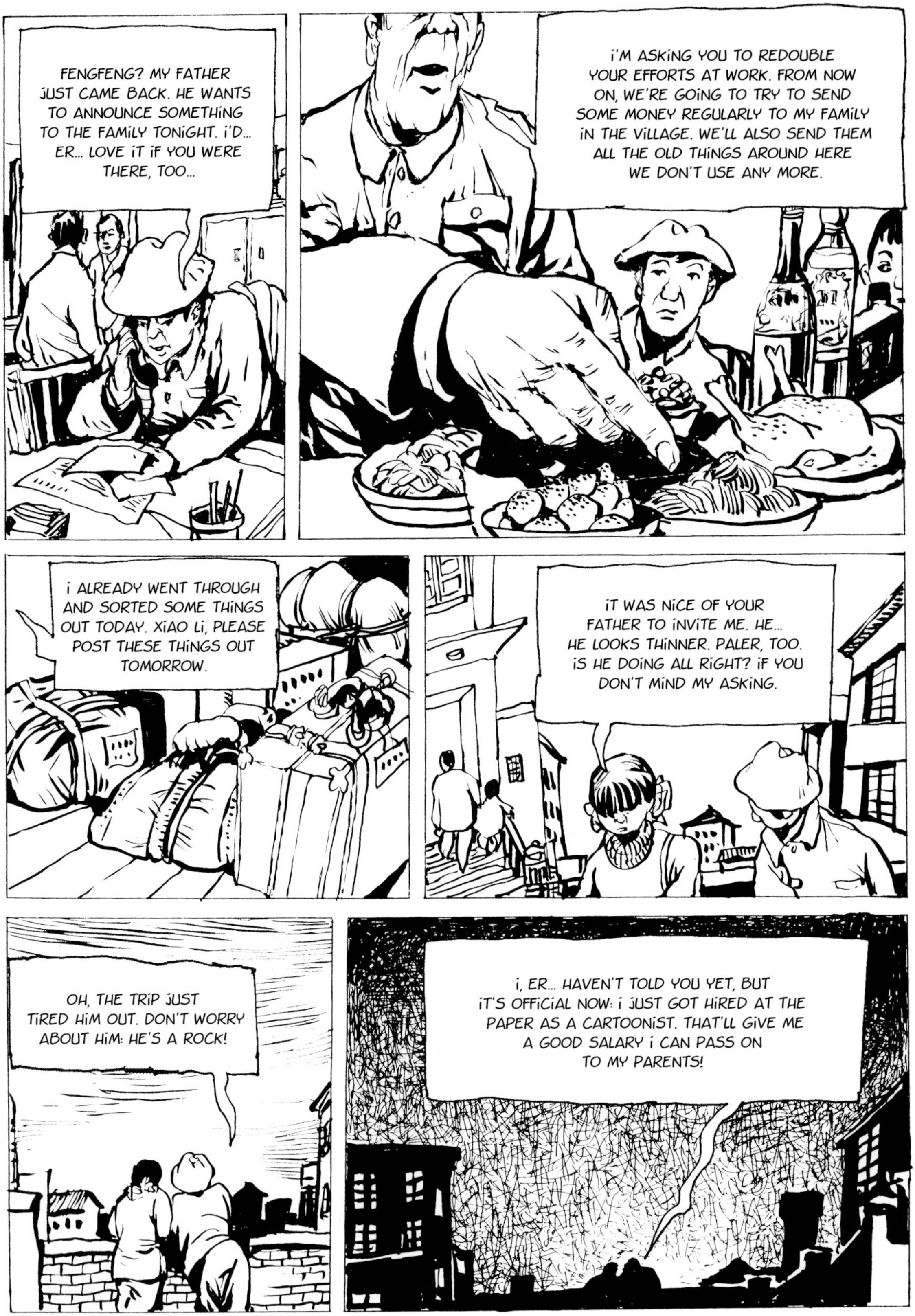
FENGFENG? MY FATHER JUST CAME BACK. HE WANTS TO ANNOUNCE SOMETHING TO THE FAMILY TONIGHT. I'D... ER... LOVE IT IF YOU WERE THERE, TOO...
I'M ASKING YOU TO REDOUBLE YOUR EFFORTS AT WORK. FROM NOW ON, WE'RE GOING TO TRY TO SEND SOME MONEY REGULARLY TO MY FAMILY IN THE VILLAGE. WE'LL ALSO SEND THEM ALL THE OLD THINGS AROUND HERE WE DON'T USE ANY MORE.
I ALREADY WENT THROUGH AND SORTED SOME THINGS OUT TODAY. XIAO LI, PLEASE POST THESE THINGS OUT TOMORROW.
IT WAS NICE OF YOUR FATHER TO INVITE ME. HE... HE LOOKS THINNER. PALER, TOO. IS HE DOING ALL RIGHT? IF YOU DON'T MIND MY ASKING.
OH, THE TRIP JUST TIRED HIM OUT. DON'T WORRY ABOUT HIM: HE'S A ROCK!
I, ER... HAVEN'T TOLD YOU YET, BUT IT'S OFFICIAL NOW: I JUST GOT HIRED AT THE PAPER AS A CARTOONIST. THAT'LL GIVE ME A GOOD SALARY I CAN PASS ON TO MY PARENTS!

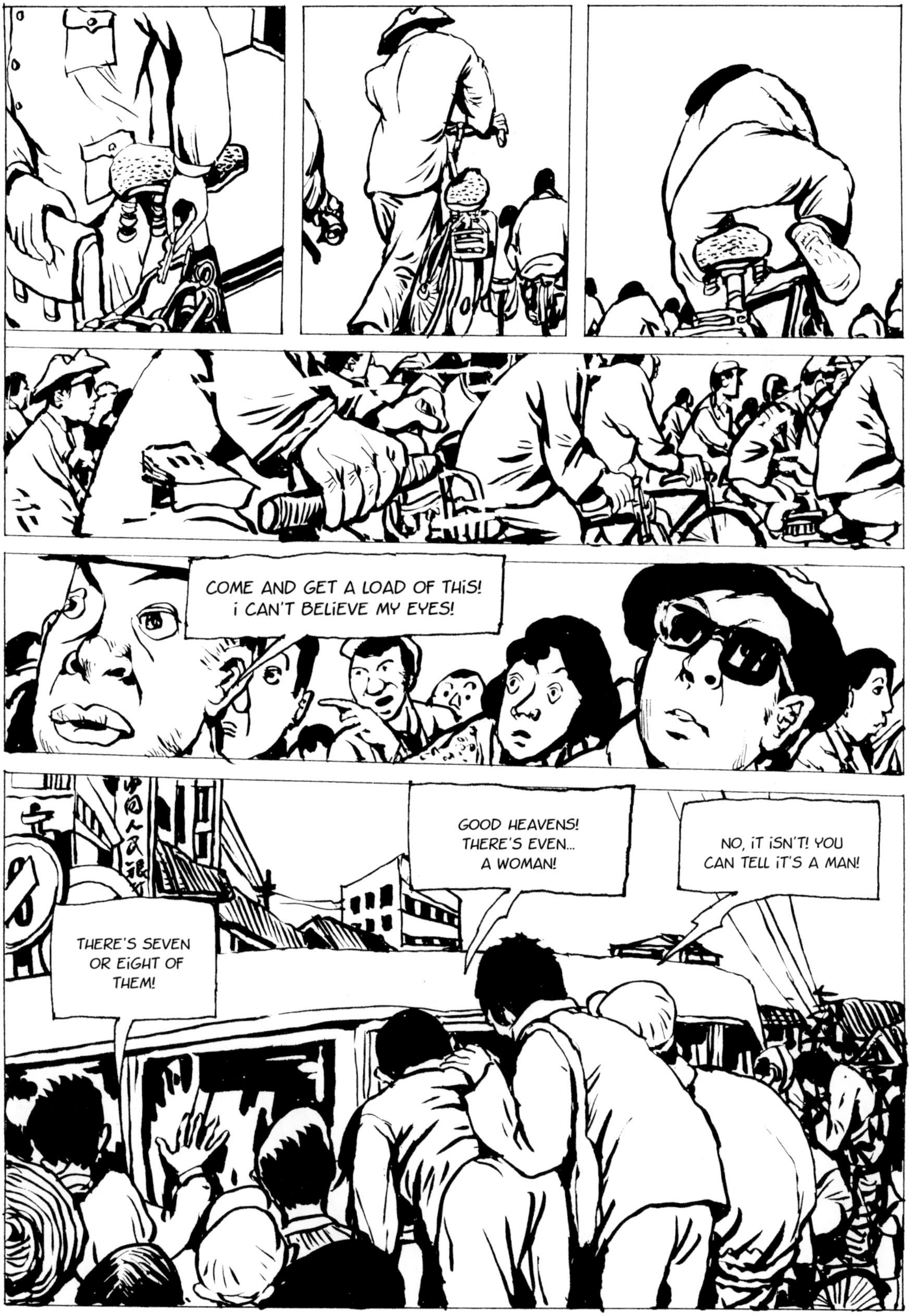
COME AND GET A LOAD OF THIS!
I CAN'T BELIEVE MY EYES!
THERE'S SEVEN OR EIGHT OF THEM!
GOOD HEAVENS! THERE'S EVEN... A WOMAN!
NO, IT ISN'T! YOU CAN TELL IT'S A MAN!

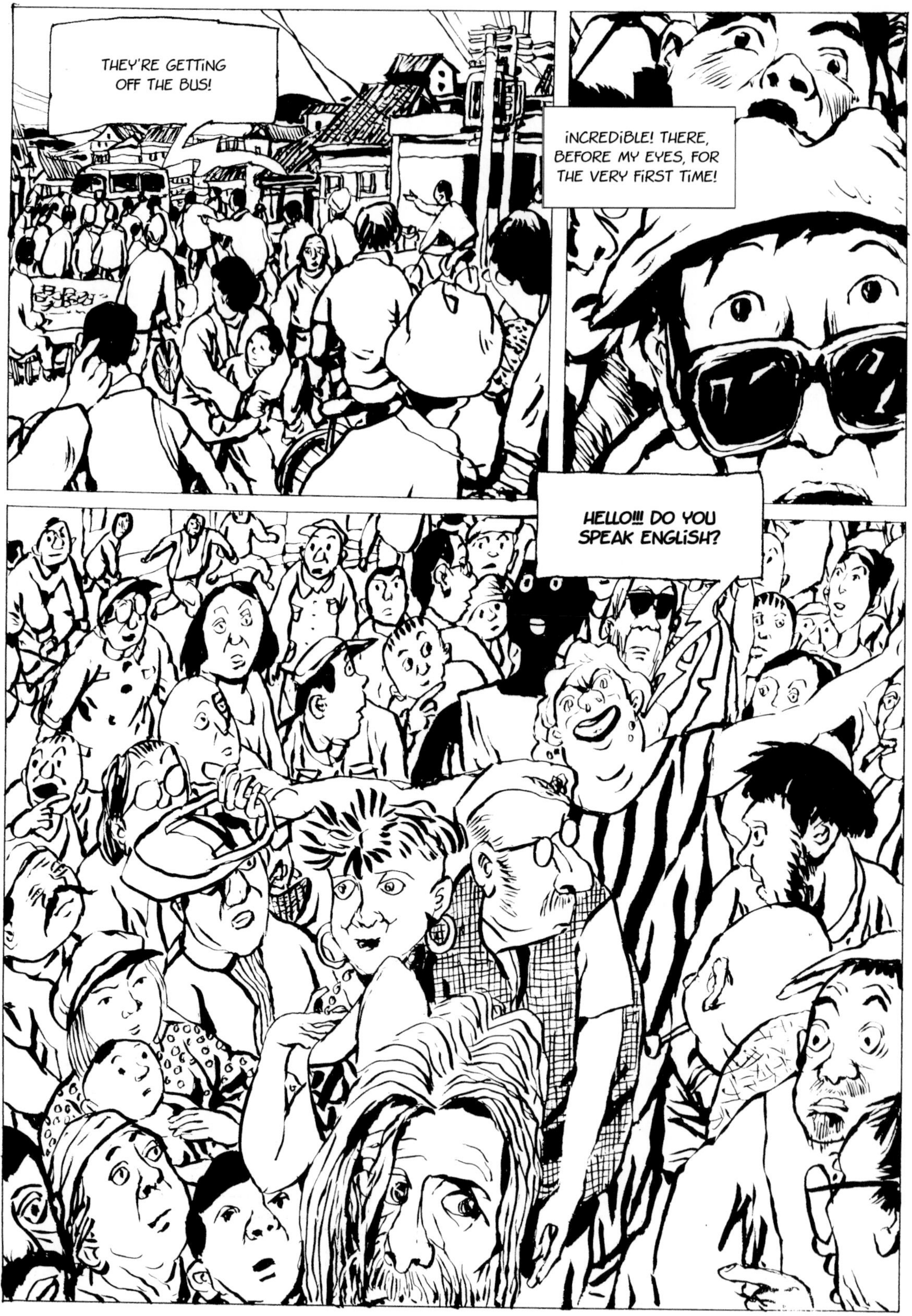
THEY'RE GETTING OFF THE BUS!
INCREDIBLE! THERE, BEFORE MY EYES, FOR THE VERY FIRST TIME!
HELLO!!! DO YOU SPEAK ENGLISH?

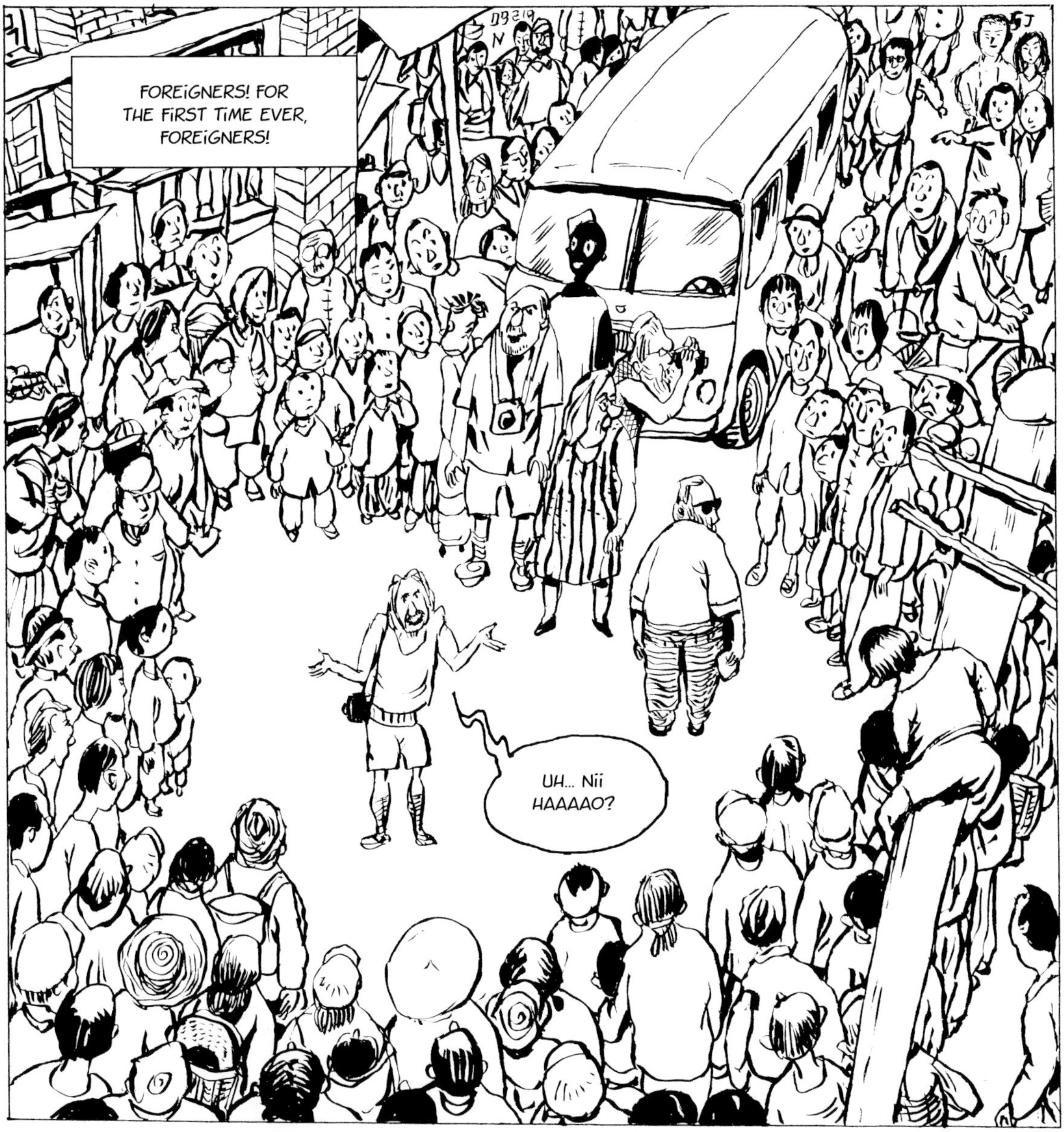
FOREIGNERS! FOR THE FIRST TIME EVER, FOREIGNERS!
UH... NII HAAAAO?

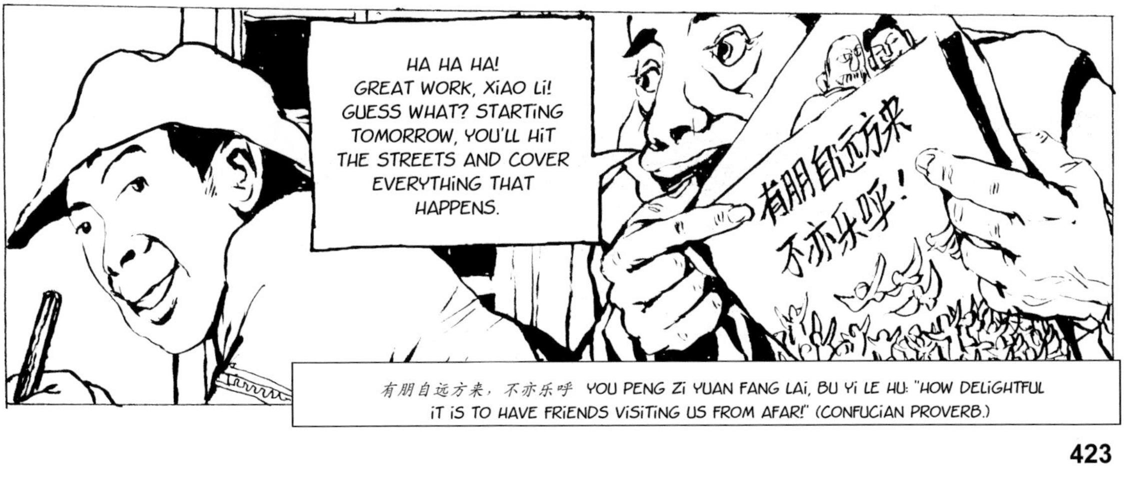
HA HA HA! GREAT WORK, XIAO LI! GUESS WHAT? STARTING TOMORROW, YOU'LL HIT THE STREETS AND COVER EVERYTHING THAT HAPPENS.
有朋自远方来
不亦乐乎！
有朋自远方来，不亦乐呼 YOU PENG ZI YUAN FANG LAI, BU YI LE HU: "HOW DELIGHTFUL IT IS TO HAVE FRIENDS VISITING US FROM AFAR!" (CONFUCIAN PROVERB.)

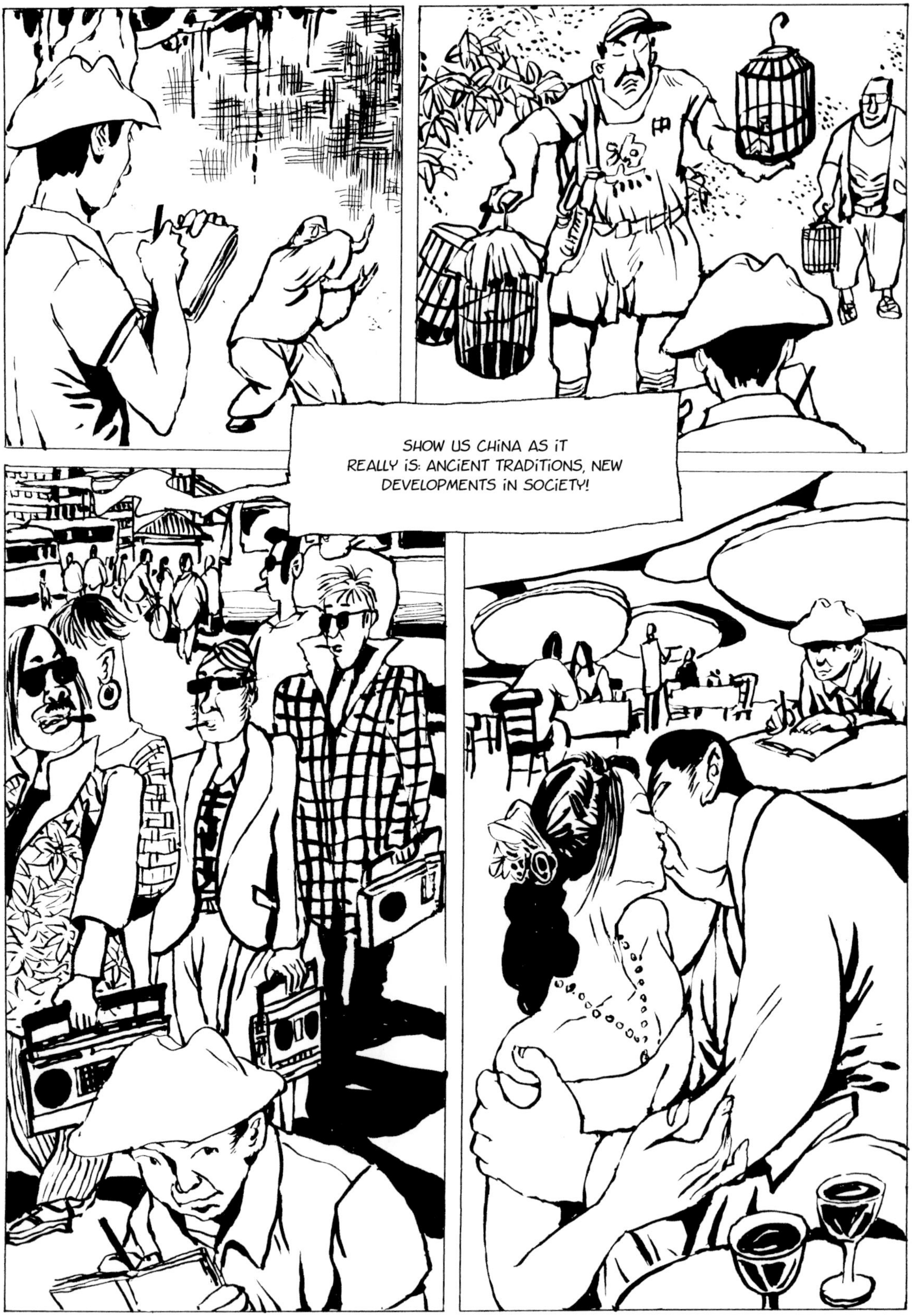
SHOW US CHINA AS IT REALLY IS: ANCIENT TRADITIONS, NEW DEVELOPMENTS IN SOCIETY!

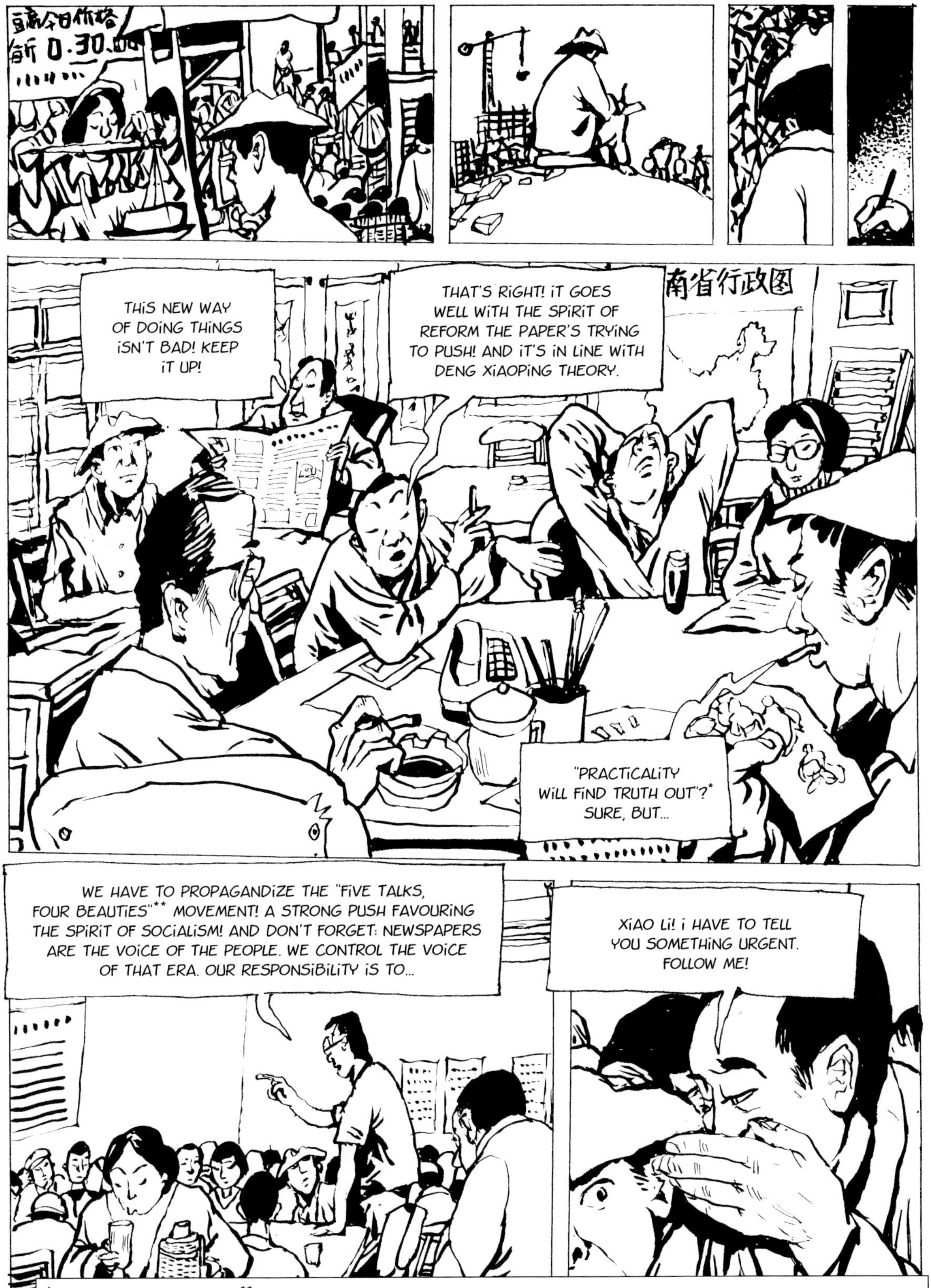
THIS NEW WAY OF DOING THINGS ISN'T BAD! KEEP IT UP!
THAT'S RIGHT! IT GOES WELL WITH THE SPIRIT OF REFORM THE PAPER'S TRYING TO PUSH! AND IT'S IN LINE WITH DENG XIAOPING THEORY.
南省行政图
"PRACTICALITY WILL FIND TRUTH OUT"?* SURE, BUT...
WE HAVE TO PROPAGANDIZE THE "FIVE TALKS, FOUR BEAUTIES"** MOVEMENT! A STRONG PUSH FAVOURING THE SPIRIT OF SOCIALISM! AND DON'T FORGET: NEWSPAPERS ARE THE VOICE OF THE PEOPLE. WE CONTROL THE VOICE OF THAT ERA. OUR RESPONSIBILITY IS TO...
XIAO LI! I HAVE TO TELL YOU SOMETHING URGENT. FOLLOW ME!

* 实事求是 SHI SHI QIU SHI. ** 五讲四美 WU JIANG SI MEI. THE FIVE TALKS: POLITENESS, CIVIL BEHAVIOUR, MORALITY, ATTENTION TO SOCIAL RELATIONS AND GOOD HYGIENE; THE FOUR BEAUTIES: BEAUTIFUL LANGUAGE, BEAUTIFUL BEHAVIOUR, BEAUTIFUL HEART AND BEAUTIFUL ENVIRONMENT.

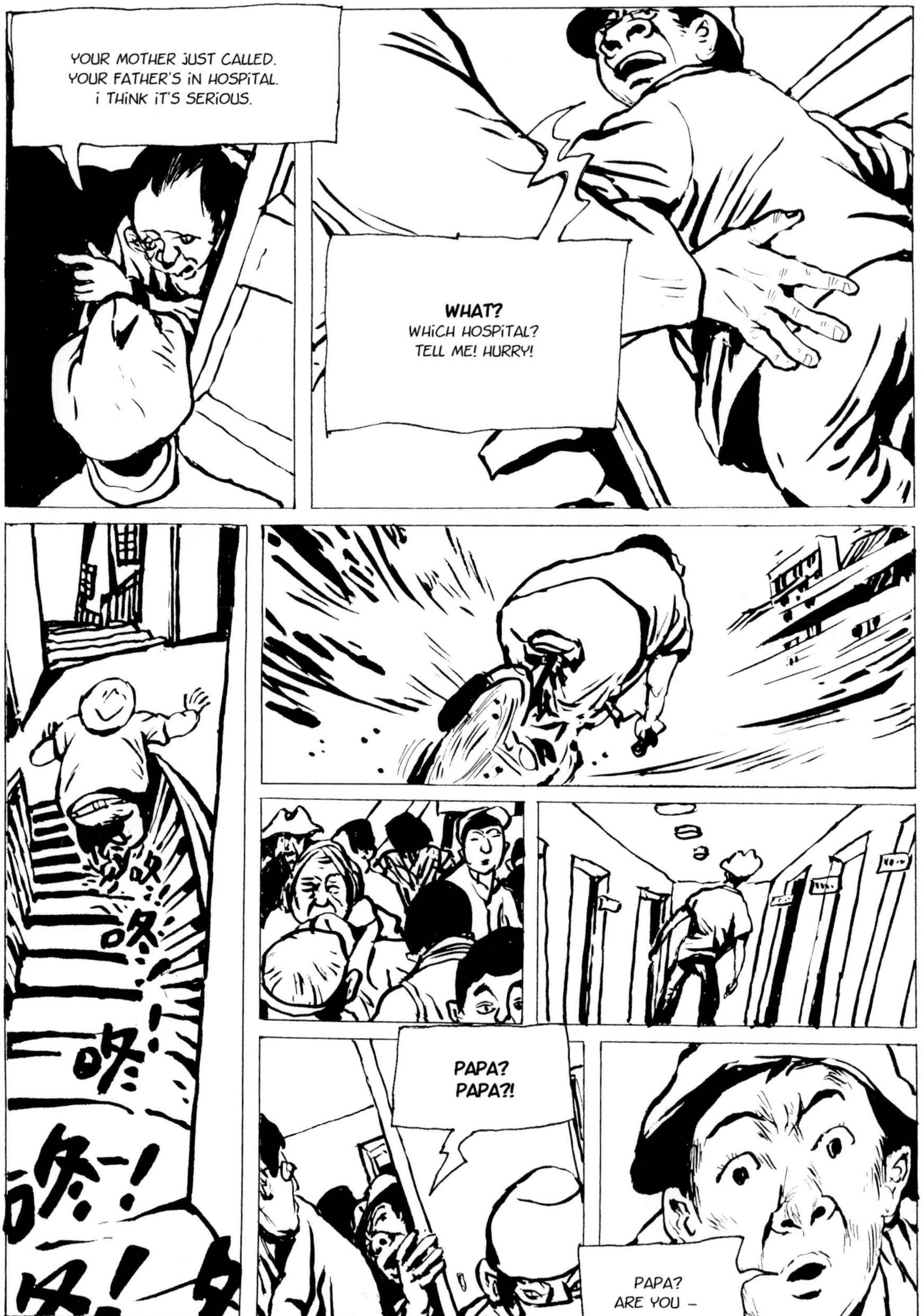
YOUR MOTHER JUST CALLED. YOUR FATHER'S IN HOSPITAL. I THINK IT'S SERIOUS.
WHAT? WHICH HOSPITAL? TELL ME! HURRY!
咚!
咚—!
PAPA? PAPA?!
PAPA? ARE YOU –

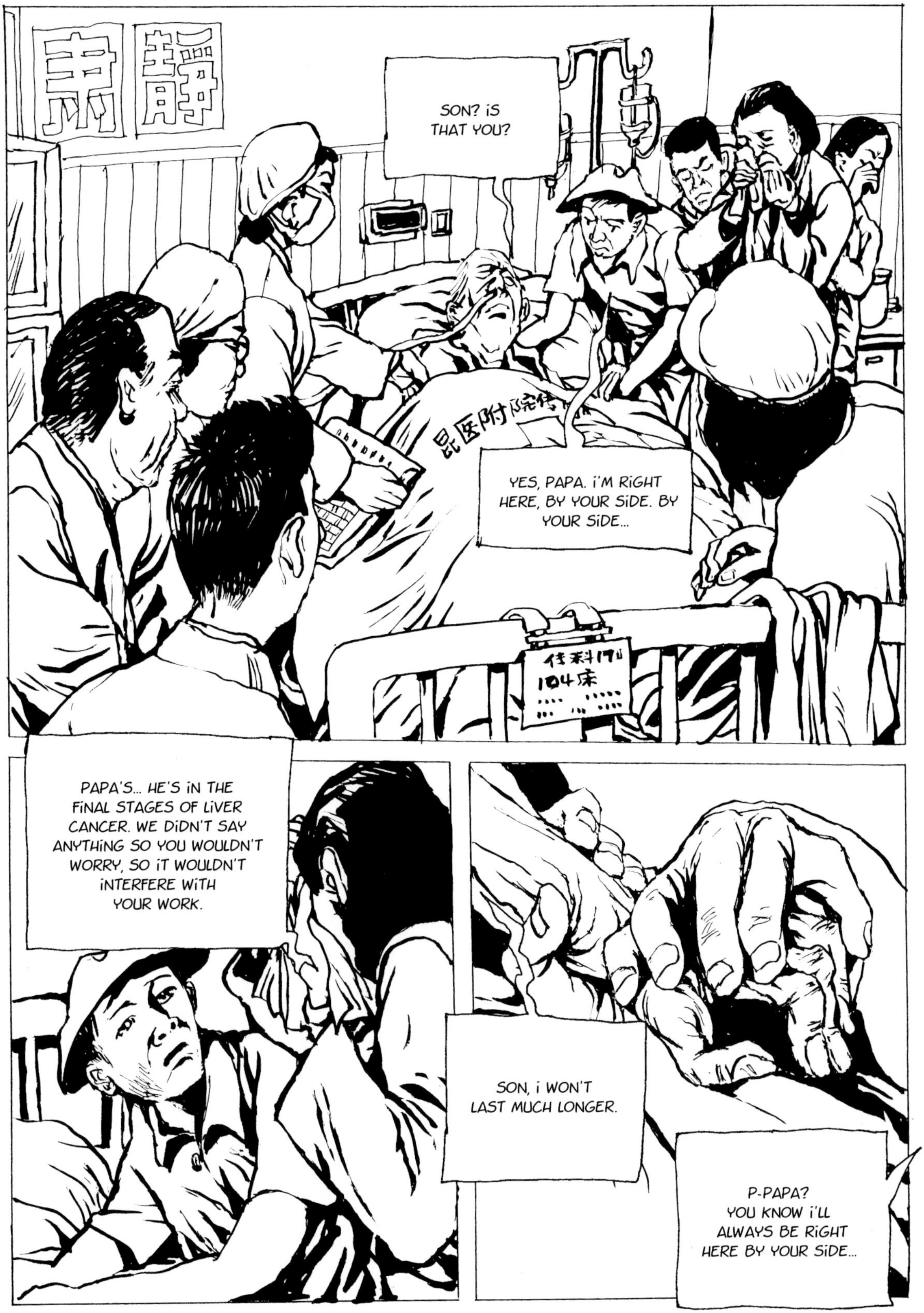
SON? iS THAT YOU?
YES, PAPA. i'M RiGHT HERE, BY YOUR SiDE. BY YOUR SiDE...
PAPA'S... HE'S iN THE FiNAL STAGES OF LiVER CANCER. WE DiDN'T SAY ANYTHiNG SO YOU WOULDN'T WORRY, SO iT WOULDN'T iNTERFERE WiTH YOUR WORK.
SON, i WON'T LAST MUCH LONGER.
P-PAPA? YOU KNOW i'LL ALWAYS BE RiGHT HERE BY YOUR SiDE...

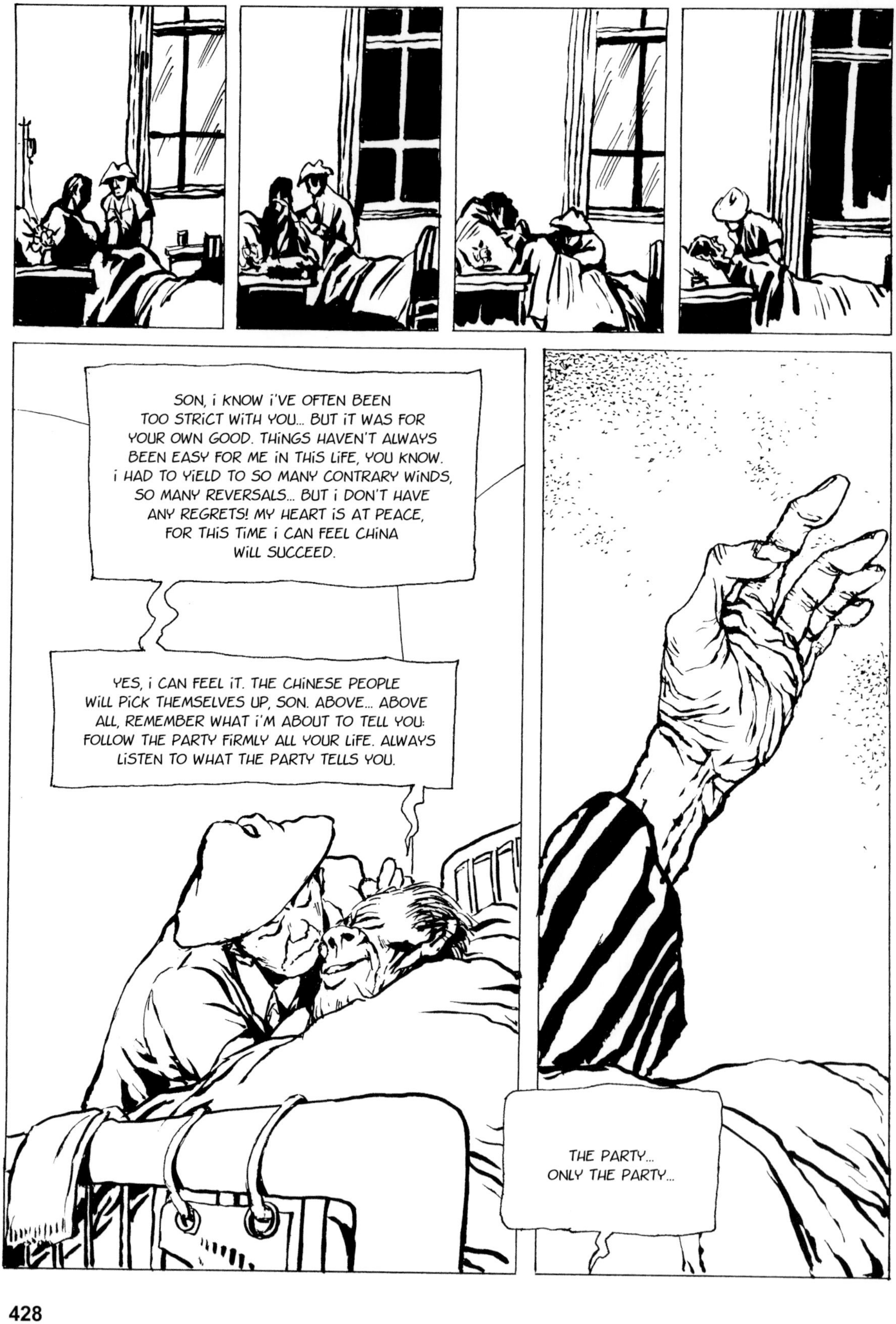
SON, I KNOW I'VE OFTEN BEEN TOO STRICT WITH YOU... BUT IT WAS FOR YOUR OWN GOOD. THINGS HAVEN'T ALWAYS BEEN EASY FOR ME IN THIS LIFE, YOU KNOW. I HAD TO YIELD TO SO MANY CONTRARY WINDS, SO MANY REVERSALS... BUT I DON'T HAVE ANY REGRETS! MY HEART IS AT PEACE, FOR THIS TIME I CAN FEEL CHINA WILL SUCCEED.
YES, I CAN FEEL IT. THE CHINESE PEOPLE WILL PICK THEMSELVES UP, SON. ABOVE... ABOVE ALL, REMEMBER WHAT I'M ABOUT TO TELL YOU: FOLLOW THE PARTY FIRMLY ALL YOUR LIFE. ALWAYS LISTEN TO WHAT THE PARTY TELLS YOU.
THE PARTY... ONLY THE PARTY...

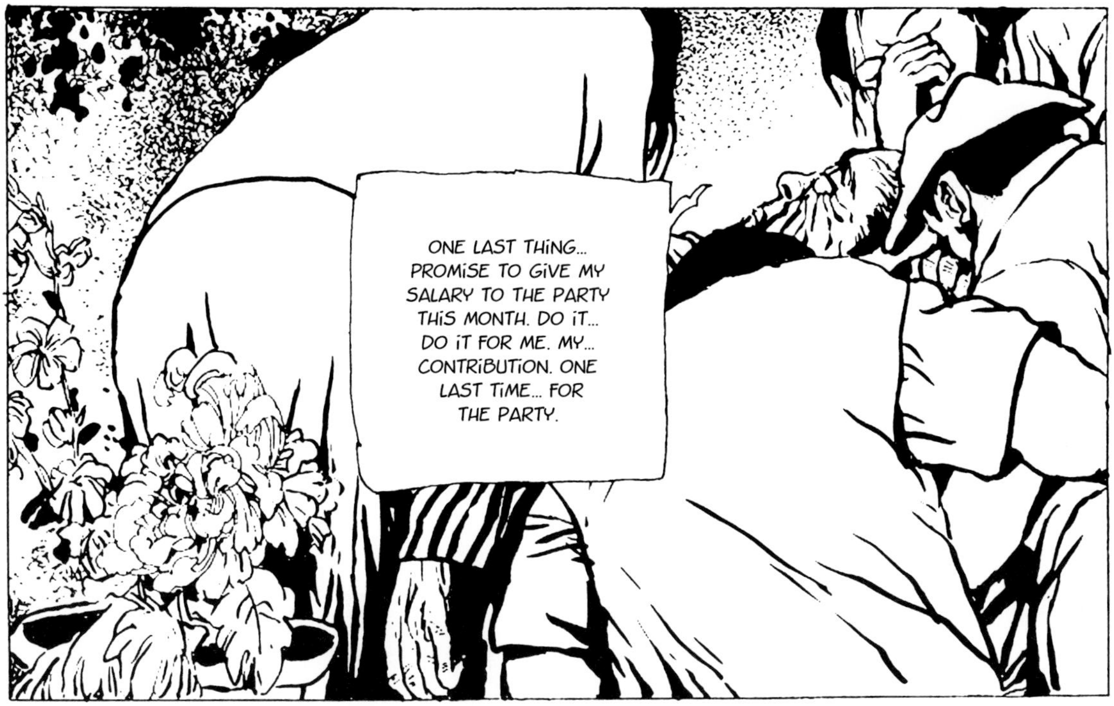
ONE LAST THING... PROMISE TO GIVE MY SALARY TO THE PARTY THIS MONTH. DO IT... DO IT FOR ME. MY... CONTRIBUTION. ONE LAST TIME... FOR THE PARTY.

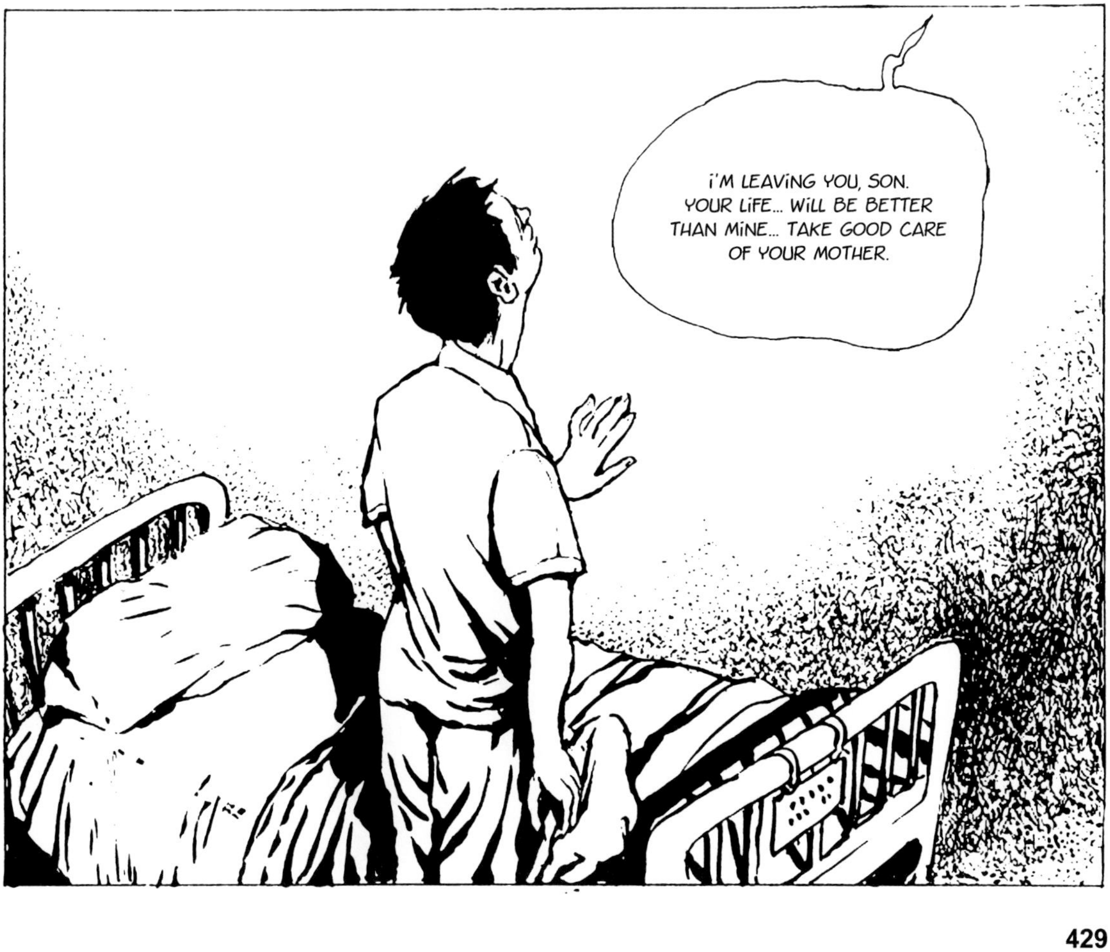
I'M LEAVING YOU, SON. YOUR LIFE... WILL BE BETTER THAN MINE... TAKE GOOD CARE OF YOUR MOTHER.

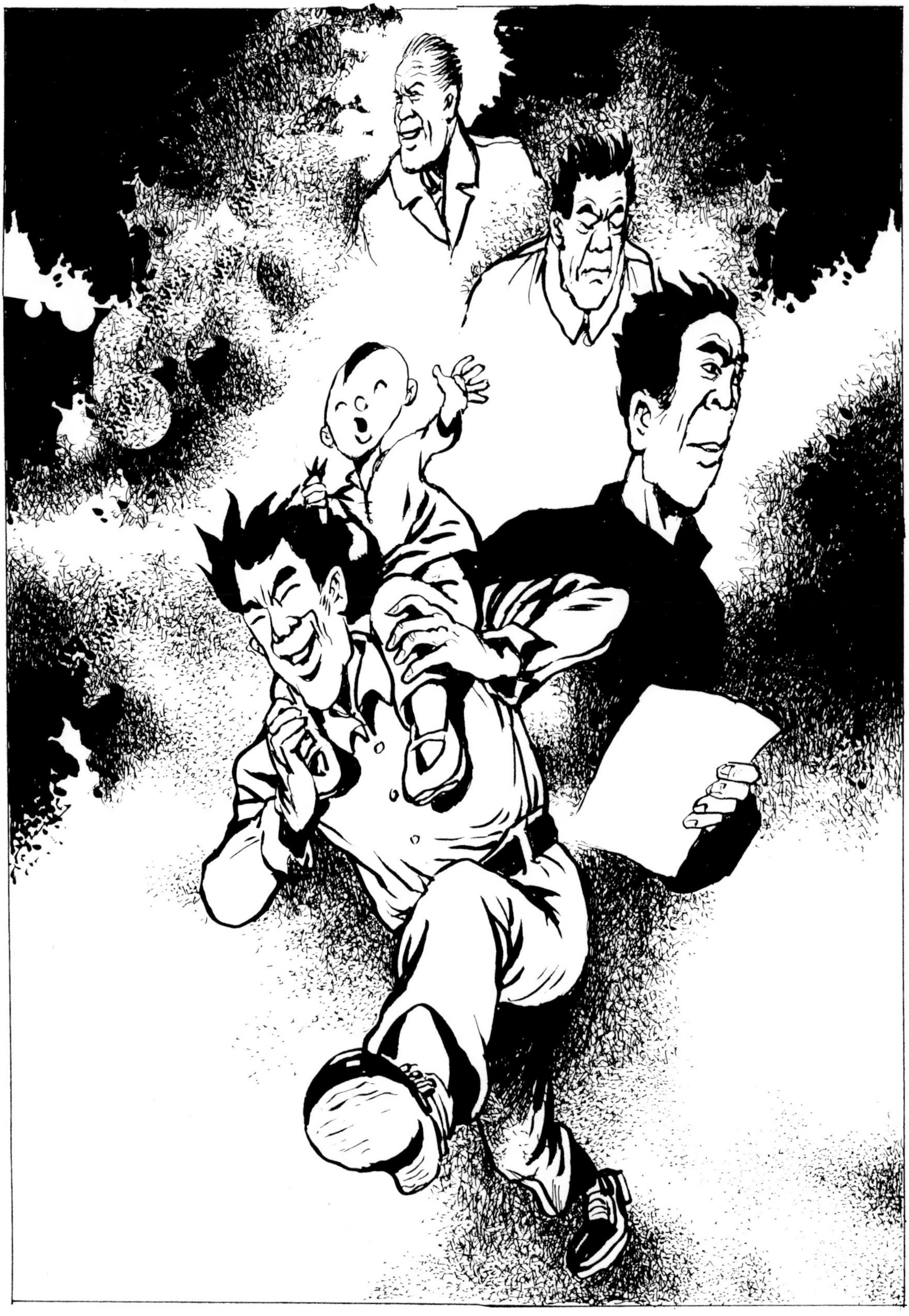

BOOK III

The Time of the Money

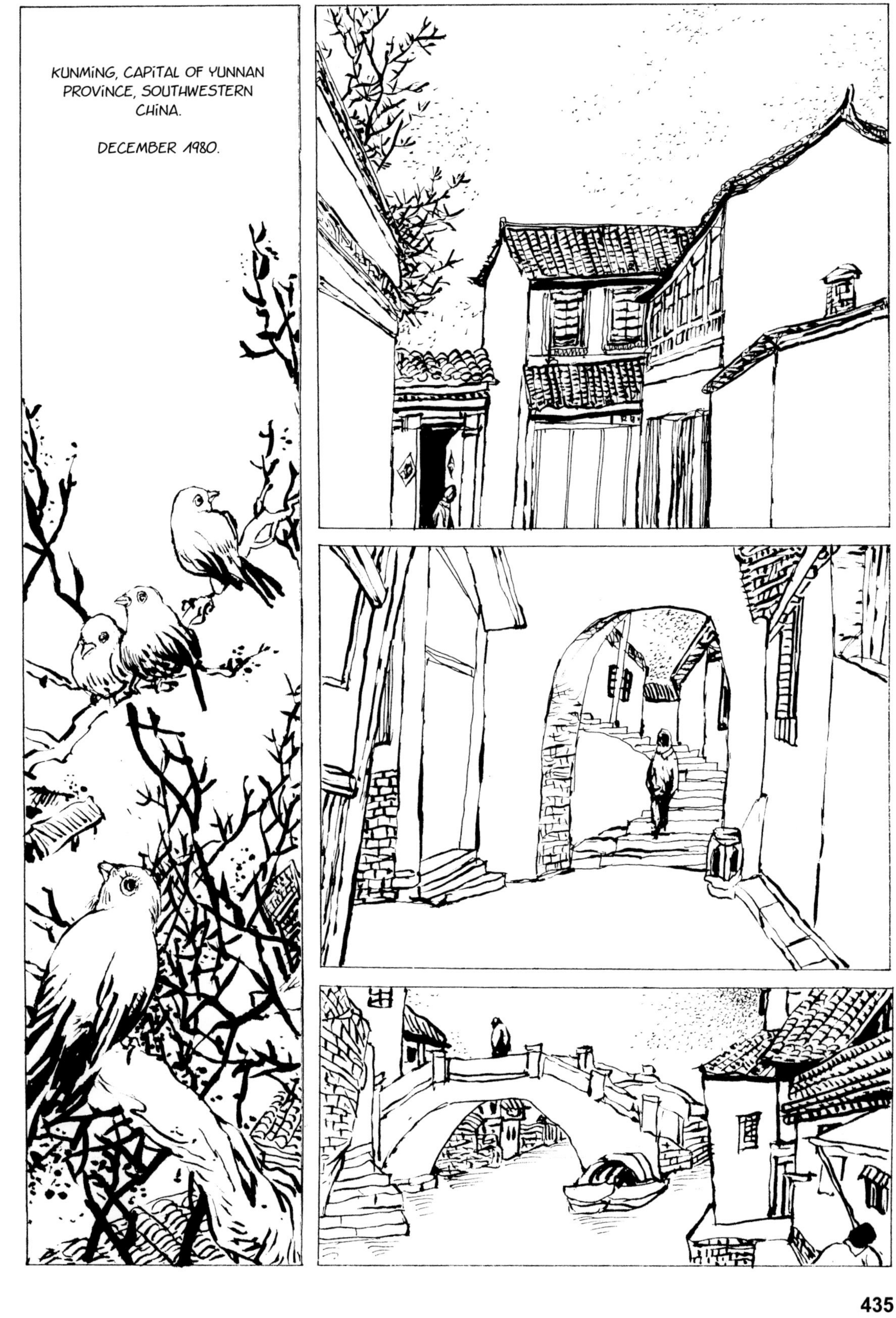
KUNMiNG, CAPiTAL OF YUNNAN PROViNCE, SOUTHWESTERN CHiNA.
DECEMBER 1980.

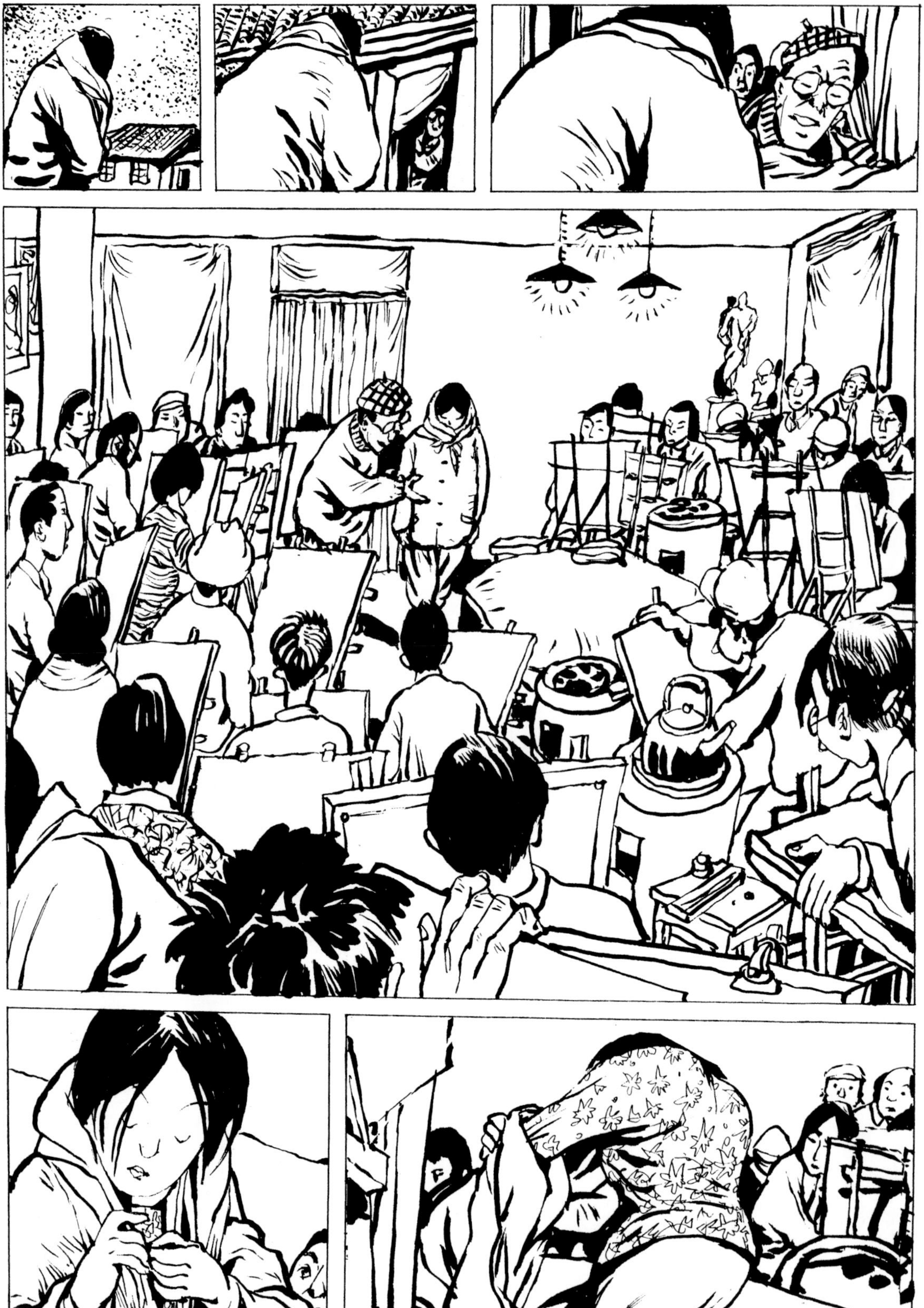

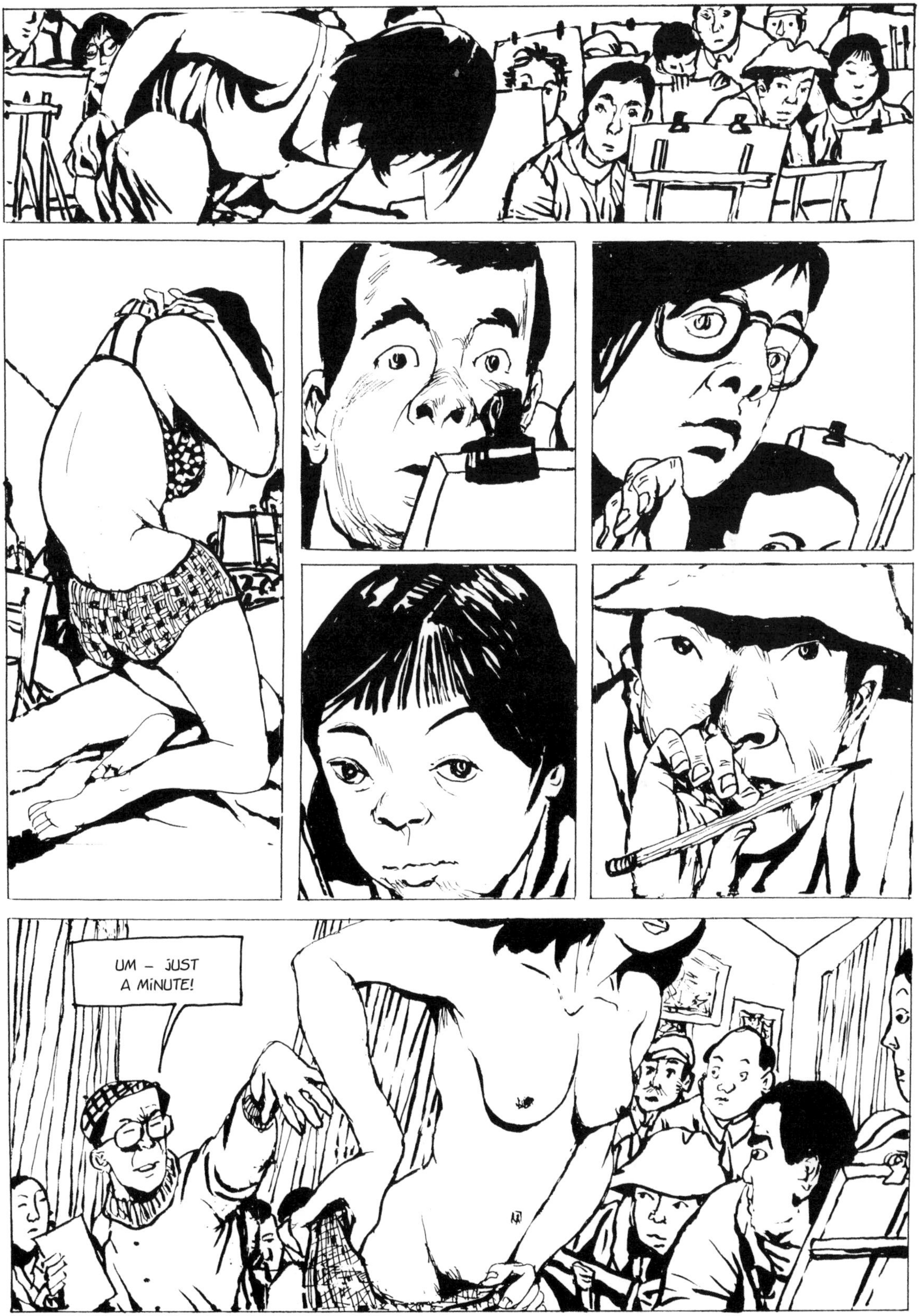
UM – JUST A MINUTE!

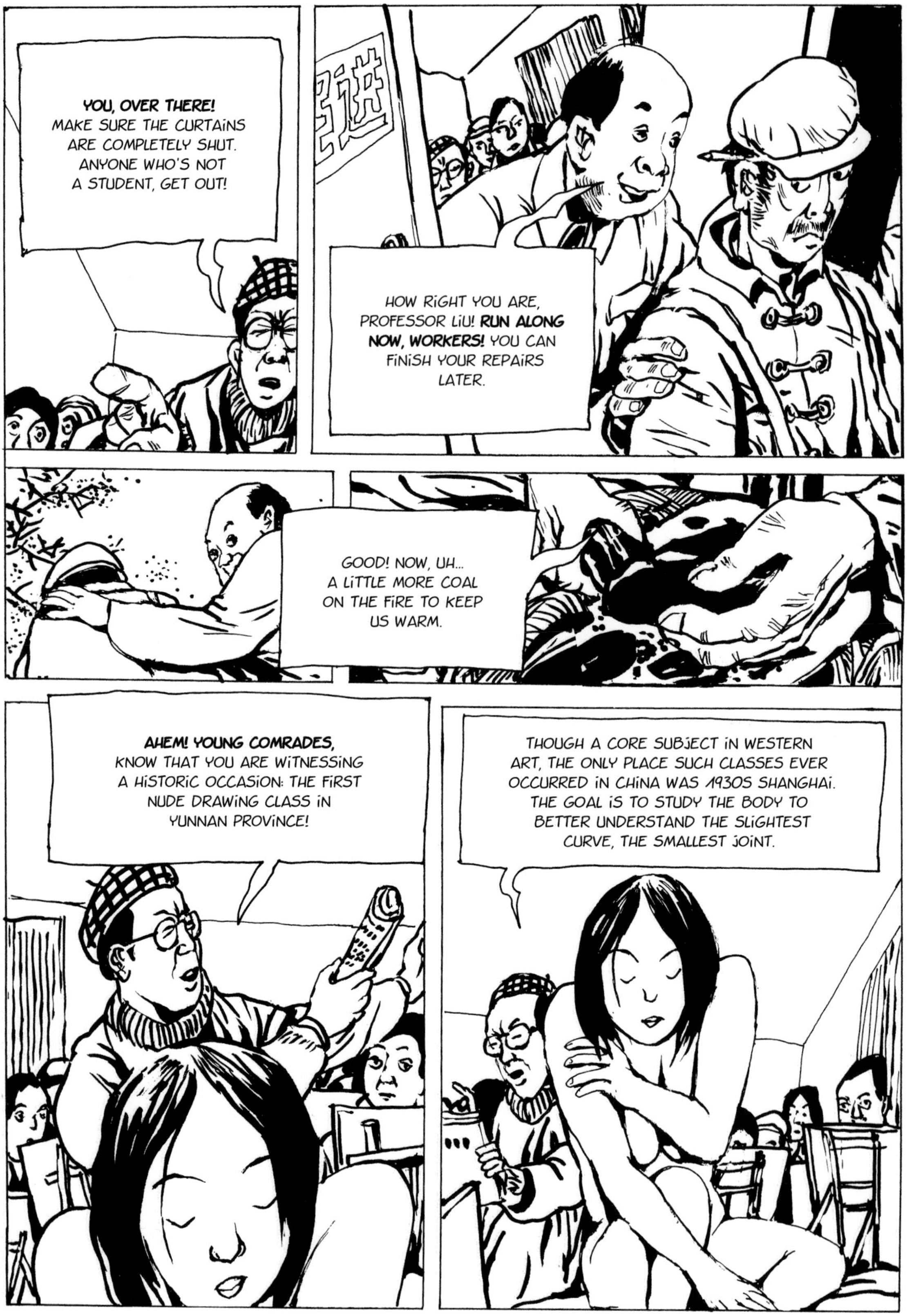
YOU, OVER THERE! MAKE SURE THE CURTAINS ARE COMPLETELY SHUT. ANYONE WHO'S NOT A STUDENT, GET OUT!
HOW RIGHT YOU ARE, PROFESSOR LIU! RUN ALONG NOW, WORKERS! YOU CAN FINISH YOUR REPAIRS LATER.
GOOD! NOW, UH... A LITTLE MORE COAL ON THE FIRE TO KEEP US WARM.
AHEM! YOUNG COMRADES, KNOW THAT YOU ARE WITNESSING A HISTORIC OCCASION: THE FIRST NUDE DRAWING CLASS IN YUNNAN PROVINCE!
THOUGH A CORE SUBJECT IN WESTERN ART, THE ONLY PLACE SUCH CLASSES EVER OCCURRED IN CHINA WAS 1930S SHANGHAI. THE GOAL IS TO STUDY THE BODY TO BETTER UNDERSTAND THE SLIGHTEST CURVE, THE SMALLEST JOINT.

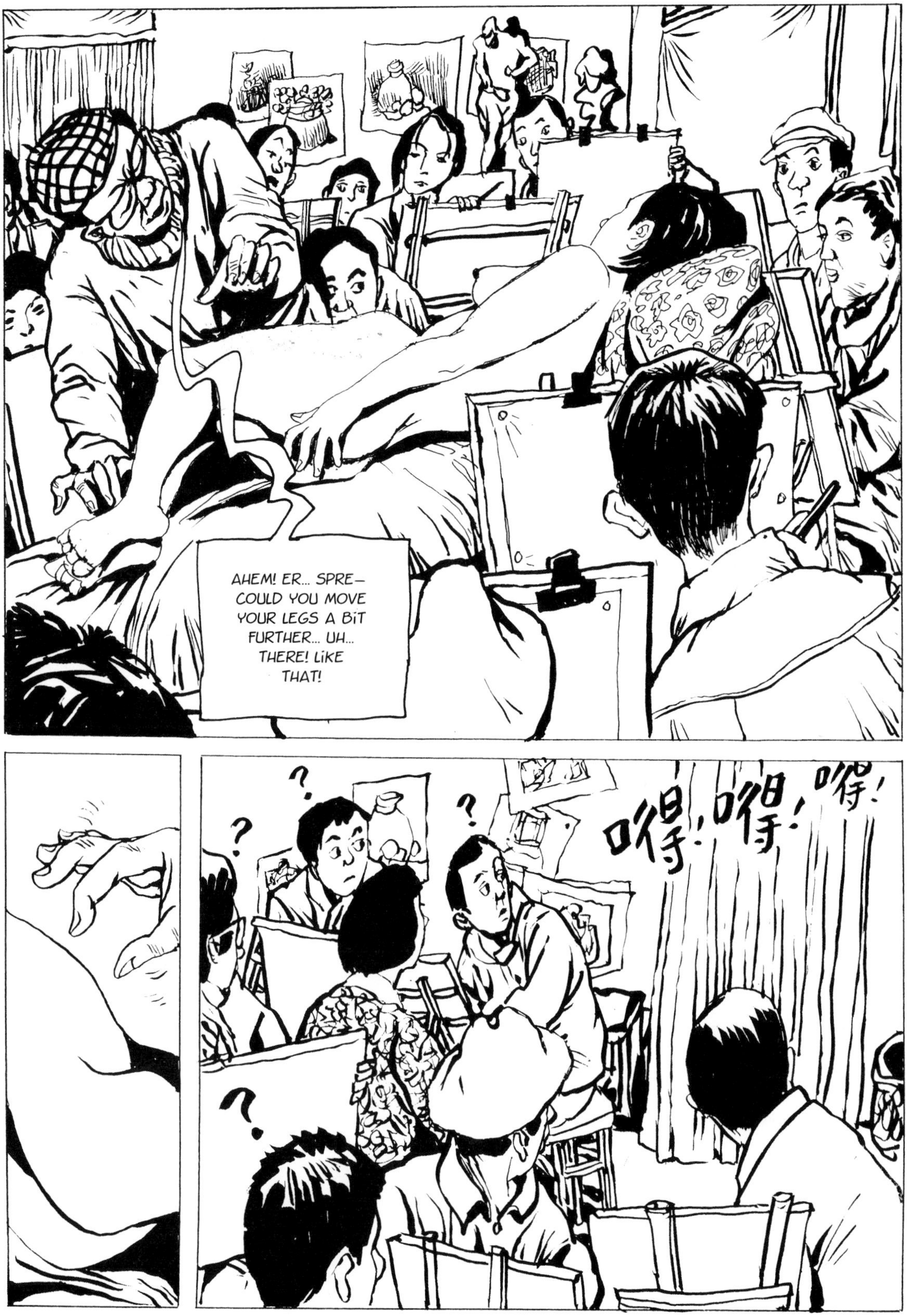

AHEM! ER... SPRE— COULD YOU MOVE YOUR LEGS A BIT FURTHER... UH... THERE! LIKE THAT!
?
?
?
?
嘚! 嘚! 嘚!

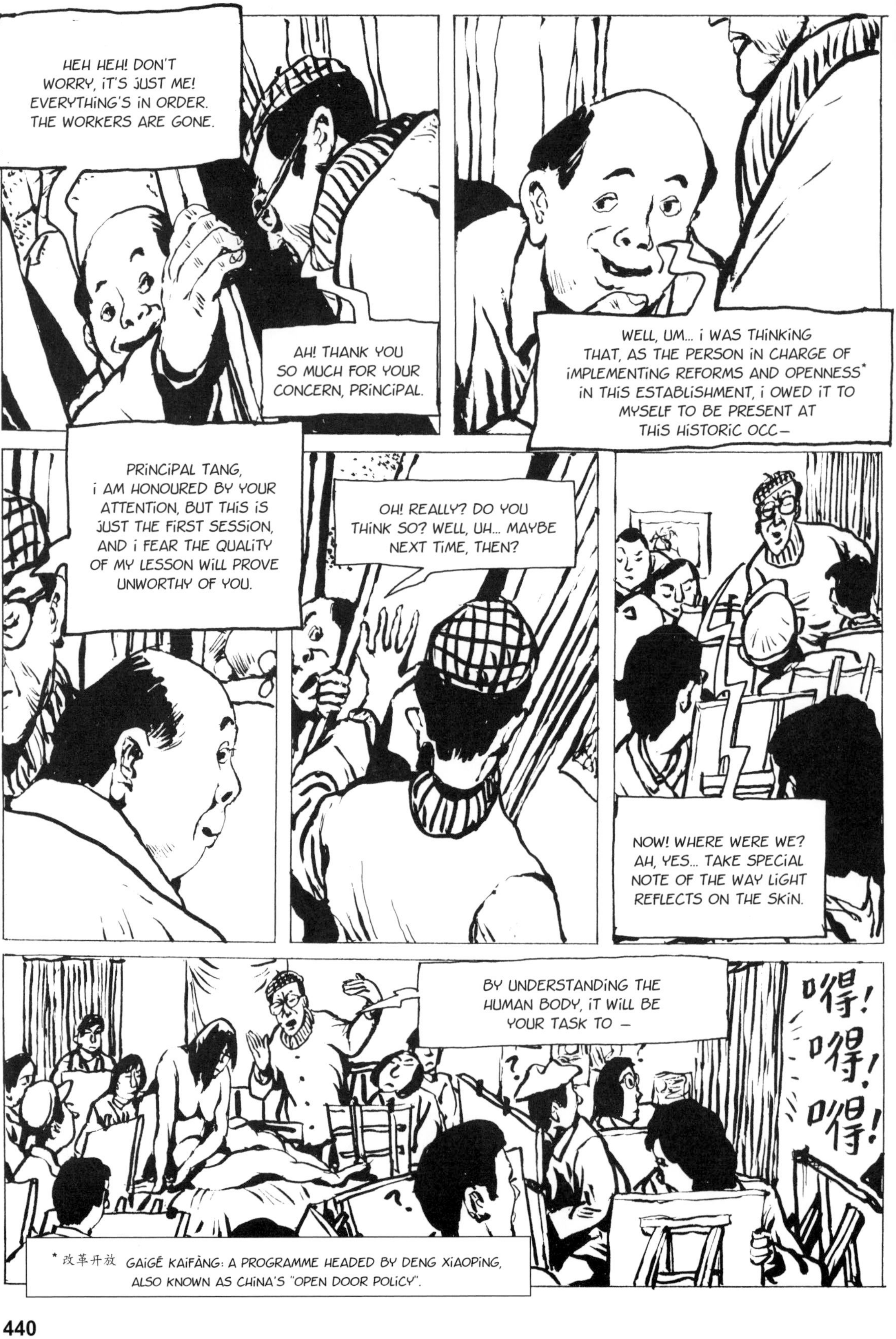
HEH HEH! DON'T WORRY, iT'S JUST ME! EVERYTHiNG'S iN ORDER. THE WORKERS ARE GONE.
AH! THANK YOU SO MUCH FOR YOUR CONCERN, PRiNCiPAL.
WELL, UM... i WAS THiNKiNG THAT, AS THE PERSON iN CHARGE OF iMPLEMENTiNG REFORMS AND OPENNESS* iN THiS ESTABLiSHMENT, i OWED iT TO MYSELF TO BE PRESENT AT THiS HiSTORiC OCC–
PRiNCiPAL TANG, i AM HONOURED BY YOUR ATTENTiON, BUT THiS iS JUST THE FiRST SESSiON, AND i FEAR THE QUALiTY OF MY LESSON WiLL PROVE UNWORTHY OF YOU.
OH! REALLY? DO YOU THiNK SO? WELL, UH... MAYBE NEXT TiME, THEN?
NOW! WHERE WERE WE? AH, YES... TAKE SPECiAL NOTE OF THE WAY LiGHT REFLECTS ON THE SKiN.
BY UNDERSTANDiNG THE HUMAN BODY, iT WiLL BE YOUR TASK TO –
嘚! 嘚! 嘚!

* 改革开放 GAiGĒ KAiFÀNG: A PROGRAMME HEADED BY DENG XiAOPiNG, ALSO KNOWN AS CHiNA'S "OPEN DOOR POLiCY".

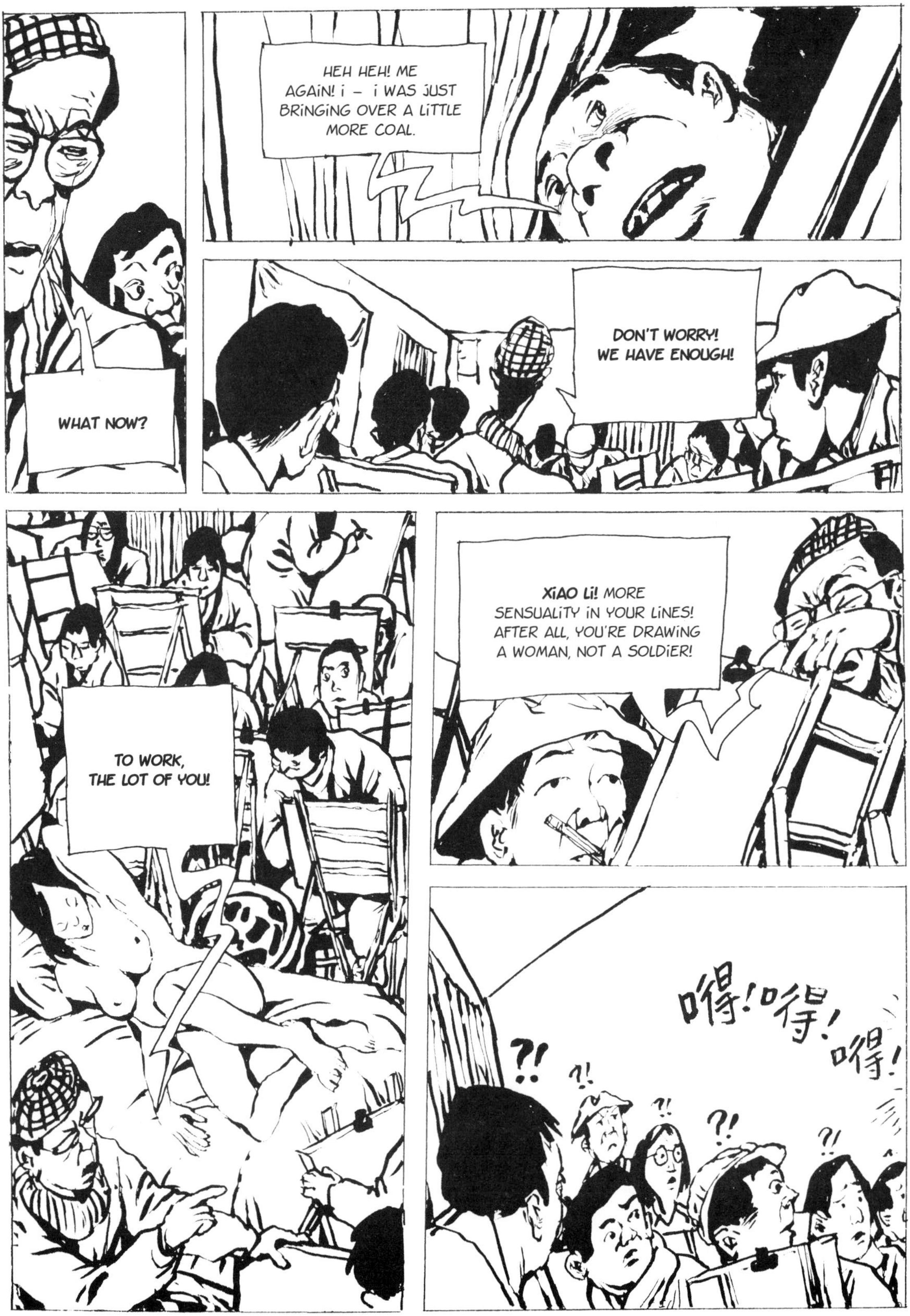
HEH HEH! ME AGAIN! I – I WAS JUST BRINGING OVER A LITTLE MORE COAL.
WHAT NOW?
DON'T WORRY! WE HAVE ENOUGH!
TO WORK, THE LOT OF YOU!
XIAO LI! MORE SENSUALITY IN YOUR LINES! AFTER ALL, YOU'RE DRAWING A WOMAN, NOT A SOLDIER!
嘚!嘚!嘚!
?!
?!
?!
?!
?!

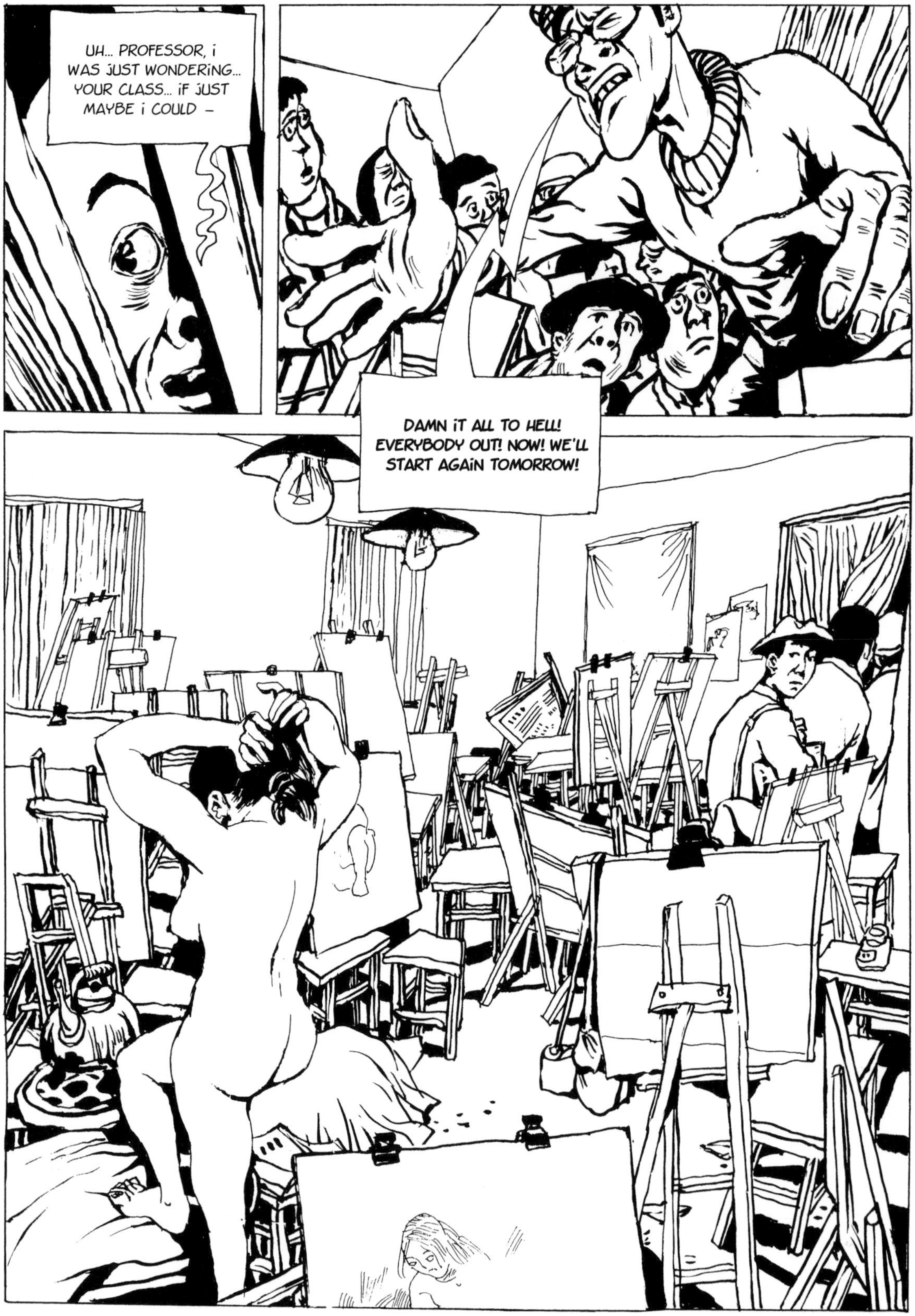
UH... PROFESSOR, i WAS JUST WONDERiNG... YOUR CLASS... iF JUST MAYBE i COULD –
DAMN iT ALL TO HELL! EVERYBODY OUT! NOW! WE'LL START AGAiN TOMORROW!

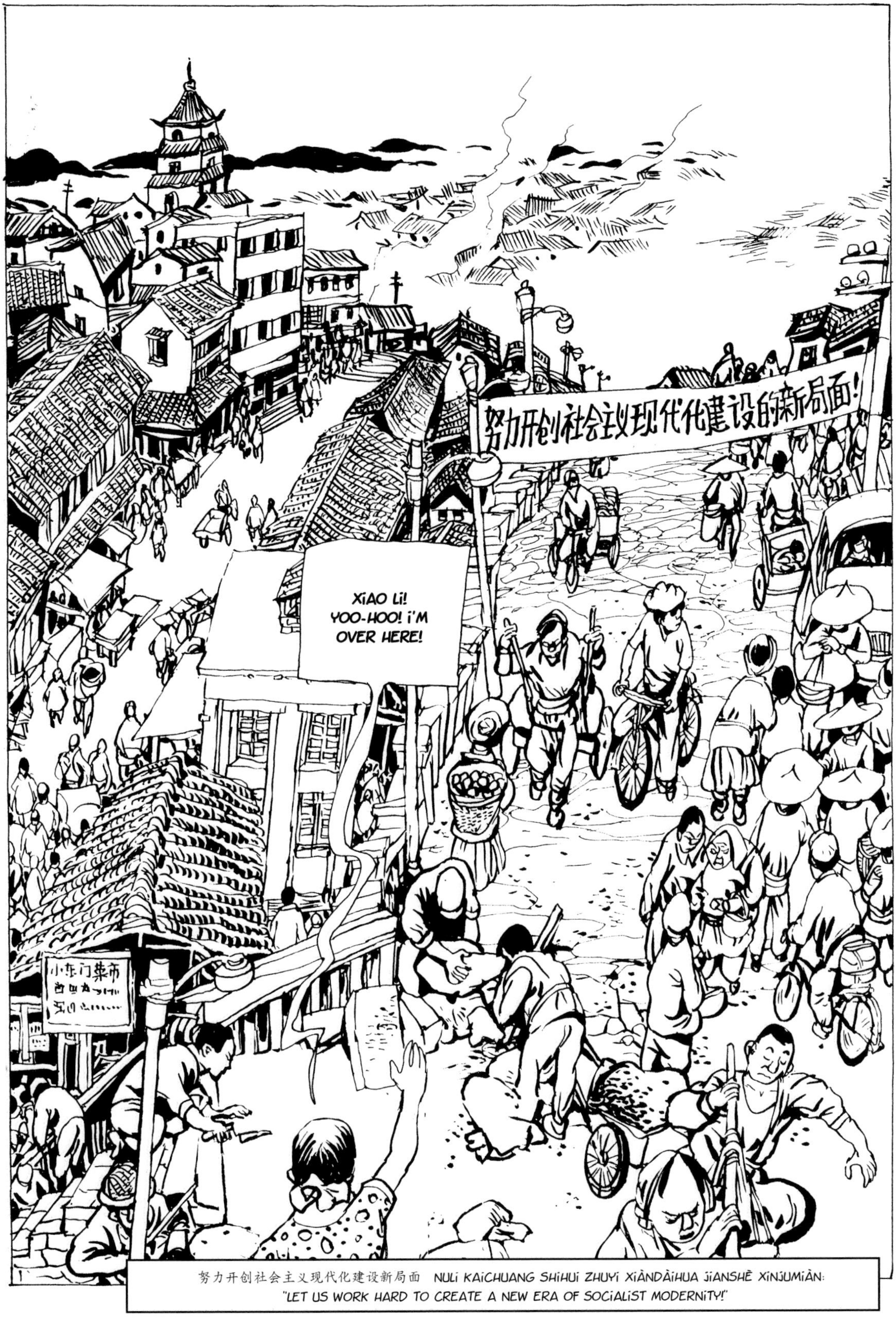
努力开创社会主义现代化建设的新局面!
XIAO LI! YOO-HOO! I'M OVER HERE!
小东门菜市
努力开创社会主义现代化建设新局面 NULI KAICHUANG SHIHUI ZHUYI XIÀNDÀIHUA JIANSHÈ XINJUMIÀN:
"LET US WORK HARD TO CREATE A NEW ERA OF SOCIALIST MODERNITY!"

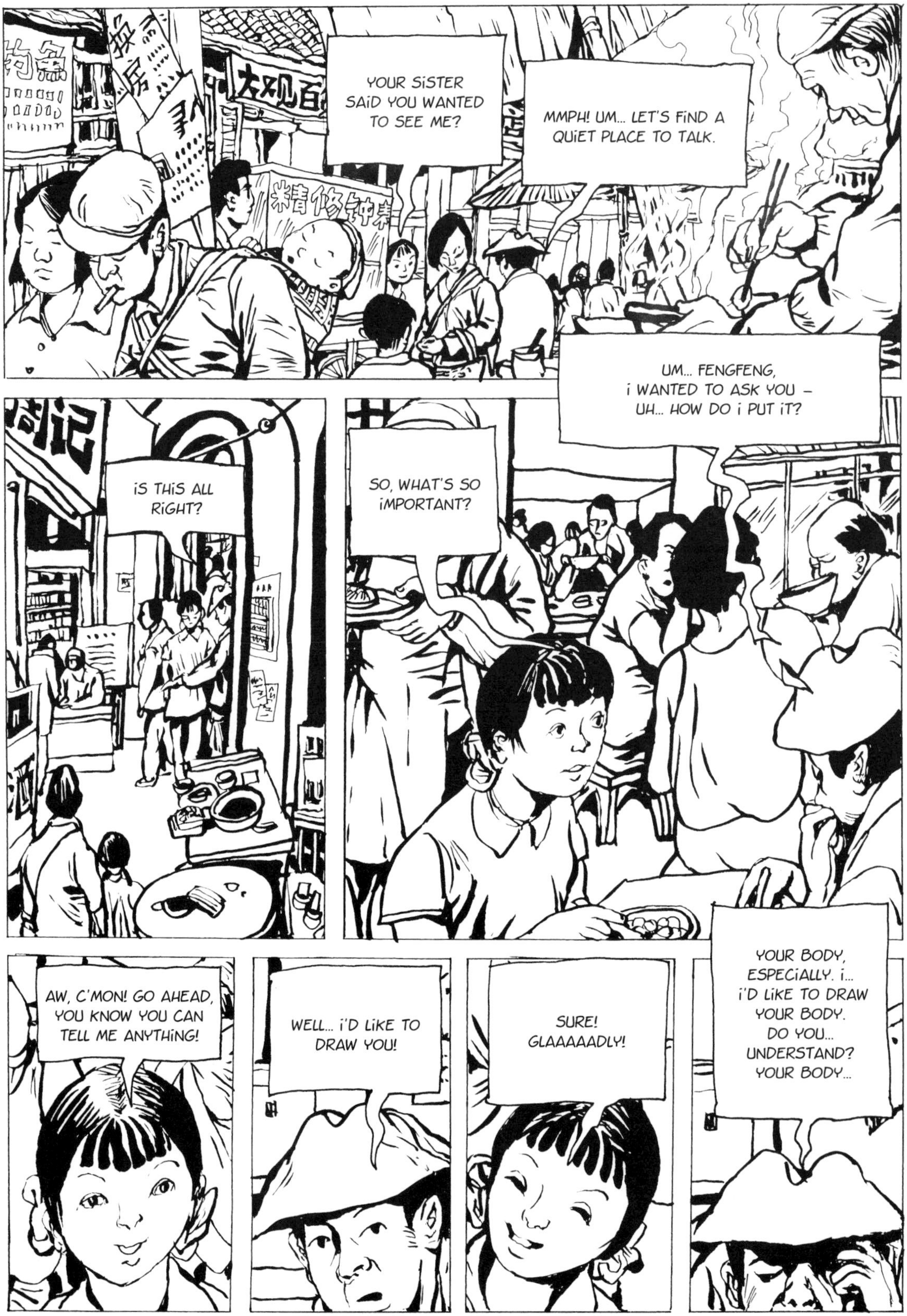

YOUR SISTER SAID YOU WANTED TO SEE ME?
MMPH! UM... LET'S FIND A QUIET PLACE TO TALK.
IS THIS ALL RIGHT?
SO, WHAT'S SO IMPORTANT?
UM... FENGFENG, I WANTED TO ASK YOU – UH... HOW DO I PUT IT?
AW, C'MON! GO AHEAD, YOU KNOW YOU CAN TELL ME ANYTHING!
WELL... I'D LIKE TO DRAW YOU!
SURE! GLAAAAADLY!
YOUR BODY, ESPECIALLY. I... I'D LIKE TO DRAW YOUR BODY. DO YOU... UNDERSTAND? YOUR BODY...

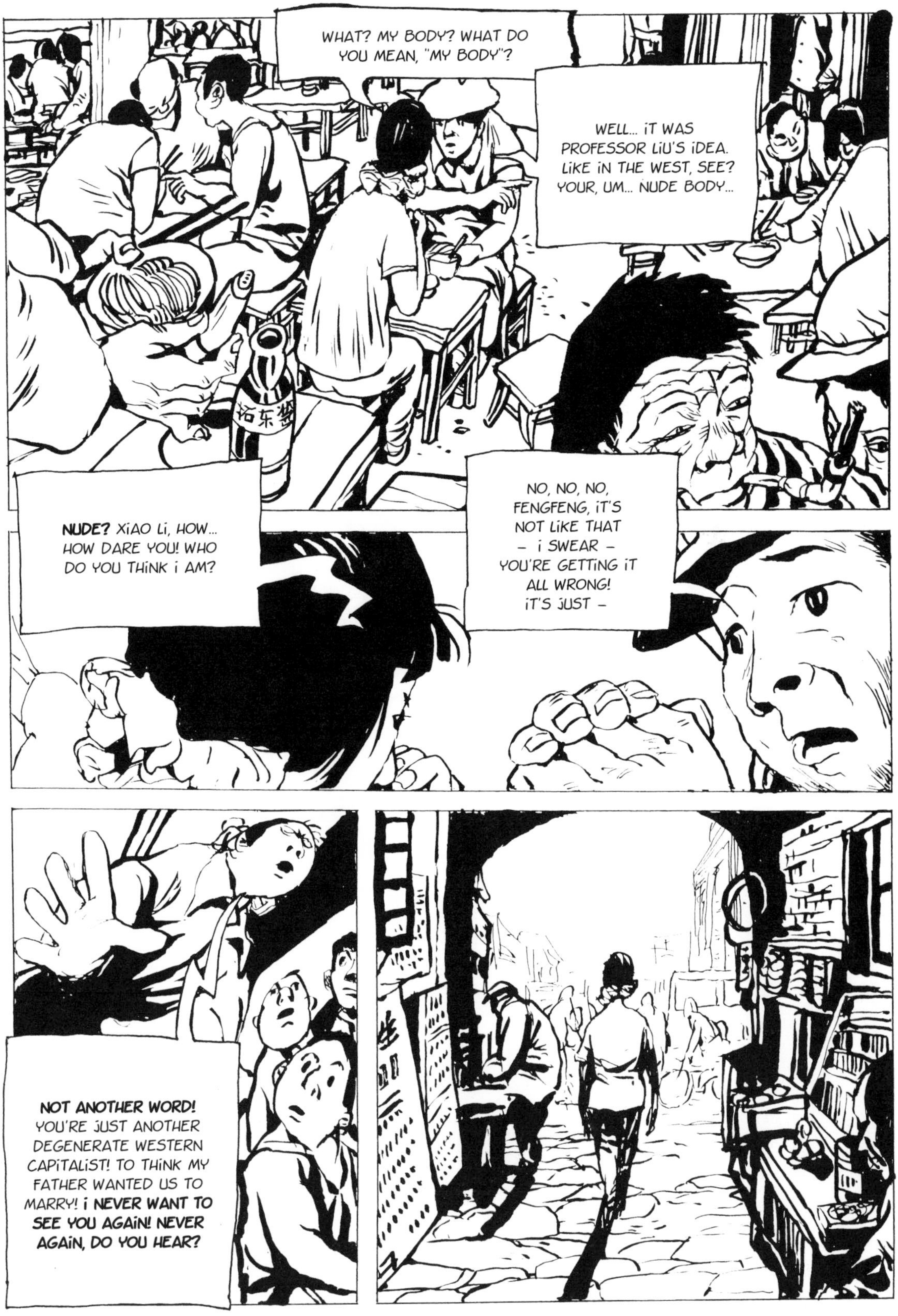
WHAT? MY BODY? WHAT DO YOU MEAN, "MY BODY"?
WELL... iT WAS PROFESSOR LiU'S iDEA. LiKE iN THE WEST, SEE? YOUR, UM... NUDE BODY...
NUDE? XiAO Li, HOW... HOW DARE YOU! WHO DO YOU THiNK i AM?
NO, NO, NO, FENGFENG, iT'S NOT LiKE THAT – i SWEAR – YOU'RE GETTiNG iT ALL WRONG! iT'S JUST –
NOT ANOTHER WORD! YOU'RE JUST ANOTHER DEGENERATE WESTERN CAPiTALiST! TO THiNK MY FATHER WANTED US TO MARRY! i NEVER WANT TO SEE YOU AGAiN! NEVER AGAiN, DO YOU HEAR?

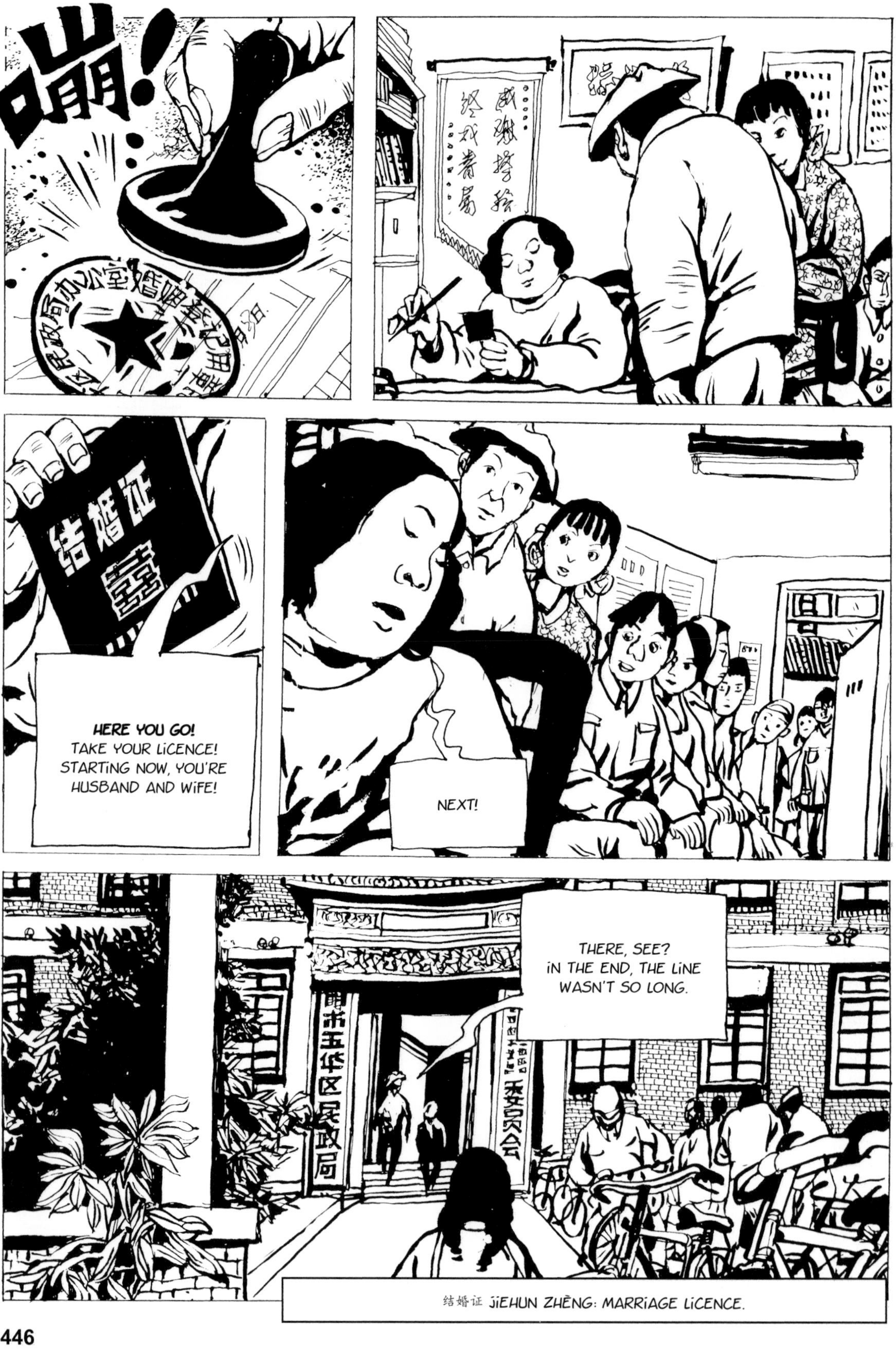
嘣!
结婚证
HERE YOU GO!
TAKE YOUR LICENCE! STARTING NOW, YOU'RE HUSBAND AND WIFE!
NEXT!
THERE, SEE? IN THE END, THE LINE WASN'T SO LONG.
结婚证 JIEHUN ZHĚNG: MARRIAGE LICENCE.

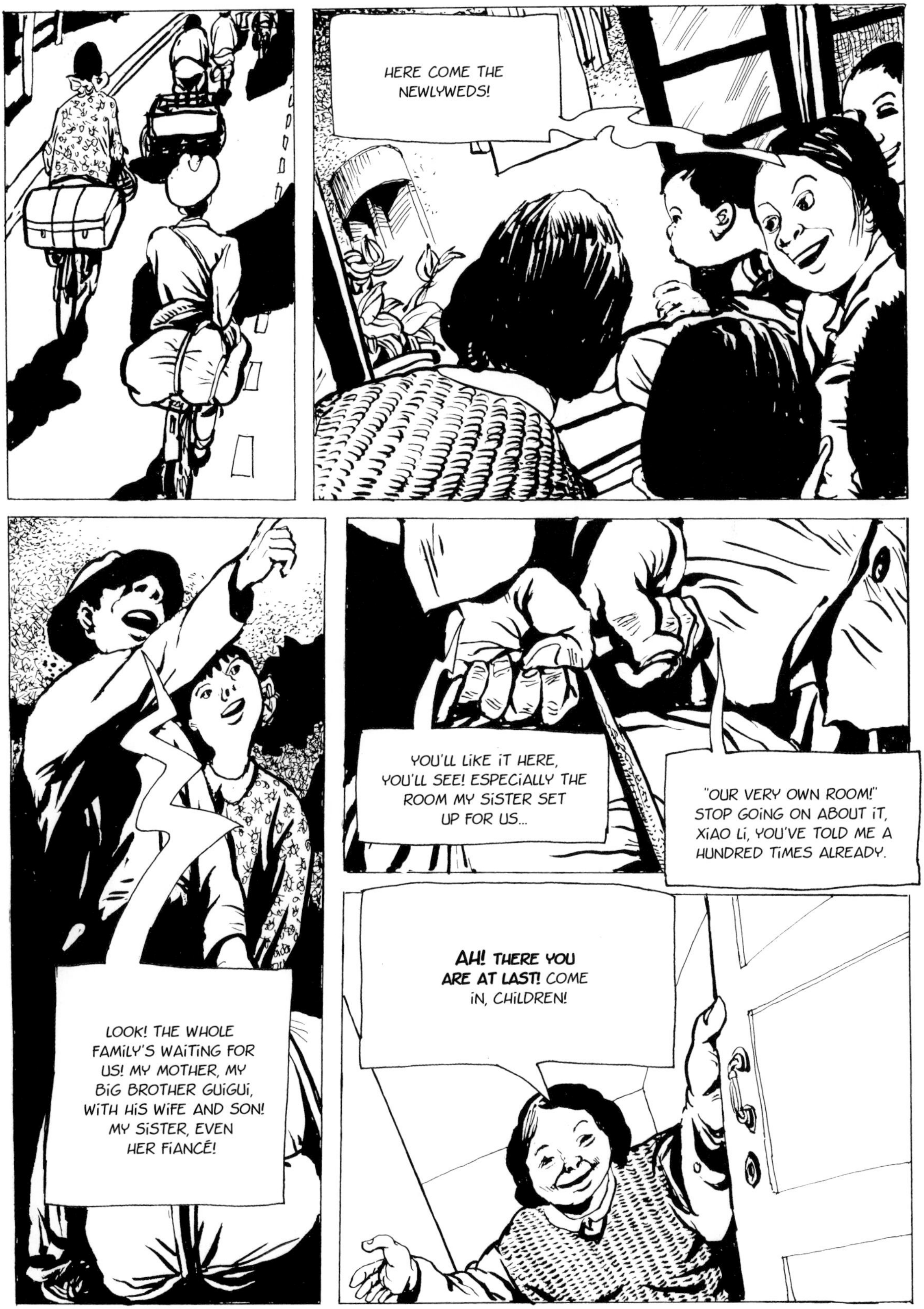
HERE COME THE NEWLYWEDS!
LOOK! THE WHOLE FAMILY'S WAITING FOR US! MY MOTHER, MY BIG BROTHER GUIGUI, WITH HIS WIFE AND SON! MY SISTER, EVEN HER FIANCÉ!
YOU'LL LIKE IT HERE, YOU'LL SEE! ESPECIALLY THE ROOM MY SISTER SET UP FOR US...
"OUR VERY OWN ROOM!" STOP GOING ON ABOUT IT, XIAO LI, YOU'VE TOLD ME A HUNDRED TIMES ALREADY.
AH! THERE YOU ARE AT LAST! COME IN, CHILDREN!

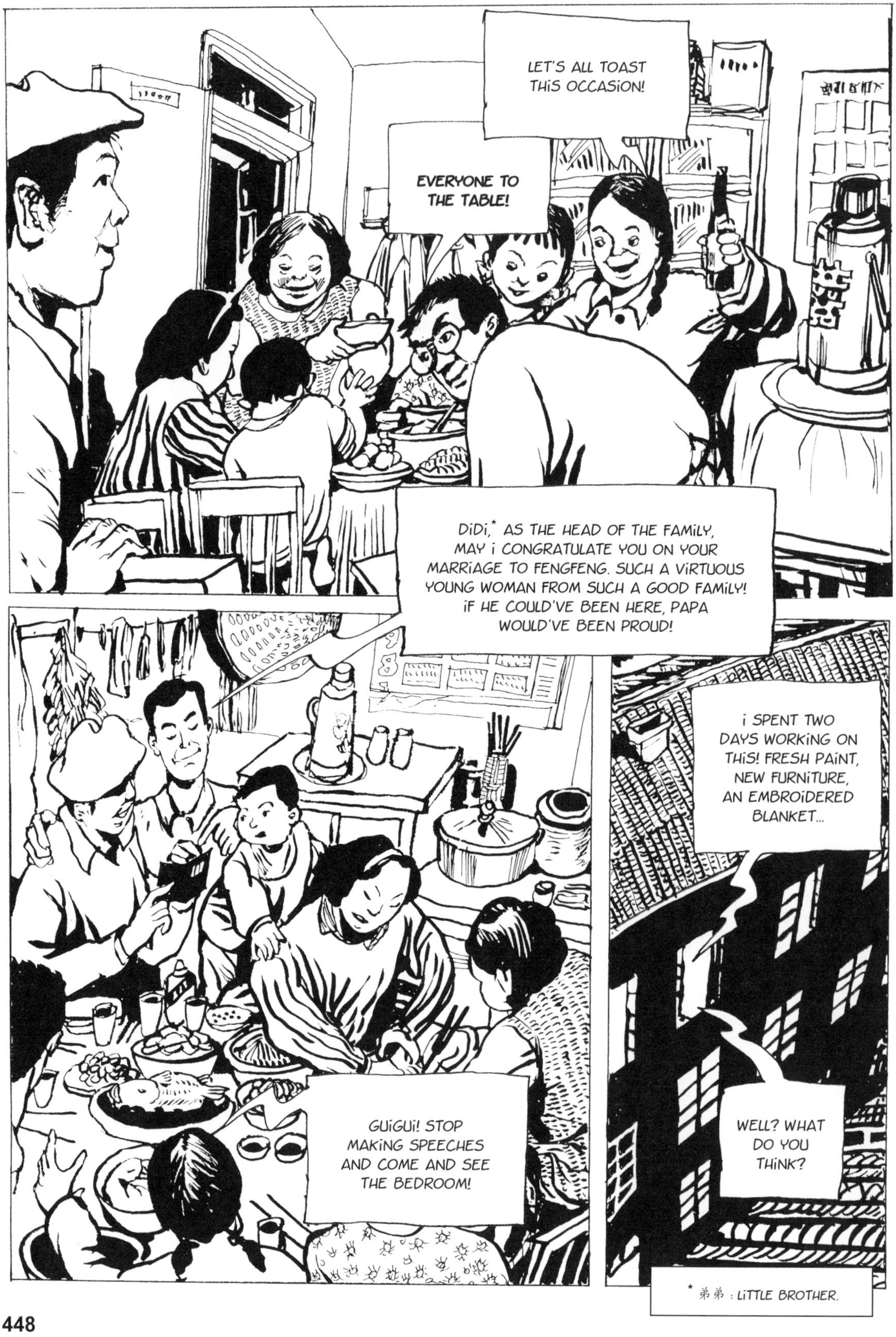
LET'S ALL TOAST THIS OCCASION!
EVERYONE TO THE TABLE!
DIDI,* AS THE HEAD OF THE FAMILY, MAY I CONGRATULATE YOU ON YOUR MARRIAGE TO FENGFENG. SUCH A VIRTUOUS YOUNG WOMAN FROM SUCH A GOOD FAMILY! IF HE COULD'VE BEEN HERE, PAPA WOULD'VE BEEN PROUD!
GUIGUI! STOP MAKING SPEECHES AND COME AND SEE THE BEDROOM!
I SPENT TWO DAYS WORKING ON THIS! FRESH PAINT, NEW FURNITURE, AN EMBROIDERED BLANKET...
WELL? WHAT DO YOU THINK?

* 弟弟 : LITTLE BROTHER.

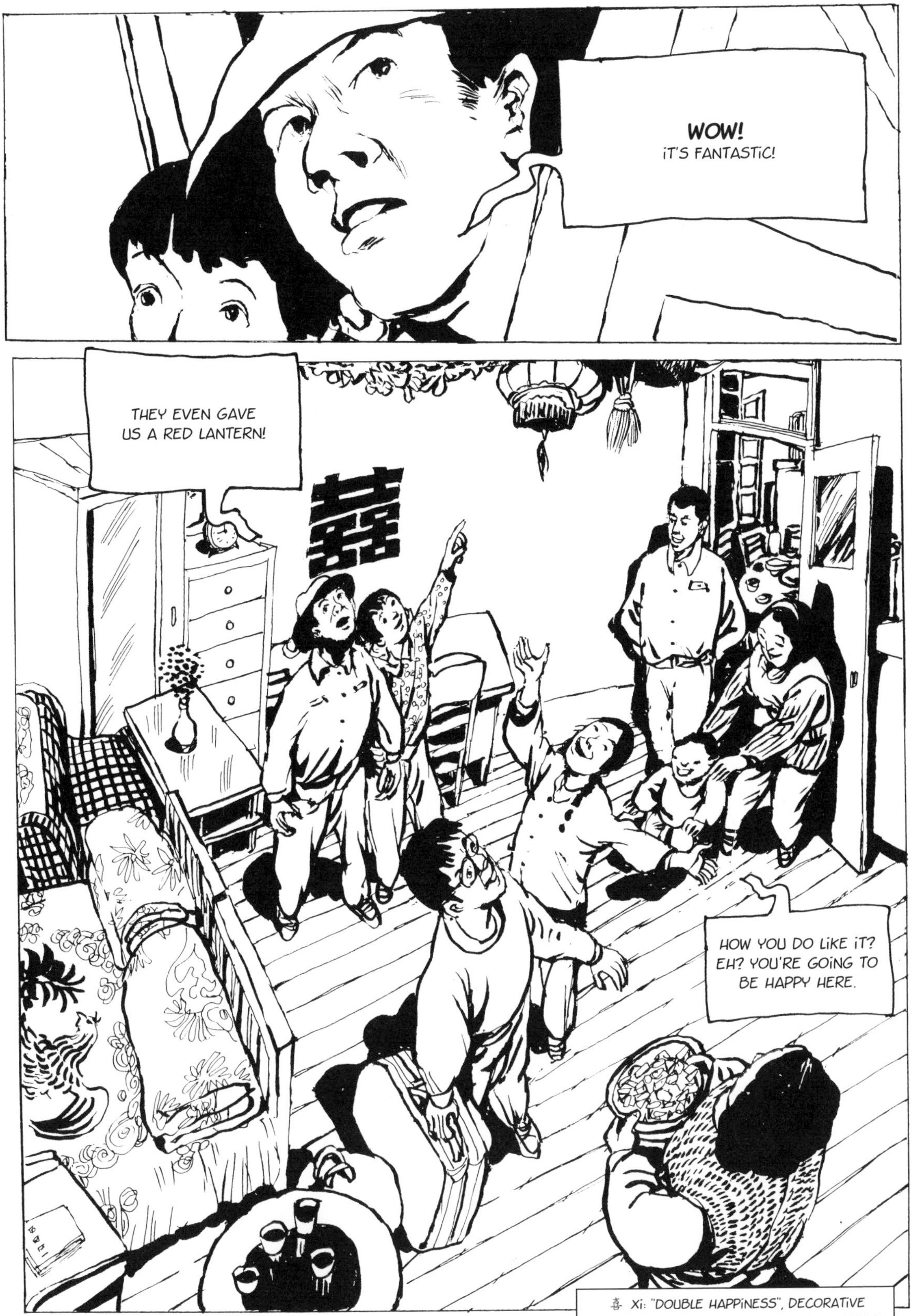
WOW!
IT'S FANTASTIC!
THEY EVEN GAVE US A RED LANTERN!
HOW YOU DO LIKE IT? EH? YOU'RE GOING TO BE HAPPY HERE.

喜 Xi: "DOUBLE HAPPINESS", DECORATIVE CHARACTER OFTEN ASSOCIATED WITH MARRIAGE.

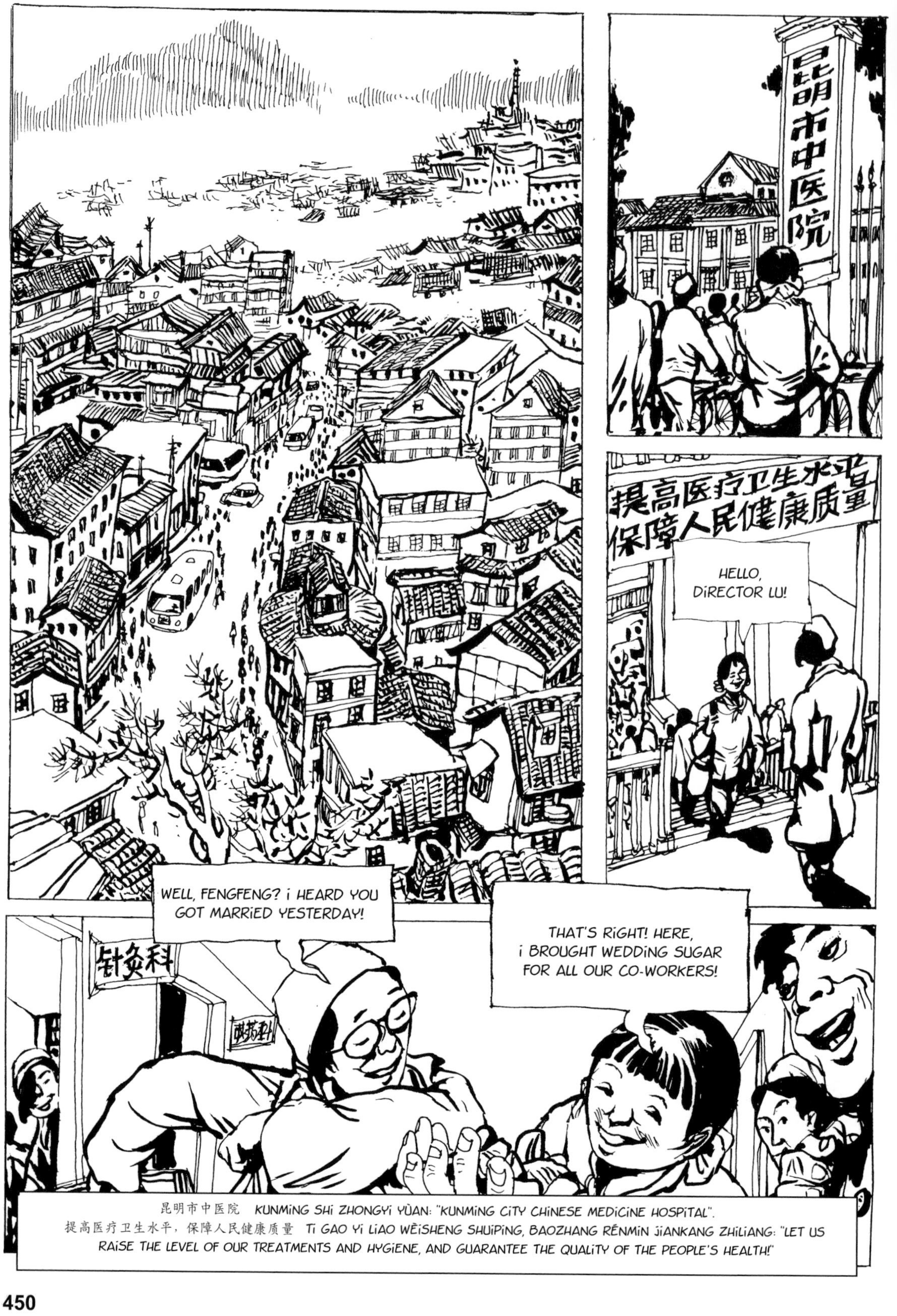

昆明市中医院
提高医疗卫生水平
保障人民健康质量
HELLO, DIRECTOR LU!
WELL, FENGFENG? I HEARD YOU GOT MARRIED YESTERDAY!
针灸科
THAT'S RIGHT! HERE, I BROUGHT WEDDING SUGAR FOR ALL OUR CO-WORKERS!

昆明市中医院 KUNMING SHI ZHONGYI YÜAN: "KUNMING CITY CHINESE MEDICINE HOSPITAL".
提高医疗卫生水平，保障人民健康质量 TI GAO YI LIAO WÈISHENG SHUIPING, BAOZHANG RÉNMIN JIANKANG ZHILIANG: "LET US RAISE THE LEVEL OF OUR TREATMENTS AND HYGIENE, AND GUARANTEE THE QUALITY OF THE PEOPLE'S HEALTH!"

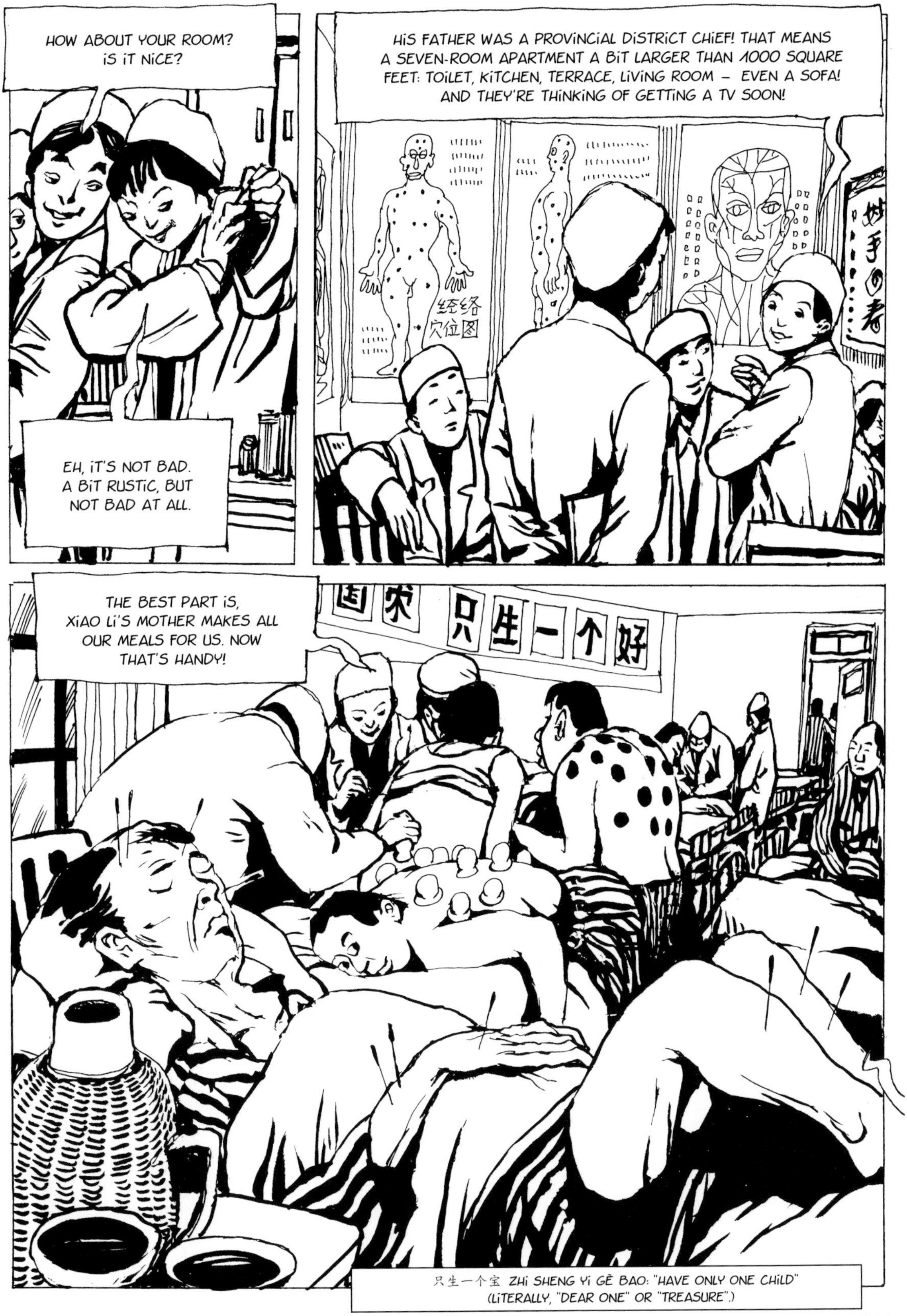
HOW ABOUT YOUR ROOM? IS IT NICE?
EH, IT'S NOT BAD. A BIT RUSTIC, BUT NOT BAD AT ALL.
HIS FATHER WAS A PROVINCIAL DISTRICT CHIEF! THAT MEANS A SEVEN-ROOM APARTMENT A BIT LARGER THAN 1000 SQUARE FEET: TOILET, KITCHEN, TERRACE, LIVING ROOM – EVEN A SOFA! AND THEY'RE THINKING OF GETTING A TV SOON!
THE BEST PART IS, XIAO LI'S MOTHER MAKES ALL OUR MEALS FOR US. NOW THAT'S HANDY!
只生一个好
只生一个宝 ZHI SHENG YI GÈ BAO: "HAVE ONLY ONE CHILD" (LITERALLY, "DEAR ONE" OR "TREASURE".)

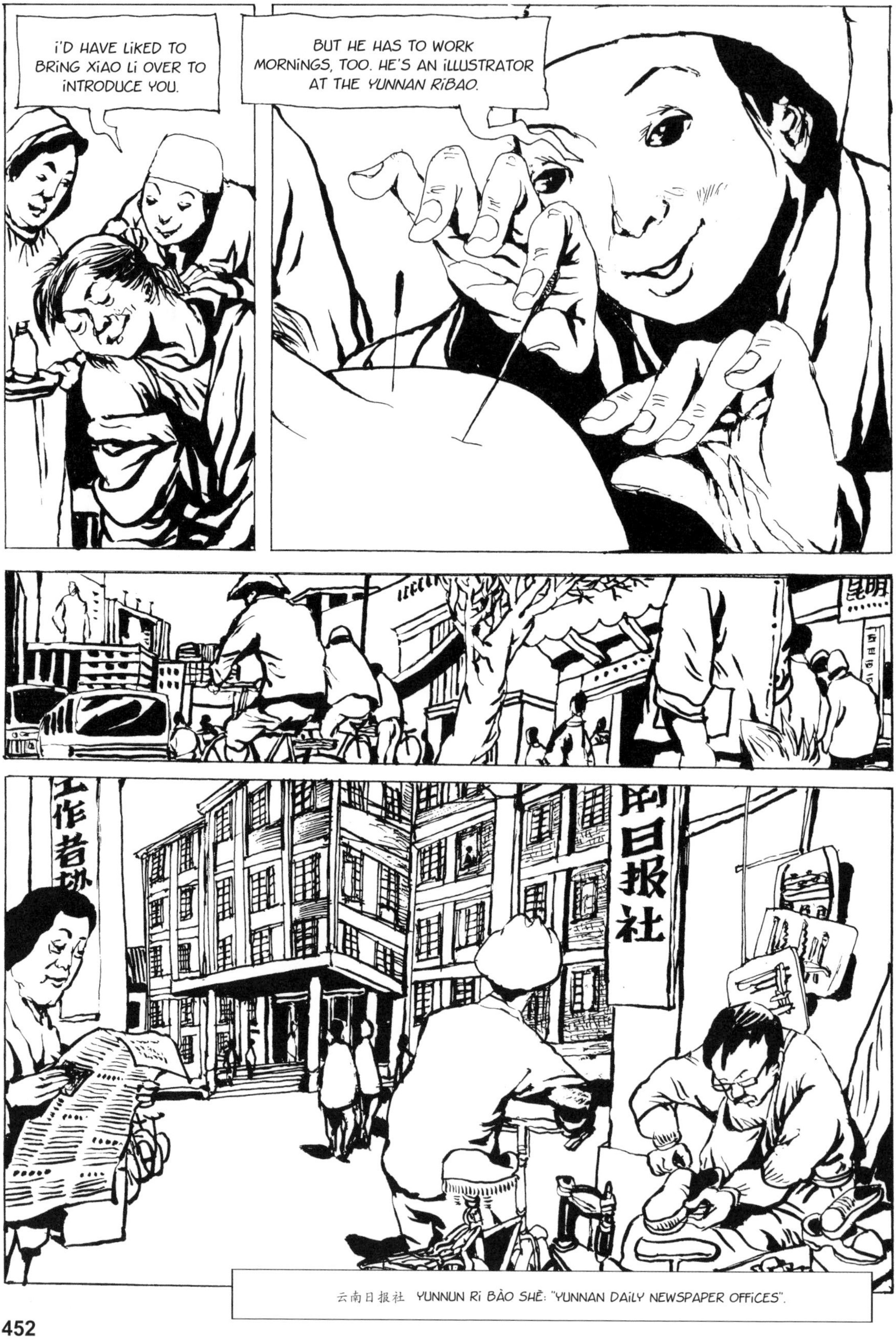
I'D HAVE LIKED TO BRING XIAO LI OVER TO INTRODUCE YOU.
BUT HE HAS TO WORK MORNINGS, TOO. HE'S AN ILLUSTRATOR AT THE *YUNNAN RIBAO*.
日报社
云南日报社 YUNNUN Ri BÀO SHÈ: "YUNNAN DAILY NEWSPAPER OFFICES".

HEY! *LAO LI!* STOP "SERVING THE PEOPLE"! WORKING DAY'S STARTED!

COMING, BOSS!

COMRADES! LOOK WHAT I BROUGHT YOU TODAY!

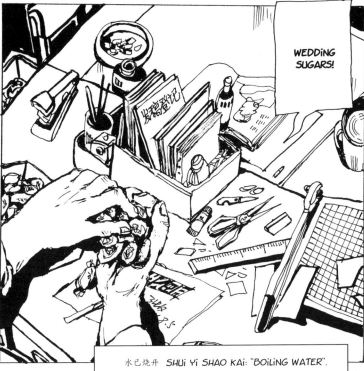

WEDDING SUGARS!

水已烧开 *SHUI YI SHAO KAI:* "BOILING WATER".

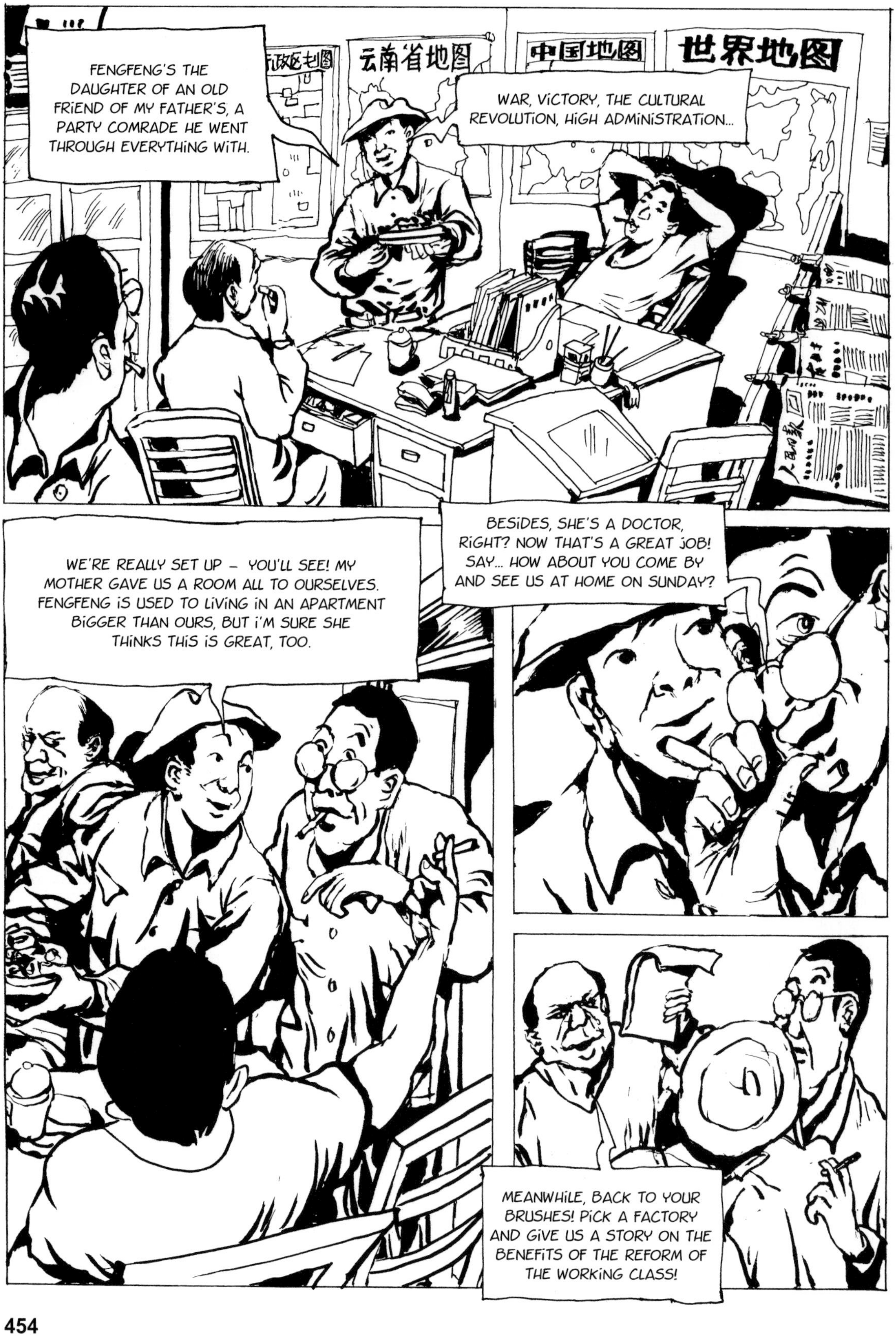

FENGFENG'S THE DAUGHTER OF AN OLD FRIEND OF MY FATHER'S, A PARTY COMRADE HE WENT THROUGH EVERYTHING WITH.
云南省地图
中国地图
世界地图
WAR, VICTORY, THE CULTURAL REVOLUTION, HIGH ADMINISTRATION...
WE'RE REALLY SET UP – YOU'LL SEE! MY MOTHER GAVE US A ROOM ALL TO OURSELVES. FENGFENG IS USED TO LIVING IN AN APARTMENT BIGGER THAN OURS, BUT I'M SURE SHE THINKS THIS IS GREAT, TOO.
BESIDES, SHE'S A DOCTOR, RIGHT? NOW THAT'S A GREAT JOB! SAY... HOW ABOUT YOU COME BY AND SEE US AT HOME ON SUNDAY?
MEANWHILE, BACK TO YOUR BRUSHES! PICK A FACTORY AND GIVE US A STORY ON THE BENEFITS OF THE REFORM OF THE WORKING CLASS!

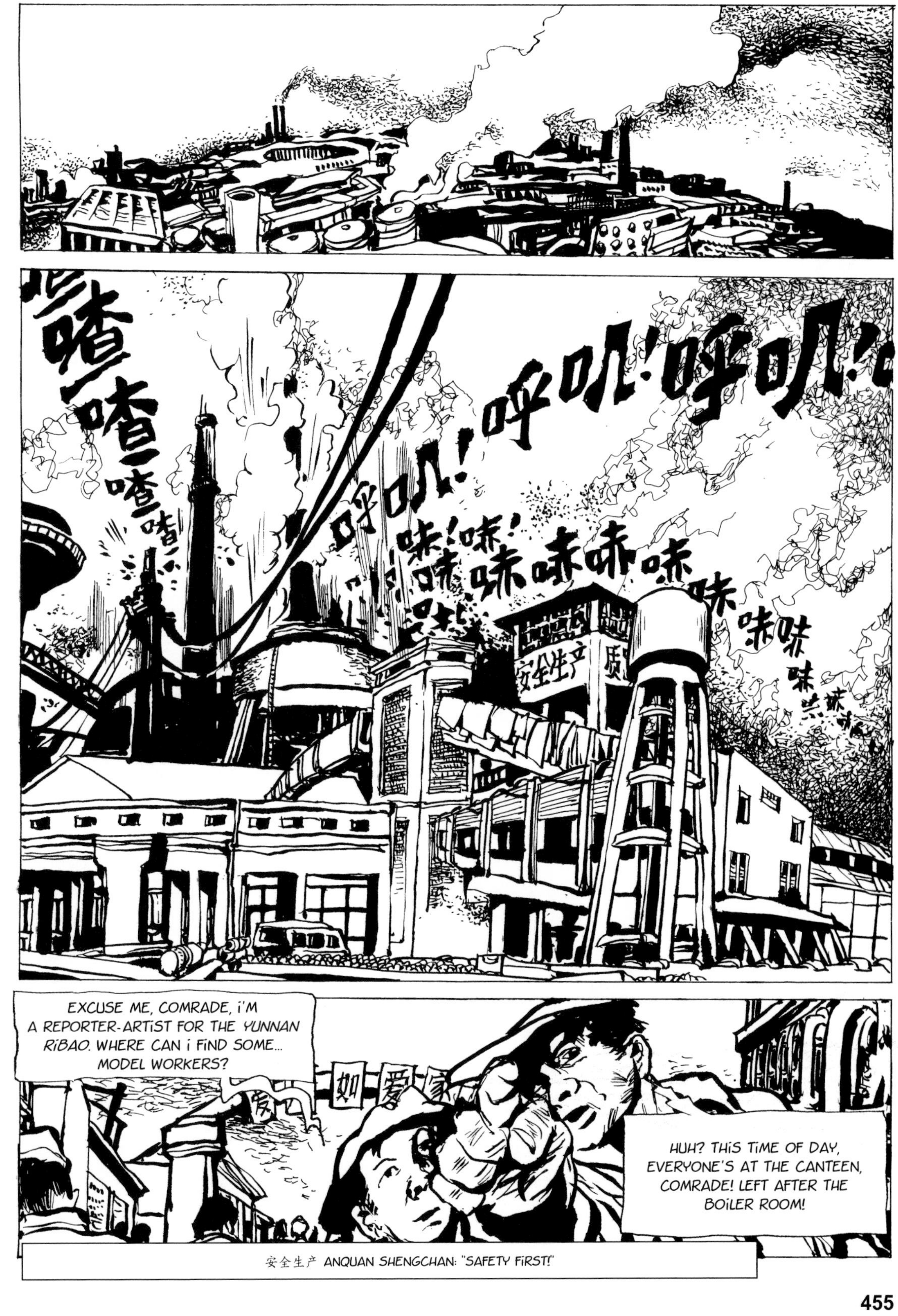
安全生产
EXCUSE ME, COMRADE, I'M A REPORTER-ARTIST FOR THE *YUNNAN RIBAO*. WHERE CAN I FIND SOME... MODEL WORKERS?
HUH? THIS TIME OF DAY, EVERYONE'S AT THE CANTEEN, COMRADE! LEFT AFTER THE BOILER ROOM!

安全生产 ANQUAN SHENGCHAN: "SAFETY FIRST!"

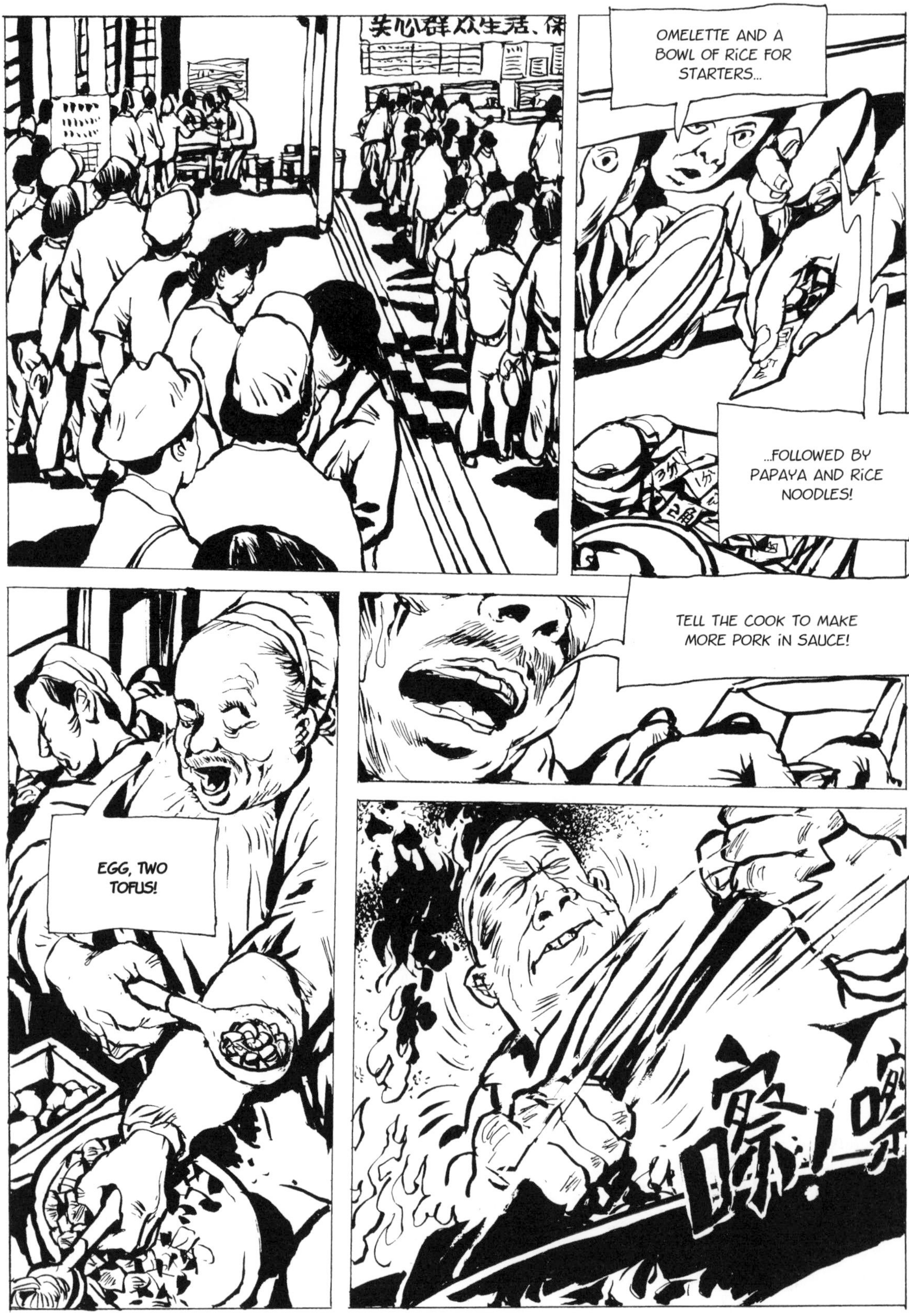
OMELETTE AND A BOWL OF RiCE FOR STARTERS...
...FOLLOWED BY PAPAYA AND RiCE NOODLES!
EGG, TWO TOFUS!
TELL THE COOK TO MAKE MORE PORK iN SAUCE!

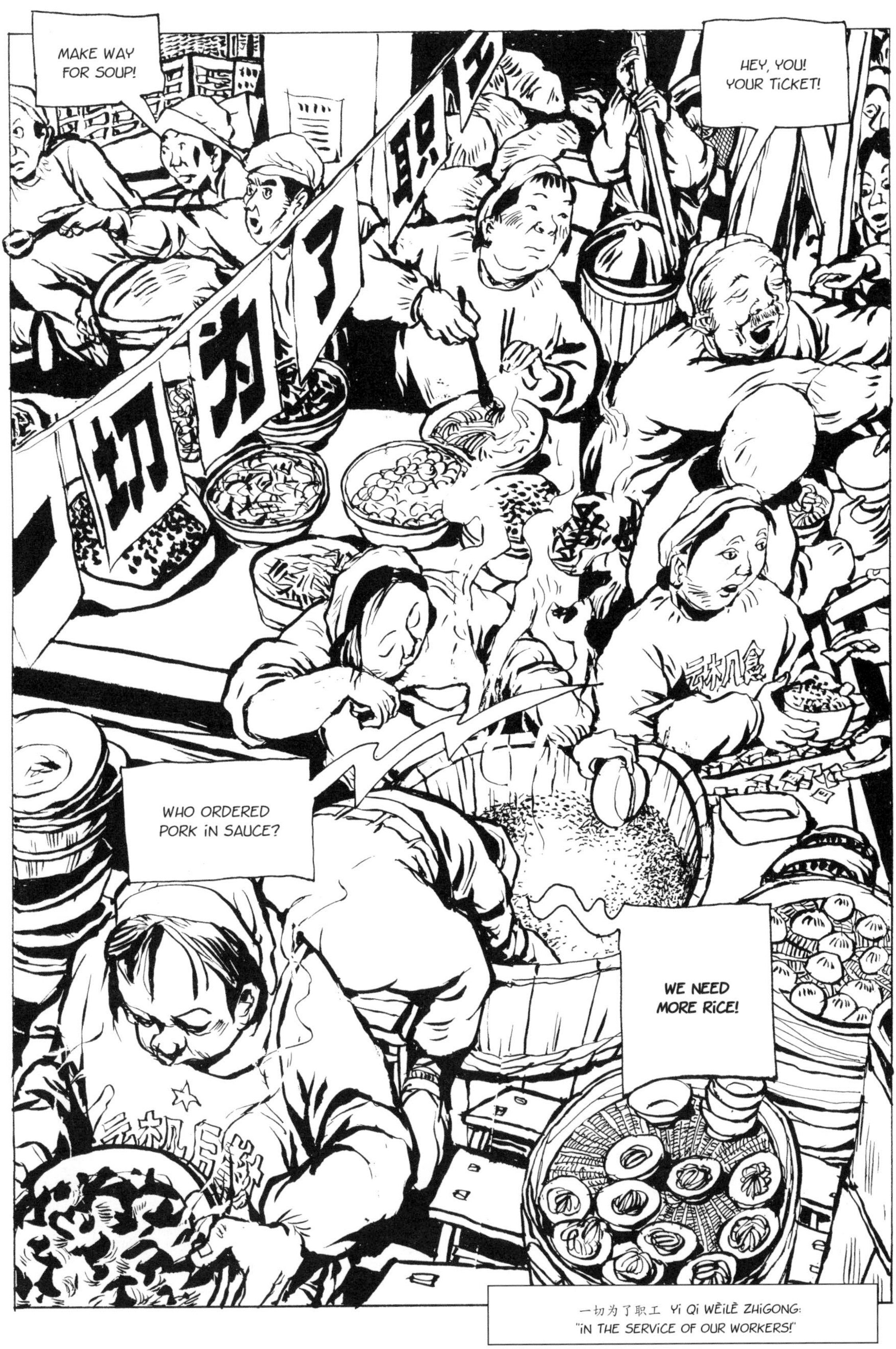
MAKE WAY FOR SOUP!
HEY, YOU! YOUR TICKET!
WHO ORDERED PORK IN SAUCE?
WE NEED MORE RICE!
一切为了职工 YI QI WÈILÈ ZHIGONG: "IN THE SERVICE OF OUR WORKERS!"

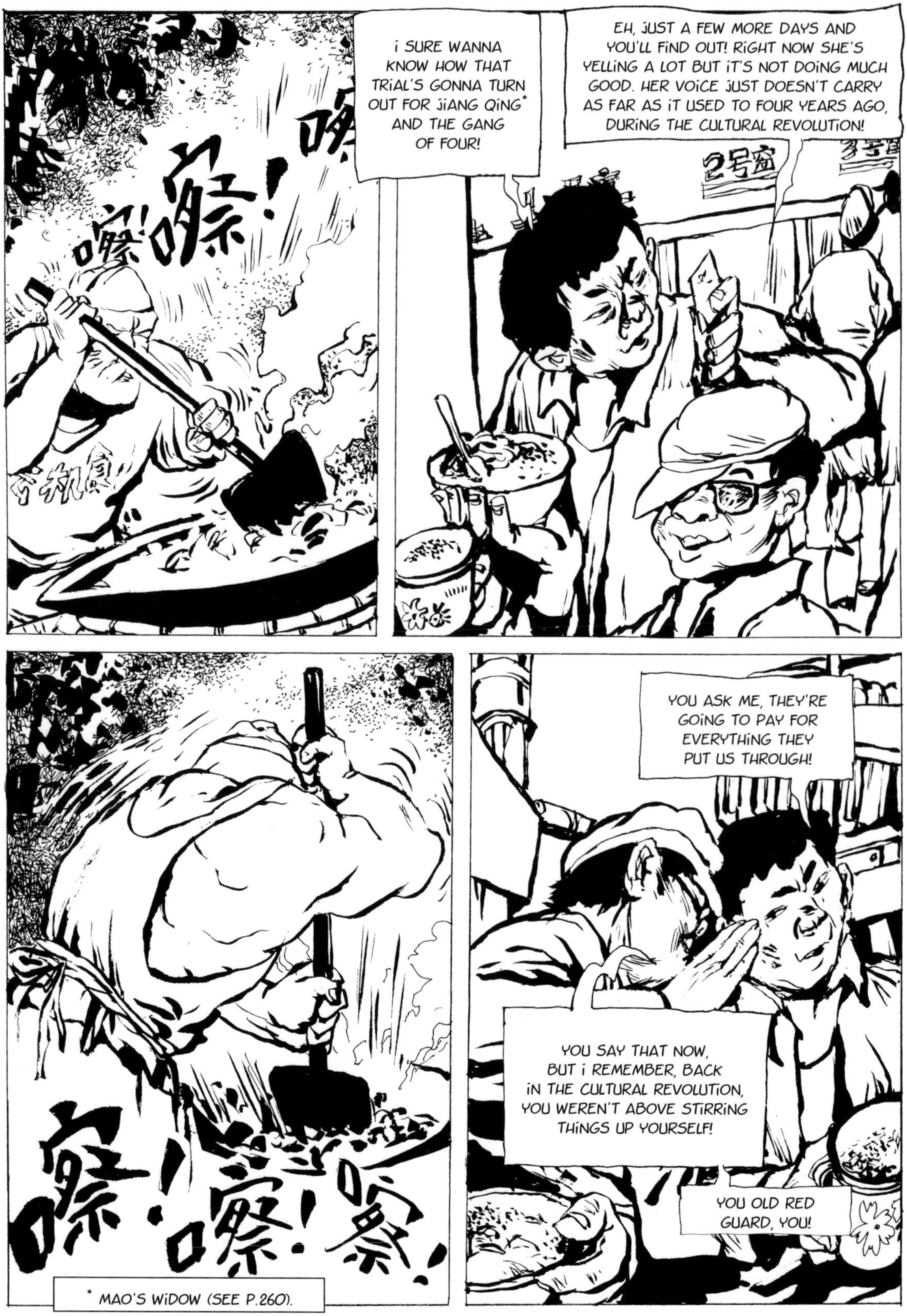
I SURE WANNA KNOW HOW THAT TRIAL'S GONNA TURN OUT FOR JIANG QING* AND THE GANG OF FOUR!
EH, JUST A FEW MORE DAYS AND YOU'LL FIND OUT! RIGHT NOW SHE'S YELLING A LOT BUT IT'S NOT DOING MUCH GOOD. HER VOICE JUST DOESN'T CARRY AS FAR AS IT USED TO FOUR YEARS AGO, DURING THE CULTURAL REVOLUTION!
YOU ASK ME, THEY'RE GOING TO PAY FOR EVERYTHING THEY PUT US THROUGH!
YOU SAY THAT NOW, BUT I REMEMBER, BACK IN THE CULTURAL REVOLUTION, YOU WEREN'T ABOVE STIRRING THINGS UP YOURSELF!
YOU OLD RED GUARD, YOU!

* MAO'S WIDOW (SEE P.260).

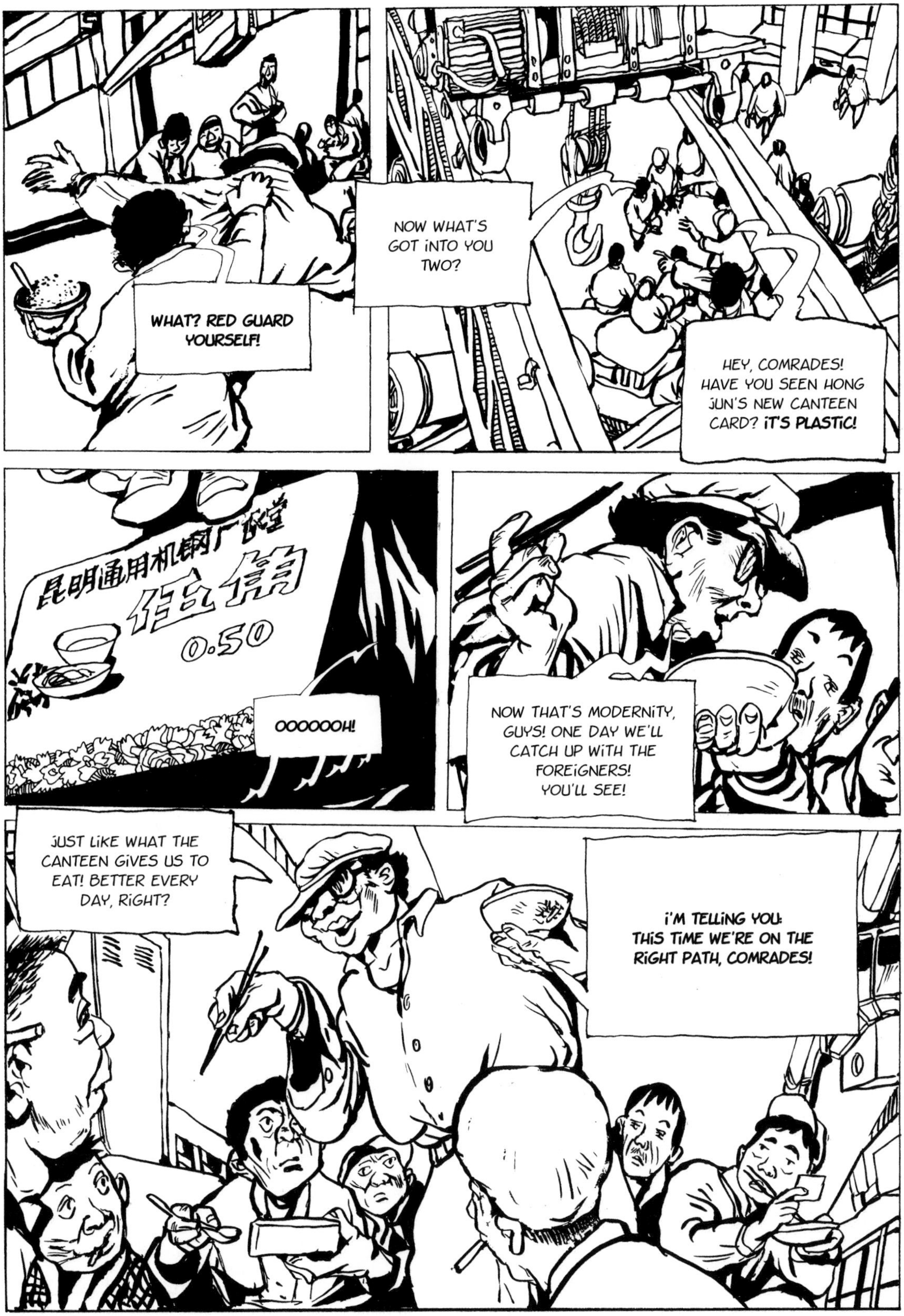
WHAT? RED GUARD YOURSELF!
NOW WHAT'S GOT INTO YOU TWO?
HEY, COMRADES! HAVE YOU SEEN HONG JUN'S NEW CANTEEN CARD? IT'S PLASTIC!
昆明通用机钢厂饭堂
0.50
OOOOOOH!
NOW THAT'S MODERNITY, GUYS! ONE DAY WE'LL CATCH UP WITH THE FOREIGNERS! YOU'LL SEE!
JUST LIKE WHAT THE CANTEEN GIVES US TO EAT! BETTER EVERY DAY, RIGHT?
I'M TELLING YOU: THIS TIME WE'RE ON THE RIGHT PATH, COMRADES!

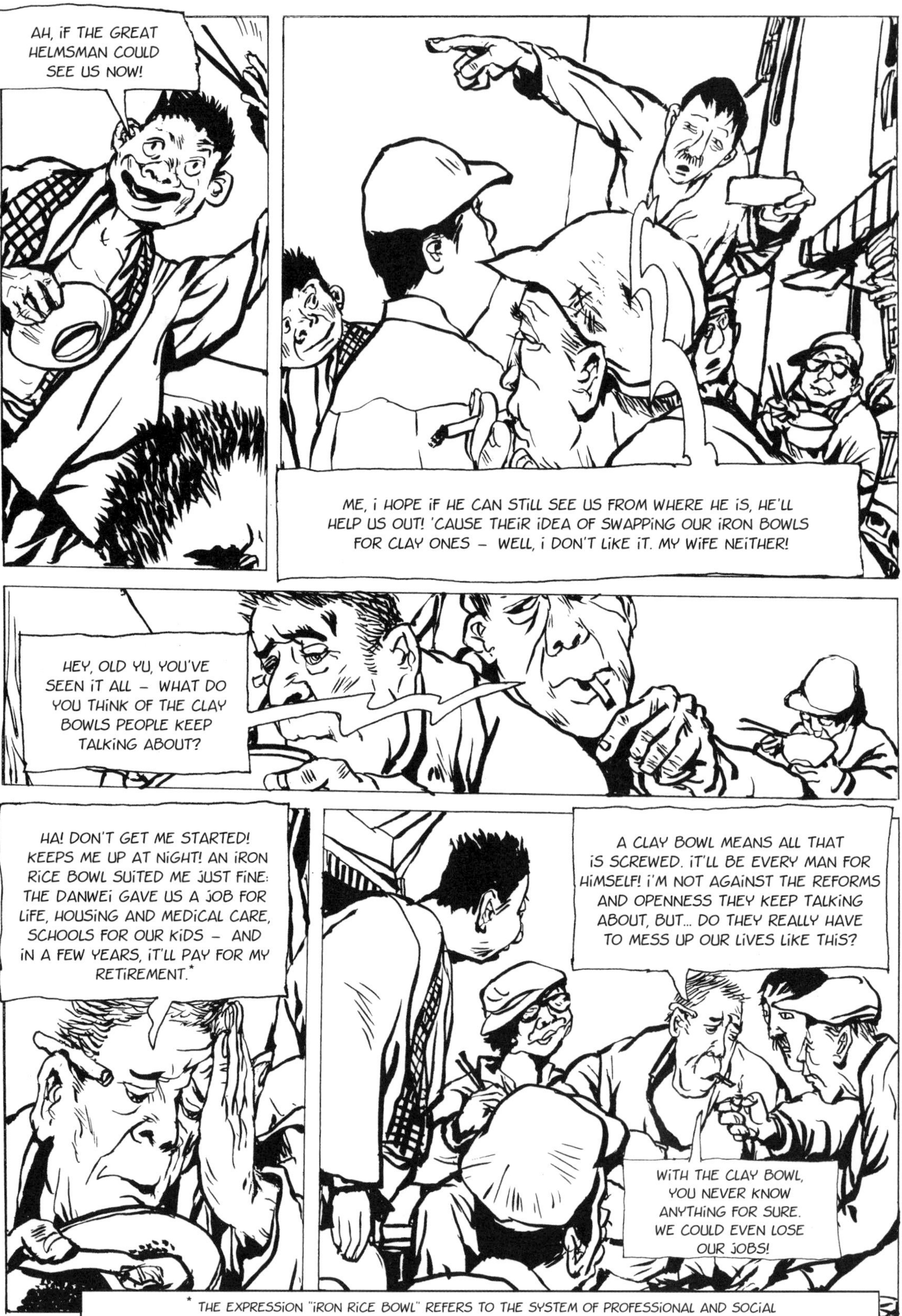
AH, IF THE GREAT HELMSMAN COULD SEE US NOW!
ME, I HOPE IF HE CAN STILL SEE US FROM WHERE HE IS, HE'LL HELP US OUT! 'CAUSE THEIR IDEA OF SWAPPING OUR IRON BOWLS FOR CLAY ONES – WELL, I DON'T LIKE IT. MY WIFE NEITHER!
HEY, OLD YU, YOU'VE SEEN IT ALL – WHAT DO YOU THINK OF THE CLAY BOWLS PEOPLE KEEP TALKING ABOUT?
HA! DON'T GET ME STARTED! KEEPS ME UP AT NIGHT! AN IRON RICE BOWL SUITED ME JUST FINE: THE DANWEI GAVE US A JOB FOR LIFE, HOUSING AND MEDICAL CARE, SCHOOLS FOR OUR KIDS – AND IN A FEW YEARS, IT'LL PAY FOR MY RETIREMENT.*
A CLAY BOWL MEANS ALL THAT IS SCREWED. IT'LL BE EVERY MAN FOR HIMSELF! I'M NOT AGAINST THE REFORMS AND OPENNESS THEY KEEP TALKING ABOUT, BUT... DO THEY REALLY HAVE TO MESS UP OUR LIVES LIKE THIS?
WITH THE CLAY BOWL, YOU NEVER KNOW ANYTHING FOR SURE. WE COULD EVEN LOSE OUR JOBS!

* THE EXPRESSION "IRON RICE BOWL" REFERS TO THE SYSTEM OF PROFESSIONAL AND SOCIAL ORGANIZATION IN USE AT THE TIME, BY WHICH THE CHINESE STATE TOOK ITS CITIZENS IN HAND FOR LIFE THROUGH THE MECHANISM OF THE WORK UNIT (单位 "DÀNWÈI") TO WHICH EACH WAS ASSIGNED.

YOU REALLY THINK IT'LL BE THAT EASY? TRY DROPPING INTO ONE AND SAYING, "HI, I SPENT MY WHOLE LIFE IN A STATE-RUN COMPANY, USED TO THE PROTECTION OF MY IRON RICE BOWL. I DON'T KNOW HOW TO DO MUCH WITH THESE FINGERS EXCEPT OPERATE MORE OR LESS OBSOLETE MACHINES..."

EH! THERE'LL ALWAYS BE WORK! IF IT SHUTS DOWN HERE, WE'LL GET HIRED SOMEWHERE ELSE! SOON THERE'LL BE LOTS OF PRIVATE COMPANIES!

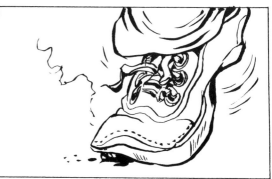

BEST NOT TO THINK ABOUT IT!

NAAAAH! YOU'RE PAINTING MUCH TOO BLEAK A PICTURE!

LOOK! AN APPROACH LIKE THIS IS ALL YOU'LL NEED.

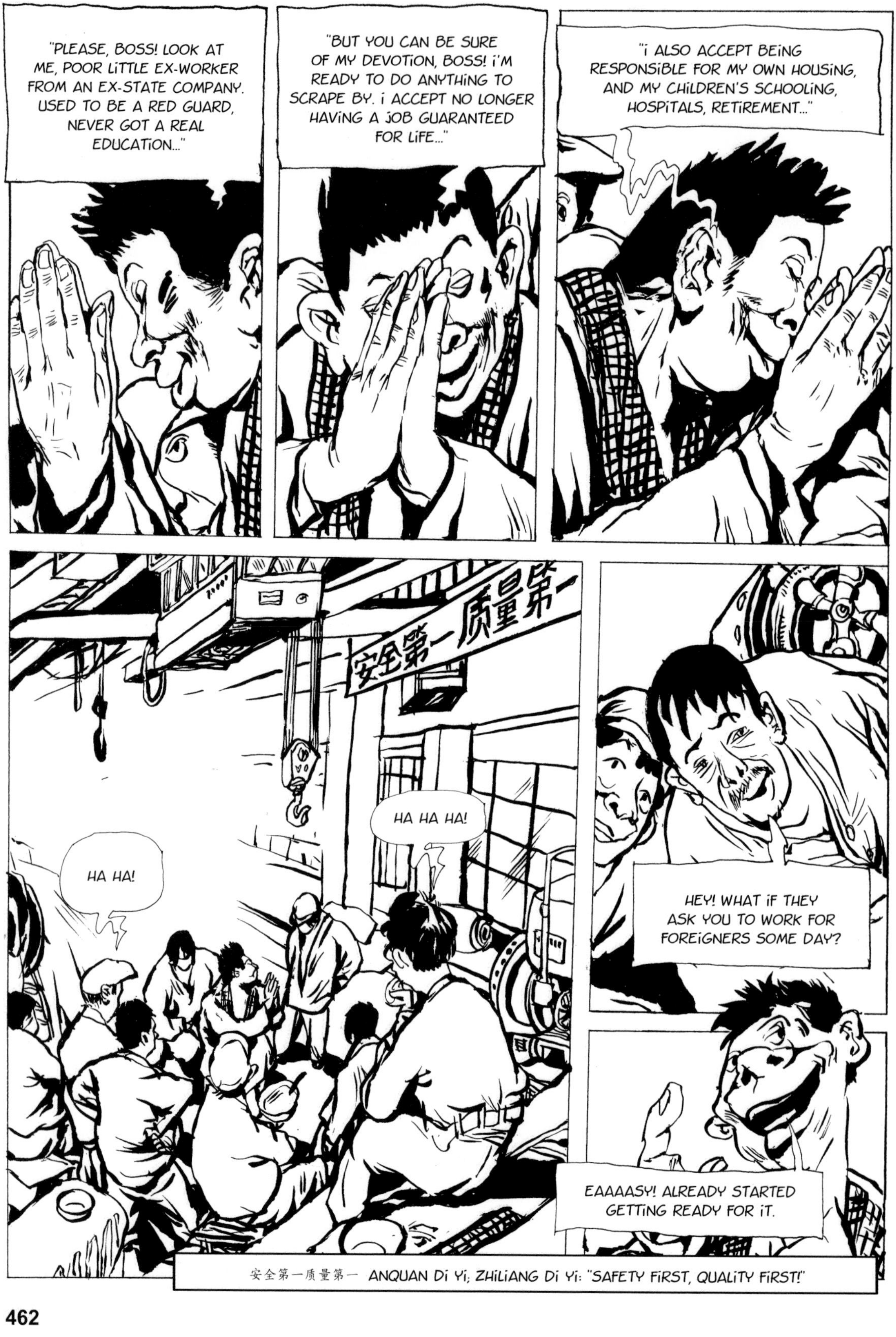
"PLEASE, BOSS! LOOK AT ME, POOR LITTLE EX-WORKER FROM AN EX-STATE COMPANY. USED TO BE A RED GUARD, NEVER GOT A REAL EDUCATION..."
"BUT YOU CAN BE SURE OF MY DEVOTION, BOSS! I'M READY TO DO ANYTHING TO SCRAPE BY. I ACCEPT NO LONGER HAVING A JOB GUARANTEED FOR LIFE..."
"I ALSO ACCEPT BEING RESPONSIBLE FOR MY OWN HOUSING, AND MY CHILDREN'S SCHOOLING, HOSPITALS, RETIREMENT..."
安全第一质量第一
HA HA!
HA HA HA!
HEY! WHAT IF THEY ASK YOU TO WORK FOR FOREIGNERS SOME DAY?
EAAAASY! ALREADY STARTED GETTING READY FOR IT.
安全第一质量第一 ANQUAN DI YI; ZHILIANG DI YI: "SAFETY FIRST, QUALITY FIRST!"

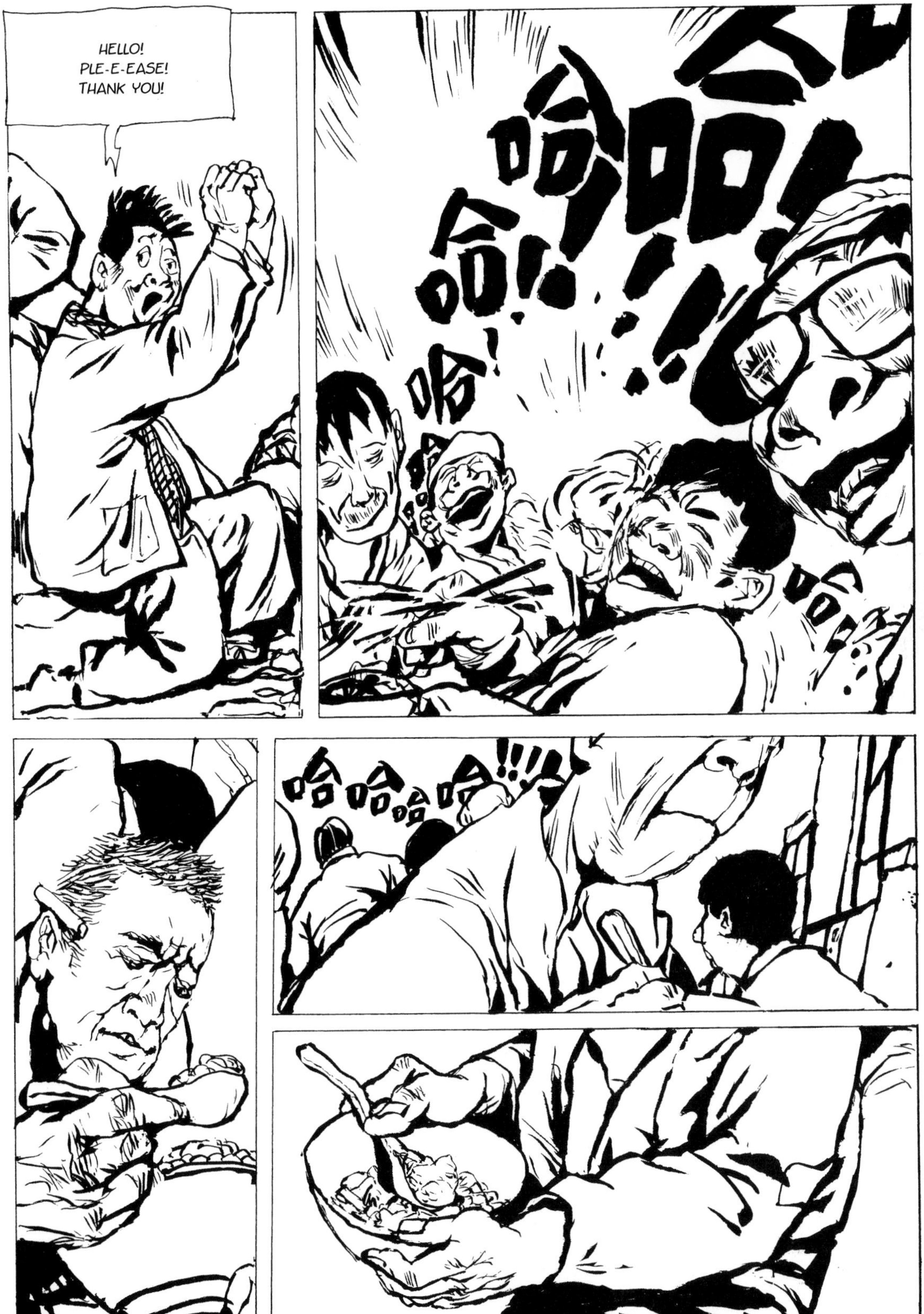
HELLO!
PLE-E-EASE!
THANK YOU!
哈!!
哈!!
哈!!
哈!
哈!
哈哈哈哈!!!!

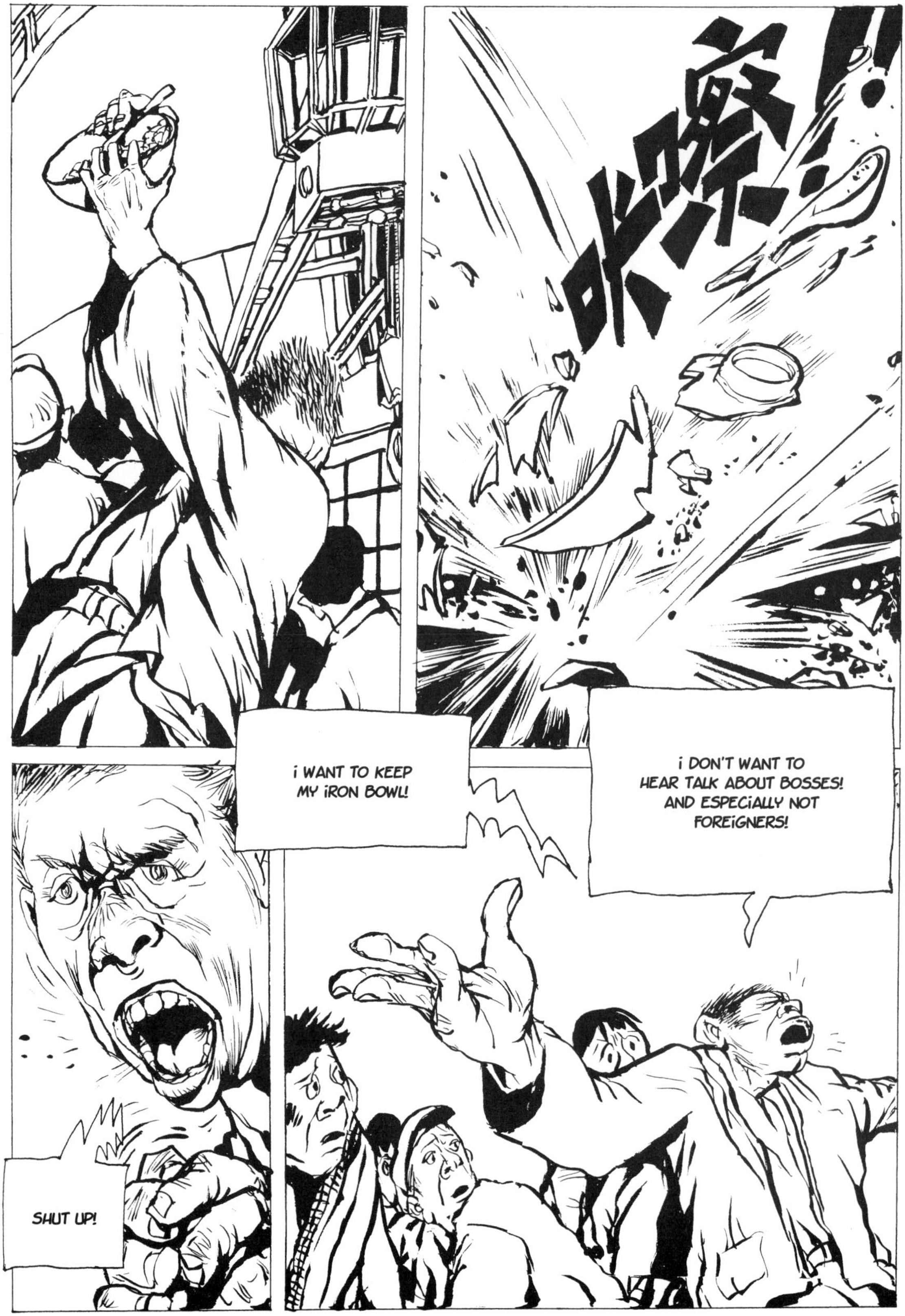

咔嚓!!
I WANT TO KEEP MY IRON BOWL!
I DON'T WANT TO HEAR TALK ABOUT BOSSES! AND ESPECIALLY NOT FOREIGNERS!
SHUT UP!

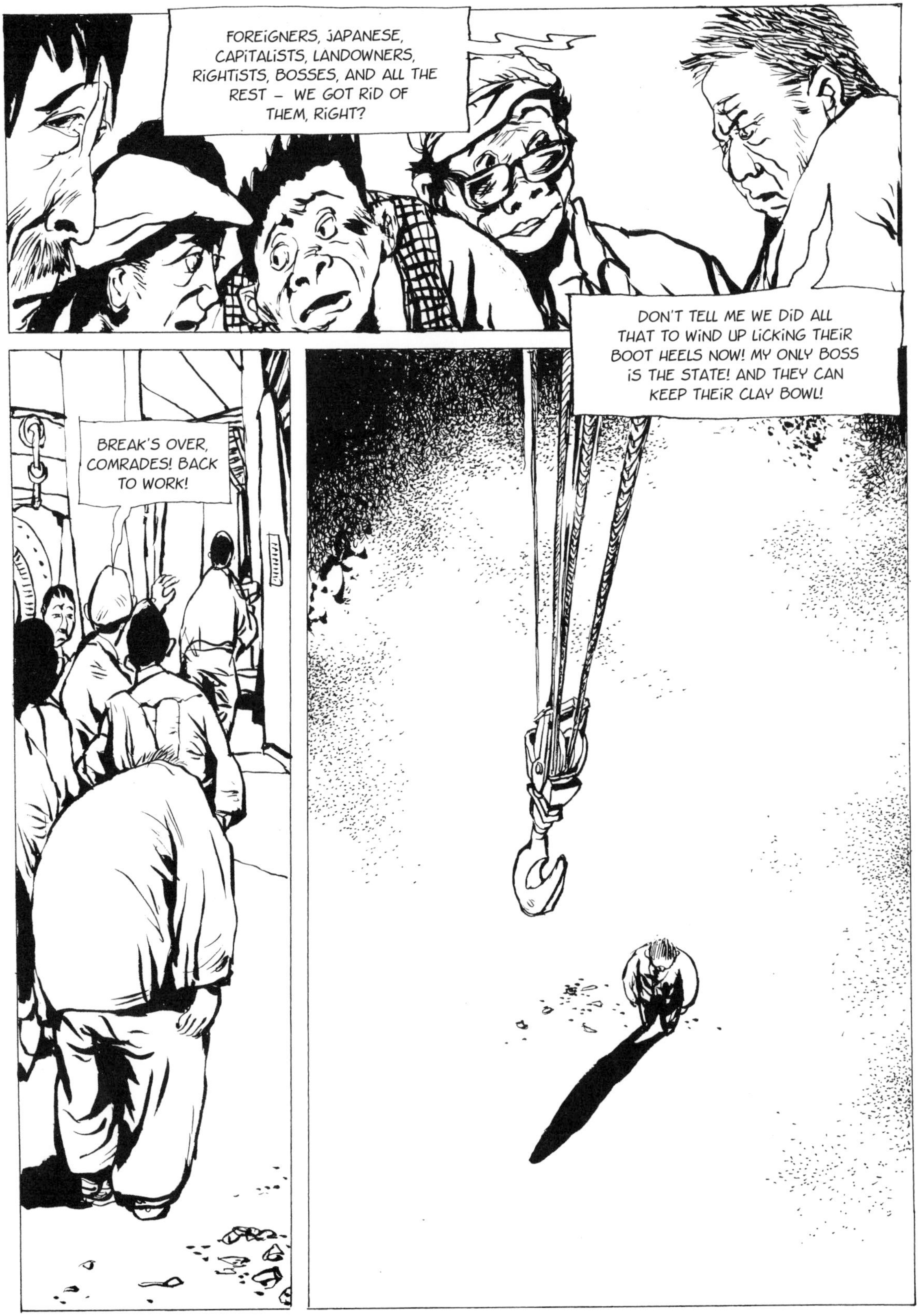
FOREIGNERS, JAPANESE, CAPITALISTS, LANDOWNERS, RIGHTISTS, BOSSES, AND ALL THE REST – WE GOT RID OF THEM, RIGHT?
DON'T TELL ME WE DID ALL THAT TO WIND UP LICKING THEIR BOOT HEELS NOW! MY ONLY BOSS IS THE STATE! AND THEY CAN KEEP THEIR CLAY BOWL!
BREAK'S OVER, COMRADES! BACK TO WORK!

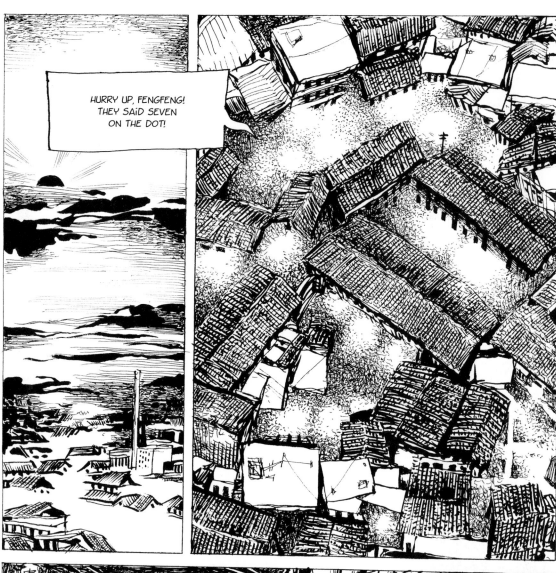

HURRY UP, FENGFENG! THEY SAID SEVEN ON THE DOT!

HERE WE ARE! THE YUNNAN *RIBAO* DORMITORIES START HERE AND GO ALL THE WAY DOWN THERE! BUREAU CHIEF WANG LIVES IN 5B WEST.

立即掀起爱国卫生运动新高潮 *Lìjí Xiānqǐ Àiguó Wēishēng Yùndòng Xīngāocháo:* "LET US CARRY THE PATRIOTIC HYGIENE CAMPAIGN TO NEW HEIGHTS RIGHT AWAY!"

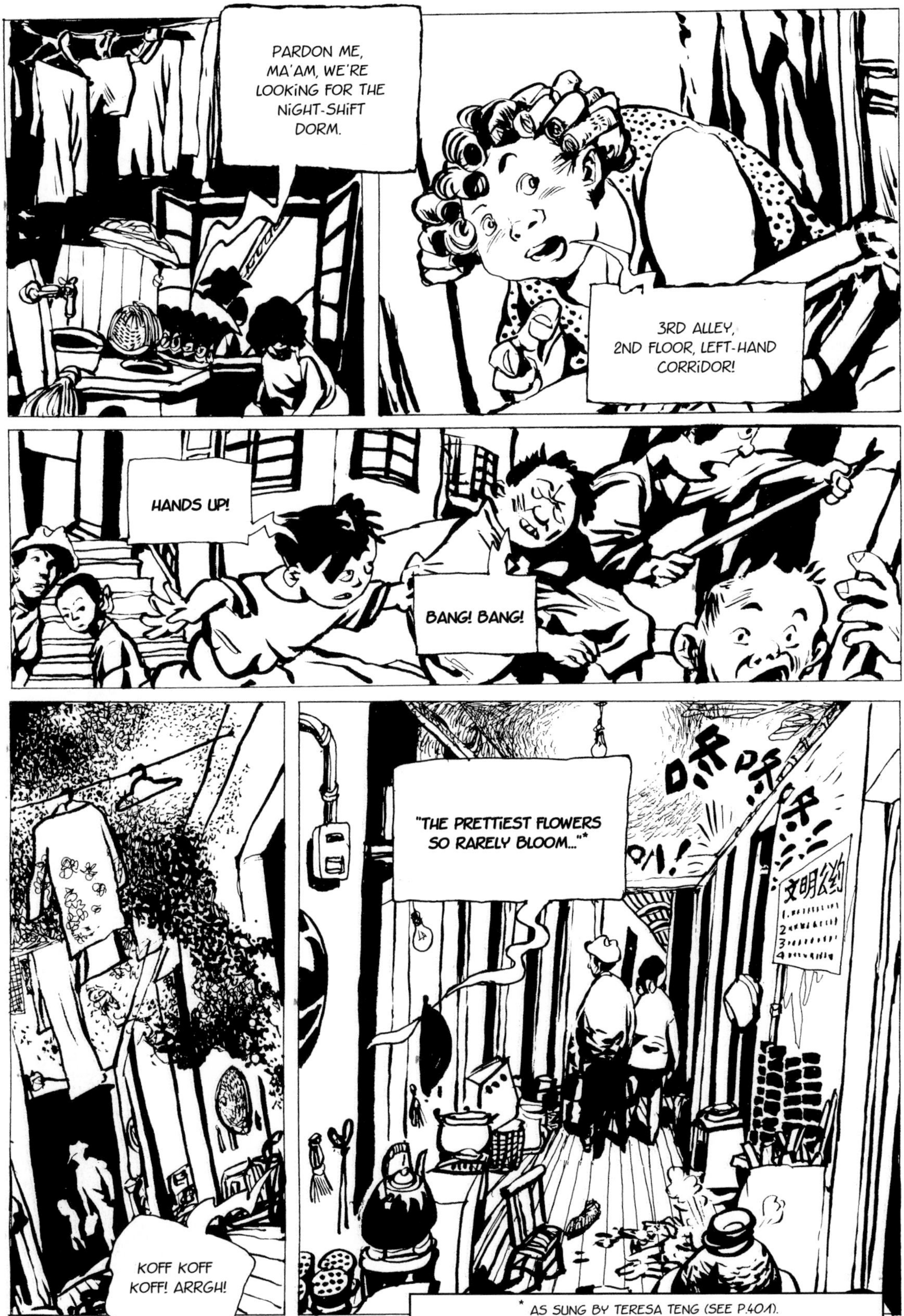
PARDON ME, MA'AM, WE'RE LOOKING FOR THE NIGHT-SHIFT DORM.
3RD ALLEY, 2ND FLOOR, LEFT-HAND CORRIDOR!
HANDS UP!
BANG! BANG!
KOFF KOFF KOFF! ARRGH!
"THE PRETTIEST FLOWERS SO RARELY BLOOM..."*
文明公约
1
2
3
4

* AS SUNG BY TERESA TENG (SEE P.401).
文明公约 WENMING GONGYUE: "HOUSE RULES" OR "CIVIL AGREEMENT".

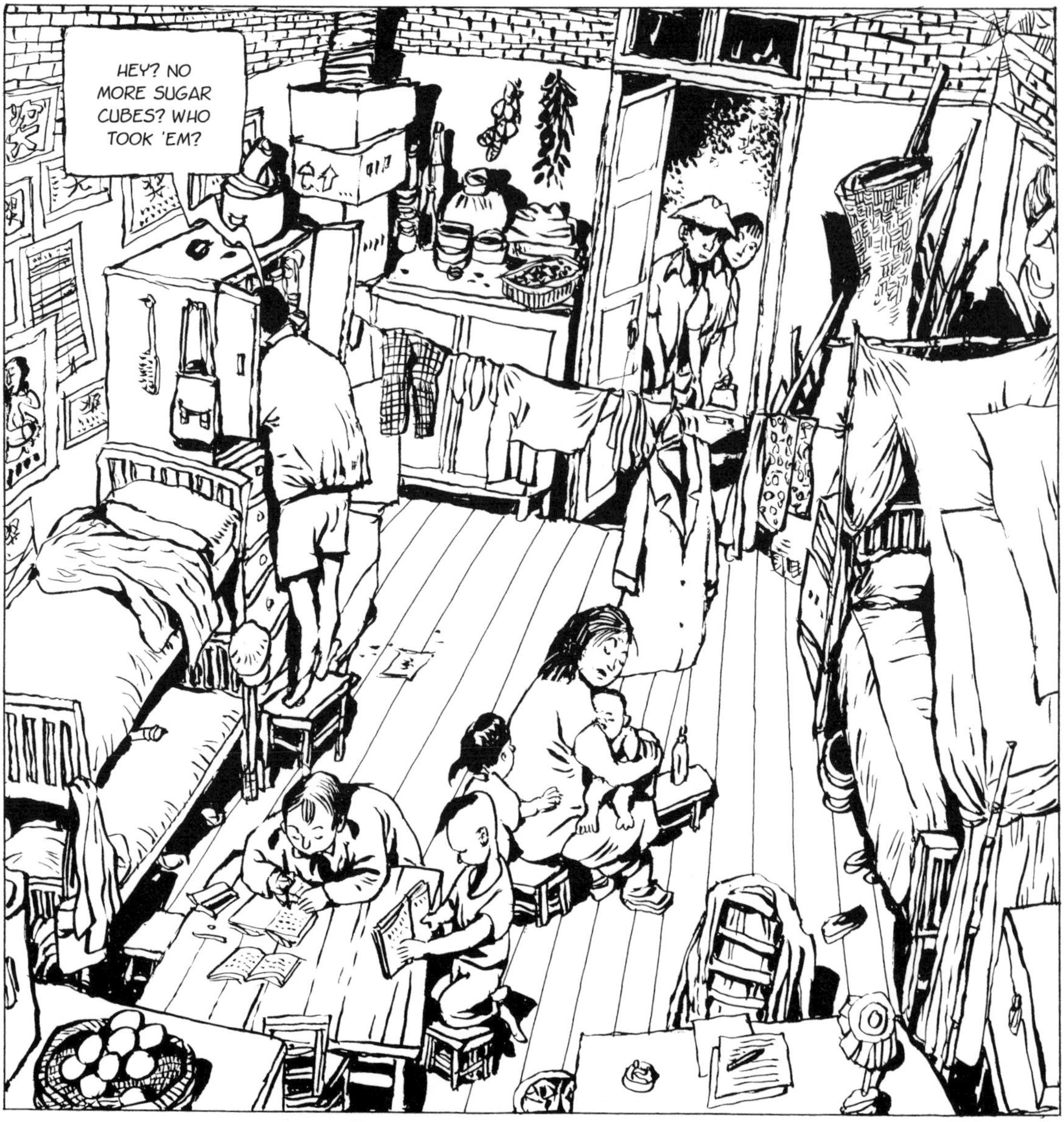
HEY? NO MORE SUGAR CUBES? WHO TOOK 'EM?

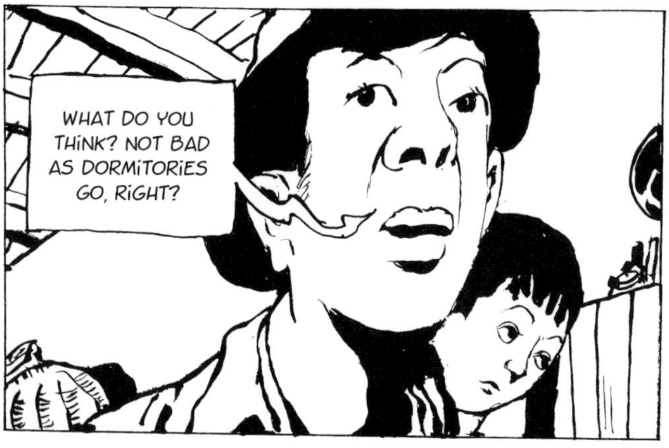
WHAT DO YOU THINK? NOT BAD AS DORMITORIES GO, RIGHT?

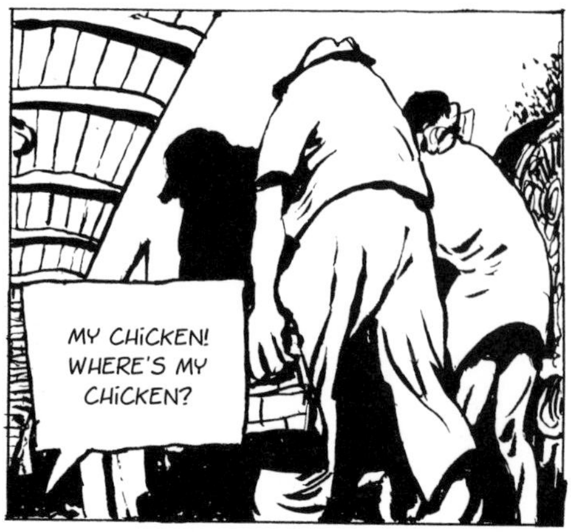
MY CHICKEN! WHERE'S MY CHICKEN?

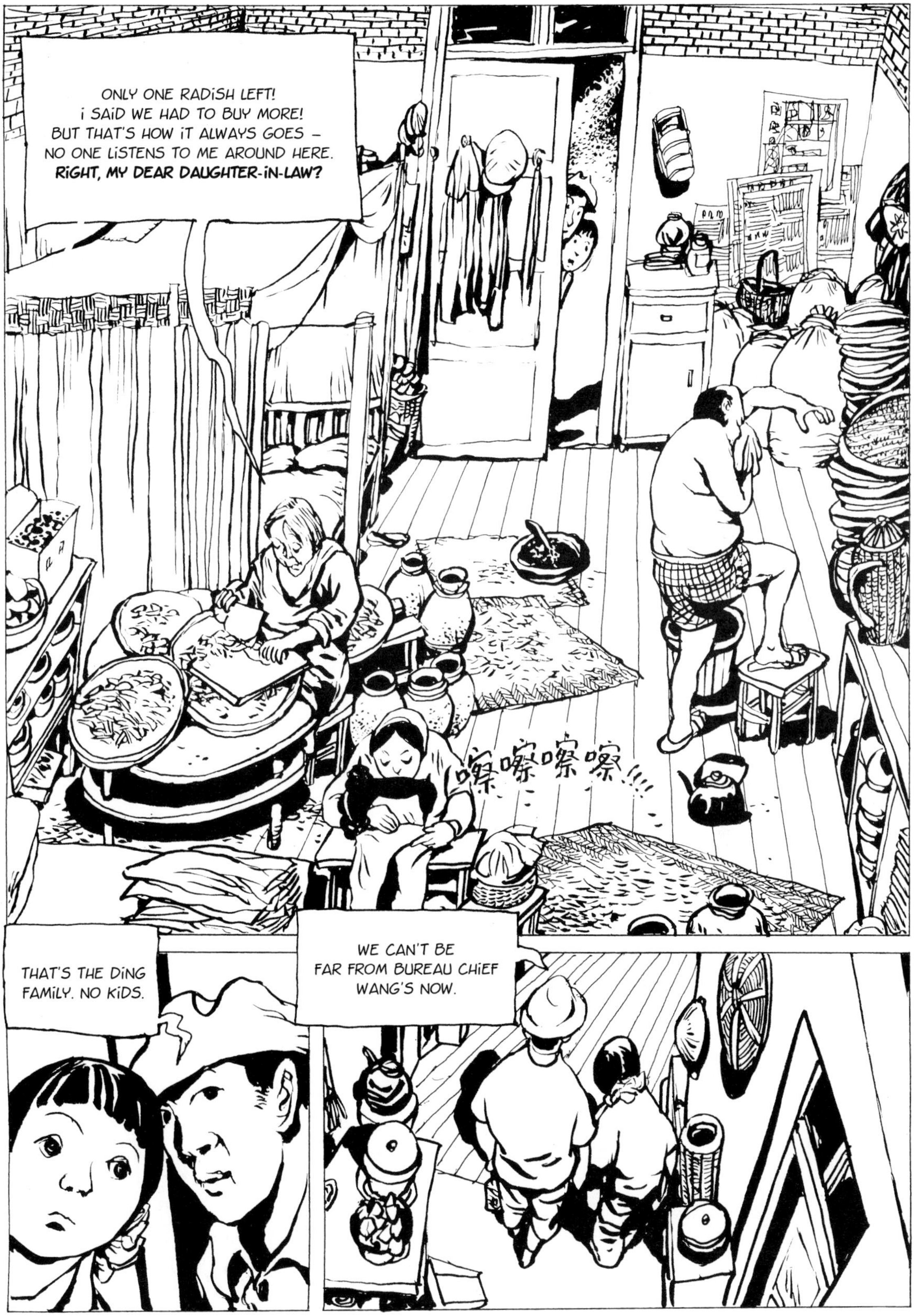
ONLY ONE RADISH LEFT!
I SAID WE HAD TO BUY MORE!
BUT THAT'S HOW IT ALWAYS GOES – NO ONE LISTENS TO ME AROUND HERE.
RIGHT, MY DEAR DAUGHTER-IN-LAW?
嚓嚓嚓嚓!!!
THAT'S THE DING FAMILY. NO KIDS.
WE CAN'T BE FAR FROM BUREAU CHIEF WANG'S NOW.

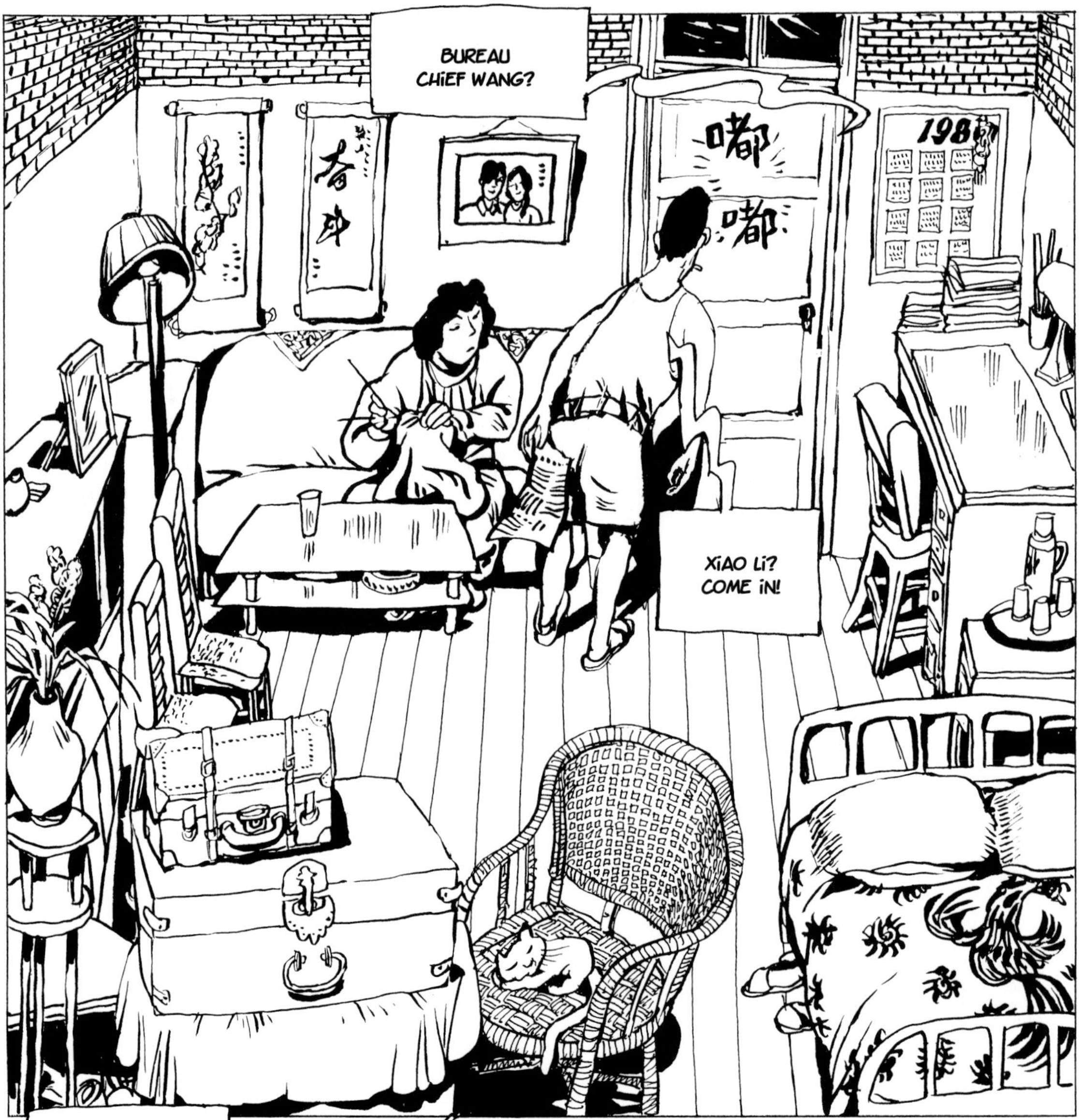
BUREAU CHIEF WANG?
嘟
嘟
XIAO LI? COME IN!

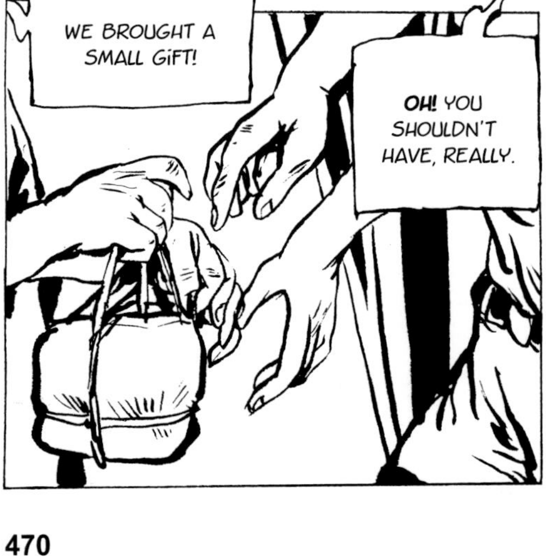
WE BROUGHT A SMALL GIFT!
OH! YOU SHOULDN'T HAVE, REALLY.

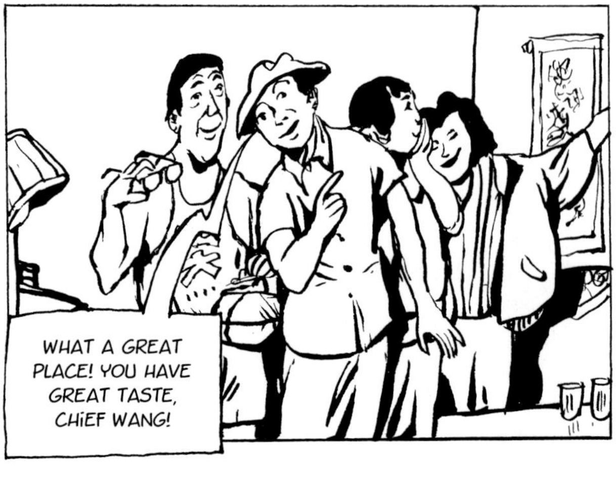
WHAT A GREAT PLACE! YOU HAVE GREAT TASTE, CHIEF WANG!

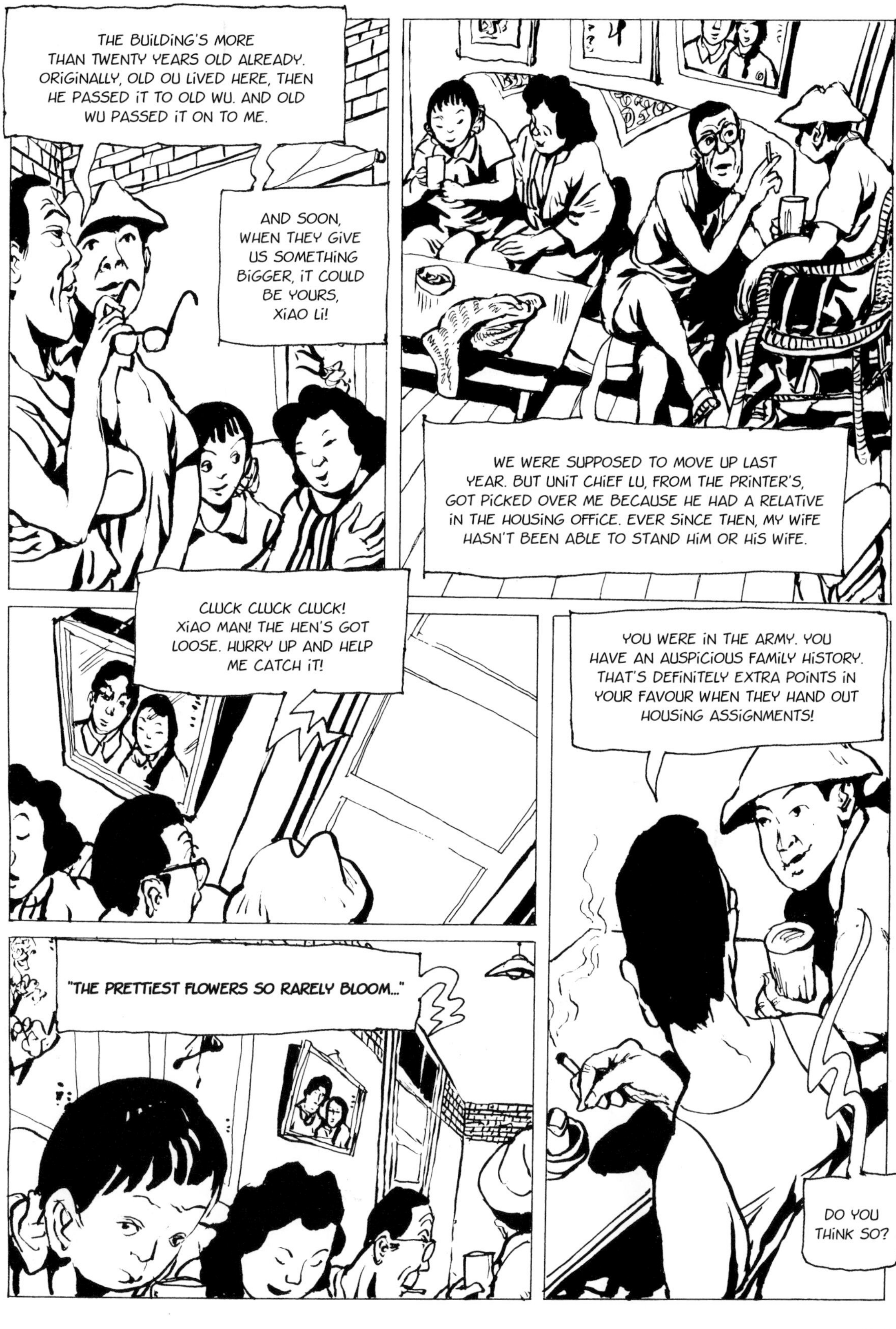
THE BUILDING'S MORE THAN TWENTY YEARS OLD ALREADY. ORIGINALLY, OLD OU LIVED HERE, THEN HE PASSED IT TO OLD WU. AND OLD WU PASSED IT ON TO ME.
AND SOON, WHEN THEY GIVE US SOMETHING BIGGER, IT COULD BE YOURS, XIAO LI!
WE WERE SUPPOSED TO MOVE UP LAST YEAR. BUT UNIT CHIEF LU, FROM THE PRINTER'S, GOT PICKED OVER ME BECAUSE HE HAD A RELATIVE IN THE HOUSING OFFICE. EVER SINCE THEN, MY WIFE HASN'T BEEN ABLE TO STAND HIM OR HIS WIFE.
CLUCK CLUCK CLUCK! XIAO MAN! THE HEN'S GOT LOOSE. HURRY UP AND HELP ME CATCH IT!
YOU WERE IN THE ARMY. YOU HAVE AN AUSPICIOUS FAMILY HISTORY. THAT'S DEFINITELY EXTRA POINTS IN YOUR FAVOUR WHEN THEY HAND OUT HOUSING ASSIGNMENTS!
"THE PRETTIEST FLOWERS SO RARELY BLOOM..."
DO YOU THINK SO?

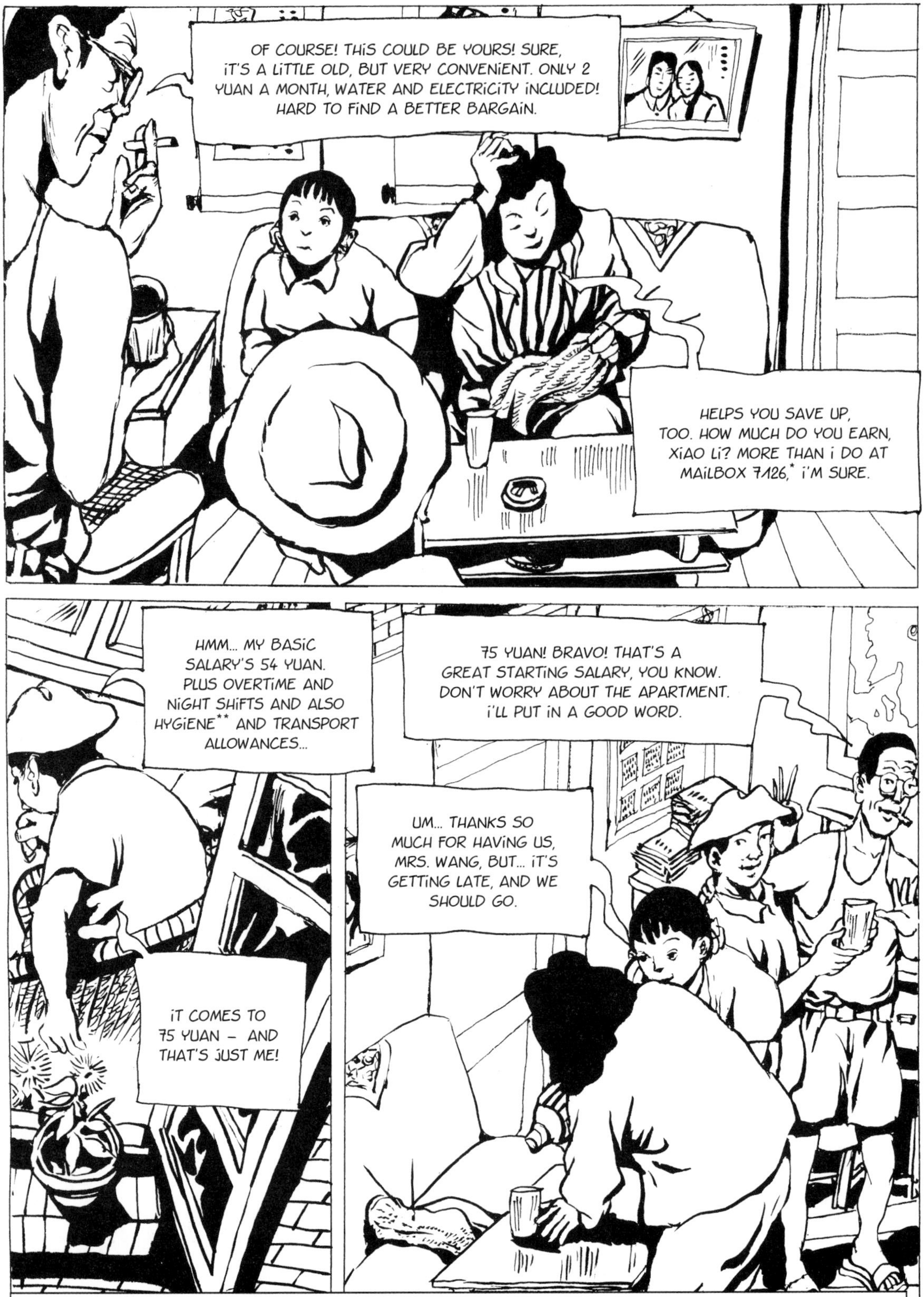
OF COURSE! THIS COULD BE YOURS! SURE, IT'S A LITTLE OLD, BUT VERY CONVENIENT. ONLY 2 YUAN A MONTH, WATER AND ELECTRICITY INCLUDED! HARD TO FIND A BETTER BARGAIN.
HELPS YOU SAVE UP, TOO. HOW MUCH DO YOU EARN, XIAO LI? MORE THAN I DO AT MAILBOX 7126,* I'M SURE.
HMM... MY BASIC SALARY'S 54 YUAN. PLUS OVERTIME AND NIGHT SHIFTS AND ALSO HYGIENE** AND TRANSPORT ALLOWANCES...
IT COMES TO 75 YUAN – AND THAT'S JUST ME!
75 YUAN! BRAVO! THAT'S A GREAT STARTING SALARY, YOU KNOW. DON'T WORRY ABOUT THE APARTMENT. I'LL PUT IN A GOOD WORD.
UM... THANKS SO MUCH FOR HAVING US, MRS. WANG, BUT... IT'S GETTING LATE, AND WE SHOULD GO.

* 信箱 XIN XIANG: LITERALLY, "MAILBOX". AN EXAMPLE OF THE SECRET FORM OF IDENTIFICATION FOR NUMEROUS ORGANIZATIONS WHOSE ACTIVITIES WERE CONSIDERED SENSITIVE.

** 卫生费 WÈISHENG FÈI: ALLOWANCES FOR PURCHASING ITEMS OF PERSONAL HYGIENE.

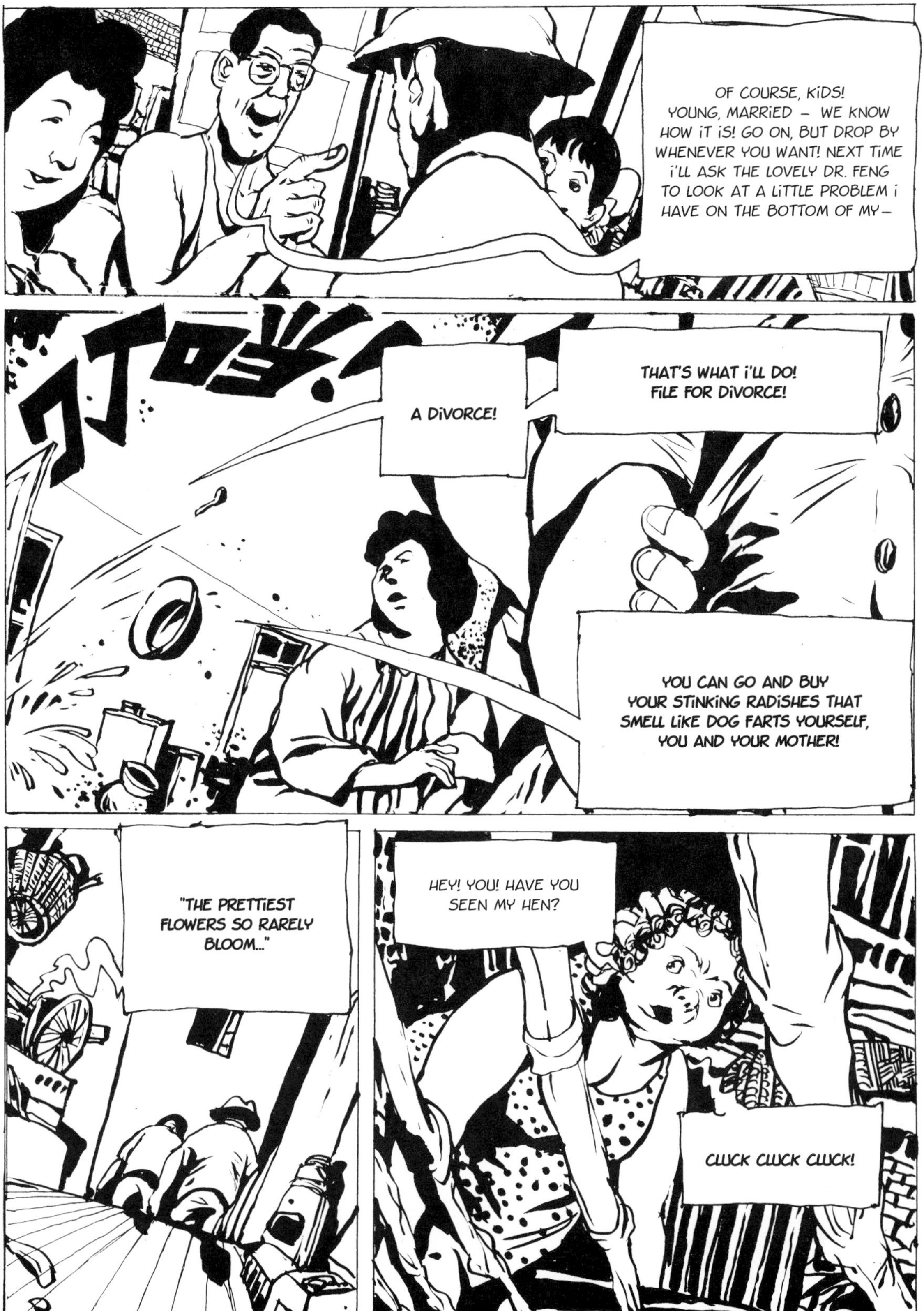
OF COURSE, KIDS! YOUNG, MARRIED – WE KNOW HOW IT IS! GO ON, BUT DROP BY WHENEVER YOU WANT! NEXT TIME I'LL ASK THE LOVELY DR. FENG TO LOOK AT A LITTLE PROBLEM I HAVE ON THE BOTTOM OF MY–
A DIVORCE!
THAT'S WHAT I'LL DO! FILE FOR DIVORCE!
YOU CAN GO AND BUY YOUR STINKING RADISHES THAT SMELL LIKE DOG FARTS YOURSELF, YOU AND YOUR MOTHER!
"THE PRETTIEST FLOWERS SO RARELY BLOOM..."
HEY! YOU! HAVE YOU SEEN MY HEN?
CLUCK CLUCK CLUCK!

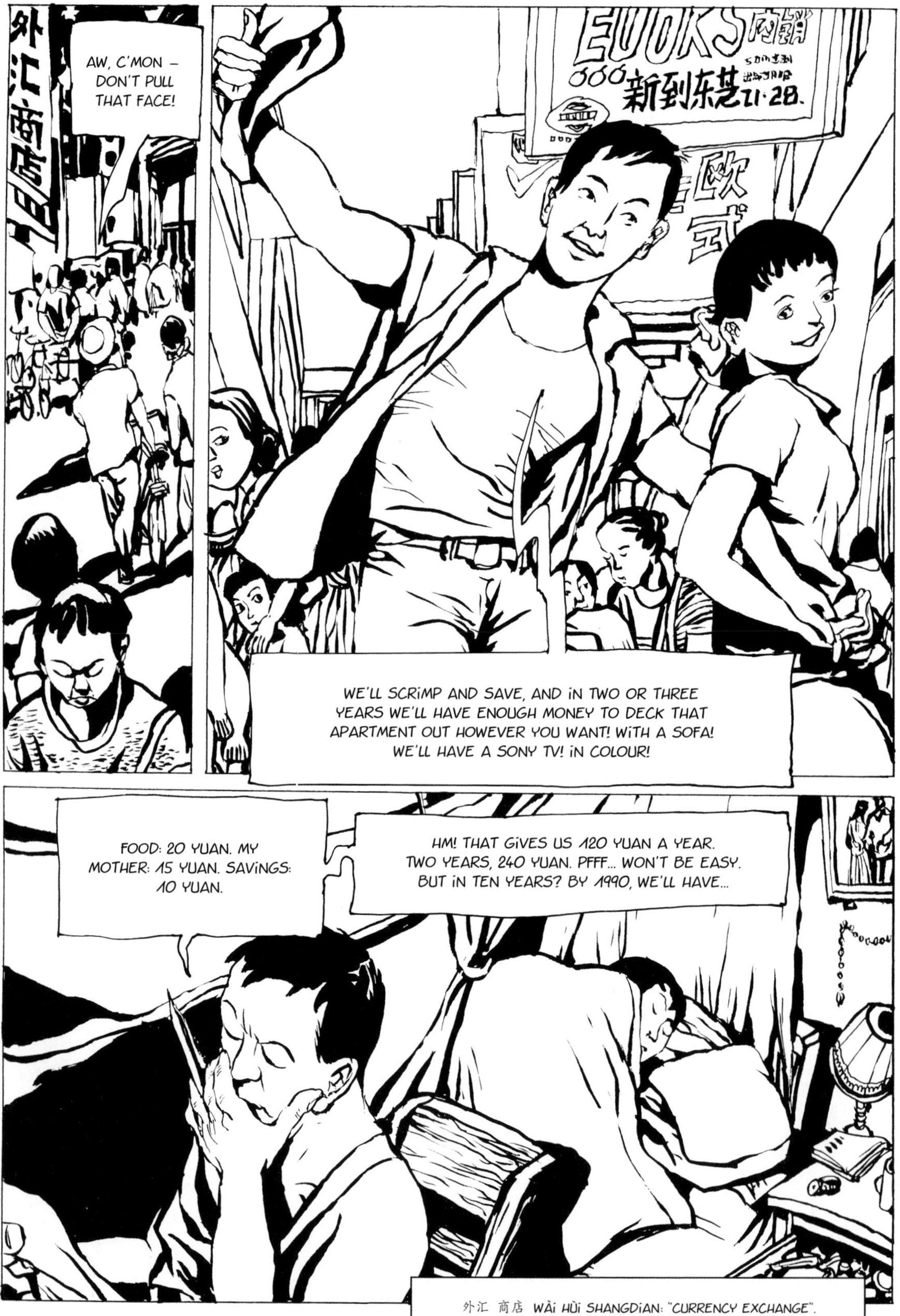
外汇商店
AW, C'MON – DON'T PULL THAT FACE!
WE'LL SCRIMP AND SAVE, AND IN TWO OR THREE YEARS WE'LL HAVE ENOUGH MONEY TO DECK THAT APARTMENT OUT HOWEVER YOU WANT! WITH A SOFA! WE'LL HAVE A SONY TV! IN COLOUR!
FOOD: 20 YUAN. MY MOTHER: 15 YUAN. SAVINGS: 10 YUAN.
HM! THAT GIVES US 120 YUAN A YEAR. TWO YEARS, 240 YUAN. PFFF... WON'T BE EASY. BUT IN TEN YEARS? BY 1990, WE'LL HAVE...

外汇 商店 WÀI HÙI SHANGDIAN: "CURRENCY EXCHANGE".

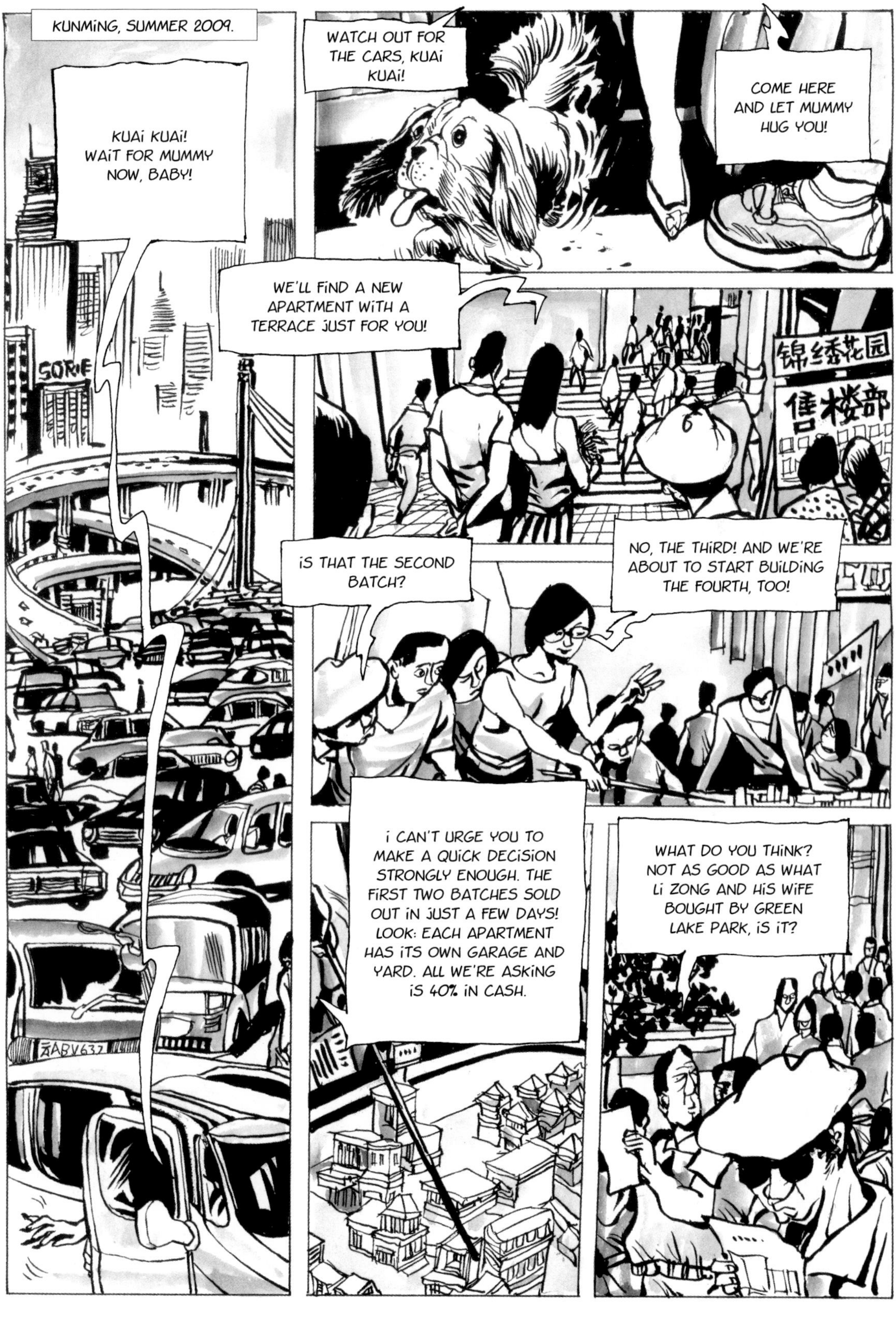
KUNMING, SUMMER 2009.
KUAI KUAI! WAIT FOR MUMMY NOW, BABY!
WATCH OUT FOR THE CARS, KUAI KUAI!
COME HERE AND LET MUMMY HUG YOU!
WE'LL FIND A NEW APARTMENT WITH A TERRACE JUST FOR YOU!
锦绣花园
售楼部
IS THAT THE SECOND BATCH?
NO, THE THIRD! AND WE'RE ABOUT TO START BUILDING THE FOURTH, TOO!
I CAN'T URGE YOU TO MAKE A QUICK DECISION STRONGLY ENOUGH. THE FIRST TWO BATCHES SOLD OUT IN JUST A FEW DAYS! LOOK: EACH APARTMENT HAS ITS OWN GARAGE AND YARD. ALL WE'RE ASKING IS 40% IN CASH.
WHAT DO YOU THINK? NOT AS GOOD AS WHAT LI ZONG AND HIS WIFE BOUGHT BY GREEN LAKE PARK, IS IT?

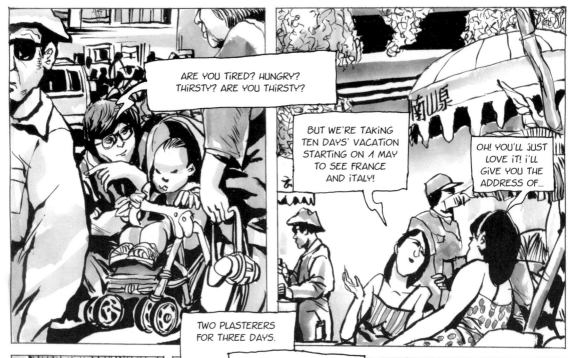

ARE YOU TIRED? HUNGRY? THIRSTY? ARE YOU THIRSTY?

BUT WE'RE TAKING TEN DAYS' VACATION STARTING ON 1 MAY TO SEE FRANCE AND ITALY!

OH! YOU'LL JUST LOVE IT! I'LL GIVE YOU THE ADDRESS OF...

TWO PLASTERERS FOR THREE DAYS.

FIVE EXPERIENCED MASONS!

FIVE CONSTRUCTION WORKERS! ROOM AND BOARD!

HAVE YOU SPOKEN WITH YOUR WIFE ABOUT THE DIVORCE?

EVERYTHING'S CHANGED SO FAST! EACH STEP WAS IMPORTANT, BUT IF I HAD TO PICK ONE DATE TO REMEMBER, IT'D BE 1982...

De Xiaoli à Lao Li: Une vie chinoise* 小李 老李

* FROM XIAO LI TO LAO LI: A CHINESE LIFE.

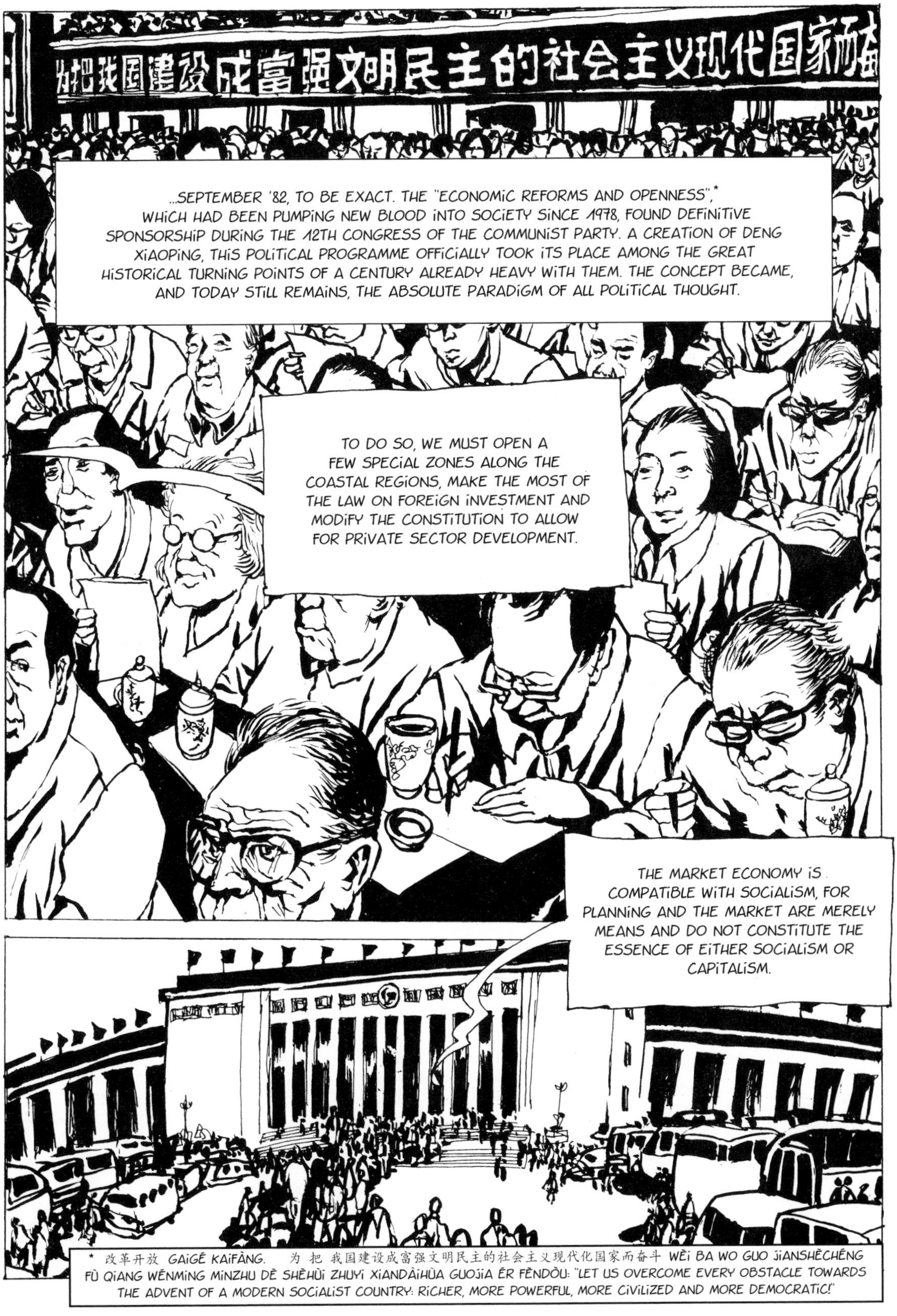
为把我国建设成富强文明民主的社会主义现代国家而
...SEPTEMBER '82, TO BE EXACT. THE "ECONOMIC REFORMS AND OPENNESS",* WHICH HAD BEEN PUMPING NEW BLOOD INTO SOCIETY SINCE 1978, FOUND DEFINITIVE SPONSORSHIP DURING THE 12TH CONGRESS OF THE COMMUNIST PARTY. A CREATION OF DENG XIAOPING, THIS POLITICAL PROGRAMME OFFICIALLY TOOK ITS PLACE AMONG THE GREAT HISTORICAL TURNING POINTS OF A CENTURY ALREADY HEAVY WITH THEM. THE CONCEPT BECAME, AND TODAY STILL REMAINS, THE ABSOLUTE PARADIGM OF ALL POLITICAL THOUGHT.
TO DO SO, WE MUST OPEN A FEW SPECIAL ZONES ALONG THE COASTAL REGIONS, MAKE THE MOST OF THE LAW ON FOREIGN INVESTMENT AND MODIFY THE CONSTITUTION TO ALLOW FOR PRIVATE SECTOR DEVELOPMENT.
THE MARKET ECONOMY IS COMPATIBLE WITH SOCIALISM, FOR PLANNING AND THE MARKET ARE MERELY MEANS AND DO NOT CONSTITUTE THE ESSENCE OF EITHER SOCIALISM OR CAPITALISM.

* 改革开放 GAIGĒ KAIFÀNG. 为 把 我国建设成富强文明民主的社会主义现代化国家而奋斗 WÈI BA WO GUO JIANSHÈCHÉNG FÙ QIANG WÉNMING MINZHU DĒ SHÈHÙI ZHUYI XIANDÀIHÙA GUOJIA ÉR FÈNDÒU: "LET US OVERCOME EVERY OBSTACLE TOWARDS THE ADVENT OF A MODERN SOCIALIST COUNTRY: RICHER, MORE POWERFUL, MORE CIVILIZED AND MORE DEMOCRATIC!"

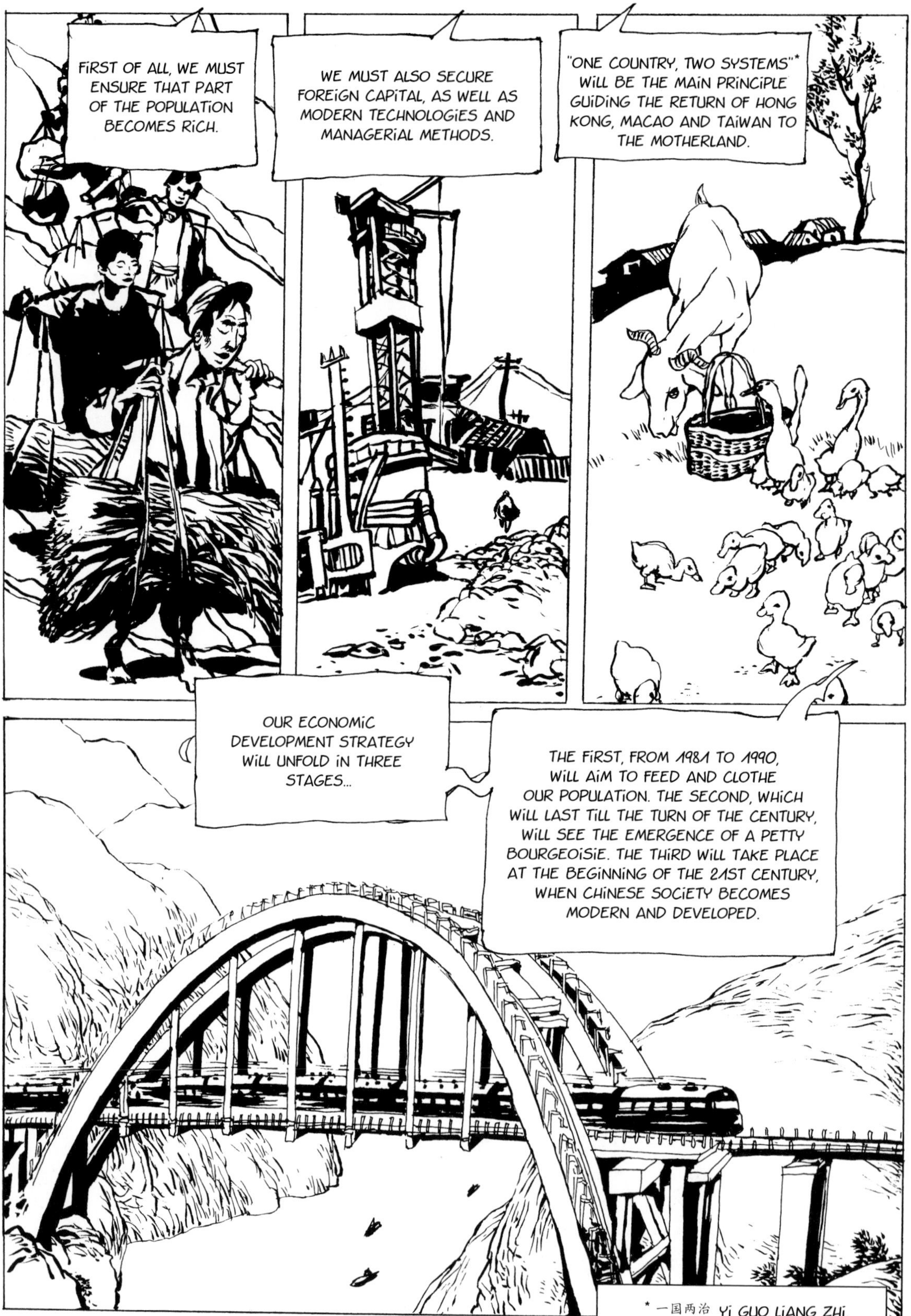
FIRST OF ALL, WE MUST ENSURE THAT PART OF THE POPULATION BECOMES RICH.
WE MUST ALSO SECURE FOREIGN CAPITAL, AS WELL AS MODERN TECHNOLOGIES AND MANAGERIAL METHODS.
"ONE COUNTRY, TWO SYSTEMS"* WILL BE THE MAIN PRINCIPLE GUIDING THE RETURN OF HONG KONG, MACAO AND TAIWAN TO THE MOTHERLAND.
OUR ECONOMIC DEVELOPMENT STRATEGY WILL UNFOLD IN THREE STAGES...
THE FIRST, FROM 1981 TO 1990, WILL AIM TO FEED AND CLOTHE OUR POPULATION. THE SECOND, WHICH WILL LAST TILL THE TURN OF THE CENTURY, WILL SEE THE EMERGENCE OF A PETTY BOURGEOISIE. THE THIRD WILL TAKE PLACE AT THE BEGINNING OF THE 21ST CENTURY, WHEN CHINESE SOCIETY BECOMES MODERN AND DEVELOPED.
* 一国两治 YI GUO LIANG ZHI.

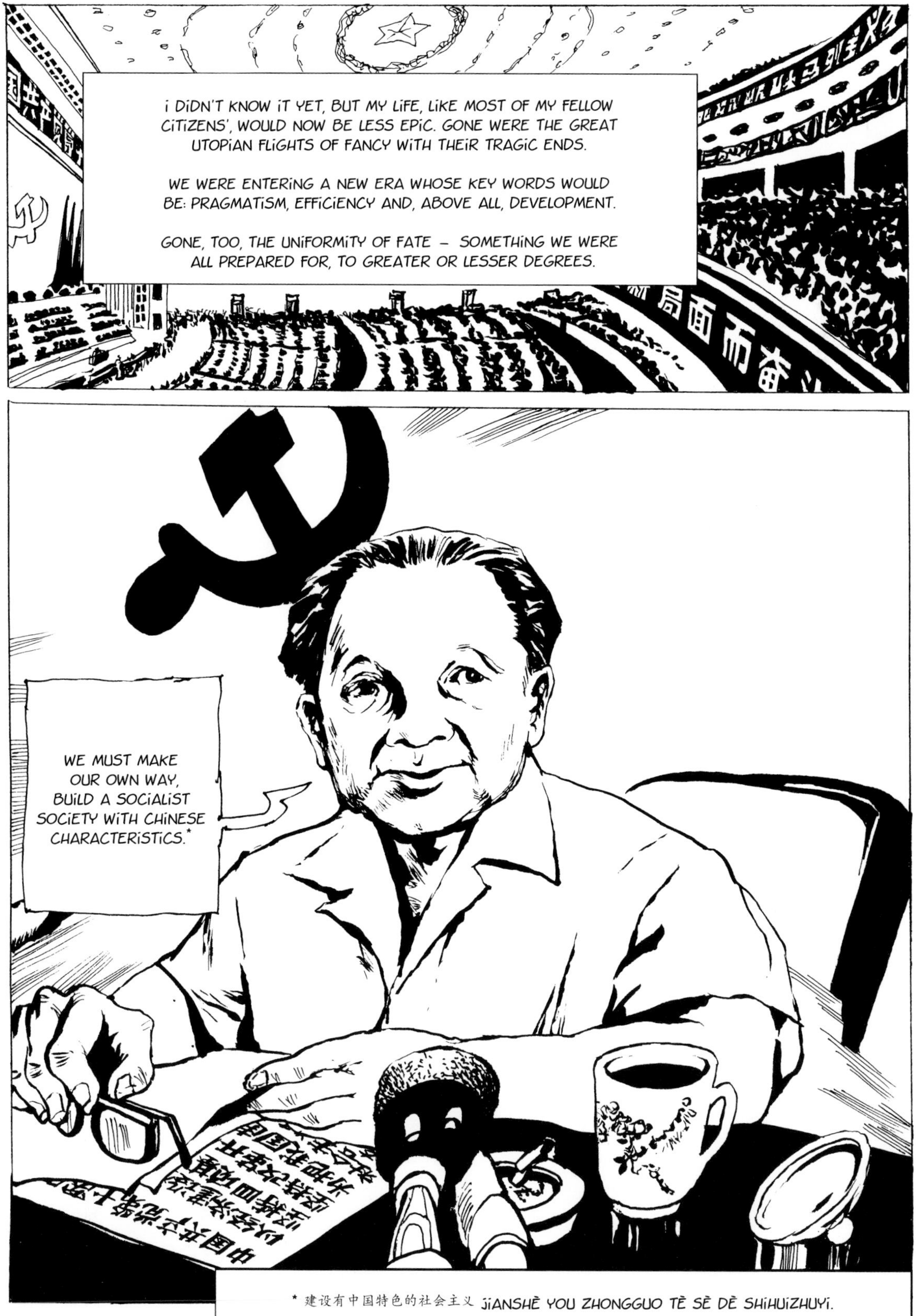
I DIDN'T KNOW IT YET, BUT MY LIFE, LIKE MOST OF MY FELLOW CITIZENS', WOULD NOW BE LESS EPIC. GONE WERE THE GREAT UTOPIAN FLIGHTS OF FANCY WITH THEIR TRAGIC ENDS.
WE WERE ENTERING A NEW ERA WHOSE KEY WORDS WOULD BE: PRAGMATISM, EFFICIENCY AND, ABOVE ALL, DEVELOPMENT.
GONE, TOO, THE UNIFORMITY OF FATE – SOMETHING WE WERE ALL PREPARED FOR, TO GREATER OR LESSER DEGREES.
WE MUST MAKE OUR OWN WAY, BUILD A SOCIALIST SOCIETY WITH CHINESE CHARACTERISTICS.*

* 建设有中国特色的社会主义 JIANSHÈ YOU ZHONGGUO TÈ SÈ DÈ SHIHUIZHUYI.

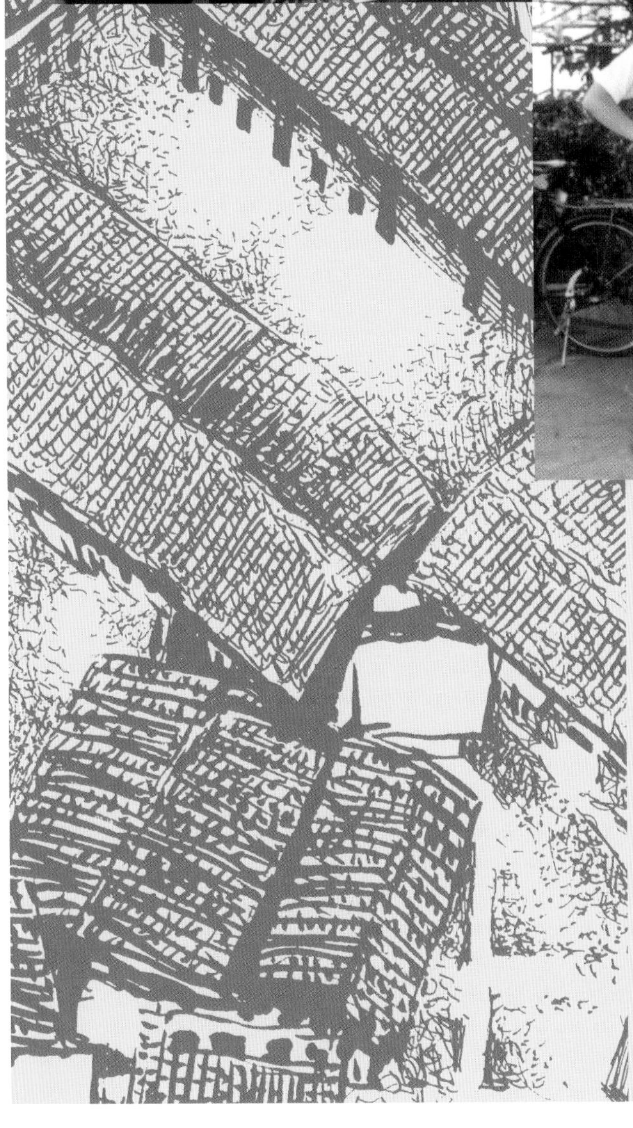

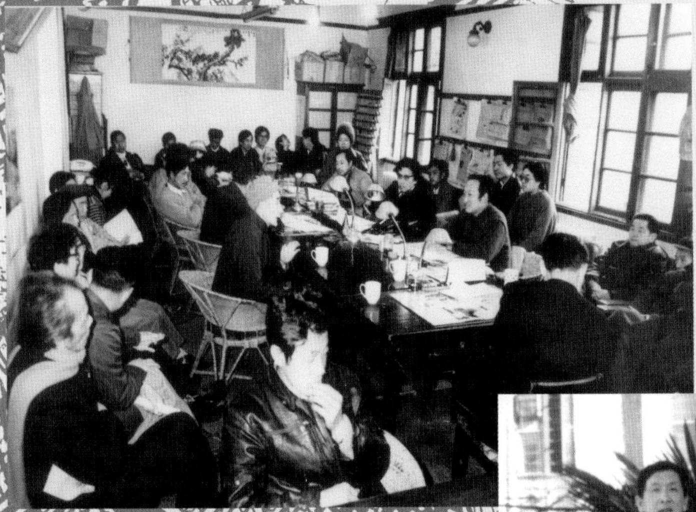

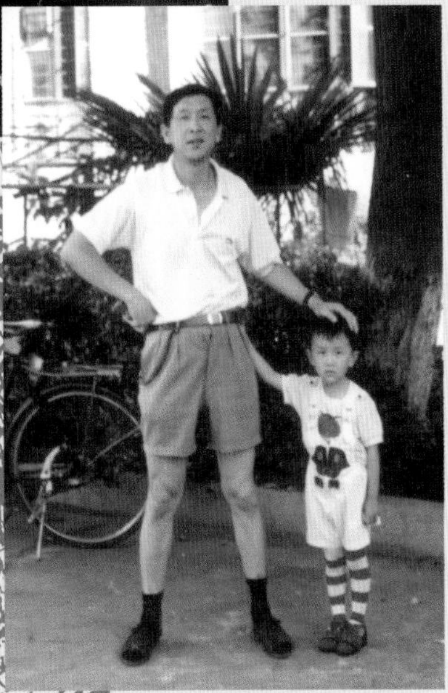

CHAPTER 7

The First Golden Bowl

再过二十年，
我们来相会，
荡起小船儿，
暖风轻轻吹，
天也新，地也新，
光荣属于八十年代的新一辈。
……

IN TWENTY YEARS,
WE WILL COME TOGETHER
ON A BOAT, TO THE RHYTHM OF THE WAVES.
A GENTLE BREEZE WILL CARESS US,
BENEATH A NEW SKY, ON A NEW WORLD;
GLORY BELONGS TO THE RISING '80S GENERATION.

(FROM THE POPULAR SONG "YOUNG FRIENDS
COME TOGETHER")

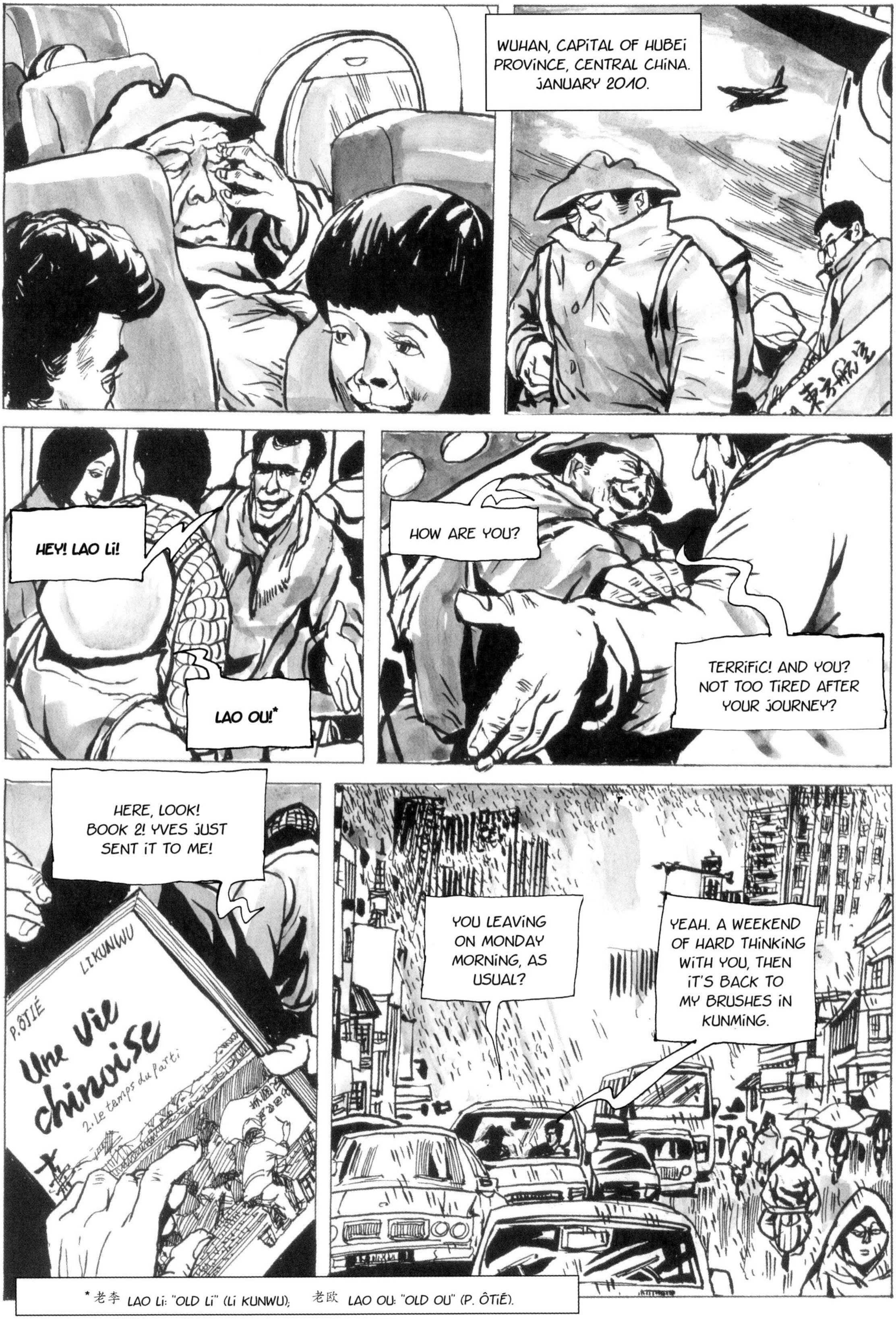
WUHAN, CAPITAL OF HUBEI PROVINCE, CENTRAL CHINA. JANUARY 2010.
HEY! LAO LI!
LAO OU!*
HOW ARE YOU?
TERRIFIC! AND YOU? NOT TOO TIRED AFTER YOUR JOURNEY?
HERE, LOOK! BOOK 2! YVES JUST SENT IT TO ME!
LIKUNWU
P. ÔTIÉ
Une vie chinoise
2. Le temps du Parti
YOU LEAVING ON MONDAY MORNING, AS USUAL?
YEAH. A WEEKEND OF HARD THINKING WITH YOU, THEN IT'S BACK TO MY BRUSHES IN KUNMING.

* 老李 LAO LI: "OLD LI" (LI KUNWU); 老欧 LAO OU: "OLD OU" (P. ÔTIÉ).

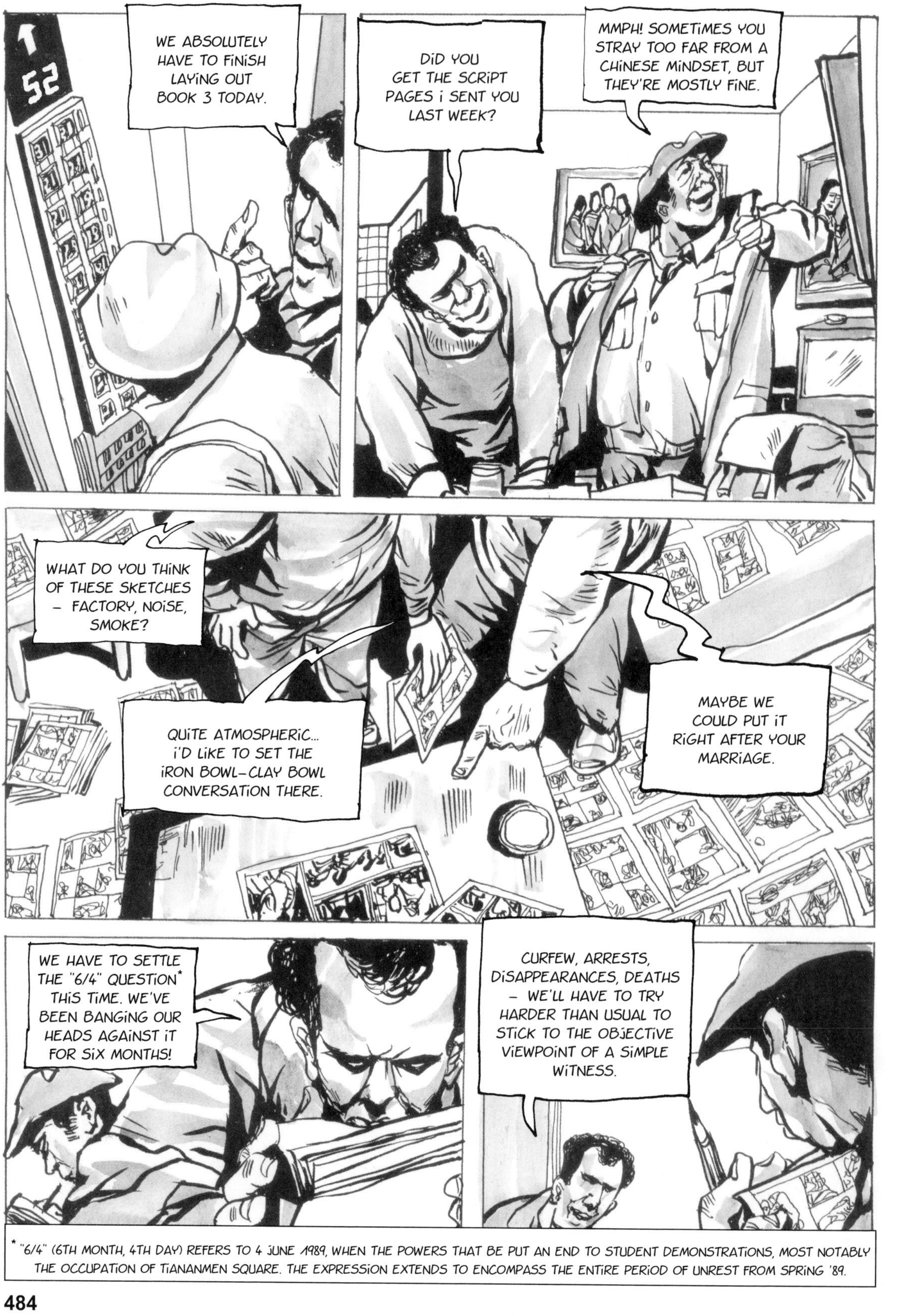

WE ABSOLUTELY HAVE TO FINISH LAYING OUT BOOK 3 TODAY.
DID YOU GET THE SCRIPT PAGES I SENT YOU LAST WEEK?
MMPH! SOMETIMES YOU STRAY TOO FAR FROM A CHINESE MINDSET, BUT THEY'RE MOSTLY FINE.
WHAT DO YOU THINK OF THESE SKETCHES – FACTORY, NOISE, SMOKE?
QUITE ATMOSPHERIC... I'D LIKE TO SET THE IRON BOWL-CLAY BOWL CONVERSATION THERE.
MAYBE WE COULD PUT IT RIGHT AFTER YOUR MARRIAGE.
WE HAVE TO SETTLE THE "6/4" QUESTION* THIS TIME. WE'VE BEEN BANGING OUR HEADS AGAINST IT FOR SIX MONTHS!
CURFEW, ARRESTS, DISAPPEARANCES, DEATHS – WE'LL HAVE TO TRY HARDER THAN USUAL TO STICK TO THE OBJECTIVE VIEWPOINT OF A SIMPLE WITNESS.

* "6/4" (6TH MONTH, 4TH DAY) REFERS TO 4 JUNE 1989, WHEN THE POWERS THAT BE PUT AN END TO STUDENT DEMONSTRATIONS, MOST NOTABLY THE OCCUPATION OF TIANANMEN SQUARE. THE EXPRESSION EXTENDS TO ENCOMPASS THE ENTIRE PERIOD OF UNREST FROM SPRING '89.

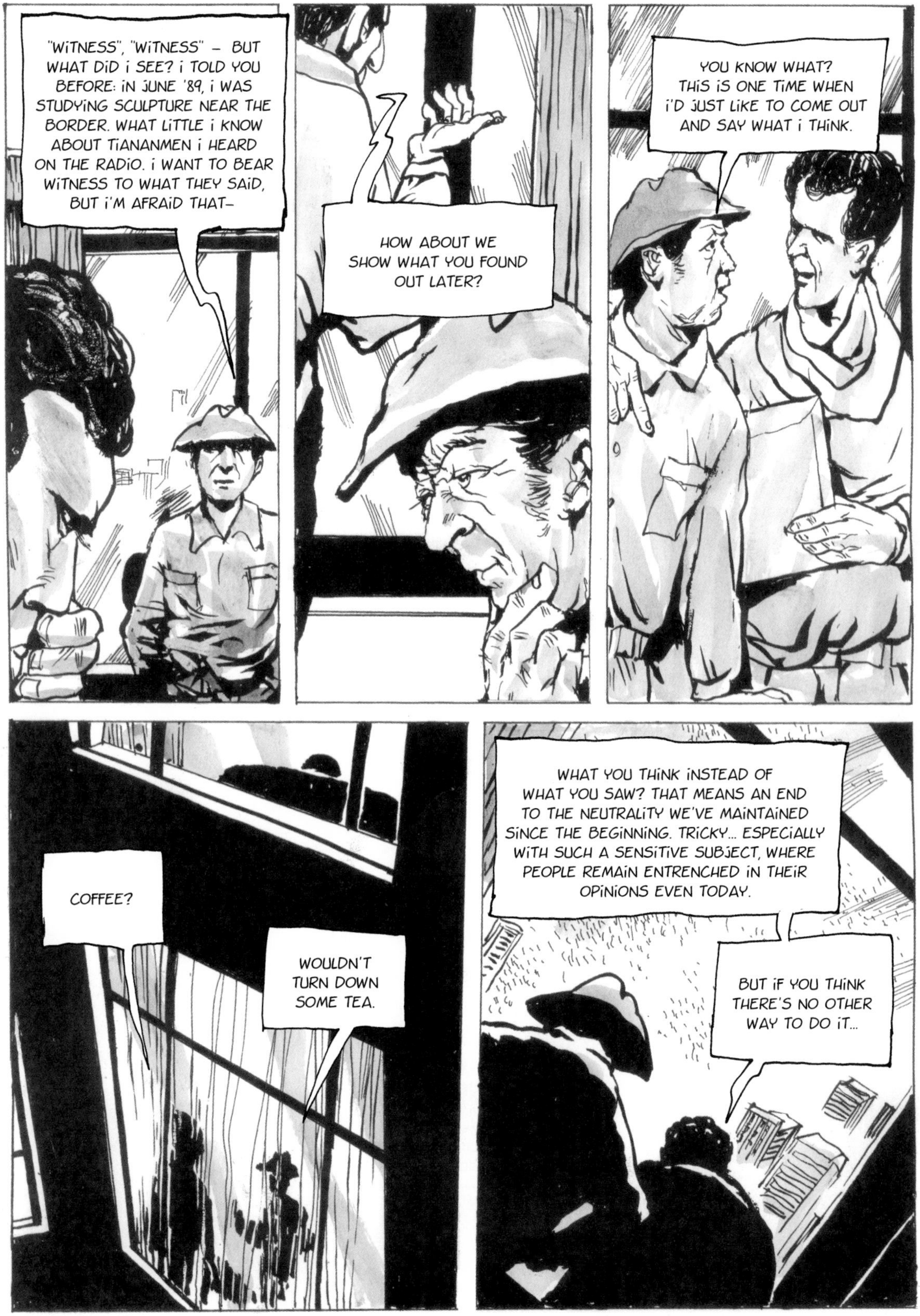
"WITNESS", "WITNESS" – BUT WHAT DID I SEE? I TOLD YOU BEFORE: IN JUNE '89, I WAS STUDYING SCULPTURE NEAR THE BORDER. WHAT LITTLE I KNOW ABOUT TIANANMEN I HEARD ON THE RADIO. I WANT TO BEAR WITNESS TO WHAT THEY SAID, BUT I'M AFRAID THAT–
HOW ABOUT WE SHOW WHAT YOU FOUND OUT LATER?
YOU KNOW WHAT? THIS IS ONE TIME WHEN I'D JUST LIKE TO COME OUT AND SAY WHAT I THINK.
COFFEE?
WOULDN'T TURN DOWN SOME TEA.
WHAT YOU THINK INSTEAD OF WHAT YOU SAW? THAT MEANS AN END TO THE NEUTRALITY WE'VE MAINTAINED SINCE THE BEGINNING. TRICKY… ESPECIALLY WITH SUCH A SENSITIVE SUBJECT, WHERE PEOPLE REMAIN ENTRENCHED IN THEIR OPINIONS EVEN TODAY.
BUT IF YOU THINK THERE'S NO OTHER WAY TO DO IT…

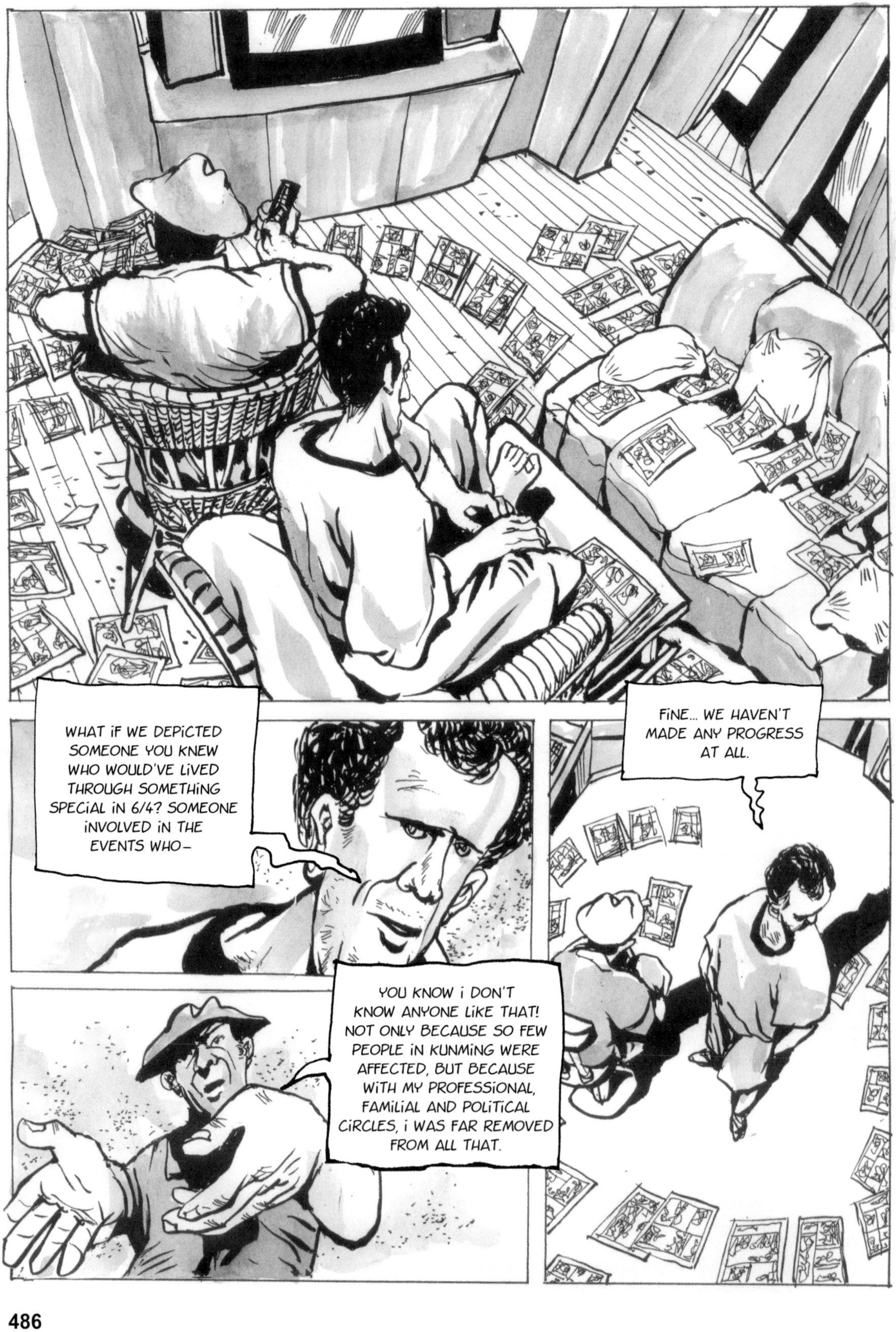
WHAT iF WE DEPiCTED SOMEONE YOU KNEW WHO WOULD'VE LiVED THROUGH SOMETHiNG SPECiAL iN 6/4? SOMEONE iNVOLVED iN THE EVENTS WHO–
FiNE... WE HAVEN'T MADE ANY PROGRESS AT ALL.
YOU KNOW i DON'T KNOW ANYONE LiKE THAT! NOT ONLY BECAUSE SO FEW PEOPLE iN KUNMiNG WERE AFFECTED, BUT BECAUSE WiTH MY PROFESSiONAL, FAMiLiAL AND POLiTiCAL CiRCLES, i WAS FAR REMOVED FROM ALL THAT.

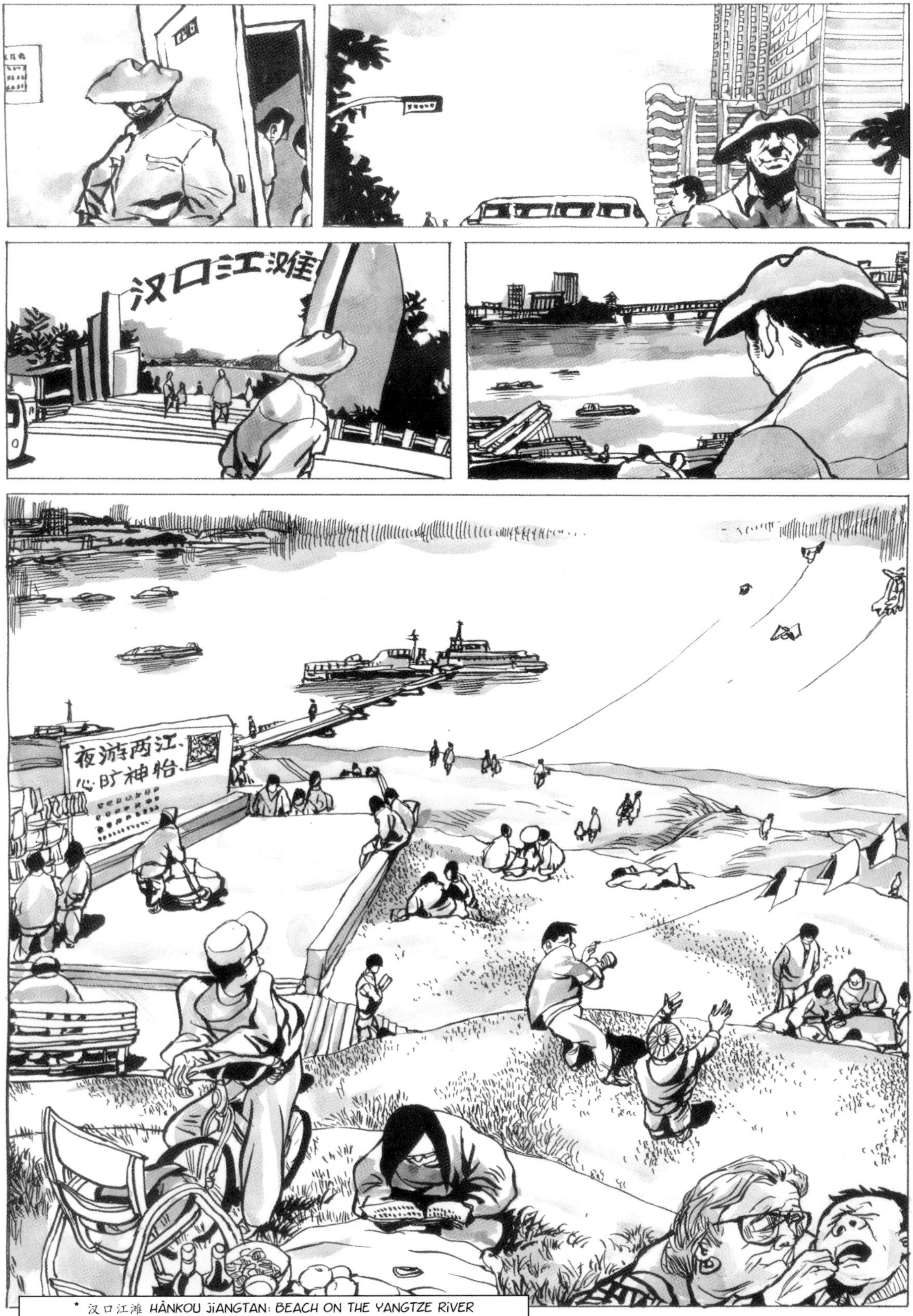
汉口江滩
夜游西江、心旷神怡。

* 汉口江滩 HÀNKOU JIANGTAN: BEACH ON THE YANGTZE RIVER IN HANKOU (WUHAN DISTRICT).

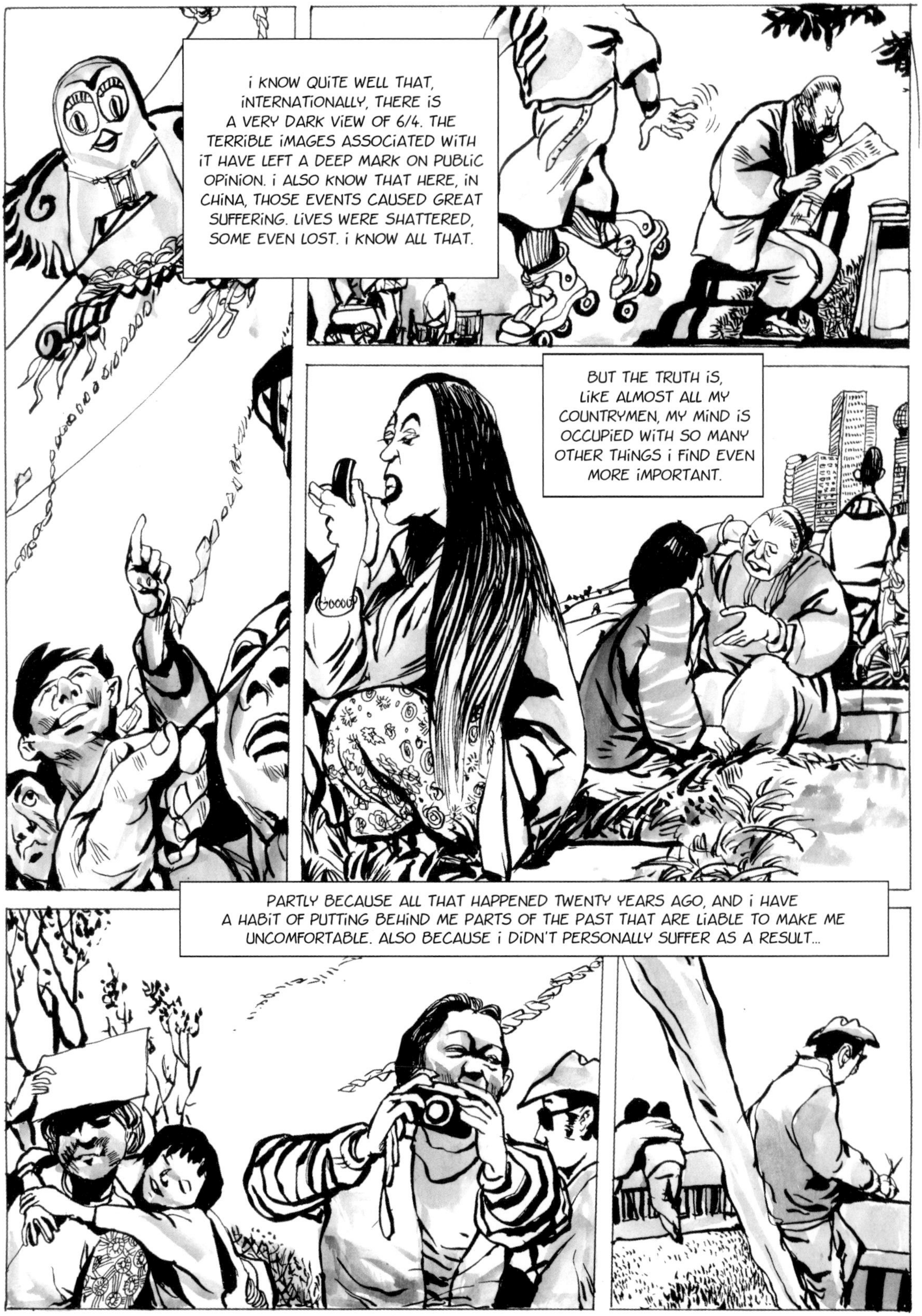
i KNOW QUiTE WELL THAT, iNTERNATiONALLY, THERE iS A VERY DARK ViEW OF 6/4. THE TERRiBLE iMAGES ASSOCiATED WiTH iT HAVE LEFT A DEEP MARK ON PUBLiC OPiNiON. i ALSO KNOW THAT HERE, iN CHiNA, THOSE EVENTS CAUSED GREAT SUFFERiNG. LiVES WERE SHATTERED, SOME EVEN LOST. i KNOW ALL THAT.
BUT THE TRUTH iS, LiKE ALMOST ALL MY COUNTRYMEN, MY MiND iS OCCUPiED WiTH SO MANY OTHER THiNGS i FiND EVEN MORE iMPORTANT.
PARTLY BECAUSE ALL THAT HAPPENED TWENTY YEARS AGO, AND i HAVE A HABiT OF PUTTiNG BEHiND ME PARTS OF THE PAST THAT ARE LiABLE TO MAKE ME UNCOMFORTABLE. ALSO BECAUSE i DiDN'T PERSONALLY SUFFER AS A RESULT...

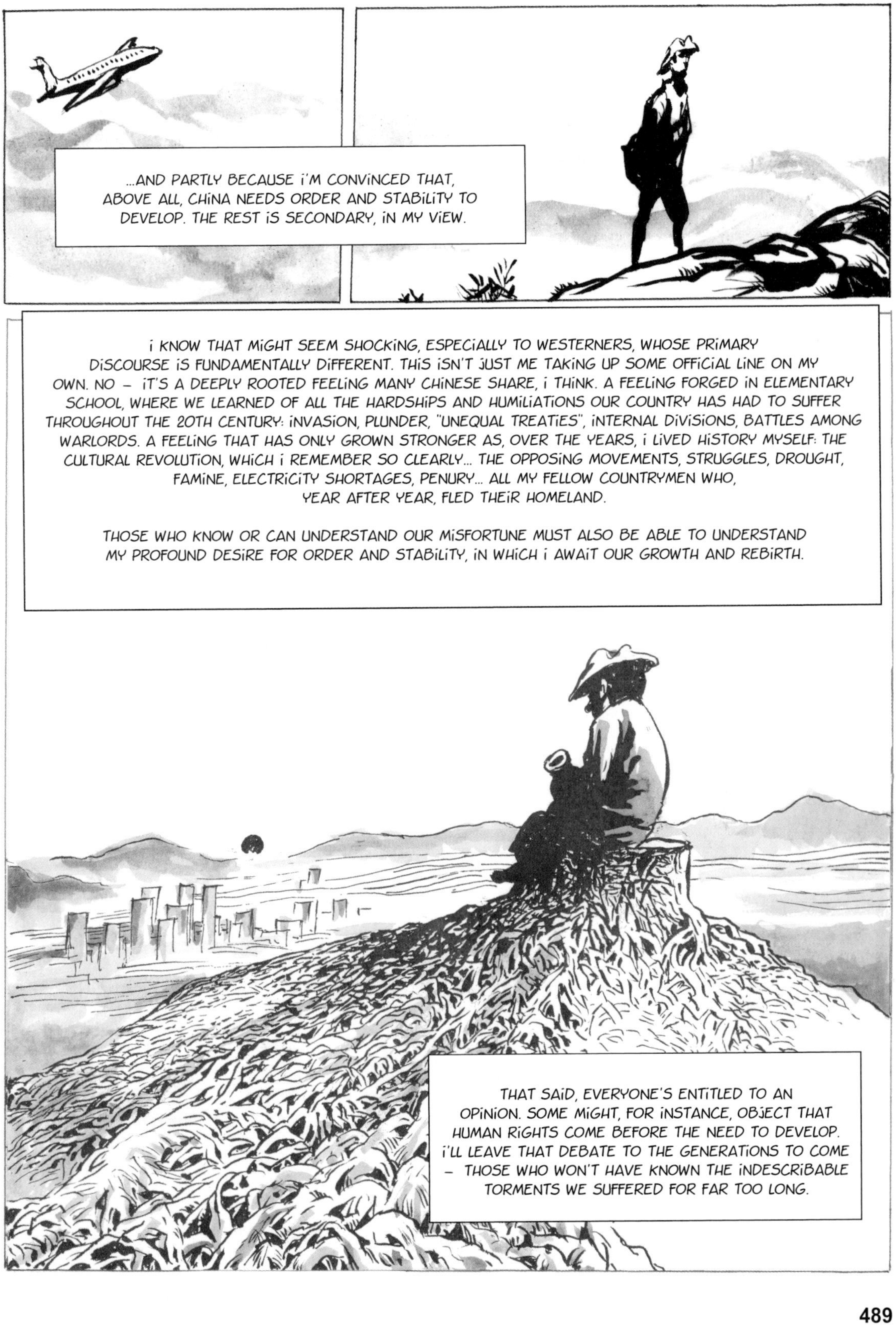
...AND PARTLY BECAUSE I'M CONVINCED THAT, ABOVE ALL, CHINA NEEDS ORDER AND STABILITY TO DEVELOP. THE REST IS SECONDARY, IN MY VIEW.
I KNOW THAT MIGHT SEEM SHOCKING, ESPECIALLY TO WESTERNERS, WHOSE PRIMARY DISCOURSE IS FUNDAMENTALLY DIFFERENT. THIS ISN'T JUST ME TAKING UP SOME OFFICIAL LINE ON MY OWN. NO – IT'S A DEEPLY ROOTED FEELING MANY CHINESE SHARE, I THINK. A FEELING FORGED IN ELEMENTARY SCHOOL, WHERE WE LEARNED OF ALL THE HARDSHIPS AND HUMILIATIONS OUR COUNTRY HAS HAD TO SUFFER THROUGHOUT THE 20TH CENTURY: INVASION, PLUNDER, "UNEQUAL TREATIES", INTERNAL DIVISIONS, BATTLES AMONG WARLORDS. A FEELING THAT HAS ONLY GROWN STRONGER AS, OVER THE YEARS, I LIVED HISTORY MYSELF: THE CULTURAL REVOLUTION, WHICH I REMEMBER SO CLEARLY... THE OPPOSING MOVEMENTS, STRUGGLES, DROUGHT, FAMINE, ELECTRICITY SHORTAGES, PENURY... ALL MY FELLOW COUNTRYMEN WHO, YEAR AFTER YEAR, FLED THEIR HOMELAND.
THOSE WHO KNOW OR CAN UNDERSTAND OUR MISFORTUNE MUST ALSO BE ABLE TO UNDERSTAND MY PROFOUND DESIRE FOR ORDER AND STABILITY, IN WHICH I AWAIT OUR GROWTH AND REBIRTH.
THAT SAID, EVERYONE'S ENTITLED TO AN OPINION. SOME MIGHT, FOR INSTANCE, OBJECT THAT HUMAN RIGHTS COME BEFORE THE NEED TO DEVELOP. I'LL LEAVE THAT DEBATE TO THE GENERATIONS TO COME – THOSE WHO WON'T HAVE KNOWN THE INDESCRIBABLE TORMENTS WE SUFFERED FOR FAR TOO LONG.

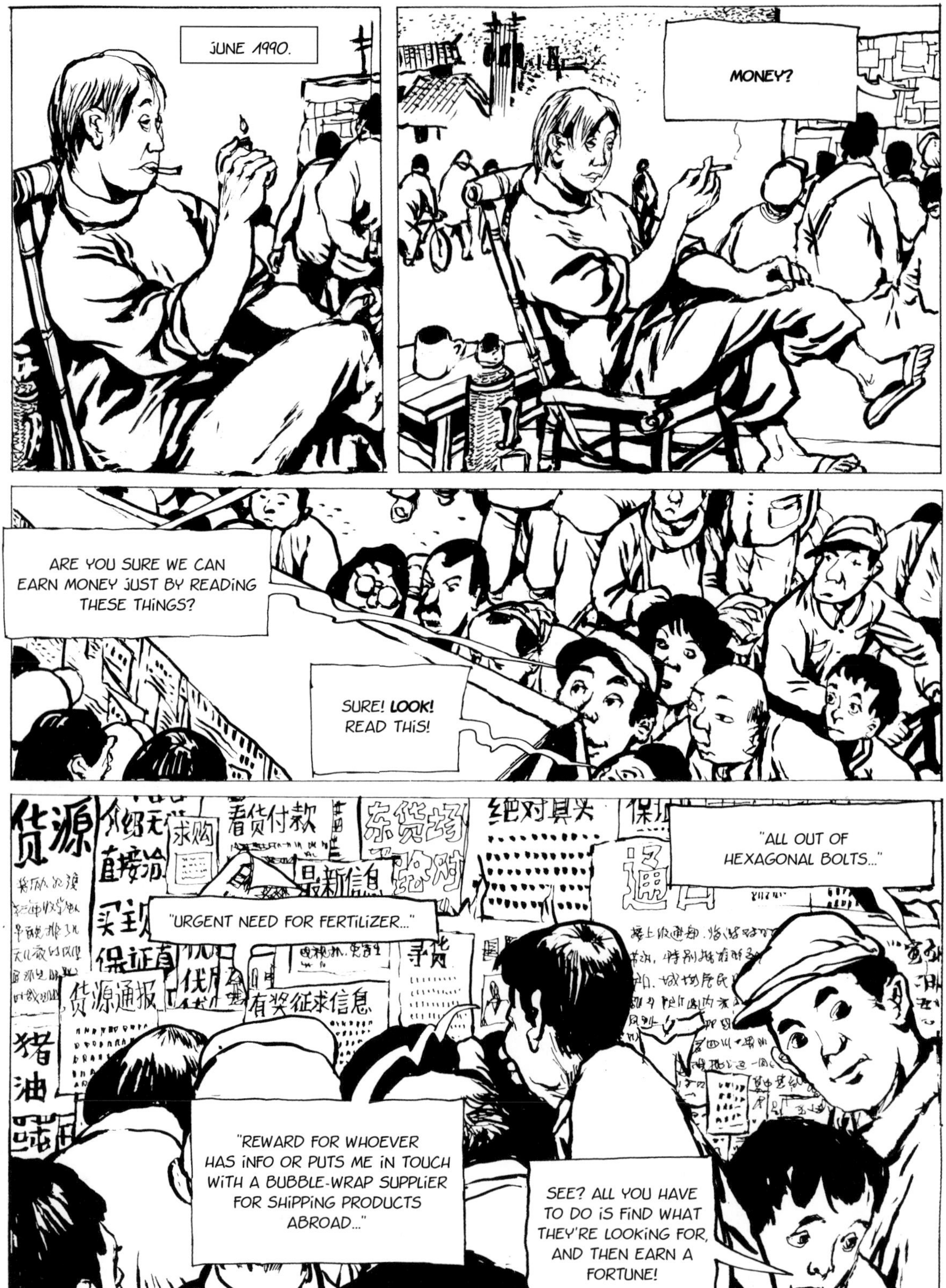
JUNE 1990.
MONEY?
ARE YOU SURE WE CAN EARN MONEY JUST BY READING THESE THINGS?
SURE! **LOOK!** READ THIS!
货源
看货付款
求购
最新信息
货源通报
有奖征求信息
"ALL OUT OF HEXAGONAL BOLTS..."
"URGENT NEED FOR FERTILIZER..."
"REWARD FOR WHOEVER HAS INFO OR PUTS ME IN TOUCH WITH A BUBBLE-WRAP SUPPLIER FOR SHIPPING PRODUCTS ABROAD..."
SEE? ALL YOU HAVE TO DO IS FIND WHAT THEY'RE LOOKING FOR, AND THEN EARN A FORTUNE!

货源 HÙO YUAN: "DIRECT FROM THE SOURCE". 直接洽谈 ZHIJIE QIA TAN: "NO MIDDLEMAN".
保证真 BAOZHÈNG ZHĒN: "CERTIFICATE OF GUARANTEE". 买主见面 MAIZHU JIANMIAN: "MEET THE BUYER".
看货付款 KÀNHÙO FÙKUAN: "PAYMENT UPON INSPECTION OF MERCHANDISE". 绝对真实 JUEDÙI ZHĒNSHI: "ABSOLUTELY TRUE".

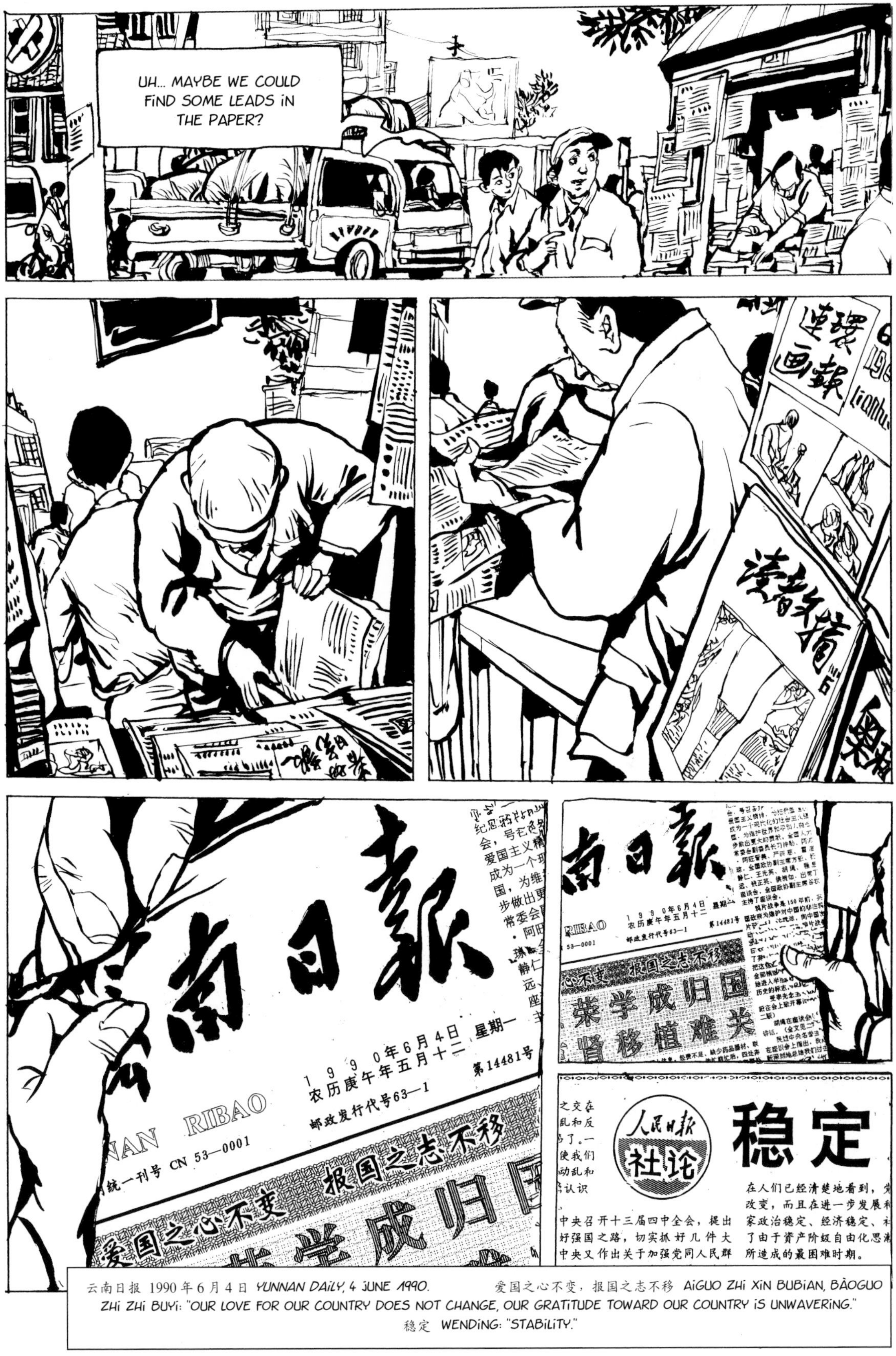
UH… MAYBE WE COULD FIND SOME LEADS IN THE PAPER?
1990年6月4日 星期一
爱国之心不变 报国之志不移
稳定

云南日报 1990年6月4日 *YUNNAN DAILY, 4 JUNE 1990.* 爱国之心不变，报国之志不移 AIGUO ZHI XIN BUBIAN, BÀOGUO ZHI ZHI BUYI: "OUR LOVE FOR OUR COUNTRY DOES NOT CHANGE, OUR GRATITUDE TOWARD OUR COUNTRY IS UNWAVERING."
稳定 WENDING: "STABILITY."

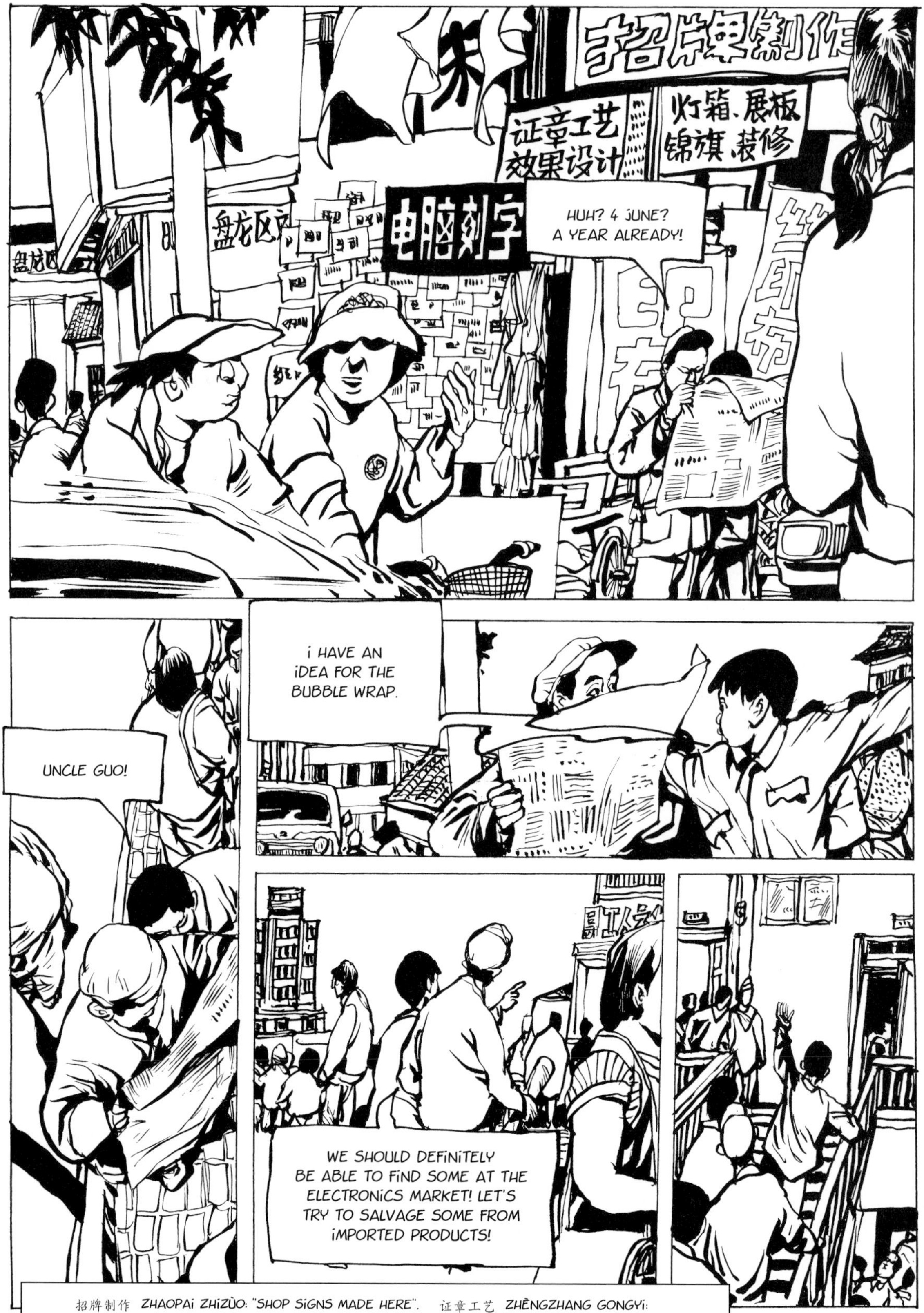
招牌制作
证章工艺
效果设计
灯箱、展板
锦旗、装修
电脑刻字
HUH? 4 JUNE? A YEAR ALREADY!
I HAVE AN IDEA FOR THE BUBBLE WRAP.
UNCLE GUO!
WE SHOULD DEFINITELY BE ABLE TO FIND SOME AT THE ELECTRONICS MARKET! LET'S TRY TO SALVAGE SOME FROM IMPORTED PRODUCTS!

招牌制作 ZHAOPAI ZHIZÙO: "SHOP SIGNS MADE HERE". 证章工艺 ZHĔNGZHANG GONGYI: "CHOPS CARVED HERE". 灯箱 DENGXIANG: "NEON SIGNS."

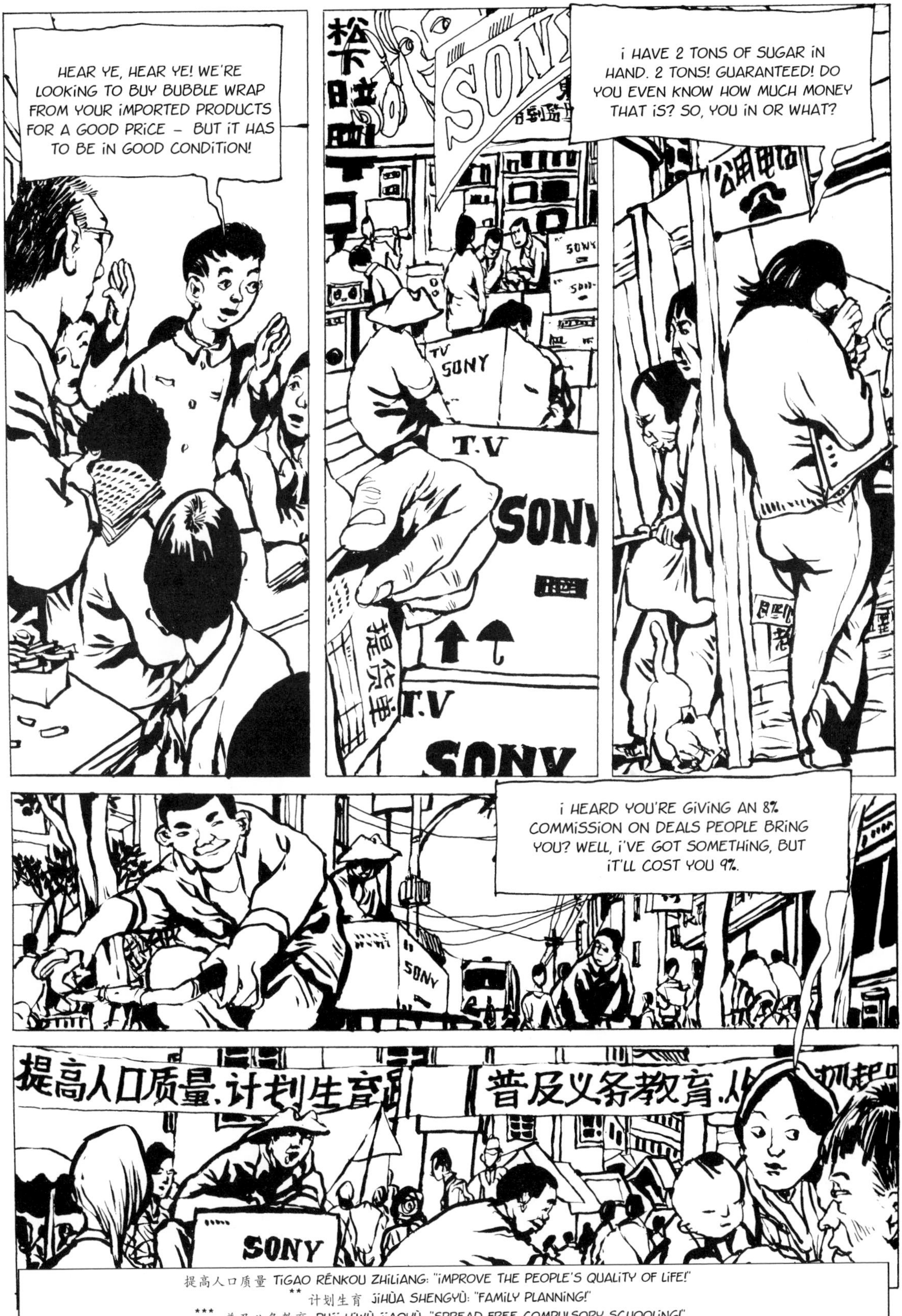
HEAR YE, HEAR YE! WE'RE LOOKING TO BUY BUBBLE WRAP FROM YOUR IMPORTED PRODUCTS FOR A GOOD PRICE – BUT IT HAS TO BE IN GOOD CONDITION!
SONY
TV SONY
T.V SONY
提货单
T.V SONY
I HAVE 2 TONS OF SUGAR IN HAND. 2 TONS! GUARANTEED! DO YOU EVEN KNOW HOW MUCH MONEY THAT IS? SO, YOU IN OR WHAT?
公用电话
I HEARD YOU'RE GIVING AN 8% COMMISSION ON DEALS PEOPLE BRING YOU? WELL, I'VE GOT SOMETHING, BUT IT'LL COST YOU 9%.
SONY
提高人口质量,计划生育
普及义务教育,
SONY
提高人口质量 TIGAO RÉNKOU ZHILIANG: "IMPROVE THE PEOPLE'S QUALITY OF LIFE!"
** 计划生育 JIHÙA SHENGYÙ: "FAMILY PLANNING!"
*** 普及义务教育 PUJI YIWÙ JIAOYÙ: "SPREAD FREE COMPULSORY SCHOOLING!"

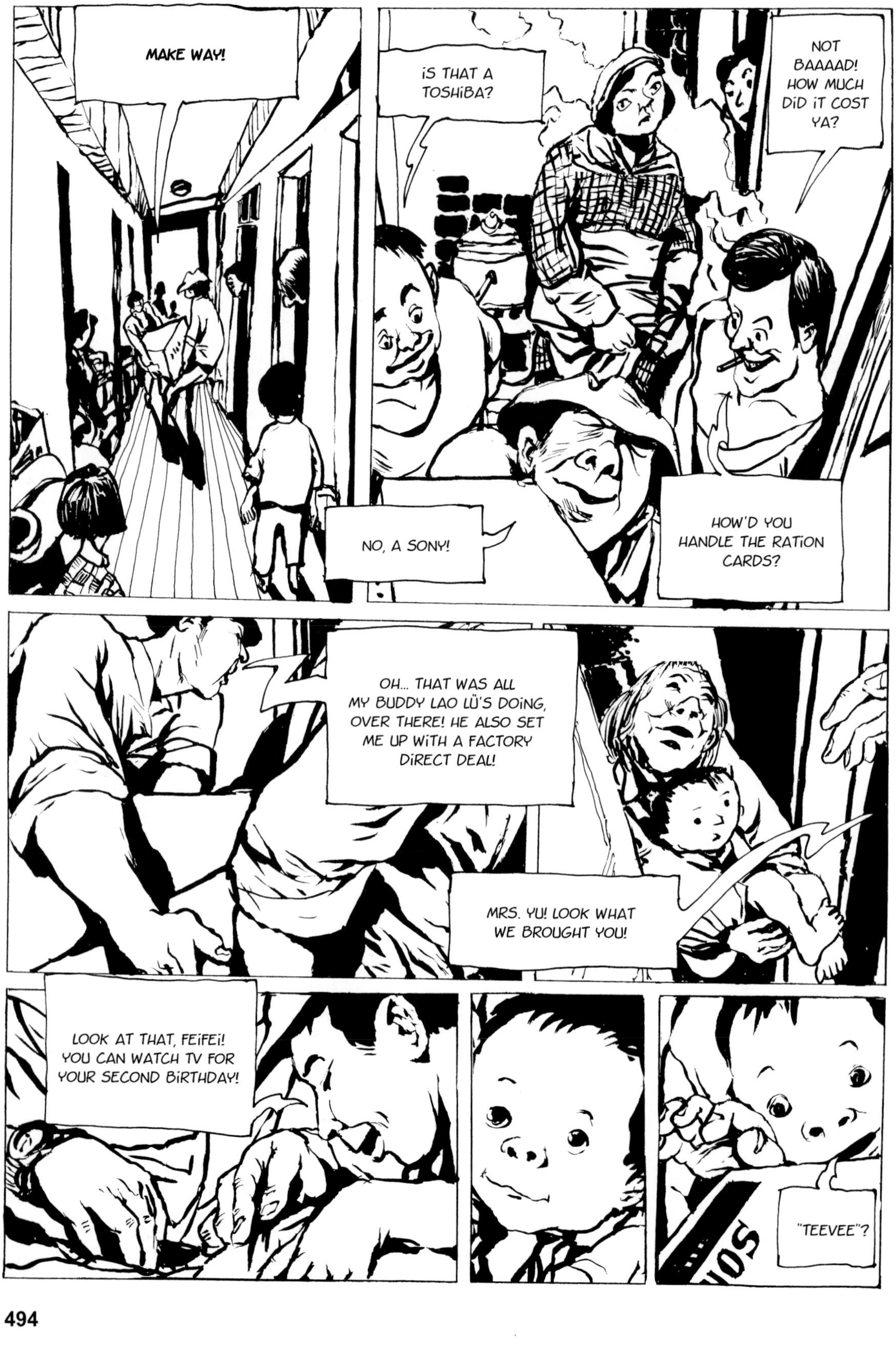
MAKE WAY!
iS THAT A TOSHiBA?
NOT BAAAAD! HOW MUCH DiD iT COST YA?
NO, A SONY!
HOW'D YOU HANDLE THE RATiON CARDS?
OH... THAT WAS ALL MY BUDDY LAO LÜ'S DOiNG, OVER THERE! HE ALSO SET ME UP WiTH A FACTORY DiRECT DEAL!
MRS. YU! LOOK WHAT WE BROUGHT YOU!
LOOK AT THAT, FEiFEi! YOU CAN WATCH TV FOR YOUR SECOND BiRTHDAY!
"TEEVEE"?

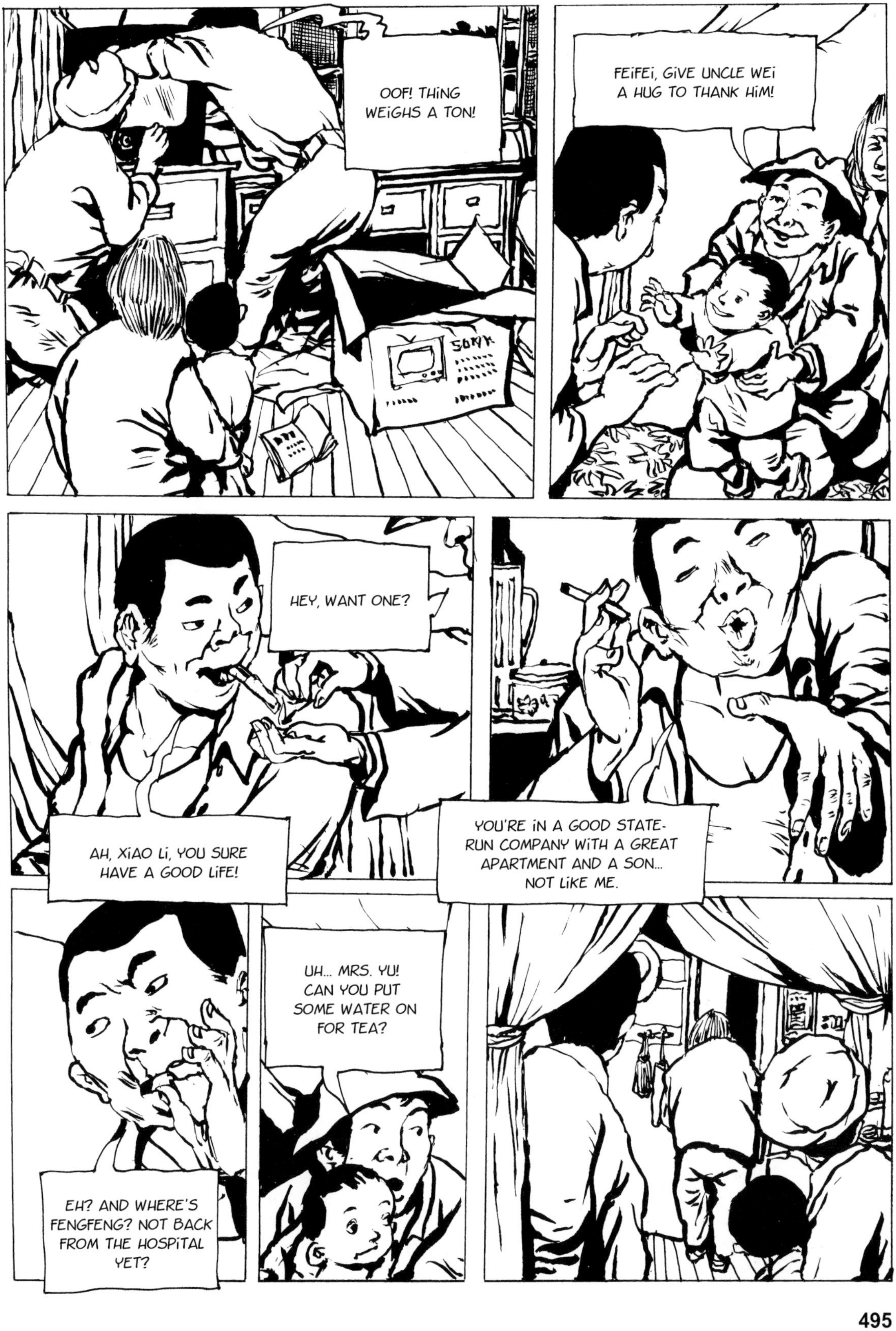
OOF! THING WEIGHS A TON!
SONY
FEIFEI, GIVE UNCLE WEI A HUG TO THANK HIM!
HEY, WANT ONE?
AH, XIAO LI, YOU SURE HAVE A GOOD LIFE!
YOU'RE IN A GOOD STATE-RUN COMPANY WITH A GREAT APARTMENT AND A SON... NOT LIKE ME.
EH? AND WHERE'S FENGFENG? NOT BACK FROM THE HOSPITAL YET?
UH... MRS. YU! CAN YOU PUT SOME WATER ON FOR TEA?

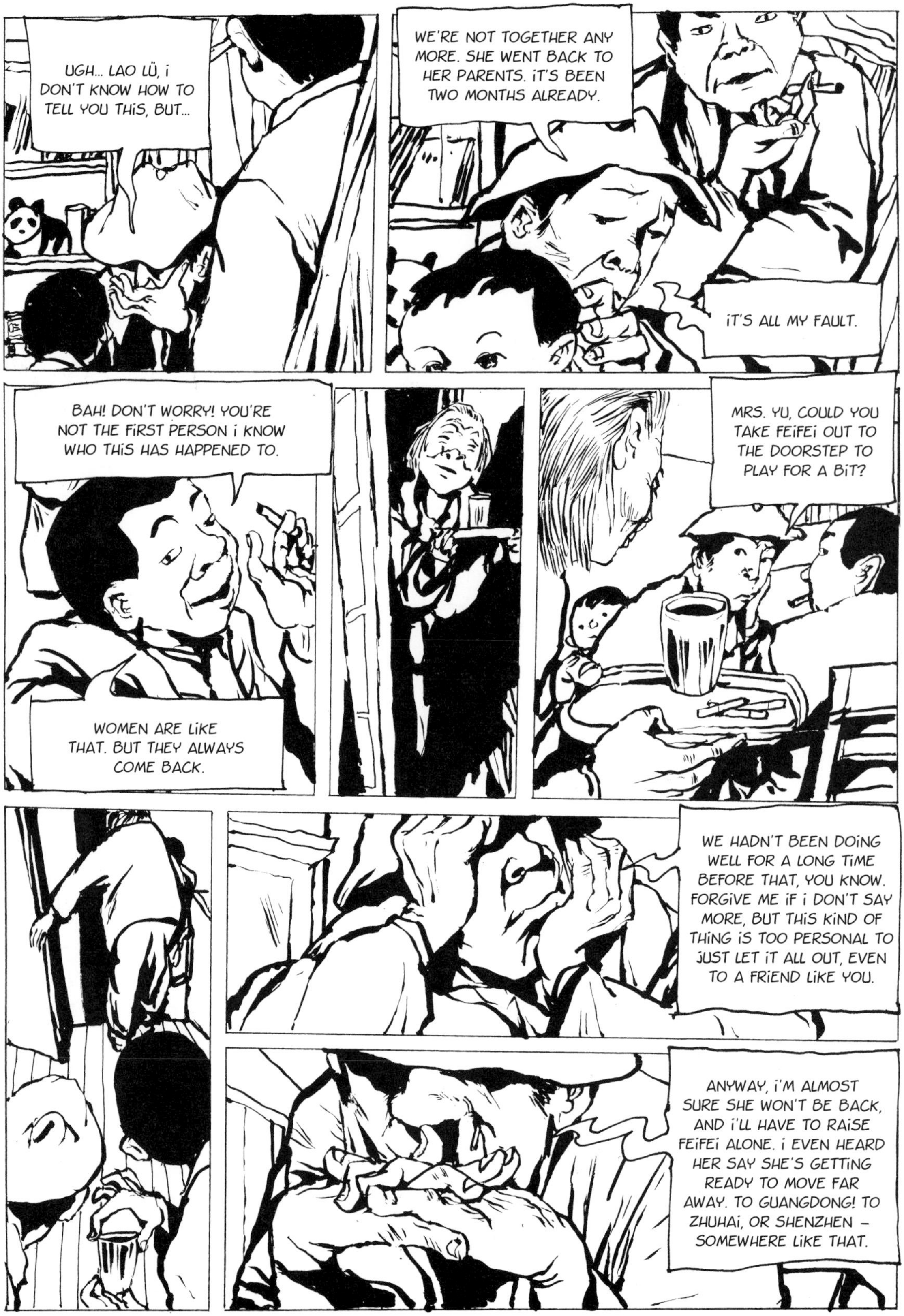
UGH... LAO LÜ, i DON'T KNOW HOW TO TELL YOU THiS, BUT...
WE'RE NOT TOGETHER ANY MORE. SHE WENT BACK TO HER PARENTS. iT'S BEEN TWO MONTHS ALREADY.
iT'S ALL MY FAULT.
BAH! DON'T WORRY! YOU'RE NOT THE FiRST PERSON i KNOW WHO THiS HAS HAPPENED TO.
WOMEN ARE LiKE THAT. BUT THEY ALWAYS COME BACK.
MRS. YU, COULD YOU TAKE FEiFEi OUT TO THE DOORSTEP TO PLAY FOR A BiT?
WE HADN'T BEEN DOiNG WELL FOR A LONG TiME BEFORE THAT, YOU KNOW. FORGiVE ME iF i DON'T SAY MORE, BUT THiS KiND OF THiNG iS TOO PERSONAL TO JUST LET iT ALL OUT, EVEN TO A FRiEND LiKE YOU.
ANYWAY, i'M ALMOST SURE SHE WON'T BE BACK, AND i'LL HAVE TO RAiSE FEiFEi ALONE. i EVEN HEARD HER SAY SHE'S GETTiNG READY TO MOVE FAR AWAY. TO GUANGDONG! TO ZHUHAi, OR SHENZHEN – SOMEWHERE LiKE THAT.

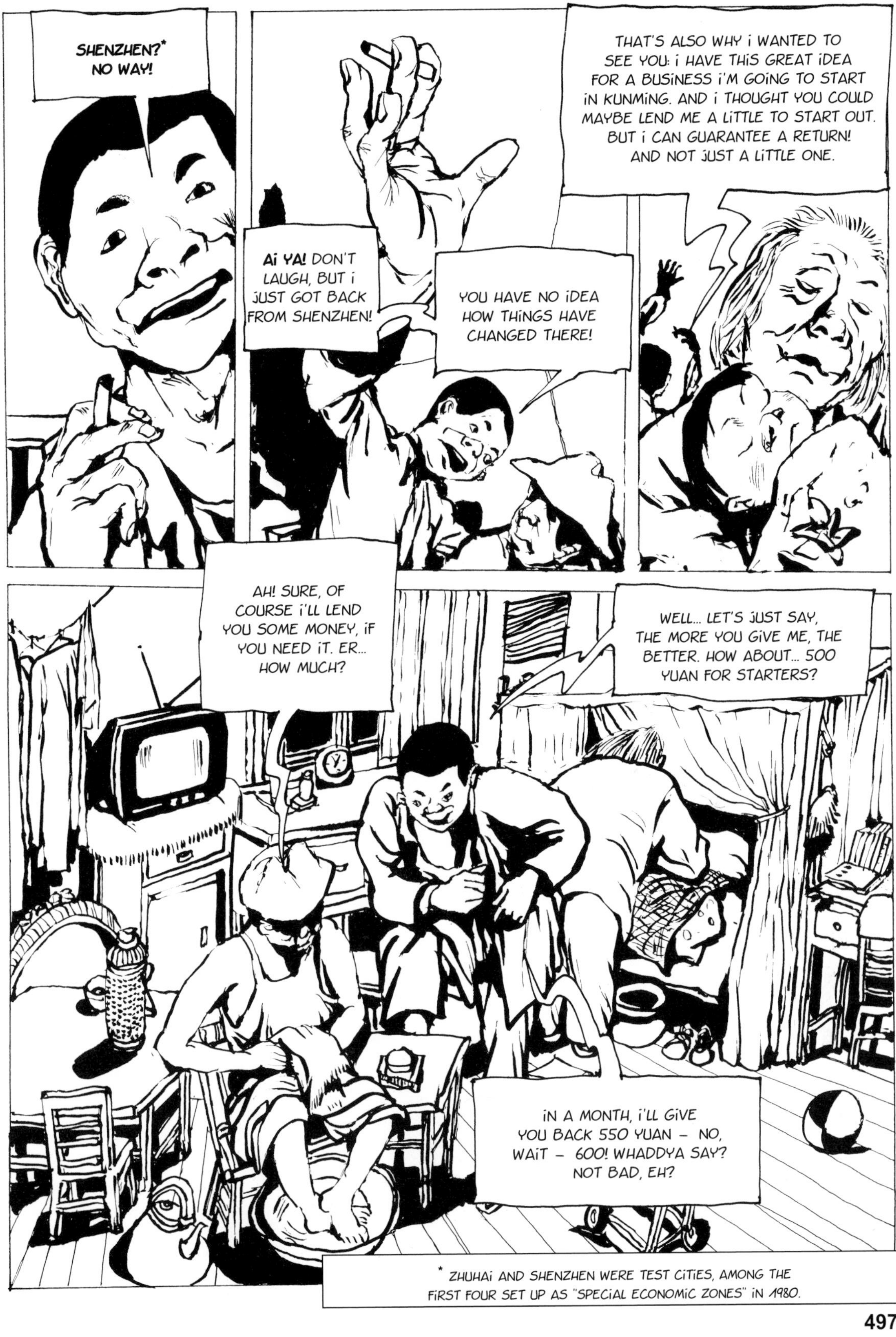
SHENZHEN?* NO WAY!
Ai YA! DON'T LAUGH, BUT i JUST GOT BACK FROM SHENZHEN!
YOU HAVE NO iDEA HOW THiNGS HAVE CHANGED THERE!
THAT'S ALSO WHY i WANTED TO SEE YOU: i HAVE THiS GREAT iDEA FOR A BUSiNESS i'M GOiNG TO START iN KUNMiNG. AND i THOUGHT YOU COULD MAYBE LEND ME A LiTTLE TO START OUT. BUT i CAN GUARANTEE A RETURN! AND NOT JUST A LiTTLE ONE.
AH! SURE, OF COURSE i'LL LEND YOU SOME MONEY, iF YOU NEED iT. ER... HOW MUCH?
WELL... LET'S JUST SAY, THE MORE YOU GiVE ME, THE BETTER. HOW ABOUT... 500 YUAN FOR STARTERS?
iN A MONTH, i'LL GiVE YOU BACK 550 YUAN – NO, WAiT – 600! WHADDYA SAY? NOT BAD, EH?

* ZHUHAi AND SHENZHEN WERE TEST CiTiES, AMONG THE FiRST FOUR SET UP AS "SPECiAL ECONOMiC ZONES" iN 1980.

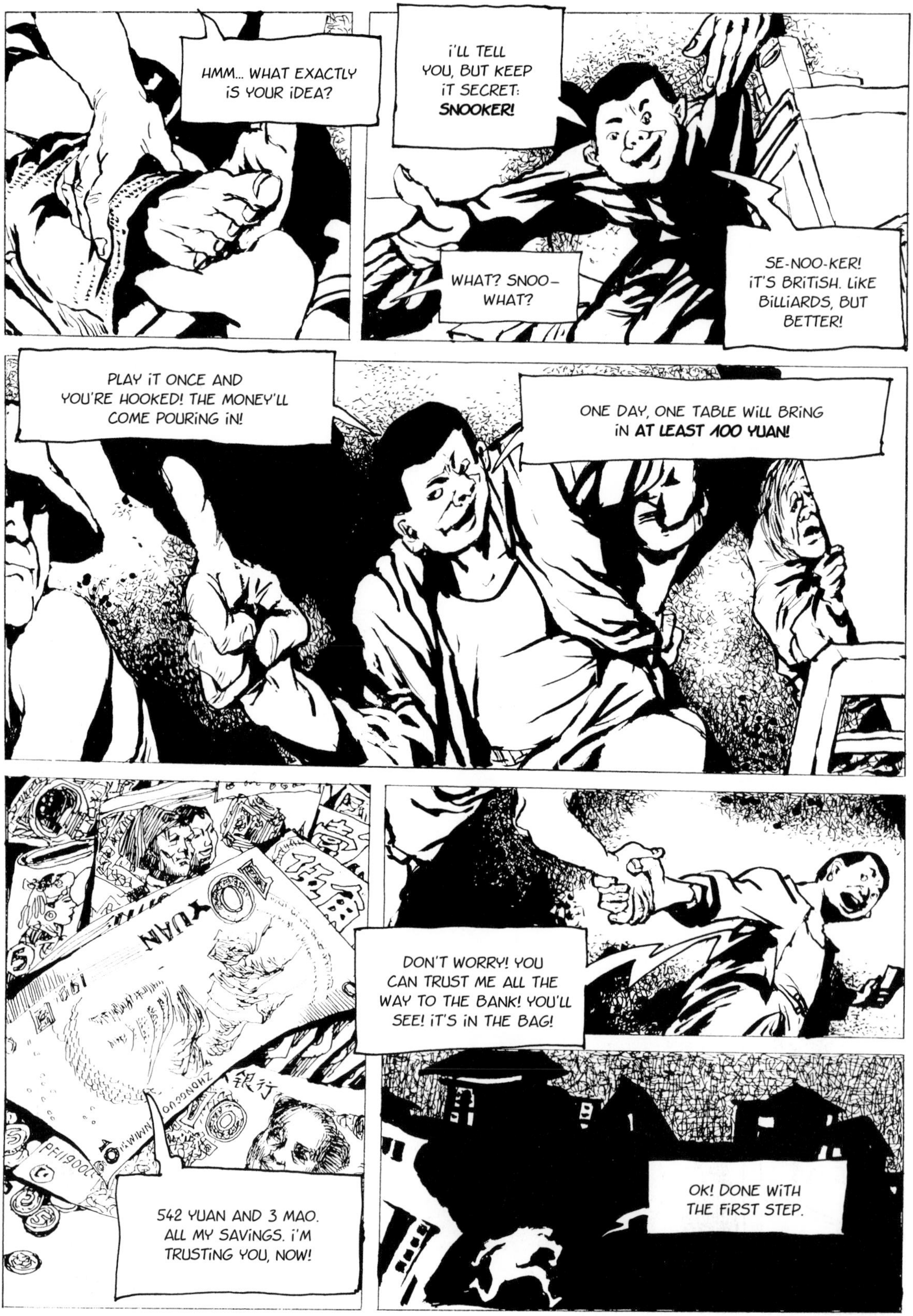
HMM... WHAT EXACTLY iS YOUR iDEA?
i'LL TELL YOU, BUT KEEP iT SECRET: **SNOOKER!**
WHAT? SNOO-WHAT?
SE-NOO-KER! iT'S BRiTiSH. LiKE BiLLiARDS, BUT BETTER!
PLAY iT ONCE AND YOU'RE HOOKED! THE MONEY'LL COME POURiNG iN!
ONE DAY, ONE TABLE WiLL BRiNG iN **AT LEAST 100 YUAN!**
YUAN
542 YUAN AND 3 MAO. ALL MY SAViNGS. i'M TRUSTiNG YOU, NOW!
DON'T WORRY! YOU CAN TRUST ME ALL THE WAY TO THE BANK! YOU'LL SEE! iT'S iN THE BAG!
OK! DONE WiTH THE FiRST STEP.

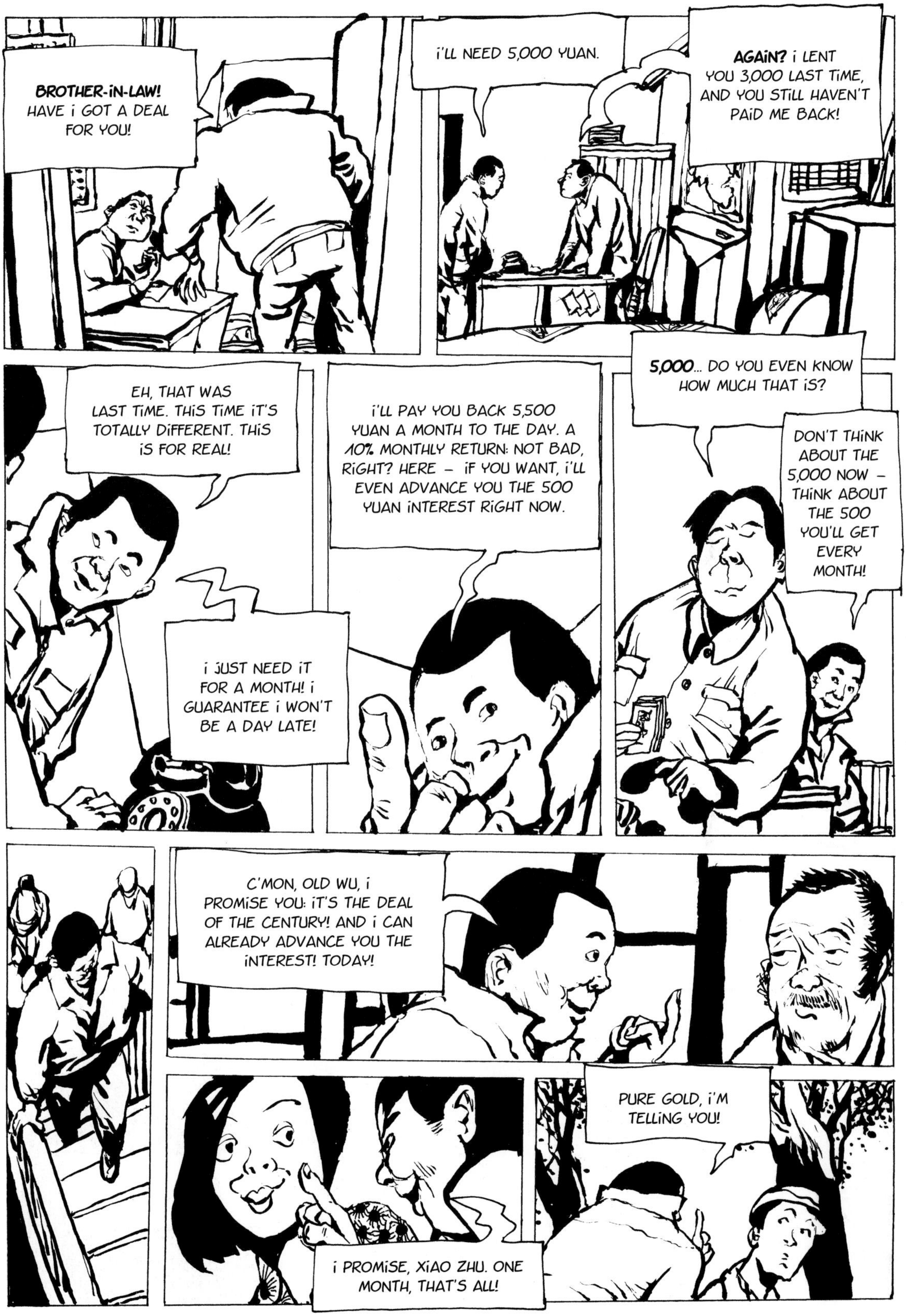
BROTHER-IN-LAW! HAVE I GOT A DEAL FOR YOU!
I'LL NEED 5,000 YUAN.
AGAIN? I LENT YOU 3,000 LAST TIME, AND YOU STILL HAVEN'T PAID ME BACK!
EH, THAT WAS LAST TIME. THIS TIME IT'S TOTALLY DIFFERENT. THIS IS FOR REAL!
I JUST NEED IT FOR A MONTH! I GUARANTEE I WON'T BE A DAY LATE!
I'LL PAY YOU BACK 5,500 YUAN A MONTH TO THE DAY. A 10% MONTHLY RETURN: NOT BAD, RIGHT? HERE – IF YOU WANT, I'LL EVEN ADVANCE YOU THE 500 YUAN INTEREST RIGHT NOW.
5,000... DO YOU EVEN KNOW HOW MUCH THAT IS?
DON'T THINK ABOUT THE 5,000 NOW – THINK ABOUT THE 500 YOU'LL GET EVERY MONTH!
C'MON, OLD WU, I PROMISE YOU: IT'S THE DEAL OF THE CENTURY! AND I CAN ALREADY ADVANCE YOU THE INTEREST! TODAY!
I PROMISE, XIAO ZHU. ONE MONTH, THAT'S ALL!
PURE GOLD, I'M TELLING YOU!

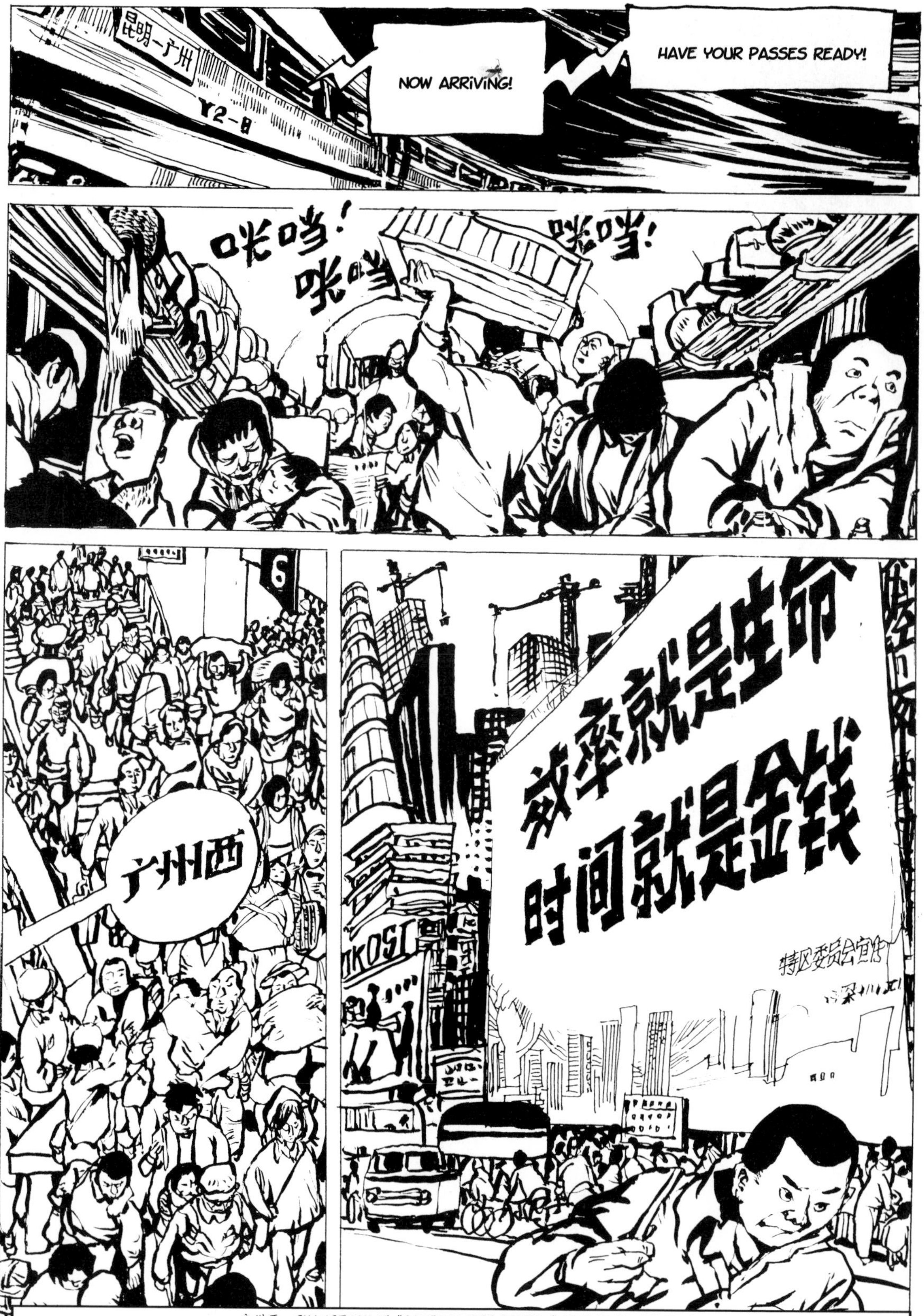

昆明—广州
NOW ARRIVING!
HAVE YOUR PASSES READY!
咣当!
咣当
咣当!
广州西
效率就是生命
时间就是金钱

广州西 GUANGZHOU XI: "CANTON WEST STATION" (SHENZHEN STATION).
效率就是生命 XIAOLÜE JIU SHI SHENGMING: "EFFICIENCY IS LIFE."
时间就是金钱 SHIJIAN JIU SHI JINGQIAN: "TIME IS MONEY."

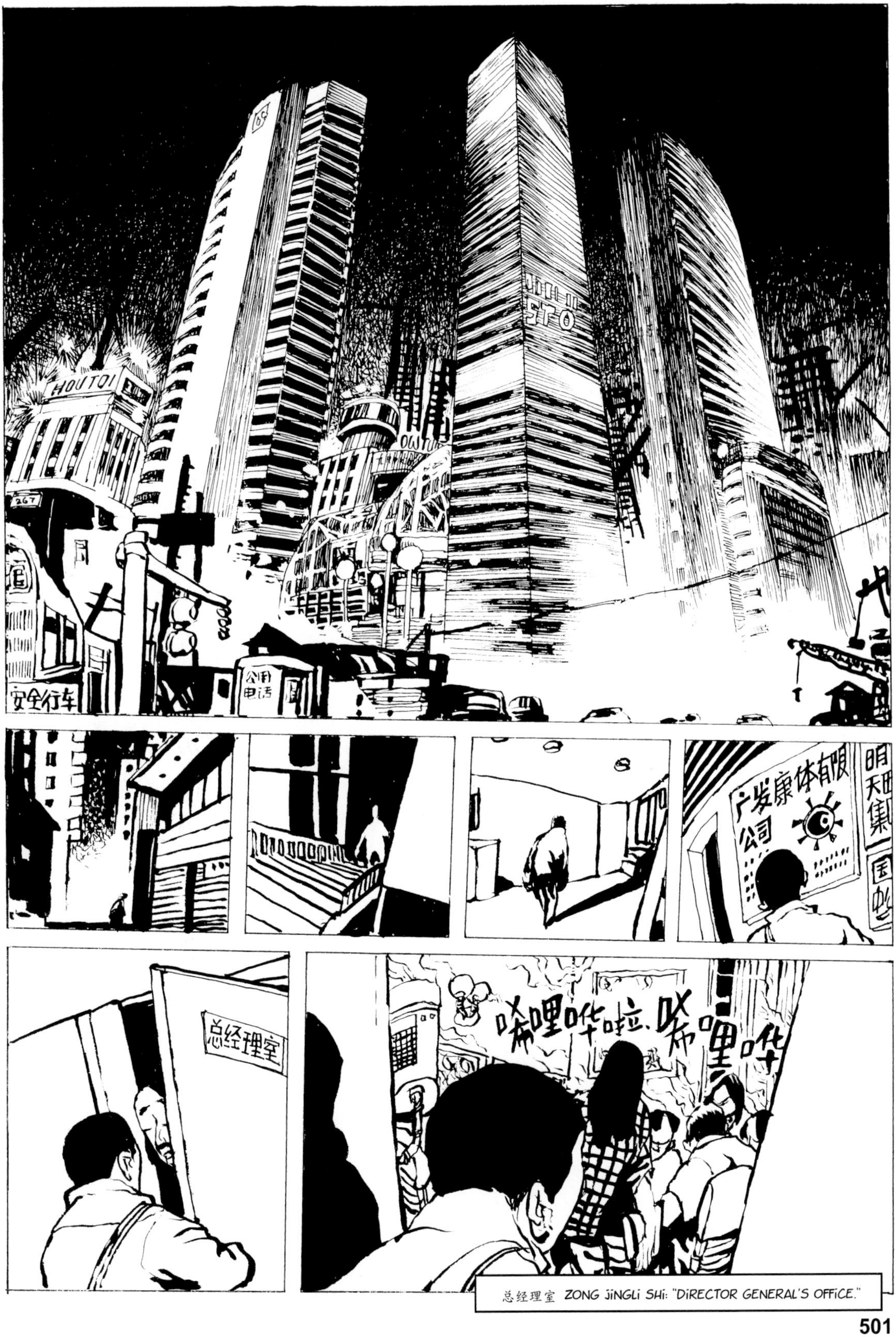
HOUTOI
267
安全行车
公用电话
广发康体有限公司
总经理室
唏哩哗啦、唏哩哗

总经理室 ZONG JINGLI SHI: "DIRECTOR GENERAL'S OFFICE."

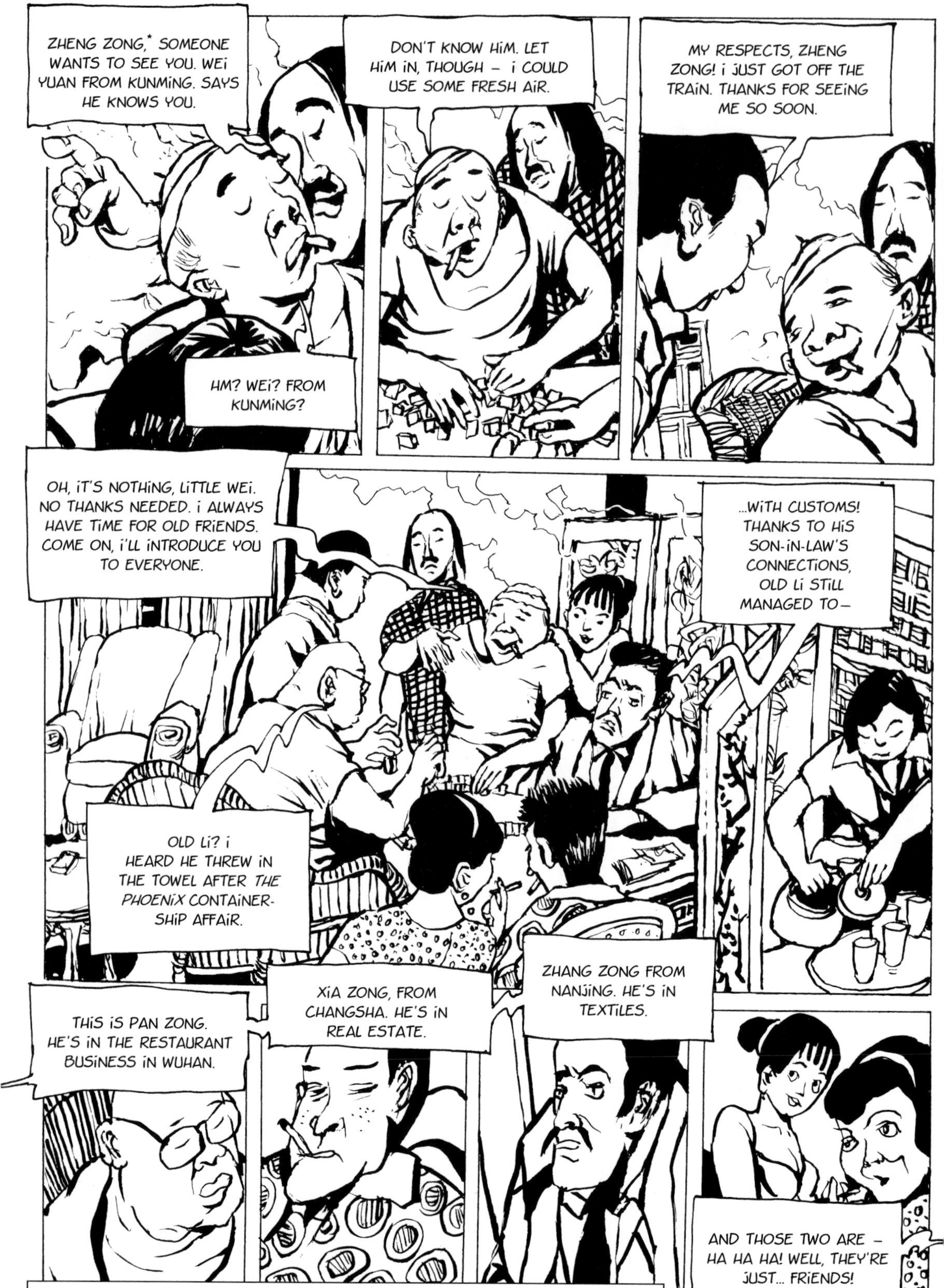
ZHENG ZONG,* SOMEONE WANTS TO SEE YOU. WEI YUAN FROM KUNMING. SAYS HE KNOWS YOU.
HM? WEI? FROM KUNMING?
DON'T KNOW HIM. LET HIM IN, THOUGH – I COULD USE SOME FRESH AIR.
MY RESPECTS, ZHENG ZONG! I JUST GOT OFF THE TRAIN. THANKS FOR SEEING ME SO SOON.
OH, IT'S NOTHING, LITTLE WEI. NO THANKS NEEDED. I ALWAYS HAVE TIME FOR OLD FRIENDS. COME ON, I'LL INTRODUCE YOU TO EVERYONE.
OLD LI? I HEARD HE THREW IN THE TOWEL AFTER *THE PHOENIX* CONTAINER-SHIP AFFAIR.
...WITH CUSTOMS! THANKS TO HIS SON-IN-LAW'S CONNECTIONS, OLD LI STILL MANAGED TO–
THIS IS PAN ZONG. HE'S IN THE RESTAURANT BUSINESS IN WUHAN.
XIA ZONG, FROM CHANGSHA. HE'S IN REAL ESTATE.
ZHANG ZONG FROM NANJING. HE'S IN TEXTILES.
AND THOSE TWO ARE – HA HA HA! WELL, THEY'RE JUST... FRIENDS!

总 ZONG: WHEN PLACED AFTER A SURNAME, THIS WORD MEANS "DIRECTOR GENERAL".

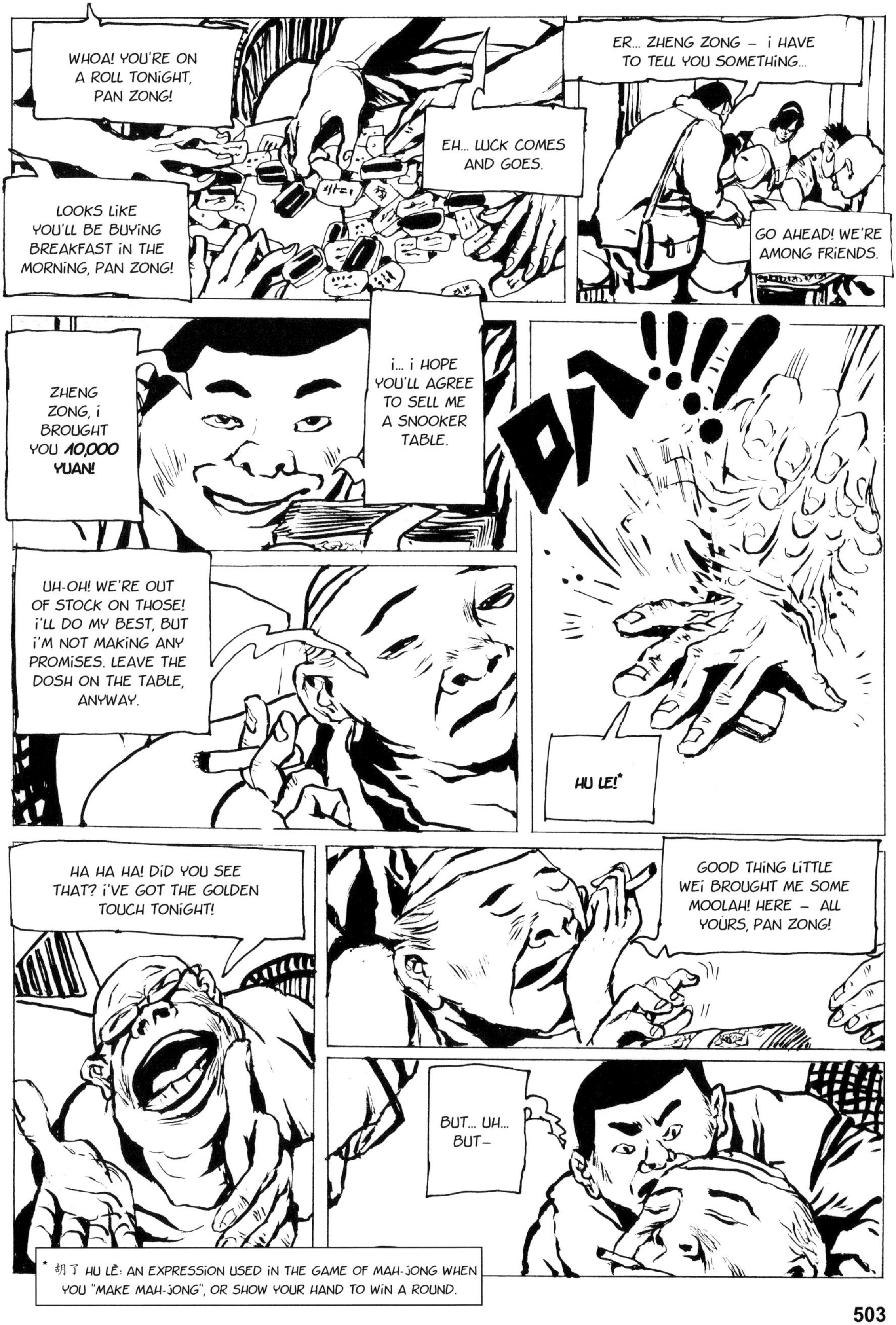
WHOA! YOU'RE ON A ROLL TONIGHT, PAN ZONG!
LOOKS LIKE YOU'LL BE BUYING BREAKFAST IN THE MORNING, PAN ZONG!
EH... LUCK COMES AND GOES.
ER... ZHENG ZONG – I HAVE TO TELL YOU SOMETHING...
GO AHEAD! WE'RE AMONG FRIENDS.
ZHENG ZONG, I BROUGHT YOU 10,000 YUAN!
I... I HOPE YOU'LL AGREE TO SELL ME A SNOOKER TABLE.
UH-OH! WE'RE OUT OF STOCK ON THOSE! I'LL DO MY BEST, BUT I'M NOT MAKING ANY PROMISES. LEAVE THE DOSH ON THE TABLE, ANYWAY.
OI!!!
HU LE!*
HA HA HA! DID YOU SEE THAT? I'VE GOT THE GOLDEN TOUCH TONIGHT!
GOOD THING LITTLE WEI BROUGHT ME SOME MOOLAH! HERE – ALL YOURS, PAN ZONG!
BUT... UH... BUT–

* 胡了 HU LÈ: AN EXPRESSION USED IN THE GAME OF MAH-JONG WHEN YOU "MAKE MAH-JONG", OR SHOW YOUR HAND TO WIN A ROUND.

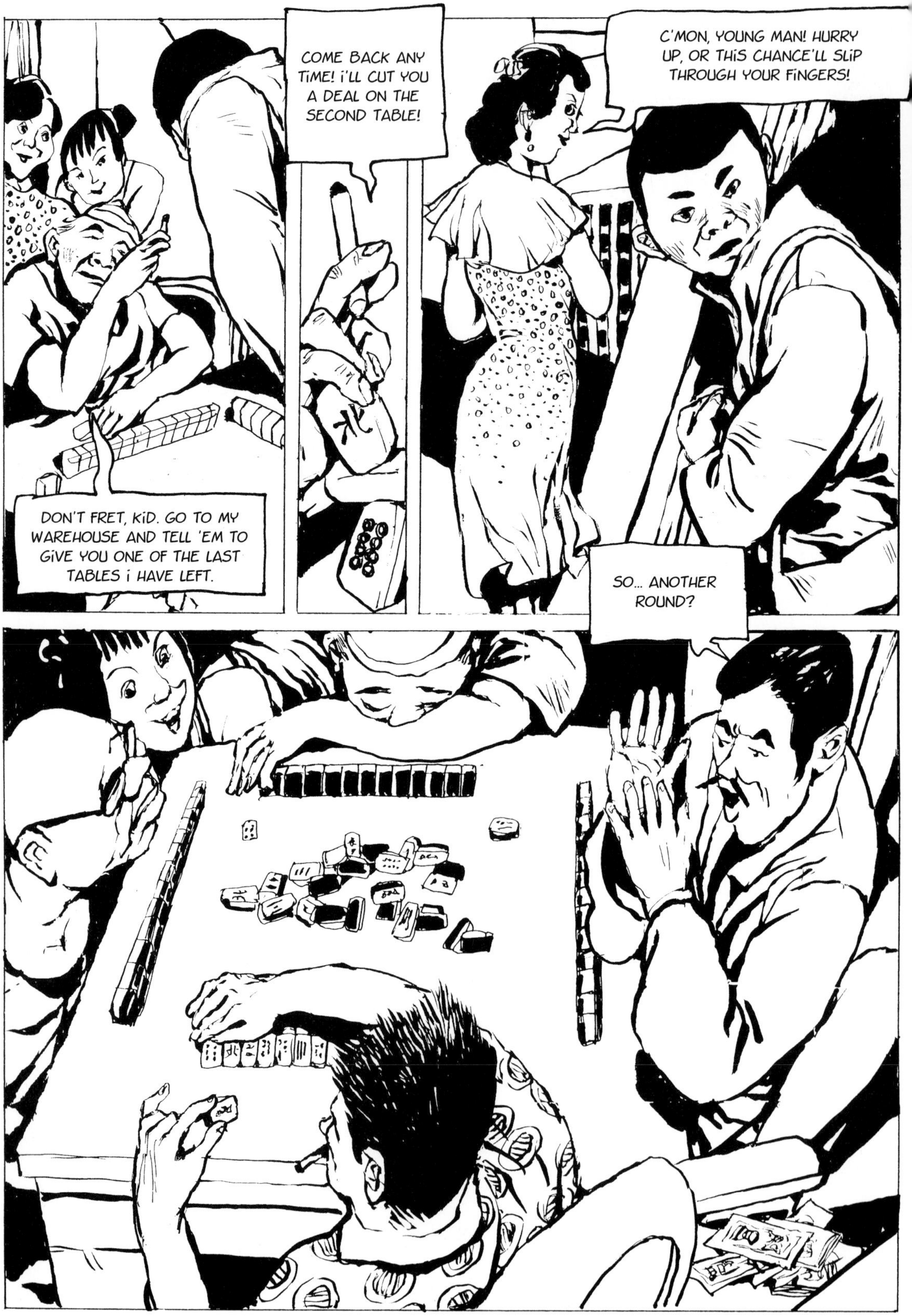
COME BACK ANY TIME! I'LL CUT YOU A DEAL ON THE SECOND TABLE!
DON'T FRET, KID. GO TO MY WAREHOUSE AND TELL 'EM TO GIVE YOU ONE OF THE LAST TABLES I HAVE LEFT.
C'MON, YOUNG MAN! HURRY UP, OR THIS CHANCE'LL SLIP THROUGH YOUR FINGERS!
SO... ANOTHER ROUND?

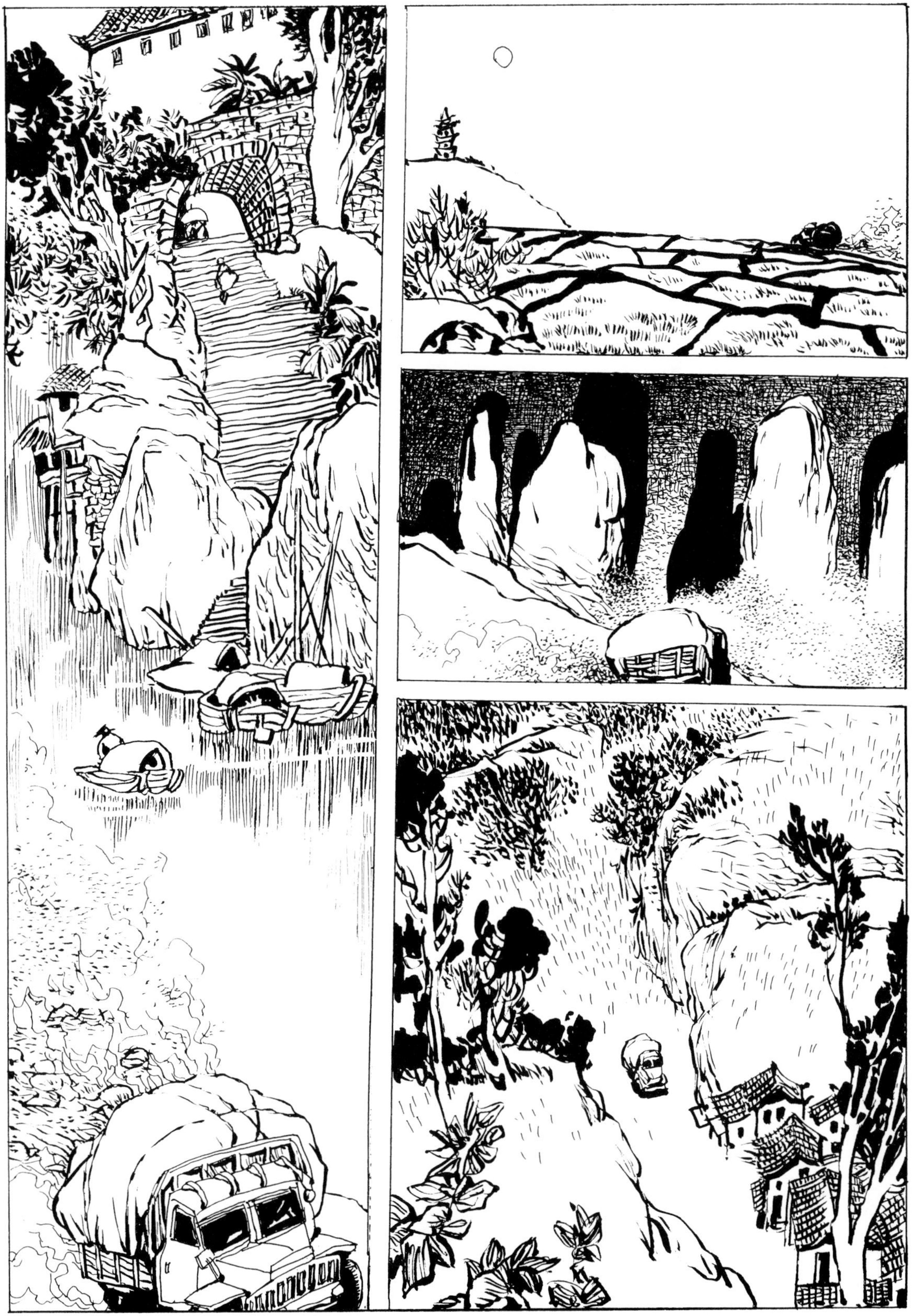

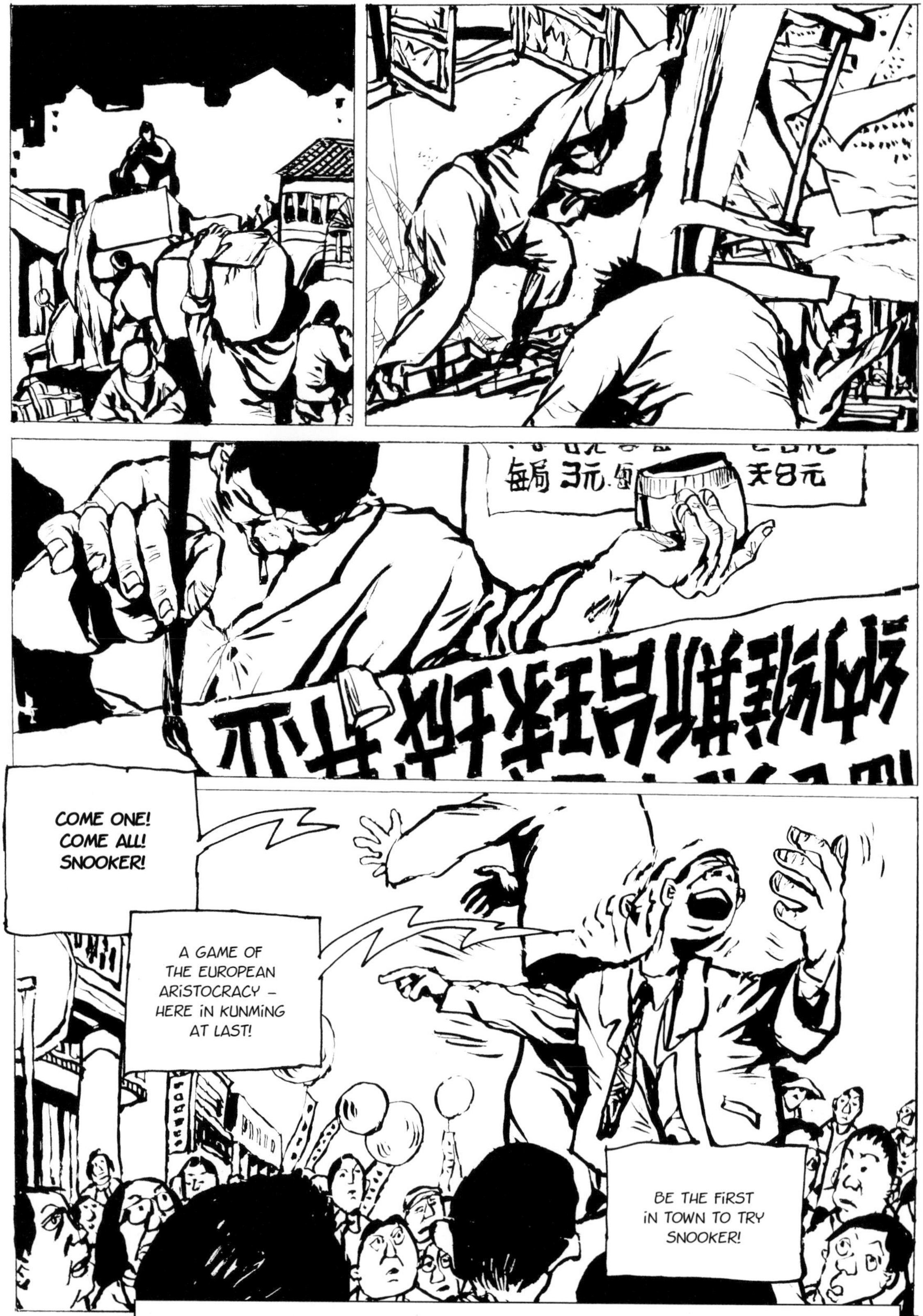
COME ONE! COME ALL! SNOOKER!
A GAME OF THE EUROPEAN ARISTOCRACY – HERE IN KUNMING AT LAST!
BE THE FIRST IN TOWN TO TRY SNOOKER!

维纳斯泰球场开业 WĒINÀSI TÀIQIUCHANG KAIYÈ: "VENUS GAME ROOM GRAND OPENING".

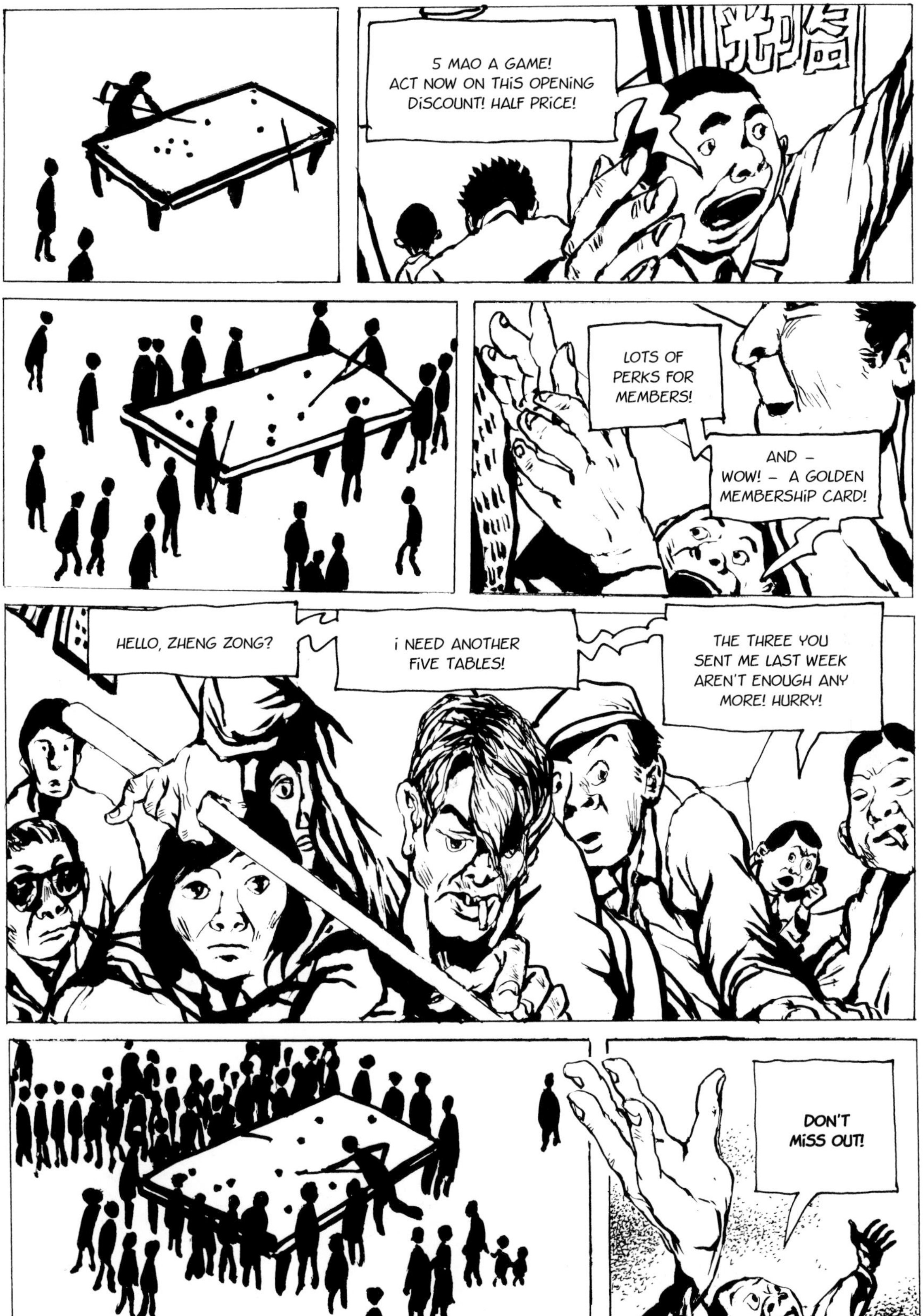
5 MAO A GAME!
ACT NOW ON THIS OPENING DISCOUNT! HALF PRICE!
LOTS OF PERKS FOR MEMBERS!
AND – WOW! – A GOLDEN MEMBERSHIP CARD!
HELLO, ZHENG ZONG?
I NEED ANOTHER FIVE TABLES!
THE THREE YOU SENT ME LAST WEEK AREN'T ENOUGH ANY MORE! HURRY!
DON'T MISS OUT!

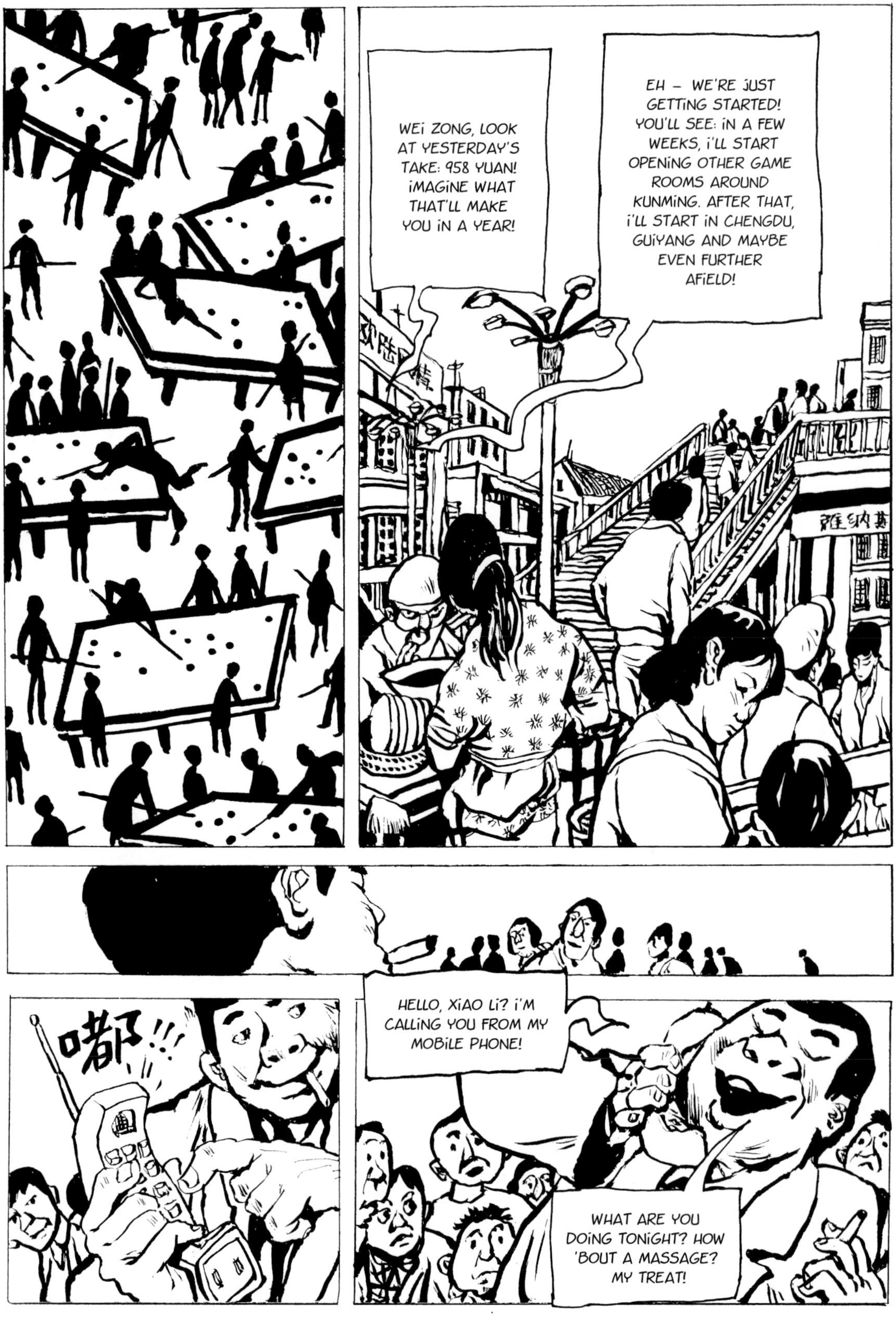
WEi ZONG, LOOK AT YESTERDAY'S TAKE: 958 YUAN! iMAGiNE WHAT THAT'LL MAKE YOU iN A YEAR!
EH – WE'RE JUST GETTiNG STARTED! YOU'LL SEE: iN A FEW WEEKS, i'LL START OPENiNG OTHER GAME ROOMS AROUND KUNMiNG. AFTER THAT, i'LL START iN CHENGDU, GUiYANG AND MAYBE EVEN FURTHER AFiELD!
嘟!!!
HELLO, XiAO Li? i'M CALLiNG YOU FROM MY MOBiLE PHONE!
WHAT ARE YOU DOiNG TONiGHT? HOW 'BOUT A MASSAGE? MY TREAT!

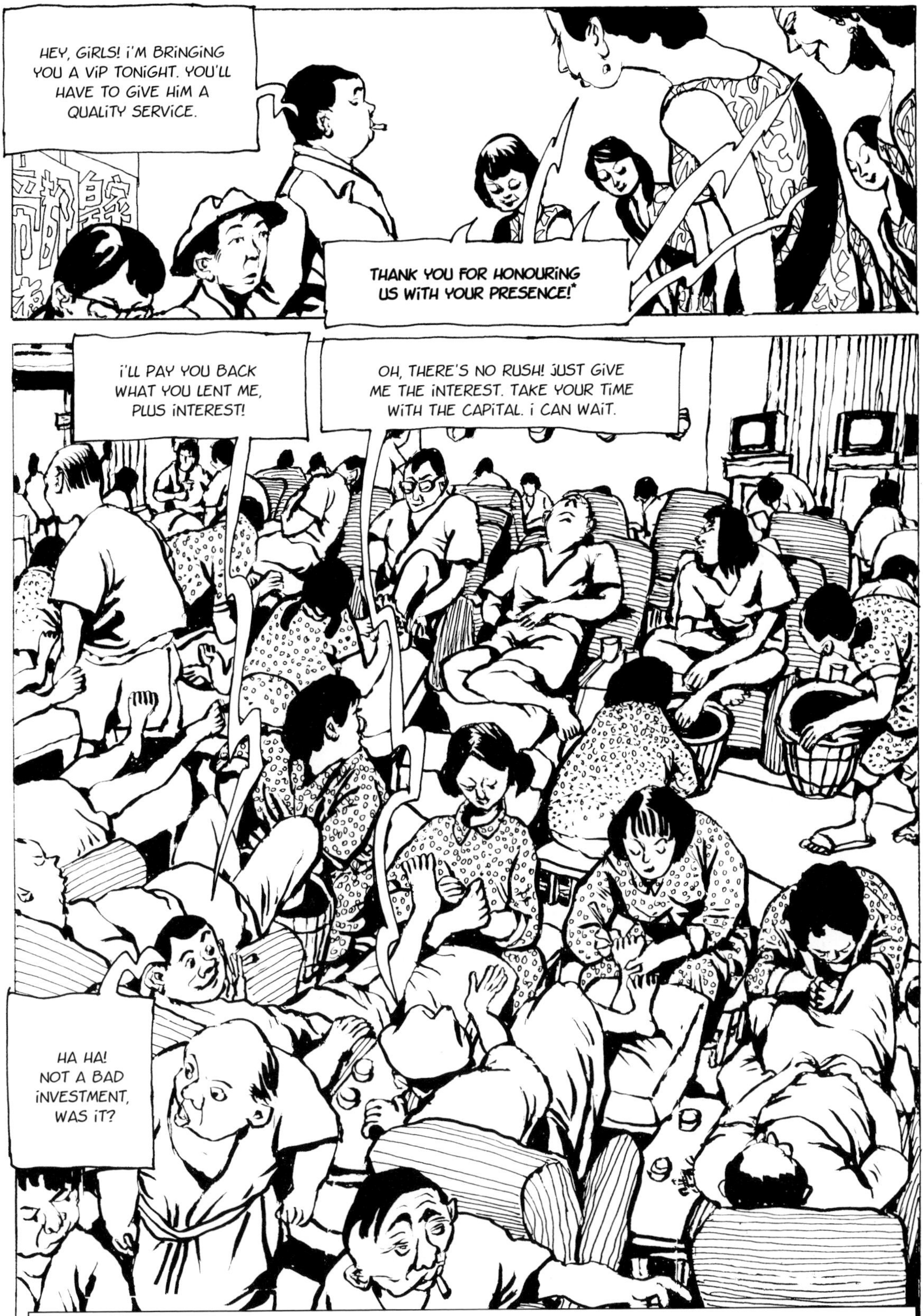
HEY, GIRLS! I'M BRINGING YOU A VIP TONIGHT. YOU'LL HAVE TO GIVE HIM A QUALITY SERVICE.
THANK YOU FOR HONOURING US WITH YOUR PRESENCE!*
I'LL PAY YOU BACK WHAT YOU LENT ME, PLUS INTEREST!
OH, THERE'S NO RUSH! JUST GIVE ME THE INTEREST. TAKE YOUR TIME WITH THE CAPITAL. I CAN WAIT.
HA HA! NOT A BAD INVESTMENT, WAS IT?

* 欢迎光临 HUANGYING GUANGLIN: CUSTOMERS ARE OFTEN GREETED WITH THIS EXPRESSION OF WELCOME UPON ENTERING SUCH AN ESTABLISHMENT.

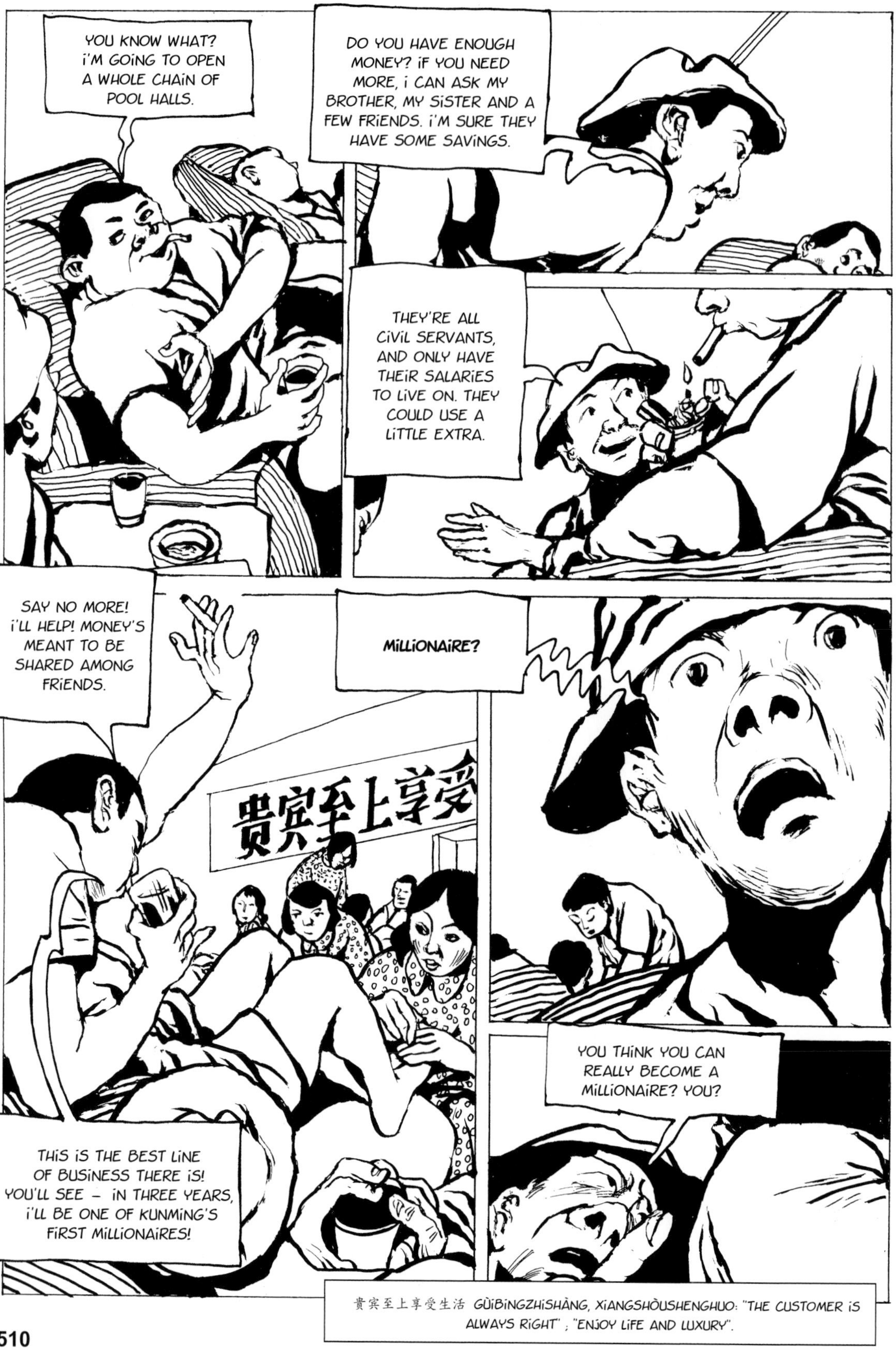
YOU KNOW WHAT? I'M GOING TO OPEN A WHOLE CHAIN OF POOL HALLS.
DO YOU HAVE ENOUGH MONEY? IF YOU NEED MORE, I CAN ASK MY BROTHER, MY SISTER AND A FEW FRIENDS. I'M SURE THEY HAVE SOME SAVINGS.
THEY'RE ALL CIVIL SERVANTS, AND ONLY HAVE THEIR SALARIES TO LIVE ON. THEY COULD USE A LITTLE EXTRA.
SAY NO MORE! I'LL HELP! MONEY'S MEANT TO BE SHARED AMONG FRIENDS.
贵宾至上享受
THIS IS THE BEST LINE OF BUSINESS THERE IS! YOU'LL SEE – IN THREE YEARS, I'LL BE ONE OF KUNMING'S FIRST MILLIONAIRES!
MILLIONAIRE?
YOU THINK YOU CAN REALLY BECOME A MILLIONAIRE? YOU?

贵宾至上享受生活 GÙIBINGZHISHÀNG, XIANGSHÒUSHENGHUO: "THE CUSTOMER IS ALWAYS RIGHT" ; "ENJOY LIFE AND LUXURY".

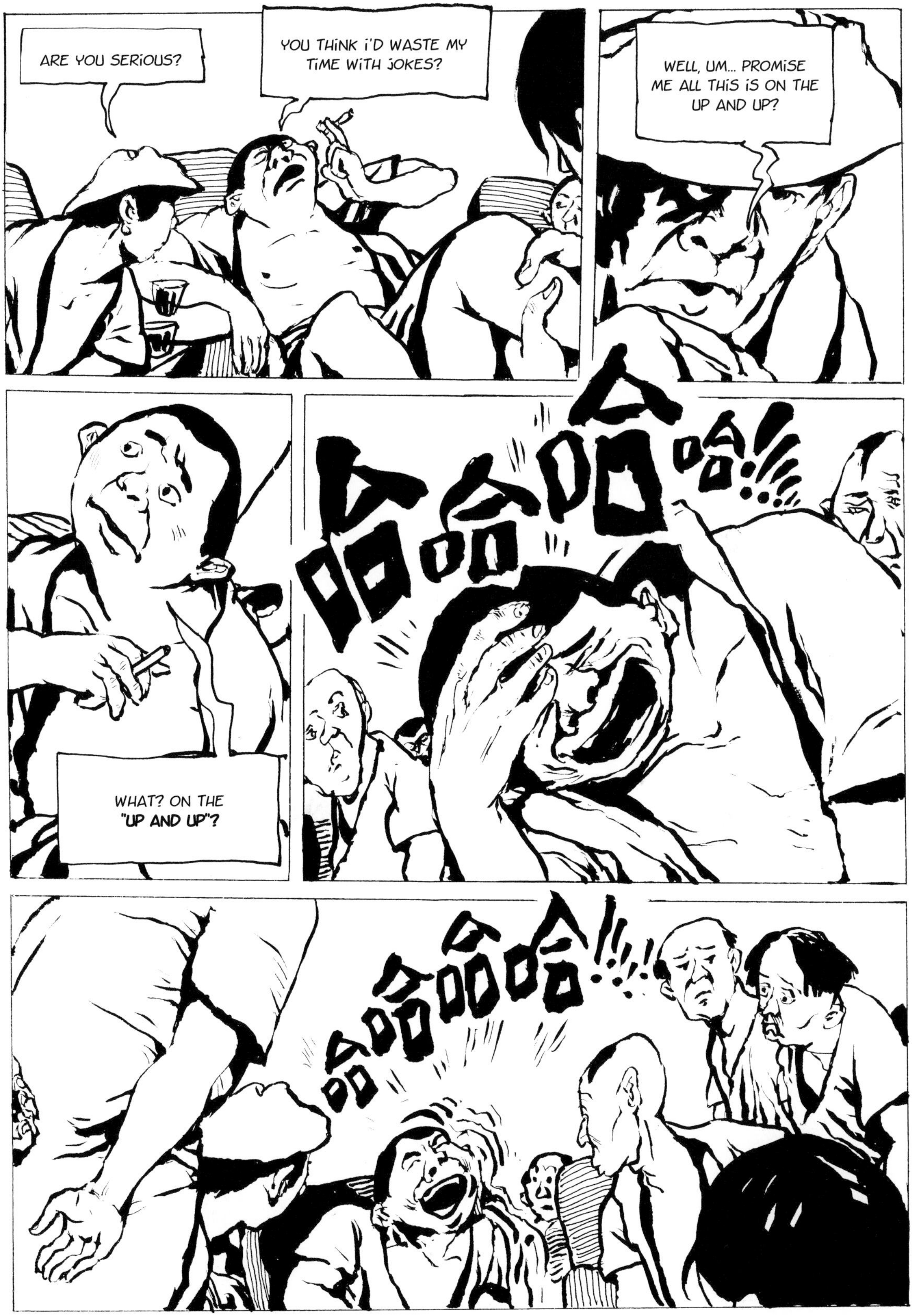
ARE YOU SERIOUS?
YOU THINK I'D WASTE MY TIME WITH JOKES?
WELL, UM... PROMISE ME ALL THIS IS ON THE UP AND UP?
WHAT? ON THE "UP AND UP"?
哈哈哈哈!!
哈哈哈哈哈!!!!!

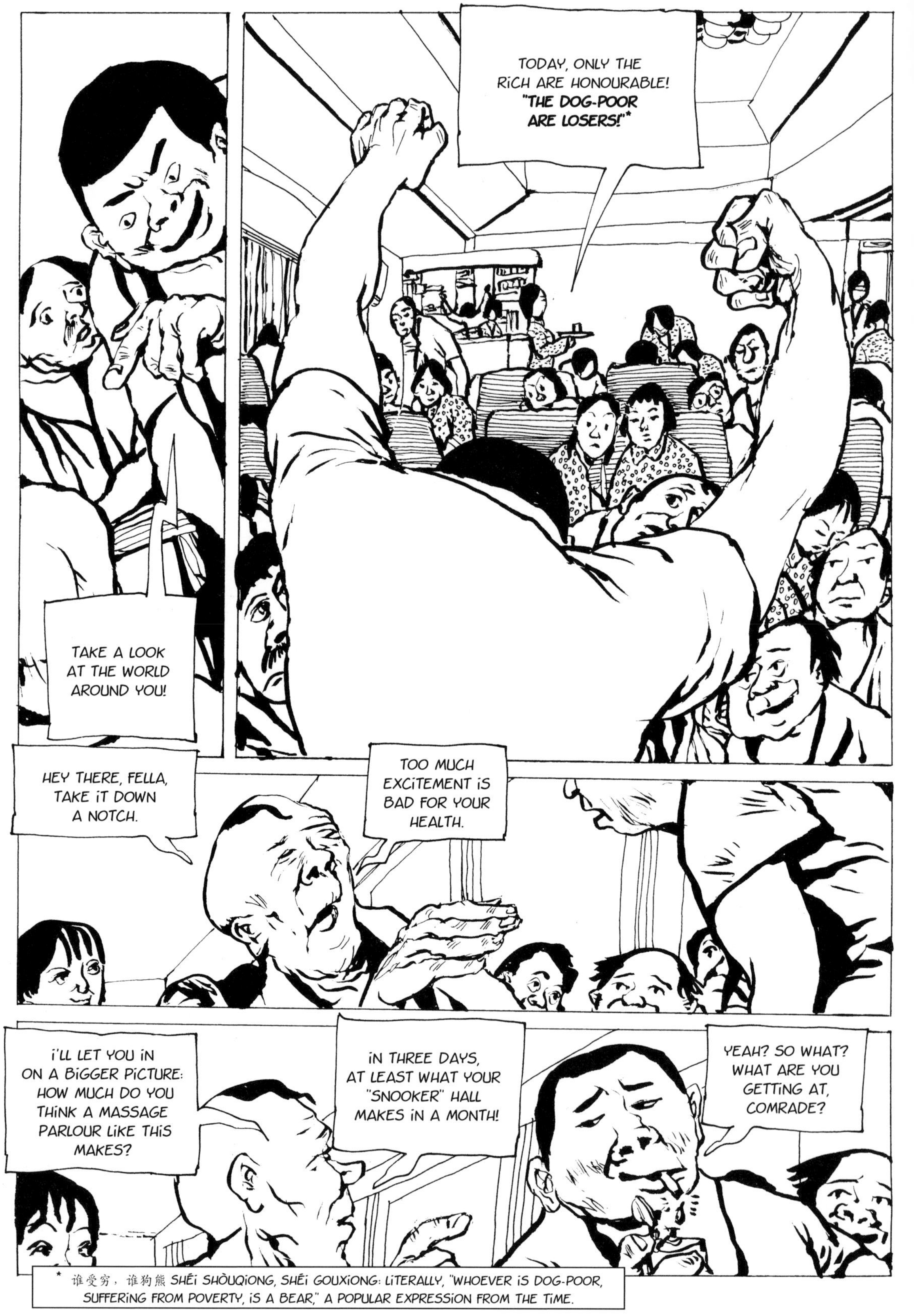
TAKE A LOOK AT THE WORLD AROUND YOU!
TODAY, ONLY THE RICH ARE HONOURABLE! "THE DOG-POOR ARE LOSERS!"*
HEY THERE, FELLA, TAKE IT DOWN A NOTCH.
TOO MUCH EXCITEMENT IS BAD FOR YOUR HEALTH.
I'LL LET YOU IN ON A BIGGER PICTURE: HOW MUCH DO YOU THINK A MASSAGE PARLOUR LIKE THIS MAKES?
IN THREE DAYS, AT LEAST WHAT YOUR "SNOOKER" HALL MAKES IN A MONTH!
YEAH? SO WHAT? WHAT ARE YOU GETTING AT, COMRADE?

* 谁受穷，谁狗熊 SHÉI SHÒUQIONG, SHÉI GOUXIONG: LITERALLY, "WHOEVER IS DOG-POOR, SUFFERING FROM POVERTY, IS A BEAR," A POPULAR EXPRESSION FROM THE TIME.

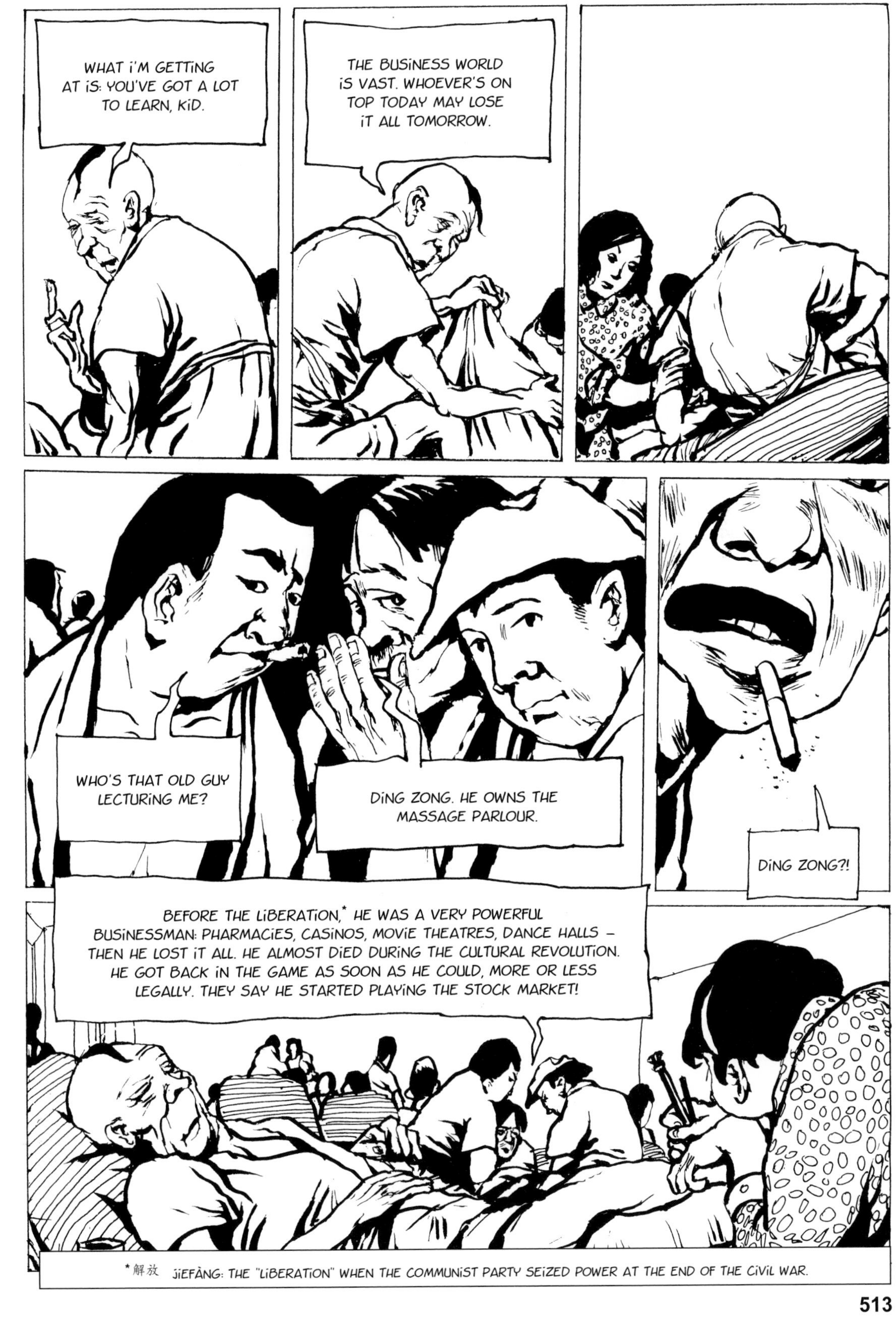
WHAT I'M GETTING AT IS: YOU'VE GOT A LOT TO LEARN, KID.
THE BUSINESS WORLD IS VAST. WHOEVER'S ON TOP TODAY MAY LOSE IT ALL TOMORROW.
WHO'S THAT OLD GUY LECTURING ME?
DING ZONG. HE OWNS THE MASSAGE PARLOUR.
DING ZONG?!
BEFORE THE LIBERATION,* HE WAS A VERY POWERFUL BUSINESSMAN: PHARMACIES, CASINOS, MOVIE THEATRES, DANCE HALLS – THEN HE LOST IT ALL. HE ALMOST DIED DURING THE CULTURAL REVOLUTION. HE GOT BACK IN THE GAME AS SOON AS HE COULD, MORE OR LESS LEGALLY. THEY SAY HE STARTED PLAYING THE STOCK MARKET!

*解放 JIEFÀNG: THE "LIBERATION" WHEN THE COMMUNIST PARTY SEIZED POWER AT THE END OF THE CIVIL WAR.

THE STOCK MARKET? WHAT'S THAT?

THE STOCK MARKET? THIS THING THAT MAKES YOUR MONEY GROW.

"MAKES YOUR MONEY GROW"? TELL ME MORE!

EASY. THERE ARE THREE WAYS OF MAKING MONEY. THE FIRST AND MOST BASIC IS WORKING BY SELLING YOUR LABOUR. PULLING A CART, BUILDING A HOUSE, OR — LIKE ME RIGHT NOW — MASSAGING YOU, FOR EXAMPLE.

YOU CAN ALSO BE A BOSS: OPEN A SHOP, START A FACTORY, OR EVEN BE A CADRE, OF COURSE. BETTER THAN JUST BEING A WORKER, BUT STILL JUST AN INTERMEDIATE STEP. NOW, THE THIRD WAY IS EVEN MORE ADVANCED.

IT'S BETTER THAN ALL THE OTHERS. GET YOURSELF A BALL OF DOUGH AND START ROLLING IT, LIKE A SNOWBALL! NOW THAT'S PLAYING THE MARKET!

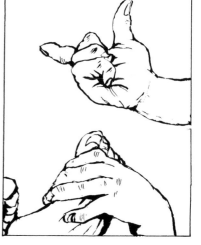

514

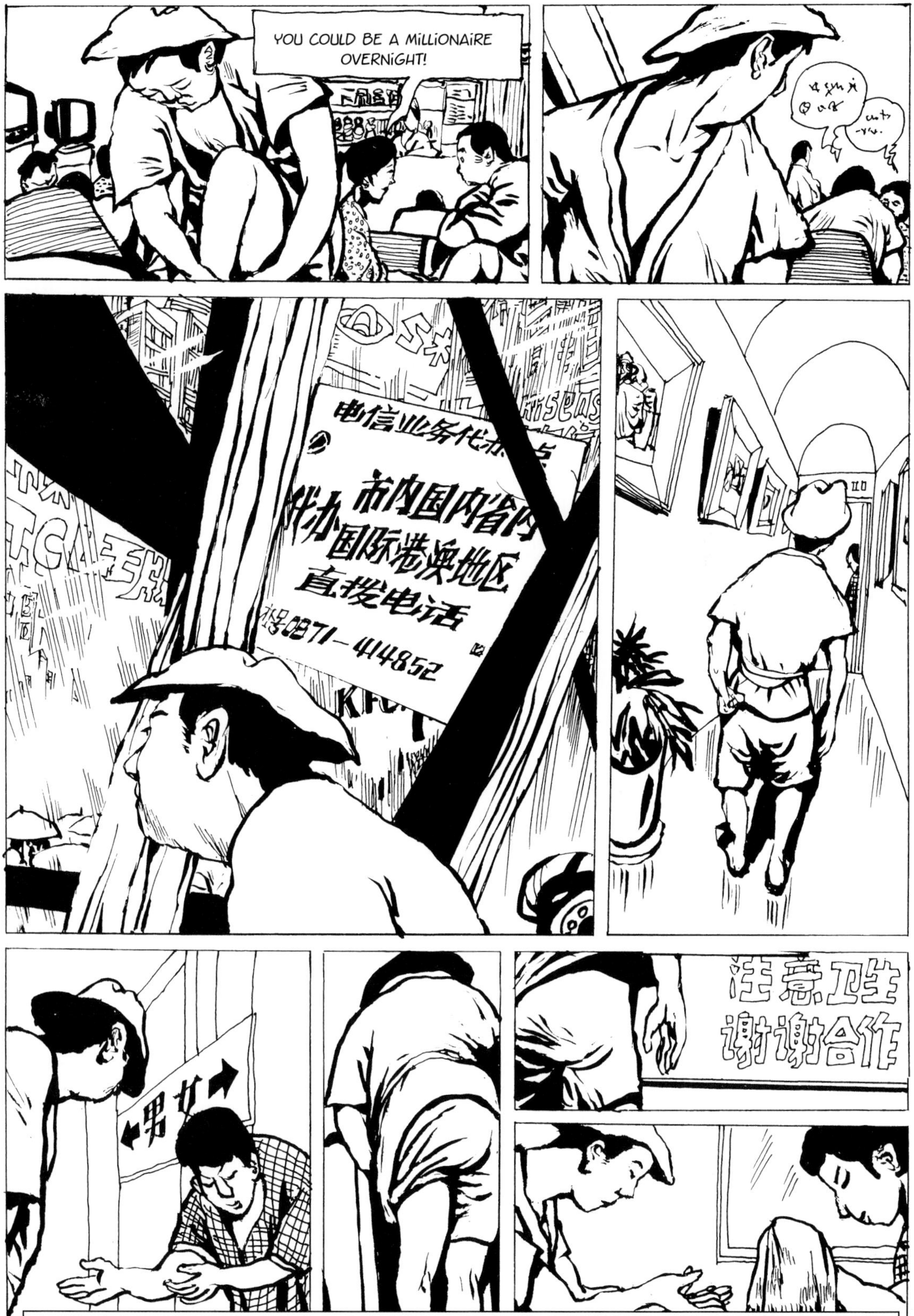

YOU COULD BE A MILLIONAIRE OVERNIGHT!
市内国内省内
国际港澳地区
直拨电话
0871-414852
男 女
注意卫生
谢谢合作

电信业务代办点。市内，国内，省内，国际，港澳地区。 直播电话 DIANXIN YÈWÙ DÀIBÀN DIAN. SHÈNÈI GUONÈI SHENGNÈI GUOJI GANGAO DIQU. ZHIBUO DIANHÙA: "EMAIL, BUSINESS, OFFICE SERVICES, TELEPHONE AND TELEGRAPH. LOCAL, PROVINCIAL, NATIONAL, INTERNATIONAL, HONG KONG, AND MACAO. DIRECT LINES."

注意卫生， 谢谢合作 ZHÙYI WÈISHENG, XIEXIE HÉZÙO: "PAY ATTENTION TO HYGIENE. THANKS FOR YOUR COOPERATION."

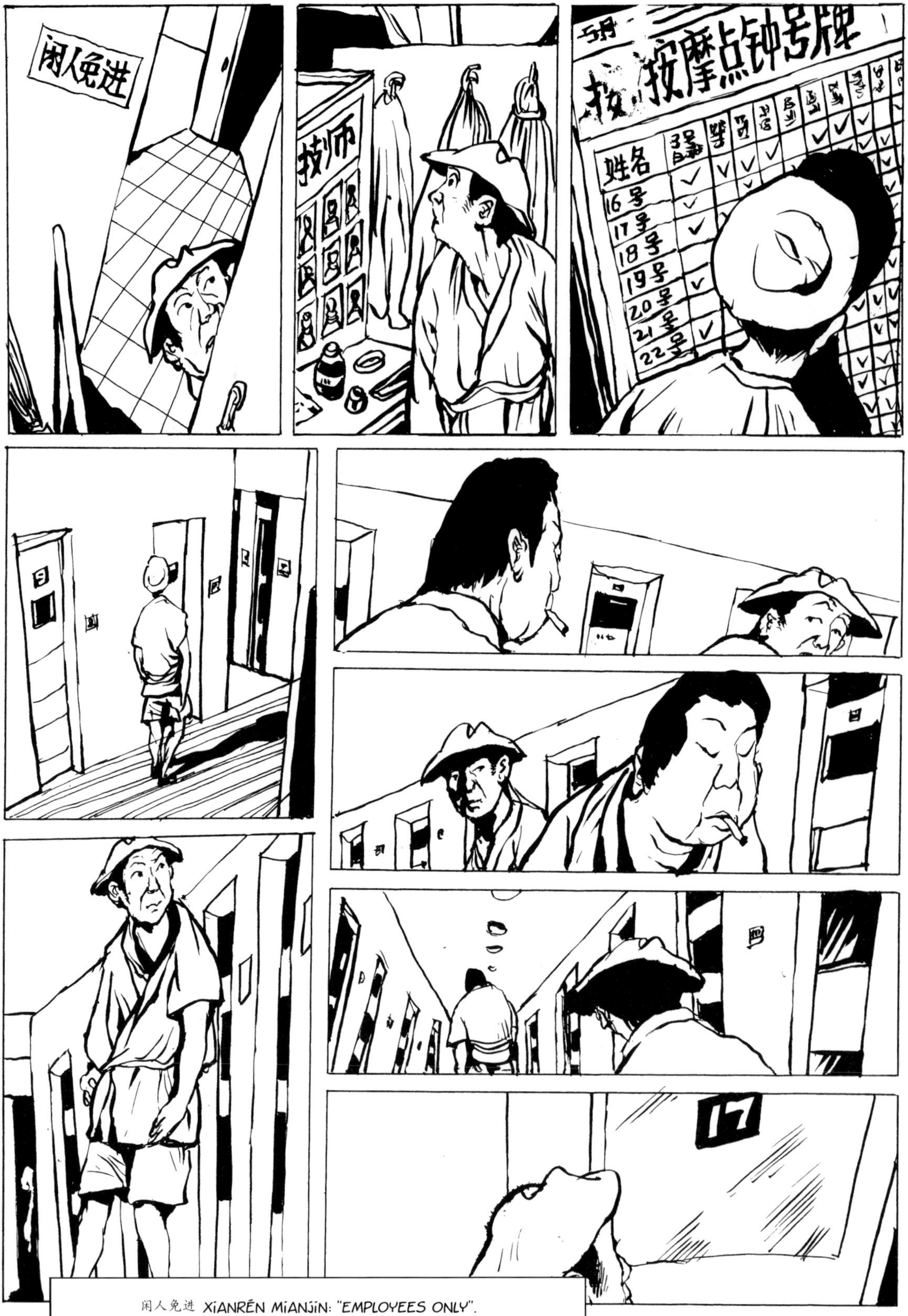
闲人免进
按摩点钟号牌
姓名
16号
17号
18号
19号
20号
21号
22号
17

闲人免进 XIANRÉN MIANJIN: "EMPLOYEES ONLY".
按摩点钟号牌 ÀNMO DIANZHONG HÀOPAI: "MASSEUSE SCHEDULE".

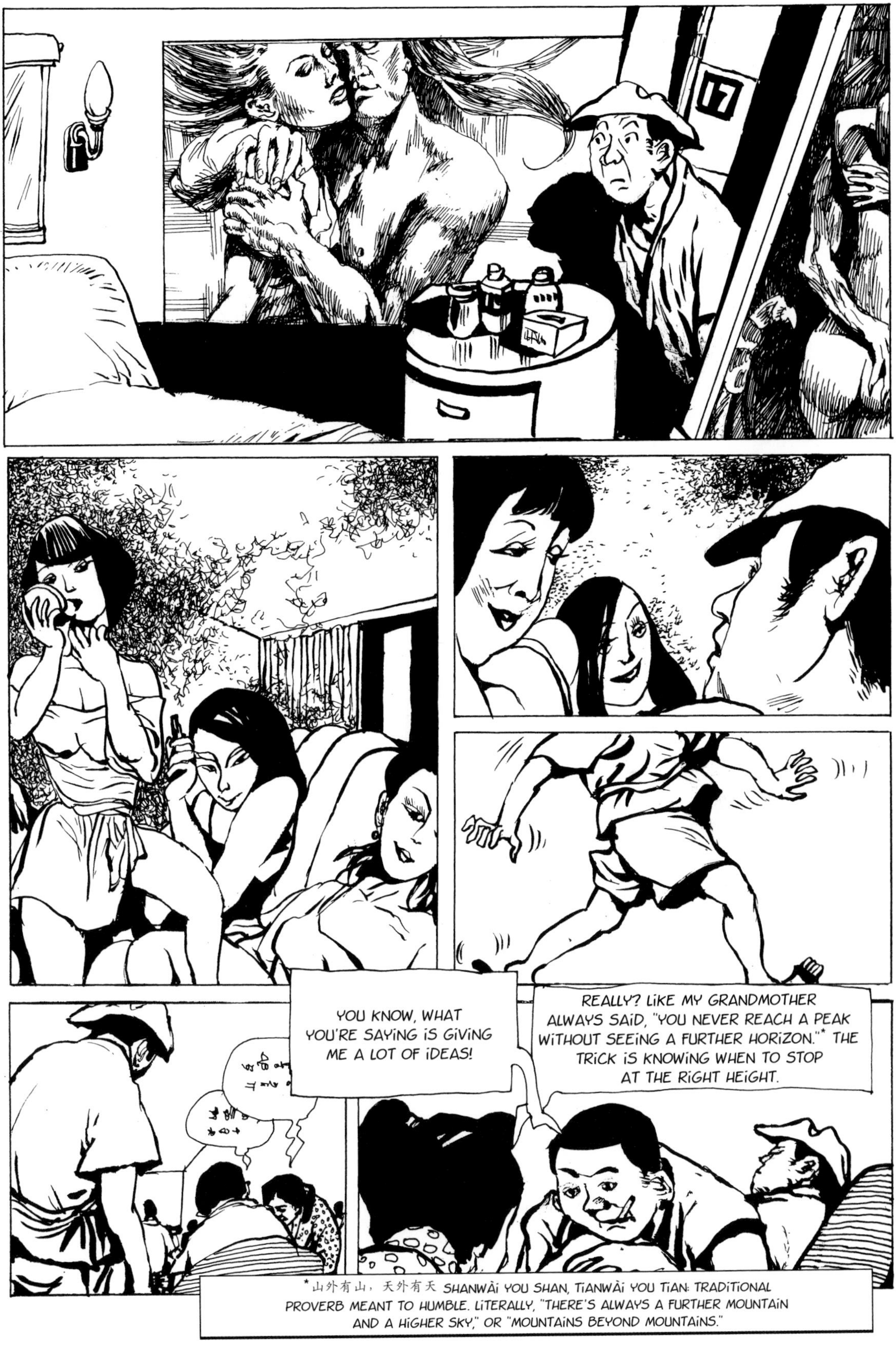
YOU KNOW, WHAT YOU'RE SAYING IS GIVING ME A LOT OF iDEAS!
REALLY? LiKE MY GRANDMOTHER ALWAYS SAiD, "YOU NEVER REACH A PEAK WiTHOUT SEEiNG A FURTHER HORiZON."* THE TRiCK iS KNOWiNG WHEN TO STOP AT THE RiGHT HEiGHT.
17

*山外有山，天外有天 SHANWÀi YOU SHAN, TiANWÀi YOU TiAN: TRADiTiONAL PROVERB MEANT TO HUMBLE. LiTERALLY, "THERE'S ALWAYS A FURTHER MOUNTAiN AND A HiGHER SKY," OR "MOUNTAiNS BEYOND MOUNTAiNS."

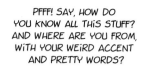

PFFF! SAY, HOW DO YOU KNOW ALL THIS STUFF? AND WHERE ARE YOU FROM, WITH YOUR WEIRD ACCENT AND PRETTY WORDS?

I'M FROM YUANYUANG DISTRICT. I'M NINETEEN; MY NAME'S LILI. IT'S NICE OF YOU TO SAY I SPEAK WELL, BUT TO BE HONEST, I NEVER GOT MUCH EDUCATION. I COME FROM A FAMILY OF POOR FARMERS. ONCE ELEMENTARY SCHOOL WAS OVER, I HAD TO GET A JOB, OF COURSE. SO I'M A MASSEUSE, TILL SOMETHING BETTER COMES ALONG. SINCE ALL I HEAR CLIENTS TALK ABOUT IS WAYS TO MAKE MONEY, IT STANDS TO REASON I'D PICK UP A FEW THINGS.

NOT THAT IT'S DONE ME MUCH GOOD YET, BUT WHO KNOWS? MAYBE ONE DAY...

YEP, ONE THING'S FOR SURE: WITH THE KIND OF CUSTOMERS YOU GET HERE, YOU'LL GET A LOT OF GOOD LEADS!

HMPH! THEY DON'T ALWAYS SAY USEFUL THINGS, BUT IT COULD HAPPEN. HERE, JUST LISTEN TO THEM TALK FOR A MINUTE.

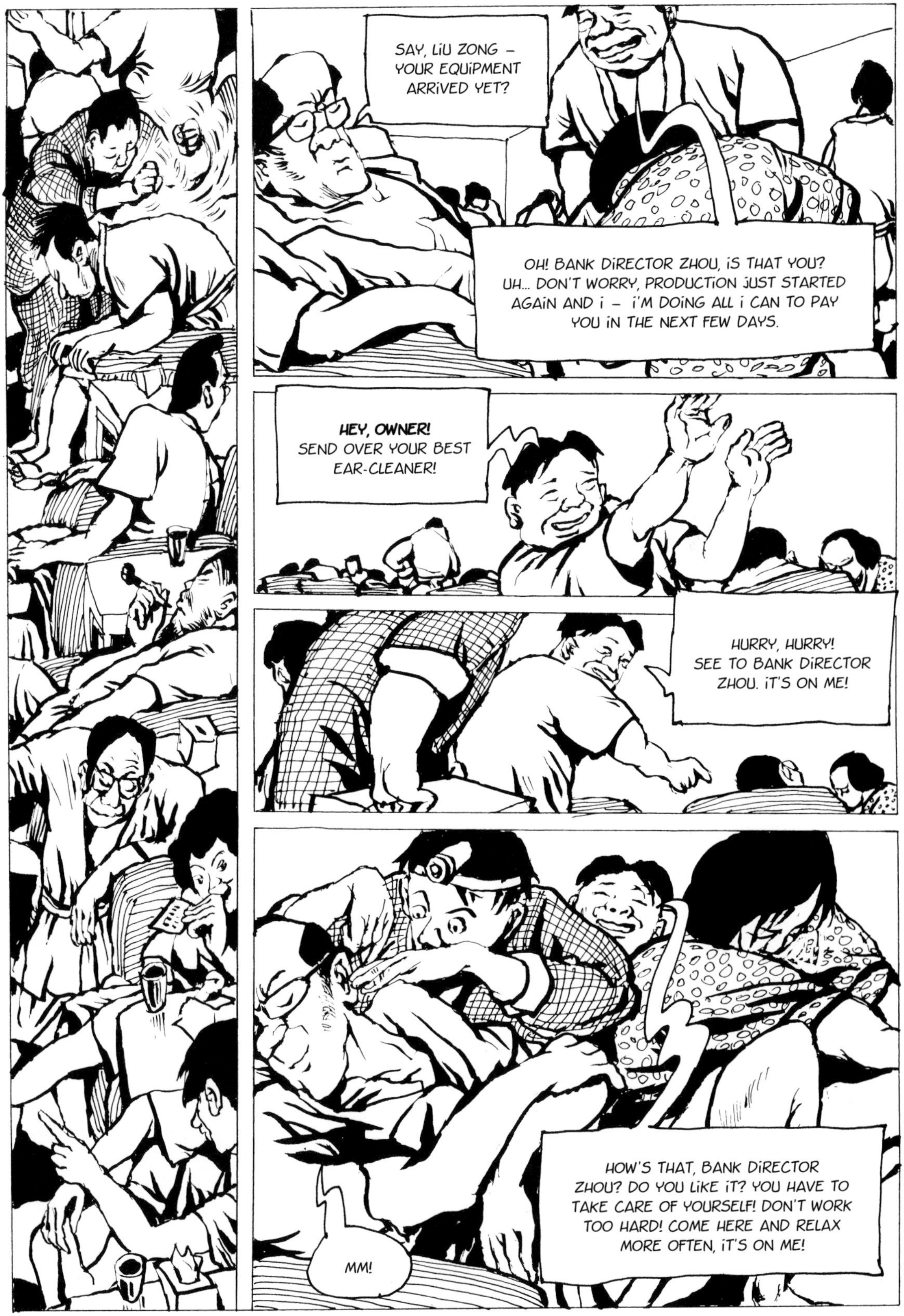
SAY, LIU ZONG – YOUR EQUIPMENT ARRIVED YET?
OH! BANK DIRECTOR ZHOU, IS THAT YOU? UH... DON'T WORRY, PRODUCTION JUST STARTED AGAIN AND I – I'M DOING ALL I CAN TO PAY YOU IN THE NEXT FEW DAYS.
HEY, OWNER! SEND OVER YOUR BEST EAR-CLEANER!
HURRY, HURRY! SEE TO BANK DIRECTOR ZHOU. IT'S ON ME!
MM!
HOW'S THAT, BANK DIRECTOR ZHOU? DO YOU LIKE IT? YOU HAVE TO TAKE CARE OF YOURSELF! DON'T WORK TOO HARD! COME HERE AND RELAX MORE OFTEN, IT'S ON ME!

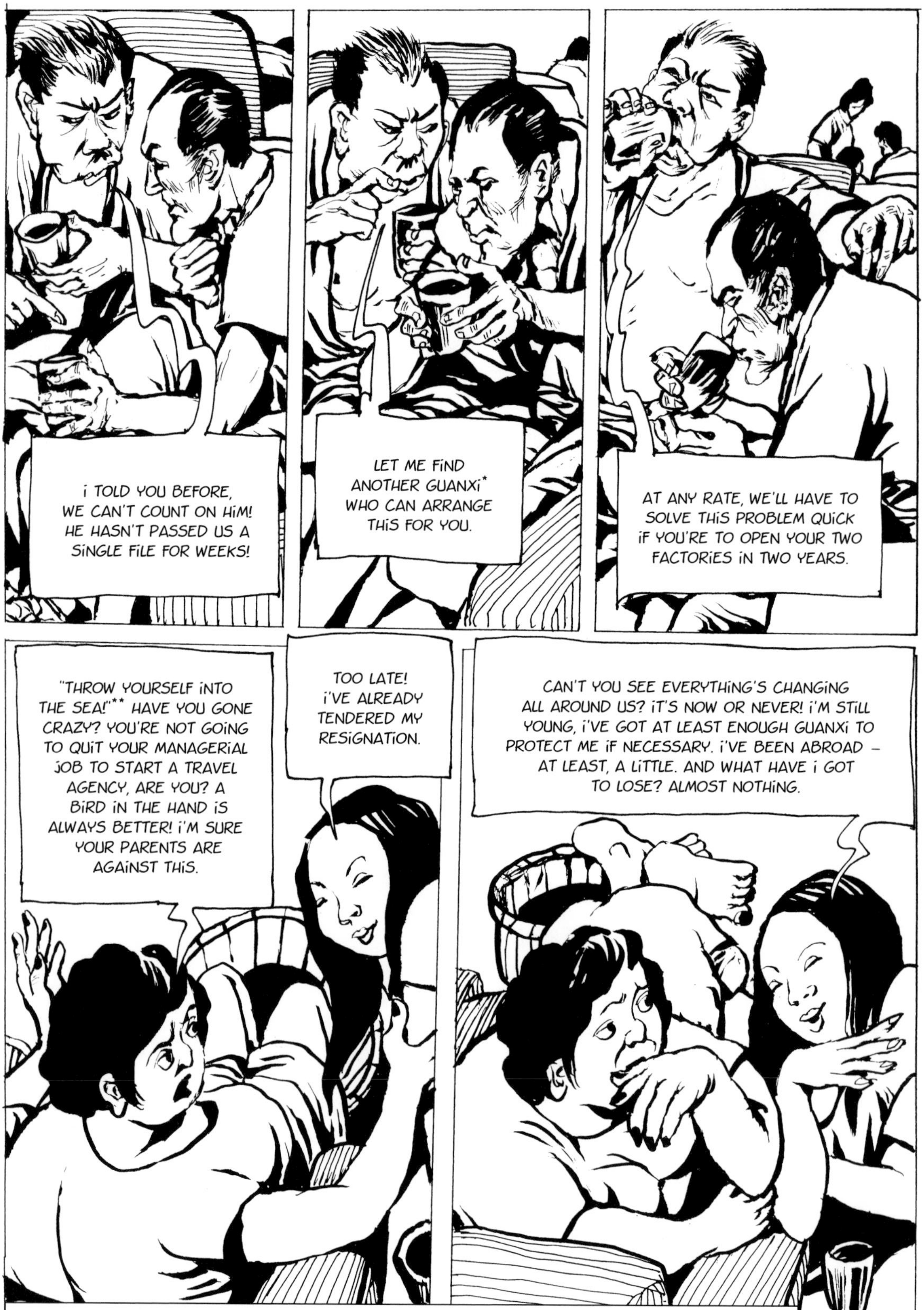
I TOLD YOU BEFORE, WE CAN'T COUNT ON HIM! HE HASN'T PASSED US A SINGLE FILE FOR WEEKS!
LET ME FIND ANOTHER GUANXI* WHO CAN ARRANGE THIS FOR YOU.
AT ANY RATE, WE'LL HAVE TO SOLVE THIS PROBLEM QUICK IF YOU'RE TO OPEN YOUR TWO FACTORIES IN TWO YEARS.
"THROW YOURSELF INTO THE SEA!"** HAVE YOU GONE CRAZY? YOU'RE NOT GOING TO QUIT YOUR MANAGERIAL JOB TO START A TRAVEL AGENCY, ARE YOU? A BIRD IN THE HAND IS ALWAYS BETTER! I'M SURE YOUR PARENTS ARE AGAINST THIS.
TOO LATE! I'VE ALREADY TENDERED MY RESIGNATION.
CAN'T YOU SEE EVERYTHING'S CHANGING ALL AROUND US? IT'S NOW OR NEVER! I'M STILL YOUNG, I'VE GOT AT LEAST ENOUGH GUANXI TO PROTECT ME IF NECESSARY. I'VE BEEN ABROAD – AT LEAST, A LITTLE. AND WHAT HAVE I GOT TO LOSE? ALMOST NOTHING.

* 关系 GUANXI: A (POTENTIALLY USEFUL) RELATIONSHIP OR "CONNECTION".

** 下海 XIA HAI: A POPULAR EXPRESSION AT THE TIME (APPLIED TO CIVIL SERVANTS WHO WENT INTO PRIVATE BUSINESS).

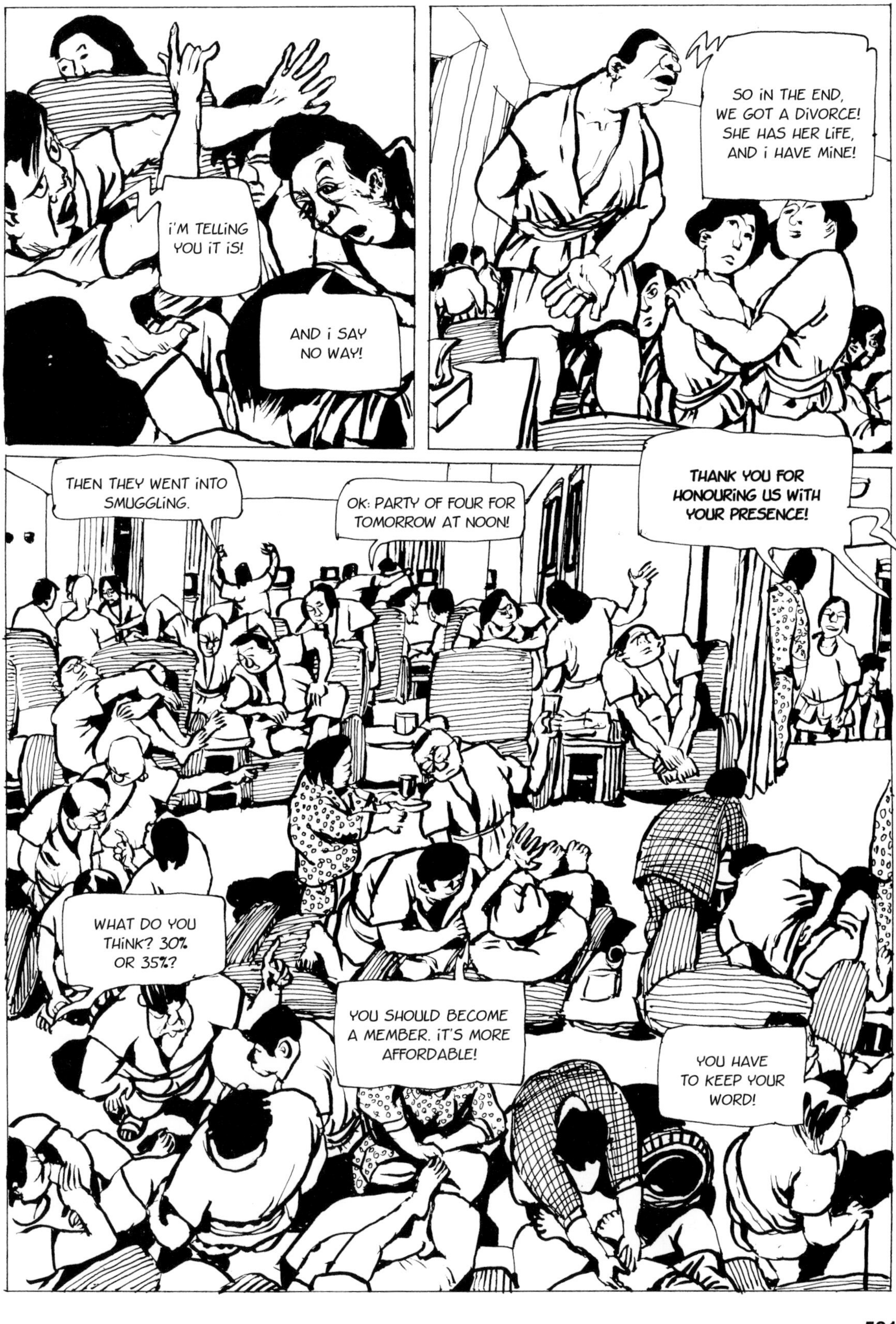
I'M TELLING YOU IT IS!
AND I SAY NO WAY!
SO IN THE END, WE GOT A DIVORCE! SHE HAS HER LIFE, AND I HAVE MINE!
THEN THEY WENT INTO SMUGGLING.
OK: PARTY OF FOUR FOR TOMORROW AT NOON!
THANK YOU FOR HONOURING US WITH YOUR PRESENCE!
WHAT DO YOU THINK? 30% OR 35%?
YOU SHOULD BECOME A MEMBER. IT'S MORE AFFORDABLE!
YOU HAVE TO KEEP YOUR WORD!

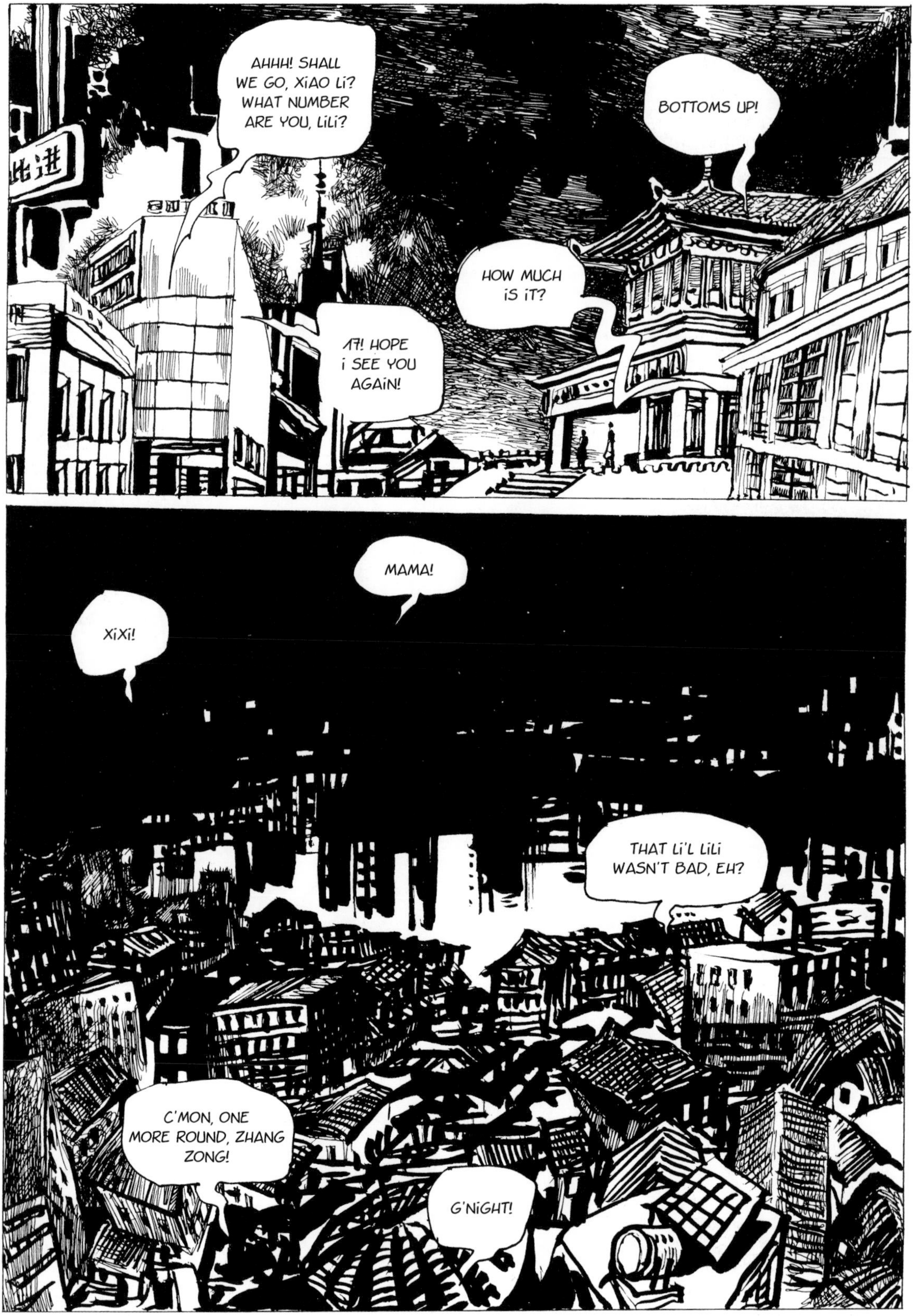
AHHH! SHALL WE GO, XIAO LI? WHAT NUMBER ARE YOU, LILI?
17! HOPE I SEE YOU AGAIN!
HOW MUCH IS IT?
BOTTOMS UP!
XIXI!
MAMA!
THAT LI'L LILI WASN'T BAD, EH?
C'MON, ONE MORE ROUND, ZHANG ZONG!
G'NIGHT!

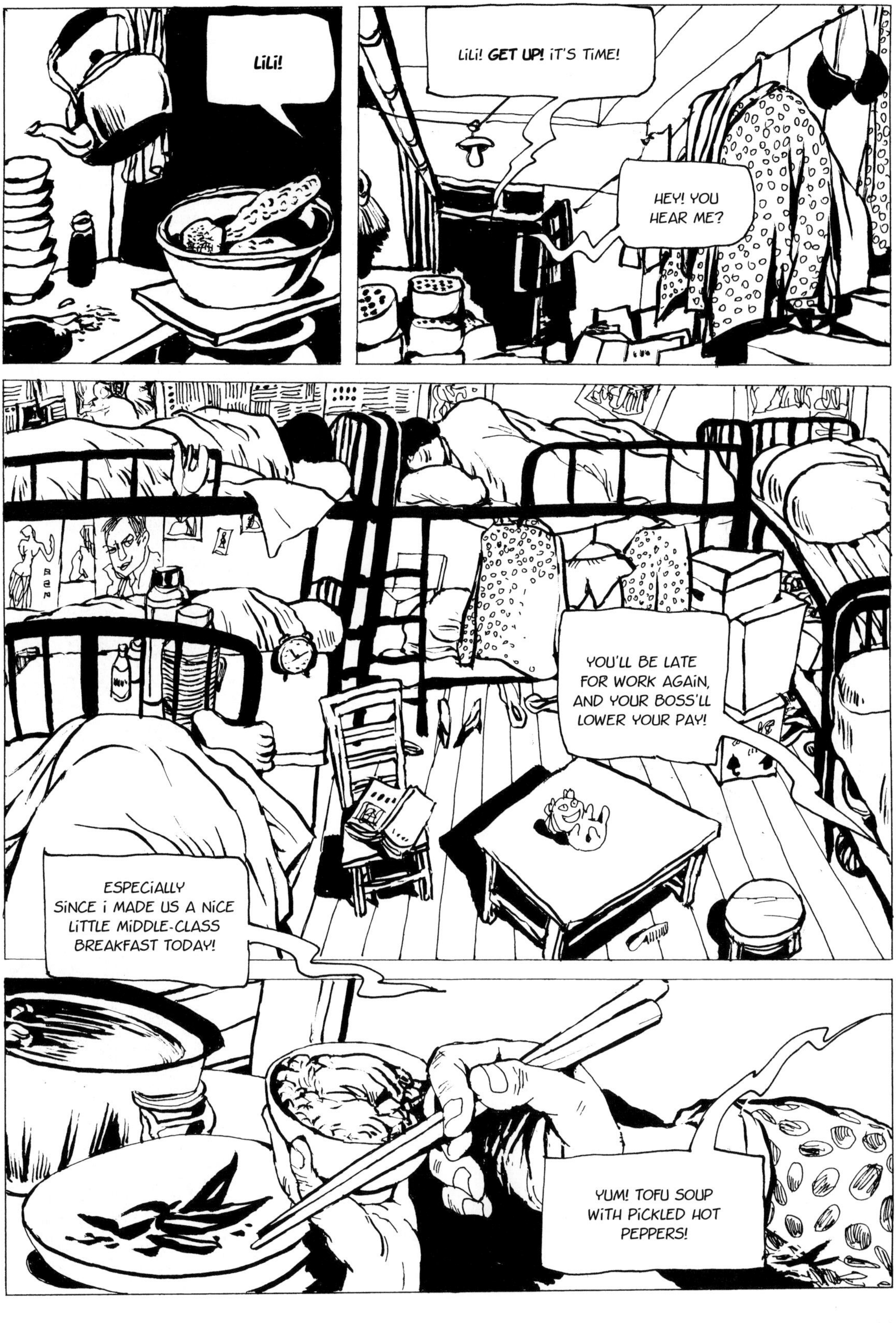
LiLi!
LiLi! GET UP! iT'S TiME!
HEY! YOU HEAR ME?
YOU'LL BE LATE FOR WORK AGAiN, AND YOUR BOSS'LL LOWER YOUR PAY!
ESPECiALLY SiNCE i MADE US A NiCE LiTTLE MiDDLE-CLASS BREAKFAST TODAY!
YUM! TOFU SOUP WiTH PiCKLED HOT PEPPERS!

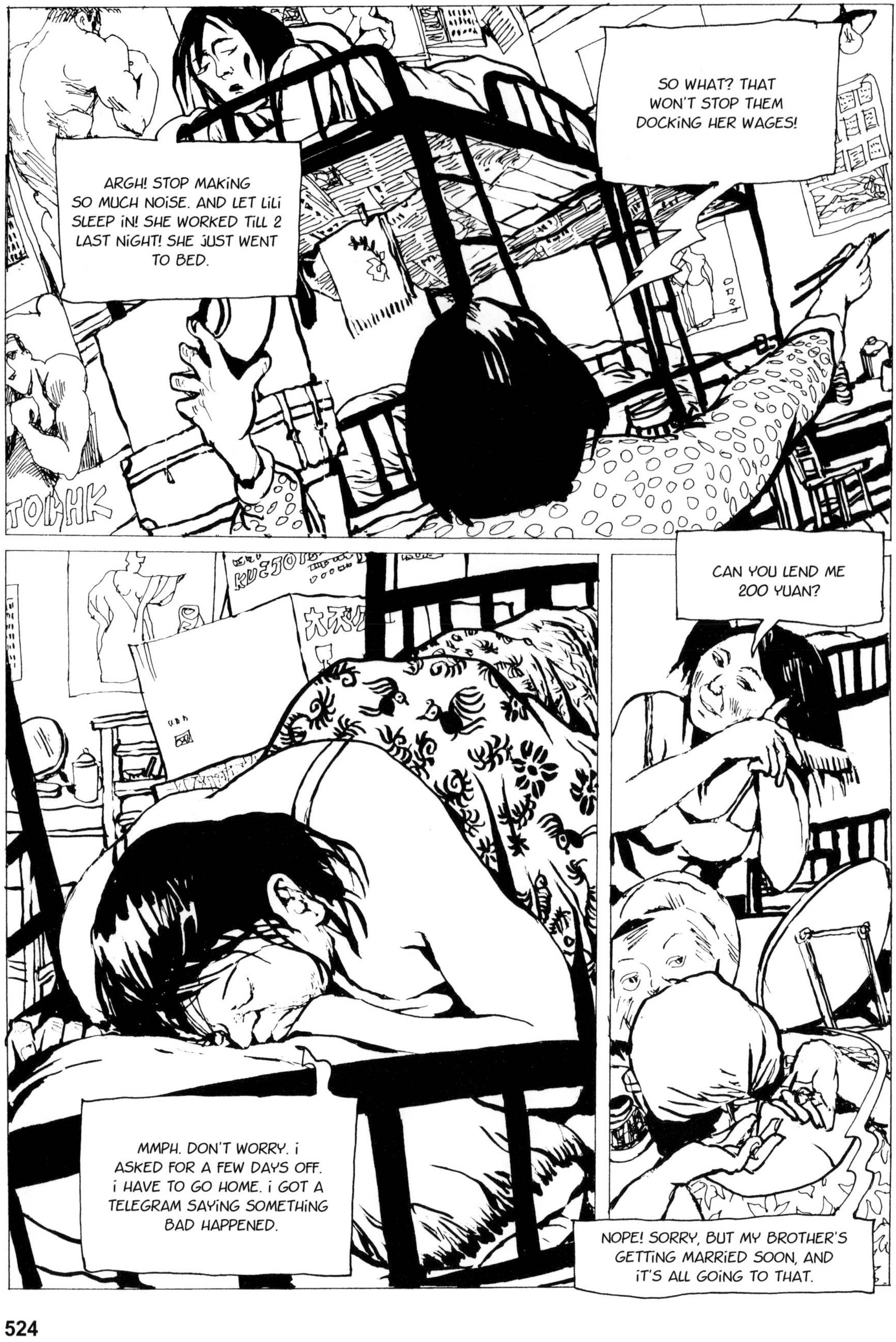

ARGH! STOP MAKING SO MUCH NOISE. AND LET LILI SLEEP IN! SHE WORKED TILL 2 LAST NIGHT! SHE JUST WENT TO BED.
SO WHAT? THAT WON'T STOP THEM DOCKING HER WAGES!
MMPH. DON'T WORRY. I ASKED FOR A FEW DAYS OFF. I HAVE TO GO HOME. I GOT A TELEGRAM SAYING SOMETHING BAD HAPPENED.
CAN YOU LEND ME 200 YUAN?
NOPE! SORRY, BUT MY BROTHER'S GETTING MARRIED SOON, AND IT'S ALL GOING TO THAT.

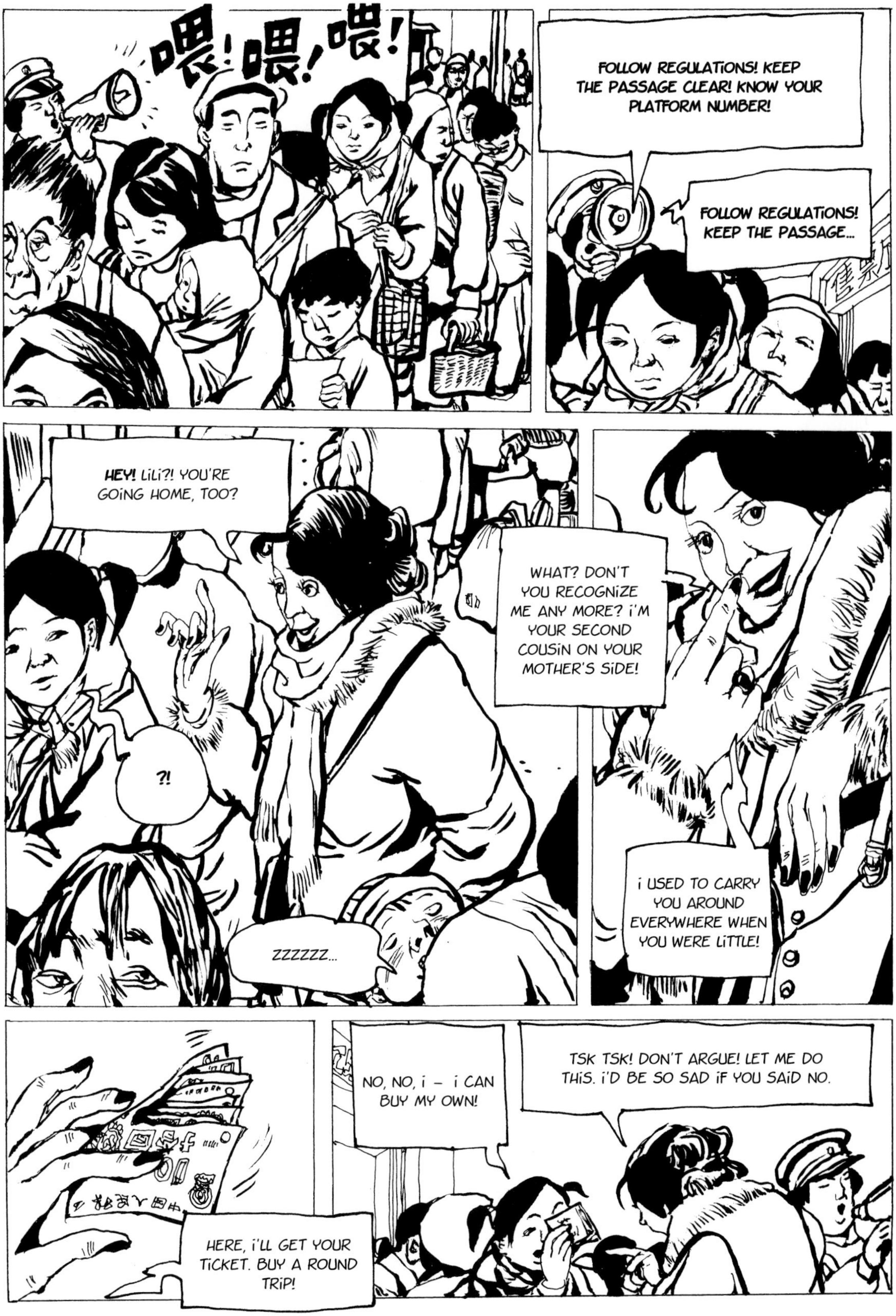
喂!喂!喂!
FOLLOW REGULATIONS! KEEP THE PASSAGE CLEAR! KNOW YOUR PLATFORM NUMBER!
FOLLOW REGULATIONS! KEEP THE PASSAGE...
HEY! LILI?! YOU'RE GOING HOME, TOO?
?!
ZZZZZZ...
WHAT? DON'T YOU RECOGNIZE ME ANY MORE? I'M YOUR SECOND COUSIN ON YOUR MOTHER'S SIDE!
I USED TO CARRY YOU AROUND EVERYWHERE WHEN YOU WERE LITTLE!
HERE, I'LL GET YOUR TICKET. BUY A ROUND TRIP!
NO, NO, I – I CAN BUY MY OWN!
TSK TSK! DON'T ARGUE! LET ME DO THIS. I'D BE SO SAD IF YOU SAID NO.

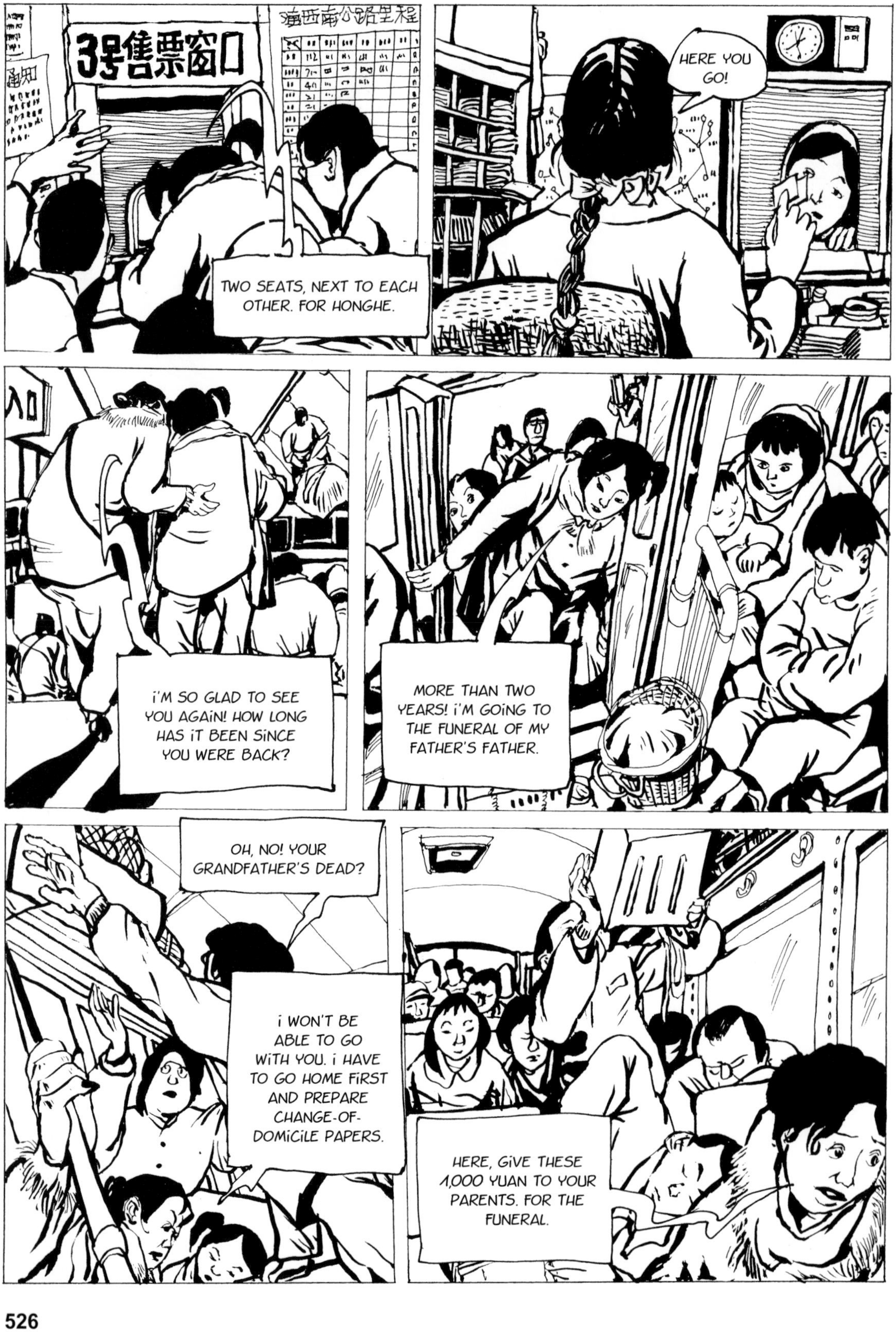
3号售票窗口
TWO SEATS, NEXT TO EACH OTHER. FOR HONGHE.
HERE YOU GO!
入口
i'M SO GLAD TO SEE YOU AGAiN! HOW LONG HAS iT BEEN SiNCE YOU WERE BACK?
MORE THAN TWO YEARS! i'M GOiNG TO THE FUNERAL OF MY FATHER'S FATHER.
OH, NO! YOUR GRANDFATHER'S DEAD?
i WON'T BE ABLE TO GO WiTH YOU. i HAVE TO GO HOME FiRST AND PREPARE CHANGE-OF-DOMiCiLE PAPERS.
HERE, GiVE THESE 1,000 YUAN TO YOUR PARENTS. FOR THE FUNERAL.

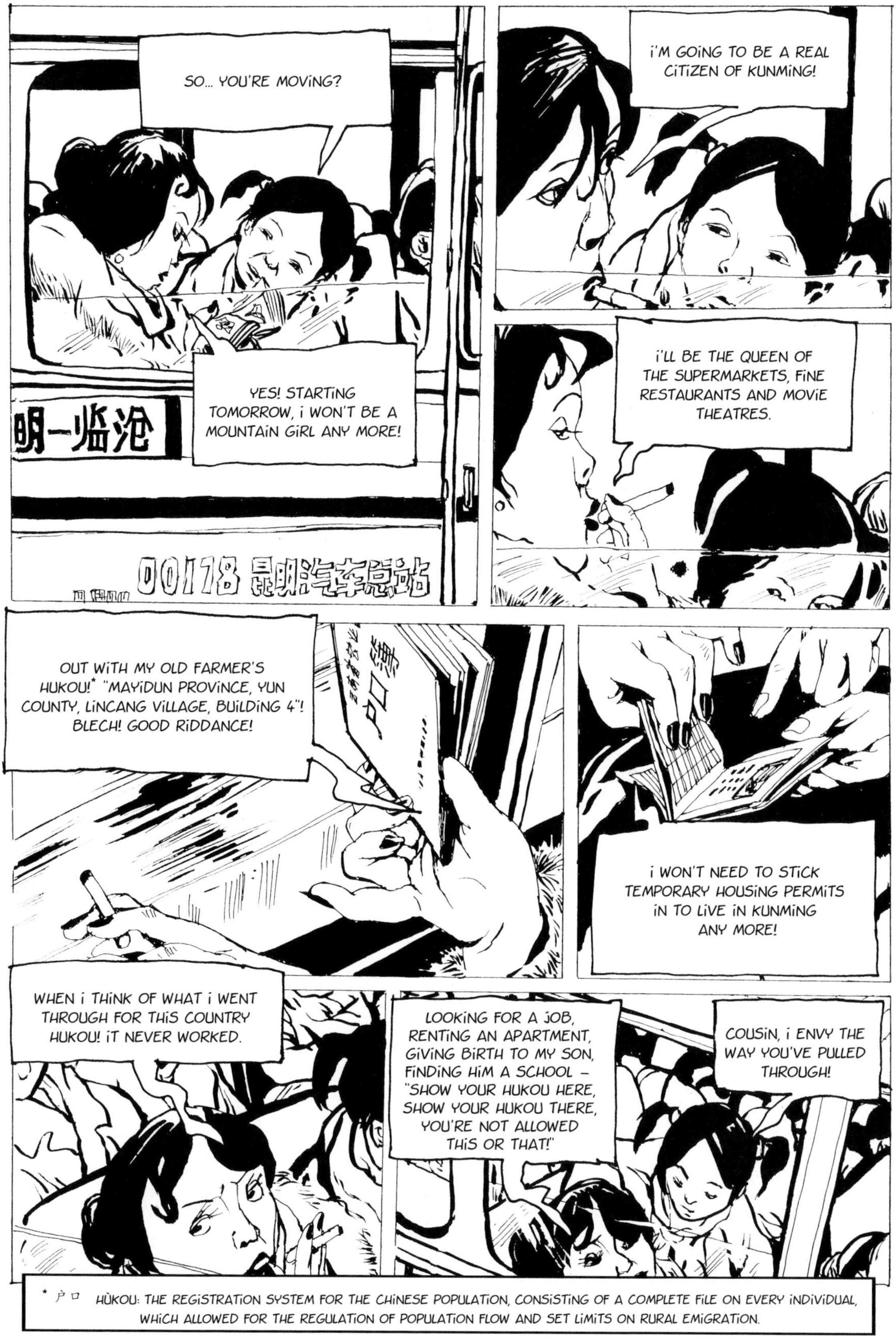
SO... YOU'RE MOVING?
YES! STARTING TOMORROW, i WON'T BE A MOUNTAIN GiRL ANY MORE!
明一临沧
00178 昆明汽车总站
i'M GOiNG TO BE A REAL CiTiZEN OF KUNMiNG!
i'LL BE THE QUEEN OF THE SUPERMARKETS, FiNE RESTAURANTS AND MOViE THEATRES.
OUT WiTH MY OLD FARMER'S HUKOU!* "MAYiDUN PROViNCE, YUN COUNTY, LiNCANG ViLLAGE, BUiLDiNG 4"! BLECH! GOOD RiDDANCE!
i WON'T NEED TO STiCK TEMPORARY HOUSiNG PERMiTS iN TO LiVE iN KUNMiNG ANY MORE!
WHEN i THiNK OF WHAT i WENT THROUGH FOR THiS COUNTRY HUKOU! iT NEVER WORKED.
LOOKiNG FOR A JOB, RENTiNG AN APARTMENT, GiViNG BiRTH TO MY SON, FiNDiNG HiM A SCHOOL – "SHOW YOUR HUKOU HERE, SHOW YOUR HUKOU THERE, YOU'RE NOT ALLOWED THiS OR THAT!"
COUSiN, i ENVY THE WAY YOU'VE PULLED THROUGH!

* 户口 HÙKOU: THE REGiSTRATiON SYSTEM FOR THE CHiNESE POPULATiON, CONSiSTiNG OF A COMPLETE FiLE ON EVERY iNDiViDUAL, WHiCH ALLOWED FOR THE REGULATiON OF POPULATiON FLOW AND SET LiMiTS ON RURAL EMiGRATiON.

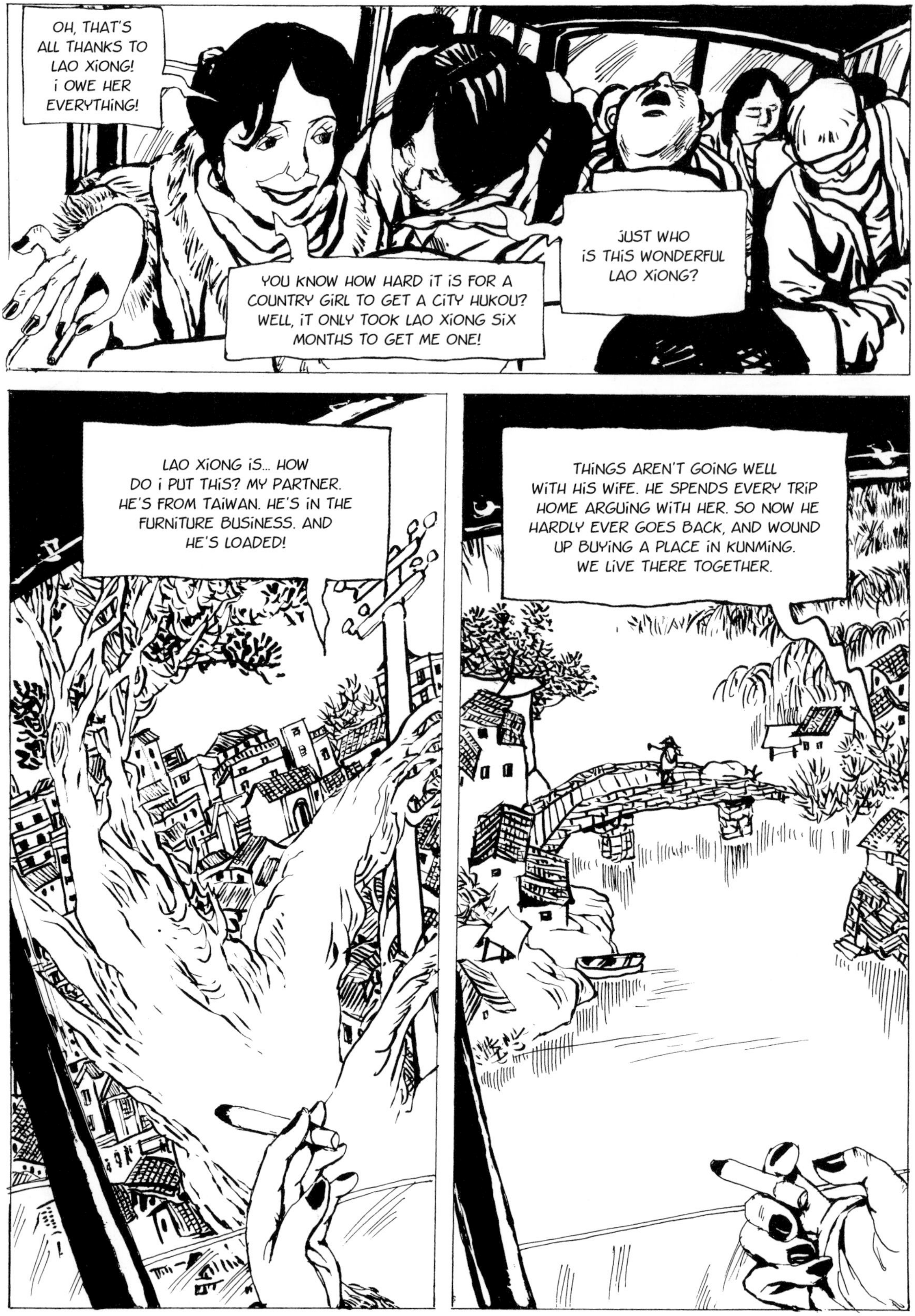
OH, THAT'S ALL THANKS TO LAO XIONG! I OWE HER EVERYTHING!
YOU KNOW HOW HARD IT IS FOR A COUNTRY GIRL TO GET A CITY HUKOU? WELL, IT ONLY TOOK LAO XIONG SIX MONTHS TO GET ME ONE!
JUST WHO IS THIS WONDERFUL LAO XIONG?
LAO XIONG IS... HOW DO I PUT THIS? MY PARTNER. HE'S FROM TAIWAN. HE'S IN THE FURNITURE BUSINESS. AND HE'S LOADED!
THINGS AREN'T GOING WELL WITH HIS WIFE. HE SPENDS EVERY TRIP HOME ARGUING WITH HER. SO NOW HE HARDLY EVER GOES BACK, AND WOUND UP BUYING A PLACE IN KUNMING. WE LIVE THERE TOGETHER.

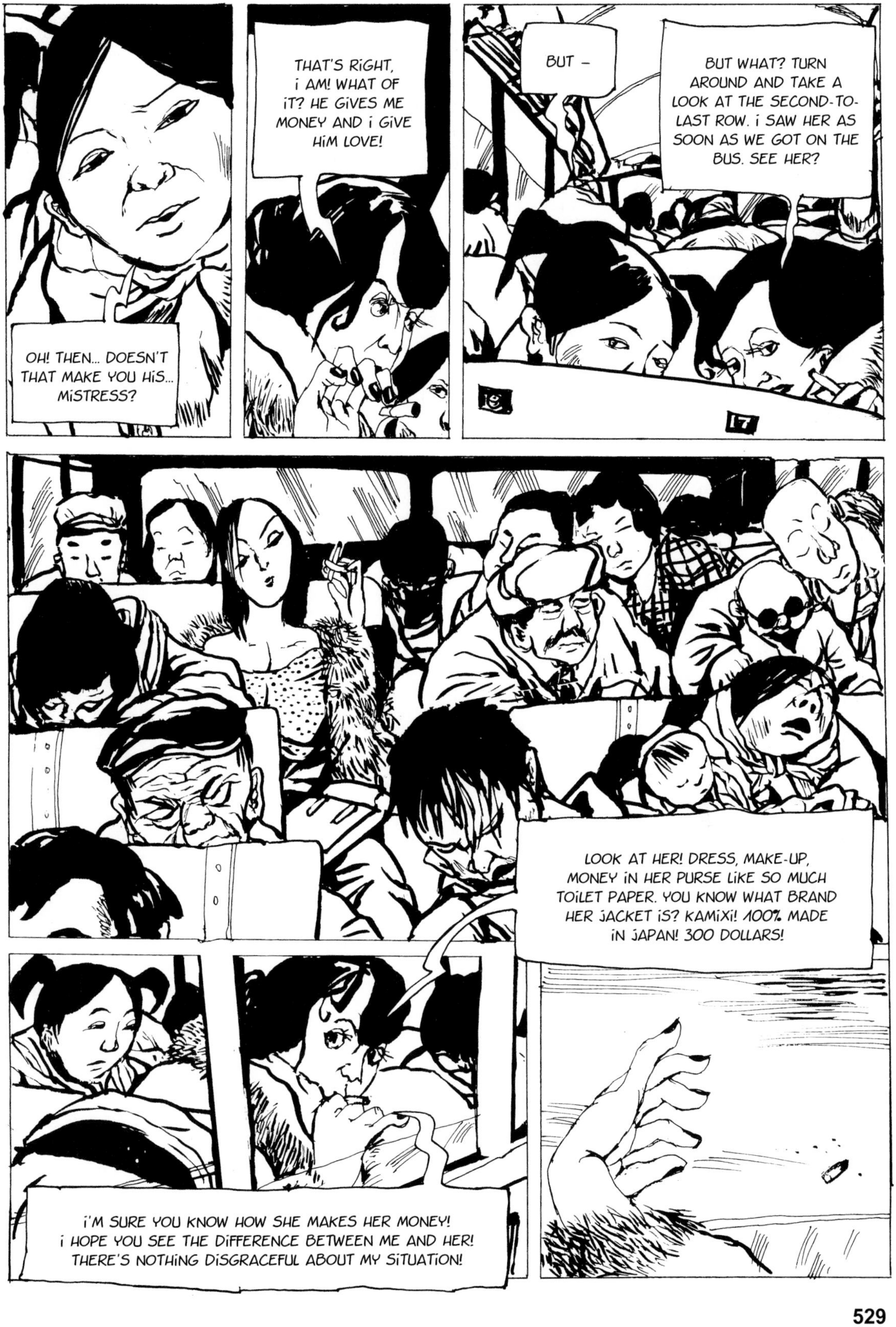
OH! THEN... DOESN'T THAT MAKE YOU HIS... MISTRESS?
THAT'S RIGHT, I AM! WHAT OF IT? HE GIVES ME MONEY AND I GIVE HIM LOVE!
BUT –
BUT WHAT? TURN AROUND AND TAKE A LOOK AT THE SECOND-TO-LAST ROW. I SAW HER AS SOON AS WE GOT ON THE BUS. SEE HER?
18
17
LOOK AT HER! DRESS, MAKE-UP, MONEY IN HER PURSE LIKE SO MUCH TOILET PAPER. YOU KNOW WHAT BRAND HER JACKET IS? KAMIXI! 100% MADE IN JAPAN! 300 DOLLARS!
I'M SURE YOU KNOW HOW SHE MAKES HER MONEY! I HOPE YOU SEE THE DIFFERENCE BETWEEN ME AND HER! THERE'S NOTHING DISGRACEFUL ABOUT MY SITUATION!

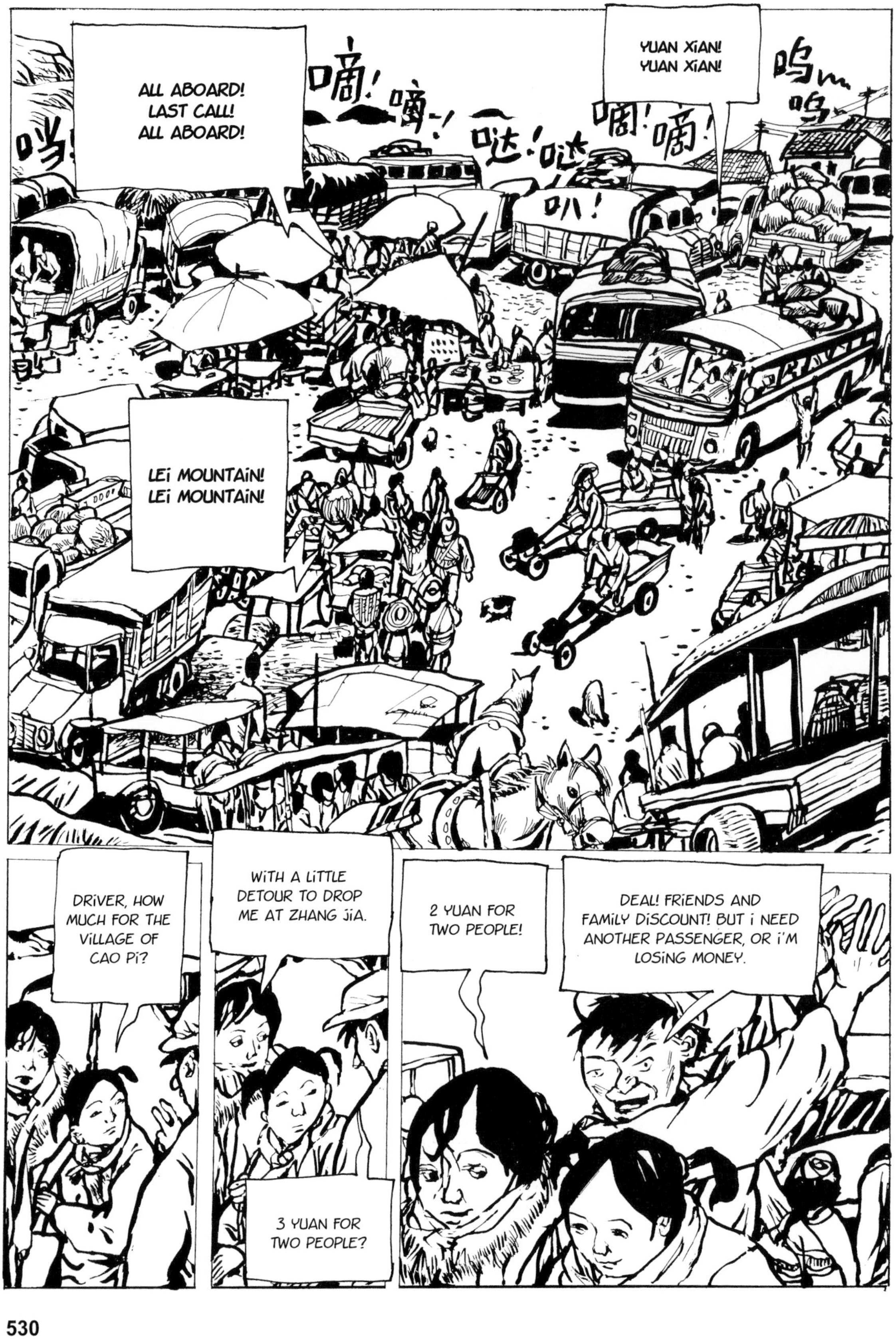
ALL ABOARD!
LAST CALL!
ALL ABOARD!
嘀!
嘀~!
哒!
哒
嘀!
嘀!
YUAN XIAN!
YUAN XIAN!
呜
呜
叭!
LEI MOUNTAIN!
LEI MOUNTAIN!
DRIVER, HOW MUCH FOR THE VILLAGE OF CAO PI?
WITH A LITTLE DETOUR TO DROP ME AT ZHANG JIA.
3 YUAN FOR TWO PEOPLE?
2 YUAN FOR TWO PEOPLE!
DEAL! FRIENDS AND FAMILY DISCOUNT! BUT I NEED ANOTHER PASSENGER, OR I'M LOSING MONEY.

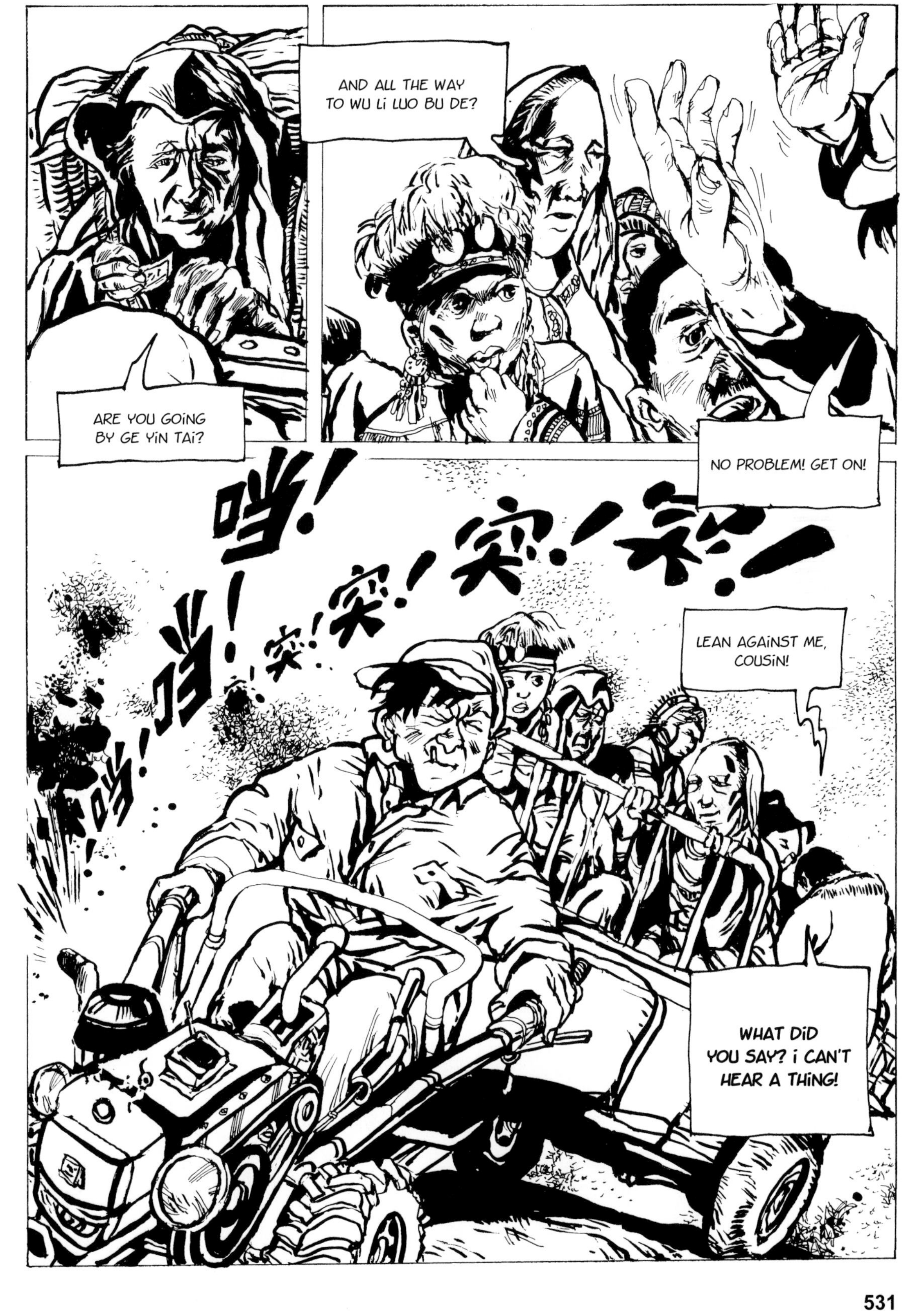
ARE YOU GOING BY GE YIN TAI?
AND ALL THE WAY TO WU LI LUO BU DE?
NO PROBLEM! GET ON!
LEAN AGAINST ME, COUSIN!
WHAT DID YOU SAY? I CAN'T HEAR A THING!

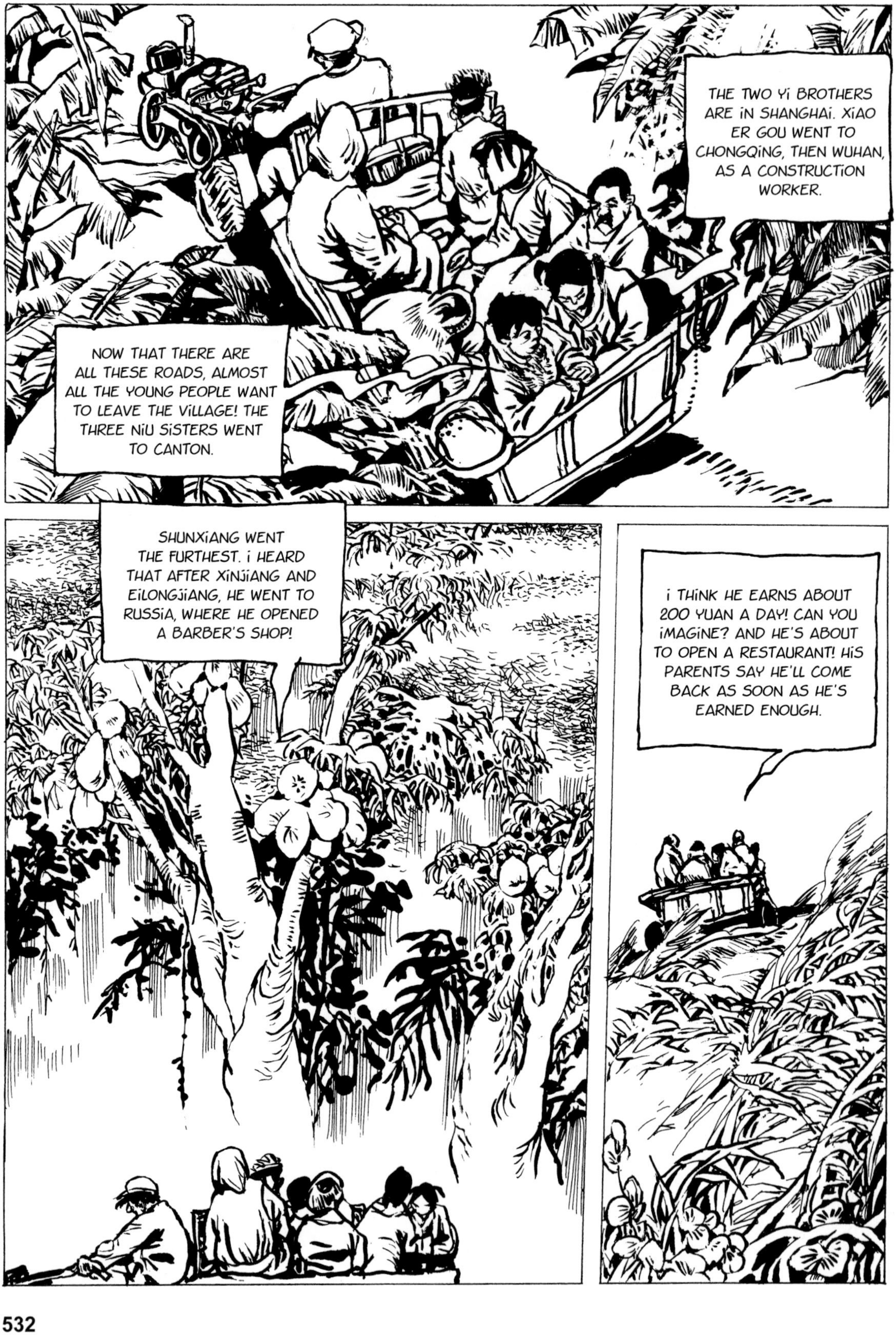
THE TWO YI BROTHERS ARE IN SHANGHAI. XIAO ER GOU WENT TO CHONGQING, THEN WUHAN, AS A CONSTRUCTION WORKER.
NOW THAT THERE ARE ALL THESE ROADS, ALMOST ALL THE YOUNG PEOPLE WANT TO LEAVE THE VILLAGE! THE THREE NIU SISTERS WENT TO CANTON.
SHUNXIANG WENT THE FURTHEST. I HEARD THAT AFTER XINJIANG AND EILONGJIANG, HE WENT TO RUSSIA, WHERE HE OPENED A BARBER'S SHOP!
I THINK HE EARNS ABOUT 200 YUAN A DAY! CAN YOU IMAGINE? AND HE'S ABOUT TO OPEN A RESTAURANT! HIS PARENTS SAY HE'LL COME BACK AS SOON AS HE'S EARNED ENOUGH.

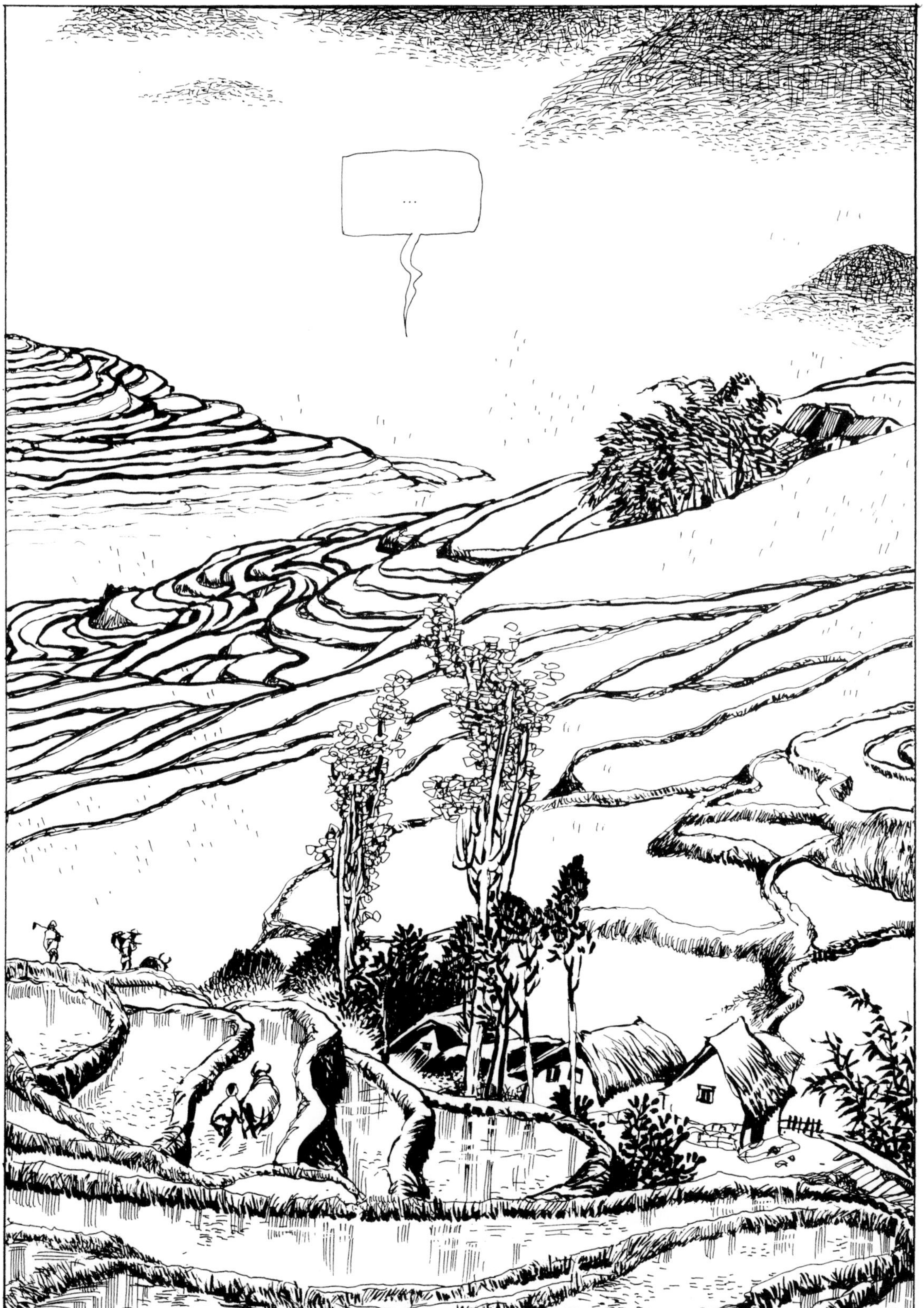
...

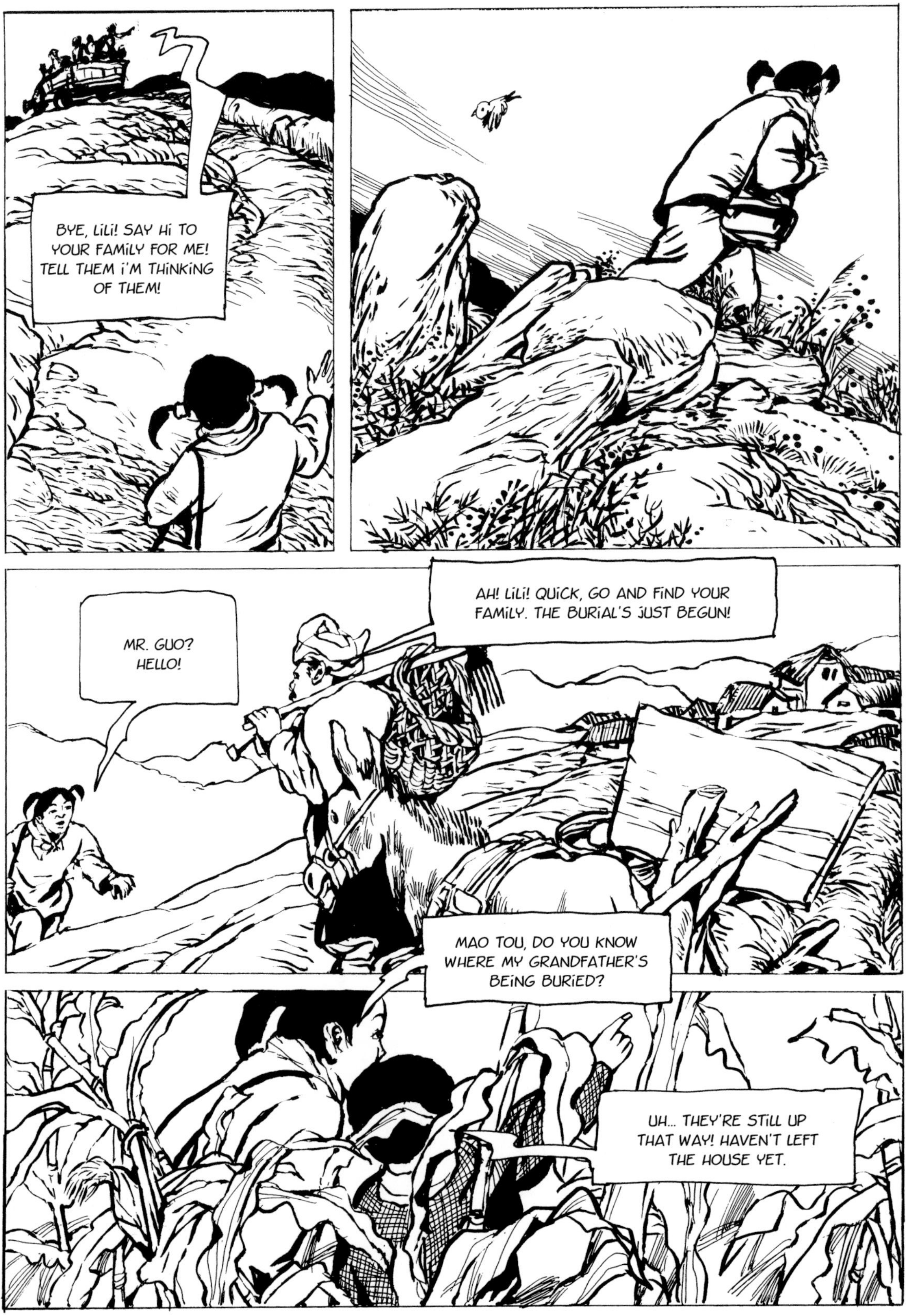
BYE, LILI! SAY HI TO YOUR FAMILY FOR ME! TELL THEM I'M THINKING OF THEM!
MR. GUO? HELLO!
AH! LILI! QUICK, GO AND FIND YOUR FAMILY. THE BURIAL'S JUST BEGUN!
MAO TOU, DO YOU KNOW WHERE MY GRANDFATHER'S BEING BURIED?
UH... THEY'RE STILL UP THAT WAY! HAVEN'T LEFT THE HOUSE YET.

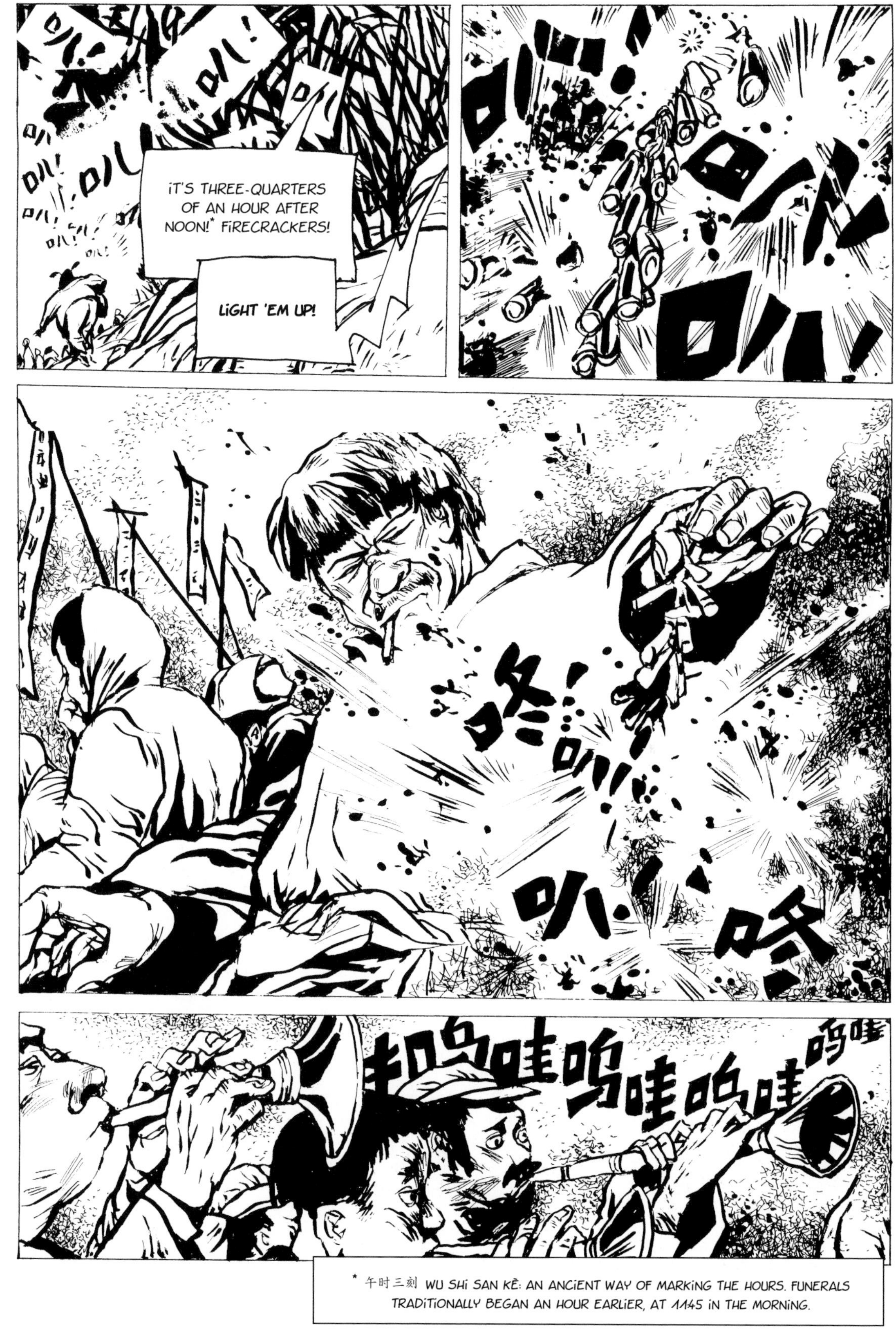
IT'S THREE-QUARTERS OF AN HOUR AFTER NOON!* FIRECRACKERS!
LIGHT 'EM UP!

* 午时三刻 WU SHI SAN KĒ: AN ANCIENT WAY OF MARKING THE HOURS. FUNERALS TRADITIONALLY BEGAN AN HOUR EARLIER, AT 11:45 IN THE MORNING.

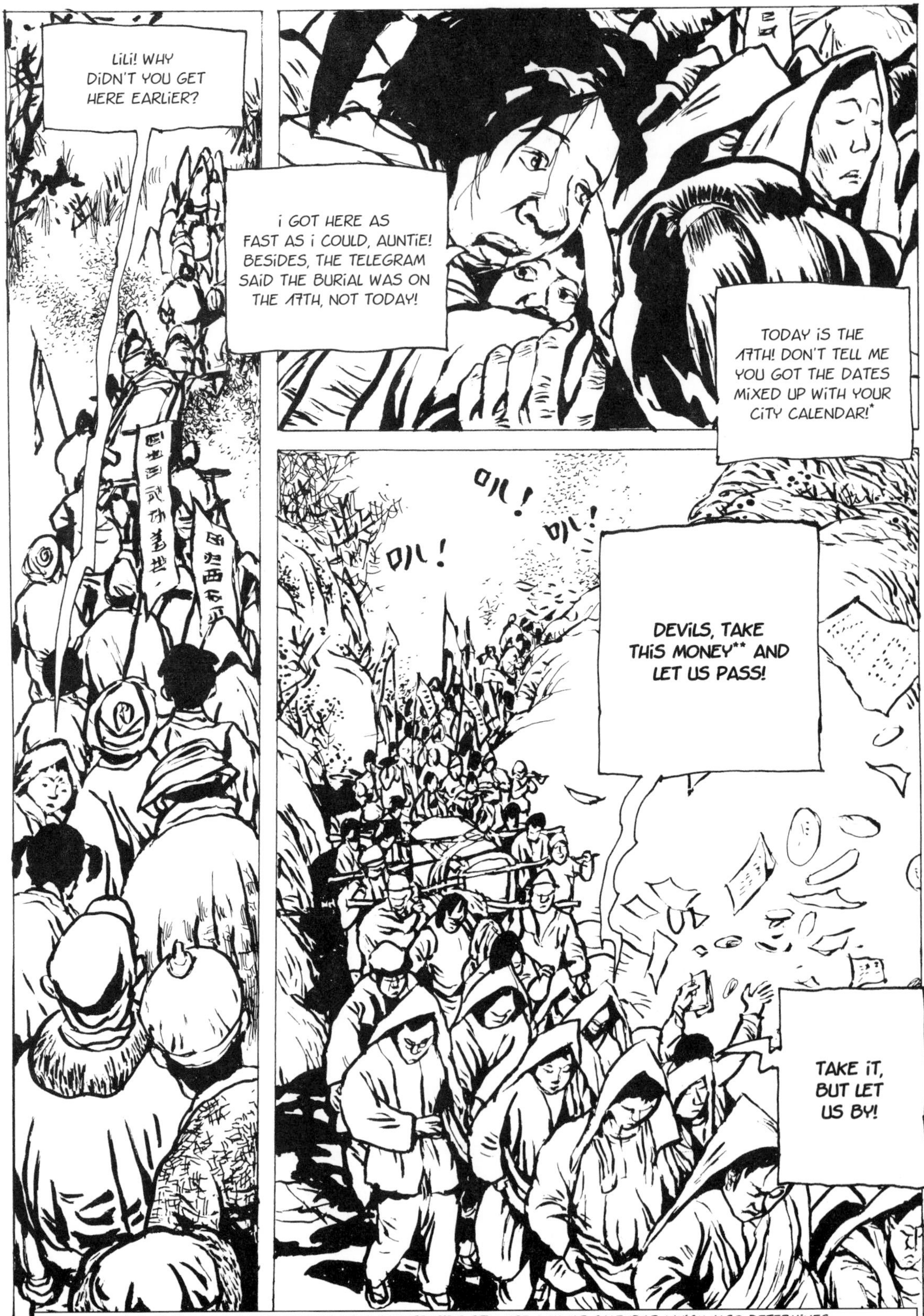
LiLi! WHY DIDN'T YOU GET HERE EARLIER?
i GOT HERE AS FAST AS i COULD, AUNTiE! BESiDES, THE TELEGRAM SAiD THE BURiAL WAS ON THE 17TH, NOT TODAY!
TODAY iS THE 17TH! DON'T TELL ME YOU GOT THE DATES MiXED UP WiTH YOUR CiTY CALENDAR!*
DEViLS, TAKE THiS MONEY** AND LET US PASS!
TAKE iT, BUT LET US BY!

* TO THiS DAY, CHiNESE PEOPLE iN THE COUNTRYSiDE STiLL USE A LUNAR CALENDAR, WHiCH ALSO DETERMiNES THE MAiN HOLiDAYS (NEW YEAR'S, THE HARVEST MOON FESTiVAL, THE LANTERN FESTiVAL, AND THE SPiRiT FESTiVAL).

** "GHOST MONEY", OR "JOSS PAPER", USED FOR BURNT OFFERiNGS AT FUNERALS.

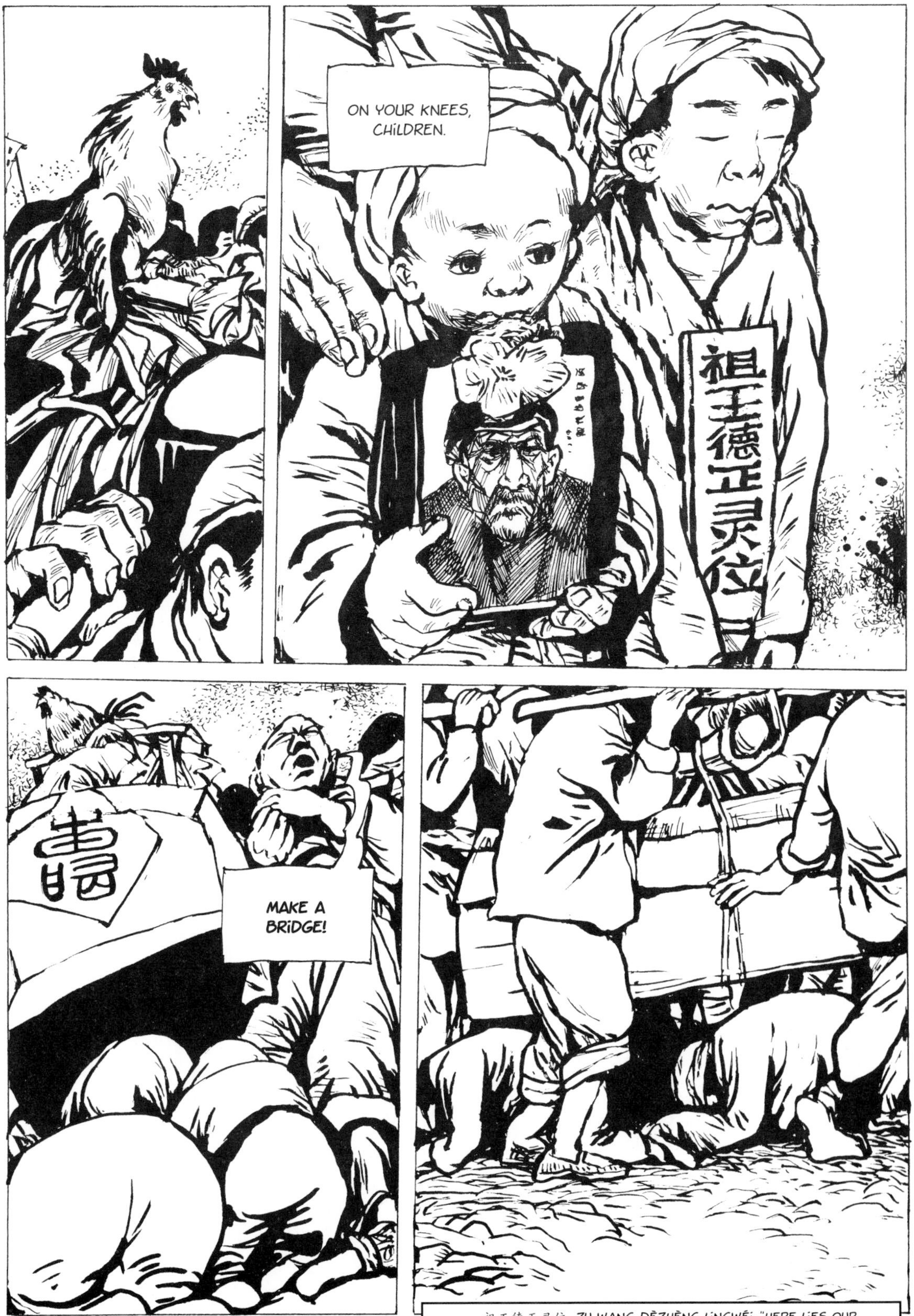
ON YOUR KNEES, CHILDREN.
祖王德正灵位
MAKE A BRIDGE!

祖王德正灵位 ZU WANG DÈZHÈNG LINGWÉI: "HERE LIES OUR ANCESTOR WANG DEZHENG".

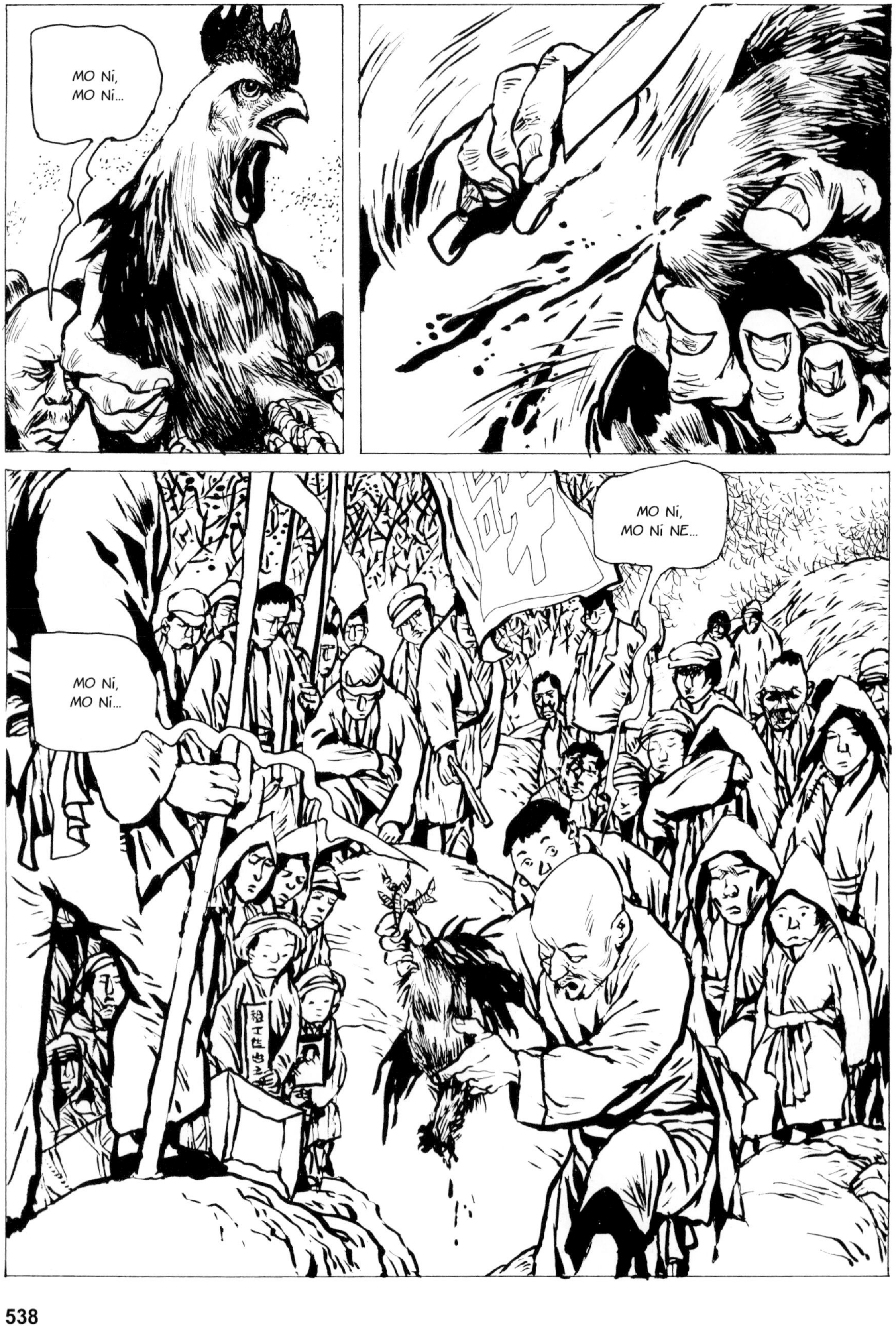
MO Ní, MO Ní...
MO Ní, MO Ní NE...
MO Ní, MO Ní...

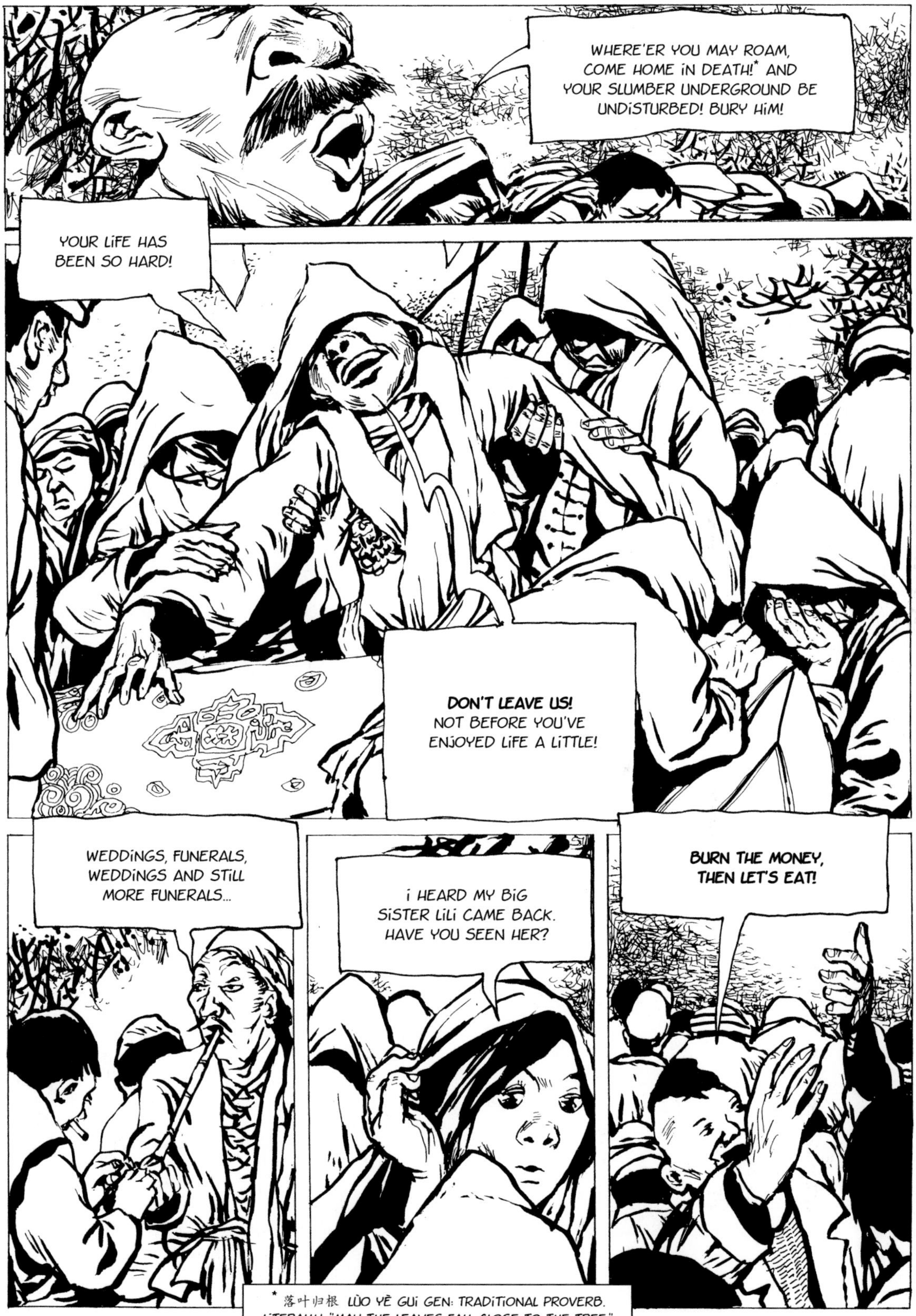
WHERE'ER YOU MAY ROAM, COME HOME IN DEATH!* AND YOUR SLUMBER UNDERGROUND BE UNDISTURBED! BURY HIM!
YOUR LIFE HAS BEEN SO HARD!
DON'T LEAVE US! NOT BEFORE YOU'VE ENJOYED LIFE A LITTLE!
WEDDINGS, FUNERALS, WEDDINGS AND STILL MORE FUNERALS...
I HEARD MY BIG SISTER LILI CAME BACK. HAVE YOU SEEN HER?
BURN THE MONEY, THEN LET'S EAT!

* 落叶归根 LÙO YÈ GUI GEN: TRADITIONAL PROVERB. LITERALLY, "MAY THE LEAVES FALL CLOSE TO THE TREE."

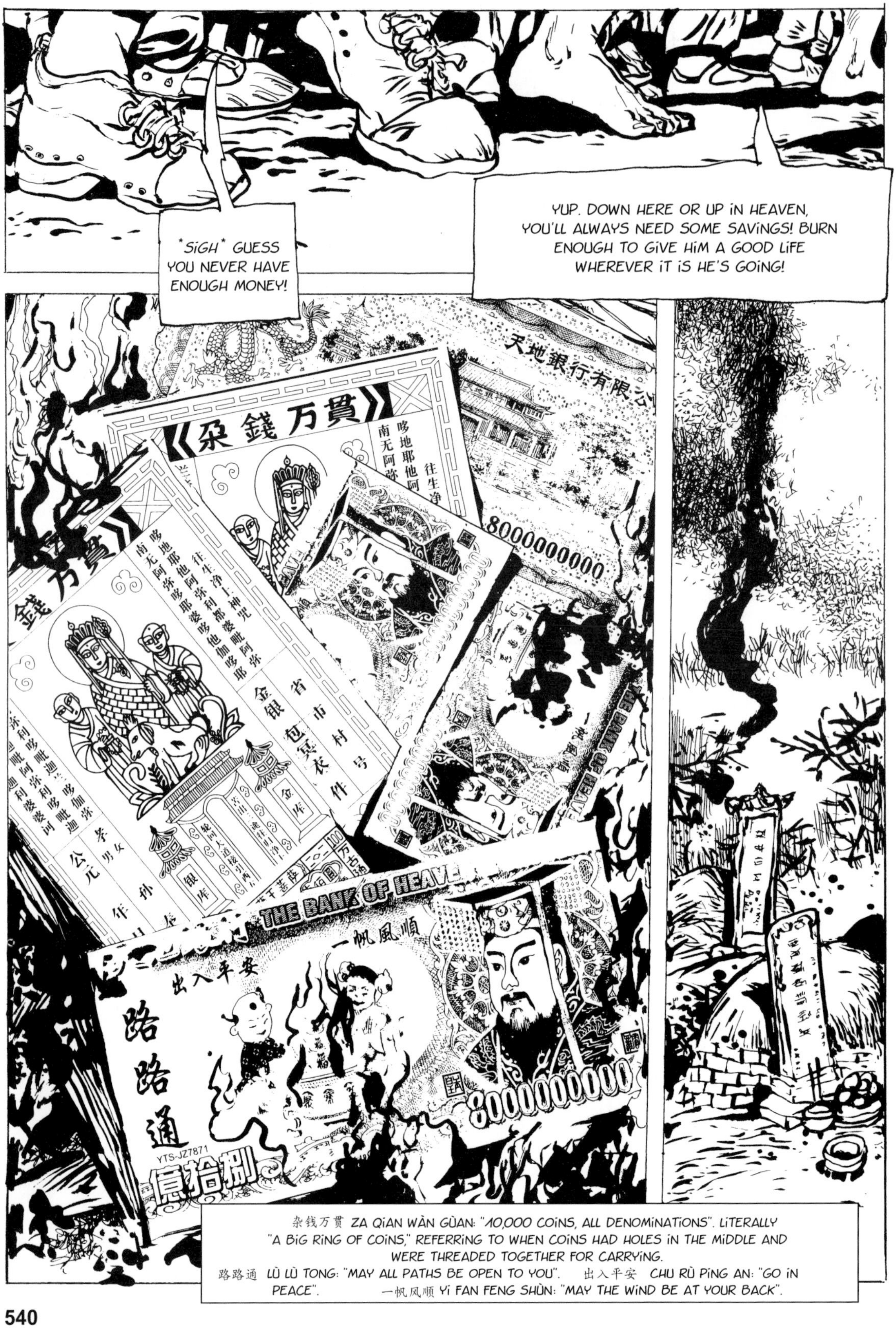
SIGH GUESS YOU NEVER HAVE ENOUGH MONEY!
YUP. DOWN HERE OR UP IN HEAVEN, YOU'LL ALWAYS NEED SOME SAVINGS! BURN ENOUGH TO GIVE HIM A GOOD LIFE WHEREVER IT IS HE'S GOING!
杂钱万贯 ZA QIAN WÀN GÙAN: "10,000 COINS, ALL DENOMINATIONS". LITERALLY "A BIG RING OF COINS," REFERRING TO WHEN COINS HAD HOLES IN THE MIDDLE AND WERE THREADED TOGETHER FOR CARRYING.
路路通 LÙ LÙ TONG: "MAY ALL PATHS BE OPEN TO YOU". 出入平安 CHU RÙ PING AN: "GO IN PEACE". 一帆风顺 YI FAN FENG SHÙN: "MAY THE WIND BE AT YOUR BACK".

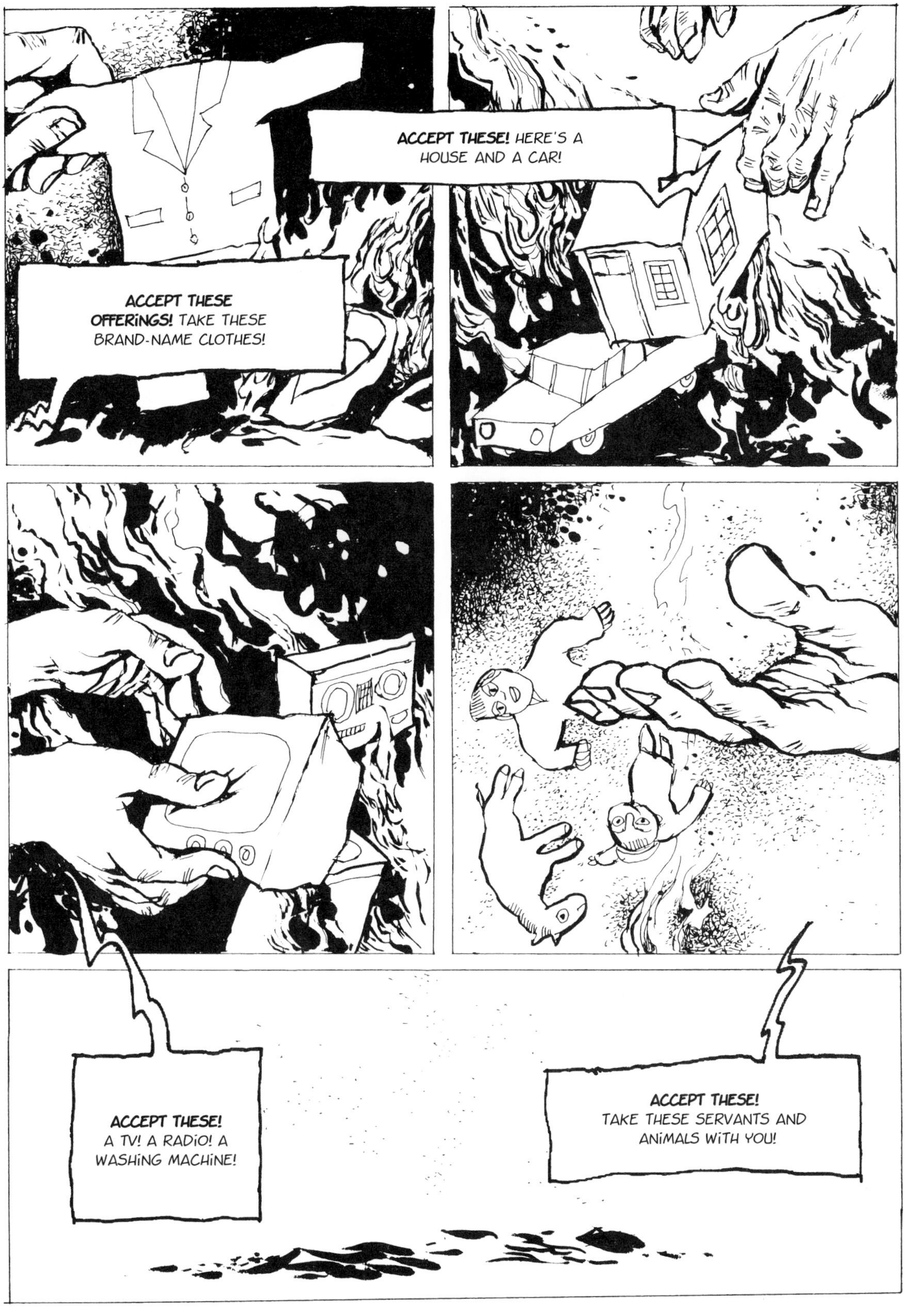

ACCEPT THESE! HERE'S A HOUSE AND A CAR!
ACCEPT THESE OFFERINGS! TAKE THESE BRAND-NAME CLOTHES!
ACCEPT THESE! A TV! A RADIO! A WASHING MACHINE!
ACCEPT THESE! TAKE THESE SERVANTS AND ANIMALS WITH YOU!

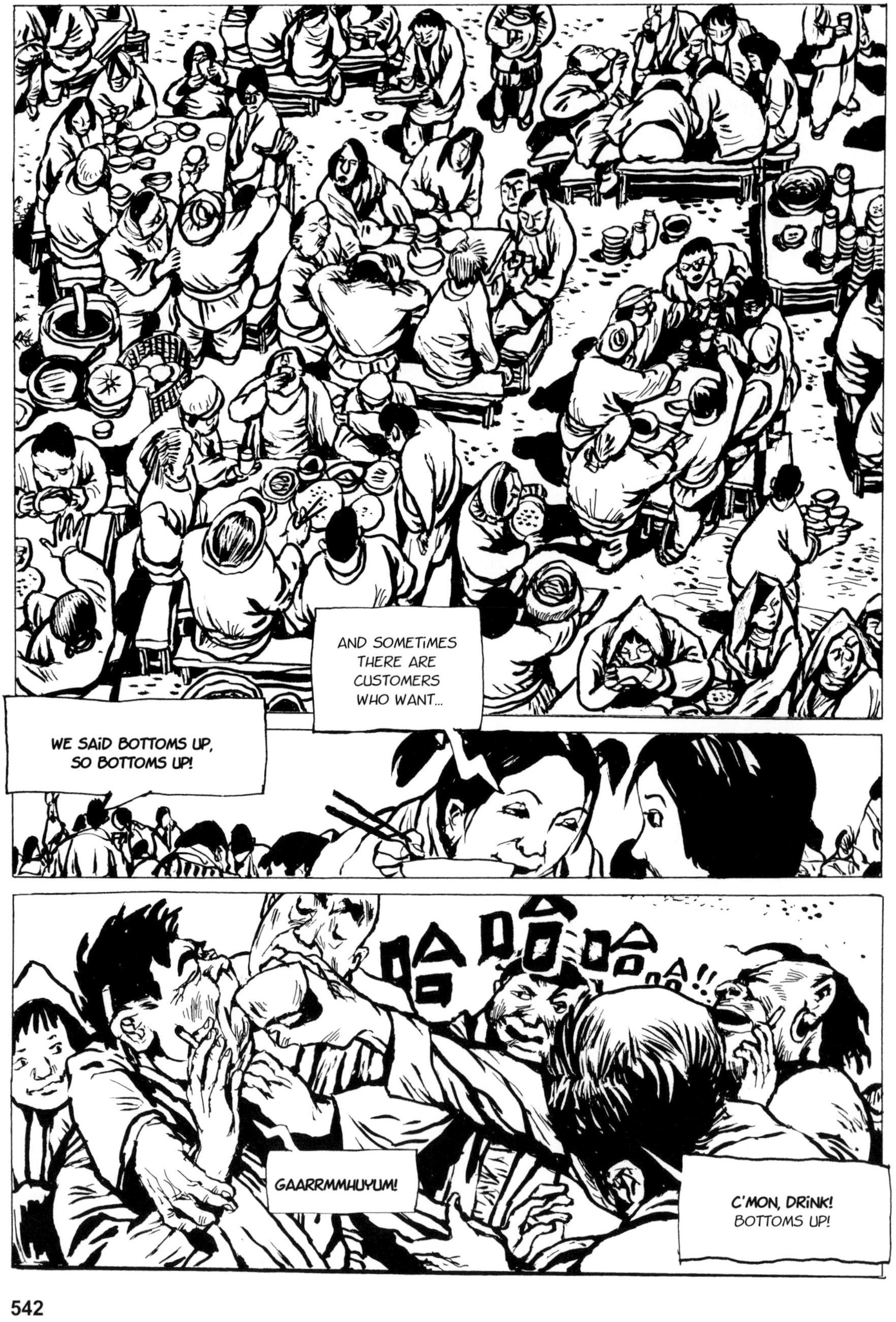
AND SOMETIMES THERE ARE CUSTOMERS WHO WANT...
WE SAID BOTTOMS UP, SO BOTTOMS UP!
GAARRMMHUYUM!
C'MON, DRINK! BOTTOMS UP!

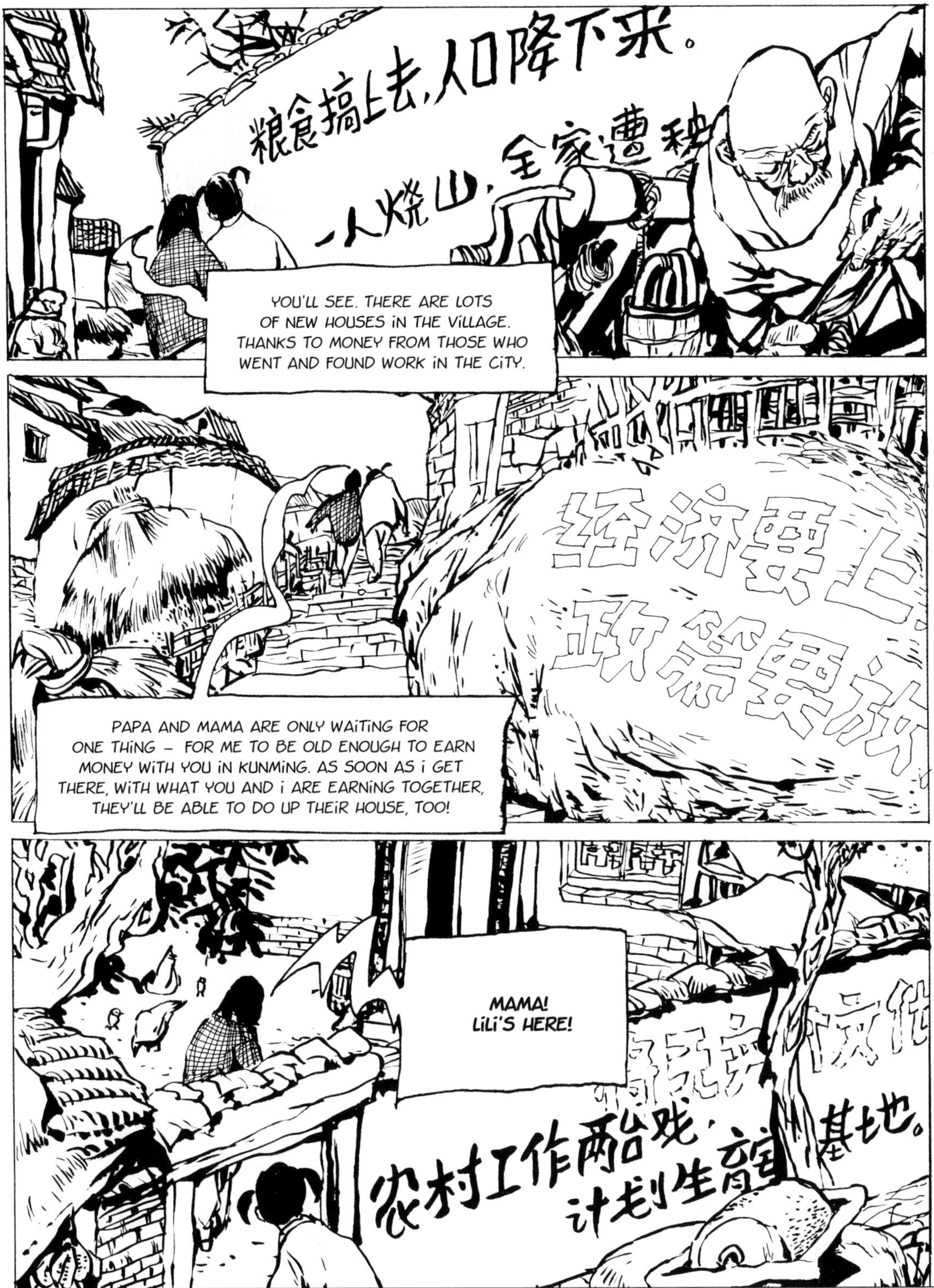
粮食搞上去,人口降下来。
一人烧山,全家遭秧
YOU'LL SEE. THERE ARE LOTS OF NEW HOUSES IN THE VILLAGE. THANKS TO MONEY FROM THOSE WHO WENT AND FOUND WORK IN THE CITY.
经济要上
政策要放
PAPA AND MAMA ARE ONLY WAITING FOR ONE THING – FOR ME TO BE OLD ENOUGH TO EARN MONEY WITH YOU IN KUNMING. AS SOON AS I GET THERE, WITH WHAT YOU AND I ARE EARNING TOGETHER, THEY'LL BE ABLE TO DO UP THEIR HOUSE, TOO!
MAMA! LILI'S HERE!

粮食搞上去,人口降下来 LIANG SHI GAO SHÀNG QÙ, RÉNKOU JIANG XIA LAI: "LET US GROW MORE GRAIN AND MAKE FEWER CHILDREN!"
一人烧山,全家遭秧 YI RÉN SHAO SAN, QUAN JIA ZAOYANG: "IF ONE PERSON BURNS THE MOUNTAIN DOWN, THE WHOLE FAMILY SUFFERS."
经济要上, 政策要放 JINGJI YÀO SHÀNG, ZHÈNGCÈ YÀO FÀNG: "LET US MAKE POLICY MORE SUPPLE TO IMPROVE THE ECONOMY!"

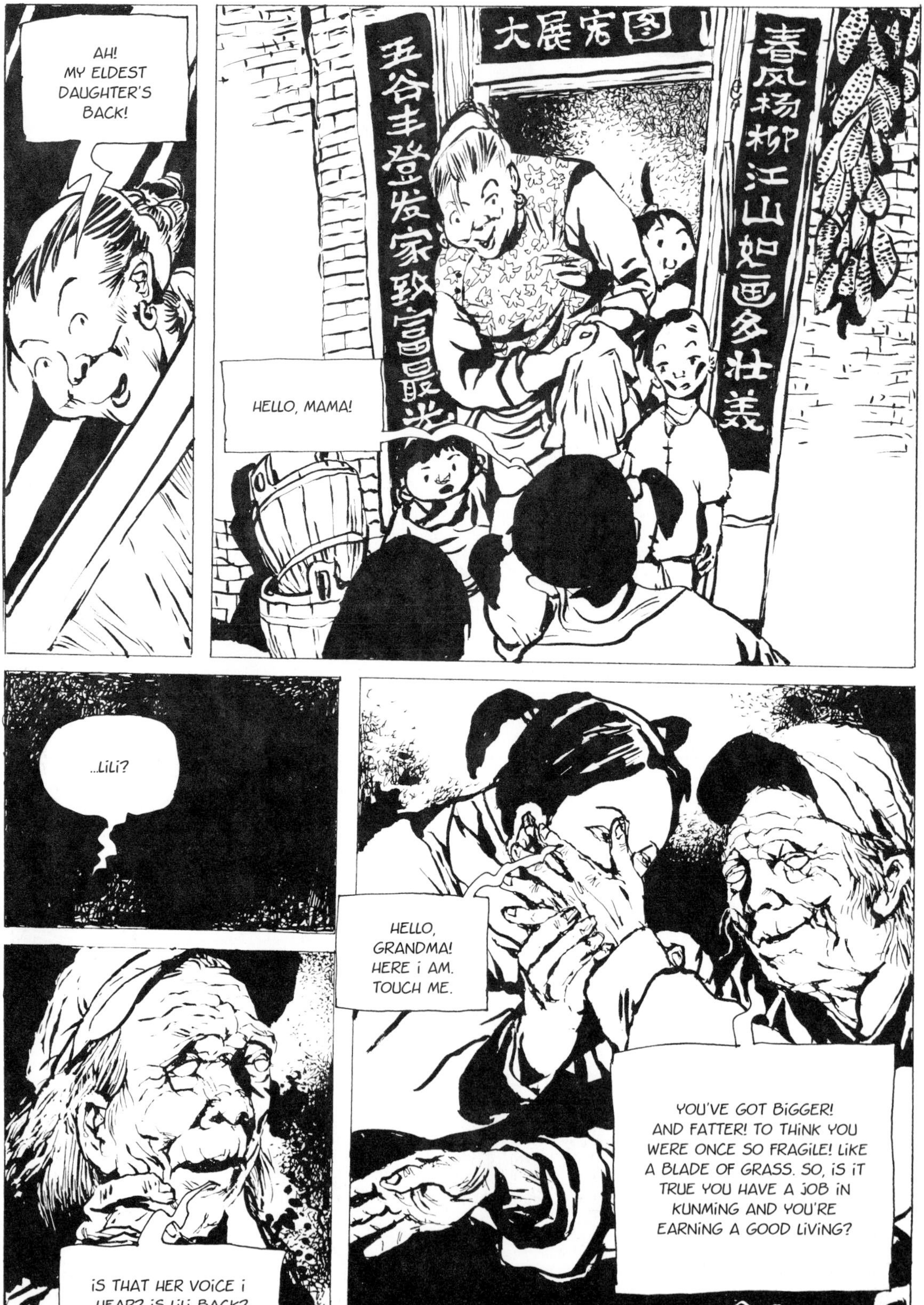
AH! MY ELDEST DAUGHTER'S BACK!
大展宏图
春风杨柳江山如画多壮美
五谷丰登发家致富最
HELLO, MAMA!
...LiLi?
HELLO, GRANDMA! HERE i AM. TOUCH ME.
iS THAT HER VOiCE i HEAR? iS LiLi BACK?
YOU'VE GOT BiGGER! AND FATTER! TO THiNK YOU WERE ONCE SO FRAGiLE! LiKE A BLADE OF GRASS. SO, iS iT TRUE YOU HAVE A JOB iN KUNMiNG AND YOU'RE EARNiNG A GOOD LiViNG?

经济要上， 政策要放 CHUN FENG YANG LiU JiANG SHAN RU HÙA DUO ZHAANG MEi: "A SPRiNG BREEZE STiRS THE WiLLOW, THE LANDSCAPE iS PRETTY AS A PiCTURE. EVERYTHiNG iS iN BOUNTiFUL BLOOM." A TYPiCAL EXAMPLE OF THE BANNERS PUT UP ON DOORWAYS AT NEW YEAR'S.

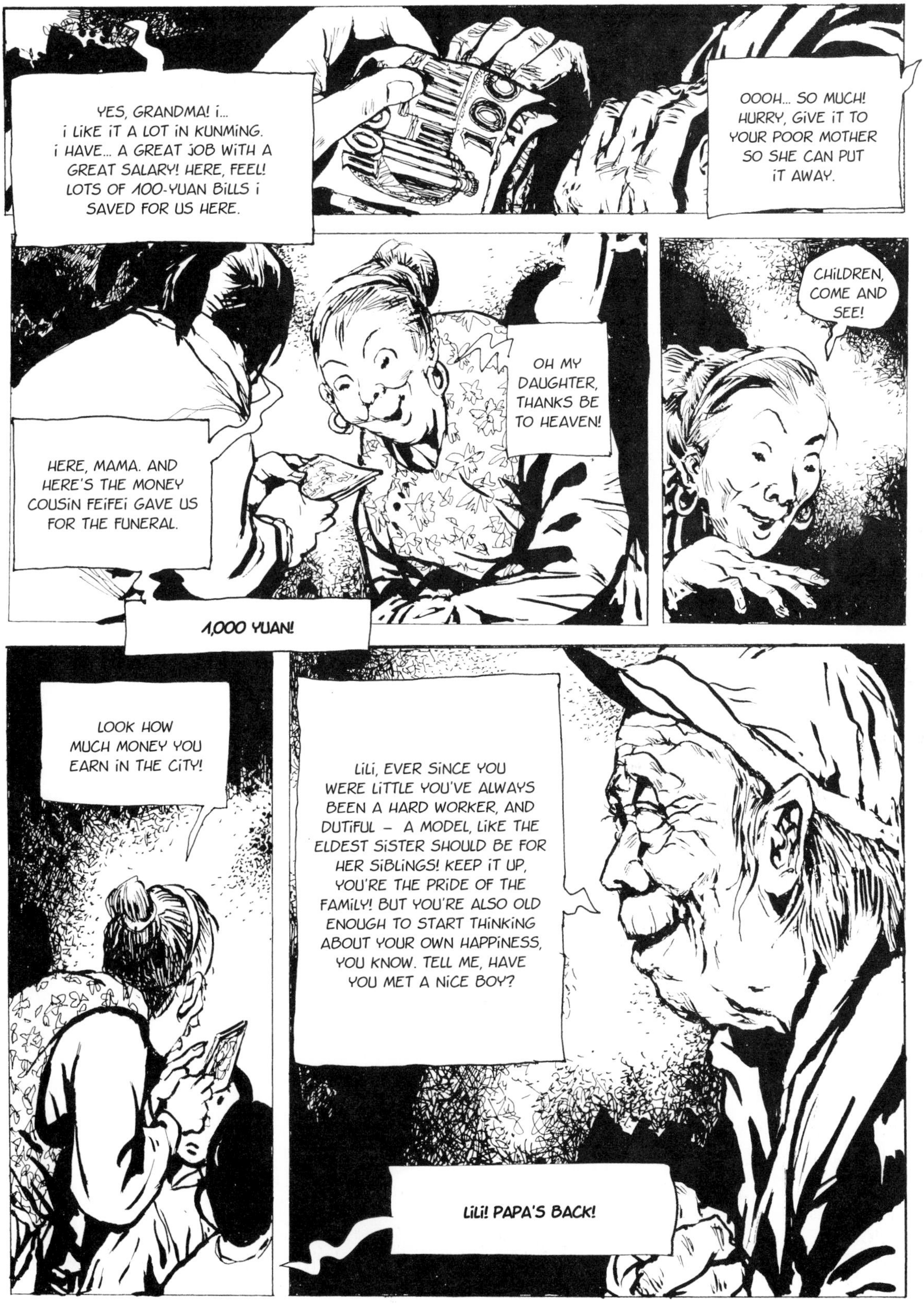
YES, GRANDMA! I... I LIKE IT A LOT IN KUNMING. I HAVE... A GREAT JOB WITH A GREAT SALARY! HERE, FEEL! LOTS OF 100-YUAN BILLS I SAVED FOR US HERE.
OOOH... SO MUCH! HURRY, GIVE IT TO YOUR POOR MOTHER SO SHE CAN PUT IT AWAY.
HERE, MAMA. AND HERE'S THE MONEY COUSIN FEIFEI GAVE US FOR THE FUNERAL.
OH MY DAUGHTER, THANKS BE TO HEAVEN!
1,000 YUAN!
CHILDREN, COME AND SEE!
LOOK HOW MUCH MONEY YOU EARN IN THE CITY!
LILI, EVER SINCE YOU WERE LITTLE YOU'VE ALWAYS BEEN A HARD WORKER, AND DUTIFUL – A MODEL, LIKE THE ELDEST SISTER SHOULD BE FOR HER SIBLINGS! KEEP IT UP, YOU'RE THE PRIDE OF THE FAMILY! BUT YOU'RE ALSO OLD ENOUGH TO START THINKING ABOUT YOUR OWN HAPPINESS, YOU KNOW. TELL ME, HAVE YOU MET A NICE BOY?
LILI! PAPA'S BACK!

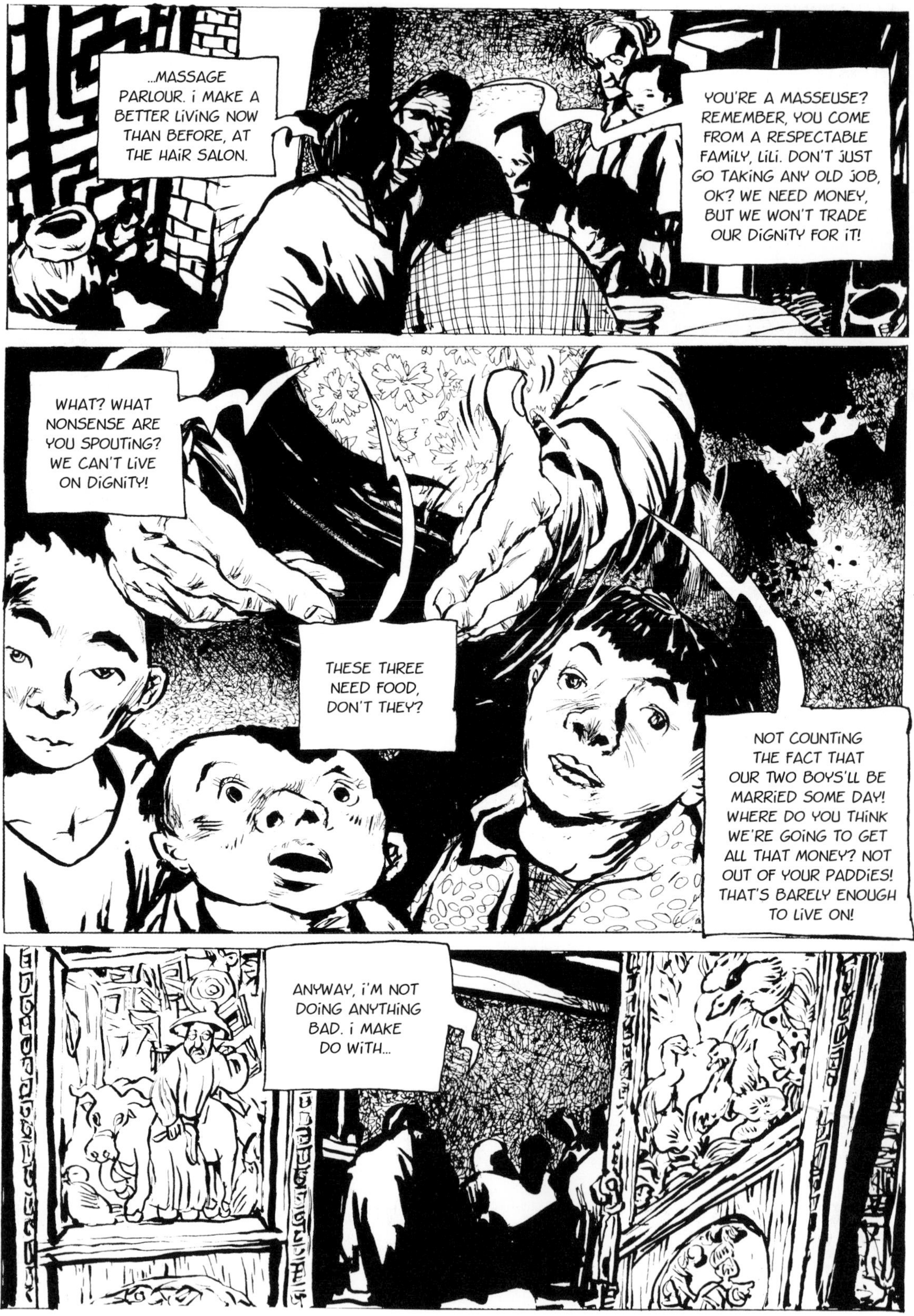
...MASSAGE PARLOUR. I MAKE A BETTER LIVING NOW THAN BEFORE, AT THE HAIR SALON.
YOU'RE A MASSEUSE? REMEMBER, YOU COME FROM A RESPECTABLE FAMILY, LILI. DON'T JUST GO TAKING ANY OLD JOB, OK? WE NEED MONEY, BUT WE WON'T TRADE OUR DIGNITY FOR IT!
WHAT? WHAT NONSENSE ARE YOU SPOUTING? WE CAN'T LIVE ON DIGNITY!
THESE THREE NEED FOOD, DON'T THEY?
NOT COUNTING THE FACT THAT OUR TWO BOYS'LL BE MARRIED SOME DAY! WHERE DO YOU THINK WE'RE GOING TO GET ALL THAT MONEY? NOT OUT OF YOUR PADDIES! THAT'S BARELY ENOUGH TO LIVE ON!
ANYWAY, I'M NOT DOING ANYTHING BAD. I MAKE DO WITH...

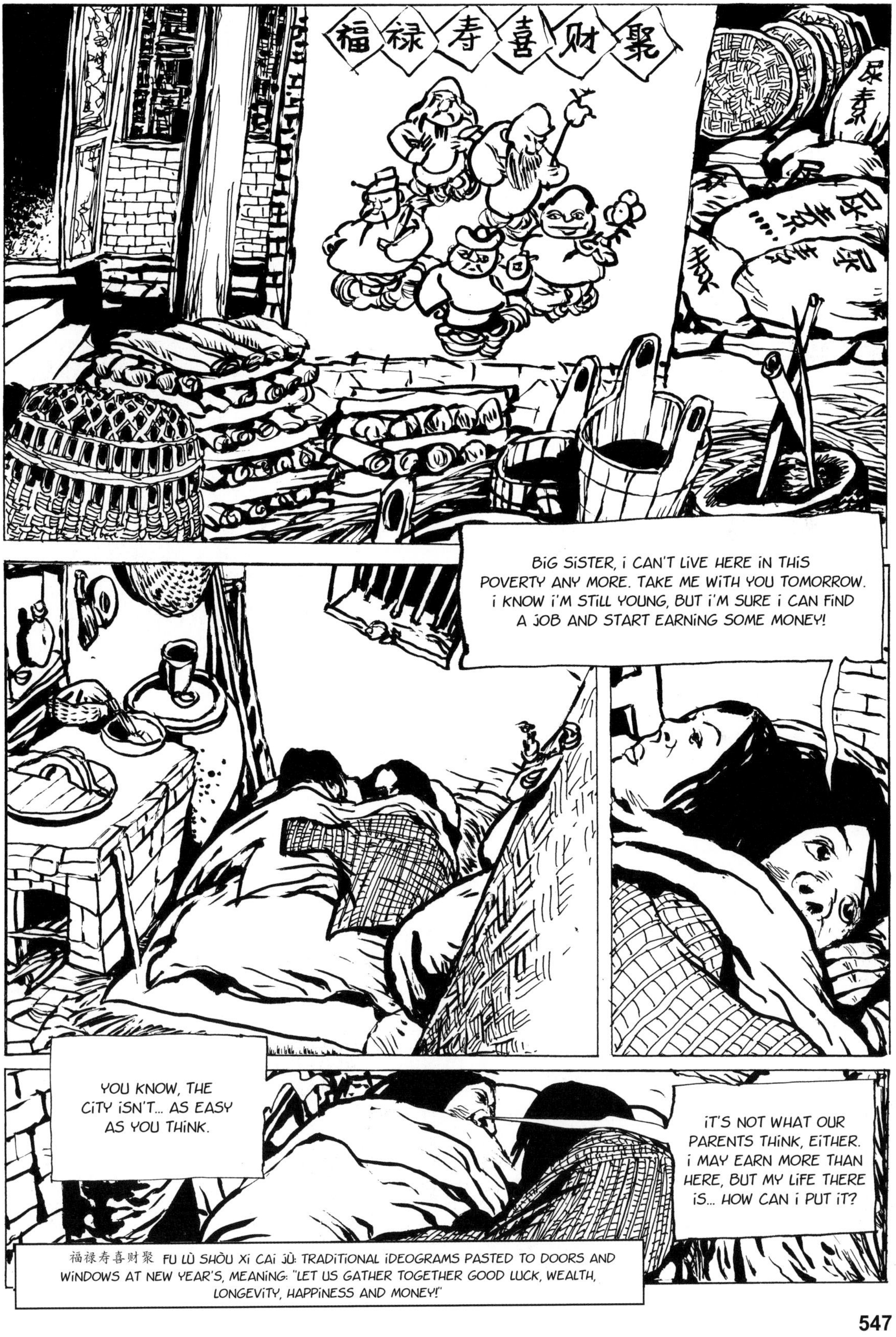
福禄寿喜财聚
尿素
BIG SISTER, I CAN'T LIVE HERE IN THIS POVERTY ANY MORE. TAKE ME WITH YOU TOMORROW. I KNOW I'M STILL YOUNG, BUT I'M SURE I CAN FIND A JOB AND START EARNING SOME MONEY!
YOU KNOW, THE CITY ISN'T... AS EASY AS YOU THINK.
IT'S NOT WHAT OUR PARENTS THINK, EITHER. I MAY EARN MORE THAN HERE, BUT MY LIFE THERE IS... HOW CAN I PUT IT?

福禄寿喜财聚 FU LÙ SHÒU XI CAI JÙ: TRADITIONAL IDEOGRAMS PASTED TO DOORS AND WINDOWS AT NEW YEAR'S, MEANING: "LET US GATHER TOGETHER GOOD LUCK, WEALTH, LONGEVITY, HAPPINESS AND MONEY!"

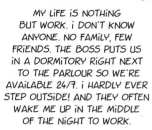

MY LIFE iS NOTHiNG BUT WORK. i DON'T KNOW ANYONE. NO FAMiLY, FEW FRiENDS. THE BOSS PUTS US iN A DORMiTORY RiGHT NEXT TO THE PARLOUR SO WE'RE AVAiLABLE 24/7. i HARDLY EVER STEP OUTSiDE! AND THEY OFTEN WAKE ME UP iN THE MiDDLE OF THE NiGHT TO WORK.

ALL THAT FOR A PiTTANCE.

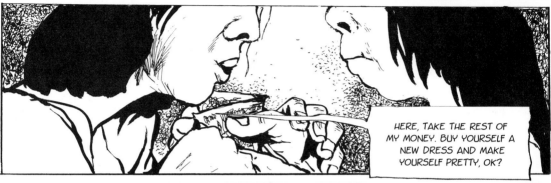

HERE, TAKE THE REST OF MY MONEY. BUY YOURSELF A NEW DRESS AND MAKE YOURSELF PRETTY, OK?

BUT DON'T THiNK ABOUT FOLLOWiNG ME TOMORROW MORNiNG. FiNiSH MiDDLE SCHOOL FiRST, AND THEN WE'LL SEE.

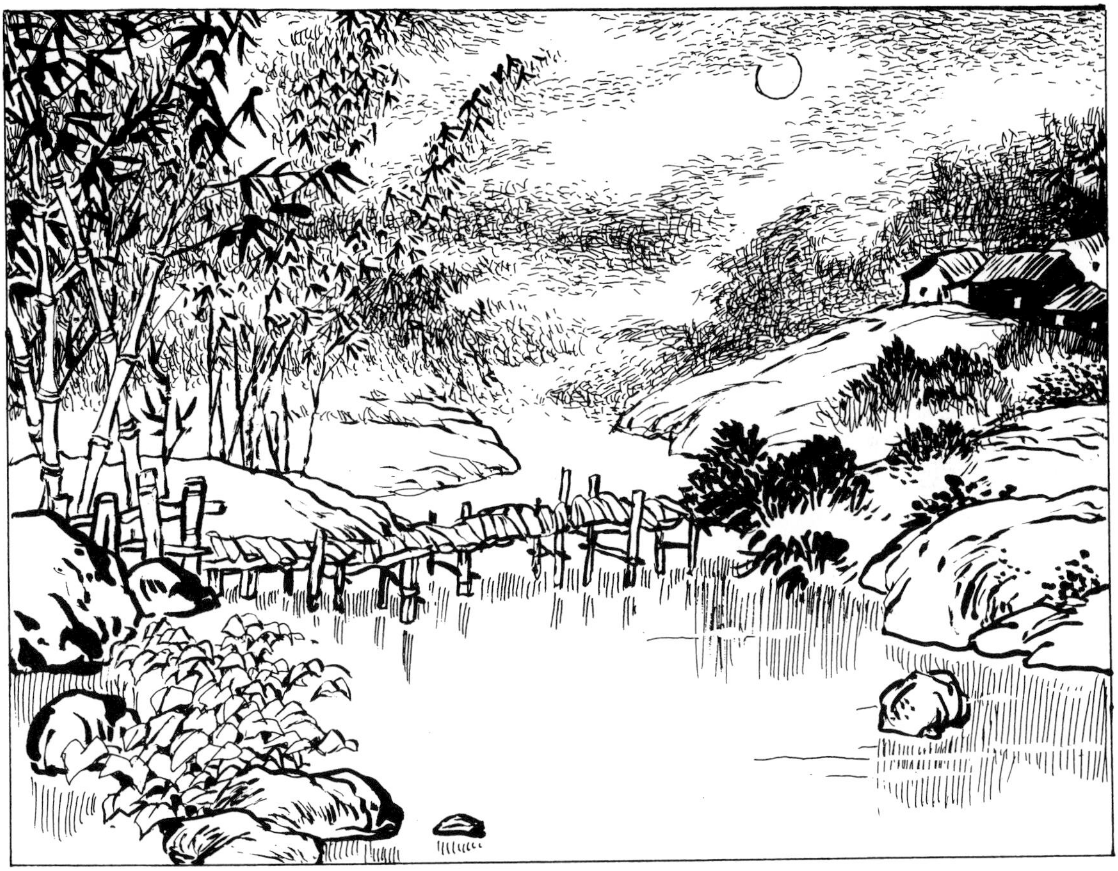

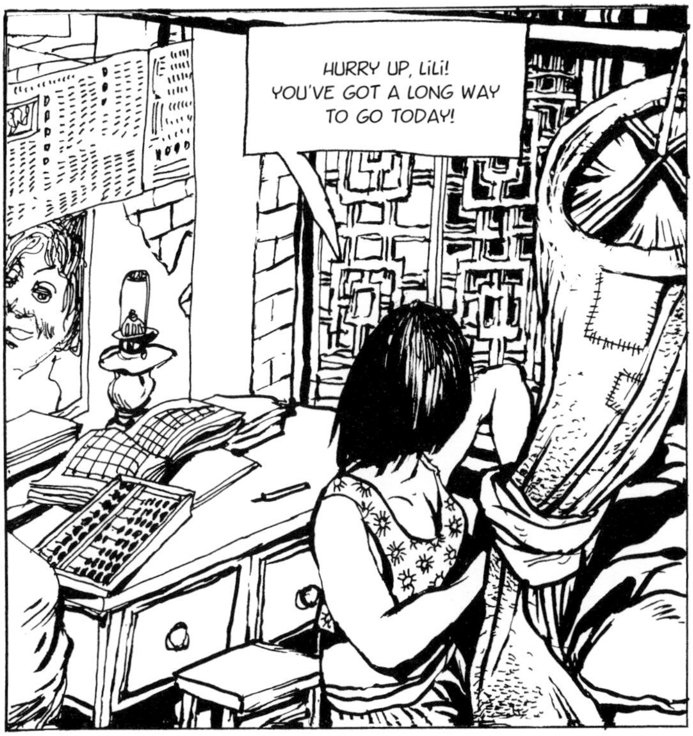
HURRY UP, LILI!
YOU'VE GOT A LONG WAY
TO GO TODAY!

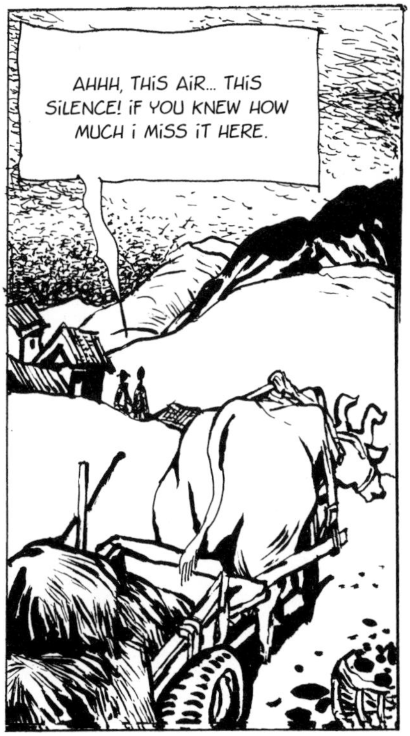
AHHH, THIS AIR... THIS
SILENCE! IF YOU KNEW HOW
MUCH I MISS IT HERE.

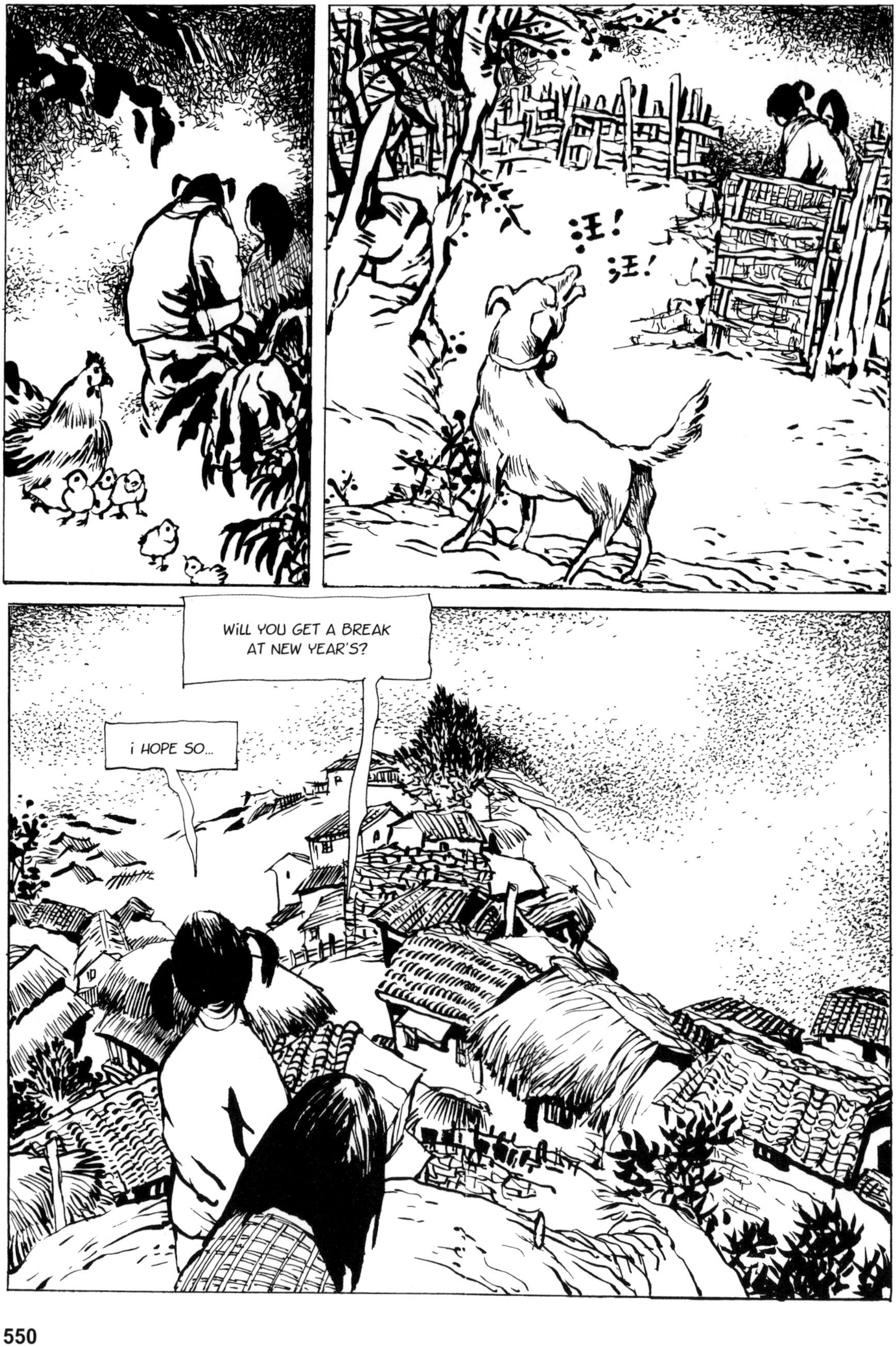
汪！
汪！
WiLL YOU GET A BREAK AT NEW YEAR'S?
i HOPE SO...

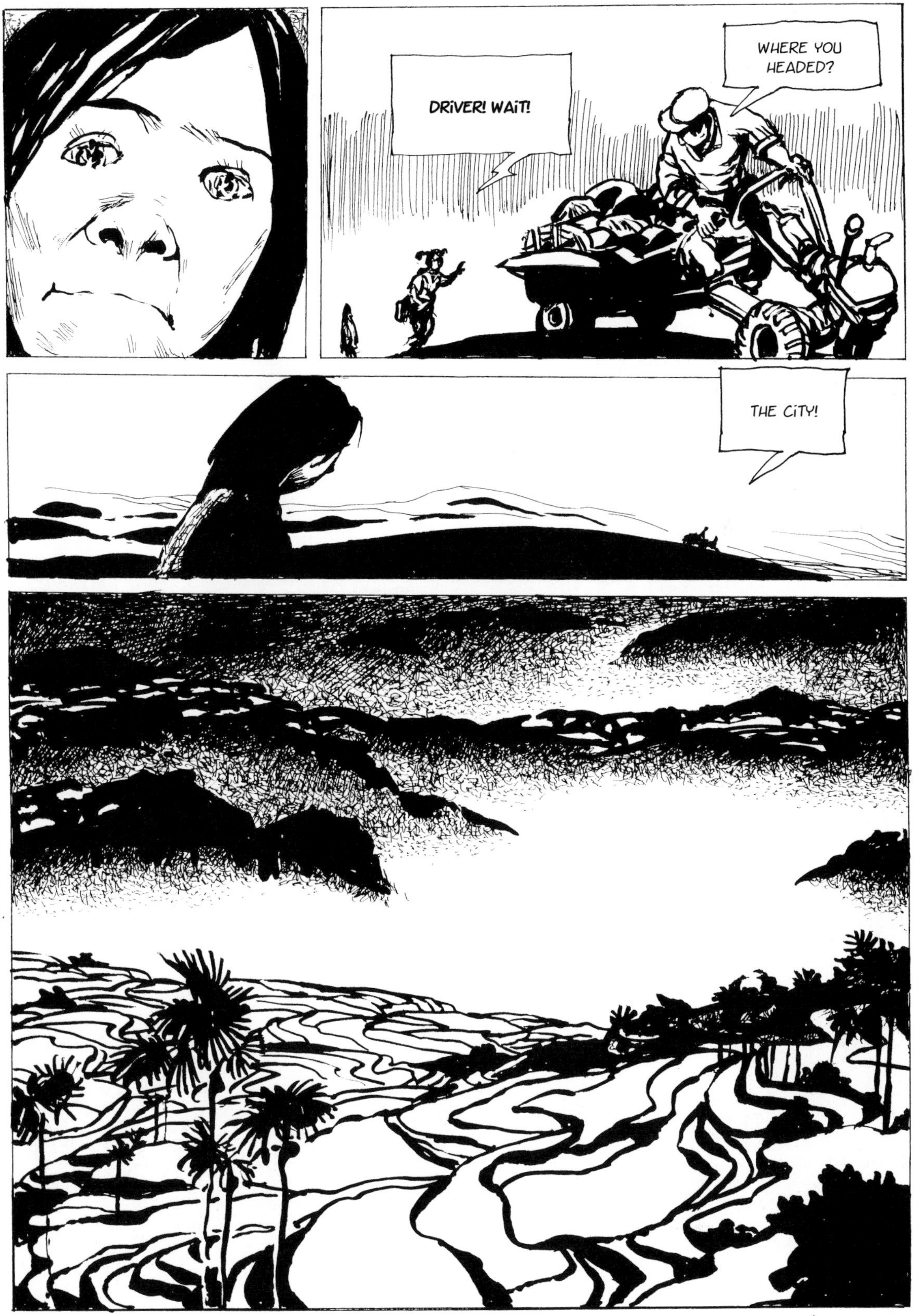
DRIVER! WAIT!
WHERE YOU HEADED?
THE CITY!

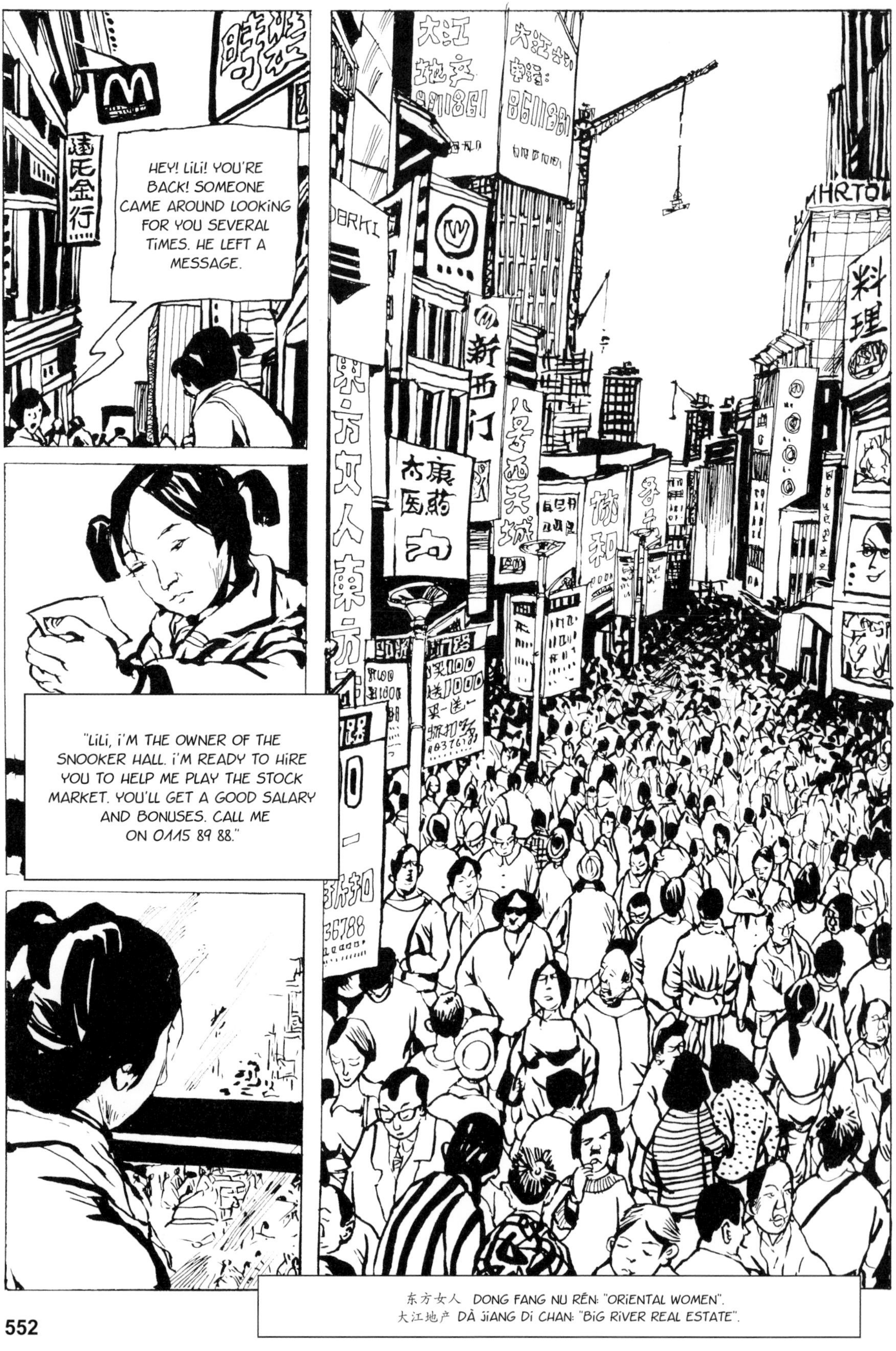
HEY! LiLi! YOU'RE BACK! SOMEONE CAME AROUND LOOKiNG FOR YOU SEVERAL TiMES. HE LEFT A MESSAGE.
"LiLi, i'M THE OWNER OF THE SNOOKER HALL. i'M READY TO HiRE YOU TO HELP ME PLAY THE STOCK MARKET. YOU'LL GET A GOOD SALARY AND BONUSES. CALL ME ON 0115 89 88."

东方女人 DONG FANG NU RÉN: "ORiENTAL WOMEN".
大江地产 DÀ JiANG Di CHAN: "BiG RiVER REAL ESTATE".

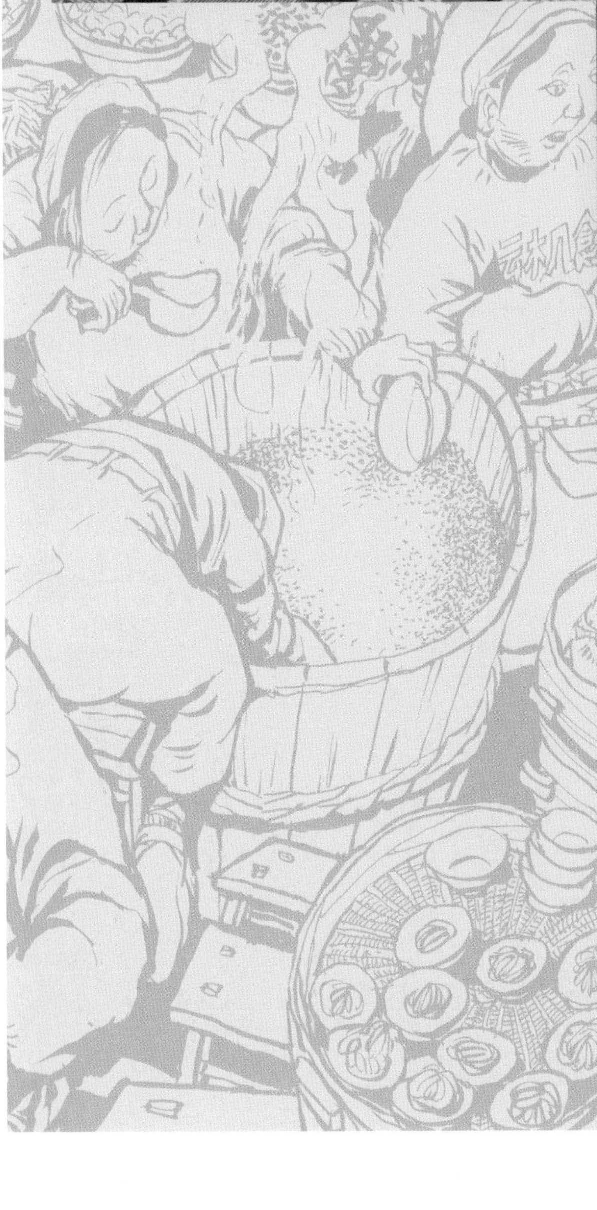

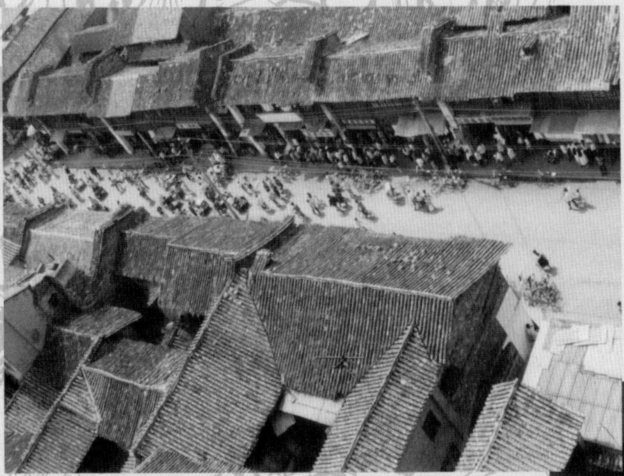

CHAPTER 8
The Character "Chai"

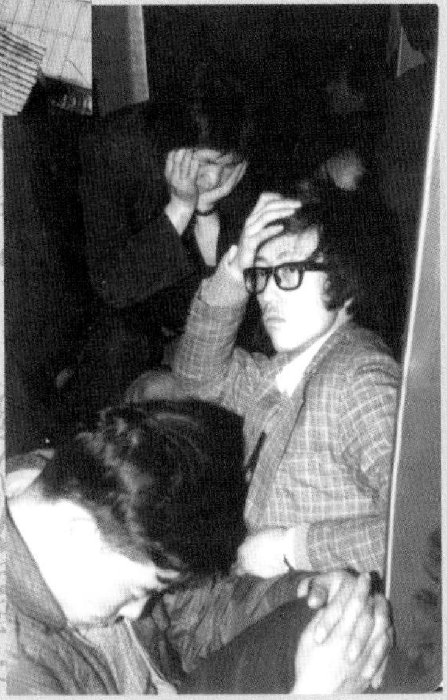

我们的家乡在希望的田野上，
炊烟在新建的住房上飘荡，
小河在美丽的村庄旁流淌……

OUR HOMELAND IS
A FIELD OF HOPE.

THE SMOKE RISING
FROM THE CHIMNEYS FLOATS
OVER NEW HOUSES.

THE BROOK FLOWS BESIDE
THE PRETTY VILLAGE.

(FROM THE POPULAR SONG
"ON THE FIELDS OF HOPE")

在希望的田野上

ZÀI XIWÀNG DĚ TIANYE SHANG.

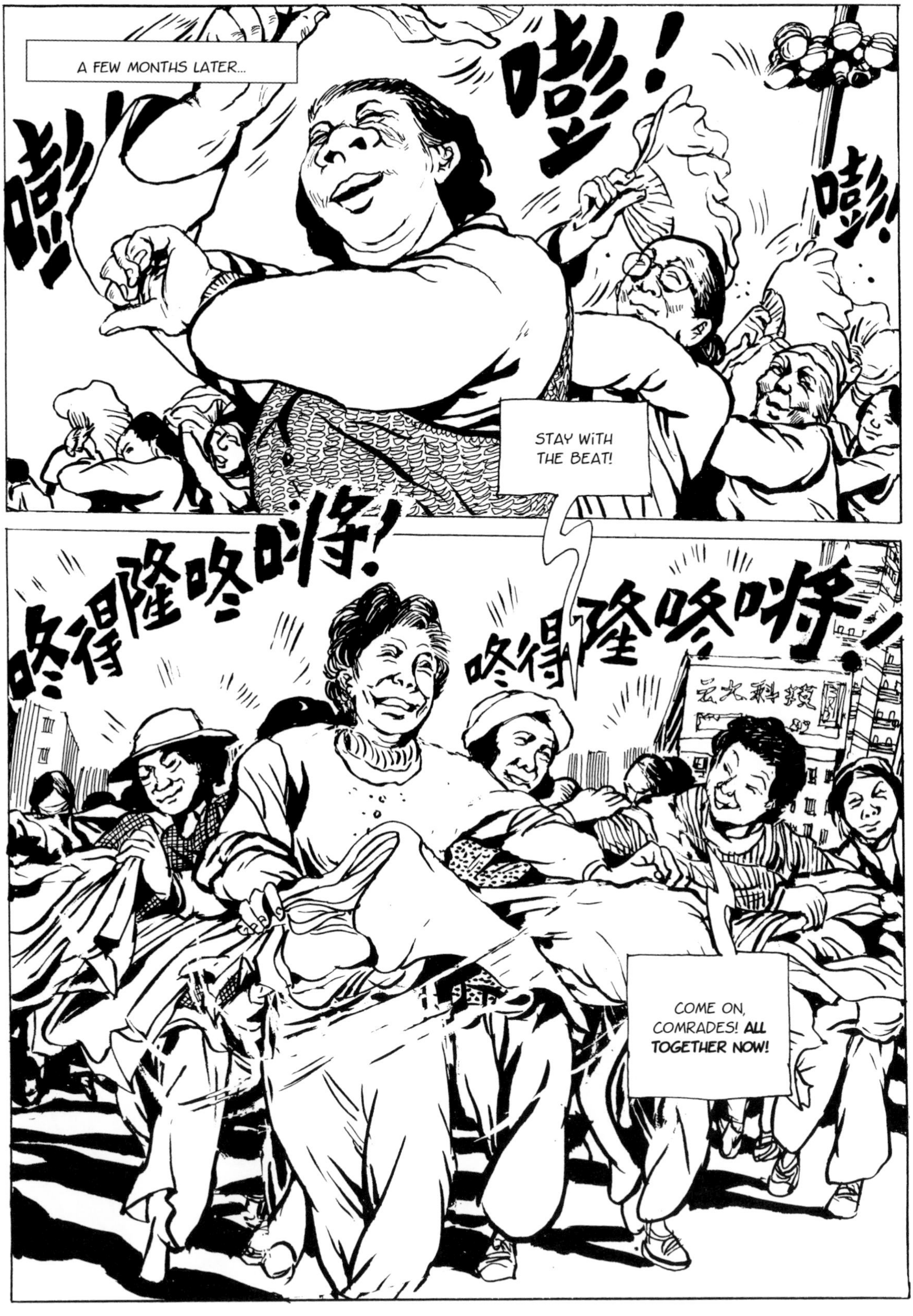
A FEW MONTHS LATER...
嘭!
嘭!
嘭!
STAY WITH THE BEAT!
咚得隆咚呛!
咚得隆咚呛!
COME ON, COMRADES! **ALL TOGETHER NOW!**

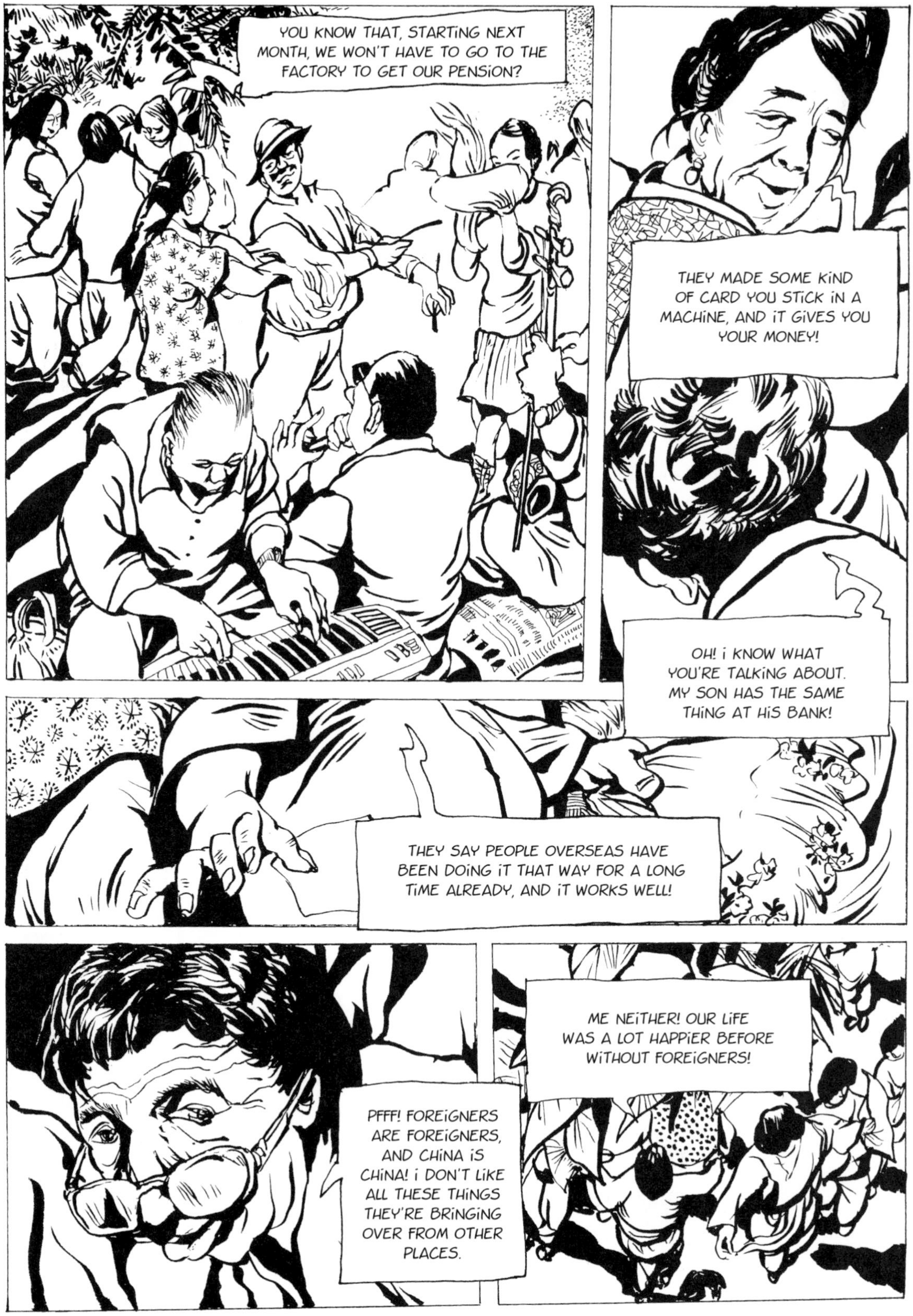
YOU KNOW THAT, STARTING NEXT MONTH, WE WON'T HAVE TO GO TO THE FACTORY TO GET OUR PENSION?
THEY MADE SOME KIND OF CARD YOU STICK IN A MACHINE, AND IT GIVES YOU YOUR MONEY!
OH! I KNOW WHAT YOU'RE TALKING ABOUT. MY SON HAS THE SAME THING AT HIS BANK!
THEY SAY PEOPLE OVERSEAS HAVE BEEN DOING IT THAT WAY FOR A LONG TIME ALREADY, AND IT WORKS WELL!
PFFF! FOREIGNERS ARE FOREIGNERS, AND CHINA IS CHINA! I DON'T LIKE ALL THESE THINGS THEY'RE BRINGING OVER FROM OTHER PLACES.
ME NEITHER! OUR LIFE WAS A LOT HAPPIER BEFORE WITHOUT FOREIGNERS!

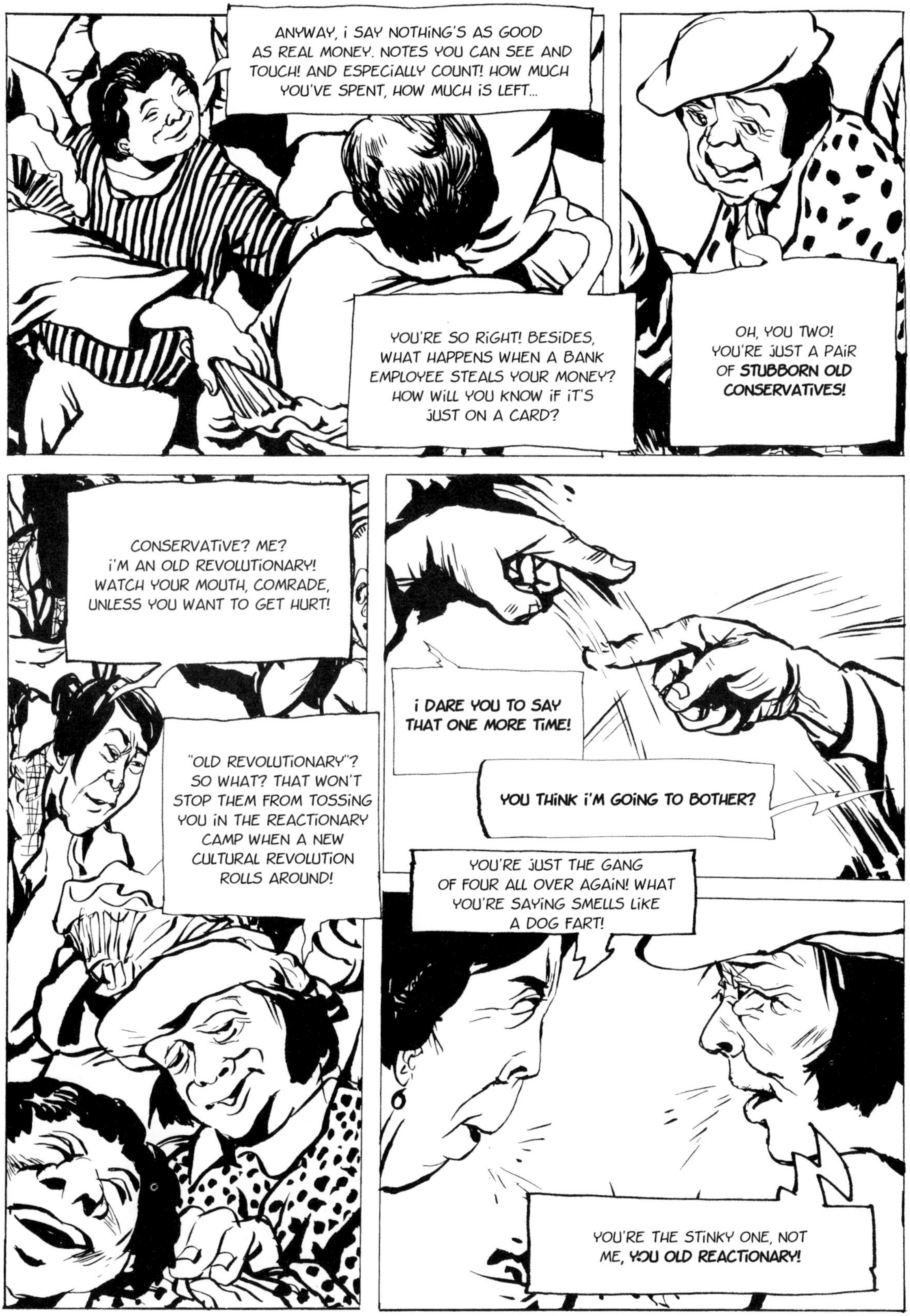

ANYWAY, i SAY NOTHING'S AS GOOD AS REAL MONEY. NOTES YOU CAN SEE AND TOUCH! AND ESPECiALLY COUNT! HOW MUCH YOU'VE SPENT, HOW MUCH iS LEFT...
YOU'RE SO RiGHT! BESiDES, WHAT HAPPENS WHEN A BANK EMPLOYEE STEALS YOUR MONEY? HOW WiLL YOU KNOW iF iT'S JUST ON A CARD?
OH, YOU TWO! YOU'RE JUST A PAiR OF **STUBBORN OLD CONSERVATiVES!**
CONSERVATiVE? ME? i'M AN OLD REVOLUTiONARY! WATCH YOUR MOUTH, COMRADE, UNLESS YOU WANT TO GET HURT!
"OLD REVOLUTiONARY"? SO WHAT? THAT WON'T STOP THEM FROM TOSSiNG YOU iN THE REACTiONARY CAMP WHEN A NEW CULTURAL REVOLUTiON ROLLS AROUND!
i DARE YOU TO SAY THAT ONE MORE TiME!
YOU THiNK i'M GOiNG TO BOTHER?
YOU'RE JUST THE GANG OF FOUR ALL OVER AGAiN! WHAT YOU'RE SAYiNG SMELLS LiKE A DOG FART!
YOU'RE THE STiNKY ONE, NOT ME, **YOU OLD REACTiONARY!**

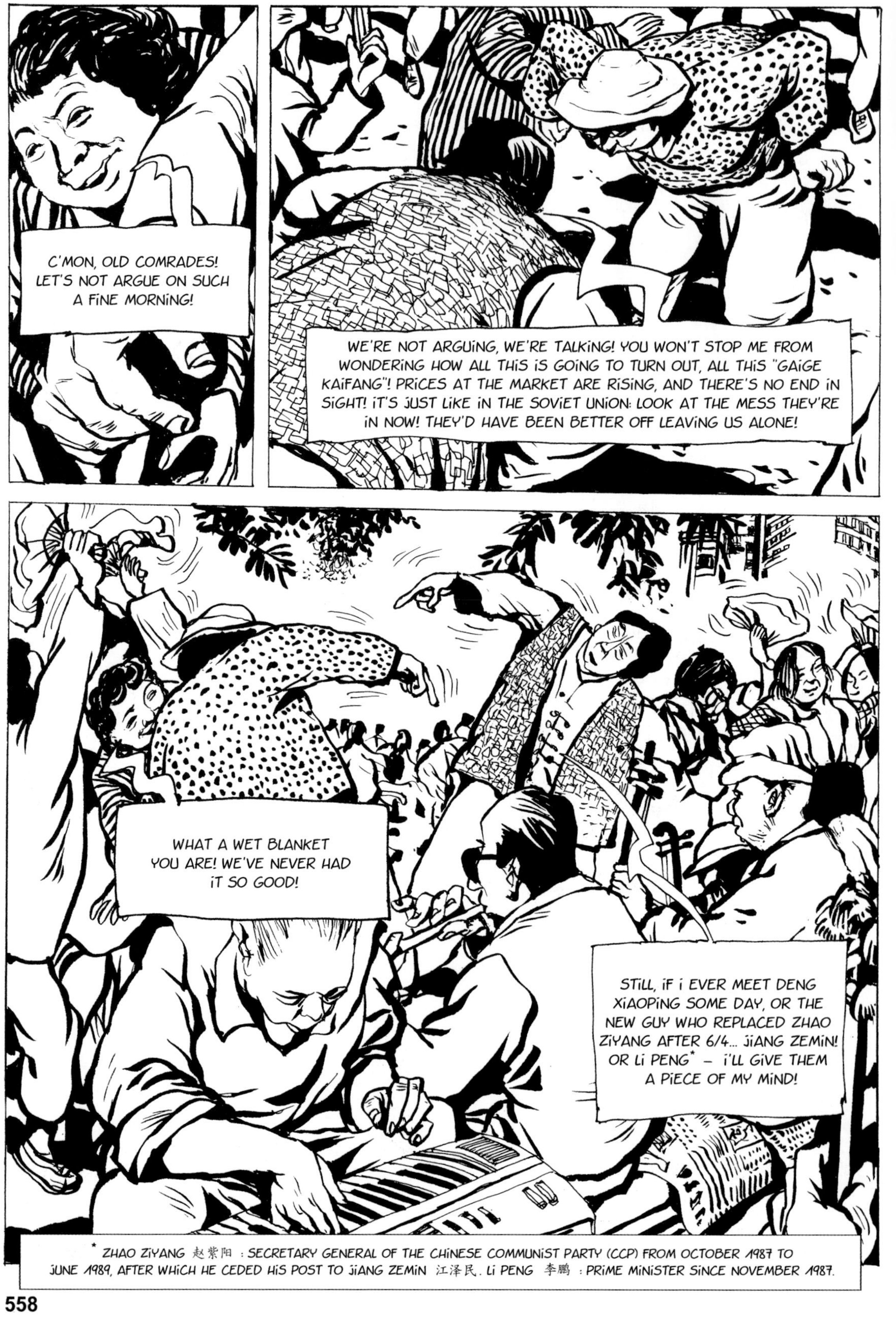
C'MON, OLD COMRADES! LET'S NOT ARGUE ON SUCH A FINE MORNING!
WE'RE NOT ARGUING, WE'RE TALKING! YOU WON'T STOP ME FROM WONDERING HOW ALL THIS IS GOING TO TURN OUT, ALL THIS "GAIGE KAIFANG"! PRICES AT THE MARKET ARE RISING, AND THERE'S NO END IN SIGHT! IT'S JUST LIKE IN THE SOVIET UNION: LOOK AT THE MESS THEY'RE IN NOW! THEY'D HAVE BEEN BETTER OFF LEAVING US ALONE!
WHAT A WET BLANKET YOU ARE! WE'VE NEVER HAD IT SO GOOD!
STILL, IF I EVER MEET DENG XIAOPING SOME DAY, OR THE NEW GUY WHO REPLACED ZHAO ZIYANG AFTER 6/4... JIANG ZEMIN! OR LI PENG* – I'LL GIVE THEM A PIECE OF MY MIND!

* ZHAO ZIYANG 赵紫阳 : SECRETARY GENERAL OF THE CHINESE COMMUNIST PARTY (CCP) FROM OCTOBER 1987 TO JUNE 1989, AFTER WHICH HE CEDED HIS POST TO JIANG ZEMIN 江泽民. LI PENG 李鹏 : PRIME MINISTER SINCE NOVEMBER 1987.

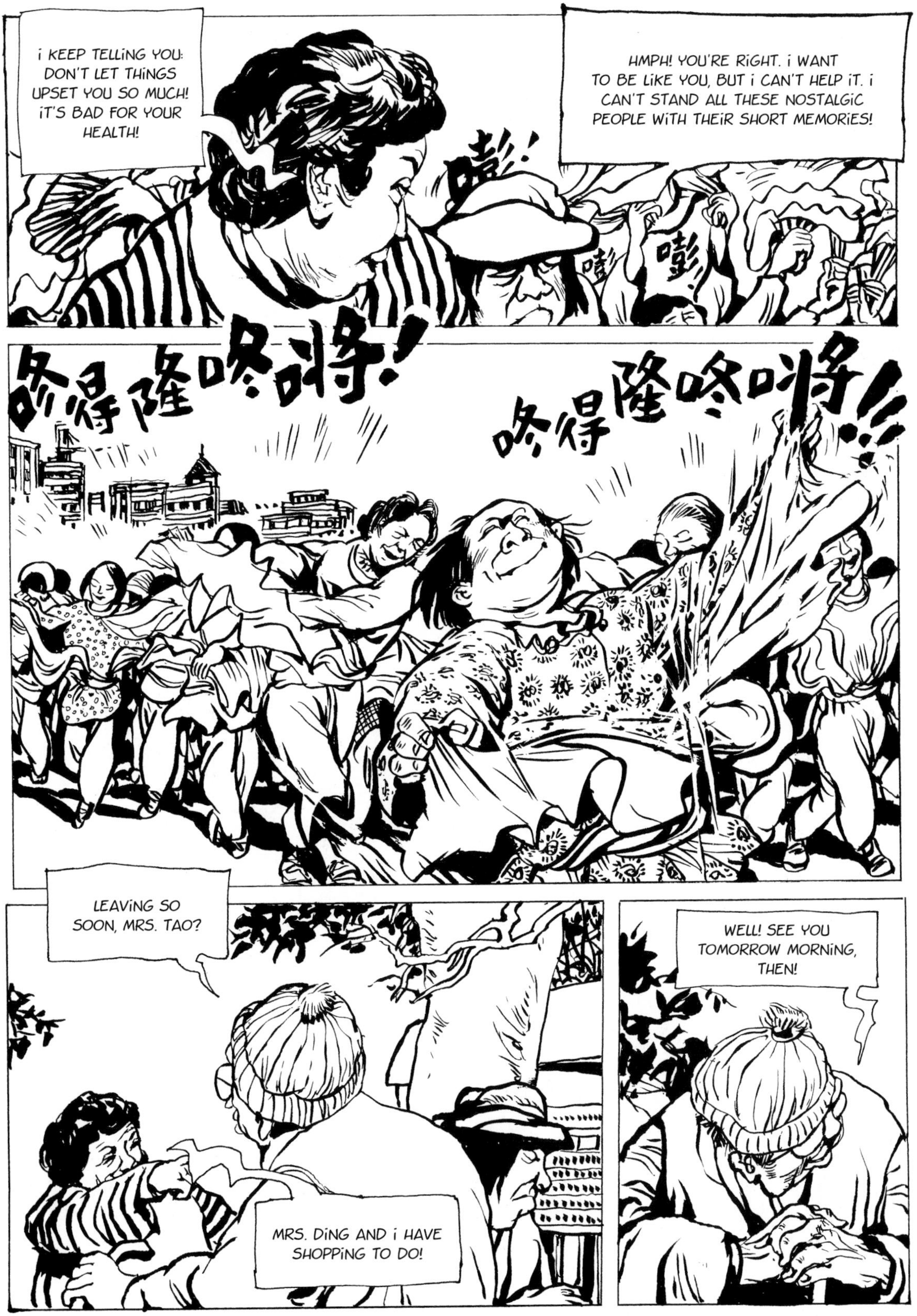

I KEEP TELLING YOU: DON'T LET THINGS UPSET YOU SO MUCH! IT'S BAD FOR YOUR HEALTH!
HMPH! YOU'RE RIGHT. I WANT TO BE LIKE YOU, BUT I CAN'T HELP IT. I CAN'T STAND ALL THESE NOSTALGIC PEOPLE WITH THEIR SHORT MEMORIES!
嘭!
嘭
嘭
咚得隆咚锵!
咚得隆咚锵!!!
LEAVING SO SOON, MRS. TAO?
MRS. DING AND I HAVE SHOPPING TO DO!
WELL! SEE YOU TOMORROW MORNING, THEN!

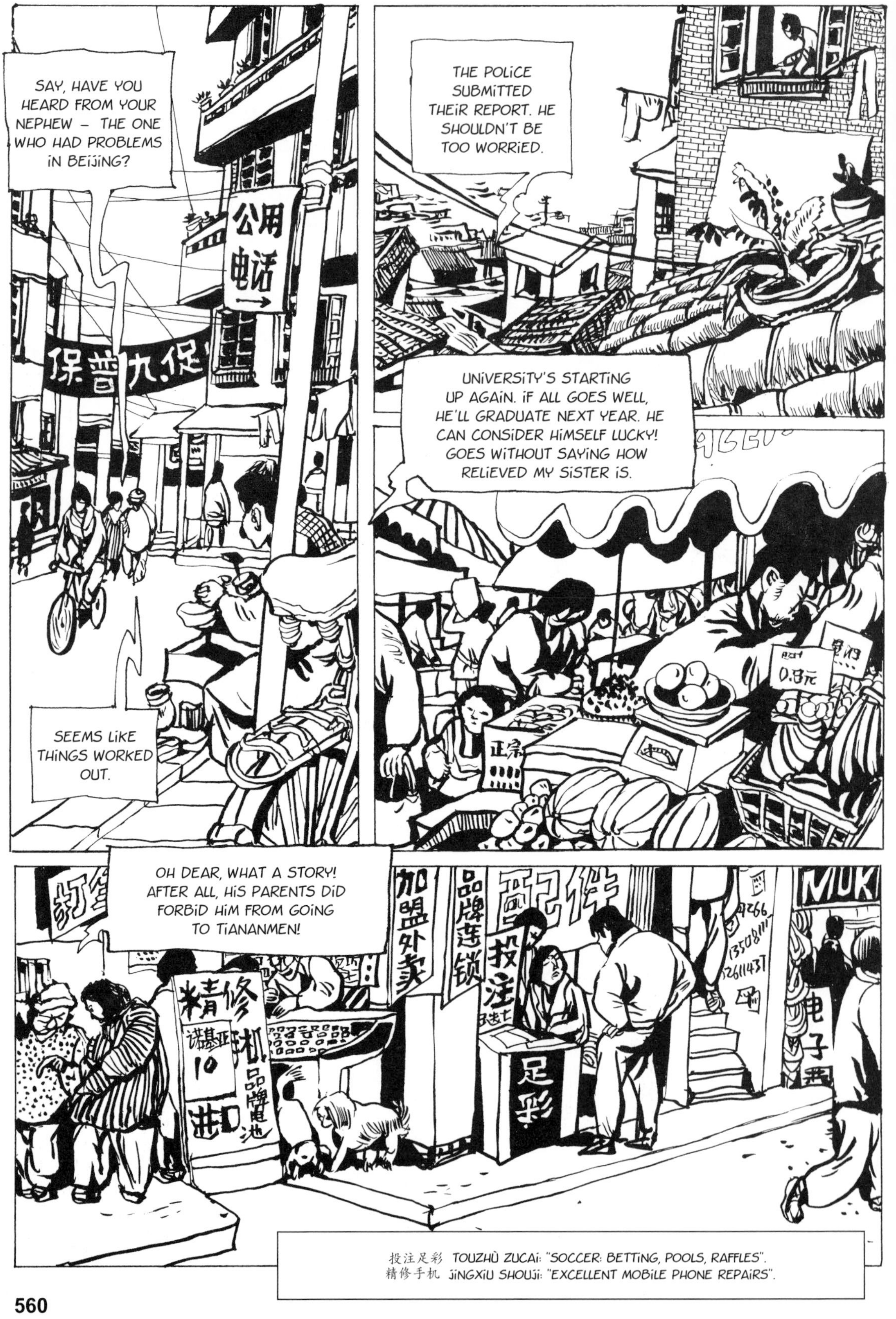
SAY, HAVE YOU HEARD FROM YOUR NEPHEW – THE ONE WHO HAD PROBLEMS IN BEIJING?
公用电话
THE POLICE SUBMITTED THEIR REPORT. HE SHOULDN'T BE TOO WORRIED.
UNIVERSITY'S STARTING UP AGAIN. IF ALL GOES WELL, HE'LL GRADUATE NEXT YEAR. HE CAN CONSIDER HIMSELF LUCKY! GOES WITHOUT SAYING HOW RELIEVED MY SISTER IS.
SEEMS LIKE THINGS WORKED OUT.
OH DEAR, WHAT A STORY! AFTER ALL, HIS PARENTS DID FORBID HIM FROM GOING TO TIANANMEN!
加盟外卖
品牌连锁
投注
足彩
电子

投注足彩 TOUZHÙ ZUCAI: "SOCCER: BETTING, POOLS, RAFFLES".
精修手机 JINGXIU SHOUJI: "EXCELLENT MOBILE PHONE REPAIRS".

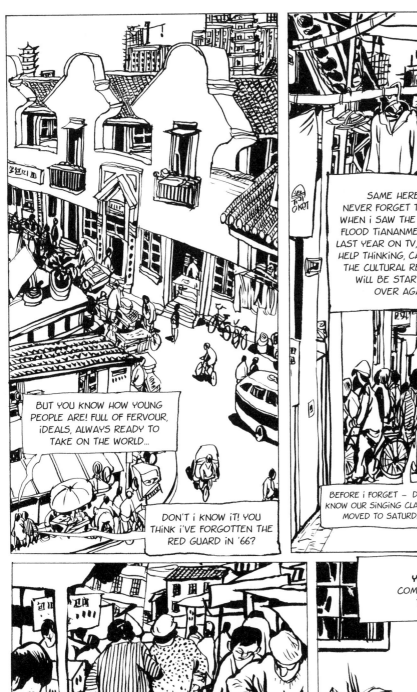

BUT YOU KNOW HOW YOUNG PEOPLE ARE! FULL OF FERVOUR, iDEALS, ALWAYS READY TO TAKE ON THE WORLD...

DON'T i KNOW iT! YOU THINK i'VE FORGOTTEN THE RED GUARD iN '66?

SAME HERE! i'LL NEVER FORGET THEM! AND WHEN i SAW THE STUDENTS FLOOD TiANANMEN SQUARE LAST YEAR ON TV, i COULDN'T HELP THiNKiNG, CAN iT MEAN THE CULTURAL REVOLUTION WiLL BE STARTiNG ALL OVER AGAiN?

BEFORE i FORGET – DiD YOU KNOW OUR SiNGiNG CLASS WAS MOVED TO SATURDAY?

OOOH! LOOK HOW PRETTY OLD WANG'S TOFU iS TODAY! BET YOU HE'LL SAY iT'S AS SOFT AND WHiTE AS A YOUNG GiRL'S SKiN AGAiN!

YOO-HOO! XiAO Li! COME AND HELP ME WiTH THE GROCERiES!

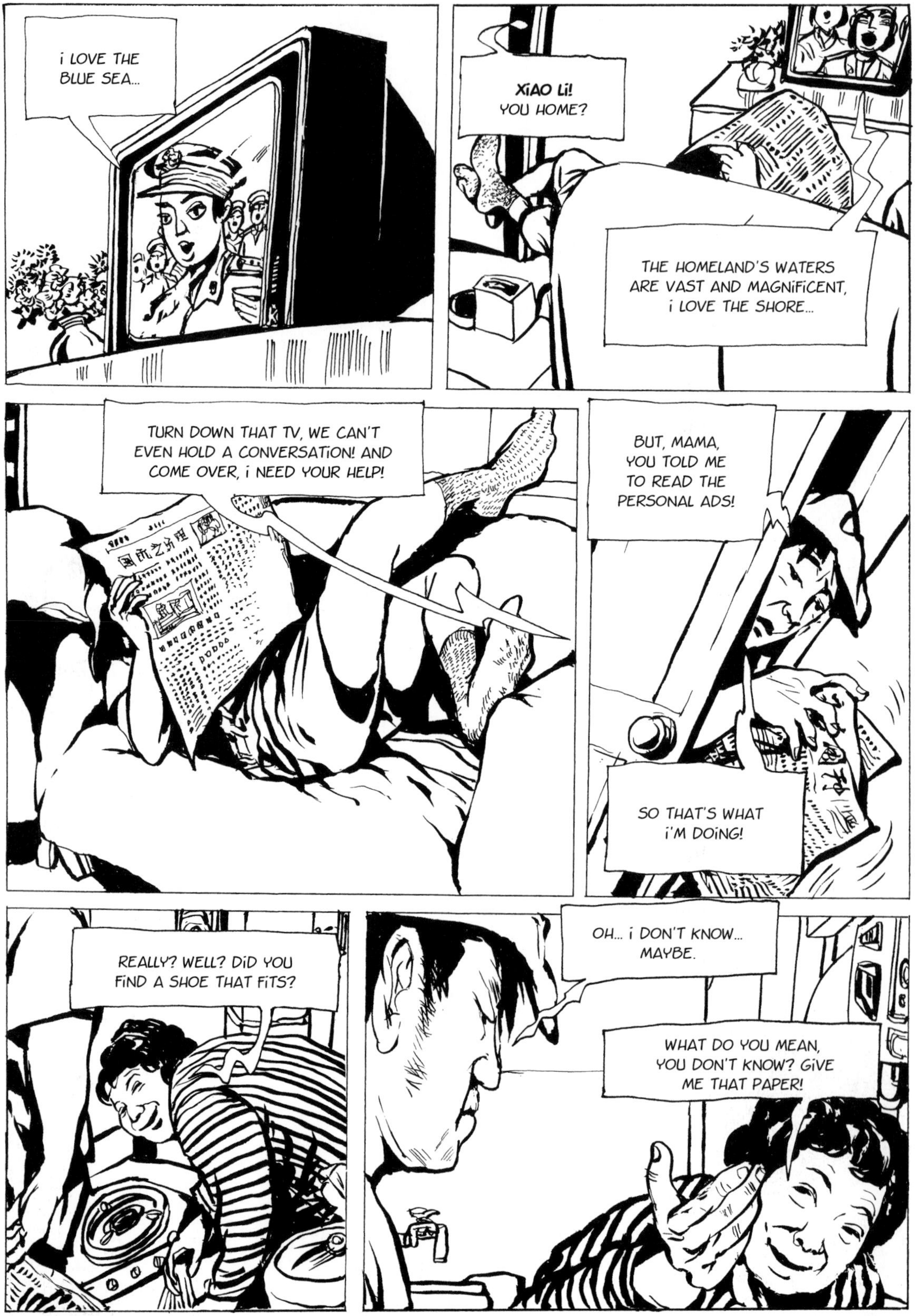
i LOVE THE BLUE SEA...
XiAO Li! YOU HOME?
THE HOMELAND'S WATERS ARE VAST AND MAGNiFiCENT, i LOVE THE SHORE...
TURN DOWN THAT TV, WE CAN'T EVEN HOLD A CONVERSATiON! AND COME OVER, i NEED YOUR HELP!
BUT, MAMA, YOU TOLD ME TO READ THE PERSONAL ADS!
SO THAT'S WHAT i'M DOiNG!
REALLY? WELL? DiD YOU FiND A SHOE THAT FiTS?
OH... i DON'T KNOW... MAYBE.
WHAT DO YOU MEAN, YOU DON'T KNOW? GiVE ME THAT PAPER!

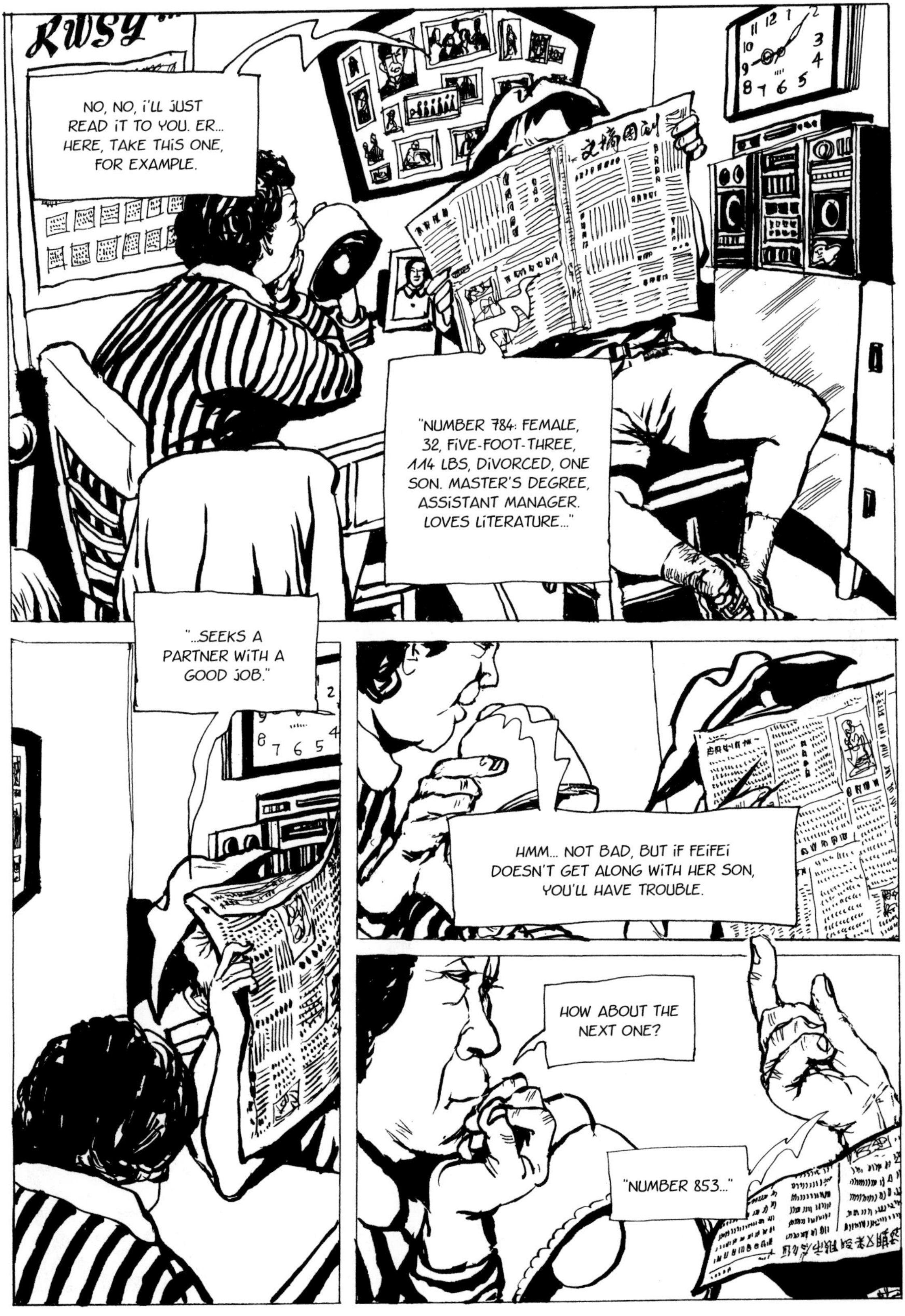
NO, NO, I'LL JUST READ IT TO YOU. ER... HERE, TAKE THIS ONE, FOR EXAMPLE.
"NUMBER 784: FEMALE, 32, FIVE-FOOT-THREE, 114 LBS, DIVORCED, ONE SON. MASTER'S DEGREE, ASSISTANT MANAGER. LOVES LITERATURE..."
"...SEEKS A PARTNER WITH A GOOD JOB."
HMM... NOT BAD, BUT IF FEIFEI DOESN'T GET ALONG WITH HER SON, YOU'LL HAVE TROUBLE.
HOW ABOUT THE NEXT ONE?
"NUMBER 853..."

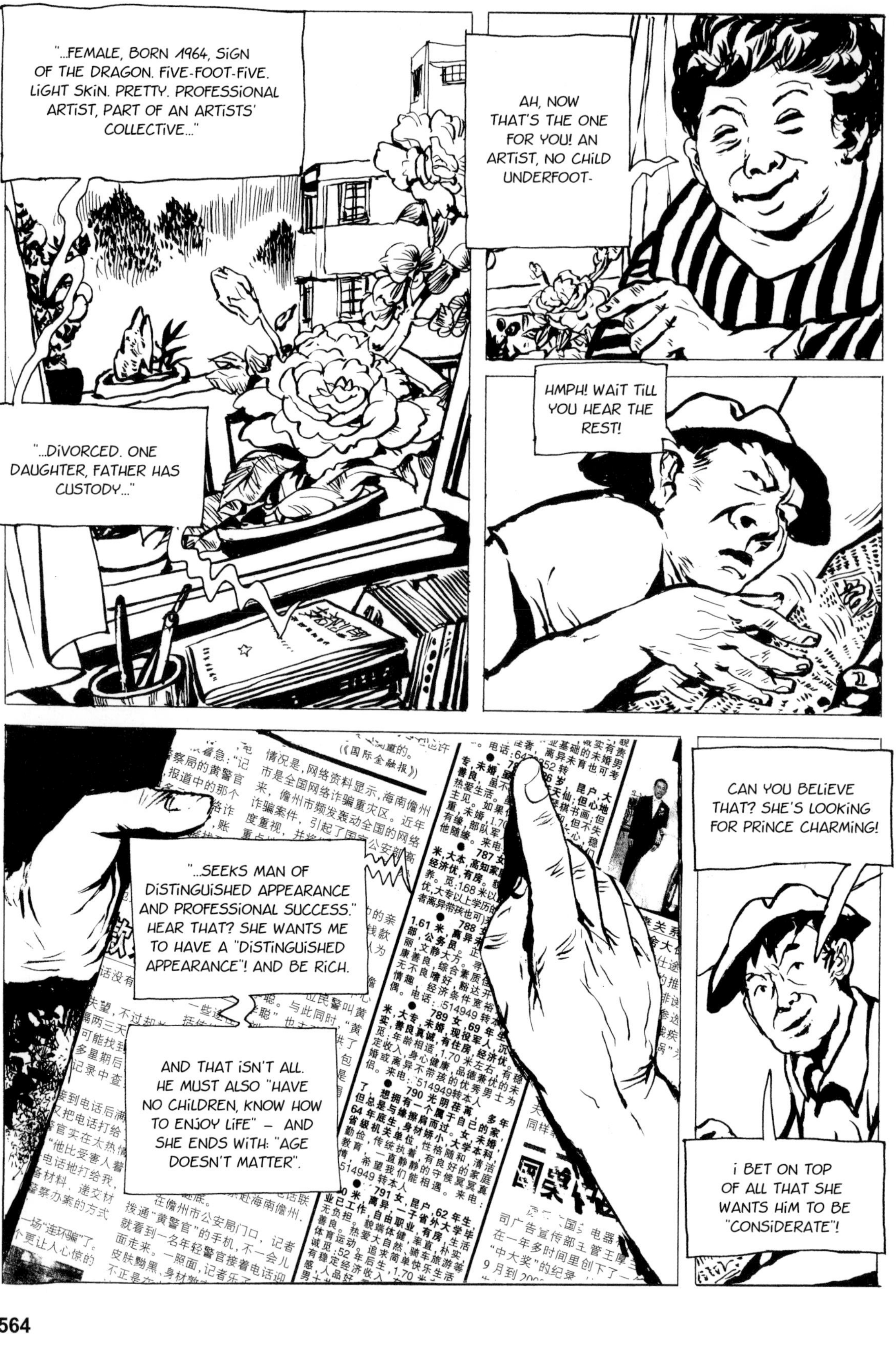
"...FEMALE, BORN 1964, SIGN OF THE DRAGON. FIVE-FOOT-FIVE. LIGHT SKIN. PRETTY. PROFESSIONAL ARTIST, PART OF AN ARTISTS' COLLECTIVE..."
AH, NOW THAT'S THE ONE FOR YOU! AN ARTIST, NO CHILD UNDERFOOT-
"...DIVORCED. ONE DAUGHTER, FATHER HAS CUSTODY..."
HMPH! WAIT TILL YOU HEAR THE REST!
"...SEEKS MAN OF DISTINGUISHED APPEARANCE AND PROFESSIONAL SUCCESS." HEAR THAT? SHE WANTS ME TO HAVE A "DISTINGUISHED APPEARANCE"! AND BE RICH.
AND THAT ISN'T ALL. HE MUST ALSO "HAVE NO CHILDREN, KNOW HOW TO ENJOY LIFE" – AND SHE ENDS WITH: "AGE DOESN'T MATTER".
CAN YOU BELIEVE THAT? SHE'S LOOKING FOR PRINCE CHARMING!
I BET ON TOP OF ALL THAT SHE WANTS HIM TO BE "CONSIDERATE"!

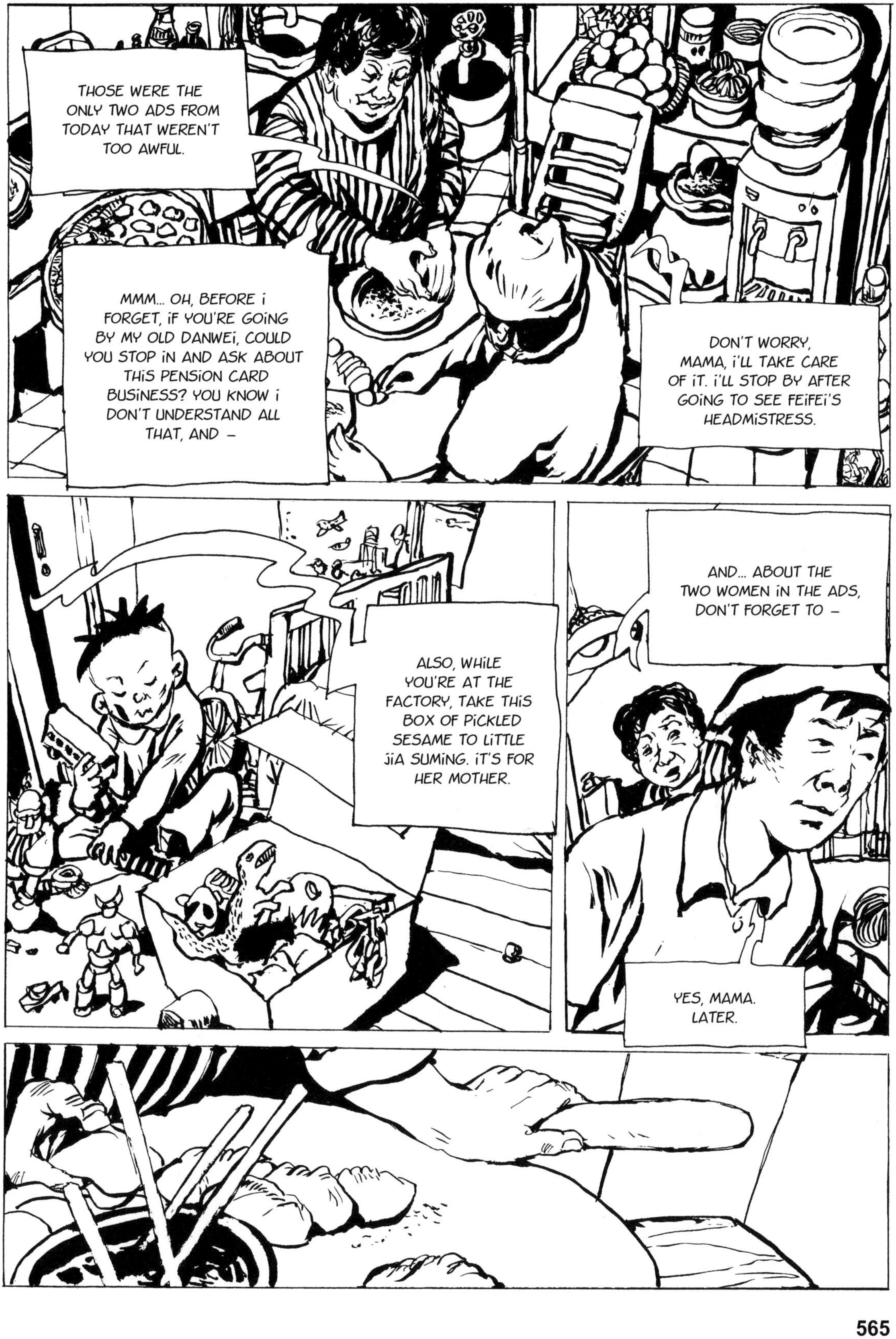
THOSE WERE THE ONLY TWO ADS FROM TODAY THAT WEREN'T TOO AWFUL.
MMM... OH, BEFORE i FORGET, iF YOU'RE GOiNG BY MY OLD DANWEi, COULD YOU STOP iN AND ASK ABOUT THiS PENSiON CARD BUSiNESS? YOU KNOW i DON'T UNDERSTAND ALL THAT, AND –
DON'T WORRY, MAMA, i'LL TAKE CARE OF iT. i'LL STOP BY AFTER GOiNG TO SEE FEiFEi'S HEADMiSTRESS.
ALSO, WHiLE YOU'RE AT THE FACTORY, TAKE THiS BOX OF PiCKLED SESAME TO LiTTLE JiA SUMiNG. iT'S FOR HER MOTHER.
AND... ABOUT THE TWO WOMEN iN THE ADS, DON'T FORGET TO –
YES, MAMA. LATER.

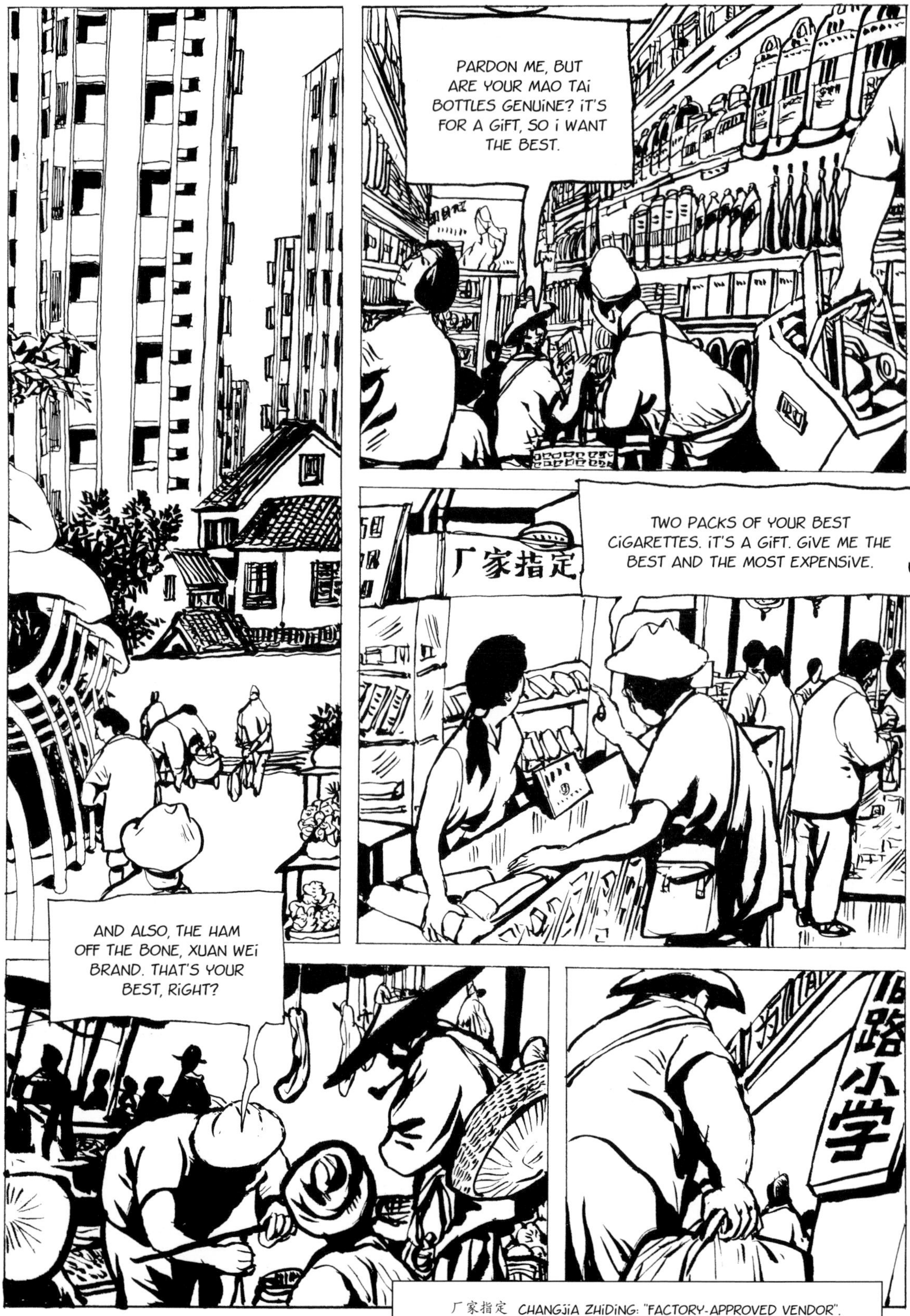
PARDON ME, BUT ARE YOUR MAO TAI BOTTLES GENUINE? IT'S FOR A GIFT, SO I WANT THE BEST.
厂家指定
TWO PACKS OF YOUR BEST CIGARETTES. IT'S A GIFT. GIVE ME THE BEST AND THE MOST EXPENSIVE.
AND ALSO, THE HAM OFF THE BONE, XUAN WEI BRAND. THAT'S YOUR BEST, RIGHT?
路小学

厂家指定 CHANGJIA ZHIDING: "FACTORY-APPROVED VENDOR".

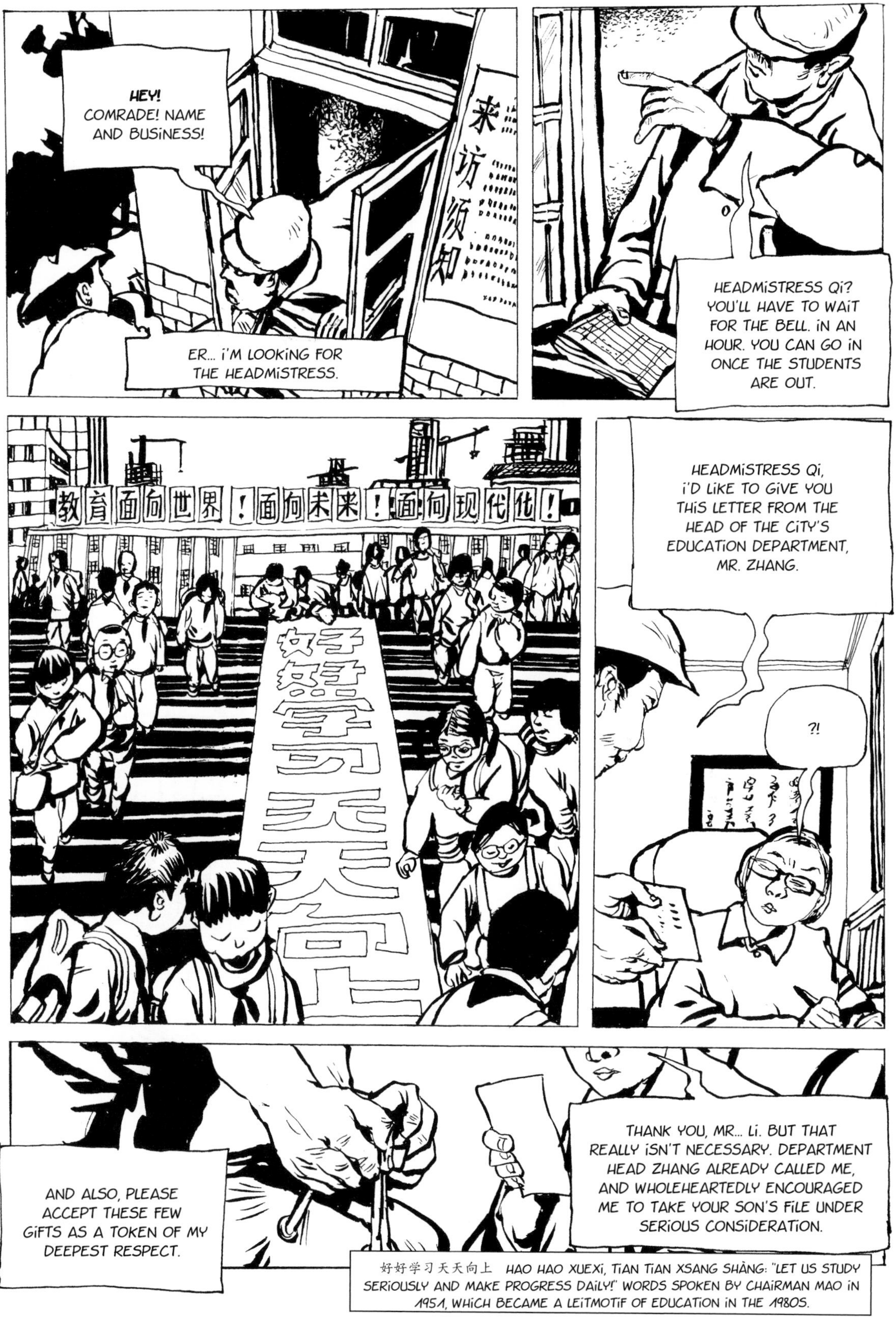
HEY!
COMRADE! NAME AND BUSINESS!
来访须知
ER... I'M LOOKING FOR THE HEADMISTRESS.
HEADMISTRESS QI? YOU'LL HAVE TO WAIT FOR THE BELL. IN AN HOUR. YOU CAN GO IN ONCE THE STUDENTS ARE OUT.
教育面向世界！面向未来！面向现代化！
好好学习天天向上
HEADMISTRESS QI, I'D LIKE TO GIVE YOU THIS LETTER FROM THE HEAD OF THE CITY'S EDUCATION DEPARTMENT, MR. ZHANG.
?!
AND ALSO, PLEASE ACCEPT THESE FEW GIFTS AS A TOKEN OF MY DEEPEST RESPECT.
THANK YOU, MR... LI. BUT THAT REALLY ISN'T NECESSARY. DEPARTMENT HEAD ZHANG ALREADY CALLED ME, AND WHOLEHEARTEDLY ENCOURAGED ME TO TAKE YOUR SON'S FILE UNDER SERIOUS CONSIDERATION.

好好学习天天向上 HAO HAO XUEXI, TIAN TIAN XSANG SHÀNG: "LET US STUDY SERIOUSLY AND MAKE PROGRESS DAILY!" WORDS SPOKEN BY CHAIRMAN MAO IN 1951, WHICH BECAME A LEITMOTIF OF EDUCATION IN THE 1980S.

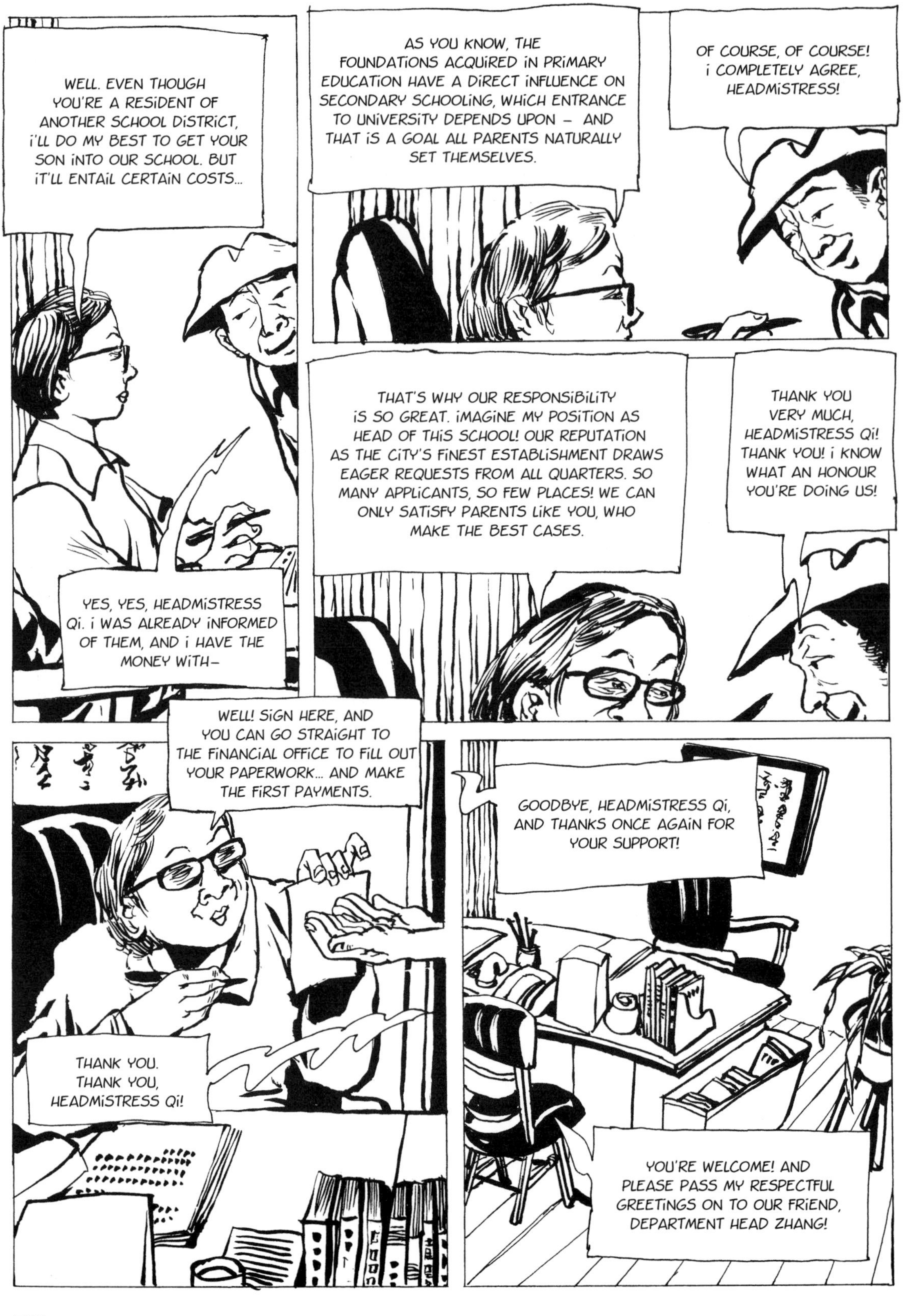
WELL. EVEN THOUGH YOU'RE A RESIDENT OF ANOTHER SCHOOL DISTRICT, I'LL DO MY BEST TO GET YOUR SON INTO OUR SCHOOL. BUT IT'LL ENTAIL CERTAIN COSTS...
YES, YES, HEADMISTRESS QI. I WAS ALREADY INFORMED OF THEM, AND I HAVE THE MONEY WITH–
AS YOU KNOW, THE FOUNDATIONS ACQUIRED IN PRIMARY EDUCATION HAVE A DIRECT INFLUENCE ON SECONDARY SCHOOLING, WHICH ENTRANCE TO UNIVERSITY DEPENDS UPON – AND THAT IS A GOAL ALL PARENTS NATURALLY SET THEMSELVES.
OF COURSE, OF COURSE! I COMPLETELY AGREE, HEADMISTRESS!
THAT'S WHY OUR RESPONSIBILITY IS SO GREAT. IMAGINE MY POSITION AS HEAD OF THIS SCHOOL! OUR REPUTATION AS THE CITY'S FINEST ESTABLISHMENT DRAWS EAGER REQUESTS FROM ALL QUARTERS. SO MANY APPLICANTS, SO FEW PLACES! WE CAN ONLY SATISFY PARENTS LIKE YOU, WHO MAKE THE BEST CASES.
THANK YOU VERY MUCH, HEADMISTRESS QI! THANK YOU! I KNOW WHAT AN HONOUR YOU'RE DOING US!
WELL! SIGN HERE, AND YOU CAN GO STRAIGHT TO THE FINANCIAL OFFICE TO FILL OUT YOUR PAPERWORK... AND MAKE THE FIRST PAYMENTS.
THANK YOU. THANK YOU, HEADMISTRESS QI!
GOODBYE, HEADMISTRESS QI, AND THANKS ONCE AGAIN FOR YOUR SUPPORT!
YOU'RE WELCOME! AND PLEASE PASS MY RESPECTFUL GREETINGS ON TO OUR FRIEND, DEPARTMENT HEAD ZHANG!

WHAT'S WRONG, MY BOY? WHAT ARE YOU...? WHY ARE YOU CRYING?

...

UH... YOU CAN TALK TO ME, YOU KNOW. i CAN... KEEP A SECRET.

iN CLASS, WE ALL PRETEND WE DON'T CARE. BUT AS SOON AS WE'RE HOME, ALL WE DO iS WORK. EVENiNGS AND SATURDAYS. SUNDAYS, TOO. i DON'T HAVE ANY FRiENDS WHO AREN'T GETTING TUTORED!

i... i'LL BE iN 9TH GRADE NEXT YEAR. MY FiRST YEAR OF HiGH SCHOOL! i'VE DONE EVERYTHING i COULD, BUT i'M NOT AT THE HEAD OF THE CLASS!

iF i'M NOT iN THE TOP FiVE, i'LL NEVER GET iNTO HiGH SCHOOL # 1. NOT EVEN HiGH SCHOOL # 8 WiLL WANT ME. WHiCH MEANS THAT iN FOUR YEARS i WON'T HAVE A HiGH ENOUGH SCORE ON THE GAOKAO* TO GET iNTO THE BEST UNiVERSiTiES!

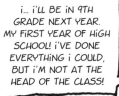

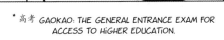

* 高考 GAOKAO: THE GENERAL ENTRANCE EXAM FOR ACCESS TO HiGHER EDUCATION.

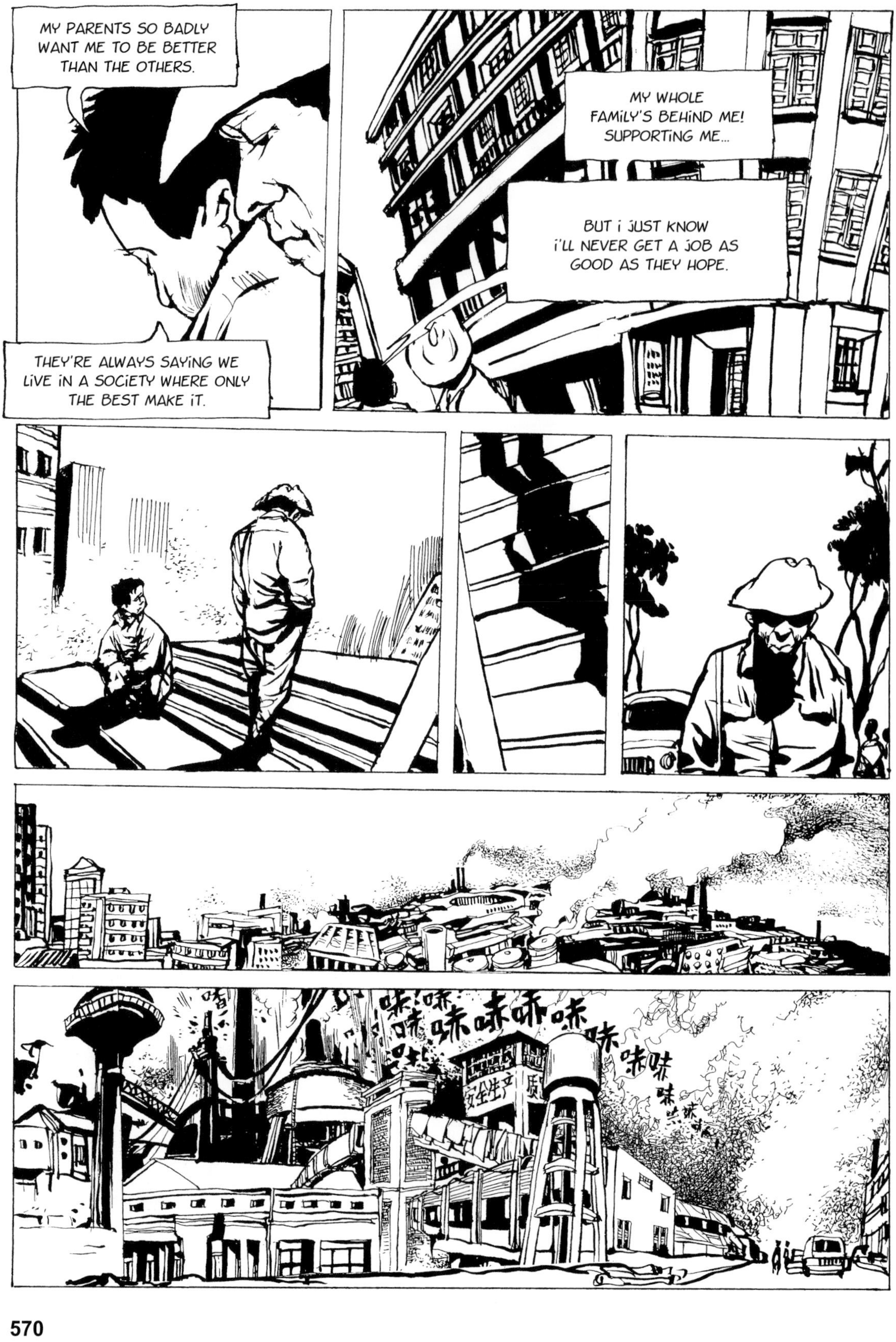
MY PARENTS SO BADLY WANT ME TO BE BETTER THAN THE OTHERS.
THEY'RE ALWAYS SAYING WE LIVE IN A SOCIETY WHERE ONLY THE BEST MAKE IT.
MY WHOLE FAMILY'S BEHIND ME! SUPPORTING ME...
BUT I JUST KNOW I'LL NEVER GET A JOB AS GOOD AS THEY HOPE.

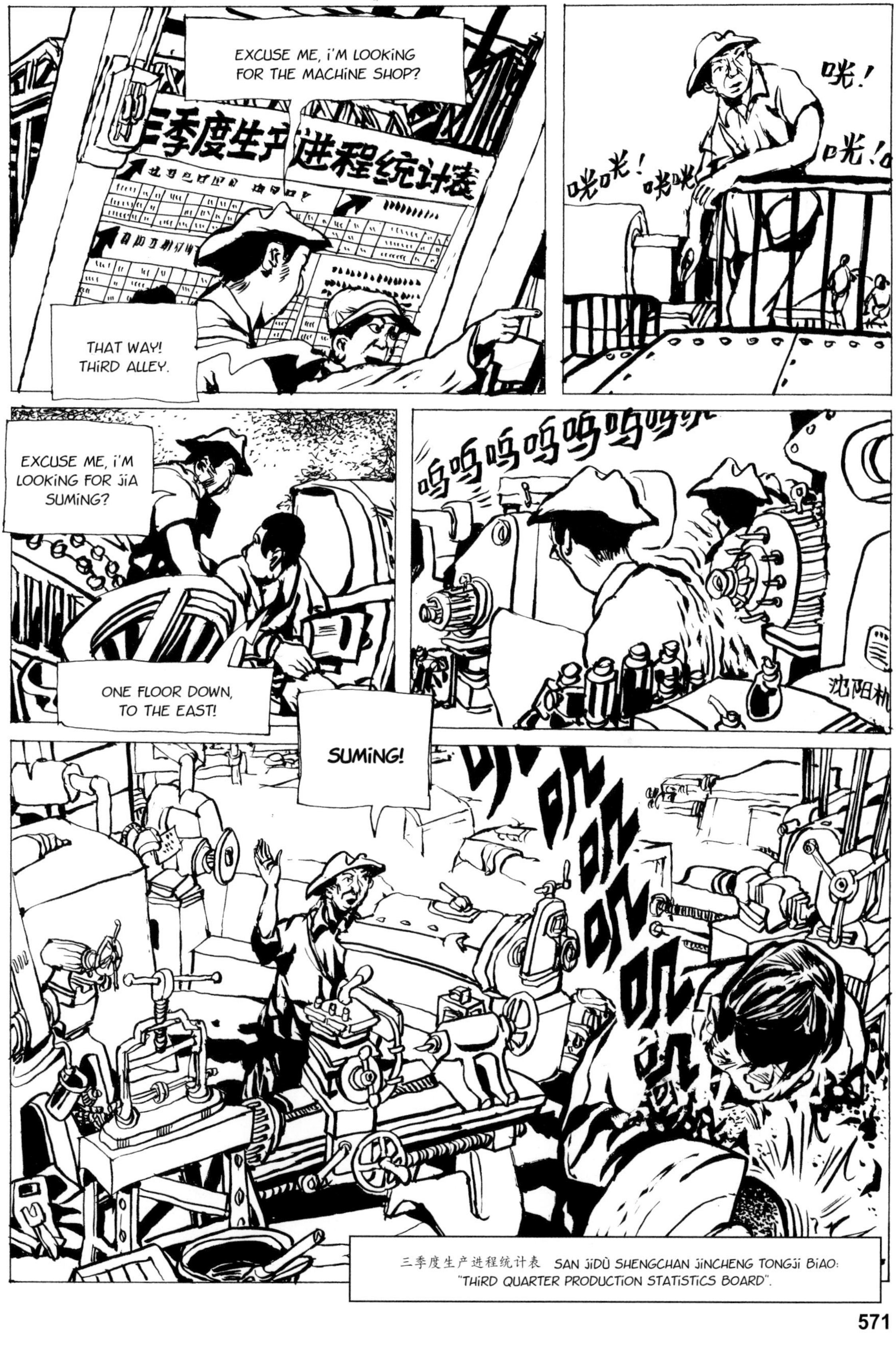
EXCUSE ME, I'M LOOKING FOR THE MACHINE SHOP?
THAT WAY! THIRD ALLEY.
咣!
咣咣!
咣咣
咣!
EXCUSE ME, I'M LOOKING FOR JIA SUMING?
ONE FLOOR DOWN, TO THE EAST!
呜呜呜呜呜呜呜
沈阳机
SUMING!

三季度生产进程统计表 SAN JIDÙ SHENGCHAN JINCHENG TONGJI BIAO: "THIRD QUARTER PRODUCTION STATISTICS BOARD".

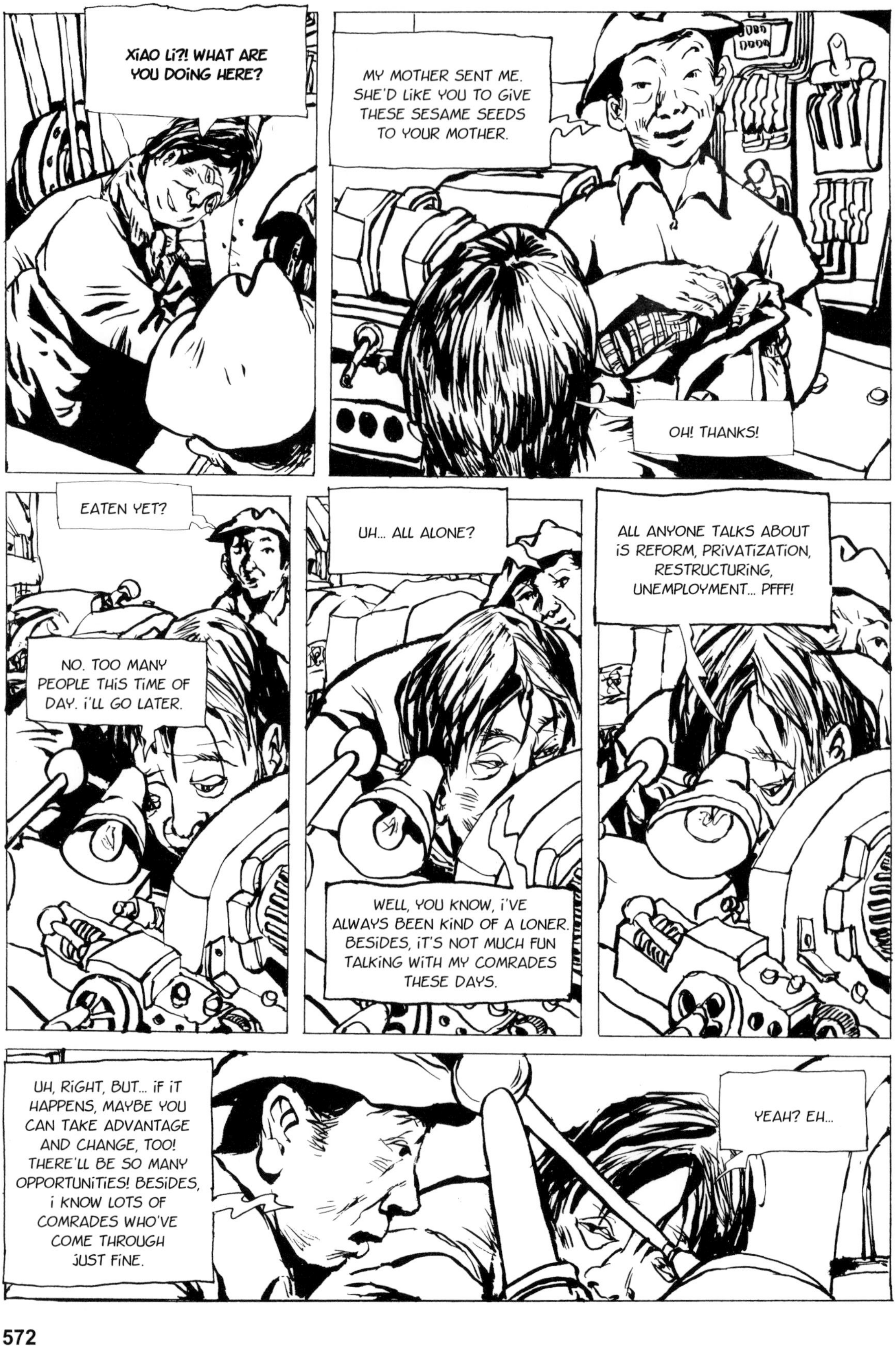
XIAO Li?! WHAT ARE YOU DOiNG HERE?
MY MOTHER SENT ME. SHE'D LiKE YOU TO GiVE THESE SESAME SEEDS TO YOUR MOTHER.
OH! THANKS!
EATEN YET?
NO. TOO MANY PEOPLE THiS TiME OF DAY. i'LL GO LATER.
UH... ALL ALONE?
WELL, YOU KNOW, i'VE ALWAYS BEEN KiND OF A LONER. BESiDES, iT'S NOT MUCH FUN TALKiNG WiTH MY COMRADES THESE DAYS.
ALL ANYONE TALKS ABOUT iS REFORM, PRiVATiZATiON, RESTRUCTURiNG, UNEMPLOYMENT... PFFF!
UH, RiGHT, BUT... iF iT HAPPENS, MAYBE YOU CAN TAKE ADVANTAGE AND CHANGE, TOO! THERE'LL BE SO MANY OPPORTUNiTiES! BESiDES, i KNOW LOTS OF COMRADES WHO'VE COME THROUGH JUST FiNE.
YEAH? EH...

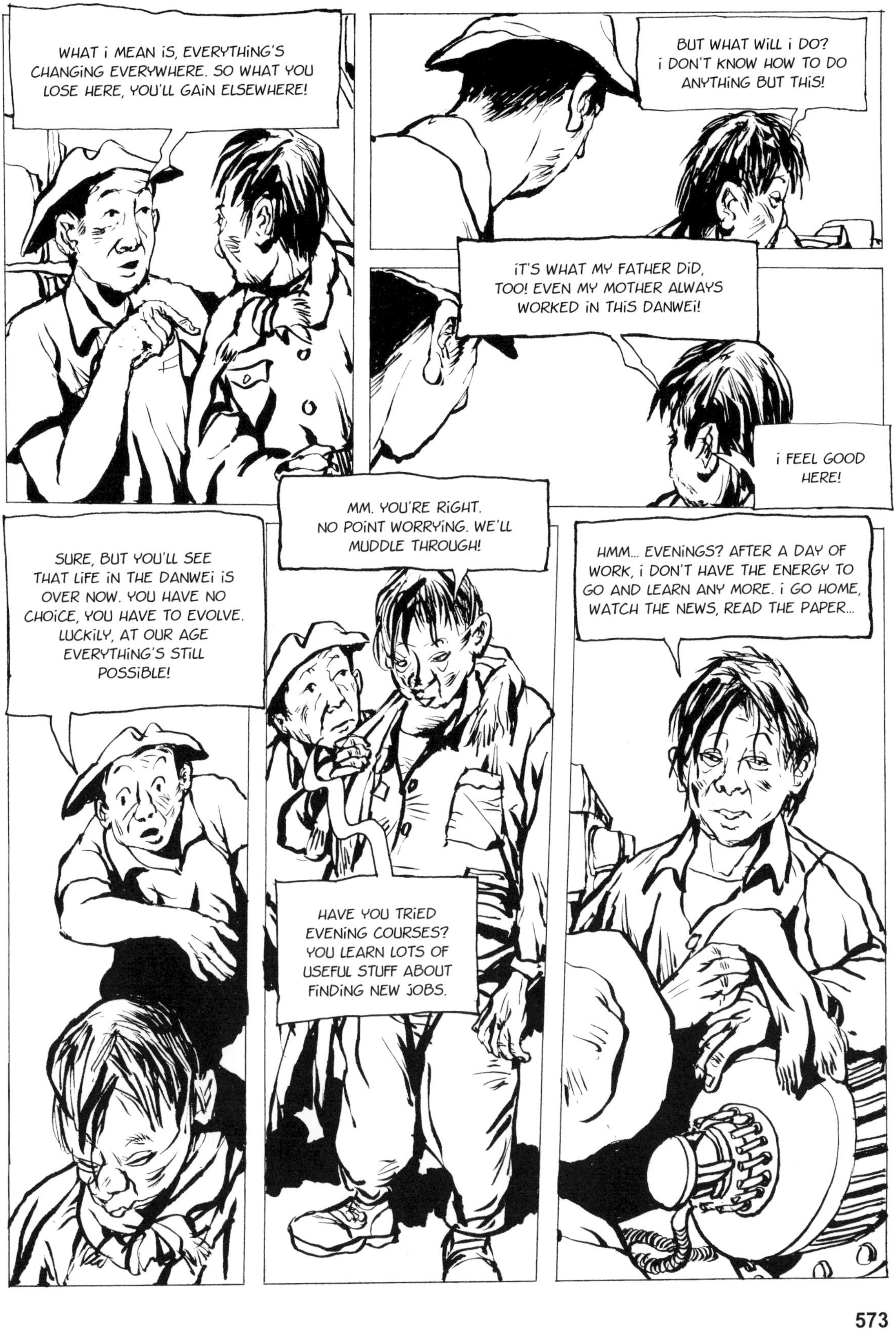
WHAT i MEAN iS, EVERYTHiNG'S CHANGiNG EVERYWHERE. SO WHAT YOU LOSE HERE, YOU'LL GAiN ELSEWHERE!
BUT WHAT WiLL i DO? i DON'T KNOW HOW TO DO ANYTHiNG BUT THiS!
iT'S WHAT MY FATHER DiD, TOO! EVEN MY MOTHER ALWAYS WORKED iN THiS DANWEi!
i FEEL GOOD HERE!
SURE, BUT YOU'LL SEE THAT LiFE iN THE DANWEi iS OVER NOW. YOU HAVE NO CHOiCE, YOU HAVE TO EVOLVE. LUCKiLY, AT OUR AGE EVERYTHiNG'S STiLL POSSiBLE!
MM. YOU'RE RiGHT. NO POiNT WORRYiNG. WE'LL MUDDLE THROUGH!
HAVE YOU TRiED EVENiNG COURSES? YOU LEARN LOTS OF USEFUL STUFF ABOUT FiNDiNG NEW JOBS.
HMM... EVENiNGS? AFTER A DAY OF WORK, i DON'T HAVE THE ENERGY TO GO AND LEARN ANY MORE. i GO HOME, WATCH THE NEWS, READ THE PAPER...

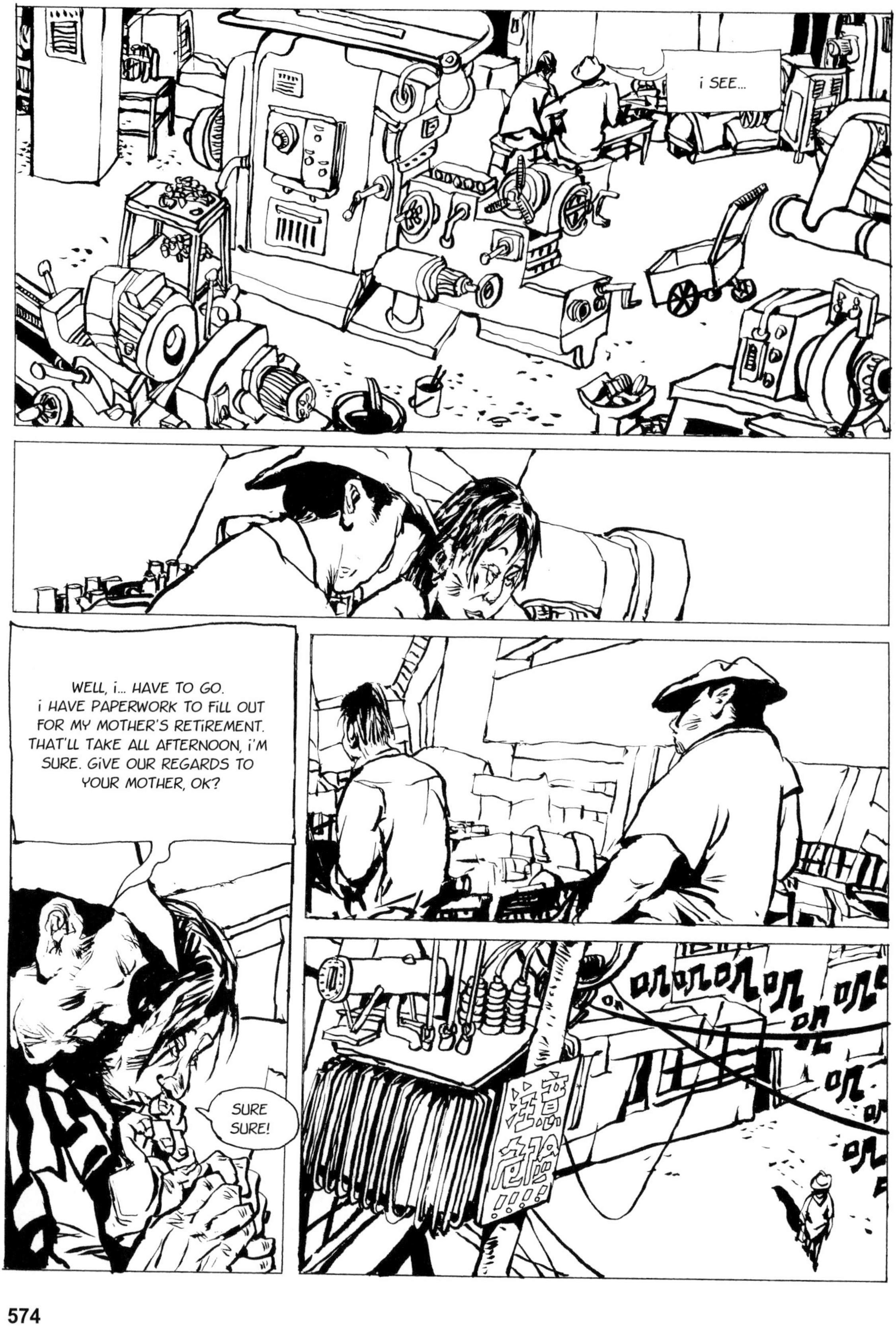
i SEE...
WELL, i... HAVE TO GO. i HAVE PAPERWORK TO FiLL OUT FOR MY MOTHER'S RETiREMENT. THAT'LL TAKE ALL AFTERNOON, i'M SURE. GiVE OUR REGARDS TO YOUR MOTHER, OK?
SURE SURE!

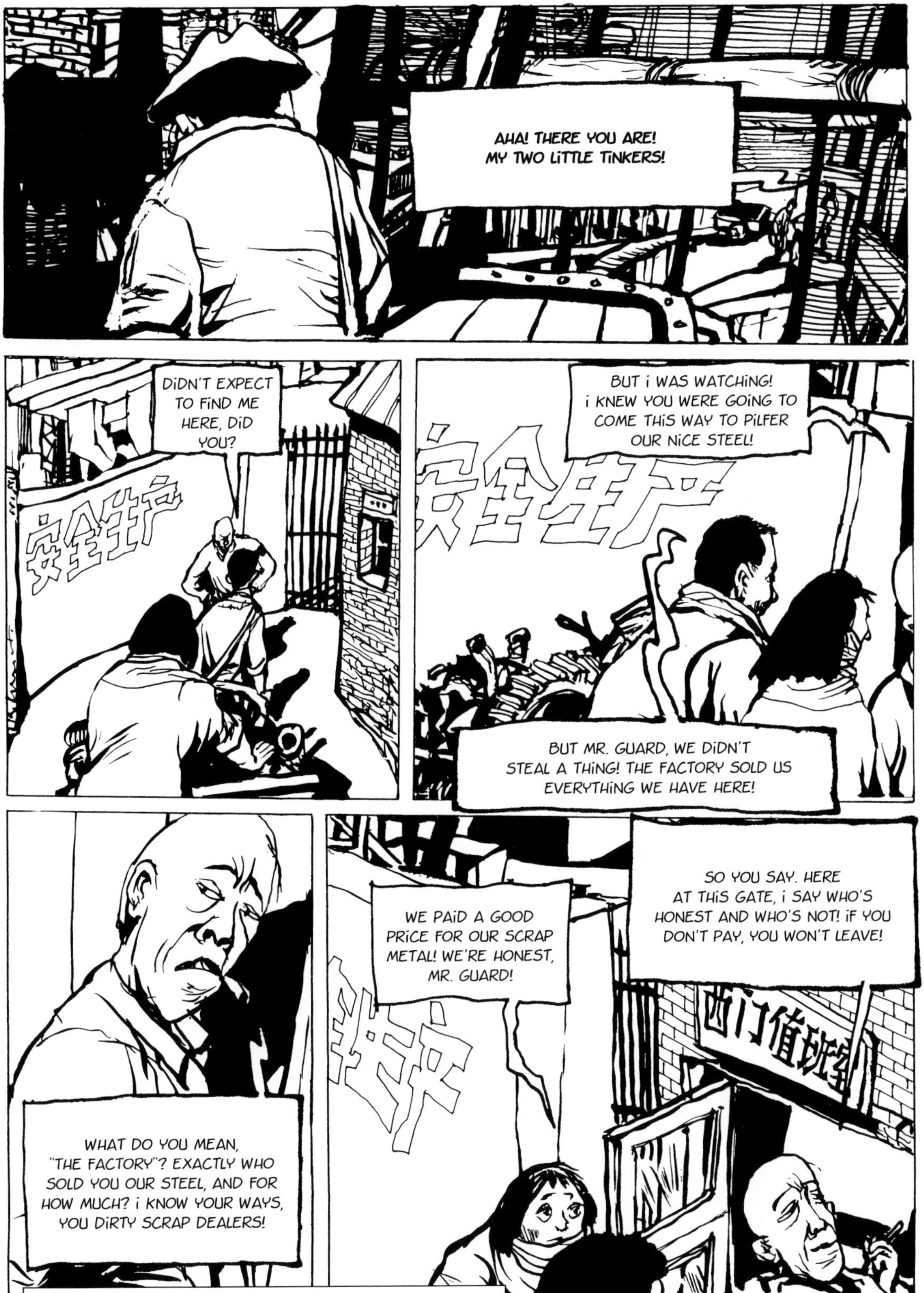

AHA! THERE YOU ARE! MY TWO LITTLE TINKERS!
DIDN'T EXPECT TO FIND ME HERE, DID YOU?
安全生产
BUT I WAS WATCHING! I KNEW YOU WERE GOING TO COME THIS WAY TO PILFER OUR NICE STEEL!
安全生产
BUT MR. GUARD, WE DIDN'T STEAL A THING! THE FACTORY SOLD US EVERYTHING WE HAVE HERE!
WHAT DO YOU MEAN, "THE FACTORY"? EXACTLY WHO SOLD YOU OUR STEEL, AND FOR HOW MUCH? I KNOW YOUR WAYS, YOU DIRTY SCRAP DEALERS!
WE PAID A GOOD PRICE FOR OUR SCRAP METAL! WE'RE HONEST, MR. GUARD!
SO YOU SAY. HERE AT THIS GATE, I SAY WHO'S HONEST AND WHO'S NOT! IF YOU DON'T PAY, YOU WON'T LEAVE!

安全生产 ANQUAN SHENGCHAN: "SAFETY FIRST".

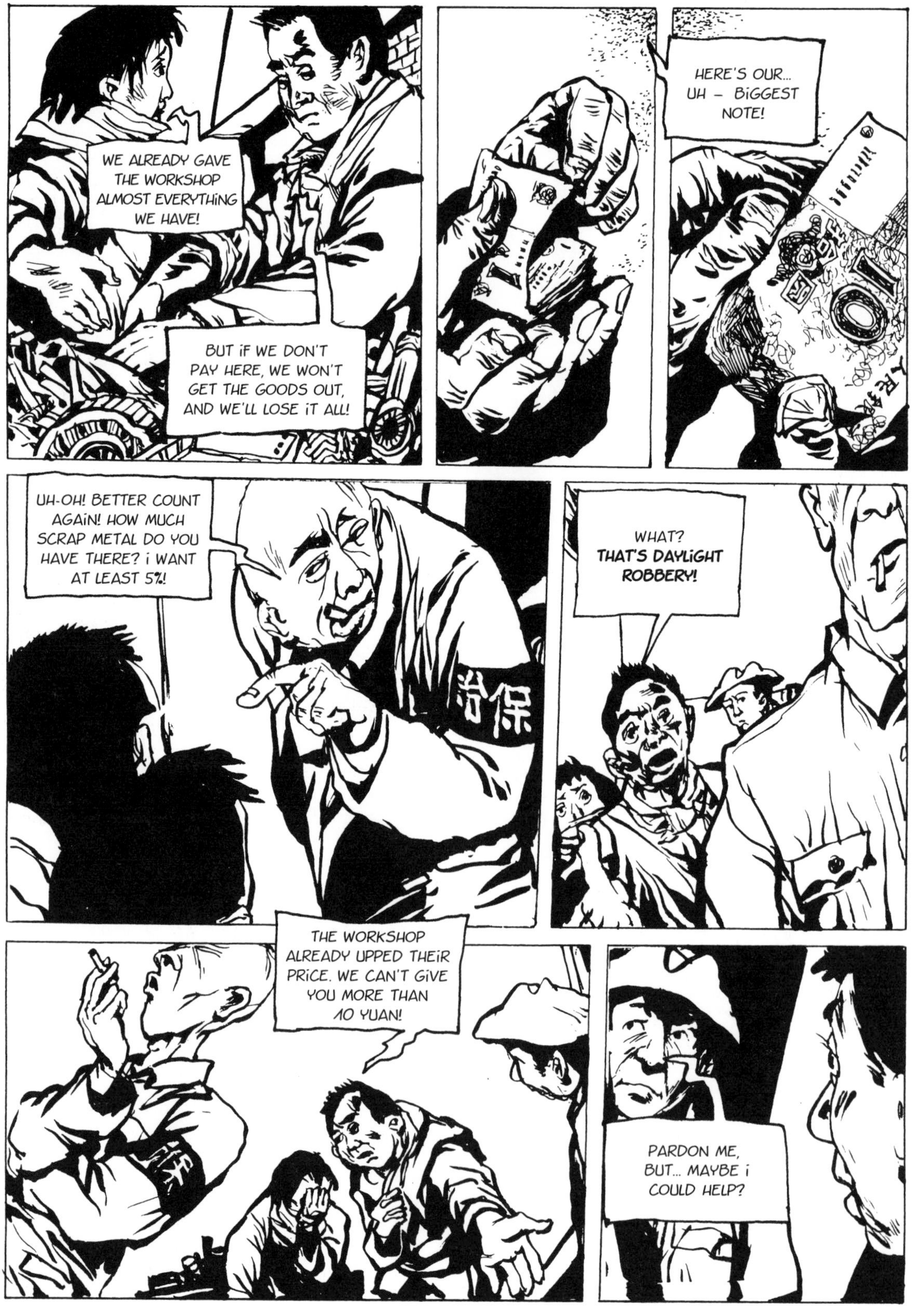
WE ALREADY GAVE THE WORKSHOP ALMOST EVERYTHING WE HAVE!
BUT IF WE DON'T PAY HERE, WE WON'T GET THE GOODS OUT, AND WE'LL LOSE IT ALL!
HERE'S OUR... UH – BIGGEST NOTE!
UH-OH! BETTER COUNT AGAIN! HOW MUCH SCRAP METAL DO YOU HAVE THERE? I WANT AT LEAST 5%!
治保
WHAT? **THAT'S DAYLIGHT ROBBERY!**
THE WORKSHOP ALREADY UPPED THEIR PRICE. WE CAN'T GIVE YOU MORE THAN 10 YUAN!
PARDON ME, BUT... MAYBE I COULD HELP?

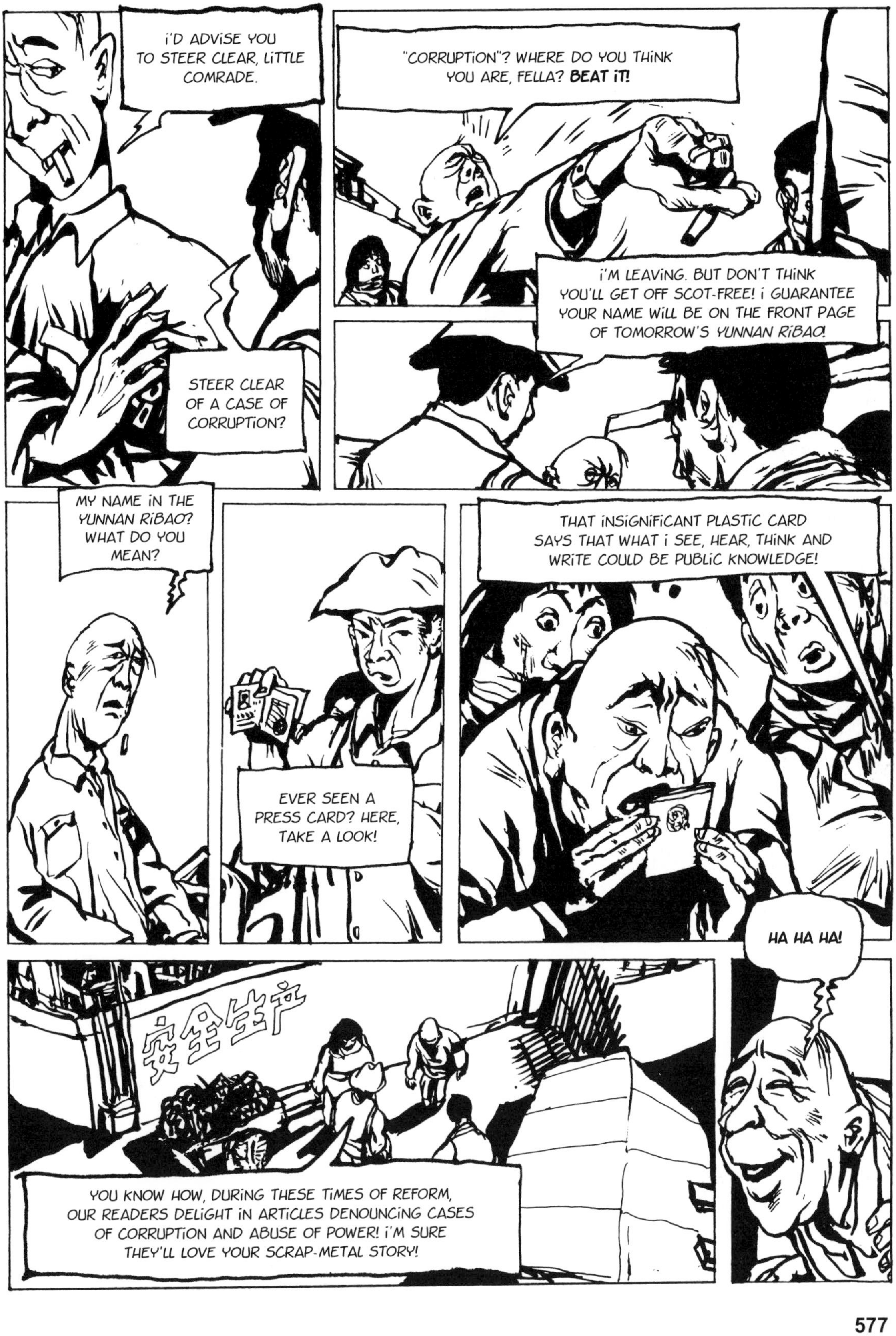
I'D ADVISE YOU TO STEER CLEAR, LITTLE COMRADE.
STEER CLEAR OF A CASE OF CORRUPTION?
"CORRUPTION"? WHERE DO YOU THINK YOU ARE, FELLA? **BEAT IT!**
I'M LEAVING. BUT DON'T THINK YOU'LL GET OFF SCOT-FREE! I GUARANTEE YOUR NAME WILL BE ON THE FRONT PAGE OF TOMORROW'S *YUNNAN RIBAO*!
MY NAME IN THE *YUNNAN RIBAO*? WHAT DO YOU MEAN?
EVER SEEN A PRESS CARD? HERE, TAKE A LOOK!
THAT INSIGNIFICANT PLASTIC CARD SAYS THAT WHAT I SEE, HEAR, THINK AND WRITE COULD BE PUBLIC KNOWLEDGE!
安全生产
YOU KNOW HOW, DURING THESE TIMES OF REFORM, OUR READERS DELIGHT IN ARTICLES DENOUNCING CASES OF CORRUPTION AND ABUSE OF POWER! I'M SURE THEY'LL LOVE YOUR SCRAP-METAL STORY!
HA HA HA!

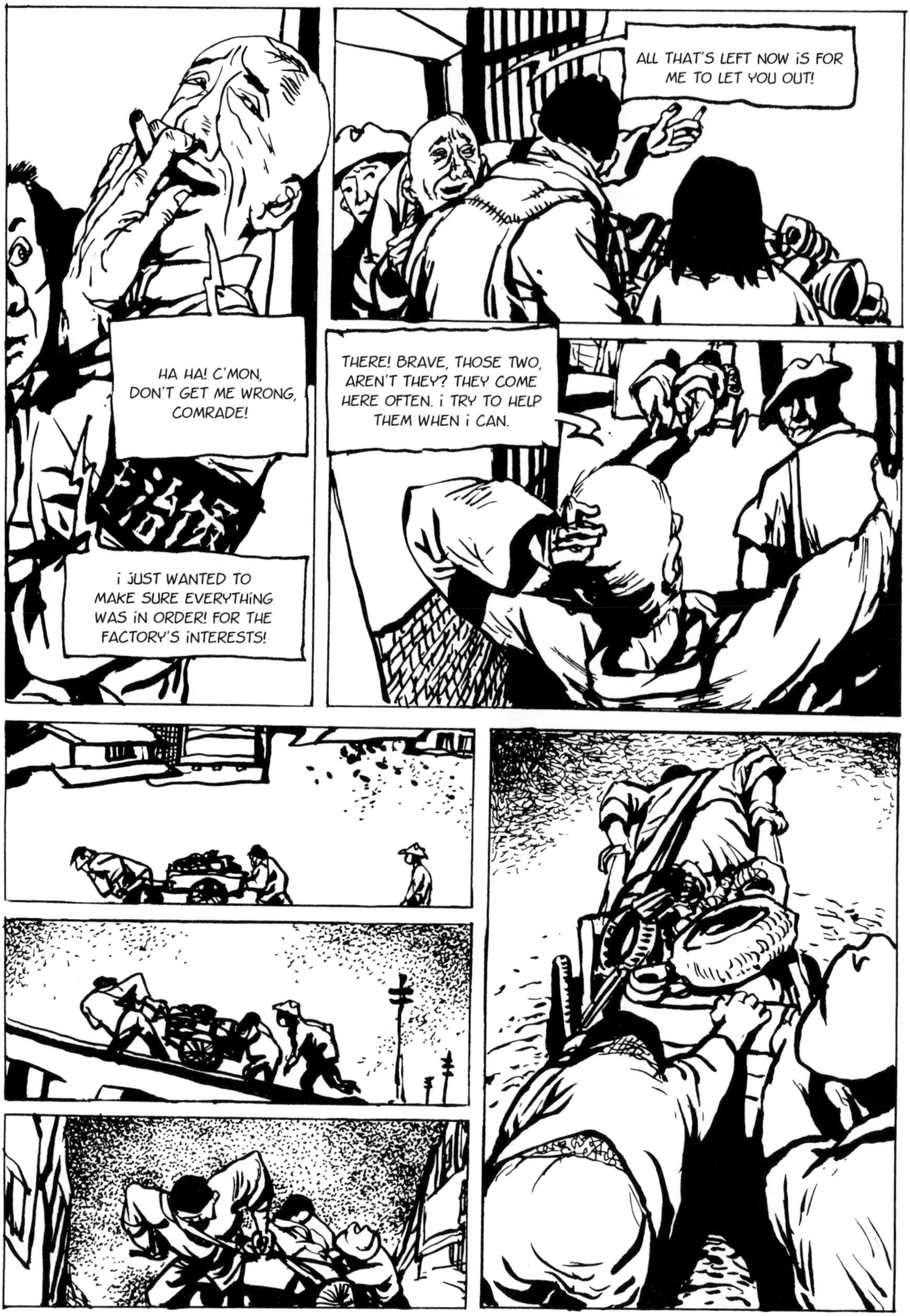
HA HA! C'MON, DON'T GET ME WRONG, COMRADE!
i JUST WANTED TO MAKE SURE EVERYTHiNG WAS iN ORDER! FOR THE FACTORY'S iNTERESTS!
ALL THAT'S LEFT NOW iS FOR ME TO LET YOU OUT!
THERE! BRAVE, THOSE TWO, AREN'T THEY? THEY COME HERE OFTEN. i TRY TO HELP THEM WHEN i CAN.

RONGYU, LOOK! iSN'T THAT A CAN OF OiL OVER THERE?

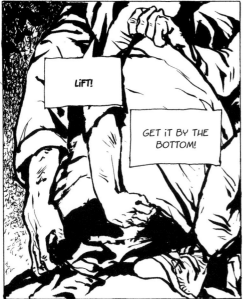

LiFT!

GET iT BY THE BOTTOM!

WAiT, i'M COMiNG!

MUST BE AT LEAST 60 OR 70 LBS!

THANKS FOR YOUR HELP, DA GE!* HERE, WiPE YOUR BROW.

AND HAVE A DRiNK!

*大哥 DÀ GE: LiTERALLY, "BiG BROTHER" (ALSO USED AS A TERM OF FLATTERY).

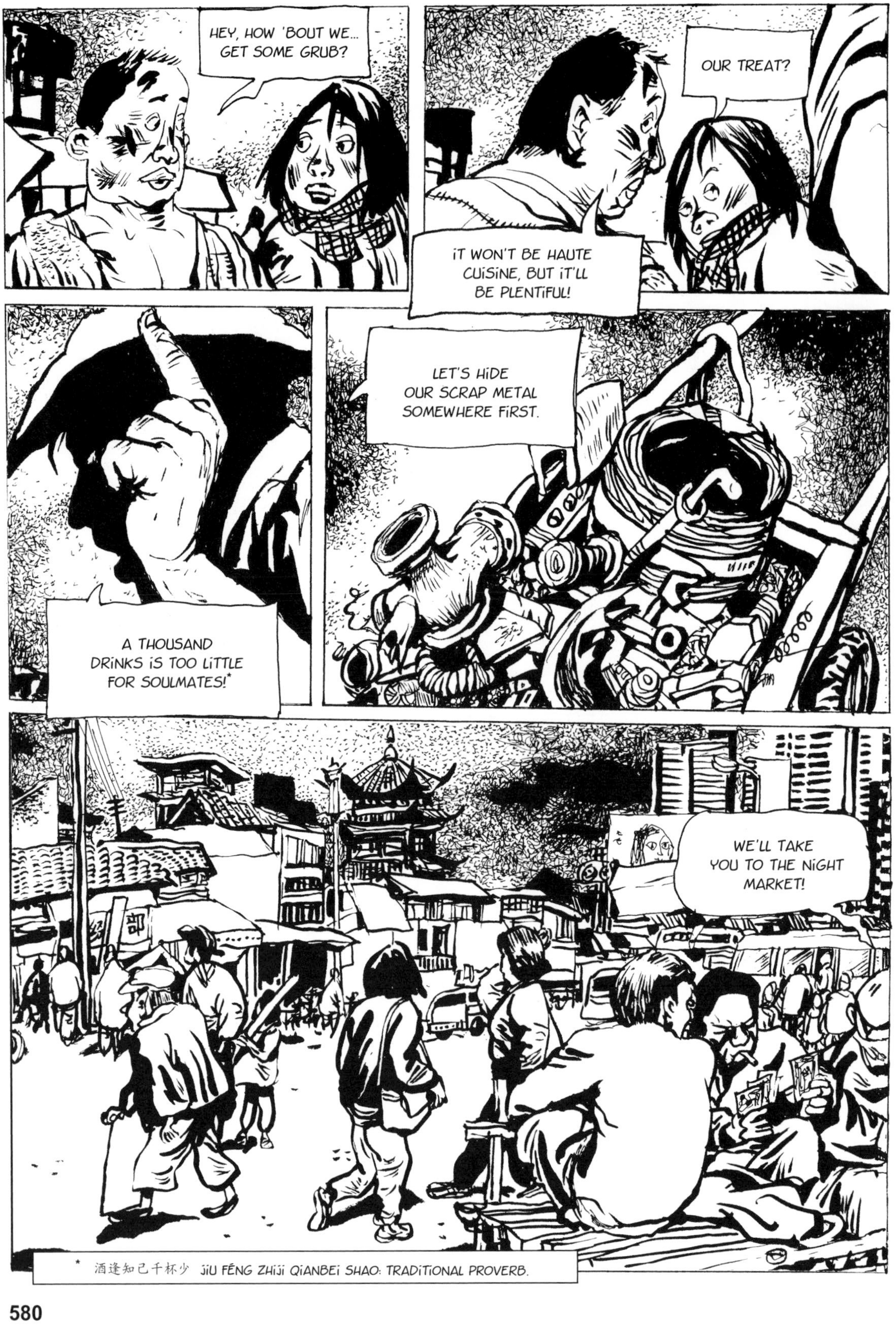
HEY, HOW 'BOUT WE... GET SOME GRUB?
OUR TREAT?
IT WON'T BE HAUTE CUISINE, BUT IT'LL BE PLENTIFUL!
A THOUSAND DRINKS IS TOO LITTLE FOR SOULMATES!*
LET'S HIDE OUR SCRAP METAL SOMEWHERE FIRST.
WE'LL TAKE YOU TO THE NIGHT MARKET!

* 酒逢知己千杯少 JIU FÉNG ZHIJI QIANBEI SHAO: TRADITIONAL PROVERB.

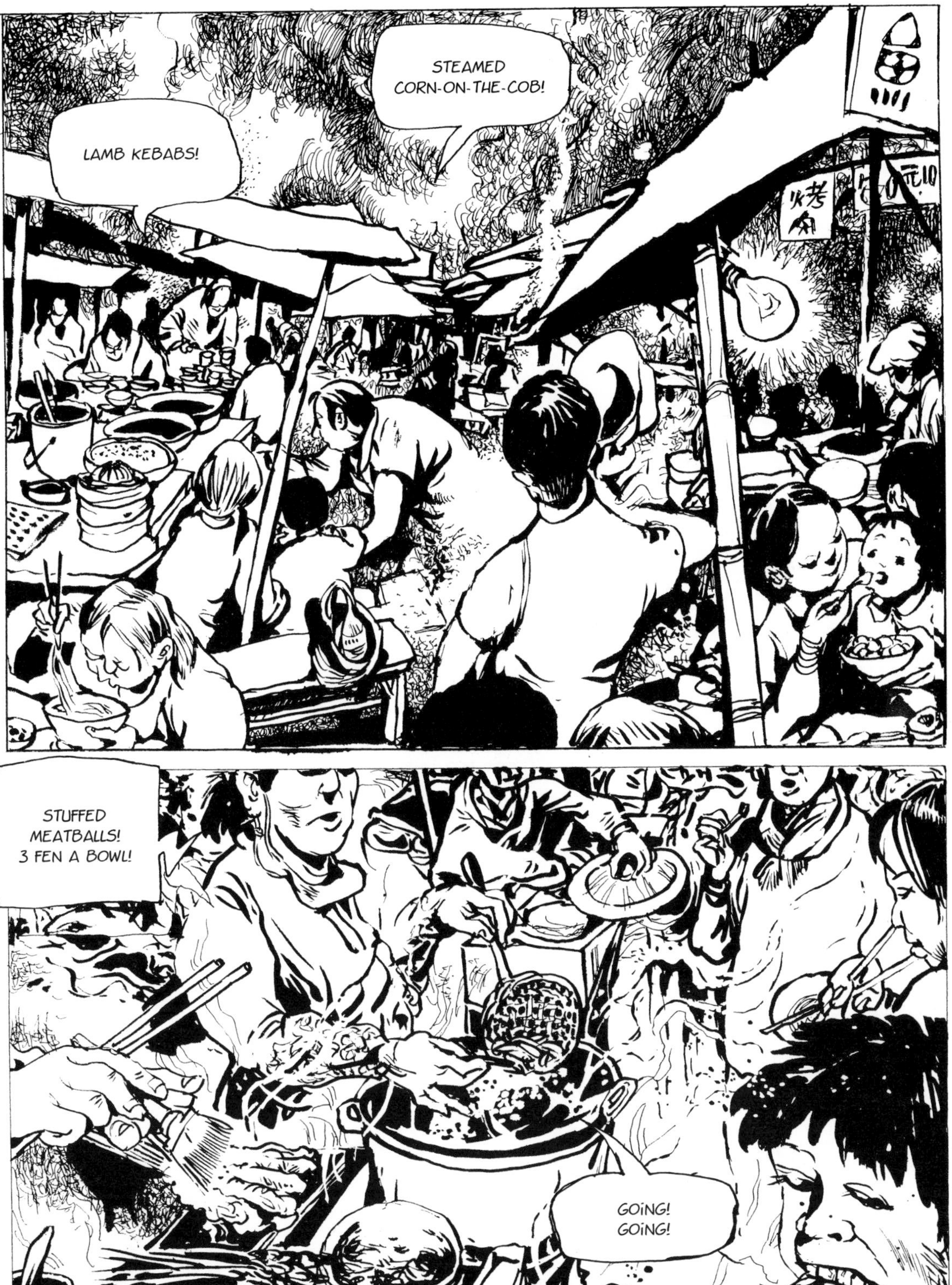
LAMB KEBABS!
STEAMED CORN-ON-THE-COB!
STUFFED MEATBALLS! 3 FEN A BOWL!
GOiNG! GOiNG!

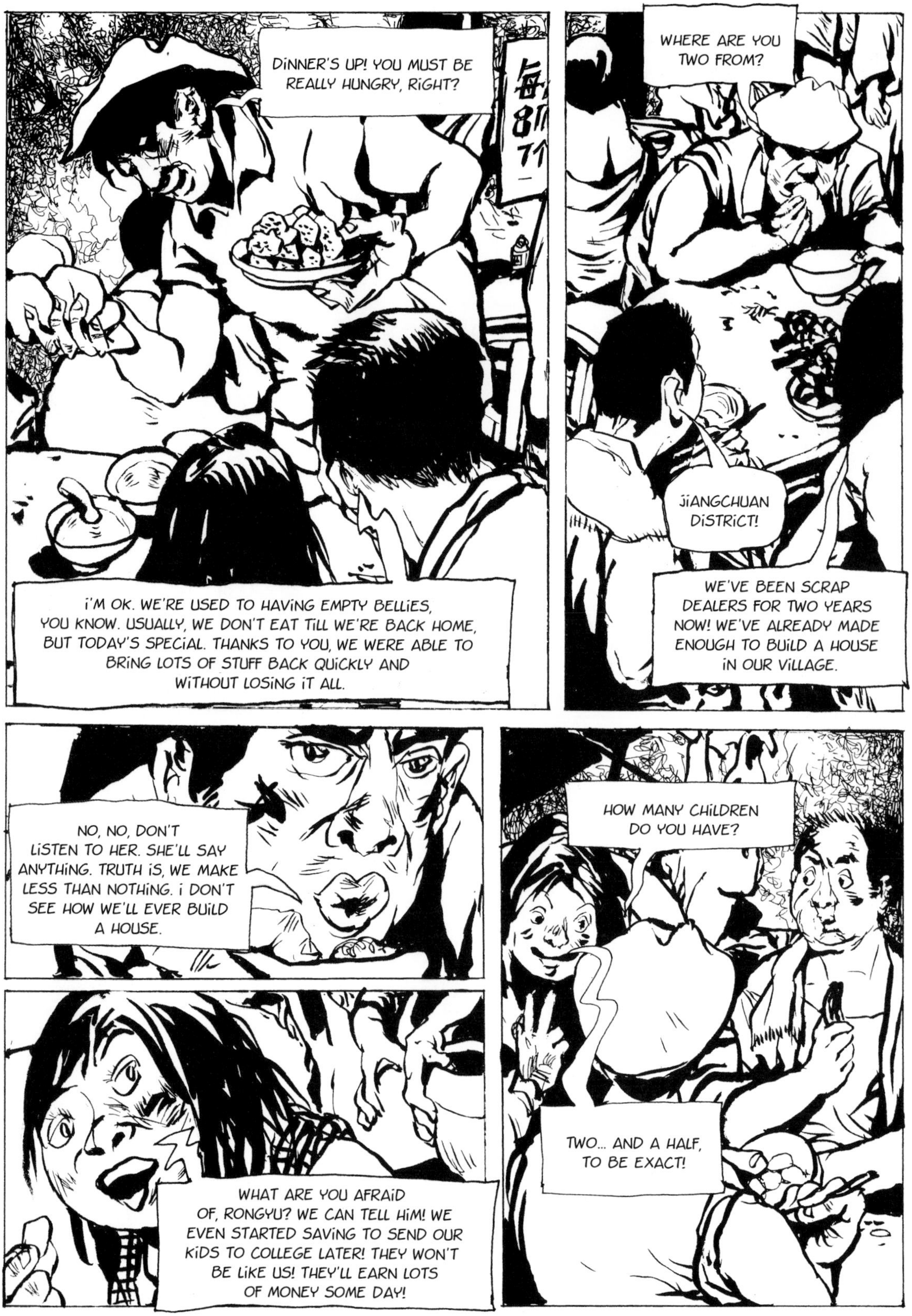
DINNER'S UP! YOU MUST BE REALLY HUNGRY, RIGHT?
I'M OK. WE'RE USED TO HAVING EMPTY BELLIES, YOU KNOW. USUALLY, WE DON'T EAT TILL WE'RE BACK HOME, BUT TODAY'S SPECIAL. THANKS TO YOU, WE WERE ABLE TO BRING LOTS OF STUFF BACK QUICKLY AND WITHOUT LOSING IT ALL.
WHERE ARE YOU TWO FROM?
JIANGCHUAN DISTRICT!
WE'VE BEEN SCRAP DEALERS FOR TWO YEARS NOW! WE'VE ALREADY MADE ENOUGH TO BUILD A HOUSE IN OUR VILLAGE.
NO, NO, DON'T LISTEN TO HER. SHE'LL SAY ANYTHING. TRUTH IS, WE MAKE LESS THAN NOTHING. I DON'T SEE HOW WE'LL EVER BUILD A HOUSE.
WHAT ARE YOU AFRAID OF, RONGYU? WE CAN TELL HIM! WE EVEN STARTED SAVING TO SEND OUR KIDS TO COLLEGE LATER! THEY WON'T BE LIKE US! THEY'LL EARN LOTS OF MONEY SOME DAY!
HOW MANY CHILDREN DO YOU HAVE?
TWO... AND A HALF, TO BE EXACT!

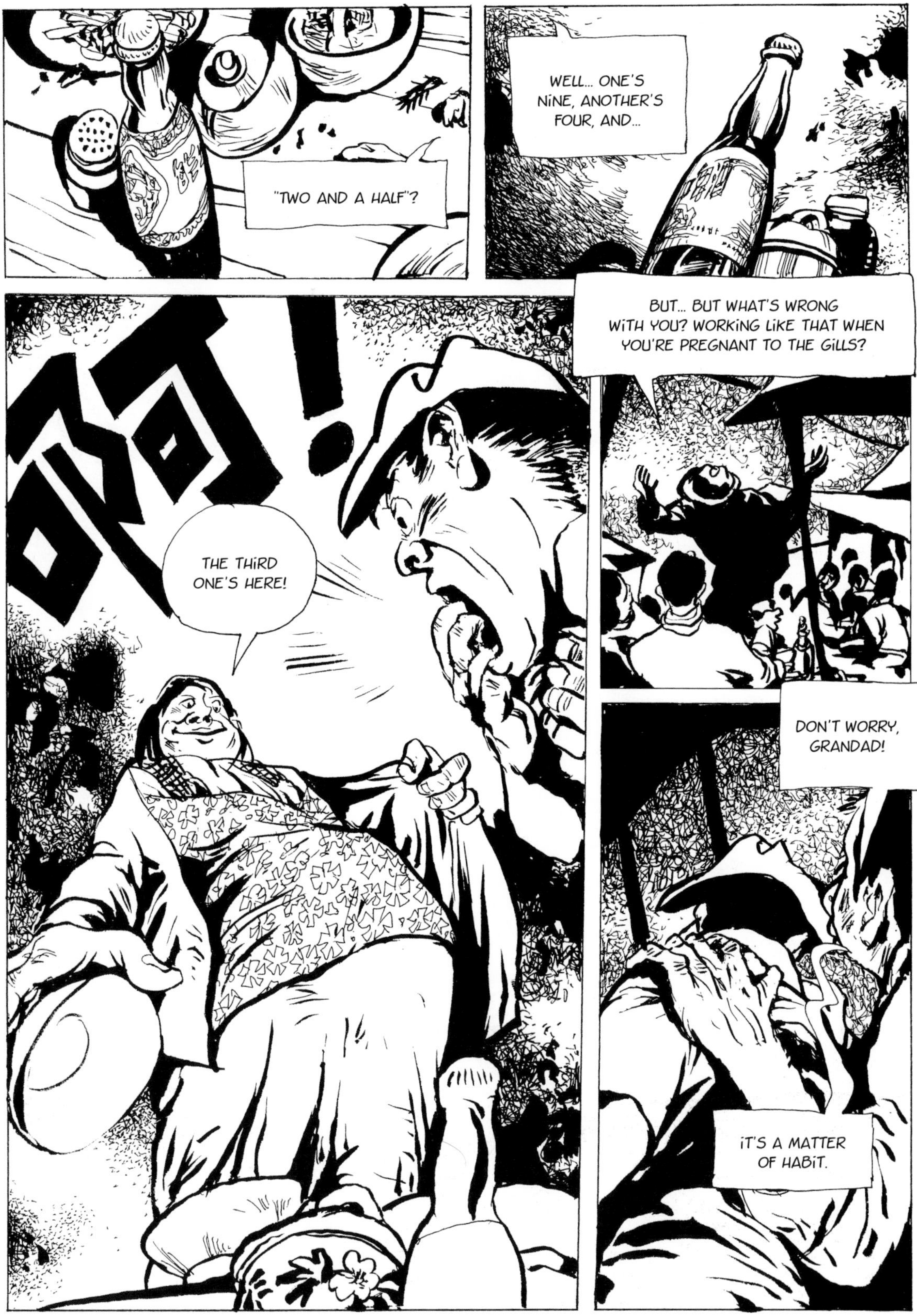
"TWO AND A HALF"?
WELL... ONE'S NINE, ANOTHER'S FOUR, AND...
THE THIRD ONE'S HERE!
BUT... BUT WHAT'S WRONG WITH YOU? WORKING LIKE THAT WHEN YOU'RE PREGNANT TO THE GILLS?
DON'T WORRY, GRANDAD!
IT'S A MATTER OF HABIT.

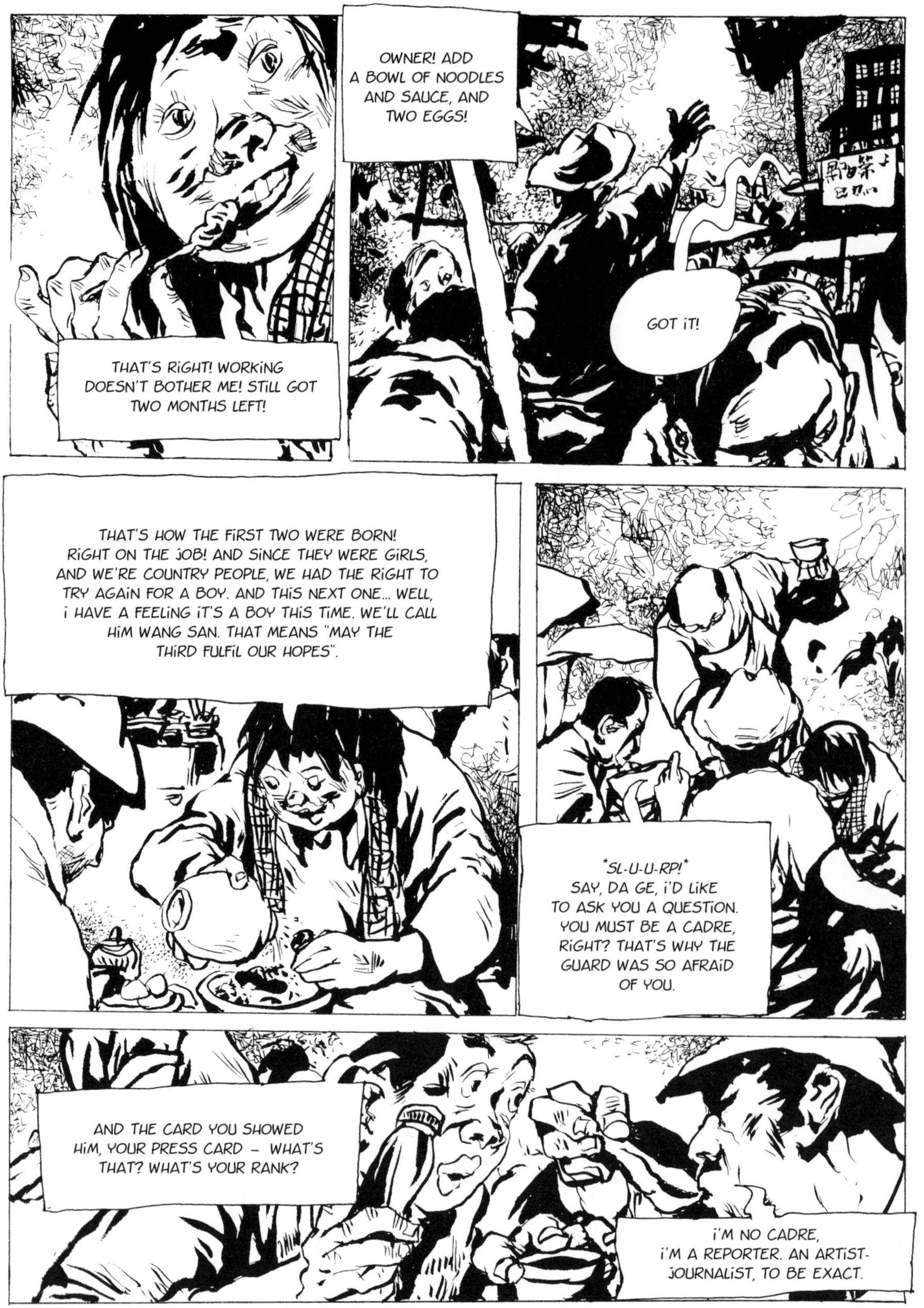
THAT'S RIGHT! WORKING DOESN'T BOTHER ME! STILL GOT TWO MONTHS LEFT!
OWNER! ADD A BOWL OF NOODLES AND SAUCE, AND TWO EGGS!
GOT IT!
THAT'S HOW THE FIRST TWO WERE BORN! RIGHT ON THE JOB! AND SINCE THEY WERE GIRLS, AND WE'RE COUNTRY PEOPLE, WE HAD THE RIGHT TO TRY AGAIN FOR A BOY. AND THIS NEXT ONE... WELL, I HAVE A FEELING IT'S A BOY THIS TIME. WE'LL CALL HIM WANG SAN. THAT MEANS "MAY THE THIRD FULFIL OUR HOPES".
SL-U-U-RP! SAY, DA GE, I'D LIKE TO ASK YOU A QUESTION. YOU MUST BE A CADRE, RIGHT? THAT'S WHY THE GUARD WAS SO AFRAID OF YOU.
AND THE CARD YOU SHOWED HIM, YOUR PRESS CARD – WHAT'S THAT? WHAT'S YOUR RANK?
I'M NO CADRE, I'M A REPORTER. AN ARTIST-JOURNALIST, TO BE EXACT.

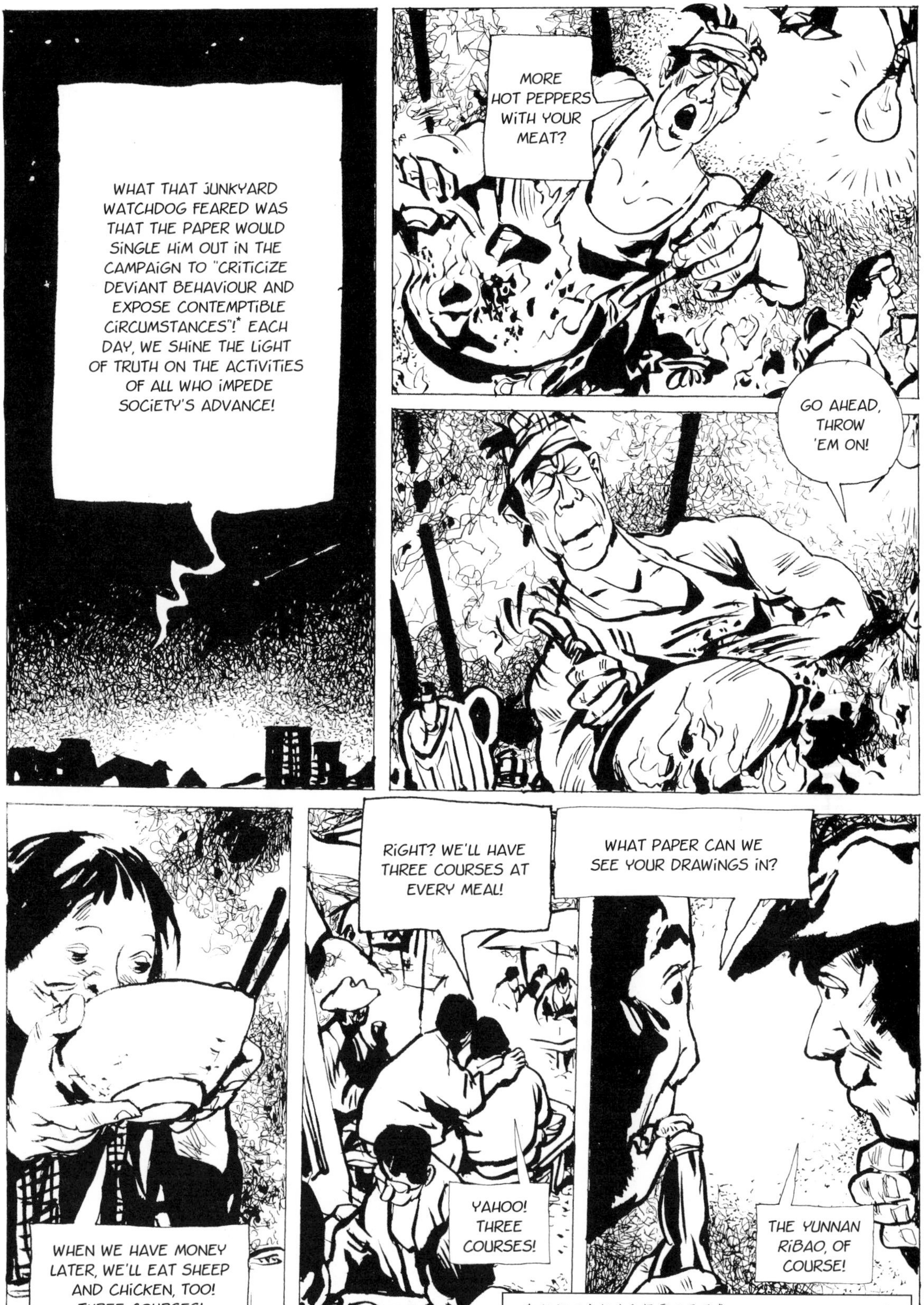
WHAT THAT JUNKYARD WATCHDOG FEARED WAS THAT THE PAPER WOULD SINGLE HIM OUT IN THE CAMPAIGN TO "CRITICIZE DEVIANT BEHAVIOUR AND EXPOSE CONTEMPTIBLE CIRCUMSTANCES"!* EACH DAY, WE SHINE THE LIGHT OF TRUTH ON THE ACTIVITIES OF ALL WHO IMPEDE SOCIETY'S ADVANCE!
MORE HOT PEPPERS WITH YOUR MEAT?
GO AHEAD, THROW 'EM ON!
WHEN WE HAVE MONEY LATER, WE'LL EAT SHEEP AND CHICKEN, TOO! THREE COURSES!
RIGHT? WE'LL HAVE THREE COURSES AT EVERY MEAL!
YAHOO! THREE COURSES!
WHAT PAPER CAN WE SEE YOUR DRAWINGS IN?
THE YUNNAN RIBAO, OF COURSE!

* 批评不良行为和揭露丑恶现象 PIPING BULIANG XINGWÉI HÉ JIELÙ CHOU È XIANXIANG.

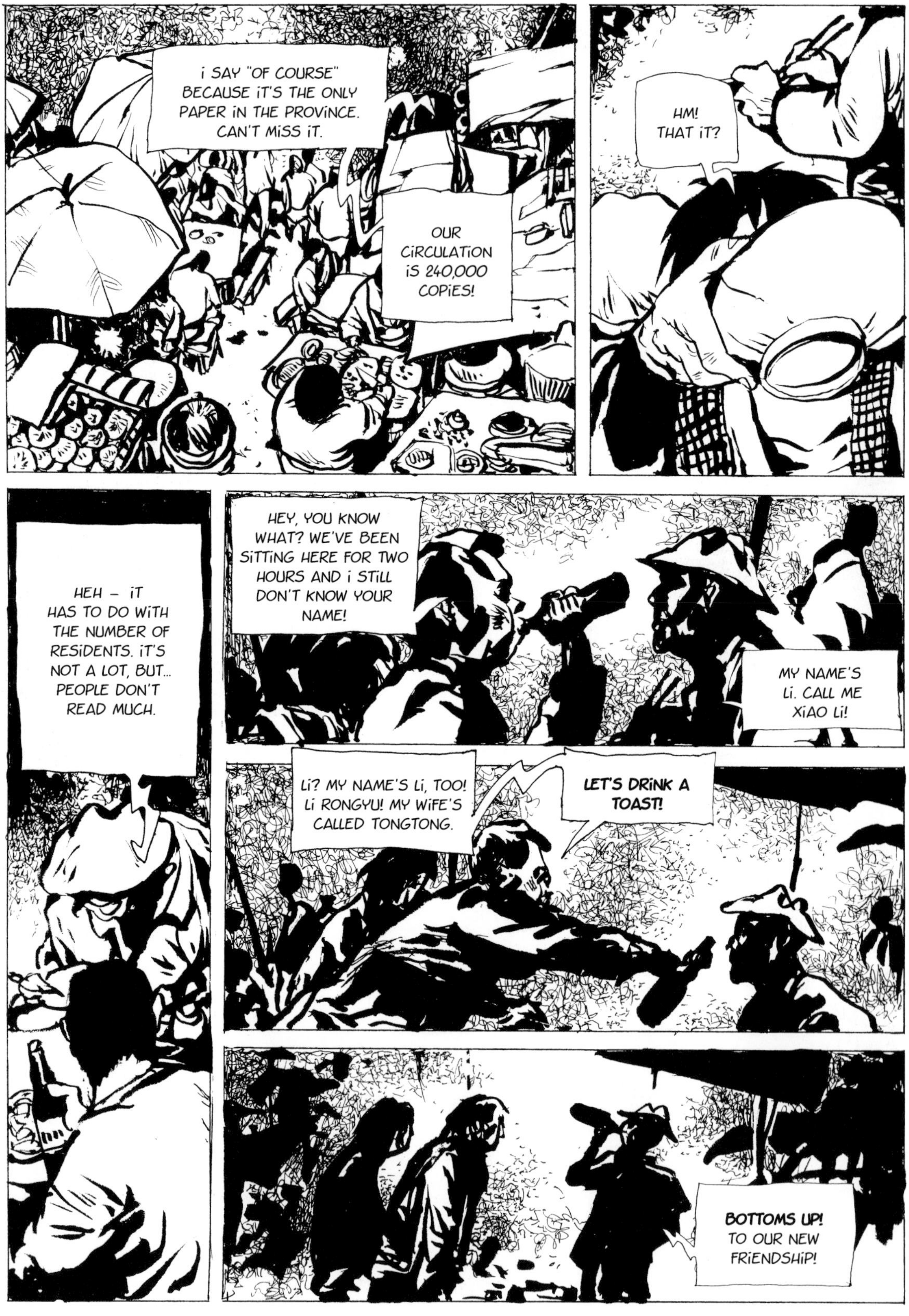

I SAY "OF COURSE" BECAUSE IT'S THE ONLY PAPER IN THE PROVINCE. CAN'T MISS IT.
OUR CIRCULATION IS 240,000 COPIES!
HM! THAT IT?
HEH – IT HAS TO DO WITH THE NUMBER OF RESIDENTS. IT'S NOT A LOT, BUT... PEOPLE DON'T READ MUCH.
HEY, YOU KNOW WHAT? WE'VE BEEN SITTING HERE FOR TWO HOURS AND I STILL DON'T KNOW YOUR NAME!
MY NAME'S LI. CALL ME XIAO LI!
LI? MY NAME'S LI, TOO! LI RONGYU! MY WIFE'S CALLED TONGTONG.
LET'S DRINK A TOAST!
BOTTOMS UP! TO OUR NEW FRIENDSHIP!

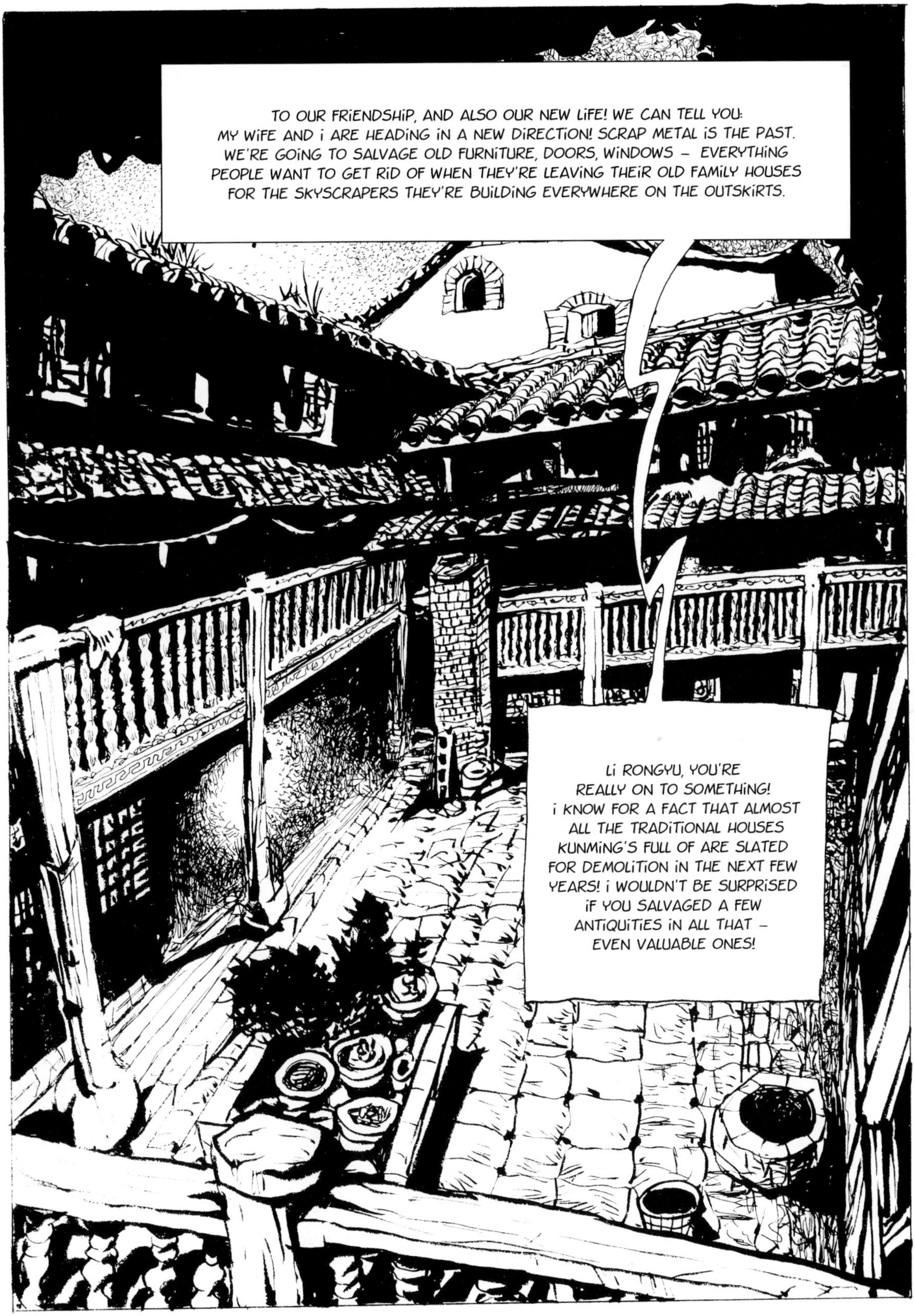
TO OUR FRIENDSHIP, AND ALSO OUR NEW LIFE! WE CAN TELL YOU: MY WIFE AND I ARE HEADING IN A NEW DIRECTION! SCRAP METAL IS THE PAST. WE'RE GOING TO SALVAGE OLD FURNITURE, DOORS, WINDOWS – EVERYTHING PEOPLE WANT TO GET RID OF WHEN THEY'RE LEAVING THEIR OLD FAMILY HOUSES FOR THE SKYSCRAPERS THEY'RE BUILDING EVERYWHERE ON THE OUTSKIRTS.
LI RONGYU, YOU'RE REALLY ON TO SOMETHING! I KNOW FOR A FACT THAT ALMOST ALL THE TRADITIONAL HOUSES KUNMING'S FULL OF ARE SLATED FOR DEMOLITION IN THE NEXT FEW YEARS! I WOULDN'T BE SURPRISED IF YOU SALVAGED A FEW ANTIQUITIES IN ALL THAT – EVEN VALUABLE ONES!

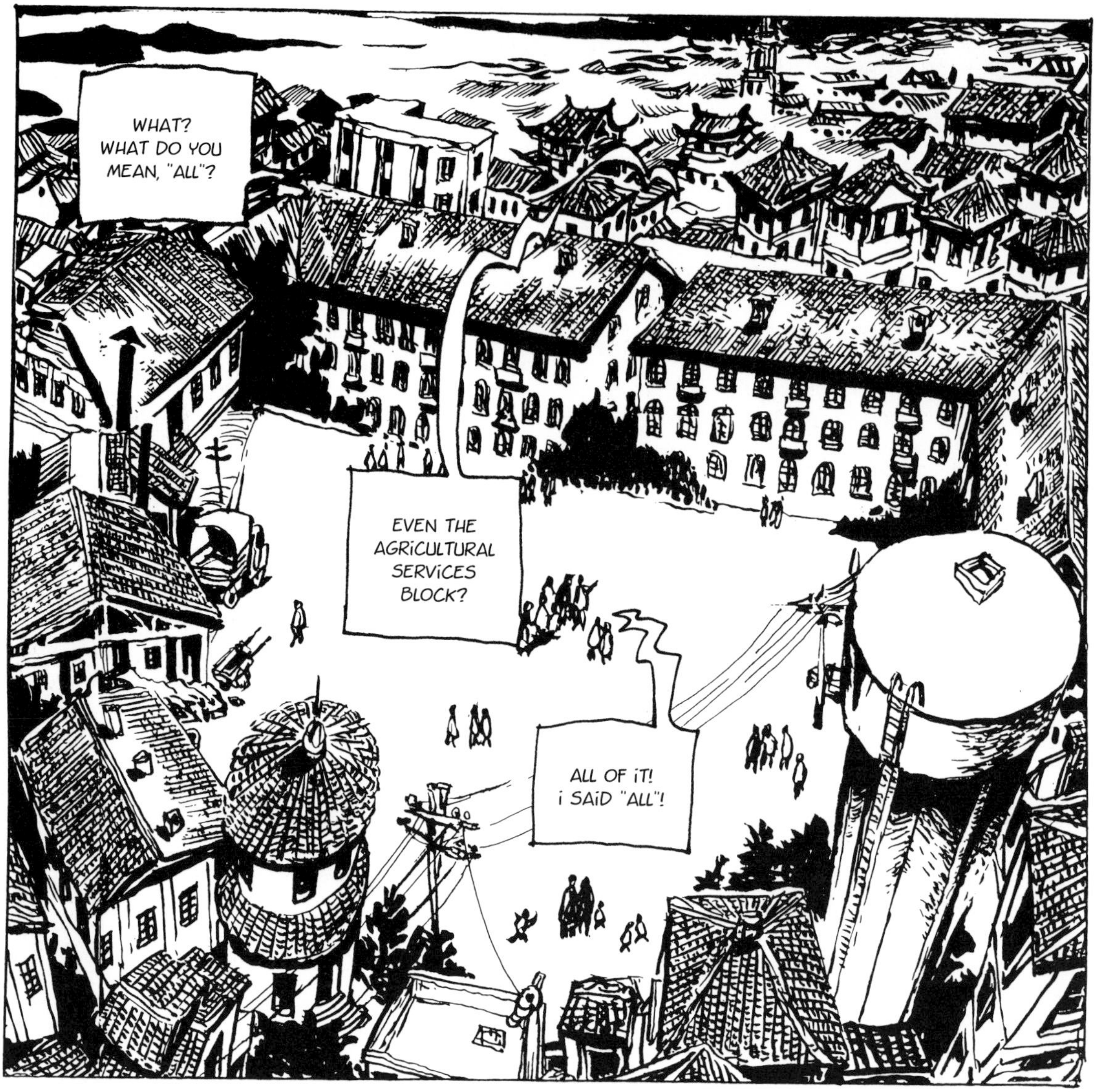
WHAT? WHAT DO YOU MEAN, "ALL"?
EVEN THE AGRICULTURAL SERVICES BLOCK?
ALL OF IT! I SAID "ALL"!

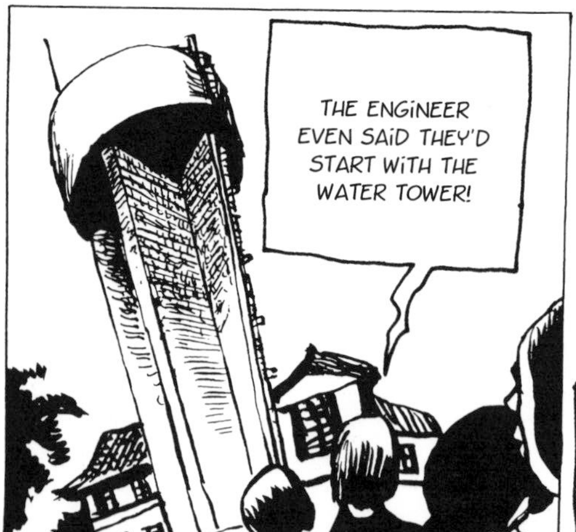
THE ENGINEER EVEN SAID THEY'D START WITH THE WATER TOWER!

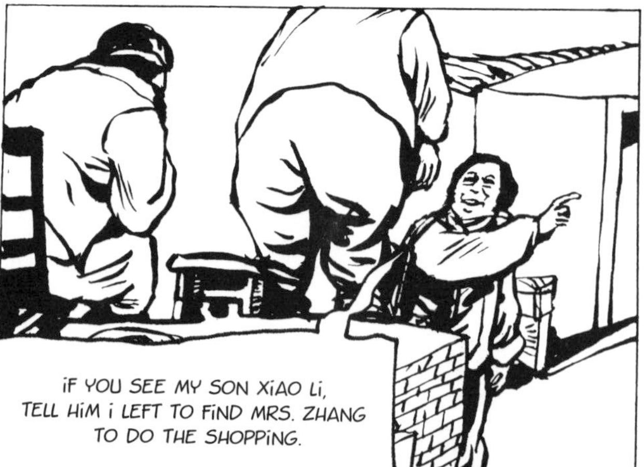
IF YOU SEE MY SON XIAO LI, TELL HIM I LEFT TO FIND MRS. ZHANG TO DO THE SHOPPING.

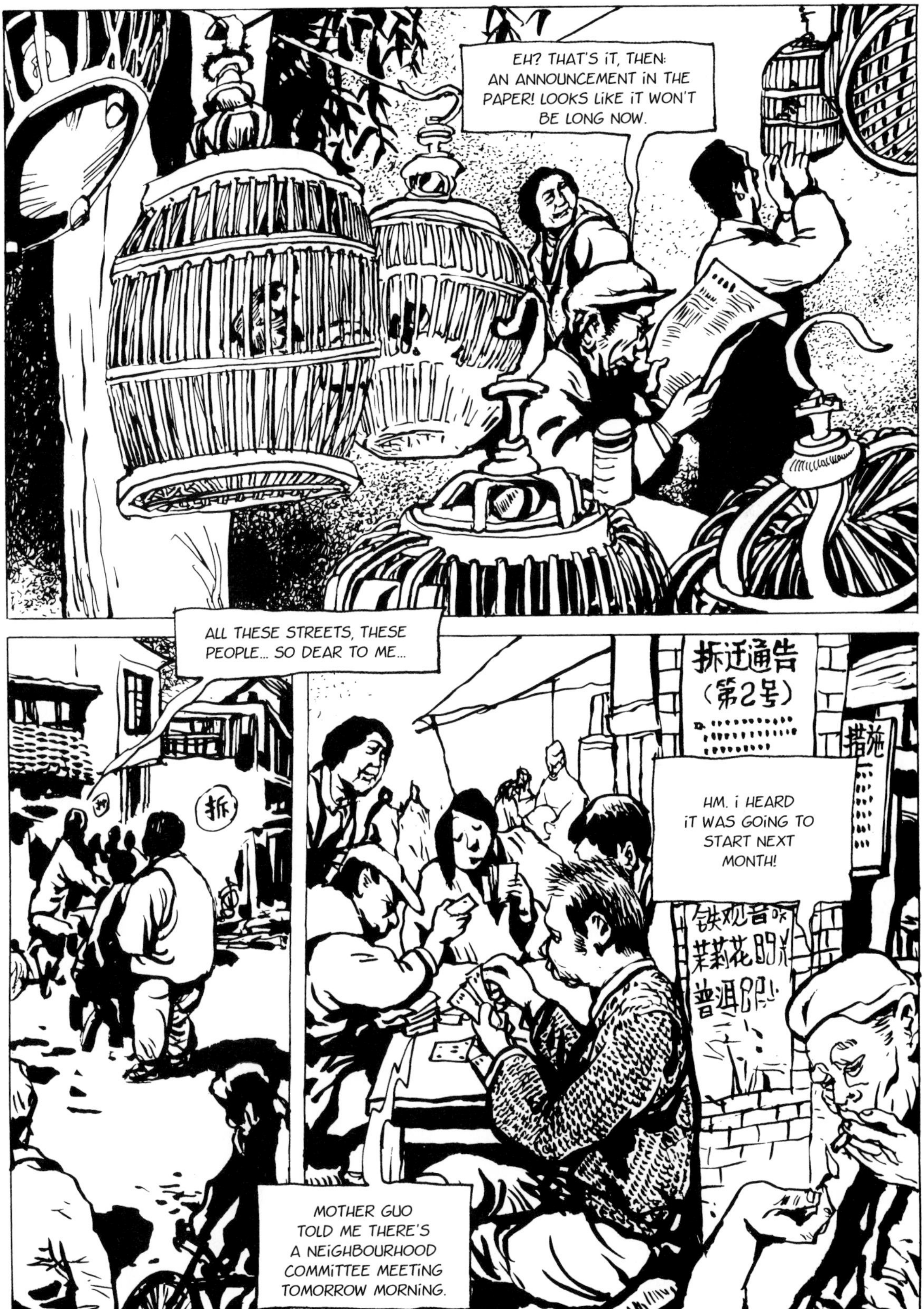
EH? THAT'S iT, THEN: AN ANNOUNCEMENT iN THE PAPER! LOOKS LiKE iT WON'T BE LONG NOW.
ALL THESE STREETS, THESE PEOPLE... SO DEAR TO ME...
拆
拆迁通告
(第2号)
措施
HM. i HEARD iT WAS GOiNG TO START NEXT MONTH!
铁观音
茉莉花
普洱
MOTHER GUO TOLD ME THERE'S A NEiGHBOURHOOD COMMiTTEE MEETiNG TOMORROW MORNiNG.

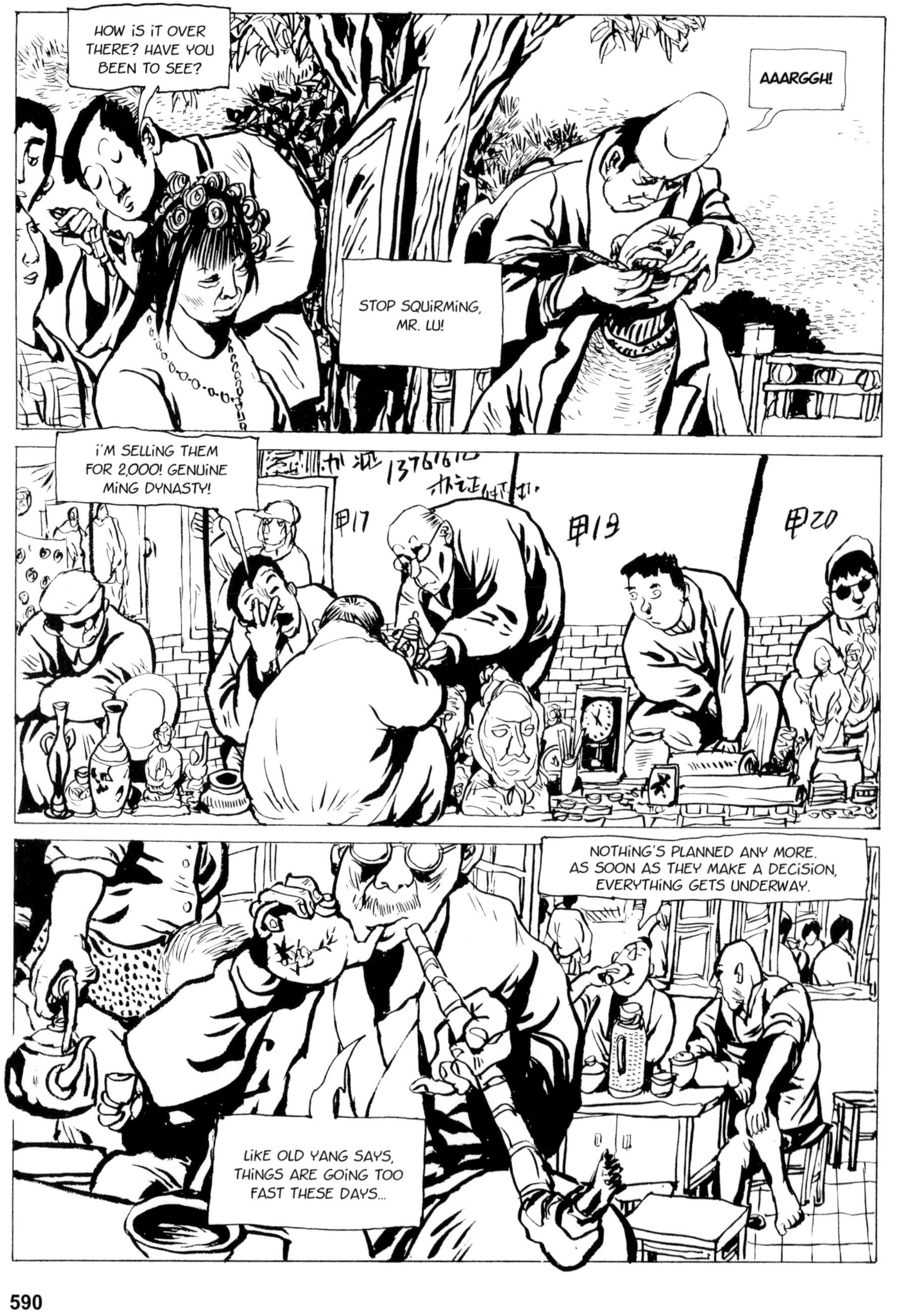
HOW iS iT OVER THERE? HAVE YOU BEEN TO SEE?
AAARGGH!
STOP SQUiRMiNG, MR. LU!
i'M SELLiNG THEM FOR 2,000! GENUiNE MiNG DYNASTY!
甲17
甲19
甲20
NOTHiNG'S PLANNED ANY MORE. AS SOON AS THEY MAKE A DECiSiON, EVERYTHiNG GETS UNDERWAY.
LiKE OLD YANG SAYS, THiNGS ARE GOiNG TOO FAST THESE DAYS...

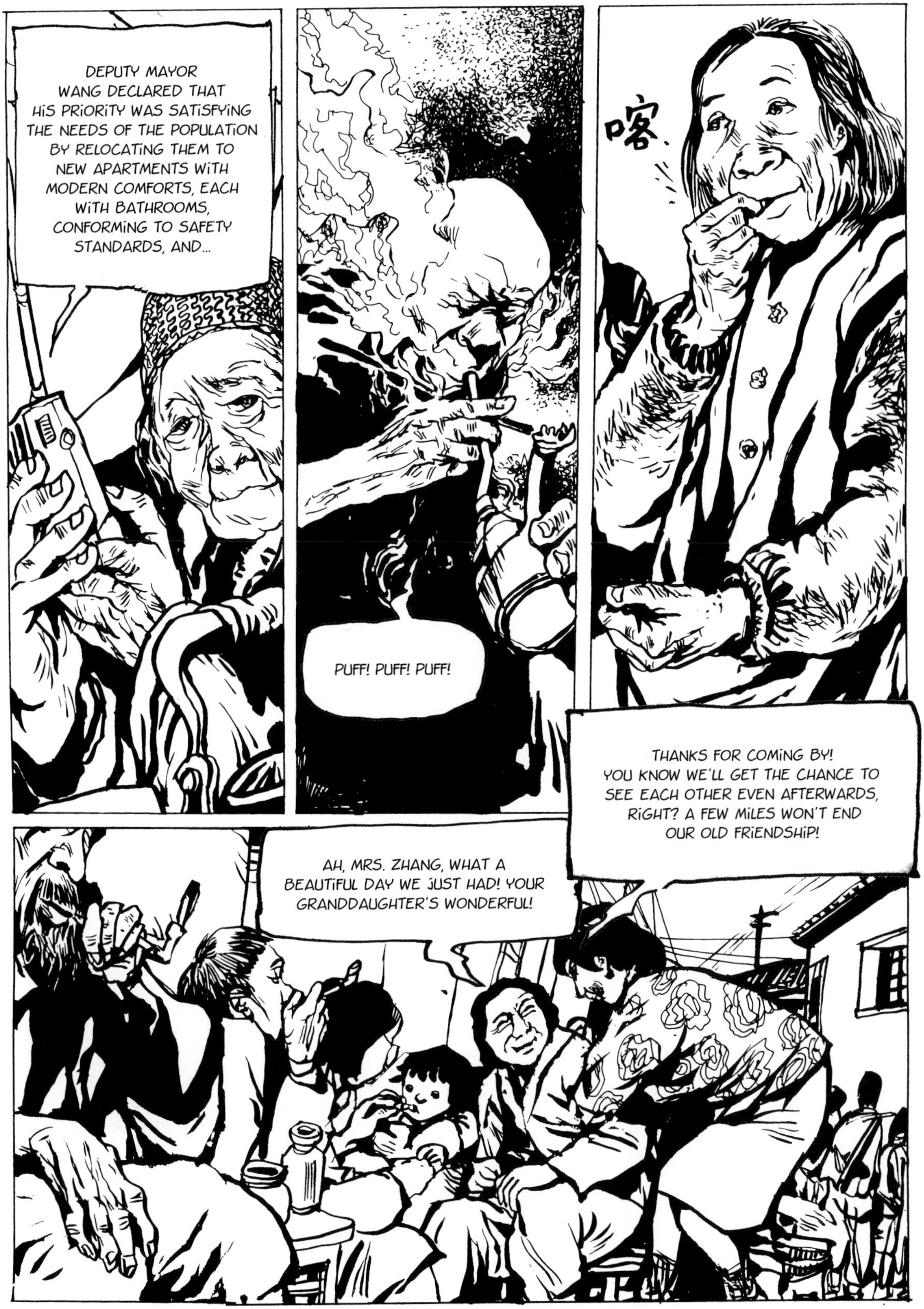
DEPUTY MAYOR WANG DECLARED THAT HIS PRIORITY WAS SATISFYING THE NEEDS OF THE POPULATION BY RELOCATING THEM TO NEW APARTMENTS WITH MODERN COMFORTS, EACH WITH BATHROOMS, CONFORMING TO SAFETY STANDARDS, AND...
PUFF! PUFF! PUFF!
喀.
THANKS FOR COMING BY! YOU KNOW WE'LL GET THE CHANCE TO SEE EACH OTHER EVEN AFTERWARDS, RIGHT? A FEW MILES WON'T END OUR OLD FRIENDSHIP!
AH, MRS. ZHANG, WHAT A BEAUTIFUL DAY WE JUST HAD! YOUR GRANDDAUGHTER'S WONDERFUL!

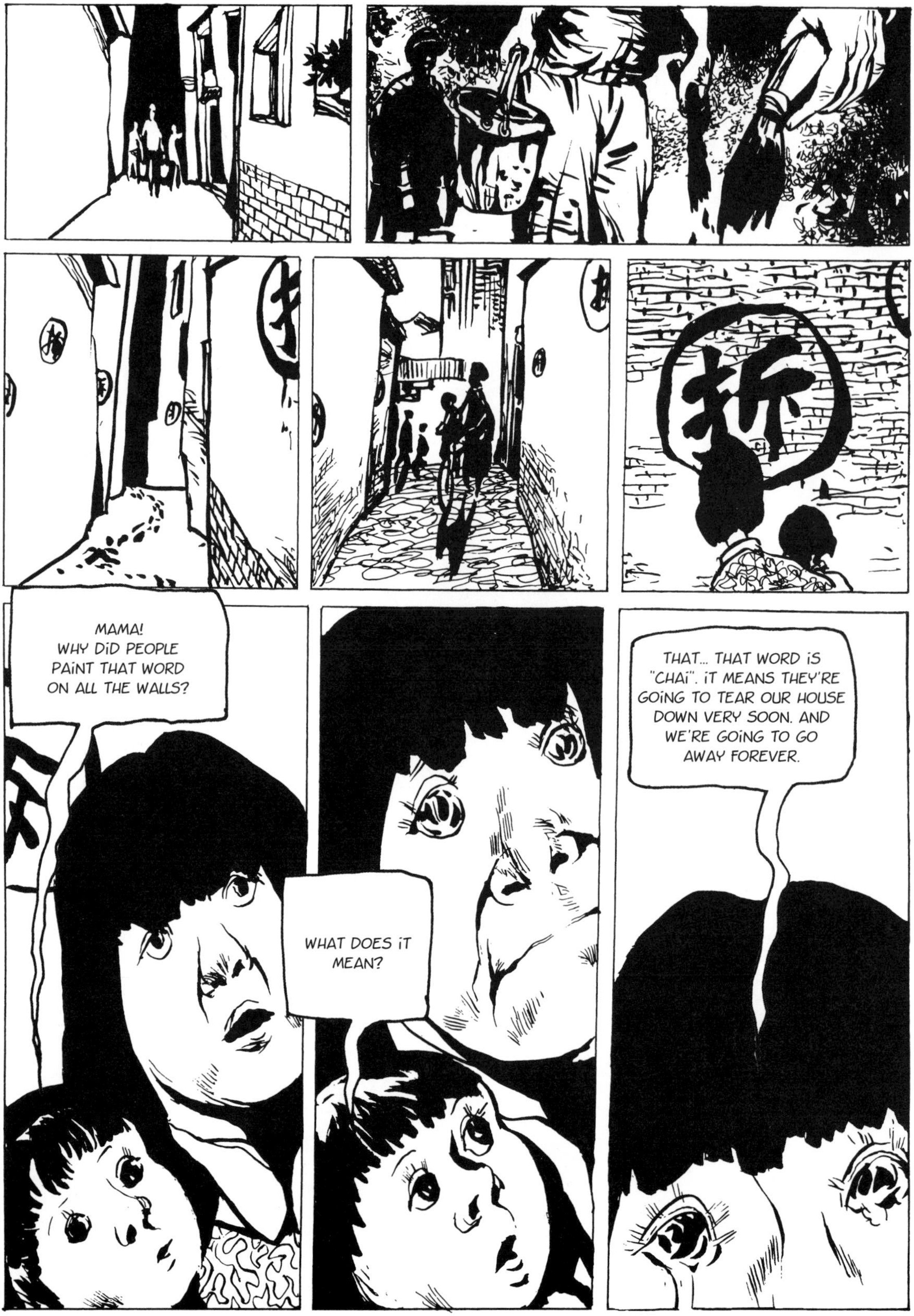
MAMA! WHY DID PEOPLE PAINT THAT WORD ON ALL THE WALLS?
WHAT DOES IT MEAN?
THAT... THAT WORD IS "CHAI". IT MEANS THEY'RE GOING TO TEAR OUR HOUSE DOWN VERY SOON. AND WE'RE GOING TO GO AWAY FOREVER.

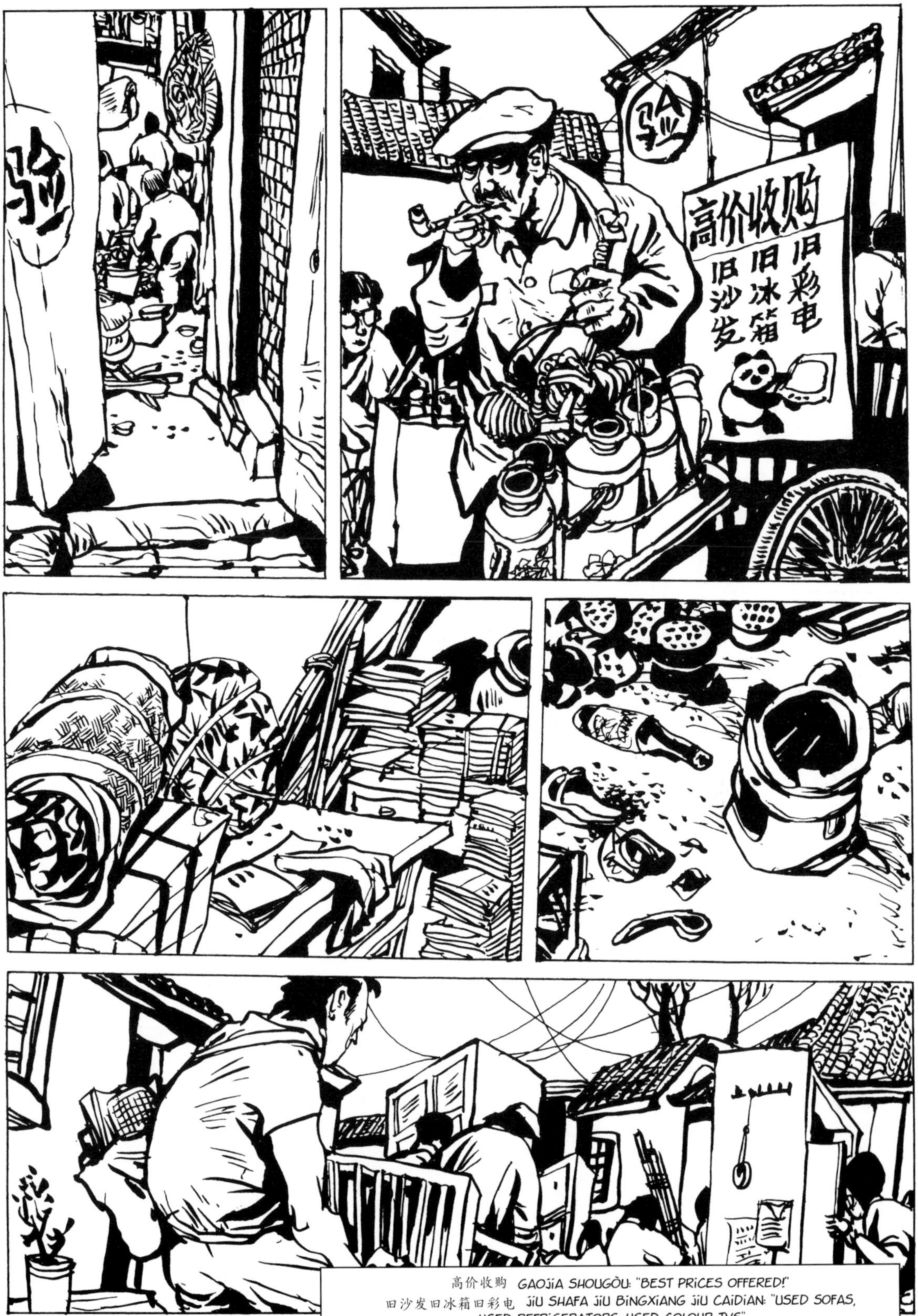
高价收购
旧彩电
旧冰箱
旧沙发
高价收购 GAOJIA SHOUGOU: "BEST PRICES OFFERED!"
旧沙发旧冰箱旧彩电 JIU SHAFA JIU BINGXIANG JIU CAIDIAN: "USED SOFAS, USED REFRIGERATORS, USED COLOUR TVS".

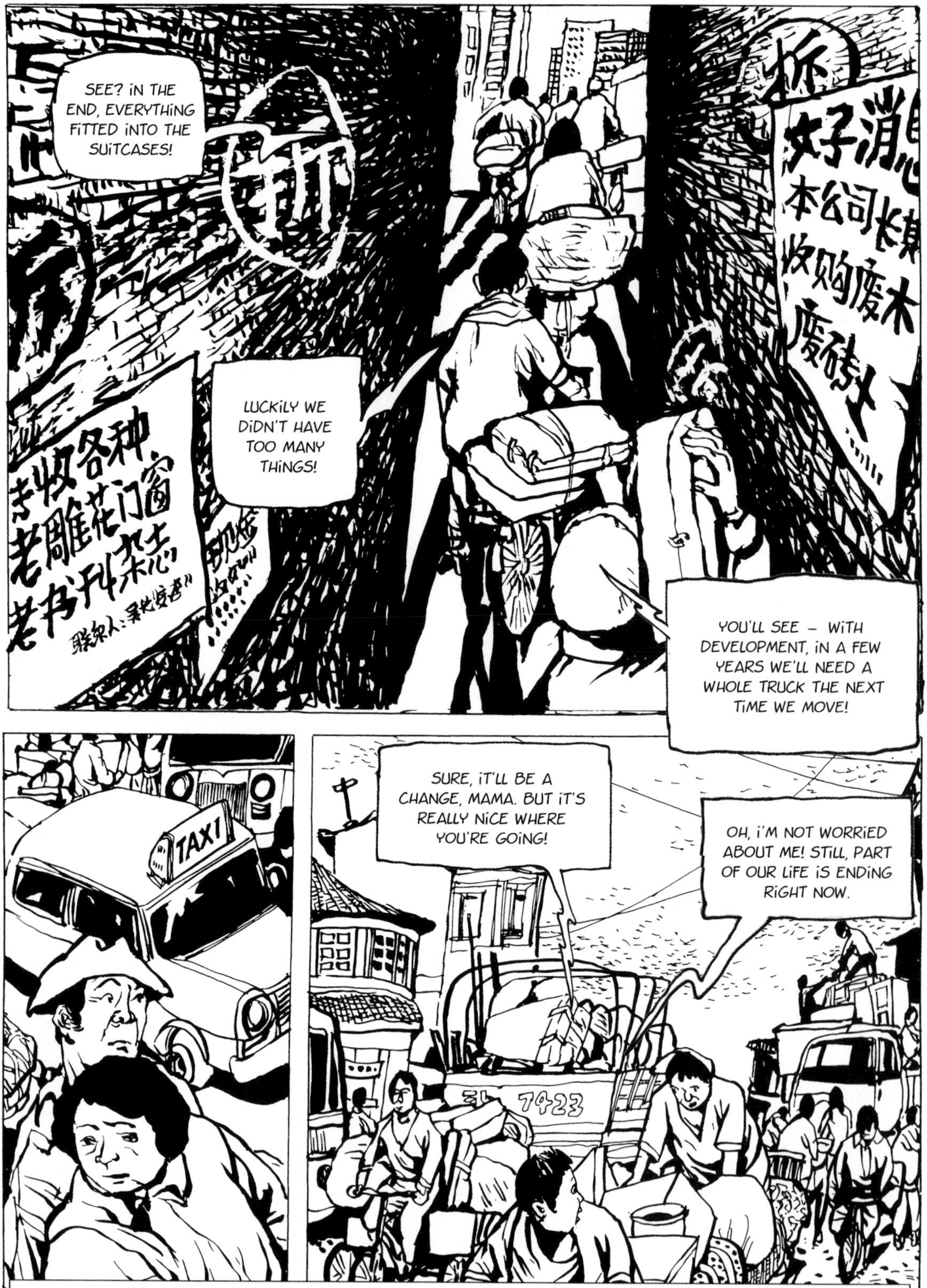
SEE? IN THE END, EVERYTHING FITTED INTO THE SUITCASES!
LUCKILY WE DIDN'T HAVE TOO MANY THINGS!
YOU'LL SEE – WITH DEVELOPMENT, IN A FEW YEARS WE'LL NEED A WHOLE TRUCK THE NEXT TIME WE MOVE!
TAXI
SURE, IT'LL BE A CHANGE, MAMA. BUT IT'S REALLY NICE WHERE YOU'RE GOING!
OH, I'M NOT WORRIED ABOUT ME! STILL, PART OF OUR LIFE IS ENDING RIGHT NOW.

* 专收各种老雕花门窗老书刊杂志 ZHUANSHOU GÈZHONG LAO DIAOHUA MÉNCHUANG LAO SHUKAN ZAZHI: "SPECIALIZE IN PURCHASING DOORS OF ALL SORTS, ANCIENT CARVED WINDOWS, OLD MAGAZINES AND NEWSPAPERS".

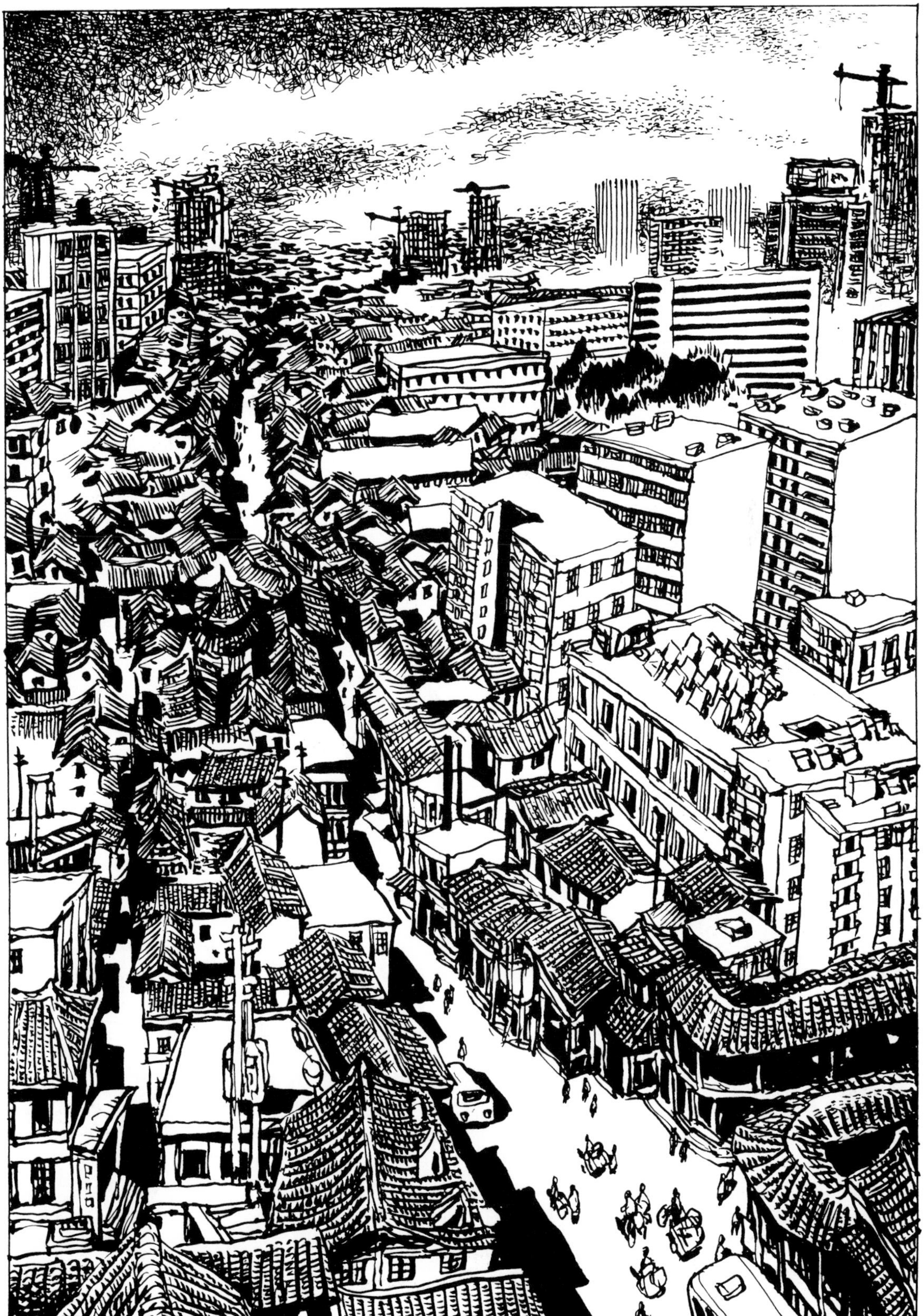

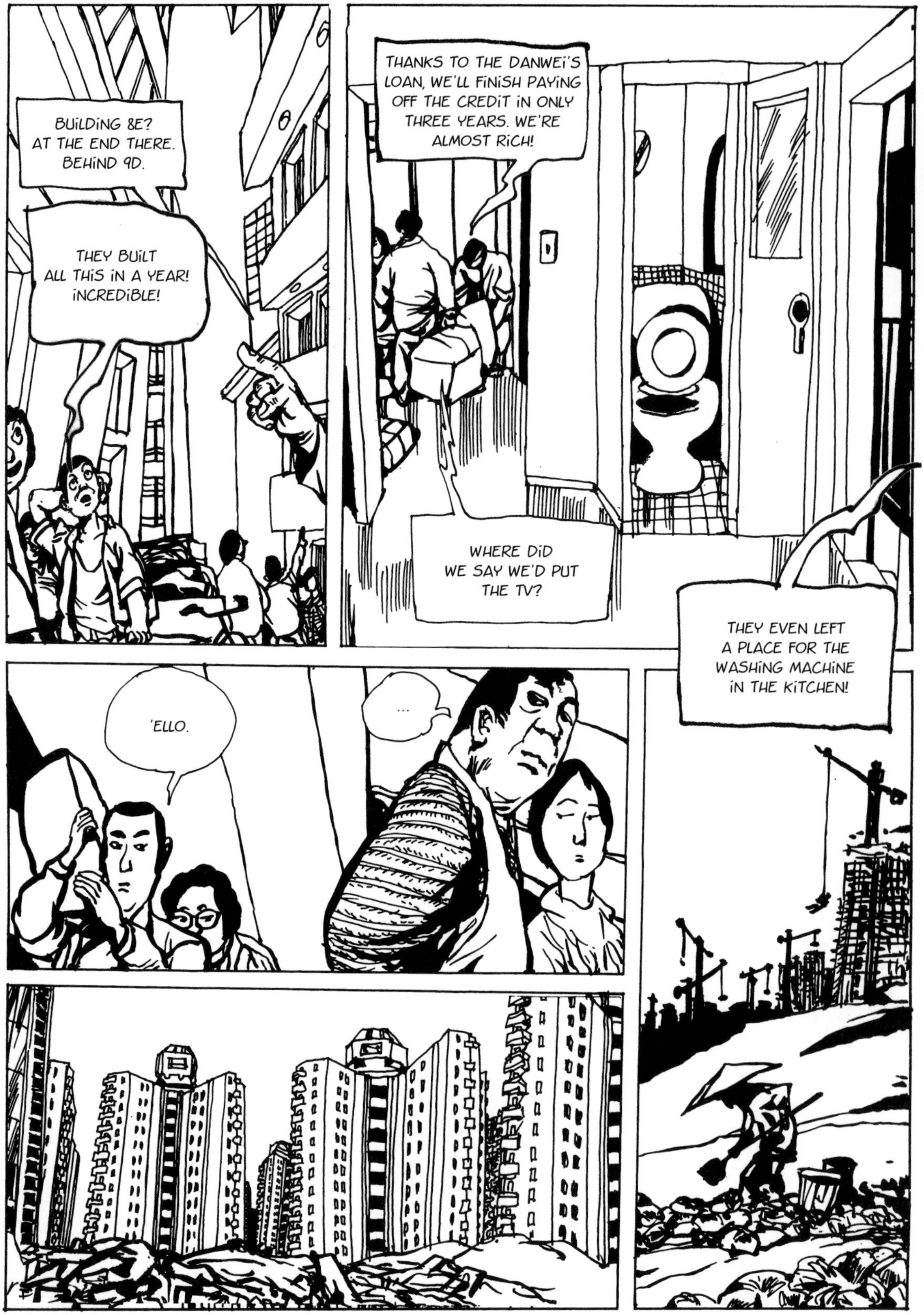
BUILDING 8E?
AT THE END THERE.
BEHIND 9D.
THEY BUILT
ALL THIS IN A YEAR!
INCREDIBLE!
THANKS TO THE DANWEI'S LOAN, WE'LL FINISH PAYING OFF THE CREDIT IN ONLY THREE YEARS. WE'RE ALMOST RICH!
WHERE DID WE SAY WE'D PUT THE TV?
THEY EVEN LEFT A PLACE FOR THE WASHING MACHINE IN THE KITCHEN!
'ELLO.
...

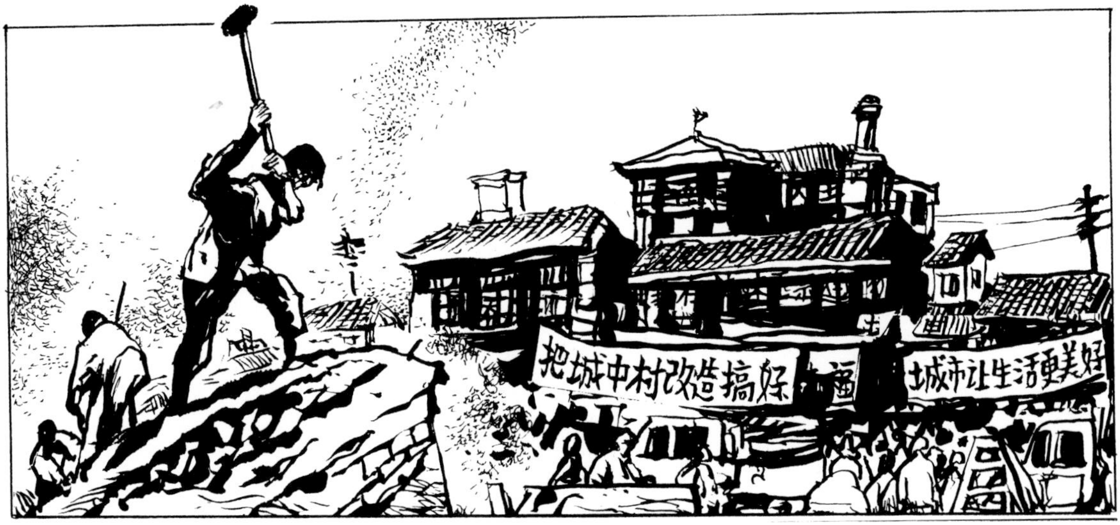
把城中村改造搞好
城市让生活更美好

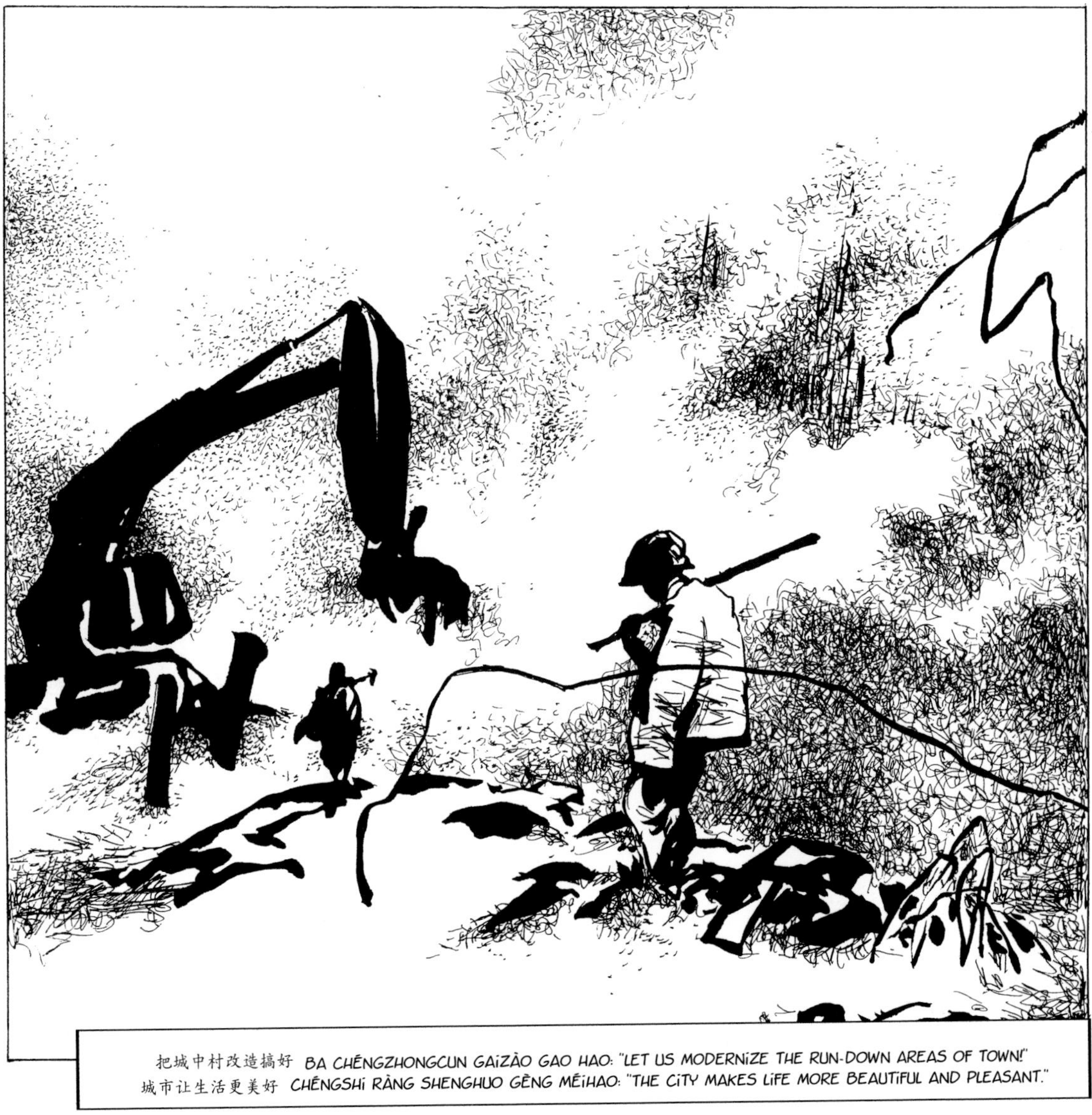

把城中村改造搞好 BA CHÉNGZHONGCUN GAIZÀO GAO HAO: "LET US MODERNIZE THE RUN-DOWN AREAS OF TOWN!"
城市让生活更美好 CHÉNGSHI RÀNG SHENGHUO GÈNG MĚIHAO: "THE CITY MAKES LIFE MORE BEAUTIFUL AND PLEASANT."

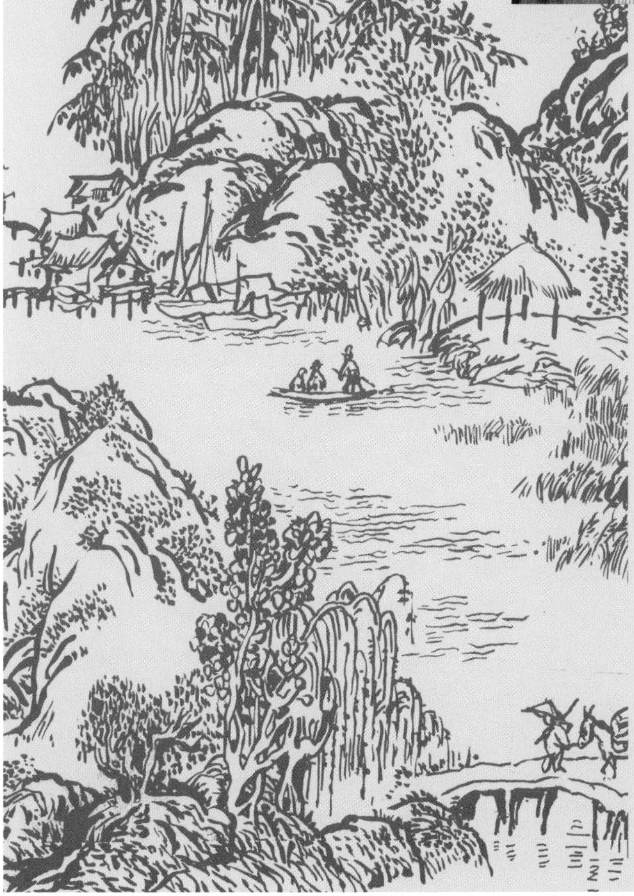

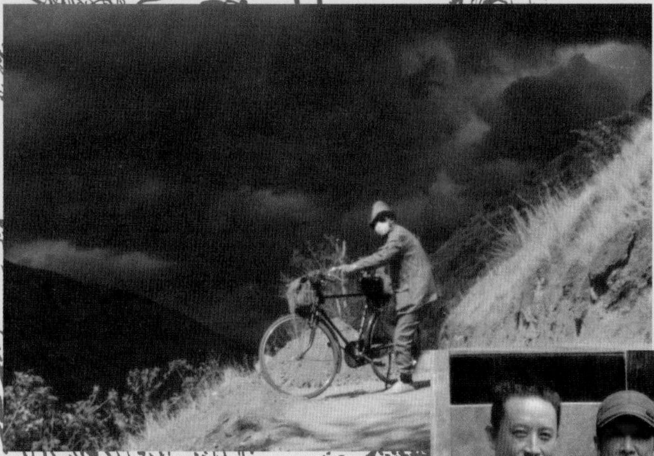

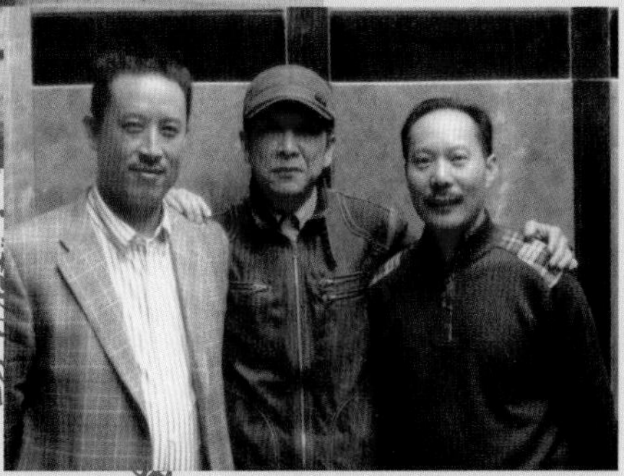

CHAPTER 9
Rebirth

曙光像轻沙飘浮在滇池上，

山上的龙门映在水中央，

渔船轻轻地随风飘荡，

渔家姑娘歌声悠扬。

……

THE GLIMMER OF DAWN
FLOATS LIKE A SILK CURTAIN
OVER LAKE DIAN.

THE DRAGON'S GATE
ON THE HILL IS REFLECTED
IN THE SURFACE OF THE WATER,

AND THE FISHING BOATS BOB
GENTLY TO THE RHYTHM OF THE BREEZE.

THE SONG OF THE MAIDENS FISHING
CARRIES FAR...

(FROM A POPULAR SONG)

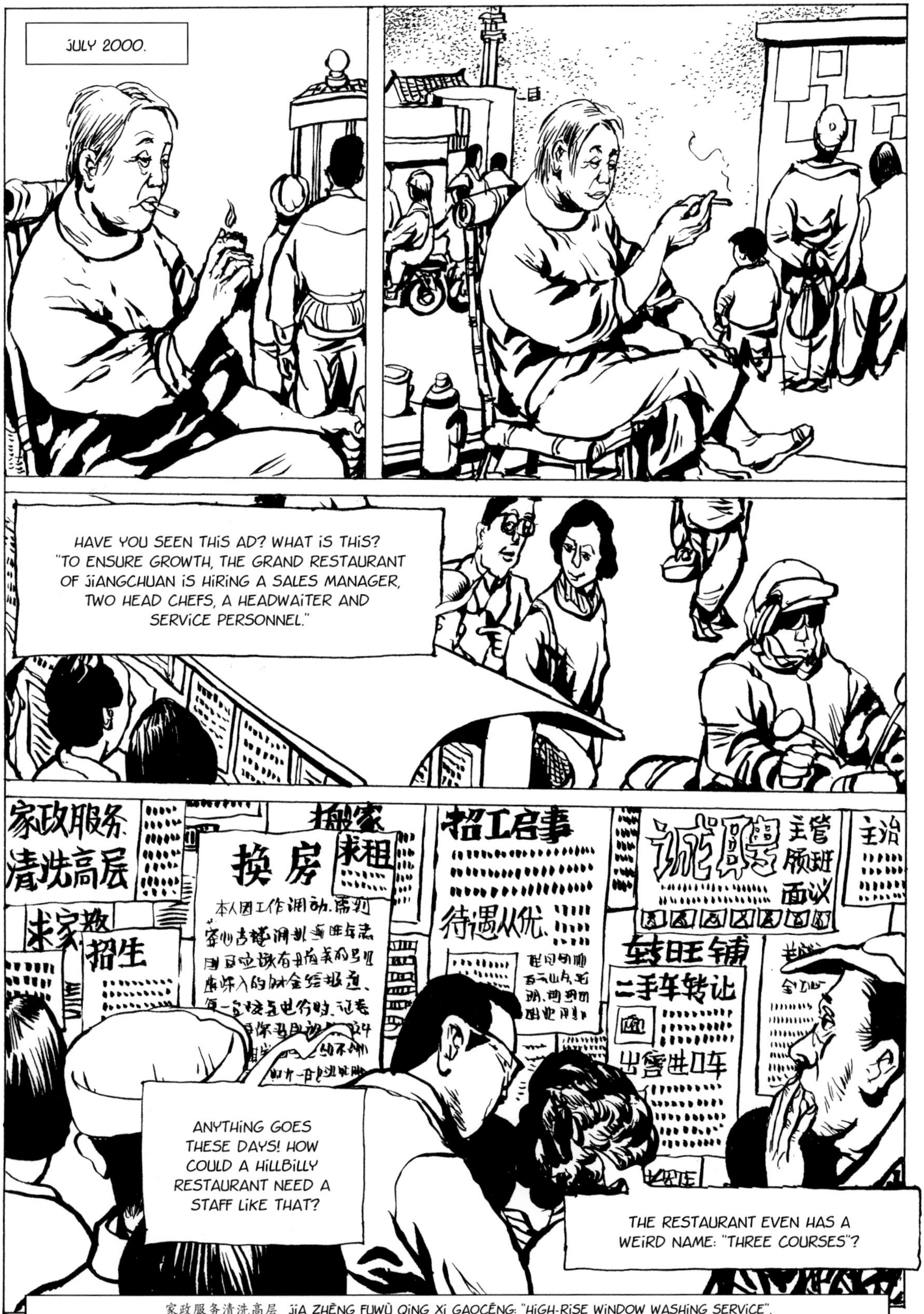
JULY 2000.
HAVE YOU SEEN THIS AD? WHAT IS THIS? "TO ENSURE GROWTH, THE GRAND RESTAURANT OF JIANGCHUAN IS HIRING A SALES MANAGER, TWO HEAD CHEFS, A HEADWAITER AND SERVICE PERSONNEL."
家政服务
清洗高层
换房
搬家
求租
招工启事
待遇从优
主管
领班
面议
主治
招生
转旺铺
二手车转让
出售进口车
ANYTHING GOES THESE DAYS! HOW COULD A HILLBILLY RESTAURANT NEED A STAFF LIKE THAT?
THE RESTAURANT EVEN HAS A WEIRD NAME: "THREE COURSES"?

家政服务清洗高层 JIA ZHĒNG FUWÙ QING XI GAOCĒNG: "HIGH-RISE WINDOW WASHING SERVICE". 换房 HÙAN FANG: "APARTMENT SWAP". 招工启事 ZHAO GONG QISHI: "NOW HIRING". 转旺铺 DÀI YÙ CONG YOU: "GOOD SALARY". 待遇从优 ZHUAN WÀNGPÙ: "LUCRATIVE BUSINESS FOR SALE". 主治 ZHU ZHI: "SPECIALIST MEDICAL TREATMENT".

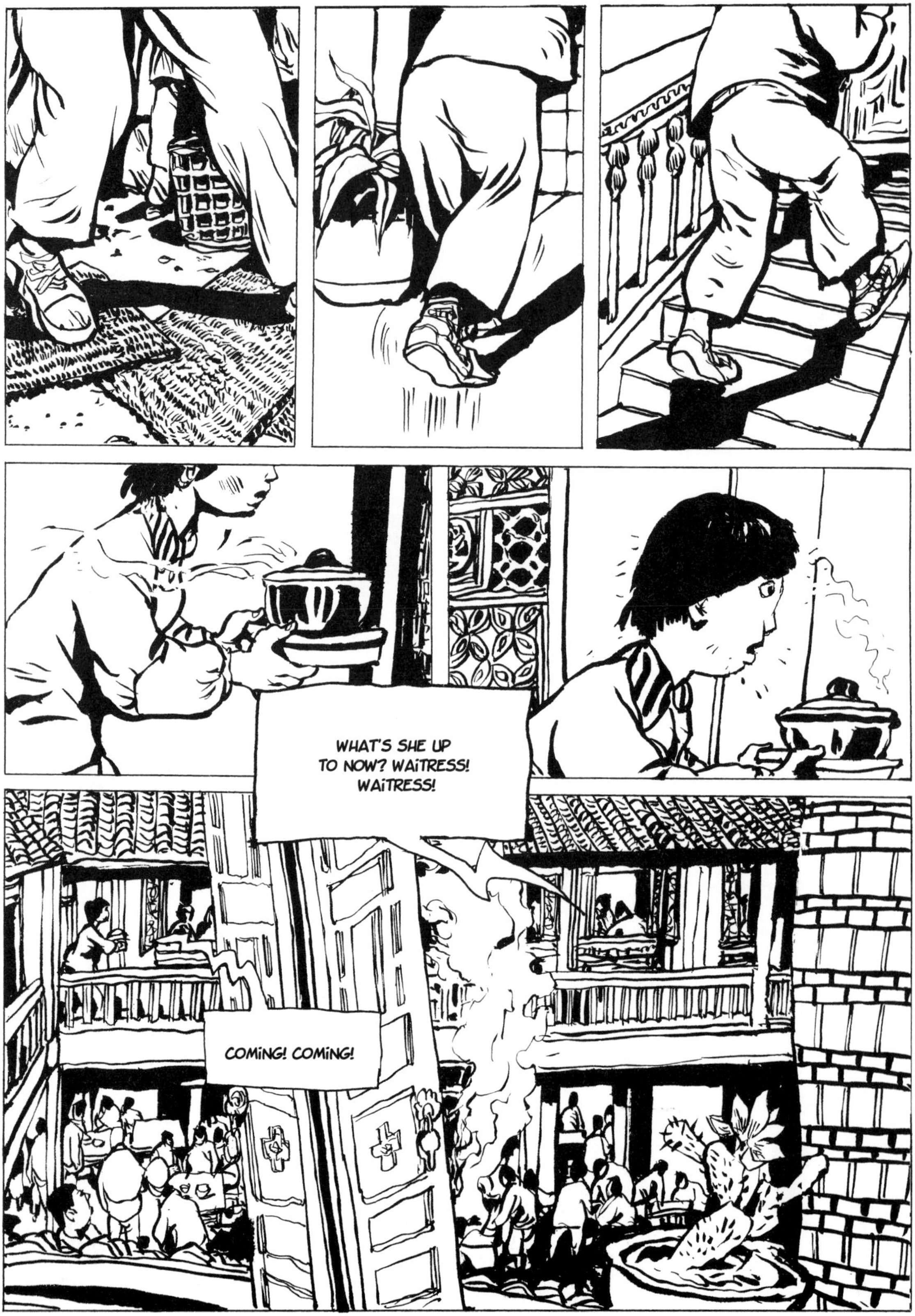
WHAT'S SHE UP
TO NOW? WAITRESS!
WAITRESS!
COMING! COMING!

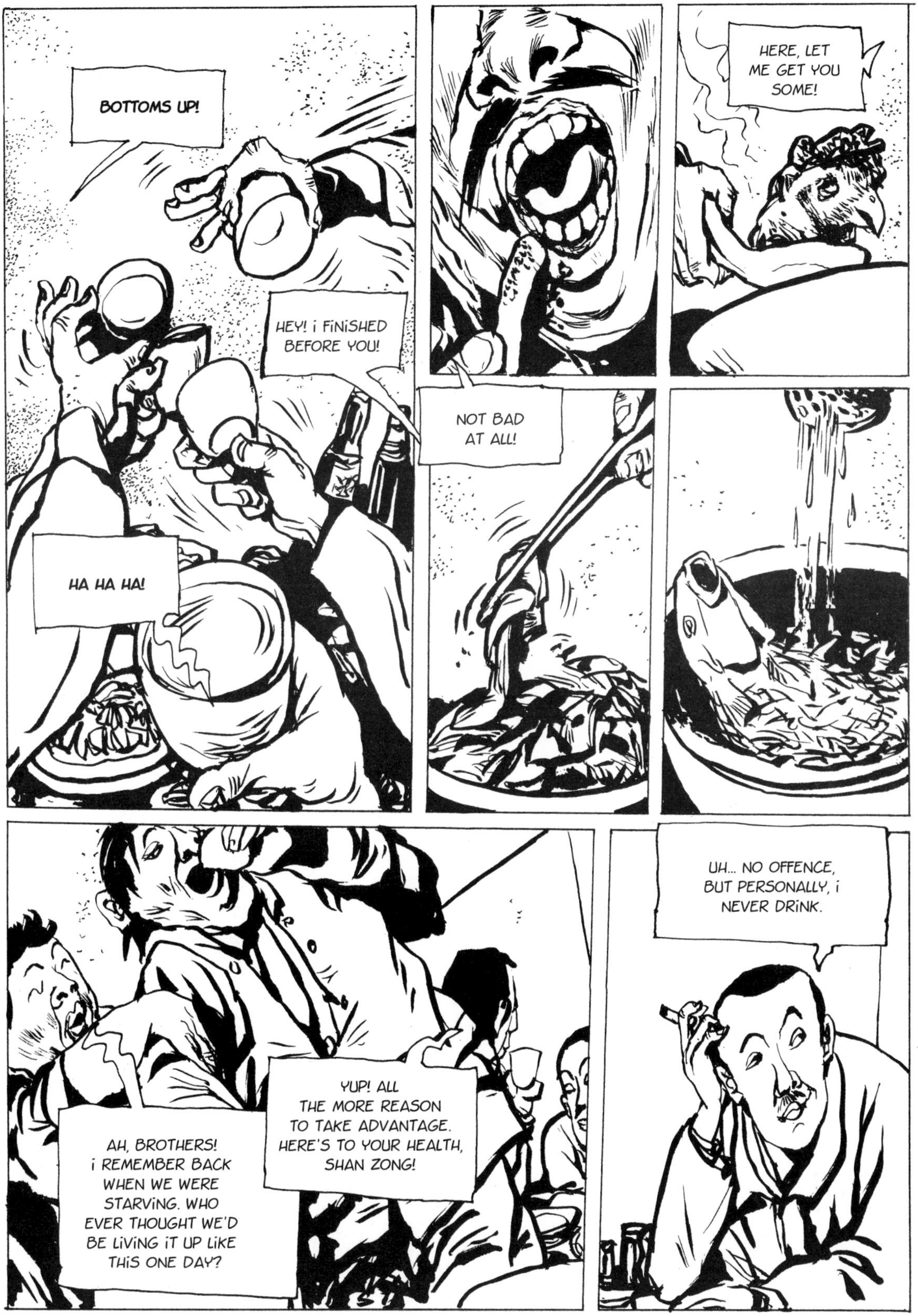
BOTTOMS UP!
HEY! i FiNiSHED BEFORE YOU!
HA HA HA!
HERE, LET ME GET YOU SOME!
NOT BAD AT ALL!
AH, BROTHERS! i REMEMBER BACK WHEN WE WERE STARViNG. WHO EVER THOUGHT WE'D BE LiViNG iT UP LiKE THiS ONE DAY?
YUP! ALL THE MORE REASON TO TAKE ADVANTAGE. HERE'S TO YOUR HEALTH, SHAN ZONG!
UH... NO OFFENCE, BUT PERSONALLY, i NEVER DRiNK.

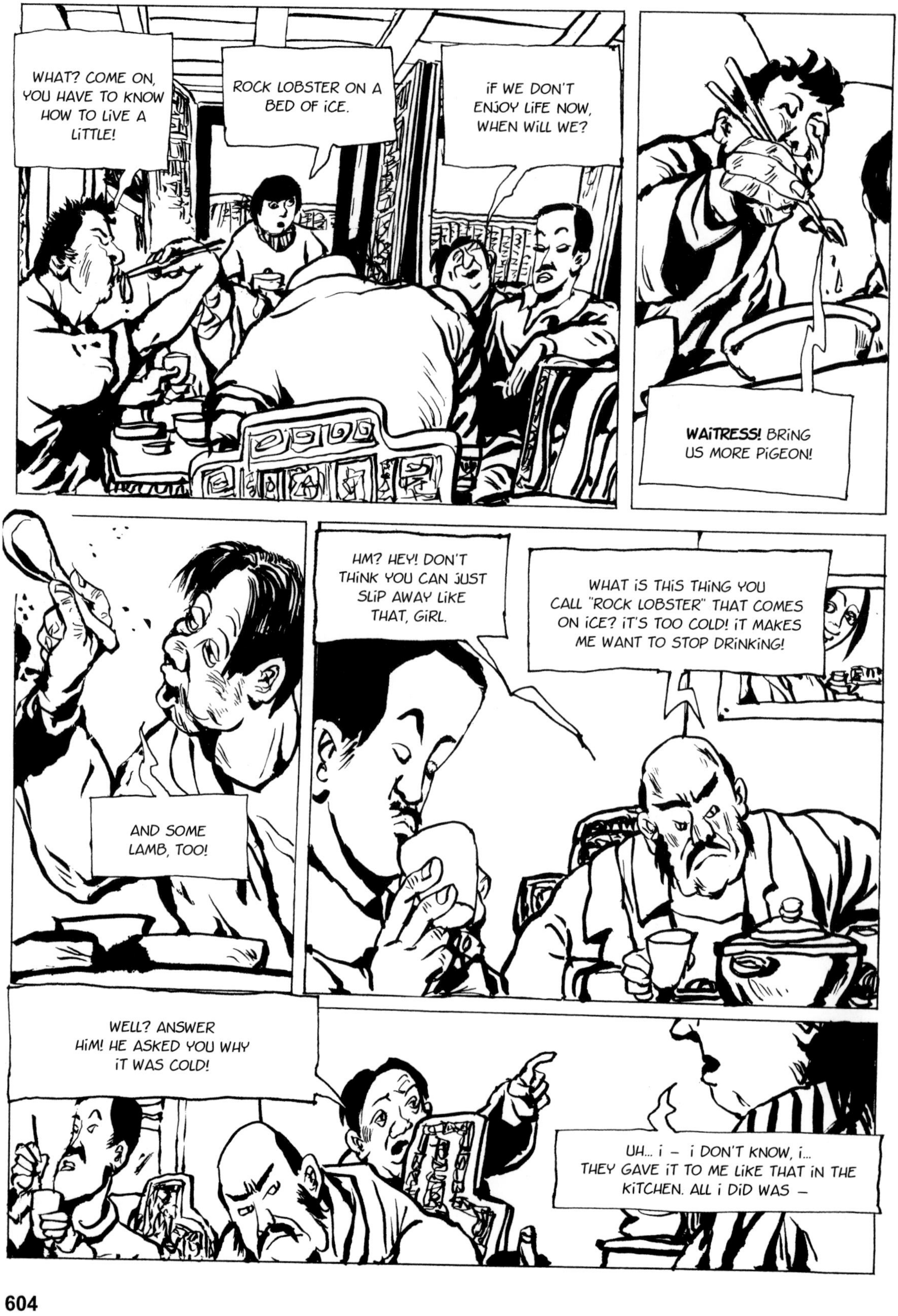

WHAT? COME ON, YOU HAVE TO KNOW HOW TO LIVE A LITTLE!
ROCK LOBSTER ON A BED OF ICE.
IF WE DON'T ENJOY LIFE NOW, WHEN WILL WE?
WAITRESS! BRING US MORE PIGEON!
AND SOME LAMB, TOO!
HM? HEY! DON'T THINK YOU CAN JUST SLIP AWAY LIKE THAT, GIRL.
WHAT IS THIS THING YOU CALL "ROCK LOBSTER" THAT COMES ON ICE? IT'S TOO COLD! IT MAKES ME WANT TO STOP DRINKING!
WELL? ANSWER HIM! HE ASKED YOU WHY IT WAS COLD!
UH... I – I DON'T KNOW, I... THEY GAVE IT TO ME LIKE THAT IN THE KITCHEN. ALL I DID WAS –

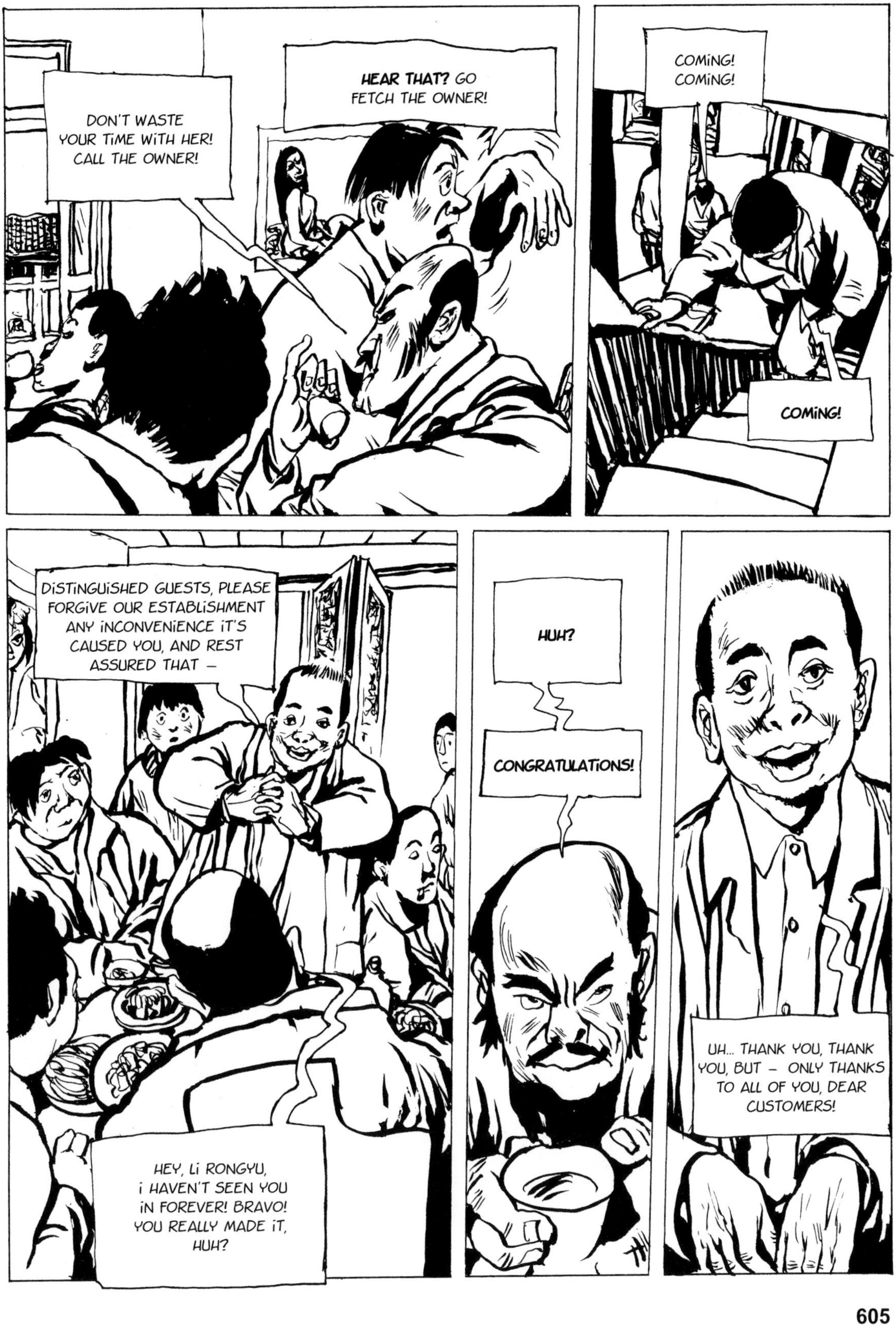
DON'T WASTE YOUR TIME WITH HER! CALL THE OWNER!
HEAR THAT? GO FETCH THE OWNER!
COMING! COMING!
COMING!
DISTINGUISHED GUESTS, PLEASE FORGIVE OUR ESTABLISHMENT ANY INCONVENIENCE IT'S CAUSED YOU, AND REST ASSURED THAT –
HEY, LI RONGYU, I HAVEN'T SEEN YOU IN FOREVER! BRAVO! YOU REALLY MADE IT, HUH?
HUH?
CONGRATULATIONS!
UH... THANK YOU, THANK YOU, BUT – ONLY THANKS TO ALL OF YOU, DEAR CUSTOMERS!

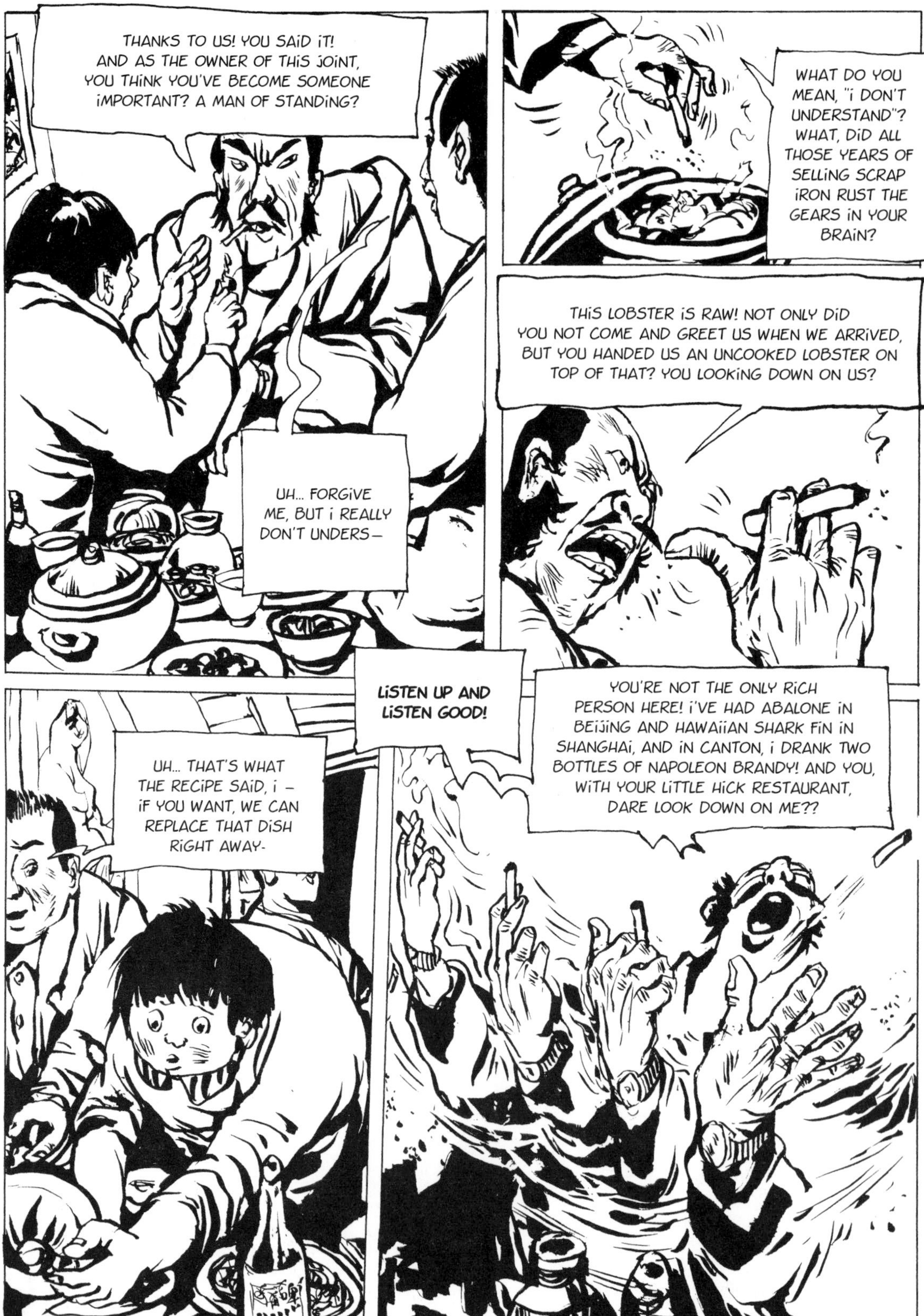
THANKS TO US! YOU SAID IT! AND AS THE OWNER OF THIS JOINT, YOU THINK YOU'VE BECOME SOMEONE IMPORTANT? A MAN OF STANDING?
UH... FORGIVE ME, BUT I REALLY DON'T UNDERS—
WHAT DO YOU MEAN, "I DON'T UNDERSTAND"? WHAT, DID ALL THOSE YEARS OF SELLING SCRAP IRON RUST THE GEARS IN YOUR BRAIN?
THIS LOBSTER IS RAW! NOT ONLY DID YOU NOT COME AND GREET US WHEN WE ARRIVED, BUT YOU HANDED US AN UNCOOKED LOBSTER ON TOP OF THAT? YOU LOOKING DOWN ON US?
UH... THAT'S WHAT THE RECIPE SAID, I — IF YOU WANT, WE CAN REPLACE THAT DISH RIGHT AWAY-
LISTEN UP AND LISTEN GOOD!
YOU'RE NOT THE ONLY RICH PERSON HERE! I'VE HAD ABALONE IN BEIJING AND HAWAIIAN SHARK FIN IN SHANGHAI, AND IN CANTON, I DRANK TWO BOTTLES OF NAPOLEON BRANDY! AND YOU, WITH YOUR LITTLE HICK RESTAURANT, DARE LOOK DOWN ON ME??

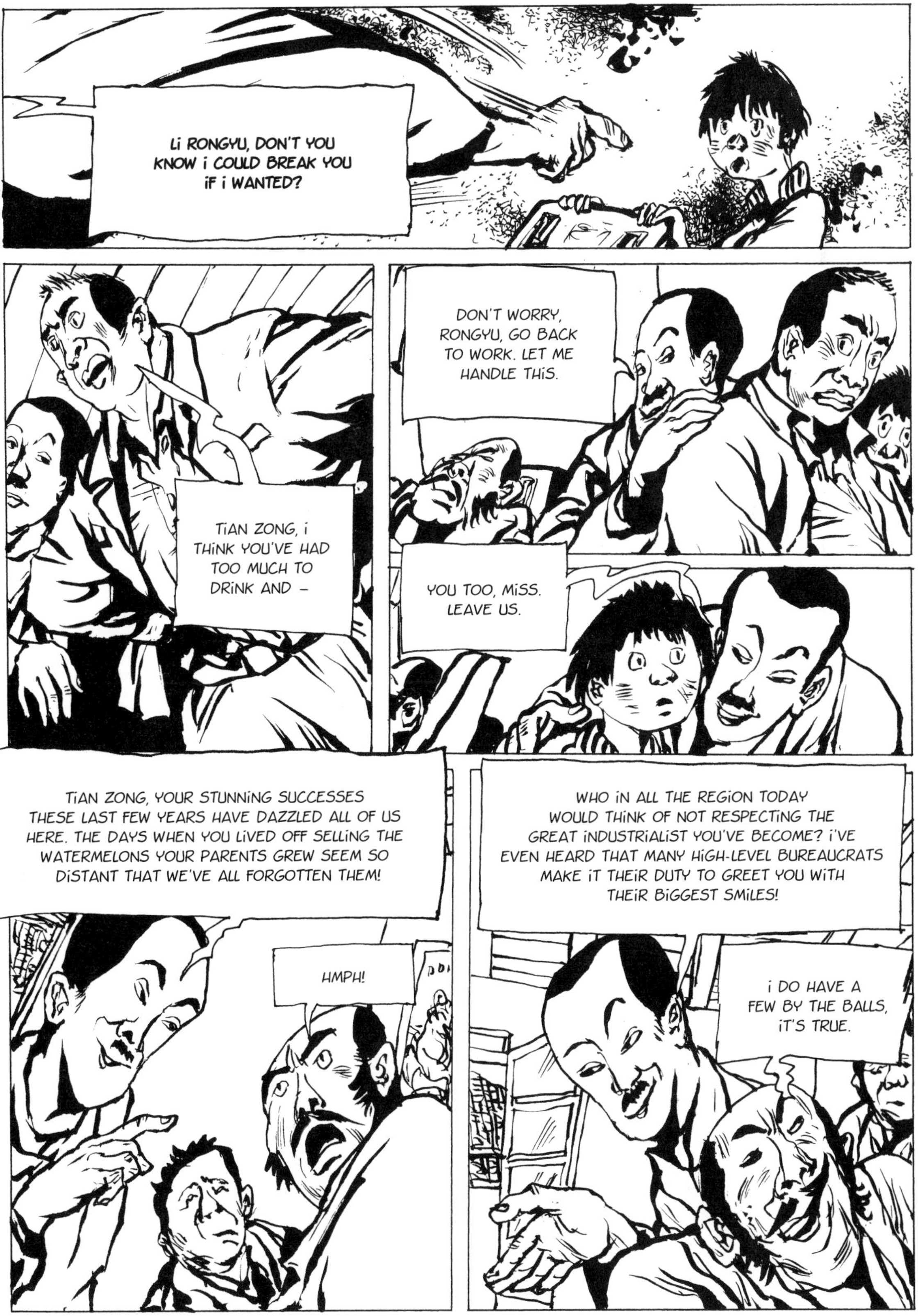
Li RONGYU, DON'T YOU KNOW i COULD BREAK YOU iF i WANTED?
TiAN ZONG, i THiNK YOU'VE HAD TOO MUCH TO DRiNK AND –
DON'T WORRY, RONGYU, GO BACK TO WORK. LET ME HANDLE THiS.
YOU TOO, MiSS. LEAVE US.
TiAN ZONG, YOUR STUNNiNG SUCCESSES THESE LAST FEW YEARS HAVE DAZZLED ALL OF US HERE. THE DAYS WHEN YOU LiVED OFF SELLiNG THE WATERMELONS YOUR PARENTS GREW SEEM SO DiSTANT THAT WE'VE ALL FORGOTTEN THEM!
HMPH!
WHO iN ALL THE REGiON TODAY WOULD THiNK OF NOT RESPECTiNG THE GREAT iNDUSTRiALiST YOU'VE BECOME? i'VE EVEN HEARD THAT MANY HiGH-LEVEL BUREAUCRATS MAKE iT THEiR DUTY TO GREET YOU WiTH THEiR BiGGEST SMiLES!
i DO HAVE A FEW BY THE BALLS, iT'S TRUE.

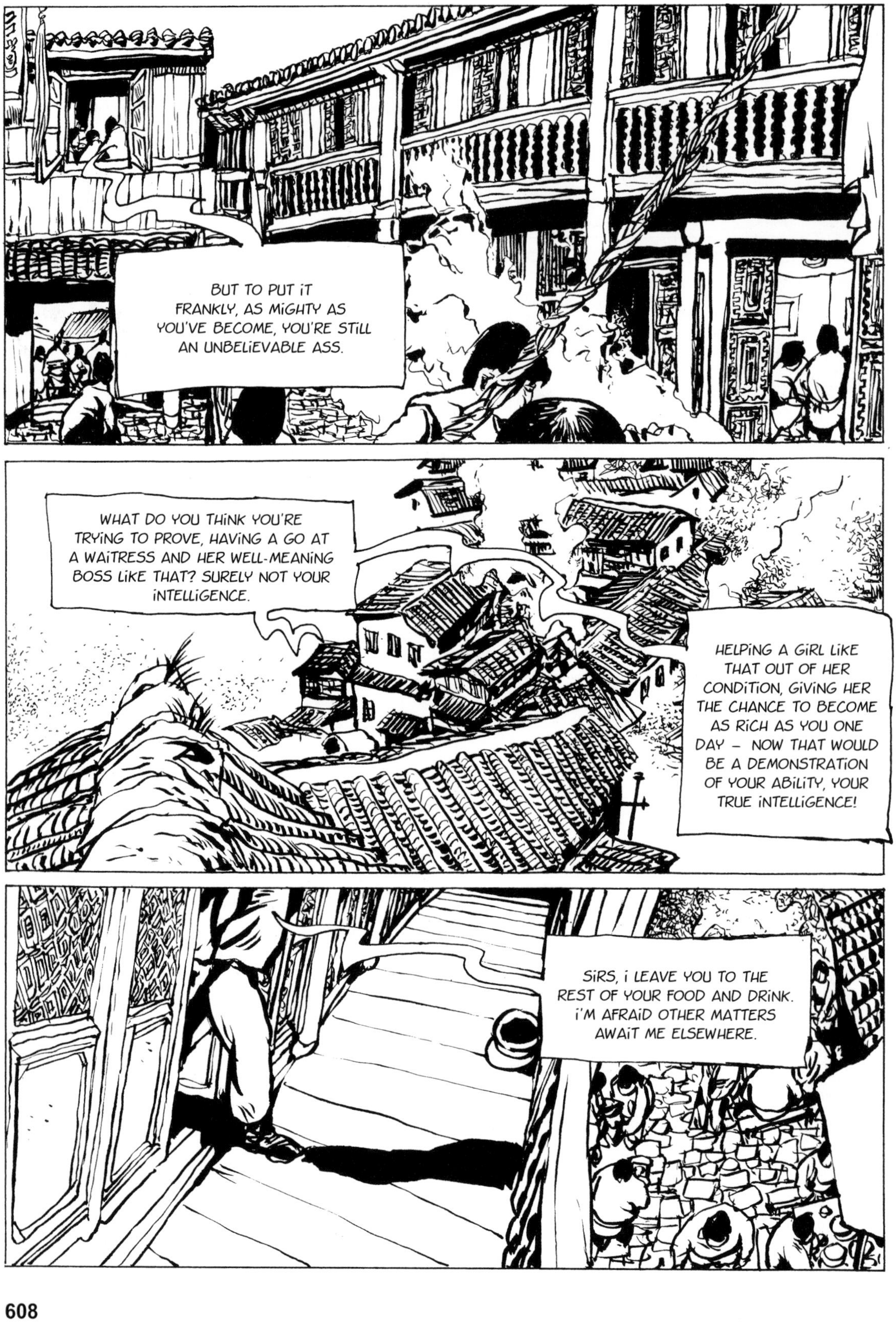
BUT TO PUT IT FRANKLY, AS MIGHTY AS YOU'VE BECOME, YOU'RE STILL AN UNBELIEVABLE ASS.
WHAT DO YOU THINK YOU'RE TRYING TO PROVE, HAVING A GO AT A WAITRESS AND HER WELL-MEANING BOSS LIKE THAT? SURELY NOT YOUR INTELLIGENCE.
HELPING A GIRL LIKE THAT OUT OF HER CONDITION, GIVING HER THE CHANCE TO BECOME AS RICH AS YOU ONE DAY – NOW THAT WOULD BE A DEMONSTRATION OF YOUR ABILITY, YOUR TRUE INTELLIGENCE!
SIRS, I LEAVE YOU TO THE REST OF YOUR FOOD AND DRINK. I'M AFRAID OTHER MATTERS AWAIT ME ELSEWHERE.

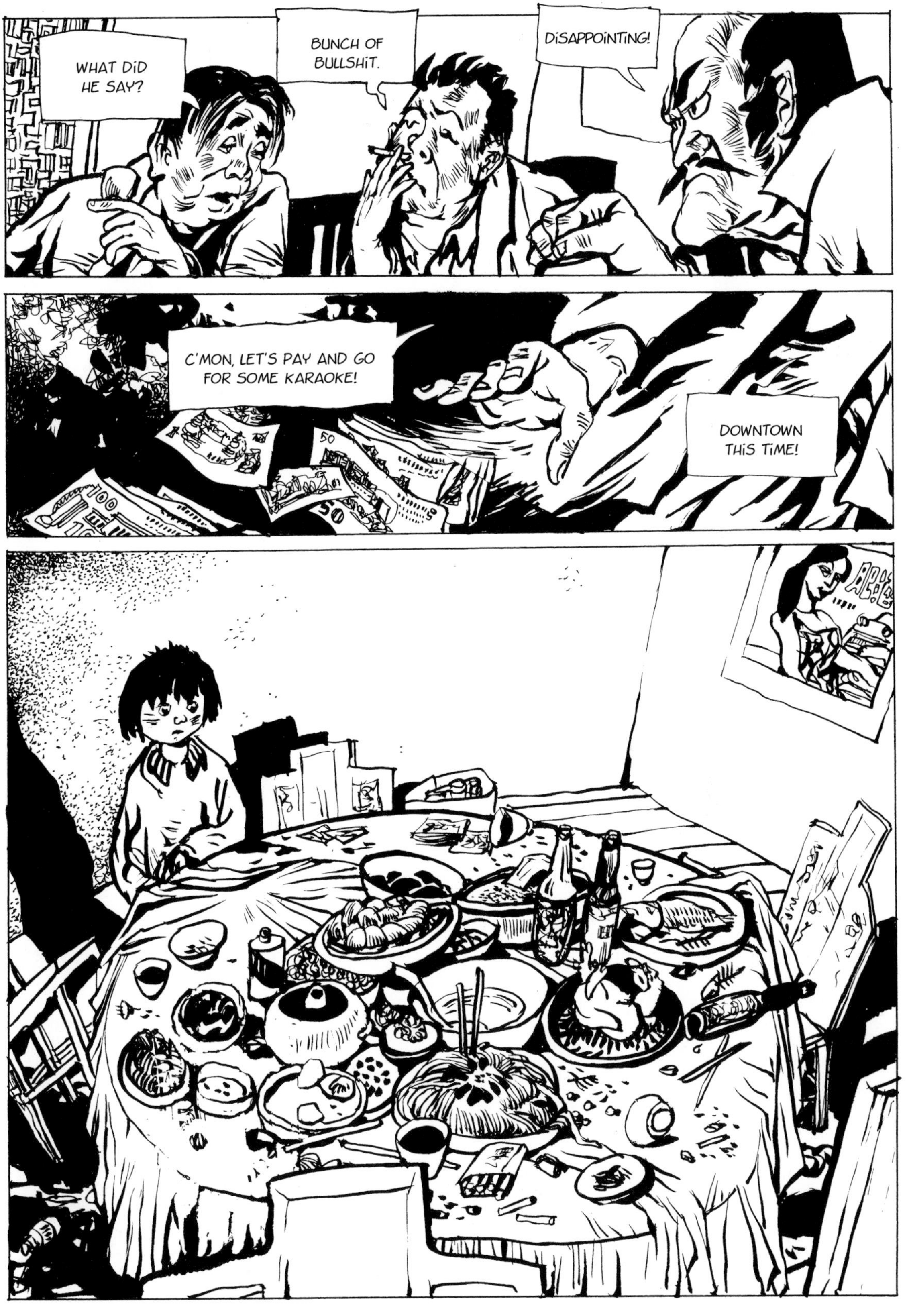
WHAT DID HE SAY?
BUNCH OF BULLSHIT.
DISAPPOINTING!
C'MON, LET'S PAY AND GO FOR SOME KARAOKE!
DOWNTOWN THIS TIME!

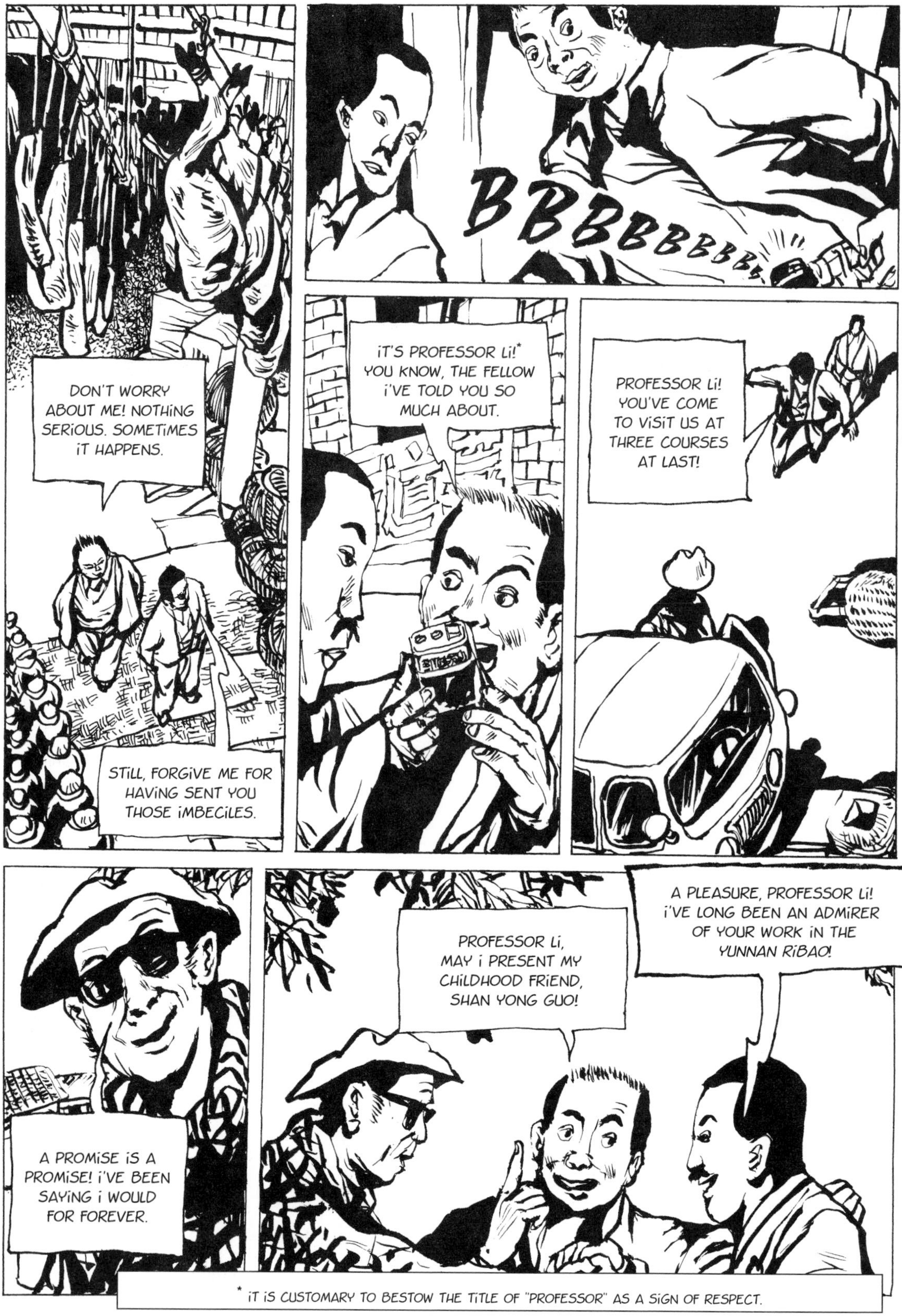

BBBBBBBBBB
DON'T WORRY ABOUT ME! NOTHING SERIOUS. SOMETIMES IT HAPPENS.
STILL, FORGIVE ME FOR HAVING SENT YOU THOSE IMBECILES.
IT'S PROFESSOR LI!* YOU KNOW, THE FELLOW I'VE TOLD YOU SO MUCH ABOUT.
PROFESSOR LI! YOU'VE COME TO VISIT US AT THREE COURSES AT LAST!
A PROMISE IS A PROMISE! I'VE BEEN SAYING I WOULD FOR FOREVER.
PROFESSOR LI, MAY I PRESENT MY CHILDHOOD FRIEND, SHAN YONG GUO!
A PLEASURE, PROFESSOR LI! I'VE LONG BEEN AN ADMIRER OF YOUR WORK IN THE YUNNAN RIBAO!

* IT IS CUSTOMARY TO BESTOW THE TITLE OF "PROFESSOR" AS A SIGN OF RESPECT.

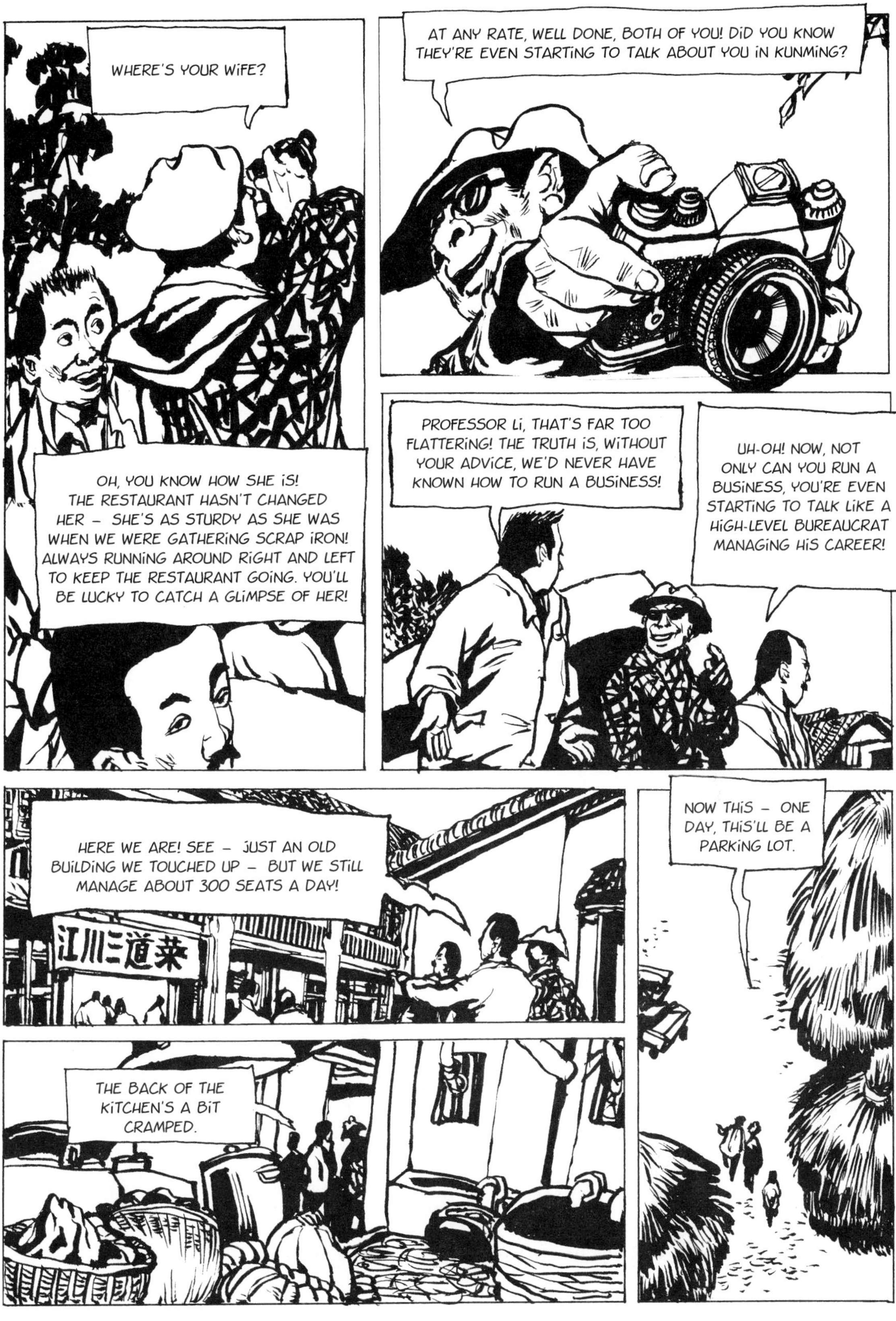
WHERE'S YOUR WIFE?
AT ANY RATE, WELL DONE, BOTH OF YOU! DID YOU KNOW THEY'RE EVEN STARTING TO TALK ABOUT YOU IN KUNMING?
OH, YOU KNOW HOW SHE IS! THE RESTAURANT HASN'T CHANGED HER – SHE'S AS STURDY AS SHE WAS WHEN WE WERE GATHERING SCRAP IRON! ALWAYS RUNNING AROUND RIGHT AND LEFT TO KEEP THE RESTAURANT GOING. YOU'LL BE LUCKY TO CATCH A GLIMPSE OF HER!
PROFESSOR LI, THAT'S FAR TOO FLATTERING! THE TRUTH IS, WITHOUT YOUR ADVICE, WE'D NEVER HAVE KNOWN HOW TO RUN A BUSINESS!
UH-OH! NOW, NOT ONLY CAN YOU RUN A BUSINESS, YOU'RE EVEN STARTING TO TALK LIKE A HIGH-LEVEL BUREAUCRAT MANAGING HIS CAREER!
HERE WE ARE! SEE – JUST AN OLD BUILDING WE TOUCHED UP – BUT WE STILL MANAGE ABOUT 300 SEATS A DAY!
江川三道菜
THE BACK OF THE KITCHEN'S A BIT CRAMPED.
NOW THIS – ONE DAY, THIS'LL BE A PARKING LOT.

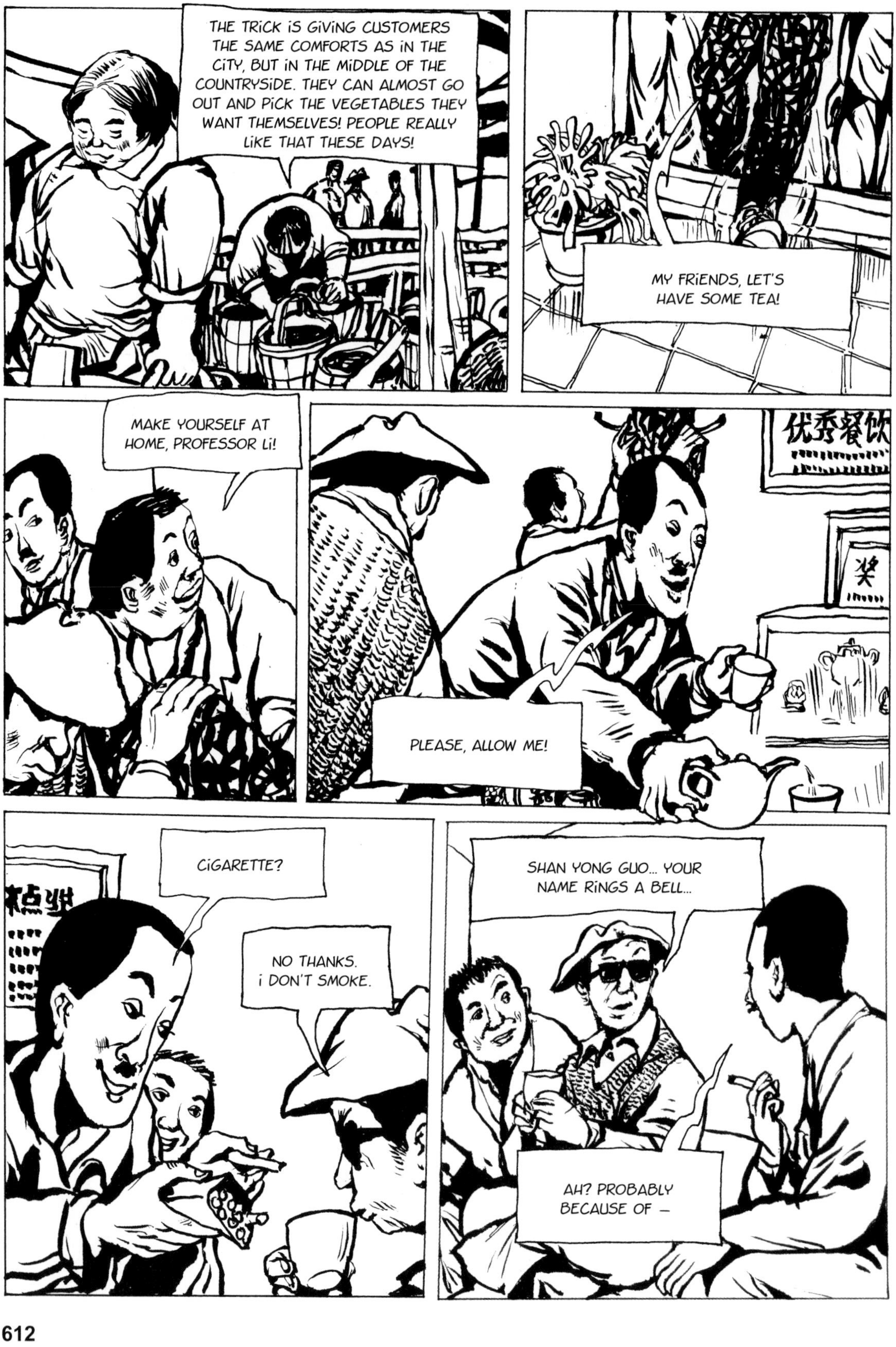
THE TRICK IS GIVING CUSTOMERS THE SAME COMFORTS AS IN THE CITY, BUT IN THE MIDDLE OF THE COUNTRYSIDE. THEY CAN ALMOST GO OUT AND PICK THE VEGETABLES THEY WANT THEMSELVES! PEOPLE REALLY LIKE THAT THESE DAYS!
MY FRIENDS, LET'S HAVE SOME TEA!
MAKE YOURSELF AT HOME, PROFESSOR LI!
优秀餐饮
奖
PLEASE, ALLOW ME!
CIGARETTE?
NO THANKS. I DON'T SMOKE.
SHAN YONG GUO... YOUR NAME RINGS A BELL...
AH? PROBABLY BECAUSE OF –

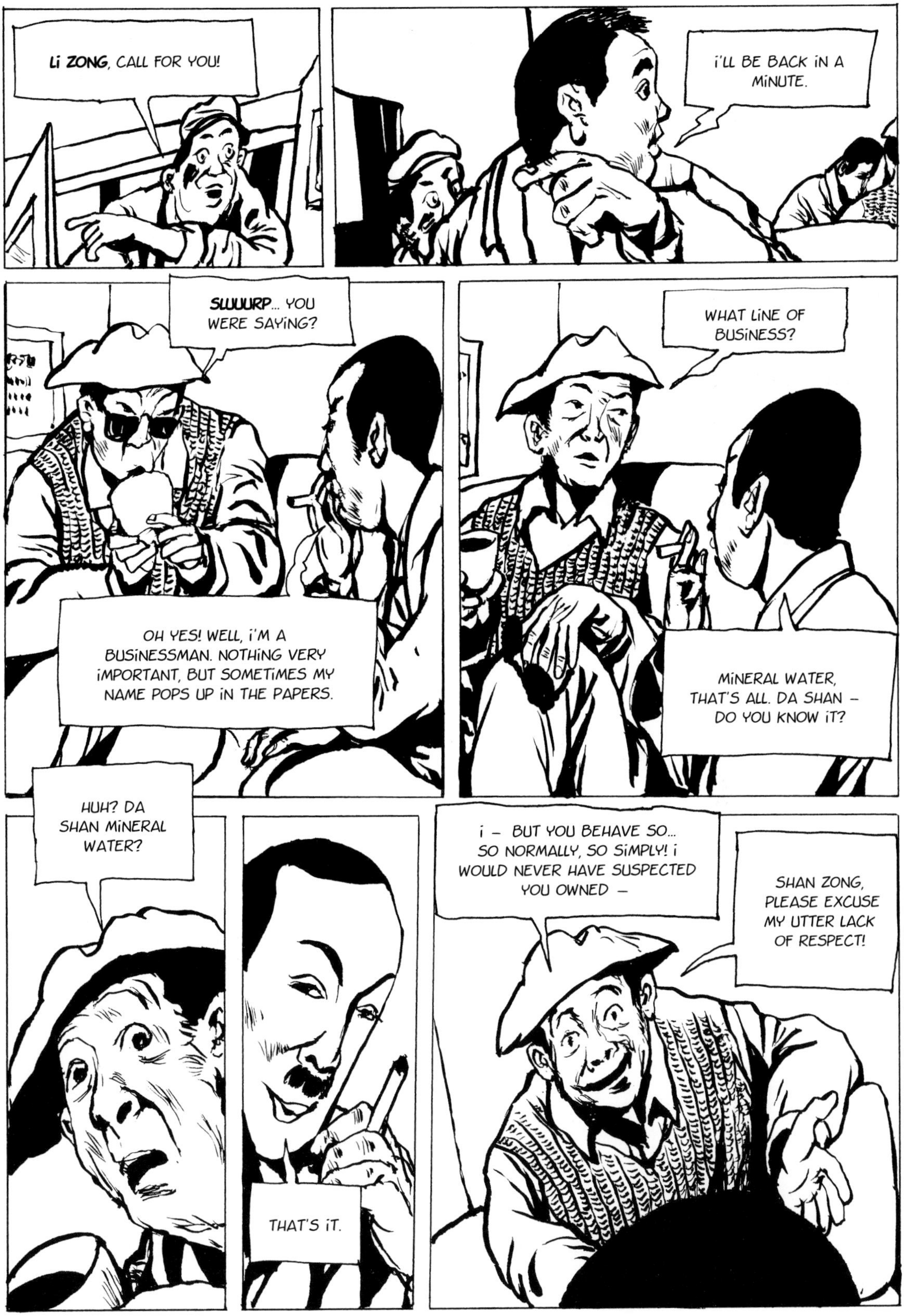
LI ZONG, CALL FOR YOU!
I'LL BE BACK IN A MINUTE.
SLUUURP... YOU WERE SAYING?
OH YES! WELL, I'M A BUSINESSMAN. NOTHING VERY IMPORTANT, BUT SOMETIMES MY NAME POPS UP IN THE PAPERS.
WHAT LINE OF BUSINESS?
MINERAL WATER, THAT'S ALL. DA SHAN – DO YOU KNOW IT?
HUH? DA SHAN MINERAL WATER?
THAT'S IT.
I – BUT YOU BEHAVE SO... SO NORMALLY, SO SIMPLY! I WOULD NEVER HAVE SUSPECTED YOU OWNED –
SHAN ZONG, PLEASE EXCUSE MY UTTER LACK OF RESPECT!

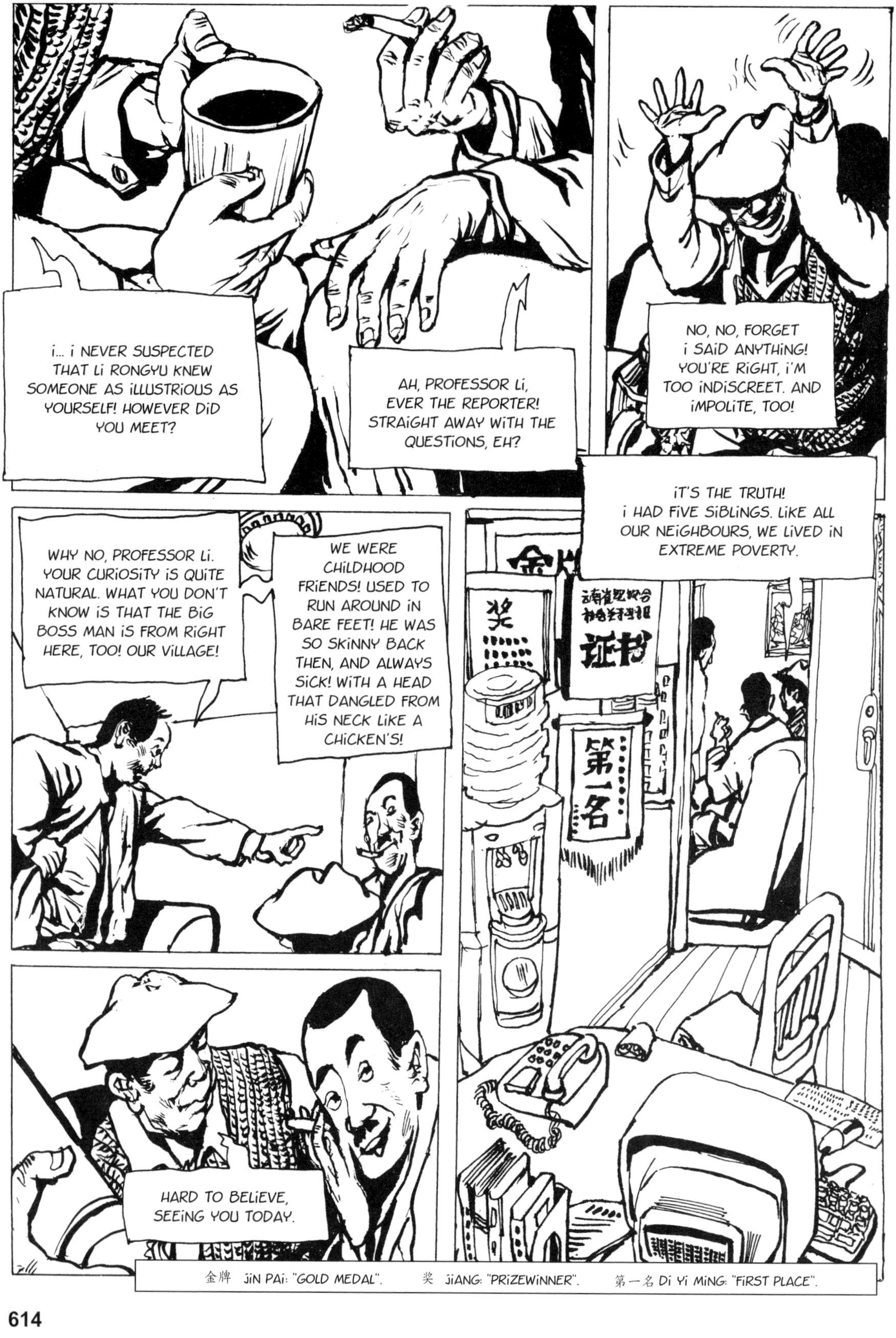
i... i NEVER SUSPECTED THAT Li RONGYU KNEW SOMEONE AS iLLUSTRIOUS AS YOURSELF! HOWEVER DiD YOU MEET?
AH, PROFESSOR Li, EVER THE REPORTER! STRAiGHT AWAY WiTH THE QUESTiONS, EH?
NO, NO, FORGET i SAiD ANYTHiNG! YOU'RE RiGHT, i'M TOO iNDiSCREET. AND iMPOLiTE, TOO!
WHY NO, PROFESSOR Li. YOUR CURiOSiTY iS QUiTE NATURAL. WHAT YOU DON'T KNOW iS THAT THE BiG BOSS MAN iS FROM RiGHT HERE, TOO! OUR ViLLAGE!
WE WERE CHiLDHOOD FRiENDS! USED TO RUN AROUND iN BARE FEET! HE WAS SO SKiNNY BACK THEN, AND ALWAYS SiCK! WiTH A HEAD THAT DANGLED FROM HiS NECK LiKE A CHiCKEN'S!
HARD TO BELiEVE, SEEiNG YOU TODAY.
iT'S THE TRUTH! i HAD FiVE SiBLiNGS. LiKE ALL OUR NEiGHBOURS, WE LiVED iN EXTREME POVERTY.
奖
证书
第一名

金牌 JiN PAi: "GOLD MEDAL". 奖 JiANG: "PRiZEWiNNER". 第一名 Di Yi MiNG: "FiRST PLACE".

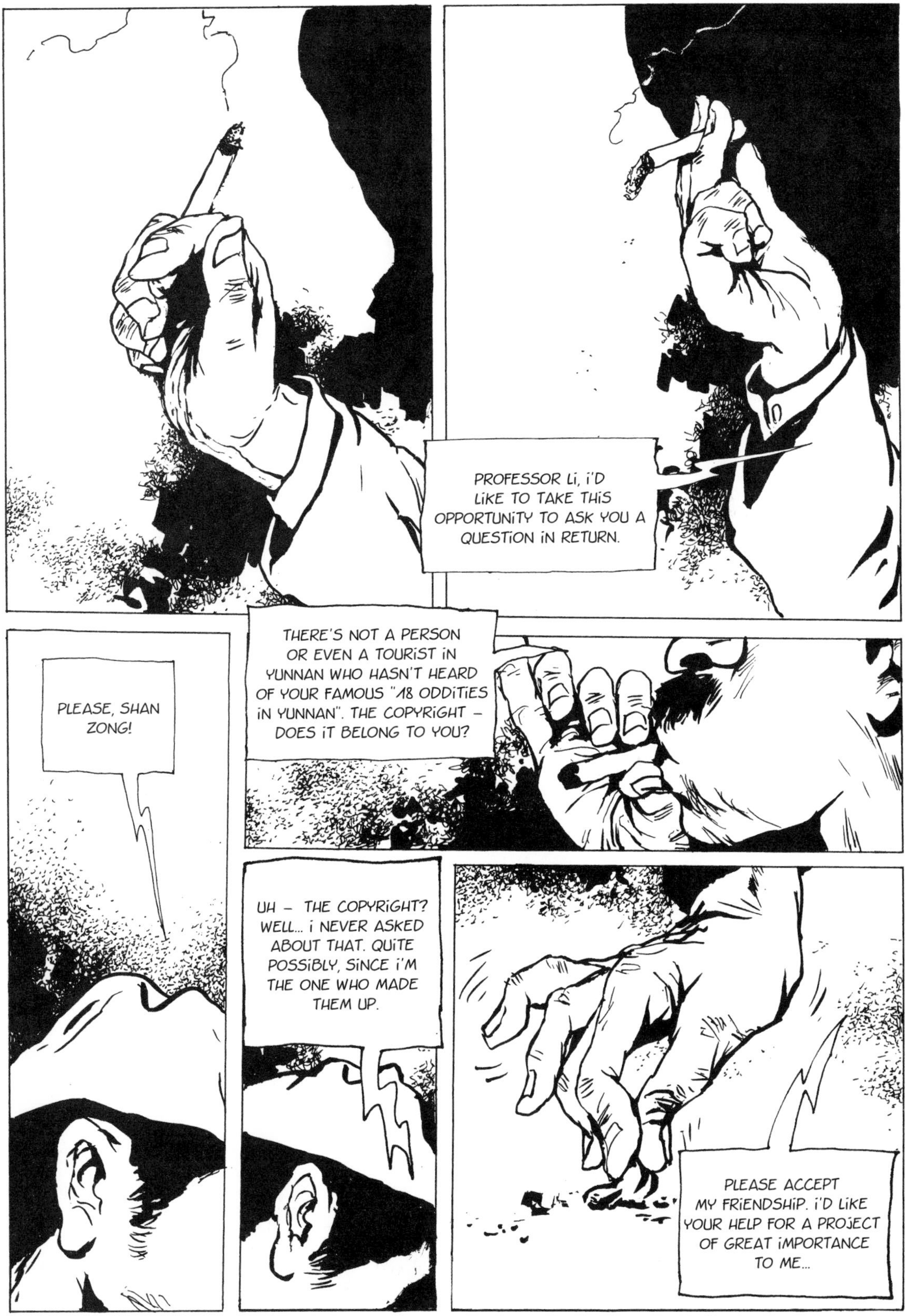
PROFESSOR Li, i'D LiKE TO TAKE THiS OPPORTUNiTY TO ASK YOU A QUESTiON iN RETURN.
PLEASE, SHAN ZONG!
THERE'S NOT A PERSON OR EVEN A TOURiST iN YUNNAN WHO HASN'T HEARD OF YOUR FAMOUS "18 ODDiTiES iN YUNNAN". THE COPYRiGHT – DOES iT BELONG TO YOU?
UH – THE COPYRiGHT? WELL... i NEVER ASKED ABOUT THAT. QUiTE POSSiBLY, SiNCE i'M THE ONE WHO MADE THEM UP.
PLEASE ACCEPT MY FRiENDSHiP. i'D LiKE YOUR HELP FOR A PROJECT OF GREAT iMPORTANCE TO ME...

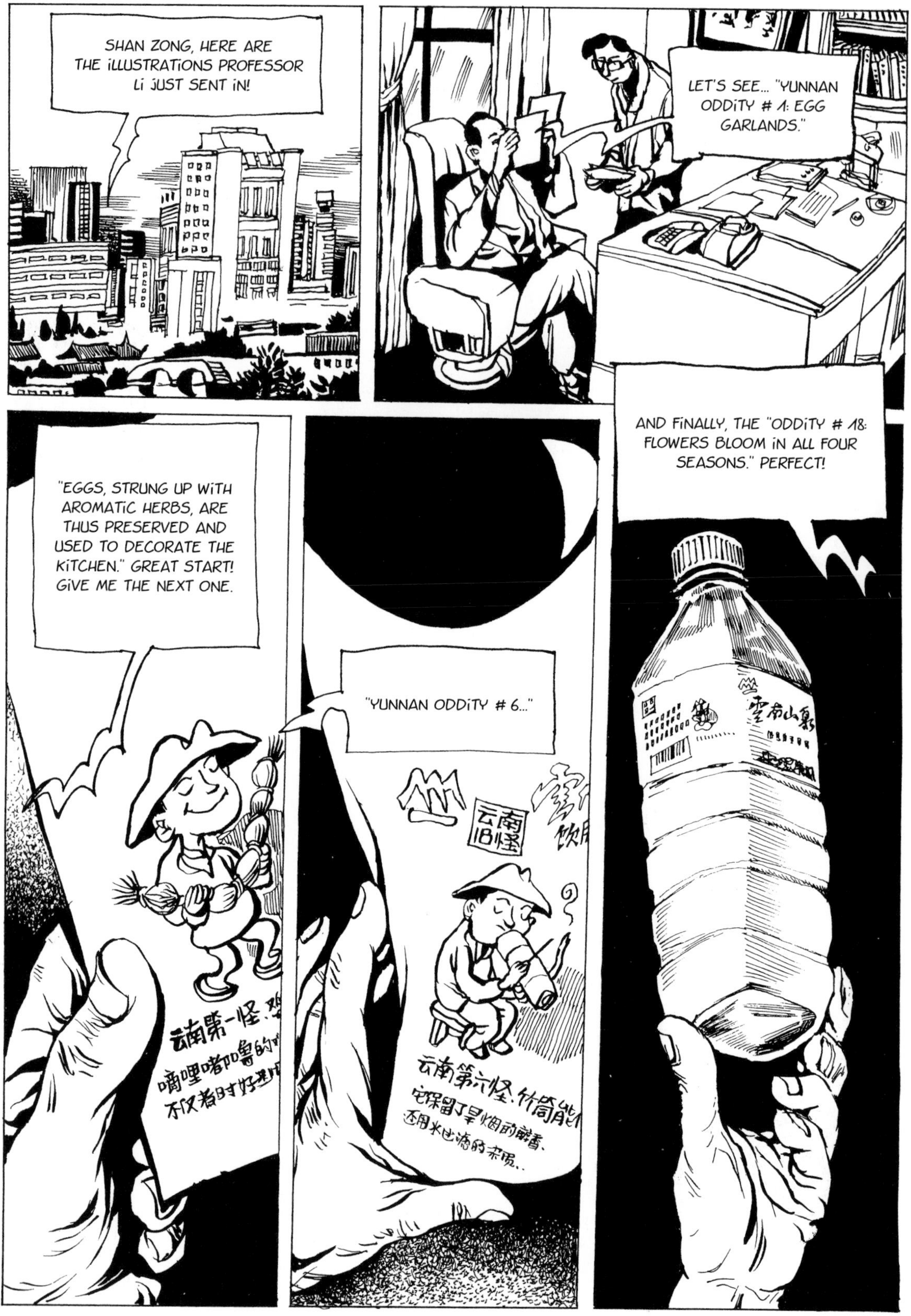
SHAN ZONG, HERE ARE THE ILLUSTRATIONS PROFESSOR LI JUST SENT IN!
LET'S SEE... "YUNNAN ODDITY # 1: EGG GARLANDS."
"EGGS, STRUNG UP WITH AROMATIC HERBS, ARE THUS PRESERVED AND USED TO DECORATE THE KITCHEN." GREAT START! GIVE ME THE NEXT ONE.
"YUNNAN ODDITY # 6..."
AND FINALLY, THE "ODDITY # 18: FLOWERS BLOOM IN ALL FOUR SEASONS." PERFECT!

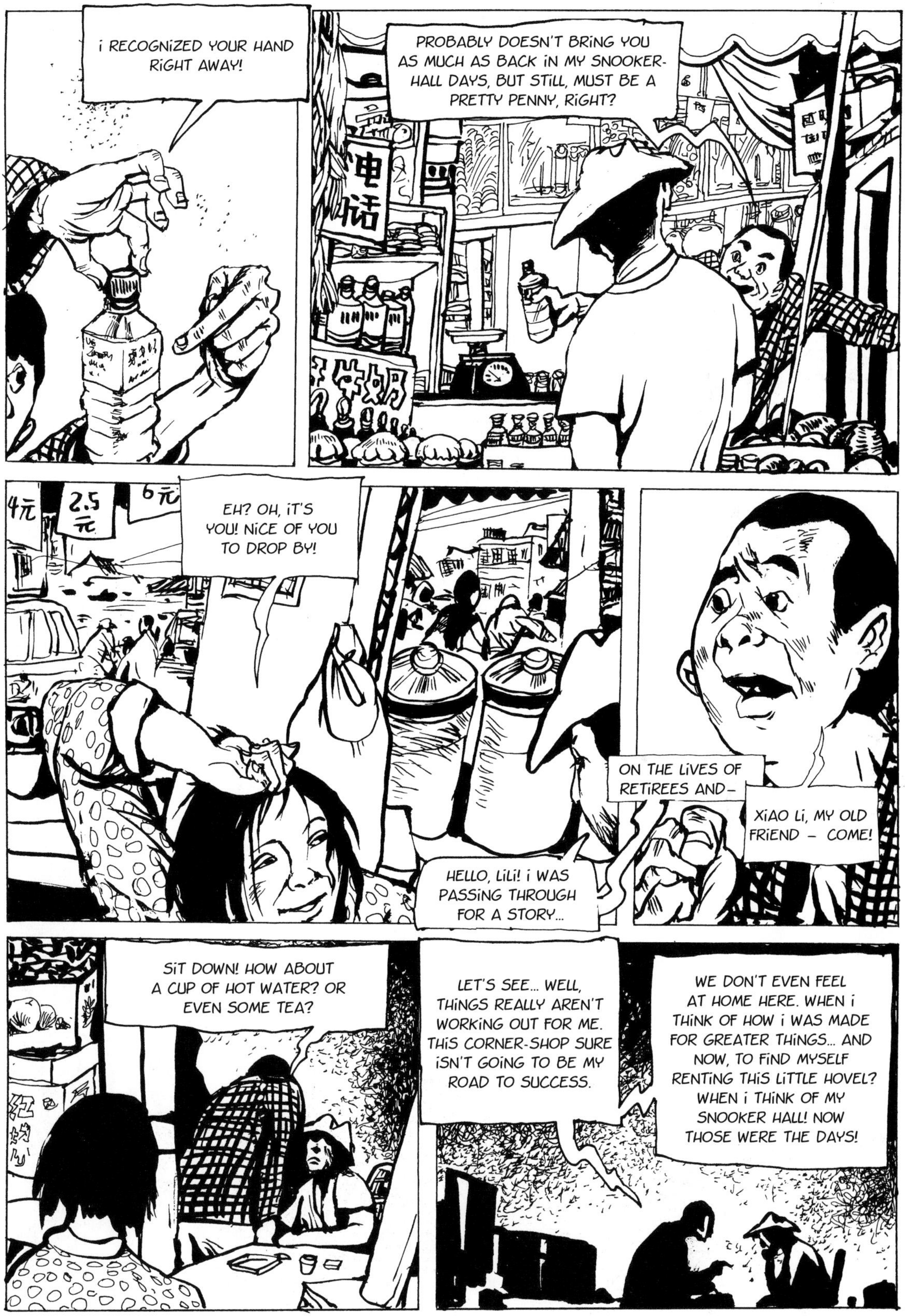

I RECOGNIZED YOUR HAND RIGHT AWAY!
PROBABLY DOESN'T BRING YOU AS MUCH AS BACK IN MY SNOOKER-HALL DAYS, BUT STILL, MUST BE A PRETTY PENNY, RIGHT?
4元
2.5元
6元
EH? OH, IT'S YOU! NICE OF YOU TO DROP BY!
HELLO, LILI! I WAS PASSING THROUGH FOR A STORY...
ON THE LIVES OF RETIREES AND–
XIAO LI, MY OLD FRIEND – COME!
SIT DOWN! HOW ABOUT A CUP OF HOT WATER? OR EVEN SOME TEA?
LET'S SEE... WELL, THINGS REALLY AREN'T WORKING OUT FOR ME. THIS CORNER-SHOP SURE ISN'T GOING TO BE MY ROAD TO SUCCESS.
WE DON'T EVEN FEEL AT HOME HERE. WHEN I THINK OF HOW I WAS MADE FOR GREATER THINGS... AND NOW, TO FIND MYSELF RENTING THIS LITTLE HOVEL? WHEN I THINK OF MY SNOOKER HALL! NOW THOSE WERE THE DAYS!

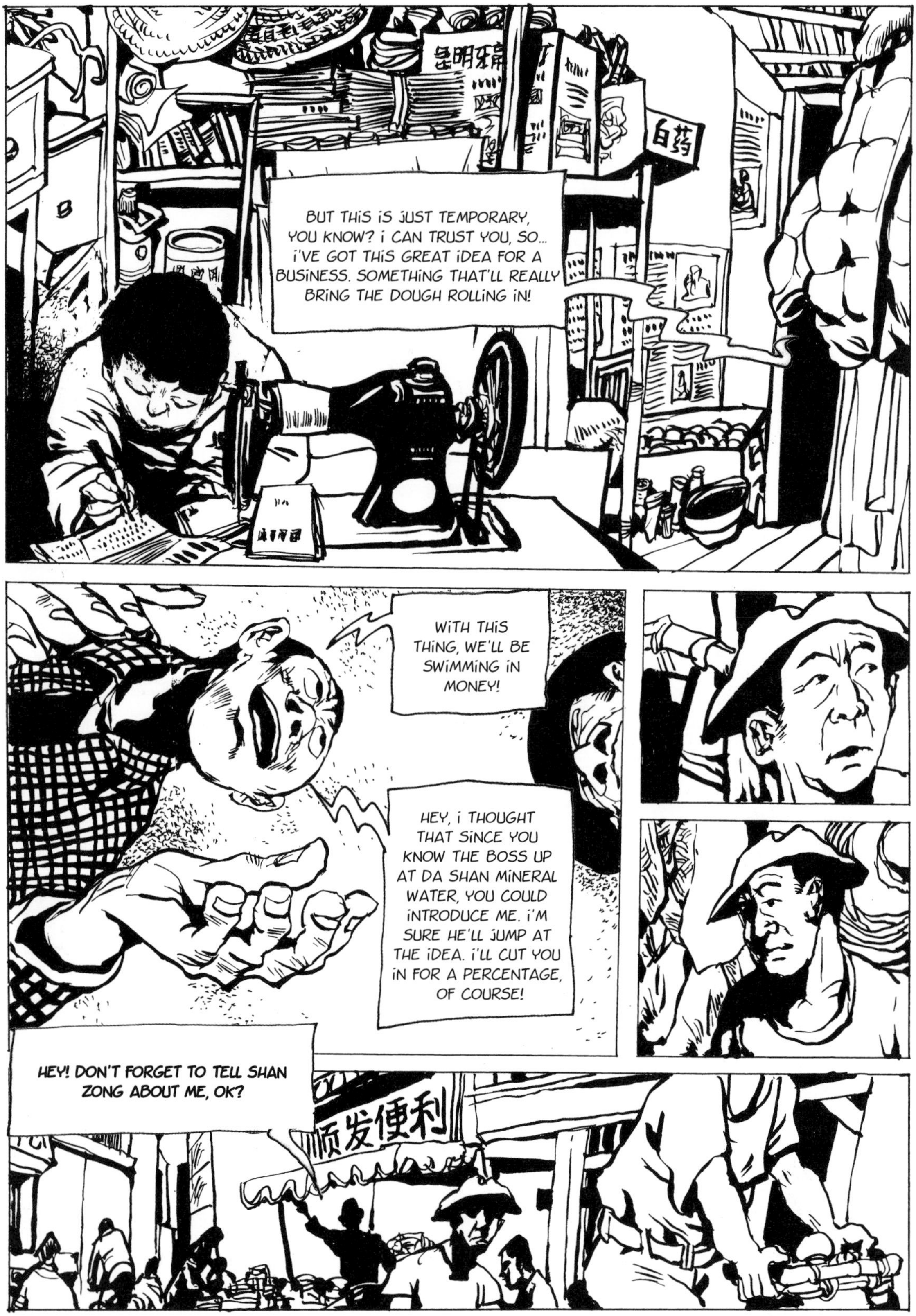

BUT THIS IS JUST TEMPORARY, YOU KNOW? I CAN TRUST YOU, SO... I'VE GOT THIS GREAT IDEA FOR A BUSINESS. SOMETHING THAT'LL REALLY BRING THE DOUGH ROLLING IN!
白药
WITH THIS THING, WE'LL BE SWIMMING IN MONEY!
HEY, I THOUGHT THAT SINCE YOU KNOW THE BOSS UP AT DA SHAN MINERAL WATER, YOU COULD INTRODUCE ME. I'M SURE HE'LL JUMP AT THE IDEA. I'LL CUT YOU IN FOR A PERCENTAGE, OF COURSE!
HEY! DON'T FORGET TO TELL SHAN ZONG ABOUT ME, OK?
顺发便利

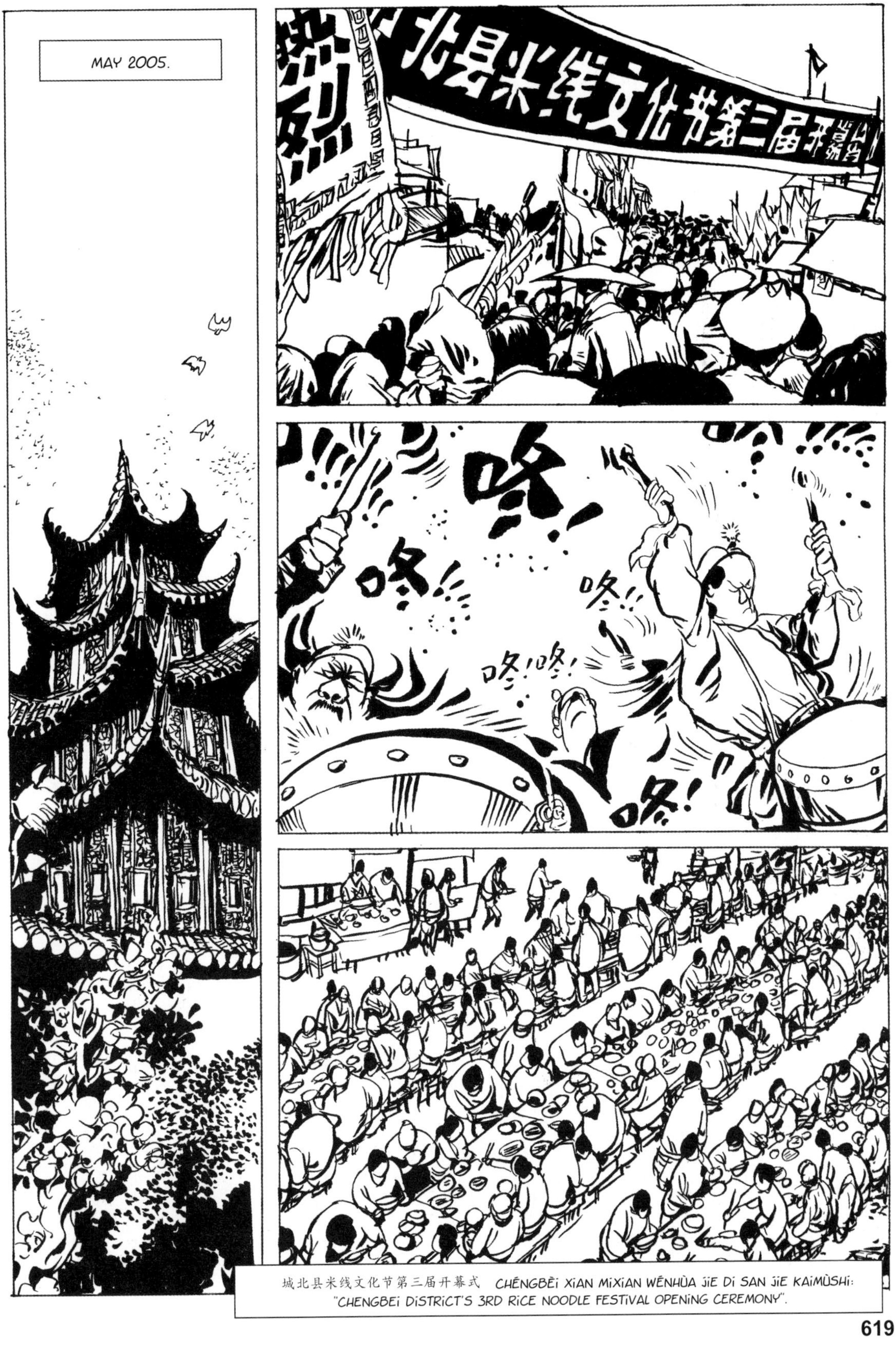
MAY 2005.
北县米线文化节第三届开
咚!
咚!
咚!
咚!咚!
咚!
城北县米线文化节第三届开幕式 CHÉNGBĚI XIAN MIXIAN WÉNHÙA JIE DI SAN JIE KAIMÙSHI:
"CHENGBEI DISTRICT'S 3RD RICE NOODLE FESTIVAL OPENING CEREMONY".

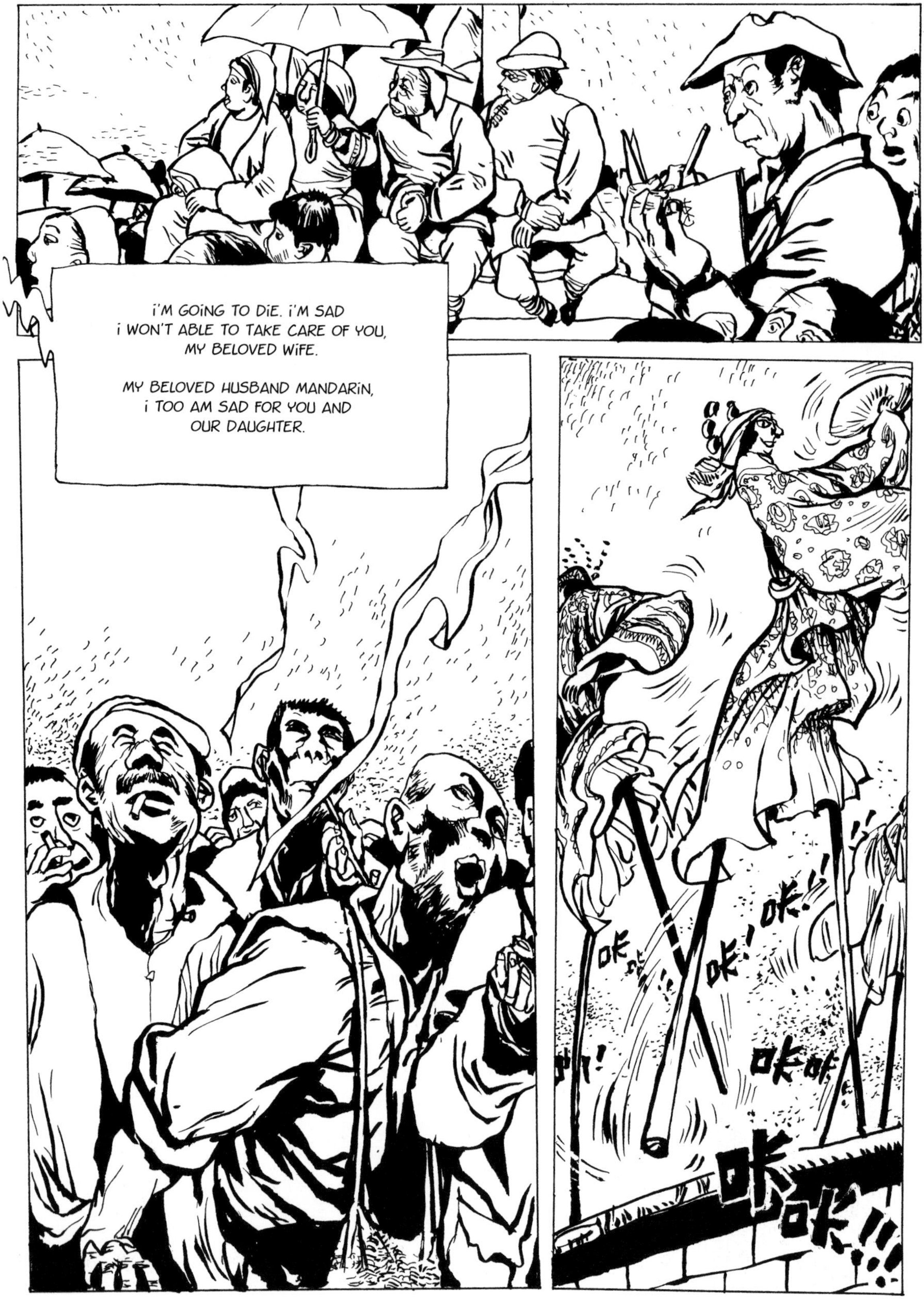
i'M GOiNG TO DiE. i'M SAD
i WON'T ABLE TO TAKE CARE OF YOU,
MY BELOVED WiFE.
MY BELOVED HUSBAND MANDARiN,
i TOO AM SAD FOR YOU AND
OUR DAUGHTER.
咔咔!!!

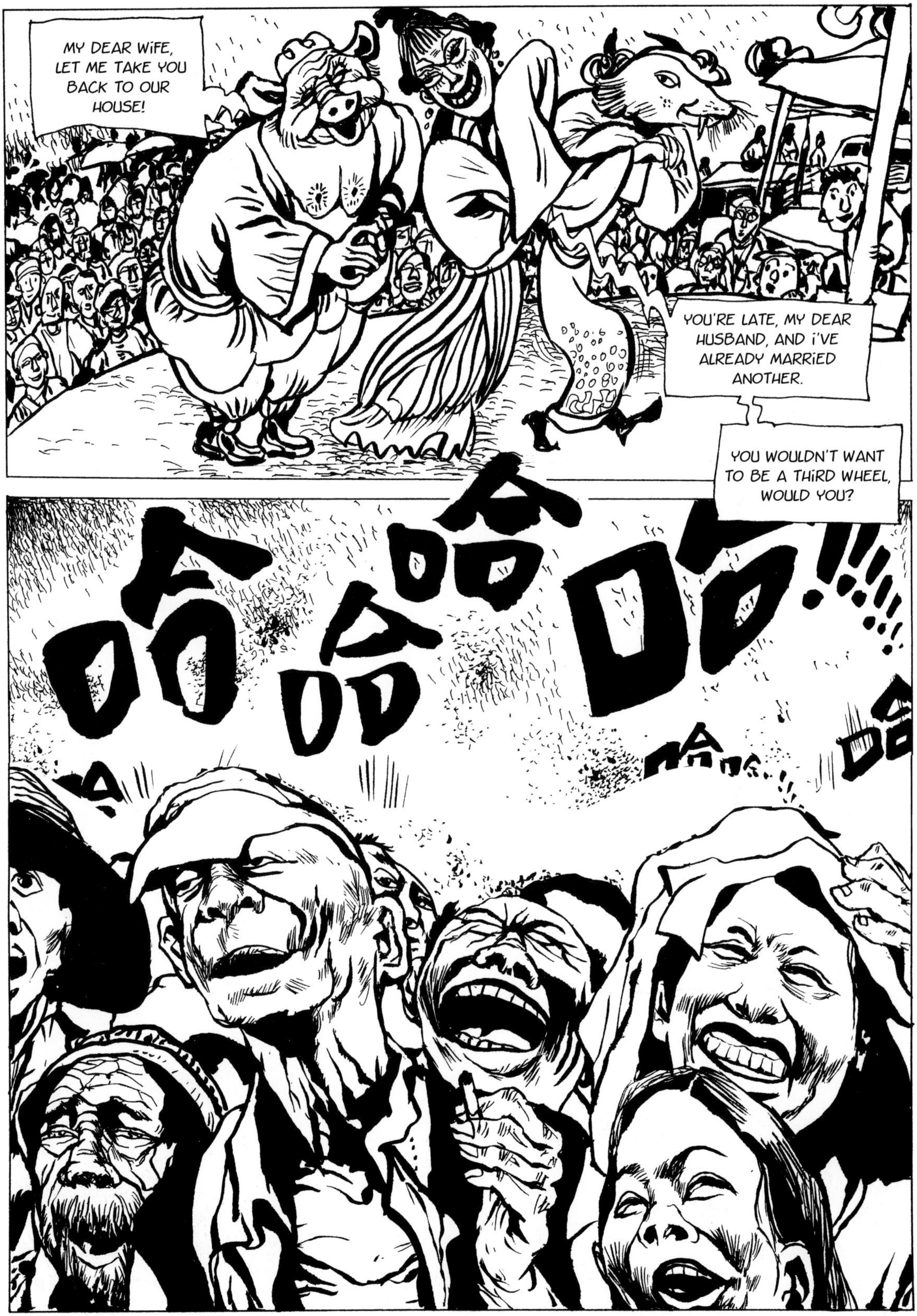
MY DEAR WIFE, LET ME TAKE YOU BACK TO OUR HOUSE!
YOU'RE LATE, MY DEAR HUSBAND, AND I'VE ALREADY MARRIED ANOTHER.
YOU WOULDN'T WANT TO BE A THIRD WHEEL, WOULD YOU?
哈哈哈!!!

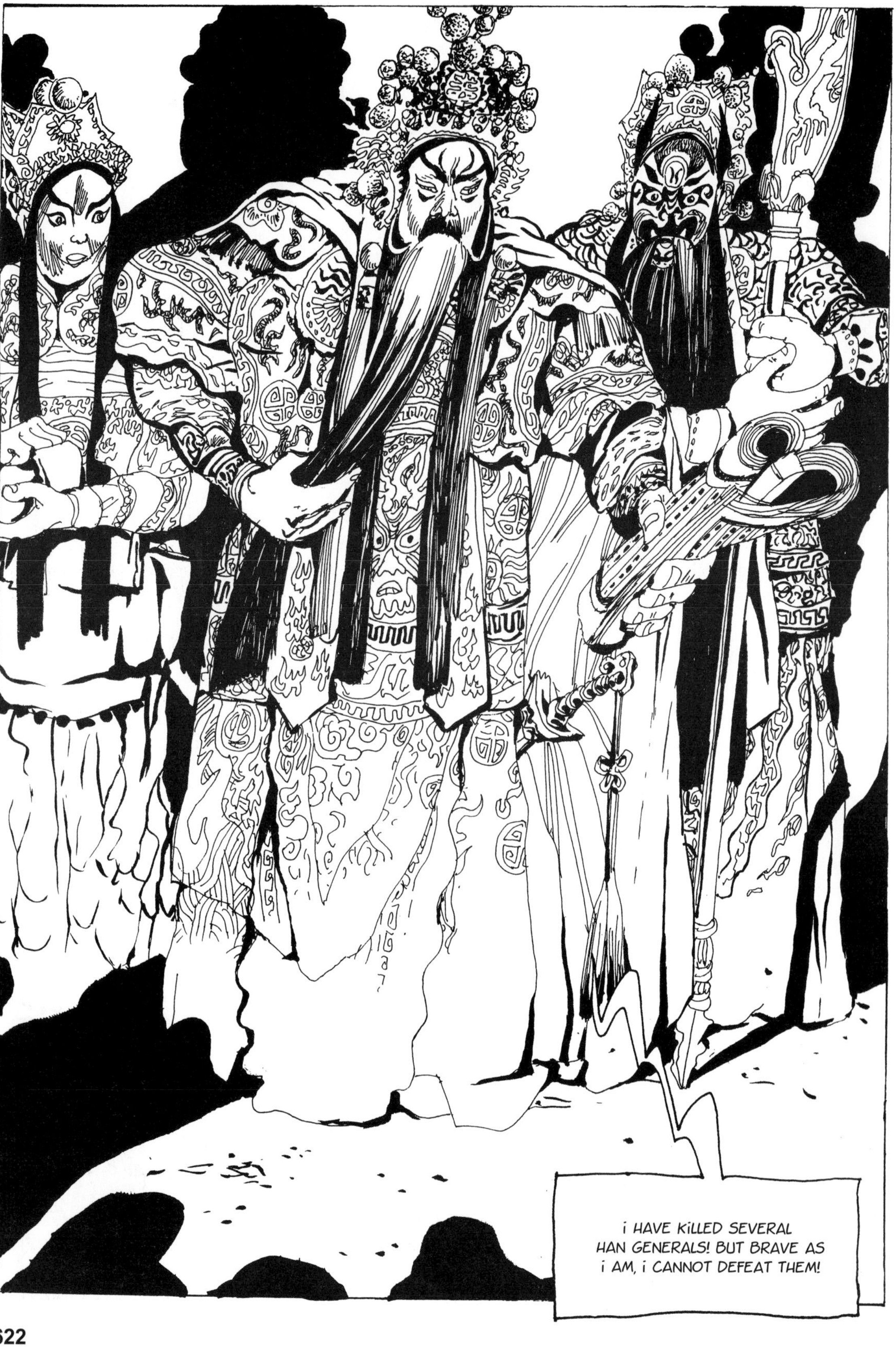
I HAVE KILLED SEVERAL HAN GENERALS! BUT BRAVE AS I AM, I CANNOT DEFEAT THEM!

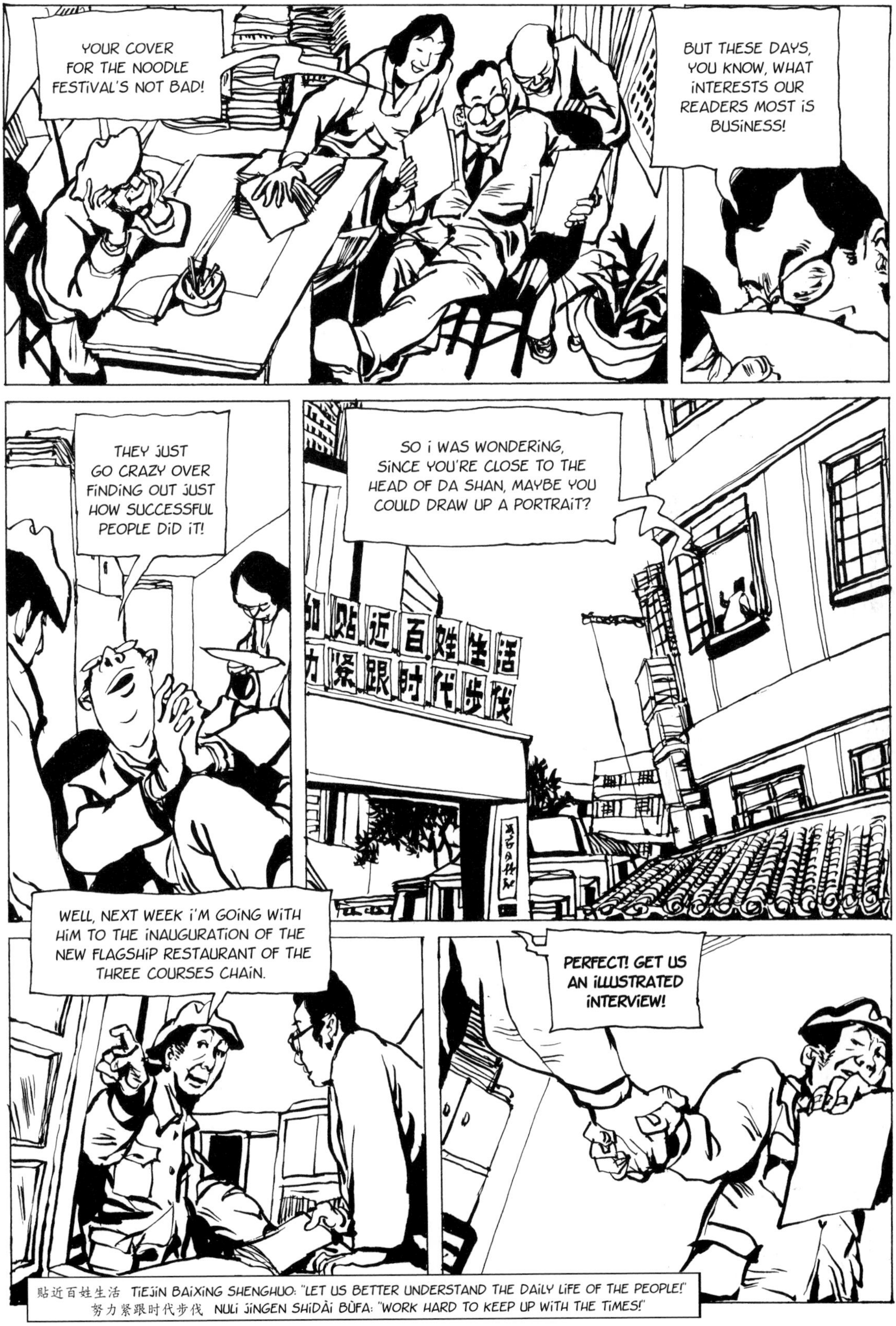

YOUR COVER FOR THE NOODLE FESTIVAL'S NOT BAD!
BUT THESE DAYS, YOU KNOW, WHAT INTERESTS OUR READERS MOST IS BUSINESS!
THEY JUST GO CRAZY OVER FINDING OUT JUST HOW SUCCESSFUL PEOPLE DID IT!
SO I WAS WONDERING, SINCE YOU'RE CLOSE TO THE HEAD OF DA SHAN, MAYBE YOU COULD DRAW UP A PORTRAIT?
贴近百姓生活
力紧跟时代步伐
WELL, NEXT WEEK I'M GOING WITH HIM TO THE INAUGURATION OF THE NEW FLAGSHIP RESTAURANT OF THE THREE COURSES CHAIN.
PERFECT! GET US AN ILLUSTRATED INTERVIEW!

贴近百姓生活 TIEJIN BAIXING SHENGHUO: "LET US BETTER UNDERSTAND THE DAILY LIFE OF THE PEOPLE!"
努力紧跟时代步伐 NULI JINGEN SHIDAI BUFA: "WORK HARD TO KEEP UP WITH THE TIMES!"

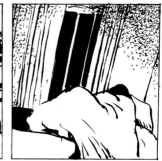

DA SHAN CORPORATE
TRAINING CENTRE

ASSEMBLE!

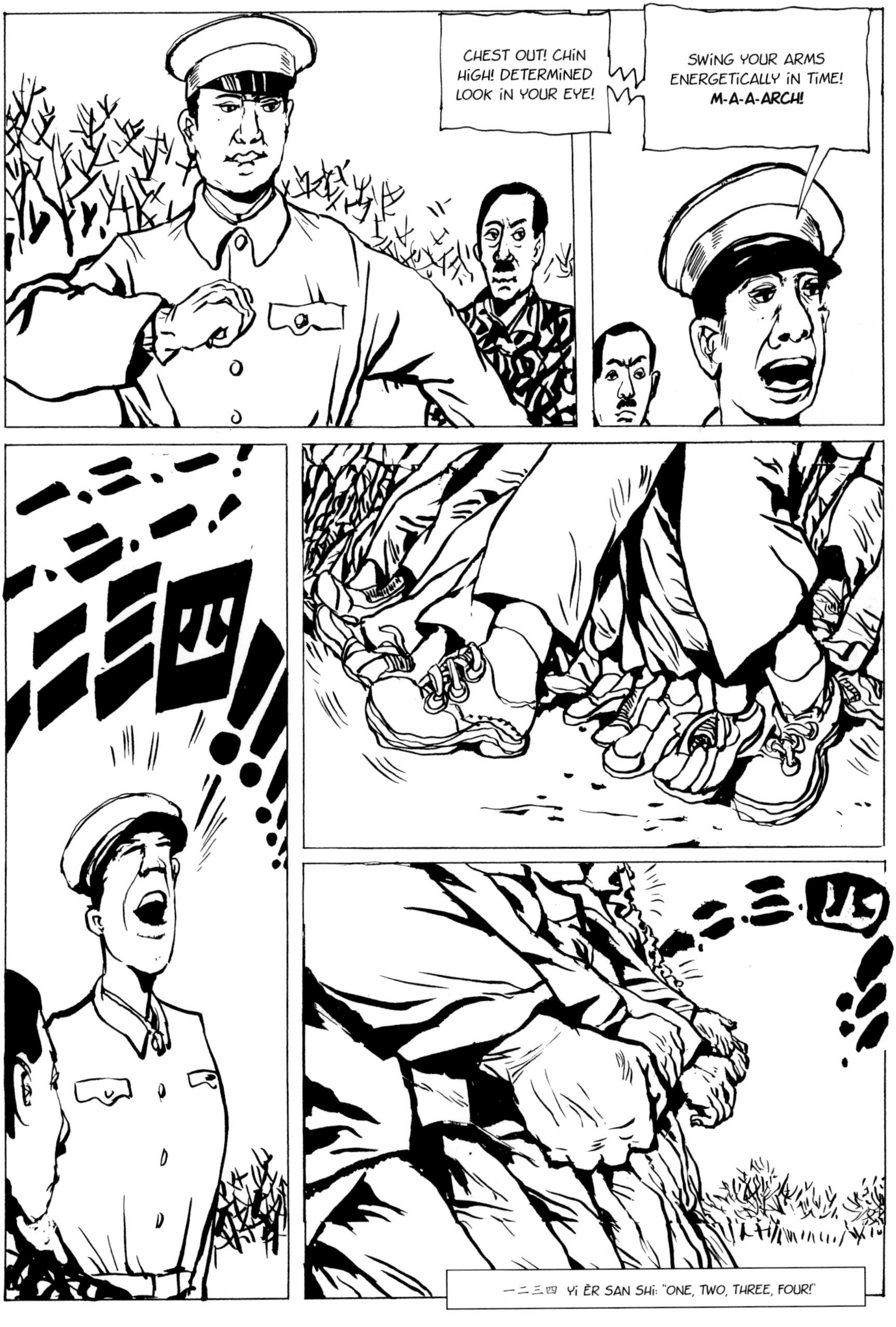
CHEST OUT! CHIN HIGH! DETERMINED LOOK IN YOUR EYE!
SWING YOUR ARMS ENERGETICALLY IN TIME! **M-A-A-ARCH!**
一、二、一！
一、二、一！
一、二、三、四！
一、二、三、四！
一二三四 YI ÈR SAN SHI: "ONE, TWO, THREE, FOUR!"

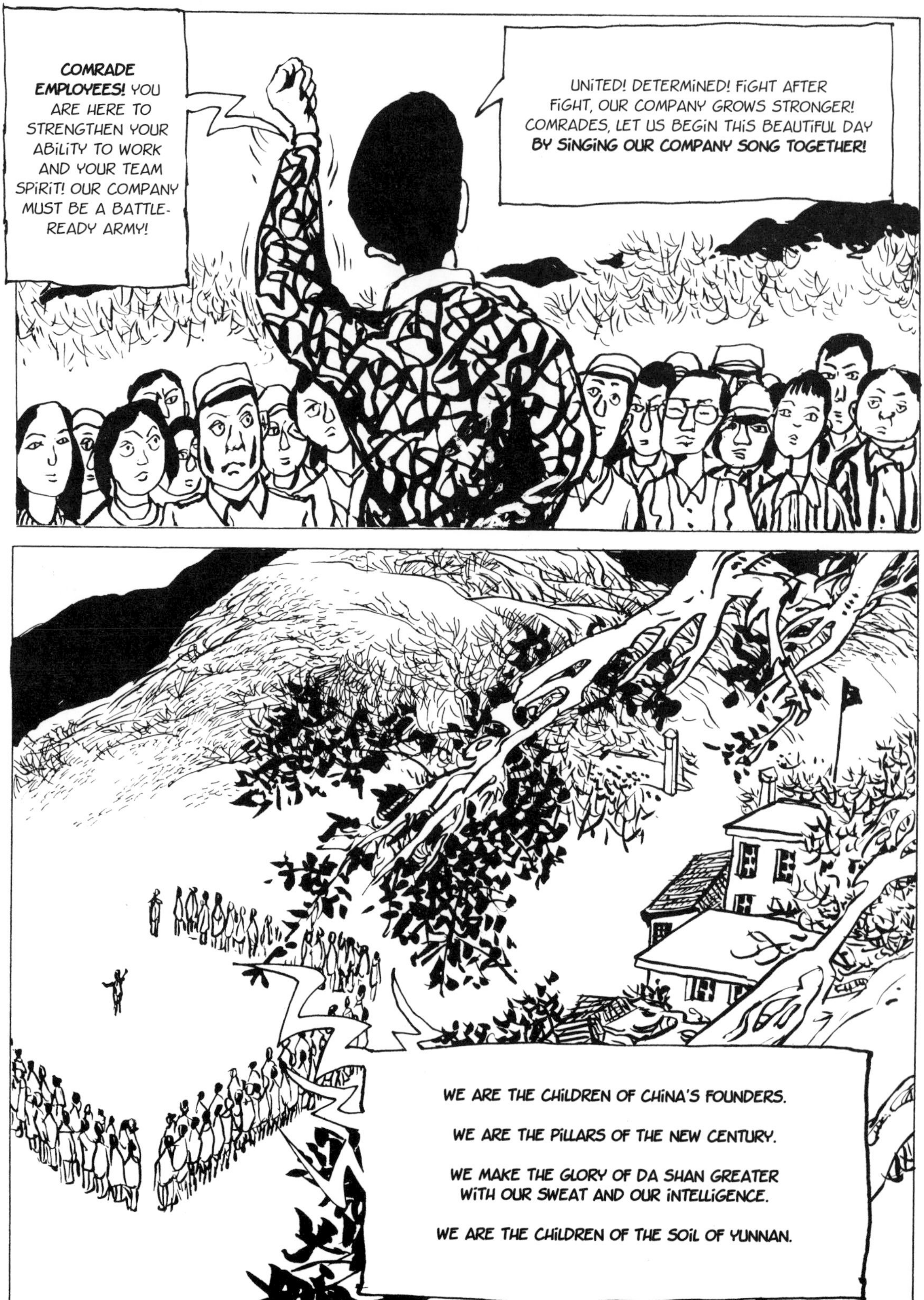
COMRADE EMPLOYEES! YOU ARE HERE TO STRENGTHEN YOUR ABILITY TO WORK AND YOUR TEAM SPIRIT! OUR COMPANY MUST BE A BATTLE-READY ARMY!
UNITED! DETERMINED! FIGHT AFTER FIGHT, OUR COMPANY GROWS STRONGER! COMRADES, LET US BEGIN THIS BEAUTIFUL DAY BY SINGING OUR COMPANY SONG TOGETHER!
WE ARE THE CHILDREN OF CHINA'S FOUNDERS.
WE ARE THE PILLARS OF THE NEW CENTURY.
WE MAKE THE GLORY OF DA SHAN GREATER WITH OUR SWEAT AND OUR INTELLIGENCE.
WE ARE THE CHILDREN OF THE SOIL OF YUNNAN.

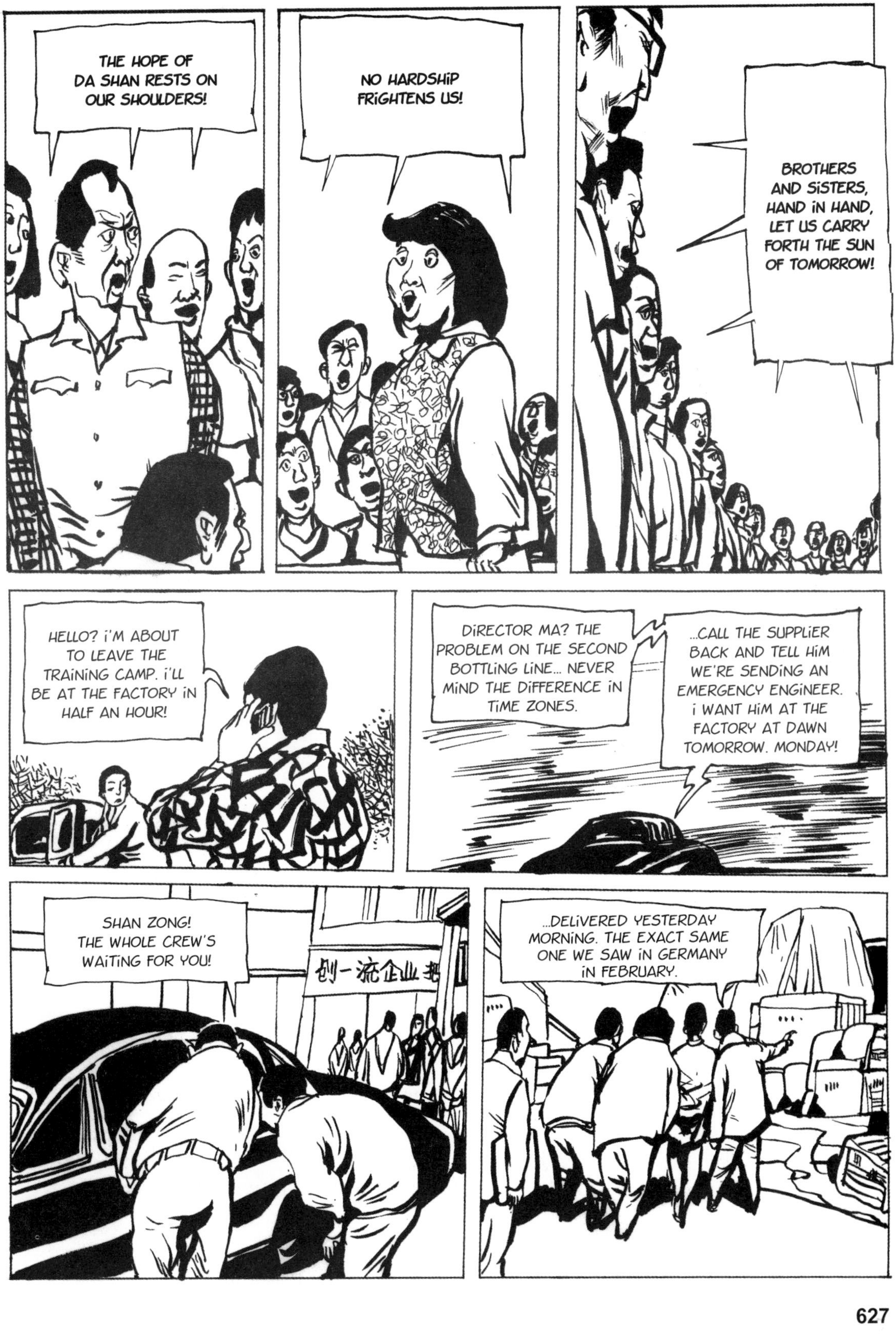
THE HOPE OF DA SHAN RESTS ON OUR SHOULDERS!
NO HARDSHIP FRIGHTENS US!
BROTHERS AND SISTERS, HAND IN HAND, LET US CARRY FORTH THE SUN OF TOMORROW!
HELLO? I'M ABOUT TO LEAVE THE TRAINING CAMP. I'LL BE AT THE FACTORY IN HALF AN HOUR!
DIRECTOR MA? THE PROBLEM ON THE SECOND BOTTLING LINE... NEVER MIND THE DIFFERENCE IN TIME ZONES.
...CALL THE SUPPLIER BACK AND TELL HIM WE'RE SENDING AN EMERGENCY ENGINEER. I WANT HIM AT THE FACTORY AT DAWN TOMORROW. MONDAY!
SHAN ZONG! THE WHOLE CREW'S WAITING FOR YOU!
创一流企业 把
...DELIVERED YESTERDAY MORNING. THE EXACT SAME ONE WE SAW IN GERMANY IN FEBRUARY.

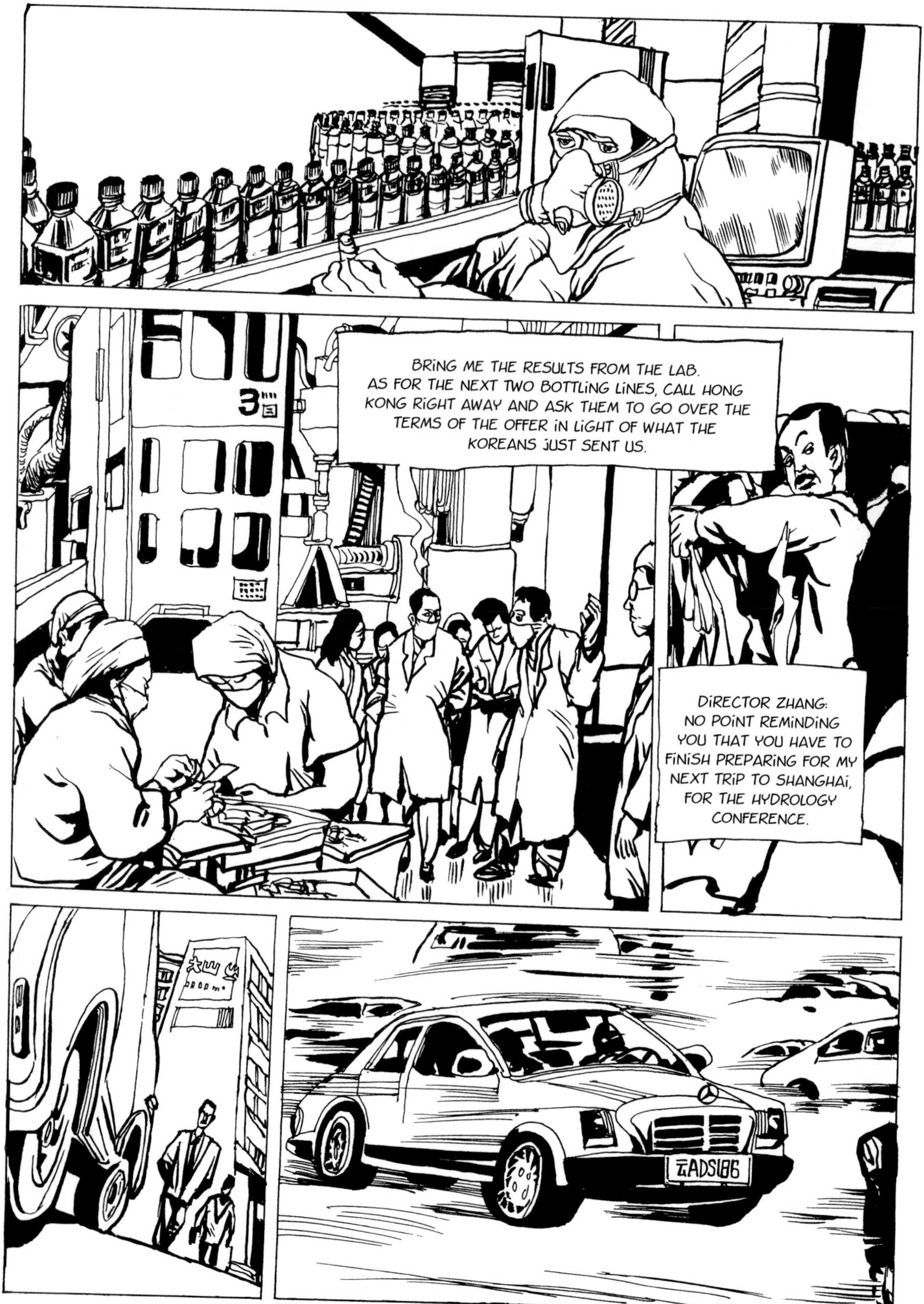
BRING ME THE RESULTS FROM THE LAB.
AS FOR THE NEXT TWO BOTTLING LINES, CALL HONG KONG RIGHT AWAY AND ASK THEM TO GO OVER THE TERMS OF THE OFFER IN LIGHT OF WHAT THE KOREANS JUST SENT US.
DIRECTOR ZHANG: NO POINT REMINDING YOU THAT YOU HAVE TO FINISH PREPARING FOR MY NEXT TRIP TO SHANGHAI, FOR THE HYDROLOGY CONFERENCE.
云ADS186

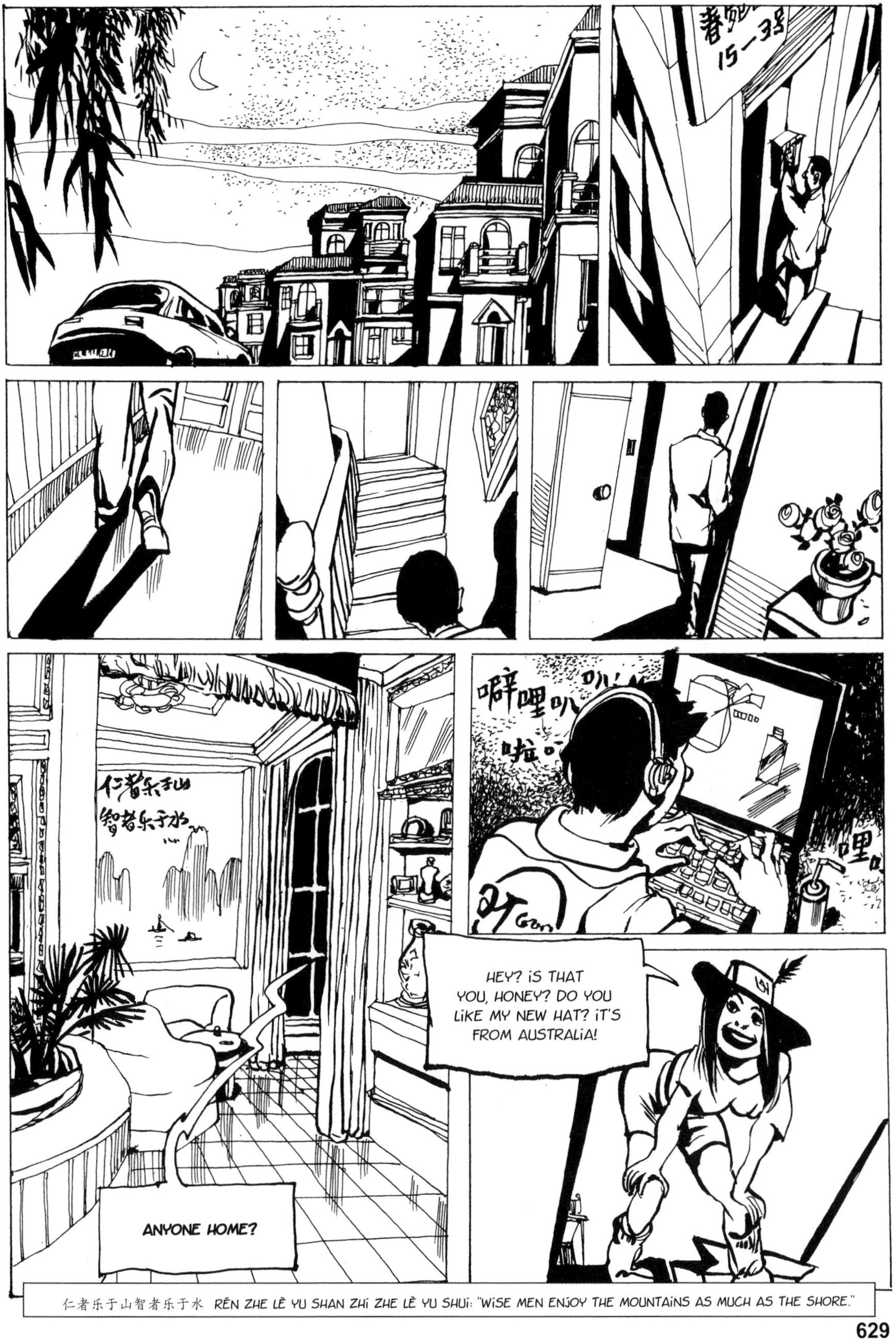
仁者乐于山
智者乐于水
ANYONE HOME?
HEY? iS THAT YOU, HONEY? DO YOU LiKE MY NEW HAT? iT'S FROM AUSTRALiA!

仁者乐于山智者乐于水 RĚN ZHE LÈ YU SHAN ZHi ZHE LÈ YU SHUi: "WiSE MEN ENJOY THE MOUNTAiNS AS MUCH AS THE SHORE."

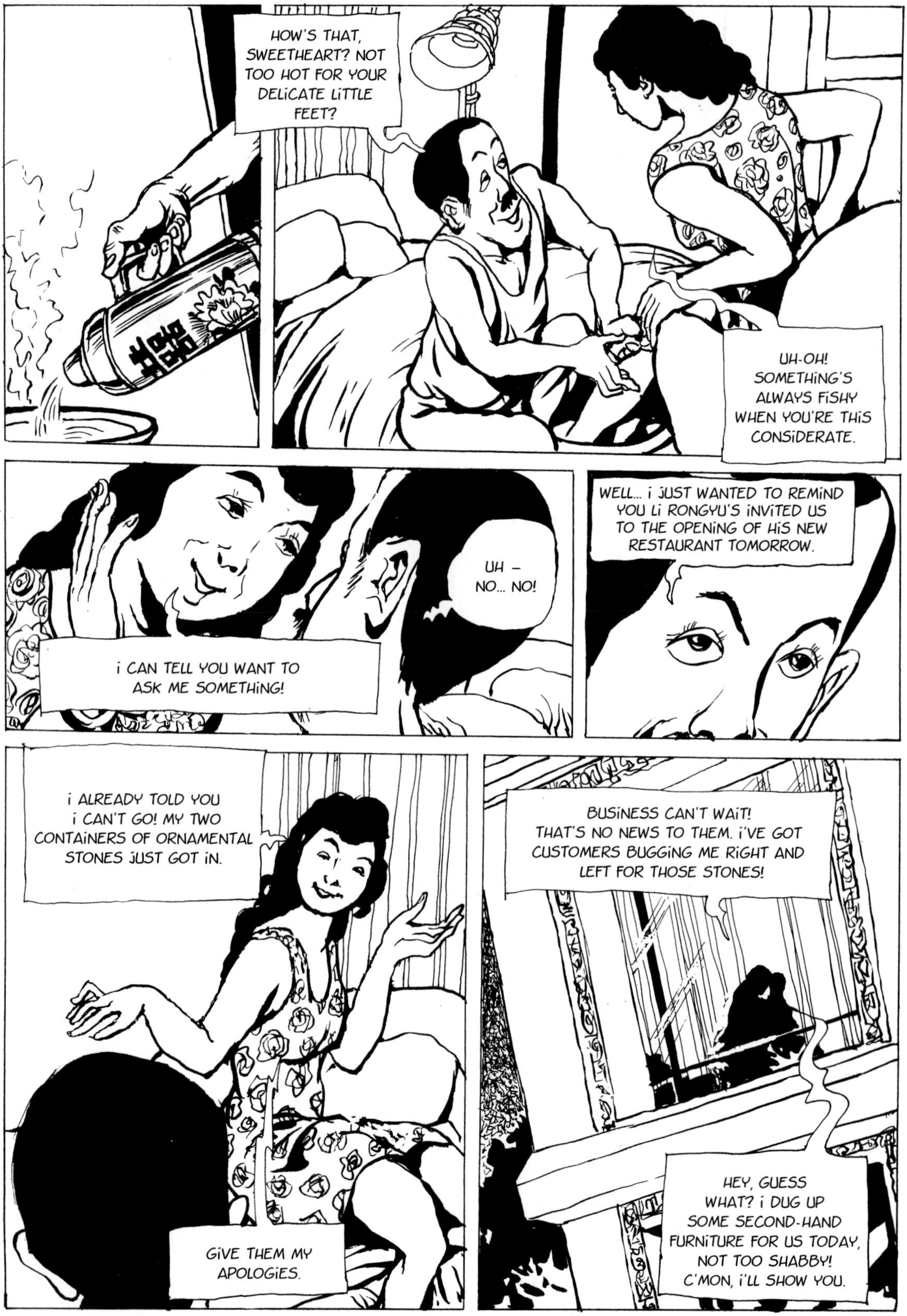
HOW'S THAT, SWEETHEART? NOT TOO HOT FOR YOUR DELICATE LITTLE FEET?
UH-OH! SOMETHING'S ALWAYS FISHY WHEN YOU'RE THIS CONSIDERATE.
I CAN TELL YOU WANT TO ASK ME SOMETHING!
UH – NO... NO!
WELL... I JUST WANTED TO REMIND YOU LI RONGYU'S INVITED US TO THE OPENING OF HIS NEW RESTAURANT TOMORROW.
I ALREADY TOLD YOU I CAN'T GO! MY TWO CONTAINERS OF ORNAMENTAL STONES JUST GOT IN.
GIVE THEM MY APOLOGIES.
BUSINESS CAN'T WAIT! THAT'S NO NEWS TO THEM. I'VE GOT CUSTOMERS BUGGING ME RIGHT AND LEFT FOR THOSE STONES!
HEY, GUESS WHAT? I DUG UP SOME SECOND-HAND FURNITURE FOR US TODAY, NOT TOO SHABBY! C'MON, I'LL SHOW YOU.

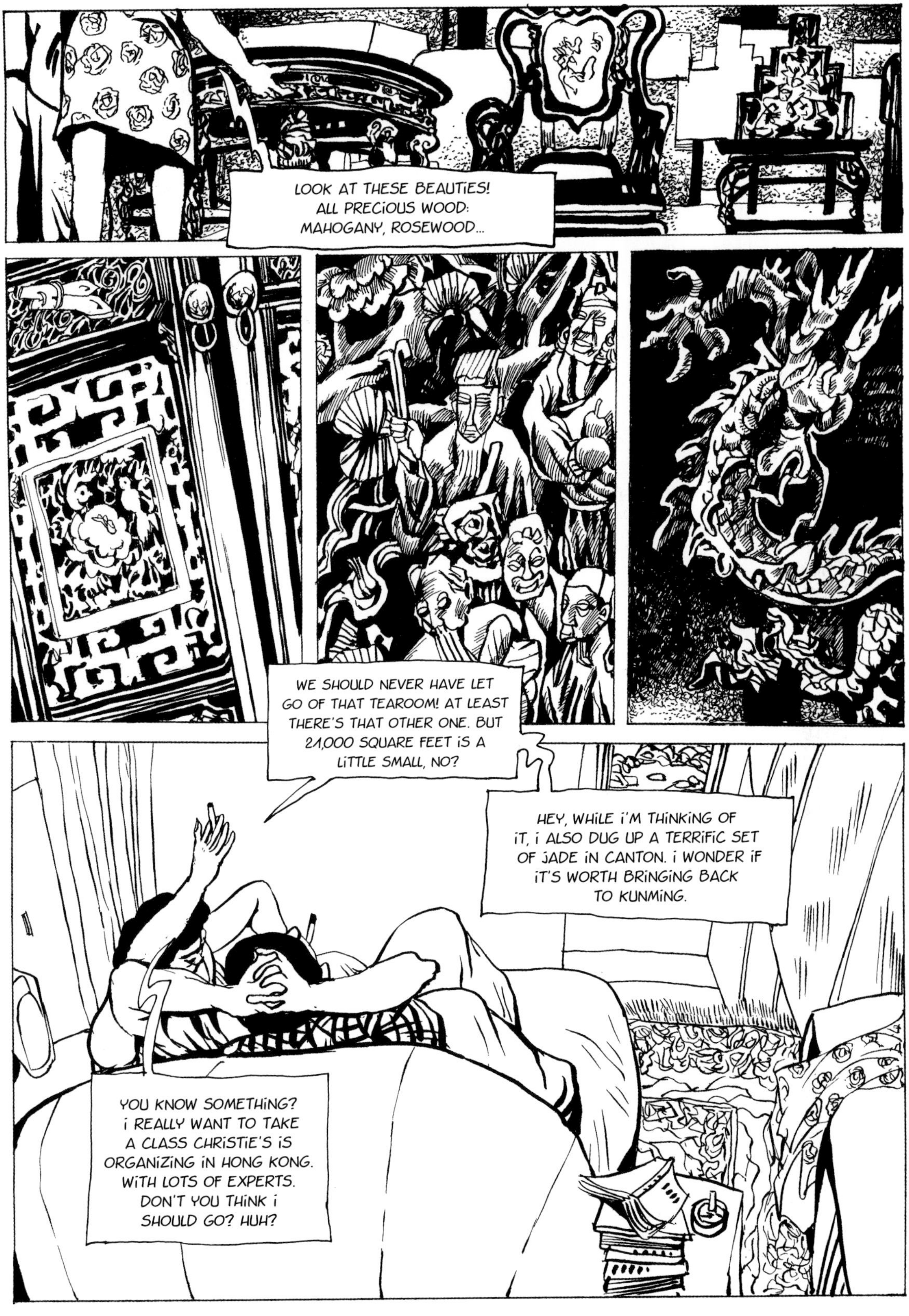
LOOK AT THESE BEAUTiES! ALL PRECiOUS WOOD: MAHOGANY, ROSEWOOD...
WE SHOULD NEVER HAVE LET GO OF THAT TEAROOM! AT LEAST THERE'S THAT OTHER ONE. BUT 21,000 SQUARE FEET iS A LiTTLE SMALL, NO?
HEY, WHiLE i'M THiNKiNG OF iT, i ALSO DUG UP A TERRiFiC SET OF JADE iN CANTON. i WONDER iF iT'S WORTH BRiNGiNG BACK TO KUNMiNG.
YOU KNOW SOMETHiNG? i REALLY WANT TO TAKE A CLASS CHRiSTiE'S iS ORGANiZiNG iN HONG KONG. WiTH LOTS OF EXPERTS. DON'T YOU THiNK i SHOULD GO? HUH?

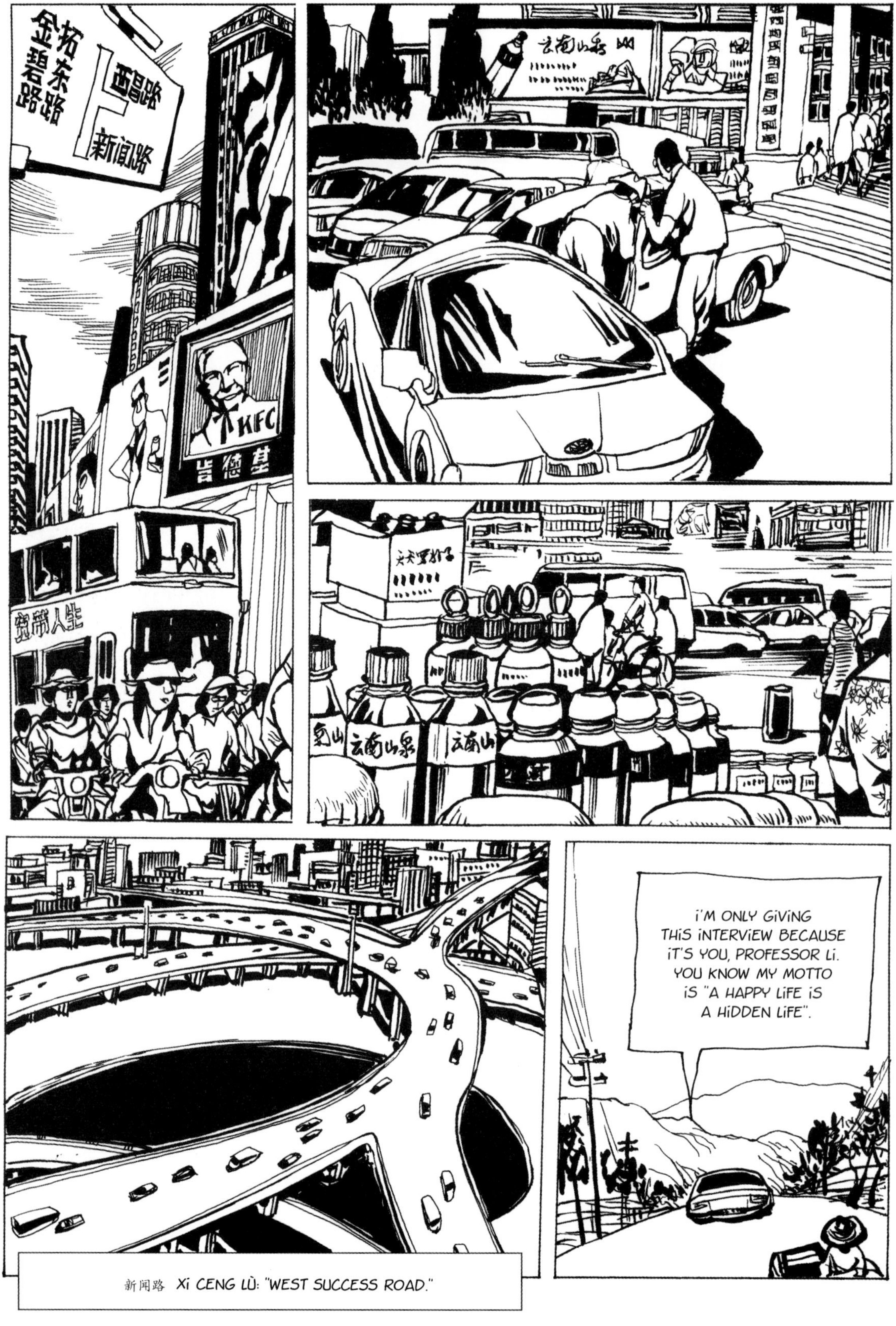
金碧路
拓东路
西昌路
新闻路
KFC
肯德基
云南山泉
I'M ONLY GIVING THIS INTERVIEW BECAUSE IT'S YOU, PROFESSOR LI. YOU KNOW MY MOTTO IS "A HAPPY LIFE IS A HIDDEN LIFE".
新闻路 Xi CENG LÙ: "WEST SUCCESS ROAD."

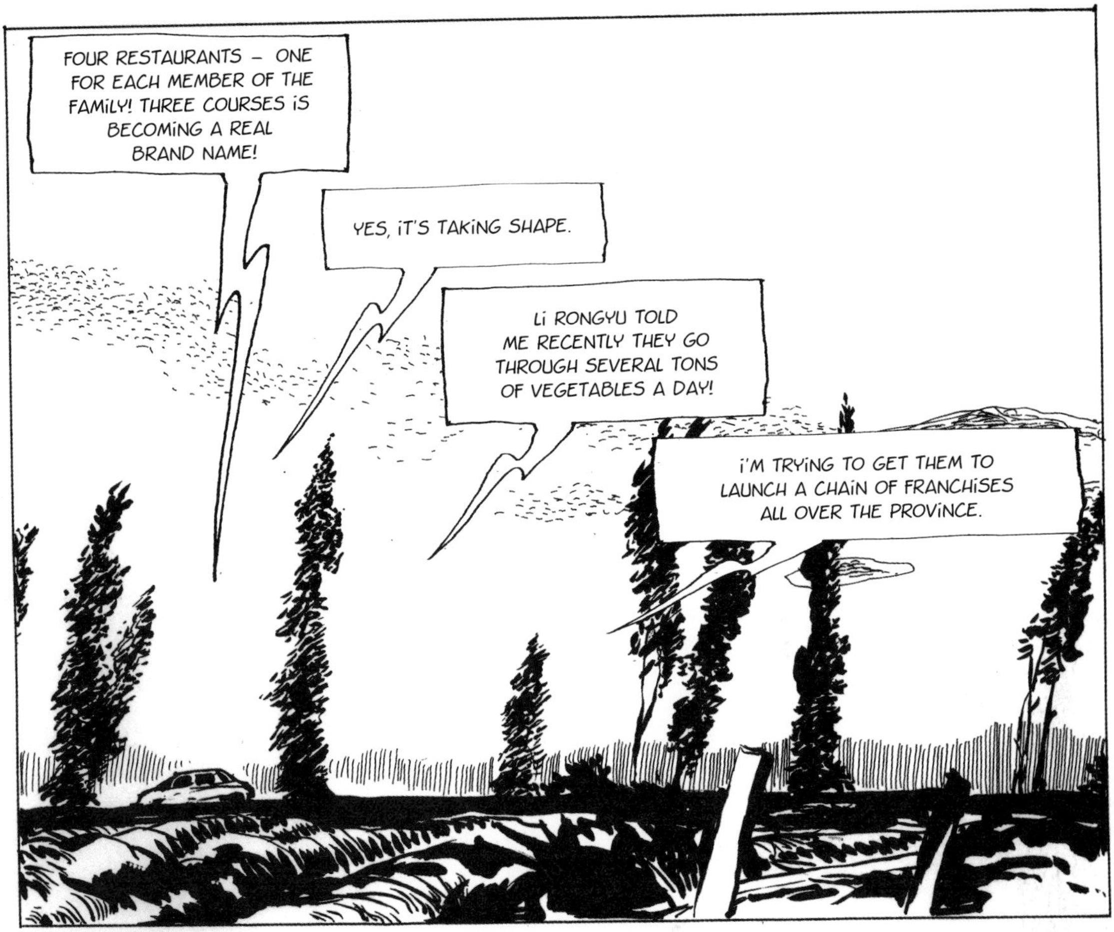
FOUR RESTAURANTS – ONE FOR EACH MEMBER OF THE FAMILY! THREE COURSES IS BECOMING A REAL BRAND NAME!
YES, IT'S TAKING SHAPE.
LI RONGYU TOLD ME RECENTLY THEY GO THROUGH SEVERAL TONS OF VEGETABLES A DAY!
I'M TRYING TO GET THEM TO LAUNCH A CHAIN OF FRANCHISES ALL OVER THE PROVINCE.

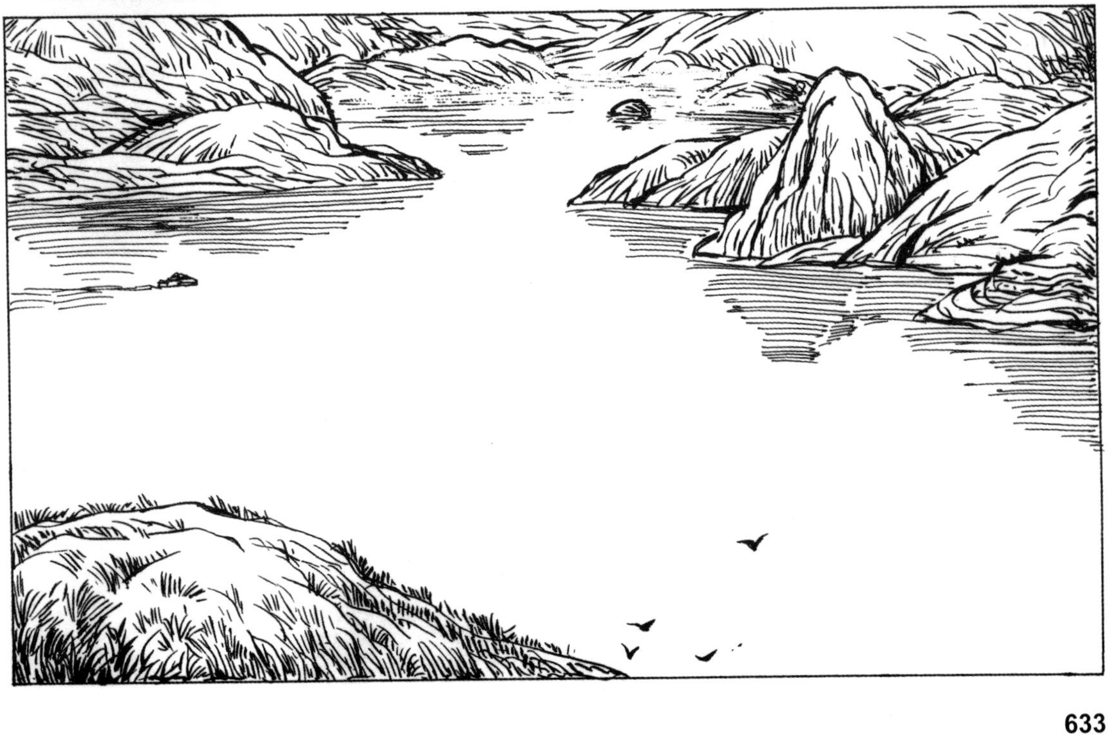

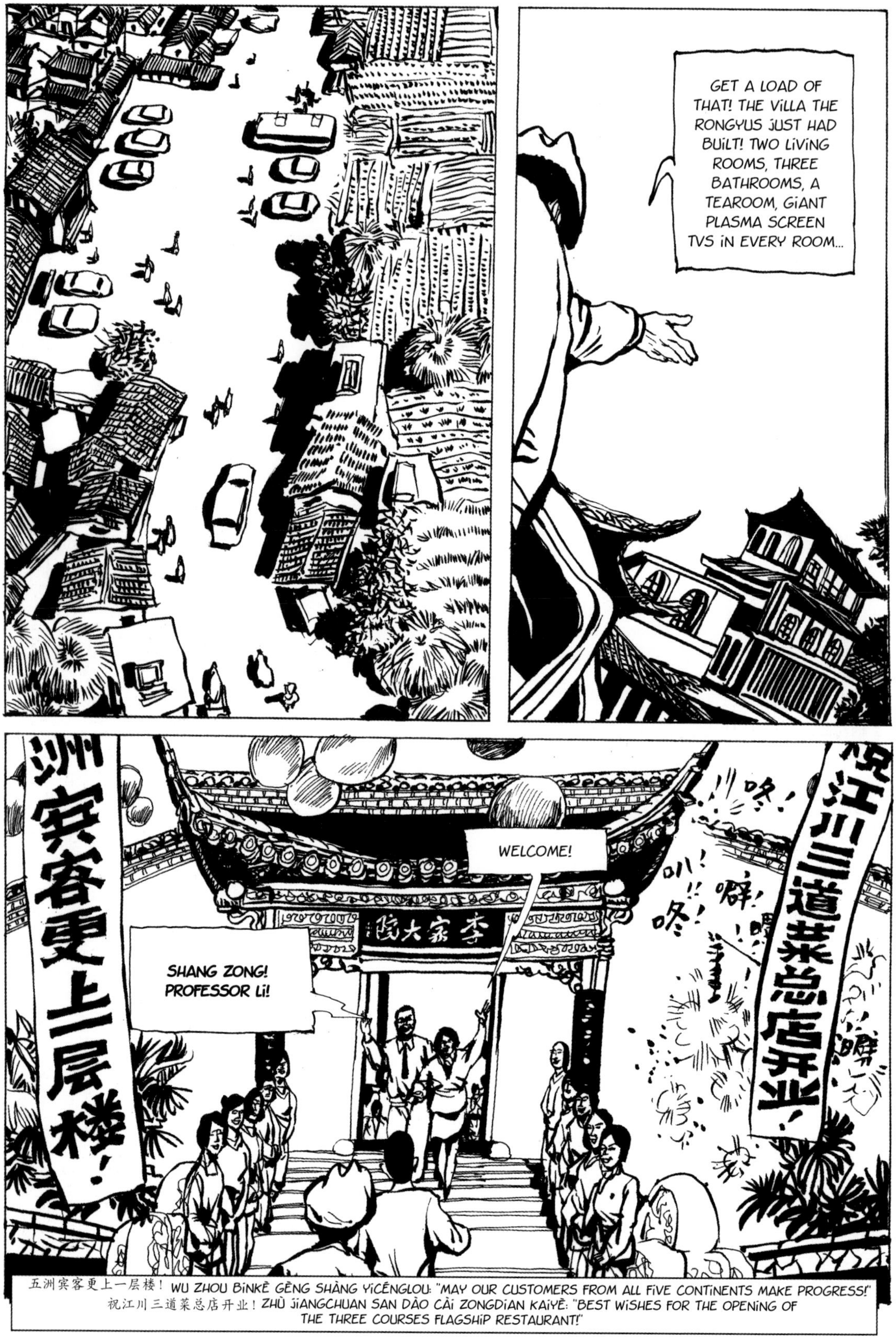
GET A LOAD OF THAT! THE ViLLA THE RONGYUS JUST HAD BUiLT! TWO LiViNG ROOMS, THREE BATHROOMS, A TEAROOM, GiANT PLASMA SCREEN TVS iN EVERY ROOM...
洲宾客更上一层楼！
李家大院
WELCOME!
SHANG ZONG! PROFESSOR Li!
江川三道菜总店开业！
咚！
叭！
咚！
噼！

五洲宾客更上一层楼！ WU ZHOU BiNKÈ GÈNG SHÀNG YiCÉNGLOU: "MAY OUR CUSTOMERS FROM ALL FiVE CONTiNENTS MAKE PROGRESS!"
祝江川三道菜总店开业！ ZHÙ JiANGCHUAN SAN DÀO CÀi ZONGDiAN KAiYÈ: "BEST WiSHES FOR THE OPENiNG OF THE THREE COURSES FLAGSHiP RESTAURANT!"

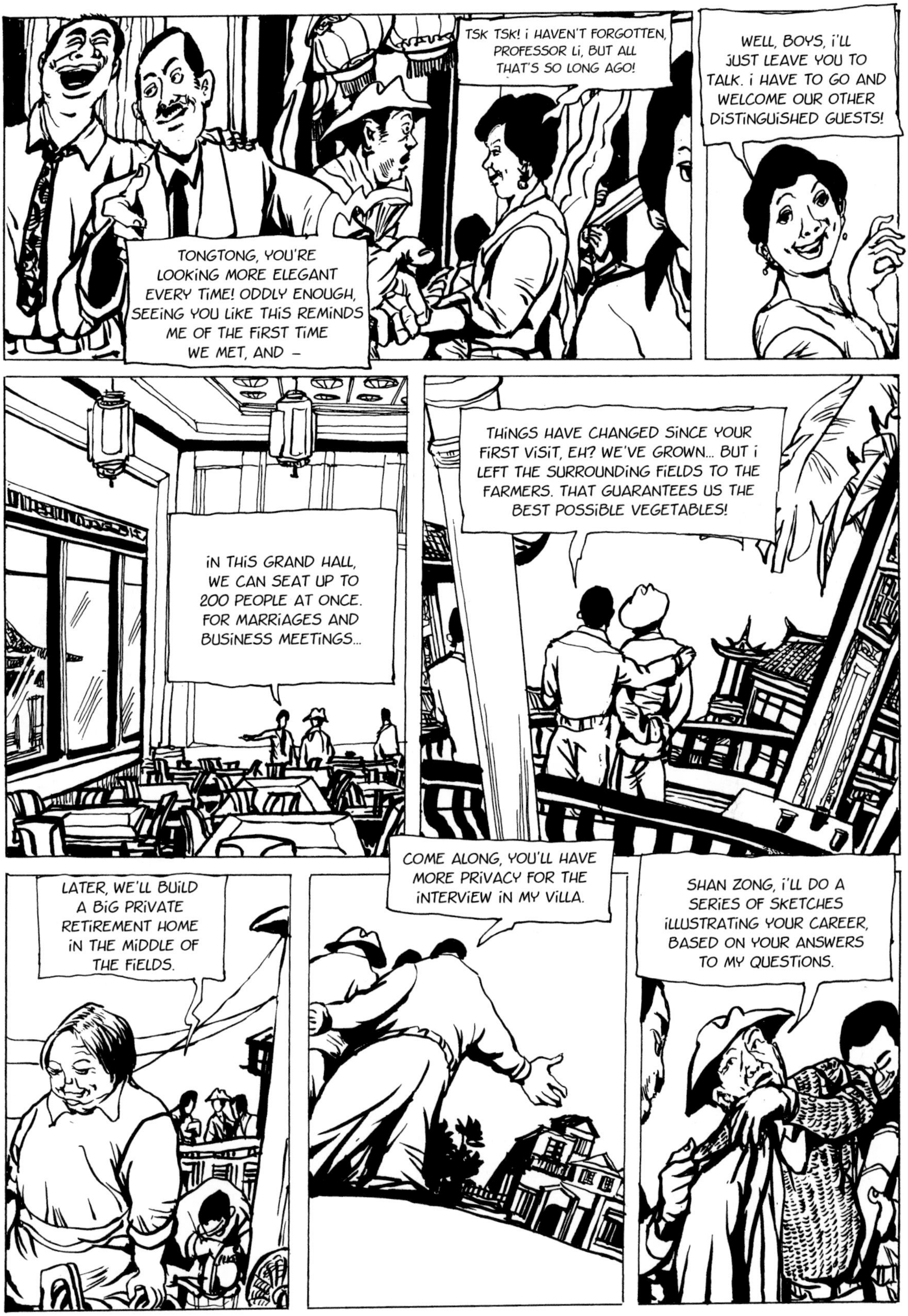
TONGTONG, YOU'RE LOOKING MORE ELEGANT EVERY TIME! ODDLY ENOUGH, SEEING YOU LIKE THIS REMINDS ME OF THE FIRST TIME WE MET, AND –
TSK TSK! I HAVEN'T FORGOTTEN, PROFESSOR LI, BUT ALL THAT'S SO LONG AGO!
WELL, BOYS, I'LL JUST LEAVE YOU TO TALK. I HAVE TO GO AND WELCOME OUR OTHER DISTINGUISHED GUESTS!
IN THIS GRAND HALL, WE CAN SEAT UP TO 200 PEOPLE AT ONCE. FOR MARRIAGES AND BUSINESS MEETINGS...
THINGS HAVE CHANGED SINCE YOUR FIRST VISIT, EH? WE'VE GROWN... BUT I LEFT THE SURROUNDING FIELDS TO THE FARMERS. THAT GUARANTEES US THE BEST POSSIBLE VEGETABLES!
LATER, WE'LL BUILD A BIG PRIVATE RETIREMENT HOME IN THE MIDDLE OF THE FIELDS.
COME ALONG, YOU'LL HAVE MORE PRIVACY FOR THE INTERVIEW IN MY VILLA.
SHAN ZONG, I'LL DO A SERIES OF SKETCHES ILLUSTRATING YOUR CAREER, BASED ON YOUR ANSWERS TO MY QUESTIONS.

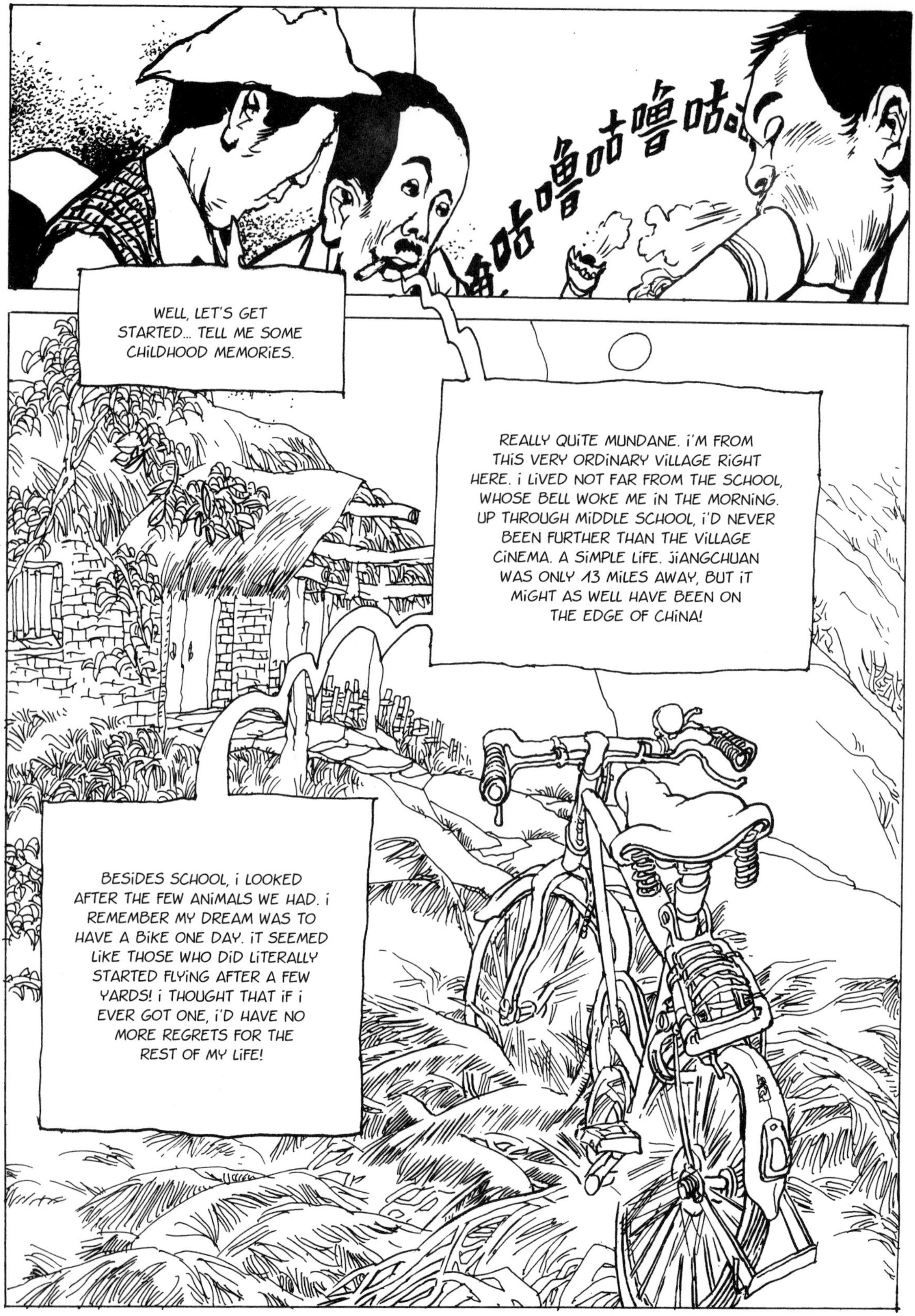
WELL, LET'S GET STARTED... TELL ME SOME CHILDHOOD MEMORIES.
REALLY QUITE MUNDANE. I'M FROM THIS VERY ORDINARY VILLAGE RIGHT HERE. I LIVED NOT FAR FROM THE SCHOOL, WHOSE BELL WOKE ME IN THE MORNING. UP THROUGH MIDDLE SCHOOL, I'D NEVER BEEN FURTHER THAN THE VILLAGE CINEMA. A SIMPLE LIFE. JIANGCHUAN WAS ONLY 13 MILES AWAY, BUT IT MIGHT AS WELL HAVE BEEN ON THE EDGE OF CHINA!
BESIDES SCHOOL, I LOOKED AFTER THE FEW ANIMALS WE HAD. I REMEMBER MY DREAM WAS TO HAVE A BIKE ONE DAY. IT SEEMED LIKE THOSE WHO DID LITERALLY STARTED FLYING AFTER A FEW YARDS! I THOUGHT THAT IF I EVER GOT ONE, I'D HAVE NO MORE REGRETS FOR THE REST OF MY LIFE!

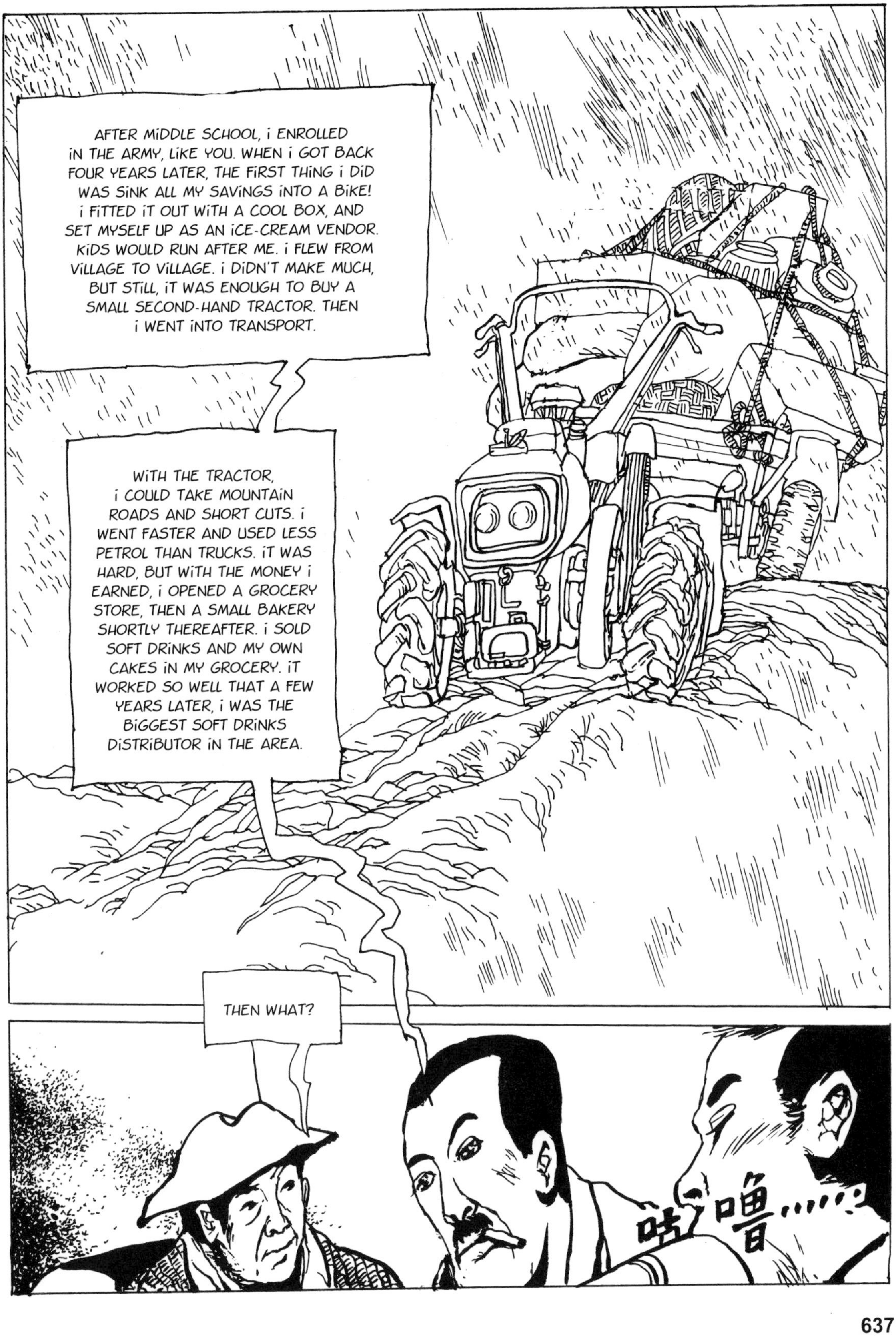
AFTER MIDDLE SCHOOL, I ENROLLED IN THE ARMY, LIKE YOU. WHEN I GOT BACK FOUR YEARS LATER, THE FIRST THING I DID WAS SINK ALL MY SAVINGS INTO A BIKE! I FITTED IT OUT WITH A COOL BOX, AND SET MYSELF UP AS AN ICE-CREAM VENDOR. KIDS WOULD RUN AFTER ME. I FLEW FROM VILLAGE TO VILLAGE. I DIDN'T MAKE MUCH, BUT STILL, IT WAS ENOUGH TO BUY A SMALL SECOND-HAND TRACTOR. THEN I WENT INTO TRANSPORT.
WITH THE TRACTOR, I COULD TAKE MOUNTAIN ROADS AND SHORT CUTS. I WENT FASTER AND USED LESS PETROL THAN TRUCKS. IT WAS HARD, BUT WITH THE MONEY I EARNED, I OPENED A GROCERY STORE, THEN A SMALL BAKERY SHORTLY THEREAFTER. I SOLD SOFT DRINKS AND MY OWN CAKES IN MY GROCERY. IT WORKED SO WELL THAT A FEW YEARS LATER, I WAS THE BIGGEST SOFT DRINKS DISTRIBUTOR IN THE AREA.
THEN WHAT?
咕噜……

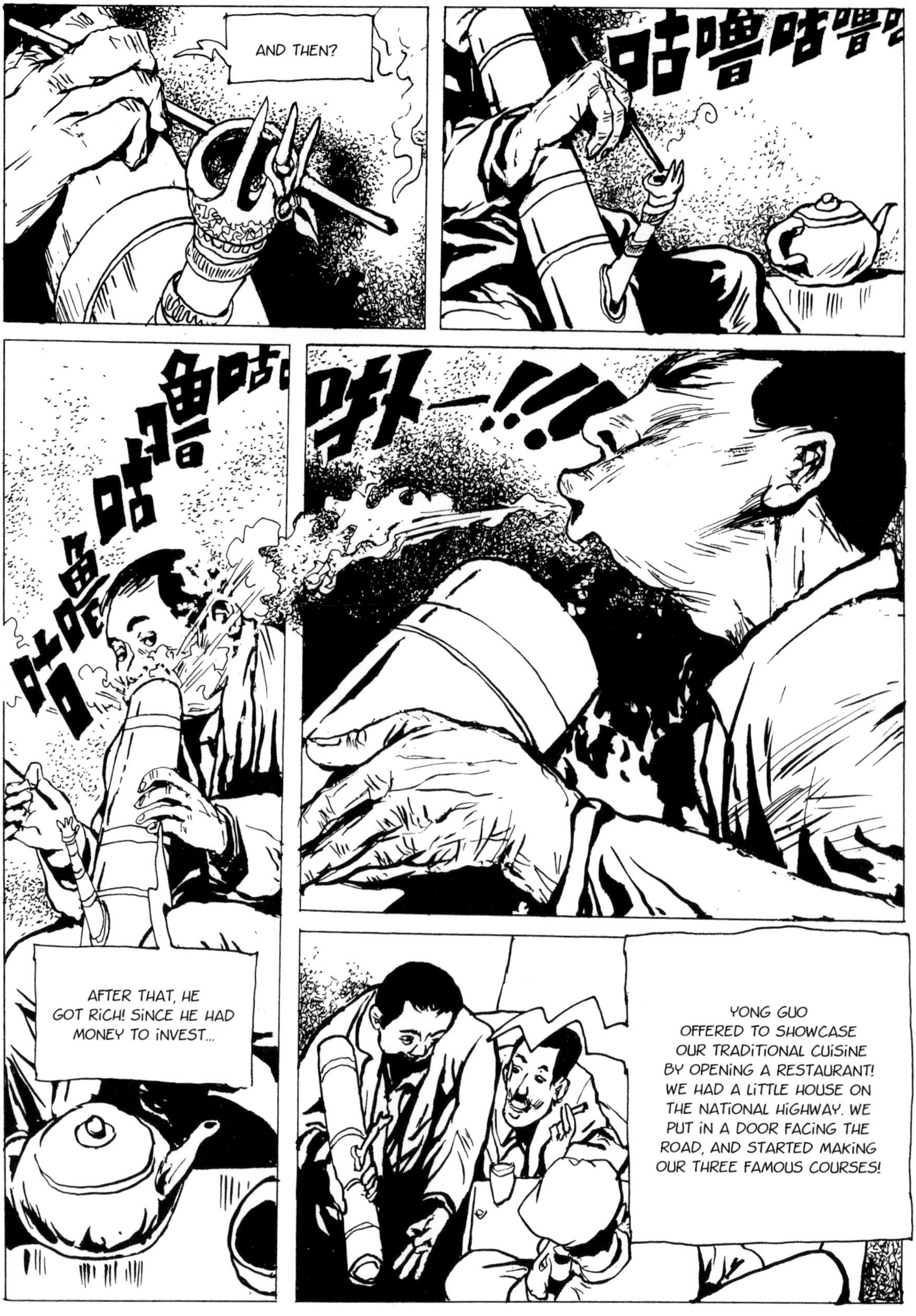
AND THEN?
咕嚕咕嚕
咕噜咕噜
AFTER THAT, HE GOT RICH! SINCE HE HAD MONEY TO INVEST...
YONG GUO OFFERED TO SHOWCASE OUR TRADITIONAL CUISINE BY OPENING A RESTAURANT! WE HAD A LITTLE HOUSE ON THE NATIONAL HIGHWAY. WE PUT IN A DOOR FACING THE ROAD, AND STARTED MAKING OUR THREE FAMOUS COURSES!

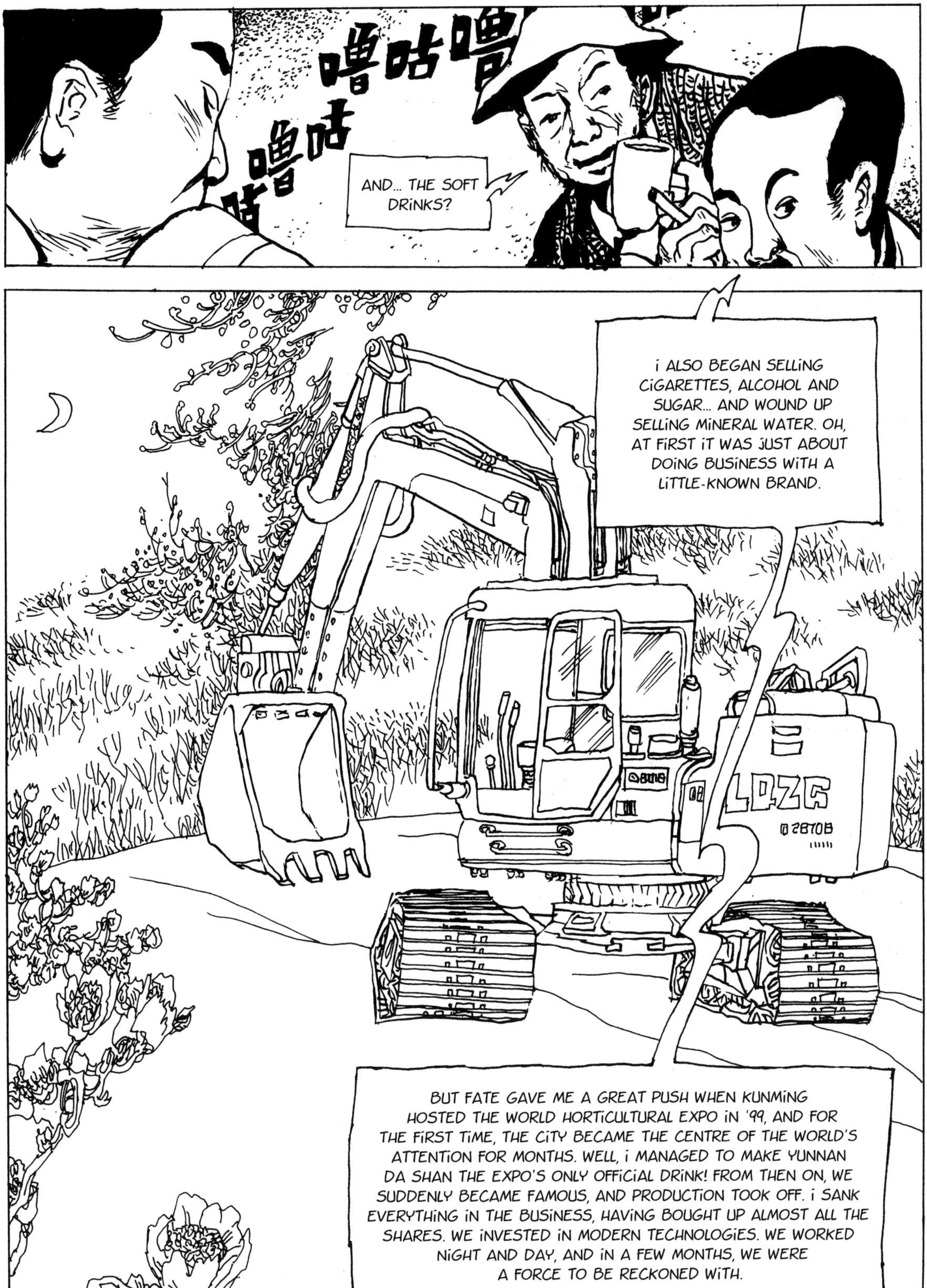
噌咕噌
噌咕
AND... THE SOFT DRINKS?
I ALSO BEGAN SELLING CIGARETTES, ALCOHOL AND SUGAR... AND WOUND UP SELLING MINERAL WATER. OH, AT FIRST IT WAS JUST ABOUT DOING BUSINESS WITH A LITTLE-KNOWN BRAND.
LQZG
BUT FATE GAVE ME A GREAT PUSH WHEN KUNMING HOSTED THE WORLD HORTICULTURAL EXPO IN '99, AND FOR THE FIRST TIME, THE CITY BECAME THE CENTRE OF THE WORLD'S ATTENTION FOR MONTHS. WELL, I MANAGED TO MAKE YUNNAN DA SHAN THE EXPO'S ONLY OFFICIAL DRINK! FROM THEN ON, WE SUDDENLY BECAME FAMOUS, AND PRODUCTION TOOK OFF. I SANK EVERYTHING IN THE BUSINESS, HAVING BOUGHT UP ALMOST ALL THE SHARES. WE INVESTED IN MODERN TECHNOLOGIES. WE WORKED NIGHT AND DAY, AND IN A FEW MONTHS, WE WERE A FORCE TO BE RECKONED WITH.

ALL THESE MEMORIES COMING BACK TODAY...

i, WHO WAS ONCE JUST ANOTHER FACELESS PEASANT, HAVE BECOME A MANUFACTURER EVERYONE RESPECTS. HMM... i HAVE MONEY AND RESPECT, BUT DEEP DOWN i FEEL WHAT'S iMPORTANT TO ME NOW GOES FAR BEYOND THAT...

IN THE END, MY FIRST BiKE WASN'T ENOUGH FOR ME. i ALWAYS WANTED MORE... WHERE WILL THiS END? DON'T i HAVE ENOUGH?

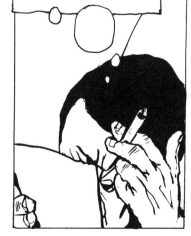

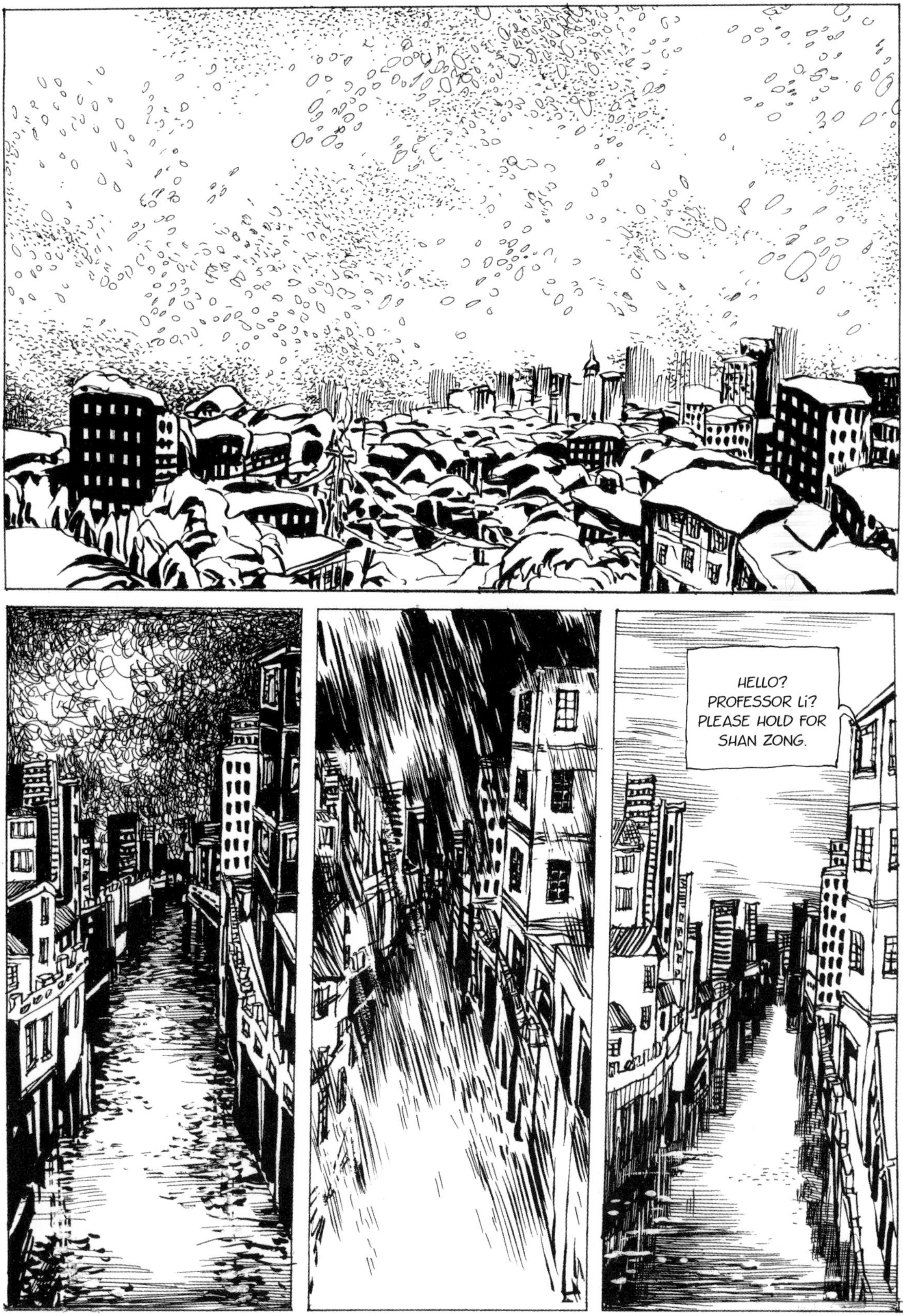
HELLO? PROFESSOR LI? PLEASE HOLD FOR SHAN ZONG.

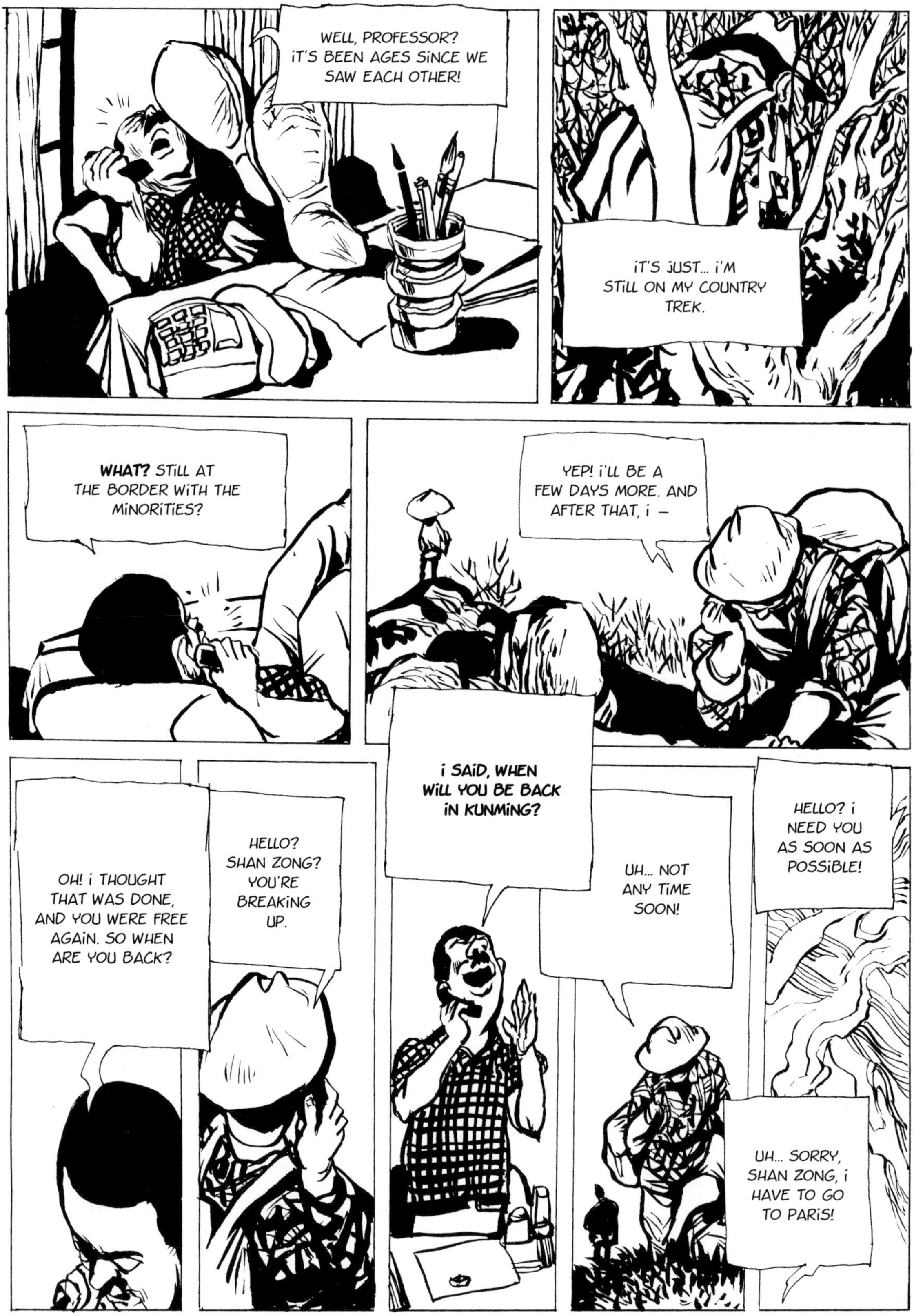

WELL, PROFESSOR? iT'S BEEN AGES SiNCE WE SAW EACH OTHER!
iT'S JUST... i'M STiLL ON MY COUNTRY TREK.
WHAT? STiLL AT THE BORDER WiTH THE MiNORiTiES?
YEP! i'LL BE A FEW DAYS MORE. AND AFTER THAT, i –
OH! i THOUGHT THAT WAS DONE, AND YOU WERE FREE AGAiN. SO WHEN ARE YOU BACK?
HELLO? SHAN ZONG? YOU'RE BREAKiNG UP.
i SAiD, WHEN WiLL YOU BE BACK iN KUNMiNG?
UH... NOT ANY TiME SOON!
HELLO? i NEED YOU AS SOON AS POSSiBLE!
UH... SORRY, SHAN ZONG, i HAVE TO GO TO PARiS!

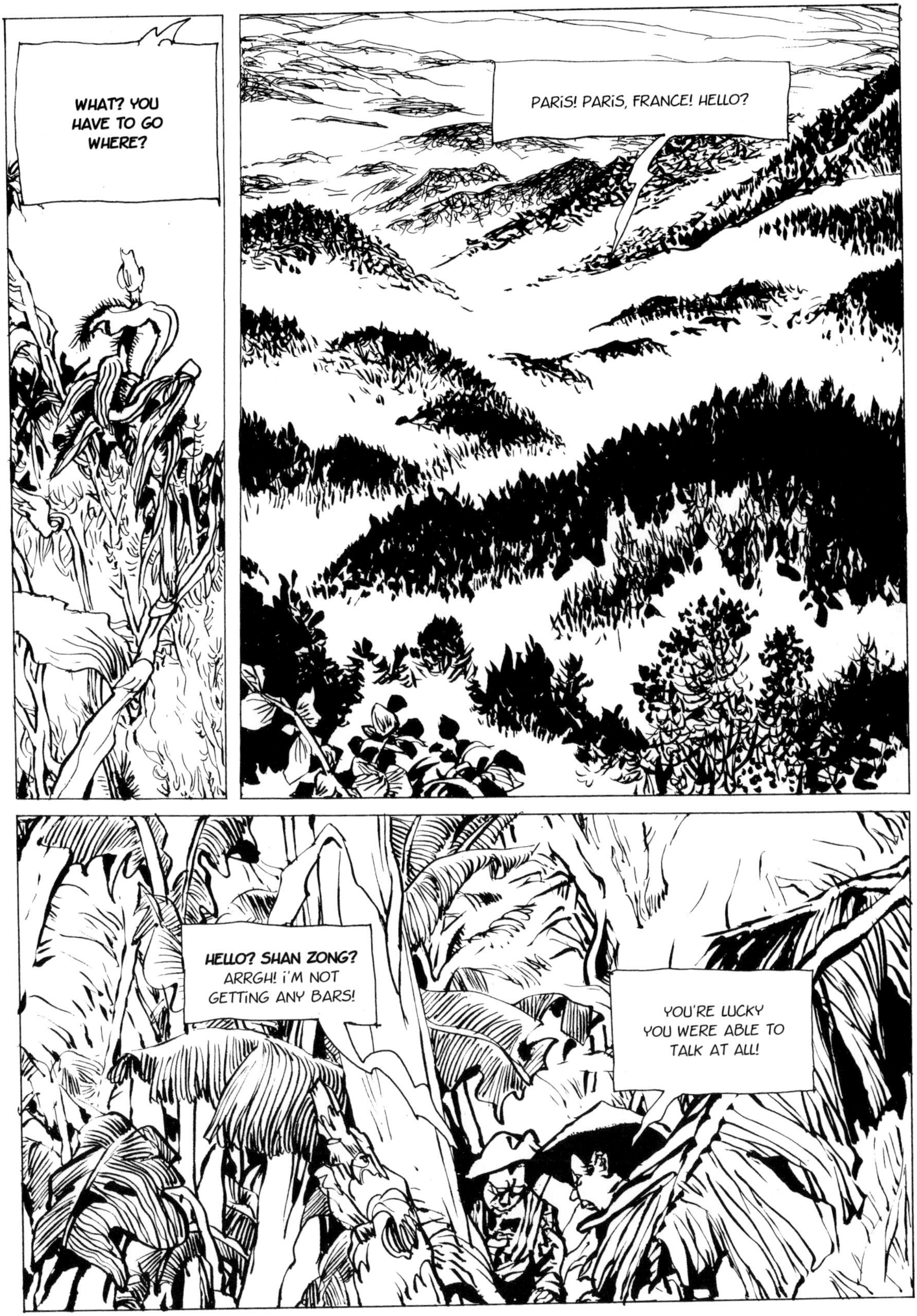
WHAT? YOU HAVE TO GO WHERE?
PARiS! PARiS, FRANCE! HELLO?
HELLO? SHAN ZONG? ARRGH! i'M NOT GETTiNG ANY BARS!
YOU'RE LUCKY YOU WERE ABLE TO TALK AT ALL!

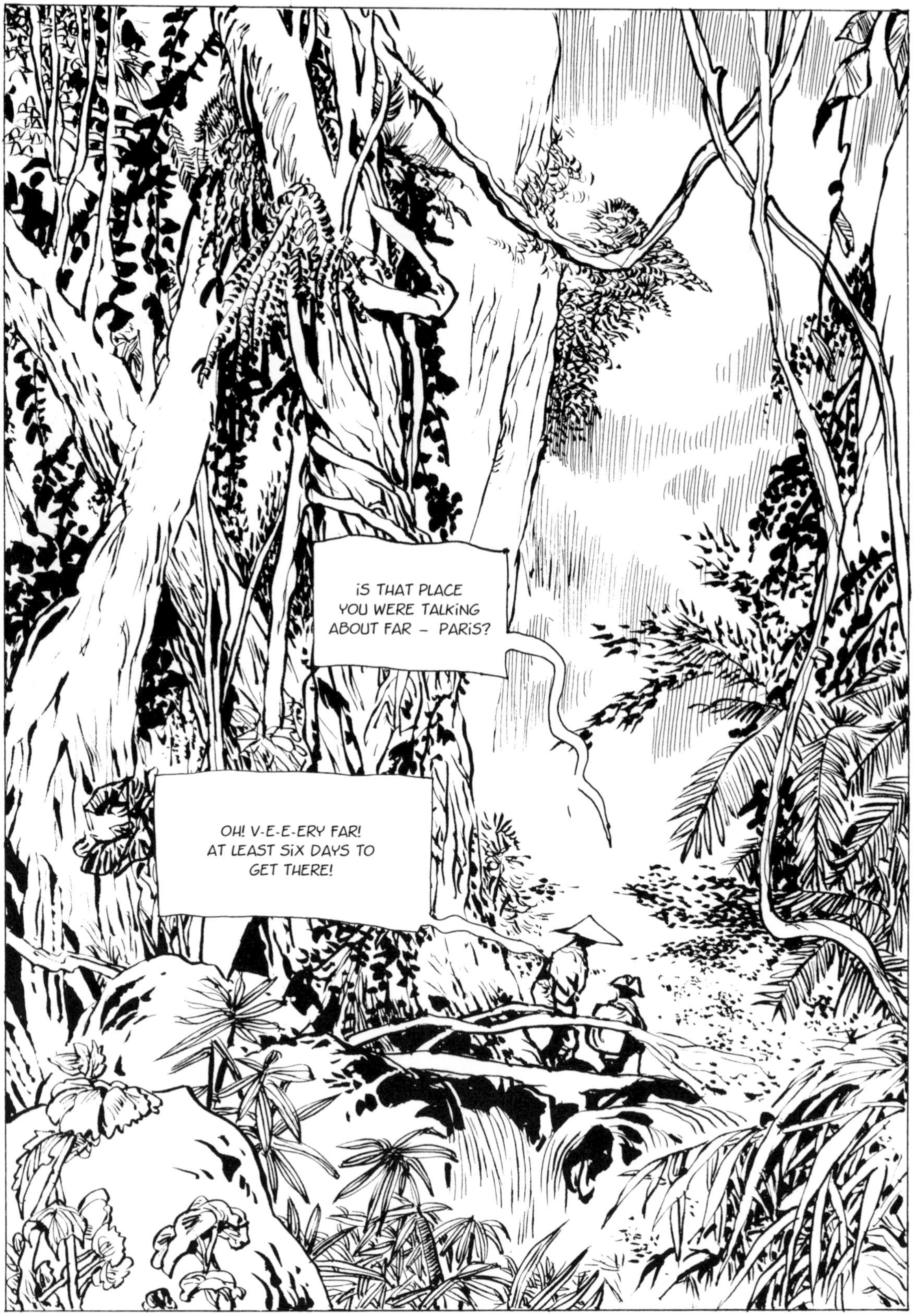
iS THAT PLACE YOU WERE TALKiNG ABOUT FAR – PARiS?
OH! V-E-E-ERY FAR! AT LEAST SiX DAYS TO GET THERE!

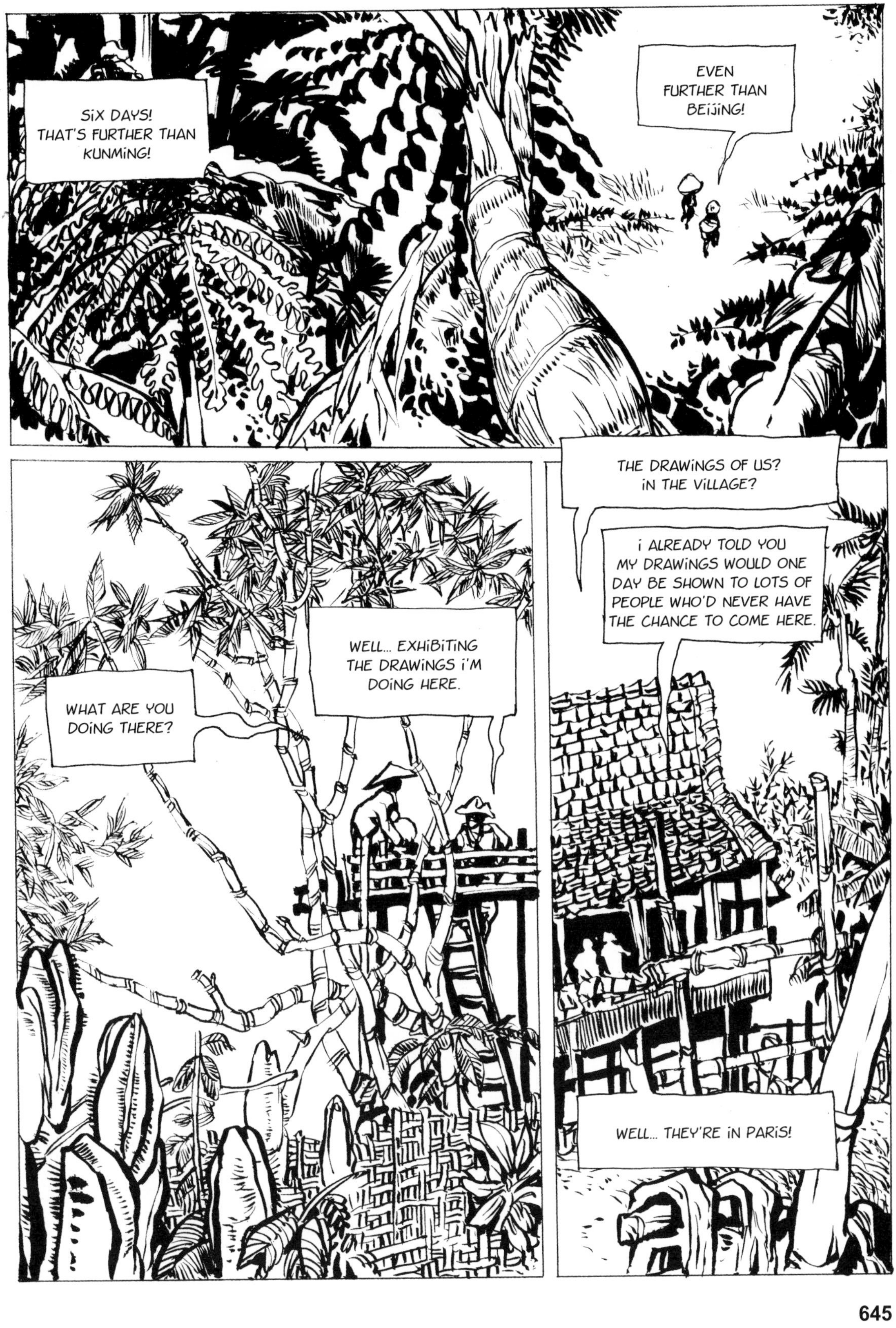

SIX DAYS! THAT'S FURTHER THAN KUNMING!
EVEN FURTHER THAN BEIJING!
WHAT ARE YOU DOING THERE?
WELL... EXHIBITING THE DRAWINGS I'M DOING HERE.
THE DRAWINGS OF US? IN THE VILLAGE?
I ALREADY TOLD YOU MY DRAWINGS WOULD ONE DAY BE SHOWN TO LOTS OF PEOPLE WHO'D NEVER HAVE THE CHANCE TO COME HERE.
WELL... THEY'RE IN PARIS!

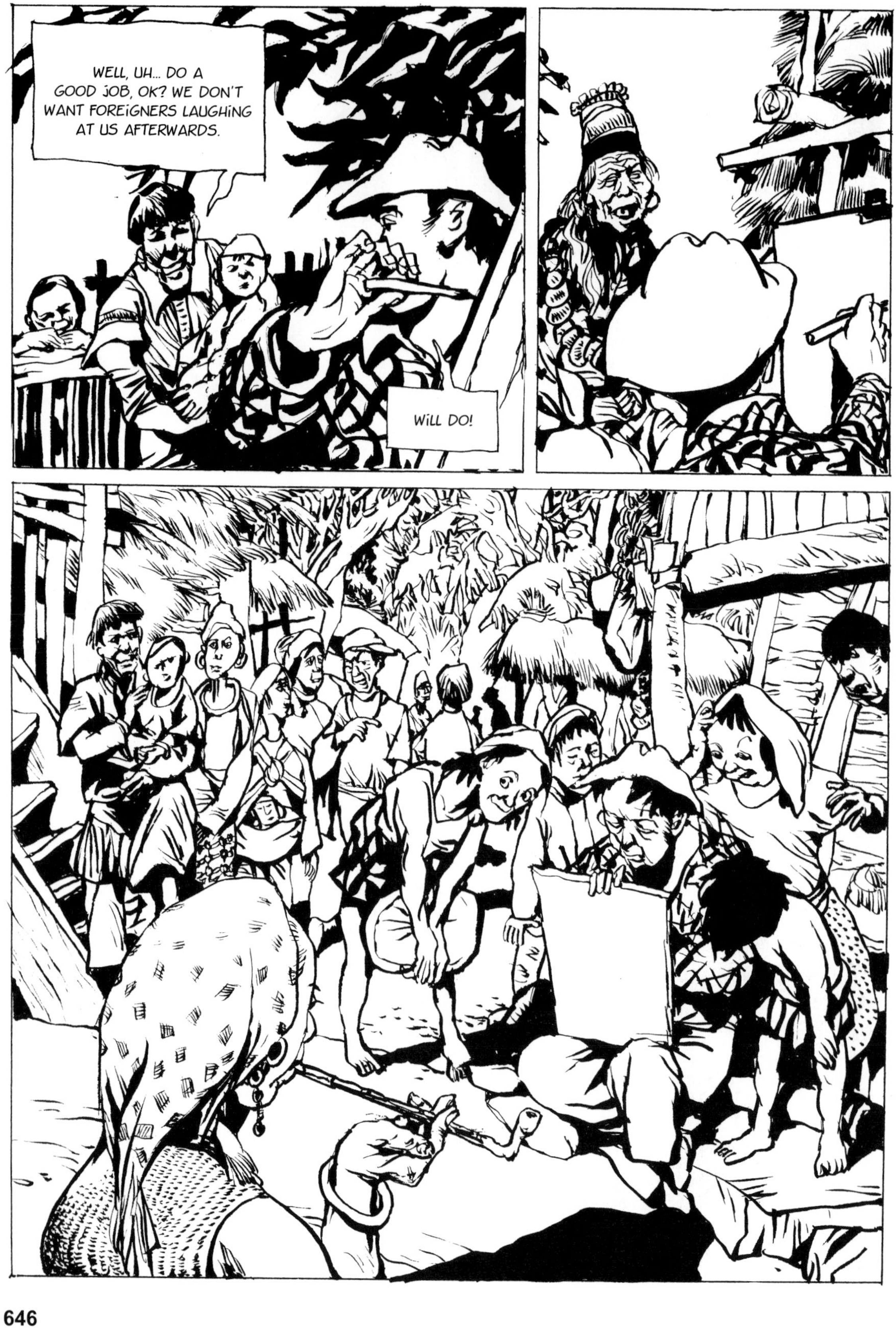
WELL, UH... DO A GOOD JOB, OK? WE DON'T WANT FOREIGNERS LAUGHING AT US AFTERWARDS.
WILL DO!

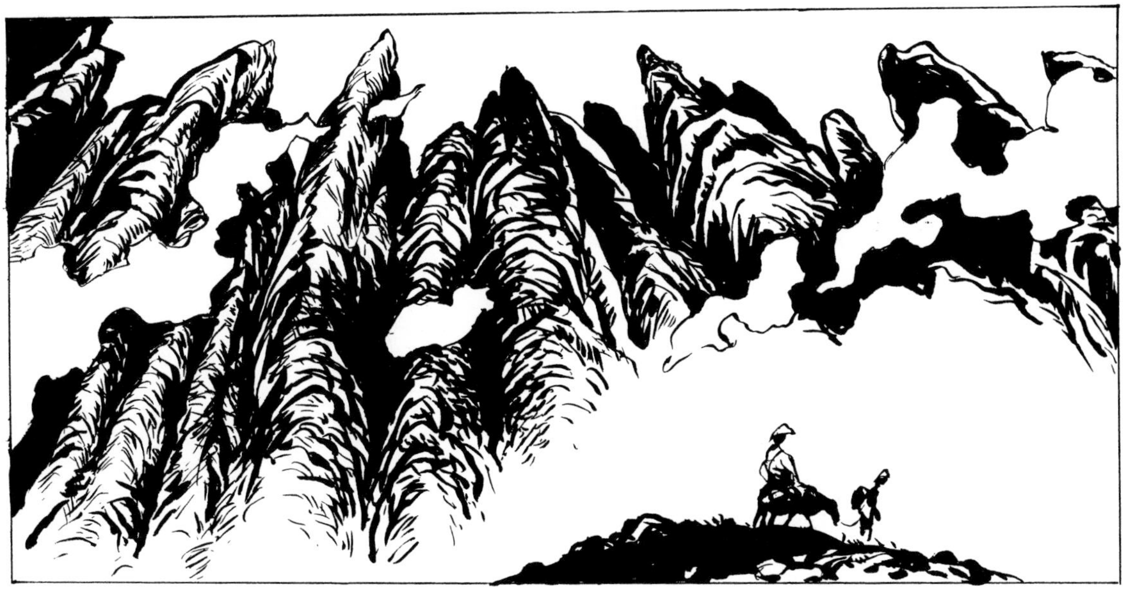

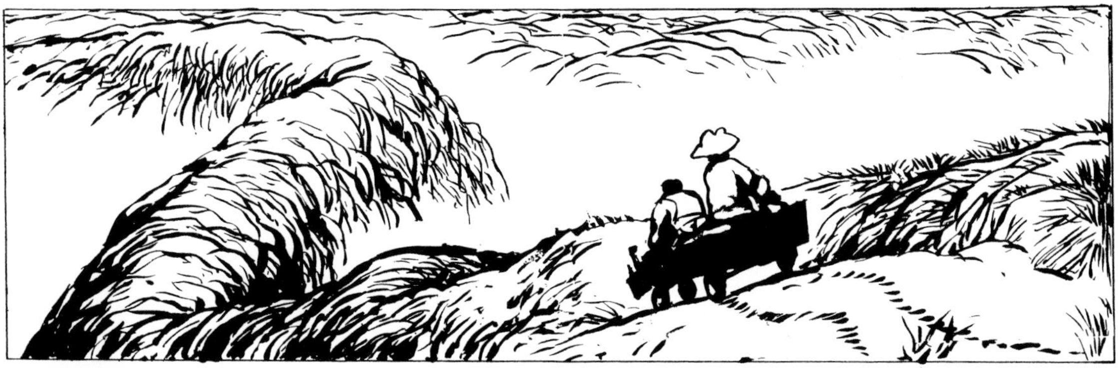

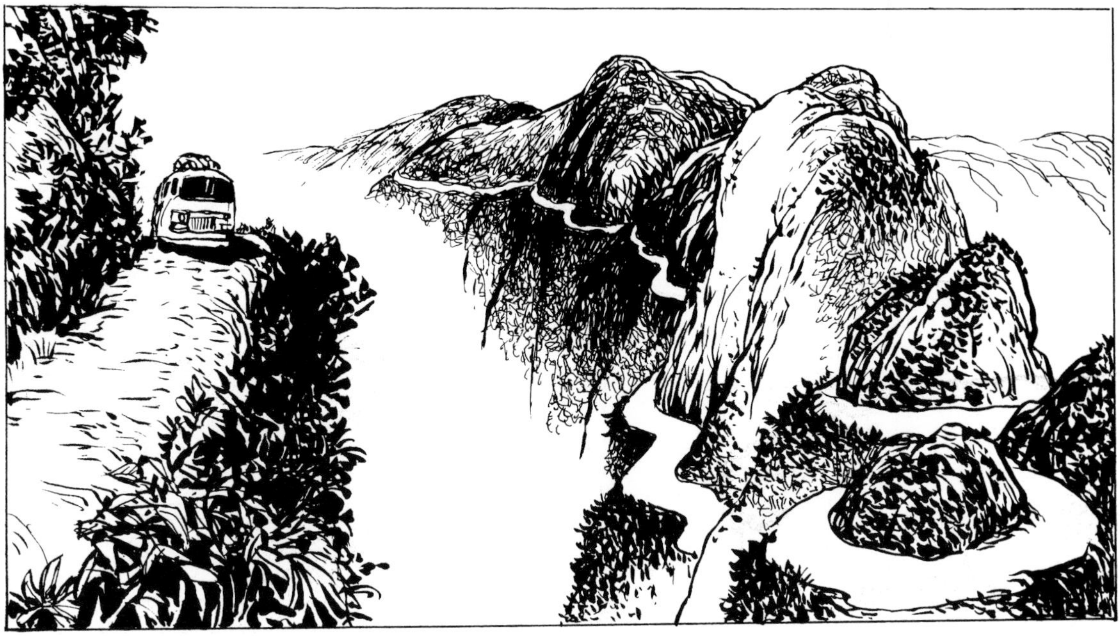

SAY, KID, IS THERE A CYBERCAFÉ IN THE VILLAGE?

HUH? OF COURSE! C'MON, I'LL TAKE YOU!

AND DO YOU, UH... KNOW YOUR WAY AROUND COMPUTERS?

SURE DO! BUT NOT AS WELL AS MY BIG BROTHER. HE KNOWS EVERYTHING! ESPECIALLY ABOUT ONLINE GAMES!

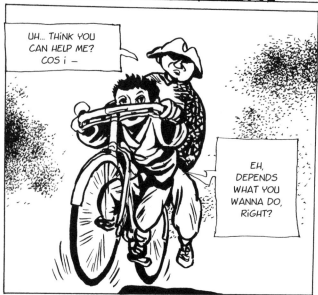

UH... THINK YOU CAN HELP ME? COS I —

EH, DEPENDS WHAT YOU WANNA DO, RIGHT?

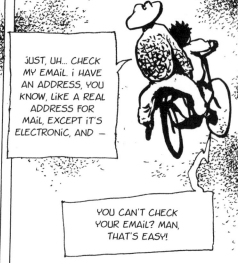

JUST, UH... CHECK MY EMAIL. I HAVE AN ADDRESS, YOU KNOW, LIKE A REAL ADDRESS FOR MAIL, EXCEPT IT'S ELECTRONIC, AND —

YOU CAN'T CHECK YOUR EMAIL? MAN, THAT'S EASY!

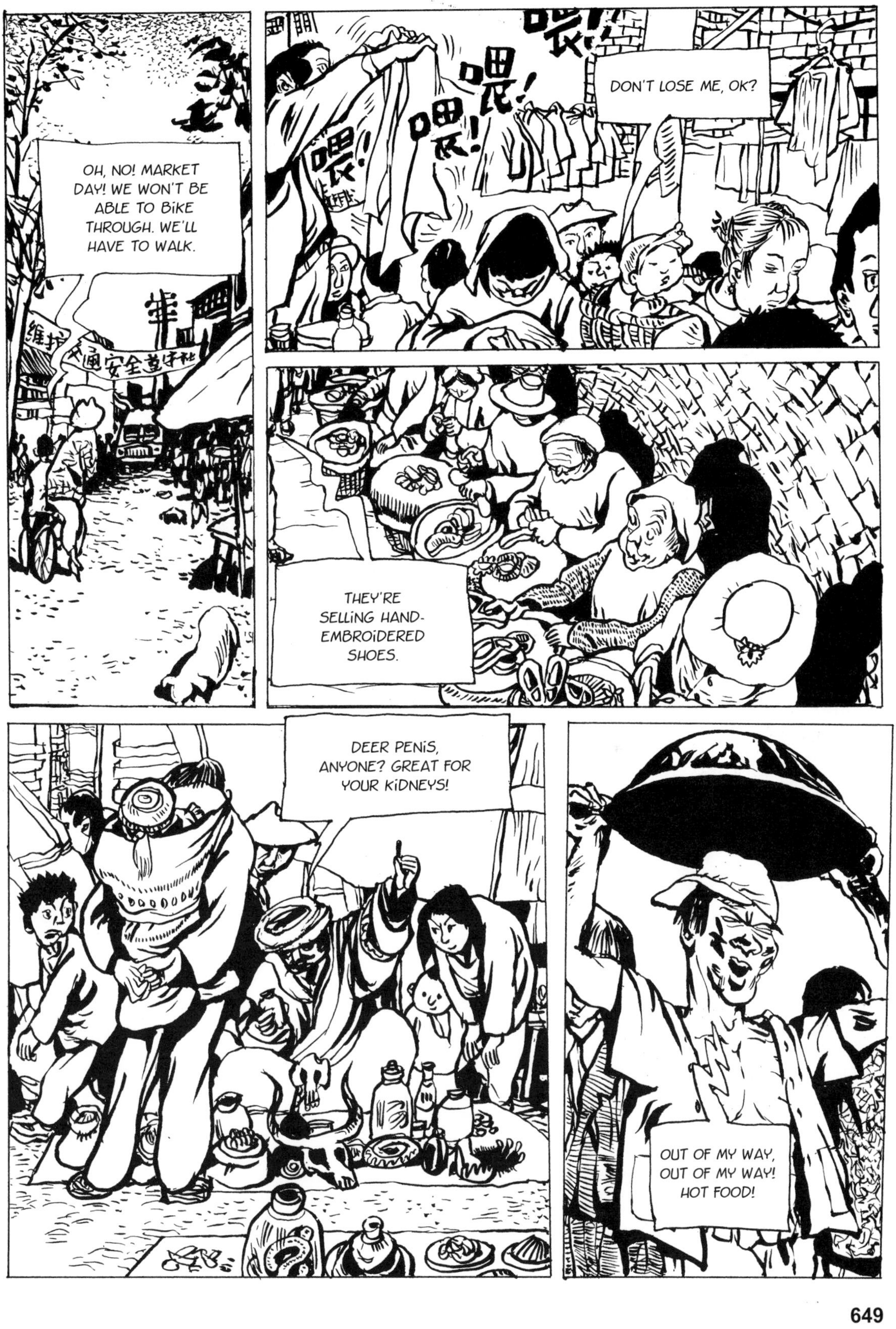
OH, NO! MARKET DAY! WE WON'T BE ABLE TO BIKE THROUGH. WE'LL HAVE TO WALK.
喂!
喂!
喂!
喂!!
DON'T LOSE ME, OK?
THEY'RE SELLING HAND-EMBROIDERED SHOES.
DEER PENIS, ANYONE? GREAT FOR YOUR KIDNEYS!
OUT OF MY WAY, OUT OF MY WAY! HOT FOOD!

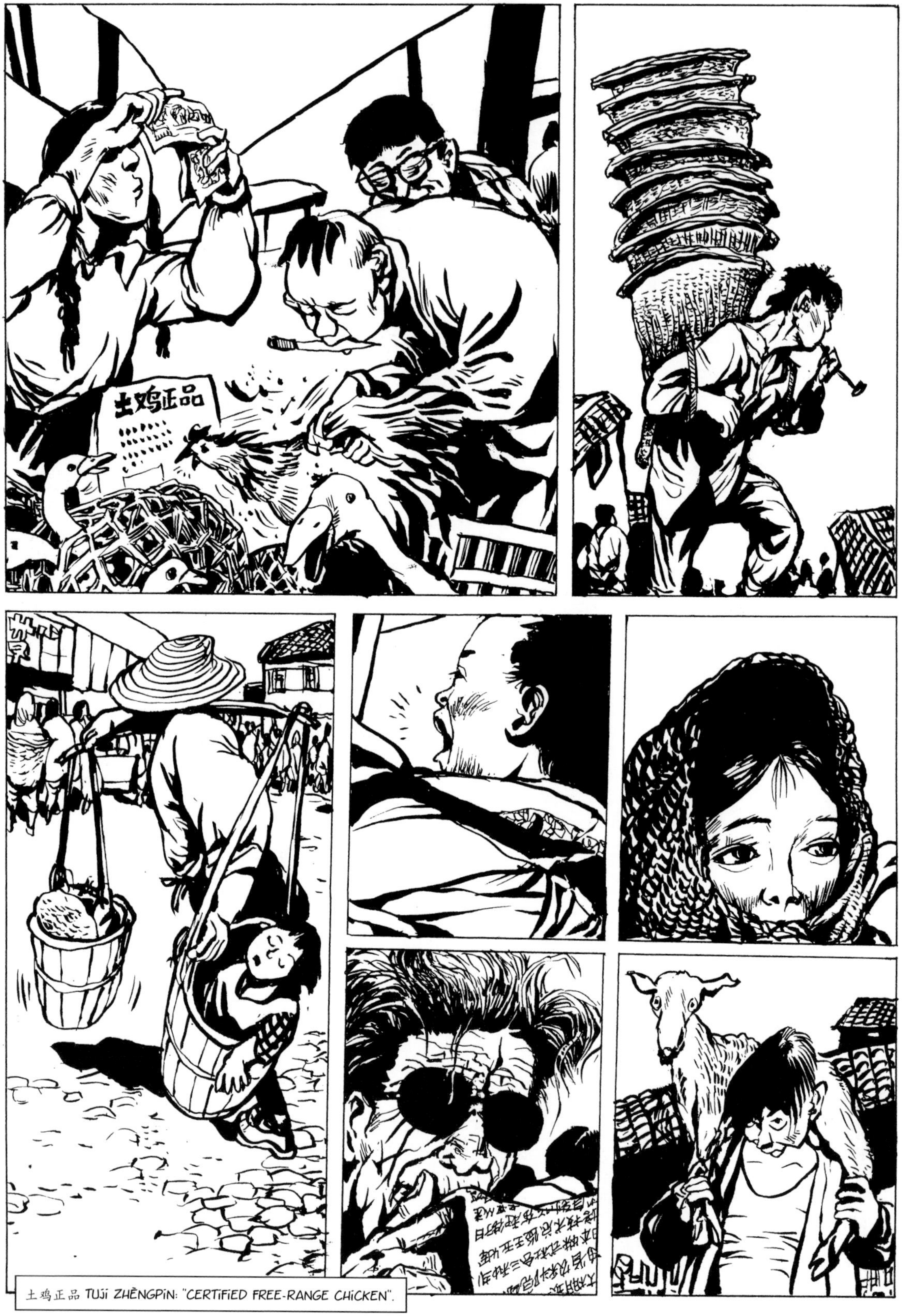
土鸡正品

土鸡正品 TUJI ZHĚNGPIN: "CERTIFIED FREE-RANGE CHICKEN".

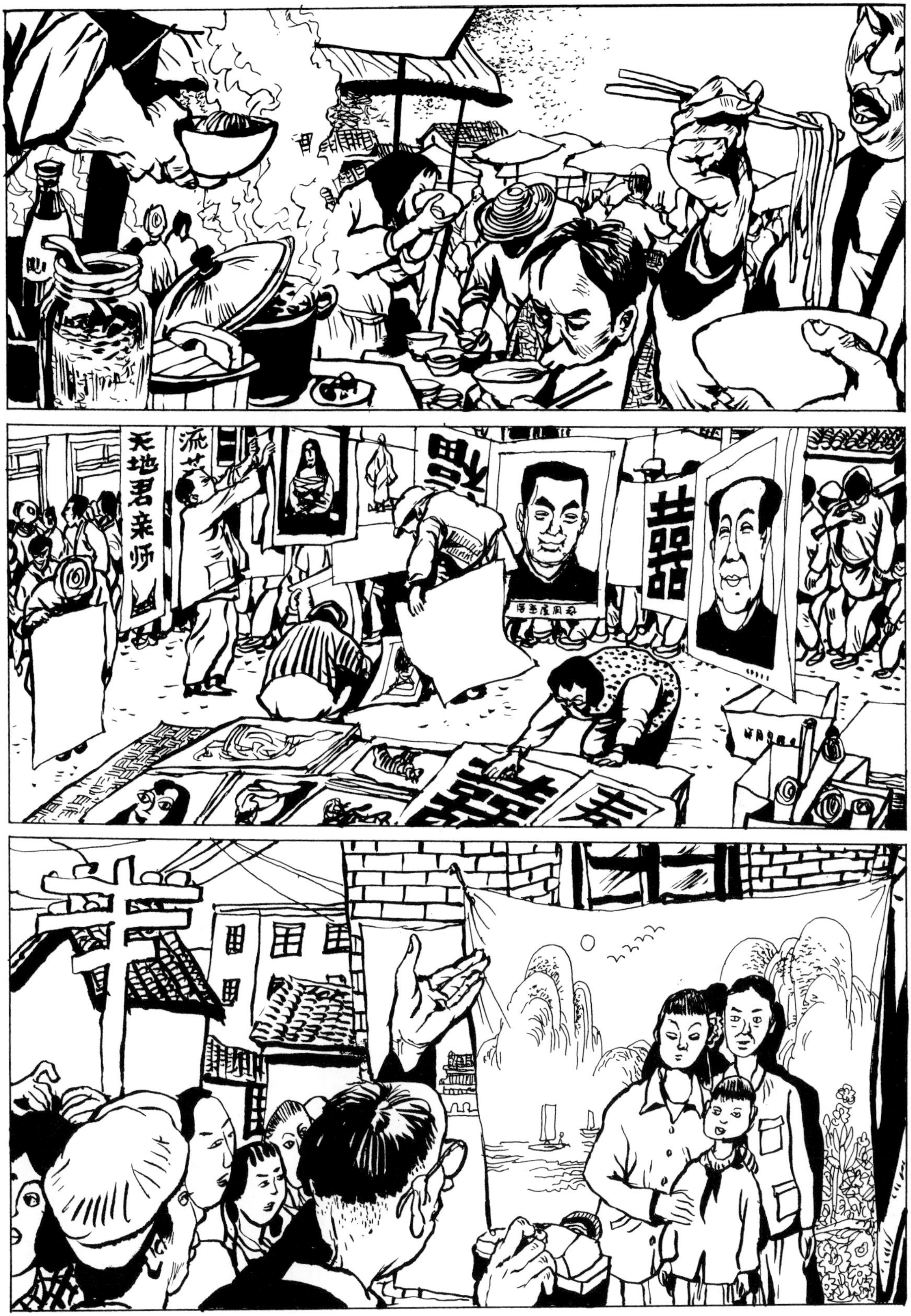
天地君亲师
囍

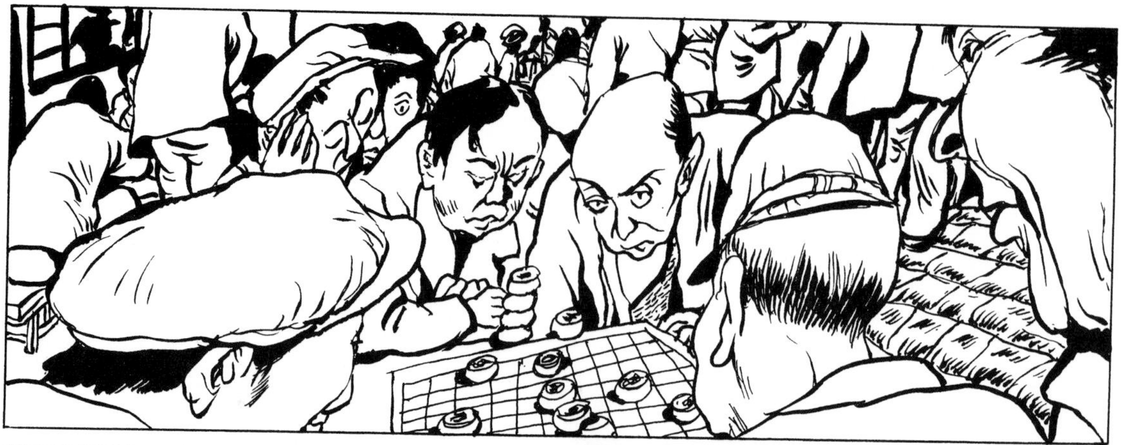

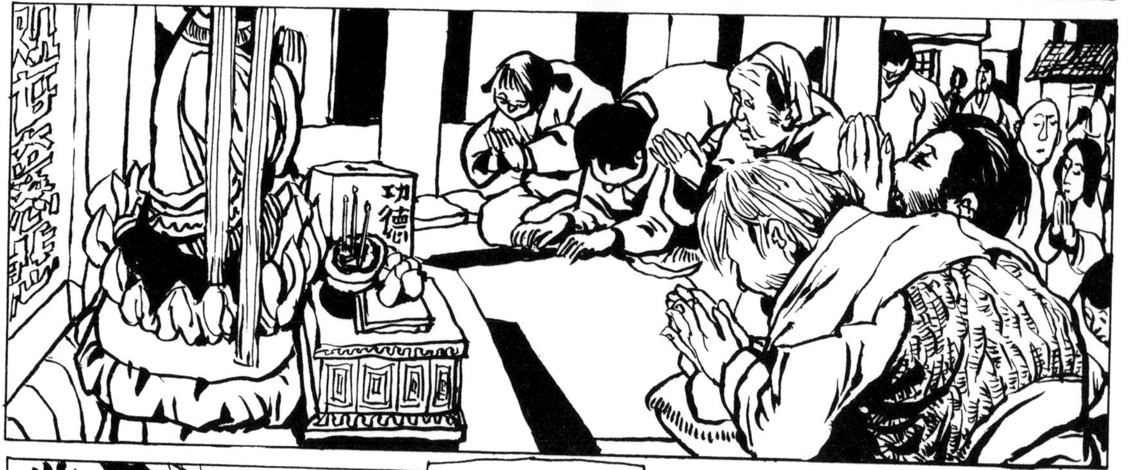
功德

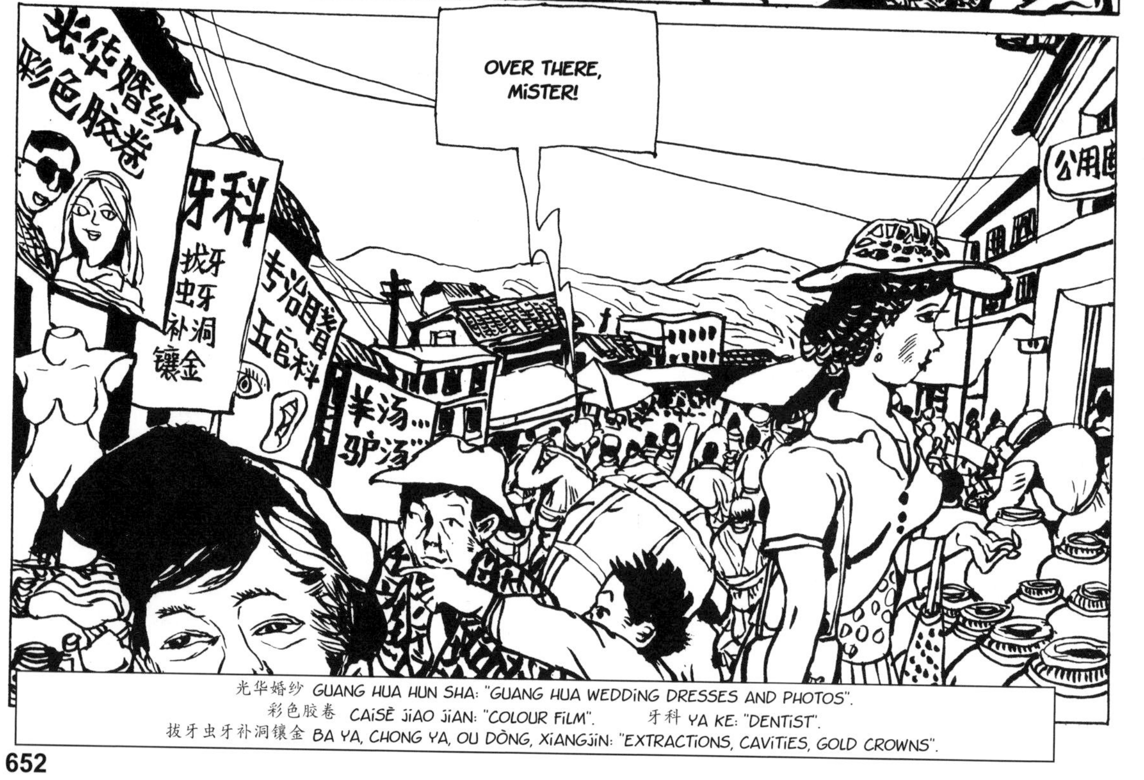
光华婚纱
彩色胶卷
牙科
拔牙
虫牙
补洞
镶金
羊汤...
驴汤
OVER THERE, MISTER!

光华婚纱 GUANG HUA HUN SHA: "GUANG HUA WEDDING DRESSES AND PHOTOS".
彩色胶卷 CAISÈ JIAO JIAN: "COLOUR FILM". 牙科 YA KE: "DENTIST".
拔牙虫牙补洞镶金 BA YA, CHONG YA, OU DÒNG, XIANGJIN: "EXTRACTIONS, CAVITIES, GOLD CROWNS".

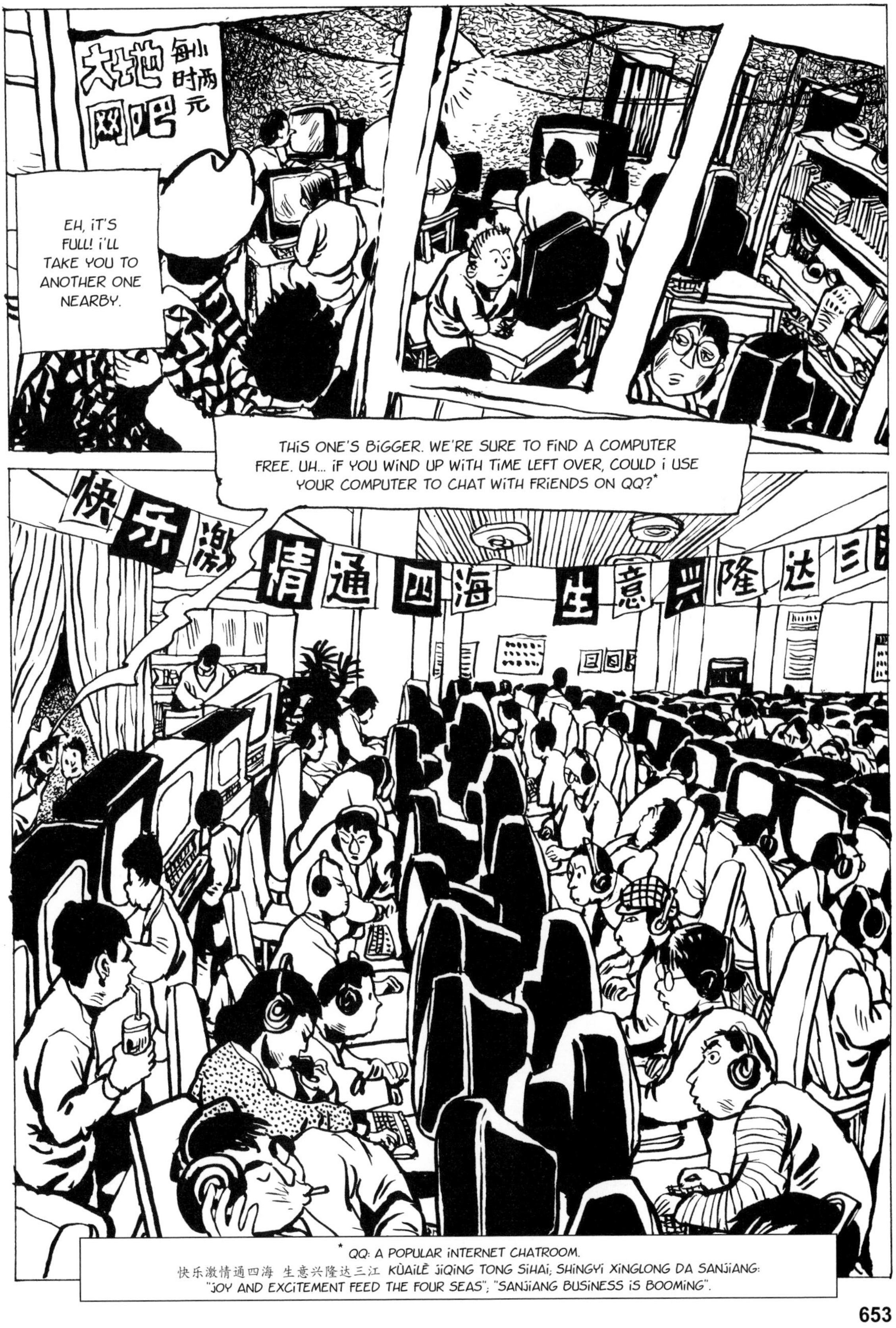
大地网吧
每小时两元
EH, iT'S FULL! i'LL TAKE YOU TO ANOTHER ONE NEARBY.
THiS ONE'S BiGGER. WE'RE SURE TO FiND A COMPUTER FREE. UH... iF YOU WiND UP WiTH TiME LEFT OVER, COULD i USE YOUR COMPUTER TO CHAT WiTH FRiENDS ON QQ?*
快乐激情通四海
生意兴隆达三

* QQ: A POPULAR iNTERNET CHATROOM.
快乐激情通四海 生意兴隆达三江 KÙAiLÈ JiQiNG TONG SiHAi; SHiNGYi XiNGLONG DA SANJiANG: "JOY AND EXCiTEMENT FEED THE FOUR SEAS"; "SANJiANG BUSiNESS iS BOOMiNG".

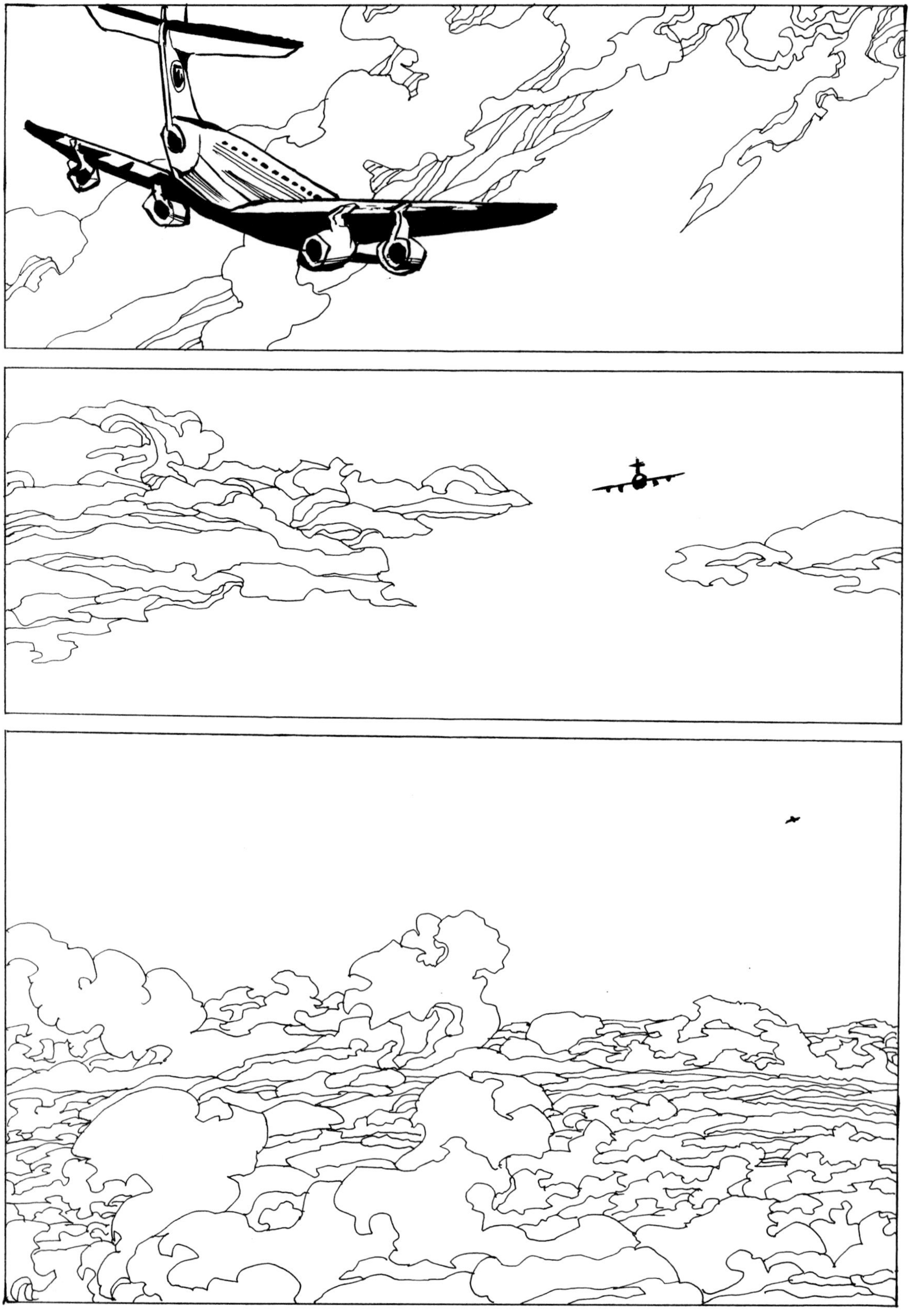

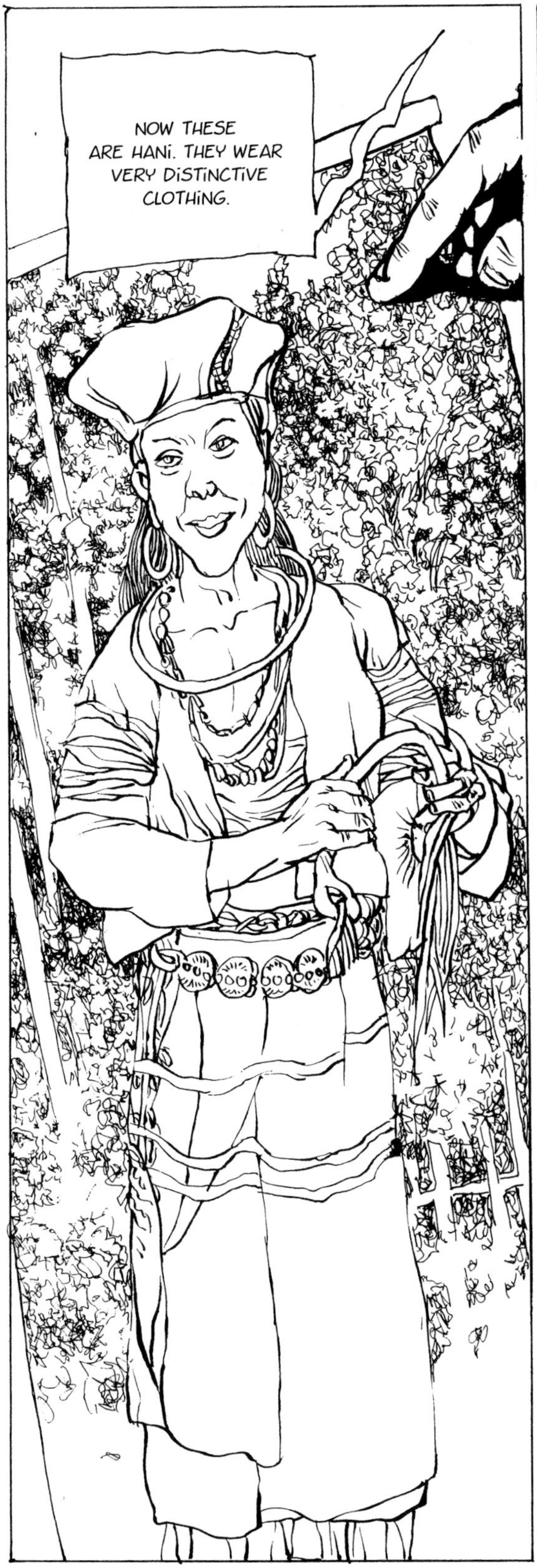
NOW THESE ARE HANI. THEY WEAR VERY DISTINCTIVE CLOTHING.

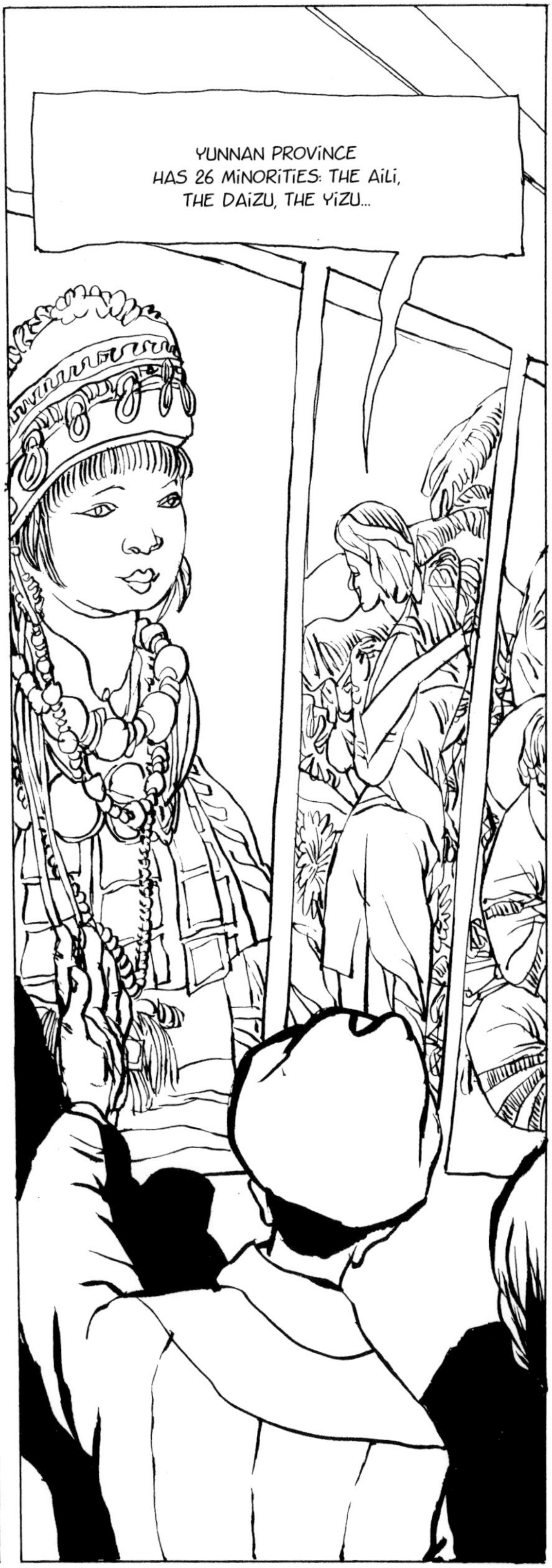
YUNNAN PROVINCE HAS 26 MINORITIES: THE AILI, THE DAIZU, THE YIZU...

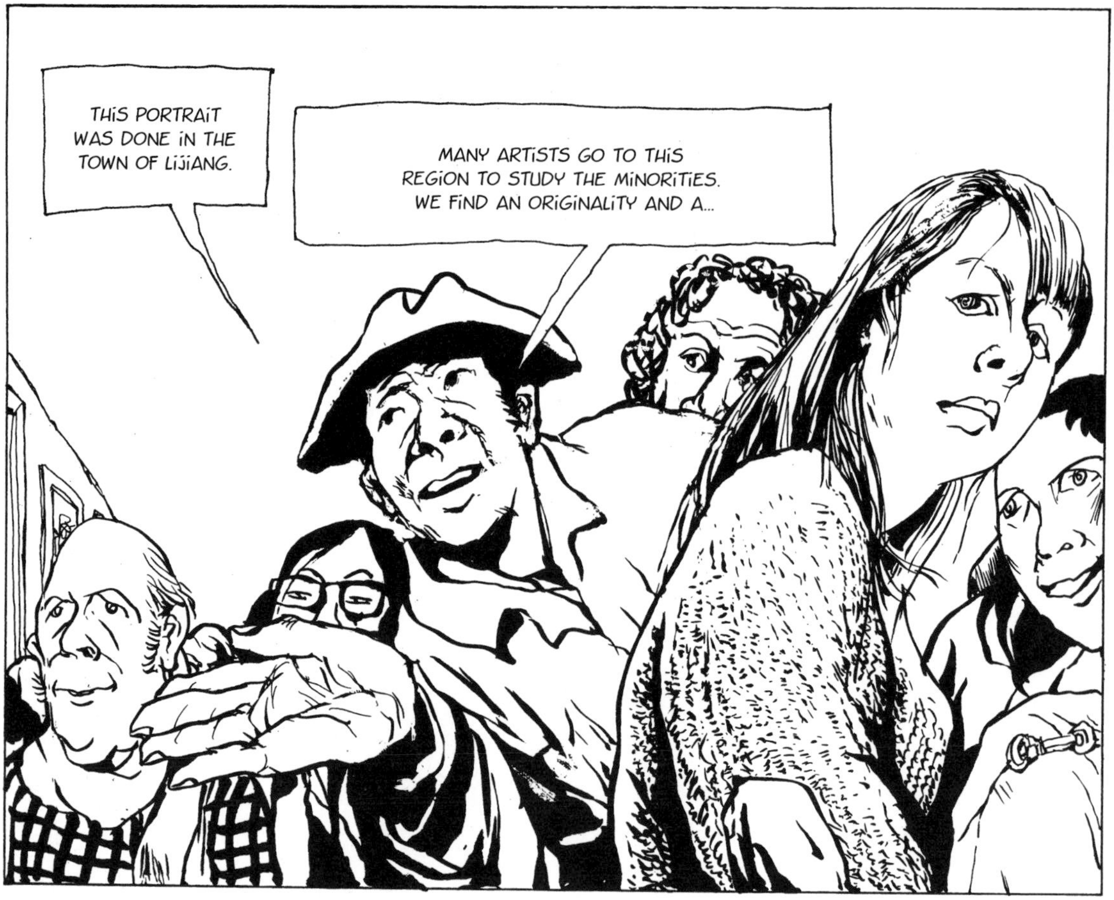
THIS PORTRAIT WAS DONE IN THE TOWN OF LIJIANG.
MANY ARTISTS GO TO THIS REGION TO STUDY THE MINORITIES. WE FIND AN ORIGINALITY AND A...

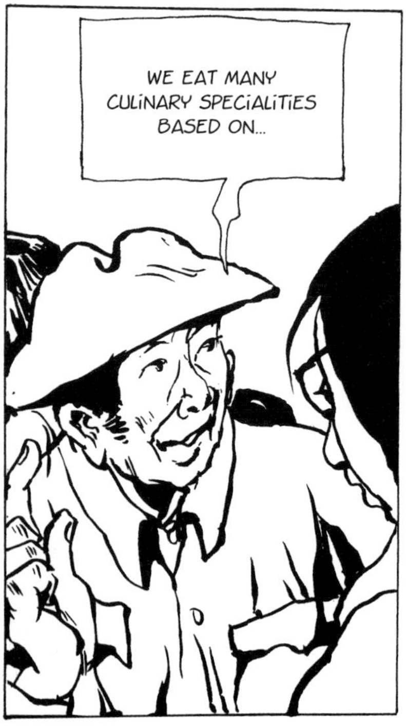
WE EAT MANY CULINARY SPECIALITIES BASED ON...

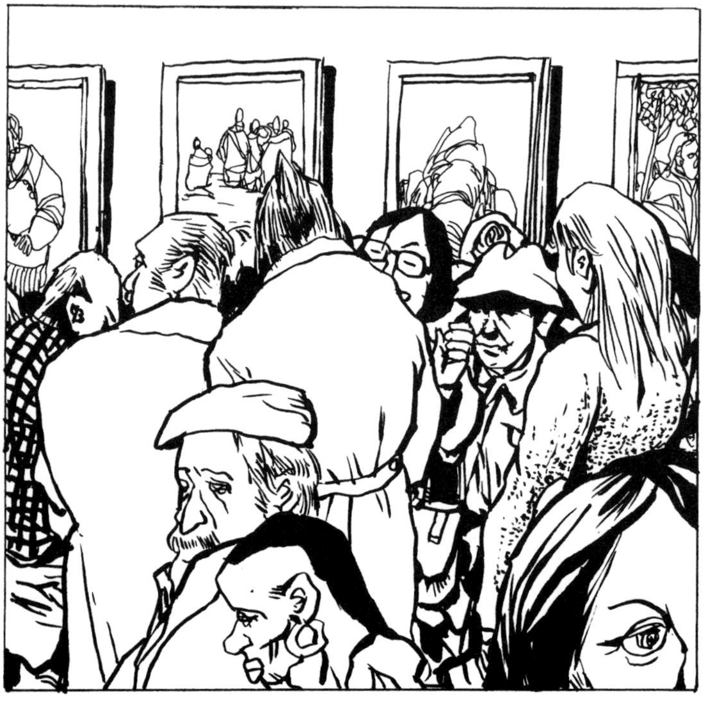

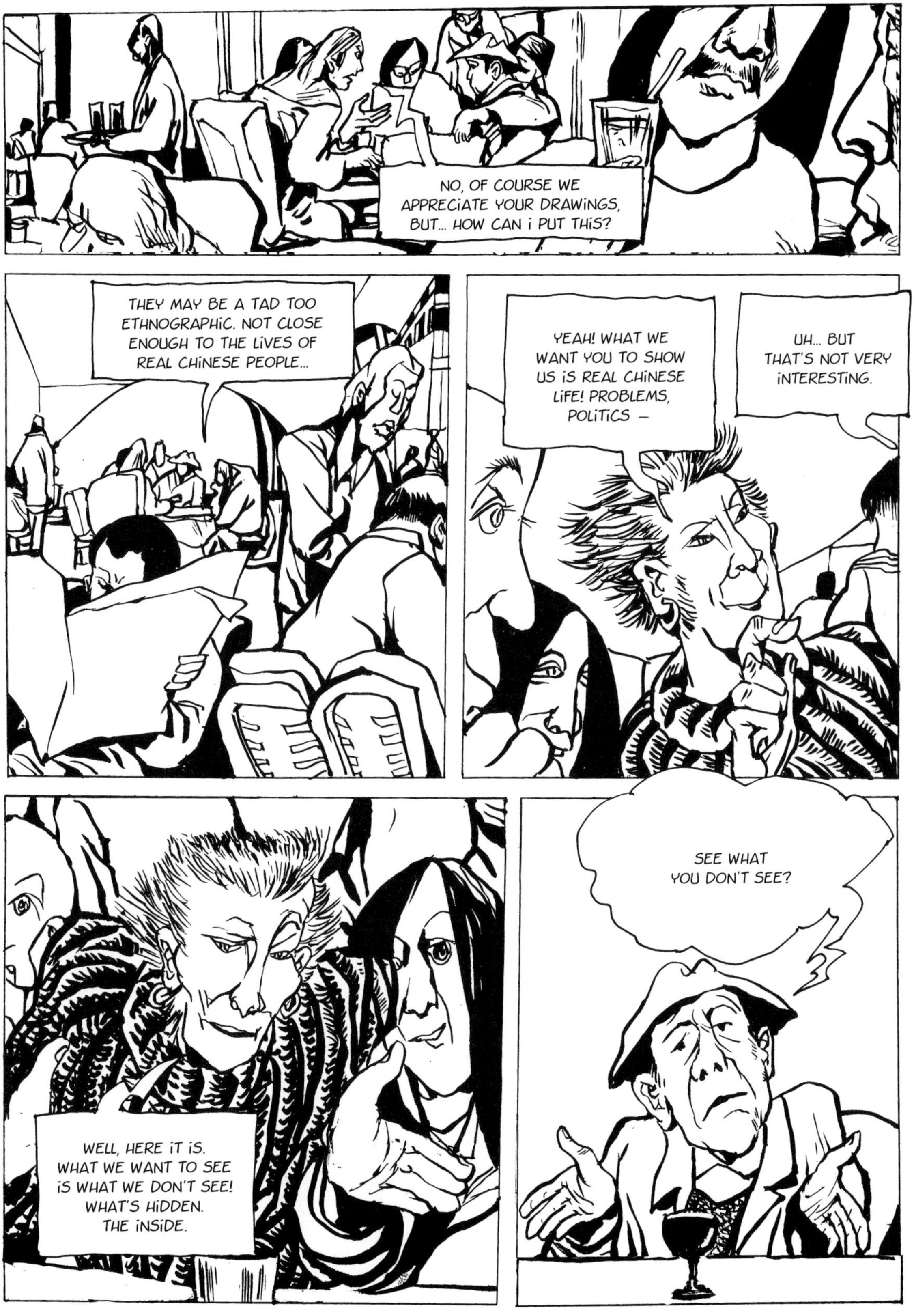
NO, OF COURSE WE APPRECIATE YOUR DRAWINGS, BUT... HOW CAN I PUT THIS?
THEY MAY BE A TAD TOO ETHNOGRAPHIC. NOT CLOSE ENOUGH TO THE LIVES OF REAL CHINESE PEOPLE...
YEAH! WHAT WE WANT YOU TO SHOW US IS REAL CHINESE LIFE! PROBLEMS, POLITICS –
UH... BUT THAT'S NOT VERY INTERESTING.
WELL, HERE IT IS. WHAT WE WANT TO SEE IS WHAT WE DON'T SEE! WHAT'S HIDDEN. THE INSIDE.
SEE WHAT YOU DON'T SEE?

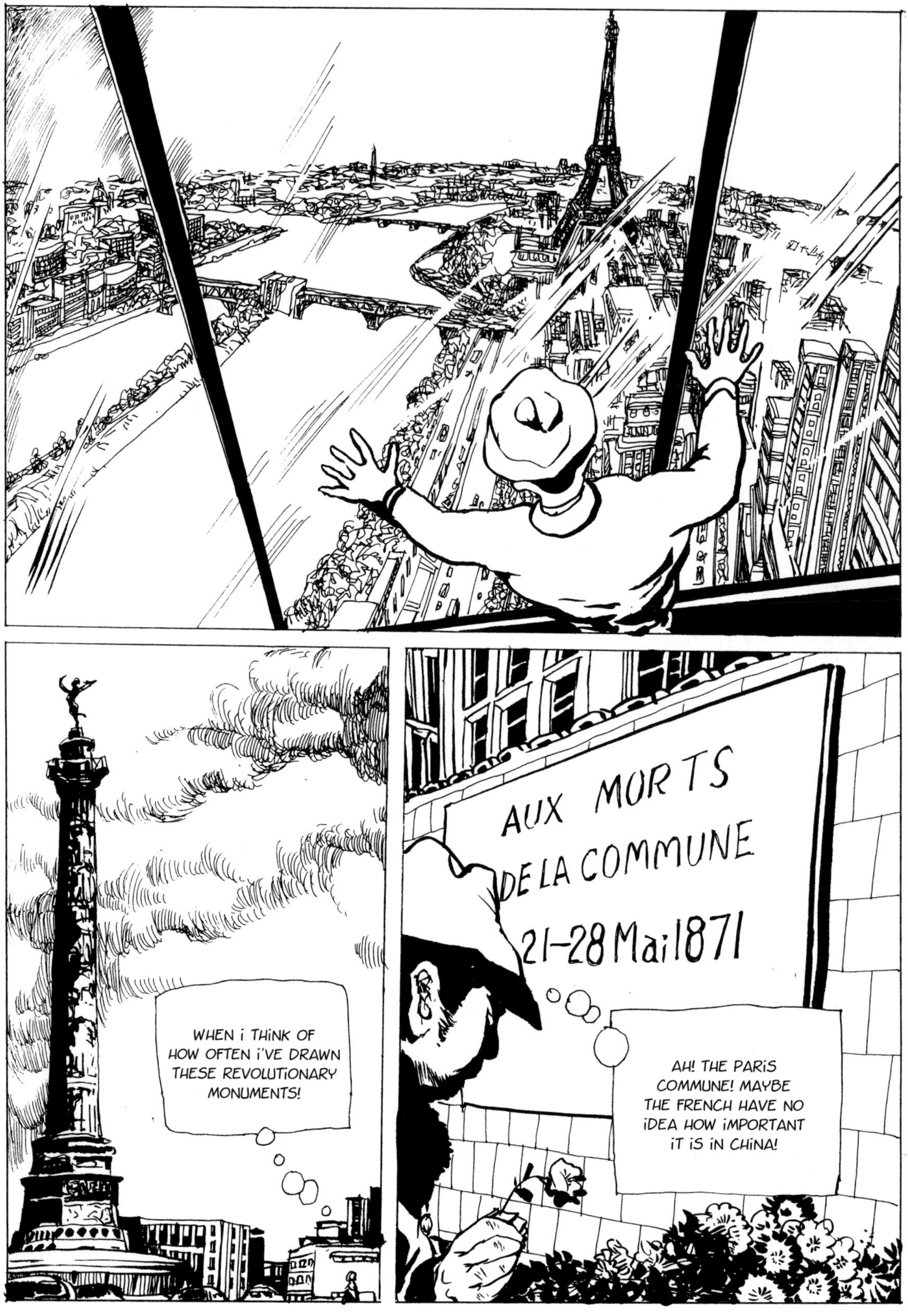

WHEN i THINK OF HOW OFTEN i'VE DRAWN THESE REVOLUTIONARY MONUMENTS!
AUX MORTS DE LA COMMUNE 21-28 Mai 1871
AH! THE PARiS COMMUNE! MAYBE THE FRENCH HAVE NO iDEA HOW iMPORTANT iT iS iN CHiNA!

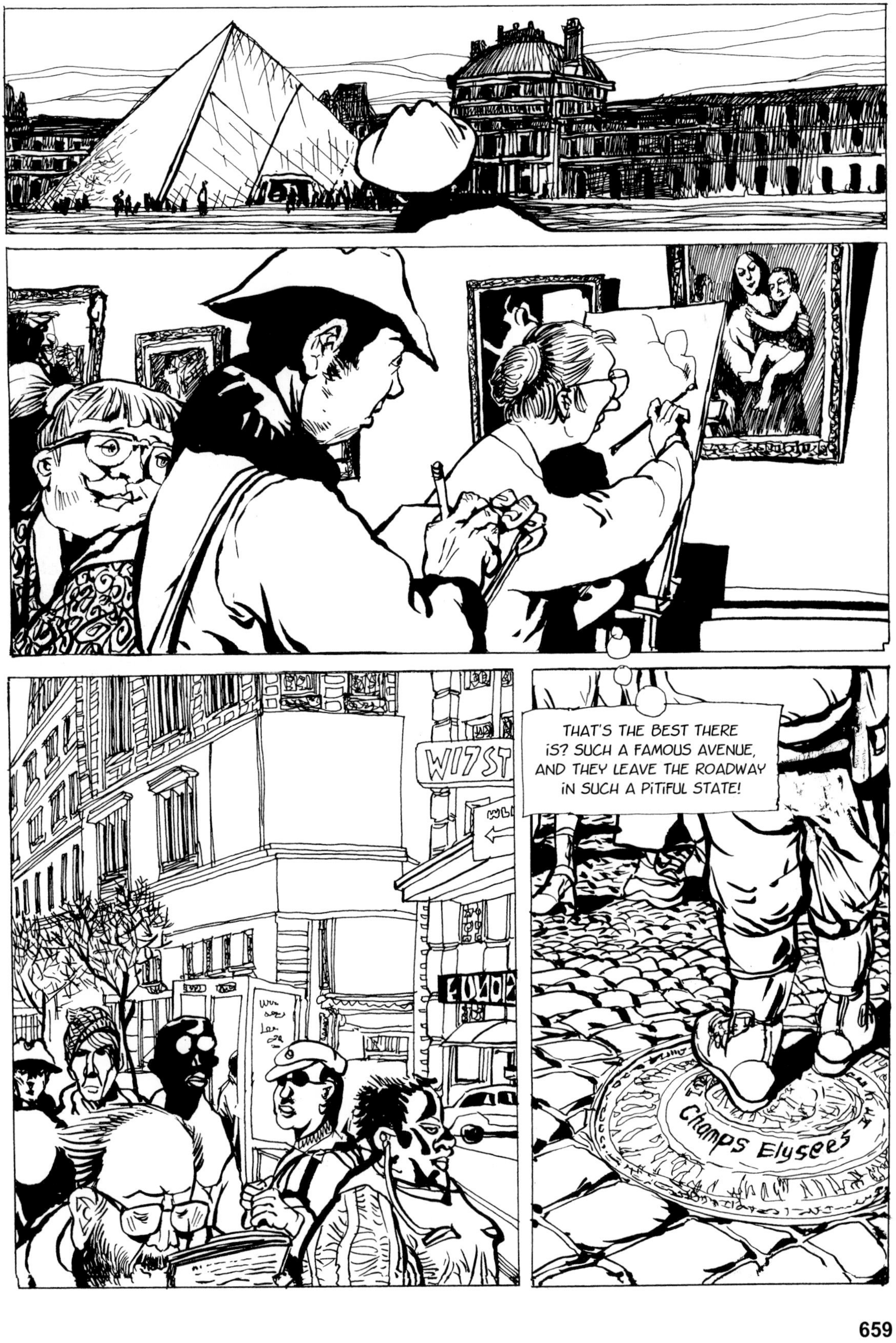
THAT'S THE BEST THERE iS? SUCH A FAMOUS AVENUE, AND THEY LEAVE THE ROADWAY iN SUCH A PiTiFUL STATE!
Champs Elysees

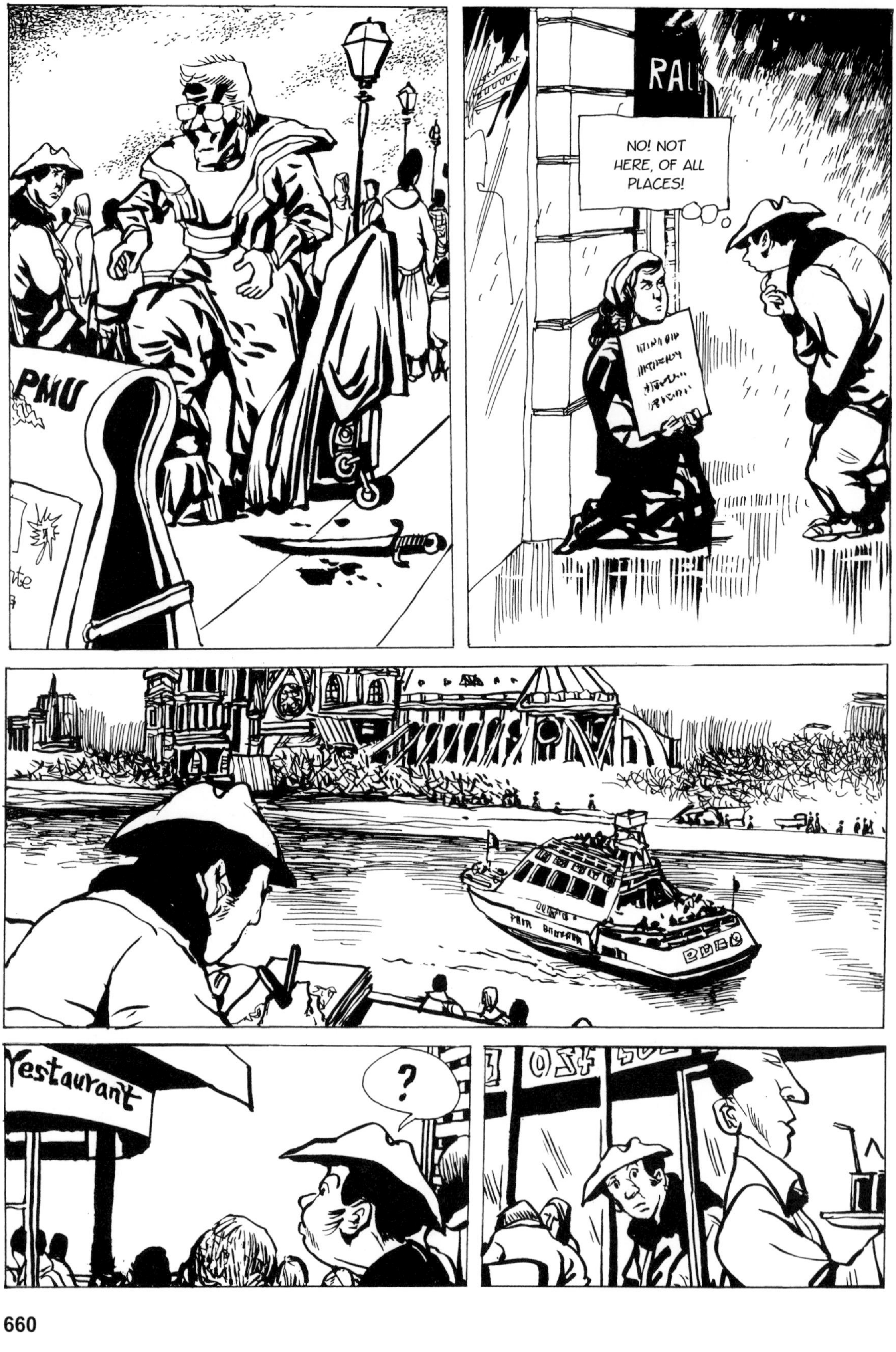
PMU
NO! NOT HERE, OF ALL PLACES!
Restaurant
?

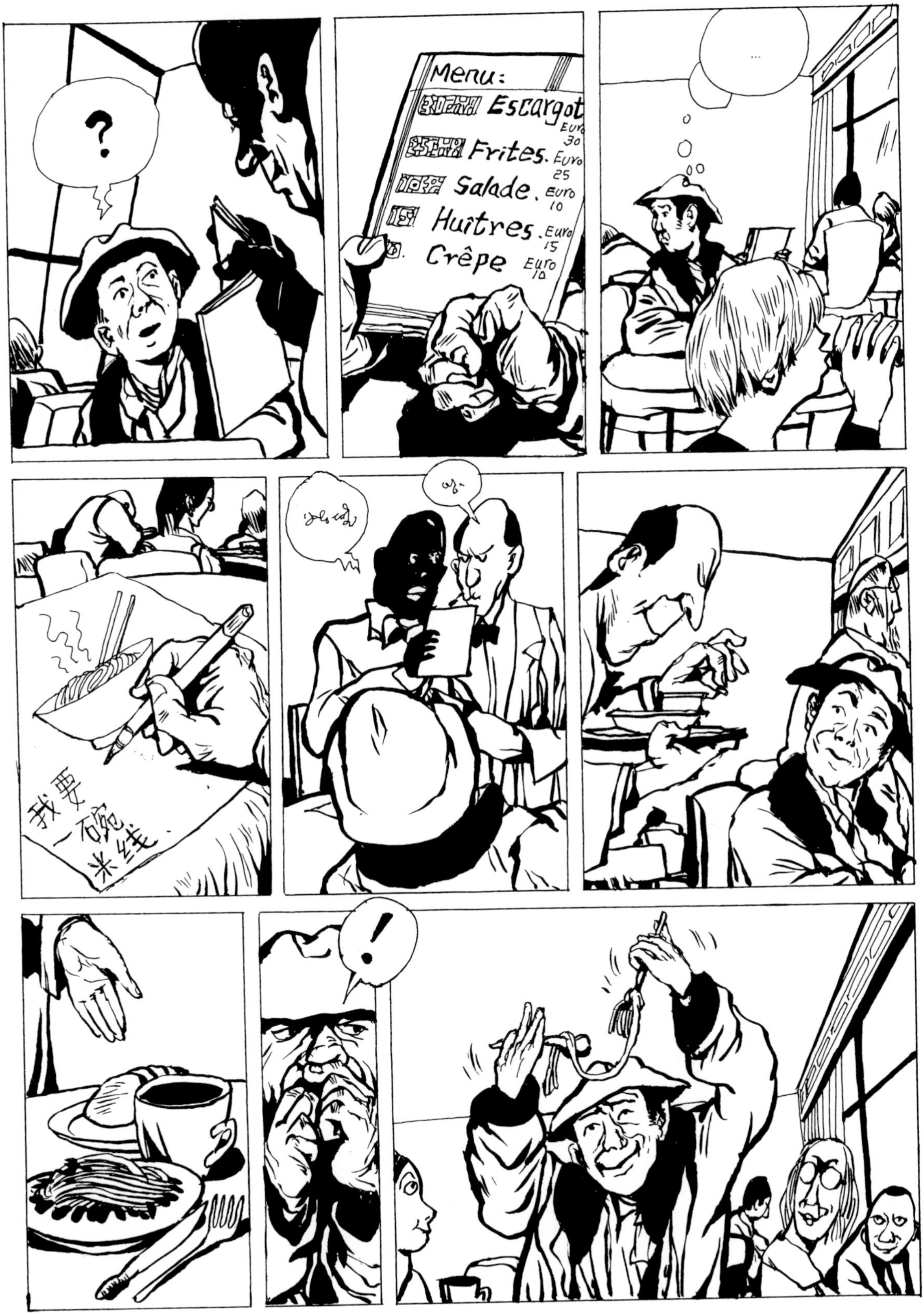
?
Menu:
Escargot Euro 30
Frites. Euro 25
Salade. Euro 10
Huitres. Euro 15
Crêpe Euro 10
...
我要一碗米线
!

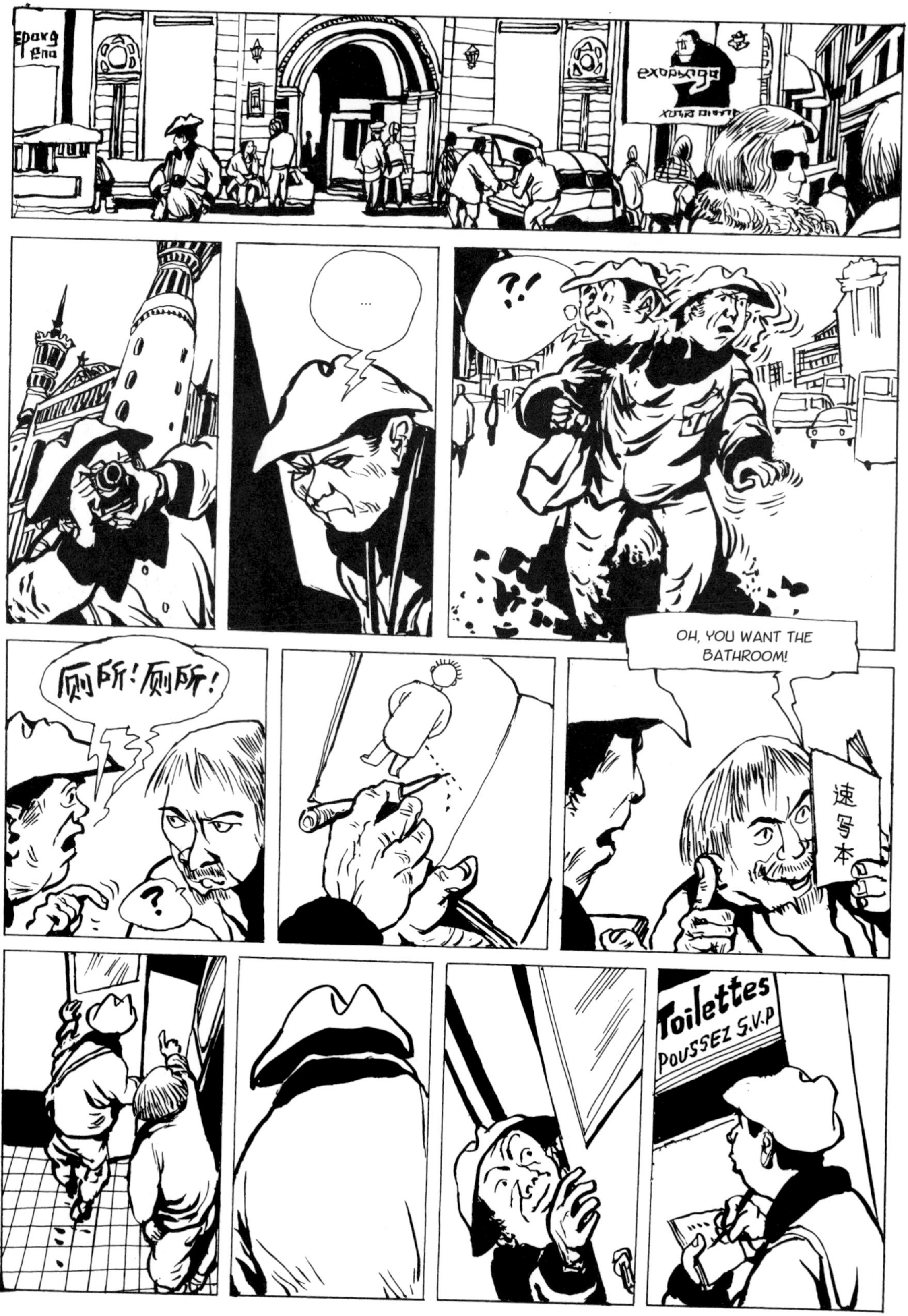
...
?!
厕所!厕所!
?
OH, YOU WANT THE BATHROOM!
速写本
Toilettes
POUSSEZ S.V.P

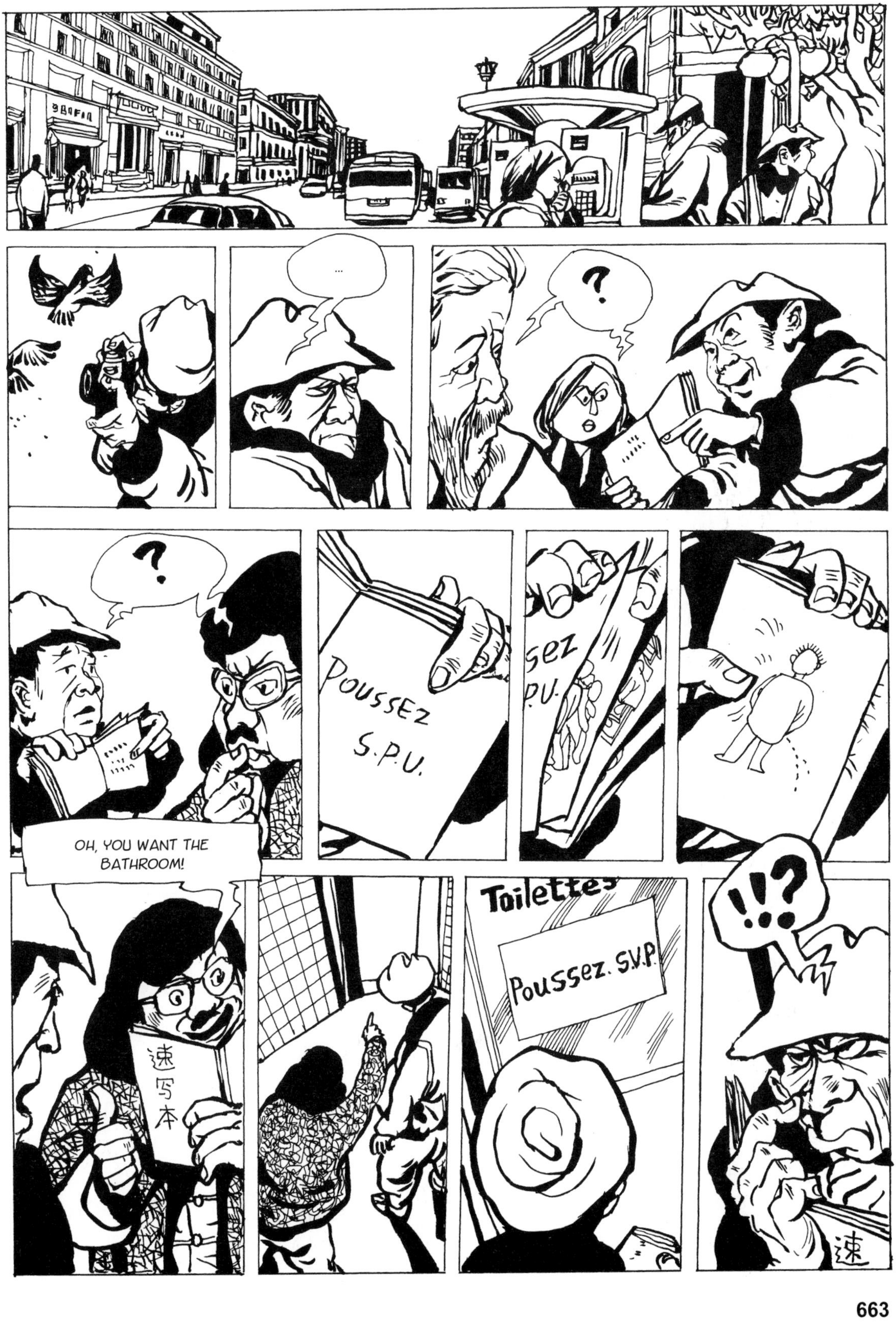

...
?
?
POUSSEZ S.P.U.
SEZ P.U.
OH, YOU WANT THE BATHROOM!
速写本
Toilettes
Poussez. S.V.P.
!!?
速

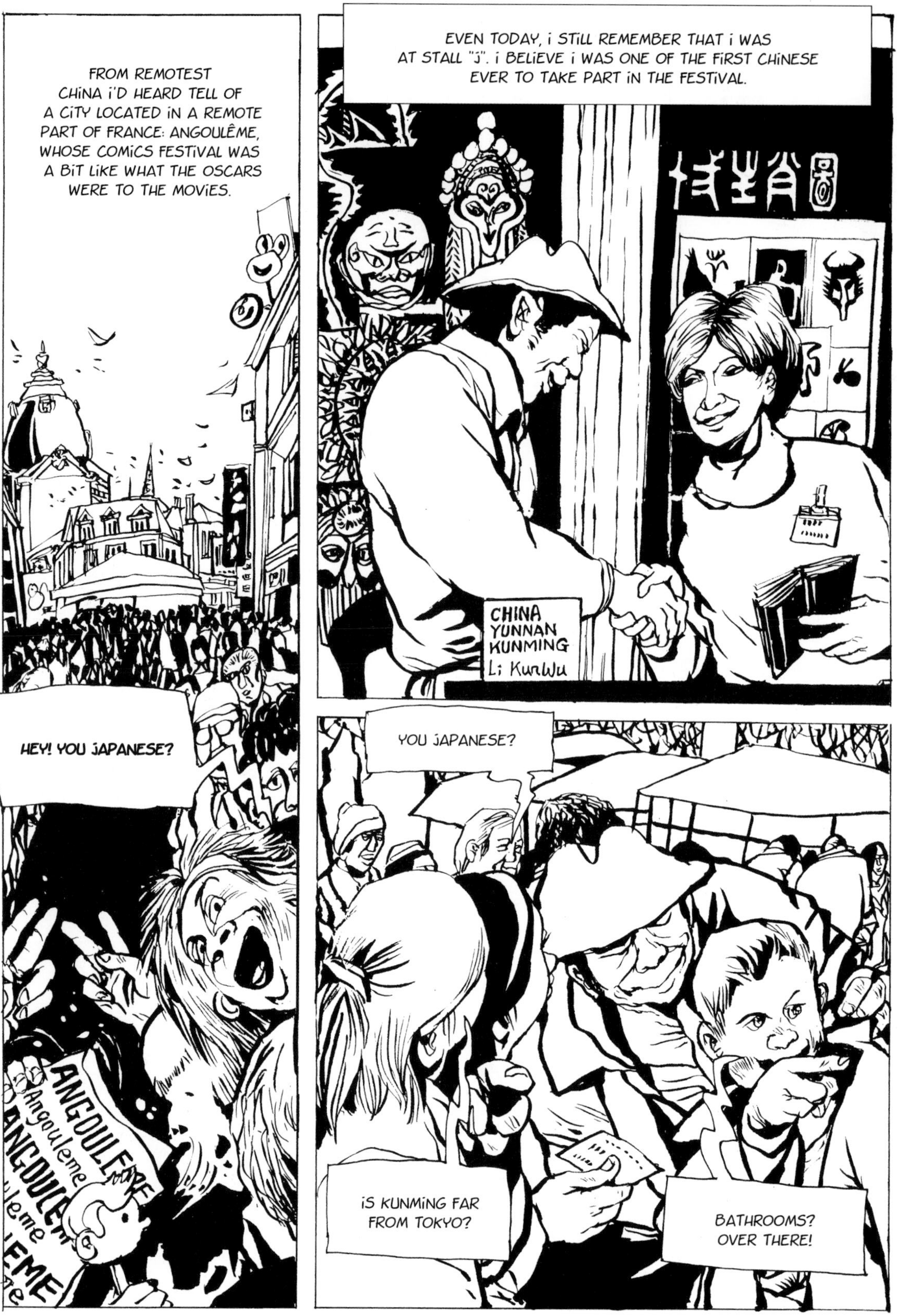
FROM REMOTEST CHINA I'D HEARD TELL OF A CITY LOCATED IN A REMOTE PART OF FRANCE: ANGOULÊME, WHOSE COMICS FESTIVAL WAS A BIT LIKE WHAT THE OSCARS WERE TO THE MOVIES.
EVEN TODAY, I STILL REMEMBER THAT I WAS AT STALL "J". I BELIEVE I WAS ONE OF THE FIRST CHINESE EVER TO TAKE PART IN THE FESTIVAL.
CHINA YUNNAN KUNMING
Li KunWu
HEY! YOU JAPANESE?
ANGOULEME
Angouleme
YOU JAPANESE?
IS KUNMING FAR FROM TOKYO?
BATHROOMS? OVER THERE!

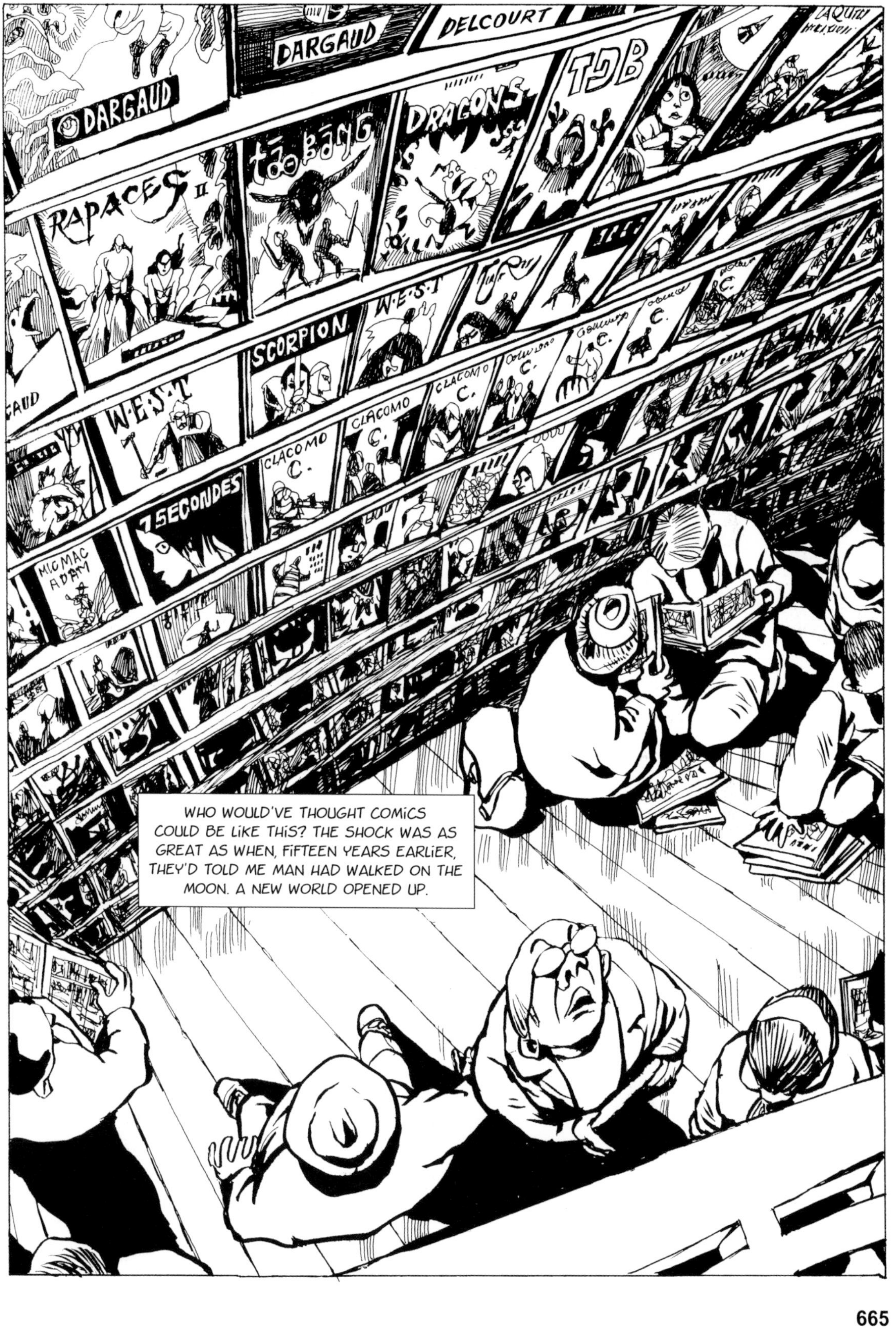
DARGAUD
DELCOURT
DARGAUD
TDB
DRAGONS
RAPACES II
SCORPION
W.E.S.T
W.E.S.T
75 SECONDES
MIC MAC ADAM
WHO WOULD'VE THOUGHT COMICS COULD BE LIKE THIS? THE SHOCK WAS AS GREAT AS WHEN, FIFTEEN YEARS EARLIER, THEY'D TOLD ME MAN HAD WALKED ON THE MOON. A NEW WORLD OPENED UP.

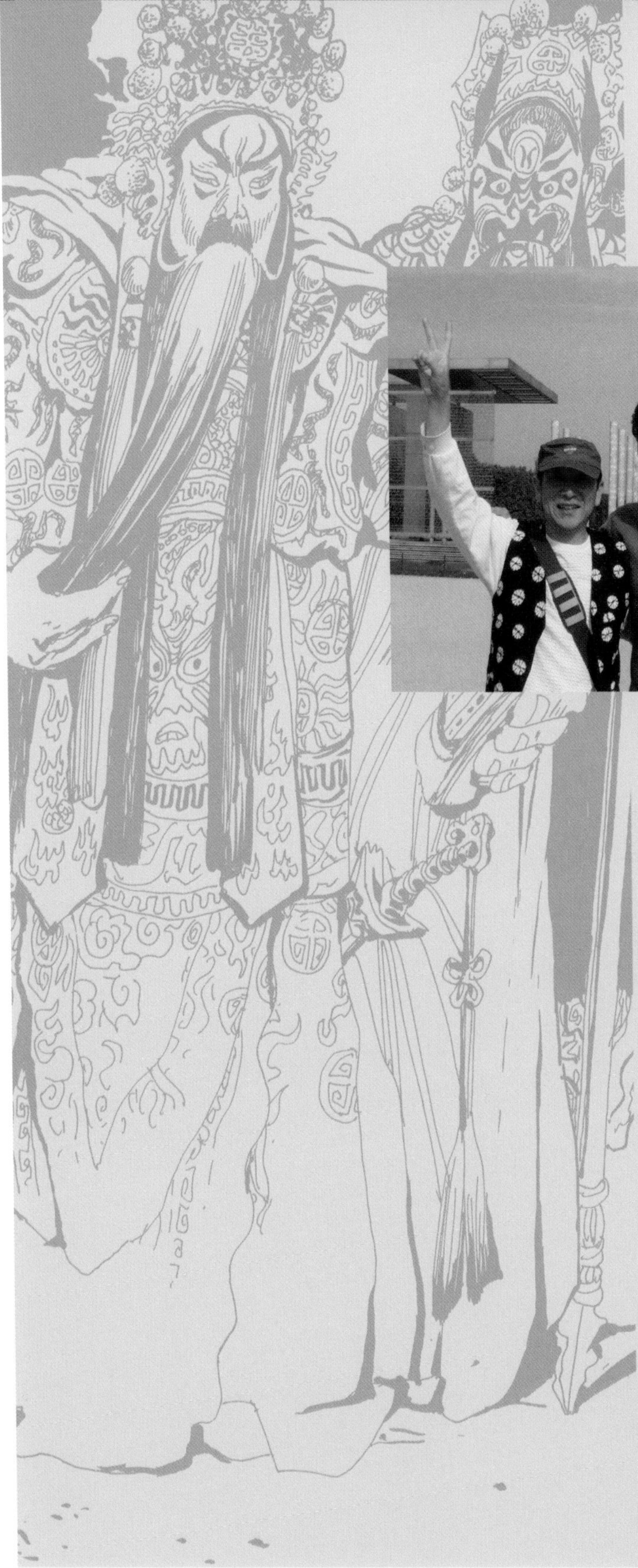

CHAPTER 10
Modern Times

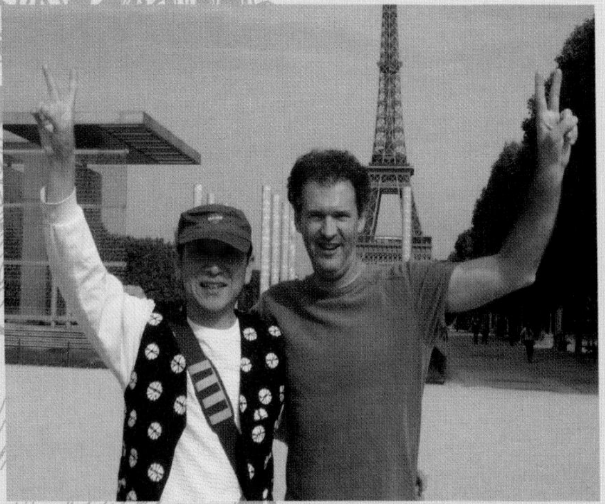

迎接另一个晨曦，
带来全新空气。
气息改变情味不变，
茶香飘满情谊。
我家大门常打开，
开放怀抱等你。
拥抱过就有了默契，
你会爱上这里。
不管远近都是客人，
请不用客气。
相约好了再一起，
北京欢迎你！
……

LET'S EMBRACE ANOTHER MORNING
AND ENJOY ITS FRESH AIR.
THINGS MIGHT BE CHANGING,
BUT OUR FEELINGS HAVEN'T.
THE FRAGRANCE OF TEA IS FILLING
US WITH FRIENDSHIP.
OUR DOOR IS ALWAYS OPEN.
WE ARE WAITING FOR YOU WITH OPEN ARMS.
AFTER A BIG HUG OF FELLOW-FEELING,
YOU'LL FEEL CLOSE TO US.
YOU'LL FALL IN LOVE WITH THIS PLACE.
GUESTS: NO MATTER WHERE
YOU'RE FROM, NEAR OR FAR,
PLEASE FEEL AT HOME.
WE PROMISED TO GET TOGETHER
HERE. SO WELCOME!
BEIJING WELCOMES YOU!

("BEIJING WELCOMES YOU", OFFICIAL SONG OF THE BEIJING OLYMPICS)

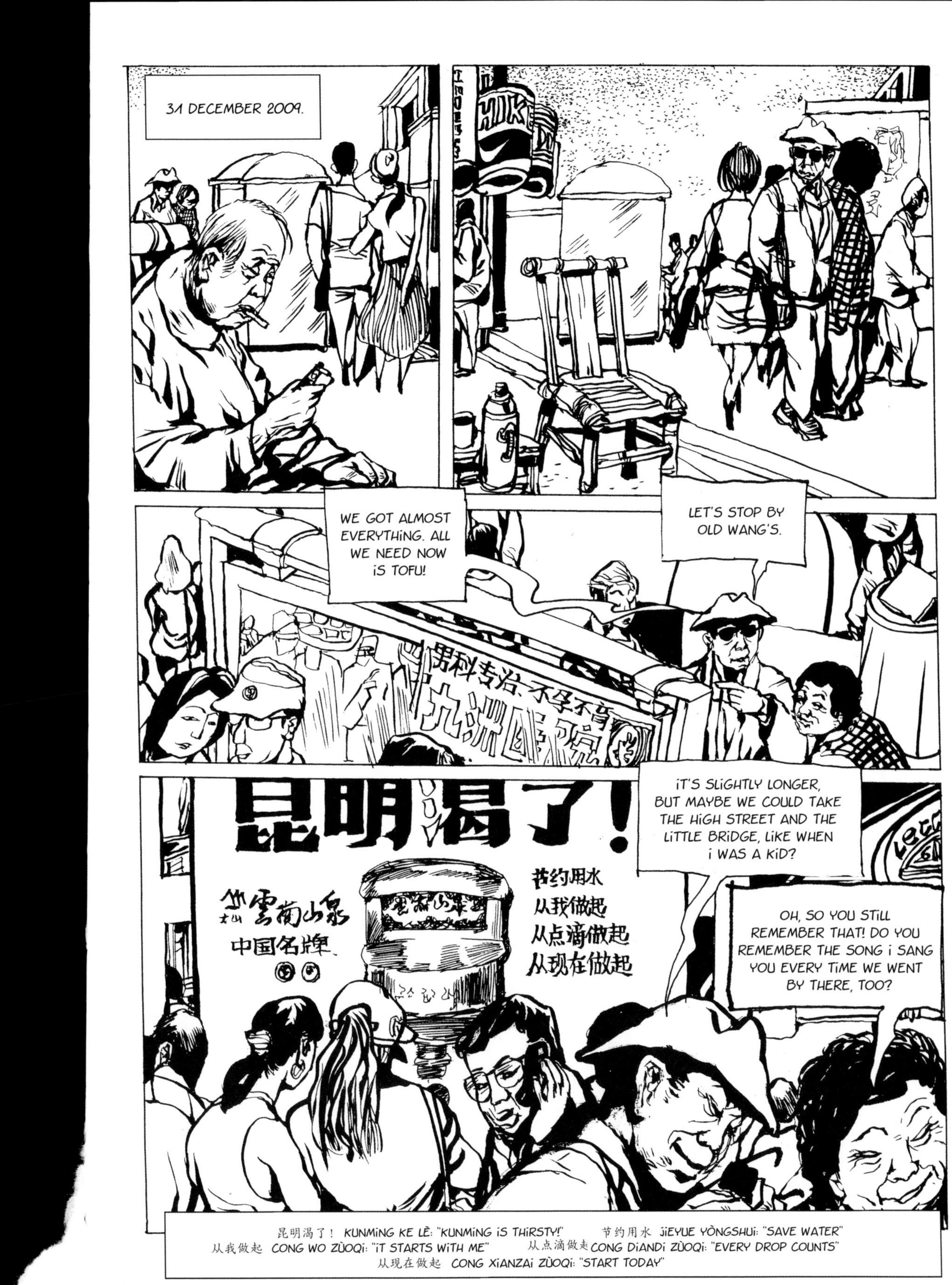
31 DECEMBER 2009.
WE GOT ALMOST EVERYTHING. ALL WE NEED NOW IS TOFU!
LET'S STOP BY OLD WANG'S.
昆明渴了！
节约用水
从我做起
从点滴做起
从现在做起
中国名牌
IT'S SLIGHTLY LONGER, BUT MAYBE WE COULD TAKE THE HIGH STREET AND THE LITTLE BRIDGE, LIKE WHEN I WAS A KID?
OH, SO YOU STILL REMEMBER THAT! DO YOU REMEMBER THE SONG I SANG YOU EVERY TIME WE WENT BY THERE, TOO?

昆明渴了！ KUNMING KE LÈ: "KUNMING IS THIRSTY!" 节约用水 JIEYUE YÒNGSHUI: "SAVE WATER"
从我做起 CONG WO ZÙOQI: "IT STARTS WITH ME" 从点滴做起 CONG DIANDI ZÙOQI: "EVERY DROP COUNTS"
从现在做起 CONG XIANZAI ZÙOQI: "START TODAY"

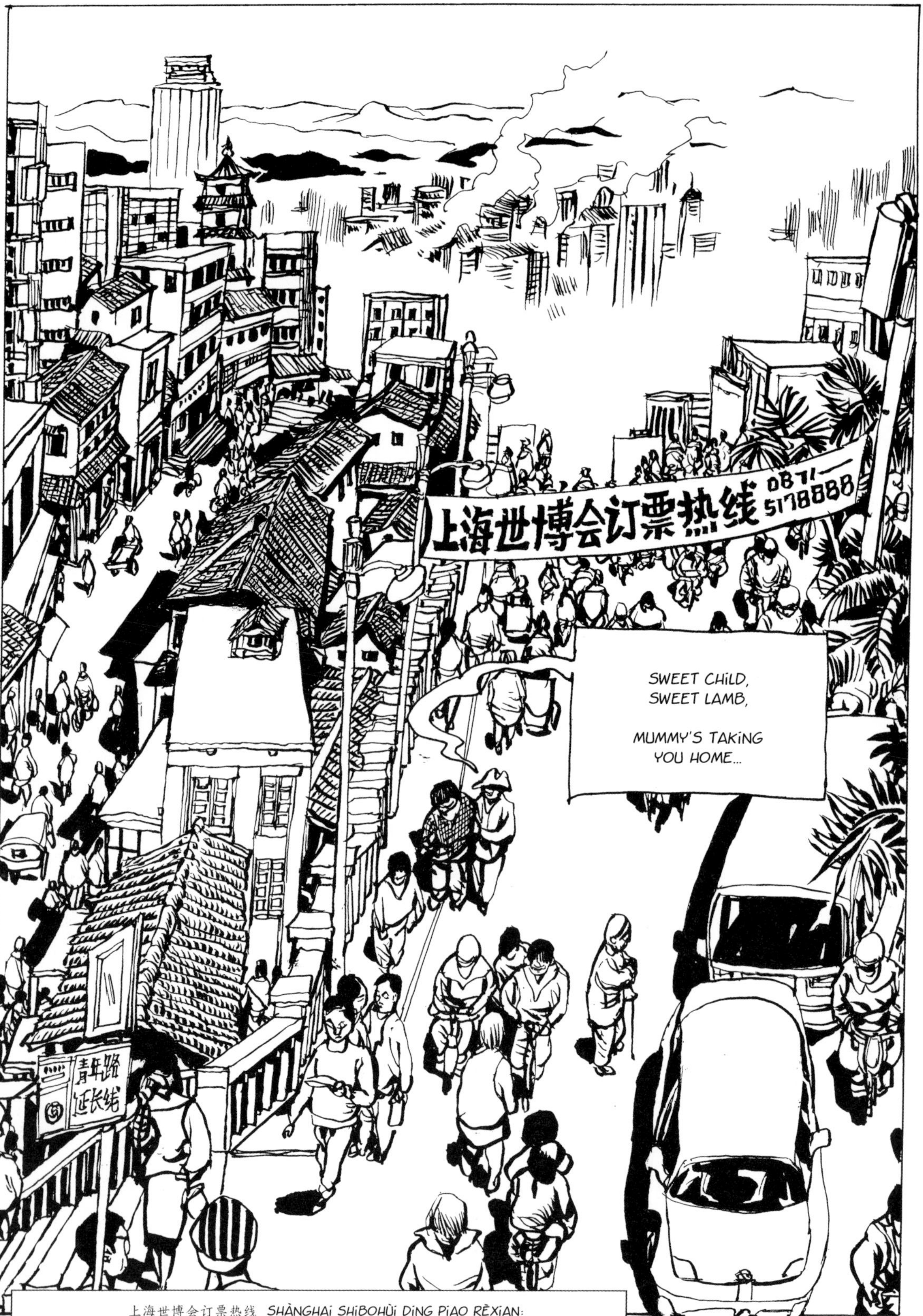
上海世博会订票热线
0871—
5178888
SWEET CHILD,
SWEET LAMB,
MUMMY'S TAKING YOU HOME...
青年路
延长线

上海世博会订票热线 SHÀNGHAI SHIBOHÙI DING PIAO RÈXIAN:
"TICKET RESERVATION HOTLINE FOR THE SHANGHAI WORLD EXPO".

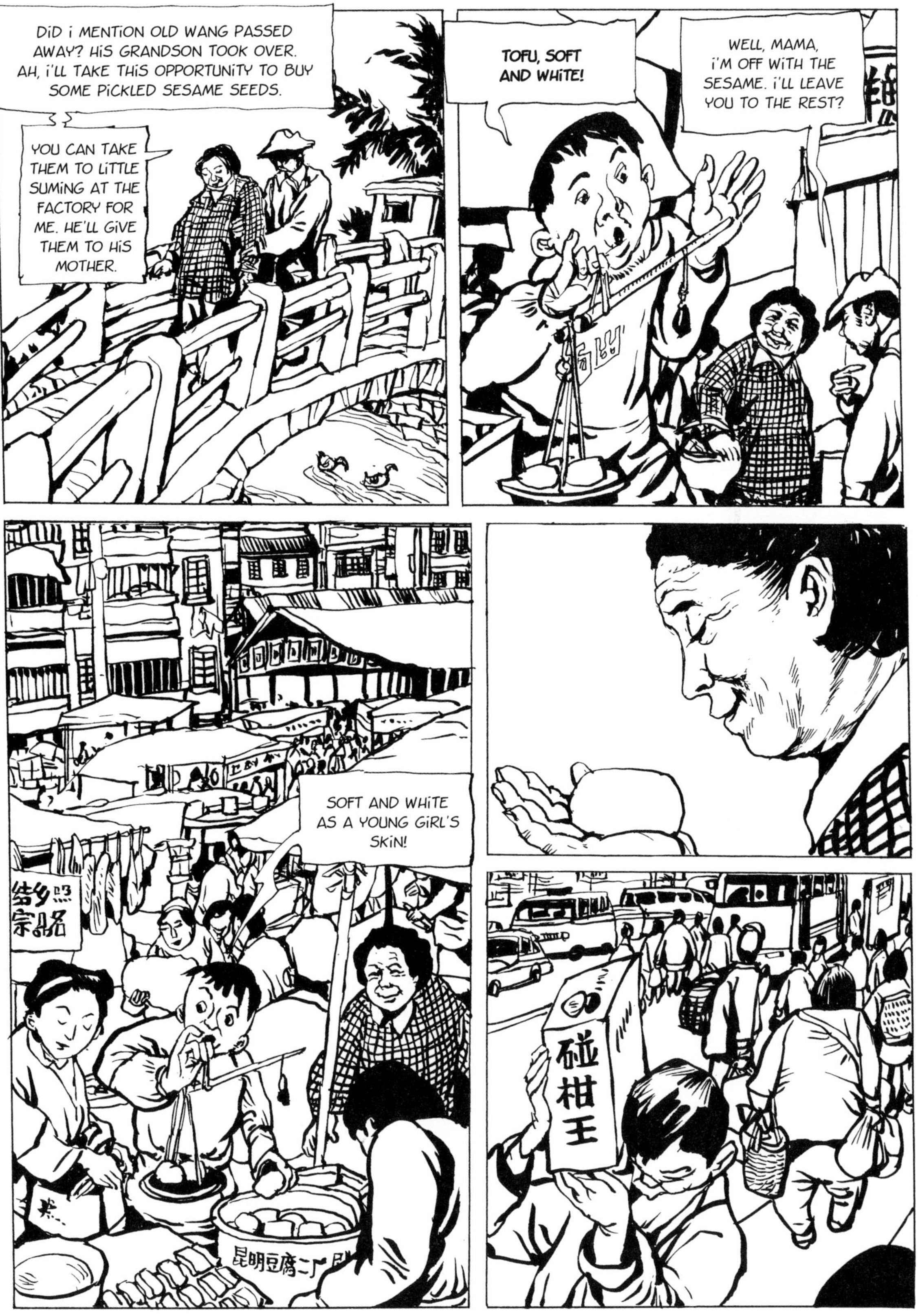

DID I MENTION OLD WANG PASSED AWAY? HIS GRANDSON TOOK OVER. AH, I'LL TAKE THIS OPPORTUNITY TO BUY SOME PICKLED SESAME SEEDS.
YOU CAN TAKE THEM TO LITTLE SUMING AT THE FACTORY FOR ME. HE'LL GIVE THEM TO HIS MOTHER.
TOFU, SOFT AND WHITE!
WELL, MAMA, I'M OFF WITH THE SESAME. I'LL LEAVE YOU TO THE REST?
SOFT AND WHITE AS A YOUNG GIRL'S SKIN!
碰柑王

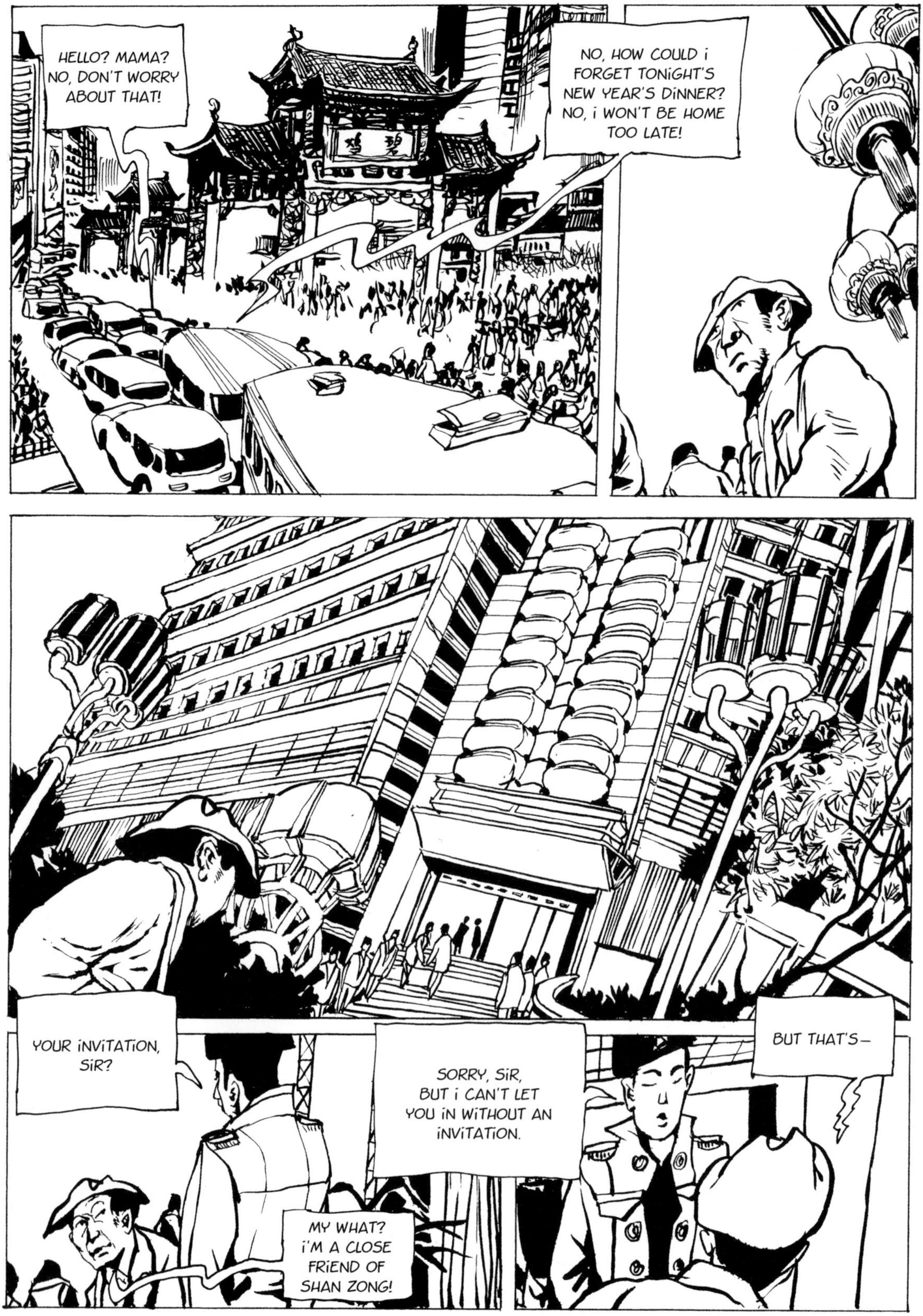
HELLO? MAMA? NO, DON'T WORRY ABOUT THAT!
NO, HOW COULD i FORGET TONiGHT'S NEW YEAR'S DiNNER? NO, i WON'T BE HOME TOO LATE!
YOUR iNViTATiON, SiR?
MY WHAT? i'M A CLOSE FRiEND OF SHAN ZONG!
SORRY, SiR, BUT i CAN'T LET YOU iN WiTHOUT AN iNViTATiON.
BUT THAT'S–

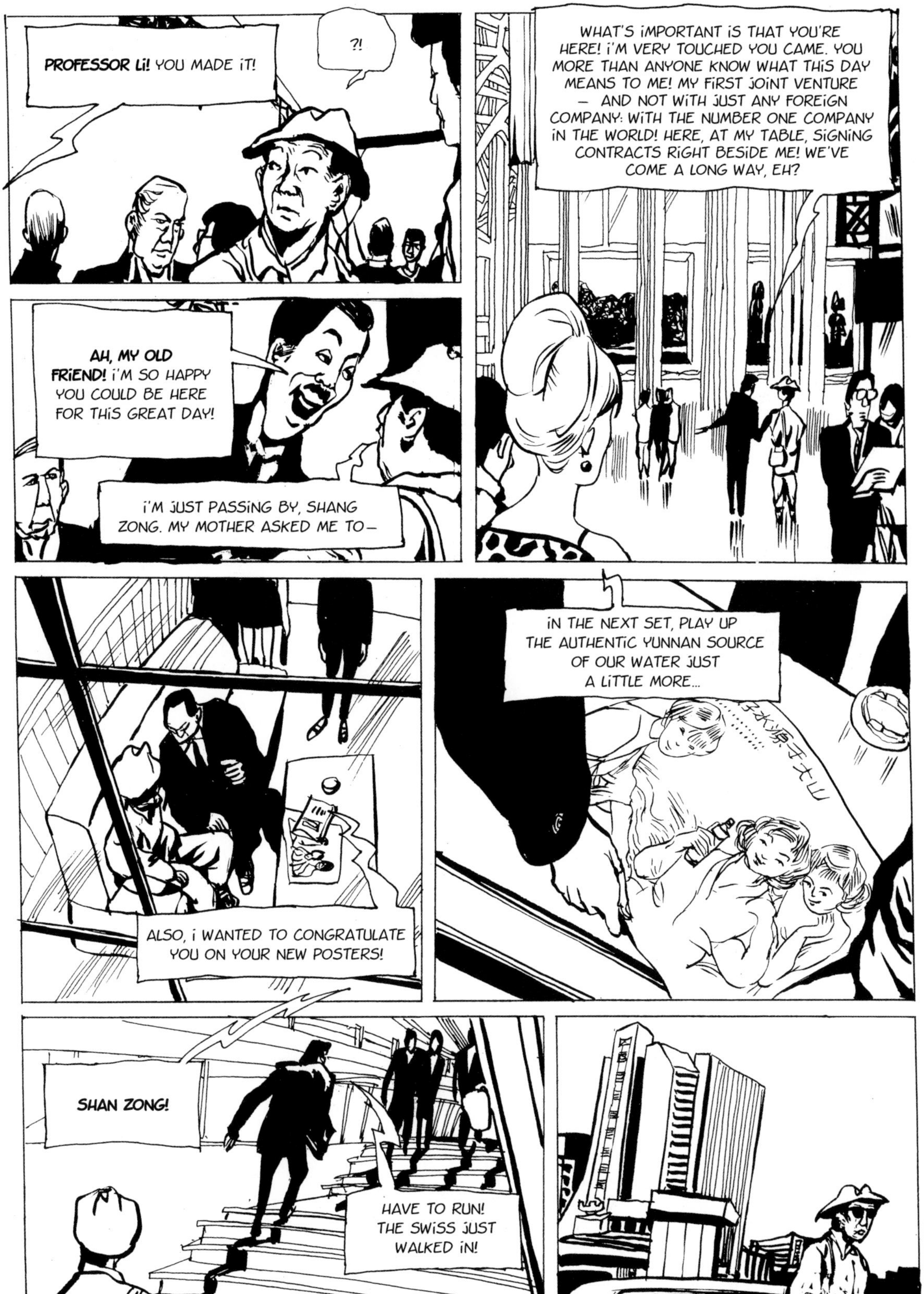

PROFESSOR Li! YOU MADE iT!
?!
WHAT'S iMPORTANT iS THAT YOU'RE HERE! i'M VERY TOUCHED YOU CAME. YOU MORE THAN ANYONE KNOW WHAT THiS DAY MEANS TO ME! MY FiRST JOiNT VENTURE – AND NOT WiTH JUST ANY FOREiGN COMPANY: WiTH THE NUMBER ONE COMPANY iN THE WORLD! HERE, AT MY TABLE, SiGNiNG CONTRACTS RiGHT BESiDE ME! WE'VE COME A LONG WAY, EH?
AH, MY OLD FRiEND! i'M SO HAPPY YOU COULD BE HERE FOR THiS GREAT DAY!
i'M JUST PASSiNG BY, SHANG ZONG. MY MOTHER ASKED ME TO–
ALSO, i WANTED TO CONGRATULATE YOU ON YOUR NEW POSTERS!
iN THE NEXT SET, PLAY UP THE AUTHENTiC YUNNAN SOURCE OF OUR WATER JUST A LiTTLE MORE...
SHAN ZONG!
HAVE TO RUN! THE SWiSS JUST WALKED iN!

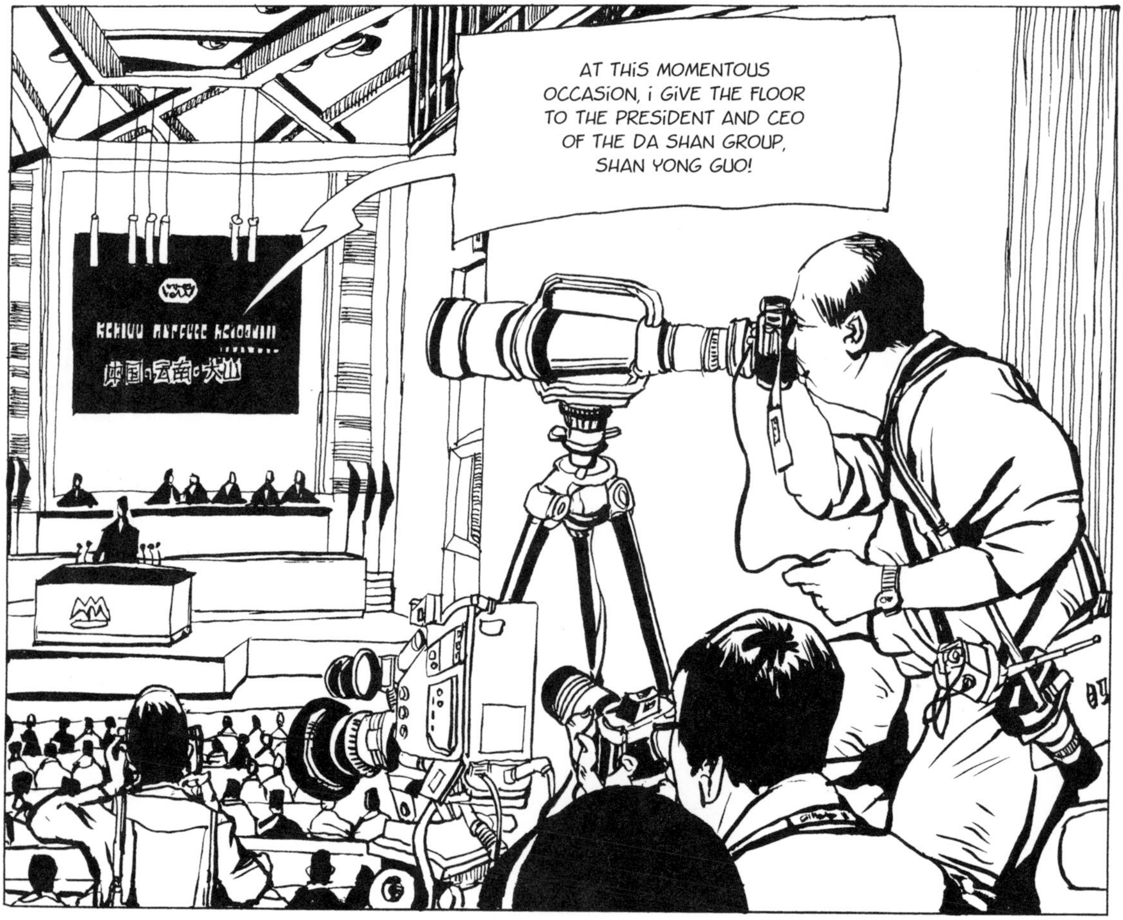
AT THIS MOMENTOUS OCCASION, I GIVE THE FLOOR TO THE PRESIDENT AND CEO OF THE DA SHAN GROUP, SHAN YONG GUO!

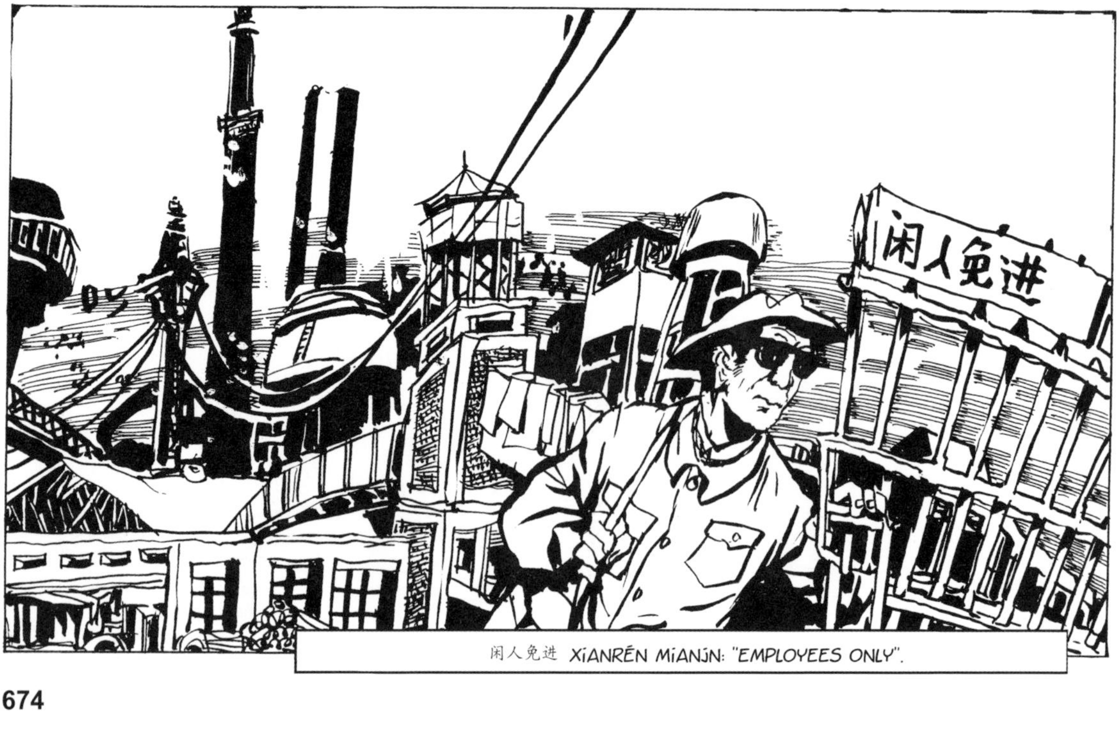
闲人免进
闲人免进 XIANRÉN MIANJN: "EMPLOYEES ONLY".

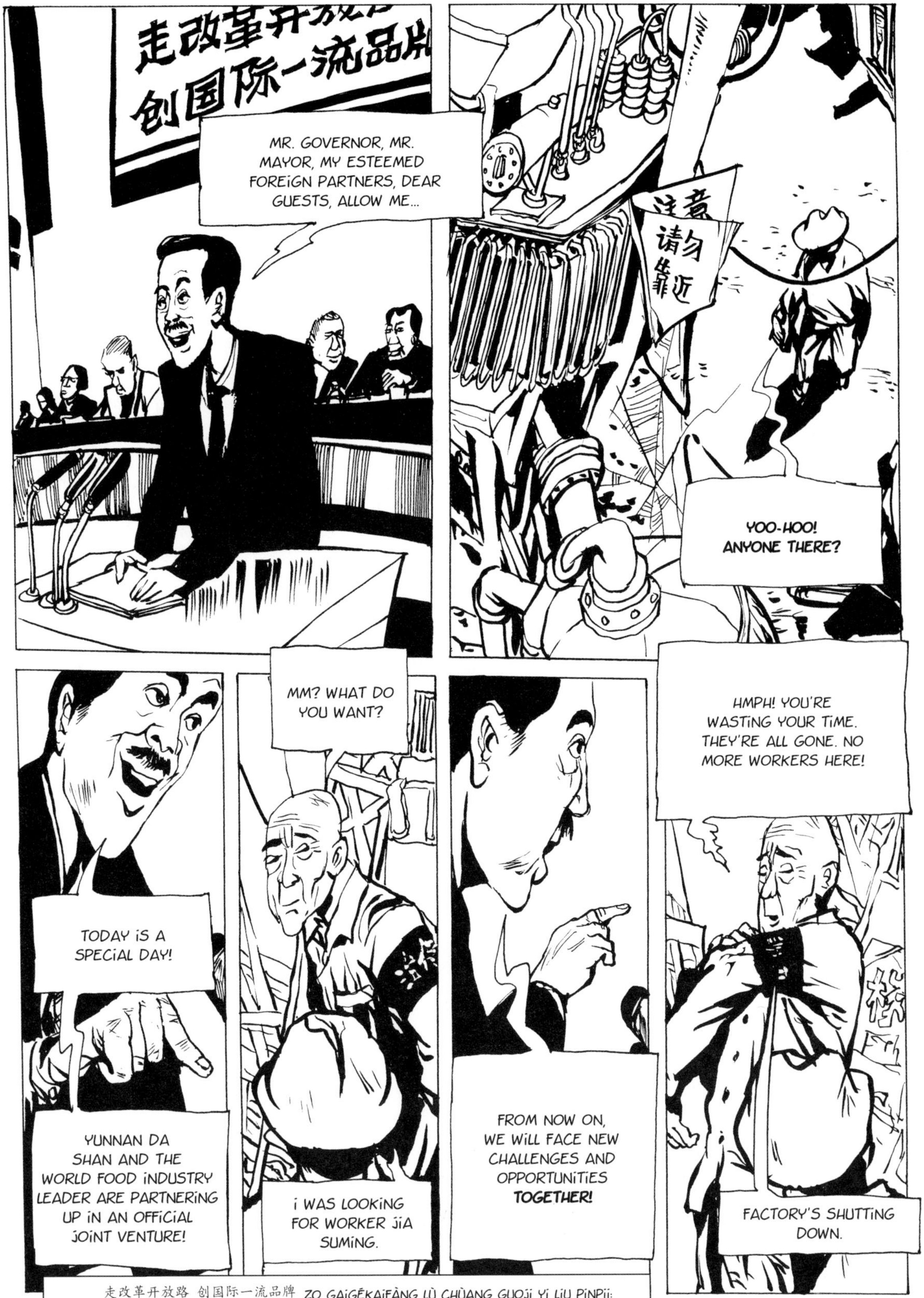
MR. GOVERNOR, MR. MAYOR, MY ESTEEMED FOREiGN PARTNERS, DEAR GUESTS, ALLOW ME...
YOO-HOO! ANYONE THERE?
TODAY iS A SPECiAL DAY!
YUNNAN DA SHAN AND THE WORLD FOOD iNDUSTRY LEADER ARE PARTNERiNG UP iN AN OFFiCiAL JOiNT VENTURE!
MM? WHAT DO YOU WANT?
i WAS LOOKiNG FOR WORKER JiA SUMiNG.
FROM NOW ON, WE WiLL FACE NEW CHALLENGES AND OPPORTUNiTiES **TOGETHER!**
HMPH! YOU'RE WASTiNG YOUR TiME. THEY'RE ALL GONE. NO MORE WORKERS HERE!
FACTORY'S SHUTTiNG DOWN.

走改革开放路 创国际一流品牌 ZO GAiGÉKAiFÀNG LÙ CHÙANG GUOJi Yi LiU PiNPii:
"LET US TAKE THE PATH OF REFORMS AND OPENNESS, AND CREATE A PREMiER GLOBAL BRAND!"

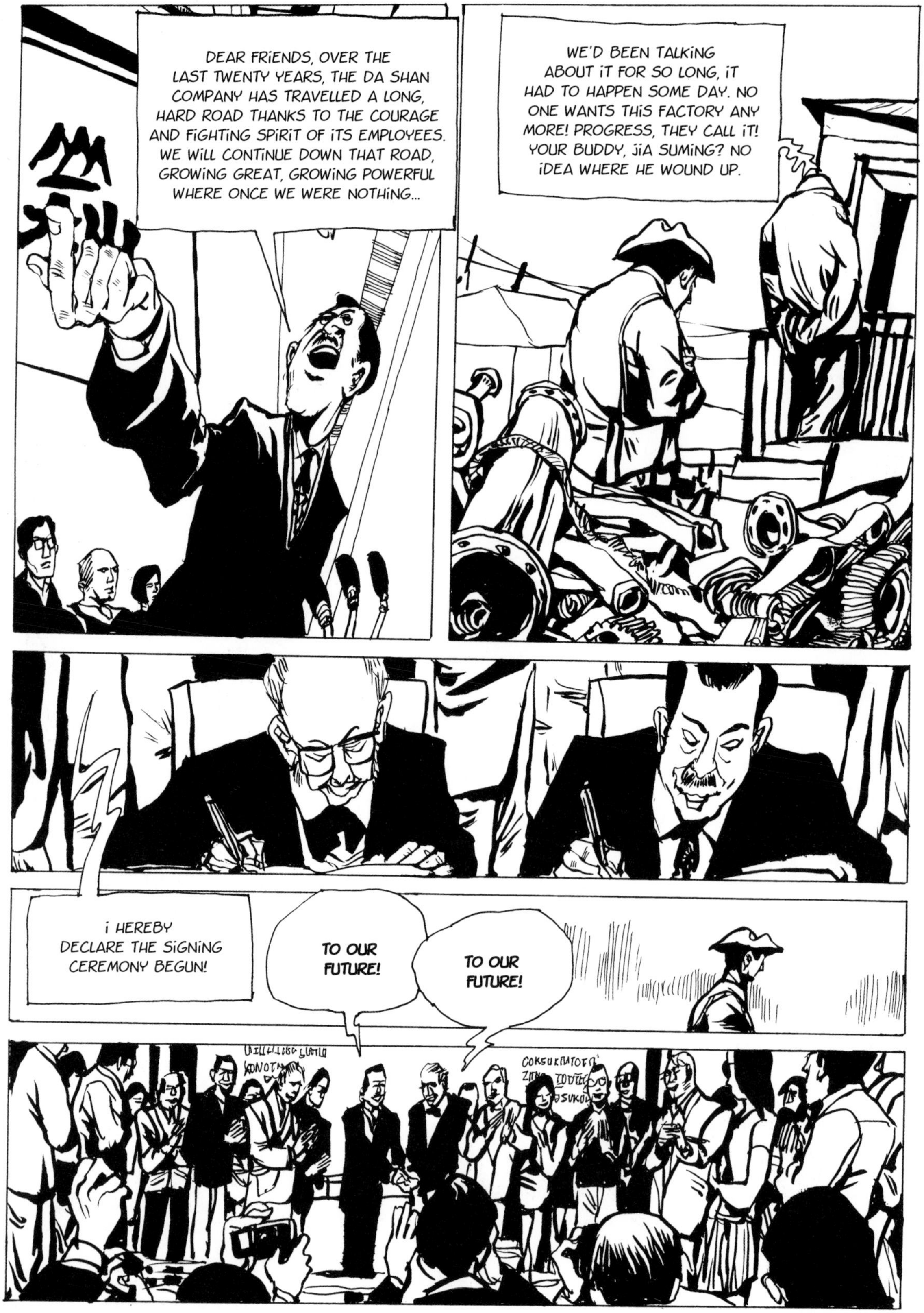
DEAR FRIENDS, OVER THE LAST TWENTY YEARS, THE DA SHAN COMPANY HAS TRAVELLED A LONG, HARD ROAD THANKS TO THE COURAGE AND FIGHTING SPIRIT OF ITS EMPLOYEES. WE WILL CONTINUE DOWN THAT ROAD, GROWING GREAT, GROWING POWERFUL WHERE ONCE WE WERE NOTHING...
WE'D BEEN TALKING ABOUT IT FOR SO LONG, IT HAD TO HAPPEN SOME DAY. NO ONE WANTS THIS FACTORY ANY MORE! PROGRESS, THEY CALL IT! YOUR BUDDY, JIA SUMING? NO IDEA WHERE HE WOUND UP.
I HEREBY DECLARE THE SIGNING CEREMONY BEGUN!
TO OUR FUTURE!
TO OUR FUTURE!

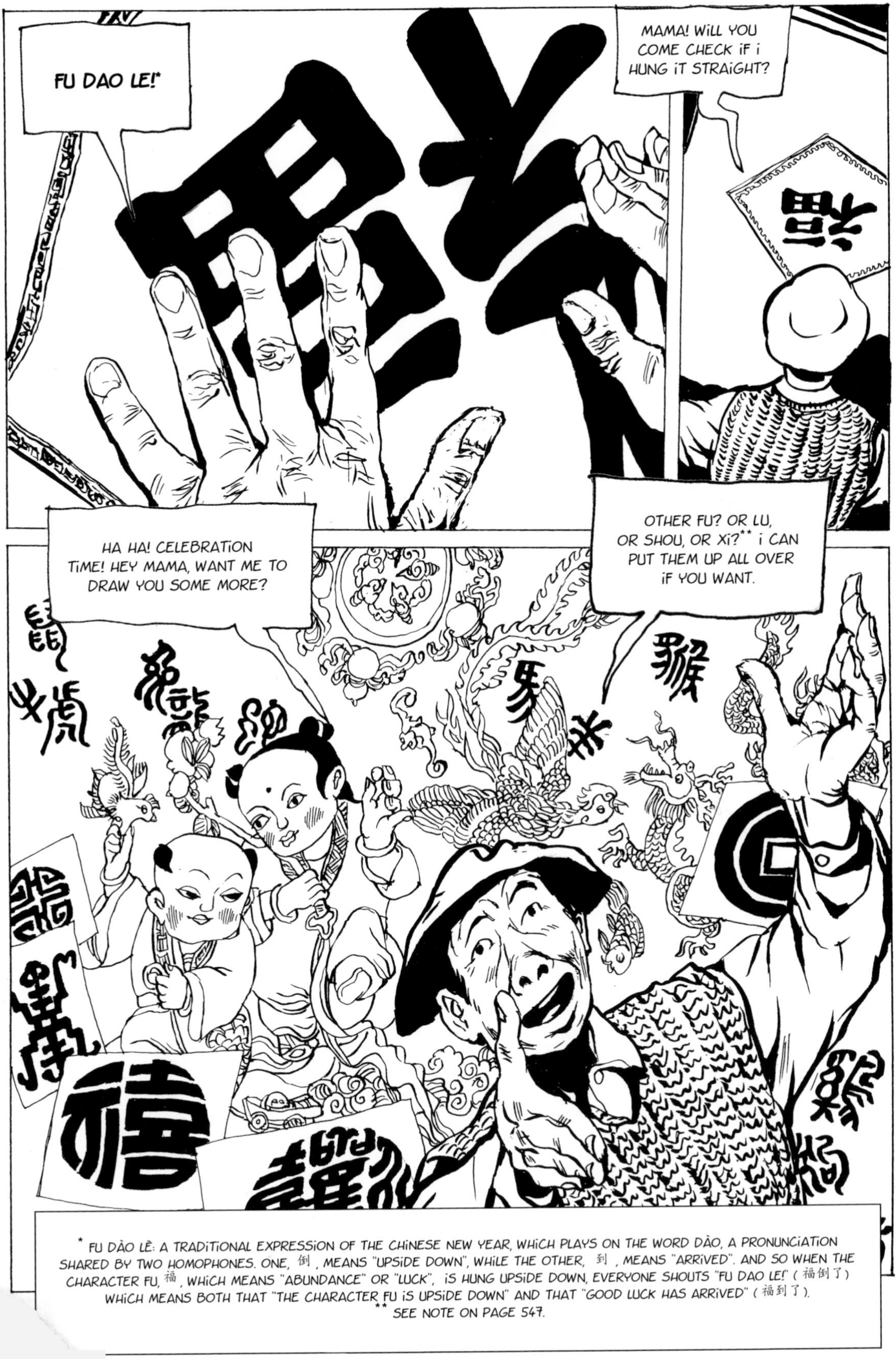
FU DAO LE!*
MAMA! WILL YOU COME CHECK IF I HUNG IT STRAIGHT?
HA HA! CELEBRATION TIME! HEY MAMA, WANT ME TO DRAW YOU SOME MORE?
OTHER FU? OR LU, OR SHOU, OR XI?** I CAN PUT THEM UP ALL OVER IF YOU WANT.

* FU DÀO LÈ: A TRADITIONAL EXPRESSION OF THE CHINESE NEW YEAR, WHICH PLAYS ON THE WORD DÀO, A PRONUNCIATION SHARED BY TWO HOMOPHONES. ONE, 倒, MEANS "UPSIDE DOWN", WHILE THE OTHER, 到, MEANS "ARRIVED". AND SO WHEN THE CHARACTER FU, 福, WHICH MEANS "ABUNDANCE" OR "LUCK", IS HUNG UPSIDE DOWN, EVERYONE SHOUTS "FU DAO LE!" (福倒了) WHICH MEANS BOTH THAT "THE CHARACTER FU IS UPSIDE DOWN" AND THAT "GOOD LUCK HAS ARRIVED" (福到了).

** SEE NOTE ON PAGE 547.

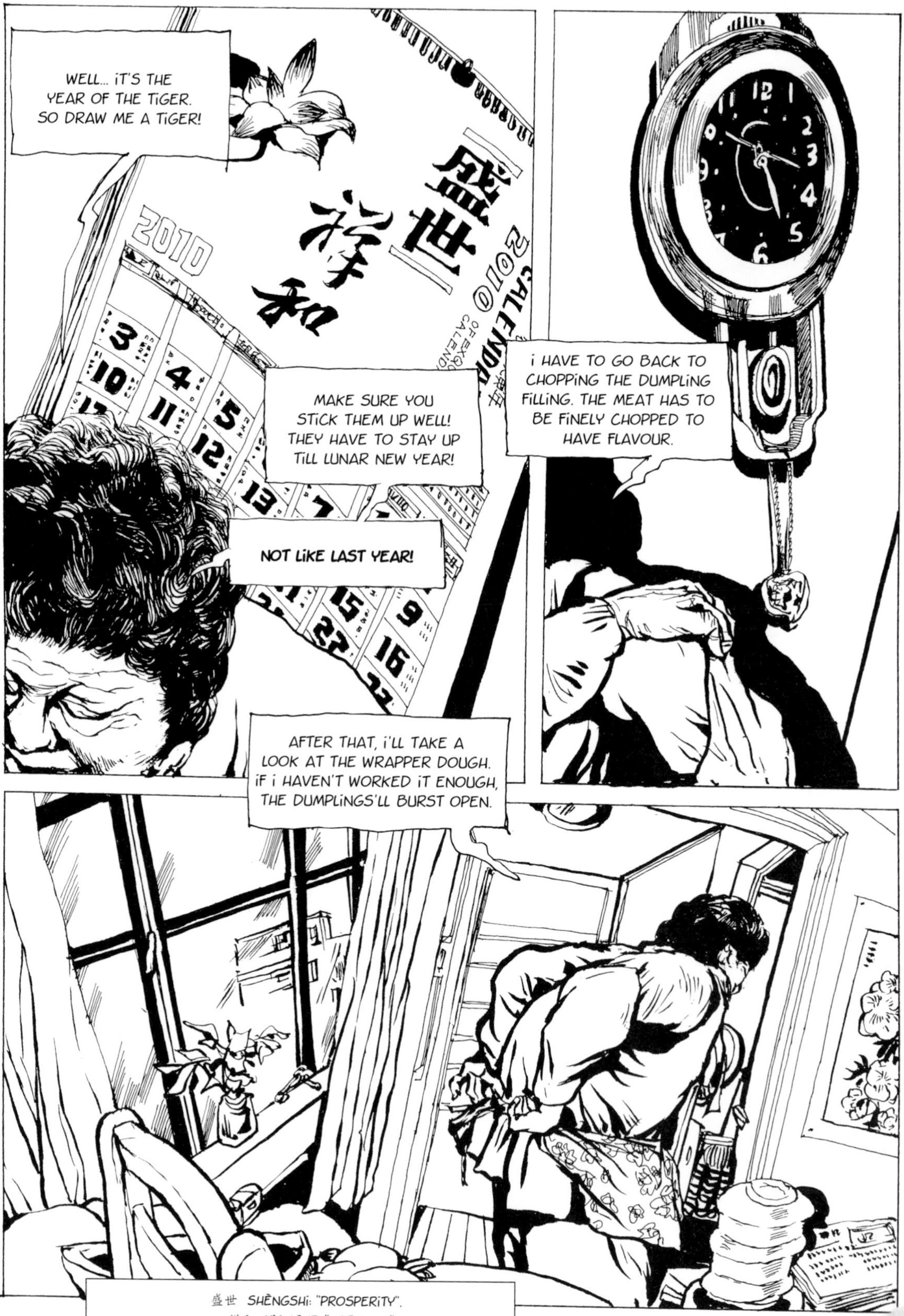
WELL... iT'S THE YEAR OF THE TiGER. SO DRAW ME A TiGER!
盛世
祥和
2010
MAKE SURE YOU STiCK THEM UP WELL! THEY HAVE TO STAY UP TiLL LUNAR NEW YEAR!
NOT LiKE LAST YEAR!
i HAVE TO GO BACK TO CHOPPiNG THE DUMPLiNG FiLLiNG. THE MEAT HAS TO BE FiNELY CHOPPED TO HAVE FLAVOUR.
AFTER THAT, i'LL TAKE A LOOK AT THE WRAPPER DOUGH. iF i HAVEN'T WORKED iT ENOUGH, THE DUMPLiNGS'LL BURST OPEN.

盛世 SHÈNGSHi: "PROSPERiTY".
祥和 XiANGHE: "HARMONY".

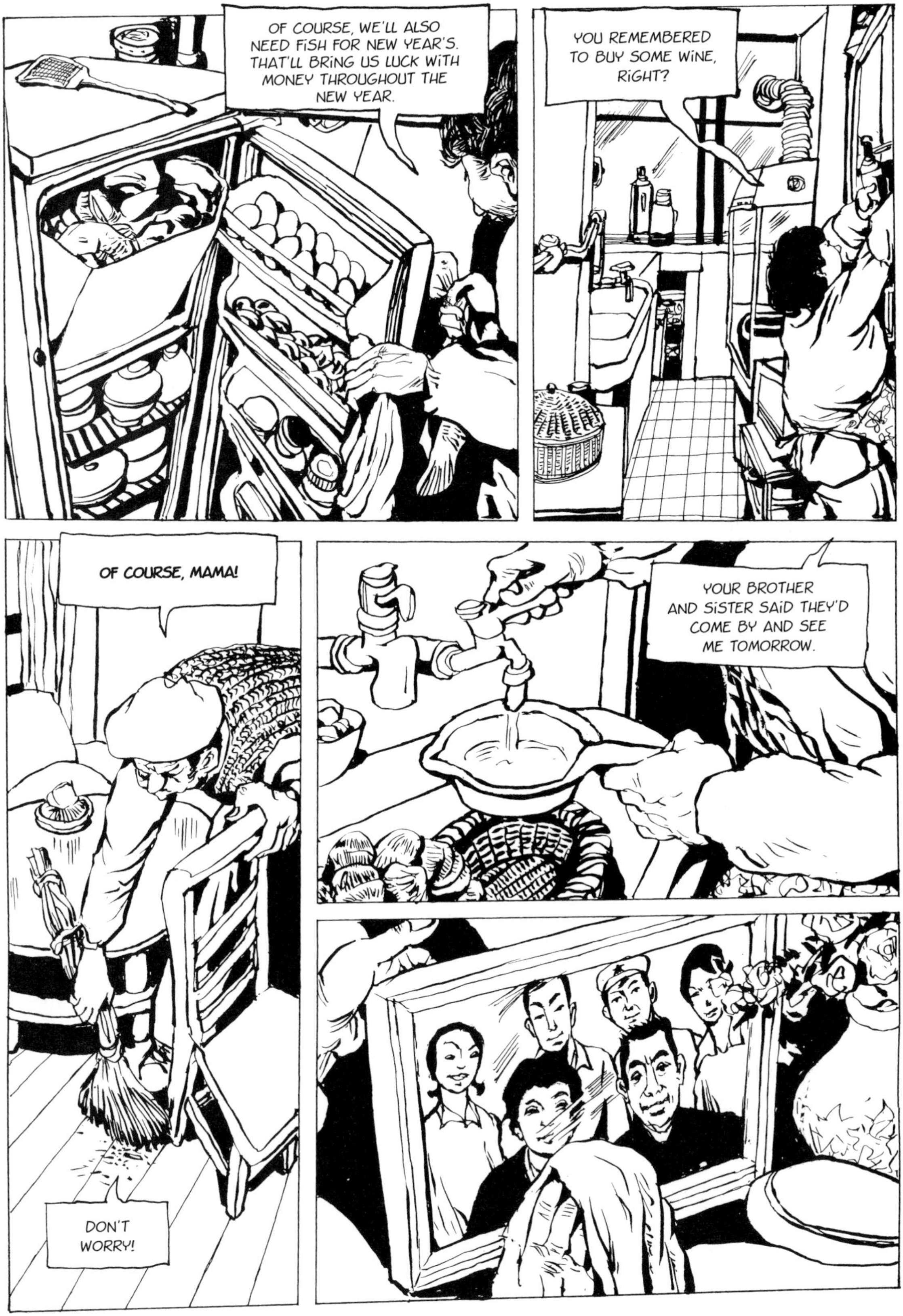
OF COURSE, WE'LL ALSO NEED FISH FOR NEW YEAR'S. THAT'LL BRING US LUCK WITH MONEY THROUGHOUT THE NEW YEAR.
YOU REMEMBERED TO BUY SOME WINE, RIGHT?
OF COURSE, MAMA!
DON'T WORRY!
YOUR BROTHER AND SISTER SAID THEY'D COME BY AND SEE ME TOMORROW.

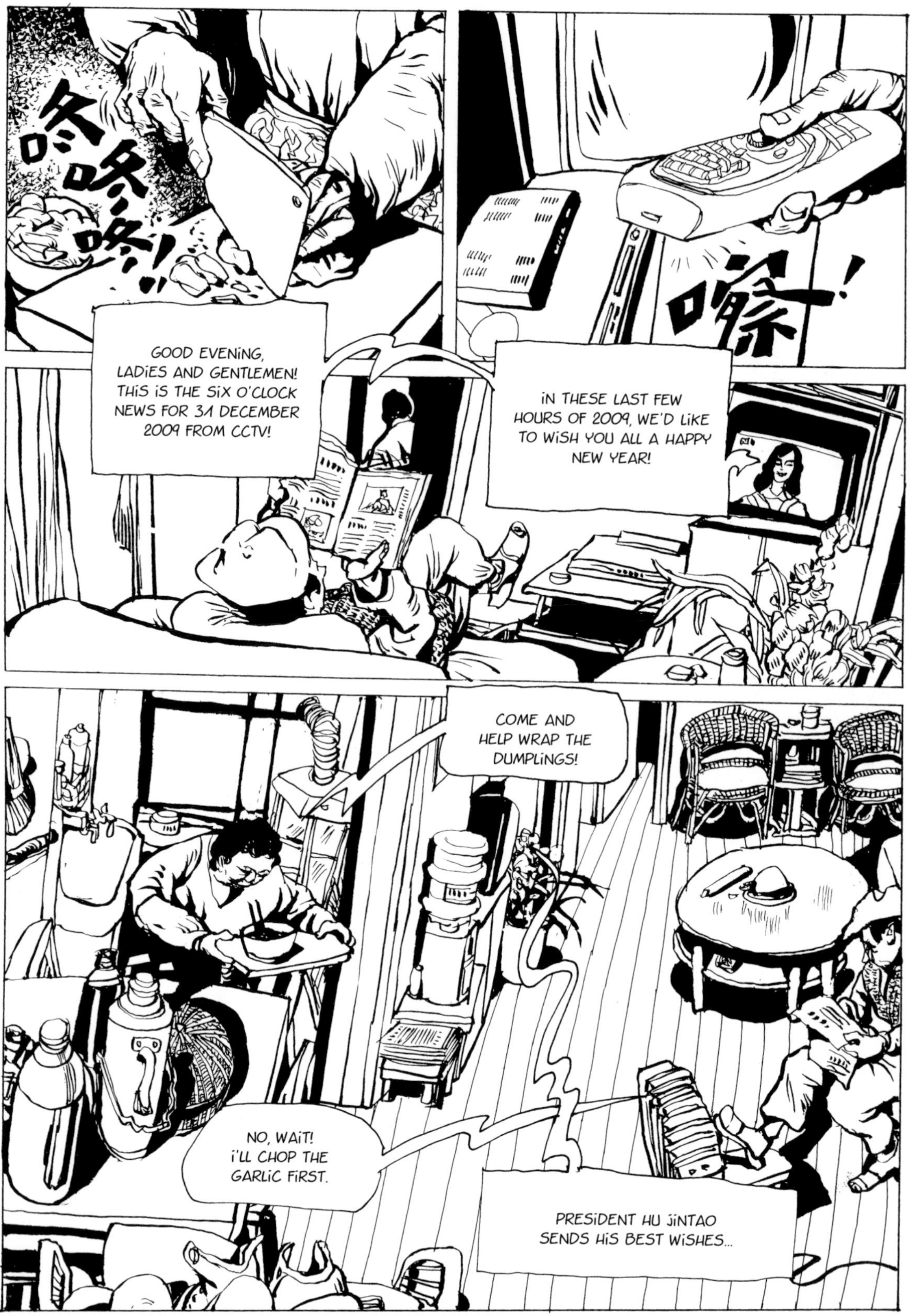

咚咚咚!!
嚓!
GOOD EVENING, LADIES AND GENTLEMEN! THIS IS THE SIX O'CLOCK NEWS FOR 31 DECEMBER 2009 FROM CCTV!
IN THESE LAST FEW HOURS OF 2009, WE'D LIKE TO WISH YOU ALL A HAPPY NEW YEAR!
COME AND HELP WRAP THE DUMPLINGS!
NO, WAIT! I'LL CHOP THE GARLIC FIRST.
PRESIDENT HU JINTAO SENDS HIS BEST WISHES...

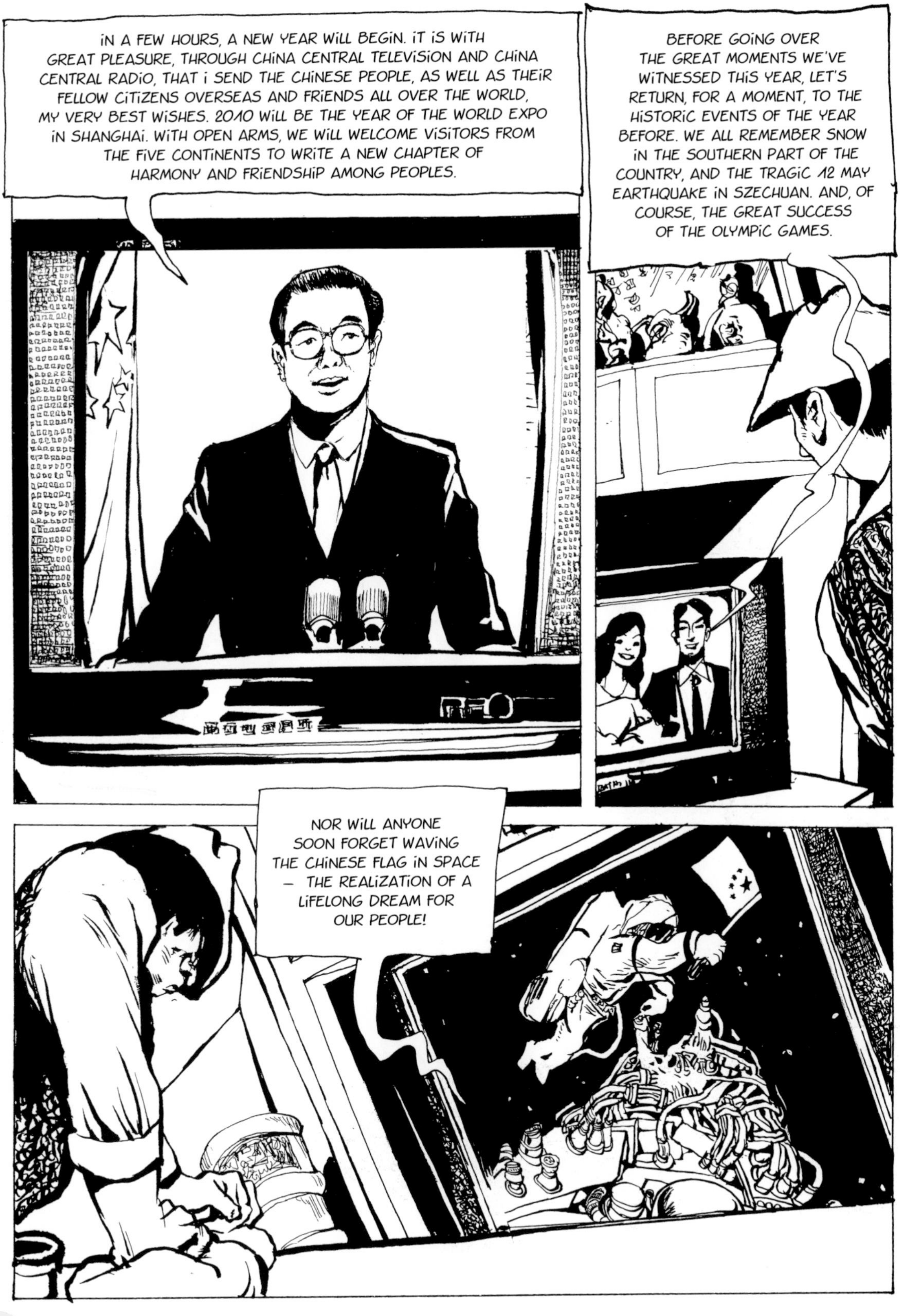
IN A FEW HOURS, A NEW YEAR WILL BEGIN. IT IS WITH GREAT PLEASURE, THROUGH CHINA CENTRAL TELEVISION AND CHINA CENTRAL RADIO, THAT I SEND THE CHINESE PEOPLE, AS WELL AS THEIR FELLOW CITIZENS OVERSEAS AND FRIENDS ALL OVER THE WORLD, MY VERY BEST WISHES. 2010 WILL BE THE YEAR OF THE WORLD EXPO IN SHANGHAI. WITH OPEN ARMS, WE WILL WELCOME VISITORS FROM THE FIVE CONTINENTS TO WRITE A NEW CHAPTER OF HARMONY AND FRIENDSHIP AMONG PEOPLES.
BEFORE GOING OVER THE GREAT MOMENTS WE'VE WITNESSED THIS YEAR, LET'S RETURN, FOR A MOMENT, TO THE HISTORIC EVENTS OF THE YEAR BEFORE. WE ALL REMEMBER SNOW IN THE SOUTHERN PART OF THE COUNTRY, AND THE TRAGIC 12 MAY EARTHQUAKE IN SZECHUAN. AND, OF COURSE, THE GREAT SUCCESS OF THE OLYMPIC GAMES.
NOR WILL ANYONE SOON FORGET WAVING THE CHINESE FLAG IN SPACE – THE REALIZATION OF A LIFELONG DREAM FOR OUR PEOPLE!

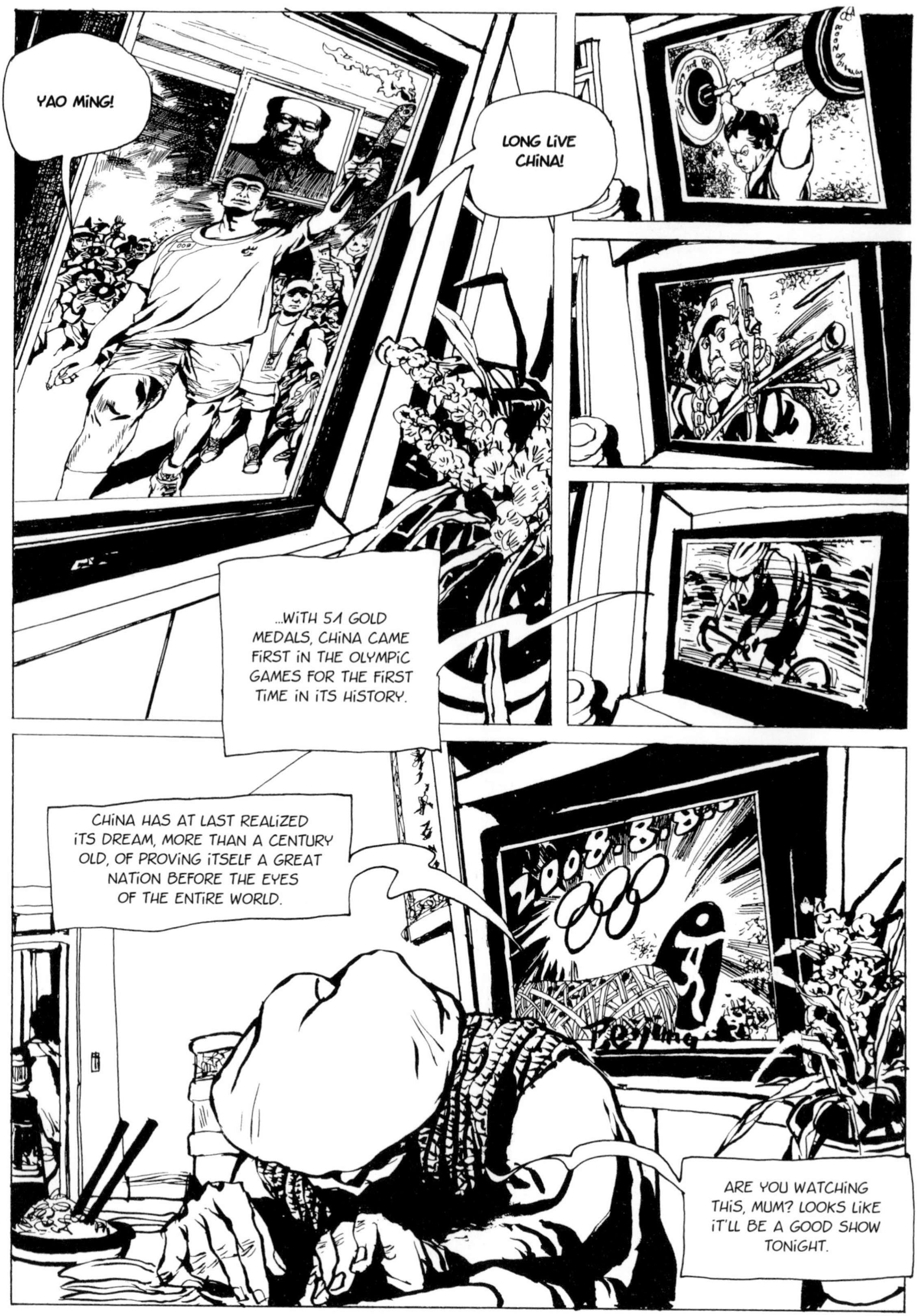

YAO MING!
LONG LIVE CHINA!
...WITH 51 GOLD MEDALS, CHINA CAME FIRST IN THE OLYMPIC GAMES FOR THE FIRST TIME IN ITS HISTORY.
CHINA HAS AT LAST REALIZED ITS DREAM, MORE THAN A CENTURY OLD, OF PROVING ITSELF A GREAT NATION BEFORE THE EYES OF THE ENTIRE WORLD.
2008.8.8.
Beijing
ARE YOU WATCHING THIS, MUM? LOOKS LIKE IT'LL BE A GOOD SHOW TONIGHT.

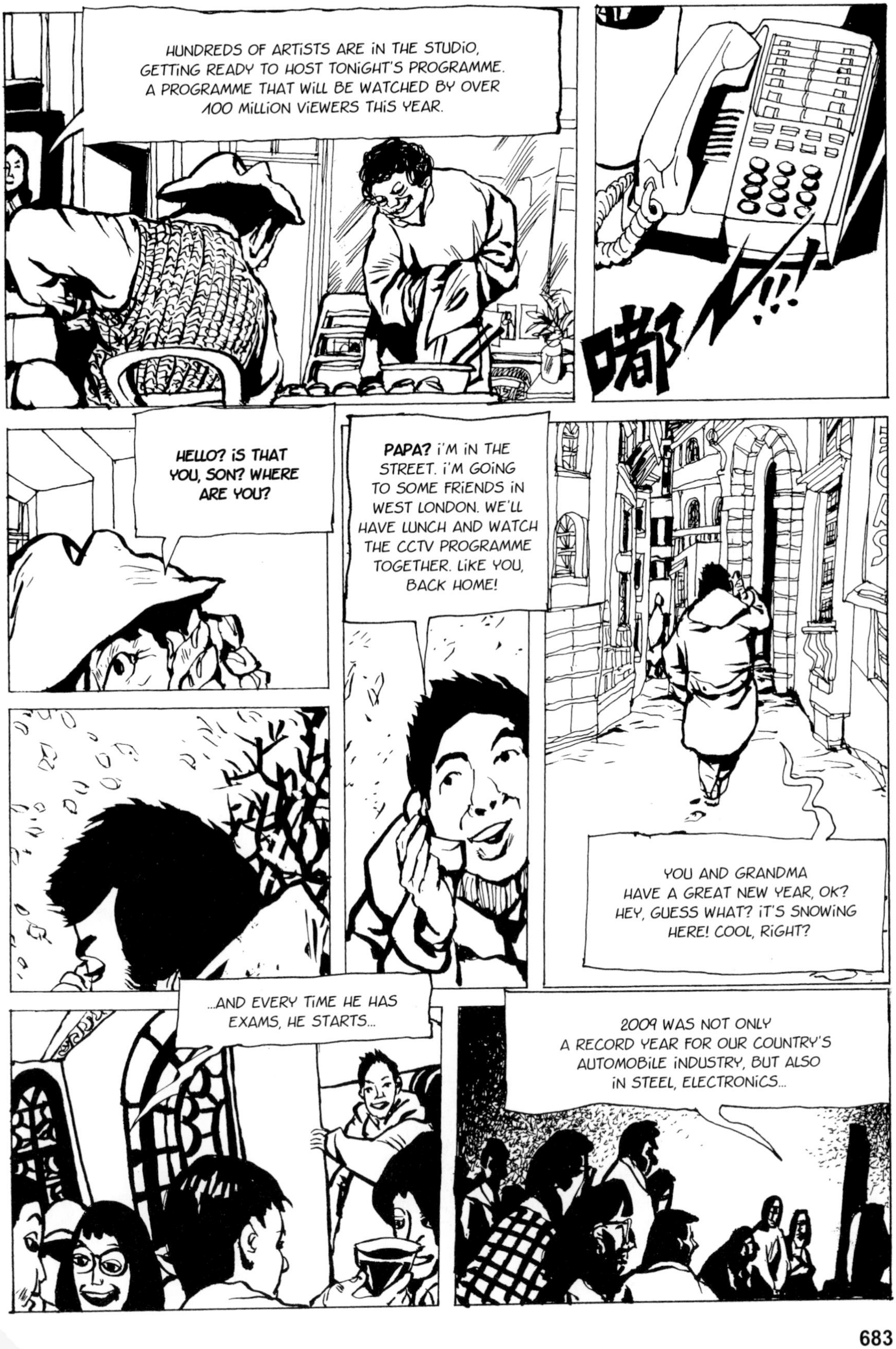

HUNDREDS OF ARTISTS ARE IN THE STUDIO, GETTING READY TO HOST TONIGHT'S PROGRAMME. A PROGRAMME THAT WILL BE WATCHED BY OVER 100 MILLION VIEWERS THIS YEAR.
嘟
HELLO? IS THAT YOU, SON? WHERE ARE YOU?
PAPA? I'M IN THE STREET. I'M GOING TO SOME FRIENDS IN WEST LONDON. WE'LL HAVE LUNCH AND WATCH THE CCTV PROGRAMME TOGETHER. LIKE YOU, BACK HOME!
YOU AND GRANDMA HAVE A GREAT NEW YEAR, OK? HEY, GUESS WHAT? IT'S SNOWING HERE! COOL, RIGHT?
...AND EVERY TIME HE HAS EXAMS, HE STARTS...
2009 WAS NOT ONLY A RECORD YEAR FOR OUR COUNTRY'S AUTOMOBILE INDUSTRY, BUT ALSO IN STEEL, ELECTRONICS...

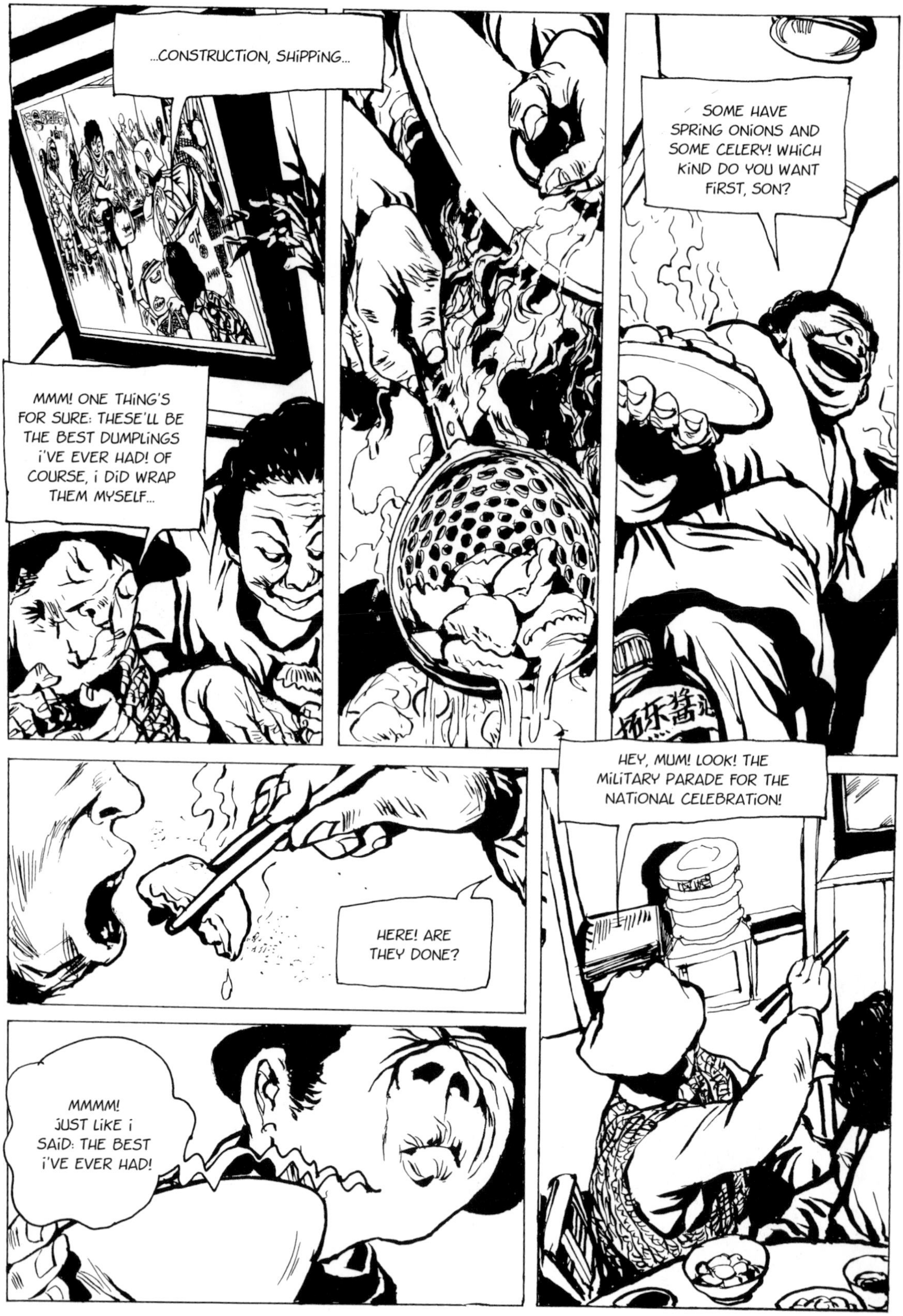
...CONSTRUCTION, SHIPPING...
MMM! ONE THING'S FOR SURE: THESE'LL BE THE BEST DUMPLINGS I'VE EVER HAD! OF COURSE, I DID WRAP THEM MYSELF...
SOME HAVE SPRING ONIONS AND SOME CELERY! WHICH KIND DO YOU WANT FIRST, SON?
HERE! ARE THEY DONE?
MMMM! JUST LIKE I SAID: THE BEST I'VE EVER HAD!
HEY, MUM! LOOK! THE MILITARY PARADE FOR THE NATIONAL CELEBRATION!

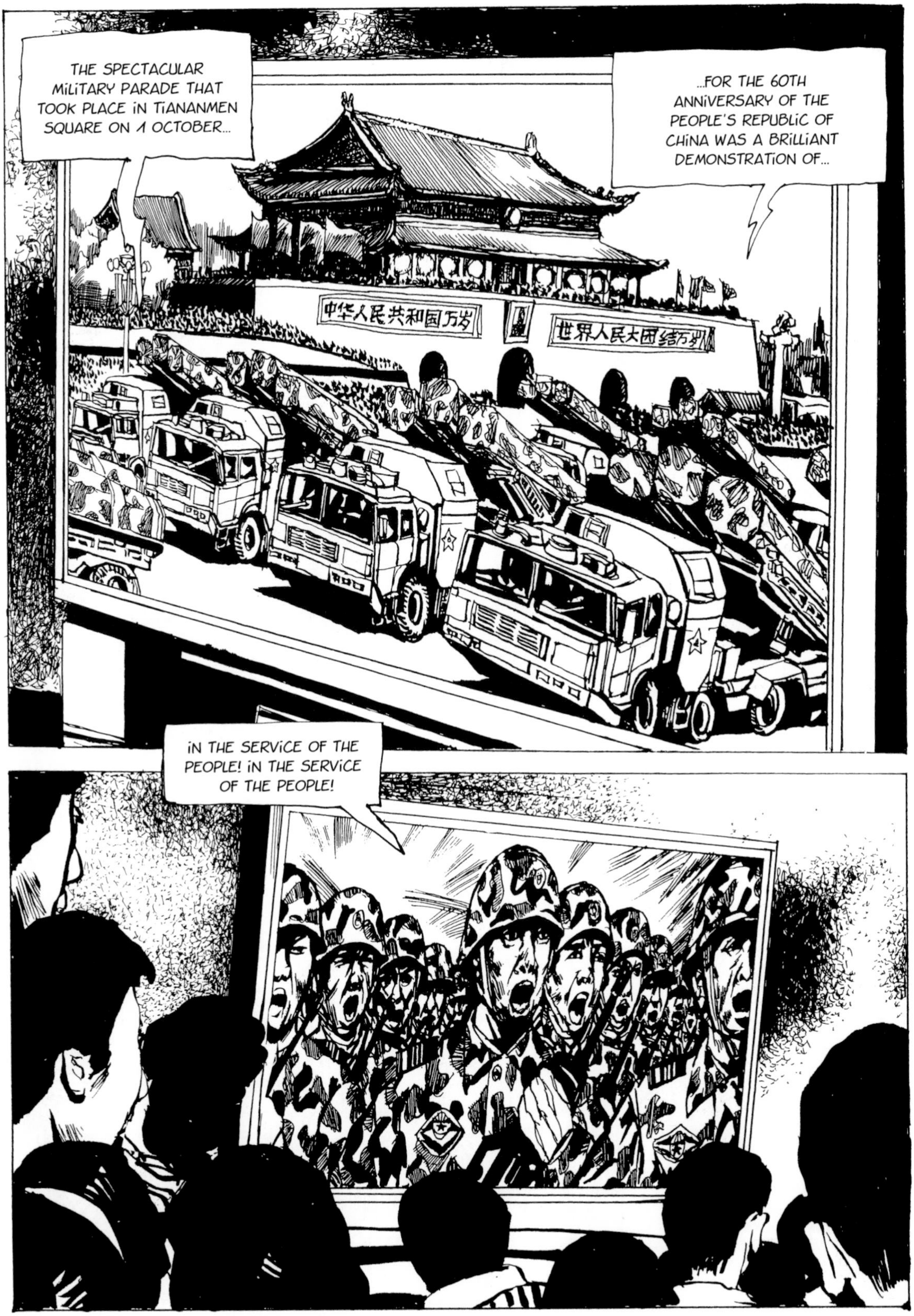
THE SPECTACULAR MILITARY PARADE THAT TOOK PLACE IN TIANANMEN SQUARE ON 1 OCTOBER...
...FOR THE 60TH ANNIVERSARY OF THE PEOPLE'S REPUBLIC OF CHINA WAS A BRILLIANT DEMONSTRATION OF...
中华人民共和国万岁
世界人民大团结万岁
IN THE SERVICE OF THE PEOPLE! IN THE SERVICE OF THE PEOPLE!

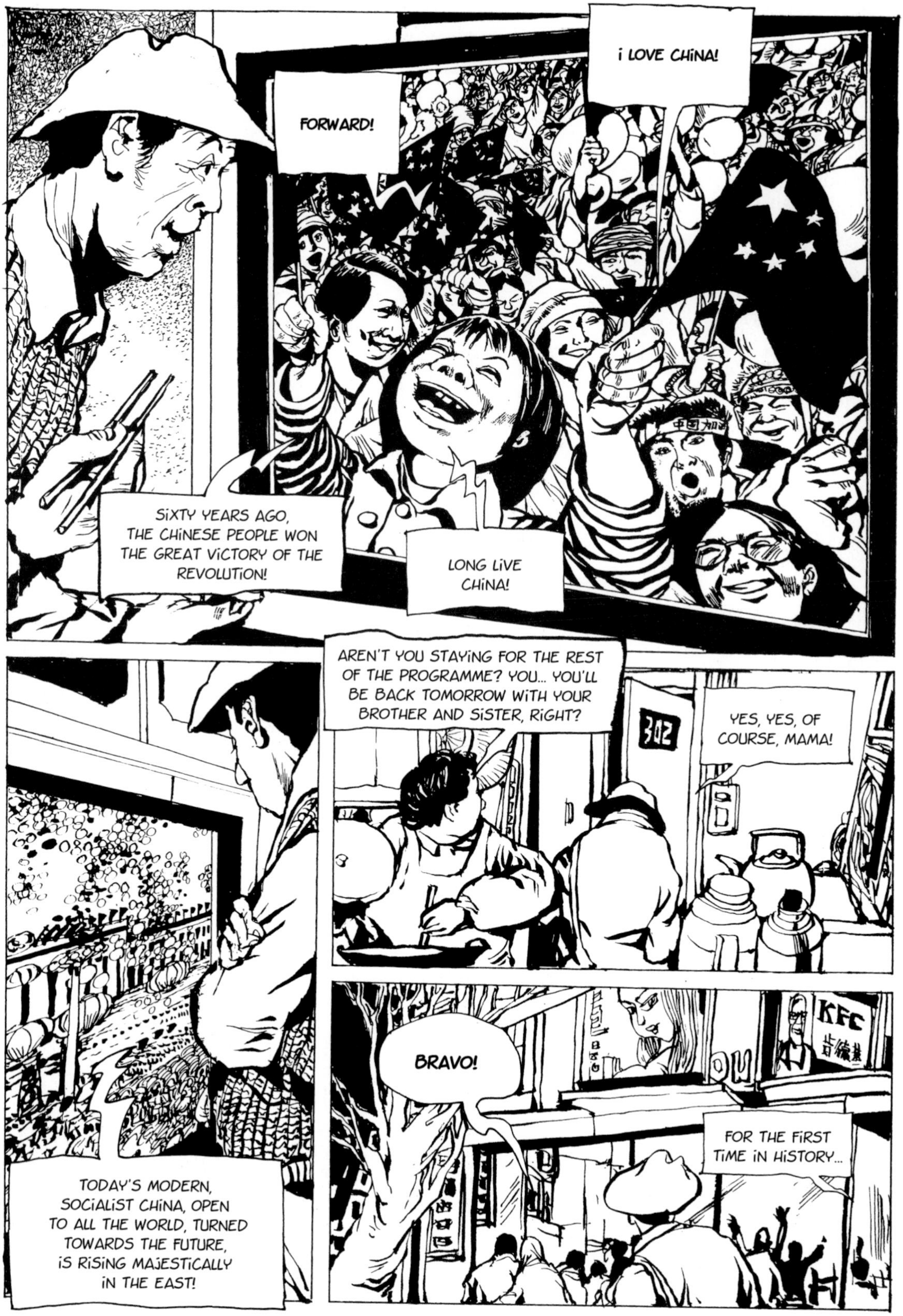

FORWARD!
I LOVE CHINA!
SIXTY YEARS AGO, THE CHINESE PEOPLE WON THE GREAT VICTORY OF THE REVOLUTION!
LONG LIVE CHINA!
TODAY'S MODERN, SOCIALIST CHINA, OPEN TO ALL THE WORLD, TURNED TOWARDS THE FUTURE, IS RISING MAJESTICALLY IN THE EAST!
AREN'T YOU STAYING FOR THE REST OF THE PROGRAMME? YOU... YOU'LL BE BACK TOMORROW WITH YOUR BROTHER AND SISTER, RIGHT?
302
YES, YES, OF COURSE, MAMA!
BRAVO!
KFC
FOR THE FIRST TIME IN HISTORY...

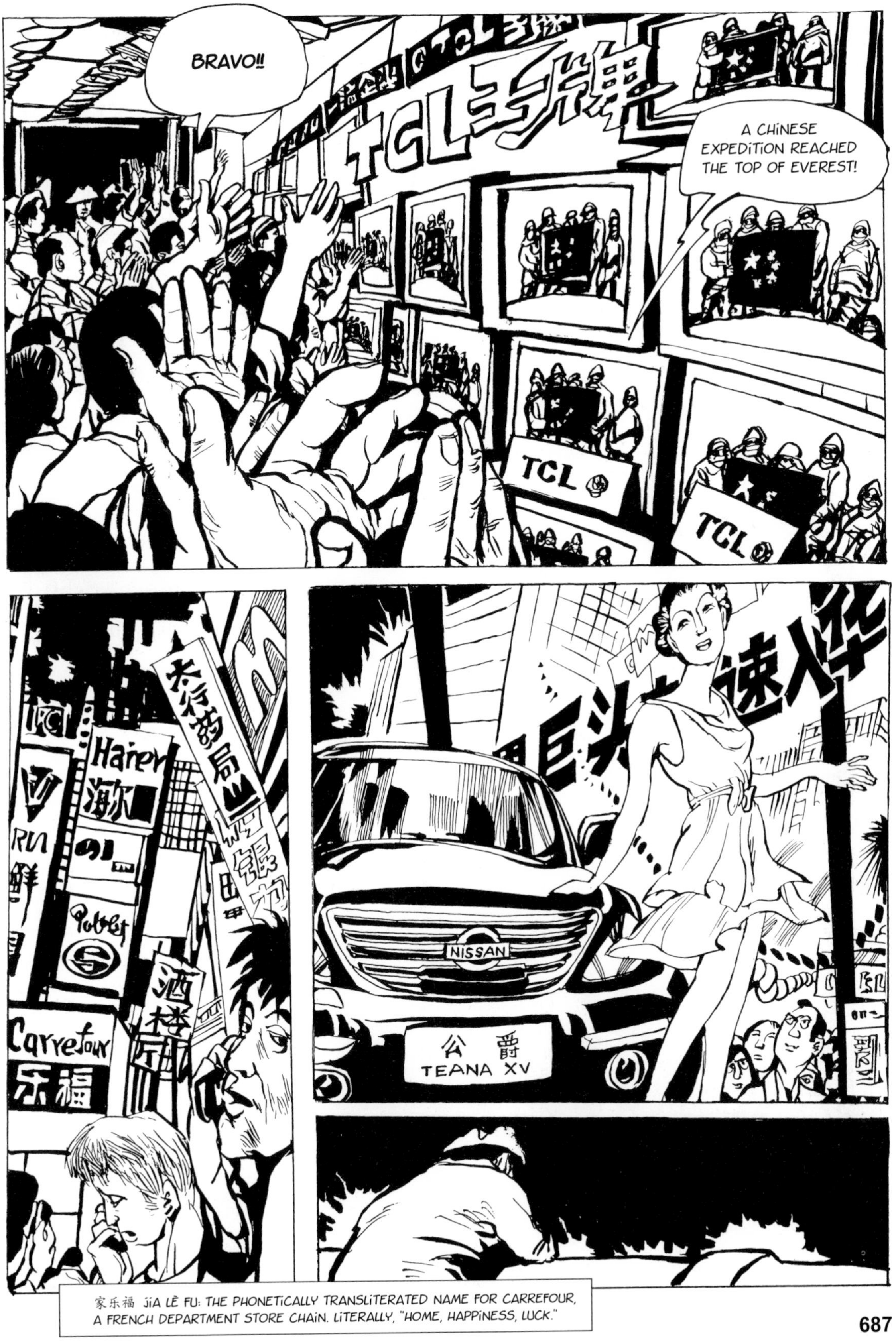
BRAVO!!
A CHINESE EXPEDITION REACHED THE TOP OF EVEREST!
TCL
TCL
TCL
Haier
Carrefour
乐福
NISSAN
公爵
TEANA XV

家乐福 JIA LÈ FU: THE PHONETICALLY TRANSLITERATED NAME FOR CARREFOUR, A FRENCH DEPARTMENT STORE CHAIN. LITERALLY, "HOME, HAPPINESS, LUCK."

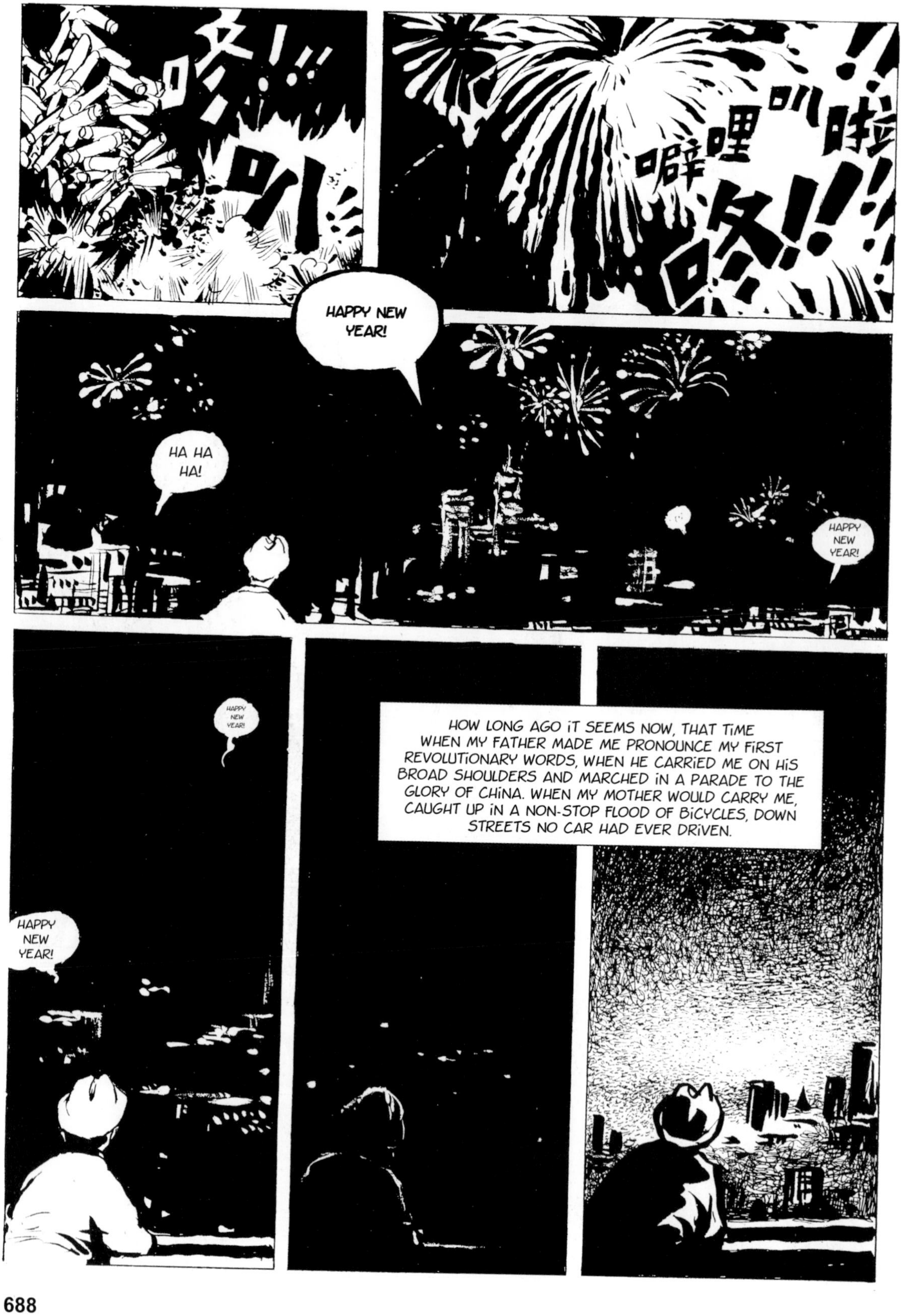

咚!!
叭!!
噼哩叭啦
咚!!
HAPPY NEW YEAR!
HA HA HA!
HAPPY NEW YEAR!
HAPPY NEW YEAR!
HAPPY NEW YEAR!
HOW LONG AGO IT SEEMS NOW, THAT TIME WHEN MY FATHER MADE ME PRONOUNCE MY FIRST REVOLUTIONARY WORDS, WHEN HE CARRIED ME ON HIS BROAD SHOULDERS AND MARCHED IN A PARADE TO THE GLORY OF CHINA. WHEN MY MOTHER WOULD CARRY ME, CAUGHT UP IN A NON-STOP FLOOD OF BICYCLES, DOWN STREETS NO CAR HAD EVER DRIVEN.

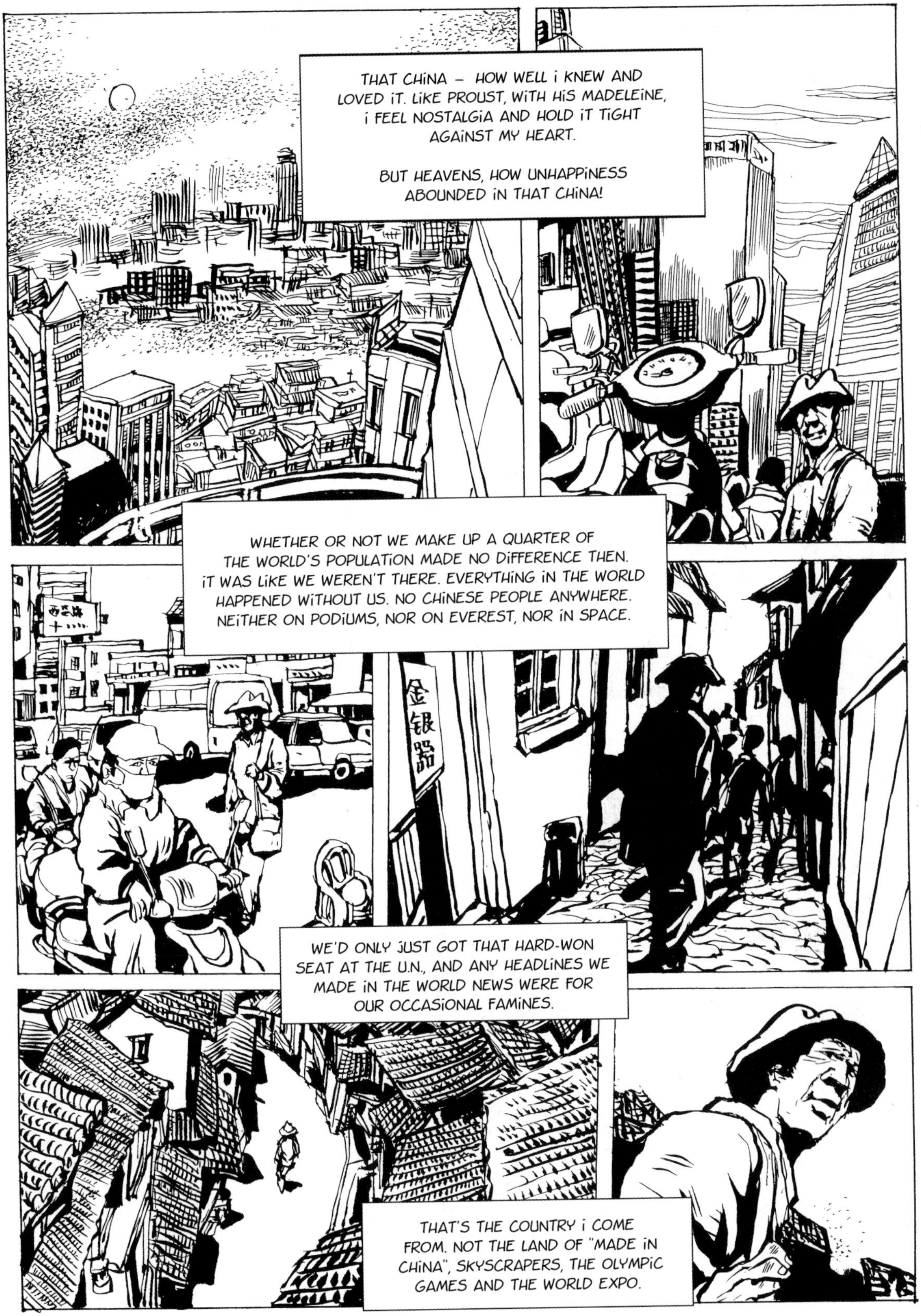
THAT CHINA – HOW WELL I KNEW AND LOVED IT. LIKE PROUST, WITH HIS MADELEINE, I FEEL NOSTALGIA AND HOLD IT TIGHT AGAINST MY HEART.
BUT HEAVENS, HOW UNHAPPINESS ABOUNDED IN THAT CHINA!
WHETHER OR NOT WE MAKE UP A QUARTER OF THE WORLD'S POPULATION MADE NO DIFFERENCE THEN. IT WAS LIKE WE WEREN'T THERE. EVERYTHING IN THE WORLD HAPPENED WITHOUT US. NO CHINESE PEOPLE ANYWHERE. NEITHER ON PODIUMS, NOR ON EVEREST, NOR IN SPACE.
金银器
WE'D ONLY JUST GOT THAT HARD-WON SEAT AT THE U.N., AND ANY HEADLINES WE MADE IN THE WORLD NEWS WERE FOR OUR OCCASIONAL FAMINES.
THAT'S THE COUNTRY I COME FROM. NOT THE LAND OF "MADE IN CHINA", SKYSCRAPERS, THE OLYMPIC GAMES AND THE WORLD EXPO.

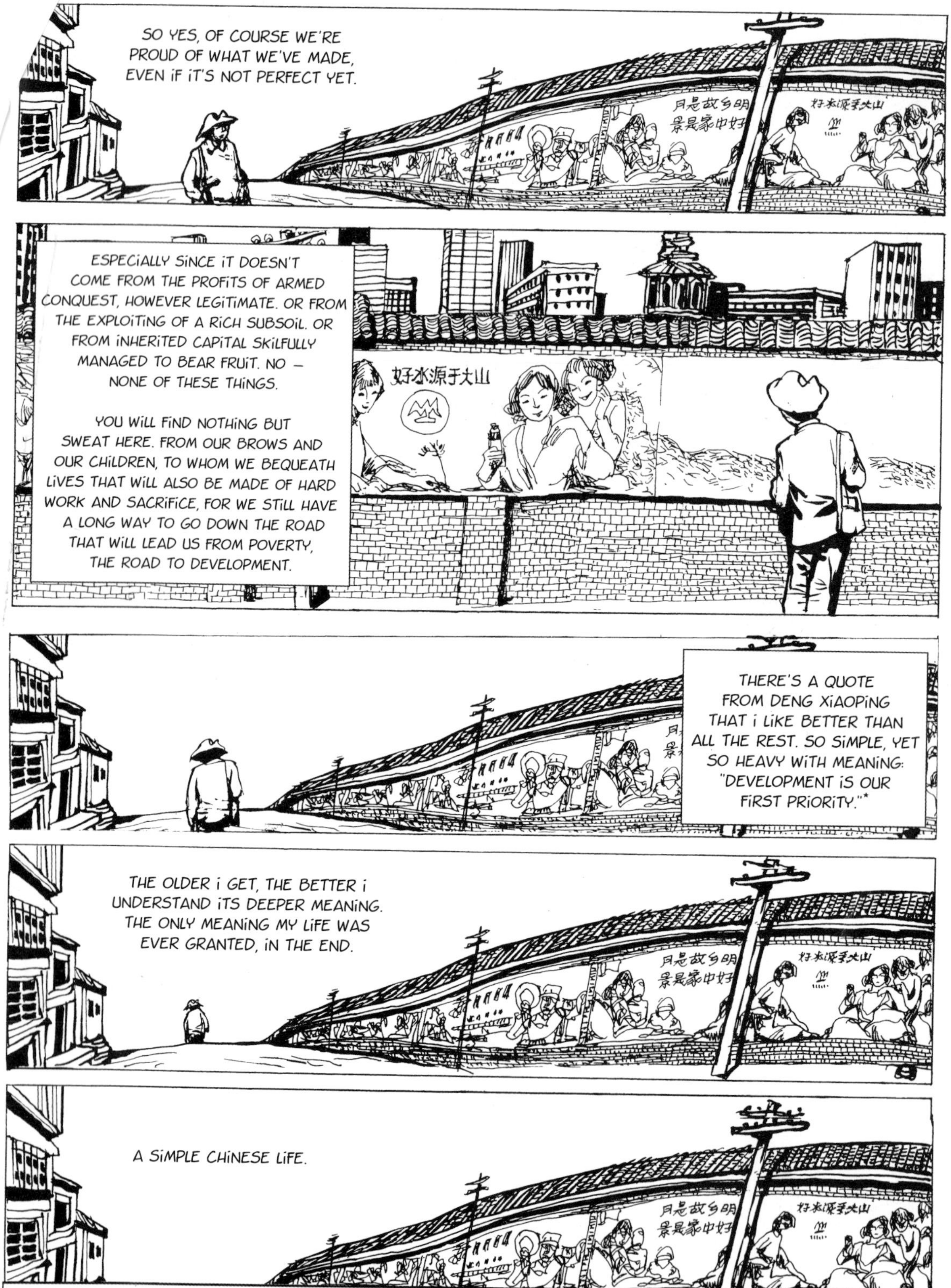
SO YES, OF COURSE WE'RE PROUD OF WHAT WE'VE MADE, EVEN iF iT'S NOT PERFECT YET.
月是故乡明
景是家中好
好水源于大山
ESPECiALLY SiNCE iT DOESN'T COME FROM THE PROFiTS OF ARMED CONQUEST, HOWEVER LEGiTiMATE. OR FROM THE EXPLOiTiNG OF A RiCH SUBSOiL. OR FROM iNHERiTED CAPiTAL SKiLFULLY MANAGED TO BEAR FRUiT. NO – NONE OF THESE THiNGS.
YOU WiLL FiND NOTHiNG BUT SWEAT HERE. FROM OUR BROWS AND OUR CHiLDREN, TO WHOM WE BEQUEATH LiVES THAT WiLL ALSO BE MADE OF HARD WORK AND SACRiFiCE, FOR WE STiLL HAVE A LONG WAY TO GO DOWN THE ROAD THAT WiLL LEAD US FROM POVERTY, THE ROAD TO DEVELOPMENT.
THERE'S A QUOTE FROM DENG XiAOPiNG THAT i LiKE BETTER THAN ALL THE REST. SO SiMPLE, YET SO HEAVY WiTH MEANiNG: "DEVELOPMENT iS OUR FiRST PRiORiTY."*
THE OLDER i GET, THE BETTER i UNDERSTAND iTS DEEPER MEANiNG. THE ONLY MEANiNG MY LiFE WAS EVER GRANTED, iN THE END.
A SiMPLE CHiNESE LiFE.

* 发展才是硬道理 FAZHAN CAi SHi YiNG DÀOLi.
月是故乡明 景是家中好 YÙE SHi FÙ XiANG MiNG JiNG SHi JiA ZHONG HAO: "THE BRiGHTEST MOON iS THAT OF THE HOMELAND"; YUE SHi GUXiANG MiNG, JiNG SHi JiAZHONG HAO: "THE PRETTiEST COUNTRYSiDE iS THAT OF THE HOMELAND."

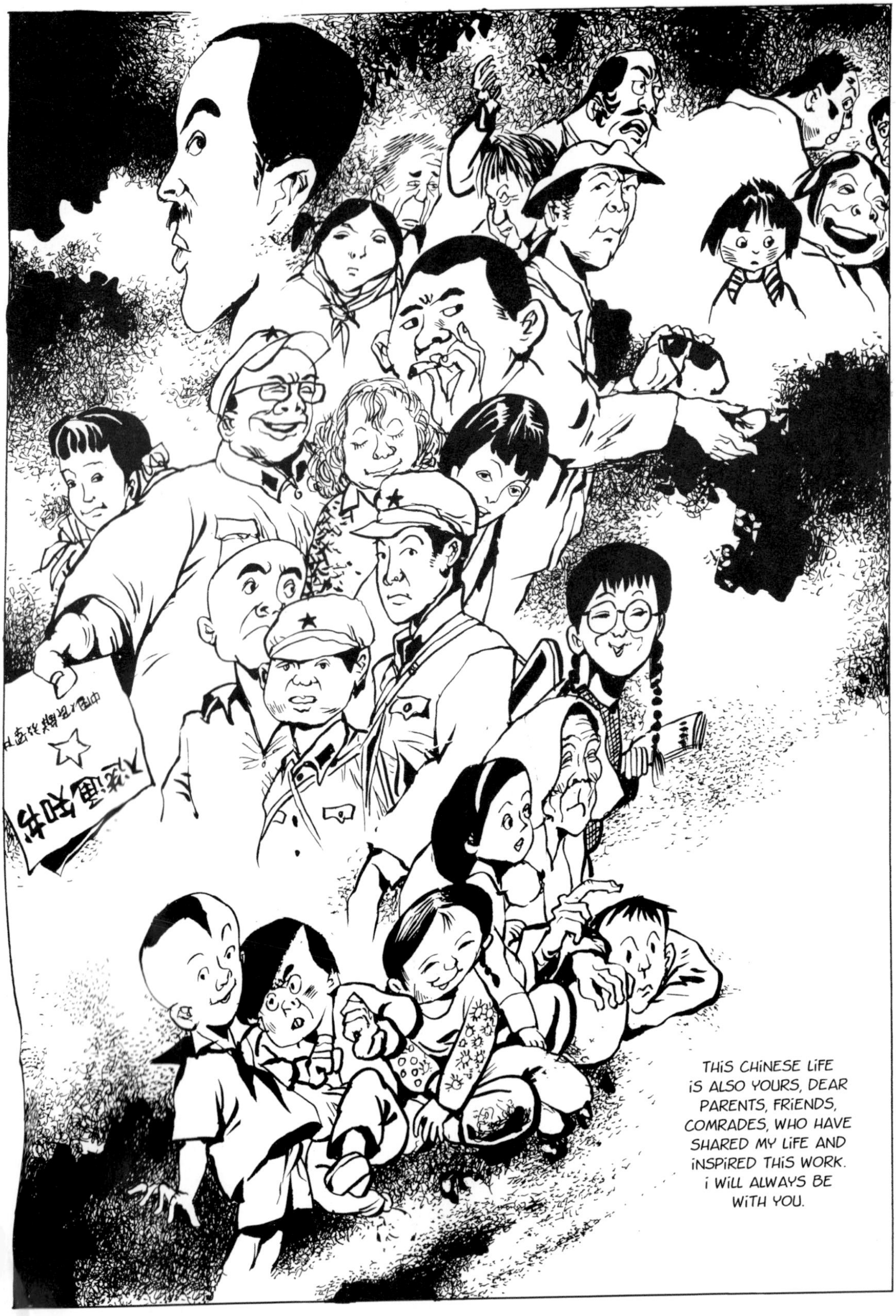
THIS CHINESE LIFE IS ALSO YOURS, DEAR PARENTS, FRIENDS, COMRADES, WHO HAVE SHARED MY LIFE AND INSPIRED THIS WORK. I WILL ALWAYS BE WITH YOU.